THE ROUTLEDGE HANDBOOK ON THE EUROPEAN NEIGHBOURHOOD POLICY

The Routledge Handbook on the European Neighbourhood Policy provides a comprehensive overview of the EU's most important foreign policy instrument, provided by leading experts in the field.

Coherently structured and adopting a multidisciplinary approach, this handbook covers the most important themes, developments and dynamics in the EU's neighbourhood policy framework through a series of cutting-edge contributions. With chapters from a substantial number of scholars who have been influential in shaping the study of the ENP, this handbook serves to encourage debates which will hopefully produce more conceptual as well as neighbourhood-specific perspectives leading to enriching future studies on the EU's policies towards its neighbourhood.

It will be a key reference point for advanced-level students, scholars and professionals developing knowledge in the fields of EU/European Studies, European Foreign Policy Analysis, Area studies, EU law, and more broadly in political economy, political science, comparative politics and international relations.

Tobias Schumacher is Chairholder of the European Neighbourhood Policy Chair at the College of Europe, Natolin, Poland. He is also an Associate Senior Research Fellow at the Centre for International Studies (CEI-IUL) at the University Institute of Lisbon, Portugal.

Andreas Marchetti is a Senior Fellow at the Center for European Integration Studies (ZEI) at the University of Bonn, Germany. He is also Founder and Director of politglott GmbH.

Thomas Demmelhuber is Professor of Middle East Politics and Society in the Department of Political Science at the Friedrich-Alexander-University of Erlangen-Nuremberg, Germany, and since 2015 he has been Visiting Professor at the College of Europe, Natolin, Poland.

'This wide-ranging volume from an expert team is an outstanding contribution to the understanding of our European neighbourhood. It covers the range of countries and issues in depth with thoughtful insights into the many policy challenges for the European Union, not least for its foreign policy and role in conflict management.'

– **Helen Wallace**, *University of Sussex, UK*

'A most indispensable reading for all those who wish to know more about one of the central features of EU foreign policy. At a time when the EU neighbourhood in both its Eastern and Southern dimensions is on fire and facing unprecedented challenges, this handbook offers the necessary keys to better understand Europe's policy in this field for the last ten years. It also helps to grasp the essential ingredients that will shape its future as Europe is struggling to stabilise its highly volatile fringes.'

– **H.E. Ambassador Pierre Vimont**, *Carnegie Europe, and former Secretary General, European External Action Service*

THE ROUTLEDGE HANDBOOK ON THE EUROPEAN NEIGHBOURHOOD POLICY

Edited by Tobias Schumacher, Andreas Marchetti and Thomas Demmelhuber

LONDON AND NEW YORK

First published 2018
by Routledge
2 Park Square, Milton Park, Abingdon, Oxon OX14 4RN

and by Routledge
711 Third Avenue, New York, NY 10017

Routledge is an imprint of the Taylor & Francis Group, an informa business

© 2018 selection and editorial matter, Tobias Schumacher, Andreas Marchetti and Thomas Demmelhuber; individual chapters, the contributors

The right of Tobias Schumacher, Andreas Marchetti and Thomas Demmelhuber to be identified as the authors of the editorial material, and of the authors for their individual chapters, has been asserted in accordance with sections 77 and 78 of the Copyright, Designs and Patents Act 1988.

All rights reserved. No part of this book may be reprinted or reproduced or utilised in any form or by any electronic, mechanical, or other means, now known or hereafter invented, including photocopying and recording, or in any information storage or retrieval system, without permission in writing from the publishers.

Trademark notice: Product or corporate names may be trademarks or registered trademarks, and are used only for identification and explanation without intent to infringe.

British Library Cataloguing in Publication Data
A catalogue record for this book is available from the British Library

Library of Congress Cataloging in Publication Data
A catalog record has been requested for this book

ISBN: 978-1-138-91372-1 (hbk)
ISBN: 978-1-315-69124-4 (ebk)

Typeset in Bembo
by Sunrise Setting Ltd, Brixham, UK

Printed and bound by CPI Group (UK) Ltd, Croydon, CR0 4YY

CONTENTS

List of figures   *x*
List of tables   *xi*
List of contributors   *xiii*
Foreword   *xxvii*
Preface   *xxix*

Introduction   1

1 The European Neighbourhood Policy: the challenge of demarcating a complex and contested field of study   3
 Tobias Schumacher

PART I
Conceptual, theoretical and legal approaches in the study of the European Neighbourhood Policy   15

2 Beyond enlargement: conceptualizing the study of the European Neighbourhood Policy   17
 Frank Schimmelfennig

3 EU actorness and the European Neighbourhood Policy   28
 Nils Hoffmann and Arne Niemann

4 The challenge of analysing the performance of the European Neighbourhood Policy   39
 Dorina Baltag and Iulian Romanyshyn

5	Power and leadership in the European neighbourhood: contending role concepts *Lisbeth Aggestam*	50
6	Realism and the European Neighbourhood Policy *Adrian Hyde-Price*	60
7	Constructivist approaches to the study of the European Neighbourhood Policy *Petr Kratochvíl and Elsa Tulmets*	70
8	The study of the European Neighbourhood Policy through the lenses of critical approaches *Åsne Kalland Aarstad and Niklas Bremberg*	81
9	Methodological and theoretical challenges to the study of the European Neighbourhood Policy *Theofanis Exadaktylos*	93
10	Legal perspectives on the study of the European Neighbourhood Policy *Peter Van Elsuwege and Roman Petrov*	105

PART II
The EU and its neighbourhood: drawing borders, shaping identities — 117

11	The construction and deconstruction of the EU's neighbourhood *Christopher Browning*	119
12	Of borders and boundaries: the neighbourhood as the EU's buffer zone *Andreas Marchetti*	130
13	The EU and the European Neighbourhood Policy: the re-making of Europe's identity *Jan Zielonka*	142
14	Strategic narratives of EU foreign policy and the European Neighbourhood Policy *Alister Miskimmon*	153
15	The challenges of a changing eastern neighbourhood *Elena Korosteleva*	167

16 The challenges of a changing southern neighbourhood 177
    Thomas Demmelhuber

PART III
European Neighbourhood Policy-making: institutional dynamics, actors and instruments **187**

17 Coherence, cohesiveness and consistency in the European
    Neighbourhood Policy 189
    Tanja Börzel and Bidzina Lebanidze

18 European Neighbourhood Policy decision-making at critical junctures:
    EU institutions, the Member States and neighbourhood countries 200
    Mark Furness

19 EU Member States and the European Neighbourhood Policy 211
    Amelia Hadfield

20 The European Parliament as an actor in its own right in
    the EU's neighbourhood 223
    Cristian Nitoiu

21 Financial instruments and the European Neighbourhood Policy 234
    Anna-Sophie Maass

PART IV
Bilateralism, region-building and conflict management in the European Neighbourhood Policy **247**

22 The European Neighbourhood Policy between bilateralism and
    region-building 249
    Federica Bicchi, Gergana Noutcheva and Benedetta Voltolini

23 The EU and civilian missions in the neighbourhood 259
    Dimitris Bouris and Madalina Dobrescu

24 The European Neighbourhood Policy and the politics
    of sanctions 270
    Clara Portela

25 Ukraine in the European Neighbourhood Policy: a paradoxical
    partner 279
    Kataryna Wolczuk

26	EU–Belarus relations in the context of the European Neighbourhood Policy *Giselle Bosse*	290
27	The European Neighbourhood Policy and Moldova: a resilient oligarchic system wedged between the EU and Russia *Florent Parmentier*	302
28	The European Neighbourhood Policy and the South Caucasus *Licínia Simão*	312
29	The European Neighbourhood Policy and EU–Maghreb relations *Irene Fernández-Molina*	324
30	EU–Mashreq relations: differentiation, conditionality and security *Peter Seeberg*	336
31	Israel and Palestine and the European Neighbourhood Policy *Patrick Müller and Sharon Pardo*	347
32	Libya and Syria: at the crossroads of European Neighbourhood Policy and EU crisis management *Nicole Koenig*	358

PART V
The European Neighbourhood Policy and sectoral cooperation   **369**

33	Deep and comprehensive free trade agreements *Bernard Hoekman*	371
34	The European Neighbourhood Policy and energy *Bernd Weber*	381
35	Migration: moving to the centre of the European Neighbourhood Policy *Florian Trauner and Jean-Pierre Cassarino*	393
36	Counter-terrorism cooperation and the European Neighbourhood Policy *Chantal Lavallée, Sarah Léonard and Christian Kaunert*	405
37	Aid in the European Neighbourhood Policy *Fabienne Bossuyt, Hrant Kostanyan, Jan Orbie and Bruno Vandecasteele*	415

PART VI
The European Neighbourhood Policy and the promotion of EU norms and values   433

38 Perceptions of the European Neighbourhood Policy and of its values and norms promotion   435
Elisabeth Johansson-Nogués

39 European Neighbourhood Policy mechanisms: conditionality, socialisation and differentiation   445
Laure Delcour and Eduard Soler i Lecha

40 Geopolitics and democracy in the European Neighbourhood Policy   456
Anna Khakee and Richard Youngs

41 Democracy promotion by functional cooperation   467
Tina Freyburg and Sandra Lavenex

42 Human rights in the European Neighbourhood Policy   481
Rosa Balfour

43 The European Neighbourhood Policy promotion of civil society   494
Silvia Colombo and Natalia Shapovalova

PART VII
The European Neighbourhood Policy and future lines of inquiry   507

44 The European Neighbourhood Policy and Islamist actors in the southern neighbourhood   509
Michelle Pace and Sarah Wolff

45 The neighbours of the EU's neighbours: overcoming geographical silos   522
Sieglinde Gstöhl and Erwan Lannon

46 The European Neighbourhood Policy and the CFSP/CSDP: from the European Security Strategy to the Global Strategy   533
Thomas Henökl

Index   *544*

FIGURES

20.1	EP electoral monitoring missions in the EU neighbourhood	228
26.1	Trade volume: EU and Belarus 2002–2015	295
26.2	EU financial assistance Belarus: 2007–2014	297
37.1	ENPI/ENI bilateral and regional allocations (in EUR million) (2007–2014)	419
41.1	Trends in the European neighbourhood	476
42.1	EIHDR funding in ENP countries, 2011–2013	485
42.2	Civil Society Facility funding in the ENP region from 2011 to 2013	486
46.1	EU strategies and reforms affecting ENP – with involved DGs	537

TABLES

2.1	Mechanisms of Europeanization	22
7.1	Constructivist positions in the study of the European Neighbourhood Policy	72
9.1	List of articles in the ENP sample (2004–2015)	95
9.2	Criteria on research design	97
9.3	Field and framework of analysis of the ENP sample	98
9.4	Actors involved ($N = 90$) and variables studied ($N = 71$)	99
12.1	Comparative data on the functioning of ENP countries as the EU's buffer zone	137
14.1	Summary of main narrative content on ENP in key EU documents	157
14.2	The identity, system and issue narratives of the EU and Russia	163
17.1	Consistency and effectiveness of the ENP	195
20.1	EP delegations for relations with ENP countries	226
21.1	Overview of allocation of funding to TACIS, MEDA, ENPI and ENI in EUR billion	236
21.2	Allocation of ENPI bilateral assistance to all ENP countries (2007–2013)	238
23.1	EU CSDP missions in the neighbourhood 2003–2016	261
29.1	Share (%) of trade with EU-28 in the Maghreb countries' total trade with the world (2014)	327
29.2	Share (%) of trade with Maghreb countries in EU-28's total trade with the world (2015)	327
29.3	EU–Maghreb relations in 2016	329
35.1	EU Member States and ENP countries participating in EU Mobility Partnerships (as of October 2016)	396
35.2	EU migration agreements with EaP countries and Russia (as of October 2016)	398
37.1	EU bilateral support to ENP countries	421
37.2	EU support to regional programmes in the eastern and southern neighbourhoods	426
37.3	Neighbourhood-wide programmes	427
37.4	Funding of cross-border cooperation	428

Tables

40.1	SPRING and Umbrella Programme Funds – application of the 'more for more' principle (in EUR million)	463
41.1	Comparative analysis	474
42.1	Priority areas of ENP	484
42.2	ENP human rights – Freedom House indicators	488

CONTRIBUTORS

Lisbeth Aggestam is Associate Professor in the Department of Political Science at the University of Gothenburg, Sweden. She has written extensively on European foreign and security policy. She is currently working on a research project entitled, 'The Leadership Paradox in EU Foreign Policy', funded by Riksbankens Jubileumsfond (RJ: P14-0030: 1).

Rosa Balfour is the Acting Director of the Europe Program at the German Marshall Fund of the United States (GMF) in Brussels, where she focuses on European foreign and security policy, including the relationship between Europe's internal politics and international relations. She has researched and published widely on issues relating to European foreign policy and external action, relations with the Mediterranean region, Eastern Europe and the Balkans, EU enlargement, European Neighbourhood Policy and on the role of human rights and democracy in international relations. Prior to joining GMF, she was a Director at the European Policy Centre (EPC), an independent think tank based in Brussels, where she headed the Europe in the World programme. She holds an MA in history from Cambridge University, and an MSc in European studies and a PhD in international relations, both from the London School of Economics and Political Science.

Dorina Baltag teaches European Studies at Maastricht University and is currently a PhD candidate at Loughborough University. Her main areas of research interest include EU foreign policy, EU diplomacy, EU performance and EU relations with Eastern Europe. Her current research, for which she obtained a Marie Curie Fellowship in 2012 (European Commission, FP7 People programme, Initial Training Network INCOOP), focuses on EU diplomatic performance in Eastern Europe with a focus on Moldova, Ukraine and Belarus. In 2016, she co-authored a book chapter in *External Governance as Security Community Building* (London: Palgrave) and co-edited a special issue, forthcoming in 2017, on 'Assessing the performance of the European Union in Central and Eastern Europe and in its Neighbourhood', *East European Politics*. Her work has been published in, among others, SWP (German Institute for International and Security Affairs) working papers (2011), INCOOP policy briefs (2013), NUPI (Norwegian Institute of International Affairs) working papers (2014) and EIoP (European Integration Online) papers (2015).

Contributors

Federica Bicchi is Associate Professor in the International Relations of Europe in the Department of International Relations at the London School of Economics and Political Science. She holds a PhD in Political Science from the European University Institute in Florence, Italy. Her research interests include EU foreign policy towards its southern neighbourhood, a topic on which she has published numerous articles and the following volumes: *European Foreign Policy Making towards the Mediterranean* (Palgrave, 2007); *The Struggle for Influence in the Middle East*, co-edited with Benoit Challand and Steven Heydemann, translated into Arabic (Palgrave, 2015); and *The Union for the Mediterranean: Continuity or Change in Euro-Mediterranean Relations?* co-edited with Richard Gillespie (Palgrave, 2012).

Tanja Börzel is Professor of Political Science and holds the Chair for European Integration at the Otto-Suhr-Institute for Political Science, Freie Universität Berlin. Her recent publications include: 'From Europeanization to diffusion', co-edited with Thomas Risse, Special Issue of *West European Politics*, (35)1, 2012; *Business and Governance in South Africa. Racing to the Top?* co-edited with Christian Thauer, (Palgrave, 2013); *Governance Transfer by Regional Organizations*, co-edited with Vera van Hüllen, (Palgrave, 2014); and *The Oxford Handbook of Comparative Regionalism* co-edited with Thomas Risse, (Oxford University Press, 2016).

Giselle Bosse is Assistant Professor and Co-Director of the MSc European Studies at Maastricht University (NL), Visiting Professor at the College of Europe (Bruges) and Research Associate at the Martens Centre for European Studies (Brussels). Her research focuses on the EU's Eastern Partnership (EaP) and policy towards autocratic regimes in Eastern Europe and Central Asia. She is currently principal investigator of a VENI research project funded by the Netherlands Organisation for Scientific Research (NWO) on 'Explaining Europe's failure to deal with autocratic regimes' (Ref. 451-12-015). Giselle Bosse has published her research *inter alia* in the *Journal of Common Market Studies*, *Geopolitics*, *Europe-Asia Studies*, and *Cooperation and Conflict*, and frequently presents her work at leading think tanks in Europe.

Fabienne Bossuyt is Postdoctoral Fellow at the Department of Political Science at Ghent University (Belgium), where she teaches and researches on the European Union's external relations, including on the European Neighbourhood Policy.

Dimitris Bouris is Assistant Professor at the Department of Political Science at the University of Amsterdam and a Visiting Professor at the College of Europe (Natolin Campus). He is the author of *The European Union and Occupied Palestinian Territories: State-building without a State* (Routledge, 2014) and the co-editor (with Tobias Schumacher) of the *Revised European Neighbourhood Policy: Continuity and Change in EU Foreign Policy* (Palgrave, 2017). He has published a number of scholarly articles in peer-reviewed academic journals as well as policy briefs and op-eds for major news and policy outlets. His research interests include state-building, conflict resolution and EU external relations.

Niklas Bremberg is Senior Research Fellow at the Swedish Institute of International Affairs in Stockholm. He is also affiliated to the Department of Government, Uppsala University, as research coordinator for the Swedish Network for European Studies in Political Science (SNES). He has published on security communities, crisis management and EU foreign and security policy, especially towards North Africa, in *Journal of Common Market Studies*, *Cooperation and Conflict*, *Mediterranean Politics* and *European Security*. His latest book is *Diplomacy and Security Community-Building: EU Crisis Management in the Western Mediterranean* (Routledge, 2016).

Contributors

Christopher Browning is Reader of Politics and International Studies at the University of Warwick, United Kingdom. He has written widely on themes exploring the politics of identity, security and region-building in Europe, with a particular focus on the constitutive power of marginal spaces and border zones. In this context he has written several pieces on EU policies towards its neighbouring regions and on the ENP more specifically. His current research focuses on the concept of ontological security and the politics of nation branding.

Jean-Pierre Cassarino is a political scientist doing research at the Institut de Recherche sur le Maghreb Contemporain (IRMC, Tunisia) on labour migration issues and international relations. Previously, he held a professorship at the Robert Schuman Centre for Advanced Studies, European University Institute (RSCAS, EUI). His research interests focus on patterns of international cooperation and state sovereignty as applied to the 'management' of international migration and asylum. Selected recent publications include: *The Drive for Securitized Temporariness* (Oxford University Press, 2013); *Readmission Policy in the European Union* (European Parliament Publications Office, 2010); *Unbalanced Reciprocities: Cooperation on Readmission in the Euro-Mediterranean Area* (Middle-East Institute, 2010).

Silvia Colombo is Senior Research Fellow in the Mediterranean and Middle East Programme at the International Affairs Institute (IAI) in Rome. An expert on Middle Eastern politics, she works on Euro-Mediterranean relations, and domestic and regional dynamics in the Arab world. She holds a PhD in Comparative Politics from the Scuola Normale Superiore of Pisa (Florence Branch) and a Master's Degree in Near and Middle Eastern Studies from the School of Oriental and African Studies (SOAS) in London.

Laure Delcour is Visiting Professor at the College of Europe, Bruges (Belgium) and a Scientific Coordinator and Senior Research Fellow under the EU-funded FP7 project 'Exploring the Security-Democracy Nexus in the Caucasus' (project CASCADE, FMSH, Paris). Her research interests focus on the diffusion and reception of EU norms and policies as part of the European Neighbourhood Policy, as well as region-building processes in Eurasia. As part of a French–British research project (EUIMPACTEAST, ANR-ESRC, 2011–2014), she has previously investigated the EU's influence on domestic change in four post-Soviet countries (Armenia, Georgia, Moldova and Ukraine). She has lectured on EU institutions and decision-making, the European Neighbourhood Policy, EU–Russia relations and Russia's foreign policy (Sciences-Po Paris, Sciences-Po Strasbourg, INALCO Paris). Laure Delcour's publications include: *The EU and Russia in their 'Contested Neighbourhood'. Multiple External Influences, Policy Transfer and Domestic Change* (Routledge, 2017); 'Beyond geopolitics: exploring the impact of the EU and. Russia in the "contested neighborhood"' (special issue co-edited with E. Ademmer and K. Wolczuk), *Eurasian Geography and Economics* (57)1, 2016.

Thomas Demmelhuber is Professor of Middle East Politics and Society in the Department of Political Science at the Friedrich-Alexander-University of Erlangen-Nuremberg (Germany) and, since 2015, Visiting Professor at the College of Europe, Natolin (Warsaw, Poland). From 2012 to 2015, he was Assistant Professor for Political Science at the University of Hildesheim. His PhD thesis on EU–Egyptian relations was awarded the German Middle East Studies Association's dissertation prize for best PhD in Middle Eastern studies (2009). Demmelhuber's research focuses on state, power and politics in the Middle East from a comparative perspective, including international actors such as the European Union.

Contributors

Madalina Dobrescu is Research Fellow at the European Neighbourhood Policy Chair, College of Europe, Natolin (Warsaw, Poland). Dr Dobrescu holds a BA in Political Science from the University of Bucharest, an MA in International Politics from the University of Manchester, and a Phd in European Studies from the London School of Economics. Her PhD thesis explored the impact of EU civilian missions in the eastern neighbourhood with a particular focus on the role of national governments and local actors in Georgia, Moldova and Ukraine in shaping the EU's contribution to conflict management and domestic reforms on the ground. Dr Dobrescu's research interests revolve around the European Union's foreign policy and in particular the Common Security and Defence Policy (CSDP), as well as processes of Europeanisation, external governance, peacebuilding and conflict resolution, all of this with respect to the Eastern dimension of the EU's Neighbourhood Policy.

Theofanis Exadaktylos is Senior Lecturer (Associate Professor) in European Politics at the Department of Politics at the University of Surrey. He has expertise in political methodology and research design in European Union studies, applying them to a range of political science issues, from foreign and security policy, the ENP, enlargement and European integration to the politics of austerity, policy implementation and political trust, populism and the extreme right, and emergence of stereotypes in times of crisis. He is also co-convening the ECPR Standing Group on Political Methodology. His book, co-edited with Claudio Radaelli, *Research Design in European Studies: Establishing Causality in Europeanization*, is an edited collection that provides different ways of ensuring methodological rigour in the study of European politics.

Irene Fernández-Molina is Lecturer in the Politics Department at the University of Exeter. Her research deals with the international relations of the Middle East and North Africa, foreign policy analysis and conflict studies, with a particular focus on the Maghreb, as well as EU foreign policy. She is the author of *Moroccan Foreign Policy under Mohammed VI, 1999–2014* (Routledge, 2015). Her most recent projects address the multilevel politics of recognition in protracted conflicts, 'subaltern' foreign policies and foreign economic policies of Southern Mediterranean countries, the international dimension of regime hybridisation, and practices of interaction between contested states and the EU.

Tina Freyburg is Professor of Comparative Politics in the School of Economics and Political Sciences at the University of St. Gallen, Switzerland. In her research she explores the chances and risks that emerge for democracy in a globalised world.

Mark Furness is Senior Researcher at the German Development Institute/Deutsches Institut für Entwicklungspolitik (DIE) in Bonn. His research and policy advisory work focuses on EU external relations, the security-development nexus, fragile and conflict-affected countries, and the Middle East and North Africa.

Sieglinde Gstöhl is Director of the Department of EU International Relations and Diplomacy Studies at the College of Europe, Bruges (Belgium). She has been Professor at the College since 2005. From 1999 to 2005, she was Assistant Professor of International Relations at Humboldt University Berlin. She holds a PhD and an MA in International Relations from the Graduate Institute of International and Development Studies in Geneva, as well as a degree in Public Affairs from the University of St. Gallen, Switzerland. She was, *inter alia*, a research fellow at the Liechtenstein-Institut in Bendern and at the Center for International Affairs at Harvard University in Cambridge and worked at the EFTA Secretariat.

Contributors

Amelia Hadfield is the Director of the Centre for European Studies at Canterbury Christ Church University, a Jean Monnet Centre of Excellence. She is also the Jean Monnet Chair in European Foreign Affairs. Her areas of interest cover European foreign policy, from security and defence to EU strategic partnerships to energy governance and neighbourhood policy. In light of recent events, this focus has widened to include the strategic implications of UK–EU relations against the backdrop of Brexit. Amelia has published and consulted widely on European and international foreign affairs, including other topics such as sovereignty, foreign policy analysis and the EU's Global Strategy.

Thomas Henökl is Senior Researcher at the German Development Institute in Bonn and Associate Professor for Public Policy at the University of Agder (Norway). He works in research and teaching in the fields of public policy and administration, ethics and integrity management, EU foreign and security policy, international cooperation and development, as well as comparative politics and organisation theory. Previously, Henökl worked for the European Commission and DG Relex (from 2011 the European External Action Service), and at the European Institute of Public Administration (EIPA).

Bernard Hoekman is Professor and Director, Global Economics at the Robert Schuman Centre for Advanced Studies, European University Institute in Florence, Italy. Prior positions include Director of the International Trade Department and Research Manager in the Development Research Group of the World Bank. He is a CEPR Research Fellow and co-directed the Trade Policy Research Network; a Visiting Professor at the School for Business, Management and Economics, University of Sussex; a Senior Associate of the Economic Research Forum for the Arab countries, Turkey and Iran; and a member of the World Economic Forum Global Future Council on International Trade and Investment. He holds a PhD in economics from the University of Michigan. Recent publications include 'The Global Trade Slowdown: A New Normal?' (CEPR and EUI, 2015) and *The World Trade Organization: Law, Economics and Politics*, with Petros Mavroidis (Routledge, 2016).

Nils Hoffmann is a PhD candidate at the Department of Political Science of the Johannes Gutenberg University Mainz, Germany. His dissertation project focuses on EU performance and effectiveness in the European Neighbourhood Policy.

Adrian Hyde-Price is Professor of International Politics in the Department of Political Science at Gothenburg University, Sweden. He has previously held a number of academic posts at universities in the UK, including Bath, Leicester, Birmingham, Southampton and Manchester. He is the Lead European Editor for the European Journal of International Security, and convenes the research seminar programme for the Centre for European Research at Gothenburg University (CERGU). His research interests focus on European security, Germany's role in Europe, the EU as an international security actor and the NATO alliance. His main publications include research monographs on 'European Security in the Twenty-First Century: the Challenge of Multipolarity', 'Germany and European Order, and 'The International Politics of East Central Europe', and edited volumes on Theorising NATO, British Foreign Policy and the Anglican Church and Europe's New Security Challenges.

Elisabeth Johansson-Nogués is Associate Professor at the Institut Barcelona d'Estudis Internationals (IBEI) in Spain and a CIS Fellow at the London School of Economics and Political Science in the UK. She is a member of the Observatory of European Foreign Policy, Barcelona,

Spain. Her research interests include the EU's foreign policy, the EU's relations with Eastern Europe and the Arab world, international security, multilateralism and regionalism. Her publications have appeared in *Security Dialogue*, *International Affairs*, *Mediterranean Politics*, and elsewhere.

Åsne Kalland Aarstad (PhD) is Advisor at the Norwegian Agency for Quality Assurance in Education (NOKUT). She defended her PhD in political science at Aarhus University in 2016. She has published on private security, maritime security and EU foreign policy in journals such as *Mediterranean Politics*, *Cooperation and Conflict* and *Crime, Law and Social Change*. She is the co-editor of *The SAGE Handbook on European Foreign Policy* (SAGE, 2015).

Christian Kaunert is Full Professor of Politics and Academic Director of the Institute for European Studies at the Vrije Universiteit Brussels. He was previously Full Professor of International Politics and Jean Monnet Chair in EU Justice and Home Affairs (July 2013), as well as the Director of the European Institute for Security and Justice at the University of Dundee. Prior to that, he was Senior Lecturer at the University of Dundee, Marie Curie Senior Research Fellow at the European University Institute Florence and Senior Lecturer in EU Politics & International Relations, University of Salford. He was awarded a prestigious Jean Monnet Chair in EU Justice and Home Affairs Policy in July 2013, and received a prestigious Marie Curie Career Integration Grant (from 2012 to 2016), as well as a Marie Curie Intra-European Fellowship (2010–2012). He has also been the Editor of the *Journal of Contemporary European Research* (JCER), Executive Committee member of the University Association for Contemporary European Studies (UACES) and an Expert for the European Parliament. He is also on the editorial board of the journal *European Politics and Society* and the *Journal of European Integration* (JEI). Prof. Kaunert holds a PhD in International Politics and an MSc in European Politics from the University of Wales Aberystwyth, a BA (Hons) European Business from Dublin City University, ESB Reutlingen and a BA (Hons) Open University. Prof. Kaunert has researched and taught in many international departments, such as Aberystwyth (Wales), ULB Brussels (Belgium, 2004, UACES Research Fellow), Maastricht (Netherlands), Salford (England), EUI Florence (Marie Curie Fellowship), and been a guest professor in Barcelona (Spain), Turin (Italy), Yerevan (Armenia, at the UNDP mission), Cairo (Egypt), Medellin, Bogota and Cali (Colombia), and Jinan (China).

Anna Khakee is Senior Lecturer and Head of the Department of International Relations, University of Malta. Prior to joining the University of Malta, she worked as a Senior Researcher at the Graduate Institute of International and Development Studies in Geneva and for several years as a consultant to think tanks and international organisations, including the Norwegian Peacebuilding Centre, FRIDE, EuroMeSCo, The Policy Practice, Geneva Centre for the Democratic Control of Armed Forces (DCAF) and the United Nations Development Program (UNDP). She has been a guest lecturer at College of Europe, Natolin (Warsaw), DiploFoundation, University Institute of Lisbon, United Nations University for Peace, Geneva Centre for Security Policy, and Geneva School of Diplomacy and International Relations. Dr Khakee has published widely, including in international journals such as *Mediterranean Politics*, *Mediterranean Quarterly* and *East European Politics and Societies*.

Nicole Koenig is Research Fellow on EU foreign and security policy as well as institutional affairs at the Jacques Delors Institut – Berlin. She has worked with several universities and think tanks, including the University of Constance, King's College London, Edinburgh University, the Institute for International Affairs in Rome and the Trans European Policy Studies Association in Brussels. Koenig holds a PhD in Politics and International Relations from Edinburgh University and the University of Cologne. She has published one monograph entitled 'EU Security Policy and Crisis Management: A Quest for Coherence' (Routledge, 2016).

Elena Korosteleva is Professor of International Politics, and Jean Monnet Chair in European Politics, School of Politics and IR, University of Kent, Canterbury. She is co-founder and co-director of the Global Europe Centre at Kent, LSE Dahrendorf Professorial Fellow and was a Visiting Professor at the College of Europe, Natolin (Warsaw) and CIFE. Korosteleva's main research interests include EU foreign policies and EU relations with the eastern neighbourhood, democracy promotion and democratisation. Among her recent publications are 'The EU and Belarus: Democracy promotion by technocratic means?' *Democratization* 2015; *The EU and its Eastern Neighbours: Towards a More Ambitious Partnership* (Routledge, 2014 paperback); and *EU Policies in the Eastern Neighbourhood: The Practices Perspective* with M. Natorski and L. Simão (Routledge, 2014).

Hrant Kostanyan is Researcher at CEPS, a Senior Key Expert at the College of Europe, Natolin (Warsaw) and an Adjunct Professor at Vesalius College, Brussels. His research focuses on EU institutions and decision-making, primarily on the European External Action Service (EEAS), the European Neighbourhood Policy (ENP) and the EU's relations with eastern neighbours and Russia. He has published extensively on EU decision-making and external policies. Hrant Kostanyan has taught courses on politics of the European Union, EU decision-making and inter-institutional relations, as well as the EU's relations with the post-Soviet space in various Master and Bachelor programmes. Kostanyan has extensive experience in speaking at international conferences and giving guest lectures and training for bureaucrats, diplomats, and members of academia and civil society.

Petr Kratochvíl works as the Director of the Institute of International Relations in Prague, Czech Republic and as a lecturer at several universities. His research interests cover theory of international relations, European integration, the role of religion in world politics and Eastern Europe. He has published more than 120 monographs, edited volumes, book chapters and articles, among others, in the *Journal of Common Market Studies*, *Journal of International Relations and Development*, *Europe-Asia Studies* and the *Journal of Communist and Post-Communist Studies*.

Erwan Lannon is Professor at the University of Ghent. He also teaches at the Bruges and Natolin campus of the College of Europe. He specialises in the EU's external relations and international and strategic relations as well as in EU institutional and constitutional law. He is active in various expert networks and worked as a consultant to several EU institutions and international organisations. He was also Director of Studies at the College of Europe, Natolin (Warsaw), a senior researcher at the European Union Institute for Security Studies (EU-ISS), and head of office within the General Secretariat of the Council the EU.

Chantal Lavallée is Marie Curie Research Fellow at the Institute for European Studies (IES) of the Vrije Universiteit Brussel (VUB). Prior to joining the IES, she was a Postdoctoral Fellow at the Institute for Strategic Research at the École Militaire (IRSEM) in Paris. She obtained her PhD in Political Science from the Université du Québec à Montréal in 2010. With a distinctive scholarship from the Government of Québec, she was also a Postdoctoral Research Fellow at the European University Institute in Florence, Italy (2010–2012). Her work examines the internal and external challenges of the EU comprehensive approach to security with a particular focus on the role of the European Commission in relation to other actors, both in security-related policy-making in Brussels and in concrete action, mainly through the European Neighbourhood Policy in the Middle East, and EU operations in the Horn of Africa and the Sahel region. She has published her research in peer-reviewed journals such as *European Foreign Affairs Review*, *Perspectives on European Politics and Society*, *Journal of Contemporary European Research* and *Études Internationales*, and edited special issues in *Politique Européenne*, *Journal of Contemporary European Research* and *Les Champs de Mars*.

Sandra Lavenex is Professor of European and International Politics at the University of Geneva, Switzerland. Her research focuses on EU external relations, international democracy promotion and migration policy.

Bidzina Lebanidze is Lecturer in the Department of Political Science at the University of Freiburg (Germany). He was PhD Candidate at the Berlin Graduate School for Transnational Studies. He holds a Master's degree in international relations from Tbilisi State University and a Bachelor's degree from Ilia State University, Tbilisi. His research interests include democratisation and regime transition studies, international and transnational relations, EU external relations, post-Soviet states, Russian foreign policy and the Southern Caucasus. Previously, he worked for the Konrad-Adenauer-Foundation and lectured at Ilia State University, Tbilisi. He has recently published articles in journals such as *Security Studies* and *Southeast European and Black Sea Studies*.

Sarah Léonard is the Head of the Department of International Affairs and the Associate Dean for Research at Vesalius College, Vrije Universiteit Brussel (Belgium). She received her PhD in International Politics from the University of Wales, Aberystwyth. Prior to joining Vesalius College, she was a Lecturer in International Security at the University of Salford, a Marie Curie Research Fellow at Sciences Po Paris and a Senior Lecturer in Politics at the University of Dundee. Her research interests lie at the intersection between Security Studies and European Union Studies. She is particularly interested in securitisation theory and the development of the European Union's internal security policies, especially those relating to asylum, migration and borders, as well as counter-terrorism. Her research has been published in journals such as the *Journal of European Public Policy*, *Cooperation and Conflict*, *Intelligence and National Security* and *International Relations*.

Anna-Sophie Maass is Post-doctoral Research Fellow in the European Neighbourhood Policy Chair at the College of Europe, Natolin (Warsaw). Prior to working at the College of Europe Natolin, she graduated with a PhD in Politics and International Relations from La Trobe University in Melbourne. Her thesis examined the reasons for the transformation of EU–Russia relations from courtship to confrontation between 1999 and 2008. Her research interest in the EU's external relations with Russia was shaped during her Bachelor and Master's degrees in European Studies at Maastricht University and at the Institut d'Etudes Politiques in Rennes. Her current research focuses on the Eastern dimension of the ENP, especially on the EU's foreign policy towards Georgia, Armenia and Ukraine. Her monograph 'EU–Russia Relations, 1999–2015. From Courtship to Confrontation' has been published in Routledge's series on Contemporary Russia and Eastern Europe, in 2017.

Andreas Marchetti is Senior Fellow at the Center for European Integration Studies (ZEI) at the University of Bonn (Germany). He is also founder and director of politglott GmbH.

Contributors

Andreas Marchetti is a graduate in political science of the University of Toulouse (Maîtrise) and the University of Bonn (MA, PhD). He previously worked as a research fellow at ZEI and as a project manager at Stiftung Mercator.

Alister Miskimmon is Professor of International Relations and Head of the School of History, Anthropology, Philosophy and Politics at Queen's University, Belfast. He works on strategic narratives, German foreign policy and European security. He is part of an EU-funded Jean Monnet Network (2015–2018) conducting research on EU crisis narratives in Ukraine and Israel/Palestine. Miskimmon's other current project is on British and Polish defense policy after the 2016 NATO summit in Warsaw, funded by the Noble Foundation. Alister Miskimmon, Ben O'Loughlin and Laura Roselle have published two books on strategic narratives, *Strategic Narratives: Communication Power and the New World Order* (New York: Routledge, 2013) and *Forging the World: Strategic Narratives and International Relations* (Ann Arbor: University of Michigan Press, 2017).

Patrick Müller is Research Fellow at the Faculty for Social Science at the University of the Basque Country/Ikerbasque Foundation for Science. His research interests include the European external relations, Mediterranean Politics and the Arab–Israeli conflict. He has published widely on these subjects including in journals such as the *Journal of European Public Policy*, the *Journal of Common Market Studies* and *Mediterranean Politics*, as well as with major international presses.

Arne Niemann is Professor of International Politics and Deputy Director of the Jean Monnet Centre of Excellence 'Europe in Global Dialogue' at the Department of Political Science of the Johannes Gutenberg University Mainz, Germany. His research focuses on European Union politics and policies, with a particular focus on the EU's external dimension.

Cristian Nitoiu is Lecturer in Politics and International Relations at Aston University. He was a Post-doctoral Fellow in EU–Russia relations and Ukraine at LSE IDEAS. He is an expert on EU and Russian foreign policy, EU–Russia relations, Eastern Europe, international relations, the European public sphere or international political communication. Before coming to Aston University and the LSE, he held research positions at Trinity College Dublin and the College of Europe, Natolin campus.

Gergana Noutcheva is Assistant Professor in International Relations and European Foreign Policy at the Political Science Department of Maastricht University, The Netherlands. She holds a PhD in International Relations from the University of Pittsburgh, USA (2006). Her research focuses on the European Neighbourhood Policy and democratisation in the Balkans and the post-Soviet space. Her articles have appeared in the *Journal of Common Market Studies*, *Journal of European Public Policy*, *West European Politics*, *East European Politics and Societies* and *Journal of European Integration*.

Jan Orbie is the Director of the Centre for EU Studies and a Professor at the Department of Political Science at Ghent University. He was a visiting scholar at Utrecht University (the Netherlands) and the ISCTE (Portugal), guest professor at Sichuan University (China) and at the University of Canterbury (New Zealand). His primary research focus is on the European Union's external relations, specifically the trade, development, social, democracy and human rights promotion dimensions. He has (co-)edited books on EU trade and development politics

(2007 and 2009), European external policies (2008) and Europe's global social policies (2008), and special issues of the *European Foreign Affairs Review* (2009 and 2011), *Res Publica* (2008), *Journal of Contemporary European Research* (2013), *Contemporary Politics* (2014), *Cambridge Review of International Affairs* (2015) and *European Politics and Society* (2016).

Michelle Pace is Professor with Special Responsibilities in EU–MENA relations at the Department of Social Sciences and Business, Roskilde University, Denmark. She is also Honorary Professor at The University of Birmingham, UK, Academic Fellow at the European Policy Centre (EPC, in Brussels) and co-editor of the peer reviewed journal *Mediterranean Politics*. She has published widely on EU–Mediterranean relations and acted as Principal Investigator on two large research projects funded by the British Academy and the Economic and Social Research Council on a '"Modern" Islamist Democracy? Perceptions of democratization in the Arab-Mediterranean world' and on 'Paradoxes and Contradictions in EU democracy promotion efforts in the Middle East', respectively. She was also Principal Investigator of two other projects: one funded by the Carlsberg foundation on 'The Struggle of State-Building in Palestine: Exploring "State-less"-Society Relations in the West Bank' (until late 2016) and the other funded by the Danish Arab Partnership Programme (DAPP) on 'Change in exile: re-invigorating principles of reform and social stability among young Syrian refugees in Denmark and Lebanon' (until July 2017).

Sharon Pardo (PhD, Ghent University, Faculty of Political and Social Studies) is a Jean Monnet Chair ad personam in European studies and the Chairperson of the Department of Politics and Government at Ben-Gurion University of the Negev (BGU). Pardo is also the Chair of the National Jean Monnet Centre of Excellence – the Centre for the Study of European Politics and Society (CSEPS), at BGU.

Florent Parmentier (PhD) is Research Associate at the Chair of Geopolitics of Ecole des Hautes Etudes Commerciales (HEC) and a lecturer at Sciences Po. He is the co-founder of eurasiaprospective.net with Cyrille Bret.

Roman Petrov holds an LL.M in EU Law (Durham University, UK, 1998), a PhD in Law (National Academy of Science of Ukraine, 2000), a PhD in Law (Queen Mary, University of London, UK, 2005) and a habilitation in Law (Law Institute at the Parliament of Ukraine, 2014). He conducted post-doctoral research as Max Weber Fellow at the European University Institute (Italy, 2006–2008) and had visiting research fellowships at the University of Heidelberg (Germany), the University of Oxford (UK), the University of Augsburg (Germany) and Ghent University (Belgium). Petrov is founder and first elected President of the Ukrainian European Studies Association. Currently Petrov is Jean Monnet Chair in EU Law and Head of the Jean Monnet Centre of Excellence at the National University 'Kyiv-Mohyla Academy' in Ukraine. Areas of Petrov's research and teaching include: EU Law, EU External Relations Law; Approximation and Harmonisation of Legislation in the EU; Rights of Third Country Nationals in the EU; and Legal Aspects of Regional Integration in the Post-Soviet Area.

Clara Portela is Assistant Professor of Political Science at Singapore Management University. She holds a PhD from the European University Institute in Florence and an MA from the Free University of Berlin. She is the author of the monograph 'European Union Sanctions and Foreign Policy' (Routledge, 2010), for which she received the 2011 THESEUS Award for Promising Research on European Integration. Her research interests include international sanctions, nuclear non-proliferation and EU–ASEAN relations. She has prepared reports for the European Parliament's Committee on Foreign Affairs (2011 and 2013) and Sub-committee on Human Rights (2007) and participated in consultative policy processes convened by the United Nations, the European Union and the Asia-Europe Meeting. Portela was a Visiting Professor at the College of Europe, Natolin (Warsaw), a Guest Professor at the University of Innsbruck, and has held visiting positions with Carleton University (Canada), the Institut d'Etudes Politiques de Grenoble (France) and Monash University (Australia), among others.

Iulian Romanyshyn teaches European Studies at Maastricht University and is also a PhD researcher at IMT Institute for Advanced Studies Lucca. In the past, Iulian was a visiting researcher at the European University Institute in Florence and the Institute for European Studies at Vrije Universiteit Brussels. In his doctoral research, Iulian studies EU effectiveness in multilateral security negotiations in the areas of arms trade, nuclear non-proliferation and space security. His broader research interests include the EU's relations with eastern neighbours, Russia and EU Arctic policy. His research has been published among others in the *Journal for Common Market Studies* and *International Journal*.

Frank Schimmelfennig is Professor of European Politics at ETH Zurich and member of the Center for Comparative and International Studies. He has published widely on the theory of European integration, EU enlargement, differentiated integration, EU democracy promotion and the Euro crisis. His most recent books are *Democracy Promotion by Functional Cooperation. The European Union and its Neighbourhood*, with Tina Freyburg, Sandra Lavenex, Tatiana Skripka and Anne Wetzel (Palgrave Macmillan, 2015) and *Differentiated Integration. Explaining Variation in the European Union*, with Dirk Leuffen and Berthold Rittberger (Palgrave Macmillan, 2013).

Tobias Schumacher is the Chairholder of the European Neighbourhood Policy Chair at the College of Europe, Natolin (Warsaw). He is also Associate Senior Research Fellow at the Centre for International Studies (CEI-IUL) at the University Institute of Lisbon. He was a John F. Kennedy Memorial Fellow at the Minda de Gunzburg Center for European Studies at Harvard University and a Visiting Professor at Ilia State University, Tbilisi. His work has been published in journals such as *Democratization, Mediterranean Politics, European Security, Global Affairs, German Journal for Politics, Economics and Culture of the Middle East, European Foreign Affairs Review, International Spectator, Insight Turkey* and others. He is the profiles editor of the peer-reviewed journal, *Mediterranean Politics*, a member of the editorial board of *Insight Turkey* and a member of the international advisory board of the *Cambridge Journal of Eurasian Studies*. His most recent co-edited book (with Dimitris Bouris) is titled *The Revised European Neighbourhood Policy. Continuity and Change in EU Foreign Policy* (Palgrave, 2017).

Peter Seeberg is Associate Professor at the Centre for Contemporary Middle East Studies, University of Southern Denmark and Director of the DJUCO-project, an academic cooperation project in Amman, Jordan, funded by the Danish Ministry of Foreign Affairs (www.djuco.org). Seeberg has published widely on the relations between EU and the Middle East, migration and security, and political conflicts related to the Mediterranean region. His most recent books are *The Levant in Turmoil. Syria, Palestine, and the Transformation of Middle Eastern Politics*, with Martin Beck and Dietrich Jung (New York: Palgrave, 2016); *Migration, Security, and Citizenship in the Middle East. New Perspectives*, with Zaid Eyadat (New York; Palgrave, 2014). His articles have appeared, among others, in *British Journal of Middle Eastern Studies, Democracy and Security*,

Democratization, *European Foreign Affairs Review*, *Mediterranean Politics*, *Middle East Critique* and *Middle East Policy*.

Natalia Shapovalova is researcher interested in EU foreign policy, civil society, democracy and human rights. She has a PhD in Politics and International Studies from the University of Warwick. In 2009–2015, she worked for FRIDE, a European think-tank based in Madrid and Brussels, analysing the EU's policies towards the eastern neighbourhood.

Licínia Simão is a Researcher at the Centre for Social Studies and Lecturer in International Relations at the University of Coimbra. She is currently the national coordinator of the CASPIAN Marie Curie Innovative Training Network. Her research interests include foreign policy analysis, security studies and EU relations with the post-Soviet space. Relevant publications include edited volumes on *Security in Shared Neighbourhoods: Foreign Policy of Russia Turkey, and the EU* with R. Piet (Palgrave Macmillan, 2017), and *The European Neighbourhood Policy in the Eastern Region: The Practices Perspective*, with E. Korosteleva and M. Natorski (Routledge, 2014), as well as several academic articles in leading peer reviewed journals, and book chapters.

Eduard Soler i Lecha is a Senior Research Fellow at the Barcelona Centre for International Affairs (CIDOB) and Lecturer on international relations at Ramon Llull-Blanquerna University and the Institut Barcelona d'Estudis Internacionals (IBEI). He is the scientific coordinator of MENARA (www.menarproject.eu), a H2020 research project on the emerging regional order in the Middle East and North Africa, and the Team Leader of El-Hiwar, a training project implemented by the College of Europe on Euro-Arab diplomacy. His main areas of expertise are geopolitics in the MENA region, Turkey and European policies towards the southern neighbourhood. He has published extensively in academic journals such as *Mediterranean Politics* and the *International Spectator* as well as in policy-oriented ones such as *Política Exterior*, *Insight Turkey* or *Foreign Affairs* (Spanish edition).

Florian Trauner is Research Professor at the Institute for European Studies and the Department of Political Science of the Vrije Universiteit Brussels. He is also Visiting Professor at the College of Europe, Natolin (Warsaw), where he teaches on immigration, asylum and border management in the EU. His research interests concern the field of European integration, in particular EU justice and home affairs (migration, asylum, Schengen, return policies and counter-terrorism), fundamental rights and rule of law promotion and EU–Western Balkans relations. Among his recent publications are *Policy Change in the Area of Freedom, Security and Justice: How EU Institutions Matter*, with Ariadna Ripoll Servent (Routledge, 2015) and 'Asylum Policy: the EU's "crises" and the looming policy regime failure', *Journal of European Integration*.

Elsa Tulmets is Associated Researcher at the Institute of International Relations in Prague, where she was a Research Fellow from 2006 to 2011, and research fellow at the French-German Centre Marc Bloch. In 2016, she was also project leader at the French-German-Polish Foundation of Genshagen. From 2012 to 2015, she was Marie Curie Fellow at CERI/Sciences Po Paris (project EUTRANSGOV), and in 2005–2006 a Jean Monnet Fellow at the European University Institute in Florence. She holds a PhD in Political Science and International Relations from Sciences Po Paris and Free University Berlin. She has taught EU external relations and European Neighbourhood Policy, *inter alia*, in Paris, Berlin, Prague and Bruges. Her publications include *East Central European Foreign Policy in Perspective: Back to Europe and the EU's Neighbourhood* (Palgrave Macmillan, 2014); the special issue 'Identity and Solidarity in Foreign

Policy: Investigating East Central European Relations with the Eastern Neighbourhood', *Perspectives* 19(2), 2011; *Rationalism and Constructivism in EU External Relations: The Case of the European Neighbourhood Policy*, with P. Kratochvíl (Nomos, 2010).

Bruno Vandecasteele is a trainee diplomat at the Belgian Foreign service. Between 2011 and 2016 he worked at Ghent University's Centre for EU Studies. He holds a doctoral degree in political science with a grant of the Research Foundation Flanders (FWO). He has teaching and research experience on decision-making in the EU, EU–Eastern Partnership relations, EU external policy, theory of European integration and transport policy in the EU.

Peter Van Elsuwege is Professor in EU law at Ghent University and co-director of the Ghent European Law Institute (GELI). He is an affiliated member of the Centre for the Law of EU External Relations (CLEER) at the Asser Institute (The Hague) and the Centre for Russian International, Socio-Political and Economic Studies (CERISE) at Ghent University. He has been Visiting Professor at the University of Tartu (Estonia), the College of Europe (Natolin campus, Warsaw) and the Moscow State University for International Relations (MGIMO). His research activities focus on the law of EU external relations. Specific attention is devoted to the legal framework of the relations between the European Union and its East European neighbours.

Benedetta Voltolini is Marie Skłodowska-Curie Research Fellow at the Centre d'études européennes, Sciences Po Paris. She holds a PhD in International Relations from the London School of Economics and Political Science. Before joining Sciences Po in September 2015, she was Lecturer in International Relations at Maastricht University, The Netherlands. Her research interests include EU external policies towards the southern neighbourhood, especially the Arab–Israeli conflict, lobbying in EU foreign policy, and processes of framing and knowledge construction.

Bernd Weber is Research Associate at the Centre de Recherches Internationales (CERI) at Sciences Po Paris. He holds a Doctoral Degree in Political Science/International Relations from Sciences Po Paris and a MA Degree in Political Science, Economic Geography and European Cultural Anthropology from Ludwigs-Maximilians University in Munich. Previously, he was Doctoral Fellow of the Oxford-Sciences Po Research Group (OXPO) at the Department of Politics and International Relations at the University of Oxford and an Associated Researcher at the Fundação Getúlio Vargas in São Paulo. His research interests include EU energy policy, energy security, European foreign policy analysis and European Neighbourhood Policy.

Kataryna Wolczuk is Professor of East European Politics at the Centre for Russian, European and Eurasian Studies, the University of Birmingham and Associate Fellow at Chatham House (Royal Institute for International Affairs), London.

Sarah Wolff is Lecturer in Public Policy at Queen Mary, University of London and Senior Associate Research Fellow at The Netherlands Institute for International Relations. She is an expert on EU public policies, Justice and Home Affairs (JHA), migration and border management policies, as well as EU–Arab Mediterranean relations. Her monograph 'The Mediterranean Dimension of the European Union's Internal Security' (Palgrave, 2012) builds upon fieldwork in Europe, Morocco, Egypt and Jordan. She received the LISBOAN Research Award 2012 for her book *Freedom, Security and Justice after Lisbon and Stockholm*, which she co-edited (Asser,

2012). In 2014–2015 she was a Fulbright-Schuman fellow at the Transatlantic Academy (Washington, DC) where she investigated the role of religion in Transatlantic Foreign policy. She was also awarded a 2014–2015 Leverhulme Research grant for research on EU Engagement with Islamist political parties in Morocco and Tunisia. Wolff holds a PhD in International Relations (LSE, 2009), an MSc in European Politics and Governance (LSE, 2004) and a BA in Public Administration (Science Po Grenoble, 1999).

Richard Youngs is Senior Associate in the Democracy and Rule of Law Program, based at Carnegie Europe. He works on EU foreign policy and on issues of international democracy. Youngs is also a Professor of international relations at the University of Warwick. Prior to joining Carnegie in July 2013, he was the director of the European think tank FRIDE. He has held positions in the UK Foreign and Commonwealth Office and as an EU Marie Curie fellow. He was a senior fellow at the Transatlantic Academy in Washington, DC, from 2012 to 2013. His latest books include *The Puzzle of Non-Western Democracy* (Carnegie, 2015); *The Uncertain Legacy of Crisis* (Carnegie, 2014); *Europe in the New Middle East* (Oxford University Press, 2014); and *Climate Change and European Security* (Routledge, 2014).

Jan Zielonka is Professor of European Politics at the University of Oxford and a Ralf Dahrendorf Professorial Fellow at St Antony's College. His previous appointments included posts at the University of Warsaw, Leiden and the European University Institute in Florence. He has published numerous works in the field of international relations, comparative politics and the history of political ideas. His current work analyses the politics of European integration and disintegration. His latest books are: *Is the EU doomed?* (Polity Press, 2014) and *Media and Politics in New Democracies. Europe in a Comparative Perspective* (Oxford University Press, 2015).

FOREWORD

Johannes Hahn, EU Commissioner for European Neighbourhood Policy and Enlargement Negotiations

To keep our policies relevant, we constantly need to challenge and develop our policy-making. Academic reflection such as in this book, which provides an excellent overview and in-depth analysis of the European Neighbourhood Policy (ENP), is a valuable tool towards this end. Such reflections were also key to the ENP Review consultation process held in 2015 and helped shape the revised policy.

The ENP was reviewed in 2015 in order to address more effectively the challenges in the neighbourhood; to better answer citizens' concerns and to better serve the interests of the European Union (EU) and of its partner countries. This reviewed policy provides the EU with the necessary tools to reach out to partner countries on key issues such as good governance, rule of law, democracy and human rights; economic development (including trade, employment, transport and connectivity, energy security and climate action); security; and migration and mobility. Above all, the EU's interest is the stabilisation of its wider neighbourhood (in political, socio-economic and security-related terms) including by addressing the root causes of the crisis and conflicts. This will also work towards the goals of the EU Global Strategy, which devotes a specific chapter on how to further state and societal resilience in the EU's broader neighbourhood.

Security is one of the key issues that came out as a priority from the ENP review. Conflicts in our wider neighbourhood have a strong impact on the EU. This means we should redouble our efforts to counter terrorist threats, prevent radicalisation, disrupt organised crime, fight cybercrime and ensure effective border management. Given the specific security challenges the region is facing, strong effort is being put into security sector reform and into working with Member States on helping to develop effective and transparent institutions in partner countries.

The EU's work on migration and mobility also aims to answer the expectations of our citizens, who rightly demand that their freedom and safety be protected. With the European Agenda on Migration, the EU aims not just to work with partner countries to support them and help them tackle the challenges of migration but also to protect freedom of movement within the EU, a huge privilege, which must not be taken for granted. At the same time we offer protection to refugees and address humanitarian needs in line with our international obligations and European values, by also using the Syria Trust Fund, Turkey Facility and the Trust Fund for Africa. The EU and its Member States are the biggest donors to the humanitarian effort to tackle the consequences of the Syrian crisis and to strengthen the resilience of surrounding countries in the region.

Good governance, rule of law, democracy and human rights remain a priority of the EU and continue to form an essential part of our political dialogue with partners, as a way to strengthen state and societal resilience and prosperity. Engagement with civil society is a fundamental element of our political dialogue and EU external assistance, because stronger civil society and institutions, as well as economic growth and job creation, are fundamental for societal and state resilience and efforts to address the root causes of conflict, fragility, instability and irregular migration.

Economic development is at the heart of our efforts for stabilisation and resilience. This includes work on economic governance, improving the business environment (including property rights, dispute mechanisms and commercial courts, which aid stability and promote growth) and job creation, especially for youth. Measures such as these will encourage trade and investment, both domestic and foreign, and stronger economic integration with the EU. In this context, the EU also makes efforts to facilitate energy connectivity and transport between the EU and ENP partners.

The EU's enhanced coordination of measures and tools cannot replace the need for policy dialogue and political will of the partner countries. Achieving resilience will always be the result of a political work of the partner countries – at both a state and societal level – rather than a matter of EU resource allocation alone, and it cannot be induced from the outside. The EU can only assist those countries willing to implement relevant resilience-enhancing policies.

Ultimately, the ENP will only succeed if the EU implements a pragmatic, tailor-made approach, which focuses on the essentials and ensures delivery on issues vital to citizens, such as liberty, security and mobility.

PREFACE

This handbook, the first of its kind on the European Union's (EU's) European Neighbourhood Policy (ENP), is an outgrowth from our years-long academic preoccupation with the EU's dynamic and multifaceted relations with its neighbours in Eastern Europe and the South Caucasus, and the Maghreb and Mashreq. Since the ENP was launched in 2003–2004, it has sparked an enormous scholarly interest, as exemplified by a rich and ever growing body of literature, and nowadays can be considered one of the most popular areas of research in the broad fields of EU external relations and EU foreign policy analysis. This is also reflected by the many courses and academic events that revolve around the analysis of ENP-related matters and that are offered by universities and research centres across EU Member States and many of the 16 ENP countries.

In the context of our research, and particularly in the framework of the many courses, seminars and lectures that we have been giving throughout the years on the ENP and its eastern and southern neighbourhoods, we noticed that while the ENP had developed into a fully-fledged field of study, its nature and analytical delineations are complex and even contested. Moreover, it has become apparent that it has developed into a multidisciplinary research field that sits on the fence between European Studies and European foreign policy analysis, International Relations, Comparative Politics, EU external relations law and even Area Studies. At least in our view, these features make the scholarly engagement with the ENP truly intriguing and fascinating. However, they are also responsible for the absence of comprehensive scholarly publications that engage with the study of the ENP holistically. In other words, accounts that simultaneously offer different conceptual and theoretical interpretations, capture the ENP's many policy dimensions and also discuss the EU's neighbourhoods as such, and how they feed into the actual shaping, making and implementation of the ENP, are still missing. This handbook aims at addressing these gaps as it is intended to serve as a single source of information that brings together 68 contributors with multiple academic backgrounds, areas of expertise and perspectives. It reaches out to a broad readership, ranging from students and scholars, to practitioners, journalists, civil society activists, and the interested public by and large. In particular, at a time when societies in most EU Member States display little appetite for potentially costly foreign policy initiatives and when the EU's neighbourhood is increasingly considered to be a 'ring of fire', we sincerely hope that this handbook will also tackle existing misconceptions and contribute to a more comprehensive understanding of the ENP and the 16 countries it reaches out to.

Preface

This book would not have been possible without the enthusiastic and strong commitment of its 68 contributors, none of whom hesitated to become part of this ambitious project when they were initially approached by us. We thank them sincerely – not only for their valuable contributions but also for their devotion and patience throughout the process of producing this book. We are also grateful to several colleagues who were willing to act as anonymous reviewers of the manuscript proposal and who read and re-read several chapters, even at short notice. Our gratitude goes also to Routledge, and in particular to Andrew Taylor and Sophie Iddamalgoda, for having been a source of enthusiasm, encouragement and professionalism. Dr Madalina Dobrescu deserves special mention for her tremendous help and feedback in crucial moments. We are truly indebted to Maja Olszewska, whose devoted and well spirited engagement with this project, and meticulous copy-editing have proved to be invaluable. Working with Maja is simply a great pleasure – she has become a trusted colleague and a dear friend. Lastly we would like to thank our families who had to put up with us reviewing or writing chapters or engaging in editorial discussions, when in fact we should have spent time with them.

We dedicate this handbook to our current and future students, hoping that they find it enriching and useful and a source of inspiration for further research into what is a truly captivating and ever evolving field of study.

Tobias Schumacher, Andreas Marchetti, Thomas Demmelhuber
Natolin, Bonn, Erlangen

Introduction

1
THE EUROPEAN NEIGHBOURHOOD POLICY

The challenge of demarcating a complex and contested field of study

Tobias Schumacher

Since the European Neighbourhood Policy (ENP) was launched in 2004 it has become one of the most popular fields of study among scholars dealing with European Union (EU) external relations and European foreign policy analysis. This is because, over the past 15 years, the ENP has become the EU's most important and wide-ranging foreign policy instrument. At the same time, being an umbrella framework and thus, as was pointed out elsewhere, 'a roof over an expanding system of functional regional integration that moves at different speeds and with different dynamics in different policy fields' (Lavenex 2008: 939), the ENP's complexity and contested nature explains why it has become a fluid object of study (Manners, 2012). Initially developed as a substitute for enlargement, aimed at providing countries at the EU's external borders, without an accession perspective, with deeper political and economic relations, the ENP features a unique combination of characteristics that are at the heart of multiple and diverse research agendas. The ENP, both as a practice and as a field of study, addresses a highly heterogeneous group of countries – Armenia, Azerbaijan, Belarus, Georgia, Moldova and Ukraine in the EU's eastern neighbourhood, and Algeria, Egypt, Israel, Jordan, Lebanon, Libya, Morocco, Palestine, Syria and Tunisia in the southern neighbourhood – that differ considerably in terms of their political, economic, social and historical development, and legacies. What is more, by subsuming a vast array of policy fields and sectors, it represents a framework of cooperation that sits on the fence between the EU's internal and external dimension and transcends the intergovernmentalism–supranationalism divide. Also, by seeking to transpose EU norms, values, rules and regulations, the ENP became an expression of, and test case for, the EU's ambition to develop further its actorness and to establish itself as a power.

Ever since the European Commission adopted its 'Wider Europe' strategy on 11 March 2003 (Commission of the European Communities 2003), the EU gradually intensified the institutionalization of relations with its 16 neighbours and created a cooperation architecture which, drawing on key mechanisms such as differentiated bilateralism, conditionality and socialization (Delcour and Soler i Lecha, this volume), culminated in the establishment of the ENP's two sub-regional components, the Union for the Mediterranean (UfM) (Bicchi and Gillespie 2012) and the Eastern Partnership (EaP) initiative (Korosteleva 2011) in 2008 and

2009. Subsequently, the EU deepened its relations with eastern neighbours, by concluding third-generation Association Agreements (AAs) with Georgia, Moldova and Ukraine in 2014 (Van Elsuwege and Van der Loo 2017; Van Elsuwege and Petrov, Wolczuk, Simão and Parmentier, all in this volume). Over the years, the ENP has been implemented through the adoption of country strategy papers, national indicative programmes and annual progress reports – in conjunction with the establishment of new financial instruments and mechanisms – the conclusion of bilaterally negotiated action plans, and, most recently, single support frameworks and association agendas. The evolution of these tools and mechanisms reflected the gradual expansion of the ENP's scope and the EU's growing ambition to transpose (parts of) its *acquis communautaire*, and to engage itself not just in crisis management and conflict prevention, as was initially envisaged by the Wider Europe strategy (Commission 2003: 9), but also in the resolution of protracted conflicts in the neighbourhood (Bouris and Schumacher 2017). The ENP's overarching and rather ambitious objective of contributing to the 'strengthening of stability, security, and well-being' of the neighbours (Commission of the European Communities 2004: 3) was best captured by Commission President Romano Prodi's – somewhat premature – pledge to offer the neighbours 'everything but institutions' (Prodi 2002) and 'a stake' in the EU's internal market (ibid.).

This rhetoric demonstrates the existence and influence of powerful path dependencies in the evolution of the ENP, as it draws considerably on the EU's enlargement policy and its inbuilt 'Europeanisation beyond Europe' (Schimmelfennig 2012a) logic. This was explicitly acknowledged in the Wider Europe strategy which stated that enlargement 'gives new impetus to the effort of drawing closer to the 385 million inhabitants of the countries who will find themselves on the [EU's] external land and sea border' and 'that the Union should take the opportunity offered by enlargement to enhance relations with its neighbours on the basis of shared values' (Commission of the European Communities 2003: 3–4). It was reiterated even more concretely in the 2004 European Neighbourhood Policy Strategy Paper, which postulated that relations with the neighbours 'will be drawing on the experience gained in supporting the process of political and economic transition, as well as economic development and modernization in the new Member States and candidate countries' (Commission of the European Communities 2004: 6). Throughout the course of time, these initial references to the EU's enlargement policy gradually disappeared from intra-EU discourses, increasing the visibility of the ENP's status as a hybrid policy framework that is rooted in enlargement logics and even practices, but *de facto* falls short of providing recipients of EU action with a membership perspective. Thus, as Schimmelfennig has pointed out, it is not surprising that the 'goals and contents of Europeanization beyond Europe [. . .] are of a more general character' (Schimmelfennig 2012a: 22) – and continue to be so – compared to Europeanization in candidate countries for EU membership.

Seen from this perspective, it can even be argued that the adoption of the 'new' ENP on 18 November 2015 and the abolition of some of the ENP's principal, enlargement-related tools, in conjunction with the downgrading of the EU's ambition to engage in the promotion of democracy, good governance, the rule of law and human rights in its neighbourhood, was a logical consequence (Delcour 2015). While this came in response to developments in a neighbourhood that is nowadays widely and narrowly perceived as a 'ring of fire' (*The Economist* 2014), it is clearly rooted in the EU's inconsistent use of positive conditionality and socialization through transgovernmental cooperation, its failure to empower civil society and other potential agents of change in the neighbourhood, as well as the EU's inability – or rather unwillingness – to offer attractive and effective substitutes for political accession conditionality (Schimmelfennig 2012a: 22; Schimmelfennig 2012b; Sasse 2008; Freyburg 2011; Baracani 2009; Bicchi 2010).

Nonetheless, and despite these recent changes, the overview of the ENP's core features above alludes to the increased relevance the policy has obtained in political and scholarly terms. Thus, at least nine observations stand out as reflecting the political debate and shaping the epistemological interest surrounding the ENP.

First, though the ENP has been exposed to considerable critique, it has shown remarkable resilience and continues to be at the centre of the EU's evolving foreign and security policy framework. On one hand, this is due to institutional path dependencies and the agency of powerful stakeholders at different levels of EU governance who succeeded in hedging their ENP-related interests through the instrumentalization, and thus preservation of existing structures and policy objectives. On the other hand, the emergence of an increasingly self-assertive Russia in the 'shared neighbourhood' (Averre 2009; Gower and Timmins 2013; Simão and Piet 2016), exhibiting features of a 'cross-conditionality' provider (Hagemann 2013), which does not hesitate to resort to violent means in the event of neighbours' non-compliance, has proved to function as a reinforcement mechanism of sorts that keeps providing the ENP – unintentionally rather than deliberately – with an important sense of meaning and thus considerable external legitimacy.

Second, since the adoption of the Wider Europe communication, the ENP's positioning in the EU's multi-level governance system, and its corresponding policy portfolio, has been systematically upgraded. This became apparent for the first time in 2004 in the framework of the Barroso I Commission which created a new Directorate General (DG), entitled External Relations and European Neighbourhood Policy, and was further accentuated in 2009 under the Barroso II Commission with the merger of the Enlargement and the ENP portfolio, thus providing the ENP with the same intra-institutional relevance as, for instance, development and humanitarian aid. Nonetheless, it was the entering into force of the Lisbon Treaty (TEU), and with it the 'constitutionalisation' (Hanf 2011: 7) of the EU's relations with its neighbours in Article 8, that represented the most symbolic upgrade. Though this 'neighbourhood clause' (ibid.) has not yet served as a legal basis for the conclusion of 'specific agreements' (Article 8(2) TEU) with the neighbours (Van Elsuwege and Van der Loo 2017), it has underpinned the creation of the Directorate General for Neighbourhood and Enlargement Negotiations (DG NEAR), thus further underlining the salience of the ENP in the EU's multi-level governance system. To date DG NEAR is the only external relations-related DG in the European Commission whose geographical mandate is explicitly spelled out in its institutional designation. At the same time, neighbourhood-related issues have come to feature on the agenda of almost every Foreign Affairs Council meeting.

Third, throughout the course of time, the ENP has been subjected to processes of technocratization and de-politicization, which are marked by a growing tendency on the part of the EU to predominantly resort to, and thus rely on, technical means and instruments to address policy issues. Arguably, this has come most visibly to the fore in the context of Euro-Mediterranean relations and the creation of the UfM in 2008, which revolves exclusively around project-based cooperation in supposedly technical policy fields and issue areas, and it is further exemplified by the ENP's recent shift towards focusing mainly on sector-specific cooperation and the creation of Deep and Comprehensive Free Trade Areas (DCFTAs) (Pace 2010; Khalifa Isaac and Kares 2017; Morillas and Soler i Lecha 2017; Cebeci and Schumacher 2017; Van der Loo 2016). This development can be attributed to the European Commission's ever expanding role in the administration and operationalization of the ENP as well as the Commission's significant policy entrepreneurship, as evidenced, for example, by the elaboration of the Wider Europe communication and the 2015 ENP review process (Kelley 2006; Furness, this volume).

Fourth, despite the growing salience of neighbourhood-related matters, the attention dedicated by the EU to the eastern and southern neighbourhoods has differed considerably throughout the ENP's life span. The EU's selective, and sometimes rather narrow, focus on regional, sub-regional or local developments, in just one neighbourhood, can be explained by distinct perceptions of EU and EU Member States' interests and priorities. Examples in this regard are manifold, but the outbreak of the Arab uprisings in early 2011 contributing to the adoption of the 'New Response for a Changing Neighbourhood', and the wars in Syria, Eastern Ukraine and Libya, leading to the 2015 ENP review, clearly stand out (Sadiki 2015; Tömmel 2013). Moreover, the fact that some of the neighbours and sub-neighbourhoods did occasionally end up at the periphery of EU interests is also due to: a) the existence of intervening external variables such as the growing role of other competing external actors like Russia, China, Saudi Arabia, Qatar, the United Arab Emirates and Turkey; b) a lack of competencies on the part of the EU; c) EU Member States' proprietorial issue- and neighbour-specific attitudes or, conversely, Member States' disinterest in ENP-related policy entrepreneurship and/or action (Schumacher, 2017); and d) neighbours' reluctance to engage actively in the ENP. As far as the southern neighbourhood is concerned, the latter clearly applies to Algeria and Lebanon, both of which, for reasons related to regime survival strategies, historical legacies and path dependencies, have displayed rather uncooperative tendencies (Van Hüllen 2015). Similarly, in the eastern neighbourhood, Azerbaijan – at least until May 2015, when it proposed the conclusion of an EU-Azerbaijan Strategic Partnership on the sidelines of the Eastern Partnership Summit in Riga – had equally demonstrated its reluctance to go beyond energy- and visa-related cooperation. As a matter of fact, so has Belarus and, to a lesser extent, Armenia, which on 21 March 2017 initialled a Comprehensive and Enhanced Partnership Agreement with the EU after President Sargsyan, in September 2013, suddenly announced Armenia's withdrawal from the envisaged AA.

Fifth, the ENP is rooted in a rather artificial notion of neighbourhood, the constituting elements of which continue to be marked by enormous political, socio-economic, cultural and security-related differences rather than by commonalities that would justify their inclusion into one overarching policy framework. In fact, prior to the adoption of Wider Europe, the EU conducted its relations with southern and eastern neighbours separately and based on different legal frameworks – AAs vs Partnership and Cooperation Agreements (PCAs) – and instruments – MEDA vs TACIS. Furthermore, the ENP has extended to countries such as Jordan, Azerbaijan and Armenia that do not share with the EU either land or sea borders, while at the same time it has been reaching out to countries that even aspire to become EU members (Georgia, Moldova, Ukraine) or have explicitly applied for membership at some point in the distant past (Morocco). Obviously, the absence of clearly defined selection criteria has left current and potential future 'neighbours' in a state of limbo with regard to their 'Europeanness'. Also, it renders the idea of 'neighbourhood', as well as the increasingly popular notion of reaching out to the 'neighbours of the EU's neighbours' (Gstöhl and Lannon 2014), as questionable, and thus continues to leave open the geographical and geopolitical rationale of the ENP. While this has made the construction of a true Euro-neighbourhood space a rather fragile, if not even unrealistic and unsustainable endeavour, the EU's ambition to strive towards 'good neighbourliness', as stipulated in Article 8 TEU, has been contradicted by the EU itself due to the application of a rather self-centred, give-and-take approach.

Sixth, it is a noteworthy coincidence that the ENP emerged at the same time as the scholarly debate on what type of power the EU is gained new ground, following some initial attempts in the 1970s and 1980s that aimed at capturing the European Community's role in world politics (Dûchene 1972; Galtung 1973) and its 'actor capability' (Sjöstedt 1977). Manners's (2002) seminal article, 'Normative power Europe: a contradiction in terms?' undoubtedly contributed to a better understanding of the EU's actorness (Jupille and Caporaso 1998; Bretherton and Vogler 2006), its identity and its corresponding attempts to practise 'discursive representation' (Diez 2005). Yet, the subsequently produced and rather inflationary number of studies that seek to understand the power characteristics of the EU, the constitutive principles underlying its expanding network of external relations, and thus how the EU's putative nature translates into what it does in particular *vis-à-vis* its neighbourhoods (Barbé and Johansson-Nogués 2008; Davis Cross and Karolewski 2017), have not only been pursued mainly along a liberalism–realism binary, but have also perpetuated a deep-rooted assumption of the EU's 'hierarchical supremacy' (Natorski 2017: 166) in EU-neighbourhood relations. While this 'centrality-superiority linkage replicates the structure of the relations established during the process of accession to the EU' (ibid.), reinforcing the 'shadow of enlargement' (Gstöhl 2017: 8) template as well as notions of EU regional normative hegemony (Haukkala 2008; Haukkala 2017), it cemented a regrettable EU-centrism in the study of the ENP, which resulted in a scholarly treatment of the EU's neighbours as mere objects rather than as subjects that possess and display distinct agency.

Seventh, the study of the ENP has become an enormously popular and important sub-strand of European foreign policy analysis. Initially, it drew on the insights of the vast body of scholarship on Europeanization, which rather quickly inspired the emergence of concepts such as external governance (Lavenex 2004; Lavenex and Schimmelfennig 2011), revolving around its 'three basic institutional constellations' (Bicchi and Lavenex 2015: 870), notably networks, hierarchy and markets. External governance proved to be an innovative attempt at inquiring into 'how EU rules travel' (Lavenex 2014) beyond the Union's borders. Yet, like the literature on norms and rules diffusion and policy transfer (Börzel and Risse 2012a; Börzel and Risse 2012b), the institutionalist-inspired external governance literature has also been faced with the challenge to go beyond accounts that blackbox the actual process of rules and norms transposition. Throughout the years, laudable analytical differentiation has indeed occurred as the modes, mechanisms and scope conditions, and/or opportunity structures of external governance, have increasingly been factored in (Lavenex 2008; Freyburg et al. 2009; Freyburg et al. 2015). However, these scholarly achievements could not offer greater clarity and systematization with regards to both the influence of structure- and agency-related factors and thus the concrete ideational and behavioural input of the recipients of EU norms and rules transfer on the actual diffusion process itself.

Eighth, this lacuna is directly related to another key feature of the European foreign policy-inspired study of the ENP in so far as the burgeoning body of relevant literature follows, implicitly or explicitly, an inside-out perspective, resulting predominantly in an academic discourse that is overwhelmingly framed, influenced and (to some extent) even determined by western, that is, EU-European scholars, who keep resorting mainly to the same academic platforms and fora for the scholarly dissemination of their findings. While this phenomenon is due to structural constraints of the current publication model and research assessment in the mainstream social sciences and beyond, revolving around quantitative metrics and thus the reinforcement of artificial (and all too often unjustified) hierarchies of publication outlets, it is rather noteworthy for two reasons. To some extent it seems to suggest that the discursive resonance of the study of the ENP in the EU's neighbourhoods and sub-neighbourhoods is rather limited because many of the EU's neighbours do not, and possibly cannot, relate to the geographical imaginary of EU institutions and EU Member States' governments and subsequent policy practices (Kuus 2015). It also seems to indicate that, provided the study of the ENP as a sub-component of EU foreign policy does resonate in academic circles in the EU's neighbourhoods, there are considerable differences in what regard the importance and relevance that scholarly communities, from within EU Member States and the EU's neighbourhoods, attribute to western mainstream academic outlets, not least as a consequence of, for example, language barriers, academic socialization and exposure to different – or sometimes even opposing – research trends and practices.

Ninth, and lastly, it is remarkable to observe that despite the growing body of European Studies literature dealing with the external image of the EU, very few studies have emerged that address perceptions of governmental and non-governmental actors in the EU's neighbourhood of both the EU and the ENP (Pardo 2014; Bolkvadze 2014; Timmermann 2014; Pardo 2015). This merits pointing out, particularly since, as was stressed by Checkel and Katzenstein (2009), the EU, and thus its identity, is constructed not only from within, but also through its engagement and interactions with its external 'Others'. In fact, this important observation was preceded by studies that demonstrated that the EU's presence (Allen and Smith 1990) and actorness (Bretherton and Vogler 2006) in the international system and thus the EU's neighbourhood are dependent 'upon the expectations and constructions of other international actors' (ibid.: 5).

This handbook is primarily meant to provide as wide an interested readership as possible with a broad and yet detailed overview of the multifaceted dimensions of the ENP since it was launched. Thus, by providing predominantly western scholars, who have been influential in shaping the study of the ENP and setting its research agenda over the past 15 years, with a platform to synthesize their findings, this handbook clearly does not remedy the inherent EU-centrism in European foreign policy analysis and, by extension, in the study of the ENP (Keulers, Fonck and Keukeleire 2016). Yet, by acknowledging the existence of the phenomenon, and by gathering a substantial number of scholars from the EU's neighbourhoods, in conjunction with scholars who have taken part in an advisory capacity in the 2015 review process of the EU, this handbook serves as an attempt to initiate a debate, which will hopefully produce more neighbourhood-specific perspectives leading to enriching future studies on the EU's policies towards its neighbourhood.

Thus, the scope of this handbook is immense and brings together scholarly voices with eclectic – and sometimes even opposing – views and standpoints on the study of the ENP, thereby transcending uniform understandings and fixed interpretations of EU action (and inaction) and behaviour *vis-à-vis* the EU's 16 neighbours. Rather than adopting one overarching conceptual and methodological approach, the 68 authors who contributed to this handbook have chosen to adopt different research perspectives, and by bringing together European Studies and European foreign policy analysis, International Relations, Comparative Politics, EU external relations law and various strands in Area Studies, this handbook mirrors the multidisciplinarity that has marked the scholarly pre-occupation with the ENP. At the same time, the 46 chapters that this volume contains are by no means considered to offer an exhaustive coverage of all aspects of the ENP, let alone discuss holistically, local and regional political, economic and security trajectories of the ENP's 16 target countries that occurred due to, or despite, the ENP's presence and implementation. Instead, the handbook's seven parts are rooted in an understanding that the ENP and the EU's neighbourhood are fluid research phenomena characterized by continuities and discontinuities that require further investigation and hence new lines of inquiry. Drawing on the most salient debates in the study of the ENP, and building on the above mentioned nine observations, the handbook is structured in seven parts as follows.

Part I provides a comprehensive overview of the most widely used conceptual and theoretical approaches to the study of the ENP. Starting with a discussion of three core concepts, notably integration, governance and Europeanization and their respective application to the

ENP, it subsequently offers an examination of the EU's actorness in the framework of the ENP, as well as a discussion of the analytical challenge of scrutinizing the ENP's performance. This is followed by analyses that discuss contending role concepts and issues such as power and leadership and that offer (neo-)realist, constructivist and critical interpretations of the ENP. Subsequently, a systematic scrutiny of the existing body of ENP literature with regard to its methodological and theoretical foundations is pursued, destined to expose current research challenges and inform about potential pitfalls and limitations. Considering that the launch of the ENP and the introduction of a separate EU Treaty provision devoted explicitly to the EU's relations with neighbouring countries sparked a considerable debate among legal scholars working on EU external relations law, Part I goes beyond a mere social science-oriented focus by also featuring a discussion of legal perspectives on the study of the ENP.

Contributions in Part II are embedded in the academic discourse on Europe's political geographies and borders, geographical imaginations of European belonging and identity, and debates on the extent to which the ENP can be considered a boundary-drawing exercise. Part II offers an examination of the construction and deconstruction of 'neighbourhood' and thus the EU's own identity, discusses the EU's conception of boundaries and the effectiveness of the ENP's geostrategic orientation, and enquires into linkages between shifts in how the EU narrates its identity and its view of the neighbourhood and the world. Also, it brings together two analyses of the many challenges the ENP is faced with in its eastern and southern neighbourhood, thus taking issue with, among others, matters related to the lack of 'positive othering' (Korosteleva, this volume) as an important benchmark in conceptualizing the outside, and processes of regional re-configuration.

Themes in Part III are concerned with European Neighbourhood Policy-making and look at institutional dynamics, actors and financial instruments. This entails an examination of concepts such as coherence, cohesiveness and consistency in the context of the ENP, as well as an inquiry into the role and influence of the European Commission, EU Member States, the European External Action Service and the European Parliament in the shaping and making of ENP-related decisions. A critical overview and discussion of financial instruments developed and used in the framework of EU-neighbourhood relations follows.

Acknowledging the intensification of the EU's relations with its 16 neighbours since 2003–2004 and the ENP's self-imposed ambition to engage in the prevention, management and resolution of conflicts in its neighbourhood, Part IV examines the interplay between bilateralism and region-building, discusses the civilian missions that the EU has deployed in its neighbourhood as instruments of conflict resolution, and provides an introduction to the EU's use of restrictive measures in the neighbourhood as well as an assessment of the policy of sanctions and of its connection to the ENP. Moreover, it depicts the evolution of the EU's bilateral relations with every single ENP country and explores the EU's attempts to establish itself as a manager of protracted and ongoing conflicts in both the eastern and southern neighbourhoods.

Part V builds on the previous section by disentangling the EU's web of relations with its 16 neighbours and focuses on core themes of bilateral sector-specific cooperation, such as trade, energy, migration, counter-terrorism and development. The need to engage in a scholarly way with these sectors is a result of the entering into force of the Lisbon Treaty in December 2009 and the review of the ENP in 2011 and 2015, all of which allowed the ENP to broaden its scope.

Part VI focuses on the EU's promotion of values and norms in its neighbourhood. How can we conceive of EU democracy promotion in the EU's neighbourhood? How does the EU export its core norms and values, as enshrined in Article 3(5), 8 and 21 TEU, and the challenges which it has faced in the framework of the ENP? Does the EU's norms and values promotion differ from neighbour to neighbour, and if it does, what explanatory factors can be identified? Mirroring the growing salience of values and norms promotion in EU external relations since the mid-1990s, and the large body of scholarship that has been generated ever since, contributions address the EU's support of good governance, rule of law, human rights and civil society in the EU's eastern and southern neighbourhoods, and also offer alternative accounts of external democracy support more generally through functional cooperation, thus reflecting more recent research trends. These analyses are preceded by an examination of perceptions of governmental and civil society stakeholders from within the neighbourhood, and of EU institutions, as well as an inquiry into some of the mechanisms and tools that underpin the ENP's norms and values promotion.

The handbook closes with Part VII, which brings together transversal themes that are deemed to be of crucial importance for the future of EU external relations in general and the implementation and impact of the ENP in particular. Tracing elements of path dependence in the development of the European Security Strategy/EU Global Strategy (EUGS) (Council of the European Union 2003; Biscop and Andersson 2007; European Union 2016) and the ENP, it analyses the extent to which the EU's foreign and security policy strategy and the ENP have co-evolved into a coherent framework for guiding policy action and whether the EUGS will facilitate the EU's acquisition and use of operational capacities and also help bridge Member States' diverging foreign policy interests towards the neighbourhood. Part VII also contains an examination of the ENP's relationship with Islamist actors in the southern neighbourhood, proposing an alternative, more open-minded and inclusive approach by the EU, and ends with an inquiry into how policy and strategic frameworks designed by the EU for its neighbours and their neighbours could be better integrated, or at least linked with one another, with a view to develop transnational and cross-regional cooperation initiatives. Based on an analysis of the 2015 ENP review and the 2016 EUGS, it is, however, concluded that the EU missed an opportunity to develop a more consistent cross-regional approach as it failed to identify new or innovative instruments to address, in concrete terms, the many challenges posed by the neighbours of the EU's neighbours.

References

Allen, D. and Smith, M. (1990) 'Western Europe's presence in the contemporary international arena', *Review of International Affairs* 16(1): 19–37.

Averre, D. (2009) 'Competing rationalities: Russia, the EU and the "Shared Neighbourhood"', *Europe-Asia Studies* 61(10): 1689–1713.

Baracani, E. (2009) 'The European Neighbourhood Policy and Political Conditionality: Double Standards in EU Democracy Promotion?', in Balzacq, T. (ed.) *The External Dimension of EU Justice and Home Affairs: Governance, Neighbours, Security*, Houndmills, Basingstoke: Palgrave Macmillan, 133–153.

Barbé, E. and Johansson-Nogués, E. (2008) 'The EU as a "modest force for good": the European Neighbourhood Policy', *International Affairs* 84(1): 81–96.

Bicchi, F. (2010) 'The Impact of the ENP on EU-North Africa Relations: The Good, the Bad and the Ugly', in Whitman, R. and Wolff, S. (eds.) *The European Neighbourhood Policy in Perspective: Context, Implementation and Impact*, Houndmills, Basingstoke: Palgrave Macmillan, 206–222.

Bicchi, F. and Gillespie, R. (eds.) (2012) *The Union for the Mediterranean*, Oxon: Routledge.

Bicchi, F. and Lavenex, S. (2015) 'The European Neighbourhood: Between European Integration and International Relations', in Jorgensen, K., Kalland Aarstad, A., Drieskens, E., Laatikainen, K. and Tonra, B. (eds.) *The SAGE Handbook of European Foreign Policy*, Thousand Oaks: Sage, 868–884.

Biscop, S. and Andersson, J. (eds.) (2007) *The EU and the European Security Strategy: Forging a Global Europe*, Oxon: Routledge.

Bolkvadze, K. (2014) "I am Georgian and Therefore I am European": Comparing Elite and Public Perceptions of Europe in Georgia, 2003–2013', in Chaban, N. and Holland, M. (eds.) *Communicating Europe in Times of Crisis. External Perceptions of the European Union*, Houndmills, Basingstoke: Palgrave, Macmillan, 197–219.

Börzel, T. and Risse, T. (2012a) 'From Europeanisation to diffusion: introduction', *West European Politics* 35(1): 1–19.

Börzel, T. and Risse, T. (2012b) 'When Europeanisation meets diffusion: exploring new territory', *West European Politics* 35(1): 192–207.

Bouris, D. and Schumacher, T. (2017) 'The 2011 Revised European Neighbourhood Policy: Continuity and Change in EU Foreign Policy', in Bouris, D. and Schumacher, T. (eds.) *The Revised European Neighbourhood Policy: Continuity and Change in EU Foreign Policy*, Houndmills Basingstoke: Palgrave Macmillan, 1–34.

Bretherton, C. and Vogler, J. (2006) *The European Union as a Global Actor*, second edition, Oxon: Routledge.

Cebeci, M. and Schumacher, T. (2017) 'The EU's Constructions of the Mediterranean (2003–2017)', *MEDRESET Working Paper* 3, April, Rome.

Checkel, J. and Katzenstein, P. (2009) (eds.) *European Identity*, Cambridge, Cambridge University Press.

Commission of the European Communities (2003) '*Wider Europe – Neighbourhood: A New Framework for Relations with our Eastern and Southern Neighbours*', COM(2003) 104 Final, Brussels, 11 March.

Commission of the European Communities (2004) European Neighbourhood Policy – Strategy Paper, Communication from the European Commission, COM(2004) 373 Final, Brussels, 12 May.

Council of the European Union (2003) *A Secure Europe in a Better World*, Brussels, 12 December.

Davis Cross, M. and Karolewski, P. (2017) 'What type of power has the EU exercised in the Ukraine–Russia crisis? A framework of analysis', *Journal of Common Market Studies* 55(1): 3–19.

Delcour, L. (2015) 'The 2015 ENP Review: Beyond Stocktaking, the Need for a Political Strategy', *CEPOB*, 1.

Diez, T. (2005) 'Constructing the self and changing others: reconsidering "Normative Power Europe"', *Millennium: Journal of International Studies* 33(3): 613–636.

Dûchene, F. (1972) 'Europe Role in World Peace', in Mayne, R. (ed.) *Europe Tomorrow: Sixteen Europeans Look Ahead*, London: Fontana.

Dûchene, F. (1973) 'The European Community and the Uncertainties of Interdependence', in Kohlstamm, M. and Hager, W. (eds.) *A Nation Writ Large? Foreign Policy Problems Before the European Community*, Houndmills, Basingstoke: Macmillan, 1–21.

European Union. (2016) *Shared Vision, Common Action: A Stronger Europe. A Global Strategy for the European Union's Foreign and Security Policy*, June, Brussels.

Freyburg, T. (2011) 'Transgovernmental networks as catalysts for democratic change? EU functional cooperation with Arab authoritarian regimes and socialization of involved state officials into democratic governance', *Democratization* 18(4): 1001–1025.

Freyburg, T., Lavenex, S., Schimmelfennig, F., Skripka, T. and Wetzel, A. (2009) 'EU promotion of democratic governance in the neighbourhood', *Journal of European Public Policy* 16(6): 916–934.

Freyburg, T., Lavenex, S., Schimmelfennig, F., Skripka, T. and Wetzel, A. (2015) *Democracy Promotion by Functional Cooperation: The European Union and Its Neighbourhood*, Houndmills, Basingstoke: Palgrave Macmillan.

Galtung, J. (1973) *The European Community: A Superpower in the Making*, London: HarperCollins.

Gower, J. and Timmins, G. (eds.) (2013) *The European Union, Russia and the Shared Neighbourhood*, Oxon: Routledge.

Gstöhl, S. (2017) 'Theoretical Approaches to the European Neighbourhood Policy', in Gstöhl, S. and Schunz, S. (eds.) *Theorizing the European Neighbourhood Policy*, Oxon: Routledge, 3–22.

Gstöhl, S. and Lannon, E. (eds.) (2014) *The Neighbours of the European Union's Neighbours: Diplomatic and Geopolitical Dimensions beyond the European Neighbourhood Policy*, Abingdon: Ashgate.

Hagemann, C. (2013) 'External Governance on the Terms of the Partner? The EU, Russia and the Republic of Moldova in the European Neighbourhood Policy', *Journal of European Integration* 35(7): 767–783.

Hanf, D. (2011) 'The ENP in the Light of the new "neighbourhood clause" (Article 8 TEU)', College of Europe Research Paper in Law – Cahiers juridiques 2(2011)

Haukkala, H. (2008) 'The European Union as a regional normative hegemon: the case of European neighbourhood policy', *Europe-Asia Studies* 60(9): 1601–1622.

Haukkala, H. (2017) 'The EU's Regional Normative Hegemony Encounters Hard Realities: The Revised European Neighbourhood Policy and the Ring of Fire', in Schumacher, T. and Bouris, D. (eds.) *The Revised European Neighbourhood Policy: Continuity and Change in EU Foreign Policy*, Houndmills, Basingstoke: Palgrave Macmillan, 77–94.

Jupille, J. and Caporaso, J. (1998) 'States, Agency and Rules: The European Union in Global Environmental Politics', in Rhodes, C. (ed.) *The European Union in the World Community*, Boulder: Lynne Rienner, 213–229.

Kelley, J. (2006) 'New Wine in Old Wineskins: Promoting Political Reforms through the New European Neighbourhood Policy', *JCMS: Journal of Common Market Studies* 44(1): 29–55.

Keulers, F., Fonck, D. and Keukeleire, S. (2016) 'Beyond EU navel-gazing: taking stock of EU-centrism in the analysis of EU foreign policy', *Cooperation and Conflict* 51(3): 345–364.

Khalifa Isaac, S. and Esmat Kares, H. (2017) 'The European community framing of the Mediterranean (1970–1990)', *MEDRESET Working Paper* 1, April, Rome.

Korosteleva, E. (ed.) (2011) *Eastern Partnership. A New Opportunity for the Neighbours?* Oxon: Routledge.

Kuus, M. (2015) 'Crafting Europe for Its Neighbourhood: Practical Geopolitics in European Institutions', in Bachmann, V. and Müller, M. (eds.) *Perceptions of the EU in Eastern Europe and Sub-Saharan Africa: Looking from the Outside In*, Houndmills Basingstoke: Palgrave Macmillan, 34–49.

Lavenex, S. (2004) 'EU external governance in "wider Europe"', *Journal of European Public Policy* 11(4): 680–700.

Lavenex, S. (2008) 'A governance perspective on the European neighbourhood policy: integration beyond conditionality?', *Journal of European Public Policy* 15(6): 938–955.

Lavenex, S. (2014) 'The power of functionalist extension: how EU rules travel', *Journal of European Public Policy* 21(6): 885–903.

Lavenex, S. and Schimmelfennig, F. (2011) 'EU democracy promotion in the neighbourhood: from leverage to governance?', *Democratization* 18(4): 885–909.

Manners, I. (2002) 'Normative power Europe: a contradiction in terms?', *JCMS: Journal of Common Market Studies* 40(2): 235–258.

Manners, I. (2012) 'As You Like It: European Union Normative Power in the European Neighbourhood Policy', in Whitman, R.G. and Wolff, S. (eds.) *The European Neighbourhood Policy in Perspective. Context, Implementation and Impact*, Houndmills Basingstoke: Palgrave Macmillan, 29–50.

Morillas, P. and Soler i Lecha, E. (2017) 'The EU's Framing of the Mediterranean (1990–2002): Building a Euro-Mediterranean Partnership', *MEDRESET Working Paper* 2, Rome.

Natorski, M. (2017) 'The Practice of EU Power Relations with International Organizations in the Neighbourhood: Imperator or Primus Inter Pares?', in Gstöhl, S. and Schunz, S. (eds.) *Theorizing the European Neighbourhood Policy*, Oxon: Routledge, 164–184.

Pace, M. (2010) 'The ugly duckling of Europe: the Mediterranean in the foreign policy of the European Union', *Journal of European Area Studies* 10(2): 189–210.

Pardo, S. (2014) 'Views from the Neighbourhood: Israel', in Chaban, N. and Holland, M. (eds.) *Communicating Europe in Times of Crisis: External Perceptions of the European Union*, Houndmills, Basingstoke: Palgrave, Macmillan, 175–196.

Pardo, S. (2015) *Normative Power Europe meets Israel: Perceptions and Realities*, Lanham, Lexington: Rowman & Littlefield.

Prodi, R. (2002) 'A wider Europe—a proximity policy as a key to stability', 5–6 December 2002, European Commission Press Database, http://europa.eu/rapid/press-release_SPEECH-02-619_en.htm, accessed 9 November 2016.

Sadiki, L. (ed.) (2015) *Routledge Handbook of the Arab Spring: Rethinking Democratization*, Oxon: Routledge.

Sasse, G. (2008) 'The European neighbourhood policy: conditionality revisited for the EU's Eastern neighbours', *Europe-Asia Studies* 60(2): 295–316.

Schimmelfennig, F. (2012a) 'Europeanization beyond Europe', *Living Reviews in European Governance* 7(1): 5–31.

Schimmelfennig, F. (2012b) 'EU External Governance and Europeanization Beyond the EU', in Levi-Faur, D. (ed.) *Oxford Handbook of Governance*, Oxford: Oxford University Press, 656–672.

Schumacher, T. (2017) 'EU Member States' Representation and Positioning and the North-South Divide in Euro-Mediterranean Affairs', in Gillespie, R. and Volpi, F. (eds.) *The Routledge Handbook of Mediterranean Politics*, London: Routledge, 85–96.

Simão, L. and Piet, R. (eds.) (2016) *Security in Shared Neighbourhoods: Foreign Policy of Russia, Turkey and the EU*, Houndmills, Basingstoke: Palgrave Macmillan.

Sjöstedt, G. (1977) *The External Role of the European Community*, Farnborough: Saxon House.

The Economist (2014) 'Europe's Ring of Fire', Charlemagne, 20 September.

Timmermann, C. (2014) 'Imagining Europe from the Outside: The Role of Perceptions of Human Rights in Europe in Migration Aspirations in Turkey, Morocco, Senegal and Ukraine', in Chaban, N. and Holland, M. (eds.) *Communicating Europe in Times of Crisis. External Perceptions of the European Union*, Houndmills, Basingstoke: Palgrave, Macmillan, 220–247.

Tömmel, I. (2013) 'The new neighborhood policy of the EU: an appropriate response to the Arab Spring?', *Democracy and Security* 9(1–2): 19–39.

Van der Loo, G. (2016) *The EU-Ukraine Association Agreement and Deep and Comprehensive Free Trade Area. A New Legal Instrument for EU Integration Without Membership*, Leiden, Boston: Brill Nijhoff.

Van Elsuwege, P. and Van der Loo, G. (2017) 'Continuity and Change in the Legal Relations Between the EU and its Neighbours: A Result of Path Dependency and Spill-Over Effects', in Bouris, D. and Schumacher, T. (eds.) *The Revised European Neighbourhood Policy: Continuity and Change in EU Foreign Policy*, Houndmills, Basingstoke: Palgrave Macmillan, 97–116.

Van Hüllen, V. (2015) *EU Democracy Promotion and the Arab Spring: International Cooperation and Authoritarianism*, Houndmills, Basingstoke: Palgrave Macmillan.

PART I

Conceptual, theoretical and legal approaches in the study of the European Neighbourhood Policy

2
BEYOND ENLARGEMENT
Conceptualizing the study of the European Neighbourhood Policy

Frank Schimmelfennig

Introduction: beyond enlargement

From its very beginning, the European Neighbourhood Policy (ENP) was designed as an alternative to enlargement. It was limited to neighbouring countries that were not designated as candidate or potential candidate countries, and it offered them participation in a variety of European Union (EU) policies without integration into the EU polity – 'sharing everything but institutions' according to Commission President Romano Prodi (Prodi 2002). The ENP reflected both the EU's reluctance to commit itself to a further expansion of its membership and its realization that the enlarged Union needed to deal with the interdependence at its prospective new borders. It was designed to create a 'ring of friends' and zone of stability beyond its formal members (ibid.). At the same time, Enlargement Commissioner Günter Verheugen announced that the new policy would 'build on the experience' of eastern enlargement (quoted in Johansson-Nogués 2007: 26), and scholars have highlighted the organizational and practical path-dependencies of enlargement in the ENP (Kelley 2006).

This chapter describes how the ENP has been conceptualized in the academic literature on the EU. I argue that we find the same mix of delimitation and path-dependency as in the politics of the ENP. On the one hand, academic observers of the ENP have not only stressed the differences between the ENP and enlargement but also distinguished the ENP from traditional foreign policy. To the extent that they theorized the ENP at all, they have often imported concepts and theoretical approaches from the study of enlargement, as well as International Relations (IR) and foreign policy analysis. Because the IR concepts are the subject of other chapters in this handbook, I will focus on the literature on European integration.[1]

The main sections of this chapter will discuss three core concepts and their application to the ENP – integration, governance and Europeanization. In adapting these core concepts to the EU's external relations, observers of European integration have benefited from the increasing political diversity within the EU – from uniform to differentiated integration and from the hierarchical 'community method' of governance to a diverse set of governance modes and Europeanization mechanisms. Whereas the European integration and enlargement literatures have traditionally focused on the dichotomy of Member States and non-member states, and have regarded other institutional arrangements as irrelevant or transitory, the ENP fits well with an emerging literature on differentiated integration, which not only studies the internal differentiation of integration among EU members but also external differentiation and the selective integration of formal non-members (Holzinger and Schimmelfennig 2012; Schimmelfennig et al. 2015). Similarly, the 'governance turn' in the study of European integration initially focused on the (multi-level) policy-making within the EU (Jachtenfuchs 2001), but has since been extended to studying governance modes and outcomes in EU relations with third countries. The ENP has been an important catalyst for the concept of external governance (Lavenex 2004; Schimmelfennig and Wagner 2004). Finally, the study of Europeanization has travelled from an exclusive focus on the Member States (Green Cowles et al. 2001) *via* the Europeanization of candidate countries (Schimmelfennig and Sedelmeier 2005a) to the European neighbourhood and beyond (Schimmelfennig 2015).

Integration, governance and Europeanization are conceptually linked but cover different aspects. Integration is mainly concerned with the level and scope of authority transfer from the state to a supranational union. Governance focuses on the forms and modes in which this authority is exercised to make binding collective rules beyond the state. Europeanization refers to the mechanisms through which European governance affects states and their policies – and the effects they produce. For each of these core concepts, the chapter will give an overview of conceptual developments, sketch theoretical arguments and summarize key findings.

Differentiated integration

Traditionally, EU studies have drawn a hard border between 'integration', reserved for the Member States of the EU, and 'external relations' with non-member states. In this conceptual dichotomy, 'enlargement' denoted the formal transition from non-member to member status or from external relations to integration. This has never been an accurate description of European integration. Since the Treaty of Rome came into effect in 1958, the EU and its predecessor organizations have developed a variety of association arrangements for non-member states, some with and some without a link to potential future membership. Early examples are the Association Agreements of the early 1960s with Greece and Turkey and the free trade agreements of the 1970s with Western European non-members. These arrangements have responded to international constellations, in which the Member States rejected enlargement and/or a non-member state refused to join, and in which both the member and the non-member state had a common interest in an institutionalized relationship that allows the non-member state to participate selectively in European integration (Schimmelfennig 2016).

During its history, the EU has thus created an ever more fine-grained system of differentiated integration for non-member states. The grades of membership in this system have been both durable and permeable. They have been durable because none of the institutional arrangements established since the early 1960s have come into disuse. At the same time, the grades have been permeable because most countries have moved up across the grades of membership – for example, Austria, Finland and Sweden, from free trade partners to Member States; and 13 Central and Eastern European countries, from trade and cooperation arrangements, *via* association and candidacy, to membership. Only a few have moved down (such as Belarus or Yugoslavia).

These developments have prompted scholars to go beyond a dichotomous conceptualization of membership and enlargement. The concepts of 'horizontal institutionalization' (Schimmelfennig and Sedelmeier 2002: 503) and 'horizontal integration' (Leuffen et al. 2013: 11–12) refer to a continuous process of territorial extension of EU norms and rules and a continuous measure of the EU's territorial scope. 'Horizontal differentiation' (Leuffen et al. 2013: 12; Schimmelfennig et al. 2015: 765) captures the fact that the states of Europe and its neighbourhood, participate selectively and at various levels of integration in EU policies. Horizontal differentiation is, of course, not limited to non-members of the EU; it extends to formal EU members who do not participate in EU policy areas such as the euro or Schengen areas.

The horizontal differentiation of European integration has boosted conceptual innovation. Terms such as 'multi-speed Europe', 'core Europe', 'variable geometry' and 'Europe à la carte' have long entered scholarly and political discourse (Stubb 1996), but mainly refer to Member States. Regarding neighbouring non-members, Christiansen et al. (2000) speak of 'fuzzy borders' and Lavenex (2011) and Schimmelfennig (2010) map them as 'concentric circles'. Categorizations of the EU as an 'empire' are also consistent with the idea of graded, differentiated membership and fuzzy, flexible borders, which are common features of empires (Beck and Grande 2011; Marks 2012; Zielonka 2006).

Measurement of differentiated integration is often based on the number or share of EU rules or policies that European states subscribe to. Such quantitative measures are only available for the differentiated integration of formal Member States (Schimmelfennig and Winzen 2014; Duttle et al. 2017), the European Economic Area (EEA) (Frommelt 2017) and to some extent the candidate countries based on the Commission's Progress Reports (Böhmelt and Freyburg 2013) and national scoreboards for the adoption of EU legislation. There are no such comparative quantitative assessments for the ENP.

Classification schemes including the ENP are therefore generally based on qualitative distinctions of the level (depth) and (policy) scope of integration. Lavenex (2011) distinguishes four circles of external governance based on the strength of regulatory and organizational ties. Gstöhl (2015) classifies the EU's expansion of economic community with regard to scope and the degree of institutionalization (a measure of depth). Schimmelfennig (2016) uses an inductive ranking of grades of membership for formal non-members – trade, cooperation, free trade, bilateralism, association, internal market (EEA) and candidacy, which can also be reconstructed as representing an increase in the level and scope of integration.

Where does the ENP fit in the concept and classification of differentiated integration? On the one hand, the ENP is generally in line with the notion and underlying rationale of horizontal, external differentiation. It provides for the selective participation of ENP countries in a wide range of EU policies. Its initial purpose, to create a 'ring of friends', is in line with the 'concentric circles' metaphor. The ENP is an open-ended process (up to a point) allowing for the progressive integration of neighbouring countries. Generally, the ENP is classified as the 'outer circle' of European integration. In Lavenex (2011), it is the circle with the weakest ties; Gstöhl (2015) classifies the ENP as having both narrow scope and low depth.

There is a problem with general classifications of the ENP because the ENP is differentiated itself. Informal differentiation across ENP countries results from the Action Plans they negotiate with the EU, which vary greatly in the scope and intensity of cooperation. Some ENP countries do not even have an Action Plan. In addition, differentiation is based on formal agreements, such as different types of bilateral agreements (Euro-Mediterranean Association Agreements, Partnership and Cooperation Agreements, and the planned Deep and Comprehensive Free Trade Areas (DCFTAs)), as well as the separate, more multilateral frameworks of the Eastern Partnership (EaP) and the Union for the Mediterranean (UfM). Differentiation has been emphasized even more as a core principle in the 2015 ENP review (Delcour 2015). Thus, the ENP is differentiated across countries and across policies. This has been corroborated in comparative analyses of integration across sectors in the ENP that highlight the variety in the scope and intensity of cooperation across issue-areas (Lavenex et al. 2009; Lavenex 2011). These features make it difficult to classify the ENP as a single grade of membership.

Finally, what explains the placement of the ENP and ENP countries in the outer circle of European integration and the low grades of membership? Generally, analyses of non-member state-differentiated integration are descriptive rather than explanatory (Lavenex 2011; Gstöhl 2015). By contrast, Schimmelfennig (2016) distinguishes between two groups of non-member countries – the 'refuser' countries that do not want (further) integration with the EU; and the 'refused' countries that are not allowed (further) integration with the EU. According to this analysis, which only includes a subset of ENP countries, the difference in good governance, between the core EU and the refuser and refused countries, explains their grade of membership. Refused countries have 'worse governance' than the EU core and move closer to the core as they improve democracy, the rule of law and government effectiveness. By contrast, refuser countries enjoy 'better governance' than the EU, and the further away they remain from the core, the better their governance is. This explanation of differentiated integration is only partly helpful in the case of the ENP countries. First, the ENP comprises both refuser countries like Armenia and Azerbaijan that have suspended their association process in 2013–2014 and countries that have been refused further integration at some time (such as Belarus or Morocco). Whereas the quality of democracy and governance largely explains the differentiation between candidate countries and Eastern Partnership countries, it does not account for the geographic reasons, for which Morocco's membership bid in 1987 was rejected, the geopolitical reasons, for which Armenia refused association, or the resource wealth that allows countries like Azerbaijan and Algeria to forego closer ties with the EU. The ENP countries are too heterogeneous to fit a single explanation of their status in Europe's system of differentiated integration.

External governance

Just as with the concept of integration, the concept of governance has traditionally been reserved for the Member States of the EU's system of 'multi-level governance' (for example, Marks et al. 1996). Within the EU, the governance concept was based on the assumption and observation that 'institutionalized forms of coordinated action that aim at the production of collectively binding agreements' (Lavenex and Schimmelfennig 2009: 795) exist outside and beyond the state (that is, in the international sphere and including non-state actors). Yet, the EU's governance does not stop at the EU's formal borders. Not only do the EU's rules and policy regimes such as commercial policy or migration policy often have an external dimension, the EU also establishes institutional arrangements with non-member countries designed to extend its internal institutions and policies, and it does so in a way that is not well-captured by the state-centric concept of 'foreign policy' or the more general term of 'international cooperation'. This is the domain of 'external governance' (Lavenex 2004; Schimmelfennig and Wagner 2004; Lavenex and Schimmelfennig 2009).

Conceptually, the literature on external governance is primarily concerned with the institutional forms and modes, in which the EU provides and extends governance beyond its formal borders. In a series of articles, Sandra Lavenex has made major contributions to the conceptualization of these forms and modes. As for the forms of external governance, she distinguishes extensions of the EU's 'regulatory boundary' and 'organizational boundary'. Whereas the regulatory boundary refers to the extension of EU rules or policies to non-member states, the organizational boundary refers to the inclusion of non-member states in EU policy-making organizations (Lavenex and Schimmelfennig 2009). Both may, but need not, shift together. In Lavenex (2011), she conceptualizes the regulatory boundary further, according to the scope of the EU *acquis* promoted, the legal quality of rules and the supervision of compliance. For the organizational boundary, she distinguishes inclusion in EU structures, inclusion in parallel structures and the main level of interaction.

In addition, and drawing on the general policy literature, we can distinguish three basic modes of external governance – hierarchy, networks and markets. Whereas hierarchy denotes a relationship of formal domination and subordination, in which external actors are obliged to harmonize their policies with EU policies, networks are characterized by the horizontal coordination of formally equal actors and markets produce rule convergence through competition (Lavenex 2009; Lavenex and Schimmelfennig 2009). Lavenex (2009) conjectures that form follows mode. In the hierarchical mode of external governance, only the regulatory boundary will be shifted. Shifting the organizational boundary in this mode would be equivalent to formal EU membership. In the network mode, both the regulatory and organizational boundaries shift towards non-member states. In contrast, the market mode does not require institutional shifts of either type to produce policy convergence.

How do these concepts apply to the ENP? With regard to the regulatory boundary, Lavenex (2011) categorizes EU external governance in relation to the ENP countries, as partially based on the *acquis* but limited to legal approximation (rather than harmonization) and political (rather than judicial) supervision. Clearly, then, the ENP as a whole, does not mirror the hierarchical mode of governance typical for EU relations with the candidate countries and the EEA. Rather, external governance in the neighbourhood is best characterized by the network mode (Lavenex 2008). Only the new DCFTAs with a few EaP countries – and potentially, Morocco and Tunisia – contain elements of hierarchical governance such as harmonization and judicial supervision (Delcour 2013; Gstöhl 2015).

Even though network governance is open to the extension of organizational boundaries, organizational inclusion has remained limited in the ENP. It started with a bilateral hub-and-spoke model, in which interaction is predominantly intergovernmental. In the meantime, the EU has selectively opened some of its agencies to ENP countries (Lavenex 2008; 2015) and established new regional (the EaP and the UfM) and sub-regional arrangements (for instance, in the Black Sea region) (Lavenex 2011).

How is the dominance of network governance in the ENP explained (Lavenex and Schimmelfennig 2009)? From an institutionalist perspective, the mode of external governance generally follows the mode of internal governance. Policies governed by networks within the EU are therefore likely to display the same features in relations with third countries. In addition, network governance is more likely to be found in technical, non-politicized policy areas (Katsaris 2016). The power-based explanation expects that the modes of governance vary with structures of power and interdependence. Whereas high and asymmetrical interdependence tends to produce hierarchical governance, medium interdependence is conducive to network governance. By contrast, the domestic-structure explanation assumes the compatibility of the governance mode with domestic structures in third countries. Here, network governance presupposes decentralized and sectorally differentiated state structures with access for experts and stakeholders.

Lavenex et al. (2009) find evidence for the institutionalist hypothesis by showing that sectoral governance modes are remarkably similar across the EU's external relations with varying groups of non-member states. In the ENP, however, even hierarchical EU policies tend to fall back on network governance by default, because the EU lacks the incentives and instruments to enforce its policies. Still, network governance in the ENP is likely to be asymmetrical because the EU benefits from superior bargaining power and resources in these networks. Finally, the lack of bureaucratic capacity and autonomy and the weakness of autonomous organized civil society actors in most ENP countries limit the potential of network governance (Lavenex 2008). In summary, even though the EU has the tendency to export its modes of governance, international or domestic constellations may get in the way. This is also true for the ENP, which often operates in network mode without the prerequisites of effective network governance.

Europeanization

The concept of 'Europeanization' is broad and has been used in diverse ways. Its uses include 'the emergence and the development at the European level of distinct structures of governance' (Risse et al. 2001: 3) and

> processes of (a) construction, (b) diffusion, and (c) institutionalisation of formal and informal rules, procedures, policy paradigms, styles, 'ways of doing things', and shared beliefs and norms, which are first defined and consolidated in the making of EU decisions and then incorporated in the logic of domestic discourse, identities, political structures and public policies.
>
> *(Radaelli 2003: 30)*

In the case of non-member states, Europeanization is limited to the transfer or 'downloading' from the EU. In terms of substance, studies of Europeanization in the ENP have focused on the EU impact at the policy level as well as democracy and human rights (Schimmelfennig 2015).

The literature on Europeanization has developed a rich set of concepts. All these concepts specify mechanisms of EU impact and the conditions under which they operate and are effective. At the same time, there is considerable conceptual overlap – and some conceptual inflation – in this literature. I therefore subsume the various typologies under a single framework illustrated in Table 2.1 (Schimmelfennig 2015).

The framework has three dimensions. First, it distinguishes Europeanization mechanisms by their institutional logic – the 'logic of consequences' or the 'logic of appropriateness' (March and Olsen 1989: 160–162). Whereas the logic of consequences assumes actors choose the behavioural option that maximizes their utility under given circumstances, the logic of appropriateness stipulates that actors choose the behaviour that is appropriate for their social role and the social norms in a given situation. Second, Europeanization can work through different channels: from the EU *via* governments or, transnationally, *via* societies. Third, Europeanization can be direct or EU driven or indirect or domestically driven.

Conditionality and socialization are the most used and compared mechanisms. Conditionality is a direct, intergovernmental mechanism based on the logic of consequences. In the conditionality mode, the EU provides non-member governments with rewards such as financial aid, market access or institutional ties on the condition that they meet the EU's demands. In addition, the EU provides states with additional resources to help them fulfil these conditions (capacity-building). The effectiveness of conditionality depends on the size of the EU's rewards and the credibility of its conditionality. On the one hand, the credibility of the threat to withhold rewards in case of non-compliance results from superior bargaining power. On the other hand, the credibility of the promise to reward compliance depends on the consistent application of

Table 2.1 Mechanisms of Europeanization

	Intergovernmental		Transnational	
	Direct	Indirect	Direct	Indirect
Logic of consequences	Conditionality	Externalization	Transnational incentives	Transnational externalization
Logic of appropriateness	Socialization	Emulation	Transnational socialization	Societal emulation

conditionality, which increases the belief of third countries that they will always and only receive the rewards when the conditions are met. In addition, target governments weigh external incentives against domestic costs. Domestic adaptation costs must not be higher than the international rewards because otherwise a rational target state of conditionality will not comply (Schimmelfennig and Sedelmeier 2005b). By contrast, socialization is based on the logic of appropriateness. It comprises all EU efforts to 'teach' EU policies – as well as the ideas and norms behind them – to outsiders, to persuade non-members that these policies are appropriate and, as a consequence, to motivate them to adopt EU policies. Rather than directly manipulating or indirectly affecting the cost benefit calculations of external actors, the EU teaches them the principles and rules of European governance. External actors adopt and comply with EU rules if they are convinced of their legitimacy and appropriateness and accept the EU's authority. This is assumed to be more likely the case if the external actors are in a novel and uncertain environment and identify with and aspire to belong to 'Europe'. A process characterized by deliberation and frequent, as well as dense, contacts between the EU and external actors is also thought to help. Finally, the high resonance of EU governance with domestic traditions, norms and practices provides favourable conditions for effective socialization (Checkel 2001; Risse 2000).

All other mechanisms of EU impact are best seen as varieties of these two fundamental logics – varieties that work more indirectly and/or transnationally than conditionality and socialization. First, in the transnational channel, the EU's conditionality and socialization can be directed at societal actors – parties, firms, interest groups, NGOs or even regional administrations – rather than central governments. According to the 'transnational incentives' mechanism, the EU provides these non-state actors with incentives to follow EU rules themselves and/or to put pressure on their governments to adopt EU rules. Likewise, 'transnational socialization' consists in persuading these societal actors of EU values, norms or policy ideas. Societal actors will then work to disseminate these ideas further domestically.

Second, we can move from the direct and intentional mechanisms of conditionality and socialization to indirect, and sometimes unintentional, mechanisms. Here, the EU's impact on third countries is a result of its capacity as a highly relevant market and system of regional governance for outsiders (Damro 2012). According to the externalization mechanism, internal EU governance may produce negative externalities towards third country governments and societal actors. External actors adopt and comply with EU rules because ignoring or violating them would generate net costs. Externalization is most noticeably produced by the EU's internal market and competition policies; firms interested in participating in the EU market must follow the EU's rules. Countries whose economies are strongly interconnected with the EU make their internal rules compatible with those of the EU. This is in line with the market mode of governance. It may affect societal actors, such as firms and business associations, as well as governments that are induced to alter their own rules and policies in line with those of the EU. In general, the effects of externalization increase with the market size of the EU and the strength of its regulatory institutions (Bach and Newman 2007). The larger the EU's share is in the foreign trade of a country, and the more binding and centralized the EU's rules are, the more this country will be subject to Europeanization pressures. In addition, high exposure to the EU and its policies and the success of such policies is likely to promote learning and lesson-drawing.

Emulation is the equivalent of externalization in the logic of appropriateness. Here, the EU's processes and policies may provide a model for other regions, states and societal actors. Non-member actors emulate the EU because they recognize EU rules and policies as appropriate solutions to their own problems. As in the case of socialization, novices in the international system and states in an uncertain environment are more likely to look for and emulate role models. They are more likely to select the EU as their model if they identify with the EU, are in close contact with the EU and find EU governance resonates with their prior beliefs and practices.

Analyses of the ENP often start from the benchmark of accession conditionality, widely considered the most effective mechanism of Europeanization beyond the Member States, and then point out that Europeanization in the ENP lags far behind and why this happens. First, and most obviously, the EU does not offer membership in the ENP. The size of the reward it can promise non-member states for Europeanizing is thus much smaller. This is especially detrimental because domestic adaptation costs in the ENP countries are very often higher than in the candidate countries – given the mostly non-democratic regimes or fragile democracies, widespread governance failure and mostly low state capacities in the ENP region. A positive cost benefit balance between international rewards and domestic costs would be difficult to achieve, even if the EU offered membership.

Second, even the smaller incentives on offer in the ENP are often not sufficiently credible. The main potential reward, liberalized access of goods and persons to the EU, has been undermined by protectionist interest groups in the EU, the exclusion of sectors such as agriculture, in which the ENP partners have a competitive edge, and fears of crime and uncontrolled immigration in the EU (Occhipinti 2007; Sedelmeier 2007; Vachudová 2007). Whitman and Wolff (2010: 12–13) conclude that 'the far-reaching benefits on offer have remained in the realm of possibilities' and are too vague and weak to wield substantial leverage and encourage painful and costly reforms. In addition, the EU offers less financial and technical support to build state capacity than in the candidate countries, although demand is higher. Whereas the liberalization of market access goes much further in the new DCFTAs, Bruszt and Langbein criticize that the EU does not provide adequate financial support to cushion the potentially disruptive effects of deep free trade in the EU's partner countries (Bruszt and Langbein 2017).

Third, 'joint ownership' is considered to undermine the effectiveness of conditionality. On one hand, 'it reduces the likelihood that bilateral Action Plans reflect the EU's objective precisely in relations with those countries which are furthest from conforming to the conditions preferred by the EU' (Sedelmeier 2007: 200). For instance, governments that do not share the EU's democracy and human rights agenda can, and do, minimize their role in their Action Plans. On the other, it is 'at odds with the tough monitoring and reporting by EU institutions that was a precondition for reform-oriented forces to mobilize pressure against reform-adverse governments in East Central European accession governments' (ibid.). By contrast, Sasse (2008; 2010) finds merit and opportunities in the ENP's 'conditionality-lite'. While she agrees that it is unlikely to produce short-term EU-driven change at the level of third country governments, ENP conditionality may serve as an external reference point for longer-term domestic political processes. In other words, it may trigger indirect externalization or imitation effects.

In the domain of human rights and democracy promotion, the literature generally agrees that EU impact in the ENP context has been weak and attributes this weakness to a variety of reasons (for an overview, consult Schimmelfennig (2015)). For one, EU democracy promotion policy has been inconsistent and incoherent; it has also been met with unfavourable conditions on the part of the ENP countries – weak resonance of democracy and human rights norms, weak European identities, weak civil societies and resistance by non-democratic regional powers. These factors undermine both conditionality- and socialization-based processes of Europeanization. An alternative approach, 'democratic governance promotion', seeks to overcome the constraints of top-down conditionality and bottom-up socialization by focusing on enhancing transparency, accountability and participation in the context of sectoral cooperation – yet the effects are limited as well (Freyburg et al. 2015; Freyburg and Lavenex, this volume).

At the level of individual policies, both the conditions and outcomes of Europeanization are more varied and positive. The upshot of recent empirical work is that explanations of Europeanization need to be located at the policy (rather than the polity or state) level and need to take into account the domestic and international policy context (Langbein and Börzel 2013). These studies still mostly rely on factors related to the conditionality mechanism but assess them for individual policies. They show that in policy areas – in which EU policy-specific incentives are strong and credible, third country dependence on the EU is high, EU rules fit with the interests of governments and informal veto players, and costs for domestic actors are not prohibitive – the EU has been able to produce policy change (for example, Ademmer and Börzel 2013; Dimitrova and Dragneva 2009; Langbein 2014). Langbein further argues that policy conditionality is more effective the more it is based not only on EU-target country intergovernmental relationships but also on 'multiple channels of interaction between external actors and domestic state and non-state actors' (2014: 165). To sum up, whereas top-down general conditionality is generally not an effective mechanism of Europeanization beyond enlargement because the ENP lacks credible incentives and moderate political costs for non-member state governments, policy-specific and multi-channel conditionality can still work if costs and benefits at the policy level are favourable.

Conclusions

This chapter has presented three concepts from EU studies – integration, governance and Europeanization – and their adaptation to the ENP context. The chapter shows that this adaptation has not only been possible but also fruitful to capture those aspects of the ENP that fit badly with a traditional international cooperation and foreign policy approach – the EU's intent to create a circle of peripheral policy integration, to include non-member states in its governance regimes, and to export its values, norms and policy rules. These concepts also help to understand that integration, governance and Europeanization do not end abruptly beyond enlargement but change and decrease gradually. And they come with hypotheses and explanations that enrich the study of the ENP theoretically.

Finally, the chapter has pointed out two limits of this extension. Conceptually, the ENP has become too diverse for single categories to apply well. ENP countries do not constitute a single circle of integration but spread out over several grades of differentiation and membership; by the same token, modes of external governance and mechanisms of Europeanization are becoming more varied as the ENP itself becomes more institutionally differentiated. Practically, the aim of integration, governance and Europeanization, without enlargement, has proven hard to attain – to the point that researchers need to be aware that, at least in some parts of the neighbourhood, these concepts may be stretched too far and risk becoming meaningless.

Note

1 See chapters by Aggestam, Hyde-Price, Kratochvíl and Tulmets, and Kalland Aarstad and Bremberg (this volume).

References

Ademmer, E. and Börzel, T. (2013) 'Migration, Energy, and Good Governance in the EU's Eastern Neighbourhood', *Europe-Asia Studies* 65(4): 581–608.
Bach, D. and Newman, A. (2007) 'The European Regulatory State and Global Public Policy: Micro-Institutions, Macro-Influence', *Journal of European Public Policy* 14(6): 827–846.

Beck, U. and Grande, E. (2011) 'Empire Europe: Statehood and Political Authority in the Process of Regional Integration', in Neyer, J. and Wiener, A. (eds.) *Political Theory of the European Union*, Oxford: Oxford University Press, 21–46.

Böhmelt, T. and Freyburg, T. (2013) 'The Temporal Dimension of the Credibility of EU Conditionality and Candidate States' Compliance with the Acquis Communautaire, 1998–2009', *European Union Politics* 14(2): 250–272.

Bruszt, L. and Langbein, J. (2017) 'Varieties of Dis-Embedded Liberalism: EU Integration Strategies in the Eastern Peripheries of Europe', *Journal of European Public Policy* 24(2): 297–315.

Checkel, J. (2001) 'Why Comply? Social Learning and European Identity Change', *International Organization* 55(3): 553–588.

Christiansen, T., Petto, F. and Tonra, B. (2000) 'Fuzzy Politics Around Fuzzy Borders: The European Union's "Near Abroad"', *Cooperation and Conflict* 35(4): 389–415.

Damro, C. (2012) 'Market Power Europe', *Journal of European Public Policy* 19(5): 682–699.

Delcour, L. (2013) 'Meandering Europeanisation: EU Policy Instruments and Policy Convergence in Georgia Under the Eastern Partnership', *East European Politics* 29(3): 344–357.

Delcour, L. (2015) 'The 2015 ENP Review: Beyond Stocktaking, the Need for a Political Strategy', *College of Europe Policy Brief* 1.15.

Dimitrova, A. and Dragneva, R. (2009) 'Constraining External Governance: Interdependence with Russia and the CIS as Limits to EU's Rule Transfer in Ukraine', *Journal of European Public Policy* 16(6): 853–872.

Duttle, T., Holzinger, K., Malang, T., Schäubli, T., Schimmelfennig, F. and Winzen, T. (2017) 'Opting Out from European Union Legislation: The Differentiation of Secondary Law', *Journal of European Public Policy* 24(3): 406–428.

Freyburg, T. Lavenex, S., Schimmelfennig, F., Skripka, T., Wetzel, A., Wetzel, A., Skripka, T. and Lavenex, S. (2015) *Democracy Promotion by Functional Cooperation: The European Union and Its Neighbourhood*, Basingstoke: Palgrave Macmillan.

Frommelt, C. (2017) *In Search of Effective Differentiated Integration: Lessons from the European Economic Area EEA)*, PhD thesis, ETH Zürich.

Green Cowles, M., Caporaso, J. and Risse, T. (eds.) (2001) *Transforming Europe: Europeanization and Domestic Change*, Ithaca: Cornell University Press.

Gstöhl, S. (2015) 'Models of External Differentiation in the EU's Neighbourhood: An Expanding Economic Community?', *Journal of European Public Policy* 22(6): 854–870.

Holzinger, K. and Schimmelfennig, F. (2012) 'Differentiated Integration in the European Union: Many Concepts, Sparse Theory, Few Data', *Journal of European Public Policy* 19(2): 292–305.

Jachtenfuchs, M. (2001) 'The Governance Approach to European Integration', *Journal of Common Market Studies* 39(2): 245–264.

Johansson-Nogués, E. (2007) 'The EU and Its Neighbourhood: An Overview', in Weber, K., Smith, Michael E. and Baun, M. (eds.) *Governing Europe's Neighbourhood*, Manchester: Manchester University Press, 21–35.

Katsaris, A. (2016) 'Europeanization Through Policy Networks in the Southern Neighbourhood: Advancing Renewable Energy Rules in Morocco and Algeria', *Journal of Common Market Studies* 54(3): 656–673.

Kelley, J. (2006) 'New Wine in Old Wine Skins: Policy Adaptation in the European Neighbourhood Policy', *Journal of Common Market Studies* 44(1): 29–55.

Langbein, J. (2014) 'European Union Governance Towards the Eastern Neighbourhood: Transcending or Redrawing Europe's East–West Divide?', *Journal of Common Market Studies* 52(1): 157–174.

Langbein, J. and Börzel, T. (2013) 'Introduction: Explaining Policy Change in the European Union's Eastern Neighbourhood', *Europe-Asia Studies* 65(4): 571–580.

Lavenex, S. (2004) 'EU External Governance in "Wider Europe"', *Journal of European Public Policy* 11(4): 680–700.

Lavenex, S. (2008) 'A Governance Perspective on the European Neighbourhood Policy: Integration Beyond Conditionality?', *Journal of European Public Policy* 15(6): 938–955.

Lavenex, S. (2009) 'Switzerland's Flexible Integration in the EU: A Conceptual Framework', *Swiss Political Science Review* 15(4): 547–575.

Lavenex, S. (2011) 'Concentric Circles of Flexible "European" Integration: A Typology of EU External Governance Relations?', *Comparative European Politics* 9(4/5): 372–393.

Lavenex, S. (2015) 'The External Face of Differentiated Integration: Third Country Participation in EU Sectoral Bodies', *Journal of European Public Policy* 22(6): 836–853.

Lavenex, S. and Schimmelfennig, F. (2009) 'EU Rules Beyond EU Borders: Theorizing External Governance in European Politics', *Journal of European Public Policy* 16(6): 791–812.

Lavenex, S., Lehmkuhl, D. and Wichmann, N. (2009) 'Modes of External Governance: A Cross-National and Cross-Sectoral Comparison', *Journal of European Public Policy* 16(6): 813–833.

Leuffen, D., Rittberger, B. and Schimmelfennig, F. (2013) *Differentiated Integration: Explaining Variation in the European Union*, Basingstoke: Palgrave.

March, J. and Olsen, J. (1989) *Rediscovering Institutions: The Organizational Basis of Politics*, New York: Free Press.

Marks, G. (2012) 'Europe and Its Empires: From Rome to the European Union', *Journal of Common Market Studies* 50(1): 1–20.

Marks, G., Scharpf, F., Schmitter, P. and Streeck, W. (eds.) (1996) *Governance in the European Union*, London: Sage.

Occhipinti, J. (2007) 'Justice and Home Affairs: Immigration and Policing', in Weber, K., Smith, M. and Baun, M. (eds.) *Governing Europe's Neighbourhood*, Manchester: Manchester University Press, 114–133.

Prodi, R. (2002) 'A Wider Europe—A Proximity Policy as a Key to Stability', *SPEECH/02/619*, 5–6 December, http://europa.eu/rapid/press-release_SPEECH-02-619_en.htm, accessed 9 November 2016.

Radaelli, C. (2003) 'The Europeanization of Public Policy', in Featherstone, K. and Radaelli, C. (eds.) *The Politics of Europeanization*, Oxford: Oxford University Press, 27–56.

Risse, T. (2000.) '"Let's Argue!" Communicative Action in World Politics', *International Organization* 54(1): 1–39.

Risse, T., Green Cowles, M. and Caporaso, J. (2001) 'Europeanizing and Domestic Change: Introduction', in Green Cowles, M., Caporaso, J. and Risse, T. (eds.) *Transforming Europe: Europeanization and Domestic Change*, Ithaca: Cornell University Press, 1–19.

Sasse, G. (2008) 'The European Neighbourhood Policy: Conditionality Revisited for the EU's Eastern Neighbours', *Europe-Asia Studies* 60(2): 295–316.

Sasse, G. (2010) 'The ENP and the EU's Eastern Neighbours: Ukraine and Moldova as Test Cases', in Whitman, R. and Wolff, S. (eds.) *The European Neighbourhood Policy in Perspective: Context, Implementation and Impact*, Basingstoke: Palgrave Macmillan, 181–205.

Schimmelfennig, F. (2010) 'Europeanisation Beyond the Member States', *Zeitschrift für Staats-und Europawissenschaften* 8(3): 319–339.

Schimmelfennig, F. (2015) 'Europeanization beyond Europe', *Living Reviews in European Governance* 10(1), http://europeangovernance-livingreviews.org/Articles/lreg-2015-1/, accessed 10 November 2016.

Schimmelfennig, F. (2016) 'Good Governance and Differentiated Integration: Graded Membership in the European Union', *European Journal of Political Research* 55(4): 789–810.

Schimmelfennig, F. and Sedelmeier, U. (2002) 'Theorizing EU Enlargement: Research Focus, Hypotheses and the State of Research', *Journal of European Public Policy* 9(4): 500–528.

Schimmelfennig, F. and Sedelmeier, U. (eds.) (2005a) *The Europeanization of Central and Eastern Europe*, Ithaca: Cornell University Press.

Schimmelfennig, F. and Sedelmeier, U. (2005b) 'Introduction: Conceptualizing the Europeanization of Central and Eastern Europe', in Schimmelfennig, F. and Sedelmeier, U. (eds.) *The Europeanization of Central and Eastern Europe*, Ithaca: Cornell University Press, 1–28.

Schimmelfennig, F. and Wagner, W. (2004) 'Preface: External Governance in the European Union', *Journal of European Public Policy* 11(4): 657–660.

Schimmelfennig, F. and Winzen, T. (2014) 'Instrumental and Constitutional Differentiation in the European Union', *Journal of Common Market Studies* 52(2): 354–370.

Schimmelfennig, F., Leuffen, D. and Rittberger, B. (2015) 'The European Union as a System of Differentiated Integration: Interdependence, Politicization, and Differentiation', *Journal of European Public Policy* 22(6): 764–782.

Sedelmeier, U. (2007) 'The European Neighbourhood Policy: A Comment on Theory and Policy', in Weber, K., Smith, M. and Baun, M. (eds.) *Governing Europe's Neighbourhood*, Manchester: Manchester University Press, 195–208.

Stubb, A. (1996) 'A Categorization of Differentiated Integration', *Journal of Common Market Studies* 34(2): 283–295.

Vachudová, M. (2007) 'Trade and the Internal Market', in Weber, K., Smith, M. and Baun, M. (eds.) *Governing Europe's Neighbourhood*, Manchester: Manchester University Press, 97–113.

Whitman, R. and Wolff, S. (2010) 'Much Ado About Nothing? The European Neighbourhood Policy in Context', in Whitman, R. and Wolff, S. (eds.) *The European Neighbourhood Policy in Perspective: Context, Implementation and Impact*, Basingstoke: Palgrave Macmillan, 3–26.

Zielonka, J. (2006) *Europe as Empire. The Nature of the Enlarged European Union*, Oxford: Oxford University Press.

3

EU ACTORNESS AND THE EUROPEAN NEIGHBOURHOOD POLICY

Nils Hoffmann and Arne Niemann

Introduction

Since its foundation, the European Community's (EC) role and impact in the international arena has been a subject of persistent debate among scholars of International Relations (IR). Classical IR theory faced a variety of issues in trying to conceptualise the EC/European Union (EU) and its external relations. Above all, the focus on statehood proved an inadequate starting point for analysis. To enable an analysis that acknowledges the EU's distinctive nature and significant differences from other international actors, scholars working on (the external dimension of) European integration quickly began to look beyond state-centric accounts.

Subsequently, a variety of studies emerged focusing primarily on the internal characteristics and processes that determine EU external policy, and shifted perceptions towards the conceptualisation of the EU as a new type of international actor that is unique. Consequently, accompanying this theoretical debate, different new concepts of the EU as an actor in international relations grew in prominence and importance in European Integration Studies. A key facet of the discussion has remained the question of what type of power the EU constitutes in international relations. The 1970s saw the emergence of the idea of the Union as a civilian power (Duchêne 1972), portraying the EU as an actor with limited military and strategic power on the one hand, but significant economic power on the other and increasingly interested in exercising its influence in world politics. The concept of a Civilian Power Europe (CPE) remains influential in academic discourse (Orbie 2006), despite recent developments in the EU's security and defence policy somewhat undermining the perception of the EU as a distinctive civilian entity in contrast to other actors (Smith 2000).

During the last decade, the notion of Normative Power Europe (NPE) – conceptualising the EU's (assumed) 'ability to define what passes for "normal" in world affairs' – has come into vogue (Manners 2002: 236). NPE has prompted a lively debate in IR and come in for its own share of criticism – for example, concerning its alleged 'Eurocentrism' (Fioramonti and Poletti 2008), its lack of precision (Sjursen 2006) and the relatively meagre findings of EU normativity in empirical studies (Niemann and de Wekker 2010). With the concept of neither Civilian nor Normative Power Europe proving entirely satisfactory, recent debate concerning the role of the EU as an international actor has attempted to reconceptualise the EU's role in international affairs – through notions such as 'integrative' (Koops 2011), 'small' (Toje 2011) or 'transformative'

(Leonard 2005) power Europe. In addition, it has been suggested – given the plethora of studies contesting the legitimacy and impact of EU foreign policy – that the discussion about what 'sort' of power or actor the EU is first requires a more systematic analysis of EU presence and actorness (and effectiveness) in international relations itself (Niemann and Bretherton 2013).

As for the European Neighbourhood Policy, the most prominent and important policy tool in the EU's dealing with its geographical proximity, the questions of EU presence and actorness seem of particular interest. Analysing EU actorness in the European Neighbourhood Policy (ENP) process and in particular extending the concept towards potential findings on effectiveness (and possibly performance), could provide a variety of outcomes and insights, improving the comparability and empirical underpinning of ENP research overall. The first part of this chapter will introduce important approaches and concepts surrounding the EU's role in IR. The second part of this chapter evaluates the potential, relevance and impact of these concepts by presenting selected literature, either explicitly or implicitly referring to the arguments and measures of the respective concepts. Finally, we draw some conclusions from our analysis.

Conceptualising the EU's role in international affairs and its external relations

The concept of presence

Through the concept of EU presence, Allen and Smith analyse the role of Western Europe in the international sphere. They argue for an understanding of the EC not as a classic international actor, but rather a presence in international affairs with a considerable degree of variation. Their central argument is that the EC is

> neither a fully-fledged state-like actor nor a purely dependent phenomenon in the contemporary international arena. Rather, it is a variable and multi-dimensional presence, which plays an active role in some areas of international interaction and a less active one in others.
>
> *(Allen and Smith 1990: 20)*

In their understanding, presence is a feature of issue-arenas or networks of activity, which influences the actions and expectations of the relevant participants. A combination of factors defines a particular presence in the international sphere, including credentials and legitimacy, the capacity to mobilise resources and the place the EC is able to occupy in the perceptions and expectations of the relevant policy-makers. The separation of presence from actorness is a prominent feature of this approach. Allen and Smith (1990) argue that although the EC cannot fulfil many criteria of actorness, it has significant 'presence' in the international system.

The concept of actorness

The debate concerning EC/EU actorness in international politics has attracted considerable scholarly attention in the past decades. Emerging from early debate about the potential international roles of the EC (Cosgrove and Twitchett 1970), the first detailed and systematic conceptualisation of the Community's international actor capability was developed by Gunnar Sjöstedt. He defines it as the 'ability to function actively and deliberately in relation to other actors in the international system' (Sjöstedt 1977: 16), recognising the ambiguous nature and confined capabilities of the EC, manifesting some characteristics of classical actors in IR while lacking others. Actorness still presumes the possession of a substantial degree of state-like properties, requiring the Community to retain, at least to some extent, the processes and rules of the state-centric international relations in order to be successful. Despite remaining influential in the literature, Sjöstedt's approach has been criticised for focusing excessively on internal characteristics, which are also difficult to operationalise and apply to specific cases (Niemann and Bretherton 2013). This has subsequently led to a variety of different approaches towards EU actorness in international affairs.

The first of these is the concept developed by Joseph Jupille and James A. Caporaso. Criticising previous contributions to the debate for their lack of clear criteria determining the status of the EU as an actor, they develop four main indicators for analysing EU actorness – recognition, authority, cohesion and autonomy (Jupille and Caporaso 1998). Recognition entails the EC's acceptance by other actors in the international system and the subsequent interaction with these actors. Authority concerns, above all, the legal competence to act on a given subject matter. The Community's authority can be viewed as the authority delegated by the Member States to EU institutions. Autonomy depicts the distinctiveness of the EC's institutional apparatus during international negotiations and the degree of discretionary goal formation, decision-making and implementation, independent of other actors. Finally, cohesion describes the ability of the Community to formulate an internally consistent position as assessed in several dimensions (Jupille and Caporaso 1998). Apart from being partly interconnected, the four indicators of actorness can be aptly operationalised for empirical research. The concept itself, despite being clearly structured, drew criticism for being relatively complex, given the fact that each of the four criteria contains several sub-criteria. Other critiques suggest that their framework is too narrowly focused, being excessively concerned with internal factors and leaving aside other important questions of EU influence, in particular those associated with the intersubjective processes that construct or constrain the exercise of power and authority in international politics (Niemann and Bretherton 2013).

For scholars attempting to develop a constructivist analysis, intersubjective processes are essential to an understanding of EU actorness. Bretherton and Vogler's (1999/2006) approach, which straddles the boundary between 'actorness' and 'effectiveness', seeks to arrive at a conceptualisation informed by this line of reasoning. Their analysis focuses on the three interrelated concepts of opportunity, presence and capability. Opportunity, 'denotes factors in the external environment of ideas and events which constrain or enable actorness' (Bretherton and Vogler 1999/2006: 24), that is, the structural context of EU action in international relations. This context is seen as a dynamic process that incorporates external perceptions and expectations of EU actorness. Presence builds upon the work of Allen and Smith (1990) and 'conceptualizes the ability of the EU, by virtue of its existence, to exert influence beyond its borders' (Bretherton and Vogler 1999–2006: 24). Representing an indication of the EU's structural power, it combines understanding of the nature and identity of the EU and the consequences of the Union's internal priorities and policies. Finally, capability is described as referring 'to the internal context of EU external action – the availability of policy instruments and understandings about the Union's ability to utilize these instruments, in response to opportunity and/or to capitalize presence' (ibid.). While capability was originally understood in terms of three categories – consistency, coherence and the availability of policy instruments – more recently Bretherton and Vogler (2008) have focused particularly on coherence.

The concept of effectiveness

To make more far-reaching claims concerning the EU's role and influence in international relations, it has been suggested that we have to go beyond the studies of actorness (or ability to act) and consider the effectiveness of EU action (Niemann and Bretherton 2013). Effectiveness is understood in terms of several sometimes complementary characteristics, with the focus on categories of 'goal-achievement' or 'problem-solving' (Young 1994; Groen and Niemann 2013). Effectiveness is notoriously difficult to analyse and assess – a problem that is not confined to the study of EU external policy. Debates about EU effectiveness have been particularly intense, reflecting a belief held by (many) IR scholars that the EU is particularly ineffective (Smith 2002).

The effectiveness of EU action has been addressed from a variety of perspectives. A prominent early example is the 'capability-expectations gap', from which the Community is supposed to suffer (Hill 1993), a contribution that has retained its relevance in the discussion on EU effectiveness also in the ENP. A contrast to Hill's rather pessimistic assessment was provided by the work of Ginsberg (2001), who analysed the EU's influence in the difficult case of former Yugoslavia. Recent analyses have tended to focus on coherence, which has been referred to as 'one of the most fervently discussed' factors associated with the effectiveness of EU external policy (Gebhard 2011: 101). It reflects the common-sense notion, frequently reiterated by EU officials, that effectiveness is enhanced when the EU 'speaks with one voice'.

The relationship between coherence and effectiveness is considered both complex and uncertain by many authors. This is perhaps unsurprising, given that the pursuit of coherence can result in outcomes reflecting a lowest common denominator consensus and, accordingly, ineffective policies and actions. In contrast, a distinct level of coherence can enhance or even trigger third party resistance and result in low effectiveness. There have been several works addressing this issue, with Bretherton and Vogler (2008) distinguishing between vertical coherence (between internal actors) and horizontal coherence (across policy domains), while Van Schaik (2013) argues that EU coherence is influenced by competence, preference homogeneity and socialisation.

Thomas (2012) proposes a parsimonious approach for conceptualising coherence by drawing on policy determinacy (reflecting how clearly and narrowly an EU policy defines the boundaries of acceptable behaviour) and policy implementation (reflecting how rigorously EU actors comply with and support the agreed policy). Highly determinate policies are likely to enhance the EU's effectiveness because they are viewed by others as reflecting a greater common commitment, which is likely to be perceived as a solid basis for good relations. In addition, when determinate policies are also regularly implemented, collective material resources and persuasive powers are deployed on behalf of common objectives (Thomas 2012). Groen and Niemann (2013) conceptualise effectiveness as the result of actorness conditioned by the opportunity structure that enables or constrains EU actions. They argue that actual effectiveness is the function of the internal factors (such as coherence and autonomy) which determine actorness, as conditioned by the constraints of the external environment.[1]

Moreover, concepts of effectiveness represent an important part, or even indicator complementary to others, in a variety of recent studies on EU performance. With limited theorising of performance in the original EU foreign policy literature, some relevant studies rely on the international regimes and organisational performance literature for their conceptualisation of performance (Jørgensen et al. 2011). There is a debate concerning EU performance in multilateral institutions, with distinct emphasis on the relevance of effectiveness as an indicator among others and the general understanding of the concept of effectiveness overall (Oberthür and Groen 2015).

The EU as an international actor in the ENP

To be able to present an appropriate overview of the EU as an actor in the ENP, we will analyse the presence of the concepts (and their sub-concepts) discussed in this chapter and in the

ENP literature, determine the extent to which they have been applied across topics and issues and try to highlight some possible shortcomings and difficulties to provide an evaluation of the general relevance and value of these concepts to ENP analysis.

The concept of presence and the ENP

Few works on the ENP have explicitly drawn on the concept of presence. An example of such explicit use of the concept is the work of Bechev (2011). Assessing the EU's widely criticised ineffectiveness and exploring the sources and dynamics of EU influence in the ENP, he identifies two modes of interaction between the EU and its neighbouring countries, "gatekeeping" and "power projection", arguing that the finding that the EU acts as much as a gatekeeper as proactive agent is in line with 'certain strands of the literature stressing the power of the Union related to its presence in the global and regional economy and politics' (Bechev 2011: 424), directly citing the work of Allen and Smith (1990) in this context. Bechev refers to Hill's (1993) notion of EU presence, implying that certain events would have either not occurred or occurred differently without the EU's existence (Bechev 2011). The occurrence of and distinction between the two faces of EU presence, passive traction and proactive engagement with its neighbours, are central to his argument (ibid.). Similarly, Jones explicitly notes the relevant literature suggesting that the EU simply manifests different forms of international actorness and presence and states that 'the EU's international actorness and presence often reflects the spread of contradictory "EU"ropean interests and activities, with a diversity of actors and processes involved in the construction of EU "international policy"'(Jones 2009: 83).

A more implicit application of the concept of EU presence is represented in the work of Jones and Clark (2008). Focusing on the role of the Commission in the external projection of Europeanisation towards the Mediterranean, they concentrate on the concept of Europeanisation, defining it as a 'legitimizing process through which the EU strives to gain meaning, actorness and presence internationally' (Jones and Clark 2008: 545). They argue that the European Commission holds a substantive role in the promotion of agreed European interests, ideas and identities and in the delivery of EU policy narratives, norms, practices and procedures on terms that are favourable for the Union. In addition, they point out that the contradictory demands of negotiating order, at both the internal and external level, critically affect the ability of the EU to produce policy outputs that 'obtain a desired policy outcome that accord the EU "presence" and "actorness" in international affairs' (Jones and Clark 2008: 546). They conclude their argument stating that, for the Commission, the promotion of its neighbourhood policy in the name of Europeanisation is central to EU actorness and international presence (Jones and Clark 2008).

Different, rather general notions on EU presence can be found in several other works related to the ENP that have no substantial connection to the actual concept (for example, Korosteleva 2011; Wolff and Peen Rodt 2010; Echeverria Jesus 2010).

The concept of actorness and the ENP

As with the concept of EU presence, the concept of EU actorness has influenced the literature on the ENP. Concerning EU actorness in relation to neighbouring countries, Bretherton and Vogler (1999/2006) describe EU actorness as problematic. In the eastern neighbourhood, despite achieving a significant presence, the adequacy of the incentives offered by the ENP to transform the region is open to question, being circumscribed by the necessity of caution in the face of Russia. In the Mediterranean, as a replacement of similar predecessors, the ENP seems impeded by problems of consistency (Bretherton and Vogler 1999/2006).

Bechev (2011) draws on the concept of actorness and the need for more EU actorness in the ENP. He explicitly refers to the works of Sjöstedt (1977), Hill (1993), and Jupille and Caporaso (1998) and defines actorness as 'the capacity to articulate and put forward, in a coherent manner, a set of material stimuli and normative demands, to reward alignment, and, possibly, to win the loyalty of elites and citizenry in "third countries"'(Bechev 2011: 419).

Another explicit reference can be found in Delcour (2007). Referring to Bretherton and Vogler's (1999/2006) understanding of actorness as being constructed through the interplay of internal political factors and the perceptions and expectations of outsiders, she argues that those elements contribute to the EU shaping its neighbours' perceptions towards the Union and the ENP as well as to the EU's influence. Tulmets (2007) also acknowledges the debate concerning EU international actorness, discussing the discourse on EU 'soft-power' and its possible potential to help the EU bridge its capability-expectations gap. Another direct reference to EU actorness can be found in Tulmets' (2008) article on EU coherence and the ENP, where the discussion concerning actorness is mentioned because of the creation of the Common Foreign and Security Policy (CFSP) and the debate accompanying this development, and the concept itself is described as the EU's 'capability to lead a coherent external action' (Tulmets 2008: 108).

Other uses of EU actorness in the ENP literature are rather implicit, often mentioning the term actorness, but not necessarily referring to a concrete concept or the general debate. Gebhard (2007) assesses EU actorness in the ENP by focusing on the 'policy appropriateness' of the ENP measures, but without directly raising the concept of EU actorness itself. In a different article, Gebhard (2010) links the discussions concerning the capability-expectations gap in the context of the credibility of EU foreign policy actorness to a perceived strategic inadequacy of the ENP, consequently developing the step from actorness to effectiveness, but without referring to an individual concrete concept of actorness.

To assess the relevance of the concept of EU actorness to the scholarly debate on the role of the EU in the ENP, it is helpful to identify a variety of sub-concepts (or variables) of actorness. In the context of this chapter and this section, we will focus on the sub-concepts presented by Jupille and Caporaso (1998). Cohesion (or coherence) is a very prominent point of interest in ENP literature (Balfour and Missiroli 2007; Tulmets 2006a, 2006b; Dannreuther 2006; Tulmets 2008; Rynning and Pihlkjaer Jensen 2010; Missiroli 2010). Going beyond the standard use of coherence, Manners (2010) is concerned with EU value/normative coherence and Bosse (2007) utilises the coherence 'of the policy discourse on the significance and substance of "shared values"'(Bosse 2007) as one criterion to judge the ability of the Union to justify its policies on the basis of its values, in order to assess the extent to which the ENP can improve existing policies towards neighbouring states. Interestingly, this approach implicitly links EU actorness to EU effectiveness. Making a similar argument by linking effectiveness to (normative) coherence, Tulmets identifies a key determinant of the success of the ENP as ensuring a minimal internal consistency and 'to enhance its expertise about neighbouring countries in order to keep and increase its legitimacy and external coherence' (Tulmets 2007: 215). A similar argument can be found with Missiroli (2010).

The other sub-concepts of Jupille and Caporaso receive less attention in the ENP literature. *Authority* can be distinctly identified in some approaches on the ENP. Browning and Joenniemi (2007: 20), for example, argue that 'the ENP enhances the imperial characteristics of the EU, with governance and authority becoming centred on the core and power and subjectivity being dispersed out to declining degrees in a series of concentric circles'. Lehne (2014) contrasts the role of EU institutions in the ENP with the enlargement process, arguing that while the Commission was accepted as most important dialogue partner by candidate countries in the latter (thus implicitly also referring to recognition and the Commission's autonomy in the process), the EU institutions lack similar authority in the context of the ENP. Other authors like Scott (2009) develop arguments on EU moral authority, but these approaches have very faint connections to the discussion on EU actorness.

In contrast to the previous sub-concepts, apart from implicit references (Lehne 2014), neither *recognition* nor *autonomy* are particularly prominent as explicit notions in the reviewed ENP literature. As for *recognition,* that is, the acceptance of and interaction with the EU by third countries, this can probably be explained by the fact that the EU's recognition is taken for granted in the literature, which therefore is not specifically discussed.

The concept of effectiveness and the ENP

EU effectiveness is a prominent and recurring point of interest for researchers in the ENP literature. This is hardly surprising, given that the ENP was explicitly introduced as an effective policy tool to establish stable and cooperative relations with neighbouring countries and to extend the momentum of the EU's recent enlargement process, consequently building on the experiences from it. Accordingly, several publications ask the key question of how effective (or ineffective) the ENP is, mostly in terms of goal-achievement on the side of the EU, but also on the side of the ENP countries.[2] In ENP literature, EU effectiveness, which usually means goal-achievement, is linked to ideas of coherence and capability, although recent concepts on institutional effectiveness and performance have attempted to widen the conceptual understanding beyond goal-achievement (Oberthür and Groen 2015).

A considerable number of articles evaluate the effectiveness of the ENP itself or aspects of it (Balfour and Missiroli 2007; Bechev and Nicolaïdis 2010; Börzel and van Hüllen 2014; Dannreuther 2006; Kelley 2006), both in terms of the Eastern Partnership (EaP) (Korosteleva 2011; 2013; Popescu and Wilson 2009) and the Union for the Mediterranean (UfM) (Aliboni and Ammor 2009; Yildiz 2012). The discussion on effectiveness or ineffectiveness of the ENP, its measures, design and impact is one of the most prominent questions raised in ENP literature overall. However, most of these studies use effectiveness rather loosely and do not draw on a conceptually embedded/enriched concept of effectiveness. A notable exception is the work by Börzel and van Hüllen (2014), who argue that it is the ENP's substantive inconsistency in seeking to promote effective and democratic governance that undermines the EU's external effectiveness.

Others describe the term effectiveness as problematic on its own, particularly referring to the debate on empirical measures of what effectiveness actually implies. Moschella suggests, for example, that the term EU effectiveness in relation to the ENP is 'used to indicate the range of domestic transformations that occur in the partner countries and that can be associated with EU leverage and incentives' (Moschella 2007: 160).

Due to the variety of problems, different understandings and assessments concerning the ENP being effective (or not), we will focus on the instances explicitly or implicitly illustrating the conceptual linkage from actorness to effectiveness in the reviewed literature. Some authors connect coherence to effectiveness with the former facilitating the latter, meaning the higher the level of coherence the greater level of effectiveness can be expected and *vice versa* (Tulmets 2008). Dannreuther (2006), for example, suggests that the ENP is the EU's attempt to promote greater coherence and consistency in its neighbourhood policy, due to a lack of effectiveness in previous policies and programmes. In contrast, Börzel and van Hüllen (2014) argue that the EU's ineffectiveness in its neighbourhood policy does not result from a lack of coherence.

Another link between actorness and effectiveness is the assessment of the relation between the concrete capability of the EU in the ENP and their own expectations and those of the neighbouring countries involved, the 'capability-expectations gap' (Hill 1993; Bretherton and Vogler 1999/2006). Here, the question of effectiveness is conceptually linked to the capability to act according to the EU's own expectations and those of their partners in the ENP. The specific relevance of questions concerning the incidence and specifications of the EU's capability-expectations gap in the ENP is presented in several publications. For example, Bosse (2007) argues that the gap between the EU's political rhetoric on shared values and its capability to enforce these values is widened rather than reduced through the ENP (Bosse 2007). Analysing the ENP's effectiveness in bridging the capability-expectations gap, Delcour and Tulmets (2009) reach a similarly negative conclusion, arguing that the way the ENP has been designed and implemented so far is aimed at fulfilling the EU's own expectations rather than those of their neighbouring countries. Comparable assessments can also be found in more recent reviews on the issue (for example, Nielsen 2013).

Conclusions

As elaborated in this chapter, the concrete circumstances, measures and levels of power enabling the EU to (effectively) act as an international player are of interest to studies concerning the ENP, and the underlying concepts of EU presence, actorness and effectiveness can be identified in a variety of ENP-related literature. These concepts (and their sub-concepts) are present in ENP-related literature, to a varied extent, with some publications explicitly referring to the conceptualisation and the respective authors and making use of their operationalisations, while others – in fact the majority – chose a more implicit approach to introduce the ideas in their derivations or line of argument. Accordingly, the topics and issues they have been applied to vary as much as the literature on the ENP itself.

Although it seems difficult to identify an overall trend with regard to both concepts and points of interest in the reviewed ENP literature, there is an observable focus towards questions of effectiveness and coherence. Effectiveness, especially, is represented explicitly in several analyses, but infrequently conceptually underpinned and/or linked to specific concepts of EU presence or actorness. Similarly, in the literature, coherence is not necessarily related to actorness or effectiveness. Moreover, only a minority of studies explicitly refer to a specific concept or definition of EU presence or actorness, or link effectiveness to either one of them, with Hills' (1993) related concept of the 'capability-expectations gap' representing an acknowledged and adopted exception.

Hence, there remains room for improvement. An increase in systematic (theory-driven and carefully operationalised) analyses of EU presence and actorness in the ENP could be of considerable value to ENP scholarship and enhance for instance the comparability and generalisability of findings. Useful operationalisations of the various sub-concepts of actorness, including the type of reference points and questions to be asked can be found for instance in Huigens and Niemann (2011). The relationship between coherence/cohesion and effectiveness has been skilfully specified and operationalised by Thomas (2012) as well as da Conceição-Heldt and Meunier (2014). Other works that indicate how effectiveness may be studied with substantial sophistication include Hegemann et al. (2013) in terms of IR more generally and Ginsberg (2001) with regard to EU foreign policy. Such steps could prove useful to mitigate the criticism concerning the descriptive nature of ENP literature and effectiveness. Making increased use of concepts – such as presence, actorness and effectiveness – in a methodologically more rigorous fashion, and possibly extending the analysis towards novel concepts like EU 'performance' might allow charting new waters in ENP research and contributing, to some extent, to theory-development in EU Studies generally.

Notes

1 The importance of such opportunity structure was first conceptualised by Bretherton and Vogler (1999/2006) and acknowledged by other authors, such as Thomas (2012).
2 We will focus on EU effectiveness, when it is explicitly or implicitly linked to EU presence, actorness or coherence. As outlined above, effectiveness in some respect builds on actorness, meaning that there needs to be a certain capacity to behave actively and deliberately in order to enable the EU to act effectively (Groen and Niemann 2013: 4). However, that does not imply that any argument concerning EU effectiveness necessarily includes deliberations on EU actorness or presence.

References

Aliboni, R. and Ammor, F. (2009) 'Under the Shadow of "Barcelona": From the EMP to the Union for the Mediterranean', *EuroMeSCo Paper* 77, January.
Allen, D. and Smith, M. (1990) 'Western Europe's presence in the contemporary arena', *Review of International Studies* 16: 19–37.
Balfour, R. and Missiroli, A. (2007) 'Reassessing the European Neighbourhood Policy', *EPC Issue Paper* 54, Brussels: European Policy Centre.
Bechev, D. (2011) 'Of power and powerless: The EU and its neighbours', *Comparative European Politics* 9(4–5): 414–431.
Bechev, D. and Nicolaïdis, K. (2010) 'From policy to polity: Can the EU's special relations with its "neighbourhood" be decentred?', *Journal of Common Market Studies* 48(3): 475–500.
Börzel, T. and van Hüllen, V. (2014) 'One voice, one message, but conflicting goals: Cohesiveness and consistency in the European Neighbourhood Policy', *Journal of European Public Policy* 21(7): 1033–1049.
Bosse, G. (2007) 'Values in the EU's Neighbourhood Policy', *European Political Economy Review* 7: 38–62.
Bretherton, C. and Vogler, J. (1999/2006) *The European Union as a Global Actor*, Abingdon: Routledge.
Bretherton, C. and Vogler, J. (2008) 'Sustainable Development Actor', in Tocci, N. (ed.) *Who is a Normative Foreign Policy Actor?*, Brussels: Centre for European Policy Studies.
Browning, C. and Joenniemi, P. (2007) 'Geostrategies of the European Neighbourhood', *DIIS Working Paper 2007/9*, Copenhagen: Danish Institute for International Studies.
Cosgrove, C. and Twitchett, K. (1970) *The New International Actors: The United Nations and the European Economic Community*, London: Macmillan.
da Conceição-Heldt, E. and Meunier, S. (2014) 'Speaking with a single voice: Internal cohesiveness and external effectiveness of the EU in global governance', *Journal of European Public Policy* 21(7): 961–979.
Dannreuther, R. (2006) 'Developing the alternative to enlargement: The European Neighbourhood Policy', *European Foreign Affairs Review* 11: 183–201.
Delcour, L. (2007) 'Does the European Neighbourhood Policy make a difference?', *European Political Economy Review* 7: 118–155.
Delcour, L. and Tulmets, E. (2009) 'Pioneer Europe? The ENP as a test case for EU's foreign policy', *European Foreign Affairs Review* 14: 501–523.
Duchêne, F. (1972) 'Europe in World Peace', in Mayane, R. (ed.) *Europe Tomorrow: Sixteen Europeans Look Ahead*, London: Fontana, 32–47.
Echeverria Jesus, C. (2010) 'The ENP and the Middle East', in Whitman, R. and Wolff, S. (eds.) *The European Neighbourhood Policy in Perspective*, Hampshire: Palgrave MacMillan, 247–257.
Fioramonti, L. and Poletti, A. (2008) 'Facing the giant: Southern perspectives on the European Union', *Third World Quarterly* (29)1: 167–180.
Gebhard, C. (2007) 'Assessing EU Actorness Towards its "Near Abroad"—The European Neighbourhood Policy', *EU Consent Occasional Paper*, Maastricht.
Gebhard, C. (2010) 'The ENP's Strategic Conception and Design', in Whitman, R. and Wolff, S. (eds.) *The European Neighbourhood Policy in Perspective*, Hampshire: Palgrave MacMillan, 89–111.
Gebhard, C. (2011) 'Coherence', in Hill, C. and Smith, M. (eds.) *International Relations and the European Union*, 2nd edition, Oxford: OUP, 101–127.
Ginsberg, R. (2001) *The European Union in International Relations: Baptism by Fire*, Lanham, MD: Rowman and Littlefield.
Groen, L. and Niemann, A. (2013) 'The European Union at the Copenhagen climate negotiations: A case of contested EU actorness and effectiveness', *International Relations* 27(3): 308–324.

Hill, C. (1993) 'The capability-expectations gap, or conceptualizing Europe's international role', *Journal of Common Market Studies* 31(3): 305–325.
Huigens, J. and Niemann, A. (2011) 'The G8 1/2: The EU's contested and ambiguous actorness in the G8', *Cambridge Review of International Affairs* 24(4): 629–657.
Jones, A. (2009) 'Questionable "actorness" and "presence": Projecting "EU"rope in the Mediterranean', in Bialasiewicz, L. et al. 'Interventions in the new political geographies of the European "neighbourhood", *Political Geography* 28: 79–89.
Jones, A. and Clark, J. (2008) 'Europeanisation and discourse building: The European Commission, European narratives and European Neighbourhood Policy', *Geopolitics* 13(3): 545–571.
Jørgensen, K., Oberthür, S. and Shahin, J. (2011) 'Assessing the EU's performance in international institutions', *European Integration* 33(6): 599–620.
Jupille, J. and Caporaso, J. (1998) 'States, Agency and Rules: The European Union in Global Environmental Politics', in Rhodes, C. (ed.) *The European Union in the World Community*, Boulder, CO: Lynne Rienner, 213–229.
Kelley, J. (2006) 'New wine in old wineskins: Promoting political reforms through the new European Neighbourhood Policy', *Journal of Common Market Studies* 44(1): 29–55.
Koops, J. (2011) *The European Union as an Integrative Power?*, Brussels: VUB Press.
Korosteleva, E. (2011) 'Change or continuity: Is the eastern partnership an adequate tool for the European neighbourhood', *International Relations* 25: 243–262.
Korosteleva, E. (2013) 'Evaluating the role of partnership in the European Neighbourhood Policy', *Eastern Journal of European Studies* 4(2): 11–36.
Hegemann, H., Heller, R. and Kahl, M. (eds.) (2013) 'Studying "Effectiveness" in International Relations', Opladen: Barbara Budrich.
Lehne, S. (2014) *Time to Reset the European Neighbourhood Policy*, Brussels: Carnegie Endowment for International Peace.
Leonard, M. (2005) *Why Europe Will Run the 21st Century*, New York: Public Affairs.
Manners, I. (2002) 'Normative power Europe: A contradiction in terms?', *Journal of Common Market Studies* 40(2): 235–258.
Manners, I. (2010) 'As You Like It: European Union Normative Power in the European Neighbourhood Policy', in Whitman, R. and Wolff, S. (eds.) *The European Neighbourhood Policy in Perspective*, Hampshire: Palgrave MacMillan, 29–50.
Missiroli, A. (2010) 'The ENP in Future Perspective', in Whitman, R. and Wolff, S. (eds.) *The European Neighbourhood Policy in Perspective*, Hampshire: Palgrave MacMillan, 259–270.
Moschella, M. (2007) 'An international political economy approach to the neighbourhood policy', *European Political Economy Review* 7: 156–180.
Nielsen, K. (2013) 'EU soft-power and the capability-expectations gap', *Journal of Contemporary European Research* 9(5): 723–739.
Niemann, A. and Bretherton, C. (2013) 'Introduction: EU external policy at the crossroads: The challenge of actorness and effectiveness', *International Relations* 27(3): 261–275.
Niemann, A. and de Wekker, T. (2010) 'Normative Power Europe? EU Relations with Moldova', *European Integration Online Papers* 14.
Oberthür, S. and Groen, L. (2015) 'The effectiveness dimension of the EU's performance in international institutions', *Journal of Common Market Studies* 53(6): 1319–1335.
Orbie, J. (2006) 'Civilian power Europe: Review of the original and current debates', *Cooperation and Conflict* 14(1): 123–128.
Popescu, N. and Wilson, A. (2009) *The Limits of Enlargement-lite: European and Russian Power in the Troubled Neighbourhood*, London: European Council on Foreign Relations (ECFR).
Rynning, S. and Pihlkjaer Jensen, C. (2010) 'The ENP and Transatlantic Relations', in Whitman, R. and Wolff, S. (eds.) *The European Neighbourhood Policy in Perspective*, Hampshire: Palgrave MacMillan, 135–160.
Scott, J. (2009) 'Bordering and ordering the European neighbourhood', *Trames* 13(3): 232–247.
Sjöstedt, G. (1977) *The External Role of the European Community*, Hampshire: Saxon House, Swedish Institute of International Affairs.
Sjursen, H. (2006) 'The EU as a "normative" power: How can this be?', *Journal of European Public Policy* 13(2): 235–251.
Smith, H. (2002) *European Union Foreign Policy: What Is It and What It Does*, London: Pluto.
Smith, K. (2000) 'The end of civilian power EU', *The International Spectator* 35(2): 11–28.

Thomas, D. (2012) 'Still punching below its weight? Coherence and effectiveness in European Union foreign policy', *Journal of Common Market Studies* 50: 457–474.
Toje, A. (2011) 'The European Union as a small power', *Journal of Common Market Studies* 49(1): 43–60.
Tulmets, E. (2006a) 'Adapting the Experience of Enlargement to the Neighbourhood Policy: The ENP as a Substitute to Enlargement?', in Kratochvil, P. (ed.) *The European Union and Its Neighbourhood*, Prague: Institute of International Relations, 29–57.
Tulmets, E. (2006b) 'Is a Soft Method of Coordination Best Adapted to the Context of EU's Neighbourhood?', in Cremona, M. and Sadurski, W. (ed.) *The European Neighbourhood Policy*, San Domenico di Fiesole: European University Institute.
Tulmets, E. (2007) 'Can the discourse on "soft power" help the EU to bridge its capability-expectations gap?', *European Political Economy Review* 7: 195–226.
Tulmets, E. (2008) 'The European Neighbourhood Policy: A flavour of coherence in the EU's external relations?', *Hamburg Review of Social Sciences* 3(1): 107–141.
Van Schaik, L. (2013) *EU Effectiveness and Unity in Multilateral Negotiations—More than the Sum of Its Parts?*, Hampshire: Palgrave MacMillan.
Wolff, S. and Peen Rodt, A. (2010) 'Lessons for the Balkans: The ENP as a Possible Conflict Management Tool', in Whitman, R. and Wolff, S. (eds.) *The European Neighbourhood Policy in Perspective*, Hampshire: Palgrave MacMillan, 113–134.
Yildiz, U. (2012) 'The Union for the Mediterranean: Why did it fail and how should it be effective?' *Uluslararası Hukuk ve Politika* 8(32): 117–148.
Young, O. (1994) *International Governance: Protecting the Environment in a Stateless Society*, Ithaca: Cornell University Press.

4
THE CHALLENGE OF ANALYSING THE PERFORMANCE OF THE EUROPEAN NEIGHBOURHOOD POLICY[1]

Dorina Baltag and Iulian Romanyshyn

Introduction: why analyse ENP performance?

Performance has been a salient issue on the agenda of European policy-makers (European Commission 2013; 2014) and remains a recurrent theme in the European Union's (EU's) strategies and policies. The European institutions have placed great emphasis on the performance and ultimate effect of their policies. The European Neighbourhood Policy (ENP) represents a framework of cooperation with the EU's southern and eastern neighbours. The ring of instability that surrounds the EU from Eastern Europe to the Caucasus, the Middle East and the Horn of Africa raises perennial questions regarding EU performance under the ENP flagship. Initially designed to promote democracy, rule of law, market economy, prosperity and stability, this policy has been reviewed twice – in 2011, in the light of the Arab uprisings; and more recently, in 2015, after Russia's destabilisation of Ukraine, in the midst of the refugee crisis and soon after the Paris terrorist attacks.

Yet, what is the purpose of reviewing ENP performance? And why analyse ENP performance at all? The primary aim is to *evaluate* the policy by taking stock of the ENP progress over time, as the reviews have done in 2011 and 2015. Examining ENP performance is also important for purposes of *monitoring* and *control*, exercised by the European Commission, in addition to European and national parliamentarians. Moreover, performance review is crucial for setting external benchmarks, as it facilitates the attempts to *compare* the ENP to the EU's other regional policies in its geographic vicinity (for example, Black Sea Synergy, Western Balkans' Stabilisation and Association Process). While the initial policy was anchored in a 'one size fits all' philosophy, the revised ENP of 2015 focuses on greater differentiation and mutual ownership tailored to reflect varying interests, ambitions and degrees of interdependence with the EU. Performance review thus is crucial for uncovering such elements of *learning* in ENP development. Finally, as the ENP priorities are shifting from democracy promotion and economic development to political and economic stability, the key question for internal decision-makers and external observers is how and to what extent the ENP performance review helps to *improve* policy in the long-run.

The aim of this chapter is to build analytical and empirical bridges between the growing literature on performance and performance measurement, and the study of the ENP. Firstly, the chapter discusses various approaches to, and perspectives on, performance drawing mostly on the literature on public administration and organisational studies. It also briefly reviews the EU studies scholarship showing that research on performance, though on the rise, still falls short of a systematic effort across different issue areas. Secondly, the chapter outlines five indicators for performance measurement – relevance, cohesion, effectiveness, impact and resilience – and discusses their application in the context of the ENP. The text then proceeds with concluding remarks on aggregate performance assessment and the broader significance of the ENP performance review.

Performance: definitions, approaches and perspectives

Generally, performance is conceived as a process of an actor executing a task or function. Scholars of public policy and comparative politics define the concept to measure the performance of political institutions in Western democracies, the management of governments or performance management (Keman 2002; Ingraham et al. 2003; Peters and Pierre 2006; Howlett and Ramesh 1995; Bouckaert and Halligan 2006). Performance measurement and evaluation is central to public administration and organisation studies literature. For an organisation, successful performance implies that a task is done effectively, efficiently, in a relevant manner to its stakeholders and with hindsight on financial viability (Lusthaus 2002). The way in which performance is assessed frequently depends on the eye of the beholder: an insider's viewpoint is operationalised in cooperation with internal actors and tends to be subjective in character, whereas an outsider's perspective is more distanced, backward-looking and concerned with the relative success of policies or actions (Versluis et al. 2011).

Performance auditors widely rely on an input–output model of process management derived from economics (Neely 2004). Accordingly, public agencies are evaluated with respect to the amount and type of resources (time, finances, expertise and other assets) that are transformed in an organised way into a product of added value. The results of this transformation process include both tangible products or outputs (number of clients served) and rather diffuse outcomes (improved quality of service). The same holds true for political systems: performance implies an evaluation of outputs and outcomes, as well as the process – the effort, efficiency and capabilities used to accomplish the outcome (Eckstein 1971; Roller 2005).

The most commonly used indicators to measure performance of public or private agencies are the 'three E's' – *economy*, *efficiency* and *effectiveness* (Pidd 2012). While economy refers to the inputs or costs of production, efficiency refers to the ratio of output produced *per* input units. Effectiveness, in turn, measures the degree to which outcomes of the process meet the objectives of the agency. Besides the 'three E's', scholars also highlight the importance of *relevance* and *financial viability* to discuss the needs of stakeholders and to assess resources (Lusthaus 2002). In the study of public policies, scholars rely on such indicators as *equity* (an extent to which benefits are equally distributed across recipients) and *political feasibility* (probability of policy being adopted in the view of political constraints). The last criterion points to the importance of the broader context and environment, including ideology and worldview, in which the performance measurement is embedded (Rossell 1993; Gutner and Thompson 2010).

The rationale behind studying EU performance in international politics stems from the academic debate which calls for increasing focus on the EU's results and achievements in world affairs (Ginsberg 2001; Mahncke 2011). As Smith put it, the academic community 'should [. . .] engage in a debate of what the EU does, why it does it, and with what effect, rather than about what it is' (Smith 2010a: 343). Yet, the scholarly research dedicated to exploring and unpacking the notion of EU performance has been scarce. Notable examples include the studies that analyse EU performance in multilateral institutions (Oberthür et al. 2013; Jørgensen and Laatikainen 2013). More common, however, is the focus on EU impact, EU role performance, EU legitimacy and EU effectiveness in international affairs (Smith 2000; Ginsberg 2001; Van Schaik 2013; Elgström and Smith 2006; Bickerton 2007; Smith 2010b; Vasilyan 2011; Smith 2013; Romanyshyn 2015; Baltag and Smith 2015).

Analysing ENP performance

As performance is an overarching and multi-dimensional concept, its application in the context of the ENP requires a selection of indicators through which the most important elements of performance can be captured and analysed. Our choice of ENP performance indicators rests upon a necessity to gauge both input (relevance, cohesion) and output (effectiveness, impact) aspects of the policy as well as its interaction with an external environment (resilience). A comprehensive and balanced assessment of performance is thus contingent upon an examination of each of the five constituent elements.

Relevance

Assessing performance in relation to ongoing relevance implies the extent to which a policy meets the needs and requirements of its stakeholders and clients and can maintain their continuous support. Performance in this sense is assessed as the ability of an organisation to keep its established goals, programmes and activities in line with the needs of its clients and stakeholders, 'organizations need to be relevant to both funders and clients, and must reconcile the differences' (Lusthaus 2002: 119). Stakeholders and clients are those most involved and with a vested interest in the outcome or contribution of the organisation (Barclay and Osei-Bryson 2010). When assessing relevance, it is important to discuss the level of satisfaction of stakeholders and clients and to note that stakeholders and clients may have similar or divergent views and expectations that can render constructive or destructive outcomes (Bourne and Walker 2006; Mitchell 2002).

Assessing relevance reflects on the position of both ENP stakeholders and clients, that is, EU Member States and ENP countries. Research on ENP identifies two blocs in relation to the emergence of the ENP and developments in ENP countries – one for the eastern neighbourhood (with most active roles attributed to Germany, Sweden, Austria, the Baltic states and Poland) and one for the Mediterranean (with most active roles attributed to France, Italy, Spain and Portugal) (Lippert 2007). While similar in many ways in their concerns regarding the neighbourhood, the divergence related to the future enlargement of the EU. The eastern bloc, and especially Poland, viewed the ENP as a vehicle to share their integration experience and benefits with the neighbours to the East (Copsey 2008). In contrast, the southern bloc was preoccupied, on the one hand, with strengthening Mediterranean ties to counterbalance the EU's pivot to the East – of importance to France – and, on the other, not to overstretch the economic benefits of the EU's internal integration (Smith 2005; Lengger 2012). As Böttger (2008) shows, Member States' core expectations regarding the ENP lay in the distinction between *democratisation* (for the eastern bloc) and *stabilisation* (for the southern bloc). If the projected functionalities of the policy were somewhat mixed at first, after the two ENP reviews in 2011 and 2015 the value that Member States attach to the ENP is openly shifting towards a security rationale. In other words, the policy is now identified as a means for stabilising borders and managing security threats emanating from the neighbourhood (Schumacher 2015; Dandashly 2015).

For some ENP countries, like Ukraine or Moldova, the launch of the ENP caused frustration as it clearly granted 'everything but the institutions' – that is, without the membership perspective they were interested in (Gordon and Sasse 2008; Malyhina 2009). To address rising European aspirations, the eastern neighbours were offered the Eastern Partnership (EaP), even though not all countries addressed shared the same level of ambition. The way they responded to the EU's offer of Association Agreements (AAs) and Deep and Comprehensive Free Trade Agreements (DCFTAs), designed as a step to advance political and economic cooperation, reflects a different degree of perceived policy relevance. While Georgia, Ukraine and Moldova signed and ratified the agreements, Armenia turned its back on the EU in the negotiation process, whereas Azerbaijan and Belarus were never genuinely interested in it. For the southern neighbours, the main interest lay in strengthening trade and economic cooperation, rather than membership or political dialogue (Comelli 2005). Some even argued that the reason why Mediterranean ENP countries signed up for the ENP (and the Union for the Mediterranean) was to legitimise their domestic autocratic regimes (Koeth 2014). Following the Arab uprisings in 2011, the EU proposed DCFTAs to its southern neighbours, an offer that appeared to be attractive for some countries in the region, of which only Morocco and Tunisia entered negotiations. The DCFTAs initiative aims at upgrading the existing legal framework for trade liberalisation with the EU established earlier as a part of the Euro-Mediterranean AAs.

Cohesion

Examining performance in relation to cohesion refers to the ability to articulate policy preferences consistently and to the consistent alignment of common policies among stakeholders, horizontally and vertically (Jupille and Caporaso 1998; Thomas 2012; Metcalfe 1994). Vertically, cohesion implies that the policies designed by Member States are in line with the overall EU policies to which they subscribe. This means that Member States are communicating and projecting to their counterparts the same goals, embracing the same vision substantiated with uniform actions. Horizontally, cohesion is about coordination, meaning that Member States need to ensure that their different policy objectives do not hamper or negate each another. The importance of cohesion in EU external relations has been reaffirmed by the Lisbon Treaty and emphasised by the High Representative of the Union for Foreign Affairs and Security Policy, Federica Mogherini, at her European Parliament hearing, and is central in the political guidelines of the Juncker-led Commission.

Scholars argue that when important national interests are at stake, Member States often opt to avoid EU-level instruments and act unilaterally according to their national economic (mainly energy and trade) or security interests (Rummel and Wiedermann 1998; Bosse and Schmidt-Felzmann 2011). For instance, regarding Belarus, while officially supporting EU political rhetoric on the application of sanctions and condemning the severe human rights violations that occurred in 2011, Member States chose to act in a manner that demonstrates their individual state interests. In this case, Germany continued to trade with Belarus regardless, Lithuania strongly opposed economic sanctions and Slovenia vetoed sanctions to secure individual trade deals (Baltag and Romanyshyn 2012). Also, Member States' views are divergent in how to deal with authoritarian regimes in the South (Del Sarto and Schumacher 2011). After the Arab uprisings, Member States disagreed on the management of illegal migration, as evidenced by divergent French and Italian positions over migrants coming from North Africa in 2011. Instead of seeking a common approach at the European level, both Member States relied on national measures, such as imposing border controls or issuing residence permits (Noutcheva 2015).

Horizontally, Member States cluster into different groups of interest (according to historical legacies, thematic or geographic affinities) and are reluctant to embrace joint ENP action. Poland, Sweden, Romania and Lithuania may coordinate together on EaP related issues like migration, minority rights or elections. Poland, the Czech Republic, Hungary and Slovakia develop cooperation with ENP countries in the Visegrad group, which is interested in democratic reform processes in these countries and has a common Visegrad Fund set up to foster civil society support. Sweden, Finland, Denmark, the United Kingdom, Ireland and the Netherlands coordinate under the Nordic Plus umbrella aiming at, for example, enhancing donor practices in ENP countries. Research on different examples shows how practical cooperation on the ground in the ENP countries results in competition among Member States (Baltag and Smith 2015). Recently, analysts discussed that Germany will be 'hitting the brakes' in leadership on ENP (Gressel 2015) and warned that the Franco-German competition might lead to different strategies within the ENP (Nougayrède 2015). It is also argued that the Union for Mediterranean is a prominent example of horizontal incohesion, as 'France's policies have in many ways resulted from its clear discomfort about Germany's growing economic and political power within Europe' (ibid.: 12).

Effectiveness

Effectiveness is a cross-cutting concept that is widely used in a variety of disciplines. The literature on public policy-making ties the notion of effectiveness to the achievement of specific policy goals, or policy implementation (Héritier 2012). The international relations literature also discusses the notion of effectiveness (Hegemann et al. 2013). Analysing the performance of international environmental regimes, Young (1999) argues that effectiveness is a multifaceted concept that may take on different forms, such as legal effectiveness (compliance with contractual obligations), economic effectiveness (the ratio between meeting objectives and amount of resources spent), normative effectiveness (achievement of justice, participation and other values) or political effectiveness (changes in the behaviour and interests of actors). A similar rational understanding of effectiveness is demonstrated by scholars working in the fields of organisational studies and public management (Lusthaus 2002; Meyer 2002). Effectiveness is understood as the ability of an organisation to successfully fulfil its objectives. Goal attainment is probably the most common interpretation of effectiveness, although its analysis can raise some challenges, especially when the goals are not clearly formulated, contradict each other, overlap or are scattered across different hierarchies of priorities (Gutner and Thompson 2010).

The central definition of effectiveness – goal attainment – is well illustrated in the study of the EU's external relations with its neighbours (Delcour 2007; Freyburg et al. 2009). Article 21(2) of the Treaty on European Union offers a broad list of the EU's goals in the international arena ranging from support for democracy and rule of law to conflict prevention and integration into the world economy. These objectives are echoed in Article 8(1), which specifically prescribes that the EU develops close and cooperative ties with neighbouring countries. The 2003 Communication of the European Commission singled out the aim of building 'a ring of friends' as a central objective of the ENP. According to the Commission, this signified 'a zone of prosperity and a friendly neighbourhood' committed to 'shared values and effective implementation of political, economic and institutional reforms' (Commission of the European Communities 2003: 4). The Strategy Paper on the ENP, which followed just one year later, put forward another formulation: 'The objective of the ENP is to share the benefits of the EU's 2004 enlargement with neighbouring countries in strengthening stability, security and well-being for all concerned' (Commission of the European Communities 2004: 3). These are the long-term strategic objectives; thus, a certain level of generality and ambiguity is natural. However, they are not necessarily in harmony with each other, which complicates the goal attainment and its assessment (Börzel and Van Hüllen 2014). How are values and normative principles that underpin the policy reconciled with interests, such as security and stability? To what extent did the notion of creating a 'ring of friends' resonate with the intention to abolish dividing lines in Europe as a main rationale of the EU enlargement process? Apart from the problem of conflicting objectives, another challenging aspect is that the objectives change over time, even on the level of strategy. The latest ENP review put forward stabilisation of the neighbourhood and comprehensive handling of instability sources as the policy's top priorities (European Commission and High Representative of the Union for Foreign Affairs and Security Policy 2015).

ENP strategic objectives have been further operationalised into several more specific short-term oriented priorities that laid the foundation for Action Plans or Association Agendas for ENP countries. Although the number and intensity of priorities in these documents vary from one country to another, all are related to the areas of political governance and economic development, reforms in the sectors of justice, energy, transport, environment and developing people-to-people contacts. An assessment of these objectives as to the extent of their fulfilment by the ENP countries is performed annually by the European Commission and (since the entry into force of the Lisbon Treaty in 2009) the EEAS, mainly in the form of annual Progress Reports. After the last ENP review, both Action Plans and Progress Reports will be replaced by new individualised instruments based on jointly agreed priorities.

Impact

Like effectiveness, the indicator of impact refers to an assessment of the output dimension of performance. Impact can be understood as an ability of a policy to address, mitigate and eradicate a given issue that triggered the policy's creation. The definition of impact as a problem-solving capacity is common in the literature on international regimes and international organisations. Scholars discuss, for example, the role of international institutions in dealing with environmental pollution, global epidemics or inter-state conflict (Young 1999; Boehmer et al. 2004). Impact can also be conflated with the notion of structural power or 'the authority and capacity to set the rules of the game and to determine how the others will play the game' (Holsti 1995: 69). In other words, an actor or policy produces an impact if it shapes a long-standing structural environment in which other actors operate (Strange 1987). Impact is not identical to effectiveness – a policy or actor can be effective without having an impact, if the goals are *status quo*-oriented or inaction is preferred. On the other hand, impact does not necessarily need to go along with goal attainment. In the latter case, it is the presence of unintended effects and unexpected consequences that is crucial in distinguishing impact from effectiveness.

Drawing on the EU's experience of the eastern enlargement, domestic change and transformation in third countries has become the main yardstick against which the EU's impact is measured (Grabbe 2006). For that purpose, ENP countries need to embark on the long-term process of convergence – Europeanisation – which implies selection, adoption and application of the EU's rules in their domestic political systems (Lavenex and Schimmelfennig 2009). If the rationale behind the ENP was to stabilise the EU's new borders (problem-solving) through promoting democracy and market economy in ENP countries (shaping structures), the EU's impact across its eastern and southern borderlands appears rather poor. Although scholars do acknowledge the EU's ability to successfully promote functional cooperation and convergence within specific policy areas, the EU is less capable of socialising political elites, changing political systems or societies at large in ENP countries (Freyburg et al. 2009; Bechev and Nicolaïdis 2010; Langbein and Wolczuk 2012). Some commentators even argue that the controversies surrounding the ENP's goals and implementation led to reverse results in the form of consolidated autocratic regimes, rather than genuine democratic change (Youngs 2009; Börzel 2010).

The ENP produced a tangible, yet unintended, effect in the relations between the EU and Russia. Although invited to partake, Russia from the outset perceived the ENP – and later the Eastern Partnership – with growing suspicion and accused the EU of having a hidden agenda aimed at pulling the former Soviet countries out of the Russian orbit of influence (Haukkala 2008). This perception of competition, in conjunction with a contest of the EU's normative power, guided most of the Kremlin's actions in the shared neighbourhood, up to the deployment of military force against neighbouring Georgia and Ukraine. Another example of ENP impact that had not been fully anticipated by EU policy-makers relates to empowerment of civil society actors. Until recently, the ENP prioritised the relationship with governments and state institutions that downplayed the role and strength of social movements and grassroots initiatives in the ENP countries. This tendency backfired and revealed weaknesses of the EU's policy considering the 'Colour Revolutions' in Eastern Europe, but most prominently after the outbreak of the Arab uprisings (Tocci and Cassarino 2011).

Resilience

Resilience derives from the assessment of the policy's potential flexibility and forward-looking quality (Versluis et al. 2011). It refers to the policy's capacity to change and adapt, and the possibility to re-engineer itself based on a learning process. The extent of policy resilience can be grasped through a set of characteristics that reflect different aspects of change – linear (predictable) or non-linear (unpredictable), incremental (evolutionary) or radical (revolutionary) (Capano 2009). Whereas policies are designed considering expected outcomes, sometimes failure of a policy creates a significant opportunity to learn and improve (Behn 2003). In addition, the driving forces of policy change can often be found in unexpected factors, contingencies and critical events, which also trigger feedback and learning processes (Evans and Reid 2014). Assessing performance in relation to resilience implies delving into a self-reflective exercise with the understanding that policy is not implemented in a vacuum – innovation and adaptation are intrinsically linked to resilience. From this standpoint, resilience refers not only to the policy's capacity to adapt to the changing conditions but also to anticipate future fluctuations and external shocks in the environment where the policy is implemented.

The ENP demonstrates varying patterns of resilience. Until the first ENP review in 2011, the policy was characterised by incrementalism and linearity fuelled mainly by the path dependency of the successfully tested toolbox of enlargement. The ENP thus at first remained immune to change; the fact that the policy lingered largely unaffected by the 'Colour Revolutions' in the post-Soviet space or the global economic and Eurozone crises well illustrates this point. This has changed, under the pressure of the external shock that occurred in form of the Arab uprisings in 2011 and a series of other critical events, ranging from Russia's aggressive behaviour in the East to the growth of the Islamic State/Da'esh and other forms of religious extremism in the South. The two ENP reviews in 2011 and 2015 – occurring within just four years – signal declining policy resilience because of the necessity to respond and adjust to the external context. 'A New Response to a Changing Neighbourhood' released by the European Commission and the EEAS in 2011 urged for wider – compared to the previous practice – application of the principles of differentiation, joint ownership and conditionality, demonstrating some elements of learning. Yet, the 2015 ENP review seems to prioritise stabilisation and security interests at the expense of other ENP principles and, by doing so, suggests a radical policy change (Schumacher 2016). As ENP resilience declines, an opportunity for alternative scenarios of development opens, casting a shadow of uncertainty and ambiguity on the future of the policy.

Conclusions

A central question in the performance analysis is how these individual performance indicators contribute to an aggregate assessment of ENP performance. Any attempt to determine an amassed performance score requires a careful balance and calibration between individual performance indicators. Based on the above discussion of input (relevance, cohesion) and output (effectiveness, impact) criteria, we conclude that the ENP underperforms, although a growing capacity to learn and adjust to external circumstances (resilience) can be crucial for the policy's improvement in times ahead. That said, it is important to note that ENP performance analysis is not an exact science, but a qualitative exercise. It is based on a researcher's judgement related to their individual view of perfect or optimal ENP performance. However, this ideal standard, against which the actual performance is assessed, should be a product of a balance between setting the bar of expectations too high and unreasonable lowering of the EU's potential ambitions. Similarly, how to establish a level playing field for the performance indicators or, alternatively, assign diverse weightings among them largely depends on a researcher's epistemological and conceptual standing with regard to the notion of performance.

It goes without saying that the benefits and findings of performance analysis are not – and should not be – restricted to the academic community alone. Above all, the main purpose of an investigation in relation to what the EU achieves and how it performs on the world stage is to better inform both policy and strategy. Is the EU fit for purpose in the neighbourhood? What and where can the EU do better? Can the EU compete in a world of growing multipolarity and interdependence? Reflecting upon the EU's performance in the neighbourhood would ultimately contribute to better strategic thinking and build clear linkages between means and ends in EU foreign policy. After all, it is not a coincidence that the 'principled pragmatism' – a guiding leitmotiv of the new EU Global Strategy – has surfaced after the reviewed ENP expressed a clear preference for pragmatic engagement with and stabilisation of the neighbourhood.

Note

1 We would like to thank the editors of the volume and Michael H. Smith for their useful comments on the earlier version of the chapter. We are also grateful to Sarah Melker for the language editing.

References

Baltag, D. and Romanyshyn, I. (2012) 'EU's Relations with Eastern Neighbours as a Showcase of the EU's Actorness', UACES Student Conference, Brussels, June.

Baltag, D. and Smith, M. (2015) 'EU and Member State diplomacies in Moldova and Ukraine: Examining EU diplomatic performance post-Lisbon', *European Integration Online Papers* 1(19): 1–25.

Barclay, C. and Osei-Bryson, K. (2010) 'Project performance development framework: An approach for developing performance criteria & measures for information systems (IS) projects', *International Journal of Production Economics* 124(1): 272–292.

Bechev, D. and Nicolaïdis, C. (2010) 'From policy to polity: Can the EU's special relations with its "neighbourhood" be decentred?', *Journal of Common Market Studies* 48(3): 475–500.

Behn, R. (2003) 'Why measure performance? Different purposes require different measures', *Public Administration Review* 63(5): 586–606.

Bickerton, C. (2007) 'The perils of performance: EU foreign policy and the problem of legitimization', *Perspectives: Review of International Affairs* 28: 24–42.

Boehmer, C., Gartzke, E. and Nordstrom, T. (2004) 'Do intergovernmental organizations promote peace?', *World Politics* 57(1): 699–732.

Börzel, T. (2010) 'The Transformative Power of Europe Reloaded: The Limits of External Europeanization', *KFG Working Paper Series* 11, February.

Börzel, T. and Van Hüllen, V. (2014) 'One voice, one message, but conflicting goals: Cohesiveness and consistency in the European Neighbourhood Policy', *Journal of European Public Policy* 21(7): 1033–1049.

Bosse, G. and Schmidt-Felzmann, A. (2011) 'The geopolitics of energy supply in the "Wider Europe"', *Geopolitics* 16(3): 479–485.

Böttger, K. (2008) 'The Development of the European Neighbourhood Policy (ENP): The EU as a Regional Power for Peace and Order?', 4th Pan-European Conference on EU Politics, University of Latvia, September.

Bouckaert, G. and Halligan, J. (2006) 'Performance: Its Measurement, Management, and Policy', in Peters, B. and Pierre, K. (eds.) *Handbook of Public Policy*, London: Sage, 443–460.

Bourne, L. and Walker, D. (2006) 'Using a visualising tool to study stakeholder influence: two Australian examples', *Journal of Project Management* 37(1): 5–21.

Capano, G. (2009) 'Understanding policy change as an epistemological and theoretical problem', *Journal of Comparative Policy Analysis* 11(1): 7–31.

Comelli, M. (2005) 'The approach of the European Neighbourhood Policy (ENP): Distinctive features and differences with the Euro-Mediterranean Partnership', *Documenti IAI* 0545.

Commission of the European Communities (2003) *Wider Europe—Neighbourhood: A New Framework for Relations with Our Eastern and Southern Neighbours*, COM (2003) 104, Brussels.

Commission of the European Communities (2004) *European Neighbourhood Policy: Strategy Paper*, COM (2004) 373, Brussels.

Copsey, N. (2008) 'Member state policy preferences on the integration of Ukraine and the other Eastern Neighbours', *SIPU Report for the Swedish International Development Agency* 26.

Dandashly, A. (2015) 'The EU response to regime change in the wake of the Arab revolt: Differential implementation', *Journal of European Integration* 37(1): 37–56.

Delcour, L. (2007) 'Does the European Neighbourhood Policy make a difference? Policy patterns and reception in Ukraine and Russia', *European Political Economy Review* 7: 118–155.

Del Sarto, R. and Schumacher, T. (2011) 'From Brussels with love: Leverage, benchmarking, and the action plans with Jordan and Tunisia in the EU's democratization policy', *Democratization* 18(4): 932–955.

Eckstein, H. (1971) *The Evaluation of Political Performance: Problems and Dimensions*, London: Sage.

Elgström, O. and Smith, M. (2006) *The European Union's Roles in International Politics: Concepts and Analysis*, London: Routledge.

European Commission (2013) 'Innovation Union Scoreboard 2013', https://ec.europa.eu/growth/tools-databases/eip-raw-materials/en/system/files/ged/69%20Innovation%20Union%20Scoreboard%202013_en.pdf, accessed 12 December 2016.

European Commission (2014) *Investment for Jobs and Growth: Promoting Development and Good Governance in EU Regions and Cities*, Brussels: Directorate General for Regional and Urban Policy.

European Commission and High Representative of the Union for Foreign Affairs and Security Policy (2015) *Joint Communication to the European Parliament, the Council, the European Economic and Social Committee and the Committee of the Regions: Review of the European Neighbourhood Policy*, JOIN (2015) 50, Brussels.

Evans, B. and Reid, J. (2014) *Resilient Life: The Art of Living Dangerously*, Cambridge: Polity.

Freyburg, T., Lavenex, S., Schimmelfennig, F., Skripka, T. and Wetzel, A. (2009) 'EU promotion of democratic governance in the neighbourhood', *Journal of European Public Policy* 16(6): 916–934.

Ginsberg, R. (2001) *The European Union in International Politics: Baptism by Fire*, Lanham: Rowman & Littlefield.

Gordon, C. and Sasse, G. (2008) *The European Neighbourhood Policy: Effective Instrument for Conflict Management and Democratic Change in the Union's Eastern Neighbourhood?*, Bozen/Bolzano: EURAC, August.

Grabbe, H. (2006) *The EU's Transformative Power: Europeanization through Conditionality in Central and Eastern Europe*, Basingstoke: Palgrave Macmillan.

Gressel, G. (2015) 'Germany and the Eastern Partnership: The View from Berlin', *ECFR Riga Series*, May.

Gutner, T. and Thompson, A. (2010) 'The politics of IO performance: A framework', *The Review of International Organizations* 5(3): 227–248.

Haukkala, H. (2008) The Russian challenge to EU normative power: The case of European Neighbourhood Policy, *International Spectator* 43(2): 35–47.

Hegemann, H., Heller, R. and Kahl, M. (2013) *Studying 'Effectiveness' in International Relations: A Guide for Students and Scholars*, Opladen: Barbara Budrich.

Héritier, A. (2012) 'Policy Effectiveness and Transparency in European Policy-Making', in Jones, E., Menon, A. and Weatherhill, S. (eds.) *The Oxford Handbook of the European Union*, Oxford: Oxford University Press, 676–689.

Holsti, K. (1995) *International Politics: A Framework for Analysis*, London: Prentice-Hall.

Howlett, M. and Ramesh, M. (1995) *Studying Public Policy: Policy Cycles and Policy Subsystems*, Oxford: Oxford University Press.

Ingraham, P., Joyce P. and Donahue A. (2003) *Government Performance: Why Management Matters*, Baltimore: Johns Hopkins University Press.

Jørgensen, K. and Laatikainen, K. (eds.) (2013) *Routledge Handbook on the European Union and International Institutions*, London: Routledge.

Jupille, J. and Caporaso, J. (1998) 'States, Agency, and Rules: The European Union in Global Environmental Politics', in Rhodes, C. (ed.) *The European Union in the World Community*, London: Lynne Rienner, 213–229.

Keman, H. (2002) *Comparative Democratic Politics: A Guide to Contemporary Theory and Research*, London: Sage.

Koeth, W. (2014) "The 'deep and comprehensive free trade agreements": An appropriate response by the EU to the challenges in its neighbourhood?', *Eipascope*: 23–30.

Langbein, J. and Wolczuk, K. (2012) 'Convergence without membership? The impact of the European Union in the neighbourhood: Evidence from Ukraine', *Journal of European Public Policy* 19(6): 863–881.

Lavenex, S. and Schimmelfennig, F. (2009) 'EU rules beyond EU borders: Theorizing external governance in European politics', *Journal of European Public Policy* 16(6): 791–812.

Lengger, M. (2012) 'The Review of the European Neighbourhood Policy—An Advocacy Coalition Explanation', ECPR Conference, University of Bremen, July.

Lippert, B. (2007) *The Discussion on EU Neighbourhood Policy—Concepts, Reform Proposals and National Positions*, Berlin/Bonn: Friedrich Ebert Stiftung, July.

Lusthaus, C. (2002) *Organizational Assessment: A Framework for Improving Performance*, Ottawa: IDRC.

Mahncke, D. (2011) 'Post-Modern Diplomacy: Can EU Foreign Policy Make a Difference in World Politics?', *EU Diplomacy Papers* 4.

Malyhina, K. (2009) 'EU Membership Ambitions: What Alternative Approaches Exist and How is the European Foreign Policy Perceived in Ukraine?', in Schäffer, S. and Tolksdorf, D. (eds.) *The EU Member States and the Eastern Neighbourhood–From Composite to Consistent EU Foreign Policy*, CAP Policy Analysis, August.

Metcalfe, L. (1994) 'International policy co-ordination and public management reform', *International Review of Administrative Sciences* 60: 271–290.

Meyer, M. (2002) *Rethinking Performance Measurement: Beyond the Balanced Scorecard*, Cambridge: Cambridge University Press.

Mitchell, H. (2002) *Strategic Worth of Human Resources: Driving Organizational Performance*, Practice Coordinator, Corporate Performance Improvement, Universalia, www.universalia.com/sites/default/files/presentations/fichiers/2002_strategicworthhr_hugmitchell.pdf.

Neely, A. (ed.) (2004) *Business Performance Measurement: Theory and Practice*, Cambridge: Cambridge University Press.

Nougayrède, N. (2015) 'France and the Eastern Partnership: The View from Paris', *ECFR Riga Series*, May.

Noutcheva, G. (2015) 'Institutional governance of European neighbourhood policy in the wake of the Arab Spring', *Journal of European Integration* 37(1): 19–36.

Oberthür, S., Jørgensen, K. and Shahin, J. (eds.) (2013) *The Performance of the EU in International Institutions*, London: Routledge.

Peters, B. and Pierre, J. (2006) *Handbook of Public Policy*, London: Sage.

Pidd, M. (2012) *Measuring the Performance of Public Services Principles and Practice*, Cambridge: Cambridge University Press.

Roller, E. (2005) *The Performance of Democracies: Political Institutions and Public Policy*, Oxford: Oxford University Press.

Romanyshyn, I. (2015) 'Explaining EU effectiveness in multilateral institutions: The case of the arms trade treaty negotiations', *Journal of Common Market Studies* 53(4): 875–892.
Rossell, C. (1993) 'Using multiple criteria to evaluate public policies: The case of school desegregation', *American Politics Quarterly* 21(2): 155–184.
Rummel, R. and Wiedermann, J. (1998) 'Identifying Institutional Paradoxes of CFSP', in Zielonka, J. (ed.) *Paradoxes of European Foreign Policy*, London: Kluwer Law, 35–52.
Schumacher, T. (2015) 'Uncertainty at the EU's borders: Narratives of EU external relations in the revised European Neighbourhood Policy towards the southern borderlands', *European Security* 24(3): 381–401.
Schumacher, T. (2016) 'Back to the Future: The 'New' ENP Towards the Southern Neighbourhood and the End of Ambition', *College of Europe Policy Brief* 1, January.
Smith, M. (2000) 'Conforming to Europe: The domestic impact of EU foreign policy co-operation', *Journal of European Public Policy* 7(4): 613–631.
Smith, K. (2005) 'The outsiders: The European Neighbourhood Policy', *International Affairs* 81(4): 757–773.
Smith, K. (2010a) 'The EU in the World: Future Research Agendas', in Egan, M., Nugent, N. and Paterson, W. (eds.) *Research Agendas in EU Studies: Stalking the Elephant*, Houndmills: Palgrave Macmillan, 329–353.
Smith, K. (2010b) 'The European Union at the Human Rights Council: Speaking with one voice but having little influence', *Journal of European Public Policy* 17(2): 224–241.
Smith, M. (2013) 'The European External Action Service and the security–development nexus: Organizing for effectiveness or incoherence?', *Journal of European Public Policy* 20(9): 1299–1315.
Strange, S. (1987) 'The persistent myth of lost hegemony', *International Organization* 41(4): 551–574.
Thomas, D. (2012) 'Still punching below its weight? Coherence and effectiveness in European Union foreign policy', *Journal of Common Market Studies* 50(3): 457–474.
Tocci, N. and Cassarino, J.-P. (2011) 'Rethinking the EU's Mediterranean Policies Post-1/11', *IAI Working Papers* 11(6), March.
Van Schaik, L. (2013) *EU Effectiveness and Unity in Multilateral Negotiations: More than the Sum of Its Parts?*, Basingstoke: Palgrave Macmillan.
Vasilyan, S. (2011) 'The external legitimacy of the EU in the South Caucasus', *European Foreign Affairs Review* 16(3): 341–357.
Versluis, E., Van Keulen, M. and Stephenson, P. (2011) *Analyzing the European Union Policy Process*, Basingstoke: Palgrave Macmillan.
Young, O. (1999) *The Effectiveness of International Environmental Regimes: Causal Connections and Behavioral Mechanisms*, Cambridge: MIT Press.
Youngs, R. (2009) 'Democracy promotion as external governance?', *Journal of European Public Policy* 16(6): 895–915.

5
POWER AND LEADERSHIP IN THE EUROPEAN NEIGHBOURHOOD
Contending role concepts

Lisbeth Aggestam

Introduction

While the nature of European power in the EU's neighbourhood has been subject to academic debate, the concept of leadership has received scant attention in academic analysis. This is surprising, given that much of what has been written about the European Union's (EU) role in the neighbourhood rests on latent assumptions of European leadership as a 'model' and 'example' – a power that attracts and inspires followers (Manners 2002; Leonard 2005; Börzel and Risse 2009). In contrast, scholars with a realist outlook on international relations point to the inherent strategic weakness of the EU as an actor and are more critical of European power and leadership in the neighbourhood (Hyde-Price 2008; Toje 2010). There is deep disagreement in the academic literature over the question of what kind of power and leadership the European Union exercises in and through the European Neighbourhood Policy (ENP) (Aggestam 2008; Nicolaidis and Whitman 2013; Sjursen 2006). This chapter seeks to go beyond the increasingly sterile debate on Europe as a power, focusing instead on the contested idea of European leadership in the neighbourhood.

Leadership is widely seen as a condition for the EU being able to act, achieve its aims and have an impact on some of the critical issues in its neighbourhood. The question of the EU's capacity for leadership has become salient in the context of the Ukraine crisis since 2014, the policy reviews of the ENP in 2015 and the adoption of the EU Global Strategy in 2016. Yet, the forms and modalities of leadership have not been subject to much analysis in the academic literature on the ENP. To address this lacuna, this chapter sketches out a framework of leadership analysis based on social role theory. The starting point in role theory is that leadership is a *relational activity* involving learning and socialization between leader and followers. It is social in the sense that leadership requires recognition (role-expectations) by multiple actors that are both internal and external to the EU. The leader–follower nexus is therefore central in the analysis of the ENP. Without followers from the EU's neighbourhood, there is no EU leadership.

This chapter argues that the EU suffers from a leadership paradox at the heart of the ENP. On the one hand, there is a drive to centralize and strengthen European leadership in response to the collective action problem of EU Member States. On the other hand, there is an accompanying historical and ideological unease at the idea of a strong European leadership role, which is the reason why the political construction of the EU consists of overlapping governance structures encouraging dispersed and fragmented leadership (Hayward 2008). There is, in other words, an inbuilt paradox between leadership effectiveness and leadership legitimacy that is manifest in the ENP. Political legitimacy is ultimately anchored at the national level, which is why the ENP must accommodate strong intergovernmental instincts and social practices derived from its Member States and ENP countries. Therefore, leadership in the ENP is a competitive activity with conflicting role expectations of how leadership should be performed and by whom.

The chapter is organized in four main parts. The next section provides a general overview of the academic debates on Europe as a power and highlights the assumptions of leadership implicit in this literature. The second part distinguishes four ways in which the concept of leadership tends to be discussed in the academic literature on the ENP. The third part focuses on the relationship between leaders and followers and outlines the key contributions role theory can make to analysing this relationship. The final part considers the question of leadership performance, drawing on Young's (1991) threefold typology of leadership.

Power and leadership

The long-standing debate on what kind of power the EU is, and how it acts in global politics and its immediate neighbourhood, contains many assumptions about European leadership. Liberal constructivists have tended to stress the significant transformative power of the Union in global affairs (Dunne 2008; Manners 2008; Börzel and Risse 2009; Smith 2010). Realists, on the other hand, have been more sceptical of the EU's leadership prospects, given its 'dwarf-like' status in a world of great powers (Hyde-Price 2008; Toje 2010). While power and leadership are closely related concepts, they are not synonymous. As MacGregor Burns (1992: 18) succinctly points out: 'All leaders are actual or potential power holders, but not all power holders are leaders'. While power has always been a pet subject in political studies of the EU, academic analysis of European leadership is patchy and underdeveloped. The aim in this section is to identify some of the underlying assumptions about leadership implicit in portrayals of Europe as a power.

The academic debate on European power is marked by different 'camp' mentalities, which reflect differing theoretical and methodological orientations. A clear distinction can be made between conceptualizations that emphasise the ideational sources of leadership (Manners 2008) and those that stress the materialist dimension (Hyde-Price 2006). This is not surprising, given that theories contain assumptions about how the world is constituted. The debate here is not a new one. It goes back to the writings of Duchêne (1972), who saw the European Community as exercising leadership by 'example', and to the writings of Bull (1982), who questioned whether this was not 'a contradiction in terms', as it overlooked the predominance of power politics in the international system. While the debate on European power has moved on, it is still permeated by the division between idealist and materialist interpretations. Idealist academics tend to see the EU as a potential or actual leader in the EU's neighbourhood and beyond; material analysts do not.

Few realists see the Union as having a great potential to exercise significant leadership in global politics. At best, they see the EU as a 'tragic actor' (Hyde-Price 2008: 29) or a 'small power' (Toje 2010). By contrast, liberal and normative theorists detect in the EU a potential for transformational leadership in global politics – particularly in its immediate neighbourhood, where its presence is most directly felt. MacGregor Burns (1992) first coined the concept of transformational leadership. It refers not to a set of specific behaviours, but rather to an ongoing process by which 'leaders and followers raise one another to higher levels of morality and motivation'. Leadership of this type is like charismatic leadership, with its focus on inspiration and example (Keane 2012).

The concepts of 'civilian power' (Maull 2005) and 'normative power' (Manners 2002) refer in part to this type of transformational leadership. According to the progenitors of these terms, the EU plays a leadership role in shaping what is considered 'normal' in world politics (Manners 2008). The underlying assumption is that the Union is a leader because other actors want to emulate its example and to follow the norms that it sets. In this sense, leadership is a relational activity and a social role. Without followers, there is no leadership.

The concept of normative power Europe (NPE) is especially associated with a cosmopolitan and moralistic world view. Normative power is 'power of an ideational nature characterised by common principles and willingness to disregard Westphalian conventions' (Manners 2002: 239). The Union exerts its power through attraction and example, rather than through traditional forms of power politics. The idea of normative power draws on a well-established tradition of progressive thought regarding European integration, by which national sovereignty will be gradually eroded and a new, post-national institutional agency established at the European level. The EU will play a decisive role within this transformed world, by shaping conceptions of what is 'normal' in the international society of the 21st century (Manners 2002; 2008: 45).

However, the concept of NPE does not shed much light on how or when the Union exercises this transformational leadership through the ENP. It does not address the internal dynamics of EU agency or how the alleged normative diffusion takes place (Aggestam 2013). One reason for this is that the unique post-national characteristics of the EU as a normative power are mainly symbolic. What the EU says or does is secondary to what it is (Manners 2008: 45). The claim to leadership is based on this symbolic power as a 'difference engine' that leads the way in a 'sea change' of transformation in global politics towards greater cosmopolitanism and universality (Manners and Whitman 2003: 380). In this view, the EU exercises a diffuse type of leadership that spreads like a 'contagion' (Manners 2002).

The concept of Europe as an ethical power (Aggestam 2008) offers a framework that incorporates the symbolic power of the EU but includes an analysis of what the Union does, as well as the sources – material as well as ideational – that underpin this agency. The EU can therefore be conceived as a 'force for good' in the neighbourhood, but one that exerts its leadership in various different ways and through a variety of policy instruments (Biscop and Renard 2012). This approach has been further developed and applied to the ENP by Barbé and Johansson-Nogués (2008). When making a moral audit of the ENP along four dimensions of ethical action (utility, values, rights and fairness), they conclude that the EU's track-record is mixed and modest in contrast to the high-flying rhetoric.

Four approaches to the study of leadership in the ENP

Leadership is a contested concept in the social sciences and it is therefore not surprising to find that concepts of European leadership in the ENP vary significantly. In this section, I suggest four dimensions to categorise leadership in relation to the study of the ENP – person, position, process and outcome (Aggestam 2015; Grint 2005). These four approaches are not mutually exclusive and a comprehensive analysis of the ENP involves incorporating elements of all four.

The first approach examines the personal characteristics and traits of individual leaders. This approach emphasises the critical role played by individuals in shaping the European integration process and the nature of the European Union as a political project, for example the historical roles played by Jean Monnet or Jacques Delors. In terms of the ENP, it draws attention to the key role played by Commissioners responsible for the shaping and execution of the ENP, such as the current Commissioner for the ENP and EU enlargement, Johannes Hahn. It also emphasises the individual role played by the High Representative of the EU for Foreign Affairs and Security Policy, Federica Mogherini, whose double-hatting as Vice-President of the European Commission is potentially significant at the strategic level (see the EU Global Strategy). In addition, it points to the importance of individuals at the national level who historically have shaped EU external policy, such as Adenauer and De Gaulle, Kohl and Mitterrand, Blair and, more recently, Merkel, Sikorski and Bildt. This focus on the role of individuals in providing effective leadership has its roots in the Platonic view of leadership. For the Greek philosopher Plato, leadership in the ideal political governance should reside with the individual that possesses the greatest knowledge, skill, power and resources to guide the action of others. This view of heroic leadership as a panacea to complex problems is still a popular conception, although what type of knowledge and skills are required may be hotly contested (Tsoukalis and Emmanaoulidis 2011). In the EU and Europe more broadly, this type of discussion is currently rife with suggestions that only if outstanding individual political leaders emerge can the herculean tasks facing Europe be solved (Stubb 2016).

The second approach focuses on leadership as a position and space from which the resources to lead originate. Formal leadership is an explicitly, often legally ascribed position of authority in a social structure, such as an organization, society and state. From this perspective, the EU presents a particularly complex picture. Leadership in the Union is dispersed, given the way it is structured in terms of an intricate pattern of multi-level governance (Lavenex 2004). In EU external relations, including the ENP, policy-making involves an interplay between elements of supranationalism and intergovernmentalism, which the Lisbon Treaty sought to simplify but has not resolved (Lavenex and Schimmelfennig 2009). In terms of the ENP, the coherence and coordination of the EU's relations with ENP countries is sometimes compromised by the way in which formal functions, such as agenda setting, policy decisions and implementation are dispersed among different actors and institutions (Börzel and van Hüllen 2014).

The third approach examines leadership as a process that involves a study of practices and types of behaviour that are used by an actor to influence and guide activities in a group towards collective goals, decisions and desired outcomes (Avery 2004: 22). In many respects, the process of decision-making and policy implementation within the EU is as important as the outcomes, given the need to involve a variety of actors. In terms of the implementation of the ENP, the task of shaping a more benign and cooperative environment to create what the 2003 European Security Strategy termed a 'ring of well-governed countries' (Council of the European Union 2003) around the EU was a gradual, incremental and long-term process. The goal of EU leadership was to frame this process through a series of structured interactions. The interaction between leader and followers is central in this approach. Without followers, there is no leadership, and the process of shaping a 'ring of friends' becomes impossible (Bosse and Korosteleva-Polglase 2009). To understand leadership properly, it is just as important to investigate the role of the followers as the role of the leader. In this sense, leadership is only possible if it is perceived as legitimate by the followers.

Finally, the fourth approach to leadership is conceived in terms of the result and outcomes leadership generates. In many ways, it would make little sense to talk of leadership if we do not include the outcome of the process. Consequently, this aspect of leadership is integral to all the approaches outlined above. However, studies that focus on outcomes tend to focus less on explaining the actual process of leadership and the interactions that are critical to it. This problem is one addressed by the literature on the capability-expectations gap (Hill 1993), that is, the gap between rhetoric and outcome in the ENP. As Bengtsson and Elgström (2011) have argued, the output legitimacy of the ENP is undermined by the conflicting goals it embodies and the inconsistency with which they are implemented (see also Korosteleva 2011; Rieker 2015). Given the EU's protectionist approach to many trade issues with the neighbourhood, the EU is sometimes criticised for acting with double standards (Youngs 2010). Moreover, the 'incoherent role performance and contradictory elements in the development of EU integration (for instance, the militarization and territorialisation of the Union) weakens its normative credibility. This, in turn, negatively affects the effectiveness of the Union as an international actor' (Bengtsson and Elgström 2011: 129).

Leadership and followership

Understanding the EU's leadership role in its neighbourhood involves a recognition that all four approaches to leadership outlined above – person, position, process and result – are essential elements of a more comprehensive analysis that goes beyond the limitations of the debate on what kind of power the EU is. Above all, understanding the EU's leadership role in the EU's neighbourhood involves focusing on the interactive element that is fundamental to leadership. Leadership is defined here as a process in which an actor seeks to influence and guide activities in a group towards collective goals, decisions and desired outcomes (Avery 2004: 22). This definition entails four components: a leader, followers, the activity of leadership (influencing and guiding) and the leader's objectives in the outcome (Parker and Karlsson 2014).

Fundamentally, leadership involves an interactive relationship between a leader and their followers (Bengtsson and Elgström 2011: 118). This relationship is shaped by the responsiveness of followers, as well as by a leader (Tallberg 2006). The emphasis on the need for leaders to have followers brings the expectations and perceptions of the EU's neighbours forward in an analysis of the ENP. Governments in the EU's neighbourhood must acknowledge the EU's vision of international order, but also the values and regime principles that it seeks to pursue (Averre 2009). More generally, the EU's leadership aspirations in the neighbourhood must be perceived as legitimate. Legitimacy is 'a generalized perception or assumption that the actions of an entity are desirable, proper, or appropriate within some socially constructed system of norms, values, beliefs and definitions' (Suchman, quoted in Hurd 1999: 387). It rests on perceptions of fairness and an evaluation of the values and norms a certain actor is associated with. Its leadership potential increases, if an actor (in the case of the ENP, the EU) is widely perceived as acting in accordance with principles of fairness and behaving in line with widely accepted ideas and norms.

The importance attached to understanding leadership in the EU's neighbourhood as an interactive process between leader and followers draws attention to leadership as a social relationship and role. As Bengtsson and Elgström (2011) note, role theory can make an important contribution to the analysis of the EU's leadership. Role theory draws on the theatrical analogy of actors playing roles on a stage with a script. Over the last decade, there has been a revival of role theory in International Relations, Foreign Policy Analysis and EU Studies (Elgström and Smith 2006; Harnisch et al. 2011; Henökl and Trondal 2015; Juncos and Pomorska 2010; Thies and Breuning 2012).

The key theoretical contribution of role theory is the way it views leadership as a relational activity between leader and follower. From this perspective, it is in the interplay and *process* of negotiations between expectations and conceptions that the meaning of leadership emerges and can be enacted upon (Winkler 2010: 78). In this sense, we could talk of the actors being involved in role-playing. Legitimate European leadership in the EU's neighbourhood is a process that is negotiated and changing with the situation, context and issues. Thus, if we wish to explain and understand how the EU's leadership role in its neighbourhood is located and eventually performed, we need to study how *role expectations* and *role conceptions* of both leaders and followers determine the process and outcome of the ENP.

Role conceptions refer to normative self-understandings an actor has of their leadership behaviour. They provide insight to how an actor responds to role demands and expectations from followers. After the 'Big Bang' enlargement of 2004, the EU began to seek a new role for itself in the EU's southern and eastern neighbourhoods (Commission of the European Communities 2003). It was based on a role conception that the EU could exert leadership as a pole of attraction and anchor of security for countries and peoples in the neighbourhood around its expanded borders: a 'force for good' (Barbé and Johansson-Nogués 2008). Given its largely civilian identity (Zielonka 1998; Maull 2005), it was also argued that the EU tended to see itself as a 'normative great power' (Bengtsson and Elgström 2011), projecting its civilizing values and norms (including democracy, human rights, rule of law, liberty and good governance) into its immediate neighbourhood (Kelley 2006).

However, there can be no leadership without role expectations from followers. Any study of leadership must take careful account of the normative ideas of leadership that potential followers have. Role expectations can be derived from the status and formal position that an actor enjoys within an organization (such as the EU), but may also be more informally derived from the position or status within the international society of states (Paul et al. 2015). Role expectations can therefore vary in terms of how formal or informal they are as well as in their specificity and scope. It is, therefore, crucial to understand the expectations held by the EU's neighbours to its south and east, if we want to understand the scope for EU leadership in the ENP. Studies indicate that there is a disparity between the EU's own role conception and role expectations held by neighbours, particularly on the issue of acting on principles of fairness and mutual interest (Bosse 2009; Seeberg 2009). Indeed, disjunctions between role conceptions and role expectations can generate role conflicts. A role conflict exists when two or more roles prescribe incompatible behaviour. The problem of role conflicts in the ENP is evident in terms of the disconnection between the EU's normative agenda (democracy and human rights promotion) and its concern for security and stability in the neighbourhood (Christou 2010; Averre 2010). It is also evident in the case of Ukraine, which held high expectations of the contribution the EU could make to its stability, security and prosperity (Natorski 2013).

Types of leadership

The ENP is an ambitious attempt by the EU to exercise leadership in its immediate neighbourhood to its east and south, using a broad array of power resources and policy instruments. Assessing the effectiveness of EU leadership involves analysing the various modes and forms of leadership it exercises. Within social role theory, the concept of role performance is used to refer to the actual leadership behaviour in a specific situational context. Clearly, evaluating actual performance is complicated and fraught with methodological difficulties, because while it can be assumed that the scope for action that a leader has is largely determined by the general role expectations that are directed towards him or her, the actual performance in terms of the precise leadership mode is highly contextual and contingent – as most academic studies will point out (Nye 2013).

Building on the classic work of Young (1991), three types of EU leadership in its neighbourhood can be identified – structural, entrepreneurial and intellectual. Structural leadership refers to both the material and non-material resources of the leader and its ability to transform these into effective political influence. 'The essential feature of structural leadership', Young argues, 'lies in the ability to translate structural power into bargaining leverage as a means of reaching agreement on the terms of constitutional contracts in social settings of the sort exemplified by international society' (1991: 289). The sources of the EU's asymmetrical structural power include the EU's market power (Damro 2012) and its ability to externalise its governance procedures and institutions (Bechev 2013; Keukeleire and Delreux 2014). Indeed, it has been argued that the EU's extensive structural power means that in its dealings with countries in the neighbourhood, it is effectively a realist actor in normative clothes (Seeberg 2009).

Entrepreneurial leadership differs from structural leadership in that it focuses more directly on the negotiating skills and capabilities of the EU. Entrepreneurial leadership refers to an actor's ability 'to frame issues in ways that foster integrative bargaining and to put together deals' that allow all parties 'to reap joint gains' (Young 1991: 293). For instance, it has been argued that the EU has played an entrepreneurial role in seeking to promote human rights and democracy in the enlargement process and the wider neighbourhood, although with varying success (Sedelmeier 2006; Youngs 2010). Indeed, the ENP itself was conceived as a 'win-win' approach, offering a mutually beneficial relationship that would create a 'ring of friends' in the EU's neighbourhood through integrative bargaining. As the European Commission stated in 2003, the initial aim of the ENP was to 'reduce poverty and create an area of shared prosperity and values based on deeper economic integration, intensified political and cultural relations, enhanced cross-border cooperation and shared responsibility for conflict prevention between the EU and its neighbours' (Commission of the European Communities 2003).

Finally, intellectual leadership refers explicitly to the EU's ability to generate norms and values that can reshape conceptions of normalcy – the idea at the heart of the concept of normative power Europe (Manners 2002). It points to a mode or type of leadership that aims at shaping the followers' preferences by providing intellectual guidance and creating new knowledge to alter existing conceptions about a phenomenon. This is done by reframing problems, by changing the perceptions of an existing problem or by providing innovative solutions to a problem (Parker and Karlsson 2014; Young 1991). Idea-based leadership is interactive and deliberative, and assumes that arguments matter and that preferences are not fixed, but change as perceptions of normalcy change (Manners 2010).

Conclusions

The ENP is an ambitious, complex and far-reaching attempt to exercise leadership by the EU in its neighbourhood. It is ambitious in terms of its aspirations to project stability, promote good governance, human rights and democracy, and generate rising prosperity and a mutually beneficial economic relationship; complex because it is a multifaceted policy that draws on a mix of power resources and policy instruments, and operates across a variety of different policy domains – economic, political, societal and cultural; and far-reaching, as a long-term, transformational project, which aims to create a 'ring of friends' around its enlarged borders (Bouris and Schumacher 2017; Rieker 2015; Whitman and Wolff 2012).

This chapter has pointed to the utility of social role theory as an analytical tool for examining the nature, dimensions and scope of EU leadership in its southern and eastern neighbourhoods. This approach focuses on the complex relationship between leaders and followers, and underlines the importance of research in the attitudes, preferences and role expectations of ENP countries. It also provides a conceptual framework for analysing role conflicts in the ENP that arise from competing objectives of stability, on the one hand, and the exercise of transformational leadership to promote democracy, human rights and economic prosperity on the other (Noutcheva et al. 2013).

References

Aggestam, L. (2008) 'Ethical Power Europe?', *International Affairs* 84(1): 1–11.
Aggestam, L. (2013) 'Global Norms and European Power', in Jorgensen, K. and Laatikaininen, K. (eds.) *Routledge Handbook on the European Union and International Institutions*, London: Routledge, 457–471.
Aggestam, L. (2015) 'Transformative Power or Political Dwarf? European Leadership and Global Imbalances', in Barkadjieva Engelbrekt, A. et al. (eds.) *The EU's Role in Fighting Global Imbalances*, Cheltenham: Edward Elgar, 16–34.
Aggestam, L. and Johansson, M. (2017) 'The Leadership Paradox in EU Foreign Policy', *Journal of Common Market Studies*, http://onlinelibrary.wiley.com/doi/10.1111/jcms.12558/epdf.
Averre, D. (2009) 'Competing Rationalities: Russia, the EU and the "Shared Neighbourhood"', *Europe-Asia Studies* 61(10): 1689–1713.
Averre, D. (2010) 'The EU, Russia and the Shared Neighbourhood: Security, Governance and Energy', *European Security* 19(4): 531–534.
Avery, G. (2004) *Understanding Leadership: Paradigms and Cases*, London: Sage.
Barbé, E. and Johansson-Nogués, E. (2008), 'The EU as a Modest "Force for Good": The European Neighbourhood Policy', *International Affairs* 84(1): 81–96.
Bechev, D. (2013) 'The EU as a Regional Hegemonon? From Enlargement to ENP', in Noutcheva, G. et al. (eds.) *The EU and Its Neighbours: Values Versus Security in European Foreign Policy*, Manchester: Manchester University Press.
Bengtsson, R. and Elgström, O. (2011) 'Reconsidering the European Union's Roles in International Relations', in Harnisch, S. et al. (eds.) *Role Theory in International Relations: Approaches and Analyses*, London: Routledge.
Biscop, S. and Renard, T. (eds.) (2012) *The European Union and Emerging Powers in the 21st Century: How Europe Can Shape a New Global Order*, Farnham: Ashgate.
Börzel, T. and Risse, T. (2009) 'The Transformative Power of Europe: The European Union and the Diffusion of Ideas', *KFG Working Paper* 1, Freie Universität Berlin.
Börzel, T. and van Hüllen, V. (2014) 'One Voice, One Message, but Conflicting Goals: Cohesiveness and Consistency in the European Neighbourhood Policy', *Journal of European Public Policy* 21(7): 1033–1049.
Bosse, G. (2009) 'Challenges for EU Governance Through Neighbourhood Policy and Eastern Partnership: The Values/Security Nexus in EU–Belarus Relations', *Contemporary Politics* 15(2): 215–227.
Bosse, G. and Korosteleva-Polglase, E. (2009) 'Changing Belarus? The Limits of EU Governance in Eastern Europe and the Promise of Partnership', *Cooperation and Conflict* 44(2): 143–165.
Bouris, D. and Schumacher, T. (eds.) (2017) *The Revised European Neighbourhood Policy: Continuity and Change in EU Foreign Policy*, Basingstoke: Palgrave.
Bull, H. (1982) 'Civilian Power Europe: A Contradiction in Terms?', *Journal of Common Market Studies* 21(2): 149–170.
Christou, G. (2010) 'European Union Security Logics to the East: The European Neighbourhood Policy and the Eastern Partnership', *European Security* 19(3): 413–430.
Commission of the European Communities (2003) *Wider Europe-Neighbourhood: A New Framework for Relations with Our Eastern and Southern Neighbours*, COM (2003) 104 Final, Brussels, 11 March.
Council of the European Union (2003) *A Secure Europe in a Better World: European Security Strategy*, Brussels, 12 December.
Damro, C. (2012) 'Market Power Europe', *Journal of European Public Policy* 19(5): 682–699.
Duchêne, F. (1972) 'Europe's Role in World Peace', in Mayne, R. (ed.) *Europe Tomorrow*, London: Fontana.
Dunne, T. (2008) 'Good Citizen Europe', *International Affairs* 84(2): 13–28.
Elgström, O. and Smith, M. (eds.) (2006) *The European Union's Roles in International Politics: Concepts and Analysis*, London: Routledge.
Grint, K. (2005) *Leadership: Limits and Possibilities*, Basingstoke: Palgrave/Macmillan.
Harnisch, S., Frank, C. and Maull, H. W. (2011) *Role Theory in International Relations*, London: Routledge.

Hayward, J. (ed.) (2008) *Leaderless Europe*, Oxford: Oxford University Press.
Henökl, T. and Trondal, J. (2015) 'Unveiling the Anatomy of Autonomy: Dissecting Actor-Level Independence in the European External Action Service', *Journal of European Public Policy* 22(10): 1426–1447.
Hill, C. (1993) 'The Capability-Expectations Gap, or Conceptualizing Europe's International Role', *Journal of Common Market Studies* 31(3): 305–328.
Hurd, I. (1999) 'Legitimacy and Authority in International Politics', *International Organization* 53(2): 379–408.
Hyde-Price, A. (2006) 'Normative Power Europe: A Realist Critique', *Journal of European Public Policy* 13(2): 217–234.
Hyde-Price, A. (2008) 'A "Tragic Actor"? A Realist Perspective on "Ethical Power Europe"', *International Affairs* 84(1): 49–64.
Juncos, A. and Pomorska, K. (2010) 'Secretariat, Facilitator or Policy Entrepreneur? Role Perceptions of Officials of the Council Secretariat', *European Integration Online Papers* 14(1), http://eiop.or.at/eiop/2010-007a.htm
Keane, E. (2012) 'Social Status, Social Closure and the Idea of a "Normative Power Europe"', *European Journal of International Relations* 19(4): 939–956.
Kelley, J. (2006) 'New Wine in Old Wineskins. Promoting Political Reforms Through the New European Neighbourhood Policy', *Journal of Common Market Studies* 44(1): 29–55.
Keukeleire, S. and Delreux, T. (2014), 'Competing Structural Powers and Challenges for the EU's Structural Foreign Policy', *Global Affairs* 1(1): 43–50.
Korosteleva, E. (2011) 'Change or Continuity: Is the Eastern Partnership an Adequate Tool for the European Neighbourhood?', *International Relations* 25(2): 243–262.
Lavenex, S. (2004) 'EU External Governance in "Wider Europe"', *Journal of European Public Policy* 11(4): 680–700.
Lavenex, S. and Schimmelfennig, F. (2009) 'EU Rules Beyond EU Borders: Theorizing External Governance in European Politics', *Journal of European Public Policy* 16(6): 791–812.
Leonard, M. (2005) *Why Europe Will Run the 21st Century*, New York: Public Affairs.
MacGregor Burns, J. (1992) *Leadership*, New York: Harper Collins Publishers.
Manners, I. (2002) 'Normative Power Europe: A Contradiction in Terms?', *Journal of Common Market Studies* 40(2): 235–258.
Manners, I. (2008) 'The Normative Ethics of the European Union', *International Affairs* 84(1): 45–60.
Manners, I. (2010) 'As You Like It: European Union Normative Power in the European Neighbourhood Policy', in Whitman, R. and Wolff, S. (eds.) *The European Neighbourhood Policy in Perspective: Context, Implementation and Impact*, Basingstoke: Palgrave Macmillan, 29–50.
Manners, I. and Whitman, R. (2003) 'The "Difference Engine": Constructing and Representing the International Identity of the European Union', *Journal of European Public Policy* 10(3): 380–404.
Maull, H. (2005) 'Europe and the New Balance of Global Order', *International Affairs* 81(4): 755–799.
Natorski, M. (2013) 'Deeds Not declarations: Ukraine's Convergence with the EU's Foreign and Security Policies Until 2010', in Noutcheva, G. et al. (eds.) *The EU and Its Neighbours: Values Versus Security in European Foreign Policy*, Manchester: Manchester University Press.
Nicolaidis, K. and Whitman, R. (eds.) (2013) 'Preface', Special Issue on Normative Power Europe, *Cooperation and Conflict* 48(2): 167–170.
Noutcheva, G., Pomorska, K. and Bosse, G. (eds.) (2013) *The EU and Its Neighbours: Values Versus Security in European Foreign Policy*, Manchester: Manchester University Press.
Nye, J. (2013) *Presidential Leadership and the Creation of the American Era*, Princeton: Princeton University Press.
Parker, C. and Karlsson, C. (2014) 'Leadership and International Cooperation', in Rhodes, R. and 't Hart, P. (eds.) *The Oxford Handbook of Political Leadership*, Oxford: Oxford University Press.
Paul, T. et al. (2015) *Status in World Politics*, Cambridge: Cambridge University Press.
Rieker, P. (ed.) (2015) *External Governance as Security Community Building—The Limits and Potential of the European Neighbourhood Policy*, London: Palgrave Macmillan.
Sedelmeier, U. (2006) 'The EU's Role as a Promoter of Human Rights and Democracy: Enlargement Policy Practice and Role Formation', in Elgström, O. and Smith, M. (eds.) *The European Roles in International Politics: Concepts and Analysis*, London: Routledge.
Seeberg, P. (2009) 'The EU as a Realist Actor in Normative Clothes: EU Democracy Promotion in Lebanon and the European Neighbourhood Policy', *Democratization* 16(1): 81–99.

Sjursen, H. (2006) 'What Kind of Power? European Foreign Policy in Perspective', *Journal of European Public Policy* 13(2): 169–181.
Smith, M. (2010) 'A Liberal Grand Strategy in a Realist World? Power, Purpose and the EU's Changing Global Role', *Journal of European Public Policy* 18(2): 144–163.
Stubb, A. (2016) 'Europe's Survival Depends on Its Leaders' Defence of Democracy', *Financial Times*, 15 September, www.ft.com/content/9e6b1338-7a98-11e6-ae24-f193b105145e.
Tallberg, J. (2006) *Leadership and Negotiation in the European Union*, Cambridge: Cambridge University Press.
Thies, C. and Breuning, M. (2012) 'Integrating Foreign Policy Analysis and International Relations Through Role Theory', *Foreign Policy Analysis* 8(1): 1–4.
Toje, A. (2010) *The European Union as a Small Power: After the Post-Cold War*, Basingstoke: Palgrave Macmillan.
Tsoukalis, L. and Emmanouilidis, J. (eds.) (2011) *The Delphic Oracle on Europe: Is There a Future for the European Union?*, Oxford: Oxford University Press.
Whitman, R. and Wolff, S. (eds.) (2012) *The European Neighbourhood Policy in Perspective: Context, Implementation and Impact*, London: Palgrave Macmillan.
Winkler, I. (2010) *Contemporary Leadership Theories: Enhancing the Understanding of the Complexity, Subjectivity and Dynamic of Leadership, Contributions to Management Science*, Heidelberg: Physica-Verlag HD.
Young, O. (1991) 'Political Leadership and Regime Formation: On the Development of Institutions in International Society', *International Organization* 45(3): 281–308.
Youngs, R. (ed.) (2010) *The European Union and Democracy Promotion*, Baltimore: John Hopkins University Press.
Zielonka, J. (2008) 'Europe as a Global Actor: Empire by Example?', *International Affairs* 84(3): 471–484.

6
REALISM AND THE EUROPEAN NEIGHBOURHOOD POLICY

Adrian Hyde-Price

Introduction

Dramatic and unsettling events in the European Union's (EU's) external neighbourhood have underscored yet again the continuing relevance and analytical utility of realist international theory. Europe's initial aspiration to surround itself with a 'ring of friends' and to export good governance, economic prosperity and stability to its neighbourhood by means of 'soft power' and normative inducements has not been realised. To the South, the so-called 'Arab Spring' has turned sour, and the continuing ramifications of the United States (US) invasion of Iraq in 2003 have led to the rapid spread of ISIS from a deeply fractured Iraq to war-ravaged Syria and Libya. The EU now faces an acute and growing threat to its security from state failure, regional conflicts and terrorism across the Middle East and North Africa. To the East, Russia's annexation of Crimea and simmering conflict in eastern Ukraine have highlighted the deeply rooted structural obstacles to political transformation, inclusive governance, economic modernisation and social justice throughout much of the post-Soviet lands. Above all, the military assertiveness, territorial aggrandisement and recidivist aspirations of Russia have shattered the fundamental strategic assumptions upon which the post-Cold War European security order has been constructed: namely, that the EU's Member States face no strategic challenges and that regional security competition has been largely tamed or muted.

The resurgence of a recidivist Russia and emergence of an 'arc of crisis' around Europe's eastern and southern borders, combined with the ineluctable process of power transition that is producing a more multipolar global order and contributing to the fraying of transatlantic bonds, have deeply affected the EU's flagship policy for shaping its external milieu – the European Neighbourhood Policy (ENP). This chapter examines the ENP from the perspective of realist international theory. It begins by outlining the main assumptions and tenets of realism, before providing an analysis and critique of the ENP from a realist perspective. It critically analyses the strategic and political objectives of the ENP in the EU's southern and eastern neighbourhoods, and includes consideration of the Eastern Partnership (EaP). The EaP was launched in 2009 and covers the six countries of Eastern Europe and the Caucasus (European Council 2011). Given the growing security competition with Russia in this region, it is argued, realist international theory has analytical traction in explaining the problems facing the implementation of this ambitious programme of collective milieu-shaping.

Realist international theory

Realism is a distinctive tradition within the academic discipline of International Relations, and one with a long and distinguished intellectual pedigree. A tradition of political thought, Michael Oakeshott has argued, is defined by the fact that 'it belongs to the nature of a tradition to tolerate and unite an internal variety, not insisting upon conformity to a single character, and because, further, it has the ability to change without losing its identity' (Oakeshott 1991: 227). Realism itself is a broad and diverse intellectual tradition, the roots of which can be traced back through Jean-Jacques Rousseau, Thomas Hobbes and Machiavelli to Thucydides and the fifth Century BC Sophists (Frankel 1996). As a tradition of thought, Realism is at one and the same time a philosophical mood or disposition, a form of practical knowledge concerned with the principles of statecraft and a social scientific research paradigm. As a *philosophical mood*, Realism is characterised by a profound scepticism of Enlightenment liberalism's optimistic belief in progress and has a more pessimistic view of human nature (Gilpin 1986: 304). It emphasises the irreducible element of tragedy in the human condition and expects the worst from people and their states, given the propensity for individual selfishness and egotism (a view rooted in the Christian notion of original sin). As a form of what Oakeshott called 'practical knowledge' (Oakeshott 1991: 225), Realism has been concerned to elucidate some *principles of statecraft* for the 'modern prince'/nation-state. Classical realists like Machiavelli, Morgenthau, Carr and Kissinger drew heavily on the history of European diplomacy in order to elaborate a set of policy guidelines characterised by an emphasis on *Realpolitik* and an eschewal of moralism in foreign policy (Morgenthau 1993: 12; Kissinger 1973; Carr 2001).

The main division in realist theory is between classical realism, which focuses on human nature and domestic regime type, and structural realism, which is a systemic theory focusing on the structural dynamics of the international system. Structural realism is a *social science research paradigm*, and provides a parsimonious theoretical analysis of international politics. It is further differentiated between the 'defensive realism' of Kenneth Waltz, which argues that states are primarily security maximisers, and the 'offensive realism' of Mearsheimer (2001: 33), which maintains that states are both security and power maximisers (Waltz 1979). More recently, neoclassical realism has emerged as a tool of foreign policy analysis, seeking to combine structural pressures with domestic level variables such as state capabilities, strategic culture and domestic politics (Rose 1998; Lobell, Ripsman and Taliaferro 2009). The argument presented here draws mainly on structural realism, but also draws on some elements of neoclassical realism and classical realist thinkers such as E.H. Carr, Hans Morgenthau and Reinhold Niebuhr (Carr 2001; Morgenthau 1993; Niebuhr 2005).

At this point, it is important to remind ourselves what theory can and cannot do. Theory provides a way of simplifying a complex reality and bringing 'order and meaning to a mass of phenomena without which it would remain disconnected and unintelligible' (Morgenthau 1993: 3). Theories serve to simplify, abbreviate and abstract reality, and provide a means of going beyond mere description and categorisation of events to explain *why* they happened. They therefore provide mental maps to navigate a complex and multifaceted reality. Consequently, one cannot have a theory of everything, and no theory can explain all aspects of a phenomena, event or case – especially something as complex and multi-level as the ENP and the Eastern Partnership, which span different sectors and levels of social life. Waltz argued that a theory can only hope to explain a few, hopefully important, aspects of an empirical puzzle, by providing a means of identifying the most significant variables. 'How do we decide which factors to include in our narratives and which to exclude', Colin Wight has written. 'Theory provides the answer. Theory is suggestive of the elements we deem important to the explanation of any given event. Different theories will explain the same events differently' (Wight 2006: 288).

Realism focuses centrally on power as the key variable in explaining international politics and global affairs (Hyde-Price 2007). Realist theory is centrally concerned with the manner in which power permeates the whole texture of international society and seeks to explore the nature of power, its distribution, various dimensions, operation and consequences. A realist analysis of the ENP and the EaP, takes as its point of departure the manner in which power relations shape the structural context in which actors interact and pursue strategies to achieve their aims and objectives. Power is arguably the most important analytical concept in Political Science and International Relations and different realist thinkers have defined power in various ways. E.H. Carr argued that power had three dimensions: economic, military and the 'power over opinion' (that is, 'soft' or 'normative' power) (Carr 2001: 102); Robert Gilpin, on the other hand, refers to three tangible capabilities: military, economic and technological (Gilpin 1981: 13–14); Kenneth Waltz argued that a state's power needed to be considered in terms of a 'basket' of different capabilities (Waltz 1979: 131); John Mearsheimer, more narrowly, argued that it was primarily military power that mattered for the balance of power (Mearsheimer 2001). This chapter utilises a more differentiated concept of power drawn from Michael Mann's concept of the 'four sources of social power' (Mann 2012): economic, political, military and ideational. These four forms of power have different logics, dynamics and functions, and interact and overlap with each other, to create a complex mosaic of power relations within which the ENP operates (Hyde-Price 2013a).

Realism, states and the European Union

The starting point for a realist analysis of the ENP/EaP is that the international system is diverse and pluralistic, with a wide variety of different states, political communities and groups, most of which have their own discrete conception of the 'good life', grounded on their own interests, norms, values and cultures. Power, wealth and influence within the international system are distributed between these actors in a highly unequal and asymmetric manner – much more so than in domestic social orders. Moreover, there are fewer constraints on the operation of power in international systems than there are in domestic social formations. Domestic political orders are usually based on deep-rooted ideational structures and social conventions, rules, norms and concepts of legitimacy that – to some extent at least – limit and constrain the operation of asymmetric power relationships. International orders are also based on a mix of power and legitimacy (Kissinger 2014), but the rules of the game tend to be weaker and more limited in scope. More importantly, international political orders lack a legitimate central authority for ensuring compliance (Waltz 1979). In this sense, whereas domestic orders are hierarchical, international orders are anarchic – they are, in Hedley Bull's resonant term, 'anarchical societies' (Bull 1977). The anarchic character of international society, along with the diversity of interests and values, makes cooperation between actors difficult to achieve. International politics is therefore characterised by elements of both cooperation and competition, and – to a greater or lesser extent – states conduct their affairs 'in the brooding shadow of violence' (Waltz 1979: 102), which – as developments in Europe's neighbourhood attest – remains a constant threat, and one inherent to the anarchic nature of the international system.

A second key tenet of realist international theory is that the most important actors in the multi-actor international system are states – not international organisations like the EU or other non-state actors. There are two reasons for this: first, states possess a range of capabilities – across the four domains of power (political, economic, military and ideational) – that international organisations lack; second, states – rather than international organisations – continue to serve as the primary focus of political loyalty and allegiance in the international system, and nationalism remains the most potent ideology of the modern age, even in contemporary Europe. The modern nation-state is still 'the human group of strongest social cohesion, of most undisputed central authority and of most clearly defined membership' (Niebuhr 2005: 56). Although the EU is clearly a significant actor in Europe's neighbourhood, its role, policies and conduct reflect the interests and preferences of its Member States – particularly those of its largest members, and those with the greatest stake in the ENP (Böttger 2010; Copsey and Pomorska 2013). States establish the context and define the rules within which the EU and the European Commission operate, and 'set the scene in which they, along with non-state actors, stage their dramas or carry on their humdrum affairs. Though they may choose to interfere little in the affairs of non-state actors for long periods of time, states nevertheless set the terms of the intercourse' (Waltz 1979: 94).

From a realist perspective, therefore, the significance of the EU, as an international actor in its neighbourhood, stems from its function as a collective institutional vehicle for the pursuit of its Member States' common interests and shared concerns (Hyde-Price 2000; 2006; 2012a, 2012b; 2013b). Member States, directly through the European Council, and indirectly through the mechanisms of multi-level governance that characterise the EU's complex institutional structure, frame the objectives and set the terms which determine the role played by the Union – primarily through the agency of the Commission – in its neighbourhood. At times, the Commission enjoys considerable leeway in designing and implementing policies within the ENP framework, particularly when it comes to the more technocratic, managerial and bureaucratic aspects of negotiating the Association Agreements (AA), the ENP 'Action Plans', and the Deep and Comprehensive Free Trade Area (DCFTA). Nonetheless, Member States have also intervened, on occasions, to the set of the political terms of reference within which the Commission operates and to establish new priorities and operating procedures. This can be seen from the French initiative for a 'Union for the Mediterranean' (Bicchi and Gillespie 2011) and the Swedish-Polish initiative for the Eastern Partnership (Korosteleva 2011), both of which reflected attempts by Member States to 'set the terms of the intercourse' between the EU and its southern and eastern neighbourhoods.

Security, milieu-shaping and norms

As a collective instrument for pursuing the common interests of its Member States in its neighbourhood, the EU's Neighbourhood Policy serves three major roles: security maximisation; milieu-shaping; and the pursuit of second order normative concerns. In an anarchical society, all states have a primary interest in their security and survival. A central objective of the ENP has been to strengthen European security by stabilising the European neighbourhood and promoting cooperative relations (Lavenex 2004: Christou 2010). This was evident from the 'Wider Europe' communication from the European Commission in 2003, which noted that the 'neighbouring countries are the EU's essential partners . . . to create an enlarged area of political stability' (Commission of the European Communities 2003b: 3). It was further underlined in the Commission's ENP Strategy Paper of 2004, which stressed 'an important priority will be the further development of a shared responsibility between the EU and partners for security and stability in the neighbourhood region' (Commission of the European Communities 2004: 13). The development of the ENP should also be viewed in the context of the December 2003 European Security Strategy, which declared that 'our task is to promote a ring of well-governed countries, to the East of the European Union and on the borders of the

Mediterranean, with whom we can enjoy close and cooperative relations' (European Council 2003: 12–13; Dannreuther 2004). The concern with security and milieu-shaping is also apparent from the 2015 ENP review and the 2016 Global Strategy (European Union 2016). Taken together, these documents reflected the shared concern of EU Member States to stabilise their external environment and thereby strengthen their security.

The second purpose of the ENP was collective milieu-shaping (European Commission 2011a; 2011b). Given the diversity and plurality of international society, all states have an interest in fostering a more benign and compatible external environment that is more amenable to their interests and concerns – particularly in regions geographically and territorially contiguous with them. Faced with a potentially hostile, unsettled and conflict-prone neighbourhood in Eastern Europe and around the southern rim of the Mediterranean, EU Member States have used the EU as an instrument of collective milieu-shaping. The concept of 'milieu-shaping' was coined by Arnold Wolfers, who argued that states not only use their power to exert direct influence and control over other actors but also seek to shape the material and strategic context within which policy options are framed and weighed (Wolfers 1962: 71–73). With the conclusion of the enlargement process, EU Member States began focusing on milieu-shaping beyond the Union's enlarged borders (Dannreuther 2004; Commission of the European Communities 2006). In 2003, the Commission outlined its initial thoughts on projecting EU commercial regulations, business practices, political values and norms into its neighbourhood in order to 'reduce poverty and create an area of shared prosperity and values based on deeper economic integration, intensified political and cultural relations, enhanced cross-border cooperation and shared responsibility for conflict prevention between the EU and its neighbours' (Commission of the European Communities 2003a; Lavenex and Schimmelfennig 2009). Collective milieu-shaping was also conceived as the central mechanism for stabilising the EU's neighbourhood, and therefore enhancing EU security (Rieker 2015; Bosse 2009).

The third collective purpose of the ENP was the promotion of EU norms and values in the neighbourhood. Realists argue that states are primarily motivated by vital national interests and above all, the security and survival of the state and the political community. However, realists also recognise that states pursue a range of second order moral and ethical issues reflecting their distinct political values, particularly when vital national interests (primarily economic or security) are not at stake. As John Mearsheimer notes, there is 'a well-developed and widely accepted body of idealist or liberal norms in international politics', and that 'most leaders and most of their followers want their state to behave according to those ideals and norms, and that state behaviour often conforms to these generalised principles' (Mearsheimer 2005: 142). The EU serves as the institutional repository of the second-order normative and ethical concerns of its Member States, including the promotion of human rights, social justice and civil liberties. In this sense, the EU is perceived by its Member States to be an 'ethical power' (Aggestam 2008; Hyde-Price 2008), and the ENP is one of the major policy instruments through which the Union seeks to export its liberal norms, values and institutions (Kelley 2006; Manners 2012).

The ENP is therefore an ambitious, long-term programme aimed at creating a 'ring of friends' around the EU's post-enlargement borders by projecting stability, good governance, the rule of law, liberal institutions and capitalist market regulations into its southern and eastern neighbourhoods. From the perspective of realist international theory, however, the ENP was – from its inception – seriously flawed in terms of its over-ambitious and contradictory goals, its unrealistic operating assumptions and its failure to recognise the continued importance of geopolitics and security competition in an anarchic international system. Realism draws attention to the inherent constraints on human agency, and the risk of unintended consequences. It therefore tends to be sceptical of over-ambitious projects for large-scale societal engineering and, as a guide to statecraft, advocates more limited, realistic goals that recognise the limited ability of outside actors to leverage events in domestic societies (Weiss 2009). Realism focuses on the strategic and political interactions between agents, and emphasises the importance of assessing the relative balance of political interests and political will. States – either individually or collectively, through institutions like the European Union – need to ensure that their goals match their capabilities and core interests, and to act decisively when their vital interests are at stake. Yet, states must also recognise the need for compromise, restraint and mutual accommodation when dealing with other political communities with their own interests and concerns. Above all, the problem inherent to over-ambitious schemes for milieu-shaping is that of unintended consequences: 'How often have statesmen been motivated by the desire to improve the world', Hans Morgenthau wrote, 'and ended by making it worse? And how often have they sought one goal, and ended by achieving something they neither expected nor desired?' (Morgenthau 1993: 6).

The antinomies of the ENP

The problem with the ENP from the outset has been that it involves conflicting goals and objectives, reflecting the diversity of interests and preferences of its Member States (Börzel and van Hüllen 2014). The ENP is designed to achieve a number of ambitious goals: building a more stable neighbourhood to enhance the security of the EU and its citizens; fostering economic cooperation, trade and investment between the EU and its neighbours; spreading good governance, the rule of law and open market regulations; and promoting EU norms and values, particularly in terms of human rights and civil liberties (Commission of the European Communities/European Commission 2007). This potpourri of diverse objectives reflects the multiple goals and competing role conceptions of the EU as a collective vehicle for the pursuit of the shared interests and preferences of its Member States. The EU is viewed by its Member States as, among other things, a strategic actor (*Europe puissance*), an economic actor, a promoter of political transformation and an 'ethical actor', with different Member States attaching importance to different role conceptions (Schumacher 2015). From a realist perspective, however, the problem is that these laudable aspirations are not always compatible and complementary. The export of liberal values and institutions can be a source of destabilising change and transformation, as long-established authoritarian regimes face the challenge of political reform. On the other hand, stabilising Europe's neighbourhood in order to enhance EU security can mean working with existing authoritarian regimes in order to manage threats and challenges such as terrorism, proliferation, regional conflicts, organised crime and migration. Deepening trade links in order to, for example, diversify the supply of EU natural gas and oil, can also mean working with regimes with dubious human rights records.

In other words, there is a profound tension at the heart of the ENP between its broad-ranging strategic goals and objectives, particularly between its more normative and ethical agenda (spreading human rights, civil liberties and democracy) and its security and economic interests (Bosse 2009; Bosse and Korosteleva-Polglase 2009; Whitman and Wolff 2012). The ENP is designed both to stabilise the neighbourhood and to transform it, but change is nearly always destabilising and disruptive. In the long term, of course, a transformed neighbourhood characterised by liberal democracy, civil liberties and open market economies would provide a conducive and benign milieu for the EU, enhancing its security and prosperity. The problem, however, is how to reach this promised land of a 'ring of well-governed friends'. The EU lacks a clear and credible strategy for managing the complexities and risks inherent to the processes of political, economic and societal transformation. There is considerable evidence to suggest that democratising regimes are more conflict-prone than authoritarian regimes, and that as authoritarian structures of power begin to unravel, long-suppressed political, ethnic, national and sectarian tensions can erupt in violence and turmoil (Mansfield and Snyder 1995). This dilemma is one that the EU has no answer to, and one which the ENP is not equipped to tackle. Morgenthau's advice is thus particularly pertinent to the ENP: 'Political realism does not require, nor does it condone, indifference to political ideals and moral principles, but it requires a sharp distinction between the desirable and the possible' (Morgenthau 1993: 7).

The return of geopolitics

The final problem facing the ENP that realist theory can elucidate is the continued importance of geopolitics. The countries of Eastern Europe in particular have long been a source of geopolitical tension and rivalry between the great powers of Europe, primarily Germany and Russia. As Henry Kissinger has observed, 'The principle cause of European conflicts in the past 150 years has been the existence of a no-man's land between the German and Russian peoples' (quoted in Hyde-Price 1996: 223). In contemporary Europe, Germany is embedded within the EU and North Atlantic Treaty Organization (NATO), and thus the principle geopolitical conflict in the region is between the Euro-Atlantic community and Russia. The enlargement of the EU and NATO has shifted the political and military balance in the region in the favour of the Western democracies, and the primary focus of geopolitical competition is now Ukraine (Hyde-Price 2007).

The ENP and the EaP can be viewed as an attempt by the EU to circumvent and transcend geopolitics by focusing on long-term milieu-shaping, utilising a mix of soft power and economic incentives (Rieker 2012). As the 2003 European Security Strategy makes clear, the ENP was presaged on the assumption of a benign and non-competitive security environment. Russia was seen as a 'partner in modernisation' for the EU and as a cooperative partner in security governance with NATO (Dettke 2011). The implementation of the ENP was seen as a largely technocratic and managerial undertaking, spreading broadly accepted regulations, norms, standards and institutions in order to reshape the neighbourhood in the image of the EU. Hence, negotiating AA was largely left to the Commission, albeit within the constraints of the mandate provided by the Member States.

What the EU collectively failed to recognise was the continued significance of geopolitics – particularly in its eastern neighbourhood. Since the early 1990s, Russia has consistently voiced its concern about NATO enlargement, and over the last decade – particularly following President Putin's second term in office – it has increasingly viewed the EU as a strategic competitor in the region (Averre 2009; 2010). Putin's government now sees the EU as a rival for market access and political influence, and as a destabilising force seeking to undermine Russia's interests through democracy promotion and regime change (Susan 2014). Russia has sought to create a geopolitical rival to the EU in the form of a Customs Union and the Eurasian Union, and exerted considerable pressure on Ukraine, Armenia and Georgia not to sign the DCFTA and Association Agreements at the time of the Eastern Partnership summit in Vilnius in November 2013 (although Armenia was the only country to succumb to this pressure at the time). With the fall of the Yanukovich regime in February 2014, Russia moved swiftly to annex Crimea and destabilise the new pro-Western government by fermenting secessionist violence in Ukraine's eastern provinces.

Russia's blatant violation of the principles and political agreements upon which the post-Cold war European security order has been based (articulated in the Helsinki Final Act and the 1990 Paris Charter for a New Europe) has been a 'game-changer' for Europe (Böttger and Jopp 2014). As the European Commission now admits, 'the EU post-Westphalian narrative built around economic strength, soft power and multilateral institutions is colliding with an international environment marked by the return of geopolitics and hard power' (Directorate-General for External Policies 2015). The Ukraine crisis has therefore constituted a wake-up call for the EU, demonstrating that geopolitics still matters (Granholm, Malminen and Persson 2014) and that a revised ENP and EU global strategy must reflect both the aspiration for a liberal international order and the continuing challenge of geopolitical rivalries and competition.

This is precisely the area where realist international theory can contribute to explaining the failures and continued challenges facing the ENP. Realism focuses on the operation of power in the international system, and provides a theoretical explanation for the continued pervasiveness of geopolitics, strategic rivalry and security competition. As John Mearsheimer notes, 'elites in the United States and Europe have been blindsided by events . . . because they subscribe to a flawed view of international politics' (Mearsheimer 2014: 78). Events in Ukraine 'show that realpolitik remains relevant', and the West should understand that 'great powers are always sensitive to potential threats near their home territory' (ibid.). Ukraine, he argues, 'serves as a buffer state of enormous strategic significance', and Russia's reaction to the prospect of an EU Association Agreement was therefore entirely logical. 'This is Geopolitics 101: great powers are always sensitive to potential threats near their home territory' (ibid.: 82).

Conclusions

Realism provides a useful tool of analysis for understanding and explaining the trials and tribulations of the ENP. With its focus on power, realism is able to elucidate the structural and systemic factors shaping the international system. It does not provide a comprehensive analysis of the ENP – but this is beyond the scope of any theory. What it does do is to shed light on a number of key aspects of the ENP, particularly the risks inherent in ambitious schemes for collective milieu-shaping, the need for all international actors to think strategically and eschew 'moralism in foreign policy', and the enduring importance of geopolitics in the EU's neighbourhood. Above all, realism reminds us that the ENP – like all of the EU's external relations – takes place 'in the brooding shadow of violence', and that long-time milieu-shaping is no substitute for a hard-headed security strategy and the capability for effective crisis management.

References

Aggestam, L. (2008) 'Ethical Power Europe?', *International Affairs* 84(1): 1–11.
Averre, D. (2009) 'Competing Rationalities: Russia, the EU and the "Shared Neighbourhood"', *Europe-Asia Studies* 61(10): 1689–1713.
Averre, D. (2010) 'The EU, Russia and the Shared Neighbourhood: Security, Governance and Energy', *European Security* 19(4): 531–534.
Bicchi, F. and Gillespie, R. (2011) 'The Union for the Mediterranean: Continuity or Change in Euro-Mediterranean Relations?', Bicchi, F. and Gillespie, R. (eds.) special issue *Mediterranean Politics* 16(1).
Börzel, T. and van Hüllen, V. (2014) 'One Voice, One Message, But Conflicting Goals: Cohesiveness and Consistency in the European Neighbourhood Policy', *Journal of European Public Policy* (21)7: 1033–1049.
Böttger, K. (2010) *Die Entstehung und Entwicklung der Europäischen Nachbarschaftspolitik: Akteure und Koalitionen* 78, Nomos.
Böttger, K. and Jopp, M. (2014) 'Plädoyer für ein Ende der Naivität: Die Ukraine-Krise und ihre Lehren für die EU-Politik', in Weidenfeld, W. and Wessels, W. (eds.) *Jahrbuch der Europäischen Integration 2014*, Baden-Baden: Nomos Verlag, 49–62.
Bosse, G. (2009) 'Challenges for EU Governance Through Neighbourhood Policy and Eastern Partnership: The Values/Security Nexus in EU–Belarus relations', *Contemporary Politics* (15)2: 215–227.

Bosse, G. and Korosteleva-Polglase, E. (2009) 'Changing Belarus? The Limits of EU Governance in Eastern Europe and the Promise of Partnership', *Cooperation and Conflict* 44(2): 143–165.

Bull, H. (1977) *The Anarchical Society: A Study of Order in World Politics*, London: Macmillan.

Carr, E. (2001) *The Twenty Years' Crisis: An Introduction to the Study of International Relations*, 2nd Edition, New York: Palgrave.

Christou, G. (2010) 'European Union Security Logics to the East: The European Neighbourhood Policy and the Eastern Partnership', *European Security* 19(3): 413–430.

Commission of the European Communities (2003a) *Paving the Way for a New Neighbourhood Instrument*, Brussels: European Commission.

Commission of the European Communities (2003b) *Wider Europe-Neighbourhood: A New Framework for Relations with Our Eastern and Southern Neighbours*, COM (2003) 104 final, Brussels, 11 March.

Commission of the European Communities (2004) *European Neighbourhood Policy Strategy Paper*, COM (2004) 373 final, Brussels.

Commission of the European Communities (2006) *Communication from the Commission to the Council and the European Parliament on Strengthening the European Neighbourhood Policy*, COM (2006) 726 final, Brussels, 4 December.

Commission of the European Communities/European Commission (2007) *Communication from the Commission: A Strong European Neighbourhood Policy*, COM (2007) 774 final, Brussels.

Copsey, N. and Pomorska, K. (2013) 'The Influence of Newer Member States in the European Union: The Case of Poland and the Eastern Partnership', *Europe-Asia Studies* 66(3): 421–443.

Dannreuther, R. (2004) *EU Foreign and Security Policy: Towards a Neighbourhood Strategy*, London: Routledge.

Dettke, D. (2011) 'Europe and Russia: From Neighbourhood Without a Shared Vision to a Modernisation Partnership', *European Security* 20(1): 127–142.

Directorate-General for External Policies (2015) *Towards a New European Security Strategy? Assessing the Impact of Changes in the Global Security Environment*, www.europarl.europa.eu/RegData/etudes/STUD/2015/534989/EXPO_STU(2015)534989_EN.pdf, accessed 15 September 2015.

European Commission (2011a) *A Medium Term Programme for a Renewed European Neighbourhood Policy (2011–2014)*, Brussels: European Commission.

European Commission (2011b) *A New Response to a Changing Neighbourhood*. Brussels: European Commission.

European Council (2003) *A Secure Europe in a Better World: European Security Strategy*, Brussels: European Council.

European Council (2011) *Joint Declaration of the Eastern Partnership Summit*, 29–30 September 2011, Warsaw: Council of the European Union.

European Union (2016) *Shared Vision, Common Action: A Stronger Europe: A Global Strategy for the European Union's Foreign and Security Policy*, Brussels.

Frankel, B. (ed.) (1996) *The Roots of Realism*, London: Frank Cass.

Gilpin, R. (1981) *War and Change in World Politics*, Cambridge: Cambridge University Press.

Gilpin, R. (1986) 'The Richness of the Tradition of Political Realism', in Keohane, R. (ed.) *Neorealism and Its Critics*, New York: Columbia University Press.

Granholm, N., Malminen, J. and Persson, G. (eds.) (2014) *A Rude Awakening: Ramifications of Russian Aggression Towards Ukraine*, Stockholm: FOI, June.

Hyde-Price, A. (1996) *The International Politics of East Central Europe*, Manchester: Manchester University Press.

Hyde-Price, A. (2000) *Germany and European Order: Enlarging NATO and the EU*, Manchester: Manchester University Press.

Hyde-Price, A. (2006) '"Normative" Power Europe: A Realist Critique', *Journal of European Public Policy* 13(2): 217–234.

Hyde-Price, A. (2007) *European Security in the Twenty-First Century: The Challenge of Multipolarity*, London: Routledge.

Hyde-Price, A. (2008) 'A "Tragic Actor"? A Realist Perspective on "Ethical Power Europe"', *International Affairs* 84(1): 49–64.

Hyde-Price, A. (2012a) 'The Future of the European Security System', *Studia Diplomatica* LXV(1): 127–139.

Hyde-Price, A. (2012b) 'Neorealism: A Structural Approach to the ESDP', in Kurowska, X. and Breuer, F. (eds.) *Explaining European Security and Defence Policy: Theory in Action*, London: Palgrave Macmillan, 16–40.

Hyde-Price, A. (2013a) 'Neither Realism nor Liberalism: New Directions in Theorizing EU Security Policy', *Contemporary Security Policy* 34(2): 397–408.

Hyde-Price, A. (2013b) 'Realism: A Dissident Voice in the Study of the CSDP', in Biscop, S. and Whitman, R. (eds.) *The Routledge Handbook of European Security*, London: Routledge, 18–27.

Kelley, J. (2006) 'New Wine in Old Wineskins. Promoting Political Reforms Through the New European Neighbourhood Policy', *Journal of Common Market Studies* 44(1): 29–55.

Kissinger, H. (1973) *A World Restored*, Gloucester, Massachusetts: Peter Smith.

Kissinger, H. (2014) *World Order: Reflections in the Character of Nations and the Course of History*, London: Allen Lane.

Korosteleva, E. (2011) 'Change or Continuity: Is the Eastern Partnership an Adequate Tool for the European Neighbourhood?', *International Relations* 25(2): 243–262.

Lavenex, S. (2004) 'EU External Governance in "Wider Europe"', *Journal of European Public Policy* 11(4): 680–700.

Lavenex, S. and Schimmelfennig, F. (2009) 'EU Rules Beyond EU Borders: Theorizing External Governance in European Politics', *Journal of European Public Policy* 16(6): 791–812.

Lobell, S., Ripsman, N. and Taliaferro, J. (2009) *Neoclassical Realism, The State and Foreign Policy*, Cambridge: Cambridge University Press.

Mann, M. (2012) *The Sources of Social Power. Volume 1*, Cambridge: Cambridge University Press.

Manners, I. (2012) 'European Union Normative Power', in Whitman, R. and Wolff, S. (eds.) *The European Neighbourhood Policy in Perspective: Context, Implementation and Impact*, London: Palgrave Macmillan, 29–50.

Mansfield, E. and Snyder, J. (1995) 'Democratization and the Danger of War', *International Security* 20(1): 5–38.

Mearsheimer, J. (2001) *The Tragedy of Great Power Politics*, New York: W.W. Norton & Co.

Mearsheimer, J. (2005) 'E.H. Carr vs Idealism: The Battle Rages On', *International Relations* 19(2): 139–152.

Mearsheimer, J. (2014) 'Why the Ukraine Crisis is the West's Fault', *Foreign Affairs* 77, September/October.

Morgenthau, H. (1993) *Politics Among Nations: The Struggle for Power and Influence*, Brief Edition, New York: McGraw-Hill.

Niebuhr, R. (2005) *Moral Man and Immoral Society*, London: Continuum, [1932].

Oakeshott, M. (1991) 'Introduction to *Leviathan*', in Fuller, T. (ed.) *Rationalism in Politics and Other Essays*, Indianapolis: Liberty Press, 221–294.

Rieker, P. (2012) 'Integration, Security and the European Neighborhood. The Importance of the ENP as a Security Policy Instrument', *Studia Diplomatica* LXV (1): 69–77.

Rieker, P. (ed.) (2015) *External Governance as Security Community Building—The Limits and Potential of the European Neighbourhood Policy*, London: Palgrave Macmillan.

Rose, G. (1998) 'Neoclassical Realism and Theories of Foreign Policy', *World Politics* 51(1): 144–172.

Schumacher, T. (2015) 'Uncertainty at the EU's Borders: Narratives of EU External Relations in the Revised European Neighborhood Policy Towards the Southern Borderlands', *European Security* 24(3): 381–401.

Susan, S. (2014) 'The EU, Russia and a Less Common Neighbourhood', *SWP Comments* 3, Stiftung Wissenschaft und Politik, Berlin.

Waltz, K. (1979) *Theory of International Politics*, Reading, MA: Addison-Wesley.

Weiss, T. (2009) 'Driving Forces of Change and Reform: Conditionality and Its Inherent Limits', in Brockmann, K. and Bosold, D. (eds.) *Democratization and Security in Central and Eastern Europe and the Post-Soviet States*, Berlin: DGAP, 19–21.

Whitman, R. and Wolff, S. (eds.) (2012) *The European Neighbourhood Policy in Perspective: Context, Implementation and Impact*, London: Palgrave Macmillan.

Wight, C. (2006) *Agents, Structures and International Relations Politics as Ontology*, Cambridge: Cambridge University Press.

Wolfers, A. (1962) *Discord and Collaboration*, Baltimore: John Hopkins University.

7
CONSTRUCTIVIST APPROACHES TO THE STUDY OF THE EUROPEAN NEIGHBOURHOOD POLICY

Petr Kratochvíl and Elsa Tulmets

Introduction

Social constructivism is a generic term that covers a large group of dynamically evolving theoretical approaches to the study of global politics, whose presence is increasingly felt not only in the field of International Relations (IR) but also in European studies. This means that there is no single social constructivist theory of international relations or of European integration. Instead, social constructivism has been undergoing a process of internal pluralization and its many branches share very little beyond the basic ontological position that global (and European) politics is socially constructed. As a result, some constructivist approaches – such as the liberal constructivism of the Wendtian type (Wendt 1999) – have become firm parts of the theoretical mainstream, while others – such as the more linguistically oriented types of constructivism (Balzacq 2007; Browning and Joenniemi 2008) – have adopted an openly critical attitude to this mainstream.

The situation in European studies is somewhat different. In the field of IR, the axis of contention has been along the cooperation vs conflict spectrum. This dichotomy and the dualistic IR historiography, with always two sides to the so-called great debates (Butterfield and Wight 1966; Wæver 2010), are also the reasons why some scholars are uncomfortable with positing social constructivism as a third approach (Walt 1998) and instead argue for a fusion of constructivism with liberalism. If this attempt was successful, the pattern of two opposing approaches would be repeated – (neo)realism standing for the stereotypical claims about the international relations as an arena of never-ending conflict with power-hungry actors vying for supremacy; and (neo)liberalism cum social constructivism showing various ways through which the conflictual nature of international relations can be mitigated or transformed outright into a more peaceful arrangement.

However, this simple narrative is flawed because there are deeper divisions which pit liberal theories against the constructivist stress on rule-following. It is no accident that in the last great debate of positivists versus post-positivists, (critical) constructivists are usually seen as siding with the post-positivist side. The emphasis on rational actors who try to maximise their utility is the fundamental axiom that unites neoliberals and neorealists. Thus, it sets both apart from constructivists and their principle of rule-following, the stress on norms and identity and the secondary nature of interests, which cannot be understood in isolation from actors' identities. Hence, the basic definition of constructivism is that it is a group of theories which claim 'that ideas matter and [. . .] the basic behavioural mode of social actors is rule-following' (Kratochvíl and Tulmets 2010: 26). In other words, rules and norms are internalized, constituting and re-constituting the actors' identities, which in turn define the appropriate action.

Our chapter is divided into four parts. First, we introduce our classification of social constructivism in the study of the European neighbourhood. Using the labels of thick and thin constructivism (I and II), we show how these three types differ and how the three theoretical perspectives influence the way in which we look at the neighbourhood. Second, we show how these three types are present in the literature on the ENP. While focusing on thick constructivism, we also dedicate attention to examples of the other two types. Third, we sum up our discussion in the conclusion.

Constructivism in European studies

In European studies, the scene is set differently. For obvious reasons, realists have had a hard time explaining European integration. They either had to give up many of the most essential tenets of realism to explain the integration process (for example, Hoffmann 1982; Grieco 1988), or they had to explain European integration as a temporary aberration from the natural condition in IR, that is, perpetual conflict, ending up with dire predictions about the gloom prospect of the European Union (EU) in the post-Cold War era (Mearsheimer 2001). As neither of the two positions is particularly convincing, the axis of cooperation vs conflict has been replaced in European studies by more nuanced categorization. Originally, the key dividing issue in European studies was the question of agency, with supranationally oriented theories defending the increasing role of the central EU institutions (Haas 1964) and intergovernmental theories downplaying this trend, instead stressing the role played by the Member States (Moravcsik 1993).

With the arrival of social constructivism to European studies in the 1990s (Checkel 1997, 1999), this dichotomy was replaced by the question about the driving force behind the integration process. Is it the utilitarian calculation (the logic of consequences) that stands behind a more integrated Union or is it shared European norms and, increasingly, a European identity that is at the root of the deepening of the integration process? While this debate rages even today, what has become clear is the fact that various constructivist concepts belong to the essential theoretical notions of European studies. 'Europeanization', 'Normative Power Europe' and 'European identity' are just a few examples of broadly constructivist terms, without which European studies would not be conceivable today.

The three types of constructivism in the study of the EU's neighbourhood

Interestingly, constructivist arguments or mid-range constructivist theories are even more strongly present in the study of EU external relations. The main reason for this is the inability of the more traditional (and more widespread) European integration approaches to successfully theorize the EU's ties with the outside world. This applies to both multi-level governance approach and liberal intergovernmentalism, which virtually exclusively focus on the internal functioning of the EU, its decision-making and the always shifting balance between the EU institutions, EU Member States and other (domestic) actors and levels of internal EU governance.

The study of the EU's neighbourhood has another additional peculiar feature, which is its dichotomous nature. It is always based on a sharp distinction between the inside and the outside. There have been several attempts to blur the conceptually sharp contours, for instance by depicting the EU and its neighbourhood as concentric circles of integration (Rupnik 2007). Another such softening of the division represent those studies that look into partial and/or transitory forms of integration, including European Economic Area Member States or the special status of candidate countries (Cremona 2004; Del Sarto and Schumacher 2005; Lavenex and Schimmelfennig 2010). However, the fundamental distinction between the EU and its neighbourhood as two separate entities (or sets of entities) has remained the basic framework for the vast majority of both academic and policy-oriented studies of the EU's external relations.

The distinction between the EU as an actor and the neighbouring actors as other actors should not be conflated with the question of agency, which is, however, often raised in this context as well. The agency question has three facets. The first refers to the distinction between agency and structure. The EU thus may be understood as an *agent* with its own intentions, policies and actions, but it can also be depicted as continental integration, that is, a background *structure*, in which other actors (such as the European Commission, Member States and neighbouring countries) operate. The second is about the subjectivity of the EU and the neighbouring countries. While the EU is almost always conceived of as an active element, as a specific subject, the neighbouring countries were – especially shortly after the conception of the ENP – considered as mere objects which are shaped by the EU's policies. The neighbouring countries lose their agency and instead turn into 'neighbourhood', a geographic connotation bound together only by the fact that it lies near the EU. The third is related to the asymmetry between the EU and its neighbours. The study of the relationship often starts from the – implicit or explicit – assumption that the EU is substantially more advanced than its neighbours, economically, politically and even culturally. Such Orientalist/post-colonial discourses (cf. Said 1979) then pertain to the overall discussions about the relations between the EU and its surrounding countries, with the EU representing the normative ideal which the other countries feel compelled to emulate.

Our subsequent discussion of the three basic constructivist types builds on the assumption that the agency of the neighbourhood (in the second sense mentioned above) is acknowledged. Indeed, recently, there has been a trend towards looking more into the motivations and attitudes of neighbouring countries and their societies (cf. Korosteleva, Natorski and Simão 2013, 2014; Delcour and Wolczuk 2015). Then, the question that ensues is: what is the main driving force of the interactions between the EU and its neighbours and what motivates both the EU and neighbouring countries to engage in their common relation.

As indicated in Table 7.1, we can distinguish four broad positions, three of which can be labelled as (at least partially) constructivist.

The first of these four positions, which can be called thick constructivism, builds on the assumption that both the EU and the neighbouring countries are rule-followers. The mutual interaction is not primarily based on the benefits they derive from the relationship, but on

Table 7.1 Constructivist positions in the study of the European Neighbourhood Policy

EU	Neighbouring countries	
	Normative actor	*Rational actor*
Normative actor	Thick constructivism	Thin constructivism I
Rational actor	Thin constructivism II	Rationalism

their identities. For instance, in this logic, the EU can engage with the neighbourhood because it corresponds to its self-image as the pole of attraction for its neighbours who "naturally" tend to adopt the EU's style(s) of governance simply because the EU is the natural role model for them. In this version of constructivism, this attitude is reciprocated by the neighbouring countries, which want to belong to 'the West', distancing themselves from their neighbours further eastwards or from their own past. The proverbial 'return to Europe', which was one of the main driving forces behind the Eastern enlargement is another case in point – references to the rich literature on the topic will be mentioned in the third section below.

However, thick constructivism does not necessarily posit a harmonious relationship supposedly based on the voluntary adoption of the EU's *acquis communautaire* or its values by the neighbours. In fact, the opposite is easily conceivable: both the EU and the countries in its neighbourhood define their policies in identity-based terms and if these identities are perceived as incompatible, then the logical result is a series of clashes in which the two normative orders compete for dominance in the contested areas. Studies which try to explain the rivalry between the EU and Russia in the neighbourhood, or which focus on the westernizing vs localizing discourses in the southern neighbourhood, often build on this point (Kratochvíl 2008a).

Thin constructivism I is the type of constructivism where the EU remains a largely normative actor, whose aim is to spread its norms and values to its neighbourhood. However, the neighbouring countries and their leaders are conceived as utilitarians, who rationally manipulate the EU by making such appeals to EU values that make it difficult for the EU to not comply with their wishes. The most well-known example of this approach is Frank Schimmelfennig's appropriation of the concept of rhetorical action and the related 'strategic use of norm-based arguments' (Schimmelfennig 2001: 48).

What is typical for thin constructivism I is a curious reversal of the agency of the EU and its neighbours compared to the previously discussed thick constructivism. Here, the EU is perceived as simply conducting its policies based on pre-established norms and it is hence largely predictable. The neighbouring countries, however, can easily change their positions, adapting their response to the normative pressure emanating from the EU in accordance with the benefits they receive from such actions. A typical example of this approach is those studies that portray the countries in the neighbourhood as those oscillating between the EU and another external actor (be it Russia in the cases of Belarus and Armenia, or other actors such as Saudi Arabia or the United States in the southern neighbourhood). While the EU was a somewhat clumsy benign hegemon here, the EU's neighbours are skilful in exploiting the EU's normative position.

The third type of constructivism, thin constructivism II, is the mirror image of thin constructivism I. Here, the main actor, the EU, is conceived as a rational actor whose aim is to spread its influence in the neighbourhood and the neighbours are unable to withstand the focused political and economic pressure of the Union. In other words, the positions are reversed here: while the EU still applies its normative instruments, its leaders are aware of the goals they want to reach in the neighbourhood (be they economic benefits for the EU or security). EU norms are not followed blindly by EU leaders, but instead carefully selected to achieve the intended goals. For instance, the EU may choose to focus on security and stability as one of the leading principles guiding its policies in the neighbourhood. Or it may prioritize transformation and Europeanization, which may be quite disruptive for the political arrangements in the neighbouring countries, thus being as directly contradictory to the emphasis on stability and security. This type of constructivism was first born in the study of EU enlargement. Various authors (cf. Ágh 1999; Kuus 2004) claim that the candidate countries were driven by identity-led motives or by the quest for legitimacy, while the EU (in this case, the European Commission) was a tough negotiator who forced the candidate countries to take unpopular steps and who imposed a number of (temporary) restrictions on the new members that were in the interest of the older EU Member States.

The three constructivist approaches are ideal types which never really exist in their pure forms. Instead, empirical studies may demonstrate that we always find a combination of them. For instance, a diachronic evolution is possible from one type to another. As we argue elsewhere (Kratochvíl and Tulmets 2010), the EU adopted a rationalist approach at the beginning of the ENP (seeking security), then gradually moved towards a more normative one, then again returning to the rationalist outlook. Another approach would be to unpack the EU as a whole – for instance, EU Member States may be more rationalist and some EU institutions (such as the European Commission) more normative or *vice versa*.

Three types of constructivism in the ENP literature: a discussion

Our discussion of the ENP literature focuses on the three types of constructivism identified above. We leave aside studies defending a strong rationalist approach, where both the EU and ENP countries follow rationalist purposes (cf. Kratochvíl and Tulmets 2010). Furthermore, we cannot mention empirical studies on the ENP, which are very often produced by think tanks and for practitioners. As they generally focus on the empirical evolutions of the ENP in the EU or in the ENP countries, they are necessary and useful for analysis, but generally do not seek or entail theoretical claims.

Publications contributing to theoretical debates are, however, not of an equal nature. Some of them prefer to discuss the general ENP framework, in terms of either foreign policy discourse or governance approaches, others also include implementation and tackle policy issues, like migration, environment, democratization, the rule of law, the fight against corruption, justice and home affairs, institution-building/good governance, conflict prevention and security. Some studies include both the East and the South, but most studies only look at one region or country of the ENP. Each of them thus sheds another light on the constructivist perspectives that one may adopt to analyse this composite policy and analytical results are not always in agreement. This short review will therefore try to give justice to some of them at least, given that due to space constraints it cannot address all of them. It partly builds on a previous attempt by Manners (2010) to categorise theoretical – and constructivist – approaches to the ENP, which we comment and update.

Thick constructivism: the EU and the neighbours as norm-driven actors

Studies representative of thick constructivism consider that both the EU and the ENP countries respond to a rule-following logic. One of the most representative approaches is Ian Manners' 'Normative Power Europe' (NPE). While Manners' thick constructivist perspective was developed for EU foreign policy in general (Manners 2002), later, the author reflected on this notion regarding the ENP more specifically (Manners 2010). For Manners, the EU of the 1990s and 2000s does not operate in the traditional context defined by military capabilities or economic calculations, as realists and liberals would have it, but rather ideas and identities gain a special position. He thus analyses the relations between the EU and its partners in normative terms, as none of them calculates whether the 'transference' of norms will bring them some benefits (Manners 2002: 245). This approach has been emulated by further studies on the normative aspects of EU external relations (Laïdi 2005, 2008) and the ENP (Bicchi 2006; Tocci 2008), which have nurtured the debate on the EU as a normative power. However, there are also combinations with the other theoretical types. While some analyses clearly match Manners' hard constructivist views, others include more soft rationalist elements in showing that the export of norms also serve the EU's own interests. A few authors, like Adler et al. (2006), Bicchi (2006), Johansson-Nogués (2008), Bosse (2008) and Wichmann (2010), have even expressed some doubts regarding the applicability of the concept of NPE to (at that time) novel EU foreign policies like the ENP. Barbé and Johansson-Nogués (2008) demonstrated particularly well that, despite the good will expressed on the EU's side to become a 'force for good', a look at implementation makes deeds contrast with words.

In reaction to criticism, Manners proposed a new way to apply his concept of NPE to the ENP. In 2010, he argued that the ENP can be approached through both causal theories and constitutive theories, a distinction that is shortly discussed and complemented below with additional references. The former explain the evolution of the ENP as the result of three determining factors: intergovernmental cooperation, supranational community and transnational processes (Manners 2010); they can be subsumed under the thin constructivism II. The latter claim that the evolution of the ENP can be best understood through three other approaches, which are mostly post-positivist, notably social constructivism, post-structural theory and critical social theory. It is in the very last category that Manners sees a space to deploy his approach. As a matter of fact, drawing on the work of critical social theorists like Craig Calhoun and Seyla Benhabib, Manners explains that

> the normative power approach attempts to strike a critical path between culturally sensitive universalism and the reification of cultural relativism in order to both critique and change the EU in world politics. [...] In order to study the EU's normative power in the ENP, it is useful to analyse and judge the ideational aspects found in EU principles, actions and impact in this policy field.
>
> *(Manners 2010: 36)*

Therefore, he explores the EU and international principles and norms that contribute to the legitimacy of the ENP, as well as the corresponding policy tools – like the reform of assistance policy – which contribute to the increase of the policy's potential coherence and consistency.

Manners' second stage of analysis focuses on the actions in the ENP, thus on 'the means through which EU normative power is enacted in ENP, in particular by looking at the processes of persuasion, engagement and differentiation' (Manners 2010: 40). For Manners, persuasion operates through language and argumentation and can shame or confer prestige, while engagement encourages dialogue and participation in relations with others. Quoting Del Sarto and Schumacher (2005), he also explains that with the launch of the ENP, the EU came out of a regionalist approach to favour a bilateral, more differentiated mode of action.

Finally, according to Manners, an analysis of NPE in the ENP requires looking at the impact of this policy, thus at the processes of socialization, ownership and conditionality. As he writes, 'to a remarkable degree, much of the recent ENP literature argues that traditional, rationalist incentive-based explanations for EU conditionality needs rethinking' (Manners 2010: 41–42), as Sasse (2008), Lavenex (2008), Epstein and Sedelmeier (2008) have argued. What this scholarship advances (see also Tulmets 2008; Kratochvíl 2008b) is that 'the ENP must be seen as a longer-term process of socialization rather than the application of shorter-term utilitarian calculation' (Manners 2010: 42). Scholars justify this point of view by pointing to the fact that the EU has institutionalized the ENP in an open-ended way, thus allowing for socialization to develop as an open-ended process supporting local ownership and positive conditionality, instead of the exclusive focus on negative conditionality (Del Sarto and Schumacher 2005; Sasse 2008). Manners criticizes this approach, which he sees as developed for the East and less so for the South. This point of view does not exactly fit with the arguments advanced by Kratochvíl in 2008, who identified in the EU discourse on the ENP the definition of the EU as a 'teacher in the East' – thus asymmetrically using law and conditionality to pressure for reforms – and a 'friend in the South' – here insisting on the equality of the partnership, at least in the official discourse (Kratochvíl 2008b: 217). It must be stressed that thick constructivist approaches can lead to differential results in their analysis, depending on whether their focus is on discourses or on policy action. Nevertheless, Manners insists on the necessity to identify critical concerns in socialization processes and whether they live up to the principles mentioned in the earlier stages of the policy (Manners 2010). This is a point which was also made elsewhere in the context of the analysis of institutional reforms in Eastern Partnership countries (Tulmets 2014a, 2014b).

We also consider post-structuralist approaches, such as the ones advanced by Diez (1999), Pace (2007) and Browning and Joenniemi (2008) as thick constructivist ones. These authors place 'theoretical emphasis on the construction of EU policies and identity in opposition to a neighbouring "other" (Manners 2010: 35). Kratochvíl's (2008a) and Haukkala's (2008, 2010) comparative analyses of EU and Russia foreign policies also follow this path, as they underline the different foreign policy identities of both the EU and Russia, which may clash when deployed in the same geographical space. This point of view, although highlighting differences between an EU norms- or values-oriented policy and the neighbours' more realist stance, focuses on foreign policy identity and on foreign policy norms. Even if the EU defines itself in relation to a different other (mainly Russia), it aims at shaping ENP countries to its image and most neighbours showing interest in sharing a free economic space with the EU (for example, Georgia, Israel, Moldova, Morocco, Ukraine) strive for reaching EU norms too. In this sense, such analyses contribute to a better understanding of EU foreign policy meta-narratives, even if their findings highlight diverging foreign policy conceptions – for example, between the EU and Russia. Studies addressing the foreign policy identity of East Central European EU members also tend to go in this direction: for many of these countries, the ENP represents a kind of 'containment' policy against Russia's influence in the 'common neighbourhood' (Fawn 2004; Made 2011; Tulmets 2014b).

It is also useful to mention post-structuralist contributions on the origins of the ENP and its sectoral developments. Balzacq (2007) used a post-structuralist approach to show how the notion of neighbours was constructed and entered the EU foreign policy discourse, for example on such issues as justice and home affairs (cf. also Wolff 2007). In a similar vein, Meloni (2008) examined the question of knowing 'who is my neighbour?', thus underlying the philosophical and even religious narratives on which the notion of 'neighbour' relies. The focus on foreign policy discourse was also useful to Jeandesboz (2007), Johansson-Nogués (2007), Pélerin (2008), and Kratochvíl and Tulmets (2010) to explain the origins of the policy and the key role played by various EU and national policy speeches in the launching phase of the ENP.

Among constructivist approaches, we distinguish further between thin constructivist approaches, which consider the EU as an identity-led actor facing rationalist neighbours, and those seeing the EU as a rationalist actor negotiating with norms-oriented actors. In practice, both approaches are complementary, as previous discussions of middle-range constructivist work have demonstrated (Kratochvíl and Tulmets 2010).

Thin constructivism I and II

Thin constructivism I can be summarized as an identity-led EU facing rationalist neighbours. Work by Schimmelfennig, Sedelmeier and Epstein (Schimmelfennig and Sedelmeier 2005; Sedelmeier 2006; Epstein and Sedelmeier 2008), which mainly deals with EU enlargement but was also adapted to the ENP, and studies by authors like Bicchi (2006), Haukkala (2008, 2010) and Sasse (2008) on the ENP, are representative of social and 'thin' constructivism (cf. Manners 2010: 35), which we label 'thin constructivism I'. We consider that these studies, and others written from a similar perspective (cf. Bosse and Korosteleva 2009), share the assumption that the EU is a norms-oriented actor bounded by its norms and rules, while ENP countries generally follow their own interests and use EU norms to constrain their action or act in line with their interests (cf. Kratochvíl and Tulmets 2010). Schimmelfennig demonstrated in the case of EU accession that the EU's use of 'rhetoric action' can reduce its room for manoeuvre once a consensus on its norms and policy obligations is agreed among EU Member States. On their side, ENP countries remain normatively unconstrained egoists – although they are in fact never free from international engagements. Not being EU members thus gives them the possibility of having some grip on the EU's norms promotion, though some authors consider that the reverse case is also possible, as thin constructivism II indicates.

Thin constructivism II assumes that we deal with a rationalist EU and normatively driven neighbours. Publications of this type consider that the EU and its Member States follow their own interests, while ENP countries express a strong will to adopt EU norms and values, or simply to follow other international norms and defend their identity. Some of these studies have drawn on the experience of EU enlargement and several others on the ENP, but in fact adopt either an institutionalist lens or a neo-Marxist approach.

Regarding the institutionalist lens, a first group of authors is mainly interested in intergovernmental cooperation, like Rynning and Jensen (2010) who follow the analytical path set by Moravcsik and Vachudova (2003) on EU enlargement. A second group of scholars, like Kelley (2006), Lavenex (2008) and Gebhard (2010), have highlighted the role of supranational institutions. A third group, like Balfour and Missiroli (2007) and Biscop (2010), have emphasized the impact of transnational actors in the ENP (cf. Manners 2010: 33). There are many other relevant publications on these issues, like those of Copsey (2007), Delcour and Tulmets (2008), Whitman and Wolff (2010), Mahncke and Gstöhl (2008), Böttger (2010), Nervi Christensen (2011) and Lannon (2012), which also highlight the more rationalist aspects (for example in terms of security) in the launching phase of the ENP and the role of EU Member States in shaping and implementing the ENP along their political and economic interests. From this perspective, while following its own interests, the EU plays the role of a 'substitute of empire', as Rupnik (2007: 38) has called it in reference to the work of Susan Strange. It can also be seen as a 'Pioneer Europe' (Delcour and Tulmets 2008) in constant search of solutions in order to adapt its norms and interests to its unstable environment, or as a 'Normative Empire Europe' (Del Sarto 2015) when promoting its norms but, at the same time, looking for the fulfilment of its own interests.

Studies adopting a neo-Marxist or neo-Gramscian approach are rarer, but are worth mentioning as, paradoxically, they also contribute to the constructivist debate on the ENP. The analyses by Bieler (2002) on EU accession and by Merlingen (2007) on the Common Foreign and Security Policy (CFSP) and EU missions in the neighbourhood are among the most representative ones. The EU is seen as another framework for the promotion of a neoliberal hegemony, which is, in turn, supported by the elites in the candidate or ENP countries in search of modernization strategies (cf. Kratochvíl and Tulmets 2010: 40–42).

Conclusions

Constructivism has become a leading theory in the study of the ENP. This trend is further reinforced by the current shift towards more attention given to the role played by the neighbourhood and to its agency. This is reflected in increasing references to 'joint-ownership' and the retreating allusions to conditionality in official (ENP) documents. Even though no 'theory of EU external relations' exists, constructivism is certainly among the most prospective contenders for this title. With its ability to explore norms and identities, as well as their change, constructivism has become an indispensable part of any study of the EU's interactions with its neighbours.

However, constructivism is comprised of a wide variety of theories that share the same ontological assumptions about the nature of the reality of IR. This means that while constructivists agree among themselves that the relations between the EU and its neighbours are socially constructed, the individual approaches differ in virtually all other aspects. Whether seeing the EU as a structural background or an active agent, whether stressing the role of one-sided conditionality and norms or the mutual constitution of identities, all these may be approached differently and still be categorized as broadly constructivist. Many constructivists are open to a pragmatic dialogue with various types of rationalism, casting utilitarian aspects of politics as just another expression of actors' identities. The challenge ahead for constructivists in EU studies is thus not their ability to incorporate rationalist insights into their theories, but rather the internal cohesion of the ever expanding constructivist camp itself.

References

Adler, E., Bicci, F., Crawford, B. and Del Sarto, R. (2006) *The Convergence of Civilizations: Constructing a Mediterranean Region*, Toronto: University of Toronto Press.

Ágh, A. (1999) 'Europeanisation of Policy-Making in East Central Europe: The Hungarian Approach to EU Accession', *Journal of European Public Policy* 6: 839–854.

Balfour, R. and Missiroli, A. (2007) 'Reassessing the European Neighbourhood Policy', *European Policy Center Issue Paper* 54, June.

Balzacq, T. (2007) 'La politique européenne de voisinage, un complexe de sécurité à géométrie variable', *Cultures & Conflits* 66: 31–59.

Barbé, E. and Johansson-Nogués, E. (2008) 'The EU as a Modest "Force for Good": The European Neighbourhood Policy', *International Affairs* 84(1): 81–96.

Bicchi, F. (2006) '"Our size fits all": Normative Power Europe and the Mediterranean', *Journal of European Public Policy* 13(2): 286–303.

Bieler, A. (2002) 'The Struggle Over EU Enlargement: A Historical Materialist Analysis of European Integration', *Journal of European Public Policy* 9(4): 575–597.

Biscop, S. (2010) 'The ENP, Security, and Democracy in the Context of the European Security Strategy', in Whitman, R. and Wolff, S. (eds.) *The European Neighbourhood Policy in Perspective*, New York: Palgrave Macmillan, 73–88.

Bosse, G. (2008) 'Justifying the European Neighbourhood Policy Based on, Shares Values: Can Rhetoric Match Reality?', in Delcour, L. and Tulmets, E. (eds.) *Pioneer Europe? Testing EU's Capacity in the Neighbourhood*, Baden-Baden: Nomos, 43–54.

Bosse, G. and Korosteleva, E. (2009) 'Changing Belarus? The Limits of EU Governance in Eastern Europe and the Promise of Partnership', *Cooperation and Conflict* 44(2): 143–165.

Böttger, K. (2010) *Die Entstehung und Entwicklung der Europäischen Nachbarschaftspolitik: Akteure und Koalitionen*, Baden-Baden: Nomos.

Browning, C. and Joenniemi, P. (2008) 'Geostrategies of the European Neighbourhood Policy', *European Journal of International Relations* 14(3): 519–551.

Butterfield, H. and Wight, M. (eds.) (1966) *Diplomatic Investigations: Essays in the Theory of International Politics*, London: Allen & Unwin.

Checkel, J. (1997) 'International Norms and Domestic Politics: Bridging the Rationalist–Constructivist Divide', *European Journal of International Relations* 3(4): 473–495.

Checkel, J. (1999) 'Social Construction and Integration', *Journal of European Public Policy* 4(6): 545–560.

Copsey, N. (2007) 'The Member States and the European Neighbourhood Policy', *European Research Working Paper Series* 20, Birmingham: European Research Institute.

Cremona, M. (2004) 'The European Neighbourhood Policy: Legal and Institutional Issues', *CDDRL Working Paper* 25, 2 November, http://iis-db.stanford.edu/pubs/20738/Cremona-ENP_and_the_Rule_of_Law.pdf.

Delcour, L. and Tulmets, E. (eds.) (2008) *Pioneer Europe? Testing EU Foreign Policy in the Neighbourhood*, Baden-Baden: Nomos.

Delcour, L. and Wolczuk, K. (2015) 'The EU's Unexpected "Ideal Neighbour"? The Perplexing Case of Armenia's Europeanisation', *Journal of European Integration* 37(4): 491–507.

Del Sarto, R. (2015) 'Normative Empire Europe: The European Union, Its Borderlands, and the "Arab Spring"', *Journal of Common Market Studies* 54(2): 215–232.

Del Sarto, R. and Schumacher, T. (2005) 'From EMP to ENP: What's at Stake with the European Neighbourhood Policy Towards the Southern Mediterranean?', *European Foreign Affairs Review* 10(1): 17–38.

Diez, T. (1999) 'Speaking "Europe": The Politics of Integration Discourse', *Journal of European Public Policy* 6(4): 598–613.

Epstein, R. and Sedelmeier, U. (2008) 'Beyond Conditionality: International Institutions in Postcommunist Europe After Accession', *Journal of European Public Policy* 15(6): 795–805.

Fawn, R. (2004) *Ideology and National Identity in Post-Communist Foreign Policies*, London/Portland: Frank Cass.

Gebhard, C. (2010) 'The ENP's Strategic Conception and Design Overstretching the Enlargement Template?', in Whitman, R. and Wolff, S. (eds.) *The European Neighbourhood Policy in Perspective*, New York: Palgrave Macmillan, 89–109.

Grieco, J. (1988) 'Anarchy and the Limits of Cooperation: A Realist Critique of the Newest Liberal Institutionalism', *International Organization* 42: 485–508.

Haas, E. (1964) *Beyond the Nation-State: Functionalism and International Organisation*, Stanford, California: Stanford University Press.

Haukkala, H. (2008) 'The European Union as a Regional Normative Hegemon: The Case of European Neighbourhood Policy', *Europe-Asia Studies* 60(9): 1601–1622.

Haukkala, H. (2010) 'Explaining Russian Reactions to the European Neighbourhood Policy', in Whitman, R. and Wolff, S. (eds.) *The European Neighbourhood Policy in Perspective*, New York: Palgrave Macmillan, 161–177.

Hoffmann, S. (1982) 'Reflections on the Nation-State in Western Europe Today', *Journal of Common Market Studies* 21: 21–37.

Jeandesboz, J. (2007) 'Labelling the Neighbourhood: Towards a Genesis of the European Neighbourhood Policy', *Journal of International Relations and Development* 10(4): 387–416.

Johansson-Nogués, E. (2007) 'The EU and Its Neighbourhood: An Overview', in Weber, K., Smith, M. and Baun, M. (eds.) *Governing Europe's Neighbourhood: Partners or Periphery?*, Macmillan: Manchester, 21–35.

Johansson-Nogués, E. (2008) 'The "Normative Power EU" Argument Revisited: The EU and the European Neighbourhood Policy', in Delcour, L. and Tulmets, E. (eds.) *Pioneer Europe? Testing EU Foreign Policy in the Neighbourhood*, Baden-Baden: Nomos, 121–132.

Kelley, J. (2006) 'New Wine in Old Wineskins: Policy Adaptation in the European Neighbourhood Policy', *Journal of Common Market Studies* 44(1): 29–55.

Korosteleva, E., Natorski, M. and Simão, L. (eds.) (2013) 'Special Issue: The European Neighbourhood Policy in the Eastern Region: The Practices Perspective', *East European Politics* 29(3): 257–375.

Korosteleva, E., Natorski, M. and Simão, L. (eds.) (2014) *EU Policies in the Eastern Neighbourhood: The Practices Perspective*, Abingdon: Routledge.

Kratochvíl, P. (2008a) 'The Discursive Resistance to EU-Enticement: The Russian Elite and (the Lack of) Europeanisation', *Europe-Asia Studies* 60: 401–426.

Kratochvíl, P. (2008b) 'Constructing the EU's External Roles: Friend in the South, Teacher in the East?', in Delcour, L. and Tulmets, E. (eds.) *Pioneer Europe? Testing EU Foreign Policy in the Neighbourhood*, Baden-Baden: Nomos, 217–227.

Kratochvíl, P. and Tulmets, E. (2010) *Constructivism and Rationalism in EU External Relations: The Case of the European Neighbourhood Policy*, Baden-Baden: Nomos.

Kuus, M. (2004) 'Europe's Eastern Expansion and the Reinscription of Otherness in East-Central Europe', *Progress in Human Geography* 28(4): 472–489.

Laïdi, Z. (2005) *La norme sans la force: l'énigme de la puissance européenne*, Paris: Presses de Sciences Po.

Laïdi, Z. (ed.) (2008) *EU Foreign Policy in a Globalised World: Normative Power and Social Preferences*, London: Routledge.

Lannon, E. (ed.) (2012) *The European Neighbourhood Policy's Challenges/Les défis de la politique européenne de voisinage*, Brussels: Peter Lang.

Lavenex, S. (2008) 'A Governance Perspective on the European Neighbourhood Policy: Integration Beyond Conditionality', *Journal of European Public Policy* 15(6): 938–955.

Lavenex, S. and Schimmelfennig, F. (eds.) (2010) *EU External Governance. Projecting EU Rules Beyond Membership*, New York: Routledge.

Made, V. (2011) 'Shining in Brussels? The Eastern Partnership in Estonian Foreign Policy', *Perspectives* 19(2): 62–83.

Mahncke, D. and Gstöhl, S. (eds.) (2008) *Europe's Near Abroad: Promises and Prospects of the EU's Neighbourhood Policy*, Brussels: Peter Lang, College of Europe Studies.

Manners, I. (2002) 'Normative Power Europe: A Contradiction in Terms?', *Journal of Common Market Studies* 40(2): 235–258.

Manners, I. (2010) 'As You Like It: European Union Normative Power in the European Neighbourhood Policy', in Whitman, R. and Wolff, S. (eds.) *The European Neighbourhood Policy in Perspective*, New York: Palgrave Macmillan, 29–50.

Mearsheimer, J. (2001) *The Tragedy of Great Power Politics*, New York: W. W. Norton.

Meloni, G. (2008) 'Who Is My Neighbour?', in Delcour, L. and Tulmets, E. (eds.) *Pioneer Europe? Testing EU Foreign Policy in the Neighbourhood*, Baden-Baden: Nomos, 35–42.

Merlingen, M. (2007) 'Everything is Dangerous: A Critique of "Normative Power Europe"', *Security Dialogue* 38(4): 435–453.

Moravcsik, A. (1993) 'Preference and Power in the European Community: A Liberal Intergovernmentalist Approach', *Journal of Common Market Studies* 31(4): 473–524.

Moravcsik, A. and Vachudova, M. (2003) 'National Interests, State Power, and EU Enlargement', *East European Politics and Societies* 17: 42–57.

Nervi Christensen, A. (2011) *The Making of the European Neighbourhood Policy*, Baden-Baden: Nomos.

Pace, M. (2007) *The Politics of Regional Identity: Meddling with the Mediterranean*, London: Routledge.

Pélerin, J. (2008) 'The ENP in Interinstitutional Competition: An Instrument of Leadership for the Commission?', in Mahncke, D. and Gstöhl, S. (eds.) *Europe's Near Abroad: Promises and Prospects of the EU's Neighbourhood Policy*, Brussels: Peter Lang, College of Europe Studies, 47–68.

Rupnik, J. (ed.) (2007) *Les banlieues de l'Europe. Les politiques de voisinage de l'Union européenne*, Paris: Presses de Sciences Po.

Rynning, S. and Jensen, C. (2010) 'The ENP and Transatlantic Relations', in Whitman, R. and Wolff, S. (eds.) *The European Neighbourhood Policy in Perspective*, New York: Palgrave Macmillan, 135–160.

Said, E. (1979) *Orientalism*, New York: Vintage Books.

Sasse, G. (2008) 'The European Neighbourhood Policy: Conditionality Revisited for the EU's Eastern Neighbours', *Europe-Asia Studies* 60(2): 265–316.

Schimmelfennig, F. (2001) 'The Community Trap: Liberal Norms, Rhetorical Action, and the Eastern Enlargement of the European Union', *International Organization* 55: 47–80.

Schimmelfennig, F. and Sedelmeier, U. (eds.) (2005) *The Europeanisation of Central and Eastern Europe*, Ithaca: Cornell University Press.

Sedelmeier, U. (2006), 'Europeanisation in New Member and Candidate States', *Living Review on European Governance* 1(3), www.livingreviews.org/lreg-2006-3, accessed 3 October 2012.

Tocci, N. (ed.) (2008) *Who is a Normative Foreign Policy Actor? The European Union and its Global Partners*, Brussels: CEPS.

Tulmets, E. (2008) 'A "Soft Power" with Civilian Means: Can the EU Bridge Its Capability-Expectations Gap in the ENP?', in Delcour, L. and Tulmets, E. (eds.) *Pioneer Europe? Testing EU Foreign Policy in the Neighbourhood*, Baden-Baden: Nomos, 133–158.

Tulmets, E. (2014a) *East Central European Foreign Policy Identity in Perspective: Back to Europe and EU's Neighbourhood*, New York: Palgrave Macmillan.

Tulmets, E. (2014b) 'L'exportation des normes "molles" dans la politique extérieure de l'UE: Un ou plusieurs modèles?', *Politique européenne* 46: 34–58.

Wæver, O. (2010) 'Towards a Political Sociology of Security Studies', *Security Dialogue* 41(6): 649–658.

Walt, S. (1998) 'International Relations: One World, Many Theories', *International Affairs* 110: 32–46.

Wendt, A. (1999) *Social Theory of International Politics*, Cambridge: McGraw-Hill Higher Education.

Whitman, R. and Wolff, S. (eds.) (2010) *The European Neighbourhood Policy in Perspective*, New York: Palgrave Macmillan.

Wichmann, N. (2010) *Rule of Law Promotion in the European Neighbourhood Policy: Normative or Strategic Power Europe?*, Baden-Baden: Nomos.

Wolff, S. (2007) 'La dimension méditerranéenne de la politique Justice et Affaires intérieures', *Cultures & Conflits* 66: 77–99.

8
THE STUDY OF THE EUROPEAN NEIGHBOURHOOD POLICY THROUGH THE LENSES OF CRITICAL APPROACHES

Åsne Kalland Aarstad and Niklas Bremberg

Introduction

The European Neighbourhood Policy (ENP) is in constant motion. The latest quest to make the ENP 'fit for purpose' (Schumacher 2015) initiated the policy's third round of revision, whose main contents were presented by the EU's High Representative for Foreign Affairs and Security, Federica Mogherini, and the Commissioner for ENP and Enlargement Negotiations, Johannes Hahn, on 18 November 2015 (EEAS 2015). The necessity of revision reflects unresolved issues, from the former revision in around 2010/2011, and new demands, stemming from the European Union's (EU's) increasingly troublesome neighbourhood, which in turn have not received enough political attention due to internal disputes and other challenges that the EU has been confronted with.

Following the Arab uprisings in 2011 and Russia's annexation of Crimea in 2014, there is an increasingly widespread notion that the ENP is failing to provide the EU and its Member States with the appropriate tools to promote stability, economic development and political reforms in neighbouring countries to the South and East of the Union (Lehne 2014; Tocci 2014). It is no doubt tempting to criticize the latest review of the ENP for its lofty language on the need to increase 'differentiation' among ENP countries, greater 'mutual ownership' between EU members and neighbours, and promoting democracy and good governance. However, what needs to be done to make the ENP 'fit for purpose' requires a more thorough critical engagement, because the question opens a series of contended queries: What is, or should be, the ENP's purpose, and do its means facilitate the desired ends?

Different theoretical approaches provide different answers. And exactly as the ENP continues to evolve, so does the study of it: new questions are being posed because of empirical developments and the application of new methods and theories. Taking a deep dive into this research field, this chapter aims to explore the application of various streams of critical theory to the study of the ENP. Existing scholarly work draws on developments of critical theorizing from a variety of academic disciplines ranging from EU studies, International Relations (IR) and critical security studies to critical geography and political sociology.

According to Bicchi and Lavenex (2015: 877–879) contemporary research on the ENP has indeed taken a 'critical turn', most notably through analyses that put power asymmetries at the centre of the analytical focus. The ENP, as both a policy and a project, has numerous symbolic and practical challenges in this regard, tied to the ability of the EU to export its own rules and practices to neighbouring countries (Del Sarto 2015). As such, the contended queries related to the ENP's means and ends constitute an important occupation of critical inquiries: what kind of power does the EU apply to exert influence in its neighbourhood; with what consequences; and how does this reflect back on the ENP's purpose and, in effect, the character of the EU itself? In this chapter, we aim to explore how critical approaches have answered these questions and discuss the extent to which critical approaches can point to alternative ways forward for the ongoing evolution of the ENP.

To achieve this aim, we have organized the chapter in four sections. The first section will explore the question of what it means to be 'critical' in social and political research, and specifically in the context of the ENP. In the second part, we will present a comprehensive review of the ENP scholarly literature, with a specific focus on the application of critical theoretical approaches. This will be followed by the third section, in which we aim to apply the insights from the critical approaches outlined above by (re-)posing the questions of where the challenges inherent to the ENP lie according to different critical approaches, and, if possible, how these assess the prospects for change. Finally, we propose future research agendas for the continued critical study of the ENP and concluding remarks.

What does it mean to apply a critical lens?

The critical research tradition is not easily defined, a challenge exacerbated by the critical tradition's own opposition to tight and rigid definitions. However, for the purposes of being able to say something meaningful about this tradition's promises and pitfalls *vis-à-vis* a policy domain such as the ENP, it is necessary to outline in greater detail "what we talk about when we talk about critical theories".

By 'critical theories' we refer, in this chapter, to a broad understanding of the term. We do not subscribe either to the straightforward – and in our opinion narrow – conflation of critical theories with variants of Marxism and Gramscianism, often capitalized as Critical Theory (as seen in Steans et al. 2005; Diez et al. 2011), or to a generic understanding of critical theories, a mere synonym for 'all things critical'. By aiming to strike in the middle, between the specific and the generic, we approach critical theories as an umbrella category for a multifaceted body of critical scholarship that aims to 'trace and challenge given limits' (Hutchings 2001: 84; for similar ideas see Aarstad 2015; Peoples and Vaughan-Williams 2010; Mutimer et al. 2013; Manners 2007).

These 'limits' can be physical, ideational and/or structural barriers that hinder societal or individual change or progress, and epistemological and ontological constraints in the language and practice of political inquiry that marginalize groups, issues areas and/or ways of thinking. It is possible to separate the critical tradition into two mainstreams that attack limitations in very different ways. The first is *mainstream critical theory* influenced by neo-Gramscianism and the Frankfurt School, in IR closely connected to the works of Robert Cox and Andrew Linklater. The second is *postmodernist approaches*, heavily influenced by sociologists such as Foucault and Derrida, and in IR closely connected with the works of R.B.J. Walker and Richard Ashley. The main dividing line between these two streams, as regards the question of alternatives, is understood as the ability and desirability of formulating alternatives to the experienced limitations. The division is grounded in ontological disagreements about the possibility of universalisms and foundations for knowledge, hence judgement calls. The neo-Gramscian and Frankfurt School traditions are widely held to have a strong emancipatory agenda, through their inquiries into how social structures cause and/or uphold inequalities, injustices and exclusions. Progress is possible by the freeing, or emancipation, from these limiting structures. The critique, as argued by Hutchings (2001: 84–85), is based on a 'better-worse judgement', which necessitates normative value commitments. However, as argued by postmodernist scholars, how do we know what the 'better' alternative to these injustices/inequalities/exclusions would look like? And whose normative value commitments are heard, whose are silenced? For the postmodernist approach, critique is not based on norms or values – and hence it does not advocate an emancipatory agenda – but on 'the necessary unsustainability of any secure ground for judgement' (Hutchings 2001: 85). The postmodern tradition, as a consequence, is often critical towards the mainstream critical tradition (Hobson 2007).

These broad brush-strokes underscore the critical research tradition's preoccupation with 'limitations', striving to both define and overcome them along two distinct streams of thought. Additionally, within these two streams – mainstream and postmodern – there is great variation. According to Peoples and Vaughan-Williams, 'there are crisscrossing lines of convergence and divergence over the object, method and implications of being "critical"'(2010: 1). A postmodern analysis inspired by Foucault's governmentality approach targeting the EU's democracy promotion in its neighbourhoods and a neo-Gramscian critique of the neoliberal ethos of the ENP both converge and diverge on matters ranging from meta-theoretical commitments to which issue areas are found relevant. They are both, however, part of a broad critical research tradition, and wrestle in their own ways with how to *reveal*, *expose* and, in the case of the latter, *overcome* limitations.

In the context of the ENP, it is important to acknowledge that a tight dividing line between these theoretical forms of critique, issued from the broad critical research tradition, and more conventional forms of policy criticism is not always clear-cut. This point is exacerbated by the fact that large swaths of the scholarly literature on the ENP have a distinct (policy) critical edge. The notion that there is a mismatch between the values that the ENP is said to embody and the practices it relies on is in many ways a starting point for scholarship on the ENP (cf. Bosse 2007; Hollis 2012). We are wary of the dangers of closing the net around a tight definition of what it means to be critical (Peoples and Vaughan-Williams 2010), and it is important to stress that the ENP is subject to various forms of critique that go beyond the parameters of this chapter. This holds true for realist contributions on the ENP, exemplified by Seeberg's (2009) critical chapter on the ENP, in which he characterizes the EU as 'a realist actor in normative clothes'. Important here, however, is that realist contributions are not interested in the multiple 'limiting' aspects of the ENP itself. Realist analyses focus on the extent to which the motives behind and formulations and consequences of given policies are on a par with the basic assumptions of realist theory: the pursuit of narrow self-interests in an anarchic structural environment (Hyde-Price 2006). In blunt terms, the realist critique of the ENP would be obsolete if the ENP mirrored the theory's basic assumptions.

State of the art

As stated above, the inconsistencies between the ENP's means and ends can be identified as a starting point for much of the ENP literature, and this focus is arguably amplified in works adopting a critical theoretical stance focusing on different aspects of the ENP and consequences of the policy in targeted neighbouring regions and countries. This can be illustrated by zooming in on two research areas. First, ever since the policy was launched, critical work has focused on the themes of identity and borders (Walters 2004; Browning and Joenniemi 2008; Scott 2009; Kratochvíl 2009; Del Sarto 2015).[1] The inconsistencies between the stated aims of the ENP and the ways in which the policy is understood to function, have led several contributions to highlight that the ENP operates on and reproduces a logic of insiders and outsiders, contrary to the publicly stated ambition of wanting to avoid creating 'sharp dividing lines' between EU Member States and EU neighbours (Dimitrovova 2008; van Houtum and Boedeltje 2011). Second, another important issue area for critical scholarship concerns the identified mismatch between the ENP's stated ambitions of democracy and human rights promotion and the practical investments and achievements in the same areas (Pace 2010). Works drawing upon Foucault and the governmentality approach have advanced novel understandings of the neoliberal logics that characterize these EU initiatives and contribute in their own right to the broader discussion on what drives EU external action in its neighbourhood (Tagma et al. 2013; İşleyen 2015a).

Identity, borders and 'borderlands'

Through discourse analyses, scholars have shown that the EU, to a large extent, depicts its vicinity as an unstable and potentially threatening place and that the ENP should therefore be understood primarily as a means to try and control it or as a way of 'othering' that serves to reify a certain notion of self (Holm 2005; Jeandesboz 2007; Horký-Hlucháň and Kratochvíl 2014; Kunz and Maisenbacher 2017). For example, Zaiotti (2007) describes the ENP as an outcome of the EU's 'gated community syndrome', which has emerged because of the 'Schengen culture of internal security' (see also van Houtum and Pijpers 2007). This and other similar accounts can be said to follow a trend established by earlier critical work on the EU, which addressed themes such as the blurring of the boundaries of internal and external security in post-Cold War Europe, the securitization of migration and the constitutive role of the Other in creating a European Self (cf. Krause and Williams 1997; Huysmans 1998; Bigo 2000; Diez 2004, 2014; Carta and Morin 2014).

Kunz and Maisenbacher (2017) make use of feminist and post-colonial works on the EU's gender-equality promotion strategy in order to contribute to the EU's identity debate. The authors argue that the EU makes use of gendered and racialized coding that frame the EU neighbourhoods as a backward Other, strengthening Europe's self-perception as the modern Self (ibid.). Not only does the EU present women in the neighbourhoods as helpless victims in need of assistance, the EU does not always live up to the seemingly universal standards it promotes. This, according to the authors, has the effect of injecting a false sense of superiority in the relationship with the partner country in question. As a consequence, the neighbouring country is brought down (ibid.), and the EU strengthens its position both as morally superior and as a necessary force for good in the region.

The issue of the EU's borders with its neighbours has also been critically interpreted by the broader ENP literature, which addresses the fuzziness of EU borders (Christiansen et al. 2000) and the dynamics of external governance (Lavenex 2004; Lavenex and Schimmelfennig 2009) by which the EU interferes with internal policies of its neighbours. The neighbourhood is understood as a set of 'regions that can be regarded as intermediate spaces between the inside and outside of the Union, and these regions have indeed become the targets of significant "policy-export"' (Christiansen et al. 2000: 389). These new understandings of borders have at their heart a

> series of new spatial imaginaries, institutional actors and cartographic experiments that point to a project in a process in which the relationships between territory, state and population are being reconfigured to produce new notions of sovereignty across more complex and multiple borders and, in some cases, beyond borders.
>
> *(Casas-Cortes et al. 2013: 37)*

The topic of the EU's border externalization, then, represents a case in which scholars adopt critical stances without necessarily engaging with the hermeneutics associated with critical theory. As mentioned previously, policy criticism outside the vocabulary of the critical theoretical research tradition represents an important facet of the ENP literature and is present in a wide number of studies focusing on various aspects of the EU's relations with its neighbours (Hollis 2012; Tocci 2014; Tocci and Voltolini 2011).

Furthermore, there are also contributions that seek to critically engage with the ENP by way of pointing out that ambiguities and inconsistencies in the policy need not only serve the economic and security interests of the EU and its Member States. In fact, it might actually open up space for partner countries to influence the development of the ENP. Browning and Joenniemi (2008: 520) argue that the academic focus on borders and bordering runs the risk of reproducing a 'fixed geopolitical vision of what the EU is about and how it aims to run and to organize the broader European space'. In fact, the ENP rather seems to be informed by a series of different geopolitical strategies with regard to the borders of the EU, which implies a more dynamic and complex relationship than perhaps many critical accounts seem to allow. It has even been suggested that EU neighbours in some regards do have a 'constitutive impact' on the nature of the ENP as it evolves over time. Drawing on a discussion on the 'power of the margins' and an analysis of Ukraine and Belarus, Browning and Christou (2010) suggest that neighbouring countries can play constitutive (and to some extent disruptive) roles in how the EU seeks to constitute its Self-identity, the identity of its Others and in turn the nature of its border with those others. They contend that

> the ENP works best in relation to a certain category of otherness [i.e. so called Willing Others] [and] relations of otherness also provide the outside with the capacity to act back on the EU and affect how the EU is itself constituted at its borders (whether, for example, it remains expansionist or if the emphasis shifts to a focus on firmer borders).
>
> *(Browning and Christou 2010: 111; see also Manners 2010)*

Democracy and human rights promotion

The identified mismatch between the ENP's words and deeds in the context of democracy and human rights promotion has in recent years given birth to an expanding research nexus of critical approaches and the ENP. It is here important to acknowledge the issue area's close connection to the broader debate on whether it is mainly values or interests that inform EU external action, which has been debated ever since Manners (2002) coined the concept of 'Normative Power Europe' (NPE) (see also Pace 2007). Many scholars have been quick to point out that the ENP is designed to serve the economic and security interests of the EU and its Member States, a criticism that is far from exclusively associated with critical theory (Hyde-Price 2006; Seeberg 2009). This is another indicator of the broader critical literature on the ENP that is not necessarily tied to the critical research tradition.

Zooming in on the latter, in recent years, and especially in the wake of Arab uprisings in 2011, discourse analysis has been employed in order to show that the EU's renewed emphasis on democracy and sustainable development rests on an unaltered liberal model of development and democratization and thus amounts to little or no change in the ENP. According to Teti, the EU's notion of democracy relies on narrow, procedural criteria, which prioritize elections and political rights over and above social and economic factors, and as such, it relegates the pursuit of these other features of democracy – economic rights, social justice, etc. – to the realms of aid or development, failing to recognize these as rights with political implications central to democracy and transitions toward it, particularly to the transition from formal to substantive democracy.

(2012: 280)

Moreover, several studies of the EU's relations with neighbouring countries, relying on some version of Foucauldian governmentality, have emerged.[2] Most of these studies do not focus specifically on the ENP but many are nonetheless relevant here as examples of critical scholarship on the EU's relations with closely situated countries. For example, Kurki's analysis of the European Instrument for Democracy and Human Rights (EIDHR) as a form of neoliberal governmentality technique is not only interesting for its account of what drives EU democracy promotion, centred on civil society, but also because it seeks to uncover 'a deep-running form of governmental control over the nature of individuals, society, and governance in target states' (2011: 351).

In a similar vein Tagma et al. (2013) argue that the EU promotes a neoliberal reform agenda to foster a mode of subjectivity among neighbouring Arab countries that is conducive to the EU's own norms and interests, seeking to subject the agency on the 'Arab street' to EU standards. The twinning arrangements that the EU supports between national administrations in Member States and ENP countries have also been analysed through a governmentality framework as a way of rendering socio-economic development in partner countries open to neoliberal governing patterns, linkages and practices (İşleyen 2015b).

These accounts provide new ways of understanding relations of dominance and power as well as the conditions under which the EU influences its neighbours.

There is, however, a tension between, on the one hand, taking Foucault's notion of neoliberal governmentality as a dispersed, multifaceted, yet historically contingent, set of practices and techniques that render certain societal outcomes possible while closing off others and, on the other, using that notion as an analytical tool and by doing so reify the EU as the source of such practices and techniques. Foucault was insistent on decentring the often taken for granted subjects of state, government and citizen (Foucault 2008). It is therefore not entirely unproblematic to ascribe power to the EU *per se* to effectively promote neoliberal reforms in partner countries in Eastern Europe and North Africa. It could instead be argued that the power of the EU needs to be decentred as well, at least for the sake of theoretical consistency. Moreover, to say something substantial about how EU actions are shaping deep-seated aspects of social life in neighbouring countries, more detailed accounts on how the initiatives and frameworks that stem from the EU are received in different local contexts are certainly needed. In this regard, Malmvig's analysis of EU-led initiatives on democracy promotion and economic reforms, while also being inspired by Foucault's notion of governmentality, is promising, as it effectively shows that governing technologies are never complete. Her analysis of 'counter-conduct' suggests that resistance to EU-led reforms by Arab neighbours

is not necessarily visible, spectacular, and direct as in the street protests, riots, and demonstrations carried out in the squares of Cairo, Istanbul, or Madrid. Counter-conduct – just as power that conducts – takes a multiplicity of localized forms, and these are sometimes mundane, trivial, and non-emancipatory.

(Malmvig 2014: 307)

Malmvig's contribution is important, especially for ENP scholars working within the critical research tradition, as it serves as a reminder of the dangers associated with reifying certain forms of (EU) power as well as idealizing certain modes of resistance. At the same time, it highlights the potential of critical approaches to provide new insights on both power and resistance.

Moreover, the proposed mismatch between words and deeds has itself been subject to critical review. Drawing upon the wave of critical scholarship analysing the EU's external relations through the application of concepts such as empire and imperialism (Behr 2007; Hooper and Kramsch 2007; Zielonka 2006, 2008, 2013), Del Sarto (2015: 12) proposes that the EU's export of rules and practices to its borderlands is 'normative indeed' – although these norms are starkly different from those associated with the NPE concept. Following this line of thought, the EU acts according to the idea that 'neighbouring countries should gradually accept a pre-defined set of EU rules and practices, without being offered any say in the EU's decision-making practices' (ibid.). This behaviour, in turn, is strongly linked to 'what the EU is' – an empire, according to the author – and the transfer of rules and practices in return contribute to the EU's perception of itself as a benevolent 'normative power'. As such, there is no mismatch between the promotion of norms and the EU's strategic/economic interests, as they are mutually compatible. Del Sarto's contribution to the critical literature on 'the EU as empire' provides new ways of analysing the drivers behind the ENP and, most notably, the nature of the EU as a global actor itself. The article's inquiry also resonates with other critical contributions to the study of the ENP that have questioned and deconstructed the EU literature's uncritical acceptance of norms and normative power as 'a good thing' (Diez 2005; Cebeci 2012), and have posed the question of why 'liberal democracy has achieved a normative status, a taken for granted state of affairs, a "naturalism"'(Pace 2009: 40).

What are the main challenges for the ENP? Insights from critical approaches

As stated in the introduction, the ENP requires a thorough critical engagement that goes beyond criticisms of lofty rhetoric. In our view, the main advantage of applying insights derived from critical approaches to the study of the ENP is not so much that they serve to underline that values and goals that might be depicted as universal are actually shaped by particular circumstances; they are not only historically contingent but also serve some political interests rather than others. Rather, critical approaches can be used to highlight that the ENP embodies ways of exercising power that goes beyond mainstream notions of power-as-capability. For example, compared to the major powers in the international system, the EU lacks military means to back up its foreign policy. Not even the power that lies in promising non-members' access, to the EU's large internal market through trade deals, is necessarily as powerful as one might think in the eyes of the neighbours, when considering the EU's protectionist tendencies (for example, in relation to agricultural trade). However, the power to shape neighbouring countries in its own image through rule transfer, technical assistance, financial support and other features inherent to the ENP is potentially more far-reaching than the display of military or economic might. Formulating conceptions of 'normal' is a powerful tool in asymmetric bilateral relations, which requires reflection from both academics and policy-makers.

Yet, there is a danger in over-stating the EU's power to influence its neighbourhood. In the aftermath of Arab uprisings and Russia's annexation of Crimea, the EU seems unable to wield any influence at all in large parts of its southern and eastern neighbourhood (Borg and Bremberg 2016). If the EU really is an empire, it would be an increasingly impotent and contested one. Of course, it can be argued that the ENP is failing exactly because it is operating on a self-regarding logic which reproduces hierarchies between EU Member States and ENP countries rather than serving to overcome them. Moreover, the inherently contested nature of European integration among the circle of EU Member States implies that the geographical and political boundaries of the 'European project' are subject to constant struggles. In this way, the ENP is not primarily about the 'others' but rather an attempt to create a sense of order in the open-ended and possibly reversible process of political and economic integration within the EU. Seen from this perspective, the ENP will never be 'fit for purpose' if its purpose is understood to be to promote democratic and economic reforms in ENP countries.

Analyses of the ENP's power-asymmetries, based on a critical engagement with the concept of power, often direct sweeping criticism of the ENP for being imperialist and self-regarding. In other words, the critique is used as a way to say something about the character of the EU as a foreign policy actor. However, critical approaches can also be used to uncover resistance and show different ways of understanding how the ENP operates, that is, to say something about the complex and diverse dynamics that the ENP can trigger in a given neighbouring country at the 'receiving end'. Discussions on the 'power of the margins' and 'counter-conduct' are examples of some of the most interesting critical works on the ENP. They point to creativity and non-conformity in the responses to the ENP by actors in neighbouring countries that are subject to the policy. In addition to the work being done in this regard by a diverse set of scholars such as Browning and Christou (2010), Manners (2010) and Malmvig (2014), we would like to add that the ENP seems to be operating on a particular kind of attraction to certain neighbours in North Africa.

In contrast to many eastern neighbours, such as Ukraine, Moldova and perhaps even Georgia, that find themselves in the frustrating situation of being potential candidates for membership at a time when EU enlargement beyond the countries in the Western Balkans seems to become ever less likely, ENP countries to the South, especially Morocco, Israel, Tunisia and Jordan, find themselves in a situation where how far their relations to the EU can develop is still open, although membership is not being offered. On the eastern side, there is the tragedy of knowing one's unfulfilled fate, whereas on the southern side, there is the attractiveness of a still undecided future (cf. Bremberg and Rieker 2016; Bremberg 2016). That, if anything, adds another nuance to the understanding of the prospects and pitfalls of the ENP in the years ahead.

Future research agendas and concluding remarks

Has the ENP provided the EU with the means to promote democracy, human rights, rule of law, good governance, market economy and sustainable development in neighboring countries? While this might have been the case in a select few instances, the previously recognizable secular trend in the wider neighborhood seems to go in the opposite direction. Some would argue that the ENP has been unable to make a positive impact in this regard due to its lacking institutional design (Lehne 2014; Tocci 2014), as opposed to others who claim that the EU never seriously intended to pursue those goals in the first place (Bosse 2007; Hollis 2012). Still others suggest that in those few cases where the ENP has helped to strengthen democratic and economic reforms, it has mainly served as a function of regime survival strategies (Van Hüllen 2015). In contrast, a large part of the critical scholarship that has been examined in this chapter would rather point out that the ENP reproduces a notion of inside/outside between EU members and partners, and that there is nothing to suggest that the latest review of the ENP would be able to overcome this.

However, it remains a challenge for mainstream critical scholarship to move beyond the assessment of faults to pointing out alternative ways forward. In our opinion, it would be a pity if critical engagement with the ENP were exclusively limited to an exercise of highlighting what is wrong and enlightening as to why this is. Naturally, the desire to move beyond critique by proposing alternatives is at odds with the postmodern critical tradition, as outlined in the beginning of this chapter. However, the mainstream critical tradition carries along a strong emancipatory agenda, and is characterized by scholarship that uses critique to advocate forms of reconstruction. According to this logic, if the ENP can be said to reproduce borders between EU Member States and ENP countries, it is not necessarily sufficient to spell out why and how this is done, and with what consequences. A critical engagement with the ENP should also show why this is undesirable and strive to come up with suggestions as to how this might be overcome in practice (Bohman 1996), drawing upon the vast body of mainstream critical approaches.

There is great potential in critical scholarship on the ENP to engage with these questions, as those closely situated countries that are part of the EU's neighbourhood are not going anywhere, and no 'policy' stemming out of Brussels will ever be able to deliver democracy and economic prosperity to the peoples of North Africa or Eastern Europe. In fact, one step forward would be, following Chantal Mouffe's idea of demanding that liberal democracy lives up to its own ideals (Mouffe 2000), to simply ask what it would take for the ENP to live up to the goals it is said to promote. To be sure, fostering a *common* area of democracy and shared prosperity is not something that can be done solely through EU tutelage.

Finally, if it is the case that the EU is losing influence in neighbouring countries due to the economic crisis in Europe, its poor handling of Arab uprisings and the conflict in Ukraine, or the fact that the balance of power is shifting away from the West to other parts of the world, then this is not something for only policy-makers to consider. Scholars must also reflect on the role of critique in an increasingly post-Western world, something which seems central to critical engagement with the ENP in the future.

Notes

1. For a recent overview of the critical literature on the bordering of Europe, see Borg (2015).
2. In its broadest sense, governmentality is concerned with 'analysing those regimes of practices that try to direct, with a certain degree of deliberation, the conduct of others and oneself' (Dean 2010: 52). On governmentality in IR, see Merlingen (2003).

References

Aarstad, Å. (2015) 'Critical Approaches', in Jørgensen, K., Aarstad, A., Drieskens, E., Laitikainen, K. and Tonra, B. (eds.) *The SAGE Handbook of European Foreign Policy*, London: Sage.
Behr, H. (2007) 'The European Union in the legacies of imperial rule? EU accession politics viewed from a historical comparative perspective', *European Journal of International Relations* 12(2): 239–262.
Bicchi, F. and Lavenex, S. (2015) 'The European Neighbourhood: Between European Integration and International Relations', in Jørgensen, K., Aarstad, A., Drieskens, E., Laitikainen, K. and Tonra, B. (eds.) *The SAGE Handbook of European Foreign Policy*, London: Sage.
Bigo, D. (2000) 'When Two Become One: Internal and External Securitisations in Europe', in Kelstrup, M. and Williams, M. (eds.) *International Relations Theory and the Politics of European Integration, Power, Security and Community*, London: Routledge.
Bohman, J. (1996) 'Critical Theory and Democracy', in Rasmussen, D. (ed.) *Handbook of Critical Theory*, Cambridge: Blackwell.
Borg, S. (2015) *European Integration & the Problem of the State*, Basingstoke: Palgrave Macmillan.
Borg, S. and Bremberg, N. (2016) 'Powerless Europe?', *Global Affairs* 2(4): 389–391.
Bosse, G. (2007) 'Values in the EU's neighbourhood policy: political rhetoric or reflection of a coherent policy?', *European Political Economy Review* 7(1): 38–62.
Bremberg, N. (2016) 'Making sense of the EU's response to the Arab uprisings: foreign policy practice at times of crisis', *European Security* 25(4): 423–441.

Bremberg, N. and Rieker, P. (2016) 'Security Community-Building in Times of Crisis: Morocco, the ENP, and Practices of Mutual Responsiveness', in Rieker, P. (ed.) *Security Communities and External Governance*, Houndmills: Palgrave.

Browning, C. and Christou, G. (2010) 'The constitutive power of outsiders: the European neighbourhood policy and the eastern dimension', *Political Geography* 29: 109–118.

Browning, W. and Joenniemi, P. (2008) 'Geostrategies of the European neighbourhood policy', *European Journal of International Relations* 14(3): 519–551.

Carta, C. and Morin, F. (eds.) (2014) *Making Sense of Diversity: EU's Foreign Policy through the Lenses of Discourse Analysis*, Farnham: Ashgate.

Casas-Cortes, M., Cobarrubias, S. and Pikles, J. (2013) 'Re-bordering the neighbourhood: Europe's emerging geographies of non-accession integration', *European Urban and Regional Studies* 20(1): 37–58.

Cebeci, M. (2012) 'European foreign policy research reconsidered: constructing an "Ideal Power Europe" through theory?', *Millennium: Journal of International Studies* 40(3): 563–583.

Christiansen, T., Petito, F. and Tonra, B. (2000) 'Fuzzy politics around fuzzy borders: the European Union's "Near Abroad"', *Cooperation and Conflict* 35(4): 389–415.

Cox, R. (1981) 'Social forces, states and world orders', *Millennium: Journal of International Studies* 10(2): 126–155.

Dean, M. (2010) *Governmentality, Power and Rule in Modern Society*, London: SAGE Publications.

Del Sarto, R. (2015) 'Normative empire Europe: the European Union, its borderlands, and the "Arab Spring"', *Journal of Common Market Studies* 54(2): 215–232.

Diez, T. (2004) 'Europe's others and the return of geopolitics', *Cambridge Review of International Affairs* 17(2): 319–335.

Diez, T. (2005) 'Constructing the self and changing others: reconsidering "normative power Europe"', *Millennium: Journal of International Studies* 33(3): 613–636.

Diez, T. (2014) 'Speaking Europe, Drawing Boundaries: Reflections on the Role of Discourse in EU Foreign Policy and Identity', in Carta, C. and Morin, F. (eds.) *Making Sense of Diversity: EU's Foreign Policy through the Lenses of Discourse Analysis*, Farnham: Ashgate, 27–41.

Diez, T., Bode, I. and da Costa, A. (2011) *Key Concepts in International Relations Theory*, London: Sage Publications.

Dimitrovova, B. (2008) 'Re-making of Europe's borders through the European Neighbourhood Policy', *Journal of Borderlands Studies* 23(1): 53–68.

EEAS (2015) *Review of the European Neighbourhood Policy*, JOIN(2015) 50 Final, Brussels, 18 November.

Foucault, M. (2008) 'The Birth of Biopolitics: Lectures at the Collège de France, 1978–79', in Senellart, M. (ed.), Burchell, G. (trans.) *The Birth of Biopolitics*, Basingstoke: Palgrave Macmillan.

Hobson, J. (2007) 'Is critical theory always for the white west and for western imperialism?', *Review of International Studies* 33(1): 91–107.

Hollis, R. (2012) 'No friend of democratization: Europe's role in the genesis of the "Arab Spring"', *International Affairs* 88(1): 81–94.

Holm, U. (2005) 'EU's neighbourhood policy: a question of space and security', *DIIS Working Paper* 22.

Hooper, B. and Kramsch, O. (2007) 'Post-colonising Europe: the geopolitics of globalisation, empire and borders: here and there, now and then', *Tijdschrift voor Economische en Sociale Geographie* 98(4): 526–534.

Horký-Hlucháň, O. and Kratochvíl, P. (2014) '"Nothing is imposed in this policy!" The construction and constriction of the European neighbourhood', *Alternatives: Global, Local, Political* 39(4): 252–270.

Hutchings, K. (2001) 'The Nature of Critique in Critical International Relations Theory', in Wyn Jones, R. (ed.) *Critical Theory and World Poltics*, Colorado/London: Lynne Rienner Publishers, 79–90.

Huysmans, J. (1998) 'Security! What do you mean? From Concept to Thick Signifier', *European Journal of International Relations* 42(2): 226–256.

Hyde-Price, A. (2006) '"Normative" power Europe: a realist critique', *Journal of European Public Policy* 13(2): 217–234.

İşleyen, B. (2015a) 'The European Union and neoliberal governmentality: twinning in Tunisia and Egypt', *European Journal of International Relations* 21(3): 672–690.

İşleyen B (2015b) 'Governing the Israeli–Palestinian peace process: the European Union Partnership for Peace'. *Security Dialogue* 46: 256–271.

Jeandesboz, J. (2007) 'Labelling the "neighbourhood": towards a genesis of the European neighbourhood policy', *Journal of International Relations and Development* 10(4): 387–416.

Kratochvíl, P. (2009) 'Discursive constructions of the EU's identity in the neighbourhood: an equal among equals or the power centre?', *European Political Economy Review* 9: 5–23.

Krause, K. and Williams, M. (eds.) (1997) *Critical Security Studies: Concepts and Cases*, London: UCL Press.

Kunz, R. and Maisenbacher, J. (2017) 'Women in the neighbourhood: reinstating the European Union's civilising mission on the back of gender equality promotion?', *European Journal of International Relations* 23(1): 122–144.

Kurki, M. (2011) 'Governmentality and EU democracy promotion: the European instrument for democracy and human rights and the construction of democratic civil societies', *International Political Sociology* 5(4): 349–366.

Lavenex, S. (2004) 'EU external governance in "wider Europe"', *Journal of European Public Policy* 11(4): 680–700.

Lavenex, S. and Schimmelfennig, F. (2009) 'EU rules beyond EU borders: theorizing external governance in European politics', *Journal of European Public Policy* 16(6): 791–812.

Lehne, S. (2014) 'Time to reset the European Neighbourhood Policy', Brussels: Carnegie Europe.

Malmvig, H. (2014) 'Free us from power: governmentality, counter-conduct, and simulation in European democracy and reform promotion in the Arab World', *International Political Sociology* 8(3): 293–310.

Manners, I. (2002) 'Normative power Europe: a contradiction in terms?', *Journal of Common Market Studies* 40(2): 235–258.

Manners, I. (2007) 'Another Europe is Possible: Critical Perspectives on European Union', in Jørgensen, K.E., Pollack. M and Rosamond, B. (eds.) *Handbook of European Union Politics*, London: Sage.

Manners, I. (2010) 'As You Like It: European Union Normative Power in the European Neighbourhood Policy', in Whitman, R. and Wolff, S. (eds.) *The European Neighbourhood Policy in Perspective: Context, Implementation and Impact*, Hampshire: Palgrave Macmillan.

Merlingen, M. (2003) 'Governmentality: towards a Foucauldian framework for the study of IGOs', *Cooperation and Conflict* 38(4): 361–384.

Mouffe, C. (2000) *The Democratic Paradox*, London: Verso.

Mustapha, J. (2013) 'Ontological theorizations in critical security studies: making the case for a (modified) post-structuralist approach', *Critical Studies on Security* 1(1): 64–82.

Mutimer, D., Grayson, K. and Beier, J. (2013) 'Critical studies on security: an introduction', *Critical Studies on Security* 1(1): 1–12.

Pace, M. (2007) 'The construction of EU normative power', *Journal of Common Market Studies* 45(5): 1041–1064.

Pace, M. (2009) 'Paradoxes and contradictions in EU democracy promotion in the Mediterranean: the limits of EU normative power', *Democratization* 16(1): 39–58.

Pace, M. (2010) 'Interrogating the European Union's democracy promotion agenda: discursive configurations of "democracy" from the Middle East', *European Foreign Affairs Review* 15(5): 611–628.

Peoples, C. and Vaughan-Williams, N. (2010) *Critical Security Studies: An Introduction*, Abingdon: Routledge.

Schumacher, T. (2015) 'How to make the European Neighborhood Policy fit for purpose', *Europe's World*, http://europesworld.org/2015/06/25/make-european-neighbourhood-policy-fit-purpose/#. Vl-ci2SrRFY, accessed 17 July 2015.

Scott, J. (2009) 'Bordering and ordering the European neighbourhood: a critical perspective on EU territoriality and geopolitics', *TRAMES: A Journal of the Humanities & Social Sciences* 13(3): 232–247.

Seeberg, P. (2009) 'The EU as a realist actor in normative clothes: EU democracy promotion in Lebanon and the European Neighbourhood Policy', *Democratization* 16(1): 81–99.

Steans, J., Pettiford, L. and Diez, T. (2005) *Introduction to International Relations: Perspectives and Themes*, Edinburg: Pearson Education Limited.

Tagma, H., Kalaycioglu, E. and Ackali, E. (2013) '"Taming" Arab social movements: exporting neoliberal governmentality', *Security Dialogue* 44(5–6): 375–392.

Teti, A. (2012) 'The EU's first response to the "Arab Spring": a critical discourse analysis of the partnership for democracy and shared prosperity', *Mediterranean Politics* 17(3): 266–284.

Tocci, N. (2014) *The Neighbourhood Policy is Dead: What's Next for European Foreign Policy Along its Arc of Instability?*, Istituto Affari Internazionali, Rome, www.iai.it/en/pubblicazioni/neighbourhood-policy-dead#sthash.5sWvWJA4.dpuf, accessed 10 July 2015.

Tocci, N. and Voltolini, B. (2011) 'Eyes wide shut: the European Union and the Arab minority in Israel', *European Foreign Affairs Review* 16(4): 521–538.

van Houtum, H. and Boedeltje, F. (2011) 'Questioning the EU's neighbourhood geo-politics: introduction to a special section', *Geopolitics* 16(1): 121–129.

van Houtum, H. and Pijpers, R. (2007) 'The European Union as a gated community: the two-faced border and immigration regime of the EU', *Antipode* 39(2): 291–309.

van Hüllen, V. (2015) *EU Democracy Promotion and the Arab Spring: International Cooperation and Authoritarianism*, Basingstoke: Palgrave Macmillan.

Vaughan-Williams, N. (2008) 'Borderwork beyond inside/outside? Frontex, the citizen–detective and the war on terror', *Space and Polity* 12(1): 63–79.

Walters, W. (2004) 'The frontiers of the European Union: a geostrategic perspective', *Geopolitics* 9(3): 674–698.

Zaiotti, R. (2007) 'Of friends and fences: Europe's neighbourhood policy and the "gated community syndrome"', *Journal of European Integration* 29(2): 143–162.

Zielonka, J. (2006) *Europe as Empire: The Nature of the Enlarged European Union*, Oxford: Oxford University Press.

Zielonka, J. (2008) 'Europe as a global actor: empire by example?', *International Affairs* 84(3): 471–484.

Zielonka, J. (2013) 'Europe's new civilizing missions: the EU's normative power discourse', *Journal of Political Ideologies* 18(1): 35–55.

9
METHODOLOGICAL AND THEORETICAL CHALLENGES TO THE STUDY OF THE EUROPEAN NEIGHBOURHOOD POLICY

Theofanis Exadaktylos

Introduction

The study of the European Neighbourhood Policy (ENP) brings together a range of lenses from sister disciplines – for example, international relations, comparative politics, area studies and foreign policy analysis. This is because the ENP, both as it was conceived in its original format and in its subsequent revision, is a policy that involves moving targets. It is a complex range of policies that involve tailor-made objectives, strategies and areas of impact. Precisely because of its complexity, the study of the ENP becomes a challenging venture as it is evident by the mapping attempt of this handbook, exploring issues related to EU foreign policy-making and implementation of the policy towards the EU's southern and eastern neighbourhoods.

First, the ENP reflects the ambition by the EU to enhance its presence in countries in its geopolitical proximity as a conflict resolution actor and a transformation innovator and, thus, covers practically any policy and cooperation area (Schumacher and Bouris 2017). As a two-way process, the policy incorporates a gamut of actors, ranging from the EU and those in the countries covered by the ENP to key international players such as the United States, Russia, China, Persian Gulf states and the United Nations, in an overt or more subtle way (Manners 2010). Therefore, the problem identified early on by Del Sarto and Schumacher (2005) persists in terms of demarcating the limits of the research object: What is it that we study?

Second, due to the diversity of countries and policy areas covered by the scope of the ENP, its study involves a diverse set of institutional settings, arrangements and processes as well as policy core beliefs, secondary beliefs and paradigms (Exadaktylos and Lynggaard 2016). The European neighbourhood is a political sphere that experiences different types of interactions and political systems (Celata and Coletti 2015), making it difficult to set up research strategies to study them: How do we study our research object?

Finally, as identified in the scope of this handbook, there is a range of multiple research agendas involved in the study of the ENP that go beyond traditional EU foreign policy and extend into studies of international relations, Europeanization and EU external governance, and area studies. Therefore, the location of the ENP research agendas, in the cross-section of different sister disciplines and approaches, sets the ground for important advancements in our understanding or explanation of the impact of this policy. Yet, this potential can only be realized if we are aware of the focal point of the ENP research agenda in terms of field and framework. In other words, the dichotomy between politics and policy as widely used in understanding studies of Europeanization (Exadaktylos and Radaelli 2012). In a similar vein, then: Does the choice of focus make a difference in the way we study the ENP?

Given the demand for methodological rigour identified in mainstream political science and international relations, as well as the turn to theoretical precision of the past decade (Sil and Katzenstein 2010), scholars working on the ENP need to be fundamentally aware of the methodological and theoretical challenges posed by our research object. In fact, due to the complexities and intricacies of the ENP and the wealth of its applications and impacts, ENP scholarship has a unique opportunity to overcome these methodological and theoretical challenges and influence researchers who face similar concerns in other areas of political science and international relations.

The purpose of this chapter is to 'interview' the existing literature on its methodological and theoretical consciousness, expose the current challenges and inform scholars of the ENP about potential pitfalls and limitations. Therefore, the chapter continues with a review of the state of the art in terms of the research object. It moves on to discuss the current challenges and concerns that stem out of this review and, finally, links these findings to the future agendas in the study of the ENP.

State of the art: methodological and theoretical consciousness in ENP

As an area of research, the ENP is comparatively new, since its first version was formally launched only in 2004, following the 'Wider Europe' communication in 2003. The new policy of the European Union that dealt with issues of its immediate neighbourhood caught the scholarship's interest from the beginning and has since been burgeoning. Starting with Lavenex (2004), who studied the external governance dimension of the 'Wider Europe' idea, and Del Sarto and Schumacher (2005), who initiated the comparative analysis with previous EU initiatives towards its neighbouring countries, the subfield has grown exponentially to more than 250 research articles at the time of writing (2016), as listed in the Web of Science, in addition to a range of edited collections, monographs and working papers. To assess the methodological and theoretical consciousness of the articles published on the ENP, we need to take stock of the awareness or explicit use and mention of certain elements pertaining to the field based on the three main questions identified in the introduction. Given the current volume of the literature, this can be possible only through a bibliometric mapping exercise. Inspired by the exercise run by Exadaktylos and Lynggaard (2016) on classic conceptions of research design and causal analysis in the study of the ENP, as well as a similar exercise on causality in Europeanization (Radaelli and Exadaktylos 2010; Exadaktylos and Radaelli 2012), which is an equally complex and multi-varied area of research, this chapter focuses more on elements that signal methodological and theoretical rigour and strong awareness of methodological trade-offs.

Hence, the literature is assessed against three sets of criteria to understand the trends and direction of the subfield corresponding with these categories: 1) methods and approaches to research; 2) field and framework of study; and 3) the politics/policy dichotomy.

The first set focuses on the way we study our research object. Given the fact that comparative typologies are difficult to establish, scholars have followed a range of different strategies to increase methodological rigour. Awareness and explicit mention of research design is therefore important. The way the cases, countries, policies and time periods under examination have been selected plays a vital role in establishing a systematic way of studying the research object. The type of research methodology employed, as well as the use and understanding of hypotheses, allows the gauging of the scope of approaches available. Finally, since the ENP has undergone one revision in 2011 and another in 2015 and the countries it is affecting have gone through significant periods of change (for example, Arab uprisings), we need to acknowledge the importance of time as a variable to determine critical junctures (cf. Pierson 2004) in the outcome of the phenomena under study.

Second, and linking further to the final point: does the choice of examination of policy or politics determine the field and framework of change on which the study wants to shed light? Because of the cross-disciplinary nature of the research agendas on the ENP, we need to understand where the body of literature is headed in terms of the subfields of political science it applies to and the methodological and theoretical constraints those subfields present.

Table 9.1 List of articles in the ENP sample (2004–2015)

ID	Author(s)	Journal	Year
1	Barbé and Johansson-Nogués	International Affairs	2008
2	Barbé et al.	Cooperation & Conflict	2009b
3	Barbé et al.	Journal of European Public Policy	2009a
4	Berg and Ehin	Cooperation & Conflict	2006
5	Börzel and Pamuk	West European Politics	2012
6	Bosse and Korosteleva-Polglase	Cooperation & Conflict	2009
7	Browning and Joenniemi	European Journal of International Relations	2008
8	Dodini and Fantini	Journal of Common Market Studies	2006
9	Epstein and Sedelmeier	Journal of European Public Policy	2008
10	Freyburg	Democratization	2011
11	Freyburg et al.	Journal of European Public Policy	2009
12	Freyburg et al.	Democratization	2011
13	Galbreath and Lamoreaux	Geopolitics	2007
14	Haukkala	Europe-Asia Studies	2008
15	Hollis	International Affairs	2012
16	Jones and Clark	Geopolitics	2008
17	Kaunert	Studies in Conflict & Terrorism	2010
18	Kelley	Journal of Common Market Studies	2006
19	Lavenex	Journal of European Public Policy	2004
20	Lavenex	Journal of European Public Policy	2008
21	Lavenex and Schimmelfennig	Journal of European Public Policy	2009
22	Lavenex and Schimmelfennig	Democratization	2011
23	Lavenex et al.	Journal of European Public Policy	2009
24	Lindstrom	Social Policy & Administration	2005
25	Sagramoso	International Affairs	2007
26	Sasse	Europe-Asia Studies	2008
27	Schimmelfennig and Scholtz	European Union Politics	2008
28	Seeberg	Democratization	2009
29	Smith	International Affairs	2005
30	Smith	Journal of European Public Policy	2011
31	Subotic	International Studies Quarterly	2011
32	Vogler	International Affairs	2005

Source: ISI Web of Science, search 'European AND neighbo* AND policy' and years 2004–2015 (October 2015).

The final set of criteria on the politics/policy dichotomy concerns the stretch of the research object. We can consider the ENP as a compound policy along the lines of EU foreign policy (Exadaktylos 2012; 2015) that comprises variables of actors, instruments, procedures and paradigms. As such, the literature on the ENP is scored on the type of actors it involves – for example, European, domestic and international actors. The type of actor involved allows us to explore the caveats in setting the analytical framework in our study. It is easy to suggest that the ENP flows out of the EU, hence, the EU – alongside its Member States – is determining the direction of the policy towards the affected countries. Yet, as Manners (2010) identified, there can be other influential political actors external to the EU engaged in the process. At the same time, we need to assess what changes or what is impacted. Therefore, the literature is scored against the policy areas the ENP seeks to influence or the domestic political elements it targets.

This chapter uses the same ENP literature sample constructed by Exadaktylos and Lynggaard (2016). Following the guidelines for running a meta-analysis (Exadaktylos and Radaelli 2009), the sample was drawn from the Social Science Citation Index (SSCI) using the terms 'European Neighbo★ Policy' from 2004, when the ENP was launched, to 2015. The sample was populated with the most highly cited articles in international peer-reviewed journals. The caveat of the sampling is that it will exclude articles published in outlets not included in the SSCI, such as the seminal article by Del Sarto and Schumacher (2005). Equally, given the regulations governing meta-analytical exercises, books, book chapters and reviews are not included in the sample. Although this method may exclude some influential or seminal pieces of work, it still provides a far-reaching overview of the literature.

Following the cleaning of the sample drawn in terms of highly cited articles, the list includes 32 articles that have attracted between 11 and 142 citations with an h-index of 21 (Exadaktylos and Lynggaard 2016).[1] Understanding that metrics come with a range of problems in terms of capturing citations – especially as academic publishing constitutes a long process – or that they represent only a small portion of the literature, they offer the opportunity of grabbing some of the most influential articles in the subfield, in terms of the orientation of the research agendas of the ENP and identifying a range of key scholars – for example, Lavenex (2004, 2008), Lavenex and Schimmelfennig (2009), Freyburg et al. (2009), Barbé et al. (2009a) or Smith (2005). The sample is listed in Table 9.1.

Mapping out the literature on ENP

This section presents the results of the bibliometric exercise. At first sight, the univariate analysis demonstrates a certain pattern of choice in the study of the ENP and largely corroborates the expectations set out above. It also demonstrates a certain degree of depth in the exploration of the policy through specific lenses and with a range of specific dynamics in mind.

In terms of methods and approaches to research, the findings confirm that the literature is not explicit about research design, although as the research object is better-defined every year, awareness increases: more recent articles seem to have picked up some of the early concerns about the study of the ENP. Yet, looking at the literature all together, the articles without clear research methods and design section form the majority. There is a direct correlation between articles in the sample, without a research design section and the absence of justification for selecting case studies: apart from two, all others have been scored as 'not justified' or 'irrelevant' (based on the way the study was set up from the outset).

It is also reasonable that the sample demonstrates a strong preference for qualitative methods. This is justified by the fact that as a subfield of EU studies it is driven by a strong qualitative tradition (Jupille 2005). There are only three studies in the sample that have a clear quantitative methodological mandate (Börzel and Pamuk 2012; Freyburg 2011; Schimmelfennig and Scholtz 2008). It is worth noting that there are a handful of studies using single-case narratives – that take a single case study and try to contribute to our deeper knowledge of a specific country that is missing from the literature (for example, Bosse and Korosteleva-Polglase (2009) on Belarus, Seeberg (2009) on Lebanon, or Sagramoso (2007) on the Caucasus). Finally, there is an interesting set of studies that manage to appropriately employ mixed methods approaches in combinations of interviews, coding of frames and qualitative content analysis. Interestingly, half of the sample contains studies that offer explicit causal hypotheses (including those where a rival hypothesis is not offered). That is a limitation in the literature that seeks to explain the impact of the ENP on both the EU Member States and the countries at the receiving end, especially on issues of democratization, institutional reform and state capacity building. Finally, what is surprising is that temporal aspects are not factored in the research. The expectation would be that since the ENP is moving goalposts as a 'living' policy that changes based on current affairs, political circumstances and EU Member States' preferences (Lavenex and Schimmelfennig 2011; Barbé and Johansson-Nogués 2008; Noutcheva 2015), the temporal effect of the application of the policy would be an important element in designing the research. Yet, even in studies that incorporate a temporal effect, it is vaguely done and in a narrative mode rather than demonstrating the causal impact. Table 9.2 presents the aggregate results from this set of criteria.

In terms of the field of study, there is a clear bias of the sample towards studying policy effects in terms of generic policy analysis. In other words, most studies attempt to analyse the effect of the implementation of the ENP, not only on the receiving countries but also on the European Union itself in terms of transforming elements of its normative power or foreign policy, or tailoring partners for cooperation alongside its own standards. Most of the studies in

Table 9.2 Criteria on research design

Research design section	
Yes, there is a section	11
No such section exists	16
There is not a clear section	5
Case selection justification	
Justified selection	12
Selection not justified	13
Justification irrelevant given the scope of the study	7
Methodological approach	
Qualitative	20
Quantitative	3
Single-case studies/narratives	4
Mixed methods	5
Causal hypotheses	
Yes, there are specific hypotheses	13
No causal hypotheses present	16
Hypotheses are present but no rival is offered	3
Time considered as variable	
Yes, specific period	2
Yes, but vaguely specified	8
No or irrelevant in the scope of the study	22

Source: Author's coding; sample size N = 32.

focus can be classified through policy analysis, comparative politics perspectives and public administration, or a combination of fields. These fields of study determine the theoretical approaches applied and the epistemological positions taken. What is interesting to observe is a cluster of articles that deal with the ENP strictly from an international relations perspective including studies referring to the construction of identities either in the EU as an actor of foreign policy (Barbé and Johansson-Nogués 2008; Browning and Joenniemi 2008; Galbreath and Lamoreaux 2007; Hollis 2012; Haukkala 2008; Smith 2011) or from the point of view of the ENP countries (Jones and Clark 2008; Subotic 2011). Given the multifaceted nature of the ENP, frequently, more than one field or framework of analysis were employed in different studies, emphasizing a potentially analytic eclectic positioning of the scholarship (Sil and Katzenstein 2010).

It is surprising that, given the extent of the ENP into areas of political economy or democratization and stabilization, there is practically no study in the sample that falls under the framework of electoral politics as such or political economy. Similarly, it is understandable that the practical nature and application of the ENP limits the intellectual stimulus on political theory studies – yet, this may well reflect the novelty of the subfield. Nonetheless, the politics dimension is not as prominent as one would hope, given the transformative nature of the ENP on the dynamics of the political systems of the affected countries. Table 9.3 summarizes these findings.

Finally, in terms of the politics/policy, the objective was twofold: (a) to assess the types of political actors the literature focused on; and (b) to examine whether it assesses variation in politics-based or policy-based variables. In terms of actors, it is not surprising that the scholarship seeks to gain knowledge of the dynamic that develops between the European Commission, the Council and other EU actors with national executives and other domestic actors. The literature is also attempting to scope the role of the United Nations, Russia and other international organizations (such as the World Trade Organization (WTO), North Atlantic Treaty Organization (NATO) or the International Monetary Fund (IMF)) in shaping the policy itself, but also in determining its outcomes (Barbé et al. 2009a; Epstein and Sedelmeier 2008; Galbreath and Lamoreaux 2007; Sagramoso 2007; Vogler 2005). Turning to what is affected, there is a clear preference for examining change in policy, especially foreign and security policy broadly defined, competition, internal market, trade and regulation, as well as refugee, asylum and migration policy. Finally, in terms of politics-level variables, there is intellectual interest in studying the impact on mainly national executives, followed by interest groups and civil society at large. Table 9.4 summarizes those findings. The left-hand column contains all actors involved (more than one could be present) and the right-hand column contains all variables examined (again, more than one observation could be noted in a study).

Table 9.3 Field and framework of analysis of the ENP sample

Field and framework	Total
Policy analysis (incl. foreign policy analysis)	18
Comparative politics, parties and government	14
International identity (incl. identity construction)	12
Public administration	6
Political economy	1

Source: Author's own scoring: N.B. N = 51 as multiple field and frameworks can be used in the context of a study.

Table 9.4 Actors involved (N = 90) and variables studied (N = 71)

Actors	Observations
European Commission	20
European Court of Justice	3
Council	9
Other EU actors	5
National executives	19
Political parties	1
Other domestic actors	8
Public opinion	2
Business groups	1
EU NGOs	1
Domestic NGOs	1
United States	1
Russia	8
United Nations	4
Other int'l actors	7

Variables	Observations
Policy-level	
Competition, internal market, trade & regulation	14
Economic policy (monetary & fiscal)	1
Energy policy	1
Environmental policy	7
Foreign & security policy	21
Refugee, asylum & migration policy	9
Social, welfare, education policy	2
Urban, regional policy	1
Politics-level	
National executives	8
National elections	1
Public opinion	1
Interest groups/civil society	5

Discussion: methodological and theoretical challenges in ENP studies

What kind of challenges does the analysis of the most frequently cited literature bring about for the study of the ENP, both theoretically and methodologically?

Returning to the questions in the beginning of the chapter, the demarcation of the research object, the ENP, is one crucial challenge. Although this is about conceptualization as well as developments in the ENP itself, it is important to note that the research surrounding the ENP has not managed to fully incorporate elements for methodological rigour. Instead, the sample demonstrated qualitative research acts as a cover-up for the lack of research. This is a general challenge in EU studies (Lynggaard et al. 2015; Rosamond 2015; Exadaktylos and Radaelli 2012) which, as a mainly policy-driven subfield, is struggling with comparative politics analysis, single-case studies and comparative case study analysis (Ragin 1987), simply because of the diverse nature of policies, countries and institutional arrangements involved. The absence of methodological rigour in the study of the ENP can be detrimental to the scholarship, which can be reduced to simple narrative accounts rather than systematic study of the stems and impact of the ENP or a perpetual navel-gazing exercise of trying to shape up new typologies.

Second, it is also hard to capture a moving target (Noutcheva 2015): the ENP has already been revised twice and its implementation depends not only on the desire and interests of the EU but also on the changing conditions in the countries at the receiving end. Events such as the Arab uprisings, the refugee crisis, the surge of terrorism and the rise of populism and right-wing extremism in Europe, constantly provide new parameters in the study of the ENP. Therefore, it becomes imperative to incorporate time as a variable and as an element of the methodological approach and introduce methods such as process tracing (Rieker 2014) that capture long-term processes. For example, Lynggaard (2012; 2015) proposes deployment of a comparative temporal approach that would create within-case variation and allow the shift away from single-case narratives. Equally, the development of proper mixed methods approaches that incorporate fuzzy sets analysis and process tracing gives the additional advantage of capturing complex processes (Kopraleva and Vink 2015).

Third, the multitude of areas covered by the ENP supports the blending of different fields and approaches. As noted in Table 9.3, articles from the sample could be scored under multiple frameworks or fields of study. This is as much of an opportunity as it is a challenge. As an opportunity, it gives scholars of the ENP the capacity to eclectically select tools and instruments of study from various toolkits, bringing together the theoretical perspectives of international relations, public policy analysis and comparative politics. The challenge is that, frequently, concepts from different areas of the discipline are not compatible with each other or do not work together from an ontological perspective (for example, social constructivism and rational choice institutionalism).

Fourth, the revision of the ENP in 2011, and the subsequent one in 2015, brought a new set of procedures, instruments, actors and norms that influence both the origins and the impact of the ENP. Since the majority of the literature explores the dynamics in the relationship between the European Commission and domestic executives on the receiving end of the ENP, it is *de facto* interested in the mechanisms by which the policy is implemented, or, the character of the policy finds its expression through network governance for example (Lavenex 2008, 2015; Katsaris 2016). In addition, given the clear bias towards studying policy effects, there is often the challenge of overcoming dependence between the variation under study and the methodological tools to study it. In other words, there may be room for cutting across methodological and theoretical traditions due to the complexity of the policy under study and the blurring between foreign and domestic or internal and external objectives (Del Sarto 2009; Lavenex and Wichmann 2009). This challenge becomes more prominent especially as the latest revised ENP turns towards security and economic and social development (European External Action Service 2015), which traditionally belong in the domestic policy sphere.

Finally, the overarching theoretical and methodological challenge, hinted by Lynggaard (2015) and Manners et al. (2015), concerns the presence of actors that are external to the ENP, the EU and the countries participating in it. The role of a range of international political actors as well as external and internal processes has been highlighted in the literature (Vogler 2005; Smith 2011; Schimmelfennig and Scholtz 2008). Therefore, it is hard to disentangle the EU effect from other parallel processes in place. Thus, studies concerned with the impact of the ENP need to be able to methodologically isolate the EU/ENP effect and theoretically frame it within the study of the ENP. The influence of the United Nations, the United States and Russia, of international social movements and civil society organizations, as well as domestic processes in the countries of the ENP, should be explicitly incorporated to allow for the development of rival hypotheses. In this regard, the ENP research agenda is not unique compared to the broader challenges in EU studies.

Conclusions

The main argument in this chapter was that increased consciousness of the theoretical and methodological choices that leads to a better demarcation of our object of study is essential. This supports the selection of cases and the construction of alternative explanations or discourses; it adds transparency to our results and helps to position different actors and processes better within the analytical framework. The bibliometric exercise exposed some of the traits of the research of the ENP as a body of literature: overall absence of research design sections, usually not well-justified case selection, studies of qualitative tradition with limited alternative explanations and absence of temporal parameters. The blending of different subfields is the one element that makes the literature unique and, at the same time, has a rich theoretical and methodological toolkit at its disposal. The plurality of actors involved in the ENP reveals a potential for a range of future agendas drilling down to the micro-level relations that develop between them in the context of the ENP. Similarly, the lack of literature covering politics-level variables opens new areas of research, which move away from the traditional foreign policy/trade and regulation/migration policy research sphere.

The theoretical and methodological challenges in the study of the ENP originate in the ENP itself. The ENP is a fairly recent (and recently twice revised) policy that cuts across different and often competing policy areas (domestic and foreign) and touches on a range of different subfields of the discipline. Therefore, the choice of focus of the research agenda defines well its ability to overcome some of these theoretical and methodological challenges. As such, it can constrain our capacity to effectively construct a toolkit for analysis. The literature has demonstrated, so far, a lack of techniques of methodological rigour, which further amplifies the effect of the volatile nature of the ENP itself and complicates its systematic study. Such an effect has the potential to marginalize the ENP agenda from mainstream political science and international relations agendas.

In responding to these theoretical and methodological challenges, the object of study still requires clear demarcation. Thus, effective and conscious methodological choices are necessary. Managing to cut across competing research traditions and transcending research silos, as well as applying complementary theoretical and analytical lenses, increases our capacity to capture the complex nature of the ENP and its multi-layered effect. Finally, given the dynamics developing among actors involved in the ENP as well as the policy–politics dichotomy, temporal parameters become even more important. Methodological innovation and mainstreaming with the broader discipline is certainly one of the answers to these challenges.

Note

1 This means that there are 21 articles with at least 21 citations.

References

Barbé, E. and Johansson-Nogués, E. (2008) 'The EU as a modest "force for good": the European Neighbourhood Policy', *International Affairs* 84(1): 81–96.

Barbé, E., Costa, O., Herranz, A. and Natorski, M. (2009a) 'Which rules shape EU external governance? Patterns of rule selection in foreign and security policies', *Journal of European Public Policy* 16(6): 834–852.

Barbé, E., Costa, O., Herranz, A., Natorski, M. and Sabiote, M. (2009b) 'Drawing the neighbours closer ... to what? Explaining emerging patterns of policy convergence between the EU and its neighbours', *Cooperation and Conflict* 44(4): 378–399.

Berg, E. and Ehin, P. (2006) 'What kind of border regime is in the making? Towards a differentiated and uneven border strategy', *Cooperation and Conflict* 41(1): 53–71.

Börzel, T. and Pamuk, Y. (2012) 'Pathologies of Europeanisation: fighting corruption in the Southern Caucasus', *West European Politics* 35(1): 79–97.

Bosse, G. and Korosteleva-Polglase, E. (2009) 'Changing Belarus? The limits of EU governance in Eastern Europe and the promise of partnership', *Cooperation and Conflict* 44(2): 143–165.

Browning, C. and Joenniemi, P. (2008) 'Geostrategies of the European neighbourhood policy', *European Journal of International Relations* 14(3): 519–551.

Celata, F. and Coletti, R. (2015) 'Beyond Fortress "EU"rope? Bordering and Cross-Bordering along the European External Frontiers', in Celata, F. and Coletti, R. (eds.) *Neighbourhood Policy and the Construction of the European External Borders*, Switzerland: Springer International Publishing, 1–26.

Del Sarto, R. (2009) 'Borderlands: The Middle East and North Africa as the EU's Southern Buffer Zone', in Bechev, D. and Nicolaïdis, K. (eds.) *Mediterranean Frontiers: Borders, Conflict and Memory in a Transnational World*, London: I.B. Tauris.

Del Sarto, R. and Schumacher, T. (2005) 'From EMP to ENP: what's at stake with the European Neighbourhood Policy towards the Southern Mediterranean?' *European Foreign Affairs Review* 10(1): 17–38.

Dodini, M. and Fantini, M. (2006) 'The EU Neighbourhood Policy: implications for economic growth and stability', *Journal of Common Market Studies* 44(3): 507–532.

Epstein, R. and Sedelmeier, U. (2008) 'Beyond conditionality: international institutions in postcommunist Europe after enlargement', *Journal of European Public Policy* 15(6): 795–805.

European External Action Service. (2015) *Joint Communication to the European Parliament, the Council, the European Economic and Social Committee and the Committee of the Regions: Review of the European Neighbourhood Policy*, JOIN (2015) 50 final, Brussels, 18 November.

Exadaktylos, T. (2012) 'Europeanization in Foreign Policy outside the Common Foreign and Security Policy', in Exadaktylos, T. and Radaelli, C. (eds.) *Research Methods in European Studies: Research Design in Europeanization*, Basingstoke: Palgrave/Macmillan.

Exadaktylos, T. (2015) 'Changing Policy Paradigms', in Jørgensen, K., Drieskens, E., Kalland Aarstad, A., Laatikainen, K. and Tonra, B. (eds.) *The SAGE Handbook of European Foreign Policy*, 2nd edition, London: Sage.

Exadaktylos, T. and Lynggaard, K. (2016) 'Research Design in the Study of the European Neighbourhood Policy', in Bouris, D. and Schumacher, T. (eds.) *The Revised European Neighbourhood Policy: Continuity and Change in EU Foreign Policy*, Basingstoke: Palgrave Macmillan.

Exadaktylos, T. and Radaelli, C. (2009) 'Research design in European studies: the case of Europeanization', *Journal of Common Marked Studies* 47(3): 507–530.

Exadaktylos, T. and Radaelli, C. (2012) 'Looking for Causality in the Literature on Europeanization', in Exadaktylos, T. and Radaelli, C. (eds.) *Research Design in European Studies: Establishing Causality in Europeanization*, Basingstoke: Palgrave MacMillan.

Freyburg, T. (2011) 'Transgovernmental networks as catalysts for democratic change? EU functional cooperation with Arab authoritarian regimes and socialization of involved state officials into democratic governance', *Democratization* 18(4): 1001–1025.

Freyburg, T., Lavenex, S., Schimmelfennig, F., Skripka, T. and Wetzel, A. (2009) 'EU promotion of democratic governance in the neighbourhood', *Journal of European Public Policy* 16(6): 916–934.

Freyburg, T., Lavenex, S., Schimmelfennig, F., Skripka, T. and Wetzel, A. (2011) 'Democracy promotion through functional cooperation? The case of the European Neighbourhood Policy', *Democratization* 18(4): 1026–1054.

Galbreath, D. and Lamoreaux, J. (2007) 'Bastion, beacon or bridge? Conceptualising the Baltic logic of the EU's neighbourhood', *Geopolitics* 12(1): 109–132.

Haukkala, H. (2008) 'The European Union as a regional normative hegemon: the case of European Neighbourhood Policy', *Europe-Asia Studies* 60(9): 1601–1622.

Hollis, R. (2012) 'No friend of democratization: Europe's role in the genesis of the Arab Spring', *International Affairs* 88(1): 81–94.

Jones, A. and Clark, J. (2008) 'Europeanisation and discourse building: the European Commission, European narratives and European Neighbourhood Policy', *Geopolitics* 13(3): 545–571.

Jupille, J. (2005) 'Knowing Europe: Metatheory and Methodology in European Union Studies', in Cini, M. and Bourne, A. (eds.) *Palgrave Advances in European Union Studies*, Basingstoke: Palgrave Macmillan.

Katsaris, A. (2016) 'Europeanization through policy networks in the southern neighbourhood: advancing renewable energy rules in Morocco and Algeria', *Journal of Common Market Studies* 54(3): 656–673.

Kaunert, C. (2010) 'Europol and EU counterterrorism: international security actorness in the external dimension', *Studies in Conflict & Terrorism* 33(7): 652–671.

Kelley, J. (2006) 'New wine in old wineskins: promoting political reforms through the new European Neighbourhood Policy', *Journal of Common Market Studies* 44(1): 29–55.

Kopraleva, I. and Vink, M. (2015) 'EU sanctions in response to intra-state conflicts: a comparative approach', *European Foreign Affairs Review* 20(3): 315–336.

Lavenex, S. (2004) 'EU external governance in "wider Europe"', *Journal of European Public Policy* 11(4): 680–700.

Lavenex, S. (2008) 'A governance perspective on the European neighbourhood policy: integration beyond conditionality?' *Journal of European Public Policy* 15(6): 938–955.

Lavenex, S. (2015) 'Experimentalist Governance in EU Neighbourhood Policies: Functionalist Versus Political Logics', in Zeitlin, J. (ed.) *Extending Experimentalist Governance? The European Union and Transnational Regulation*, Oxford: Oxford University Press.

Lavenex, S. and Schimmelfennig, F. (2009) 'EU rules beyond EU borders: theorizing external governance in European politics', *Journal of European Public Policy* 16(6): 791–812.

Lavenex, S. and Schimmelfennig, F. (2011) 'EU democracy promotion in the neighbourhood: from leverage to governance?' *Democratization* 18(4): 885–909.

Lavenex, S. and Wichmann, N. (2009) 'The external governance of EU internal security'. *European Integration* 31(1): 83–102.

Lavenex, S., Lehmkuhl, D. and Wichmann, N. (2009) 'Modes of external governance: a cross-national and cross-sectoral comparison', *Journal of European Public Policy* 16(6): 813–833.

Lindstrom, C. (2005) 'European Union policy on asylum and immigration. Addressing the root causes of forced migration: a justice and home affairs policy of freedom, security and justice?' *Social Policy & Administration* 39(6): 587–605.

Lynggaard, K. (2012) 'Discursive Institutional Analytical Strategies', in Exadaktylos, T. and Radaelli, C. (eds.) *Research Design in European Studies: Establishing Causality in Europeanization*, Basingstoke: Palgrave MacMillan, 85–104.

Lynggaard, K. (2015) 'The Blurred Boundaries and Multiple Effects of European Integration and Globalisation', in Lynggaard, K., Manners, I. and Löfgren, K. (eds.) *Research Methods in European Union Studies*, Basingstoke: Palgrave MacMillan, 237–251.

Lynggaard, K., Manners, I. and Löfgren, K. (2015) 'Crossroads in European Union Studies', in Lynggaard, K., Manners, I. and Löfgren, K. (eds.) *Research Methods in European Union Studies*, Basingstoke: Palgrave MacMillan, 3–17.

Manners, I. (2010) 'As You Like It: European Union Normative Power in the European Neighbourhood Policy', in Whitman, R. and Wolff, S. (eds.) *The European Neighbourhood Policy in Perspective: Context, Implementation and Impact*, Basingstoke: Palgrave MacMillan, 29–50.

Manners, I., Lynggaard, K. and Löfgren, K. (2015) 'Research Strategies in European Union Studies: Beyond Dichotomies', in Lynggaard, K., Manners, I. and Löfgren, K. (eds.) *Research Methods in European Union Studies*, Basingstoke: Palgrave MacMillan, 309–321.

Noutcheva, G. (2015) 'Institutional governance of European neighbourhood policy in the wake of the Arab Spring'. *Journal of European Integration* 37(1): 19–36.

Pierson, P. (2004) *Politics in Time: History, Institutions and Social Analysis*, Princeton: Princeton University Press.

Radaelli, C. and Exadaktylos, T. (2010) 'New Directions in Europeanization Research', in Egan, M., Patterson, W. and Nugent, N. (eds.) *Research Agendas in EU Studies: Stalking the Elephant*, Palgrave MacMillan.

Ragin, C. (1987) *The Comparative Method: Moving Beyond Qualitative and Quantitative Strategies*, Berkeley: University of California Press.

Rieker, P. (2014) 'The European Neighbourhood Policy: an instrument for security community building', *NUPI Working Paper*, Oslo.

Rosamond, B. (2015) 'Methodology in European Union Studies', in Lynggaard, K., Manners, I. and Löfgren, K. (eds.) *Research Methods in European Union Studies*, Basingstoke: Palgrave MacMillan, 18–36.

Sagramoso, D. (2007) 'Violence and conflict in the Russian North Caucasus', *International Affairs* 83(4): 681–705.

Sasse, G. (2008) 'The European Neighbourhood Policy: conditionality revisited for the EU's Eastern neighbours', *Europe-Asia Studies* 60(2): 295–316.

Schimmelfennig, F. and Scholtz, H. (2008) 'EU democracy promotion in the European neighbourhood: political conditionality, economic development and transnational exchange', *European Union Politics* 9(2): 187–215.

Schumacher, T. and Bouris, D. (2017) 'The 2011 Revised European Neighbourhood Policy: Continuity and Change in EU Foreign Policy', in Bouris, D. and Schumacher, T. (eds.) *The Revised European Neighbourhood Policy: Continuity and Change in EU Foreign Policy*, Basingstoke: Palgrave Macmillan.

Seeberg, P. (2009) 'The EU as a realist actor in normative clothes: EU democracy promotion in Lebanon and the European Neighbourhood Policy', *Democratization* 16(1): 81–99.

Sil, R. and Katzenstein, P. (2010) *Beyond Paradigms: Analytic Eclecticism in the Study of World Politics*, Basingstoke: Palgrave Macmillan.

Smith, K. (2005) 'The outsiders: the European Neighbourhood Policy', *International Affairs* 81(4): 757–773.

Smith, M. (2011) 'A liberal grand strategy in a realist world? Power, purpose and the EU's changing global role', *Journal of European Public Policy* 18(2): 144–163.

Subotic, J. (2011) 'Europe is a state of mind: identity and Europeanization in the Balkans', *International Studies Quarterly* 55(2): 309–330.

Vogler, J. (2005) 'The European contribution to global environmental governance', *International Affairs* 81(4): 835–850.

10
LEGAL PERSPECTIVES ON THE STUDY OF THE EUROPEAN NEIGHBOURHOOD POLICY

Peter Van Elsuwege and Roman Petrov

Introduction

The launch of the European Neighbourhood Policy (ENP) and the introduction of a separate European Union (EU) Treaty provision devoted to the EU's relations with neighbouring countries sparked the interest of legal scholars. Four recurring themes can be identified. First, specific attention has been devoted to the legal nature, methodology and institutional structure of the ENP. Building upon comparisons with the EU's enlargement policy, the ENP is essentially regarded as an attempt to overcome the fragmentation of competencies in the field of EU external relations (Cremona and Hillion 2006; Van Vooren 2012). Second, a doctrinal discussion about the actual meaning and implications of the new neighbourhood clause could be observed. Such clause was first introduced in the Draft Treaty establishing a Constitution for Europe and after the non-ratification of this document, transferred to the Treaty of Lisbon to become Article 8 of the Treaty on European Union (TEU). This new provision raised multiple questions concerning, *inter alia*, the relationship with the other Treaty provisions on EU external action and the possibility of using it as a specific legal basis for the conclusion of new types of agreements with neighbouring countries (Hanf 2011; Van Elsuwege and Petrov 2011; Hillion 2014; Comelli 2014). Third, the upgrade of the bilateral legal relations – from Partnership and Co-operation Agreements to Association Agreements (AAs) – with Ukraine, Moldova and Georgia, is the most significant evolution in the legal relations with ENP countries. Whereas the concept of 'association' is nothing new in the EU's external relations practice, not even in the neighbourhood with numerous southern ENP countries already having concluded AAs in the 1990s, the new agreements bring certain innovations that are partly borrowed from other policy areas and partly result from the specificities of the ENP. The provisions on the establishment of Deep and Comprehensive Free Trade Areas (DCFTAs) are certainly the most innovative, raising questions about the extent to which this arrangement can be regarded as 'a new legal instrument for EU integration without membership' (Van der Loo 2016a). Fourth, EU rule export to neighbouring countries is a core element of the ENP. The mechanisms and principles underlying this process, as well as the actual implications for the national legal systems and judiciaries of the neighbouring countries, formed the object of several legal studies (Van Elsuwege and Petrov 2014; Dragneva and Wolczuk 2011). In what follows, the main discussions and perceptions in the legal literature dealing with the ENP are spelled out along the four identified themes.

Legal nature, methodology and institutional aspects of the ENP

During its formative years, the ENP was regarded as an attempt to overcome the complexities of the EU's pillar-structure and evolve towards a more coherent external action (Auvret-Finck 2006; Van Vooren 2012). As argued by Cremona and Hillion (2006), the ENP objectives could be related to competencies under the old first pillar (such as economic integration, environment protection and energy policy), the second pillar (such as conflict prevention, foreign policy cooperation and non-proliferation of weapons of mass destruction) and the third pillar (cooperation on organised crime and terrorism). Proceeding from a broad conception of security, the ENP thus cut across the EU's traditional division of competencies.

It has been noted that the ENP's ambition to establish a coherent overarching policy framework for the EU's relations with neighbouring countries followed the failed attempt to develop a network of Common Strategies (Lannon and Van Elsuwege 2003; Cremona and Hillion 2006). In December 1998, in anticipation of the entry into force of the Amsterdam Treaty, the Vienna European Council announced the adoption of such Common Strategies with Russia, Ukraine, the Mediterranean and the Western Balkans. Despite the actual adoption of Common Strategies on Russia and Ukraine in June and December 1999 and for the Mediterranean in June 2000, this approach quickly became obsolete. The absence of clear priorities and operational action points were deemed to be major weaknesses that could be explained by the fact that the Common Strategies were legally adopted within the framework of the EU's Common Foreign and Security Policy (CFSP) (Maresceau 2004). The ENP, on the other hand, started without an explicit basis in the EU Treaties and aimed to transcend the EU's pillar structure. This explains the close connection – in terms of instruments and methodology – between the ENP and the EU's enlargement policy. The latter is, by its very nature, an integrated external policy in the sense that it does not belong to the CFSP or to any of the Union's specific external policy competencies. It entails the promotion of the EU's norms and values to candidate countries based on a gradually developed pre-accession strategy. The soft law instruments developed within that context, most notably the Accession Partnerships, proved very useful tools that could be easily adopted and adapted without falling into the pitfalls of competence-related struggles (Van Vooren 2012). From a legal perspective, it therefore made sense to transplant the instruments and methodologies of what was perceived to be a very successful enlargement policy to the ENP.

Whereas the similarities between the EU's enlargement and neighbourhood policies have a clear legal rationale, the limitations of this approach were also quickly noticed in legal literature. These included, among others, the inherent tensions between the ENP's strategic tools of differentiation, joint ownership and conditionality (Van Elsuwege 2012; Cremona and Hillion 2006), the absence of concrete benchmarks in the ENP's soft law instruments (Ghazaryan 2014; Van Vooren 2012; Del Sarto and Schumacher 2011) and the lack of tangible long-term alternatives to the membership perspective (Gstöhl 2012). It has also been argued that the ENP's methodology is based on some flawed assumptions about the existence of shared values and the link between the export of the EU's *acquis* and the promotion of democratic values (Kochenov and Basheska 2016).

The implications of a neighbourhood clause in the Treaty on European Union

The Treaty of Lisbon introduced a so-called 'neighbourhood clause' in the primary law of the Union, more precisely in Article 8 TEU. This provision empowers the EU to 'develop a special relationship with neighbouring countries, aiming to establish an area of prosperity and good neighbourliness, founded on the values of the Union and characterised by close and peaceful relations based on cooperation' (Art. 8 (1) TEU). For this purpose, it may conclude 'specific agreements' with the countries concerned, which may contain 'reciprocal rights and obligations as well as a possibility of undertaking activities jointly' (Art. 8 (2) TEU).

The actual implications of this vaguely formulated provision are far from clear and have led to different interpretations in legal doctrine. According to Hillion (2014: 13), Article 8 TEU establishes a constitutional basis for EU norms export, endowing the Union with an explicit 'transformative mandate' in relation to its neighbourhood. He stresses the mandatory character and the normative dimension of the EU's neighbourhood competence:

> While Articles 3(5) and 21(3) TEU foresee that the external action of the Union should be guided by the values of the Union, in the context of Article 8 TEU, EU action aims at asserting them actively, with a view to ingraining them within the (constitutional) systems of neighbouring countries. Thus, in the neighbourhood, respect for the values of the Union becomes the aim of, rather than the pre-condition for, EU engagement.
>
> *(ibid.: 20)*

On the other hand, it has been argued that the drafting of Article 8 TEU was closely connected with the establishment of the ENP and, therefore, essentially codifies the ENP's conditionality approach (Van Elsuwege and Petrov 2011; Comelli 2014).

The specific characteristics of Article 8 TEU, including its position within the Treaties and political inspiration, raise questions about its potential applicability in practice. The question of whether Article 8 (2) TEU may be used as a legal basis for a distinct type of international agreements is subject to discussion. One possible approach is to regard the introduction of Article 8 (2) TEU as a reaction to the inflation of classical AAs in the past decades. From this perspective, the purpose of Article 8 (2) TEU is to create a *lex specialis* to Article 217 of the Treaty on the Functioning of the European Union (TFEU) allowing for a specific form of association, reserved for the Union's neighbours and underlining the specific importance of the EU's neighbourhood relations (Hanf 2011). However, Article 8 (2) TEU may also be regarded as a potential alternative to formal association (Van Elsuwege and Petrov 2011). Traditionally, AAs with European countries are often perceived as a stepping-stone to EU membership. For instance, all Central and Eastern European countries (CEECs) first concluded such type of agreements – called Europe Agreements (EAs) – before their accession to the Union, and the Stabilisation and Association Agreements (SAAs) with the Western Balkan countries all include specific references to their potential membership perspectives. Hence, Article 8 (2) TEU may foster contractual relations between the EU and its neighbouring countries without the political connotations of association.

A third interpretation is that, given the absence of specific procedural guidelines, Art. 8 (2) TEU cannot be used as an autonomous substantive legal basis. Its general wording and unusual location under Title I, 'common provisions' of the TEU, point in the latter direction (Van Elsuwege and Petrov 2011). From this perspective, Article 8 TEU is essentially a political provision, the significance of which for the practical development of the EU's neighbourhood relations is questionable. The new generation of AAs between the EU and some Eastern Partnership (EaP) countries (Ukraine, Moldova and Georgia) seems to support this presumption, since none of these agreements is based on Article 8 (2) TEU (Van der Loo, Van Elsuwege and Petrov 2014). It is not to be ignored that this provision is used in relation to other neighbours of the Union, such as Russia, Switzerland or the micro-states, which are not necessarily interested in formal association with the EU. Despite the close connection between the ENP and the genesis of Article 8 TEU, neighbouring countries outside the ENP have not been excluded from its geographical scope of application (Van Elsuwege and Petrov 2011).

Rather than providing a new type of integration arrangement, which stops short of accession but goes beyond existing forms of partnership and association, Article 8 TEU only institutionalises the ambiguity that also characterises the ENP. Apart from the uncertain procedural requirements for the application of this provision, it appears that most of the neighbouring countries are not interested in this formula. Ukraine strongly opposed any reference to the term 'neighbourhood' or 'neighbouring country' in the context of the ENP (Hillion 2007: 170). Moreover, the special relationship envisaged under Article 8 TEU lacks exclusivity. It is not at all clear what kind of specific benefits it offers to neighbouring countries in comparison to traditional association or even partnership agreements. The focus on conditionality and the vague reference to 'good neighbourliness' makes this new type of agreement not very attractive either. Finally, it remains to be seen to what extent the objective of creating 'reciprocal rights' would allow the neighbouring countries to contribute effectively to the development of the bilateral relationship. As a result, the neighbourhood clause may be regarded as a symbolic or 'utopian' provision which does not solve the complexities relating to the search of an appropriate legal basis for the conclusion of international agreements with neighbouring countries (Blockmans 2011).

Upgrading the bilateral legal framework of relations with the neighbouring countries

Upgrading the Partnership and Cooperation Agreements (PCAs) – which had been signed in the 1990s with all post-Soviet countries, except the Baltic States – was devised as a major 'carrot' for the EU's eastern neighbours that take part in the ENP. This process formally started with the adoption of negotiating directives for an 'enhanced agreement' between the EU and Ukraine in January 2007. After an initial period of uncertainty about the legal status of the new contractual relationship, a Joint Declaration, adopted at the 9 September 2008 EU–Ukraine summit, made an end to speculation when it announced that 'the new agreement between the EU and Ukraine will be an association agreement' (Council of the European Union 2008). The offer of association was extended to interested eastern ENP countries in the framework of the Eastern Partnership (Lannon and Van Elsuwege 2012). This resulted in the signature of a new generation of AAs with Ukraine, Moldova and Georgia on 27 June 2014.

The new AAs essentially aim to deepen the political and economic relations between Ukraine, Moldova and Georgia and the EU – through the establishment of an enhanced institutional framework and innovative provisions on regulatory and legislative approximation. The ambition to establish DCFTAs, leading to the associated countries' gradual (but partial) integration in the EU internal market, is significant. The AAs belong to the selected group of so-called 'integration-oriented agreements', that is, agreements including principles, concepts and provisions of EU law that are to be interpreted and applied as if the third state is part of the EU (Maresceau 2011).

The AAs are unique in many respects and can be characterised by three specific features: *comprehensiveness*, *complexity* and *conditionality* (Van der Loo, Van Elsuwege and Petrov 2014). First, the AAs are *comprehensive framework agreements* covering the entire spectrum of bilateral relations. Hence, they include provisions dealing with the whole array of EU activities, including cooperation and convergence in the field of Common Foreign and Security Policy (CFSP), as well as cooperation in the area of freedom, security and justice (AFSJ). Second, the *complexity* of the AAs is not only related to their comprehensive scope but also to their level of ambition,

Legal perspectives

the aim to achieve the associated countries' economic integration in the EU internal market through the establishment of DCFTAs. The objective of 'deep' integration requires extensive legislative and regulatory approximation, including sophisticated mechanisms to secure the uniform interpretation and effective implementation of relevant EU legislation (Van der Loo 2014). Last, the AAs are based on a strict *conditionality* approach. The preamble to the agreements explicitly states that

> political association and economic integration of [Ukraine, Moldova, and Georgia] within the European Union will depend on progress in the implementation of the current agreement as well as [their] track record in ensuring respect for common values, and progress in achieving convergence with the EU in political, economic and legal areas.

This link between the third country's performance and the deepening of the EU's engagement is a key characteristic of the ENP and the EaP. Whereas this principle has so far been applied based on soft-law instruments such as Action Plans and the Association Agendas, it is now encapsulated in legally binding bilateral agreements.

Two different forms of conditionality can be distinguished. On the one hand, the AAs include several provisions related to the associated countries' commitment to the common values of democracy, rule of law and respect for human rights and fundamental freedoms (Ghazaryan 2015). On the other hand, the part on the DCFTA is based on an explicit 'market access conditionality', implying that additional access to a section of the EU Internal Market will only be granted if the EU decides, after a strict monitoring procedure, that the legislative approximation commitments are adequately implemented (Van der Loo, Van Elsuwege and Petrov 2014).

An outstanding legal question concerns the potential direct effect of the new AAs in the EU legal order (Van der Loo, Van Elsuwege and Petrov 2014). Over the years, the European Court of Justice (ECJ) has developed a consistent practice of accepting the direct effect of bilateral agreements on the condition that the provisions invoked are clear and unconditional (Maresceau 2013). If the agreement contains a formulation excluding the direct applicability of the agreement or the direct effect of some of its provisions, the situation is different. The latter is the case for certain trade-related aspects of the AAs (such as the dispute settlement mechanism for the DCFTA part and WTO-like commitments in the fields of establishment and services). This practice, which can also be observed in other recently concluded EU free trade agreements, avoids the possibility of circumventing the non-direct effect of WTO commitments in the EU legal order (Semertzi 2014).

More debatable is the statement included in the Council decisions on the signing and provisional application of the AAs that '[t]he Agreement shall not be construed as conferring rights or imposing obligations which can be directly invoked before Union or Member State courts or tribunals' (Council of the European Union 2014). The question arises as to what extent such a unilateral declaration, which is not part of the agreement itself, precludes the direct effect of the AA's clear and unconditional provisions. This issue is particularly relevant with regard to the non-discrimination clause included in Article 17 (1) of the EU–Ukraine AA, which provides that

> [s]ubject to the laws, conditions and procedures applicable in each Member State and the EU, treatment accorded to workers who are Ukrainian nationals and who are legally employed in the territory of a Member State shall be free of any discrimination based on nationality, as regards working conditions, remuneration or dismissal, compared to the nationals of that Member State.[1]

In *Simutenkov*, the ECJ concluded that an identically worded provision of the PCA with Russia 'has direct effect, with the result that individuals to whom that provision applies are entitled to rely on it before the courts of the Member States' (European Court of Justice 2005). Precluding a similar right for Ukrainian nationals would, therefore, lead to a very paradoxical situation. It would imply that an old PCA, with Russia having relatively limited ambitions of partnership, would have more far-reaching direct legal implications than a far more ambitious AA with Ukraine (Van der Loo, Van Elsuwege and Petrov 2014).

The legal developments in the framework of the EaP are also relevant for the EU's southern neighbours. Nevertheless, there are obvious differences between the relationships those two groups of countries have with the EU. Most significantly, the Mediterranean countries already concluded Euro-Mediterranean Association Agreements (EMAAs) in the wake of the 1995 Barcelona Declaration (Hakura 1997; Pieters 2010). Despite far-reaching ambitions of trade integration, including the progressive establishment of a Free Trade Area (FTA) by 2010, the scope and contents of the EMAAs was rather limited. They essentially provided for trade liberalisation of manufactured goods with limited market opening for agricultural goods, services and establishment. Over the years, the legal framework has been gradually updated based on sectoral agreements, which were added as Protocols to the respective EMAAs (Van der Loo 2016b). For instance, the EU concluded bilateral agreements on agricultural, processed agricultural and fisheries products with several Mediterranean countries, including Israel, Egypt, Morocco, Jordan and the Palestinian Authority. In addition, Dispute Settlement Protocols have been concluded with Tunisia, Jordan, Egypt, Lebanon and Morocco to replace the diplomatic dispute settlement procedure in the EMAAs with a more sophisticated mechanism of dispute settlement implying 'a quasi-judicial model of trade adjudication' (ibid.: 14).

Despite those upgrades, the EMAAs are still less developed in comparison to the AAs with Ukraine, Moldova and Georgia. For instance, the EMAAs hardly regulate important issues such as public procurement, intellectual property rights, technical barriers to trade or sanitary and phytosanitary measures. Moreover, they only include a 'best endeavour clause' with respect to legislative approximation, in comparison to the detailed provisions on approximation in the DCFTA chapter of the AAs (Van der Loo 2016b). It was only after the 'Arab Spring' of 2011 that the prospect of a DCFTA was offered to a selected group of Mediterranean countries (Lannon 2011). In December 2011, the Council of the European Union (2011) adopted negotiating directives for DCFTAs with Jordan, Egypt, Tunisia and Morocco. Actual negotiations were launched with Morocco in March 2013 and with Tunisia in October 2015. At the time of writing, preparations for the start of negotiations with Jordan were still ongoing, whereas this option was no longer realistic for Egypt due to the instable political situation in the country. Moreover, the negotiations with Morocco were put on hold due to a General Court ruling in *Front Polisario* v. *Council*. In this case, the court partially annulled the Council Decision concluding the agreement on agricultural, processed agricultural and fisheries products with Morocco because the Council failed to consider the potential human rights implications for the population of the Western Sahara (General Court 2015). In a fierce reaction, the Moroccan government decided to temporarily suspend all contacts with the EU. In February 2016, the Council lodged an appeal against the General Court's judgement before the EU Court of Justice. It is unlikely that the DCFTA negotiations with Morocco will resume while there is no final decision on this issue. Moreover, given the different political and legal context, it has been argued that the DCFTA deal with the EaP countries cannot simply be transposed to the southern neighbourhood (Van der Loo 2016b). In this context, it is noteworthy that the 2015 ENP review explicitly recognised the need for more flexibility, pointing at 'the possibility to sign Agreements on Conformity Assessment and Acceptance (ACAAs)' (European Commission/High Representative of the Union for Foreign Affairs and Security Policy 2015), among other things. This type of agreement, which has been concluded with Israel in the form of a Protocol to the EMAA (Council of the European Union 2013), aims at the elimination of technical barriers to trade in specific sectors.

The promotion of EU values and the export of EU legislation

Legislative approximation and the application of shared norms and values is a key objective of the EU's relations with its neighbours. What started based on vaguely formulated 'approximation clauses', gradually but surely developed into one of the most important dimensions of the EU's external action (Dragneva and Wolczuk 2011; Van Elsuwege and Petrov 2014). The ENP and the EaP essentially aim at the export of the EU's norms and values to create prosperity, stability and security on the entire European continent.

Whereas the EU *acquis* plays a significant role as a source of inspiration for legislative reform in all neighbouring countries, effective implementation and application of EU rules remains a crucial challenge (Harpaz 2014; Delcour and Wolczuk 2013). The complexity and dynamic nature of the *acquis*, the (lack of) institutional coordination, limited implementation capacities, and the social and economic cost of approximation, as well as political sensitivities in ENP countries, are the key variables explaining the difficulties of legal approximation in practice (Delcour and Wolczuk 2013). Significantly, the costs of approximation are borne not only by state authorities but also by non-state actors, such as business operators, who need to adjust their production to new regulations. Hence, the more detailed the approximation requirements, the higher the implementation costs. This explains why the costs for implementing the DCFTAs, as foreseen under the AAs with Ukraine, Moldova and Georgia, are likely to be higher in comparison to less far-reaching bilateral agreements with other neighbouring countries. The result is a so-called 'cost–benefit disparity' with high costs of legal approximation in the short term and benefits from facilitated access to the EU internal market in the long term (ibid: 18).

With respect to the challenge of effective implementation, the role of the judiciary can hardly be underestimated. Only when national judges manage to apply the approximated national legislation considering the wording and spirit of the original EU *acquis*, and follow the dynamic development of EU law, can the objective of (economic) integration without membership be achieved without undermining the uniform application of EU legal norms and principles (Petrov 2015). For the EU's eastern neighbourhood, it has been found that national Constitutional Courts and national administrative courts are pioneers when it comes to the acceptance of EU legal norms and principles as a persuasive source of reference for the interpretation of approximated national legislation (Van Elsuwege and Petrov 2014; Petrov and Kalinichenko 2011). They can be considered as the most progressive and outward looking judicial bodies, which do not hesitate to apply sources of international and European law to fill gaps in national legal regulation. Judges of lower domestic courts often lack the necessary training in EU law to ensure the consistent and correct application of EU law.

The assumption that the export of the EU's *acquis* contributes to the export of the EU's values has been contested (Kochenov 2014; Ghazaryan 2014; Poli 2016). The EU's norms export in the context of the ENP goes beyond the Union's legislation *senso strictu* and also entails the 'values-based *acquis*', often borrowed from the Council of Europe or the Organisation for Security and Co-operation in Europe, as far as the eastern neighbours are concerned, and from the United Nations with respect to the southern neighbours. After the 'Arab Spring', the Council of Europe and the EU jointly developed the South Programme to support democratic reforms in the Southern Mediterranean (Council of Europe 2016). However, there is no automatic connection between EU rules and values. Exporting the Union's sectoral and internal market *acquis* does not necessarily imply that the neighbouring countries become exemplary democracies. The discrepancy between rules and values has been illustrated in the academic literature on EU rule of law export (Pech 2012; Van Elsuwege and Burlyuk 2016). It has also been argued that there is a gap between EU statements on the promotion of its values abroad and internal practices of EU Member States, putting the legitimacy of the EU's external action under pressure (Gatti 2016).

Conclusions

The ENP occupies a particular place within the EU's external action. In contrast to other EU external policies such as the CFSP, the Common Commercial Policy, development co-operation or humanitarian aid, it is not subject to explicit competence delimitations. Similar to the EU's enlargement policy, the ENP is of a horizontal nature. Hence, the close connections between the methodology and instruments used in the framework of the ENP and in the context of the EU's pre-accession strategy can be explained from a legal perspective.

Since the entry into force of the Treaty of Lisbon, the special nature of the ENP has also been reflected in Article 8 TEU. Even though the geographical scope of this provision is broader than the ENP – since it refers to 'neighbouring countries' in general – the link between its incorporation in the Treaties and the emergence of the ENP cannot be ignored. As a result, Article 8 TEU is generally considered as the constitutional basis for further development of an assertive neighbourhood policy. Nevertheless, the vague formulation of this neighbourhood clause, as well as the unclear procedural requirements for the conclusion of the special agreements foreseen under Article 8 (2) TEU, reduce its significance in practice. This is particularly the case since Article 8 TEU did not play any role in the process, leading to the conclusion of a new generation of AAs with Ukraine, Georgia and Moldova. These AAs include some innovative features. They are comprehensive framework agreements, based on an advanced form of conditionality and including a complex mixture of provisions on legislative approximation. The part on the establishment of DCFTAs is the most far-reaching, providing for the partial integration of the associated countries in the EU internal market.

The review of the ENP in 2015 put forward a more pragmatic approach towards the neighbouring countries (European Commission/High Representative of the Union for Foreign Affairs and Security Policy 2015). It gives the ENP countries the opportunity to opt for cooperation in specific areas or sectors of interest. Accordingly, the revised ENP aims at further differentiation and greater mutual ownership. This is deemed important for the development of bilateral relations with those ENP countries that are not interested in adopting EU rules and standards and/or are involved in alternative regional integration projects. In this respect, the ambition of the ENP to address 'the neighbours of the neighbours' raises interesting questions about the future development of the EU's legal framework for relations with the Eurasian Economic Union and its participating EaP countries, Armenia and Belarus (Delcour et al. 2015). It may lead to the negotiation of a new generation of enhanced partnership agreements, which may accommodate most of the ENP objectives and priorities but without the legal approximation requirements inherent to the contractual relations between the EU and associated ENP countries. Together with the upgrading of the EMAAs, the revision of the remaining PCAs with the non-associated eastern neighbours may therefore be regarded as important challenges for the future.

Note

1 In this respect, it also noteworthy that the AAs with Georgia and Moldova do not even include a comparable provision on the non-discrimination of legally employed workers.

References

Auvret-Finck, J. (2006) 'Vers une cohérence accrue des relations extérieures de l'Union: l' example de la politique européenne de voisinage', *Revue des Affaires Européennes* 16(2): 313–329.

Blockmans, S. (2011) 'Friend or Foe? Reviewing EU Relations with its Neighbours Post-Lisbon', in Koutrakos, P. (ed.) *The European Union's External Relations a Year after Lisbon*, CLEER Working Papers 2011/13, 113–114, www.asser.nl/cleer/publications/cleer-papers/, accessed 4 January 2016.

Comelli, M. (2014) 'Article 8 TEU and the Revision of the European Neighbourhood Policy', in Rossi, L. and Casolari, F. (eds.) *The EU after Lisbon: Amending or Coping with the Existing Treaties?* New York: Springer, 267–289.

Council of Europe (2016) 'South Programme: A flagship EU-CoE joint programme supporting democratic governance in the Southern Mediterranean', www.coe.int/en/web/programmes/south-programme, accessed 27 November 2016.

Council of the European Union (2008) *EU-Ukraine Summit*, doc. 12812/08, 9 September.

Council of the European Union (2011) *Free Trade Agreements with Southern Mediterranean Countries*, doc. 18685/11, 14 December.

Council of the European Union (2013) *Decision of 20 November 2012 on the Conclusion of a Protocol to the Euro-Mediterranean Agreement Establishing an Association between the European Communities and their Member States, of the One Part, and the State of Israel, of the Other Part, on Conformity Assessment and Acceptance of Industrial Products*, OJ L1/1.

Council of the European Union (2014) *Decision of 16 June 2014 on the Signing, on Behalf of the European Union, and Provisional Application of the Association Agreement between the European Union and the European Atomic Energy Community and their Member States, of the One Part, and Georgia, of the Other Part*, OJ L 261/1.

Cremona, M. and Hillion, C. (2006) '*L'Union fait la force?* Potential and limitations of the European Neighbourhood Policy as an integrated EU Foreign and Security Policy', *EUI Working Paper Law*, http://cadmus.eui.eu/handle/1814/6419, accessed 4 January 2016.

Del Sarto, R. and Schumacher, T. (2011) 'From Brussels with love: leverage, benchmarking, and the action plans with Jordan and Tunisia in the EU's democratisation policy', *Democratization* 18(4): 932–955.

Delcour, L. et al. (2015) 'The implications of Eurasian integration for the EU's relations with the countries in the post-Soviet space', *Studia Diplomatica* 58(1): 5–34.

Delcour, L. and Wolczuk, K. (2013) *Approximation of the National Legislation of Eastern Partnership Countries with EU Legislation in the Economic Field*, Brussels: European Parliament Committee on Foreign Affairs.

Dragneva, R. and Wolczuk, K. (2011) 'EU Law Export to the Eastern Neighbourhood and the Elusive Demand for Law', in Cardwell, P. (ed.) *EU External Relations Law and Policy in the Post-Lisbon Era*, The Hague: Asser/Springer, 217–240.

European Commission/High Representative of the Union for Foreign Affairs and Security Policy (2015) *Review of the European Neighbourhood Policy*, JOIN(2015) 50 final, Brussels.

European Court of Justice (2005) Case C-265/03, *Simutenkov v. Real Federacion Española de Fùtbol* [2005] ECR I-02579.

Gatti, M. (2016) 'The log in your eye: is Europe's external promotion of religious freedom consistent with its internal practice?', *European Law Journal* 22(2): 250–267.

General Court (2015) *Front Polisario v. Council* EU:T:2015:953.

Ghazaryan, N. (2014) *The European Neighbourhood Policy and the Democratic Values of the EU*, Oregon: Hart Publishing.

Ghazaryan, N. (2015) 'A new generation of human rights clauses? The case of Association Agreements in the eastern neighbourhood', *European Law Review* 40(3): 391–410.

Gstöhl, S. (2012) 'What is at Stake in the Internal Market? Towards a Neighbourhood Economic Community', in Lannon, E. (ed.) *Challenges of the European Neighbourhood Policy*, Brussels-Berlin: Peter Lang, 85–108.

Hakura, F. (1997) 'The Euro-Med policy: the implications of the Barcelona declaration', *Common Market Law Review* 34(2): 337–366.

Hanf, D. (2011) 'The ENP in the light of the new neighbourhood clause', in Lannon, E. (ed.) *Challenges of the European Neighbourhood Policy*, Brussels-Berlin: Peter Lang, 109–125.

Harpaz, G. (2014) 'Approximation of laws under the European Neighbourhood Policy: the challenges that lie ahead', *European Foreign Affairs Review* 19(3): 429–452.

Hillion, C. (2007) 'Mapping-out the new contractual relations between the European Union and its neighbours: learning from the EU-Ukraine "enhanced agreement"', *European Foreign Affairs Review* 12(2): 169–182.

Hillion, C. (2014) 'Anatomy of EU Norm Export Towards the Neighbourhood: The Impact of Article 8 TEU', in Van Elsuwege P. and Petrov R. (eds.) *Legislative Approximation and Application of EU Law in the Eastern Neighbourhood of the European Union: Towards a Common Regulatory Space?* Oxon: Routledge, 13–20.

Kochenov, D. (2014) 'The Issue of Values', in Van Elsuwege, P. and Petrov, R. (eds.) *Legislative Approximation and Application of EU Law in the Eastern Neighbourhood of the European Union: Towards a Common Regulatory Space?* Oxon: Routledge, 46–62.

Kochenov, D. and Basheska, E. (2016) 'ENP's Values Conditionality from Enlargements to Post-Crimea', in Poli, S. (ed.) *The EU and its Values in the Neighbourhood*, Oxon: Routledge, 145–166.

Lannon, E. (2011) 'An Economic Response to the Crisis: Towards a New Generation of Deep and Comprehensive Free Trade Areas with the Mediterranean Partner Countries', in *The Euromed Region after the Arab Spring and the new Generation of DCFTAs*, Brussels: European Parliament Committee on International Trade, 37–63.

Lannon, E. and Van Elsuwege, P. (2003) 'The EU's Emerging Neighbourhood Policy and its Potential Impact on the Euro-Mediterranean Partnership', in Xuereb, P. (ed.) *Euro-Med Integration and the Ring of Friends: The Mediterranean's European Challenge*, Malta: EDRC, 21–84.

Lannon, E. and Van Elsuwege, P. (2012) 'The Eastern Partnership: Prospects of a New Regional Dimension within the European Neighbourhood Policy', in Lannon, E. (ed.) *The European Neighbourhood Policy's Challenges*, Brussels: Peter Lang, 285–322.

Maresceau, M. (2004) 'EU Enlargement and EU Common Strategies on Russia and Ukraine: An Ambiguous yet Unavoidable Connection', in Hillion, C. (ed.) *EU Enlargement: A Legal Approach*, Oxford and Portland Oregon: Hart Publishing, 181–219.

Maresceau, M. (2011) 'Les accords d'intégration dans les relations de proximité de l'Union européenne', in Blumann, C. (ed.) *Les frontières de l'Union européenne*, Bruxelles: Bruylant, 151–192.

Maresceau, M. (2013) 'The Court of Justice and Bilateral Agreements', in Romas, A., Levits E. and Bot, Y. (eds.) *The Court of Justice and the Construction of Europe: Analyses and Perspectives on Sixty Years of Case-law*, The Hague: Asser Press, 693–717.

Pech, L. (2012) 'Rule of law as a guiding principle of the European Union's external action', *CLEER Working Papers* 2012/3, www.asser.nl/cleer/publications/cleer-papers/, accessed 4 January 2016.

Petrov, R. (2015) 'Constitutional challenges for the implementation of Association Agreements between the EU and Ukraine, Moldova and Georgia', *European Public Law* 21(2): 241–254.

Petrov, R. and Kalinichenko, P. (2011) 'The Europeanization of third country judiciaries through the application of the EU acquis: the cases of Russia and Ukraine', *International and Comparative Law Quarterly* 60(2): 325–353.

Pieters, K. (2010) *The Integration of the Mediterranean Neighbours into the EU Internal Market*, The Hague: Asser Press.

Poli, S. (ed.) (2016) *The EU and its Values in the Neighbourhood*, Oxon: Routledge.

Semertzi, A. (2014) 'The preclusion of direct effect in the recently concluded EU free trade agreements', *Common Market Law Review* 51(4): 1125–1158.

Van der Loo, G. (2014) 'The EU-Ukraine Deep and Comprehensive Free Trade Area: A Coherent Mechanism for Legislative Approximation?' in Van Elsuwege, P. and Petrov, R. (eds.) *Legislative Approximation and Application of EU Law in the Eastern Neighbourhood of the European Union: Towards a Common Regulatory Space?*, Oxon: Routledge, 63–88.

Van der Loo, G. (2016a) *The EU–Ukraine Association Agreement and Deep and Comprehensive Free Trade Area: A New Legal Instrument for EU Integration without Membership*, Boston-Leiden: Brill.

Van der Loo, G. (2016b) 'Mapping out the Scope and Contents of the DCFTAs with Tunisia and Morocco', *EuroMeSCO Paper* 28.

Van der Loo, G., Van Elsuwege, P. and Petrov, R. (2014) 'The EU-Ukraine Association Agreement: Assessment of an Innovative Legal Instrument', *EUI Working Papers Law* 2014/09, http://cadmus.eui.eu/handle/1814/32031, accessed 4 January 2016.

Van Elsuwege, P. (2012) 'Variable Geometry in the European Neighbourhood Policy: The Principle of Differentiation and its Consequences', in Lannon, E. (ed.) *The European Neighbourhood Policy's Challenges*, Brussels: P.I.E. Peter Lang, 59–84.

Van Elsuwege, P. and Petrov, R. (2011) 'Towards a new generation of agreements with the neighbouring countries of the European Union? Scope, objectives and potential application of Article 8 TEU', *European Law Review* 36(5): 688–703.

Van Elsuwege, P. and Petrov, R. (eds.) (2014) *Legislative Approximation and Application of EU Law in the Eastern Neighbourhood of the European Union: Towards a Common Regulatory Space?* Oxon: Routledge.

Van Elsuwege, P. and Burlyuk O. (2016) 'Exporting the Rule of Law to the EU's Eastern Neighbourhood: Reconciling Coherence and Differentiation', in Poli S. (ed.) *The EU and its Values in the Neighbourhood*, Oxon: Routledge, 167–182.

Van Vooren, B. (2012) *EU External Relations Law and the European Neighbourhood Policy: A Paradigm for Coherence*, Oxon: Routledge.

PART II

The EU and its neighbourhood
Drawing borders, shaping identities

11
THE CONSTRUCTION AND DECONSTRUCTION OF THE EU'S NEIGHBOURHOOD

Christopher Browning

Introduction

Since its founding as the European Economic Community in 1957, the history of the European project has been one of both steadily deepening levels of integration and steadily expanding membership. From an original six members in 1957, the 2004 enlargement brought the number of members to 25, with Romania, Bulgaria and Croatia joining subsequently. While all the enlargements have raised important issues, the 2004 enlargement was particularly significant. This was because, although debates about the Union's continuing ability to take on new members have always been aired, the 2004 enlargement process resulted in a definitive policy stance that future enlargements would be few and far between. With an unprecedented ten new members to be integrated, it was argued that the Union's borders needed to be delimited once and for all if the European Union (EU) was to have any hope of preserving its democratic legitimacy and of remaining bureaucratically functional. Thus, in 2003, the European Commission issued a communication on the 'Wider Europe Neighbourhood' calling for 'A New Framework for Relations with our Eastern and Southern Neighbours' (Commission of the European Communities 2003). By 2004, the Wider Europe initiative had transformed into the European Neighbourhood Policy (ENP).

Although enlargement was perceived as challenging the EU's democratic legitimacy and bureaucratic functionality, the ENP's introduction created its own challenges, principal of which concerned security. Despite having gradually evolved its own security and defence dimensions, the EU's primary security enhancing capabilities have been overwhelmingly connected to the processes of further integration and enlargement (Wæver 1996; 1998). In other words, the promise of future enlargement and inclusion within the European club has been used to promote stability beyond the EU's borders. With further enlargement now precluded, there was therefore concern as to how stability and security might be maintained in future.

Responding to this challenge is at the heart of the ENP, with this aspiration already clearly articulated in the Commission's 2003 communication on the Wider Europe, which called for the EU 'to develop a zone of prosperity and a friendly neighbourhood – "a ring of friends" – with whom the EU enjoys close, peaceful and co-operative relations' (Commission of the European Communities 2003: 4). As will become evident, the mechanisms through which the ENP has sought to do this share much with the previous enlargement policy, focused as it is on offering a closer relationship with the Union in return for adherence to EU norms. However, with membership off the agenda, the carrot is smaller, with Association Agreements (AAs) and Deep and Comprehensive Free Trade Areas (DCFTAs) providing the closest possible relationship the EU presently has on offer (European Commission and High Representative of the EU for Foreign Affairs and Security Policy 2015: 7). Neighbours will remain neighbours.

As Schumacher (2015: 386) argues, the references to 'good neighbourliness' (but also to the 'neighbourhood' and the 'ring of friends') within the ENP, reflect the EU's perceived need for a new narrative for the post-enlargement environment. The ENP, however, did not just respond to a perceived narratological absence. The chapter argues that it has also functioned as a supreme geopolitical constitutive act, with the naming of the 'neighbourhood' in the ENP introducing a geopolitical imaginary of the nature of Europe. In other words, the ENP is premised on a geopolitical vision of what we might term a 'hub-and-spoke' Europe. In this imaginary, the EU is located at the centre, a presumed pole of attraction and source of order (and ordering). In contrast, the EU's neighbourhood – destined to remain formally excluded – appears as a kind of buffer zone or marchland (Browning and Joenniemi 2008; Walters 2004) to the chaos lying beyond. As will become evident, however, in the EU's ENP discourse, the friendliness of the neighbourhood countries cannot be taken as given, but is primarily related to how far they find the EU attractive and wish to draw closer to it *via* active engagement with the ENP and their appropriation of EU norms through it.

Despite appearances, however, and despite its predominant position in respect of the neighbourhood, the chapter argues that the EU's ability to impose on its neighbours the geopolitical imaginary of European space embedded within the ENP is restricted. The fact that, in 2015, the ENP was undergoing its second revision since its implementation in 2004 is indicative of this, with the background documents noting its various failures and limitations to date. The chapter therefore demonstrates that those in the neighbourhood have had considerable ability to 'bite back' (Parker 2000) and impact on the core. In doing so, they can exert influence on the EU, not least in terms of how it conceives of itself, its security environment and the very idea of Europe and Europeanness that underpins this.

The chapter begins by outlining the EU's geopolitical vision of Europe and its construction of the neighbourhood in the ENP in more detail. It then examines the ENP in practice, before a final section explores the 'partners' role in impacting back on the ENP and the construction of Europe in the policy. The chapter concludes with a few reflections on the most recent EU documents in preparation for a new ENP and the extent to which they are opening to a different vision of the EU's relationship with its neighbourhood.

Of mindscapes and geopolitical imaginaries

As a policy targeted at partners beyond its borders, the ENP is inevitably imbued with an idealization of European space. To this extent, it betrays a mindscape and geopolitical vision. The concept of mindscape refers to how actors generate geospatial visions that come to frame both their perception of and responses to their environment. Once constructed they provide 'a mental map, a way of looking at things and one's environment, whilst also becoming prescriptive of how to move through the mindscape' (Browning and Lehti 2007: 695; Liulevicius 2000: 151). To this extent mindscapes perform an ordering function, establishing grounds on which actors can understand the nature of the situation they face, distinguish between the 'normal' and 'abnormal', and provide an impulse for action as mindscapes entail a vision of what 'ought' to be (Eglitis 2004: 8–10).

The mindscape of the ENP comprises at least four elements. First, it is premised on a teleological vision that positions the EU at the forefront of a universal developmental model, and representative of what is quintessentially 'normal'. This model is premised around open economies, de-bordering and democratic governance. It is assumed that this model of liberal economic and political governance is universally attractive, that the tide of history is going this way and that this is the form of order and society to aspire to. Intimately connected is the second element, which is the assumption that while the model itself is attractive, so too is the EU. Therefore, it is expected that outsiders will aspire to a closer relationship with the Union – either through membership or, failing that, through some form of association. Derivative of this is the third element, which is that the world beyond the EU's borders is a world of risks, instability and insecurity. The mindscape is therefore one differentiating a safe inside from a potentially chaotic, threatening and 'abnormal' outside, an outside that needs to be tamed (that is, through the ENP) and/or kept at arm's length.

Lastly, despite the universalist claims surrounding the EU's developmental model, the ENP itself rests on a restricted and geocultural conception of Europeanness that is highly particularistic. This conception is evident in the subdivision of the EU's neighbourhood into a 'European East' (where the 'Europeanness' of partners like Ukraine is taken for granted) and a 'non-European South' (where the 'Europeanness' of partners like Morocco is rejected[1]) within the policy and the development of different policy instruments within the ENP for dealing with them – the Eastern Partnership (EaP) and the Union for the Mediterranean.

The above claims can obviously be contested at an empirical level. For instance, the idea that the EU has a singular developmental model to offer is open to question (Kurki 2013) and is something returned to later. The same applies to embedded conceptions of Europeanness, of who qualifies or does not qualify for inclusion in this privileged category. This is evident in internal EU disputes over Turkey's European credentials, debates that often hinge on disagreements as to whether the core characteristics of Europeanness should be culturally, racially, religiously or geographically determined.

Setting those issues aside, the key point to note is that this mindscape has tended to foster an imperial vision of how the EU views its relationship with its outside, and with its neighbourhood more specifically (Del Sarto 2016). The mindscape places the EU at the apex of a hierarchy, dispensing wisdom. For instance, as stated in Article 8(1) of the Treaty on European Union, the sense of 'good neighbourliness' aspired for in the ENP is generated and 'founded on the values of the Union'. Elsewhere, these values are stipulated in terms of 'a shared commitment to the universal values of human rights, democracy and the rule of law' (European Commission and High Representative of the EU for Foreign Affairs and Security Policy 2013: 14), although in its implementation the EU places at least as much emphasis on fostering open liberal market economies. The point, as Schumacher (2015: 386) notes, is that Article 8 refers 'exclusively to the values of the EU (the self) and not the other', with this becoming 'an important tool in the EU's discursive efforts of self-presentation and of delineating boundaries of inclusion and exclusion'. EU norms, values and practices are essentially seen as non-negotiable, with the ENP imbued with an imperial impulse – to reproduce itself on the outside, while keeping the borders between inside and outside in place.

The notion that the mindscape of the ENP entails an imperial impulse is important and can be contrasted with other geopolitical visions often ascribed to the EU, be it of the EU coalescing into a unified Westphalian state-like actor with a unified and impermeable border regime, a currency and army, or of the EU promoting the postmodern neomedievalization of Europe into an area of multidimensional overlapping spaces and networks (Browning 2005). Elements of all three can be detected in the ENP but an imperial vision of the Union extending its influence, norms and practices beyond its borders is arguably the overriding impulse (Browning and Joenniemi 2008).

The ENP in 'imperial' practice

While the mindscape sketched above emphasizes the EU as a beacon and agent of (imperial) transformation, this imperative is further supported by two other important constitutive narratives related to the EU as a peace project and the integration–security dilemma raised by the decision to delimit final borders for the Union. Starting with the second, the challenge facing the EU has been how to avoid alienating its neighbours, how to promote reform within them and how to avoid the EU's external border becoming a line of exclusion and negative othering, now that enlargement is off the agenda. As Jeandesboz (2007) argues, in the debates framing the constitution of the ENP this has essentially translated into the neighbourhood being viewed as a source of threats to the EU and the need to avoid any negative spill-over into the Union. Such threats have generally been understood in terms of illegal immigration, terrorism, organized crime, communicable diseases and social ills associated with poverty. With the disciplining mechanism of enlargement off the agenda, the outside has therefore become a space to be kept outside and guarded against, but also managed in such a way as to keep it friendly (Pardo 2004). Instead of establishing a Westphalian border of total exclusion, Del Sarto and Schumacher (2005) argue the emphasis has been on turning the neighbourhood into a buffer zone. The ENP therefore seeks to blur the border with the EU's neighbours in some spheres of activity as a way of making them responsible for controlling their borders furthest from the Union, thereby pushing the threatening outside further away.

This security imperative driving engagement with the neighbours is, in turn, supported by a deeper ontological narrative of self-identity that depicts the EU as fundamentally a project for bringing peace and stability to the continent. This has created a sense of moral imperative and duty determining that the EU cannot be satisfied with its own internal achievements. Instead, it also needs to organize the space beyond its borders, spreading European values in a broader effort of creating a 'Europe whole and free' (Browning and Joenniemi 2008: 524, 532; Schumacher 2015: 384–385).

In practical terms, the ENP has been designed to respond to these imperatives by offering the 'opportunity of closer economic integration with the EU and the prospect of increased access to the EU's Internal Market' in return for 'the implementation of challenging political, economic and institutional reforms and a commitment to common values' (European Commission and High Representative of the EU for Foreign Affairs and Security Policy 2015: 2). The EU emphasizes it is not seeking to 'impose a model or a ready-made recipe for political reform' and has argued that the ENP can be differentiated to respond to the partners' different ambitions (European Commission and High Representative of the EU for Foreign Affairs and Security Policy 2011: 2–3). EU discourse on the ENP is therefore replete with notions of voluntarism, while asserting that in principle everything is possible but institutions (that is, membership).

Even so, the ENP's normative aspirations are clear. Thus, in 2011 the ENP's commitment to transformative change in the neighbourhood was upgraded to an emphasis on promoting not just democracy but 'deep democracy' (European Commission and High Representative of the EU for Foreign Affairs and Security Policy 2011). As Kurki notes, deep democracy seems to combine a concern with institutions and elections with a more wholesale 'reform of societies' economic, civic, cultural and political structures'. Indeed, she argues that the policy is becoming notably embedded with neoliberal preferences and tendencies as the policy increasingly emphasizes economic rights and calls for economic liberalization (Kurki 2013: 153–154). The latter is evident, for example, in the more recent advent of DCFTAs and visa free regimes for the most willing partners (European Commission and High Representative of the EU for Foreign Affairs and Security Policy 2015: 2).

While there is nothing forced about the ENP, the policy strapline that the ENP offers 'more for more' (a closer relationship in return for more change) is clearly designed as a form of strategic leverage premised on the EU's continuing reliance on principles of conditionality that have served it well in the enlargement process. As the European Commission and EU's High Representative put it:

> Increased EU support to its neighbours is conditional. It will depend on progress in building and consolidating democracy and respect for the rule of law. The more and faster a country progresses in its internal reforms, the more support it will get from the EU.

The carrot of 'more' EU is therefore seen to offer leverage over the partners, while the flip side of conditionality is not simply that those who fail to reform will get less, but that 'where reform has not taken place, the EU will reconsider or even reduce funding' (European Commission and High Representative of the EU for Foreign Affairs and Security Policy 2011: 3). Such progress (or lack thereof) is measured against Action Plans (or Association Agendas for those partners who have signed AAs) that ENP countries are required to negotiate and agree with the Commission on an individual bilateral basis. By constituting the ENP around a set of carrots and sticks the EU is therefore establishing criteria and conditions that the partners need to meet to become fully embedded as part of the EU's 'ring of friends'.

Therefore, despite the voluntarism, the EU's prescription of norms and emphasis on conditionality as an enforcement mechanism in the ENP does inscribe the policy with hierarchical and imperial tendencies. Thus, there is little doubt as to who is expected to learn from whom, or of the fact that the EU positions itself as more advanced and temporally ahead on a range of measures. This makes the frequent references to joint ownership and partnership in ENP documents disingenuous. Reflecting on the EU's relationship with Ukraine in the ENP, Kurki notes that there has been notably little discussion of what 'shared values' like democracy might mean, with the EU largely 'dictating to Ukraine' democracy support requirements in a manner 'which is clearly not in line with pluralism or debate' (Kurki 2013: 165).

This approach has not been entirely successful. As the Commission itself has noted, the 'more for more' strategy 'has not always contributed to an atmosphere of equal partnership and has not always been successful in providing incentives [for] further reforms in the partner countries' (European Commission and High Representative of the EU for Foreign Affairs and Security Policy 2015: 4). Indeed, it is reasonable to wonder whether an equal partnership is even feasible in a situation where the values to be promoted have been predetermined by the more powerful party. The approach, however, also has other constitutive effects. For instance, it has the effect of promoting a hierarchy of otherness, with this operating in two respects. First, at the broadest level, the ENP's very existence is indicative that the partners of the neighbourhood are viewed not only as geographically closer to the EU than those that lie at a greater distance but also potentially as normatively more similar (or able to be made so). However, while their status as (potential) 'friends' is what draws them closer, it also constitutes their otherness, not least by designating them as more foreign than the few remaining prospective candidate countries for membership, though arguably less foreign than those that are not part of the ENP.

Second, in providing for differentiation between partners the conditionality mechanism also has the potential of constituting ENP countries as being friendly/threatening to the EU relative to each other depending on their willingness to buy into the ENP's normative transformative vision. In short, friendliness in the ENP is primarily related to how far the partners find the EU attractive and wish to draw closer to it *via* active engagement. The danger is that this reduces friend–threat calculations down to assessments of others' desire to become like us and the EU's ability to reproduce itself on its outside (Browning and Christou 2010). This is also significant in that as the ENP is embedded with a mindscape that assumes the universal attraction of both the values the EU claims to stand for and of the EU itself, then any rejection of the ENP (or failure to actively embrace its transformative agenda) is liable to pose an ontological challenge to the EU by questioning the EU's own self-understanding as a model to be aspired to and emulated by all.

The constitutive power of neighbours

This last point is significant as it suggests that although the mindscape of the ENP is impregnated with a normatively imperializing geopolitical vision, with the EU seeking to expand its influence beyond its border by normalizing its conception of good governance for those beyond, this is a two-way relationship, with the EU also vulnerable to the partners' actions. This is to say that the partners also have constitutive power to impact on the nature of the ENP, and therefore on conceptions of the nature of the border, the EU's sense of self-understanding and its perception of the security environment it faces. As Parker (2000; 2008) puts it, marginal actors often have the capacity to 'bite back', often in unanticipated ways. For instance, the very fact that the ENP presumes that the EU is sufficiently attractive that the partners will sign up to its preconditions, even despite the carrot of membership having been withdrawn, assigns the partners a power of 'recognition/non-recognition'. While active engagement with the ENP signifies recognition and an endorsement of EU conceptions of self-identity as a benevolent peace project, non/restricted-recognition *via* limited engagement and enthusiasm for the ENP puts such claims in question.

It is therefore not surprising that in EU discourse the partners have increasingly become located along a spectrum from willing to unwilling others, depending on their acceptance of the ENP's Europeanizing agenda. One consequence of this is that the partners' differential willingness to respond to the EU's overtures in the ENP has impacted on the openness and reciprocity the EU is willing to countenance with its neighbourhood partners. For example, despite rejections of its Europeanness, the EU has been willing to reward Morocco with participation in various EU programmes, a mobility partnership and a DCFTA, a level of engagement that has so far eluded some of the other partners. Through its attempts at extending EU norms of governance, the ENP has not resulted in uniform borders, but significant plurality. Moreover, the character of the EU's neighbourhood as a buffer zone to that which lies beyond has also tended to take on a different complexion between the eastern and southern dimensions of the policy as the 'European aspirations' of some of the Eastern partners (such as Georgia, Moldova and Ukraine) remain acknowledged in their respective AAs, while such possibilities go unmentioned in agreements with the southern partners.

The EU has therefore begun to talk about the need for the ENP to embrace '*some kind of variable geometry with different kinds of relationships for those partners that choose different levels of engagement*' (original emphasis) (European Commission and High Representative of the EU for Foreign Affairs and Security Policy 2015: 7), thereby explicitly acknowledging the ability of the partners to frame the EU's geometry at its borders. However, as the EU has also been forced to acknowledge, it is not only the partners that have this capacity but those beyond as well. Thus, the EU has recognized that other actors have also become increasingly involved in the region (not least Turkey and Russia), which 'may also make the EU less attractive as a model and partner'. This will require the EU to reflect on how to have a more multilateral policy approach, involving and working with, more systematically than it does now, the other actors working in the neighbourhood in addressing, together with partner countries themselves, issues of shared interest.

(European Commission and High Representative of the EU for Foreign Affairs and Security Policy 2013: 22)

The top-down imperial mindscape and geopolitical vision of the ENP therefore encounters significant obstacles on the ground. This can be further demonstrated with a more direct comparison of the ENP in both the southern and eastern parts of the EU's neighbourhood.

As noted, the EU has never seriously considered the southern partners of the ENP as (potential) European countries. As such, their otherness and non-inclusion as members has been presumed from the start. At the same time, this constitutive move is reinforced by the fact that (aside from Morocco in 1987) the southern partners also have not expressed any aspiration for membership, let alone constituted their own self-identities in terms of Europeanness.

On its inception, however, it was also clear that in the post-9/11 context, questions of security dominated EU concerns with respect to the South in the ENP. A key question was therefore how the EU would use the ENP to address the various security problems it saw as emanating from the region. In this respect, Malmvig (2006) notes that, historically, EU policy towards the Mediterranean has tended to be driven by a tension between contradictory security discourses. The liberal security discourse has emphasized the promotion of democracy and human rights, with the belief that the absence of democracy, the rule of law, basic freedoms and economic growth has created fertile ground for the emergence of threats of terrorism, radicalization, migration and organized crime. From this perspective, the very existence of authoritarian regimes in the region, and their reliance on cronyism, corruption, repression and violence, is central to the problem that needs to be tackled. Diametrically opposed to this is what Malmvig terms a cooperative security discourse that sees these authoritarian regimes as partners in tackling common challenges, including terrorism, radicalism, weapons of mass destruction, organized crime and illegal migration. The record, particularly since 9/11, Malmvig contends, suggests that the EU has generally prioritized stability and regime security over promoting democracy and human rights, the suggestion being that the prospects of the ENP promoting transformation in the EU's southern neighbourhood have therefore been slim.

Importantly, the southern ENP countries themselves have reinforced this view and the cautious approach the ENP initially adopted. Thus, although a closer relationship with the EU is perceived as offering some (mainly economic) benefits, the ENP's references to democratization and transformation are viewed suspiciously and even as a source of threat to regime security. Hence, while the ENP speaks of the need for cooperation in matters of security, it is not always clear that the EU and its partner regimes in the South identify threats in the same way. These tensions over security perceptions have impacted on the potential impact of the ENP and have affected the nature and logic of the neighbourhood border zone created. In the South, the border has therefore been primarily viewed by the EU as a border between safety and threat and as a line of control and exclusion, the EU goal essentially being one driven by logics of 'containment' (Walters 2004: 692).

It is important to note that the first revision of the ENP took place in 2011 in the wake of the so-called 'Arab Spring' and was to a large degree inspired by it. Acknowledging the limited successes of the original ENP in 'incentivizing authoritarian regimes in the south to embark on wide-ranging political and economic reforms' (Schumacher 2015: 382), Schumacher argues that the new ENP sought to place greater emphasis on the liberal security discourse of democratization.

Thus, Stefan Füle, the Commissioner for Enlargement and Neighbourhood Policy, stated shortly after the overthrow of President Ben Ali in Tunisia that 'the assumption that authoritarian regimes were a guarantee of stability in the region . . . [was] . . . short-termism' (quoted in Schumacher 2015: 387–388). There was clearly a sense, therefore, that the 'Arab Spring' might be capitalized on. The subsequent retrenchment of the presumed 'democratic' uprisings, the reassertion of authoritarian rule in many of the southern partners, the intensification of the trans-Mediterranean migration crisis, the civil wars in Libya, Syria and the rise of ISIS/ISIL, however, have considerably dampened the initial optimism of 2011. Thus, ENP progress reports with respect to the EU's southern neighbourhood continue to be notable for their recognition of a lack of progress in implementing the ENP's agenda of normative transformation.

In comparison, the EU's approach to its eastern neighbourhood looks subtly different. One major reason for this concerns the fact that the Europeanness of the eastern partners is not questioned and their membership aspirations are acknowledged in the AAs. For the most part, the eastern ENP countries have also sought to strategically mobilize their Europeanness in ways arguably uncomfortable for the Union. Thus, while the EU has seen the ENP as offering an alternative to membership, several of the eastern partners have refused to let the issue lie. Continually asserting their European credentials – be it culturally or through gradual economic and democratic transformation as stipulated in the ENP Action Plans – has been a way to keep enlargement on the agenda.

There are parallels here to the 2004 EU enlargement process, where Schimmelfennig (2004) argues that the prospective members could keep enlargement on the agenda by consistently referring to the EU's own constitutive discourse as a peace project open to all in Europe. Failure to enlarge, he suggests, would have spurred an ontological crisis for the EU. In a similar vein, the leaders of Ukraine's 'Orange Revolution', in 2004–2005, presented the revolution as indicative of their European credentials, with these claims endorsed by EU leaders. Likewise, Ukrainian leaders have insisted that their signing of an Association Agreement with the EU would be 'without prejudice' to their further European aspirations (Runner 2008). Thus, while the eastern partners are implicitly depicted as lagging behind and therefore as somewhat 'inferior' and 'backward', they have managed to avoid being excluded with the potential to become fully European *via* membership (Tiirmaa-Klaar 2006).

There is another important element at play in the EU's eastern neighbourhood, which concerns important changes to the geopolitical landscape since the ENP first emerged as a consequence of Russia's increasing assertiveness. The result is that the ENP is no longer the only game in town, with a choice of models now available to states in the neighbourhood. To be sure, Russia's assertiveness also entails a carrot and stick approach. The stick has been seen in the context of its military intervention in Georgia in 2008 and the annexation of Crimea in 2014 and the subsequent and ongoing conflict in Ukraine – all events sparked by concerns in Moscow about what they see as key states in their own sphere of influence/near abroad (a more pejorative label for neighbourhood) orienting too closely to the West. The carrot, by contrast, is evident in the creation of the Eurasian Economic Union (EEU) as a competitor to the ENPs Eastern Partnership.

The result has been a certain amount of recognition that the eastern neighbourhood has become a zone of geopolitical competition between the EU and Russia for the attention of the region's states. For example, the fact that, at the last minute, Armenia did not, as expected, sign the agreement in September 2013 it had negotiated with the EU for an AA/DCFTA, but instead decided to join Russia's EEU, demonstrates that the EU cannot presume its power of attraction will win out in this competition (European Commission and High Representative of the EU for Foreign Affairs and Security Policy 2014: 5). As the EU notes, for the partners 'there is a choice to be made' because joining the EEU precludes further integration with the EU through a DCFTA (European Commission and High Representative of the EU for Foreign Affairs and Security Policy 2013: 22). This can sound slightly threatening or admonishing to the partners as they make their decision; however, the flip side is that it also stands as an injunction for the EU to offer sufficiently attractive carrots, if it does not wish the eastern neighbourhood to fall more under Russian influence. It is therefore notable not only that the EU signed an Association Agreement with Ukraine on 27 June 2014, just over a month after Russia's annexation of Crimea, but also that it asserted that 'the Association Agreement does not constitute the final goal in the EU-Ukraine cooperation' (European Commission and High Representative of the EU for Foreign Affairs and Security Policy 2014: 3). Membership, therefore, potentially remains on the agenda. What this suggests, however, is that eastern ENP countries possess considerable leverage as, in different ways, the EU and Russia compete for their attentions.

Conclusions

The chapter has argued that the ENP has served an important geopolitical constitutive function, re-imagining Europe in terms of an EU core, surrounded by a buffer zone of a so-called 'ring of friends', beyond which lies a more threatening world. The ENP has therefore aspired to be a policy of geopolitical ordering. It has also been argued that the mindscape underpinning the ENP has imbued it with an imperial geopolitical impulse because of the EU's assumption that its norms, values and practices – and therefore the EU itself – are inherently attractive and desired by others. The ENP therefore results in the border with the partners being blurred to some extent, but with this border now appearing like a colonial frontier, in which the EU projects itself into the space beyond, pacifying and assimilating it to a degree by defining the bounds of appropriate behaviour and practice (Walters 2004: 687). However, as the mindscape of the ENP differentiates the EU's neighbourhood into an Eastern European zone and a southern non-European zone, it also provides the buffer zone of the neighbourhood with a differentiated character and where, in the South, a threat-defence mindset appears more in evidence.

It has been shown that the neighbours also have considerable ability to 'bite back' – by their power of (non-)recognition, their willingness or otherwise to endorse the EU's transformative normative agenda and, not least, their ability to play the EU off against contending visions offered by those beyond the neighbourhood. As they do this, they can impact the nature of Europe in construction, the nature of its borders of inclusion/exclusion and the bases on which conceptions of security/threat are defined. What is clear is that the positions of the neighbours have resulted in a much more variegated ENP than was initially outlined by the EU and one in which it has become relevant to speak of an emerging variable geometry along the EU's borders.

In conclusion and writing in a context in which the ENP has just undergone its second round of revisions since its initial framing in 2003/2004, a few words about the possible future of the ENP are merited. Most notable is that there is much more soul-searching evident in the most recent EU documents released in preparation for the new ENP than at other times. Previous documents, for example, have often noted the limited progress of partners in implementing the reform agendas agreed in their individual action plans, but with the response essentially being that the partners must therefore try harder to meet 'their commitment to achieving the objectives jointly agreed with the EU' (European Commission and High Representative 2013 of the EU for Foreign Affairs and Security Policy: 21).[2] Statements released in 2015 suggest a more reflective view is becoming dominant. For example, a joint consultation paper on behalf of the Commission and the High Representative recognizes that the ENP 'has not always been able to offer adequate responses [. . .] to the changing aspirations of our partners', that 'not all partners seem equally interested in a special partnership with the EU under the model of pluralism and integration' and that '[t]he approach of "more for more" [. . .] has not always been successful in providing incentives' (European Commission and High Representative of the EU for Foreign Affairs and Security Policy 2015: 2, 4). This shows clear recognition that the EU's power of attraction – particularly in view of the economic crisis affecting the Eurozone – may have diminished, but also that the conditionality mechanism is not working. Indeed, the document goes on to acknowledge '[t]he lack of a sense of shared ownership' (European Commission and High Representative of the EU for Foreign Affairs and Security Policy 2015: 4) on the part of the partners, a point further reflected in Commissioner Johannes Hahn's desire 'to see a more equal partnership' (quoted in European Commission 2015). As the European Commission and High Representative of the EU for Foreign Affairs and Security Policy put it, there is a need to enhance the sense of shared ownership and to develop ways of working 'that are seen as more respectful by partners and demonstrate a partnership of equals' (2015: 9).

Such reflections are welcome. They indicate understanding that the EU no longer gets to unilaterally set the agenda of the future of Europe and there is a certain amount of self-realization that the EU can appear arrogant, imposing and imperialistic to outsiders. Whether their goals can be realized is, however, a more difficult proposition. This is because, despite the apparent *mea culpa* evident in such statements, it is also the case that the EU continues to remain deeply attached to its reformist agenda in its neighbourhood. How willing, therefore, is the EU likely to be in developing a genuinely equal dialogue with respect to the very framing of the values and norms that should underpin the ENP? This is not a technical question, but one that gets right to the heart of core elements of the EU's *raison d'être* and sense of self. Opening such questions therefore highlights precisely the extent to which the (de)construction of the EU's neighbourhood and the (de)construction of the EU itself are mutually implicated.

Notes

1 This reflects historical practice. For instance, in 1987 Morocco's application for membership was rejected simply on the grounds of it not being a European country (Neumann 1998).
2 Insofar as the EU has engaged in introspection this has been confined to largely technical reflections as to whether the ENP instruments and mechanisms might be tweaked (European Commission and High Representative of the EU for Foreign Affairs and Security Policy 2013: 21).

References

Browning, C. (2005) 'Westphalian, Imperial, Neomedieval: The Geopolitics of Europe and the Role of the North', in Browning, C. (ed.) *Remaking Europe in the Margins: Northern Europe After the Enlargements*, Aldershot: Ashgate, 85–101.

Browning, C. and Christou, G. (2010) 'The Constitutive Power of Outsiders: The European Neighbourhood Policy and the Eastern Dimension', *Political Geography* 29(2): 109–118.

Browning, C. and Joenniemi, P. (2008) 'Geostrategies of the European Neighbourhood Policy', *European Journal of International Relations* 14(3): 519–552.

Browning, C. and Lehti, M. (2007) 'Beyond East–West: Marginality and National Dignity in Finnish Identity Construction', *Nationalities Papers* 35(4): 691–716.

Commission of the European Communities (2003) *Wider Europe Neighbourhood: A New Framework for Relations with Our Eastern and Southern Neighbours*, COM (2003) 104 final, Brussels.

Del Sarto, R. (2016) 'Normative Empire Europe: The European Union, Its Borderlands, and the Arab Spring', *Journal of Common Market Studies* 54(2): 215–232.

Del Sarto, R. and Schumacher, T. (2005) 'From EMP to ENP: What's at Stake with the European Neighbourhood Policy Towards the Southern Mediterranean?', *European Foreign Affairs Review* 10(1): 17–38.

Eglitis, D. (2004) *Imagining the Nation: History, Modernity and Revolution in Latvia*, University Park: Pennsylvania State University Press.
European Commission (2015) 'Towards a New European Neighbourhood Policy: The EU Launches a Consultation on the Future of Its Relations with Neighbouring Countries', *Press Release*, Brussels, 4 March.
European Commission and High Representative of the EU for Foreign Affairs and Security Policy (2011) *A New Response to a Changing Neighbourhood: A Review of European Neighbourhood Policy*, COM (2011) 303, Brussels.
European Commission and High Representative of the EU for Foreign Affairs and Security Policy (2013) *Joint Communication to the European Parliament, the Council, the European Economic and Social Committee and the Committee of the Regions: European Neighbourhood Policy: Working Towards a Stronger Partnership*, Brussels: JOIN (2013) 4 final.
European Commission and High Representative of the EU for Foreign Affairs and Security Policy (2014) *Joint Communication to the European Parliament, the Council, the European Economic and Social Committee and the Committee of the Regions: Neighbourhood at the Crossroads: Implementation of the European Neighbourhood Policy in 2013*, JOIN (2014) 12 final, Brussels.
European Commission and High Representative of the EU for Foreign Affairs and Security Policy (2015) *Joint Consultation Paper: Towards a New European Neighbourhood Policy*, JOIN (2015) 6 final, Brussels.
Jeandesboz, J. (2007) 'Labelling the "Neighbourhood": Towards a Genesis of the European Neighbourhood Policy', *Journal of International Relations and Development* 10(4): 387–416.
Kurki, M. (2013) *Democratic Futures: Revisioning Democracy Promotion*, London: Routledge.
Liulevicius, V. (2000) *War Land on the Eastern Front: Culture, National Identity, and German Occupation in World War I*, Cambridge: Cambridge University Press.
Malmvig, H. (2006) 'Caught Between Cooperation and Democratization: The Barcelona Process and the EU's Double-Discursive Approach', *Journal of International Relations and Development* 9(4): 343–370.
Neumann, I. (1998) 'European Identity, EU Expansion and the Integration/Exclusion Nexus', *Alternatives* 23(3): 397–416.
Pardo, S. (2004) 'Europe of Many Circles: European Neighbourhood Policy', *Geopolitics* 9(3): 731–737.
Parker, N. (2000) 'Integrated Europe and Its "Margins": Action and Reaction', in Parker, N. and Armstrong, B. (eds.) *Margins in European Integration*, Houndmills: Macmillan, 3–27.
Parker, N. (2008) A Theoretical Introduction: Spaces, Centers and Margins', in Parker, N. (ed.) *The Geopolitics of Europe's Identity: Centers, Boundaries, and Margins*, Houndmills: Palgrave Macmillan, 3–23.
Runner, P. (2008) 'Brussels to Recognize European Aspirations of Post-Soviet States', www.euobserver.com/24/27167, 24/11/08, accessed November 2008.
Schimmelfennig, F. (2004) *The EU, NATO and the Integration of Europe*, Cambridge: Cambridge University Press.
Schumacher, T. (2015) 'Uncertainty at the EU's Borders: Narratives of EU External Relations in the Revised European Neighbourhood Policy Towards the Southern Borderlands', *European Security* 24(3): 381–401.
Tiirmaa-Klaar, H. (2006) 'EU's Governance Methods in Its Neighbourhood Policy', Paper Presented at the CEEISA Annual Conference, Tartu, 25–27 June.
Wæver, O. (1996) 'European Security Identities', *Journal of Common Market Studies* 34(1): 103–132.
Wæver, O. (1998) 'Insecurity, Security and Asecurity in the West-European Non-War Community', in Adler, E. and Barnett, M. (eds.) *Security Communities*, Cambridge: Cambridge University Press, 69–118.
Walters, W. (2004) 'The Frontiers of the European Union: A Geostrategic Perspective', *Geopolitics* 9(3): 674–698.

12
OF BORDERS AND BOUNDARIES
The neighbourhood as the EU's buffer zone

Andreas Marchetti

Introduction

The European Neighbourhood Policy (ENP) has frequently been described as successor to the European Union's (EU) enlargement policy (Comelli 2004; Dannreuther 2006), thereby placing it in a context of European expansion. Although, in contrast to enlargement, the ENP does not aim at the advancement of the EU's geographic borders, it is a policy promoting or even projecting European interests, norms and principles in its geographic vicinity. Hence, despite covering almost the entire neighbourhood to the East and the South of the EU and of its current (potential) candidates, the ENP does not include Western European neighbours, like Switzerland or Norway. This selective definition of 'neighbourhood' has long been associated with an agenda of creating a sort of buffer zone around the EU to protect it from negative outside developments. Discussing the notion of the ENP as an effort to establish a European buffer zone, the chapter will first focus on the academic debate related to the general conception of borders and boundaries underlying the ENP. It will then consider major policy documents giving guidance to the ENP to assess how far such interpretations match with the actual formulation of the ENP. The chapter concludes by displaying empirical data on major issues put forward by the EU when conceptualising the ENP in order to scrutinise in how far ENP countries can truly be considered a buffer zone from an EU point of view.

Conceptualising borders, boundaries and buffers

From an International Relations (IR) perspective, the EU has been hard to define: established based on the will of its constituting Member States, it displays features of a confederation just as much as of a federation. As such, it does not match with the traditional idea of a state-centred international order, nor does it correspond to the conventional set-up of international organisations, meaning intergovernmental organisations. Having been characterised as a multilevel system of governance, the EU is now referred to as a *sui generis* construction. Due to various seminal works (Sjöstedt 1977; Allen and Smith 1990; Jupille and Caporaso 1998; Bretherton and Vogler [a]1999; [b]2006), looking not only at what the EU is but also at what it does, a focus on the EU's actions – and its actorness – has become more prominent, resulting in considering the EU as an international actor in its own right (Hill et al. 2017). Against this background, the view of the

EU as a normative actor, coined 'Normative Power Europe' by Manners (2002), promoting its core values and principles beyond its own territory and acting as a 'force for good' (Barbé and Johansson-Nogués 2008), has continuously but not exclusively been competing with traditional, namely neo-realist perspectives, arguing that the EU – just like other international actors – is pursuing its own interests, or rather those of its Member States (Hyde-Price 2006).

With these two main strands interpreting the EU's international behaviour, conceptions of sovereignty and of strict border demarcation have been less important for the overall analysis of the EU than for the traditional IR perspective on states,[1] despite borders constituting an important element of the European construction. With the integration of the Schengen *acquis*, the EU has *de facto* internalised the logic of a nation states' concept of borders; in addition, eastern enlargement and then the formulation of the ENP – with an increasingly wary Russia looking at NATO's and the EU's eastbound policies – have advanced considerations of borders and of geography. Hence, scholars have seen geopolitics come back to Europe, some depicting the initial draft of the ENP (Commission of the European Communities 2003) even as the Union's 'first geostrategic document' (Guérot and Witt 2004: 11). Along these lines, Browning and Joenniemi (2008) have proposed to systematise the way the EU is conceiving its borders by referring to three geopolitical models that have been evoked to seize the ultimate character of the EU. The first model is 'Westphalian' in nature, implying that in the EU, in analogy to sovereign states, '[p]ower [. . .] is seen as held at the centre but as applied consistently over the territory up to the border, where one sovereign territoriality meets another' (ibid.: 522). The second model, labelled 'Imperial', 'depicts EU governance in terms of a series of concentric circles', where power is 'located at the centre in Brussels and dispersed outwards in varying, multi-layered and declining degrees' (ibid.: 522–524). The third model is depicted as 'medieval', 'with power no longer fixed on a single centre [. . .], but as being far more regionalized and corresponding to logics of transnationalism and network governance' (ibid.: 525).

Based on the three geopolitical models and drawing largely on Walters (2004), Browning and Joenniemi (2008) describe four possible geostrategies to manage the EU's borders. Whereas a 'networked (non)border' follows a deterritorialised logic, aiming at transcending borders by developing networks of shared responsibilities between insiders and outsiders, the geostrategy of the 'march' strives for the establishment of a – potentially dynamic – protective zone between the inside and the outside, labelled 'interzone' or 'buffer zone' (ibid.: 527). In contrast, the geostrategy of a 'colonial frontier', based on power asymmetries between the inside and the outside, aims at shaping the outside according to the inside's preferences with the perspective of ultimately incorporating the outside. Therefore, the colonial frontier strategy can be quite dynamic, whereas a 'limes' strategy has a rather consolidating character, considering an existing border as permanent and at the same time, building on asymmetries to shape the outside according to the inside's preferences (ibid.: 529).

With respect to the ENP, Browning and Joenniemi (2008) concede that the way the EU manages its borders and deals with ENP countries does not correspond to only one of the models and strategies outlined, but varies according to time and space. Although they identify an overall imperial tendency, to the East, they see the EU oscillating between a limes and a colonial frontier strategy, including elements of a march with a buffer zone to Russia, whereas to the South, they detect a more pronounced limes strategy, underlining a rather Westphalian understanding of the EU (ibid.: 537–538). This assessment of intertwined and even fluctuating approaches hints at a non-coherent set-up of the ENP, which is largely reflected in the academic literature on the subject by pointing to numerous dilemmas, contradictions or paradoxes inherent to the policy. From an IR perspective, the ENP features both rationalist and constructivist qualities, frequently associated with a friction between the EU's (realist) security and (normative) democratisation agenda *vis-à-vis* neighbouring countries (Bosse 2009; Eris, 2012; Pace 2007). In this context, authors also point to a discrepancy in time, with security being frequently a short-term preoccupation, whereas democratisation often constitutes a long-term strategy, despite the latter also aiming at reducing 'economic, social and demographic security threats' (Khalifa Isaac 2013: 41), the EU is seen prioritising (short-term) security gains over (long-term) engagement for democratic transformation (Börzel and van Hüllen 2014; Hollis 2012; Marchetti 2012). The application of both inclusionary and exclusionary logics within the ENP reinforces this assessment (Bengtsson 2008; Joenniemi 2012), underscored by a discourse of dialogue and cooperation in contrast to the parallel articulation of a hierarchy between the EU and neighbours, going as far as claiming neighbours' inferiority (Bechev and Nicolaïdis 2010; Boedeltje and van Houtum 2011).

The outlined dilemmas are echoed, in the absence of a scholarly consensus labelling what the ENP entails for the way the EU is dealing with borders. Whereas the above concept of 'networked (non)border' is hardly taken up explicitly, scholars point to the EU resorting to network governance (Bosse and Korosteleva-Polglase 2009). Despite the semantic suggestion of networks bringing together entities on equal footing, Lavenex and Wichmann highlight that, with respect to existing power asymmetries, network governance can also be interpreted as a 'vehicle for policy transfer through "softer" means' (Lavenex and Wichmann 2009: 99). Similarly, Dimitrovova argues that the EU applying conditionality *vis-à-vis* neighbours is 'more typical of some types of empires than of networks' (Dimitrovova 2012: 255). This interpretation links the consideration of networks to literature conceptualising the EU as an empire (Zielonka 2006).[2] Such an imperial modelling of the EU can be coupled with claims that the EU is managing its borders in a (neo-) 'colonial' way (Boedeltje and van Houtum 2011), while authors also underline that the EU itself is wary of such an assessment (Dimitrovova 2012; Pace 2010). In addition, such interpretations are undisputed as others oppose considering the EU an empire (Haldén 2011) and reject viewing the ENP as an 're-enactment of "coloniality"' (Scott 2005: 434). At the same time, Boedeltje and van Houtum (2011) concede that the ENP, aiming at 'Europeanisation' beyond the EU, is not about the EU expanding geographically but more about 'reinforcing its own external borders' (ibid.: 143), thereby also highlighting the fuzziness in the use of concepts – as such a terminology of consolidation, according to Browning and Joenniemi (2008), would be associated with a 'limes' rather than with a 'colonial' strategy. Whereas this latter term is rarely taken up, just as the concept of the 'march' is practically absent from academic discussion, numerous authors refer to the ENP as a policy favouring the establishment of a 'buffer zone' by the EU (Boedeltje 2012: 15; Boedeltje and van Houtum 2011: 142; Zaiotti 2007: 149), or detect at least a 'buffering logic' (Del Sarto and Schumacher 2005: 26). With reference to Immanuel Wallerstein's concept of world-economy – without assuming a neo-Marxist perspective – this buffer zone has also been understood as 'semi-periphery' (Marchetti 2006: 17–18) between the EU and neighbours' neighbours and beyond.

Beyond terminology, most authors share the analysis that the ENP is a hybrid policy, reinforcing and weakening the relevance of physical borders and thereby contributing to 'blurred boundaries' (Grant 2006; Del Sarto and Schumacher 2005: 25–26; Joenniemi 2012: 37). As the ENP pushes the functional (legal) boundaries of EU influence beyond its physical (institutional) borders (Lavenex 2004), it creates what can be labelled EU 'borderlands' (Del Sarto 2010: 151–152) or described as 'flexible spaces' (Boedeltje 2012: 5). Despite acknowledging the existence of strong asymmetries between the EU and its neighbours, the majority of authors do not see effects of 'Europeanisation' or 'externalisation' taking place in an environment of strict dependency but rather of interdependence (Bengtsson 2008; Scott 2005; Marchetti 2006: 17–18), ranging from specifications of 'asymmetric interdependence' (Börzel and van Hüllen 2014: 1041; Kahraman 2005: 5; Lavenex and Wichmann 2009: 84–85) to going as far as arguing for 'mutual interdependence' (Scott 2009: 236–238; 2011).[3]

It is not surprising that, according to these broadly accepted findings, scholars have come up with labels such as 'hybrid geopolitics' (Scott 2009: 238) or 'soft geopolitics' (Dimitrovova 2012: 253) to describe what is considered particular about the EU's approach in its neighbourhood. How much the EU is eventually following tendencies of 'gatekeeping' more than those of 'power projection' (Bechev 2011) continues to be an issue for debate, with authors also concluding that, despite all 'softness' and openness to 'cooperation', the EU is still nothing but 'a realist actor in normative clothes' (Seeberg 2009: 95), leading back to controversies of rational vs constructivist and realist vs normative interpretations of the EU (Kratochvíl and Tulmets 2010). To reconcile these, Del Sarto proposes to consider the EU as a 'normative empire' (Del Sarto 2016: 216), arguing that the EU's 'utility-maximizing strategies' and its 'norm-based behaviour' eventually 'interlock and reinforce each other' (ibid.: 227), by exemplifying that

> exporting rules and practices to neighbouring states is a cost-efficient way of seeking to stabilize the periphery, while advancing the security and economic interests of the EU [. . . , with t]he logic of empire [being] clearly reinforced by the EU's civilizing mission, which derives from the Union's specific raison d'être: namely to prevent the recurrence of war through growing economic interdependence.
>
> (Del Sarto 2016: 227)

In essence, this concept proposes the notion of empire, less as a model of what the EU is and more as a mode of how the EU acts. Hence, Del Sarto contents herself with labelling the EU as an 'empire of sorts' and points to the potential limits of such an analogy, particularly when looking at the EU's internal functioning (Del Sarto 2016: 223). Following her argument, one would nonetheless need to add to the presented geostrategies a 'neo-imperial border'[4] strategy: based on the conception of the EU as a postmodern Empire *sui generis*,[5] lacking a clear-cut 'territorial fixity', but rather following a 'heterogeneous spatial logic' itself (Dimitrovova 2012: 252), such a strategy can be understood as an effort to establish semipermeable borders through the export of rules and practices, at the same time granting benefits to neighbours, including dosed access to the EU – as neighbours' well-being and cooperation is crucial for the EU's pursuit of its own interests under the conditions of asymmetric interdependence.[6]

The implicit buffering agenda of the ENP

Perfectly backed by central documents giving strategic orientation to the ENP is the scholarly assessment that enlargement has been the EU's reflective starting point in forging a policy towards its 'new' neighbours, even before the 'big bang' enlargement of 2004. The prominent and explicit reference to enlargement in the 'Wider Europe' communication (Commission of the European Communities 2003: 3–4) makes this just as clear as the 'European Neighbourhood Policy Strategy Paper' published a year later (Commission of the European Communities 2004: 2, 6). With the further elaboration and operationalisation of the ENP, the reference to enlargement has become less relevant, despite the fact that the policy – initially at least – draws considerable inspiration from enlargement. Being classified as the Union's 'most successful foreign policy instrument' (Commission of the European Communities 2003: 5), enlargement policy was predestined to serve as the model for the ENP. Beyond explicit policy choices, this inspiration from enlargement can also be explained by recalling that the Commission's Directorate-General (DG) for Enlargement mainly elaborated the initial drafts of the ENP before the policy moved on to the DG for External Relations (Kelley 2006). Even with the transfer to today's European External Action Service, headed by the Union's High Representative for Foreign Affairs and Security Policy, Federica Mogherini, the link to enlargement remains institutionally visible, as the policy is also within the portfolio of the Commissioner for European Neighbourhood Policy and Enlargement Negotiations, Johannes Hahn.

On the policy level, the initial inspiration from enlargement led to the ENP as a sort of 'enlargement light' policy. However, the ENP encountered difficulties 'in developing "silver" or "bronze" carrots, which fall short of offering the "golden" carrot of prospective membership' (Dannreuther 2006: 189), especially as the perspective to 'share everything but institutions' as formulated by Commission President Prodi (2002) was eventually not taken up in guiding documents. Likewise, whereas the Commission in its Wider Europe communication offered ENP countries 'the prospect of a stake in the Internal Market' by explicitly enumerating the 'four freedoms' (Commission of the European Communities 2003: 4), the formula of 'a stake in the Internal Market' reappears in later documents without specifying how far this could possibly go. In addition, the EU has been highlighting from the beginning that the ENP is distinct from enlargement, and at the same time differentiating between European neighbours (to the East) without a membership perspective 'in the medium-term' and non-European neighbours (to the South) for whom '[a]ccession has been ruled out' (ibid.: 5). Therefore, despite drawing on enlargement and continuously speaking of 'partners' and 'partnership', all central ENP documents display a distinction between insiders (the EU and candidates) and outsiders (neighbours and other third countries) (Smith 2005). Taken together, these features themselves already point to geopolitical considerations, although these are implicit rather than explicit. However, the rarely spelled out 'geopolitical imperative' (Council of the European Union 2007: 2) of the ENP becomes evident by not only looking closely at ENP related communications but also by including central statements on the EU's foreign policy orientation as a whole. As the latter do not consider ENP countries as one of their main addresses they are much less reticent in this respect. With regard to neighbours, the European Security Strategy (ESS) of 2003, for example, adopted after the Wider Europe communication and before the European Neighbourhood Policy Strategy Paper, clearly states that 'geography is still important' (Council of the European Union 2003: 7). It also articulates the European demand that neighbours should eventually form a 'ring of well governed countries' (ibid.: 8) around the EU. In the Wider Europe communication the idea is formulated much more inclusively by promoting a 'ring of friends' (Commission of the European Communities 2003: 4), to fall back into the lines of the ESS with the European Neighbourhood Policy Strategy Paper, a year later, by citing its claim to promote 'a ring of well governed countries' (Commission of the European Communities 2004: 6). Despite these differences in tone, the 'ring of' rhetoric relates to the geographic space around the EU and is essentially geopolitical.

Nonetheless, the pursuance of a geostrategic foreign policy approach *via* the ENP appears less evident in its beginnings than today. In 2003–2004, the ENP set out to promote 'stability, security and well-being for all concerned' (Commission of the European Communities 2004: 3). These aims, presented as being 'mutual' or 'shared' (Commission of the European Communities 2003: 6), were to be achieved on the basis of equally 'shared' (ibid.: 9) or 'common values' (Commission of the European Communities 2004: 3), despite the acknowledgment that neighbours had a rather mixed, if not deficient, record when it comes to '[d]emocracy, pluralism, respect for human rights, civil liberties, the rule of law and core labour standards' (Commission of the European Communities 2003: 7). This is why the EU made it clear from the start that the 'level of the EU's ambition in developing links with each partner through the ENP will take into account the extent to which common values are effectively shared' (Commission of the European Communities 2004: 13), thereby pointing to the potential application of conditionality by the EU.

Likewise, the EU initially avoids postulating a hierarchy between the ENP's objectives by making clear that all – stability, security, prosperity and values – are interlinked (Commission of the European Communities 2003). With the first review of the ENP in 2011 coinciding with the Arab uprisings (Bouris and Schumacher 2017), there appears to be a shift in the EU's approach with values becoming more prominent, setting a normative hierarchy in an alleged effort to make up for the EU's negligence in this respect so far: 'The EU [. . .] will insist that each partner country's reform process reflect a clear commitment to universal values that form the basis of our renewed approach' (European Commission and High Representative of the European Union for Foreign Affairs and Security Policy 2011: 2–3). This 'normative turn' has led Bauer to conclude that the EU reversed 'the logic of the ENP' from 'economic cooperation leading to democracy' to 'democratisation lead[ing] to economic prosperity' (2013: 7). The assessment, however, can claim relevance for the intermediate period between the 2011 and the 2015 review of the ENP, as the latter reshuffles priorities and rearranges the hierarchy between the ENP's aims, by now formulating that 'the new ENP will take stabilisation as its main political priority' (European Commission and High Representative of the Union for Foreign Affairs and Security Policy 2015: 2), despite the continuously articulated conviction of the importance of values by the EU. This 'realist turn' is resonated in the European Union's Global Strategy by recalling that 'internal and external security are ever more intertwined: our security at home entails a parallel interest in peace in our neighbourhood and surrounding regions' (European Union 2016: 14), which then leads it to postulate that '[s]tate and societal resilience is our strategic priority in the neighbourhood' (ibid.: 25).

With the 2015 ENP review, the EU dissolves the link that existed to the initial enlargement logic. Whereas such logic could be considered part of a larger colonial frontier strategy, aiming at a later incorporation of (at least eastern) ENP countries into the EU, the approach that has prevailed since 2015 – in the ENP review as well as the 2016 EU Global Strategy – is that of a neo-imperial border strategy. This is clear when one looks at the details of the EU's offer. Despite partner rhetoric and highlighting interdependencies, it's the EU that constantly demands alignment of neighbours to EU rules and practices (Del Sarto 2016). This 'process of EU non-territorial expansionism' (Dimitrovova 2012: 254) is accompanied by complementing it with buffering elements, derived from the 'stabilisation' or 'resilience' imperative. Including neighbours in European efforts for 'migration management' (European Commission and High Representative of the European Union for Foreign Affairs and Security Policy 2011: 12), and preventing the 'spill-over of insecurity' (European Union 2016: 30) by granting support and economic benefits for ENP countries, fit well into this image.

ENP countries as weak buffer

Although an implicit buffering agenda can be identified within central EU documents on the ENP, empirical evidence on whether the ENP is generating these effects is limited, given the overall difficulty in determining the overall impact of the ENP (Baltag and Romanyshyn in this volume). Despite this deficiency, a comparative analysis of transnational indices, touching upon issues the EU is concerned with when conceptualising its neighbourhood, can at least highlight how far ENP countries do or do not serve as a buffer for the EU, without identifying the ENP's specific share in this. Assuming a buffering role of ENP countries from an EU point of view, two buffering types are observable. Following a logic of 'negative buffering', the prevention of security threats to the EU should translate into ENP countries being marked more by terrorism, conflicts and migration than the EU, but less than their respective neighbours (dilution of problems). 'Negative buffering' could also be considered at work in cases where ENP countries serve as a barrage (holding up of problems), although this would then imply pressure on ENP countries going beyond the stress faced by the EU and by their respective neighbours. Whereas the former would therefore indicate a rather sustainable buffer, the latter – due to the high pressure on ENP countries – would have to be considered more fragile. In any case, it is expected that 'negative buffering' would be complemented by a logic of 'positive buffering', marked by socio-economic performance and governance structures of ENP countries being relatively stronger than in the case of their neighbours, but still being weaker than within the EU. In such case, ENP countries could be considered to be – at least to a certain degree – in a position to cope with problems the EU intends to hold off, thereby vindicating approaches to share benefits with ENP countries to empower them for this task.

Within the scope of this chapter, an assessment as to whether ENP countries factually constitute a buffer zone along the lines indicated can only be cursory in nature. Nonetheless, even a limited comparison of transnational indices as provided in Table 12.1 reveals several features whose persistence would need to be tested in a more coherent and substantial manner in future research. Besides providing data for the EU, ENP countries – for the sake of geography, including Turkey as well as Russia – and neighbours' neighbours, the column to the left designates the type of indicator, that is, whether a functioning buffer would follow a positive or negative logic. It also designates the general gradation that could be expected from a functioning buffer – in the case of 'negative buffering' this column is again subdivided, helping to identify a more sustainable (left) and a more fragile situation (right).

Looking first into the representation of data potentially indicating 'positive buffering', the overall picture is that of an EU being clearly distinguishable from its neighbours in terms of human development – including socio-economic development – and democratic governance. Both the United Nations Development Programme's (2016) 'Human Development Index' and Freedom House's (2017) 'Freedom in the World' highlight the degree to which the EU is to be considered a centre distinct from its surroundings. In addition, according to the data, neighbours can generally be considered more developed and more attached to democratic values than their neighbours, marking them indeed as a sort of semi-periphery between the EU and the (less developed) periphery and thereby fulfilling attributions as formulated when conceptualising them as a buffer. Although this is particularly striking with Africa, a closer look at the available data highlights that this assessment is not unflawed. Despite displaying higher human development than their sub-Saharan neighbours, neither Algeria nor Libya perform better in terms of democratic governance, thereby factually perforating the intended 'ring of well governed countries' (Council of the European Union 2003: 8). This is even more striking when looking at war-torn Syria, performing considerably worse in terms of human development and democratic governance than any of its neighbours, negating the factual existence of a ring around the EU again in the Eastern Mediterranean.

When it comes to examining 'negative buffering', the perforation of the ring around the EU becomes even more evident. Although the EU can indisputably be identified as the stable and secure centre, already the neighbourhood is considerably conflict-ridden and not overwhelmingly diluting stability and security problems but itself subject to major concerns: the Fund for Peace's (2016) 'Fragile States Index' points to the high pressure faced by ENP countries just as the Heidelberg Institute for International Conflict Research's (2017) 'Conflict Barometer' illustrates the high intensity of conflicts in numerous ENP countries. Both indices illustrate widespread instability in the EU's immediate neighbourhood, mainly to the South (Libya, Syria and their surroundings) but also to the East (Ukraine), and also point to the fragility of ENP countries to form a reliable ring around the EU.

With the referenced indices highlighting the factual perforation of the intended ring around the EU, it is fair to say that the actual performance of ENP countries as a buffer is weak, if one does not even subscribe to the more pessimistic view that ENP countries actually form a 'ring of

Table 12.1 Comparative data on the functioning of ENP countries as the EU's buffer zone

Coding of charts

type	EU												
expected gradation	MA	DZ	TN	LY	EG	PS IL JO		LB	SY	TR	GE AM AZ	RU	UA	MD	BY
	MR	ML	NE	TD	SD	SA		IQ			IR				

Human Development Index (0., data for 2015, United Nations Development Programme 2016)

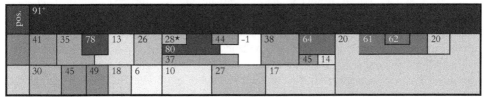

[+] Score for EU weighted by author.

Freedom in the World (aggregate score for all categories, data for 2016, Freedom House 2017)

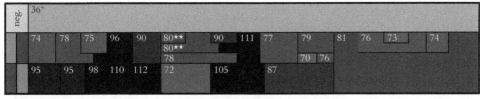

★ Score for West Bank. [+] Score for EU weighted by author.

Fragile States Index (data for 2015, Fund for Peace 2016)

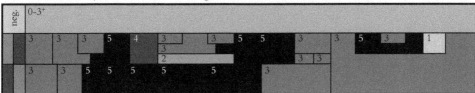

★★ Score for Israel includes West Bank. [+] Score for EU weighted by author.

Conflict Barometer (data for 2016, Heidelberg Institute for International Conflict Research 2017)

[+] Score range indicated for EU by author.

fire' (*The Economist* 2014) around the EU. On the one hand, this assessment can serve as a rational justification for the 'securitisation' of the EU's policy towards its neighbours by now privileging stability and security over other objectives, as is the case where deficiencies have come to the fore. On the other hand, the EU has a particularly weak track record when it comes to hard security in the neighbourhood as it has frequently let other actors take the lead here (Bauer 2013). It also needs to be acknowledged that until now the overall policy in the neighbourhood has only been of limited effectiveness due to conflicting goals (Börzel and van Hüllen 2014) or restrictive spending (Bicchi 2014). How far the EU's new prioritisation, as laid out in the 2015 ENP review and the 2016 Global Strategy, will eventually make a difference remains to be seen.

Conclusions

The ENP is a hybrid policy, which can be considered geopolitical in nature and geostrategic in orientation. This orientation is frequently more implicit than explicit and remains somewhat blurred – just as the EU's borders have become increasingly blurred with the EU exporting rules and practices to its neighbourhood while at the same time maintaining areas, like security or migration, where a rather strict conception of external borders continues to apply. In this context, different geostrategies to manage the EU's borders have been proposed and identified, oscillating mainly between a limes strategy, trying to clearly draw a line between the EU and its neighbours, and a colonial frontier strategy, eventually granting incorporation of neighbours into the EU. Overall, the geostrategic approach of the EU can best be conceived as a neo-imperial border strategy, characterised by the creation of semipermeable borders *via* the ENP, leading to the factual emergence of EU borderlands, following the implicit objective of serving as the EU's buffer zone to the more precarious periphery. In reality, ENP countries are far from forming a democratic, prosperous, peaceful and stable ring around the EU. With several neighbours featuring severe deficiencies with regard to the EU's intentions, the ring as conceived by the ENP can at most be considered a weak buffer today.

Notes

1 For a broader IR perspective on the shifting meaning of international borders – or 'frontiers' – see Anderson 1996, who also considers the process of European regional integration.
2 Zielonka (2006) actually conceptualises the EU as a neo-medieval empire, thereby bringing together two of the three models put forward by Browning and Joenniemi (2008), while rejecting a Westphalian reading.
3 In contrast, Eriş (2012: 250) is making a case for dependence from the EU.
4 In a further effort to concretise this notion, it would be necessary to clearly differentiate such a neo-imperial approach from allegations of neo-imperialist politics (cf. Scott 2005: 430).
5 As a matter of fact, Joenniemi sees 'neighbouring' as a vehicle that 'enables the EU to retain its quality as something *sui generis* and exceptional in character' (Joenniemi 2012: 44).
6 Such a conception can be informed by drawing on ideas of the 'cosmopolitanization' of borders (Rumford 2006b: 190–191) – based on an understanding of their frequent shifting and their dividing as well as connecting features (Rumford 2006a: 133) – or on concepts such as those of 'homogeneous empire', pursuing a logic of integration, and of 'multicultural empire', following a logic of difference (Dimitrovova 2012).

References

Allen, D. and Smith, M. (1990) 'Western Europe's Presence in the Contemporary International Arena', *Review of International Studies* 16(1): 19–37.
Anderson, M. (1996) *Frontiers: Territory and State Formation in the Modern World*, Cambridge: Polity.

Barbé, E. and Johansson-Nogués, E. (2008) 'The EU as a Modest "Force for Good": The European Neighbourhood Policy', *International Affairs* 84(1): 81–96.

Bauer, P. (2013) 'European-Mediterranean Security and the Arab Spring: Changes and Challenges', *Democracy and Security* 9(1–2): 1–18.

Bechev, D. (2011) 'Of Power and Powerlessness: The EU and Its Neighbours', *Comparative European Politics* 9(4): 414–431.

Bechev, D. and Nicolaïdis, K. (2010) 'From Policy to Polity: Can the EU's Special Relations with Its "Neighbourhood" be Decentred?', *Journal of Common Market Studies* 48(3): 475–500.

Bengtsson, R. (2008) 'Constructing Interfaces: The Neighbourhood Discourse in EU External Policy', *Journal of European Integration* 30(5): 597–616.

Bicchi, F. (2014) 'The Politics of Foreign Aid and the European Neighbourhood Policy Post-Arab Spring: "More for More" or Less of the Same?', *Mediterranean Politics* 19(3): 318–332.

Boedeltje, F. (2012) 'The Other Spaces of Europe: Seeing European Geopolitics Through the Disturbing Eye of Foucault's Heterotopias', *Geopolitics* 17(1): 1–24.

Boedeltje, F. and van Houtum, H. (2011) 'Brussels is Speaking: The Adverse Speech Geo-Politics of the European Union Towards Its Neighbours', *Geopolitics* 16(1): 130–145.

Börzel, T. and van Hüllen, V. (2014) 'One Voice, One Message, but Conflicting Goals: Cohesiveness and Consistency in the European Neighbourhood Policy', *Journal of European Public Policy* 21(7): 1033–1049.

Bosse, G. (2009) 'Challenges for EU Governance Through Neighbourhood Policy and Eastern Partnership: The Values/Security Nexus in EU–Belarus Relations', *Contemporary Politics* 15(2): 215–227.

Bosse, G. and Korosteleva-Polglase, E. (2009) 'Changing Belarus? The Limits of EU Governance in Eastern Europe and the Promise of Partnership', *Cooperation and Conflict* 44(2): 143–165.

Bouris, D. and Schumacher, T. (2017) *The Revised European Neighbourhood Policy: Continuity and Change in EU Foreign Policy*, London: Palgrave Macmillan.

Bretherton, C. and Vogler, J. ([a]1999, [b]2006) *The European Union as a Global Actor*, [a]London/[b]Abingdon: Routledge.

Browning, C. and Joenniemi, J. (2008) 'Geostrategies of the European Neighbourhood Policy', *European Journal of International Relations* 14(3): 519–551.

Comelli, M. (2004) 'The Challenges of the European Neighbourhood Policy', *The International Spectator* 39(3): 97–110.

Commission of the European Communities (2003) *Wider Europe—Neighbourhood: A New Framework for Relations with Our Eastern and Southern Neighbours*, COM (2003) 104 final, Brussels, 11 March.

Commission of the European Communities (2004) *European Neighbourhood Policy Strategy Paper*, COM (2004) 373 final, Brussels, 12 May.

Council of the European Union (2003) *A Secure Europe in a Better World: European Security Strategy*, Brussels, 12 December.

Council of the European Union (2007) *Strengthening the European Neighbourhood Policy—Presidency Progress Report (10874/07)*, Brussels.

Dannreuther, R. (2006) 'Developing the Alternative to Enlargement: The European Neighbourhood Policy', *European Foreign Affairs Review* 11(2): 183–201.

Del Sarto, R. (2010) 'Borderlands: The Middle East and North Africa as the EU's Southern Buffer Zone', in Bechev, D. and Nicolaïdis, K. (eds.) *Mediterranean Frontiers: Borders, Conflicts and Memory in a Transnational World*, London: I.B. Tauris, 149–167.

Del Sarto, R. (2016) 'Normative Empire Europe: The European Union, Its Borderlands, and the "Arab Spring"', *Journal of Common Market Studies* 54(2): 215–232.

Del Sarto, R. and Schumacher, T. (2005) 'From EMP to ENP: What's at Stake with the European Neighbourhood Policy Towards the Southern Mediterranean?', *European Foreign Affairs Review* 10(1): 17–38.

Dimitrovova, B. (2012) 'Imperial Re-Bordering of Europe: The Case of the European Neighbourhood Policy', *Cambridge Review of International Affairs* 25(2): 249–267.

Eri, Ö. (2012) 'European Neighbourhood Policy as a Tool for Stabilizing Europe's Neighbourhood', *Southeast European and Black Sea Studies* 12(2): 243–260.

European Commission and High Representative of the European Union for Foreign Affairs and Security Policy (2011) *A New Response to a Changing Neighbourhood*, COM (2011) 303 final, Brussels.

European Commission and High Representative of the Union for Foreign Affairs and Security Policy (2015) *Review of the European Neighbourhood Policy*, JOIN (2015) 50 final, Brussels.

European Union (2016) *Shared Vision, Common Action: A Stronger Europe. A Global Strategy for the European Union's Foreign and Security Policy*, Brussels.

Freedom House (2017) Subcategory Scores for Countries and Territories, https://freedomhouse.org/sites/default/files/FH_Aggregate_Category_and_Subcategory_Scores_FIW2003-FIW2017.xls, accessed 29 April 2017.

Fund for Peace (2016) Fragile States Index 2016, http://fsi.fundforpeace.org/library/fragilestatesindex-2016.xlsx, accessed 29 April 2017.

Grant, C. (2006) *Europe's Blurred Boundaries: Rethinking Enlargement and Neighbourhood Policy*, London: Centre for European Reform.

Guérot, U. and Witt, A. (2004) 'Europas neue Geostrategie', *Aus Politik und Zeitgeschichte* 54(17): 6–12.

Haldén, P. (2011) 'Understanding the EU, the US and Their External Spheres of Rule: Republican Synergies, Destructive Feedbacks and Dependencies', *Journal of Political Power* 4(3): 433–450.

Heidelberg Institute for International Conflict Research (2017) *Conflict Barometer 2016*, Heidelberg: Heidelberg Institute for International Conflict Research.

Hill, C., Smith, M. and Vanhoonacker, S. (2017) *International Relations and the European Union*, Oxford: Oxford University Press.

Hollis, R. (2012) 'No Friend of Democratization: Europe's Role in the Genesis of the "Arab Spring"', *International Affairs* 88(1): 81–94.

Hyde-Price, A. (2006) '"Normative" Power Europe: A Realist Critique', *Journal of European Public Policy* 13(2): 217–234.

Joenniemi, P. (2012) 'Turning into a Sovereign Actor? Probing the EU Through the Lens of Neighbourhood', *Geopolitics* 17(1): 25–46.

Jupille, J. and Caporaso, J. (1998) 'States, Agency, and Rules: The European Union in Global Environmental Politics', in Rhodes, C. (ed.) *The European Union in the World Community*, London: Lynne Rienner, 213–229.

Kahraman, S. (2005) 'The European Neighbourhood Policy: The European Union's New Engagement Towards Wider Europe', *Perceptions* 10(4): 1–28.

Kelley, J. (2006) 'New Wine in Old Wineskins: Promoting Political Reforms Through the New European Neighbourhood Policy', *Journal of Common Market Studies* 44(1): 29–55.

Khalifa Isaac, S. (2013) 'Rethinking the New ENP: A Vision for an Enhanced European Role in the Arab Revolutions', *Democracy and Security* 9(1–2): 40–60.

Kratochvíl, P. and Tulmets, E. (2010) 'Constructivism and Rationalism as Analytical Lenses: The Case of the European Neighbourhood Policy', *Politics in Central Europe* 6(1): 22–40.

Lavenex, S. (2004) 'EU External Governance in "Wider Europe"', *Journal of European Public Policy* 11(4): 680–700.

Lavenex, S. and Wichmann, N. (2009) 'The External Governance of EU Internal Security', *Journal of European Integration* 31(1): 83–102.

Manners, I. (2002) 'Normative Power Europe: A Contradiction in Terms?', *Journal of Common Market Studies* 40(2): 235–258.

Marchetti, A. (2006) *The European Neighbourhood Policy: Foreign Policy at the EU's Periphery*, Bonn: Center for European Integration Studies.

Marchetti, A. (2012) 'The EU's Relations with Its Mediterranean Neighbours in a Regional Perspective', in Calleya, S. and Wohlfeld, M. (eds.) *Change and Opportunities in the Emerging Mediterranean*, Malta: Mediterranean Academy of Diplomatic Studies, 397–412.

Pace, M. (2007) 'Norm Shifting from EMP to ENP: The EU as a Norm Entrepreneur in the South?', *Cambridge Review of International Affairs* 20(4): 659–675.

Pace, M. (2010) 'The European Union, Security and the Southern Dimension', *European Security* 19(3): 431–444.

Prodi, R. (2002) 'A Wider Europe—A Proximity Policy as the Key to Stability', *Speech* /02/619, Brussels.

Rumford, C. (2006a) 'Rethinking European Spaces: Territory, Borders, Governance', *Comparative European Politics* 4(2): 127–140.

Rumford, C. (2006b) 'Borders and Rebordering', in Delanty, G. (ed.) *Europe and Asia Beyond East and West*, Abingdon: Routledge, 181–192.

Scott, J. (2005) 'The EU and "Wider Europe": Toward an Alternative Geopolitics of Regional Cooperation?', *Geopolitics* 10(3): 429–454.

Scott, J. (2009) 'Bordering and Ordering the European Neighbourhood: A Critical Perspective on EU Territoriality and Geopolitics', *TRAMES* 13(3): 232–247.

Scott, J. (2011) 'Reflections on EU Geopolitics: Consolidation, Neighbourhood and Civil Society in the Reordering of European Space', *Geopolitics* 16(1): 146–175.

Seeberg, P. (2009) 'The EU as a Realist Actor in Normative Clothes: EU Democracy Promotion in Lebanon and the European Neighbourhood Policy', *Democratization* 16(1): 81–99.

Sjöstedt, G. (1977) *The External Role of the European Community*, Farnborough: Saxon House.

Smith, K. (2005) 'The Outsiders: The European Neighbourhood Policy', *International Affairs* 81(4): 757–773.

The Economist (2014) 'Europe's Ring of Fire: The European Union's Neighbourhood is More Troubled than Ever', 20 September, www.economist.com/node/21618846, accessed 15 May 2017.

United Nations Development Programme (2016) *Human Development Report 2016: Human Development for Everyone*, New York: United Nations Development Programme.

Walters, W. (2004) 'The Frontiers of the European Union: A Geostrategic Perspective', *Geopolitics* 9(3): 674–698.

Zaiotti, R. (2007) 'Of Friends and Fences: Europe's Neighbourhood Policy and the "Gated Community Syndrome"', *Journal of European Integration* 29(2): 143–162.

Zielonka, J. (2006) *Europe as Empire: The Nature of the Enlarged European Union*, Oxford: Oxford University Press.

13
THE EU AND THE EUROPEAN NEIGHBOURHOOD POLICY
The re-making of Europe's identity

Jan Zielonka

Introduction

Initially, only six states decided to integrate, but after successive waves of enlargement the present day European Union (EU) has twenty-eight states covering much of Europe's space. Each enlargement represented an import not only of new states but also of new institutional structures, political and economic preoccupations, as well as political cultures. Each enlargement has also implied new neighbours and these neighbours have again presented the EC/EU with new opportunities and challenges. In this sense, the history of European integration can be described as a continuous process of identity formation prompted by successive waves of enlargement (Piedrafita and Torreblanca 2005; Sedelmeier 2003).

Territorial enlargement went hand in hand with functional enlargement. Integration has progressively moved to new functional fields – from trade and agriculture to industrial competition, justice and home affairs, monetary and social matters and even defence and foreign policy (Blockmans and Prechal 2008). Neither the widening of the Union nor its deepening had a clear point of arrival. No one knows where Europe ends and functional integration may bring about different outcomes ranging from a European super-state to a hybrid institutional maze.

Widening and deepening have never been smooth but they progressed nevertheless for five decades, despite occasional pauses and contestations. However, the process of widening and deepening has been stalled, if not reversed, over recent years with serious implications for the EU identity formation. The ENP, designed as a 'softer' version of widening than enlargement, has failed to meet its prime objectives. In fact, the EU is now facing movement in the opposite direction as exemplified by the results of the Brexit referendum. Deepening is also under threat; a possible collapse of the integrated institutional frameworks of the single currency and Schengen is now being publicly contemplated. Public support for integration is relatively low and Eurosceptic parties have won elections to the European Parliament in such crucial states as France and the United Kingdom.[1] Formally, nation states are still the key decision-making actors within the EU, but they seem to be less and less in control of economic flows, communication and migration. All these developments have a profound impact on EU borders and by extension its identity.

In this chapter, I will examine three basic issues. First, I will explore the relationship of boundary-making and identity construction. Second, I will analyse the EU's discourse and policy towards its vast and ever changing neighbourhood. Third, I will examine how recent external shocks – the global financial crisis, violent conflicts in the neighbourhood and migration flows – have influenced the EU's borders and identity.

In conclusion, I will argue that the EU's strength rested not only on material or institutional capabilities but also on the set of norms and values it proposed: the rule of law, democracy, solidarity and open borders most prominent among them. The EU envisaged Europe as an growing integrated space, where people can move freely and enjoy a similar set of economic, social and political rights. This vision of common European norms is now in tatters because of external shocks, for which the EU was unable to find adequate answers. The failure of the ENP is an illustrative example of how the predicament of Europe's identity formation impacted on the EU's foreign policy.

Borders and identity

The term 'identity', like all terms in social sciences, is imprecise and subject to different interpretations. Psychologists, sociologists, lawyers and political analysts talk differently about identity (Guild 2004). In European studies, identity is not only about shared values but also about a certain kind of community that lives on a certain territory (Kastoryano 2008). However, the relationship between community, values and territory has always been somewhat ambiguous. External borders of the EU define this territory and community, but these borders are not fixed and hard. Values can be shared across EU borders, but only EU citizens enjoy the rights granted by EU treaties. In an open-ended, multi-layered and multi-cultural polity such as the EU, identity cannot be simple and straightforward. Yet identity requires some common sense of political belonging, which is often related to territory.

As Pierre Manent argued:

> Instituting a political order, prior to consulting the will of any individuals, requires first the staking out of a common territory. A common territory is the barest requirement of a political community, to be sure, but it is also in a sense the most necessary . . . . While I readily admit that one can renounce the nation as a political form, I do not believe that people can live long within civilization alone without some sense of political belonging (which is necessarily exclusive), and thus without some definition of what is held in common.
>
> *(Manent 1996: 7–8)*

When identity is constructed in relation to space, we cannot but focus on borders. Borders delimit individual spaces, but they are not just lines on a map. They represent complex institutions determining the link between the territory, authority and rights. Borders define arrangements for market transactions, coercion powers, politico-administrative entitlements and communication clusters. These arrangements can be formal or informal to various degrees, but they are not given or stable; they are subject to historical change driven by technological, economic, social, cultural, political and military developments.

Foreign policy specialists feel comfortable with the notion of borders. After all, without borders it would be difficult to distinguish what is foreign and what is domestic. Foreign policy is principally geared to implementing a set of interests defined territorially, even though it is increasingly difficult to provide a 'territorial defence' or enhance economic interests of a certain territory only, national or European.

Foreign policy specialists feel less comfortable with the notion of identity, despite the growing popularity of such terms as soft power or cultural diplomacy (Nye 2004; Melissen 2005). The way foreign policy specialists handle identity issues is chiefly through the demarcation and enforcement of legal, administrative and military boundaries. Boundary construction helps to identify those on behalf of whom foreign policy is being conducted and those who are on its receiving end, friends and enemies alike.

Of course, anthropologists or sociologists use a different notion of borders. For them, borders are also about binary distinctions – us/them, inside/outside, here/there – but their focus is more on people rather than states (Newman 2006: 147–148). Anthropologists argue that personal borders determine our daily practices more than legal or institutional ones. Sociologists emphasize cultural borders such as language (Barbour and Carmichael 2000; Carsten 2000). In fact, the linguistic border is difficult to trespass for many people, with implications for mutual communication.[2] The EU has twenty-four official languages, which explains why so many trans-border agreements are being 'lost in translation'. DG Translation within the European Commission has translated 2.30 million pages in 2014 at a cost of EUR330 million.[3] German may well be the most widely used mother tongue, but only 18 per cent of Europeans speak German; 51 per cent of Europeans speak English of some sort but this has not led to a genuine pan-European press, for instance.[4]

For political theorists, borders reflect, first of all, power relationships. Boundary making is thus about creating hierarchies and dependencies. It is also about creating rules and order. Max Weber and different generations of his disciples – Charles Tilly, Stein Rokkan or Stefano Bartolini – argued that the whole history of human organizations could largely be read as a series of continuing efforts to bring territorial borders to correspond to and coincide with systemic functional boundaries and to be in line with the consolidated socio-political hierarchies of corresponding populations (Tilly 1975; Rokkan et al. 1987; Bartolini 2005).

This process of boundary making has a profound, but not mechanical, impact on identity formation. The history of states, for instance, shows two distinct patterns. Sometimes state borders have been set to reflect prevalent cultural patterns related to language, ethnicity or cultural myths. At other times, it was the other way around. As Massimo d'Azeglio famously observed, during the nineteenth century: 'We have made Italy. Now we must make Italians' ('*L'Italia è fatta. Restano da fare gli italiani*').[5]

The interplay between border making and identity formation is particularly complex in the case of the EU. This is because the scope and nature of EU borders were always highly ambiguous and subject to contestation and change. There is no rational or 'natural' way to draw boundaries of the EU. The scope of borders depends on the degree of diversity the EU can 'digest' in political, legal and economic terms. External pressures also define the scope of EU borders. The EU's enlargement to Southern Europe and then to Central and Eastern Europe was driven by a mixture of geopolitical and economic considerations, which were not always widely shared among European electorates. Cultural factors were important, but not decisive, in the EU's border formation. Otherwise, a country of Tolstoy, Tchaikovsky and Dostoyevsky would be seriously considered as a potential EU member.

The nature of EU borders has not been straightforward either. There was always a heated discussion on whether these borders ought to be relatively open or closed, soft or hard. Economists argued that it is disadvantageous and impractical to hamper cross-border movement of capital, goods, services and labour.[6] Security specialists, on the other hand, contested the notion of open or porous borders (Caparini and Otwin 2006).[7] Political leaders shifted between these two extreme positions depending on circumstances and audiences. Each terrorist attack reinforced the notion of sealed borders, but successive political upheavals in neighbouring countries demanded more open borders for either humanitarian or political reasons.

The EU's boundary policy had numerous practical and symbolic implications. Each new territorial acquisition has been studied by neighbouring states and people, sometimes evoking hope and sometimes suspicion. Each EU enlargement represented an import of diverse political, legal and economic cultures creating new challenges and opportunities. Hardening of EU borders pleased anti-immigration campaigners, but angered human right campaigners. The Schengen regime was viewed by some as a symbol of free travel and by some as a symbol of exclusion (Grabbe 2000).

All this has shaped the EU's identity, although in a rather messy manner. Ever changing EU borders, in terms of scope and nature, complicated if not frustrated the identity formation process. The opening of EU internal borders has not necessarily resulted in a fusion of cultural identities. Most EU citizens retain strong national affiliations and loyalties. But the policy of closing EU external borders has not necessarily resulted in greater security, while antagonizing the EU's neighbours.

A series of external shocks in the early twenty-first century – financial, security and migratory – have exposed the weakness of the EU border policies and caused a profound identity crisis. The EU's borders proved unable to protect Europe's citizens from either 'pre-modern' or 'post-modern' pressures. On the one hand, we see a resurgence of national power politics benefiting strong states such as Germany, Russia or Turkey and, on the other, a cascading globalization benefiting such transnational actors as financial speculators or human traffickers. Many European citizens found themselves without effective means of protection and they began to lose a sense of common destiny. With no clear answer as to who 'we' are within the EU, it is hard to design foreign policies in any meaningful way (Guéhenno 1998). In other words, the EU's fuzzy borders generated a fuzzy European identity with serious foreign policy implications.

Imperial foreign policies and the fuzziness of identities

These EU foreign policies also contributed to the fuzziness of borders and identity. The EU has tried to embrace neighbouring states, rather than insulating itself from them through a policy of deterrence and containment. This has been done for a variety of reasons. The war in Yugoslavia demonstrated that the EU can scarcely insulate itself from major conflicts on its doorsteps and it lacks the military means that would allow it to practice an effective policy of deterrence and containment. In addition and probably more crucially, sealing borders was impractical in the age of economic globalization and internet communication. Democracy and good governance have been the best means of preventing the spread of violence in neighbouring countries. A meaningful promotion of democracy and good governance required various forms of trans-border cooperation, if not integration (Dimitrova and Pridham 2007; Freyburg et al. 2015). Last, after the fall of the Berlin Wall, citizens of Central and Eastern Europe embraced the notions of democracy and the free market as part of their 'return' to Europe strategy. It was difficult to leave this quest unanswered despite the initial scepticism (Vachudova 2005).

Enlargement of the EU has therefore become the official EU policy, and when it became domestically unpopular it was replaced by the ENP, with the same rhetoric and rationale. 'Everything but institutions' was the famous term coined by the President of the European Commission, Romano Prodi, to distinguish between the enlargement and neighbourhood policy (that is, the ENP).[8] Although neighbours were no longer guaranteed EU membership, they were still offered EU help on similar conditions as was the case with the enlargement policy. The more neighbours embraced EU laws and regulations, the more barriers to trans-border cooperation were promised to be lifted.

The EU's expectations of states participating in the ENP framework have not necessarily been more modest than in the case of prospective EU members. For instance, after the Arab 'Spring', the prime EU objective in the region has become so-called 'deep democracy', which demanded from Arab partners not just free elections but also profound political reforms, institution building, fighting against corruption, an independent judiciary and support to civil society.[9]

The ENP framework, like the enlargement one, represented an unusual way of carrying out foreign policies; the instruments applied towards neighbours were largely 'domestic' and the policy blurred the distinction between internal and external matters.

EU policies towards neighbours were more about creating a 'borderless' Europe than a 'fortress' Europe as envisaged by the paradigm of deterrence and containment. True, borders were blurred rather than totally open for countries taking part in the ENP framework, but the intention was to gradually get rid of borders, not to reinforce them (Del Sarto 2015; Armstrong and Anderson 2007). The official ENP rhetoric talked about an 'undivided', 'wider' Europe, 'a ring of friends', 'trans-European networks' and pan-European 'zones of prosperity'. This rhetoric emphasized that EU borders are anything but sealed. The policy was to promote trans-border 'connectivity' and 'mobility'.[10] This trans-border connectivity and mobility was the way to make neighbours secure, prosperous and stable. It was seen to be the answer to a range of social and economic problems confronting neighbours: exclusion, peripherality and lack of competitiveness (Jensen and Richardson 2004). It was a means to make EU foreign policy effective and in tune with the requirements of modernity and globalization.

This EU policy obviously blurred not only the notion of borders but also the meaning of EU membership. In an 'undivided' Europe, composed of numerous cross-border networks, the difference between ENP partners, candidates for EU membership and full-fledged EU members could not be sharp. This EU policy has also blurred the notion of the EU's identity. In an undivided Europe composed of numerous cross-border networks, identity was perceived as multi-level, open-ended and variable. Outsiders were would-be insiders, norms were universal and borders were zones of interaction (Delanty and Rumford 2005).

It is often suggested that the process of European integration resembles a state building process, but the evidence presented so far suggests that integration resembles an empire building process. In other words, to understand the EU policy of borders and its subsequent implications for the EU's identity, we need to apply an imperial rather than statist paradigm (Zielonka 2006). While states usually have hard and fixed external borders, empires have soft borders undergoing regular enlargements. The EU is obviously a prototype of the latter. The distinction between 'foreign' and 'domestic' affairs is clear in typical states, but this is not the case in empires where the distinction between the centre and the periphery is more pronounced. Again, the latter situation could be observed in the case of the EU, especially within the ENP framework. Various types of state borders – cultural, legal, economic and military – usually overlap. The central government of a classical state is fully in charge of these borders and the territory within them. In the case of empires (and the EU) we observe disassociation between authoritative allocations, functional competencies and territorial constituencies. Instead of a clear hierarchical structure, in empires we have the interpenetration of various types of political units and loyalties. The EU shares this imperial feature too. The multiple, open-ended and variable identities observed in the EU are also more common in empires than states.

Moreover, the EU justifies or rationalizes its policies towards neighbours in a way characteristic of empires (Del Sarto 2016). Put differently, the EU official discourse resembles the ideology of empire and its civilizing mission (Zielonka 2013). The neighbourhood is being portrayed as an unstable and underdeveloped periphery that needs to be taken care of lest it become a source of political or economic turmoil. The EU, by contrast, is being portrayed as a benevolent and rational actor congruent with the deeper forces of modernization and cross-border integration. As such, it is well equipped to act as an agent of peace, democracy, sustainable growth and good governance in the vast area falling under the ENP. As was often claimed, the EU represents a normative power 'civilizing' the external environment. It installs order, promotes development, constructs viable institutional structures and spreads rules of legitimate behaviour. The fact that this noble self-vision was not always shared by EU neighbours does not undermine the importance of the EU civilizing mission.

Civilizing missions are not merely rhetorical exercises: they try to convince the peripheries that imperial policies are beneficial for them, not merely for the imperial centre. They make the peripheries comply rather than rebel. They create normative bonds between the peripheries and the metropolis.

Civilizing missions are also important for the formation of the imperial identity. They help empires to define their vision of the world and their own role in it. They also help to identify and explain the purpose of imperial policies. As Thomas Diez put it in the contemporary European context:

> the discourse of the EU as a normative power constructs a particular self of the EU (and it is indeed perhaps the only form of identity that most of the diverse set of actors within the EU can agree on), while it attempts to change others through the spread of particular norms.
>
> *(Diez 2005: 614)*

Failure of the imperial 'dream'

The ENP has clearly failed to live up to its promise. As a 2015 study of the German Marshall Fund put it:

> The European Neighbourhood Policy (ENP) is in tatters. When launching this regional framework for its neighbours in 2004, the EU stated that its ambition was to surround itself with a 'ring of friends', a zone of well-governed, stable and prosperous states, with whom the EU has close and cooperative ties. Little over a decade later, instead, realities in the European neighbourhood resemble a veritable ring of fire, with regional challenges and pressures on Europe greater than ever before.
>
> *(Inayeh and Forbrig 2015: 1; see also Juncos and Whitman 2015)*

The 2015 Policy Memo by the European Council on Foreign Relations was equally critical about the ENP's legacy. The ENP's aim was to 'encircle the EU by a ring of prosperous, stable and friendly countries', but the paper concludes that after a decade since the ENP was launched, the EU 'finds itself in a neighbourhood characterized by conflict, counter-revolution and resurgent extremism' (Witney and Dennison 2015: 1).

The question is, what went wrong and what are the implications for the EU's identity? Explanations of the ENP's failure range from technical to institutional, cultural to existential. Technical explanations focus on an incorrect policy blueprint of the ENP. EU policies towards neighbours were too rigid and technocratic, it is argued. Sixteen different neighbours have all too often been subjected to the same policy framework with little space for differentiation and flexibility (Koenig 2016; Lehne 2014).

Institutional explanations point to inadequate procedures for responding to foreign policy emergency situations and to the lack of military instruments for coping with local violence in the neighbourhood. EU institutional priorities also seemed misguided. For instance, it has been pointed out that the EU's major preoccupation was migration rather than democracy, good governance, economic development and social justice (Noutcheva 2015; Lavenex 2011).

Cultural explanations point to the EU's difficulty in exporting norms for which there was little demand in the neighbourhood. For instance, it is difficult to promote democracy in countries where liberal and secular values are not widely shared. As Olivier Roy has argued:

> The democratization movement in the Arab world came precisely after thirty years of what has been called the 'return of the sacred', an obvious process of re-Islamization of everyday life, coupled with the rise of Islamist parties . . . There was no flowering of 'liberal Islam' preceding the spread of democratic ideas in the Middle East. There are a few reformist religious thinkers who are lauded here and there in the West, but none has ever had much popular appeal in any Arab country.
>
> *(Roy 2012: 6)*

Existential explanations point to a profound crisis of European integration which undermined the EU's ability to shape its external environment. Some analysts argue that the EU is already in the process of disintegration, but even less dramatic assessments agree that the EU became inward looking, lost its 'sex appeal' and betrayed the values it was preaching to neighbours (Gstöhl 2016; Bosse 2007). No wonder the EU is having problems in getting its foreign policies off the ground, let alone forging its civilizing mission.

An introverted, conflicted and paralysed EU does not match the vision of an open, if not borderless, Union actively promoting democracy, stability and a friendly neighbourhood. Today 'unity in diversity' seems to be an empty slogan and the EU lacks a recognizable 'self' that would make people stick to the Union in difficult times. The crisis has also undermined, if not discredited, the EU's modernist notion of administrative competence and social progress. It showed that traditional notions of loyalty, trust and affection are still important, but found chiefly in nation states and not in cross-border regions and networks. The assertion of power politics within the EU at the expense of the power of laws and moral norms has also had serious identity implications. Let's examine how developments on the ground began to question the proclaimed common values and community spirit of the EU.

Over the last decade or so, the EU has experienced a series of external shocks. The most crucial were geopolitical (in Eastern Europe, the Middle East and North Africa), financial and migratory. The origins and scenarios of these shocks were complex, but they all have pulled EU Member States apart, complicating a process of joint European interest and identity formation. A major cleavage has emerged between the creditor and the debtor states within the EU, between states welcoming refugees and those resisting them, between those concerned with Eastern Europe and those concerned with the Southern Mediterranean. What is more, all these groups are split still further into many sub-groups, each fiercely arguing their partisan case. At stake is equal access to EU decision-making and resources. At stake is also the mutual trust needed for any meaningful cooperation, especially in difficult times. The EU can hardly forge an effective foreign policy if Member States are suspicious of each other's intentions and have little confidence that their differences can be bridged by accommodation and compromise. The result is a general paralysis of decision-making, a concentration on EU internal matters and a neglect of the external environment. It is not surprising therefore that the EU is increasingly introverted and passive towards its neighbourhood.

The domestic situation in numerous EU Member States has also deteriorated. Excessive debt, low or even negative growth and mounting social problems have elevated to prominence anti-establishment parties on the left and right of the political spectrum. Liberal norms have been questioned and even compromised in some cases. In short, the EU has lost its power of example and legitimacy to promote liberal values abroad. The EU can hardly 'preach' liberal democracy to neighbours if neo-fascist parties are winning ever more parliamentary seats in some of the Member States, if EU governments constrain the freedom of the media or if they undermine the judicial independence.

Also, the EU cannot promote a vision of an open Europe if its external borders are being sealed by hastily erected walls and barbed wire fences. Even internal EU borders are being reinstated between individual Member States in response to terrorism and refugee flows.

The handling of the Euro has also questioned if not contradicted basic values of solidarity and social justice within the EU. Eurozone policies towards Greece and other insolvent Eurozone members have been found rigid and stingy, if not dictatorial, by many independent observers.[11] They exacerbated social problems without necessarily providing a solution for debt problems. Can neighbours still believe that integration is beneficial for weak and strong states alike? If EU Member States do not treat each other as friends, will neighbours receive any better treatment? If the solidarity principle does not apply to EU Member States, can it apply to non-members?

Moreover, it is not easy to maintain that the EU represents a community based on law. Today, crucial decisions within the EU are being made in an informal mode in Berlin, with little input from formal institutions from Brussels. New treaties are written with only some states in mind and they envisage numerous forms of punishment and external forms of interference that are widely seen as arbitrary. Institutions not properly grounded in EU law, such as the Eurogroup, are playing a major role with no written rules of conduct, let alone public scrutiny. If rule of law does not prevail within the EU, can it prevail in a wider European framework? Can neighbours believe that the import of EU laws will help them in eradicating shady informal deals and power politics?

In sum, a series of external shocks have not only undermined the EU's ability to act in the neighbourhood; they also questioned the normative rationale of the EU's Neighbourhood Policy. The EU's civilizing mission has begun to look increasingly utopian and less legitimate or sincere.

Conclusions: empire without a purpose

The EU's current problems emerge more from ideational than material factors. The EU is still a very wealthy actor despite all the problems related to the common currency. It has not been destroyed by any war or invasion. The problems emerge crucially from the failure of norms and visions that kept the EU together. This is the reason why the EU found it difficult to identify viable collective responses to a series of external shocks. The EU prided itself on being based on law, democracy, social justice and solidarity. It stood for open borders and regional integration. Trans-border trade, mobility and communication were the means to overcome historic fears and cultural prejudices. These common European values have inspired ever greater numbers of European nations. Even more of them decided to give up traditional sovereignty by joining European institutional structures, the EEC and then the EU and the Euro. Others were looking at these structures with admiration, if not jealousy. They either aspired to join these structures or to imitate them.

The failure of this inspiring common European identity has been a blow to the integrative system. Some will argue that the EU's peculiar identity was always artificial because it was imposed on Europeans from the top with little grassroots authentic engagement. Others will argue that the EU's normative vision was not supported by adequate institutions and material resources. Yet others will point to global trends which undermined European identity formation. In their view, a civilian power such as the EU could probably not survive the rise of terrorism, religious fundamentalism and political despotism in its environment.

However, it is hard to deny that European integration, understood as both deepening and widening, has been a success for several decades. The ENP has been the last and probably the least successful chapter of the otherwise plausible agenda. EU leaders and civil servants can hardly be blamed for everything that went wrong in Europe over recent years. However, we should point to cases of the compromising if not violating of norms and values that were the pillars of European integration. A divided, conflicted, inward-looking and selfish Europe has something to do with their political choices. It didn't have to be that way.

Notes

1 EurActiv (2014) 'Eurosceptics make controversial return to EU Parliament', www.euractiv.com/section/eu-elections-2014/news/eurosceptics-make-controversial-return-to-eu-parliament/.
2 For an interesting discussion about the relationship between language and borders, see the special issue of the *International Journal of the Sociology of Language*: www.degruyter.com/view/j/ijsl.2014.2014.issue-227/issue-files/ijsl.2014.2014.issue-227.xml.
3 Source: http://ec.europa.eu/dgs/translation/faq/index_en.htm.
4 Ibid. See also Eurobarometer, 'Europeans and their languages', http://ec.europa.eu/public_opinion/archives/ebs/ebs_386_en.pdf.
5 'Massimo D Azeglio nell "Enciclopedia Treccani"', *Treccani.it*, accessed 23 November 2015.
6 See, for example, EU business, 'EU Single Market – benefits', www.eubusiness.com/topics/sme/eu-single-market-guide/, or European Commission (2012) 'Twenty Years of the European Single Market', ec.europa.eu/internal_market/publications/docs/20years/key-points-web_en.pdf.
7 See also *EUobserver*, 'Terrorists gain "advantage" from EU open borders', https://euobserver.com/migration/133123.
8 Prodi (2002) 'A Wider Europe - A Proximity Policy as the key to stability', http://europa.eu/rapid/press-release_SPEECH-02-619_en.htm.
9 European Union (2011) *Remarks by the EU High Representative Catherine Ashton at the Senior Officials' Meeting on Egypt and Tunisia*. A 069/11, Brussels, 23 February. See also Stefan Füle (2011) *Strengthening Cooperation on Democracy Support*, SPEECH/11/179, 2nd Transatlantic Dialogue Conference, Brussels, 15 March. For a different view, see Bouris and Schumacher (2016), Del Sarto (2016).
10 Günter Verheugen, *The European neighbourhood policy*, speech/04/141, Prime Ministerial Conference of the Vilnius and Visegrad Democracies: 'Towards a Wider Europe: the new agenda', Bratislava, 19 March 2004.
11 *The Guardian*, 2015, 'Treatment of Greece and the future of the European project', www.theguardian.com/world/2015/jul/01/treatment-of-greece-and-the-future-of-the-european-project. See also 'German MP slams creditors for Greece's unfair treatment', www.sigmalive.com/en/news/greece/131501/german-mp-slams-creditors-for-greeces-unfair-treatment.

References

Armstrong, W. and Anderson, J. (eds.) (2007) *Geopolitics of European Union Enlargement: The Fortress Empire*, London: Routledge.
Barbour, S. and Carmichael, C. (2000) *Language and Nationalism in Europe*, Oxford: Oxford University Press.
Bartolini, S. (2005) *Restructuring Europe: Centre Formation, System Building, and Political Structuring between the Nation State and the European Union*, Oxford: Oxford University Press.
Blockmans, S. and Prechal, S. (2008) *Reconciling the Deepening and Widening of the European Union*, The Hague: Asser Press.
Bosse, G. (2007) 'Values in the EU's Neighbourhood Policy: Political Rhetoric or Reflection of a Coherent Policy?', *European Political Economy Review* 7(1): 38–62.
Bouris, D. and Schumacher, T. (eds.) (2016) *The Revised European Neighbourhood Policy: Change and Continuity in EU Foreign Policy*, Basingstoke: Palgrave.

Caparini, M. and Otwin, M. (2006) *Borders and Security Governance: Managing Borders in a Globalised World*, Geneva Centre for the Democratic Control of Armed Forces (DCAF), Zürich: Lit.

Carsten, J. (2000) *Cultures of Relatedness: New Approaches to the Study of Kinship*, Cambridge: Cambridge University Press.

Delanty, G. and Rumford, C. (2005) *Rethinking Europe: Social Theory and the Implications of Europeanization*, London: Routledge.

Del Sarto, R. (ed.) (2015) *Fragmented Borders, Interdependence and External Relations: The Israel–Palestine–European Union Triangle*, New York: Palgrave Macmillan.

Del Sarto, R. (2016) 'Normative Empire Europe: The European Union, Its Borderlands, and the "Arab Spring"', *Journal of Common Market Studies* 54(2): 215–232.

Diez, T. (2005) 'Constructing the Self and Changing Others: Reconsidering "Normative Power Europe"', *Millennium – Journal of International Studies* 33(3): 613–636.

Dimitrova, A. and Pridham, G. (2007) 'International Actors and Democracy Promotion in Central and Eastern Europe: The integration model and its limits', *Democratization* 11(5): 91–112.

Freyburg, T. Lavenex, S., Schimmelfennig, F., Skripka, T., Wetzel, A., Wetzel, A., Skripka, T. and Lavenex, S. (2015) *Democracy Promotion by Functional Cooperation: The European Union and Its Neighbourhood*, New York: Palgrave Macmillan.

Grabbe, H. (2000) 'The Sharp Edges of Europe: Extending Schengen Eastwards', *International Affairs* 76(3): 519–536.

Gstöhl, S. (2016) 'The Contestation of Values in the European Neighbourhood Policy: Challenges of Capacity, Consistency and Competition', in Poli, S. (ed.) *The European Neighbourhood Policy – Values and Principles*, London: Routledge, 58–78.

Guéhenno, J.-M. (1998) 'A Foreign Policy in Search of a Polity', in Zielonka, J. (ed.) *Paradoxes of European Foreign Policy*, The Hague: Kluwer Law International, 25–34.

Guild, E. (2004) *The Legal Elements of European Identity: EU Citizenship and Migration Law*, The Hague: Kluwer Law International.

Inayeh, A. and Forbrig, J. (eds.) (2015) 'Reviewing the European Neighbourhood Policy: Eastern Perspectives', *Europe Policy Paper* 4, Washington, DC: German Marshall Fund of the United States.

Jensen, O. and Richardson, T. (2004) *Making European Space: Mobility, Power and Territorial Identity*, London: Routledge.

Juncos, A. and Whitman, R. (2015) 'Europe as a Regional Actor: Neighbourhood Lost?', *Journal of Common Market Studies* 53(S1): 200–215.

Kastoryano, R. (2008) 'Europe: Space, Territory and Identity', in Laible, J. and Barkey, H. (eds.) *European Responses to Globalization*, Bingley, UK: Emerald Group Publishing Limited, 93–110.

Koenig, N. (2016) 'Taking the ENP Beyond the Conception-Performance Gap', *Policy Paper* 160, Berlin: Jacques Delors Institut.

Lavenex, S. (2011) 'A Governance Perspective on the European Neighbourhood Policy: Integration beyond Conditionality?', *Journal of European Public Policy* 15(6): 938–955.

Lehne, S. (2014) 'Time to Reset the European Neighbourhood Policy', Carnegie Europe, http://carnegieeurope.eu/publications/?fa=54420.

Manent, P. (1996), 'On Modern Individualism', *Journal of Democracy* 7(1): 3–10.

Melissen, J. (ed.) (2005) *The New Public Diplomacy: Soft Power in International Relations*, Basingstocke: Palgrave.

Newman, D. (2006) 'The Lines that Continue to Separate Us: Borders in Our "Borderless" World', *Progress in Human Geography* 30(2): 143–161.

Noutcheva, G. (2015) 'Institutional Governance of European Neighbourhood Policy in the Wake of the Arab Spring', *Journal of European Integration* 37(1): 19–36.

Nye, J. (2004) *Soft Power: The Means to Success in World Politics*, New York: Public Affairs.

Piedrafita, S. and Torreblanca, J. (2005) 'The Three Logics of EU Enlargement: Interests Identities and Arguments', *Politique Européenne* 15(1): 29–59.

Rokkan, S. and Urwin, D. (1987) *Centre-Periphery Structures in Europe*, Frankfurt: Campus Verlag.

Roy, O. (2012) 'The Transformation of the Arab World', *Journal of Democracy* 23(3): 5–18.

Sedelmeier, U. (2003) 'EU Enlargement, Identity and the Analysis of European Foreign Policy: Identity Formation Through Policy Practice', *EUI Working Papers*, Robert Schuman Centre for Advanced Studies.

Tilly, C. (ed.) (1975) *The Formation of Nation States in Western Europe*, Princeton: Princeton University Press.

Vachudova, M. (2005) *Europe Undivided: Democracy, Leverage and Integration After Communism*, Oxford: Oxford University Press.
Witney, N. and Dennison, S. (2015) 'Europe's Neighbourhood: Crisis as the New Normal', *ECFR Policy Memo*, London.
Zielonka, J. (2006) *Europe as Empire: The Nature of the Enlarged European Union*, Oxford: Oxford University Press.
Zielonka, J. (2013) 'Europe's New Civilizing Missions: The EU's Normative Power Discourse', *Journal of Political Ideologies* 18(1): 35–55.

14
STRATEGIC NARRATIVES OF EU FOREIGN POLICY AND THE EUROPEAN NEIGHBOURHOOD POLICY

Alister Miskimmon

Introduction

The European Union (EU) is confronted with an extremely challenging neighbourhood. In its own words, the EU is faced with an 'arc of instability' on its borders (Mogherini 2015: 1). These challenges demand an EU response. For most of the post-Cold War period, the EU has relied on the power of attraction to expand its membership, broaden its scope and stabilise post-Cold War Europe. However, the EU faces significant internal challenges affecting the extent to which it can project a coherent foreign policy response to instability in its region. Foreign policy, an area which the EU states and central institutions have consistently struggled with, is key to understanding the evolution of European Neighbourhood Policy (ENP). The EU's complex and contested internal politics and the difficulty of projecting a narrative that articulates the EU's role in the neighbourhood space have challenged the EU's credibility as a regional actor (Jones and Clark 2008). Despite these impediments, the EU has sought to find a way to influence the course of emerging events and the actors beyond the EU's borders. This chapter examines how the EU has sought to craft a strategic narrative of its neighbourhood, to shape its regional milieu.

The EU's post-Cold War narrative of deepening its cooperation and widening its membership as part of a strategy to stabilise Europe, has been central to its development (Manners and Murray 2016; Della Sala 2010). EU enlargement has been an effective means to encourage political and economic adaptation in neighbouring states. Narratives have also been used strategically by candidate countries to reinforce their claims to membership and ensure the EU delivers on its promises, most visible in the 'return to Europe' narrative of candidate states in Central and Eastern Europe (Schimmelfennig 2003). The ENP has been directed at expanding EU influence in countries without this membership perspective. Schumacher (2015) has highlighted four strategic narratives projected by the EU in its wider neighbourhood, designed to expand its influence. These are the threat/risk narrative and the duty and opportunity narrative in EU external relations and EU foreign policy, the EU as a promoter of peace narrative, the EU and its contribution to good neighbourliness narrative and, finally, the EU and the well-being of people narrative. These strategic narratives have raised expectations of the EU's activities in the neighbourhood and created expectations in third countries of what their cooperation with the EU might bring. Echoing Hill's (1993) oft-cited 'capabilities-expectations gap', Celata and Colletti argue that

> The ENP generated, more generally, a gap between the expectations raised by the policy and the EU's 'capacity to deliver'. The adoption of the narratives of enlargement and integration [. . .] creates ambiguity and false expectations regarding what the final aims of the policy are and what it is effectively able to 'deliver'.
>
> *(2015: 6)*

Rather than the transformational aims outlined in the official strategic narrative of the ENP, the EU has consistently favoured stability over radical change in its neighbourhood, as the list of challenges creating this 'arc of instability' has grown (Mogherini 2015; Börzel and van Hüllen 2014). More fundamentally, the EU's ability to shape its regional milieu has become more limited (Epstein and Jacoby 2014), which is exacerbated by the gap between what the EU says and what the EU does. This is apparent in the case of ENP in which Schumacher suggests that there has been a 'shift from focusing on external effectiveness to self-presentation and identity' (Schumacher 2015: 396). This chapter outlines the challenges surrounding the EU's efforts to influence its neighbourhood through the projection of strategic narratives. Despite the EU's resources, it has failed to outline a settled narrative of its identity and its narrative of order in the region, and has found it difficult to have a coherent narrative on the events that have destabilised the region. This greatly limits the EU's ability to play a shaping role in the region and challenges its own internal identity in the face of foreign policy change.

Strategic narratives

Strategic narratives have become central to how policy makers seek to exert influence in international affairs (House of Lords 2014; Rudd 2015). They can also provide a framework for forging shared meaning and understanding between actors (Miskimmon, O'Loughlin and Roselle 2013; 2017). Della Sala suggests that 'every form of social organization requires narratives to give it meaning and to provide a reason for being' (Della Sala 2010: 1; Polletta 1998). As a collective actor, the EU's meta-narrative of overcoming the divisions of Europe after World War II has been central to this story of becoming, until challenged by counter-narratives forged in the eurocrisis, the momentous Brexit vote and by the impact of mass migration in the wake of instability on Europe's borders. Foreign policy narratives do not exist without the hard power realities that underpin them. The EU is characterised by the diversity of narratives of European integration from its citizens and by the many actors vying to shape the EU's foreign policy (Lacroix and Nicolaïdis 2010; Zielonka 2014). There are also diverse narratives of the EU and its foreign policy, emanating from academic scholarship – for example, Civilian Power (Duchêne 1972; 1973), Ethical Power Europe (Aggestam 2008), Normative Power Europe (NPE) (Manners 2002) – all descriptions of the EU's foreign policy, which could be read as narratives. Each of these narratives evokes conceptions of the EU's collective identity, guides for the EU's role in the world and what kind of international order the EU should strive for. They suggest expectations of how the EU will act in its foreign policy. How the EU and its Member States seek to narrate its identity, their vision of international order and their position on the challenges the EU faces in the region are central to understanding how the EU seeks to position itself in international affairs. The EU's Global Strategy of 2016 is the EU's latest attempt to narrate its role in the world to foster internal foreign policy cohesion and project external influence.

We understand this conceptually through strategic narratives, which we define as, ' . . . a means by which political actors attempt to construct a shared meaning of international politics to shape the behaviour of domestic and international actors' (Miskimmon, O'Loughlin and Roselle 2013: 2). These narratives are generated to build domestic cohesion and external influence. We suggest narratives come in three main forms. First, identity narratives: actors give meaning to themselves and to others, through narratives. A state's self-identification as a Great Power will drive it to act according to this identity in international affairs. External perceptions of states, such as how others perceive Russia's or China's emergence, will affect how other states respond. Second, system narratives: how an actor conceives of international order will have a major impact on the types of policies they will pursue. There are many narratives of the international system – the Cold War, narratives of the emergence of the BRICS (Brazil, Russia, India, China and South Africa) and a new multipolar world order. For the ENP, the EU has never managed to forge a narrative of the EU and the region that expands its influence and binds third countries to it (Browning and Christou 2010). Third, policy or issue narratives: these narratives focus on a challenge, policy or event – how actors seek to give meaning to events through narrative defines how they respond. Actors seek narrative alignment across these three domains. For instance, the NPE narrative contends that the EU's influence emerged by being an example of how a peaceful, prosperous polity could develop through rejecting war to settle differences between its members (Manners 2002). The core values of NPE – including human rights, good governance and the importance of social and environmental protection – would inspire emulation and a steady stream of European states willing to join.

We highlight three reinforcing processes of strategic narratives. The formation of narratives, the projection of narratives and the reception of narratives (Miskimmon, O'Loughlin and Roselle 2013; 2017). Who forms the EU's strategic narrative on ENP remains contested and problematic. The European External Action Service (EEAS), led by Federica Mogherini, must work hand in hand with the European Commission and the Member States, with the associated risk of projecting mixed messages, which has led some to claim that the EU projects little overall coherence in ENP (Bertelsmann Stiftung 2015). Adding to this complexity, different directorates within the Commission are involved in the ENP and the problem of coordination between these different actors and interests has not been fixed by the establishment of the EEAS. Forging a unified strategic narrative of ENP is further complicated by Member States' foreign policy narratives. With these structural weaknesses in mind, the EU's 2015 strategic review, which led to the EU's global strategy, called for greater efforts to overcome the complexity of forging a common position arguing that

> In a more connected, contested and complex world, we need a clear sense of direction. We need to agree on our priorities, our goals and the means required to achieve them. We must refine the art of orchestration of the polyphony of voices around the table and the panoply of instruments at our disposal. We need a common, comprehensive and consistent EU global strategy.
>
> *(Mogherini 2015)*

The resultant 2016 EU Global Strategy is an attempt to deal with this polyphony and diversity of opinion (Tocci 2016). The formation and projection of the EU's strategic narrative is, therefore, suffused with political infighting. Thus, the projection of the EU's foreign policy narrative is often considered to be a process of masking internal divisions among Member States and EU institutions, rather than an exercise in exerting external influence (Nicolaïdis and Howse 2002). The EU foreign policy narrative is an amalgam of different, often competing, voices within

Brussels and narratives emanating from Member States' capitals. Contestation over 'whose story wins' (House of Lords 2014: 53; Nye 2013), therefore takes place both within the EU and externally. Coordination is the major challenge EU foreign policy narrative formation and projection face. On technical aspects of ENP, a bureaucratic, legalistic narrative is most prominent. On issues of overtly 'high politics', the narrative is driven by Member States' interests (Howorth 2017). These bureaucratic and political narratives have clashed, however, on issues such as continuing EU–Russia scientific cooperation, despite EU sanctions on Russia being simultaneously in place over the conflict in Ukraine (Forsberg and Haukkala 2016). This lack of a joined policy has amplified incoherent narratives on the issues, such as the Ukraine conflict, which will be explored below.

Despite the challenges which the EU faces to project a compelling narrative in its neighbourhood, Drezner argues that articulating a strategy can have a positive effect. He argues that, '[. . .] it can drive home messages about a country's intentions to domestic and foreign audiences' (Drezner 2011: 58). The EU is clearly experiencing a period of deep uncertainty. This uncertainty manifests itself with the growing questioning of the benefits of European integration, and uncertainty about the EU's ability to shape and help pacify the space beyond the EU's borders. Drezner goes on to argue that

> A grand strategy consists of a clear articulation of national interests married to a set of operational plans for advancing them . . . strategic narratives are offered as coherent explanations connecting past policies with future ones. Either way, a well-articulated grand strategy can offer an interpretative framework that tells everybody, including foreign policy officials themselves, how to understand the administration's behavior.
> *(Drezner 2011: 58)*

A strategic narrative on the ENP, therefore, could serve as a framework for action for those involved in delivering the objectives of neighbourhood policy. But it also explains for non-EU states for why the EU has acted in the neighbourhood as it has and how it understands its future involvement.

The EU has begun a gradual, but important, shift in its narrative on the ENP since the beginning of thinking about neighbourhood in the 1990s (see Table 14.1). Moving from a general narrative of promoting universal rights and technical cooperation, such as in the Euro-Mediterranean Partnership, the EU's narrative has become one of being ready to draw distinctions in relations with individual partners. Initially, the ENP was viewed as an attempt to educate countries in the region who aspired to be more like the EU (Browning and Joenniemi 2008; Dimitrovova 2012). The impact of the EU's influence on non-EU states is quite mixed (Björkdahl et al. 2015), often characterised by selective adaptation to EU norms and uneven implementation and enforcement of rules in third countries (Lavenex and Schimmelfennig 2009; 2011; Acharya 2004).

In the review of the ENP carried out in 2015, the resulting joint communication states:

> The EU's own stability is built on democracy, human rights and the rule of law and economic openness and the new ENP will take stabilisation as its main political priority in this mandate.
> *(European Commission and High Representative of the European Union for Foreign Affairs and Security Policy 2015)*

Differentiation and greater mutual ownership will be the hallmark of the new ENP, recognising that not all partners aspire to EU rules and standards and reflecting the wishes of each country

Table 14.1 Summary of main narrative content on ENP in key EU documents

	EU identity narratives	System narratives	ENP policy narratives
Euro-Mediterranean Partnership, 1995	An actor fostering cooperation; A partner for neighbouring states.	Promote regional security through de-militarisation; Strategic importance of the Mediterranean space; Bilateral ties; Aim to turn the Mediterranean space in to an area of dialogue, exchange and cooperation to guarantee peace, stability, prosperity.	Highlights economic and social development; Focus on social, cultural and human capital.
'Wider Europe', 2003	Emerging, weighty player in Europe post-2004 enlargement; ENP states as EU's 'essential partners'; Promoter of regional and intra-regional cooperation; Provider of vision for neighbourhood.	Enlargement is changing the continent; Borders are changing in Europe; Interdependence with neighbourhood; No new dividing lines in Europe.	Russia, western NIS, Southern Mediterranean states to have stake in EU internal market; Common interests with neighbouring states; Proximity, prosperity, poverty; Conflict prevention; Differentiated, progressive and benchmarked approach.
European Security Strategy, 2003	EU as promoter of peace and prosperity; EU as a Global Player; Ready to share responsibility in the world; Potential to be formidable force for good in the world.	Stable environment, though challenges will remain; Challenges largely within states, rather than between states; Terrorism, WMDs, regional conflict, state failure, organised crime are major challenges; Mediterranean facing economic stagnation, social unrest, unresolved crises; EU desires a rules-based order; Multilateralism.	No new dividing lines post-EU enlargement; Promotion of stability in states on EU's borders; Consider broader engagement with Arab states; Continued engagement with Mediterranean partners in Euro-Mediterranean Partnership.

(Continued)

Table 14.1 (continued)

	EU identity narratives	System narratives	ENP policy narratives
ENP Review, 2011	The EU is rising to challenges of neighbourhood; EU as the main trading partner.	Conflict is defining the neighbourhood; Destabilisation in Southern Mediterranean.	ENP understood as alignment of the EU Member States' bilateral efforts to support political objectives; Limited success supporting political reforms; Greater differentiation between partner states; Conditionality; Building deep democracy, civil society; political and security cooperation; economic and social development; trade; Strengthening Eastern Partnership; Union for the Mediterranean; European Neighbourhood Instrument.
ENP Review, 2015	Need for stronger EU foreign policy.	Neighbourhood less stable than 10 years ago; Economic and social pressures, irregular migration and refugee flows, security threats; Variations in engagement with the EU; Impact of major economic crisis.	UfM and Eastern Partnership strengthens approach; ENP has not served EU interests; Integration of ENP with overall foreign policy interests of EU; Greater involvement of EU Member States; Stability promotion; Differentiation, focus, flexibility, ownership and visibility.
EU Global Strategy, 2016	EU's unique advantage to cope with complex, contested world; EU as a contested union; Largest global donor; Leader in development and humanitarian assistance; Inflexible actor; EU perceived as less prosperous; Temporarily tarnished reputation due to eurocrisis; EU is less influential than it could be.	Changing global order; Connected, contested and complex world; Power shifts and power diffusion; Challenges overwhelmingly in neighbourhood; Globalisation as both good and bad; Geo-economic pressures; Growth in ungoverned spaces in Mediterranean; BRICS do not have common values or interests.	Forging a new social contract with EU citizens through foreign policy; Need special relationship with neighbours; ENP fostering reform minded citizens in neighbourhood.

concerning the nature and focus of its partnership with the EU. The EU alone cannot solve the many challenges of the region and there are limits to its leverage, but the new ENP will play its part in helping to create the conditions for positive development (ibid.:2).

This narrative shift towards interest-driven stabilisation promotion is a major change to previous articulations of the ENP narrative. Biscop has consistently argued that the ENP should be driven more by strategic calculation due to the challenges it faces in the eastern and southern neighbourhood (Biscop 2015). ENP is now part of the foreign policy narrative of the EU as a clear indication of the move towards a more interest-driven stance. The EU Global Strategy 2016 cements this development, which outlines a narrative to frame this move towards what it defines as 'principled pragmatism' (Biscop 2016: 1; European Union 2016). This is detailed in a clear shift in the EU's narrative from stressing the promotion of rules and norms to the stabilisation of incumbent regimes. Börzel argues that this more pragmatic posture is evidenced with the EU more interested in good governance in the neighbourhood than in promoting radical democratic transformation, as promised at the genesis of the ENP (Börzel 2015).

Reception in the study of strategic narratives highlights the challenges political actors have in influencing others (Miskimmon, O'Loughlin and Roselle 2013). This is where the inconsistencies of the EU's identity, system and issue narratives are exposed to criticism and divergent interpretations. This has the impact of limiting the EU's influence and calls into question the legitimacy of the EU as a foreign policy actor. Attempts to influence neighbourhood countries to implement democratic and economic reforms, in line with the EU's core ENP narrative, have proved problematic, putting the EU's narrative into question. In the case of Tunisia in the first decade of the twenty-first century, Mohamed Zayani argues that

> Western interests in preserving the existing power structure trumped the advancement of human rights and the institutionalization of democracy [. . .] The Western inclination to prioritize stability over the promotion of democracy favoured a de facto complicity that was in line with national interests. Although concerned about human rights violations, the West was disinclined to exert real pressure to reform or undermine the regime. Likewise, the regime's lack of progress toward – and indeed, conscious moves to undermine – real democratic reform and its imposition of constraints on individual liberty and on civil society did not lessen European support for Tunisia's bid for an advanced status within the EU.
>
> *(Zayani 2015: 50)*

This is a direct challenge to the EU's identity narrative. The 2016 EU Global Strategy indicates an acceptance of this criticism and a more realistic framing of the EU's expectations of ENP countries. In the time between the beginning of the strategic review and the final wording of the global strategy, alongside the stabilisation narrative, a parallel narrative of resilience emerges. With stabilisation of the neighbourhood as the explicit EU goal, resilience in partner states is presented to achieve this. The strategy outlines that, 'State and societal resilience is our strategic priority in the neighbourhood' (European Union 2016: 25). This narrative shift could have the potential to have greater alignment between the EU's identity narrative and its issue narrative, by reducing expectations on the EU to prioritise human rights and democracy promotion in its foreign policy towards the neighbourhood.

System narratives focus on the type of international order an actor wants. The EU has situated the ENP in wider narratives of its neighbourhoods, with the overriding aim of stabilisation, above the aim of normative influence. However, outlining a longer-term narrative of the regional order is more complicated. Indeed, even when Russia's actions in Ukraine since

2014 threatened the established regional order in Eastern Europe, the EU was unable to respond. As Juncos and Whitman have argued,

> Despite this being the one region where one would expect the EU to have some clout, the EU's political and economic influence in its neighbourhood was marginal in 2014. Furthermore, the foundations of the post-Cold War regional order within which the EU is embedded were called into question by the Russian Federation's use of force to seize Crimea from Ukraine, its increasing meddling in enlargement politics and the emergence of non-state actors such as ISIS with the capacity to overturn the authority and rule of existing nation-states. The EU's milieu-shaping goals and instruments are not equipped for these challenges. An EU response equivalent to the magnitude of these challenges did not take shape during the course of the year.
>
> (Juncos and Whitman 2015: 212)

The EU has not outlined a long-term system narrative of its neighbourhood. Indeed, Haukkala suggests that the EU has been unwilling to consider the strategic implications of its policies in this space and has not developed long-term thinking to guide its activities (Haukkala 2016: 654). The EU Global Strategy 2016 is the latest attempt by the EU to outline its view of the world and its place within it. The EU's narrative stresses

> A multilateral order grounded in international law, including the principles of the UN Charter and the Universal Declaration of Human Rights, is the only guarantee of peace and security at home and abroad. A rules-based global order unlocks the full potential of a prosperous Union with open economies and deep global connections, and embeds democratic values within the international system.
>
> (European Union 2016: 15–16)

The EU Global Strategy outlines a narrative of the world as a 'complex world of global power shifts and power diffusion' (European Union 2016: 16). This system narrative portrays the EU as an upholder of values in a world where not all states share its views. While this situation continues, it will pursue a policy of 'principled pragmatism' (Biscop 2016:1), to ensure it can achieve its aims. However, the Russian annexation of Crimea demonstrates how big a challenge the EU faces to uphold a rules-based conception of international order in its neighbourhood (Kuzio 2017).

The EU Global Strategy makes it clear that the EU faces competition to shape the regional order. The strategy tells a story of a world that is increasingly marked by competition, with new actors wanting what they see as their rightful say in international affairs. Similarly, Schweller suggests that the plurality of narratives of the emerging international order is causing major disruption. He argues that

> Profound dislocations throughout the global system are causing the narrative of world politics to become an increasingly fragmented and disjointed story. Like a postmodern novel, the plot features a wild menagerie of wildly incongruent themes and unlikely protagonists, as if divinely plucked from different historical ages and placed in a time machine set for the third millennium.
>
> (Schweller 2014: 9)

The EU must confront alternative narratives from other players in its neighbourhood. In addition, the EU is projecting its narrative of international order within a complex media ecology that is characterised by an increasing number of voices transmitted through the internet and social media, which has transformed the ways in which states must communicate. Soft power ultimately rests on communication and the new media ecology has opened new ways for state and non-state actors to communicate with target audiences, and to challenge the communication of others (Roselle, Miskimmon and O'Loughlin 2014). The EU faces vigorous challenges to its foreign policy narrative that have the potential to undermine its efficacy as a foreign policy actor (Tonra 2011). Rejection of the EU's narrative of international order is highlighted in narrative de-alignment with other major players, which can be seen in the Ukraine conflict and the EU's relations with Russia.

We have examined problems with the EU's identity, issue and system narratives, rooted in problems of diversity and inconsistency, and a gap between how the EU narrates order and its capacity to influence it. Together, these imply difficulties for the EU in aligning narratives across those three levels of analysis and action and presenting a coherent story of its place in the world to other powers. To illustrate these difficulties, we shall investigate one ENP instance of the EU responding to its narrative struggle in detail, the case of Ukraine.

The case of Ukraine

The conflict that emerged in Ukraine in 2014 is a good example of how narrative de-alignment between actors shapes responses to events and restricts the resolution of crises and conflicts (Miskimmon and O'Loughlin 2014). It also highlights the internal contradictions in the EU's own strategic narrative formation and the difficulties the EU faces in influencing its neighbourhood. The EU has faced considerable challenges in forging a collective foreign policy narrative on Ukraine. As outlined above, the EU's strategic narrative is generally characterised by polyphony, rather than a single voice, greatly complicating its ability to respond coherently to crises. International organisations often struggle to overcome their internal plurality of voices in forging a strategic narrative. The EU is not alone in facing this predicament (Singh 2017). Nevertheless, the conflict has in many ways resulted in a modest galvanisation of the ENP, albeit within the confines of the continued structural fragilities of EU foreign policy cooperation. This has impacted on the formation of the EU's identity narrative as a foreign policy actor. The Ukraine conflict and the EU's limited response has been a test for the EU's identity narrative as a regional pacifier and upholder of universal values. In its narration of the conflict, it sought to bridge the inconsistencies between its identity narrative and its actions, to reinforce its ontological security in the face of foreign policy change (Subotic 2016).

In the face of the challenge posed by instability on its borders, the EU's identity narrative has developed throughout the conflict. A new identity of an emerging global player, no longer able to avoid its international responsibility, has become evident. This has emerged alongside a shifting system narrative, which reflects a more pragmatic role for the EU in international affairs. The new system narrative has several core components. First, the EU continues to view international order in terms of interdependence of major powers. Stable relations, with a focus on partnership with other major powers, are central to a robust international order. Strategic partners are central to this narrative. Third, consistent with its traditional narrative of the international system, the EU asserts that international order should be founded on good governance, the rule of law, democratic principles and human rights. The major shift in the system narrative is a move towards conceiving the world as increasingly complex and contested – emerging narratives challenging the EU's conception of international order are to be forcefully challenged (High Representative of the Union for Foreign Affairs and Security Policy 2015; European Union 2016).

These identity and system narratives inform and are influenced by the continuing conflict in Ukraine and are explicit in the EU's issue narrative of the conflict. The EU faced considerable criticism of its involvement. Applebaum (2014) argues that the general acceptance in the West of a post-Cold War narrative of Russian decline has masked the emergence of a more authoritarian Russia, evidence of which can be seen in the Ukraine conflict. She suggests that the acceptance of the narrative of Russian decline has meant that the West has found it difficult to respond to Russian president Putin's more assertive behaviour. Former German Chancellor, Gerhard Schröder, even suggested that the West had been partly responsible for Russia's actions by pushing Russia into a corner through the EU's and NATO's expansionist policies (Kirschbaum 2014). Nevertheless, the EU continues to stress the comprehensive approach to crises in its narrative on ENP, where solutions are not conceived solely in military terms. Secondly, the EU outlines that it should promote its interests and values and encourage others to share those. These values challenge those of Russia and their alternative conceptions of freedom, sovereignty, security and human rights. Third, the EU has explicitly stated that it is in strategic competition with the BRICS (Mogherini, 2015). Fourth, Russia is acting illegally in Ukraine (European Union 2016: 33). Finally, as with NATO's issue narrative on Ukraine, the bilateral relations with Russia are increasingly strained.

Differences and similarities between the EU and Russian positions are recognisable in how they have sought to narrate the conflict. Vieira argues that Russia's narrative has changed from a narrative stressing efficiency in business relations with the West and a narrative of global connectivity, to one which returns to stressing the importance of Russia's 'near abroad' and a narrative that casts Russia a counterweight to the EU (Vieira 2016a, 2016b). Vieira suggests that this re-emergence of a narrative of the near abroad contributed to Moscow's more forceful policy towards Ukraine. Russia's identity narrative under president Putin has stressed Russia as a global player, a proud civilisation with a substantial heritage in culture and scientific discovery, which has been deliberately excluded by the West. There is some overlap with the EU in how Russia narrates international order. President Putin has stressed the need for a Common European Home, a narrative harking back to the end of the Cold War, aimed at preventing the emergence of new dividing lines in Europe after the fall of the Iron Curtain and a narrative which is prominent in the ENP. Putin has also projected a narrative of the BRICS and the emergence of a polycentric world, less centred on Europe, which is also a narrative present in the EU Global Strategy. However, Putin's narrative is more forcefully expressed in the idea of 'competitive struggle' (*konkurentnaya borba*), which is understood as a deliberate attempt to counter the influence of the West. A communication strategy challenging Western narratives is central to this strategy (Szostek 2016). President Putin has called for an international order based on the centrality of international law founded on state sovereignty, as a direct challenge to the interventionist policies of the West. Narratives on the Ukraine conflict itself display significant de-alignment between the EU and Russia. Russia's narrative on Ukraine emphasises the deliberate attempts by the EU to project a narrative of Russian aggression, dangerous propagandising on Russia's part and deliberate attempts to paint Russia as an enemy. Russia also sought to use its system narrative of the importance of international law to criticise Western interference in Ukraine and disrespect for the democratic freedom of Ukrainians (Haukkala 2015; 2016).

The identity, system and issue narratives of the EU and Russia are summarised in Table 14.2.

This de-alignment led to a substantial shift in public opinion in Russia on the EU, changing from a largely positive outlook towards the EU to a negative stance (Lipman 2016) – thus making EU efforts to influence domestic opinion in Russia very constrained. While Russia's attempts to reinforce its great power narrative had positive effects domestically, with public opinion supportive of the government, they had negative effects internationally, by hampering attempts for political

Table 14.2 The identity, system and issue narratives of the EU and Russia

	Identity	System	Issue
EU	New identity narrative of an emerging global player; Ever closer union – despite the challenges of the eurocrisis and Brexit; The EU demonstrates by example the benefits of democracy and human rights.	World characterised by demands of interdependence; Relations with others central to stable international order, based on partnership; Founded on governance, rule of law, democracy, human rights – and principled pragmatism with reluctant states; World increasingly contested and complex – alternative narratives emerging should be challenged.	Comprehensive approach to crisis management; Promoting interests and universal values; Russia undermining freedom, sovereignty, security and minority rights; Strategic competition with BRICS; Russian aggression in Ukraine; Russia acting illegally; Russian is conducting hybrid war; Russia is no longer a 'strategic partner'.
Russia	Russia as a Global Player; Civilisation with heritage of culture and science; Excluded and badly treated by the West.	For a Common European Home – a common economic and humanitarian space (Putin); Europe less central to world order – emergence of BRICS; Return of East/West confrontation in Europe; Polycentric world order; International order should have a legal framework, founded on state sovereignty. Russia is part of a 'competitive struggle' (*konkurentnaya borba*) with the West.	Western media propagating new Cold War narrative; EU/NATO not respecting freedom of Ukrainian people; Absence of strategic trust in EU/Russia relations; EU exaggerates friend/foe narrative; Sanctions unjust, not merited. *Coup d'état* in Ukraine supported by outsiders; Western provocation and flouting of international law; Russia helping Ukraine to overcome crisis.

agreement between the EU and Russia (Szostek 2014; 2016). Despite the diplomacy of the Minsk agreements (Bentzen and Anosovs 2015), no unified narrative of the conflict shared by the main actors has emerged. In response to this, the EU has sought to address the inconsistencies within its own identity and issue narrative of the conflict to defend its limited response. This is in line with wider shifts in the EU's narrative on the ENP, which has focused on reinforcing the EU's own identity narrative in the face of the complex challenges it faces (Schumacher 2015).

The strategic narratives of the EU and Russia above indicate areas where there is overlap and scope for potential agreement. The EU shares Russia's system narrative understanding of the emerging world order as one of multiple powerful leading actors. They also emphasise the importance of an international order that should be based on a legal framework and they both narrate their identities as being global players. Focusing on these narratives could uncover areas of agreement that would open space for wider agreement on international crises they are both confronting.

Conclusions

The EU's strategic narrative of ENP is a central pillar of the EU's emerging foreign policy. The EU has found it challenging to outline a narrative of its role in the neighbourhood that is both domestically accepted and externally persuasive. Indeed, the 'intolerable incongruities' (Bially Mattern 2005: 99) of the EU's strategic narrative have been damaging to the EU's international credibility and given its critics within EU Member States ample material to challenge its claim to be an emerging foreign policy actor. Jones and Clark (2008) assert that the EU's efforts to Europeanise its neighbourhood to reinforce legitimacy within the EU and to promote regional influence limited the EU's actorness in the neighbourhood. Partly responsible for this inability to construct an effective strategic narrative are the continued structural limitations the EU faces. The EU is a hybrid actor – partly supranational, partly intergovernmental – that plays an inhibiting role in forging a united foreign policy. The EU does not have a strategic narrative that aligns across its narrative of identity and its narrative of the regional order. This is exposed in the issue narrative of ENP in which its approach to the region does not align with the identity and system narratives it projects. This opens the EU to criticism for not living up to the commitments it makes.

Shifts in how the EU narrates its identity, its view of the international system and the development of ENP have gone hand in hand with the changing role of the EU in the neighbourhood since the 1990s. The change in identity narrative has involved a more pronounced articulation of the EU's role in the world and outlined associated claims on greater international influence. The EU's narrative of the international system has changed over time from a relatively stable view of the neighbourhood to concerns over instability. The EU now understands the international system as one characterised by global connectivity, polycentrism and competition. Finally, the narrative of ENP itself has changed from one hopeful of transformation to one acknowledging the challenges of altering the status quo and a stress on EU interests when dealing with ENP partner states.

References

Acharya, A. (2004) 'How ideas spread: whose norms matter? Norm localization and institutional change in Asian regionalism', *International Organization* 58(2): 239–275.
Aggestam, L. (2008) 'Introduction: Ethical power Europe?', *International Affairs* 84(1): 1–11.
Applebaum, A. (2014) 'How he and his cronies stole Russia', *New York Review of Books,* 18 December, www.nybooks.com/articles/archives/2014/dec/18/how-he-and-his-cronies-stole-russia/.

Bentzen, N. and Anosovs, E. (2015) 'Briefing: Minsk peace agreement: Still to be consolidated on the ground', European Parliament Research Service, 12 February, www.europarl.europa.eu/EPRS/EPRS-Briefing-548991-Minsk-peace-summit-FINAL.pdf.

Bertelsmann Stiftung (2015) 'The EU Neighbourhood in shambles', www.bertelsmann-stiftung.de/de/publikationen/publikation/did/the-eu-neighbourhood-in-shambles/

Bially Mattern, J. (2005) *Ordering International Politics: Identity, Crisis, and Representational Force*, New York: Routledge.

Biscop, S. (2015) 'Game of zones: Power struggles in the EU's neighbourhood', *Global Affairs* 1(4–5): 369–379.

Biscop, S. (2016) 'The EU Global Strategy: Realpolitik with European Characteristics', *Security Policy Brief* 75, Brussels: Egmont Institute.

Björkdahl, A., Chaban, N., Leslie, J. and Masselot, A. (eds.) (2015) *Importing EU Norms: Conceptual Framework and Empirical Findings*, New York: Springer.

Börzel, T. (2015) 'The noble West and the dirty rest? Western democracy promoters and illiberal regional powers', *Democratization* 22(3): 519–535.

Börzel, T. and van Hüllen, V. (2014) 'One voice, one message, but conflicting goals: Cohesiveness and consistency in the European Neighbourhood Policy', *Journal of European Public Policy* 21(7): 1033–1049.

Browning, C. and Christou, G. (2010) 'The constitutive power of outsiders: The European Neighbourhood Policy and the eastern dimension', *Political Geography* 29(2): 109–118.

Browning, C. and Joenniemi, P. (2008) 'Geostrategies of the European Neighbourhood Policy', *European Journal of International Relations* 14(3): 519–551.

Celata, F. and Coletti, R. (2015) 'Beyond Fortress "EU"rope? Bordering and Cross-Bordering Along the European External Frontiers', in Celata, F. and Coletti, R. (eds.) *Neighbourhood Policy and the Construction of the European External Borders*, New York: Springer, 1–25.

Della Sala, V. (2010) 'Political myth, mythology and the European Union', *JCMS* 48(1): 1–19.

Dimitrovova, B. (2012) 'Imperial re-bordering of Europe: The case of the European Neighbourhood Policy', *Cambridge Review of International Affairs* 25(2): 249–267.

Drezner, D. (2011) 'Does Obama have a grand strategy: Why we need doctrines in uncertain times', *Foreign Affairs* 90(57): 57–68.

Duchêne, F. (1972) 'Europe's Role in World Peace', in Mayne, R. (ed.) *Europe Tomorrow: Sixteen Europeans Look Ahead London*, London: Fontana.

Duchêne, F. (1973) 'The European Community and the Uncertainties of Interdependence', in Kohlstamm, M. and Hager, W. (eds.) *Nation Writ Large: Foreign Policy Problems Before the European Communities*, London: Macmillan.

Epstein, R. and Jacoby, W. (2014) 'Eastern enlargement ten years on: Transcending the East–West divide?', *JCMS* 52(1): 1–16.

European Commission and High Representative of the European Union for Foreign Affairs and Security Policy (2015) *Review of the European Neighbourhood Policy*, JOIN (2015) 50 Final, Brussels, 18 November.

European Union (2016) *Shared Vision, Common Action: A Stronger Europe. A Global Strategy for the European Union's Foreign and Security Policy*, Brussels: European Union.

Forsberg, T. and Haukkala, H. (2016) *The European Union and Russia*, Basingstoke: Palgrave Macmillan.

Haukkala, H. (2015) 'From cooperative to contested Europe? The conflict in Ukraine as a culmination of a long-term crisis in EU–Russia relations', *Journal of Contemporary European Studies* 23(1): 25–40.

Haukkala, H. (2016) 'A perfect storm; or what went wrong and what went right for the EU in Ukraine', *Europe-Asia Studies* 68(4): 653–664.

High Representative of the Union for Foreign Affairs and Security Policy (2015) *The European Union in a Changing Global Environment: A More Connected, Contested and Complex World*.

Hill, C. (1993) 'The capability-expectations gap, or conceptualizing Europe's international role', *JCMS* 31(3): 305–328.

House of Lords (2014) *Persuasion and Power in the Modern World*, London: The Stationery Office, www.publications.parliament.uk/pa/ld201314/ldselect/ldsoftpower/150/150.pdf.

Howorth, J. (2017) "Stability on the borders": The Ukraine crisis and the EU's constrained policy towards the eastern neighbourhood', *JCMS* 55(1): 121–136.

Jones, A. and Clark, J. (2008) 'Europeanisation and discourse building: The European Commission, European narratives and European Neighbourhood Policy', *Geopolitics* 13(3): 545–571.

Juncos, A. and Whitman, R. (2015) 'Europe as a regional actor: Neighbourhood lost?', *JCMS* 53(1): 200–215.

Kirschbaum, E. (2014) 'Putin's apologist? Germany's Schröder says they're just friends', *Reuters*, 27 March, www.reuters.com/article/ukraine-russia-schroeder-idUSL5N0MN3ZI20140327.

Kuzio, T. (2017) 'Ukraine between a constrained EU and assertive Russia', *JCMS* 55(1): 103–120.
Lacroix, J. and Nicolaïdis, K. (2010) *European Stories: Intellectual Debates on Europe in National Contexts*, Oxford: Oxford University Press.
Lavenex, S. and Schimmelfennig, F. (2009) 'EU rules beyond EU borders: Theorizing external governance in European politics', *Journal of European Public Policy* 16(6): 791–812.
Lavenex, S. and Schimmelfennig, F. (2011) 'EU democracy promotion in the neighbourhood: From leverage to governance?', *Democratization* 18(4): 885–909.
Lipman, M. (2016) 'What Russia thinks of Europe', European Council on Foreign Relations, 2 February, www.ecfr.eu/article/commentary_what_russia_thinks_of_europe5084#.VrjuVm1zvE4.gmail.
Manners, I. (2002) 'Normative power Europe: A contradiction in terms?', *JCMS* 40(2): 235–258.
Manners, I. and Murray, P. (2016) 'The end of a noble narrative? European integration narratives after the Nobel Peace Prize', *JCMS* 54(1): 185–202.
Miskimmon, A. and O'Loughlin, B. (2014) 'Weaponising information: Putin, the West and competing strategic narratives of Ukraine', *European Geostrategy*, 18 December, www.europeangeostrategy.org/2014/12/weaponising-information-putin-west-competing-strategic-narratives-ukraine/.
Miskimmon, A., O'Loughlin, B. and Roselle, L. (2013) *Strategic Narratives: Communication Power and the New World Order*, New York: Routledge.
Miskimmon, A., O'Loughlin, B. and Roselle, L. (eds.) (2017) *Forging the World: Strategic Narratives and International Affairs*, Ann Arbor: University of Michigan Press.
Mogherini, F. (2015) 'The European Union in a changing global environment: A more connected, contested and complex world', https://europa.eu/globalstrategy/en/file/12/download?token=0QM7p8iJ.
Nicolaïdis, K. and Howse, R. (2002) 'This is my EUtopia . . .': narrative as power', *JCMS* 40(4): 767–792.
Nye Jr, J. (2013) 'Transcript of Witness Testimony to the House of Lords Select Committee on Soft Power and UK Influence', 15 October, www.parliament.uk/documents/lords-committees/soft-power-uk-influence/uc151013Ev10.pdf.
Polletta, F. (1998) 'Contending stories: Narrative in social movements', *Qualitative Sociology* 21(4): 419–446.
Roselle, L., Miskimmon, A. and O'Loughlin, B. (2014) 'Strategic narrative: A new means to understand soft power', *Media, War & Conflict* 7(1): 70–84.
Rudd, K. (2015) 'How Ancient Chinese thought applies today', *New Perspectives Quarterly* 32 (2015):8–23.
Schimmelfennig, F. (2003) *The EU, NATO and the Integration of Europe: Rules and Rhetoric*, Cambridge: Cambridge University Press.
Schumacher, T. (2015) 'Uncertainty at the EU's borders: Narratives of EU external relations in the revised European Neighbourhood Policy towards the southern borderlands', *European Security* 24(3): 381–401.
Schweller, R. (2014) *Maxwell's Demon and the Golden Apple: Global Discord in the New Millennium*, Baltimore, MA: Johns Hopkins University Press.
Singh, V. (2017) 'Beyond Neoliberalism: Contested Narratives of International Development', in Miskimmon, A., O'Loughlin, B. and Roselle, L. (eds.) *Forging the World: Strategic Narratives and International Affairs*, Ann Arbor: University of Michigan Press, 134–163.
Subotic, J. (2016) 'Narrative, ontological security, and foreign policy change', *Foreign Policy Analysis* 12: 610–627.
Szostek, J. (2014) 'Russia and the news media in Ukraine a case of "Soft Power"?', *East European Politics & Societies* 28(3): 463–486.
Szostek, J. (2016) 'Defence and promotion of desired state identity in Russia's strategic narrative', *Geopolitics*, DOI: 10.1080/14650045.2016.1214910.
Tocci, N. (2016) 'The making of the EU global strategy', *Contemporary Security Policy* 37(3): 461–472.
Tonra, B. (2011) 'Democratic foundations of EU foreign policy: Narratives and the myth of EU exceptionalism', *Journal of European Public Policy* 18(8): 1190–1207.
Vieira, A. (2016a) 'Eurasian integration: Elite perspectives before and after the Ukraine crisis', *Post-Soviet Affairs* 32(6): 566–580.
Vieira, A. (2016b) 'Ukraine, Russia and the strategic partnership dynamics in the EU's eastern neighbourhood: Recalibrating the EU's "self", "we" and "other"', *Cambridge Review of International Affairs* 29(1): 128–150.
Zayani, M. (2015) *Networked Publics and Digital Contention: The Politics of Everyday Life in Tunisia*, Oxford: Oxford University Press.
Zielonka, J. (2014) *Is the EU Doomed?*, Cambridge: John Wiley & Sons.

15
THE CHALLENGES OF A CHANGING EASTERN NEIGHBOURHOOD

Elena Korosteleva

Introduction

In this chapter, we will examine the challenges posed by the changing eastern neighbourhood and the (in)adequacy of the European Union's (EU) response to this dynamic and volatile region.

Ever since the launch of the European Neighbourhood Policy (ENP) in 2004 and the Eastern Partnership (EaP) Initiative in 2009, the EU has been seeking ways to make its policies more sustainable – that is, more effective and legitimate – in the increasingly complex and contested environment (European External Action Service 2015) of the eastern region. In its reflective endeavours, as this chapter argues, the EU has undergone at least three paradigmatic shifts in its strategic approach to the region, which included: regional differentiation, diversification of policy instruments, extending outreach to all-level actors and fine-tuning the budget. And yet, by the EU's own admission, over a decade on, 'today's neighbourhood is less stable than it was ten years ago', being permeated by ever more complex and security-predicated challenges such as 'the crisis in Georgia in 2008 [and] the ongoing conflict in Ukraine' (European Commission and High Representative of the European Union for Foreign Affairs and Security Policy 2015a: 2).

The slow and uneven progress of reform in the eastern neighbourhood has been further exacerbated by the growing influence of the Eurasian Economic Union (EEU) – the initiative instigated by Kazakhstan in 2007 and actively driven by Russia ever since (Dragneva and Wolczuk 2013). The EEU comes to offer a contrasting regional alternative to that of the EaP (Delcour 2008) and has succeeded in diluting neighbours' commitment and swaying allegiances away from the EU course.

In this unfolding 'arc of crisis running across its neighbourhood' (Juncos and Whitman 2015: 200), the EU now finds itself confronted by multiple economic, political and, especially, security challenges – for the large share of which it blames 'an increasingly assertive Russian foreign policy', seeing it as a primary cause of instability, 'security threats and diverging aspirations' (European Commission and High Representative of the European Union for Foreign Affairs and Security Policy 2015a: 2) in the region. The escalating EU–Russia stand-off is deeply disturbing in its implications for the region, not to mention the broken global order, proliferation of frozen conflicts and continuing loss of human lives.

While some of the EU's blame attribution may be justifiable, and it is indeed shocking to witness 'the use of state power [by Russia] to alter borders and impose its will on its neighbours' (Juncos and Whitman 2015: 200), in the post-Cold War European order, the underlying causes of instability are far more complex than is currently understood. This chapter argues that in this increasingly inter-connected and unstable global order, the blame could be equally assigned to *both* the EU and Russia, for their neglect of '*the other*' and, especially, of the less-protected recipient-countries of the region. First, we will briefly review the EU's reflective attempts to adjust its policy to the eastern neighbourhood and the latter's variable response and commitment to reform. Second, we will contend that the EaP has effectively been developing almost in parallel and, yet, until recently, unaware of the engendered Eurasian economic space – often a spoiler to European integration. Drawing on the above, the chapter will conclude that, while a domestic landscape and specific problems of the region – associated with engrained corruption, Soviet legacies and differing cultural affinities – are relevant for explaining a slow progress of change, they may be peripheral to the wider picture. A larger underlying concern for the wider region is the lack of *positive othering* in the EU's (and Russia's) foreign policy, which would involve not just an acknowledgement or recognition of differences but, more importantly, would become a process of learning about one another to transcend them. In the absence of the latter, power relations, as the EU's case testifies, would continue to perpetuate the same old fallacy – a Self-centred understanding of the *outside* and the ensuing perception of the latter as different, inferior and potentially as a threat, generated by the rejection of the *other*.

Setting the scene: the Eastern Partnership as EU Governance

The EU has come a long way in spearheading a new approach to the outside, and its neighbourhood. Its modus operandi in the eastern region has progressed from standard Partnership and Cooperation Agreements (PCAs) of the mid-1990s to more novel and advanced forms of cooperation – the Association Agreements (AAs) – in 2014, under the framework of the ENP/EaP. This demonstrates the EU's *reflective* way of structuring its regional presence, which is often defined in the scholarly and policy debates as 'External Governance', signifying, in the EU context, an effort to coordinate and control its external environment, by way of extending its internal rule structures and practices to the outside world (Lavenex 2004; Kohler-Koch and Rittberger 2006; Börzel 2010; Gänzle 2009). We will briefly examine some major milestones in the evolution of EU governance driven by ENP countries' response and engagement with the EaP, to uncover some *persistent disconnects* and challenges, which contribute to the rising volatility and insecurity in the EU's neighbourhood.

Our tentative analysis suggests that the EU has undergone at least three *paradigmatic shifts* in re-structuring its relations with the eastern neighbourhood, to make its policy more effective and legitimate. And yet, with each attempt, the EU seems to find itself further away from the very objectives it had originally set to pursue in the neighbourhood – that is, to bring prosperity, stability and security and to have a ring of well-governed states on the EU's doorstep (Council of the European Union 2003).

The first *paradigmatic shift* associates with a move *away* from enlargement towards a new policy instrument and strategy – the ENP – launched in 2004 after some considerable deliberations (Korosteleva 2011). While the policy aims were comprehensive and laudable, its vision and strategy were effectively curtailed by the success of the enlargement policy, at the time seen as 'unarguably the most successful foreign policy instrument' (Commission of the European Communities 2003: 5), in trying to model the new instrument on its design. Consequently, without much contextualisation, the EU's relations with the new neighbourhood assumed an 'enlargement-light' format of transferring the EU *acquis communautaire* – a so-called '*inside-out approach*' (Lavenex and Schimmelfennig 2010) – executed *via* strict conditionality in the membership-void circumstances (Delcour 2008). The prevalent features of EU governance included:

- a hierarchical mode of coordination favouring executive bias and bilateral communication with national governments;
- a binary way of inculcating EU normative practices: 'take-it' or 'leave-it' approach without accounting for regional socio-cultural differences;
- a prescriptive governance approach delivered as a rule *via* strict conditionality and disciplinary actions (sanctions, naming-and-shaming and other means of economic/political statecraft).

This EU approach could be termed as 'disciplinary governance', which, while successful in the case of enlargement, bore only limited effect on the neighbourhood. Instead, it registered some (minor) enthusiasm but, mostly, much disappointment and disaffection across the region.[1] Furthermore, it also generated some tacit resistance, especially at the public level, and even rejection in some exceptional cases (for example, Belarus and Azerbaijan). Overall, the policy was excessively prescriptive, inflexible and declarative, causing a discomforting sense of inferiority and power asymmetry in the ENP countries' relations with the EU, which considerably nudged the latter to reconsider its approach (Kelley 2006; Raik 2006; Korosteleva 2012).

In response to this rather disfavoured and poorly received policy, EU governance was subsequently revisited during 2006–7 and a more comprehensive policy iteration emerged by 2008 (Commission of the European Communities 2007). The EU sought to offer adjustments to the policy's instruments and policy outreach, to generate interest and involve new stakeholders for reform in the region. The new iteration was a second paradigmatic shift in EU governance. It brought about an important change: regionalisation of the policy and a more differentiated focus on the regional specificities (Commission of the European Communities 2008). The new approach was also associated with more decentring and more active ENP countries' participation in the policy process. Most notably, since 2009, the EU relations with the eastern neighbours envisaged more collaboration over different levels and across the region. This was initialled *via* a dual-track approach, which was meant to diversify channels of engagement and communication and to target those other than government actors in the recipient countries. This tool paved the way for the rise of civil society as an influential agency for promoting reforms in the neighbourhood. During this period (2008–11), the EU modus operandi was often seen as transitional – that is, experiential but not necessarily correcting the less effective forms of engagement. The EU governance of this period could be described as 'deliberative' rather than strictly disciplinary, affording – alongside some traditional forms of control and conditionality – greater input and ENP countries' involvement in the processes of policy negotiation and implementation (Delcour 2011). Yet, as the developments in the region indicated, captured by the Commission's Progress Reports and wider research, the policy continued to yield only a limited appeal, even among the most advanced and relatively committed partners of European integration – Ukraine, Georgia and Moldova. Notably, not only did a wider analysis of the region (Korosteleva et al. 2014; Kostanyan and Delcour 2014) underscore the growing necessity to differentiate and contextualise the policy – to understand how and why each ENP country differs in their needs and challenges – it also demonstrated persistently low levels of awareness and interest in the EU among the general population, concomitant with growing levels of policy dissatisfaction among the governing elites of the region. Many saw the EaP as incapable of catering for their differing aspirations and growing security concerns

(Korosteleva 2013; 2014). Dissatisfaction was further propelled by a discomforting sense of perceived rivalry between the EU and Russia in the eyes of the regional players, which was not visible to the EU, but which was palpable for the ENP countries who were increasingly pressured by the newly launched Eurasian Customs Union (ECU). The challenge for the EU was to find a new format to re-connect and reinforce neighbours' commitment to the EU course. Furthermore, the EU had to start recognising the presence and active interest of other geostrategic actors in the region, which was vigorously demonstrated by Russia's first assertive border challenge in Georgia in August 2008.

The third crucial shift in the evolution of EU governance came about in 2011, and was reflected in the newly revised neighbourhood strategy (European Commission and High Representative of the European Union for Foreign Affairs and Security Policy 2011). The strategy placed more emphasis on 'common interest' than 'common values' and 'the spirit of shared ownership and mutual accountability' (Council of the European Union 2011: 1). It also intended to offer greater diversification of EU instruments and higher financial commitment. Furthermore, the strategy also pioneered a more technocratic approach, in the form of new roadmaps and association agendas for individual countries, to see if this more transactional and low politics approach could reconcile some growing geopolitical tensions in the region. Additionally, instead of further policy contextualisation, some new policy instruments were put in place to garner even wider outreach than ever before – this time engaging all levels of society, from grassroots NGOs and local authorities to regional and national level government agents and businesses. This approach not only consolidated the know-how of the EU governance framework, building on its progress and policy failure; it also brought together an incredible machinery of EU tools and instruments – 'more for more' – which, if connected to the needs and interests of the recipient parties, had the potential to alter the political landscape of the eastern neighbourhood (Korosteleva et al. 2014). This new EU governance approach, which was more 'from a distance' and less intrusive and allowed for more local ownership, signified a breakthrough in the EU external approach, taking it to a new level plain. The main pioneering features of this new governance model included:

- control from a distance and only of the pertinent, allowing for more local ownership, agenda input and tailored solutions;
- a complex matrix of 'enablement' premised on voluntary engagement and rational freedom of choice, aiming to lock ENP countries in the perpetual mode of 'more for more cooperation';
- engagement of all levels of society: from civil society, business and education actors to local/regional authorities, national governments, parliaments and media representatives, thus generating all-inclusive grounds for mutual learning and socialisation into European norms and standards;
- 'optimal (rather than binary) space' between 'the permitted' and 'the prohibited', allowing neighbours to approximate rather than fully replicate European norms and values, thus accounting for and preserving their 'cultural space' as well;
- development of a dual track of engagement: making the bilateral track more technocratic (for example, roadmaps) and the multilateral track more 'political' to generate a sense of community and, this way, re-engineer public behaviour in the neighbourhood.

The EU has pioneered and applied, one of the principal (and latest) modalities of the EU engagement in the neighbourhood – AAs – to the ENP/EaP frontrunners, Ukraine, Moldova and Georgia. This modality was explicitly more technocratic, offering, on the one hand, an ensemble of a-political instruments and knowledge transfer to help the countries with their target reforms but, on the other, protruding the same old principle of convergence with the EU-centred norms and rules, without further contextualisation and attention to the emergent regional geopolitics. In this sense, these 'new' and potentially effective modalities simply became the embodiment of the 'old wine in new wineskins' (Kelley 2006) and, more than ever before, encapsulated the EU's parochial and endogenous style of governance – that is, treating external problems with internal solutions (Lavenex 2004), which may not always be best-suited for dealing with normatively divergent and contested environments.

This chapter argues that, while trying to be reflective in its undertakings in the eastern region, the EU has attempted to address the challenges and problems in the neighbourhood one-sidedly, failing to understand the reciprocal nature of power relations and, more notably, that its internal solutions may not necessarily be best suited for solving external regional complexities, as best exemplified by the situation in Ukraine (Dutkiewicz and Sakwa 2015; House of Lords 2015). In fact, while perfecting this complex machinery of enablement and outreach under the AA which, if implemented, could arguably offer 'a quantum leap towards the real transformation in that post soviet space' (Füle 2013a), it could be argued that the EU may have been producing some of the regional challenges itself by being excessively Eurocentric in its external relations. It may even be argued that this 'inside-out' approach has misjudged Ukraine's readiness to take the EU up on its offer, as part of the wider geostrategic regional dilemma, which subsequently ensured the escalation of conflict and the emergence of new dividing lines in the EaP region.

With all the changes in the neighbourhood and their continuing resentment and limited support for the EaP's objectives, the EU had to continue searching for a more refined and tailored strategy to engage. The newly revised ENP (European Commission and High Representative of the European Union for Foreign Affairs and Security Policy 2015b) places more emphasis on further differentiation and a more transactional/technocratic approach to the region. Yet, there is little reassurance that it may work better on its fourth substantive iteration, premised on two main assumptions – the EU's continued neglect of the developments in the Eurasian economic space and the un-learned lessons of Ukraine, which are explored in the following sections.

Contesting the scene: the Eurasian Union as Russia's geopolitical challenge

The EU has clearly underestimated the increasingly influential regional economic project of Eurasian integration, driven by Russia.

Following the dissolution of the Soviet Union and the subsequent inter-state integration tendencies – especially in economic and humanitarian fields (Delcour 2008) – in 2007, Russia, Belarus and Kazakhstan, at the latter's initiative, inaugurated the ECU, a Russian-led, region-building project in the post-Soviet space as an alternative to the EU. The construction of the ECU, and the subsequent EEU, allegedly emulates the EU's supranational structures (Dragneva and Wolczuk 2013), and has moved considerably, from signing the initial treaty on the ECU Commission and Common Territory (2007) to establishing the ECU in 2011, and a single economic space (SES) in 2012, which was soon heralded by the launch of the EEU in 2015, with further expansion of its membership to include Armenia and Kyrgyzstan. Highlighting the pace of this fast-growing regional integration, Vladimir Putin commented:

> It took Europe 40 years to move from the European Coal and Steel Community to the full European Union. The establishment of the Customs Union and the Common Economic Space is proceeding at a much faster pace because we could draw on the

experience of the EU and other regional associations. We see their strengths and weaknesses. And this is our obvious advantage since it means we are in a position to avoid mistakes and unnecessary bureaucratic superstructures.

(Putin 2011)

The key features of this alternative regional integration project include market harmonisation and interest-driven multilateral partnerships, often led by Russia, with the consent of other signatories. Since its launch, this regional project has not yet been recognised by the EU or the US. At the same time, as Dragneva and Wolczuk (2013) contend, given that the ECU and SES had developed alongside Russia's WTO accession in 2012, further developments within the EEU are likely to adhere to WTO legal provisions.

Russia's special interests in fostering closer cooperation with its neighbours have been *de jure* stipulated in its foreign policy strategies of 1993 and 1998, and reinforced further by pre-existing cultural affinity and growing cooperation across the region. The EU advancement in Ukraine, Moldova and Georgia, requiring signature of the legally binding AAs, was bound to antagonise Russia and cause an open conflict of interest between the two competing power modalities.

The EaP and the ECU, by their intentions, are not necessarily dissimilar, especially in their rhetorical projections as regional economic projects by their respective protagonists – the EU and Russia. At the same time, the process of their realisation points to an enduring practice of contestation between them which by 2014 was articulated into a discourse of incompatibility. This sense of rivalry between the two regional powers in the neighbourhood has been registered by public opinion (Korosteleva 2013; 2014) as 'alarming' and unconducive to the future sustainability of the region and which, as developments in Ukraine illustrate, may lead to long-term instability and conflict in the neighbourhood, as well as disruption of global order. Both projects effectively target an overlapping zone of interest – the eastern neighbourhood – which is framed in somewhat conflicting terms by the EU and Russia. The former refers to the region as 'shared neighbourhood', *de facto* extending the EU governance bias towards the region. Conversely, Russia, from the early 2000s, has been methodically depicting the region as 'common' rather than 'shared', with subtle but crucial difference, which invokes an alternative meaning – of a no man's land – for the same region (Shishkina 2013). More importantly, these terms of reference have been significantly politicised in the Russian media, adversely affecting perceptions as well as prospects for future cooperation across the region.

Furthermore, both the EU and Russia claim to have an overlapping 'grand vision' for the region, especially in terms of their prospective inter-regional economic cooperation. The Commission, for example, contends: 'Our vision is that these agreements should contribute in the long term to the eventual creation of a common economic space from Lisbon to Vladivostok, based on WTO rules' (Füle 2013b). In a similar manner, at the inception of the project, Vladimir Putin, the then Prime Minister, insisted that

> we suggest a powerful supranational association capable of becoming one of the poles in the modern world and serving as an efficient bridge between Europe and the dynamic Asia-Pacific region [. . .]. Alongside other key players and regional structures, such as the European Union, the United States, China and APEC, the Eurasian Economic Union will help ensure global sustainable development.
>
> (Putin 2011)

This overlapping 'grand rhetoric' of the EU and Russia falls short when it comes to its implementation, resembling more a tug-of-war than partnership for regional modernisation.

While the EU demands convergence with its *acquis*, which is claimed to be incompatible with the EEU standards, Russia, although envisaging a prospective application of the WTO rules to the EEU, operates more through compulsion and dependency arguments bearing the mark of Soviet times.

Finally, both the EU and Russia clearly recognise each other's presence and interests in the region, often stipulated in their respective official discourses. At the same time, in this acknowledgement of interests, they fail to understand, let alone facilitate, the need for interface and trialogue over and with the region. Instead, they continue their advancement of overlapping but disjoined projects in the region, which in 2013, owing to their highly politicised focus on economic integration, led to the eruption of conflict in Ukraine. While recognising the region's historical complexity, the EU efforts fall short of discernment and resemble more of an 'ostrich' approach in a blinkered pursuit of its technocratic governance. Even in 2013, in the midst of the emerging tensions in the wider region, the EU approach remained unaltered: while negotiating the divisive AA and Deep and Comprehensive Free Trade Agreement (DCFTA) with Ukraine, the EU also had separate talks with Russia on a 'new' PCA agreement, to belatedly consider 'provisions for greater convergence of the regulatory framework between the EU and Russia', which did not aim to defuse regional tensions caused by the alleged 'incompatibility' of the two economic projects, but rather 'to generate stability and predictability for both Russian and European Union companies' (Füle 2013b). The decision to finally triangulate the EU and Russia's intensions with Ukraine came rather late in 2014, because of war and negotiated ceasefire in Ukraine, whereby the DCFTA implementation by the latter was agreed to be delayed by six months, on Russia's demands (Council of the European Union 2014). At the same time, while the Commission proposed establishing official contacts with the EEU to start negotiations on harmonisation of respective free trade agreements between the EU and the EEU – and even to use Armenia as a test ground – the EU and Member States are far from reaching consensus on their future dealings with the EEU and especially on how to work with Russia.

Due to above developments, one could question the grand vision of the EU and Russia *vis-à-vis* their respective regional projects in the neighbourhood. Two manifestations become apparent.

First, in their self-centred projections, both the EU and Russia have been negligent of each other's rationalities over the contested region. The EU focused on the default assumption that the exposure of Ukraine and others to the future benefits of the EU and the prospect of a 'ring of well-governed countries' (centred on the EU) would enable recipients to unequivocally legitimise the European course. This was clearly an error of judgement, not only in terms of the timing to harvest allegiances but also, more essentially, in failing to factor Russia into the EU's expansionist normative *modus operandi*.

Second and most significantly, both powers evidently failed to understand the region itself and its historical urge for complementary rather than dichotomous relations with the wider Europe. As our research findings indicate (Korosteleva 2013; 2014), both powers yield similarly appealing offers in the eastern neighbourhood, which, instead of mobilising binary loyalties, foster an ambivalence of choice for the peoples in the region: in 2013–14 a healthy plurality (40 per cent on average) of the polled respondents across Belarus and Moldova, indicated attractiveness of both regional projects. Furthermore, a temporal cross-regional comparison (Korosteleva 2012) reveals that both powers appeal to the residents of the region, in their own, complementary way: while the EEU is important for energy security and trade, the EaP and the EU have stronger clout in promoting functional government and effective sector-specific cooperation. Enforcing a dichotomous choice on the region, not yet ready for making these commitments through their internalised norms of behaviour, testifies to the profound lack of understanding the Other – the EaP countries – including their needs and aspirations. The error of judgement by the EU and the loss of control by Russia are, in an equal measure, the causalities of the decision-making process, which occurred in the vacuum of correlated knowledge, resulting in unnecessary politicisation and subsequent securitisation of the contestable narratives, as the case of Ukraine has demonstrated.

The bigger question here is whether and how the EU and Russia's discourses could be defused in their rhetorical furnishings, to return to a zone of peace and cooperation. As our comparative research findings indicate (Korosteleva 2012; 2013; 2014), the normative framing of discourses continues to conflict in a profound way but they are not necessarily insurmountable. Both powers profess, and are associated with, differing sets of values which in turn support and engineer different behavioural patterns and expectations. Notably, the EU is clearly identified as a liberal democratic model, premised on the values of democracy, human rights, market economy and the lack of corruption; and the spatial analysis of 2009 and 2014 public associations indicated a relative endurance of this model in people's mindsets. At the same time, the EEU and Russia, in the respondents' eyes, offer a mix of qualities, a hybrid case, which could be referred to as a social protective model, but which could potentially approximate the EU, especially the values of market economy, stability, economic prosperity and security and at the same time retain its cultural uniqueness. As the 2014 findings explicitly highlight, there is more proximity in these values than was publicly purported in the earlier days of the EaP, which could avail some prospects for economic cooperation if mutually agreed rules were to be considered.

Conclusions: *positive othering* as a missing variable

The above discussion calls for the need to reverse our attention away from a changing neighbourhood and more towards the politics of the EU (and of Russia) as a source of challenges, instability and insecurity for the region. This chapter argues that it is precisely the lack of *positive othering*, involving engagement between the EU and Russia – both *vis-à-vis* each other and also in relation to their target countries – that continues to wreak havoc with peoples' daily lives and cause confusion to their sense of belonging and purpose.

The EU has come a long way to acknowledge *the Other* as an important referent in defining the outside. And yet, the conventional reading of *othering* still occurs mainly through the lens of *the Self*, whereby the presence of *the Other* is only instrumental to aid the construction of *the Self* in its external projection. From this perspective, *the Other* is recognised as relevant but different, and thus, as David Campbell put it, in need of being 'enfram[ed], limit[ed] and domesticat[ed] a particular identity' (1992: 158) by way of reaching out and shaping it to the image of *the Self*.

As attested by the case of Ukraine, these readings of *the Other* do not only exclude it from the picture as an important transformative player but also generate an asymmetrical and exclusionary view of power relations, which in the case of the contested neighbourhood may lead to conflict and even war.

In an increasingly changing global order, where one's authority is no longer a given, and one's normative appeal can no longer be taken for granted, recognition and acknowledgement of *the Other* as a different kind is not enough. What is needed, instead, is more innovative thinking about the relational meaning of the outside to the inside, in which one would 'focus less on difference than on variety' (Smith 1996: 22–23). In this case, if sufficient attention is given to re-contextualising the other – the contested neighbourhood – they may no longer appear *as different* when compared, but rather simply as *distinct*, relying much on their intrinsic value and spatial positioning.

When applied to the EU, under the EaP, it is not the difference that matters between the EU and its eastern neighbours and the normative mileage between cultural heritage and historical achievements on both sides. Rather, it is the relational space that brings both the EU and the EaP region together, into a single environment and defines them not in opposition or asymmetry to one another, but rather through their distinctive individual 'worth', their value, which requires mutual recognition of their respective normalities, for their subsequent reciprocal alignment. As Haukkala puts it: 'the Union should consider a neighbourhood policy that is based less on heavy normative convergence and harmonisation and more on tangible cooperation with more modest rhetoric and clearer material incentives' (2008: 1618).

Working with *the Other* thus becomes a learning process, which no longer simply entails recognition and even acceptance of differences pertaining to values, traditions and patterns of behaviour. Rather, this new learning should be about establishing a new value of *the Self and the Other* co-jointly and placing them in the context of reciprocal interests. In the case of the EU–Russia relations in the neighbourhood, a compatible economic space, for the benefit of all, may prove just as valid for every party, as is a prospect of membership for those who aspire.

Note

1 'Synopsis of Findings', ESRC project (RES-061-25-0001); Korosteleva (2012).

References

Börzel, T. (2010) 'European Governance: Negotiation and Competition in the Shadow of Hierarchy', *Journal of Common Market Studies* 48(2): 191–219.

Campbell, D. (1992) *Writing Security. United States Foreign Policy and the Politics of Identity*, Minneapolis: University of Minnesota Press.

Commission of the European Communities (2003) *Wider Europe-Neighbourhood: A New Framework for Relations with our Eastern and Southern Neighbours*, COM (2003) 104 final, Brussels, 11 March.

Commission of the European Communities (2007) *A Strong European Neighbourhood Policy*, COM (2007) 774 final, Brussels, 5 December.

Commission of the European Communities (2008) *Eastern Partnership*, COM (2008) 823 final, Brussels, 3 December.

Council of the European Union (2003) *A Secure Europe in a Better World: European Security Strategy*, Brussels, 12 December 2003.

Council of the European Union (2011) Joint Declaration of the Eastern Partnership Summit, Warsaw, 29–30 September 2011, Presse 341, 14983/11.

Council of the European Union (2014) *Joint Statement of the Council and the Commission on the EU–Ukraine Association Agreement*, Brussels, 29 September.

Delcour, L. (2008) 'A Missing Eastern Dimension? The ENP and Region-Building in the Post-Soviet Space', in Delcour, L. and Tulmets, E. (eds.) *Pioneer Europe? Testing European Foreign Policy in the Neighbourhood*, Baden-Baden: Nomos, 135–156.

Delcour, L. (2011) 'The Institutional Functioning of the Eastern Partnership: An Early Assessment', *Eastern Partnership Review* 1, Tallin: Estonian Centre of Eastern Partnership.

Dragneva, R. and Wolczuk, K. (eds.) (2013) *Eurasian Economic Integration: Law, Policy and Politics*, London: Edward Elgar Publishers.

Dutkiewicz, P. and Sakwa, R. (2015) *Eurasian Integration – The View from Within*, London: Routledge.

European Commission and High Representative of the European Union for Foreign Affairs and Security Policy (2011) *A New Response to a Changing Neighbourhood*, COM (2011) 303 final, Brussels, 25 May.

European Commission and High Representative of the European Union for Foreign Affairs and Security Policy (2015a) *Towards a New European Neighbourhood Policy*, JOIN (2015) 6 final, 4 March.

European Commission and High Representative of the European Union for Foreign Affairs and Security Policy (2015b) *Review of the European Neighbourhood Policy*, JOIN (2015) 50 Final, Brussels.

European External Action Service (2015) *The European Union in a Changing Global Enviornment: A More Connected, Contested and Complex World*, Brussels, June.

Füle, S. (2013a) 'Ambitions of EU and East Partners for the Vilnius Summit', *Speech*/13/477, Brussels, 28 May.
Füle, S. (2013b) Statement on the Pressure Exercised by Russia on Countries of the Eastern Partnership, Speech/13/687, Strasburg, September.
Gänzle, S. (2009) 'EU Governance and the European Neighbourhood Policy: A Framework for Analysis', *Europe-Asia Studies* 61(10): 1715–1734.
Haukkala, H. (2008) 'The European Union as a Regional Normative Hegemon: The Case of European Neighbourhood Policy', *Europe-Asia Studies* 60(9): 1601–1622.
House of Lords (2015) *The EU and Russia: Before and Beyond the Crisis in Ukraine*, EU Committee, 6th Report of Session 2014–2015.
Juncos, A. and Whitman, R. (2015), 'Europe as a Regional Actor: Neighbourhood Lost?', *Journal of Common Market Studies* 53: 200–215 (Annual Review).
Kelley, J. (2006) 'New Wine in Old Wineskins: Promoting Political Reforms through the New ENP', *Journal of Common Market Studies* 44(1): 29–55.
Kohler-Koch, B. and Rittberger, B. (2006) 'Review Article: The "Governance Turn" in EU studies', *Journal of Common Market Studies* 44: 27–49.
Korosteleva, E. (2011) *The Eastern Partnership Initiative: A New Opportunity for the Neighbours?*, London: Routledge.
Korosteleva, E. (2012) *The EU and Its Eastern Neighbours: Towards a More Ambitious Partnership?*, London: Routledge.
Korosteleva, E. (2013) 'Belarus and the Eastern Partnership: A National Values Survey', *GEC policy brief*, University of Kent.
Korosteleva, E. (2014) 'Moldova's Values Survey: Widening a European Dialogue', *GEC policy brief*, University of Kent.
Korosteleva, E., Natorski, M. and Simão, L. (eds.) (2014) *EU Policies in the Eastern Neighbourhood: The Practices Perspective*, London: Routledge.
Kostanyan, H. and Delcour, L. (2014) 'Towards a Fragmented Neighbourhood: Policies of the EU and Russia and their Consequences for the area that lies in between', *CEPS Essays* 17, 17 October.
Lavenex, S. (2004) 'EU External Governance in "Wider Europe"', *Journal of Public Policy* 11(4): 680–700.
Lavenex, S. and Schimmelfennig, F. (2010) (eds.) *EU External Governance: Projecting EU Rules Beyond Membership*, London and NY: Routledge.
Putin, V. (2011) 'A New Integration Project for Eurasia: The Future in the Making', *Izvestia*, 3 October.
Raik, K. (2006), 'The EU as a Regional Power: Extended Governance and Historical Responsibility', in Mayer, H. and Vogt, H. (eds.) *A Responsible Europe? Ethical Foundations of EU External Affairs.* Basingstoke: Palgrave Macmillan, 76–98.
Shishkina, O. (2013) *Vneshnepoliticheskie Resursy: Rossiya I ES na prostranstve 'obshchego sosedstva'*, Moskva: Aspect Press.
Smith, M. (1996) 'The EU and a Changing Europe: Establishing the Boundaries of Order', *Journal of Common Market Studies* 34(1): 5–28.

16
THE CHALLENGES OF A CHANGING SOUTHERN NEIGHBOURHOOD

Thomas Demmelhuber

Introduction

The European Neighbourhood Policy (ENP) correlates with the 2003 European Security Strategy (ESS). Despite being different and independent policy initiatives, the ESS aimed at nurturing a ring of well-governed states beyond European Union (EU) border lines, that is, focusing predominantly on the EU's neighbourhood (Council of the European Union 2003; Commission of the European Communities 2003; Demmelhuber and Kaunert 2014). From early 2017 and the time of finalizing this chapter, the risk of violent conflicts, civil wars and weak states with dysfunctional societies in the southern neighbourhood and corresponding security threats, including political challenges for the ENP, are hardly new and have existed since the beginning of the ENP in 2003 (Commission of the European Communities 2003).

While, at first glance, the years since the beginning of the Arab uprisings in 2010 seem to top these regular assessments in EU documents of instability, turmoil and violence in the southern neighbourhood, core questions remain: Are there substantial changes regarding the challenges for the EU in the Southern Mediterranean, or do pathways of continuity predominate? Which role do the Arab uprisings eventually play? The academic observer might be inclined to identify the Arab uprisings as the most important trigger for a changing southern neighbourhood and regional order of the Middle East, fundamentally challenging the ENP and even having an impact on the ENP revisions in 2011 and 2015 (High Representative of the European Union for Foreign Affairs and Security Policy and European Commission 2011; 2015). This chapter builds on a slightly different reasoning. It is based on the premise that new and old challenges of a changing southern neighbourhood are interlinked with earlier events in the region that were externally initiated by the US-led Operation Iraqi Freedom of 2003 and its subsequent regional fallout.[1] As a caveat, this chapter focuses on the Southern Mediterranean encompassing all ENP (associated) countries. Yet, this focus would be impossible without referring to Southern Mediterranean states' incorporation in regional networks, organizations and dynamics of the wider Middle Eastern region. This explains why the term 'neighbourhood' in this chapter refers to an even wider neighbourhood understanding than that given by the ENP framework.

Analytical narratives and argument

The controversial debate that preceded and followed the military intervention in Iraq, and the subsequent regime change in 2003, was a milestone for intensified talks on a common EU strategy on defence and security issues and the conviction that such a manifestation of weakness of EU foreign policy should never happen again (Youngs 2014). For the Middle East and the southern EU neighbourhood, the forced regime change in Iraq was a turning point in terms of a modified organization of power within the countries as well as a creeping re-configuration of the regional order. Based on this point of departure, three analytical narratives are developed in this chapter to identify, by way of conclusion, the spectrum of challenges that the EU is facing with its southern neighbours.

First, the fall of the regime of Iraqi president Saddam Hussein in 2003 was initiated by military coercion and was – independent of the underlying and vividly debated motives – the result of boosted democracy promotion efforts on behalf of the Bush administration (2001–2009) in the aftermath of the 9/11 attacks on the US mainland. This was seriously echoed by the region's autocrats, who suddenly displayed strong enthusiasm for political reform, using a broad array of democratic vocabulary. In a nutshell, despite the 'theatre of democratic reform', state and power were re-negotiated or were exposed to an 'authoritarian upgrading' (Heydemann 2007) for the sake of authoritarian durability. Second, traditional leading powers, such as Egypt, Syria and Iraq, were significantly weakened and other state actors such as the monarchies of the Arab peninsula have been filling this strategic void, associated with even stronger hegemonic aspirations. This went along with a strategic gain in actor quality for the Islamic Republic of Iran in view of the fellow Shia government in Iraq since the 2005 elections. The regime in Tehran tries to translate this political and strategic clout into an even stronger strategic presence in its vicinity at the expense of others, such as Saudi Arabia. Third, the proliferation of new non-state actors, with the so-called Islamic State (IS) or the Kurds in Syria and Iraq, may be only fully understood through the prism of those pathways of change and continuity that began in and around Iraq since 2003. It is on the basis of these three narratives that the challenges of a changing southern neighbourhood for the ENP can be sufficiently grasped and interpreted.

Following these analytical narratives, the dynamics of the Arab uprisings are a significant challenge for the EU as they stand for a chain of events that further boosted a process of re-configuration of the regional order that had already started in previous years. By elaborating on these three narratives of regional change and continuity rather inductively, this chapter aims (1) at concluding that the regional order is in flux, with significant implications for the ENP and (2) at mirroring the developed challenges with EU policy responses (for example, 2011 and 2015 ENP reviews and the 2016 EU's Global Strategy).

Iraq, the regional fallout and Arab uprisings

The call for international support of the Iraq intervention on behalf of the Bush administration brought into focus the weakness and discord of EU foreign policy in 2003 (Youngs 2004). Donald Rumsfeld, the former US defence secretary, is still widely cited with his derogative distinction in an 'old' versus 'new' Europe to praise the support of several, in particular Middle and Eastern European countries (with Poland, Bulgaria, Romania and Ukraine leading the way) next to EU members such as the United Kingdom, Italy, Spain, the Netherlands and Denmark (Carney 2011: 34–123). Rumsfeld made his remarks in response to a French–German agreement to work together in opposing the military intervention in Iraq (*The Guardian* 2003). Meanwhile, back in 2003, there was hardly any dispute that, officially, US foreign policy followed a multifaceted agenda in Iraq, which was vividly oscillating between the Global War on Terror (including the fight against the proliferation of weapons of mass destruction) and a more normative agenda (for example, Bush's 'forward strategy of freedom'). This normative agenda was shaped by a democratization rhetoric that became a strategic source of reasoning when the arguments about weapons of mass destruction and Saddam Hussein's support of international terrorism failed to materialize and were replaced by a more nuanced democracy promotion rationale (Bunce and Wolchik 2007).

Despite this huge gap between words and action, there was indeed a tangible 'Middle East push' (Carothers 2007: 4) and an 'expansive rhetoric on democracy promotion' (ibid.) not only *vis-à-vis* Iraq. There was also a more active rhetoric that targeted traditional US allies in the region, such as Egypt. In the words of former President Bush: 'The great and proud nation of Egypt has shown the way toward peace in the Middle East and now should show the way toward democracy in the Middle East' (National Endowment for Democracy 2003). The lack of actions on the ground and continuing good security relations with the region's autocrats have been widely discussed by the scholarly literature and encompass a broad spectrum of explanatory factors as to why, in some cases, possible modes of leverage were used and in others not (Bronson 2006; Brownlee 2012; Levitsky and Way 2010).

In retrospective, the Iraq intervention has left one essential legacy regarding the organization of state and power in the region. The global discourse on democracy promotion accelerated the acknowledgement of the region's autocrats that they must invest more in political reform. It aimed at consolidating their power base and at garnering a more legitimate basis of their respective regimes to minimize the risk of eventually becoming the next target of a more nuanced regime change discourse by external powers. Until 2011, Arab regimes felt obliged to embark on a process of comprehensive political and economic reform and extended their toolbox of regime survival by forms of electoral competition and participation that should foster their power base and re-formulate their individual legitimacy recipe. This was very much in line with the strategies of international democracy promotion actors, including the US and the EU, and their obvious bigotry regarding the decisive momentum of elections (National Endowment for Democracy 2003; Pace 2010). As a result, the Arab world's autocratic regimes were characterized by a functional incorporation of liberal elements into an authoritarian setting, though without any implementation of democratic procedures (Pripstein Posusney and Penner Angrist 2005; Bellin 2004). Despite this 'theatre of reform', new spaces of dissent for contentious politics emerged, which served as decisive learning processes for activists and civil society groups when protests erupted and people called for the fall of regimes in the early days of 2011 (Albrecht 2015). This was further accompanied by a preceding 'media revolution' that had already been initiated in the mid–1990s with the Qatari satellite broadcaster *al-Jazeera* forcing national media landscapes to adapt rapidly in terms of the format and quality of their respective programmes (Lynch 2007). Later, the diffusion of the internet and social media sites prepared the ground for the respective regimes to find themselves in a defensive and passive position, giving them only responsive modes of action. For too long, they underestimated the potential of internet-based media as a political tool of mobilization, articulation and coordination (Badr 2013) and failed to benefit from a proactive use of social media as a platform of agency and self-promotion (Badr and Demmelhuber 2014). Meanwhile, EU foreign policy and the international community remained inconsistent when the results of the democratic processes did not fit other, more dominant, foreign policy principles. Hence, the lack of international acceptance of the elections for the Palestinian Legislative Council in 2006 – with Hamas winning most of the votes – called into question the credibility of EU foreign policy that did not match words with deeds (Pace 2010).

At the same time, the Arab uprisings have shown that many of these strategies of regime survival eventually failed. It was in the republics where the legitimacy crisis was too strong, with

Tunisia and Egypt being the 'frontrunners'. Both Tunisia and Egypt underwent a regime change, though with different results. Only Tunisia entered successfully an open-ended path of democratization, while Egypt witnessed a setback into autocratic regime practices after two military *coup d'états* in 2011 and 2013. Despite these different pathways of political change, that is, democratic versus autocratic transformation, the underlying causes for regime change in Tunisia and Egypt were similar. Above all, the gap between the formal democratic character of the constitutional order, and a political reality that turned this very character into its opposite, was too comprehensive (along with miserable governance performances).

However, not all republics witnessed a regime change. There were also republics of authoritarian resilience, such as Algeria, in which the collective memory of the civil war in the 1990s seemed to keep the populace aloof from widespread protest and the ruling elites in their presumed rightful place. Furthermore, since then, countries like Syria, Yemen and Libya have not only been in danger of falling apart through civil war, but have also reflected new geopolitical realities in the region and beyond (including the external interventions of international and regional actors such as Russia and Turkey). At the same time, there were political entities struggling with the project of state building since democratic procedures within their political elites were at stake (Iraq, Palestine and Lebanon). Ultimately, the Arab monarchies seemed to be the shelter of regional stability. They attempted, from Morocco to Jordan to the Gulf, to accommodate varying public pressure for change with political and constitutional reforms, in addition to generous direct payments to their citizens. Empirically, one might be inclined to conclude that the monarchies were equipped with more effective modes of regime legitimacy (Derichs and Demmelhuber 2014). Conceptually, it is the understanding of legitimacy as a fluid concept, including a broad spectrum of legitimation strategies, that may explain why some regimes prevailed and others failed. At the same time, other explanatory approaches may also be considered such as structuralist approaches that attribute explanatory power to variables like 'rent income' (Brownlee, Masoud and Reynolds 2013: 29–44).

Put differently, seen from the perspective of early 2017, the Arab uprisings stand for several pathways of change and continuity that determine a re-ordering of the whole region, thus encompassing spaces without functioning statehood (Libya, Syria and Yemen) or limited statehood (for example, Egypt/Sinai, Iraq).

Actor quality, regional hegemons and non-state actors

Since the beginning of the Euro-Mediterranean Partnership (EMP), also known as the Barcelona Process, in 1995 and ever since the ENP was initiated in 2003, Egypt has been treated as the informal leader of the ENP countries in the Southern Mediterranean. This practice was even formalized with the Union for the Mediterranean (UfM) and the appointment of Egypt as its first co-presidency (Demmelhuber and Marchetti 2011). For the EU, Egypt was a natural hub regarding its role as 'chief negotiator' in the Middle East Peace Process (MEPP), its geographic size, its demographic weight and its strategic position bridging the Middle East and North Africa. This coincided with Egypt's strong self-perception as the political and cultural leader of the entire Arab region, a constructed regional leadership narrative that successfully disguised its strategic loss of actor quality that had already become apparent long before (ibid.).

Due to the fallout of both oil crises following the 1973 Yom Kippur/October War, the subsequent surge of capital flows to the oil exporting countries boosted state and regime capacities of the resource-rich monarchies on the Arab peninsula. Saudi Arabia has gained enormous actor quality as a regional power at the expense of traditional powers such as Egypt, Syria and Iraq (Hertog 2010). Saudi Arabia's fiscal power is meanwhile more explicitly translated into hegemonic aspirations with a nuanced articulated agenda of interests and much more independent pursuit (for example, 2015 military intervention in Yemen). Of course, this goes along with a significantly increased reluctance of US foreign policy under both Obama administrations to get involved in the region's cleavages and conflicts. By now, Saudi Arabia is the only Arab country that is a member of the G20 that rose to global importance after the US mortgage subprime crisis in 2007 and the subsequent world financial crisis. Evidence for the loss of Egypt's regional leadership capacity may also be found in the country's gradual marginalization as a broker in the MEPP when the Saudi-initiated Abdullah peace plan of 2002 – initially published by the then Saudi crown prince Abdullah *via* New York Times columnist, Thomas Friedman – obtained the backing of the whole Arab League and became later known as the 'Arab Peace Initiative'. The latter was also re-endorsed in 2007 on the Arab League summit in the Saudi capital Riyadh (Maddy-Weitzman 2010).

The early days of the Arab uprisings seemed to temporarily change this loss of actor quality, at least for Egypt, while Iraq and Syria, both in domestic turmoil after 2003 and 2011 respectively, were implicitly wiped off the political map (that is, as active subjects of regional politics). Egypt appeared to be once again a self-declared frontrunner of regional change, now a frontrunner of democracy, leading short-term President Mohamed Morsi trying to revive Egypt's role as the leader in Arab and Middle Eastern politics, despite any strategic, political or economic clout (Grimm and Roll 2012). This short illusion of a comeback as a regional role model of democracy finally vanished when, in 2013, the Egyptian military, with comprehensive political and financial backing from Saudi Arabia, the United Arab Emirates and Kuwait, as well as the support of large segments of Egypt's business elite, disempowered Morsi and his government in another *coup d'état*. Eventually, it culminated in the 'enthronisation' of the new presidency of former Army General Abdel Fattah al-Sisi (Albrecht and Bishara 2011).

Saudi Arabia is the leading actor in this 'reactionary' bottom-line of the Arab uprisings. The kingdom intends to shape the results on the ground and acts like a 'gravity centre of authoritarian rule' (Kneuer and Demmelhuber 2016) that tries to have an impact on the organization of state and power in its geopolitical proximity for the sake of regional regime stability and also for the sake of a certain kind of regime convergence. Sub-regional organizations such as the Gulf Cooperation Council (GCC), the *de facto* 'club of authoritarian monarchies', are hereby used as transmission belts and learning rooms of influence (ibid.). The 2013 GCC intervention in Bahrain that helped the ruling Al Khalifa family crack down on nation-wide protests and the GCC involvement in Yemen since 2015, speak volumes about how the GCC embodies the formal framework for the dissemination of Saudi interests in its geopolitical neighbourhood that is additionally directed against any signs of a growing Iranian presence in the Middle East. The toppling of the Iraqi regime in 2003, the first elected Shia government in Bagdad in 2005, and the engagement of Iranian foreign policy in the Middle East through proxy actors (such as Hizbullah in Lebanon), stand for the collision of Saudi interests with Iranian interests, both derived from self-declared hegemonic aspiration in their geopolitical proximity.

The re-configuration of the regional order has been creating multiple power vacuums that non-state actors could fill, most notably since 2014, with IS being able to seize power in large parts of Syria and Iraq at the expense of Syria's Assad regime, the heterogeneous Syrian opposition and the Iraqi central government. It has led to a multi-level alliance of international actors and regional actors fighting IS with hitherto only limited though increasing success. Here again, the vacuum that allowed IS in Syria and Iraq to emerge is rooted in the post-2003 years in Iraq, namely in the costly fight against Sunni insurgents after the initiated full-scale De-Baathification of Iraq's military, security apparatus and bureaucracy on behalf of the coalition forces' military administration in Bagdad (Sissons and al-Saiedi 2013; Buchta 2015).

Known previously as al-Qaida in Iraq, after the killing of al-Zarqawi (leader of al-Qaida's branch in Iraq) in 2006, various factions succeeded in a re-organization and founded the 'Islamic State in Iraq' (since 2013, 'Islamic State in Iraq and the Levant'). Subsequently, they gave themselves a new label with varying theological reasoning and a different strategic understanding of how to fight alleged infidels (including Shiites) within and beyond the region. In this power vacuum and vanishing state power, the Kurds have been on the rise in Syria and Iraq, though with different political institutions and actors at play (including different militant wings). This dynamic received a specific boost in the aftermath of Iraqi state building efforts after the toppling of Saddam Hussein and a new constitution that allowed the proclamation of autonomous regions. The federalist character of the Iraqi constitution, that never fully materialized, set the ground for a formalized Kurdish autonomy. In 2015, this call for more autonomy witnessed further momentum with Kurdish Peshmerga units from Iraqi Kurdistan fighting the so-called Islamic State hand in hand with a loose international coalition generously supported by this coalition with arms shipments (Natali 2015).

Conclusions: changing challenges?

This chapter argues that the re-configuration of the EU's southern neighbourhood and the whole region started long before the historic events of the Arab uprisings unfolded. Though the push for this re-configuration coincided with the formulation of the ESS and the ENP, the impetus came from another externally induced event in the region. The military intervention in Iraq by US-led coalition forces set the ground for a regional re-ordering and a modified organization of political power. Domestically, autocrats of the region felt the need to go ahead with a more comprehensive rhetoric of political reform, which opened new spaces for debate and opposing voices, including newly initiated spaces and platforms of interaction. Regionally, the Iraq war created territorial spaces without functioning statehood, which, in turn, laid the ground for tremendous shifts in regional politics with new powerful non-state actors entering the scene and challenging a regional state order that was for too long considered stable.

In view of this overarching challenge, EU foreign policy toward the Southern Mediterranean still seems to be dominated by policy field-related actions instead of a more nuanced cause-related approach. The search for a common EU response in view of the 2015 migration crises exemplifies this. Yet the policy ignores the underlying causes of this migration pressure that constitutes much more pressing challenges. Providing support for state building is going to be the key challenge for the ENP in the years to come, as the 2015 ENP review clearly states that in 'the next three to five years, the most urgent challenge in many parts of the neighbourhood is stabilisation' (High Representative of the European Union for Foreign Affairs and Security Policy and European Commission 2015: 3). Building a security and bureaucracy apparatus and thus relevant institutions is one of the most serious challenges in those countries that underwent regime change and ended up with an erosion of state order because of rivalling non-state actors or weak state institutions (ibid.). Yet, in Brussels, this is obviously considered and planned within the given political map. Boosting the security dimension of state actors that are not able to fulfil relevant state functions might be the wrong answer or even a waste of effort. These statehood-based challenges for the ENP are not only consequences of the Arab uprisings; they are also deeply rooted in decades-old regional conflicts with the Arab–Israeli conflict leading the way. The official EU narrative on a two-state solution neglects the *de facto* state power of Hamas in Gaza since the elections of 2006. It also neglects lessons of history that suggest a state with a lack of territorial contiguity (West Bank and Gaza) may hardly survive in the long run (for example, Pakistan and Bangladesh, 1947–1974).

Despite state building measures being the priority issue in countries like Libya, turning a blind eye to the content of how political power is organized and how political power is justified would repeat mistakes of the past. The self-critical 2011 ENP review was progressive by stressing the fundamental need 'to support progress towards deep democracy' (High Representative of the European Union for Foreign Affairs and Security Policy and European Commission 2011: 3). In contrast, the ENP review from 2015 falls back into the dark years of muddling through with the region's dictators for the sake of short-term stability. The section on 'how politics should be organised' is hidden in section four with a rather passive and defensive vocabulary, that 'democracy will continue to be an agenda item in our political dialogue with all partners in mutually agreed formats' (High Representative of the European Union for Foreign Affairs and Security Policy and European Commission 2015: 5–6). State building does not only imply state power and territorial integrity. It also implies fostering the capacity of the state to build legitimate, efficient state institutions that allow any state and its government to generate a minimum of 'output legitimacy'. For the EU, it will remain a crucial challenge in the Southern Mediterranean and beyond to identify a middle ground between looking for a modified regional state order and maintaining a focus on the normative foreign policy goals as enshrined in the Treaty on European Union. The answer to this will be found in even more bilaterally tailored approaches in view of the multifaceted trajectories of change and continuity in the Southern Mediterranean and the whole region, in order to overcome a past 'policy conundrum' that has been oscillating between bilateralism and multilateralism with varying focal points. 'Principled Pragmatism' (European Commission 2016: 8), as suggested by the EU's Global Strategy, will certainly not help to overcome this past 'policy conundrum'. EU foreign policy had already lost much credibility in the years prior to the Arab uprisings, as it too often ignored the normative values in its partnerships with autocratic regimes, forgot possible modes of negative and positive conditionality and caused a weaker EU stance on issues of what legitimate political rule should look like.

Despite a tangible consensus for more country-specific approaches and policy solutions (Del Sarto and Schumacher 2005), as stressed by the 2016 Global Strategy calling for tailor-made policy packages (European Commission 2016), the formulation of coherent EU responses has become more challenging in view of four additional pitfalls that affect the credibility of EU policy negatively. First, we have been witnessing substantial democratic regression in the EU itself with cases of media tutelage or attempts to circumvent the separation of powers (such as Hungary and Poland). Second, this goes hand in hand with EU accession talks with Turkey, despite questionable democratic performance alone in view of the Copenhagen Criteria (democratic governance, market economy and intent to accept the *acquis communautaire*) that were the prerequisite for launching membership talks in 2005. Third, due to diverging pathways of the Arab uprisings, the EU must find a credible compromise to support and sufficiently honour, for example, Tunisia's democratization steps or Morocco's endogenous reform steps. At the same time, in other countries, it may not cherish an illusion that there will be a democratic opening with an actor constellation on the partner side that only speaks a democratic language for the sake of autocratic regime survival (such as Egypt). And fourth, the Arab uprisings have accelerated a dynamic that has been visible since the early 2000s: democracy promotion as an internationally accepted foreign policy goal is faced with increasingly tougher competition by those autocratic countries that do not only try to inhibit democracy promotion efforts but try to actively promote the dissemination of autocratic elements, ideas and norms in their geopolitical proximity as a kind of alternative language of government (such as Saudi Arabia or Qatar).

Note

1 For a geographical overview of involved ENP countries, see: http://ec.europa.eu/economy_finance/international/neighbourhood_policy/index_en.htm, accessed 28 December 2015.

References

Albrecht, H. (2015) *Raging Against the Machine: Political Opposition Under Authoritarianism*, Chapel Hill: Syracuse University Press.
Albrecht, H. and Bishara, D. (2011) 'Back on Horseback: The Military and Political Transformation in Egypt', *Middle East Law and Governance* 3(1–2): 13–23.
Badr, H. (2013) 'Battleground Facebook: Contestation Mechanisms in Egypt's 2011 Revolution', in Berenger, R. (ed.) *Social Media Go to War: Rage, Rebellion and Revolution in the Age of Twitter*, Washington, DC: Spokane, 399–422.
Badr, H. and Demmelhuber, T. (2014) 'Autoritäre Regime, Neue Medien und das Regimedilemma', *Zeitschrift für Internationale Beziehungen* 21(1): 143–160.
Bellin, E. (2004) 'The Robustness of Authoritarianism in the Middle East: Exceptionalism in Comparative Perspective', *Comparative Politics* 36(2): 139–157.
Bronson, R. (2006) *Thicker than Oil: America's Uneasy Partnership with Saudi Arabia*, New York: Oxford University Press.
Brownlee, J. (2012) *Democracy Prevention: The Politics of the U.S.–Egyptian Alliance*, New York: Cambridge University Press.
Brownlee, J., Masoud, T. and Reynolds, A. (2013) 'Why the Modest Harvest?', *Journal of Democracy* 24(4): 29–44.
Buchta, W. (2015) *Terror vor Europas Toren: Der Islamische Staat, Iraks Zerfall und Amerikas Ohnmacht*, Frankfurt/Main: Campus.
Bunce, V. and Wolchik, S. (2007) 'Bringing Down Dictators: American Democracy Promotion and Electoral Revolutions in Postcommunist Eurasia', *Working Paper Series* 5, Mario Einaudi Center for International Studies, Cornell University, Ithaca, 1–25.
Carothers, T. (2007) *U.S. Democracy Promotion During and After Bush*, Washington, DC: Carnegie Endowment for International Peace.
Carney, S. (2011) *Allied Participation in Operation Iraqi Freedom*, Washington, DC: Center of Military History, United States Army.
Commission of the European Communities (2003) *Wider Europe – Neighbourhood: A New Framework for Relations with Our Eastern and Southern Neighbours*, COM (2003) 104 final, Brussels, 3 March.
Council of the European Union (2003) *A Secure Europe in a Better World: European Security Strategy*, Brussels: Council of the European Union.
Del Sarto, R. and Schumacher, T. (2005) 'From EMP to ENP: What's at Stake with the European Neighbourhood Policy Towards the Southern Mediterranean?', *European Foreign Affairs Review* 10(1): 17–38.
Demmelhuber, T. and Marchetti, A. (2011) 'Die Union für das Mittelmeer: Ambitionen und Realität – eine ernüchternde Zwischenbilanz der französisch-ägyptischen Präsidentschaft', *Integration* 34(2): 132–147.
Demmelhuber, T. and Kaunert, C. (2014) 'The EU and the Gulf Monarchies: Normative Power Europe in Search of a Strategy', *Cambridge Review of International Affairs* 27(3): 574–592.
Derichs, C. and Demmelhuber, T. (2014) 'Monarchies and Republics, State and Regime, Durability and Fragility in View of the Arab Spring', *Journal of Arabian Studies* 4(2): 180–194.
European Commission (2016) *Shared Vision, Common Action: A Stronger Europe. A Global Strategy for the European Union's Foreign and Security Policy*, Brussels: European Commission.
Grimm, J. and Roll, S. (2012) 'Egyptian Foreign Policy under Mohamed Morsi: Domestic Considerations and Economic Constraints', *SWP Aktuell* 35, Berlin: German Institute for International and Security Affairs.
High Representative of the European Union for Foreign Affairs and Security Policy and European Commission (2011) *A New Response to a Changing Neighbourhood*, COM (2011) 303 final, Brussels, 25 May.
High Representative of the European Union for Foreign Affairs and Security Policy and European Commission (2015) *Towards a New European Neighbourhood Policy*, JOIN (2015) 6 final, 4 March.
Hertog, S. (2010) *Princes, Brokers and Bureaucrats: Oil and the State in Saudi Arabia*, Ithaca: Cornell University Press.

Heydemann, S. (2007) 'Upgrading Authoritarianism in the Arab World', *Analysis Paper* 13, The Saban Center for Middle East Policy at the Brookings Institution, October.

Kneuer, M. and Demmelhuber, T. (2016) 'Gravity Centres of Authoritarian Rule: A Conceptual Approach', *Democratization* 23(5): 775–796.

Levitsky, S. and Way, L. (2010) *Competitive Authoritarianism: Hybrid Regimes after the Cold War*, New York: Cambridge University Press.

Lynch, M. (2007) *Voices of the New Arab Public: Iraq, al-Jazeera, and Middle East Politics Today*, New York: Columbia University Press.

Maddy-Weitzman, B. (2010) 'Arabs vs. the Abdullah Plan', *Middle East Quarterly* 17(3): 3–12.

Natali, D. (2015) 'The Kurdish Quasi-State: Leveraging Political Limbo', *The Washington Quarterly* 38(2): 145–164.

National Endowment for Democracy (2003) *Remarks by President George W. Bush at the 20th Anniversary of the National Endowment for Democracy*, Washington, DC, 6 November, www.ned.org/remarks-by-president-george-w-bush-at-the-20th-anniversary/, accessed 31 December 2015.

Pace, M. (2010) 'Interrogating the European Union's Democracy Promotion Agenda: Discursive Configurations of Democracy from the Middle East', *European Foreign Affairs Review* 15(5): 611–628.

Pripstein Posusney, M. and Penner Angrist, M. (eds.) (2005) *Authoritarianism in the Middle East: Regimes and Resistance*, Boulder: Lynne Rienner.

Sissons, M. and al-Saiedi, A. (2013) *A Bitter Legacy: Lessons of De-Baathification in Iraq*, New York: International Center of Transitional Justice.

The Guardian (2003) 'France and Germany unite against Iraq war', in: www.theguardian.com/world/2003/jan/22/germany.france, last accessed 30 December 2016.

Youngs, R. (2004) 'Europe and Iraq: From Stand-off to Engagement?', *FRIDE Policy Paper, Working Paper* 45, June.

Youngs, R. (2014) *The Uncertain Legacy of Crisis: European Foreign Policy Faces the Future*, Washington, DC: Brookings Institution Press.

PART III

European Neighbourhood Policy-making

Institutional dynamics, actors and instruments

17
COHERENCE, COHESIVENESS AND CONSISTENCY IN THE EUROPEAN NEIGHBOURHOOD POLICY

Tanja Börzel and Bidzina Lebanidze

Introduction

This chapter explores the extent to which cohesiveness, coherence and consistency of the European Neighbourhood Policy (ENP) matter for its effectiveness. Much of the academic literature argues that a lack of coherence circumscribes the transformative power of the European Union (EU) in its neighbourhood (da Conceição-Heldt and Meunier 2014; Baracani 2009; Noutcheva 2014). We will argue, in contrast, that problems of consistency caused by conflicting goals undermine the EU's capacity to promote democracy in the post-Soviet and the Southern Mediterranean space. Whenever the EU applies political conditionality as the key instrument of its external democracy promotion, we see a democratic breakthrough, or higher degree of democratic quality, in ENP countries. The problem is that the EU selectively sanctions non-compliance with its democracy standards. To account for the EU's inconsistency, we identify the presence of endogenous democratic processes and low risks of political instability as two necessary conditions for the EU to apply political conditionality. If either of them is absent, the EU acts as a *status quo* power, prioritizing (authoritarian) stability over uncertain (democratic) change.

The chapter starts with outlining the conceptual differences between coherence, cohesiveness and consistency. The second and third sections explore the evolution of the ENP regarding its coherence and consistency, respectively. We will show that consistency, rather than coherence, accounts for the varying effectiveness of the ENP. The chapter concludes with a summary of the most important arguments on when and why the EU pursues a consistent approach in its ENP and how this affects the EU's overall effectiveness in promoting domestic change in its neighbourhood.

Coherence, cohesiveness and consistency

In EU studies, coherence, cohesiveness and consistency are three concepts that are most commonly attributed to the EU's foreign policy actorness. A clear differentiation between the three is a complex task, not least because they are often used as synonyms, or as interrelated concepts, both in the academic literature and in the EU's official documents (Thomas 2012, 458; Koops and Varwick 2011; van Vooren and Wessel 2014).

Many authors understand coherence as the capability of the EU to overcome institutional complexities and 'speak with a single voice' in the foreign policy arena (da Conceição-Heldt and Meunier 2014; Noutcheva 2014; Thomas 2012). For instance, Thomas speaks of 'the adoption of determinate common policies and the pursuit of those policies by EU Member States and institutions' (2012: 458). In this context, policy determinacy (clarity of articulation of EU goals) and political cohesion (unity among EU actors) are considered as two main dimensions of coherence (Thomas 2012: 459–60). Similarly, Jopp and Schlotter define coherence as 'contradiction-free foreign policy' (Koops and Varwick 2011: 123). Closely related to coherence is the term 'internal cohesiveness' introduced by da Conceição-Heldt and Meunier (2014). Internal cohesiveness refers to the 'degree to which decision-making rules produce a single message spoken with a single voice' (da Conceição-Heldt and Meunier 2014: 963).

Both coherence and cohesiveness see the complexities of institutional governance of the ENP behind the EU's failure to transform its neighbourhood. Following this argument, 'the institutional pluralism of EU foreign policy-making' (Noutcheva 2014: 21), which is often characterized as 'a high number of actors with a low level of political power' (Bicchi 2014: 320), weakens the actorness of the EU and, hence, the EU's transformative power. In the Southern Mediterranean, for instance, the EU's relative effectiveness in shaping the migration and trade policies of its southern neighbours, especially prior to the 'Arab Spring', is attributed to the unity of the EU Member States. The EU's diminished influence on democracy and conflict, by contrast, is due to the disagreements among its Member States (Noutcheva 2014: 34).

Consistency means that EU policies in one area should not undercut policies in other areas (da Conceição-Heldt and Meunier 2014: 963). The concept is generally used in the literature in combination with 'conditionality' – the main instrument of the EU to promote democracy and good governance in third countries in exchange for certain incentives (Luckau 2011; Schimmelfennig 2008). 'Accession conditionality' links the EU's 'golden carrot' of a membership perspective to compliance with the Copenhagen Criteria (democracy, human rights, rule of law), on the one hand, and the adoption of the *acquis communautaire*, on the other. Since the ENP does not entail close institutional integration, it must offer neighbouring countries other incentives in return for domestic reforms, such as advanced access to the EU's single market, liberalization of visa regimes and increased financial aid (Langbein and Börzel 2013). In the context of this 'neighbourhood conditionality' (Borell et al. 2012: 75), consistency presupposes that the promotion of democracy, human rights, the rule of law and the fight against corruption are not compromised by other foreign policy goals of the EU, such as stability, energy security or trade. The most prominent example of ENP inconsistency is what Jünemann described as the democratization-stability dilemma (Jünemann 2004; cf. Youngs 2002). Since most of the EU's neighbours are non-democratic countries, democratization is likely to trigger instability, leading to the failure of state institutions or even to the state's erosion, at least in the short run, which is exactly the opposite of what the EU intends to achieve in its neighbourhood. Thus, promoting democratic governance, on the one hand, and effective governance aiming at securing peace and stability, on the other, may become conflicting objectives of the ENP (Börzel and van Hüllen 2014a; Grimm and Leininger 2012). The consistency of the ENP tends to fall victim to the democratization-stability dilemma (Börzel and van Hüllen 2014a; 2011).

To summarize, whereas coherence and cohesiveness describe the quality of the EU as a unitary foreign policy actor, consistency refers to the degree to which different foreign policy goals of the EU may contradict each other. While coherence and cohesiveness are virtually synonymous, consistency is a distinct concept and builds a second analytical dimension of the external effectiveness of the EU.

In the remainder of this chapter, we analyse how the coherence and consistency of the ENP evolved and how they have affected the effectiveness of the EU in transforming its southern and eastern neighbourhood.

ENP South

For decades, the EU maintained a 'Faustian bargain' with autocratic rulers from its southern neighbourhood. Non-democratic regimes in the EU's southern neighbourhood have worked with the EU on fighting illegal migration, combating terrorism and maintaining peace and stability on the southern flanks of the EU (Dandashly 2014), although often they could not achieve more than a 'façade of stability' (Lynch 2013: 63). The EU reciprocated by offering increased economic incentives while its attempt at democracy promotion remained feeble (van Hüllen 2015). The strategic interaction of the EU with southern ENP countries before the outbreak of the 2011 Arab uprisings indicates the EU's prioritization of security and stability interests over democracy promotion.

The EU has tried to position itself as a democracy promoter in its southern neighbourhood. Its official discourse has been consistent in emphasizing the mutually reinforcing and complementary objectives of achieving democracy, security and economic prosperity, both before and after the 'Arab Spring' (Noutcheva 2014). The ENP Action Plans negotiated between the EU and southern ENP countries, based on the principle of joint ownership, included many vaguely defined references to issues of democracy, human rights and the rule of law (Börzel and van Hüllen 2014a). However, there has been a big discrepancy between official discourse and the actual level of implementation (Noutcheva 2014; Börzel, Risse and Dandashly 2014). In practice, the primary focus was on the EU's security concerns, while issues related to democracy and the rule of law were 'deprioritized' (Dandashly 2014: 40).

In the wake of the Arab uprisings, the EU promised to review its policy framework. The 'short-termism' of supporting authoritarian regimes as the only 'guarantee of stability in the region' (Füle 2011) was to give way to the EU's promotion of 'deep democracy' by providing the so-called 'three M's' – money, market access and mobility (Ashton 2011). The EU launched several new programmes including 'A Partnership for Democracy and Shared Prosperity with the Southern Mediterranean' (European Commission 2011) and stepped up its financial assistance for the region (European Commission 2014).

However, the Arab uprisings of 2011 heightened the threats of instability, uncontrolled migration and the prospects of long-term power struggles between different groups in the EU's southern neighbourhood countries. Thus, the EU quickly switched back to its business as usual approach (Teti, Thompson and Noble 2013). Although the EU had adjusted much of its rhetoric, its goals have remained 'security and stability-driven', prioritizing 'security concerns' over uncertain democratic openings (Dandashly 2014: 38). Migration is a case in point. Arab protests in 2011 resulted in the abolition of the migration control deals the EU had struck with the toppled dictators (Noutcheva 2014). Accordingly, the first objective of the EU in the post-'Arab Spring' southern neighbourhood was to re-establish border controls and pacify its southern flank. Rather than a lack of coherence, it is the inconsistency of the ENP that undermines the EU's effectiveness in bringing change to its southern periphery. The 'Arab Spring' has significantly heightened the risks of instability, while not bringing more democracy to the region. Except for Tunisia, the protests have ended up in state erosion (Libya), civil war (Syria) or authoritarian backlash (Egypt). With endogenously driven processes of democratic change being weak in most of the Southern Mediterranean countries and their statehood being challenged by rivalling factions, transnational terrorist networks and competing regional powers, the EU has become even less inclined to engage in democracy promotion (Börzel and van Hüllen 2014a; cf. van Hüllen 2015). With its 'well-established political parties, strong unions and highly educated middle class' (Dandashly 2014: 41), Tunisia has been the only country where the constellation of domestic actors was favourable enough to meet EU political conditionality. Thus, probably also due to cooperation between old and new elites, which allowed former regime members to re-occupy influential power positions, Tunisia has remained sufficiently stable, has had some 'governance capacities' and has possessed pro-democratic domestic agents that external actors could empower (Börzel, Risse and Dandashly 2014: 151). Accordingly, Tunisia has been the main target of the EU's democracy promotion. But, even there, support for democratic reforms has been limited and the main areas of cooperation remained economic development and migration control.

To conclude, the consistency of the ENP's southern dimension has been challenged by low levels of political liberalization and, after the outbreak of Arab uprisings, also by limited degrees of statehood in the Southern Mediterranean. Not only does the political and economic situation in Southern Mediterranean countries generate illegal migration and asylum seeking, but also the incumbent regimes are no longer willing to control, or capable of controlling, their borders to stop the refugee flows from all over the African continent (Dandashly 2014). Border security and maintenance of stability have become the single most important concern of the EU in its southern neighbourhood. While the EU has been consistent in prioritizing stability over democracy, Member States at times disagree on how to cope with the risks of instability challenging the coherence of the EU. The EU failed to speak with a single voice either on the issue of military intervention in Libya or the debate on possible no-fly zones in Syria. Overall, however, the effectiveness of the ENP in the EU's southern neighbourhood is undermined much more by problems of consistency rather than coherence.

ENP East

The effectiveness of the ENP in the post-Soviet space has been equally as limited as in the Southern Mediterranean. Not only have most of the eastern ENP countries not made much progress towards democracy (Börzel 2014); they have also experienced a high degree of political and social instability, as well as military conflicts with Russia or with each other. The presence of secessionist enclaves has further undermined their statehood. Instead of becoming a peaceful, stable and prosperous 'ring of friends', the region has ultimately ended up in another 'ring of fire' (Speck 2015).

With its eastern neighbours, the EU has remained as coherent in formulating an official discourse of transformation as it has in the case of its southern neighbours. It has also managed to preserve its unity in periods of crisis or during important decisions. This resulted, however, in the EU taking a rather reactive approach, trying to adjust its policies to events unfolding on the ground, on which it had no considerable influence due to its overall low profile in the region. For instance, during his 2004 visit to the South Caucasus countries, European Commission president, Romano Prodi, declared that the EU would not act as a conflict mediator in Georgia or between Armenia and Azerbaijan (RFE/RL 2004). In the following years, the EU ignored multiple requests from Georgian leaders for the internationalization of the conflicts in Abkhazia and South Ossetia through deploying an EU monitoring mission, at least on the borders (Börzel and Lebanidze 2015). Similarly, except for a few trust-building programmes with moderate funding, such as the European Partnership for the Peaceful Settlement of the

Conflict over Nagorno Karabakh (EPNK)[1], the EU avoided direct involvement in the Nagorno-Karabakh conflict and instead supported the OSCE Minsk Group (Babayan 2011). With the 2008 Russia–Georgia war, the EU became one of the main Western security and political actors in the South Caucasus region (Ashton 2010). It increased the conflict-related financial support to Georgia and quickly deployed the European Union Monitoring Mission (EUMM) to oversee the fulfilment of the ceasefire agreement between Russia and Georgia, which was negotiated by the then French President Nicolas Sarkozy who at the time of the conflict held the rotating EU presidency (Friedman 2008).

A few years later, another military conflict erupted in the EU's eastern neighbourhood, this time between Ukraine and Russia. In early 2014, Russia annexed the Crimean Peninsula and supported and supplied the secessionist movements in Eastern Ukraine. Due to its geographic proximity and Ukraine's close relations with several central European EU Member States, the Ukrainian conflict has been attracting much more attention in the EU than the Russia–Georgia War (Corboy, Courtney and Yalowitz 2014). The destabilizing role of Russia in the shared neighbourhood has provoked a harsh response by the EU (EurActiv 2015b). Similar to the Russia–Georgia war, the EU has played an important role in temporarily ending the fighting by negotiating two ceasefires (Minsk I and Minsk II) between the conflict parties, helping to stabilize the conflict zones. The EU has also increased financial support to Ukraine and signed the Association Agreement (AA) with the Ukrainian government. Finally, the EU, together with the US, imposed financial and economic sanctions on Russia, a step that would have been unimaginable a few years earlier due to diverging opinions among EU Member States regarding the treatment of Russia (EurActiv 2015a).

Overall, the EU has been keener to engage in unfolding political-security processes in its eastern neighbourhood compared with the southern neighbourhood countries – despite greater challenges to its coherence. Eastern and Central European EU Member States, many of which are known for their hawkish position towards Russia, have often been at odds with more reluctant Western European Member States – with Germany trying to reconcile the opposing camps. In some cases, the EU blatantly failed to speak with one voice. For instance, conciliatory remarks of the Energy Commissioner and representatives of Member States praising cooperation with Azerbaijan on energy (EEAS 2011; 2015) have often overshadowed the criticism of Baku's democratic record in official documents and resolutions adopted by the European Commission (2015) and the European Parliament (2014; 2015). This may be less an issue of coherence, but a self-assessment of the EU as lacking the transformative power *vis-à-vis* energy-rich Azerbaijan (Kobzova and Alieva 2012). To avoid jeopardising its energy and security interests, the EU has paid no more than lip service to the promotion and protection of democracy, human rights, and the rule of law. By contrast, where the EU has felt capable of making a difference, it has usually managed to reach a compromise between Member States and the EU institutions and speak with a single voice.

In terms of the democratization-stability dilemma, the EU has been pursuing a more balanced approach *vis-à-vis* eastern ENP countries than its Southern Mediterranean neighbours. While still prioritizing stability, political conditionality has played a more prominent role due to more favourable domestic conditions. First, although the eastern neighbours have not been necessarily more stable than Mediterranean ENP countries, the large inflows of migrants due to other geographic, but also demographic and political, conditions have been far less of an issue (cf. Fargues 2013). Second, according to most democracy indices, on average, eastern ENP countries have been more democratic than the southern neighbourhood countries (Börzel and van Hüllen 2014a). Third, as most of the EU's eastern neighbours consider themselves European, the EU's external legitimacy has been higher in eastern ENP countries than in the southern neighbourhood countries (Börzel and van Hüllen 2014b; Techau 2014).

Despite these more favourable domestic conditions, the EU has not consistently applied political conditionality to encourage democratic change. In the case of Armenia and Azerbaijan, the EU has consistently prioritized security over democracy. For energy-rich Azerbaijan, this is hardly surprising, since EU officials deem political conditionality unlikely to make a difference (Kobzova and Alieva 2012). So why hurt the EU's economic and security interests? Armenia, in contrast, is a country suffering from structural poverty, with no possession of mineral resources. It has a vibrant civil society and some of the largest anti-autocratic mass protests in the whole eastern neighbourhood (Levitsky and Way 2010). Yet, despite the presence of a strong domestic demand for democratic change, the EU has never invoked political conditionality against Armenia's semi-autocratic government. Rather, its focus has been on the normalization of relations between Armenia and Turkey or the preservation of the frozen state of the conflict over Nagorno-Karabakh (RFE/RL 2010).

Georgia and Ukraine provide some evidence for the EU's use of political conditionality, which has not always been consistent but rather effective. During the electoral revolutions in the early 2000s, the EU and the US empowered opposition movements, youth groups, and civil society actors through various capacity-building measures and criticized the corrupt and authoritarian regimes for flawed elections (Börzel, Pamuk and Stahn 2009; Wilson 2007). In Georgia's 2003 'Rose Revolution', the EU even employed financial sticks, postponing the disbursement of new credits, which caused the budget crisis that helped bring down the Shevardnadze regime (RFE/RL 2002a; 2002b). A few years later, the EU and the US again stepped up their democratizing pressure in both countries. In Georgia, the EU managed to persuade the incumbent regime to participate in the electoral power transition (Börzel and Lebanidze 2015). In Ukraine, the EU criticized the authoritarian roll-back of democratic reforms by newly elected president Victor Yanukovych, and used the negotiation process on the AA to address the lack of democratic change – especially the issue of selective justice. President Yanukovych refused to bow to EU pressure and turned towards Russia instead. However, his decision sparked the large-scale pro-European protests that came to be known as 'Euromaidan', which resulted in a power change with Victor Yanukovich fleeing the country in early 2014 (Marples and Mills 2015).

To summarize, Ukraine and Georgia are the only eastern ENP countries where the EU has repeatedly applied political conditionality. We should not overestimate the influence of the EU in the 'Colour Revolutions' and during the 'Euromaidan'. Yet, the critical position of the EU, with other Western actors, has empowered pro-democratic reform coalitions in Georgia and Ukraine (cf. Wilson 2007). This points to the importance of endogenous democratic processes as a major scope condition for consistency of the ENP and its effectiveness. In Ukraine and Georgia, mass mobilization pushed for democratic change or supported political elites with pro-European reform agendas. In Armenia, the democratic opposition has not been strong enough to override security concerns regarding Nagorno-Karabakh, which orients political elites towards Russia (Babayan 2015). In Azerbaijan and Belarus, finally, political opposition has been weak and the incumbents have never shown any interest in democratic change (Wilson 2011; Kobzova and Alieva 2012). Like its Southern Mediterranean neighbours, the EU's potential to empower democratic forces has been largely absent or circumscribed by the EU's own interest in stability and security in the countries.

Next to the democratization-stability dilemma, the asymmetric dependency of neighbouring countries on the EU has also mitigated the ENP's consistency and effectiveness. The EU notoriously failed to trigger democratic change in Belarus, even though Belarus has been the only country in both neighbourhood spaces that has been under consistent democratizing pressure of the EU since the inception of the ENP. The main factor, which has undermined the application of political conditionality, has been the role of Russia, which has been

Table 17.1 Consistency and effectiveness of the ENP

Consistency	Effectiveness	
	Democratic opening/democratization	Authoritarian stability/authoritarian backlash
Political conditionality	Georgia 2003, 2011–2015 Moldova 2009–2015 Ukraine 2005–2015 Tunisia 2011–2015	Belarus Egypt 2011-2012
Stability/security over democracy		Armenia Azerbaijan Georgia (2004–2010) Algeria Egypt (2003–2011; 2013–2015) Jordan Lebanon Morocco Palestine

bolstering the autocratic regime of Belarus and has made it largely immune to EU pressure (Ambrosio 2009; Tolstrup 2009).

Table 17.1 looks for correlation between the consistency and effectiveness of the EU in the ENP countries. As we can see, in most cases, the EU has prioritized stability and security over democracy, stabilizing rather than transforming the authoritarian structures. However, in the few cases in which the EU decided to invoke political conditionality in response to authoritarianism, democratic forces have prevailed. Countries that have been targeted by EU political conditionality are considered today as having more democratic development in both regions (post-'Arab Spring' Tunisia in the South, and Georgia, Moldova and Ukraine in the East). Belarus and Egypt are two exceptions that confirm the rule. In both countries, the effects of EU political conditionality were mitigated by the weakness of democratic forces, the threat of political instability and the role of illiberal regional powers.

Correlation does not equal causality. It could be that the EU only applies political conditionality where the risk of failure is low, given the presence of strong democratic forces and a low risk of political instability.

Conclusions: the EU's Neighbourhood Policy – inconsistent or Machiavellian?

This chapter discussed the ENP in terms of its coherence and consistency. We argue that the EU's transformative power in its neighbourhood is curbed by a lack of consistency rather than coherence. Whereas the EU has maintained a relatively stable degree of coherence, the inconsistency stemming from the pursuit of conflictual goals has often undermined the effectiveness of the ENP. The democratization-stability dilemma also explains the inter-regional differences we observe. In its southern neighbourhood, except for Tunisia, the EU has hardly applied political conditionality. During the 2011 'Arab Spring', the EU reluctantly accepted the changed environment and committed itself to supporting democratic change. However, the change in discourse has not resulted in a real policy change. The EU continues to prioritize stability over democracy. Despite the formal suspension of dialogue under the ENP, its tacit acceptance of the *coup d'état* by the Egyptian military against the democratically elected government of President

Morsi in Egypt in 2013 is a case in point. In its eastern neighbourhood, by contrast, the EU has sought to strike a better balance between preserving stability and promoting democratic change. The inter-regional differences are related to differences in domestic structures. First, the endogenously driven processes of democratization have been more pronounced in the East than in the South. As a result, the potential for incumbent elites trying to lock-in democratic change and for the EU to empower democratic opposition parties, is greater. Second, the EU enjoys greater public support in the East than in the South. Most of the social protests in eastern ENP countries, including the so called 'Colour Revolutions' in Georgia and Ukraine and the recent protests of 'Euromaidan', were inherently pro-European in nature. The protesters aspired to an increased role of the EU in domestic matters and, ultimately, for EU membership. In contrast, the 2011 Arab uprisings did not call for a clear foreign policy orientation. Moreover, protesters in Arab countries made it clear from the beginning that these revolutions were 'theirs' and that external actors had better stay out (Techau 2014). As one author has observed, in contrast to the protest movements in Central Europe and the former Soviet space, 'for Arabs, the ouster of decades-old dictators did not go hand-in-hand with a return to Europe' (Asseburg 2013: 57). Thus, unlike in eastern ENP countries, the EU's soft power in its southern neighbourhood has been more limited and the preconditions for democratization less straightforward, which further decreased the EU's appetite for applying political conditionality.

Overall, we draw the following conclusions regarding the ENP's coherence, consistency and effectiveness. First, in terms of policy formulation, the EU has been a coherent actor in setting foreign policy goals and asserting itself as a transformative power (Anderson 2008). This is not to say that the decision-making process has always been easy, but the EU has been able to balance different positions and achieve compromises among the Member States, for instance by simultaneous launching the Union for the Mediterranean and the Eastern Partnership. Second, in terms of policy implementation, the EU has also been consistent in pursuing its goals of stability and peace in the neighbourhood. Third, the democratization-stability dilemma has been the main reason behind the much-criticized inconsistency of the EU – which has often resulted in a large discrepancy between policy formulation and policy implementation. The EU has acted as a transformative power supporting democratization by applying political conditionality, but only under certain conditions: the presence of an endogenous democratic process and the absence of any serious risks of instability and political disorder. Otherwise, the EU consistently prioritized security and stability over democratization. Since domestic conditions are unfavourable in the EU's eastern and even more so in its southern neighbourhood, the EU tends to be a stabilizing rather than transformative power, supporting authoritarianism instead of promoting democracy. Yet this inconsistency does not result from a lack of coherence or other malfunctions in the process of EU's foreign policy making: rather, it stems from a deliberate trade-off between pursuing short-term stability and security goals and promoting long term domestic change.

Note

1 EPNK stands for European Partnership for the Peaceful Settlement of the Conflict in Nagorno-Karabakh: www.epnk.org/.

References

Ambrosio, T. (2009) *Authoritarian Backlash: Russian Resistance to Democratization in the Former Soviet Union*, Farnham: Ashgate Pub. Co.
Anderson, S. (2008) *Crafting EU Security Policy: In Pursuit of a European Identity*, Boulder, Colo: Rienner.

Ashton, C. (2010) 'Remarks at the Munich Security Conference', www.consilium.europa.eu/uedocs/cms_Data/docs/pressdata/EN/foraff/112774.pdf, accessed 4 August 2013.

Ashton, C. (2011) 'What Next in North Africa?', www.nytimes.com/2011/03/19/opinion/19iht-edashton19.html, accessed 14 October 2015.

Asseburg, M. (2013) 'The Arab Spring and the European response: The international spectator', *International Spectator* 48(2): 47–62.

Babayan, N. (2011) Armenia: Why the European Neighbourhood Policy has Failed, www.fride.org/publication/892/armenia:-why-the-european-neighbourhood-policy-has-failed.

Babayan, N. (2015) *Democratic Transformation and Obstruction: EU, US, and Russia in the South Caucasus*, London: Routledge.

Baracani, E. (2009) 'The European Neighbourhood Policy and Political Conditionality: Double Standards in EU Democracy Promotion?', in Balzacq, T. (ed.) *The External Dimension of EU Justice and Home Affairs: Governance, Neighbours, Security*, Basingstoke: Palgrave Macmillan, 111–132.

Bicchi, F. (2014) 'The politics of foreign aid and the European Neighbourhood Policy post-Arab Spring: "More for more" or less of the same?', *Mediterranean Politics* 19(3): 318–332.

Borell, M., Boschma, R. Monastiriotis, V. and Wesselink, E. (2012) 'Report on ENP Policy Concerning Its Objectives and Policy Measures over Time', www.ub.edu/searchproject/wp-content/uploads/2012/02/SEARCH-Deliverable-1.2_DEF.pdf, accessed 19 October 2015.

Börzel, T. (2014) 'Coming Together or Drifting Apart? Political Change in New Member States, Accession Candidates, and Eastern Neighbourhood Countries', *MAXCAP Working Paper* 3, Berlin: Freie Universität Berlin.

Börzel, T. and Lebanidze, B. (2015) 'European Neighbourhood Policy at the Cross-Roads: Evaluating the Past to Shape the Future', *MAXCAP Working Paper* 12, Berlin: Freie Universität Berlin.

Börzel, T. and van Hüllen, V. (2011) 'Good Governance and Bad Neighbors? The Limits of the Transformative Power of Europe', *KFG Working Paper Series* 35, http://userpage.fu-berlin.de/kfgeu/kfgwp/wpseries/WorkingPaperKFG_35.pdf.

Börzel, T. and van Hüllen, V. (2014a) 'One voice, one message, but conflicting goals: Cohesiveness and consistency in the European Neighbourhood Policy', *Journal of European Public Policy* 21(7): 1033–1049.

Börzel, T. and van Hüllen, V. (2014b) 'State-building and the European Union's fight against corruption in the Southern Caucasus: Why legitimacy matters', *Governance* 27(4): 613–634.

Börzel, T., Pamuk, J. and Stahn, A. (2009) 'Democracy or Stability? EU and US Engagement in the Southern Caucasus', in Magen, A., Risse, T. and McFaul, M. (eds.) *Promoting Democracy and the Rule of Law: American and European Strategies*, New York: Palgrave Macmillan, 150–184.

Börzel, T., Risse, T. and Dandashly, A. (2014) 'The EU, external actors, and the Arabellions: Much ado about (almost) nothing', *Journal of European Integration* 37(1): 135–153.

Corboy, D., Courtney, W. and Yalowitz, K. (2014) 'Hitting the Pause Button: The "Frozen Conflict" Dilemma in Ukraine', http://nationalinterest.org/feature/hitting-the-pause-button-the-frozen-conflict-dilemma-ukraine-11618, accessed 28 October 2015.

da Conceição-Heldt, E. and Meunier, S. (2014) 'Speaking with a single voice: Internal cohesiveness and external effectiveness of the EU in global governance', *Journal of European Public Policy* 21(7): 961–979.

Dandashly, A. (2014) 'The EU response to regime change in the wake of the Arab revolt: Differential implementation', *Journal of European Integration* 37(1): 37–56.

EEAS (2011) 'Commission President Barroso to Travel to Azerbaijan and Turkmenistan', Press Release, Baku, 12 January, http://eeas.europa.eu/delegations/azerbaijan/documents/press_releases/president_barroso_to_travel_to_azerbaijan_and_turkmenistan.pdf, accessed 28 October 2015.

EEAS (2015) 'EU Top Official to Visit Azerbaijan', Press Release, Baku, 11 February, http://eeas.europa.eu/delegations/azerbaijan/documents/press_releases/2015/20150211_eu_top_official_to_visit_azerbaijan.pdf, accessed 28 October 2015.

EurActiv (2015a) 'Think Tanks: Russia will Make New Attempt to Divide the EU', www.euractiv.com/sections/global-europe/think-tanks-russia-will-make-new-attempt-divide-eu-318749, accessed 28 October 2015.

EurActiv (2015b) 'West's Ties with Russia Frozen after Year of Ukraine Conflict', www.euractiv.com/sections/europes-east/wests-ties-russia-frozen-after-year-ukraine-conflict-313540, accessed 29 January 2016.

European Commission (2011) *A Partnership for Democracy and Shared Prosperity with the Southern Mediterranean*, COM (2011) 200 final.

European Commission (2014) *Implementation of the European Neighbourhood Policy Statistical Annex*, SWD (2014) 98 final.
European Commission (2015) *ENP Country Progress Report 2014 – Azerbaijan*, MEMO/15/4688, http://europa.eu/rapid/press-release_MEMO-15-4688_de.htm.
European Parliament (2014) *European Parliament Resolution of 18 September 2014 on the Persecution of Human Rights Defenders in Azerbaijan*, 2014/2832 (RSP), www.europarl.europa.eu/sides/getDoc.do?pubRef=-//EP//TEXT+TA+P8-TA-2014-0022+0+DOC+XML+V0//EN.
European Parliament (2015) *European Parliament Resolution of 10 September 2015 on Azerbaijan*, 2015/2840(RSP), www.europarl.europa.eu/sides/getDoc.do?pubRef=-//EP//NONSGML+TA+P8-TA-2015-0316+0+DOC+PDF+V0//EN.
Fargues, P. (2013) 'EU Neighbourhood Migration Report 2013', http://cadmus.eui.eu/bitstream/handle/1814/27394/MPC_NeighMigration.pdf?sequence=5.
Friedman, G. (2008) 'The German Question', www.stratfor.com/weekly/20081006_german_question, accessed 28 October 2015.
Füle, Š. (2011) 'Speech on the Recent Events in North Africa', http://europa.eu/rapid/press-release_SPEECH-11-130_de.htm.
Grimm, S. and Leininger, J. (2012) 'Not all good things go together: Conflicting objectives in democracy promotion', *Democratization* 19(3): 391–414.
Jünemann, A. (ed.) (2004) *Euro-Mediterranean Relations after September 11: International, Regional, and Domestic Dynamics*, London: Frank Cass.
Kobzova, J. and Alieva, L. (2012) 'The EU and Azerbaijan: Beyond Oil', www.ecfr.eu/page/-/ECFR57_EU_AZERBAIJAN_MEMO_AW.pdf, accessed 3 June 2015.
Koops, J. and Varwick, J. (2011) *The European Union as an Integrative Power: Assessing the EU's 'Effective Multilateralism' Towards NATO und the United Nations*, Brussels: VUB Press.
Langbein, J. and Börzel, T. (eds.) (2013) 'Introduction: Explaining policy change in the European Union's eastern neighbourhood', *Europe-Asia Studies* 65(4): 571–580.
Levitsky, S. and Way, L. (2010) *Competitive Authoritarianism: Hybrid Regimes after the Cold War*, New York: Cambridge University Press.
Luckau, P. (2011) 'Matching deeds to words? The principle of conditionality in the EU's contractual relations with the Western Balkans', PhD Thesis, Free University Berlin.
Lynch, M. (2013) *The Arab Uprising: The Unfinished Revolutions of the New Middle East*, New York: Public Affairs.
Marples, D. and Mills, F. (eds.) (2015) *Ukraine's Euromaidan: Analyses of a Civil Revolution*, Stuttgart: ibidem Press.
Noutcheva, G. (2014) 'Institutional governance of European Neighbourhood Policy in the wake of the Arab Spring', *Journal of European Integration* 37(1): 19–36.
RFE/RL (2002a) 'Newsline – July 1, 2002', www.rferl.org/content/article/1142707.html, accessed 4 August 2013.
RFE/RL (2002b) 'Newsline – October 10, 2002', www.rferl.org/content/article/1142777.html, accessed 4 August 2012.
RFE/RL (2004) 'Newsline – September 21, 2004', www.rferl.org/content/article/1143247.html, accessed 29 March 2012.
RFE/RL (2010) 'Oppositionist Slams Western "Double Standards"', www.armenialiberty.org/content/article/2260641.html, accessed 28 October 201.
Schimmelfennig, F. (2008) 'EU political accession conditionality after the 2004 enlargement: Consistency and effectiveness', *Journal of European Public Policy* 15(6): 918–937.
Speck, U. (2015) 'EU Faces Tough Choices in the Neighbourhood', https://euobserver.com/opinion/128728, accessed 17 October 2015.
Techau, J. (2014) 'What if the EU Had Reacted Strategically to the Arab Spring?', http://carnegieeurope.eu/publications/?fa=54672, accessed 14 October 2015.
Teti, A., Thompson, D. and Noble, C. (2013) 'EU democracy assistance discourse in its new response to a changing neighbourhood', *Democracy and Security* 9(1–2): 61–79.
Thomas, D. (2012) 'Still punching below its weight? Coherence and effectiveness in European Union Foreign Policy', *Journal of Common Market Studies* 50(3): 457–474.
Tolstrup, J. (2009) 'Studying a negative external actor: Russia's management of stability and instability in the "Near Abroad"', *Democratization* 16(5): 922–944.
van Hüllen, V. (2015) *EU Democracy Promotion and the Arab Spring: International Cooperation and Authoritarianism*, Basingstoke: Palgrave Macmillan.

van Vooren, B. and Wessel, R. (2014) *EU External Relations Law: Text, Cases and Materials*, Cambridge: Cambridge University Press.
Wilson, A. (2007) 'Ukraine's orange revolution, NGOs and the role of the West', *Cambridge Review of International Affairs* 19(1): 21–32.
Wilson, A. (2011) *Belarus: The Last European Dictatorship*, New Haven: Yale University Press.
Youngs, R. (2002) 'The European Union and democracy promotion in the Mediterranean: A new or disingenuous strategy?', *Democratization* 9(1): 40–62.

18
EUROPEAN NEIGHBOURHOOD POLICY DECISION-MAKING AT CRITICAL JUNCTURES

EU institutions, the Member States and neighbourhood countries

Mark Furness

Introduction

Political decisions, particularly those regarding complex institutionalised policy frameworks with a perspective of several years, tend to be taken at critical junctures (Capoccia and Kelemen 2007). The 2015 European Neighbourhood Policy (ENP) review has been the fourth such critical juncture in the life of the European Union's (EU's) Neighbourhood Policy since its launch in 2003, the creation of the Union for the Mediterranean (UfM) and the Eastern Partnership (EaP) in 2008–2009 and the ENP review conducted just before the 'Arab Spring' in 2010 and early 2011. Each occasion has seen the EU institutions, EU Member State governments and neighbouring countries engage in a process of reflection, proposal, counter proposal and negotiation before deciding on the ENP's future.

This chapter addresses two questions with regard to ENP decision-making. The first is descriptive: how does the process through which decisions are taken work, formally and informally? In exploring this process the chapter aims to shed some light on the arcane world of decision-making in EU foreign relations. The second question is analytical and addresses this handbook's central aim of evaluating the ENP as a political process. Has the decision-making process produced a policy framework that advances a convincing strategy from the EU's perspective, while satisfying the interests of neighbouring countries in engagement with the EU?

The academic literature that documents, analyses and explains political decision-making is vast, but research has largely followed one of two broad groups of approaches. Some analyses have used formal theories that second-guess or predict decisions and their outcomes with various techniques, including models that process indicators representing aspects of a decision-making process. Others have worked with so-called behavioural theories, which 'trace decisions empirically to find out what actually happens rather than what is expected to happen' (Pettigrew 1973: 5). As with formal models, the process-tracing approach typically accounts for the influence of key factors, including interests, power, ideology, individual and collective problem-solving, information availability and the organisational structure of decision-making processes. Decisions are usually shaped by a) interests and b) opportunity, moderated by constraints including the interests of others, the 'rules of the game' (formal and implicit), other contextual factors such as perceived urgency and uncertainty about outcomes leading to risk-averse behaviour (North 1997: 2–8).

This chapter aims to show how the ENP decision-making process works at critical junctures by tracing the 2015 ENP review. The focus is on key EU-level, Member State and neighbouring country actors involved in the process, their interests and the formal and informal processes through which they interact. ENP decision-making is a good example of 'network governance' in action (Jordan and Schout 2006). Formal processes are usually put in train by a policy entrepreneur, which in the EU is normally a Member State or group of Member States, for foreign policy initiatives, or the Commission, for community policy initiatives. Subsequent EU-level decision-making is often characterised by informal interactions that exploit 'grey areas' in formal procedures (Christiansen and Neuhold 2013). Institutional actors, such as the European Commission, the European Parliament (EP) or the European External Action Service (EEAS) can use these grey areas for their own agendas (Henökl 2015). In the case of the ENP, Member States have played a strong role as policy entrepreneurs at critical junctures, while the policy itself has been designed and implemented mainly by the Commission, using the tools of EU enlargement that are under Commission competence. Since 2011, the EEAS has had a formal joint decision-making role that, in practice, has been limited to providing political guidance and public diplomacy.

Regarding outcomes, this chapter provides support to Tsebelis' (1995) hypothesis that policy changes, in complex political systems with a large number of veto players, are rarely revolutionary. As they are made by men and women operating in bureaucratic decision-making environments, they tend to be both path-dependent and risk-averse. The ENP has been no exception throughout its history: critical junctures have arisen when events in the neighbourhood forced EU policy-makers to rejig the policy framework to make it more effective, without challenging its core rationale or its basic function.

ENP decision-making at critical junctures

The original ENP was driven by changes within the EU itself, especially the 'big bang' enlargement of May 2004, which added 10 new EU Member States. Decisions taken at that time were based on the enlarged EU's interests amid a political atmosphere characterised by confidence in the Union that, according to its 2003 Security Strategy, had 'never been so prosperous, so secure and so free' (European Council 2003: 1). The initial impetus for the ENP came from the UK, which, in a 2002 letter to the Spanish EU Presidency, called for cohesive policy towards eastern neighbours that matched the Barcelona Process for the Southern and Eastern Mediterranean (Copsey 2007). The EU-level institutions, especially DG Relex and DG Enlargement in the European Commission, then took on the task of designing the policy framework in detail.

2003: the 'ring of friends'

The 2003 ENP was modelled on enlargement policy, which had incentivised political and economic transformation in eight former communist countries in Eastern and Central Europe. The enlargement model was adapted for neighbouring countries, not only because it had been successful but also because the European Commission and Council Secretariat officials that designed the policy framework preferred to recycle decision-making procedures and substantive policies that they were used to using (Copsey 2007). As a result, the ENP looked a lot like enlargement policy in terms of its language, its emphasis on values and its attempted use of conditionality and socialisation to incentivise the reforms the EU considered desirable (Kelley 2006).

The decision-making process that produced the original ENP did not involve much consultation with neighbouring countries. Rhetorically, the ENP strengthened the ownership of neighbours through negotiated Action Plans that detailed reforms and responsibilities for both parties. In practice, however, the Action Plans were framed by pre-existing bilateral Association Agreements (AAs) (in the South) and Partnership and Cooperation Agreements (PCAs) (in the East). The scope for neighbouring countries to negotiate on the overarching ENP policy framework was limited. Just as southern neighbours felt that the Euro-Mediterranean Partnership (EMP) had proceeded without sufficient consultation, the project of creating a 'ring of friends' launched in 2004 was regarded as a consolation prize, especially by Ukraine and Moldova, which had hopes of accession to the EU (Johansson-Nogués 2004).

It quickly became clear that the ENP faced major challenges for which it was ill-equipped to deal. As Del Sarto and Schumacher noted, 'the "Wider Europe – Neighbourhood" policy was *not* designed to address socio-economic problems in the EU's periphery' (2005: 19), but rather the interests of the EU and its members in regional security, economic opportunities and border control. Moreover, the ENP's core assumption – that enlargement had proved the universal success of the EU's political-economic model and the institutions on which it was based – was flawed. Accordingly, predictions that the EU's efforts to practice 'external governance' by leveraging reforms using 'positive conditionality' would be ineffectual without the EU membership perspective proved prescient (Lavenex 2004).

2008–2009: the Union for the Mediterranean and the Eastern Partnership

The second major critical juncture for the ENP came in 2008–2009 with the *de facto* split of the framework into the UfM and the EaP. Again, a major Member State turned out to be the key policy entrepreneur, when Nicolas Sarkozy called for a Mediterranean Union during the 2007 French presidential campaign. The deadlock in EU relations with the Arab world provided Sarkozy with a golden opportunity. Indeed,

> the importance of the French initiative, in its original form, lay in the tacit recognition that [. . .] the major objectives outlined in the Barcelona Declaration of 1995 have remained elusive, especially in regard to the ultimate goals of prosperity, security and political reform.
>
> *(Gillespie 2008: 277)*

Sarkozy's proposal was controversial in that it not only ignored eastern neighbours and (initially) even non-Mediterranean EU members but also compromised EU accession negotiations with Turkey and threatened to weaken the ENP through its vision of a union of nation-states with only a minor role for the EU institutions (Lippert 2007).

As with the United Kingdom's call for strong conditions in the 2003 ENP, Sarkozy's original idea was substantially watered down by intra-EU negotiations, this time flavoured by fierce German resistance (Schumacher 2011). Consultations with Southern Mediterranean countries were limited until the major decisions about the policy framework had been taken. The UfM, launched during the French EU Presidency in July 2008, focused on concrete projects and reflected diminishing ambition on the EU side for fostering regionalism in the Middle East and North Africa (MENA) (Bicchi 2012). Nevertheless, like the ENP and the Euro-Mediterranean Partnership before it, the UfM was underpinned by the functionalist logic of enlargement, in the idea that progress in areas of common interest would eventually lead to progress on more sensitive governance and even political issues (Holden 2012). By focusing on areas where ENP countries could agree, the UfM was considered less vulnerable to failure because of areas where neighbours did not agree.

Meanwhile, the idea that relations between the EU and eastern and southern neighbours should be differentiated had already firmed during the 2007 German EU Council Presidency. In response to a Polish–Swedish initiative, the European Council decided, in May 2008, to establish an eastern partnership as a regional component of the ENP. However, the ENP's vision of a harmonious future received an immediate reality check when war in Georgia broke out during the 2008 summer Olympics. The EaP has since proved mostly irrelevant to the 'frozen conflicts' in the South Caucasus, while Belarus has remained stubbornly immune to the EU's power of attraction (Bosse 2012). The EU's influence in Moldova, Ukraine and Georgia has been greater because, even though Russia's presence looms large, significant sections of the elites of these countries want to be closer to the EU politically and economically, even as popular support for the EU has waned (Freyburg et al. 2011).

2011: the 'Arab Spring' and the 'New Response'

The 2011 'Arab Spring' uprisings caught Europe by surprise, despite signs there was something brewing in a region characterised by economic stagnation, demographic imbalances, unaccountable political systems and ageing autocratic leaders. The total irrelevance of the ENP in the early days of the Arab uprisings, combined with the impulse to 'do something' in support of grassroots movements agitating for democratic change, prompted the EU to take stock of its activities in the MENA in response to momentous events that Europeans were both inspired and alarmed by.

The 2011 ENP review was different to the 2003 and 2008–2009 critical junctures, in that the policy entrepreneur was situated at the EU level. It was not driven by Member States but rather by the European Commission, with support from the newly launched EEAS. The review was launched in mid-2010 and inputs from the 27 Member States, neighbouring countries, civil society and academia had just been compiled when the Tunisian revolution broke out in December (Tocci 2011). The Commission's response to events was then quickly revised with even less consultation with MENA neighbours than in 2008. In the words of one Commission official, 'suddenly the revision was on the website' (interview, 1 July 2015).

In May 2011, the High Representative for Foreign Affairs and Security Policy/Vice President of the European Commission (HR/VP), Catherine Ashton, and the Commission published 'A New Response to a Changing Neighbourhood' (European Commission/High Representative of the European Union for Foreign Affairs and Security Policy 2011). The document did not examine the policy framework's core premises or the usefulness of the enlargement-based instruments through which it was implemented. Rather, as Schumacher pointed out, the outcomes of the 2011 review were 'as much the result of the outbreak of Arab uprisings in early 2011 as it was a consequence of pre-existing structural problems and challenges in the EU's southern borderlands' (Schumacher 2015: 382). The 'New Response' re-iterated the EU's reliance on positive conditionality through the 'more for more' approach, and was followed up with diplomatic overtures in support of democratic processes, especially in Tunisia, Egypt and Libya.

An extra EUR1 billion was promised, although this was merely a re-budgeting of existing funds and well short of an amount that could incentivise consolidation of the democratic wave that the EU professed to support. The 'New Response' eventually proved toothless when the Egyptian military's overthrow of the country's elected Muslim Brotherhood government in mid-2013 went unchallenged by the EU (Börzel, Risse and Dandashly 2015). HR/VP Ashton's high-profile and symbolic visits to imprisoned Egyptian president Morsi aside, the EU and its Member States accepted the overthrow of a democratically elected government as the price of short-term stability in a key neighbouring country.

The 2015 ENP review

The 'Arab Spring' did not transform the EU's southern neighbourhood in a liberal democratic direction, as many had hoped for. Rather, popular uprisings stalled (or never got going) across most of this geographic space, were reversed by the return to military government in Egypt, and descended into violent nightmares in Libya and Syria. When new European Commission President, Jean-Claude Juncker, took office in November 2014, Tunisia was the only country still in transformation towards democracy, albeit vulnerable to terrorism and chaos. In the East, the situation was similarly problematic with war in Eastern Ukraine and Russia's annexation of Crimea. Inside the EU, uneasiness with enlargement amid the ongoing Euro crisis also undermined the ENP's support.

In Brussels, the feeling in late 2014 was that a review was overdue, a decade after the ENP's launch, especially as the 2011 review had been cosmetic. Senior EU policy-makers considered that the ENP had become little more than a reporting exercise, done by the EU at the expense of neighbours' involvement. There was also honest reflection that the policy framework itself was flawed. DG Neighbourhood and Enlargement Negotiations (NEAR) director-general, Christian Danielsson, told an interviewer,

> The idea was to have a ring of friends who would integrate with us but not become EU members. That was rather patronizing, with the EU telling everyone what to do because we believed they wanted to be like us.
>
> *(quoted in Taylor 2015)*

The Juncker Commission decided to conduct a full consultation process inside and outside of the EU, already with the intention to 'slim down the vast, vague policy of the past, the huge tool box with everything in it' (interview with EEAS official, 2 July 2015). The Commission and the EEAS opened the consultation in March 2015 with a Communication that asked fundamental questions, like whether there should be one ENP or different policies for the East and South. It also signalled a new approach by inviting inputs on security and migration, sectors which had previously been excluded (European Commission/High Representative of the European Union for Foreign Affairs and Security Policy 2015a).

The 2015 ENP review: actors and interests

As in 2003 and 2008–2009, key Member States provided the impetus for the 2015 ENP review. Against the background of war in Ukraine, and stalled transformation processes in other neighbouring countries, the German, French and Polish Foreign Ministers adopted the Weimar Declaration on the ENP in April 2014. The declaration called for the adaptation of the ENP in response to challenges in the East and South, and stressed the importance of flexible finance, better crisis response and improved compatibility with Member State policies (Auswärtiges Amt 2014). Following the Weimar Declaration, Member States kept a close eye on the review, and nearly all prepared non-papers, often in collaboration with other Member States. For example, a German memo to the EU Council Secretariat argued that closer harmonisation of the ENP and the CFSP would make the ENP more political, rather than development oriented, while improving the coherence of Member State and EU-level activities (EU Council Secretariat 2015). The April 2015 EU Foreign Affairs Council outcome document duly called for closer coordination between ENP and wider CFSP/Common Security and Defence Policy (CSDP) activities (European Council 2015).

At the EU level, the Weimar Declaration was taken up enthusiastically by the new Juncker Commission. Commission President Juncker included the ENP in his '10 points' list of priorities for his presidency (Juncker 2014). New Enlargement/Neighbourhood Commissioner, Johannes Hahn, wanted to make an impact after taking office, and DG NEAR's capacities had increased with the transfer of the EuropeAid units for the ENP from DG Development and Cooperation (DEVCO) in November 2014 (interview with Commission official, 1 July 2015). For the Commission, the ENP was a core part of the EU's global engagement, both for proximity reasons and because of the Commission's long-standing role (partly taken up by the EEAS from 2011) in making and implementing policies that bridge CFSP and Community competencies.

For the EEAS, the main interest in the review was in its geostrategic implications and links to crisis response strategies for Syria, Libya and Ukraine, conducted in parallel to the ENP review process (interviews with EEAS officials, 30 June 2015). The principal interest shared by the EEAS and DG NEAR has been in increasing financial flexibility under the new framework. The proposal for the 2014–2020 Multiannual Financial Framework (MFF) was drawn up in 2012, when there was no conflict in Ukraine, developments in Libya were promising and migration was not at the crisis levels of 2015. According to officials, the Commission has had to manage the many demands on the European Neighbourhood Instrument (ENI) by shifting funds allocated to one partner to another in response to shifting priorities. In 2012, the budget for Syria was EUR 38 million. This was increased to EUR 90 million in 2014, but EUR 20 million was reportedly cut from programmes in Morocco and further savings were made elsewhere, including in Development Cooperation Instrument allocations to Asia and Latin America (interviews, 30 June and 1 July 2015). Commission and EEAS officials expressed shared views that this situation is unsustainable in the medium term, given increasing demands created by neighbourhood crises: they have pushed for the creation of new instruments with greater flexibility, such as the multi-donor Madad Trust Fund in response to the Syria crisis, to which other EU Member States and Turkey have contributed (European Commission 2015).

The EP's key message was that the ENP should keep the basics, even though in 10 years it has not generated the 'ring of friends'. Parliamentarians called for the ENP to engage more with political issues through EU Special Representatives and to take the neighbours of the neighbours into account, as these countries also have influence on the European neighbourhood (European Parliament 2015a). The EP had bureaucratic interests also, which it tried to push, through its efforts to change the ENI regulation, and thereby increase influence over the whole ENP review (interview with EP official, 1 July 2015).

ENP countries expressed interests in the 2015 review more strongly than at earlier junctures. According to Commission officials who took part in the Riga and Barcelona summits and other negotiations, the neighbours wanted a policy reflecting what they desire from their relations with the EU: aid, trade and visas (interview, 1 July 2015). Beyond this general interest there was a broad spectrum of objectives among ENP countries: some preferred a closer relationship with

Europe while others did not want much engagement at all. Countries with specific interests, such as energy, education, fisheries or agriculture have tried to strengthen the protocols on these sectors and make them more concrete (interviews with EC and EEAS officials, 30 June to 2 July 2015).

The 2015 ENP review: formal and informal processes

The 2015 ENP review has mostly been an executive process, conducted by the Commission with EEAS support. Member States took part in the official consultation, European Council meetings during the process, and the high-level meetings with ENP countries in Barcelona, Riga and Beirut. This official process was conducted through a series of formal and informal decision-making steps that eventually resulted in the Communication on the revised ENP released on 18 November 2015.

The ENP review was conducted through a wide formal consultation with EU member governments, the EP, partner country governments, civil society, experts and the interested public, who were asked for their views on the ENP's strengths and weaknesses and their recommendations for its future. EU Member States expressed their views both in writing and through the Council of Permanent Representatives before the consultation paper was drafted and circulated. Nearly all EU Member States submitted or contributed to proposals in response to the consultation paper. Officials described the consultation process inside the EU as 'unprecedented this time' (interview with Commission official, 2 July 2015); 245 inputs on the consultation paper were received before the deadline on 30 June 2015.

The review also featured extensive formal consultation with ENP partner governments. The process started in earnest ahead of the 13 April 2015 Euro-Mediterranean Foreign Ministers' meeting in Barcelona, which was the first such gathering since the launch of the UfM in 2008. The summit sent a strong signal to the neighbouring country governments that the EU was serious about the ENP, and the neighbours were reportedly pleased that the EU was asking (interview with EEAS official, 2 July 2015).

The degree of responsiveness to the consultation was also unprecedented. At the multilateral level, the Arab League participated actively in the process, producing a position paper focused on migration (League of Arab States 2015). All bilateral ENP countries prepared their own papers and a joint paper, coordinated by ambassadors in Brussels, was tabled at the Euro-Mediterranean summit in Beirut on 6 July 2015. The joint paper called for the EU to abandon unilateral policies and conditionality and focus on mutual interests. It reminded the EU that ENP countries faced challenges that require them to safeguard stability, a coded reference to the EU's democracy promotion efforts in the region. It called for increased EU pressure on Israel, including through recognition of Palestine. It also called for the EU to increase financial support and not to divert development funds for humanitarian purposes, while simplifying technical and procedural processes for accessing EU funds (Arab ENP Partners 2015). Although the paper was light on detail, it was taken as an important signal to the EU that the Arab neighbours were committed to the ENP (interview with Commission official, 2 July 2015).

As the review was conducted, the Commission and the EEAS had the task of drafting a policy paper based on the consultations. Formally, this was a co-process between the EEAS and the Commission, but DG NEAR had the right of initiative. A joint Commission/EEAS Task Force was created, consisting of seven senior managers and two heads of unit (one each from DG NEAR and the EEAS), who acted as secretaries and were responsible for drafting. The Task Force oversaw the work of four thematic working groups – one each on differentiation, focus, ownership and visibility, and the flexibility of financial instruments. The first two were chaired by the EEAS, the others by DG NEAR. The working groups were made up of officials from the EEAS and DG NEAR, as well as from other EU services, including DEVCO, Humanitarian Affairs, and the Foreign Policy Instruments service. The second draft of the final communication was already completed before the consultation process closed on 30 June (interview with Commission official, 1 July 2015).

Informal processes were also very important in shaping decision-making. EEAS officials claimed credit for making the process more political, even though DG NEAR was *de facto* in the lead. HR/VP Federica Mogherini's office provided political guidance and Mogherini herself was active behind the scenes, in particular on the review's fit with broader EU global strategy discussions encompassing CFSP, CSDP, ENP, development, climate change and trade policies (Mogherini 2015). The recollection of one EEAS official was that 'at the beginning there was no margin for politicians. Mogherini said this is what we have to change.' The official remembered a meeting early in the process where the Commission tabled a 'big pile of documents telling everyone what to do,' to which 'we said you have to put questions not answers'. DG NEAR officials reportedly revised their proposal, after which 'meetings were organised where everyone congratulated the Commission for doing this' (interview with EEAS official, 2 July 2015).

These kinds of frank exchanges were taken in a positive spirit by EU officials. Some compared the 2015 ENP review to the 2003 European Security Strategy, which was written by Javier Solana's team with little discussion. The mood in the Juncker Commission has been more team-oriented with extensive exchange among Commission DGs, services and the EEAS. As one official put it, there were 'lots of different inputs into the ENP this time, because we want to make it much more about EU policies' (interview with Commission official, 2 July 2015). There was, nevertheless, an implicit understanding of the informal division of labour. Although the 18 November publication was a joint Communication, senior DG NEAR officials held the pen. As one official put it, 'NEAR is drafting, and when you draft, you push' (interview, 1 July 2015).

Formally, the EP had a scrutiny function, a budget function and a political message function in the review process. The EP was not invited to Commission/EEAS consultations with the Foreign Affairs Council but was formally consulted in parallel. Foreign Affairs Committee Chairman Elmar Brok discussed the ENP review with Commissioner Hahn and HR/VP Mogherini, and Mogherini's Foreign Affairs Committee Parliamentary briefings included updates on the ENP. Some special committees, consisting of small groups of MEPs with security clearances, met Mogherini for oral briefings on crisis response, and EEAS and Commission officials attended Parliamentary working group briefings (interview with EP official, 1 July 2015).

The EP also played an important informal role in decision-making, both inside and outside the EU. The EP's influence was less direct than that of the Commission or the EEAS and operated mostly through the political pressure of strong messages. As one EP official put it, 'it is better for the EEAS and the Commission if the Parliament is fully supportive' (interview, 1 July 2015). In order that this support be negotiated and communicated, a huge network of influences operated behind political level meetings. MEPs reportedly met informally with Commissioners and their cabinets, as well as with colleagues in Member States – dialogues which EP officials regarded as 'good and fruitful' (interview, 1 July 2015). MEPs also worked with neighbouring countries through mechanisms like the EuroNest (EaP) and Euro-Mediterranean parliamentary assemblies and the UfM Rapporteur.

The EP's Foreign Affairs Committee produced a report on the ENP review in April 2015, following work from the President's policy unit and parliamentary working groups (European Parliament 2015a). The report was amended many times to reflect the EP's broad range of views before being voted on in July 2015. The resulting resolution stressed the strategic importance of the ENP for the EU, proposed that the policy be more focused, flexible and politically driven, and called for EU special representatives to be appointed for the East and the South. The Resolution also called for the EU to 'match the ambitions of reinforced engagement in its neighbourhood with sufficient financing' (European Commission/High Representative of the European Union for Foreign Affairs and Security Policy 2015b).

The 2015 ENP review: outcomes

The revised ENP, launched on 18 November 2015, resulted from a process shaped by multiple actors engaging in formal and informal decision-making procedures that encourage risk-averse behaviour and path dependency rather than a clear focus on problem-solving. The EU retreated from proposing models for its neighbours, instead concentrating on cooperation in areas where there are concrete interests on both sides. European interests, especially in regional stability, security and controlled migration, were outlined much more explicitly than before. Mutual interests in trade, investment and energy cooperation were also highly prominent, as they have been since the beginning of the ENP in 2003. For ENP countries, the policy represented a menu *à la carte*: the thematic pillars outlined different cooperation models from which neighbours may choose, from a Deep and Comprehensive Free Trade Agreement to cooperation in one or two sectors (European Commission/High Representative of the European Union for Foreign Affairs and Security Policy 2015b).

The 2015 ENP is nevertheless a more focused and realistic cooperation framework than its predecessors. Parts that worked well were retained: one important success of the ENP has been in improving administrative structures, processes and standards in sector-specific governance fields, such as aviation, customs and border protection, and the environment (Carp and Schumacher 2015). The difference this time was that the neo-functionalist premise that sectoral relationships would eventually lead to reforms that would transform neighbouring countries in the EU's image, and progressively integrate them with the EU itself, was softened.

Indeed, the most remarkable feature of the new ENP was the scaling-back of the EU's ambitions in the neighbourhood, reflecting the reality acknowledged by Commissioner Hahn that most of the ENP countries were not interested in becoming 'more European' (Hahn 2015). While Commission officials argued that the EU has not given up on values that have always guided the EU's policy, they recognised that the EU was overambitious regarding its clout, and not focused enough, particularly regarding the most difficult ENP countries (interview with Commission official, 20 November 2015). References to democracy, good governance and human rights remained prominent in the November 2015 Communication, with specific focus on programmes supporting the judiciary, accountable public administration and civil society – all areas where the EU has extensive expertise (European Commission/High Representative of the European Union for Foreign Affairs and Security Policy 2015b). Nevertheless, the most political idea at the heart of the ENP – the transformational power of Europe – all but disappeared amid the pragmatism (Furness and Schäfer 2015).

Conclusions

Returning to the questions posed at the outset, the process-tracing approach has revealed that the formal and informal processes of EU external policy decision-making are symbiotic and mutually reinforcing. Formal rules and competencies structure informal interactions, which are essential for producing a policy framework that EU-level actors, Member States and neighbouring country governments can accept as worthwhile and legitimate. It is clear, however, that the

ENP decision-making process is an example of a multi-actor, bureaucratic process from which revolutionary outcomes should not be expected. Three of the four critical junctures in the ENP's evolution have been initiated by Member States, but the European Commission is still the main EU-level player in the decision-making process and the EEAS a supporting actor despite the HR/VP's high public profile. Although the 2015 review process has been more inclusive than in the past regarding engagement with ENP countries, it was conducted against the background of crisis in the neighbourhood and in the EU, and in a spirit of realism, pragmatism and consolidation, rather than transformation.

Has this decision-making process produced a policy framework that is convincing from the perspective of the EU and interesting for the neighbours? The effectiveness of the ENP in both its design and implementation is explored in rich detail elsewhere in this handbook. The main point here is whether the 2015 framework is an improvement on what emerged from decision-making processes at earlier critical junctures. The EU's implicit strategy of influence by persuasion has not changed. What has changed is the level of ambition. The biggest incentive the EU could offer to reform neighbouring countries in its own image was membership of the club itself. The reformed ENP reflects the realisation that the EU's 'soft power' political influence in neighbouring countries is limited, and that it cannot provide enough incentives to underwrite democratic transformation in the neighbourhood. It is, nevertheless, likely that the revised ENP will be more successful than its predecessors at achieving its objectives, because the objectives themselves are less ambitious.

References

Arab ENP Partners (2015) 'Arab ENP Common Position Paper', Beirut 24 June.
Auswärtiges Amt (2014) 'Building a stronger compact with our neighbours: A new momentum for the European Neighbourhood Policy – Statement by the Foreign Ministers of the Weimar Triangle, 1 April 2014', www.auswaertiges-amt.de/sid_AADF2882595D970725C21C4CF8F21877/EN/Infoservice/Presse/Meldungen/2014/140401-Erkl_Weimar.html?nn=473058, accessed 15 October 2015.
Bicchi, F. (2012) 'The Union for the Mediterranean, or the Changing Context of Euro-Mediterranean Relations', in Bicchi, F. and Gillespie, R. (eds.) *The Union for the Mediterranean*, London: Routledge, 1–17.
Börzel, T., Risse, T. and Dandashly, A. (2015) 'Responses to the "Arabellions": The EU in comparative perspective – Introduction', *Journal of European Integration* 37(1): 1–17.
Bosse, G. (2012) 'A partnership with dictatorship: Explaining the paradigm shift in European Union policy towards Belarus', *Journal of Common Market Studies* 50(3): 367–384.
Capoccia, G. and Kelemen, D. (2007) 'The study of critical junctures: Theory, narrative, and counterfactuals in historical institutionalism', *World Politics* 59(3): 341–369.
Carp, S. and Schumacher, T. (2015) 'From survival to revival: The Riga Summit 2015 and the revised ENP', *Egmont Security Policy Brief* 65, July.
Christiansen, T. and Neuhold, C. (2013) 'Informal politics in the EU', *Journal of Common Market Studies* 51(6): 1196–1206.
Copsey, N. (2007) 'The Member States and the European Neighbourhood Policy', *University of Birmingham European Research Working Paper Series* 20.
EU Council Secretariat (2015) 'Harmonising ENP and CFSP', *Meeting Document* 68/15.
European Commission (2015) 'Managing the refugees crisis: Immediate operational, budgetary and legal measures under the European Agenda on Migration (Annex 6)', COM (2015) 490 Final, *Press Release*, 23 September.
European Commission/High Representative of the European Union for Foreign Affairs and Security Policy (2011) *A New Response to a Changing Neighbourhood: A Review of European Neighbourhood Policy*, COM (2011) 303 Final, 25 May.
European Commission/High Representative of the European Union for Foreign Affairs and Security Policy (2015a) *Joint Consultation Paper: Towards a New European Neighbourhood Policy*, JOIN (2015) 6 Final.

European Commission/High Representative of the European Union for Foreign Affairs and Security Policy (2015b) *Review of the European Neighbourhood Policy*, JOIN (2015) 50 Final, Brussels, 18 November.

European Council (2003) *A Secure Europe in a Better World – European Security Strategy*, Brussels, 12 December.

European Council (2015) Outcome of the 3382nd Council Meeting, Luxembourg: Foreign Affairs, 20 April.

European Parliament (2015a) *Draft Report on the Review of the European Neighbourhood Policy*, (2015/2002(INI), Committee on Foreign Affairs, Rapporteur: Eduard Kukan.

European Parliament (2015b) *European Parliament Resolution of 9 July 2015 on the Review of the European Neighbourhood Policy*, (2015/2002(INI)).

Freyburg, T., Lavenex, S., Schimmelfennig, F., Skripka, T. and Wetzel, A. (2011) 'Democracy promotion through functional cooperation? The case of the European Neighbourhood Policy', *Democratization* 18(4): 1026–1054.

Furness, M. and Schäfer, I. (2015) 'The 2015 European Neighbourhood Policy review: More realism, less ambition', *German Development Institute Column*, 26 November.

Gillespie, R. (2008) 'A 'Union for the Mediterranean' . . . or for the EU?', *Mediterranean Politics* 13(2): 277–286.

Hahn, J. (2015) 'Theorizing the European Neighbourhood Policy', Speech at College of Europe, Bruges, 17 September, www.coleurope.eu/events/international-conference-theorizing-european-neighbourhood-policy, accessed 28 January 2016.

Henökl, T. (2015) 'How do EU foreign policy-makers decide? Institutional orientations within the European external action service', *West European Politics* 38(3): 679–708.

Holden, P. (2012) 'A New Beginning? Does the Union for the Mediterranean Herald a New Functionalist Approach to Co-operation in the Region?', in Bicchi, F. and Gillespie, R. (eds.) *The Union for the Mediterranean*, London: Routledge, 155–169.

Johansson-Nogués, E. (2004) 'A 'ring of friends'? The implications of the European neighbourhood policy for the Mediterranean', *Mediterranean Politics* 9(2): 240–247.

Jordan, A. and Schout, A. (2006) *The Coordination of the European Union: Exploring the Capacities of Networked Governance*, Oxford: Oxford University Press.

Juncker, J. (2014) 'A New Start for Europe: My Agenda for Jobs, Growth, Fairness and Democratic Change', Opening Statement in the European Parliament Plenary Session, Strasbourg, 22 October, http://ec.europa.eu/priorities/sites/beta-political/files/juncker-political-guidelines_en.pdf, accessed 27 January 2016.

Kelley, J. (2006) 'New wine in old wineskins: Promoting political reforms through the new European neighbourhood policy', *Journal of Common Market Studies* 44(1): 29–55.

Lavenex, S. (2004) 'External governance in "Wider Europe"', *Journal of European Public Policy* 11(4): 680–700.

League of Arab States (2015) *The New European Neighbourhood Policy: Arab Position with Regard to Migration*, non-paper.

Lippert, B. (2007) 'The EU neighbourhood policy – profile, potential, perspective', *Intereconomics* 42(4): 180–204.

Mogherini, F. (2015) 'Preface', in Misseroli, A. (ed.) *Towards an EU Global Strategy: Background, Process, References*, Paris: EU Institute for Security Studies.

North, D. (1997) 'The Contribution of the New Institutional Economics to an Understanding of the Transition Problem', *UNU-WIDER Annual Lecture* 1, March.

Pettigrew, A. (1973): *The Politics of Organizational Decision-Making*, London: Tavistock.

Schumacher, T. (2011) 'Germany and Central and Eastern European countries: Laggards or veto-players?', *Mediterranean Politics* 16(1): 79–98.

Schumacher, T. (2015) 'Uncertainty at the EU's borders: Narratives of EU external relations in the revised European Neighbourhood Policy towards the southern borderlands', *European Security* 24(3): 381–401.

Taylor, P. (2015) 'EU 'ring of friends' turns into ring of fire', Reuters, 27 September, www.reuters.com/article/2015/09/27/us-europe-migrants-neighbourhood-analysi-idUSKCN0RR09020150927, accessed 30 September 2015.

Tocci, N. (2011) 'State (un)Sustainability in the Southern Mediterranean and Scenarios to 2030: The EU's Response', *MEDPRO Policy Paper* 1/August, updated April 2012.

Tsebelis, G. (1995) 'Decision making in political systems: Veto players in presidentialism, parliamentarism, multicameralism and multipartyism', *British Journal of Political Science* 25(3): 289–325.

19
EU MEMBER STATES AND THE EUROPEAN NEIGHBOURHOOD POLICY

Amelia Hadfield

Introduction

Gone are the heady days of a 'ring of friends', inspired by the goals of fostering stability, security and prosperity in a shared neighbourhood. Despite low-level 'positive developments' in a few of the countries of the European Neighbourhood Policy (ENP), the general trend is a problematic one. As the European Union's (EU's) report of 2015 concedes, 'conflict, rising extremism and terrorism, human rights violations and other challenges to international law, and economic upheaval' have produced a series of regional disturbances that have shaken the ENP to its core, in terms of both its cause and its consequences (European Commission and High Representative of the Union for Foreign Affairs and Security Policy 2015: 2). Seen as 'idealistic in its conception as it was timid and insufficient in its implementation', the ENP has emerged as a poorly crafted EU foreign policy, and the EU itself culpable of having 'greatly overestimated its own influence and underestimated the structural problems and risks in its neighbourhood' (Lehne 2015).

As an area of scholarship, the ENP offers a wide variety of entry points. This chapter focuses on the various national positions of EU Member States (EUMS) relative to the goals of the ENP (Delcour and Tulmets 2008), in which the benefits of policy entrepreneurship balance against the risks of regional patronage in constructing forms of political and economic cooperation in Europe's eastern and southern neighbourhood (Schumacher, Bouris and Olszewska 2016). Other perspectives examine the conceptual and empirical challenges of the ENP (Whitman and Wolff 2010), its normative inconsistency (Whitman 2011), its policy content (Balfour 2012; Huber 2012) and its performance in the wake of key negative reviews (Gillespie 2013). Most of these explorations share the same overarching view of the ENP. First, as a macro-strategy, the ENP remains riddled by internal contradictions, existing as neither enlargement *stricto sensu* nor an explicitly articulated foreign policy (Melo 2014). Second, as illustrated below, EUMS themselves remain imperfectly connected to the overall project of neighbourhood in terms of specific policy competence and broader geopolitical objectives. These and other problems have their roots in a crisis of faith between the two sides, in terms of both missed opportunities to promote reform within ENP countries and a failure to align the different national interests of EUMS with the key goals of the ENP. The result was a series of incoherent EU messages, which subsequently failed to catalyse the promotion of genuine regional progress in key areas. From conflicting goals of democratisation versus stabilisation (Youngs 2002; Schlumberger

2006; Bicchi 2010) to appropriate neighbourhood incentives (Schimmelfennig 2011) to the awkward process of balancing generic goals against the need for differentiation, the overwhelming message is that of an absent policy at EU level, and a relentlessly geostrategic approach to the ENP by EUMS themselves. Conflicting policy motivations among EUMS as to the actual purpose of the ENP, alongside an inability to promote a shared rather than individuated sense of policy entrepreneurship, resulted in the principle of neighbourhood being fractured as a foreign policy in general, and obliquely 'upheld only at the EU level' (Kostanyan 2015: 2). Despite major revisions in 2011 and 2015, major gaps remain in establishing genuinely cooperative attitudes between EUMS on the transformative goals and practicality of the ENP. As the 2011 New Response to a Changing Neighbourhood made clear,

> rising to the challenge requires that EU and Member States policies be much more closely aligned than in the past, in order to deliver the common message and the coherence that will make our actions effective. EU instruments and policies will be effective only if properly backed by Member States policies.
> *(European Commission and High Representative of the Union for Foreign Affairs and Security Policy 2011: 5)*

Despite such warnings, the ENP remains blighted by incoherent goals and inconsistent implementation. After a brief survey of its salient aspects, the chapter devotes itself to exploring the symbiotic connection between the construction of the ENP and the consequent impact of its uneasy implementation upon national geopolitical aspirations. In doing so, the chapter references both the specific and the regional foreign policy aspirations that key EUMS have attempted to upload into the overall structure of the ENP, as well as ways in which the ENP has subsequently been downloaded by EUMS as a positive and/or negative mode of EU actorness. It concludes with a brief analysis of the apparent shift to a pragmatic, traditional foreign policy, based on ranked preferences within the neighbourhood and the interests rather than the core values of the EU.

Paradoxical beginnings and regional tensions

The ENP is replete with paradoxes. It is at once an inherited policy born out of previous attempts at giving meaning to north–south relations across the Mediterranean, and a novel attempt to deal with east–west post-enlargement relationships: simultaneously, it is a single policy structure encompassing sixteen states, and a regional duopoly with a variety of subsets, both security-driven and reformist in its origins, comprising both means and ends in its objectives (Youngs 2002).

Designed as a tool to accompany the EU's post-enlargement environment, the ENP emerged in 2004, as a method of ensuring both independent progress, and regional progressiveness in pursuit of coherence in a shared 'neighbourhood' (Bauer 2013). Viewing its new neighbours as simultaneously problematic and prospective, the 2003 'Wider Europe' communication attempted to convert European neighbours, both remote and proximate, into 'a ring of friends' (Commission of the European Communities 2003: 4), while also institutionalising a buffer zone for the EU, managed by variable integration on offer for like-minded neighbours. Despite its many ambiguities, the Commission's goals for the ENP remained unashamedly ambitious: emerging over time as a novel form of remote control foreign policy, managed *via* a loosely applied logic of enlargement covering sixteen states, complemented by normative demands and annual report requirements (Gillespie 2013).

EUMS were (and remain) far more geopolitical in orientation, and arguably more security-driven than the 'reform-transform' narratives initially envisaged by the European Commission (Schumacher 2015). Where the latter focused on the collective take-up of a value-based nexus as a way of positively regarding its neighbours, EUMS demands of the ENP range from improved border security to stabilised hotspots to enabling ambitions for a regional patron (shepherding mid-range economic integration and even long-term integration of certain states and key regions). EUMS inputs have produced both 'important semantic nuances' in foundational ENP documents regarding the classification of states as 'neighbours' or 'partners' and the operational ambiguity that has become the hallmark (and possibly the undoing) of the ENP (Cadier 2013: 53). In this way, the ENP's initial lack of clarity proved politically useful for the range of desires propounded separately by EUMS.

EUMS like Poland, in favour of the principle of widening, are generally supportive of a deeper and more proactive ENP that actively supports the Eastern Partnership subset; those like France are eager to convert a former *domaine privé* into a space for regional leadership; others like the UK, whose geopolitical vision for a 'distinct and durable policy' spurred on the initial idea of the ENP in 2002, regard it as a mode of increasing the strategic depth in Europe's complex outer provinces, while distracting the Commission from assorted integrationist projects (Solana and Patten 2002). Nowhere is this clearer than in the proliferation of groups and subgroups that reflect national ambitions of key EUMS.

In 2008, the Union for the Mediterranean (UfM) was launched to develop 'political cooperation', based on 'regional and sub-regional projects that are more concrete and visible to the citizens of the region' (Commission of the European Communities 2008). Driven from the outset by French President Nicolas Sarkozy's proposal on a Mediterranean Union, the UfM's output as a regional catalyst has been uneven at best (Gillespie 2013; Bicchi 2010), as the original proposal on Mediterranean Union was already seen as diverting 'political energy and credibility from ENP' in pursuit of a 'parallel EU' (Lippert 2008: 15). This spurred criticism from various EUMS: not only did Spain view the French proposal as undermining both the Barcelona Process in general and Spanish leadership in particular (Soler i Lecha 2009: 162); central, eastern and northern EUMS felt excluded from the proposal, not least because Germany had not been included in Sarkozy's initiative. Tenacious German diplomacy, based on its own interests in the Mediterranean, helped to produce a workable balance, leading to the transformation of Sarkozy's Mediterranean Union into a broader 'Union for the Mediterranean'.

Similar entrepreneurial imperatives from Britain, Sweden and Poland played a key role in the founding of the Eastern Partnership one year later. British goals in the neighbourhood have historically revolved around enhancing trade dynamics in southern, and then eastern, regions supporting projects that favour geopolitical widening over institutional deepening, and supportive dialogue frameworks with partners like NATO and the US, in order to concretise its identity as something of a foreign policy bridge. British and Swedish interests, in a balanced approach to a wider neighbourhood, overlapped felicitously in 2002, with Foreign Minister, Jack Straw's vision of a permanent structure to include eastern states, including Ukraine, Moldova and Belarus; this was strongly supported by Sweden who called for a 'broader and more active policy towards our neighbours [. . .] from Russia and Ukraine to the Mediterranean' (Johansson-Nogués 2015: 139). The UK and Sweden pushed the vision ahead to the 2009 Prague summit, with the result of making a clear geopolitical split between the ENP's southern and eastern flanks as the key hallmark of the 'overarching framework for the EU's policy towards its eastern neighbours ever since' (Hug 2015: 4).

EUMS fingerprints are more than evident in the construction of the ENP's two groupings: a Mediterranean coalition led by France, together with Italy, Spain, Portugal and, to a lesser extent,

Greece and the Benelux-countries, is being confronted with German, Swedish, Polish, Lithuanian and Romanian demands for a dedicated eastern grouping. Divided between its southern and eastern domains, the ENP was by 2008–2009 riven by the geopolitical 'uploads' of EUMS, who regarded the project as a convenient macrocosm of their own national imperatives, as well as a regional crucible for post-enlargement security and development. A paradoxical project, balancing the overzealous regional ambitions of the Commission, and the clashing, policy entrepreneurialism of the EUMS, the ENP was unable to construct a simple, coherent and above all independent structure for ENP countries themselves. Instead, something of a 'neighbourhoods quarrel' marked EUMS politics, between 'promoters of the Mediterranean pillar [. . . and] supporters of the Eastern dimension' who also 'endeavoured to introduce a semantic differentiation between "European neighbours" (East) and "Neighbours of Europe" (South)' (Cadier 2013: 54). The following cases look at key EUMS – notably France, Germany and Poland (as leader of the Visegrad Group), whose impact upon the ENP, specifically in terms of their policy entrepreneurship, has affected the project most profoundly (Börzel 2010; Grimm and Leininger 2012).

France: red in tooth and claw

Due to French strategic interests in the Mediterranean and Africa, France unsurprisingly promoted the southern dimension of the ENP, while Germany's interests in the East reflected both their economic interests and security requirements (Del Sarto and Schumacher 2005; Bosse 2007; Bicchi 2010; Nougayrède 2015). Although France has attempted to remain equitable in its approval of both the EaP and the UfM – provided both dimensions receive equal attention and funding – its key demand that the ENP not be used as an instrument of long-term accession has clouded its ability to operate judiciously in support of both flanks, and to cooperate effectively with Germany regarding EaP support. France has veered between a resuscitated national economy permitting security expansion, the need to push for unilateral solutions in the Sahel and increasing uncertainty about how to tackle with real efficacy any of the chronic causes of volatility across North Africa in the wake of the 'Arab Spring', and the profound impact of the 2015 terrorist attacks.

France's continuing economic strength has arguably underwritten its increasingly extensive international agenda. This agenda has not involved the resuscitation of the UfM project, or an uplift in support to critical aspects of the ENP *via* key bilaterals – either during or after the Arab uprisings in 2011 (Schumacher 2015). Its preference for 'the diplomatic leverage provided by the projection of military force and by the country's status as both a nuclear power and a permanent member of the UN Security Council' (Heisbourg 2015), along with interventions in Mali, Libya and Syria, has kept France in the top tier of coalition-building, but visibly external to the EU's Common Foreign and Security Policy (CFSP), to which the ENP is also linked. Instead, having abjured its initial desire to operate as a key regional patron, France appears 'manifestly uninterested in both the regional and individual demands of the ENP', and more keen on crafting an internationally oriented profile, even if operating in roughly the same geographic area.[1]

Two changes should be noted, and both may foster a change of attitude regarding neighbourhood engagement, as well as galvanising the national agenda in terms of French identity and European boundaries. The first involves the migration crisis of the summer of 2015, in which thousands of displaced and migrating individuals from North Africa and Syria, as well as the Sahel, Iraq and Afghanistan and further afield, travelled to various EUMS and border crossings. The second was the Paris terrorist attacks of 13 November 2015, carried out by an ISIL-affiliated group with French and Belgian origins. The first stems from remote problems with proximate consequences for France and other EUMS; the second has a profoundly proximate impact despite remote roots. Taken together, France confronts an uncomfortable dual logic in which migrants and asylum seekers – from or transiting the Mediterranean – view Europe as the solution, while terrorist forces regard it as the root of the problem. Although it makes for uncomfortable dynamics, the origins of both are clearly rooted in the neighbourhood and, specifically, the attitude and impact of EUMS' policies towards it. France neither begat nor warranted the vendetta-like backlash of ISIL. France was not singled out; it was merely first in line – as the March 2016 attacks in Belgium demonstrated. Equally, France may have been targeted not merely because of its infelicitous associations in the Maghreb and the Levant but because of the complex inside/outside tensions that this continues to foster in terms of French integration, and its foreign policy agenda more broadly. Due to its actions in Mali, Libya and Syria, France is ironically perceived by outsiders – whether they be passive or active in their opprobrium of France – as the archetype interventionist European state, despite its acting in the neighbourhood in a way that neither represents Union interests (that is, outside CFSP and ENP structures) nor reflects Union perceptions of the neighbourhood itself (neither intervention nor crisis management has yet been placed into ENP support structures).

More emphatically, the neighbourhood has forced the EU onto the back foot, and transformed the overall logic of the ENP itself (Börzel 2010). From the perspective of neighbourhood geopolitics, tackling ISIL will remain both a national and an international issue, managed by France with willing partners in Europe, NATO and the US, while migration and asylum solutions will require more formidable support of emergent EU legislation in this area, and a more committed approach to tackling the sources of migratory displacement.

Schumacher argues for the importance of narratives in deconstructing EU external relations, and their ability to provide 'coordinative and communicative discourse[s]' (2015: 383). Particularly salient for France's recalibrated ENP relationship are the 'threat/risk' and the 'duty and opportunity' narratives (ibid.: 384). The former focuses on the exposure to 'broad, multi-dimensional, border-transcending risks' requiring the EU, and France as a neighbourhood patron, to 'develop and apply comprehensive capabilities and policies in order to ensure its own security and development' while the latter flags the challenges of 'extending EU systems of governance' in either norm-based or more pragmatic methods, depending on the specific requirements of North African and Middle Eastern states (ibid.: 385). As intimated by the EU's Global Strategy (European External Action Service 2016), leading EUMS like France are in the forefront of providing both '[s]tate and societal resilience [as a] strategic priority in the neighbourhood', and to reach out to the '[m]any people within the scope of the European Neighbourhood Policy (ENP) both to the east and to the south [who] wish to build closer relations with the Union' (ibid.: 25). However, to do so, France needs to redefine its global agenda within the perimeters of its own neighbourhood, and clarify the as-yet undefined connections between EU foreign, security and defence policy, the ENP, the UfM and the emergent themes of state and societal resilience. Doing so may encourage France to gradually support the argument 'that the security and stability of Europe's environment cannot be carved up into different geographical directions, but must be viewed as one single, whole problem that has to be tackled from all sides with equal motivation' (Nougayrède 2015; see also Nitoiu 2013). Equally, recasting the Common Security and Defence Policy within the ENP may prove too ambitious for France, which has been singularly agnostic on both these projects for the past decade (Dempsey 2015).

Germany: the frustrated fulcrum

As Europe's largest economy, Germany has operated as a financial stabiliser during the Eurocrisis and, along with the European Commission, as a catalyst to promote open attitudes and policies to tackle the migration crisis of 2015–2016. Like France, it too has adopted various roles in the construction of ENP subgroups, supporting the EaP, along with initiators Sweden and Poland. Unlike France, Germany has maintained its attention of and support toward the eastern neighbourhood, and worked to galvanise other EUMS supportive of the EaP coalition. German and EU-level foreign policy strategies generally coincide in terms of their integrationist designs on proximate states; this extends to the promotion of key EU norms in the interests of local stability, and broader regional security (Youngs 2002; Bosse 2007; Börzel 2010). This also makes central the role that Germany plays within the eastern flank of the ENP and, as argued by Meckel et al. (2012) makes the ENP the broadest instrument of EU foreign policy within the German arsenal of externalities. This was certainly the logic at work during the 2007 German Presidency of the EU where a new 'ENP plus' scheme was proposed to highlight the importance of the eastern neighbourhood in promoting the overall security of the EU (Copsey 2007). Comprising a range of states that were both European neighbours and neighbours of Europe, the overall thrust was to offer to the former the prospect of deeper integration with the EU while recognising the limits of the ENP, regarding long-term EU accession.

Bridge-building between east and west is a natural extension of the Cold War interlocutor identity foisted upon a divided Germany, and the city of Berlin. *Ostpolitik* has since shifted from careful management of increasingly incommensurate ideologies to a pragmatic balancing of Russo-German cooperation (Stelzenmüller 2009). With the iterative developments of EU enlargement, NATO enlargement and ultimately the construction of the ENP, pursuing a 'Russia first' policy has proved increasingly problematic (Shapovalova and Kapuśniak 2011). Unsurprisingly, Russia has perceived European enlargement as institutionalised encroachment, NATO enlargement as regional infringement and the ENP as a soft-power attempt by the EU at converting its former provinces into a westward-facing buffer zone, gradually integrating them into the economic and political domain of the EU. Germany has found itself having to negotiate increasing Russian intransigence to the East with its own geopolitical and geo-economic interests (Kempe 2006). None of these can be readily discounted, and the ENP complicates each of these categories of east–west connection. Russia provides a substantial market for German manufacturers, while Germany provides a reciprocal market for Russian gas exports. The problem is one of attitude. Before 2008, post-Cold War *Ostpolitik*, first under Chancellor Gerhard Schröder, and then under Chancellor Angela Merkel, was supported by the 'German foreign policy elite', still driven by Cold War mentalities. A portion – though by no means all – of this same elite has been somewhat reluctant to shift in their support for Russia (Gressel 2015). Both eastern and southern neighbourhoods allow Germany to act as a regional microcosm, pushing forward EU-level narratives, including, for example, the EU as a 'promoter of peace' (Nitoiu 2013), the EU as a 'democratizing force' (Pace 2009) and particularly the 'good neighbourliness' narrative which, as Schumacher explains, ranges from simply legitimating EU engagement with third countries to 'a vast spectrum of areas of potential engagement' (Schumacher 2015: 386).

Two things have begun to erode this structure: the place of the EaP within German foreign policy; and the steadily worsening relations between both Germany and Russia, and between Russia and the EU as a whole. Both changes have complicated matters for Germany, and its position of post-Cold War interlocutor. Germany's natural interest is to focus both through its own foreign policy initiatives and through EU-level externalities, like the ENP first and foremost on the eastern neighbourhood as a whole, with the prime goal of ensuring stable relations with it, and with Russia itself, and to encourage greater cooperation with and among other EUMS in this task. Germany's response to the Russian invasion of Georgia was renewed engagement with the eastern dimension of the ENP, emerging – along with Sweden and

Poland – as a 'driver of ENP', and positioning the ENP 'as a central priority of EU foreign policy' (Lippert 2008: 1; Schimmelfennig and Scholtz 2008).

The economic dynamics of Europe's neighbourhood are key to unlocking the attitudes of Germany, in its overall engagement with the area. From a trade-based perspective, Russia and neighbourhood states operate as a key market for German manufacturers (Cadier 2013). Eastern states are equally, if not more, dependent on Germany. Energy security, however, remains the severest dilemma for Germany. Concurrent with the goals of the 2014 European Energy Security Strategy and the 2015 European Energy Union, all EUMS and the EU, are working to increase their respective energy security, specifically their independence from key suppliers. Germany, and more broadly Europe, remains firmly connected to Russian gas imports *via* the 2005 Nordstream Gas Pipeline. Equally, the pipeline allows Germany to increase its own energy security independent of its eastern partners, both in the EU and in the neighbourhood beyond. Nordstream (and the proposed Nordstream II) locks Russia into a viable structure of European imports, but as an offshore route through the Baltic Sea, rather than an onshore pipeline across eastern transit states including Ukraine, and allows an exclusive non-transit relationship between Russia and Germany (Korosteleva 2012). Germany now faces the unenviable position of leading and maintaining the EU's sanctions against Russia, including robust bilateral support of Ukraine, while still positioning itself viably for post-sanction bilaterals with Russia, which may restore east–west energy security while deeply shaking the geopolitical requirements of EUMS and ENP states in between.

Germany faces tough choices in terms of its role within the EaP. The May 2015 EaP Summit in Riga highlighted the paradox of German foreign policy, being both 'too progressive and too conservative to come up with new policy ideas for the European Neighbourhood Policy' (Gressel 2015). German progressiveness pushed through key reforms in the wake of the Eurozone crisis, drove forward the much-needed humanitarian approach to the summer 2015 migration crisis, with Chancellor Merkel 'integrating other EU countries into a specifically German approach', by defending the choice of EaP states to push through incentives like visa liberalisation and Deep and Comprehensive Free Trade Agreement (DCFTA) implementation (Perthes and Kaim 2015). Germany's Foreign Minister Steinmeier coordinated 'the EU approach toward Moscow [. . .] despite immense differences among the 28 Member States over Russia' (ibid.). Equally, this leadership role *vis-à-vis* Russia has not translated into management of the EaP, with, 'some parts of the German foreign policy elite [. . .] still haunted by the ghosts of the old *Ostpolitik*' (Gressel 2015), preferring a conservative attitude to EaP reform, and emphasising rapprochement with Russia.

Contemporary German approaches to the neighbourhood remain wide-ranging. Supporting continued Polish leadership of the EaP allows for continuity of existing German policy to the East among a range of like-minded states, including Poland, Sweden, Romania and the Baltic countries. In addition, German existential difficulties with its eastern neighbours, both proximate and remote, indicate its current preference for balancing reformist policies that allow Ukraine to receive sustained political support from the EU, but in a way that does not significantly alter Kyiv's current economic dependence upon Russia (Börzel and van Hüllen 2011). Further, the 2015–2016 migration crisis has presented Germany with a new opportunity to shift its attention to more regional and international challenges. This shift comes with its own problems. Germany's acceptance of hundreds of thousands of Syrian refugees, its support for humanitarian assistance to Syria, and the subsequent shift in terms of domestic attitudes to these decisions have securitised not only much in the way of attitudes to neighbourhood, but practicalities in terms of its policies (including increased efforts by the German security services to monitor and stem the flow of foreign fighters from Germany to Syria and Iraq). This has caused Germany to connect more strongly to the geopolitical problems of the neighbourhood, but rather less to the ENP programme.

Poland: leading multiplicity in the Visegrad Group

The Eastern Partnership (EaP) is linked intrinsically to Poland's foreign policy preferences, illustrated by Poland tabling the 2008 EaP Joint Proposal with Sweden. Neighbourhood itself remains a long-held national ambition, with Poland being '[t]he only country that expressed a serious interest in shaping the ENP before 2004', having adopted the operative term 'Eastern Dimension' as early as 1998 (Kratochvíl 2007: 191). The key objective was to shift the perceived favouritism in financial resources from their ineffective use supporting southern 'neighbours of Europe' to a more robust geopolitical structure buoying 'European neighbours' (Cadier 2013: 54). In doing so, Poland could also count on the support of the Visegrad Group. This group, often referred to as the 'V4', is made up of Poland, Hungary, the Czech Republic and Slovakia, and emerged unofficially in the early 2000s as something of a European subset to assist neighbouring states that were facing the same integrationist challenges of joining both NATO and the EU (Wagrowska 2009; Börzel and van Hüllen 2011). As there are divisions within the V4 regarding relations with Russia and Ukraine, and indeed attitudes toward the EU itself, the V4 is a diverse coalition displaying a range of attitudes to the ENP and the EaP (Cianciara 2009). While not precisely a foreign policy truism, EUMS from the 2004 and 2007 waves of accession 'are usually seen as the most emphatic bloc of proponents of further enlargement' and as such 'are often attributed with almost metaphysical unity in their attitudes towards the East' (Kratochvíl 2007: 191). What bound the four together as a group was their abiding dissatisfaction with the ENP before the construction of the EaP as a dedicated eastern bloc, their embedded distrust of Russia, with Hungary under Orbán being a possible exception and their general support for a transformative EaP (Dettke 2011). Further, the UfM proposal brought the four together in their determination to prevent marginalisation of the eastern component of the ENP, by 'provid[ing] a crucial opportunity to lobby for enhanced EU cooperation with the eastern neighbourhood' and by ensuring that the EaP fostered genuine regional cooperation rather than the more ambiguous and slow moving UfM structure (Cianciara 2009: 5). Equally, what divides the four are the differentiated visions of the EU that they have accrued, independently of their group identity, and the knock-on impacts this has for a variegated approach to the neighbourhood.

In this constellation, Poland has managed to spearhead the V4, and to assure its role as regional patron (along with Sweden) of an eastern dimension including Ukraine, Belarus and Moldova because – qua Kratochvíl – both goals reinforced 'the newly rediscovered Polish self-understanding as a regional power whose main tasks include the democratisation of Eastern Europe' (Kratochvíl 2007: 192). This places both the EaP and its tools that permit '[m]odernisation and democratisation of the region' (ibid.) centrally within Polish foreign policy, as well as allowing it to act as sponsor of Ukrainian membership for more than a decade. Having avoided the broader tides of recession that swept across the EU due to the 2008 financial crisis (Smolar 2015), Poland's political and economic clout has allowed it to become the quintessential eastern EUMS, defining and defending its own foreign policy credentials. Poland in general, and the V4 more broadly, have in this capacity operated as an eastern forum for the requirements of states within the EaP, chiefly by 'vigorously oppos[ing] all attempts to cast the nascent ENP [and its EaP component] as a substitute for enlargement' (Kratochvíl 2007: 193). More recently, its own expanding foreign and security policy portfolio, as well as its historic intransigence regarding Russia (and occasionally awkward attitudes to Germany) has led Poland to begin to platform its own distinctly national approaches to key regions, as well as rehearsing the broader palette of EU reforms (Shapovalova and Kapuśniak 2011).

The V4 retain a clear interest in maintaining positive relations with their various eastern neighbours, although this has fluctuated over the years, when group members were taken up with their own integration challenges, transforming the V4's rationale from a direct, group-based catalyst for specific eastern transformations to a loose coordinator of the broader needs of the region. The V4's difficulty is, of course, marshalling a common viewpoint (Wagrowska 2009; Börzel and van Hüllen 2011). The internal differences of the V4 frequently threaten any coherent message that it attempts to transmit to troubled regions, and risks institutionalising a radically unbalanced series of Eastern European approaches to the EaP overall. In this respect, Russian pugnaciousness has proved a convenient external threat allowing the V4 to close ranks in terms of Ukraine (again, Hungary proving something of a sceptical exception to this attitude), not only due to increased levels of perceived threat but also because of the large number of Ukrainian minorities in each of the V4 territories, as well as their own ethnic groupings within Ukraine.

For Poland, Russian aggression has transformed national views regarding European security; a poll conducted in April 2014 concluded that 47% of the Polish public felt their country's independence to be threatened by a combination of Russian belligerence and fragmented attitudes to European security (Smolar 2015). Accordingly, there have been noticeable attitudinal changes among younger generations, increasingly focusing on the need for Poland's independent development set against a decreasing interest in the EU (Smolar 2015; Korosteleva 2012). The broader picture is more significant. The EaP has transformed from an EU-level foreign policy project to a deeply politicised issue with significant local implications. Poland's task has been to prevent EU backtracking on the admittedly ambiguous promises of the ENP regarding post-Soviet republics, while ensuring that support for the EaP and Ukraine remains strong. Its toughest diplomatic challenge is to rebuff the suspicion that the current situation was caused by the EaP, by emphasising the overarching role of Russia in militating against the West (Buras 2015). From the Polish perspective, the EaP is and remains a successful policy, with new DCFTAs operating to viably transform the governance structures of Moldova, Ukraine and Georgia (ibid.). Unsurprisingly, Poland operates as regional patron not merely of the EaP, but the implementation of EaP tools, chiefly the DCFTAs, as well as maintaining sectoral dialogues, hosting regular summits and other meeting formats (Whitman and Wolff 2010; Buras 2015). Given the strong economic ties between Polish and some neighbourhood markets, Polish emphases regarding EaP transitions may encourage Poland to favour its economic potential as much as its transformed political potential.

For Poland and its Visegrad partners, ensuring the equal distribution of both support and funds between the eastern-oriented EaP and the Mediterranean-oriented UfM has been a prime goal from the outset (Cianciara 2009). Accordingly, V4 perspectives of the UfM both confirm and deny the geopolitical tensions between the two regions. Initially, V4 states, led by Poland, regarded the Mediterranean 'through the perspective of its eastern neighbourhood and the possible threats [believing] that the new union could pose to its strategic interests in this area [. . .] strongly correlated with the attempts to promote EU policy towards the East' (Cianciara 2009: 17). Gradually, the benefits of instituting more effective forms of cooperation with the southern dimension have emerged, and a geopolitical equilibrium has been achieved by supporting key areas that include ongoing support for the Balkans (led by Hungary), broad-ranging security policy and energy security issues.

Conclusions

Present analysis of the ENP from 2003 to the November 2015 Review, and the June 2016 EU Global Strategy, illustrate a significant shift from idealised ambition to localised pragmatism, from unwieldy, if laudable, value-based blueprints to interest-driven actions geared to visible reforms based on viable incentives. EUMS activity is therefore likely to be divided between taking the lead on the instruments of stability, and the 'longer-term structural objectives' of the ENP that can emerge only following a stabilised neighbourhood – not unlike the security-development nexus that now dominates in EU development policy (Lehne 2015). The dynamics of policy entrepreneurship also illustrate that attempts by EUMS to upload their national ambitions to the overall ENP framework, rather than download EU-level objectives into their individual approaches to neighbourhood, remain the primary mode of policy construction for the ENP. This has produced a series of contradictory approaches that have not always been artfully pulled together at EU level, and resulted in incoherent objectives across the ENP, and selective policies towards its regional subsets and individual ENP partners.

Having singularly 'failed in its goal of building a ring of well-governed states around the EU' (Leigh 2015), the ENP Review of 2015 suggests that EU attitudes to its neighbourhood should be 'more pragmatic, differentiated and focused than its predecessors' (Kostanyan 2015: 1). Indeed, the key leitmotif here is not pragmatism but differentiation: a tailor-made approach that targets the genuine requirements in key ENP states but which *simultaneously* enables EUMS to retain strategic interests in a Europeanised sense and (where necessary) a clearer sense of local ownership in overseeing such transformations. The ENP is emphatically a symbiotic structure designed to balance regional needs against established expectations; as such, 'keeping the ENP intact is a necessary condition for maintaining solidarity among EUMS, some of which prioritise the East over the South and *vice versa*. Incorporating strong differentiation in the policy addresses the diverse needs and desires of a variety of neighbours' (ibid.: 1–2) as well as of its EU-based architects.

Note

1 Anonymised interview by author, 5 December 2015, with staff members of the European External Action Service responsible for ENP, Brussels.

References

Balfour, R. (2012) 'EU conditionality after the Arab Spring', *Papers IEMed* 16, IEMed, Barcelona.
Bauer, P. (2013) 'European-Mediterranean security and the Arab Spring: changes and challenges', *Democracy and Security* 9(1–2): 1–18.
Bicchi, F. (2010) 'Dilemmas of implementation: EU democracy assistance in the Mediterranean', *Democratization* 17(5): 976–996.
Börzel, T. (2010) 'The transformative power of Europe reloaded: the limits of external Europeanization', *KFG Working Papers*, Research College 'The Transformative Power of Europe', Freie Universität Berlin.
Börzel, T. and van Hüllen, V. (2011) 'Good governance and bad neighbours? The limits of transformative power Europe', *KFG Working Papers*, Research College 'The Transformative Power of Europe', Freie Universität Berlin.
Bosse, G. (2007) 'Values in the EU's neighbourhood policy: political rhetoric or reflection of a coherent policy?', *European Political Economy Review* 7(2): 38–62.
Buras, P. (2015) 'Poland and the Eastern Partnership: the view from Warsaw', European Council on Foreign Relations, 19 May, www.ecfr.eu/article/commentary_poland_and_the_eastern_partnership_the_view_from_warsaw3038, accessed 30 November 2015.
Cadier, D. (2013) 'Is the European Neighbourhood Policy a substitute for enlargement?', in LSE IDEAS Report *The Crisis of EU Enlargement*, November, www.lse.ac.uk/IDEAS/publications/reports/pdf/SR018/Cadier_D.pdf.
Cianciara, A. (2009) *The Union for the Mediterranean and the Eastern Partnership: Perspectives from Poland, Czech Republic and Hungary*, Warsaw: Institute of Public Affairs.
Commission of the European Communities. (2003) *Wider Europe – Neighbourhood: A New Framework for Relations with our Eastern and Southern Neighbours*, COM (2003) 104 final, Brussels.

Commission of the European Communities. (2008) *Barcelona Process: Union for the Mediterranean*, COM (2008) 319 final, Brussels.

Copsey, N. (2007) 'The Member States and the European Neighbourhood Policy', *European Research Working Papers* 20, European Research Institute, Birmingham, www.download.bham.ac.uk/govsoc/eri/working-papers/wp20-copsey.pdf, accessed 30 November 2015.

Del Sarto, R. and Schumacher, T. (2005) 'From EMP to ENP: what's at stake with the European Neighbourhood Policy towards the Southern Mediterranean?', *European Foreign Affairs Review* 10(1): 17–38.

Delcour, L. and Tulmets, E. (2008) *Pioneer Europe?: Testing EU Foreign Policy in the Neighbourhood*, Baden-Baden: Nomos.

Dempsey, J. (2015) 'France and Germany to Europe's rescue?', Carnegie Europe, 30 November, http://carnegieeurope.eu/strategiceurope/?fa=62118, accessed 30 November 2015.

Dettke, D. (2011) 'Europe and Russia: from neighborhood without a shared vision to a modernization partnership', *European Security* 20(1): 127–142.

European Commission and High Representative of the Union for Foreign Affairs and Security Policy. (2011) *A New Response to a Changing Neighbourhood*, COM (2011) 303, Brussels.

European Commission and High Representative of the Union for Foreign Affairs and Security Policy. (2015) *Review of the European Neighbourhood Policy*, JOIN (2015) 50 final, Brussels.

European External Action Service. (2016) *Shared Vision, Common Action: A Stronger Europe. A Global Strategy for the European Union's Foreign and Security Policy*, Brussels.

Gillespie, R. (2013) 'The European Neighbourhood Policy and the challenge of the Mediterranean Southern Rim', in Telò, M. and Ponjaert, F. (eds.) *The EU's Foreign Policy: What Kind of Power and Diplomatic Action?*, Farnham: Ashgate, 121–134.

Gressel, G. (2015) 'Germany and the Eastern Partnership: the view from Berlin', *Commentary*, European Council on Foreign Relations, 19 May, www.ecfr.eu/article/commentary_germany_and_the_eastern_partnership_the_view_from_berlin3027, accessed 30 November 2015.

Grimm, S. and Leininger, J. (2012) 'Not all good things go together: conflicting objectives in democracy promotion', *Democratization* 19(3): 391–414.

Heisbourg, F. (2015) 'Letter from Paris', Carnegie Europe, 27 February, http://carnegieeurope.eu/strategiceurope/?fa=59193, accessed 30 November 2015.

Huber, D. (2012) 'Mixed signals still? The EU's democracy and human rights policy since the outbreak of the Arab Spring', *Working Paper* 13, IAI, Rome.

Hug, A. (2015) *Trouble in the Neighbourhood? The Future of the EU's Eastern Partnership*, London: The Foreign Policy Centre.

Johansson-Nogués, E. (2015) 'Sweden: A "supporting actor" to the EU?', in Behr, T. and Tiilikainen, T. (eds.) *Northern Europe and the Making of the EU's Mediterranean Policies: Normative Leaders or Passive Bystanders?*, Farnham: Ashgate, 131–146.

Kempe, I. (2006) 'The German impact on the European Neighbourhood Policy', *Foreign Policy in Dialogue* 7(19): 26–33.

Korosteleva, E. (2012) *The European Union and Its Eastern Neighbours: Towards a More Ambitious Partnership?*, London and New York: Routledge.

Kostanyan, H. (2015) 'The European Neighbourhood Policy reviewed: will pragmatism trump normative values?', *CEPS European Neighbourhood Watch* 121, December.

Kratochvíl, P. (2007) 'New EU members and the ENP: different agendas, different strategies', *Intereconomics*, July/August, www.dokumenty-iir.cz/CV/Kratochvil/New_EU_Members.pdf, accessed 30 November 2015.

Lehne, S. (2015) 'Toward a European Neighbourhood realpolitk?', Carnegie Europe, 19 November, http://carnegieeurope.eu/strategiceurope/?fa=62029, accessed 30 November 2015.

Leigh, M. (2015) 'New policies urgently needed for EU neighbourhood', The German Marshall Fund of the United States, 18 November, www.gmfus.org/blog/2015/11/18/new-policies-urgently-needed-eu-neighborhood, accessed 24 February 2017.

Lippert, B. (2008) 'European Neighbourhood Policy: many reservations – some progress – uncertain prospects', *International Policy Analysis*, June, http://library.fes.de/pdf-files/id/ipa/05426.pdf, accessed 30 November 2015.

Meckel, M. , Milbradt, G., Pflüger, F., Schwarz-Schilling, C., Steenblock, R., Süssmuth, R., Verheugen, G. and Voigt, K. (2012) 'Deutsche Außenpolitik und Östliche Partnerschaft', *DGAPstandpunkt*, February, https://dgap.org/de/article/getFullPDF/20492, accessed 30 November 2015.

Melo, F. (2014) 'Perspectives on the European Neighbourhood Policy failure', *Journal of European Integration* 36(2): 189–193.

Nitoiu, C. (2013) 'The narrative construction of EU in External Relations', *Perspectives on European Politics and Society* 14(2): 240–255.

Nougayrède, N. (2015) 'France and the Eastern Partnership: the view from Paris', European Council on Foreign Relations, 19 May, www.ecfr.eu/article/commentary_france_and_the_eastern_partnership_the_view_from_paris3033#, accessed 30 November 2015.

Pace, M. (2009) 'Paradoxes and contradictions in EU democracy promotion in the Mediterranean: the limits of EU normative power', *Democratization* 9(1): 39–58.

Perthes, V. and Kaim, M. (2015) 'Letter from Berlin', Carnegie Europe, 9 January, http://carnegieeurope.eu/strategiceurope/?fa=57660, accessed 30 November 2015.

Schimmelfennig, F. (2011) 'How substantial is substance? Concluding reflections on the study of substance in EU democracy promotion', *European Foreign Affairs Review* 16(5): 727–734.

Schimmelfennig, F. and H. Scholtz. (2008) 'EU democracy promotion in the European Neighbourhood: political conditionality, economic development and transnational exchange', *European Union Politics* 9(2): 187–215.

Schlumberger, O. (2006) 'Dancing with wolves: dilemmas of democracy promotion in authoritarian contexts', in Jung, D. (ed.) *Democratization and Development: New Political Strategies for the Middle East*, Basingstoke: Palgrave Macmillan, 33–60.

Schumacher, T. (2015) 'Uncertainty at the EU's borders: narratives of EU external relations in the revised European Neighbourhood Policy towards the southern borderlands', *European Security* 24(3): 381–401.

Schumacher, T., Bouris, D. and Olszewska, M. (2016) 'Of policy entrepreneurship, bandwagoning and free-riding: EU Member States and multilateral cooperation frameworks for Europe's southern neighbourhood', *Global Affairs* 2(3): 259–272.

Shapovalova, N. and Kapuśniak, T. (2011) 'Is Poland still committed to the Eastern neighbourhood?', *FRIDE* 91, August, http://fride.org/download/PB_91_Poland.pdf, accessed 30 November 2015.

Smolar, E. (2015) 'Letter from Warsaw', Carnegie Europe, 5 June, http://carnegieeurope.eu/strategiceurope/?fa=60322, accessed 30 November 2015.

Solana, J. and Patten, C. (2002) *'Wider Europe', Joint letter to the Danish Presidency*, 7 August.

Soler i Lecha, E. (2009) 'The French presidency of the EU and the Union for the Mediterranean: forced Europeanisation?', in *Mediterranean Yearbook*, IEMed and CIDOB, Barcelona, 161–64, www.iemed.org/anuari/2009/aarticles/a161.pdf, accessed 24 February 2017.

Stelzenmüller, C. (2009) 'Germany's Russia question: as new Ostpolitik for Europe', *Foreign Affairs* 88(2): 89–100.

Youngs, R. (2002) 'The European Union and democracy promotion in the Mediterranean: A new or disingenuous strategy?', *Democratization* 2(1): 40–62.

Wagrowska, M. (2009) 'Visegrad security policy: how to consolidate its own identity', *International Issues & Slovak Foreign Policy Affairs* 18(4): 31–43.

Whitman, R. (2011) *Normative Power Europe: Empirical and Theoretical Perspectives*, Basingstoke: Palgrave Macmillan.

Whitman, R. and Wolff, S. (2010) *The European Neighbourhood Policy in Perspective: Context, Implementation and Impact*, Basingstoke: Palgrave Macmillan.

20
THE EUROPEAN PARLIAMENT AS AN ACTOR IN ITS OWN RIGHT IN THE EU'S NEIGHBOURHOOD

Cristian Nitoiu

Introduction

During the last five years, due to the multiple crises erupting in the region, the European Union's (EU's) neighbourhood has transformed from a 'ring of friends' to a 'ring of fire' (Taylor 2015). Simultaneously, the European Parliament (EP) was successful in enhancing its ability to influence the foreign policy of the EU. The adoption of the Lisbon Treaty played a key role in this process as it enlarged the EP's formal prerogatives and gave members of the EP (MEPs) a better voice in external relations (Servent 2014). Since the mid-1990s, the EP has been aiming to increase its ability to shape EU foreign policy and becoming an actor in its own right. It has done this in three main ways: firstly, the EP has gradually constructed an original type of parliamentary diplomacy which draws on its strengths; secondly, it has mediated between (and bargained with) other EU institutions constructing a distinct identity; thirdly, MEPs have constantly advocated for more legal competencies to be allotted to the EP by the EU's treaties. The latter means has recently registered noticeable results, whereby the adoption of the Lisbon Treaty aimed to reduce the democratic deficit of the EU (and of its foreign policy) and highlighted the EP's role in assuring democratic legitimacy. Hence, the EP has gained various competencies in foreign policy with the adoption of the Lisbon Treaty, even though it is still falling far behind the power of national parliaments in Member States.

While the literature on the EP's role in international relations has started to develop in the last decade, especially following the adoption of the Lisbon Treaty (Nitoiu and Sus 2017; Servent 2014; Stavridis and Irrera 2015), the role of the EP in the EU's neighbourhood is still understudied. Nevertheless, since the outbreak of the 'Arab uprisings' and the conflict in Ukraine, the EP has been an active advocate of a stronger EU presence in the neighbourhood, especially in dealing with security issues. In analysing the role of the Parliament as an actor in its own right in the EU's neighbourhood, this chapter will focus on the parliamentary diplomacy which the EP has developed. The main tools used by the EP to bolster its parliamentary diplomacy include: the activity of EP delegations in ENP countries, official visits, sending messages through reports and resolutions, hosting delegations from the region, organising informal or fact finding missions, participating in electoral monitoring missions alongside other institutions, interparliamentary groups, establishing parliamentary cooperation with other legislative bodies, and the activity of EP party groups. The chapter will focus on some of these aspects and will also provide empirical insights by analysing the Cox–Kwasniewski mission to Ukraine as a prime example of the EP's parliamentary diplomacy. Before discussing these aspects, the chapter will focus on the role of the EP in EU foreign policy generally.

Locating the EP in EU foreign policy

Traditionally, the EP has had limited power in influencing the foreign policy of the EU. In this sense, it differs from national parliaments, which have the power to hold governments accountable and direct the scrutiny of the general public towards executives. While in nation states, parliaments do not play a primary role in the construction of foreign policy, they have a powerful position to keep in check executives and promote their own initiatives – which may or may not overlap with those of the government. The EP's power relations with other institutions, on the other hand, are much more asymmetrical than in the case of national parliaments. The Commission and the Council have been – for the larger part of the existence of the EU – the main actors (if not at times sole actors) driving its foreign policy. Just like national parliaments, the EP draws its legitimacy from direct elections. However, it suffers a legitimacy crisis, as turnouts for elections across Member States are very low in comparison to national elections. This raises serious concerns regarding MEPs' legitimacy to act on behalf of EU citizens. Nevertheless, the EP does provide a platform for groups from all 28 Member States to voice their concerns, making it a valuable forum, even though it is not representative in absolute terms for the whole of the EU citizenry.

The EP has recently managed to increase its powers to shape EU foreign policy since the adoption of the Lisbon Treaty, by engaging on a path towards institutionalising both formal and informal avenues for influence. Most notably, the EP has enhanced its prerogatives in relation to international trade in two key areas: the process of negotiation and the ratifying mechanisms of trade agreements (Woolcock 2010). Moreover, the EP has gained powers and influence over the adoption of legislation in this policy area, but it is not yet involved in any way in its implementation. Two other areas of foreign policy where the EP's activity has been salient are international arms control and disarmament processes. With respect to these, it is concerned with the control of small arms and light weapons at the international level and the non-proliferation of weapons of mass destruction (Barbé and Herranz-Surrallés 2008). MEPs gained the ability to vote on the EU's budget (including external relations), which can give the EP influence on how the EU's foreign policy is financed. For instance, the EP voted on the European Neighbourhood Instrument (ENI), the financial instrument (2014–2020) of the European Neighbourhood Policy (ENP). At the same time, the EP now also gives its consent for international agreements signed by the EU – this is particularly relevant in the EU's neighbourhood, as MEPs must vote on Association Agreements (AAs) and other types of agreements with states in the region.

The EP has also managed to go beyond the new legal prerogatives inscribed in the Lisbon Treaty. For example, in the case of the SWIFT negotiations, Servent (2014) shows that MEPs managed to put significant pressure on the Commission and the Council, forcing them to include the EP as an actor in its own right in the revision and negotiations of the deal with the United States (US). There is also an expectation that the EP will continue to push for more legal competencies to be allotted to it (in future revisions of EU treaties or by rulings of the European Court of Justice) and will try to make use of its present competencies, extending them through informal means (Stavridis and Irrera 2015).

The EP's parliamentary diplomacy

For the last two decades, the EP has been working to enhance its role in foreign policy by developing an original type of parliamentary diplomacy. According to Thym (2008: 20), the EP's international efforts are, for example, enhanced by its communication strategy where its influence in the real world is further increased by the publicity of its debates and the easy electronic accessibility of its reports, which contrast with the "secretive" decision-making procedures in the Council'. Parliamentary delegations and missions often allow MEPs to express freely their positions and concerns, without being constrained by cumbersome diplomatic customs or the need to converge with the approaches of Member States. The EP also regularly hosts high-level international speakers, and through its Sakharov prize has managed to put the international spotlight on a series of deteriorating human rights situations in the EU's neighbourhood and around the world – for example Belarus, Somalia or Egypt (Caballero-Bourdot 2011). In what follows, the section will explore various aspects of the EP's parliamentary diplomacy in the neighbourhood: cooperation with other legislative bodies (parliamentary cooperation), the role of EP delegations for relations with ENP countries, election monitoring missions and the EP's official discourse.

Parliamentary cooperation

The EP can set up interparliamentary forums with parliaments from other states or international organisations. This allows the EP to get better insight into the challenges and practices of other parliaments, and increased expertise on interacting with the respective countries or international organisations. In the EU's neighbourhood, the EP is part of two interparliamentary assemblies: the Parliamentary Assembly of the Union for the Mediterranean (PA-UfM) and EURONEST. The former comprises 280 members, consisting of members of parliament from EU Member States, the EP and non-EU Mediterranean countries, meeting in plenary session at least once a year. It was initially established in 2004 as the Euro-Mediterranean Parliamentary Assembly (EMPA), as part of the Barcelona Process and then incorporated into the Union for the Mediterranean. It has been hailed as a forum where Mediterranean countries could act on equal footing and interact in an effective manner with the EU (Pace and Stavridis 2010). However, the PA-UfM has often been criticised for its inactivity and unambitious response to key developments in the region, especially to the 'Arab uprisings' (Völkel 2013). At the same time, the assembly was, many times in the past, transformed into a battleground where national representatives presented competing narratives in order to influence the views of their counterparts from the EU (Stavridis and Pace 2009; 2011). The parliamentary assembly has also been criticised for its lack of democratic legitimacy, as many members from the Southern Mediterranean countries have traditionally been less accountable to their electorates (Pace and Stavridis 2010).

EURONEST was established in 2011 and reunites members of parliaments of Eastern Partnership (EaP) countries and the EP. Even before this date, the EP was collaborating on a bilateral basis with these parliaments through Parliamentary Cooperation Committees. EURONEST is constituted of 10 members from each EaP country and 60 EP members. Belarus was suspended from EURONEST in 2011 due to its low democratic standards. The EURONEST has plenary sessions on a yearly basis (except 2014), with sessions alternating between Brussels and Strasbourg on the one hand and EaP countries on the other. The number of resolutions[1] issued at these plenary meetings has remained constant over time, most of them focusing on key issues shared by the countries in the eastern neighbourhood, such as energy security, regional security challenges, economic cooperation or strengthening civil society.

Country specific resolutions have focused on former Ukrainian Prime Minister Yulia Tymoshenko, the Armenian genocide, or the Nadiya Savchenko case.

EP delegations

The EP frequently receives delegations from third party states. It can therefore play an important role as these encounters have (at least in theory) the potential to socialise representatives from ENP countries into the overall culture of the EP and to raise its foreign policy profile. Even more importantly, the EP itself sends parliamentary delegations to third party states and international organisations. Their role is to enhance information about other countries, and to communicate the EP's (and the EU's) policy, while also aiming to strike cooperation with other parliaments. Delegations provide crucial information for debates in the Committee on Foreign Affairs and the plenary as well as for parliamentary resolutions (Viola 2000).

In central and Eastern European Member States, EP delegations played a major role in confidence building in the run up to their accession to the EU. Similarly, this has also been the case in Ukraine, Georgia and Moldova during the negotiations of AAs. However, MEPs and EP delegations have sometimes been criticised for speaking outside the mandate of the EP and voicing their views as if they represented those of the EP or the EU (Feliu and Serra 2015). Visits by EP delegations in ENP countries can have a salient role in increasing the EP's visibility and reputation. In most cases, MEPs are seen both as representatives of the EP and as messengers of the EU (Fiott 2015). Even though MEPs might not hold extensive powers or prerogatives, their presence is frequently covered by local and national media in the countries they visit. In the EU's neighbourhood, EP delegations have frequently aimed at supporting countries in the region on their path to democratisation and providing positive reinforcement to political and civil society actors with European aspirations (Stavridis and Manoli 2011).

The EP has a more complex system of delegations with the countries in the eastern neighbourhood than with those in the southern neighbourhood, preferring to put the latter in broad geographical groups (Table 20.1). To the East, over the last years, the delegation for relations with Belarus has had an active role in meeting with civil society organisations and members of the democratic opposition. It meets with these stakeholders regularly in Brussels and Strasbourg, providing advice and support. However, the delegation has not been able to establish official contacts with the government or parliament in Belarus, and has regularly been denied visas to enter the country. The delegation frequently issues statements criticising the treatment of the

Table 20.1 EP delegations for relations with ENP countries

Eastern neighbourhood
Delegation for relations with Belarus
Delegation to the EU-Armenia and EU-Azerbaijan Parliamentary Cooperation Committees and the EU-Georgia Parliamentary Association Committee
Delegation to the EU-Moldova Parliamentary Association Committee
Delegation to the EU-Ukraine Parliamentary Association Committee
Southern neighbourhood
Delegation for relations with Israel
Delegation for relations with the Maghreb countries and the Arab Maghreb Union (Algeria, Morocco, Libya and Tunisia)
Delegation for relations with the Mashreq countries (Egypt, Jordan, Lebanon and Syria)
Delegation for relations with Palestine

opposition and of civil society, pointing especially at politically motivated trials or convictions. In contrast, the delegations for relations with the EU-Georgia, EU-Ukraine and EU-Moldova Parliamentary Association (former Cooperation) Committees have maintained active partnerships with national authorities, supporting the negotiations for AAs and the adoption of various reforms (especially in the justice system) – with common sessions taking place once or twice a year in Brussels or the capitals of the three countries. In Ukraine, during Viktor Yanukovich's presidency, the delegation played an active role in criticising the government for the imprisonment of various politicians – including former Prime Minister (PM) Yulia Timoshenko – and for the decreasing democratic standards of the country.

The delegation for relations with the Maghreb countries (Algeria, Morocco, Libya and Tunisia) meets with parliamentary groups from each of them (separately) annually. During the last five years, the delegation has been especially active in relation to Libya and the country's role in migrant and refugee issues (even though following the removal of Gadhafi it has been difficult for the delegation to locate the most appropriate and legitimate Libyan counterparts). In Algeria, the delegation focused on fostering contacts with members of the opposition and civil society, more broadly aiming to improve the human rights situation in the country. In Morocco and Tunisia, the delegation also focused on deepening economic relations between the two countries and the EU. In the case of Morocco, the EP interparliamentary group for Western Sahara (with over 100 members from all EP political groups) has been active in criticising the government for its actions against the Saharawi people and human rights activists (Algeria Press Service 2015; European Parliament 2015a). The delegation for relations with the Mashreq countries was one of the first to be set up by the EP in the wake of its first direct elections in 1979. The delegation covers cooperation with parliamentary groups from four countries: Egypt, Jordan, Lebanon and Syria. Since the 'Arab uprisings', the delegation has been active in monitoring the refugee and humanitarian situations in the four countries. Due to the instability of the region, the delegation has only rarely met with official authorities in past years. Egypt and Syria were the key priorities of the delegation for the last five years in view of intense political instability and ongoing conflicts. In the southern neighbourhood, the EP also has two separate delegations for Israel and Palestine, which meet on a regular basis (two to three times a year) with parliamentarians from both sides – even though those from Palestine have encountered various difficulties in travelling to Brussels or Strasbourg in the past. Recently, the delegations were active in mediating between the Palestinian Authority and Israel during the Gaza war of 2014. The delegations laid the groundwork for the EP resolution on the recognition of Palestine (European Parliament 2014b) – following it, the EP established the 'Parliamentarians for peace' initiative with members from European, Israeli and Palestinian parliaments to complement EU diplomatic efforts.

Through its delegations, the EP maintains strong relations with various civil society groups throughout the world. For example, Diedrichs (2004) showed that EP political groups have played a crucial role in enhancing the EP's presence in third countries. Zammit finds that the EP's socialist group has been particularly active in shaping the EP's policies towards the Euro-Mediterranean space. It has achieved this by addressing 'holistically the whole region urging attention to the social dimension, and a diplomatic approach that is multilateral in nature and inclusive of all actors' (2010: 9). In practice, it formed and supported various delegations around the region, which managed to feed into EP policy initiatives based on detailed analyses of the particularities and challenges faced by the countries in the region (Di Paola 2003). On the other hand, the European People's Party has focused on conferences, seminars and workshops for local actors in the region in a bid to establish or enhance its presence (Zammit 2010).

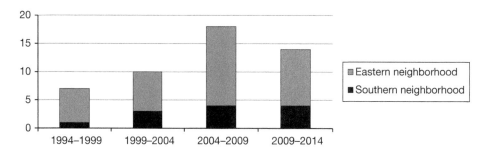

Figure 20.1 EP electoral monitoring missions in the EU neighbourhood

EP election monitoring missions

The EP has been participating in election observation since 1994, either by joining the EU's Election Observation Missions in North Africa, and in other non-neighbourhood third countries, or in the post-Soviet space in cooperation with the parliamentary assemblies of the Organization for Security and Co-operation in Europe (OSCE) and the Council of Europe, together with the OSCE Office for Democratic Institutions and Human Rights (ODIHR). As the EP does not have sufficient resources for autonomous missions, it mostly relies on the capacities of the institutions it collaborates with, which gives it a weak position to influence the overall work of such missions. Gawrich (2015) argues that the EP's presence in electoral monitoring missions is more symbolic, as it failed to invest in becoming a leading actor in the field within the EU. The EP's participation in electoral monitoring missions in the EU's neighbourhood reached its peak during the 2004–2009 term (Figure 20.1). The EP has been monitoring in several countries in the neighbourhood, with a greater frequency in the East. Nevertheless, the EP has been a marginal actor, for example, during the crucial 2014 presidential elections in Ukraine, the EP had only seven members out of a total of 1,200 observers (European Parliament 2014a).

The EP frequently adopts resolutions addressing the way the ENP has been implemented and concerning its future prospects, together with a series of resolutions that target the EU's bilateral relations with ENP countries. Resolutions highlight the overall discourse of the EP and the messages it seeks to send to other institutions, the Member States or to the public, civil society or non-EU actors. While analysing resolutions does not provide for significant data about the influence of the EP on the EU's approach towards neighbours, it highlights the way in which MEPs seek to shape the Union's foreign policy agenda. As with other resolutions on foreign policy, those concerning the EU's neighbourhood are initially discussed in the Committee on Foreign Affairs.[2] Based on discussions in the committee, a rapporteur is appointed to draft the resolution. Amendments are added by other MEPs and then debated and voted in plenary session, which decides on the final version of the resolution.

An analysis of resolutions (Nitoiu 2016), relating to the EU's neighbourhood adopted by the EP in its latest term (2009–2014) shows that:

- MEPs emphasised the EU's aspiration to enhance its presence in the international arena. A stronger EU involvement in the neighbourhood was advocated by the EP (for example, European Parliament 2013b);
- The EP enthusiastically supported the idea that the EU should play an enhanced role in world politics;

- The EP pushed for a stronger role for itself in shaping the EU's policy towards the neighbourhood in a series of issue areas, that is, democracy, human rights, rule of law, conflicts and stability in the neighbourhood, or the need to revise the ENP;
- The EP tried to construct for itself an enhanced role in pushing for the EU to become a stronger actor in terms of conflict management in the neighbourhood (European Parliament 2012). This was highlighted by both its very strong language and its demands on other EU institutions to include it in the policy-making process;
- The EP was adamant in claiming that it should be afforded a more important role in the 2011 review of the ENP (European Parliament 2011). This implied emphasising the lack of success of the EU's approach towards the neighbourhood. The EP argued that the ENP could be made more efficient at promoting the EU's values only if the EP had a more central role in the decision-making process;
- In terms of a specific focus, states experiencing conflicts, political crises or human rights violations were particularly addressed by EP's resolutions: these include Azerbaijan, Belarus, Egypt, Libya or Syria.

The Cox–Kwasniewski mission as prime instance of EP parliamentary diplomacy

The Cox–Kwasniewski mission is a salient example of the EP's foreign policy actorness. The mission was facilitated by a minor crisis in relations between the EU and Ukraine, which started with the alienation of Russia after the adoption of the EaP and the election of Yanucovich as president in early 2010. The trial of former PM Timoshenko, which started in late 2010, put into question the independence of the justice system and threatened to damage the negotiations of the AA. This paved the way for the EP to propose an EP mission as part of its diplomatic efforts and as a way of complementing the EU's overall approach in Ukraine, *inter alia* to put AA negotiations back on track (Nitoiu and Sus 2017).

The mission was announced on 16 May 2012, in the wake of a meeting between Ukrainian PM Mykola Azarov and EP President Schulz. It was headed by two high profile envoys, who were Pat Cox (former president of the EP from Ireland) and Aleksander Kwasniewski (former President of Poland). It was initially to last for two weeks to observe Timoshenko's trial[3] until it was supposed to end. However, the trial dragged on due to political reasons and the mission was subsequently prolonged. Timoshenko's trial put into question the separation of powers and the judiciary's independence; it also highlighted low professional standards and lack of respect for human rights, as Timoshenko was repeatedly denied adequate medical treatment in prison. The mission started on 11 June 2012 and eventually lasted for 18 months with Cox and Kwasniewski visiting Ukraine a total of 27 times (Cox 2014). The mission initially only attended court hearings and evaluated trial documents, raising doubts regarding the standards of the judicial process (European Parliament 2013a). However, the mission broadened its scope as it increasingly criticised the Ukrainian government for the state of the penitentiary system, particularly because Cox and Kwasniewski aimed at improving Timoshenko's conditions of detention.[4]

The EU Foreign Affairs Council, on 10 December 2012, praised and welcomed the mission's conduct and the way it was contributing to the EU's foreign policy (Council of the European Union 2012). The mission gained significance by the fact that the EU linked the improvement of rule of law standards to the negotiation of the AA. In turn, this made the mission an integral part of the EU's approach towards Ukraine. Besides its work on the Timoshenko case, the mission had a measure of success as it led to the release of a series of prisoners who were thought to have been incarcerated for political reasons – for example, former Defence Minister Ivashchenko and former Interior Minister Lutsenko. The mission also focused on selective justice and the electoral law and constantly called on the Ukrainian government for improvements. The mission released its report shortly before the 18 November 2013 EU Foreign Affairs Council, which was supposed to adopt a final decision on the signing of the AA with Ukraine (Council of the European Union 2013). Its recommendation, that is, that Ukraine had to continue working on solving the issues of selective justice (subject to political pressure), was included in the conclusions of the Council (European External Action Service 2013).

The mission provided the EU with some sort of justification to re-intensify the dialogue with Ukraine due to the crisis surrounding the negotiations of the AA. It was an expression of the EP's goal to shape EU foreign policy in Ukraine and can be perceived as a product of the constraints and opportunities offered by the negotiations for the AA.[5] Insulated from inter-institutional power games in the EU over leading the policy towards Ukraine, the Cox–Kwasniewski mission managed to reopen communication between Brussels and Kyiv, by holding a dialogue with involved parties.[6] Gradually, the mission proved its usefulness and became a prime hub of the EU in dealing with Ukraine (Nitoiu and Sus 2017). By having two high-level politicians in charge of the mission, the EP (and the EU for that matter) managed to put a face to its policy in Ukraine. Hence, the mission is a prime example of the EP's potential to solve an external crisis by ways of parliamentary diplomacy. It is a tool that complemented the official efforts of the Commission, the European External Action Service (EEAS) and the Member States in Ukraine.

Conclusions

Even though the EP is the most representative and democratic EU institution, it still suffers from low legitimacy. This is mainly caused by the EP's widespread disconnect from European citizens, expressed in constant low turnouts for EP elections. At the same time, as is demonstrated in a recent study of democratic legitimacy and foreign policy, EP involvement in foreign policy has drawn on citizens' support for a stronger EU in foreign policy matters (Nitoiu 2015) – similar to the permissive consensus which accompanied European integration for a long time, ever since its beginnings (Hooghe and Marks 2009). Given the fact that EU citizens share a low interest in the EU's approach towards its neighbours, it is unclear whether the EP can significantly enhance the legitimacy of the EU's policy in its neighbourhood. Moreover, the Cox–Kwasniewski mission strikes through its apparently undemocratic nature, as decisions about the day-to-day activities of the mission were not accountable to the EU or Ukraine. The mission thus had virtually a *carte blanche* to set up its own meetings, design its strategy and decide on the range of actors it chose to engage with, all of which created the perfect context for the mission to expand its remits.

The adoption of the Lisbon Treaty enlarged the area of formal competencies of the EP in foreign policy and paved the way for MEPs to enhance the Parliament's influence through informal means. However, in the EU's neighbourhood, the EP still lacks formal prerogatives. As the region is transforming from a 'ring of friends' to a 'ring of fire' (Taylor 2015), the EP can prove its worth for the EU and progress towards becoming an actor in its own right by developing innovative solutions to the multiple crises the EU is facing. One such innovative solution was the Cox–Kwasniewski mission – which is testimony to the EP's ability to shape EU foreign policy through parliamentary diplomacy. The EP indeed has sent more *ad hoc* missions to deal with crises in the EU's neighbourhood. Mostly, these missions (made up primarily by members of EP delegations for relations with the country in question) merely assess the situation on the ground: for example, during the last five years there have been numerous fact finding missions in southern ENP countries that assessed the immigration situation, while in the eastern neighbourhood most missions focused on assessing the state of reforms in the rule of law. However, unlike other examples, the Cox–Kwasniewski mission managed to become an integral part of the EU's diplomatic efforts in the country (Nitoiu and Sus 2017).

Lastly, the EP was an integral part of the consultation process for the revision of the ENP, published in November 2015 (Delcour 2015). During the consultation process, which led up to publication, the EP hosted a series of events with stakeholders from ENP countries, such as political actors, civil society actors or business networks. The EP generally supported the revision proposed by the Commission and the EEAS and stressed the importance of its parliamentary diplomacy for fostering regional integration (European Parliament 2015b; 2015c). Even though it is difficult to predict whether the EP will play a more significant role in the neighbourhood, the EEAS' and Commission's inclusive approach during the consultations, as well as the recognition of the utility of the Cox–Kwasniewski mission for EU diplomacy, testify to the EP's growing ability to be an actor in its own right in the neighbourhood.

Notes

1 www.euronest.europarl.europa.eu/euronest/cms/cache/offonce/home/pid/19.
2 The Committee on Foreign Affairs plays a crucial role, if not the most salient, in shaping the EP's approach in foreign policy. Members are usually chosen according to their expertise and experience of working with EU partners. The committee contracts academics to draft assessments on the situation in various places around the world (including the neighbourhood), usually focusing, for example, on democracy promotion, the state of human rights, migration or terrorism.
3 She was convicted in October 2011 for abuse of power over the contract signed in 2009 (during her time as PM) for natural gas with Russia. She then appealed in December 2011, but her appeal was delayed until August 2012.
4 Interview with Aleksander Kwasniewski, Warsaw, 8 December 2015.
5 Interview with EEAS official, via phone, 4 December 2015.
6 Interview with a staff member of Aleksander Kwasniewski's office, Warsaw, 10 November 2015.

References

Algeria Press Service. (2015) 'European Parliament's Western Sahara Intergroup Set Up', www.aps.dz/en/world/6219-european-parliament%E2%80%99s-western-sahara-intergroup-set-up, accessed 23 January 2016.
Barbé, E. and Herranz-Surrallés, A. (2008) 'The Power and Practice of the European Parliament in Security Policies', *RECON Report* 6, ARENA, Oslo.
Caballero-Bourdot, C. (2011) 'Interparliamentary Scrutiny of the CFSP: Avenues for the Future', *Occasional Paper* 94, Institute for Security Studies, Paris.
Council of the European Union. (2012) 'Press Release from the 3209th Meeting', 17438/12, 10 December.
Council of the European Union. (2013) 'Press Release from the 3273th Meeting', 17438/12, 18–19 November.
Cox, P. (2014) 'The Ukrainian Crisis and Geopolitics: An echo from the past or the shape of things to come?', Speech at The Institute of International and European Affairs, 23 October, www.iiea.com/ftp/Publications/The%20Ukrainian%20Crisis%20and%20Geopolitics_An%20echo%20from%20the%20past%20or%20the%20shape%20of%20things%20to%20come_Pat%20Cox_IIEA-2014.pdf, accessed 28 December 2015.
Delcour, L. (2015) 'The 2015 ENP Review: Beyond Stocktaking, the Need for a Political Strategy', *College of Europe Policy Brief* 1, December.
Diedrichs, U. (2004) 'The European Parliament in CFSP: More than a Marginal Player?', *The International Spectator* 39(2): 31–46.
Di Paola, S. (2003) 'International Treaty-Making in the EU: What Role for the European Parliament?', *The International Spectator* 38(2): 75–90.

European External Action Service. (2013) 'Cox and Kwaśniewski: The European Parliament Monitoring Mission to Ukraine Should Continue its Work', 16 October, http://eeas.europa.eu/delegations/ukraine/press_corner/all_news/news/2013/2013_10_16_4_en.htm, accessed 23 January 2016.

European Parliament. (2011) *European Parliament Resolution of 14 December 2011 on the Review of the European Neighbourhood Policy*, 2011/2157(INI), 14 December.

European Parliament. (2012) *European Parliament Resolution of 22 November 2012 on the Implementation of the Common Security and Defence Policy*, 2012/2138(INI), 22 November.

European Parliament. (2013a) 'Cox-Kwaśniewski Monitoring Mission to Ukraine Extended', *Press Release*, 18 April, www.europarl.europa.eu/former_ep_presidents/president-schulz/en/press/press_release_speeches/press_release/2013/2013-april/html/cox-kwa-niewski-monitoring-mission-to-ukraine-extended, accessed 23 January 2016.

European Parliament. (2013b) *European Parliament Recommendation to the High Representative of the Union for Foreign Affairs and Security Policy and Vice President of the European Commission, to the Council and to the Commission of 13 June 2013 on the 2013 Review of the Organisation and the Functioning of the EEAS*, 2012/2253(INI), 13 June.

European Parliament. (2014a) 'Report of the Election Observation Mission to the Ukrainian Presidential Election', 25 May, www.europarl.europa.eu/intcoop/election_observation/missions/2009-2014/2014_05_25_ukraine.pdf, accessed 23 January 2016.

European Parliament. (2014b) *European Parliament Resolution of 17 December 2014 on Recognition of Palestine Statehood*, 2014/2964(RSP), 17 December.

European Parliament. (2015a) *European Parliament Resolution of 30 April 2015 on the Imprisonment of Workers and Human Rights Activists in Algeria*, 2015/2665(RSP), 30 April.

European Parliament. (2015b) 'Report on the Review of the European Neighbourhood Policy', 2015/2002(INI), 19 June.

European Parliament. (2015c) *European Parliament Resolution of 9 July 2015 on the Review of the European Neighbourhood Policy*, 2015/2002(INI), 9 July.

Feliu, L. and Serra, F. (2015) 'The European Union as a "Normative Power" and the Normative Voice of the European Parliament', in Stavridis, S. and Irrera, D. (eds.) *The European Parliament and Its International Relations*, Abingdon: Routledge, 17–34.

Fiott, D. (2015) 'The Diplomatic Role of the European Parliament's Parliamentary Groups', *European Policy Analysis*, 3epa.

Gawrich, A. (2015) 'The European Parliament in International Election Observation Missions (IEOM): Division of Labour or Decreased Influence?', in Stavridis, S. and Irrera, D. (eds.) *The European Parliament and Its International Relations*, Abingdon: Routledge, 121–142.

Hooghe, L. and Marks, G. (2009) 'A Postfunctionalist Theory of European Integration: From Permissive Consensus to Constraining Dissensus', *British Journal of Political Science* 39(1): 1–23.

Nitoiu, C. (2015) *The EU Foreign Policy Analysis: Democratic Legitimacy, Media, and Climate Change*, New York: Palgrave Macmillan.

Nitoiu, C. (2016) 'Framing the EU's Policy Towards the Neighbourhood: The strategic Approach of the Seventh European Parliament (2009–2014)', *Cambridge Review of International Affairs*: 1–17. doi: 10.1080/09557571.2016.1233937.

Nitoiu, C. and Sus, M. (2017) 'The EP's Diplomacy – A Tool for Projecting EU Power in Times of Crisis? The Case of the Cox–Kwasniewski Mission', *Journal of Common Market Studies* 55(1): 71–86.

Pace, R. and Stavridis, S. (2010) 'The Euro-Mediterranean Parliamentary Assembly, 2004–2008: Assessing the First Years of the Parliamentary Dimension of the Barcelona Process', *Mediterranean Quarterly* 21(2): 90–113.

Servent, A. (2014) 'The Role of the European Parliament in International Negotiations after Lisbon', *Journal of European Public Policy* 21(4): 568–586.

Stavridis, S, and Irrera, D. (eds.) (2015) *The European Parliament and Its International Relations*, Abingdon: Routledge.

Stavridis, S. and Manoli, P. (2011) 'The Parliamentary Dimension of Regionalism: Comparing Experiences in Europe's Neighbourhood', in Warleigh-Lack, A., Robinson, N. and Rosamond, B. (eds.) *New Regionalism and the European Union: Dialogues, Comparisons and New Research Directions*, Abingdon: Routledge, 218–235.

Stavridis, S. and Pace, R. (2009) 'The EMPA and Parliamentary Diplomacy in the Mediterranean: A Preliminary Assessment', in Stavridis, S. and Sola, N. (eds.) *Factores Políticos y de Seguridad en el Área Euro-Mediterránea*, Zaragoza: Prensas Universitarias de Zaragoza, 125–148.

Stavridis, S. and Pace, R. (2011) 'Assessing the Impact of the EMPA's Parliamentary Diplomacy in International Conflicts: Contribution or Obstacle?', in Clariana, G. (ed.) *The Euro-Mediterranean Assembly*, Barcelona: Marcial Pons, 59–105.

Taylor, P. (2015) 'EU "Ring of Friends" Turns into Ring of Fire', Reuters, 27 September, www.reuters.com/article/us-europe-migrants-neighbourhood-analysi-idUSKCN0RR09020150927, accessed 23 January 2016.

Thym, D. (2008) 'Parliamentary Involvement in European International Relations', *WHI – Papers 5*, Walter Hallstein-Institut, Berlin.

Viola, D. (2000) *European Foreign Policy and the European Parliament in the 1990s: An Investigation into the Role and Voting Behaviour of the European Parliament's Political Groups*, Aldershot: Ashgate.

Völkel, J. (2013) 'Underrated Legislations: Arab Parliaments Could Play a Crucial Transformational Role', openDemocracy, 23 April, www.opendemocracy.net/jan-v%C3%B6lkel/underrated-legislations-arab-parliaments-could-play-crucial-transformational-role, accessed 23 January 2016.

Woolcock, S. (2010). 'The Treaty of Lisbon and the European Union as an Actor in International Trade', *ECIPE Working Paper 1*, European Centre for International Political Economy, Brussels.

Zammit, G. (2010) 'Reconsidering the Role of Parties at the European Level: Constructing Actorness for the Christian Democrat and Socialist Party Groups in the European Parliament Using an International Relations Framework', PhD thesis, University of Sheffield.

21
FINANCIAL INSTRUMENTS AND THE EUROPEAN NEIGHBOURHOOD POLICY

Anna-Sophie Maass

Introduction

In 2003, the European Commission announced that the reduction of poverty, the creation of an 'area of shared prosperity and values based on deeper economic integration, intensified political and cultural relations, enhanced cross-border cooperation and shared responsibility for conflict prevention' are at the core of the European Union's (EU) development of relations with its eastern and southern neighbours (Commission of the European Communities 2003: 9). In return for successful implementation of political and economic reforms, the EU offers 'concrete benefits and preferential relations' to its neighbours (ibid.). Over a decade after the EU developed these objectives for relations with its neighbours, the European Neighbourhood Policy's (ENP's) ambitions to create peace and stability have been put to a hard test. The migration crisis and the conflict in Ukraine, in the aftermath of Crimea's annexation by Russia in March 2014, are merely two in a series of examples demonstrating the tremendous challenges the ENP is faced with.

The aim of this chapter is two-fold. On the one hand, it gives an overview of both the ENP's current financial instruments and their objectives, which form the backbone of facilitating the financing of projects focusing primarily on economic and institutional transformation, humanitarian aid, security and development. Due to the limited scope of this chapter, the financial instruments that provide the largest funding, namely the European Neighbourhood and Partnership Instrument (ENPI) and the European Neighbourhood Instrument (ENI), and their predecessors, will be examined.[1] Additionally, the Madad Trust Fund, established by the EU to tackle the extensive humanitarian and economic spill-overs of the Syrian war, will be included in this analysis to understand the dynamics of recently established financial instruments available for some of the EU's neighbours affected by the fallouts of the war in Syria. This chapter sketches the evolution of these instruments and simultaneously examines the underlying motivations for their establishment. On the other hand, it seeks to elucidate both the benefits and shortcomings of these financial instruments. Several mid-term evaluation reports are examined to demonstrate the instruments' merits and their limitations. However, this approach is limited for two reasons. First, some of these evaluation reports offer limited data that could illuminate the implementation of the financial instruments. Second, the evaluation report for the budgetary period of 2014–2020 is limited, due to the continuing budgetary cycle at the time of writing this chapter. As a result, this chapter does not claim to offer an exhaustive analysis of both potential advantages and structural obstacles offered by the financial instruments, which could undermine both their implementation and the fulfilment of their wide-ranging objectives as anticipated at the time of their establishment, but is a first attempt to address critically a hitherto rather under-researched, though considerably important, component of EU-neighbourhood relations.

The evolution of financial instruments used in the framework of the ENP

The Technical Assistance to the Commonwealth of Independent States (TACIS)

TACIS was launched in the 1990s to support the six ENP countries – Armenia, Azerbaijan, Belarus, Georgia, Moldova and Ukraine – as well as Kazakhstan, Kyrgyzstan, Mongolia, Russia, Tajikistan, Turkmenistan and Uzbekistan, with the implementation of their respective Partnership and Cooperation Agreements (PCAs) with the EU. The establishment of the TACIS programme in 1991, aimed at 'enhancing the [Commonwealth of Independent States (CIS)] transition process' to market economies and democratic societies as well as counterbalancing the 'political [. . .] economic and social vacuum', which existed after the Soviet Union's collapse (Frenz 2016; Regulation TACIS).

Structural amendments to TACIS were undertaken in two distinct phases to render its implementation more efficient. According to a leader of diverse monitoring projects implemented in the framework of TACIS, the scheme's evolution was characterised by two phases (Frenz 2016). First, between 1991 and 1999, ministries from the CIS countries formulated funding requests for projects submitted to TACIS. The European Commission examined the requests based on 'often scarcely existing information' (European Commission 2015b; Frenz 2016), resulting in delays in the implementation. These delays, in both the evaluation of funding bids and the actual implementation of projects sponsored by TACIS, are shortcomings of this financial instrument because they hamper the attainment of its goals. Second, between 2000 and 2006, a dialogue between CIS countries' ministries and the European Commission emerged, seeking to understand domestic circumstances and formulate targeted responses. The cooperation between the Commission and the CIS became structured by the establishment of EU delegations fostering 'improved project identification, planning and supervision' (ibid.). This was a benefit in terms of ensuring the implementation of projects funded under TACIS. To improve the conditions for the fulfilment of TACIS objectives, the duration of the projects funded by this scheme was prolonged, from the initial funding of projects from 18 to 24 months (Commission of the European Communities 1997).

As Table 21.1 demonstrates, TACIS encompassed a budget of EUR7.3 billion for 15 years, which 'may still be considered limited' (Frenz 2016) when considering the scope of the challenges which had to be addressed, such as the sponsoring of projects in 'five priority areas': training, energy, transport, financial services and food distribution (European Commission 2015b) in the 13 countries benefiting from the scheme. Despite some initial controversy regarding the creation of a joint instrument for both neighbourhoods, TACIS and the *mesures d'accompagnements* (MEDA), a financial instrument dedicated to the Euro-Mediterranean Partnership (EMP), merged into the ENPI in the EU's budgetary period from 2007 until 2013.[2]

The mesures d'accompagnements (MEDA)

About five years after the implementation of TACIS, MEDA, which was targeted at economic reform, sustainable economic and social development, as well as regional and transnational

Table 21.1 Overview of allocation of funding to TACIS, MEDA, ENPI and ENI in EUR billion

	1995–1999	2000–2006	2007–2013	2014–2020
TACIS	4.221 (1991–1999)	3.1	TACIS and MEDA were replaced by ENPI in January 2007.	
MEDA	3.4	5.35 approximately		
ENPI	ENPI and ENI were not in place yet. ENPI was created in 2007. ENI was established in 2014.		11.2 approximately	ENPI ceased to exist in 2007.
ENI				15.4

Source: Table created by author based on Benč (2008) and Perchoc (2015).

cooperation for countries of the Southern Mediterranean space, was established. MEDA delineated diverse guidelines regarding financial cooperation in the EMP (Schumacher 2005). The official MEDA goals were threefold: to support the process of transition; to support regional integration; and to help maintain social cohesion (Holden 2003). Four years after its implementation, the second phase of MEDA started (EUR-Lex. Access to European Union Law. MEDA Programme 1996). The delay in the full operationalisation before the end of the EMP was due to the prevalence of diverging interests of Member States in the Council of Ministers (Schumacher 2005). In addition to these diverging interests, as a potential shortcoming in the operationalisation of this instrument, the allocation of funds to projects sponsored by MEDA was a pitfall in the structure of this instrument. In MEDA II, EUR 29 million was allocated for civil society and human rights projects (Bicchi 2009). EUR 20 million was donated to a project in Egypt supporting children at risk, whereas merely EUR 2 million was spent on the promotion of democracy and human rights in Jordan (ibid.) This large discrepancy in the funds donated was not addressed by merging both MEDA and TACIS into the ENPI.

The European Neighbourhood and Partnership Instrument (ENPI)

The ENPI became operational in 2007 and was valid until 2013, before it evolved into the most recently established financial instrument, the ENI (Council of the European Union 2013). The ENPI's overall aim was to establish an 'area of prosperity and friendly neighbourliness involving the EU and [the ENP members]' (Regulation No. 1638). It aimed at sustainable development, legal and political approximation to the *acquis communautaire*, while tackling shortcomings in cross-border cooperation on the EU's external frontiers, enhancing the EU's Action Plans with all ENP countries and Russia (ibid.; Balfour and Rotta 2005) and establishing a functioning market economy (Poli 2016). The aforementioned objectives were fulfilled at Community level, rather than by the EU Member States alone, due to the scope of the intended goals (Regulation (EC) No 1638/2006). According to the regulation that established the ENPI, 'the privileged relationship' between the EU and its neighbours 'should build on commitments to common values, including democracy, the rule of law, good governance and respect for human rights' (ibid.). The references to common values in EU documents, delineating the external relations with its neighbours, raises the question of how these values were defined, given the possibility of discrepancies between the EU and some of its neighbours regarding the ideational basis for their relations. At the same time, it remains questionable how the attainment of common values would be measured (Del Sarto and Schumacher 2011).[3] In turn, this raises doubts as to whether the EU would undertake certain measures in case of the neighbours' non-compliance with some of these values.

Both the diverse themes and the extensive geographical areas covered by the ENPI were likely to enhance a lack of flexibility in formulating targeted responses to emerging crises. Funds could not be implemented *ad hoc* in response to evolving crises in the EU's neighbourhood, such as the various political and economic repercussions of the war in eastern Ukraine, because their implementation was based on the planning documents between the ENP country receiving the fund and the donor. However, an advantage of the planning document was its intention to ensure a framework for the equal distribution of funds. The implementation of the ENPI faced several challenges. Seeking to assess the implementation of projects sponsored by the ENP's financial instrument, the EU applied criteria established by the Organisation for Economic Co-operation and Development (OECD) – relevance, effectiveness, efficiency, impact and sustainability – to measure competence in aid and development policy. According to the mid-term evaluation report on cross-border cooperation financed under the ENPI, the broad thematic scope of policy objectives was a challenge (The European Union's FWC COM 2013). Simultaneously, the 'thematic shifts between priorities as programme partners adjusted the policy objectives to reflect the needs of the programme area [. . .] hampered' the 'assessment of relevance' (ibid: 10). The 'lack of consistency in terminology and/or numbering order between programme priorities and policy objectives created difficulties in identifying common indicators for the monitoring of projects and programmes [as well as] for the implementation at the policy level' (ibid.). The limited budgetary scope of the instrument, which is not compatible with the scale of challenges and expectations in the EU's neighbourhood, is a shortcoming of the ENPI, when taking the enormous capital demand of all neighbours – East and South – into consideration. This limited availability of funds persisted despite an increase of allocation to the ENPI by 32 per cent, compared with the allocated funds for both MEDA and TACIS for the budgetary cycle from 2000 until 2006 (European Commission 2014). EUR11.2 billion were made available for the budgetary period 2007–2013 (see Table 21.2). This budget accounted for 'both national and multi-country programmes' (ibid.) and the allocation of these funds is based on annual and multi-annual programmes, including cross-border cooperation (Poli 2016: 43).

Despite the OECD's indicators applied by the EU to measure competence in aid and development policy, the ENPI's evaluation report alluded to inherent limitations in assessing the capabilities in these policies. The report acknowledged the difficulty in measuring effectiveness 'in a fully reliable manner due [to] the lack of indicators especially at the level of outcomes' (The European Union's FWC COM 2013: 10). The European Commission's awareness of the limitations in this regard was toned down by the Commission's remaining 'high level of confidence in the programme design' (ibid.). This difficulty in measuring also applies when seeking to assess the 'impact of the effects' (ibid.).[4] The last two criteria applied for measuring the initial results of the projects carried out by the ENPI seem to overlap and thus raise the question of whether they are appropriate for the mid-term evaluation of the instruments. In a separate evaluation report of the ENPI, which did not merely focus on cross-border cooperation but on the instrument's overall activities, the results indicated disparities of priorities between regions and countries (European Commission 2014). To address this shortcoming, the Commission stated that a stronger focus on sustainability and addressing differences in 'willingness' and 'institutional/human capacities of regional partners' was crucial, while 'considering cooperation with countries with a stronger political will' (ibid.). The emphasis on assessing differences is reflected in the concept of differentiation at the core of the second ENP review, which was published in November 2015 (European Commission 2015a; Delcour 2015; Schumacher 2016). The Commission's recommendation to direct only fractions of the ENPI's support to reform-inclined governments seemed to defeat one of the main principles of the ENP, namely to create a ring of well-governed neighbours, referring to all countries incorporated in this policy. Additionally, the direction of the policy's resources to some of the ENP countries might

Table 21.2 Allocation of ENPI bilateral assistance to all ENP countries (2007–2013)

Eastern neighbourhood	Net contribution
Armenia	EUR 281.5 million
Azerbaijan	EUR 143.5 million
Belarus	EUR 94.2 million
Georgia	EUR 452.1 million
Moldova	EUR 560.9 million
Ukraine	EUR 1,005.6 million

Southern neighbourhood	Net contribution
Algeria	EUR 366.1 million
Egypt	EUR 1,007 million
Israel	EUR 13.5 million
Jordan	EUR 589 million
Lebanon	EUR 388 million
Libya	EUR 83 million
Morocco	EUR 1,431.1 million
Palestine	EUR 2,051.7 million
Syria	EUR 358 million
Tunisia	EUR 775 million

Source: Table created by author based on European Commission (2014).

result in greater disparities regarding socio-economic developments, both in the medium and long term. In the budgetary period from 2014 to 2020, the ENPI was succeeded by the ENI.

The European Neighbourhood Instrument (ENI)

The ENI came into effect in March 2014 to support the ENP countries until 2020 (Poli 2016). Russia had assumed a special status in both the ENPI and the ENI: according to the EU regulation establishing the ENI, Russia has a 'specific status' as 'both a Union neighbour and a strategic partner in the region' (European Parliament 2014). Therefore, Russia benefits from support for cross-border cooperation between Member States and partner countries and Russia along the external borders of the Union, instead of receiving the same wide-ranging support as the ENP countries (ibid.).

The ENI's budget for the period until 2020 boasts EUR 15.4 billion and thus 'provides the bulk of funding' to the ENP countries (European Commission 2015a). Aiming at

> contributing to achieve an area of shared prosperity and good neighbourliness in the partner countries by developing a special relationship founded on cooperation, peace and security, mutual accountability and a shared commitment to the universal values of democracy, the rule of law and respect for human rights.
>
> *(ibid.)*

The ENI reflects the idea of 'values' as mentioned in Article 8 of the Treaty of Lisbon (European Union 2007). This reference to shared values raises the question of how these values were defined, also due to potential discrepancies in the EU on the ideational foundations of its relations with ENP countries – a critique also raised in the section on the ENPI.

The European Commission and the ENP countries structure their cooperation in the ENI along the objectives of the UN Millennium Development Goals (MDGs), which were recently renamed Sustainable Development Goals. They set out diverse and ambitious objectives, primarily aimed at the reduction of international poverty by 50 per cent between 2015 and 2030 (United Nations 2016). Over a decade ago, the MDGs had already been widely criticised for the mismatch between their ambitious objectives and the lack of measures to fulfil these goals (Saith 2006).

No less difficult than measuring the fulfilment of the MDGs is assessing the implementation of the ENI's objectives. Even though the ENI regulation states that 'indicators' should be used to 'measure the achievement of the specific objectives' (Regulation (EU) No 232/2014), which 'shall be predefined, clear, transparent and, where appropriate, country-specific and measurable, [including] monitored democratic elections, respect for human rights and fundamental freedoms [. . .] [and] an independent judiciary' (ibid.), the extensive thematic and geographic scope of the ENI's intended goals renders the monitoring of their implementation more difficult.

The ENI offers 'innovative features', such as cooperation between EU Member States and partner countries, which share a common border with the EU; support of partners that have demonstrated their intention to improve good governance; and the development of close cooperation between EU Member States, beneficiary countries and the Technical Assistance and Information Exchange (TAIEX), intended to create political and economic cooperation – especially regarding the approximation and adoption of EU law and the corresponding enforcement.

At the time of writing this chapter, it is too premature to assess, based on the ENI's mid-term review, whether the projects funded by the ENI have met their intended objectives as the evaluation is anticipated to be completed in the second quarter of 2017 (European Commission 2015c).

Madad Trust Fund

The Madad Trust Fund does not fall into the same category as the classical financial instruments of the ENP. It is the first Trust Fund the EU ever established, aimed at tackling the fallouts of the Syrian war. At the same time, the management of the distribution of financial means differs from other financial instruments. Trust Funds enable the 'pooling of huge volumes of aid from different sources. [They] are governed by a specific legal arrangement between donors, which specifies governance procedures, financial and operational reporting requirements, and spending priorities' (Hauck 2015). Unlike with 'pre-programmed EU instruments, [. . .] funding can shift between and among countries' thus creating 'more flexibility' in response to the crisis in Syria (Cabinet of the Commissioner for the ENP and Enlargement Negotiations 2016). This flexibility in funding is a major benefit of the fund compared to the regular financial instruments discussed. The fact that it has been established for the Syria crisis makes it a tailor-made fund, which can address the specific problems of Syria's neighbours in a targeted way and is a further advantage of this Fund.

The Trust Fund's establishment in December 2014 was to 'provide a coherent, comprehensive and joint aid response to the war in Syria by focusing on stabilisation, resilience and recovery needs of refugees from Syria in neighbouring countries' (Cabinet of the Commissioner for the ENP and Enlargement Negotiations 2016). By September 2016, the Fund had a budget of EUR736 million, though merely EUR70 million are provided by the EU Member States (European Commission 2016). This contribution reflects a shortcoming of the Fund in the sense that the Member States' relative low level of contribution, compared with the overall budget available in the fund, reflects a considerable lack of commitment on their part. To the extent that Member States have displayed their willingness to commit themselves financially, they have made their financial contributions conditional on the implementation of projects by their national agencies and NGOs. Inevitably, this is likely to sideline the European Commission's role regarding coordinating the Fund. It needs to be acknowledged that it is one of the 'biggest EU responses to the Syrian refugee crisis' (ibid.). The Fund has allocated EUR150 million for projects related to education, while resources are also spent on improved access to health care, ameliorated water and sewage water infrastructure, and 'support to resilience, economic opportunities and social inclusion' (ibid.). The Fund is administered by the Commission and financial contributors to the fund convene in its operational board, which decides on funding bid proposals for the sponsoring of prospective projects (Henökl and Stemberger 2016). The Commissioner for the ENP and Enlargement Negotiations, Johannes Hahn, argues that the Madad Trust Fund 'has already shown its capacity to deliver in a quick and efficient manner' (Hahn 2015). Despite the advantage of a financial instrument tailor-made to address the manifold consequences of the Syrian war, Hahn's reference to the success of the Madad Trust Fund should not be overestimated, but rather needs to be put into perspective. Due to the continuation of the war in 2016 and 2017, the scope of the humanitarian disaster is likely to exceed the financial capacity of the Madad Trust Fund. Also, Madad requires negotiations between the Directorate General for the European Neighbourhood Policy and Enlargement (DG NEAR), the Directorate General for European Civil Protection and Humanitarian Aid Operations (ECHO), the Directorate General Migration and Home Affairs (HOME) and DEVCO, the EEAS and EU Member States and thus is exposed to divergences of interests, potentially resulting in the emergence of bottlenecks and delays in disbursement. EU Member States donate, and have a right to vote and observe the decisions regarding the implementation of projects sponsored by the Madad Trust Fund (ibid.). Lastly, as the implementation of the Fund is undertaken in cooperation with the EU and UN agencies, the latter of which prepare statistics for the EU's estimation of allocating funds, the EU is dependent on the provision and accuracy of externally generated information.

Despite its advantages, the Madad Fund is faced with a budgetary and procedural limitation. Being mainly supported by the EU's budget, it also depends on both Member States' and other donors' contributions (Henökl and Stemberger 2016). With the urgent need to address the root causes and effects of the Syrian war in light of the refugee crisis, which not only affected ENP countries but also EU Member States, the European Commission 'exerted pressure on the latter to assume responsibility and increase their contributions' (Hauck et al. 2015: 5). This was ineffective, as in September 2016 contributions by EU Member States amounted to just EUR72 million (European Commission 2016). The Fund's objective to quickly respond to 'political pressures [. . .] entails the risk that valuable lessons of international cooperation are forgotten' (Hauck et al.). The insufficient donations, as well as the need to spend money swiftly and flexibly in response to emerging large-scale crises, raise doubts about the Trust Fund's success as the appropriate tool of 'addressing the root causes of conflict [. . .] sudden migration, and assisting the transition of conflict prone countries towards resilience and development' (ibid.).

Institutional advantages and shortcomings of the financial instruments

The development and implementation of some of the financial instruments, brought about deliberations regarding potential shifts in the EU's inter-institutional balance of power. In 2007, at the time of the development of the ENPI, the European Parliament's concern was that its input to the deliberations on ENPI-funded projects could be marginalised. It perceived the extensive 'geographical scope' concerning both 'general objectives and global allocations' as undermining its ability to both prioritise cooperation and allocate financial means to themes and regions (Canciani 2007: 150; Kaminska 2017). This search for ownership, inherent in the inter-institutional balance of power, is a potential shortcoming, given that the institutions' focus on their engagement in the decision-making process might result in delays in the implementation of the instruments.

Taking the example of the ENI, this brief section seeks to answer the question of whether a shift in the EU's inter-institutional balance of power resulted in delays in the implementation of this financial instrument. An example of a shift in the EU's inter-institutional balance of power was a new provision in the ENI regulation concerning the European Commission's and the Parliament's exchange regarding this instrument. The annex to the European Parliament's resolution in December 2013, on the proposal for a regulation of the Parliament and the Council regarding the launch of the ENI, delineates the Commission's 'strategic dialogue' with the Parliament on 'ENI programming documents before they are finalised'(European Parliament 2013).[5] The annex states that the Commission will deliver documents regarding the 'programming with thematic priorities, possible results, choice of assistance modalities and financial allocations for such priorities' (ibid.). In a potential attempt to maintain the European Parliament's say regarding the implementation of the ENI, the annex states that the 'European Commission will take into account the position expressed by the European Parliament on the matter' and 'will conduct a strategic dialogue with the European Parliament in preparing the mid-term review [. . .] before any substantial revision of the programming documents during the period of validity of this regulation' (ibid.). In the context of these internal deliberations, some discrepancies among the EU's institutions regarding the implementation of financial instruments became visible.

The internal dynamics of projects implemented by the ENI were improved. 'Partnership Priorities', the EU's political objectives to ENP partner countries, as set out by the ENI regulation, 'frame the prioritisation of assistance during programming of the ENI [. . .] in a more clear-cut way than in the past' (ibid.). At the same time 'this new clarity on what the political objectives are, will either limit the EEAS' or the Commission's possibility to interpret more freely what should go into the ENI programming documents' (ibid.). However, this change 'did not result in delays regarding the implementation of assistance carried out under the ENI'. The ENP revision of November 2015 introduced a 'flexibility cushion', which is a reserved amount of funds to be allocated for 'unforeseen needs' (ibid.). New

> modalities for implementation of assistance through Trust Funds as well as the EU's integrated approach proposed in the [EU's] Global Strategy [on the EU's Foreign and Security Policy] [. . .] provide [opportunities] for a more responsive and coherent EU engagement, drawing on all of its resources in a more conscious way.
>
> *(ibid.)*

Simultaneously, the ENP's revision implied a shift of focus of the ENP from being purely a 'development cooperation instrument [to] a part of the external policy of the [EU]'[6]. According to a member of the Cabinet of the Commissioner for the ENP and Enlargement, the shift of the ENP from development cooperation to part of the EU's external policy 'inevitably means that the EEAS is the prime player in the EU's external relations'. Surprisingly, despite this crucial role played by the EEAS in the ENP, the member of the Cabinet of the Commissioner states that 'the key role of the Commission is confirmed and acknowledged' in the overall framework of the ENP[7]. Nonetheless, the role of both the EEAS and the European Commission as crucial actors in the ENP alludes to a blurry division of competencies between both institutions. This absence of a clear delineation of responsibilities might result in delays in the implementation of aspects belonging to the ENP's policy domain. At the same time, occasional divergences might occur regarding the division of competencies between the EEAS and the Commission on one hand and the EU Member States and the institutions on the other, not least with regard to the identification of priority areas for funding of projects under the ENI's umbrella.

Conclusions

This chapter sought to fulfil two objectives. First, it provided an overview of the ENP's major financial instruments and their objectives as the underpinnings of enabling the financing of projects aimed at economic, social and humanitarian development in the EU's neighbourhood. Second, it aimed at demonstrating both benefits and shortcomings of the ENP's financial instruments. It was shown that the advantage of these instruments is their continuous evolution in response to the emerging needs of the EU's neighbouring countries since the 1990s. Structured cooperation between the Commission and the CIS under TACIS, and the creation of financial instruments targeting specific regions, created the potential for a more tailor-made approach to the financing of individual projects.

Despite the advantage of these instruments, several shortcomings persist. First, due to the extensive geopolitical and economic repercussions of the Syria war, the Madad Fund has to address the need for an extensive financial contribution by a diverse range of donors to address the conflict's wide-ranging negative spill-overs. By its nature, a trust fund requires contributions from the EU's budget as well as EU Member States and other donors. The latter have not been forthcoming in contributing to this budget. The sustainability of the Fund in the long-term is dependent on donors. In the case of MEDA there was another shortcoming, notably a large discrepancy in the allocation of funds to countries benefiting from this scheme (Bicchi 2009). This discrepancy had not been addressed by the merger of MEDA and TACIS into the ENPI (ibid.). Second, the inter-institutional balance of power within the EU regarding its involvement in the implementation of financial instruments can hamper financial instruments' streamlined implementation.

The ENP review of November 2015 seeks to further facilitate the implementation of financial instruments in the future. It called for increased flexibility in implementing projects sponsored in the framework of the financial instruments. Simultaneously, the review expressed the EU's 'commitment of substantial resources to support the major stabilisation challenge in the neighbourhood' with the funds for ENI for the budgetary period from 2014 until 2020 (European Commission 2015a). Additionally, the EU seeks to obtain funding from international financial institutions. This potentially increased financial contribution is due to the fact that the needs of the neighbouring countries exceed the financial resources of both the EU and its Member States. As a result, the European Commission intends to develop alternatives which will 'better and more efficiently address the financial needs of neighbourhood countries' (ibid.). However, in order to maximise these resources and make EU contributions more 'visible', 'improved donor coordination' is necessary. The 2015 review refers to the EU's response to Ukraine and the Syria conflict as well as the Madad Trust Fund, as examples of how the 'EU's financial instruments can react quickly and flexibly' while acknowledging that more needs to be done to 'accelerate assistance', such as the creation of a 'flexibility cushion' in the ENI to set aside resources to be used for 'unforeseen needs' during conflict and post-conflict situations (ibid.).[8]

The latest example in the EU's attempt at developing further plans aimed at contributing to developing the EU's relations with neighbouring states is the European External Investment Plan for Africa and the neighbourhood countries, which was launched in September 2016. It aims at working towards the fulfilment of the Sustainable Development Goals as well as 'strengthening partnerships' (European Commission 2017). One of the underlying motivations for the Plan's launch was the contribution to 'sustainable growth' and job creation. Thus, one of the advantages of this Plan is that it is specifically directed at the needs of Africa and the neighbourhood countries. The former have not been addressed by the financial instruments, given their focus on the ENP countries. Therefore, this investment plan can be regarded as complementary to rather than a substitution of the financial instruments of the ENP.

Future research on country specific projects which were funded by these instruments (Bicchi and Voltolini 2013), is likely to provide detailed insights regarding further advantages and potential disadvantages of the instruments.[9] It needs to assess the implementation of specific projects sponsored by the instruments in respective countries of both the eastern and the southern neighbourhoods. It will not only identify further benefits and shortcomings but also identify other factors either facilitating or undermining the operationalisation of the instruments complementing the ones identified in this chapter.

Notes

1 For an overview of some further financial contributions to the neighbourhood see 'The EU a major donor', www.enpi-info.eu/ENI, accessed 11 July 2016.
2 Interview with member of the Cabinet of the Commissioner for the ENP and Enlargement Negotiations 2016. Conducted on 6 and 7 July 2016.
3 This was the subject in Del Sarto, R. and Schumacher, T. (2011).
4 According to this evaluation report, *effectiveness* delineates the extent to which each programme achieves or is likely to achieve the programme objectives (p.10). *Outcomes* are described with the synonym of benefits (p.44). *Impact* entails 'the intermediate and longer-term effects or outcomes of an intervention' (p. 59).
5 Interview with an EEAS official. Conducted on 18 November 2016.
6 Interview with member of the Cabinet of the Commissioner for the ENP and Enlargement Negotiations. Conducted on 5 July 2016.
7 Ibid.
8 Interview with EEAS official, conducted on 15 July 2016.
9 At the time of finalising this chapter (December 2016), research on projects funded by the EIDHR exists. For further reference, see: Bicchi and Voltolini (2013).

References

Balfour, R. and Rotta, A. (2005) 'Beyond enlargement. The European Neighbourhood Policy and its tools', *International Spectator* 40(1): 7–20.
Benč, V. (2008) 'ENP financial instruments: need for a change', *International Issues & Slovak Foreign Policy Affairs* XVII(4): 78–90.
Bicchi, F. and Voltolini, B. (2013) 'EU democracy promotion in the Mediterranean: what relationship with the Arab Uprisings?', *Democracy and Security* 9(1): 80–99.
Bicchi, F. (2009) 'Democracy assistance in the Mediterranean: an overview', *Mediterranean Politics* 14(1): 61–78.
Canciani, E. (2007) 'European financial perspective and the European Neighbourhood and Partnership Instrument', *Mediterranean Politics Panorama*: Med. 2007: 148–152.
Commission of the European Communities. (1997) 'TACIS Interim Evaluation. Synthesis Report', July, http://ec.europa.eu/europeaid/how/evaluation/evaluation_reports/reports/tacis/951415_en.pdf, accessed 6 May 2016.
Commission of the European Communities. (2003) *Communication from the Commission to the Council and the European Parliament. Wider Europe-Neighbourhood: A New Framework for Relations with Our Eastern and Southern Neighbours*, COM (2003) 104 final, Brussels, 11 March.
Council of the European Union. (2013) *Joint Declaration of the Eastern Partnership Summit*, Vilnius, 17130/13 (OR.en) PRESSE 516, 28–29 November, www.consilium.europa.eu/uedocs/cms_Data/docs/pressdata/EN/foraff/139765.pdf, accessed 18 April 2016.
Delcour, L. (2015) 'The 2015 ENP Review: Beyond Stocktaking, the Need for a Political Strategy', *College of Europe Policy Brief Series*, Bruges, December.

Del Sarto, R. and Schumacher, T. (2011) 'From Brussels with love: leverage, benchmarking, and the action plans with Jordan and Tunisia in the EU's democratization policy', *Democratization* 18(4): 932–955.

EUR-Lex. Access to European Union Law. (2014). *Regulation (EU) No 232/2014 of the European Parliament and of the Council of 11 March 2014 establishing a European Neighbourhood Instrument*, Official Journal of the European Union. L 77/27, 15 March 2014.

EUR-Lex. Access to European Union Law. (2006). *Regulation (EU) No 1638/2006 of the European Parliament and of the Council of 24 October 2006 laying down general provisions establishing a European Neighbourhood and Partnership Instrument*, Official Journal of the European Union, L 310/1, 9 November 2006.

European Commission. Press Release Database. *Regulation (EU) No 2157/91 of 15 July 1991. Technical Assistance to the Commonwealth of Independent States (TACIS)*.

European Commission. (2013) 'European Neighbourhood Policy and Enlargement Negotiations. Civil Society. Civil Society Facility', http://ec.europa.eu/enlargement/policy/policy-highlights/civil-society/index_en.htm, accessed 27 September 2016.

European Commission. (2014) *European Neighbourhood and Partnership Instrument, 2007–2013. Overview of Activities and Results*, https://ec.europa.eu/europeaid/sites/devco/files/overview_of_enpi_results_2007-2013_en_0.pdf, accessed 24 April 2017.

European Commission. (2015a) *Joint Communication to the European Parliament, the Council, the European Economic and Social Committee and the Committee of the Regions. Review of the European Neighbourhood Policy*, JOIN(2015) 50 Final, Brussels.

European Commission. (2015b) 'TACIS', http://europa.eu/rapid/press-release_MEMO-92-54_en.htm, accessed 22 September 2016.

European Commission. (2015c) *Evaluation Roadmap. ENI Mid-Term Review. Evaluation of the European Neighbourhood Instrument (ENI) 2014-2020 in Support of the Mid-term Review*, http://ec.europa.eu/smart-regulation/roadmaps/docs/2017_near_002_evaluation_eni_en.pdf, accessed 14 July 2016.

European Commission. (2016) 'European Neighbourhood Policy and Enlargement Negotiations. EU Regional Trust Fund in Response to the Syrian Crisis', http://ec.europa.eu/enlargement/neighbourhood/countries/syria/madad/index_en.htm, accessed 28 September 2016.

European Commission. (2017) 'State of the Union 2016: European External Investment Plan: Questions and Answers', http://europa.eu/rapid/press-release_MEMO-16-3006_en.htm, accessed 1 February 2017.

European Union (2007). *Treaty of Lisbon amending the Treaty on European Union and the Treaty establishing the European Community, signed at Lisbon, 13 December 2007*.

EUR-Lex. Access to European Union Law. MEDA Programme. (1996). *Council Regulation (EC) No 1488/96of 23 July 1996 on financial technical measures to accompany MEDA the reform of economic and social structures in the framework of the Mediterranean partnership*.

European Parliament (2013) *Annex to the legislative resolution P7_TA(2013)0567. European Neighbourhood Instrument. European Parliament legislative resolution of 11 December 2013 on the proposal for a regulation of the European Parliament and of the Council establishing a European Neighbourhood Instrument (COM(2011)0839-c7-0492/2011-2011/0405(COD))*.

European Parliament (2014) *Regulation (EU). No 232/2014 of the European Parliament and of the Council of 11 March 2014 establishing a European Neighbourhood Instrument*.

Frenz, A. (2016) 'The European Commission's Tacis Programme. 1991–2006. A Success Story', OSCE, www.osce.org/eea/34459?download=true, accessed 4 May 2016.

Hahn. J. (2015) Live EC Press Conference Commissioners Johannes Hahn and Christos Stylianideseu Aid for the Syria Crisis – EU Trust Fund and Immediate Humanitarian Assistance, European Commission, Audiovisual Services, 1 December, http://ec.europa.eu/avservices/video/player.cfm?ref=I113348, accessed 10 May 2016.

Hauck, V., Knoll, A. and Herrero Cangas, A. (2015) 'EU Trust Funds – Shaping More Comprehensive External Action?', *Briefing Note* 81, European Centre for Development Policy Management, 20 November 2015.

Henökl, T. and Stemberger, A. (2016) 'EU policies in the Arab world: update and critical assessment', *European Foreign Affairs Review* 21(2): 227–250.

Holden, P. (2003) 'The European Community's MEDA aid programme: a strategic instrument of civilian power?', *European Foreign Affairs Review* 8(3): 347–363.

Interviews with a member of the Cabinet of the Commissioner for the ENP and Enlargement Negotiations (2016). Interviews conducted via email in July 2016.

Kaminska, J. (2017) 'The European Parliament and the Revised ENP', in Bouris, D. and Schumacher, T. (eds.) *The Revised European Neighbourhood Policy. Continuity and Change in EU Foreign Policy*, Palgrave Macmillan, 135–151.

Perchoc, P. (2015) 'The European Neighbourhood Policy. European Parliament. In-Depth Analysis', PE 569.048, European Parliamentary Research Service, October.

Poli, S. (2016) 'Promoting EU Values in the Neighbourhood Through EU Financial Instruments and Restrictive Measures', in Poli, S. (ed.) *The European Neighbourhood Policy-Values and Principles*, London and New York: Routledge, 33-57.

Regulation (EU) No 1638/2006 of the European Parliament and of the Council of 24 October 2006 laying down general provisions establishing a European Neighbourhood and Partnership Instrument, Official Journal of the European Union, L 310/1, 9 November 2006.

Regulation (EU) No 2157/91 of 15 July 1991. Technical Assistance to the Commonwealth of Independent States (TACIS).

Regulation (EU) No 232/2014 of the European Parliament and of the Council of 11 March 2014 establishing a European Neighbourhood Instrument, Official Journal of the European Union. L 77/27, 15 March 2014.

Saith, A. (2006) 'From universal values to Millennium Development Goals: lost in translation', *Development and Change* 37(6): 1167–1197.

Schumacher, T. (2005) 'Die Europaeische Union als internationaler Akteur im Suedlichen Mittelmeerraum. "Actor Capability" und EU-Mittelmeerpolitik', in Schumacher, T. *Die EU als internationaler Akteur im Mittelmeerraum zwischen 1996 und 2000: Die EU-Mittelmeer-Politik im Rahmen der Euro-Mediterranen Partnerschaft*, Baden Baden: Nomos.

Schumacher, T. (2016) 'Back to the Future: The 'New' ENP towards the Southern Neighbourhood and the End of Ambition', *College of Europe Policy Brief Series*, Bruges, January.

The European Union's FWC COM. (2013) [Framework contract Commission], Studies and Technical Assistance in All Sectors, Mid-Term Evaluation of Cross-Border Cooperation Programmes under the European Neighbourhood and Partnership Instrument (ENPI) 2007–2013, Final Report. Vol. 1.

United Nations (2016) 'We can end poverty. Millennium Development Goals and Beyond 2015', www.un.org/millenniumgoals/, accessed 3 July 2016.

PART IV

Bilateralism, region-building and conflict management in the European Neighbourhood Policy

22
THE EUROPEAN NEIGHBOURHOOD POLICY BETWEEN BILATERALISM AND REGION-BUILDING

Federica Bicchi, Gergana Noutcheva and Benedetta Voltolini

Introduction

Since its beginning, the European Neighbourhood Policy (ENP) has sparked debates about how the EU envisages relations with its neighbourhood. One of the most contested aspects has been the relationship between bilateralism, multilateralism and region-building, and how these different forms of political relations interact and, ideally, ensure harmonious relations between the EU and its neighbours. As this chapter shows, and the revised ENP (launched in November 2015) has confirmed, the EU has relied consistently on bilateralism, but it has also engaged with region-building in its neighbourhood. Region-building displays a different trajectory in its eastern and southern components, with the emphasis shifting from region-building to bilateralism in the South, whereas region-building has increased in relevance in the East. This chapter provides an overview of the interplay between bilateralism and region-building across time and in the shadow of power asymmetries in the area.

The literature on bilateralism, multilateralism and region-building (or its proxy concept, regionalism) is broad, especially related to the EU (for example, Börzel and Risse 2016; Laatikainen and Smith 2006; Telò 2014). Essentially, bilateralism centres on relations between two sovereign actors and its centrality in international politics has often been emphasised, for instance, to highlight its recent rise in trade agreements world-wide (Heydon and Woolcock 2009). Multilateralism and region-building are often associated with the policies of the EU, which is the most fully-fledged example of the construction of a prosperous region. Multilateralism has also attracted attention in relation to the more restrictive concept of 'effective multilateralism' that the EU included in the 2003 European Security Strategy (European Council 2003; Renard 2015). By working together with the US and often within the UN, as well as by intentionally building a broader coalition of actors, the EU has been considered to act multilaterally to better perform in contemporary international affairs. Region-building brings multilateralism to a further level, by putting the construction of a (political) region as the end goal of cooperation. While regionalism has been defined as 'a primarily state-led process of building and sustaining formal regional institutions and organizations among at least three states' (Börzel and Risse 2016: 7), region-building is often used, as here, to indicate more generally an open-ended political project encouraging social, economic and political interactions, which can ultimately affect the identity of participants. It is in this sense that the EU has often been considered a promoter of regional endeavours (Adler et al. 2006), not just exporting its own model to the rest of the world but also expanding to include parts of it as its neighbourhood. More broadly, the literature on comparative regionalism has highlighted regional integration as the best way to ensure peace, stability and prosperity, stressing that this has always been an important feature of EU foreign policy (Börzel and Risse 2009). Much remains to be understood about how these political phenomena interact, the extent to which they are compatible, complementary or in opposition, and, ultimately, how power relations affect their interaction. The ENP is a perfect case within which to see these processes at work, in the interplay between bilateralism and region-building.

The main tenets of the ENP display a mix of bilateralism, multilateralism and region-building. Based on bilateral agreements and subsequent Action Plans, the ENP promotes not only bilateral engagement between the EU and its neighbours but also multilateral cooperation and – to a lesser degree – cooperation between its neighbours, with a varying degree of region-building. The official position of the EU is that 'the ENP is chiefly a bilateral policy between the EU and each partner country', but is 'complemented by regional and multilateral co-operation initiatives' (European Commission 2013), such as the Eastern Partnership (EaP), the Union for the Mediterranean (UfM) and the Black Sea Synergy.

Combining bilateralism and region-building, has been a constant challenge in EU external relations. In the East, the EU founded its relations with the former Soviet states on bilateralism, not only after their independence in the early 1990s (Delcour 2011a) but also during the early years of the ENP. Since the late 2000s, the EU has started to promote and support regional initiatives in the region, with the launch of the Black Sea Synergy and of the EaP, with the aim of complementing the bilateral track. In contrast, in the southern neighbourhood, region-building proved to be largely incompatible with bilateral relations between countries bordering the Mediterranean. Before the ENP, the EU was engaged in a process of region-building in the Mediterranean with the Euro-Mediterranean Partnership (EMP), launched in 1995.[1] As the EMP was unable to impress any independent momentum to regional dynamics, bilateralism came to the fore with the ENP, while the UfM, launched in 2008, did not restore a credible region-building project.

Both bilateral and regional initiatives are characterised by the evident asymmetry of the relationship that has been crystallised in subsequent policies through the projection of EU norms, rules and practices onto the neighbouring countries. But while the EU has often used power asymmetries to set the pace of relations, it has also had to respond to the diverging views of its neighbours and to stress different modalities of interaction at different times.

The following analysis is structured as follows. The first section shows the centrality of bilateralism in the ENP, as well as the uneven impact of the EU on neighbouring countries. The subsequent section analyses regional initiatives in the neighbourhood and shows how region-building developed in different ways, with the Mediterranean being an early target and the eastern neighbourhood a latecomer. In the concluding section, we reflect on regionalism and bilateralism in the shadow of power asymmetries.

The ENP and bilateralism

The ENP is based primarily on bilateral instruments and incentives, which include market opening, financial assistance and visa facilitation between the EU and individual neighbour countries. Cooperation between the EU and each of its neighbours, centres on Partnership and

Cooperation Agreements or Association Agreements and Action Plans, which are at times also complemented by Readmission Agreements, Mobility Partnerships, Visa Liberalisation Action Plans and memoranda of understanding – in which the specificities of each individual case are considered. Differentiation among countries has thus become the main feature of the ENP (Del Sarto and Schumacher 2005).

In the academic literature, this emphasis on bilateralism has been mirrored by an increasing number of contributions on the EU's impact (or lack of) on individual cases. Through the lenses of external governance, or with a specific focus on democracy promotion (Kelley 2006; Lavenex 2011; Lavenex and Schimmelfennig 2009), a large part of the literature has focused on the EU's attempts to shape its eastern and southern neighbours according to its model, with a view to creating a 'ring of friends' and ensuring stability.

Conditionality, the main bilateral mechanism of exerting influence on ENP countries, has relied on the EU's superior power resources, but it has often proved unsuited to the context of the neighbourhood, as acknowledged in the revised ENP of 2015. First, scholars have repeatedly pointed out that incentives offered by the EU are much weaker in comparison to the accession 'carrot' and vaguely formulated, without specifying a tangible package of benefits that can stimulate economic and political change in ENP states (Weber, Smith and Baun 2007; Whitman and Wolff 2010). Second, the conditions attached are similarly fuzzy, leaving the process open-ended and with a lot of room for negotiation of EU-compliant reforms (Noutcheva, Pomorska and Bosse 2013). This practice of 'conditionality-lite' (Sasse 2008) reduces the EU's leverage on disinclined ENP governments and seriously undermines the effectiveness of EU policy, especially in areas such as democracy and rule of law. In the East, positive change has happened in cases where pro-reform constituencies within domestic regimes have managed to exploit EU help to push the domestic establishment into adopting partial reforms (Langbein and Wolczuk 2012). Similarly, there have been instances where domestic actors have abused the EU support in order to cement the status quo and avoid democratisation (Börzel and Pamuk 2012). In the South, the EU's backing of authoritarian rulers before the Arab uprisings has undermined its subsequent efforts to support democratisation (Pace 2010). Where democratic advances have occurred, the primary demand for change has come from within, and the EU's support has been limited and only partially welcome (Dandashly 2015). The bilateral instruments have proved futile altogether in improving the quality of democratic governance in both neighbourhoods.

In the absence of credible 'stick' mechanisms, the EU has reinforced the rhetoric on 'equal' partnership, counting on exerting influence and power in softer ways and through more cooperative means. These are meant to take place at the transnational level through trans-governmental exchanges and/or cross-border civil society cooperation. The dense institutionalised network of contacts in the ENP framework facilitates this practice, although many have questioned the equal terms of exchanges and pointed to the power asymmetry in the relationship between the EU and its neighbours (Bechev and Nicolaïdis 2010; Korosteleva 2011).

While the emphasis of the external governance literature remains on the bilateral dimension of the ENP, and how the EU spreads its regulatory framework *via* bilateral agreements, it is also interesting to note that these actions can lead to the blurring of borders and the creation – maybe unintended – of a regional area that is integrated into the EU's legal framework in different ways. This point echoes the main ideas of the literature on empires. The ENP favours the creation of a hub-and-spoke model that allows the centre to control the peripheries to its own advantage (Zielonka 2008). Put differently, EU bilateral relations are aimed at exporting norms and practices to the neighbourhood, leading to the creation of 'borderlands'. Neighbouring countries are thus included into the EU's system to different degrees and comply with the norms and practices that the EU imposes, which are non-negotiable (Del Sarto 2016).

In trade, for example, the EU has negotiated bilateral Deep and Comprehensive Free Trade Areas (DCFTAs) in the framework of Association Agreements with Ukraine, Georgia and Moldova, which commit them to implement considerable parts of the EU *acquis* in areas such as service sector liberalisation, public procurement, competition policy, intellectual property, investment protection, environmental protection and phytosanitary standards. The same template of trade agreements is currently considered for the Mediterranean countries with negotiating directives already issued for Morocco, Tunisia, Jordan and Egypt, although the rationale for adopting the EU *acquis* in these domains is far from obvious (Van der Loo 2015). With their legally binding provisions on regulatory approximation, the DCFTAs embody the EU vision of progressively linking ENP countries to the Internal Market. When implemented, they will put in place a hub-and-spoke system of differentiated market integration, with the EU at the core and neighbours gravitating around it and participating to varying degrees in the common regulatory space.

With migration, the EU has negotiated bilateral Mobility Partnerships with Tunisia, Morocco and Jordan, promising opportunities for legal migration against control of irregular migration. Many of these partnerships have remained on paper and are equivalent to declarations of intent, which – especially in the current climate of permanent migration crisis – do not seem viable in the short term. The EU has also concluded Visa Liberalisation Action Plans with Georgia, Ukraine and Moldova, which have already led to visa-free travel in the Schengen area for Moldovan citizens. Readmission Agreements form part of these bilateral measures in both neighbourhoods. In the framework of these bilateral instruments, the EU has tried to export to ENP countries its practices and systems in areas such as border management, detection and fighting of irregular migration, document security and asylum policy (Noutcheva 2015). The outcome of these bilateral arrangements conforms to the centre-periphery pattern – the EU sitting at the centre and dictating the terms of reform in the periphery, as well as controlling movements of particular members of the periphery closer to the core.

The bilateral regimes the EU has put in place with ENP countries in various policy areas have resulted in differentiation and the revised ENP of 2015 points in the same direction. Neighbours move at different speeds and with different purposes towards the EU-defined regulatory space and – to an extent – blur the borderlines between insiders and outsiders. The revised ENP further strengthens bilateral cooperation and it will further differentiate among EU neighbours, by providing neighbours with more of a say in the decision about priorities. Within the overarching goal of stability in the neighbourhood, the EU intends to promote a tailor-made approach – or rather, a 'made-to-measure' one (Dworkin and Wesslau 2015) – that responds to the individual needs and priorities of each neighbour. The EU will deal with each ENP country based on fewer and commonly defined priorities, thus reflecting neighbours' aspirations and increasing ownership on their side (European Commission 2015b). Differentiation among bilateral relations between the EU and its neighbours will be the name of the game for the foreseeable future.

Regionalism in the East and the South

While the instruments of the ENP are primarily bilateral, the EU's wider relations with its neighbours have also displayed a distinct regional dimension at specific points in time. The EU is often presented as being pre-disposed to spreading regionalism owing to its own experience with regional integration (Börzel and Risse 2009). Indeed, the EU has launched or helped the initiation of various regional and sub-regional initiatives in its neighbourhood and beyond but, as we are going to show, these are not the only instrument of EU foreign policy, or consistently supported. These regional cooperation schemes fall within two broad categories: region-building initiatives – promoting cooperation across the border between the EU and a set of neighbours – and region-building initiatives supporting regional cooperation within a set of neighbours, separately from the EU (cf. Tsardanidis 2011; Cottey 2012). With the first category, the EU is in the driver's seat, sets the priorities of regional cooperation and manages the network of regional exchanges, with a view to thicken interactions with its neighbours. With the second category, the EU assists existing regional cooperative endeavours by helping local actors to launch mutually beneficial projects in different sectors (Tassinari 2006). Examples of the former include the EMP, the UfM as originally intended and the EaP. Examples of the latter include the Black Sea Synergy and EU support for regional initiatives in the Southern Mediterranean such as the Arab Maghreb Union and the Agadir initiative. The EU has used existing economic and political power asymmetries to incentivise regional cooperative behaviour among countries that otherwise would not have cooperated, owing to bilateral disputes, regional rivalries and/or societal animosities. In this sense, EU-backed region-building is an important instrument for fostering stability and security in the neighbourhood.

Region-building at the border

The interaction between bilateralism and region-building has been different in the southern and eastern neighbourhoods. In the South, cooperation aiming at region-building predates the creation of the ENP, while in the East it has followed the ENP establishment.

The EMP was conceived as a multilateral and comprehensive initiative that aimed to tie the southern neighbours into a regional project potentially affecting not just the peace and prosperity of actors involved but also their identity. Despite the initial enthusiasm, the EMP's ambitious plans were unable to build a region as promised, or to create independent momentum to the region-building project. Several reasons have been pointed out. Bilateral and sub-regional initiatives have taken over the multilateral dimension (Barbé and Herranz-Surrallés 2010). Due to the asymmetry between the parties, the EMP was sometimes portrayed as a form of hegemony, which enabled the EU to pursue its economic and political goals (Holden 2009; Philippart 2003). Finally, more critical assessments argue that the EMP was based on a narrative of 'otherness', so that Mediterranean countries are used to strengthen the EU's own identity in opposition to the Arab other (Pace 2006).

Given the perceived limitations of the EMP, the launch of the UfM in 2008 was meant to breathe new life into the regional initiative. Focusing on project-based initiatives among willing countries, the UfM has highlighted the *à la carte* nature of cooperation that has characterised EU policies in its southern neighbourhood since the beginning of the ENP, thus leading to a *de facto* scaling down of EU ambitions in the region (Barbé and Herranz-Surrallés 2010; Bicchi 2014). The UfM, based on more members than the EMP,[2] has fostered initiatives among countries that share common problems and have functional complementarities and common visions (Bicchi 2011), but sectoral cooperation has been hampered by more politicised issues, from the Arab–Israeli conflict to competing national interests (Holden 2011). The establishment of a co-presidency *de facto* representing the Arab countries has not overcome the asymmetry in the relationship between the EU and Middle East and North African (MENA) countries (Cardwell 2011).

In the East, the multilateral channel of engaging ENP countries was not considered a fruitful avenue at the start, not least because imagining a geographically compact region, with sufficient distinctiveness, was not so easy. Only in 2009 did the EU's policy in the East acquire a more pronounced regional dimension with the launch of the high-profile regional initiative, the EaP, notably at a time when Russia's resurgence in the shared neighbourhood started to become real.

The EU thus felt compelled to upgrade its relationship with the eastern neighbours and offer more tangible prospects for their participation in its own regional project. The EaP has an innovative multilateral track, meant to bring together the EU and the eastern neighbours at all levels – governments, parliaments, municipalities, civil society organisations – to discuss the eastern neighbours' progressive integration in the EU policy space. Although it is intended to implement the principle of joint ownership of the ENP in practice, first appraisals have indicated that the exchanges in the different forums are not devoid of hierarchy (Delcour 2011b). In other words, while the official aim is to engage neighbours as equals and give them a real chance in co-determining the outcome of cooperation the EaP reproduces existing bilateral patterns of domination and subordination.

Russia has also viewed the EU's approach of gradually drawing the eastern neighbours closer to its regulatory and normative space, as an attempt to control an area that Russia sees as belonging to its own 'sphere of influence' (Averre 2009; Casier 2013). It has, in turn, launched its own regional integration schemes targeting the eastern neighbours and mirroring the EU's regional initiatives. The Eurasian Economic Union, centred on Russia and aimed at regionally integrating the former Soviet states, has thus emerged as a competing regional project in the eastern neighbourhood, forcing neighbours to choose between two legally and economically incompatible schemes (Dragneva and Wolczuk 2013). While the methods of attracting participants in these regional initiatives differ a great deal, with the EU inviting participation and Russia threatening to retaliate against non-participation, the choice of Belarus and Armenia to opt in to the Russia-steered regional bloc highlights the importance of cultural affinities, historical ties and emotional affiliations for regional cooperation in addition to the material incentives and disincentives offered by external parties (Keukeleire and Petrova 2014).

Compared to the EMP, the EaP is a less ambitious initiative that has a complementary, yet secondary, role to the bilateral ENP track: it has not raised unrealistic expectations about what it can achieve. The EMP was a new and substantial initiative by the EU, with the aim of engaging with MENA countries when Arab–Israeli peace seemed possible. It was loaded with high hopes for peace, political change and economic development. The subsequent launch of the UfM came at a time when the peace process had collapsed and its early beginnings were fraught with difficulties. Further developments in the Middle East and North Africa made it even more difficult to reach its original objectives. In fact, neither the EMP nor the UfM and the EaP can be credited with any concrete results, although their usefulness might be found eventually not in the outcome of cooperation but in the process of engagement and the active EU attempt at socialising the neighbours into the European way of governing various policy sectors.

Region-building beyond the EU

In 2008, the EU introduced region-building initiatives beyond its borders in both the East and the South, although neither case was particularly successful.

The EU decided to support cooperative schemes within the eastern neighbourhood by establishing the so-called Black Sea Synergy. This was the first EU attempt to do anything on a regional basis in the East and a departure from the predominant bilateral mode of engaging the eastern neighbours (Delcour 2011a). It was welcome as an additional tool of influencing developments in a region where the EU's absence was acutely felt (Tassinari 2006). The Synergy tries to invigorate existing cooperative initiatives in the wider region surrounding the Black Sea and to encourage the development of bottom-up projects in various sectors. However, there is a wide consensus that the Black Sea cooperation is not functioning well, although explanations for this vary. The EU attributes its own limited impact to the 'weak political commitment' (European

Commission 2015a: 10) of the littoral states. Some scholars point to the new geopolitical context, with several actors vying for influence (Tsantoulis 2009), while others see the difficulties of imagining a territorial space united by a common history and identity (Triantaphyllou 2009).

In the southern neighbourhood, there have been some minor attempts by the EU to promote intra-Arab cooperation. The EMP already viewed South–South integration as one of its priorities, as highlighted for instance by the system of pan-Euro-Mediterranean cumulation of origin.[3] Even the UfM, which – at least on paper – aimed at relaunching the region-building project of the EMP, favoured the establishment of sub-regional initiatives. Despite limited progress, the EU has supported, and still supports, regional initiatives beyond the EU. It supports the Agadir Agreement, signed in 2004 among Egypt, Jordan, Morocco and Tunisia, which is supposed to be the basis for a free trade area among these countries. Moreover, after the Arab uprisings, the EU has reiterated its support for regional integration in the Maghreb. In the 2012 Communication on the Maghreb, the Commission and the European External Action Service (EEAS) expressed their full support to the Arab Maghreb Union (AMU) – created in 1989, among Algeria, Libya, Mauritania, Morocco and Tunisia, to foster regional integration according to the European model (Legrenzi and Calculli 2013; European Commission and European External Action Service 2012). Dating back to 1990, the 5+5 Dialogue is a political initiative among geographically close states of the two shores of the Mediterranean Sea – including France, Italy, Malta, Spain and Portugal on the one hand, and Algeria, Libya, Mauritania, Morocco and Tunisia on the other – establishing a forum for discussion. Despite these efforts, cooperation on the southern shore of the Mediterranean remains limited due to competition between countries, political hostilities and the EU's bilateral policy (Jolly 2014).

Generally, although there are differences in the motivation and the circumstances in which the EU has engaged regionally with the two neighbourhoods, the methods of engagement and the results to date show remarkable similarities. Above all, the hierarchical way of constructing regional partnerships observed in both the East and the South confirms the importance of power asymmetries between the EU and the neighbours, and casts doubt on the joint ownership rhetoric the EU has developed around these regional schemes, making it difficult to imagine how genuine dialogue could occur. The revision of the ENP of November 2015 mentioned regional cooperation and thematic frameworks to address issues of regional interest, such as migration, energy and security, by the inclusion of the neighbours of the EU's neighbouring countries. But the emphasis remains on bilateral cooperation and further differentiation, perpetuating tensions with region-building aspirations.

Conclusions: interaction in the shadow of power asymmetries

Bilateralism, multilateralism and region-building characterise, to different extents, the EU's engagement in its neighbourhood. These political processes occur in a context characterised by profound power asymmetries. First, the relations between the EU and its neighbours, whether in multilateral or bilateral forms, are strongly asymmetrical. The EU is generally in a stronger position, even when there is an attempt to develop 'true' partnerships, like the EMP (Adler et al. 2006) or the EaP (Korosteleva 2011). Second, the EU tends to project its model, rules and norms onto its neighbours – whether this is done to spread its values (Manners 2002), to pursue its interests (Hyde-Price 2006; Seeberg 2009) or to promote its model of regional integration (Börzel and Risse 2009; Telò 2014). However, neighbours are not devoid of agency. Time and again – and most visibly during the 2015–2016 migration crisis – they have set the agenda along different lines than those embraced by the EU.

Bringing the notion of power back in the discussion is helpful, to conceptualise and explore the structural asymmetry and patterns of domination that exist between the EU and its neighbours. While the idea of a Normative Power Europe (NPE) (Manners 2002) has long dominated the debate, realist understandings have looked at how the EU attempts to shape the regional context so that the milieu is favourable to the economic, political and security interests of European states (Hyde-Price 2006). Others have mainly criticised the EU for its rhetoric of partnership and equality, which has not been matched by its practice – norms are either used strategically (Youngs 2004) or as a disguise for the pursuit of material and security-related goals (Seeberg 2009). The degree of reflexivity the EU has applied to its relations with its neighbours has been low (Bicchi 2006) and the consultation process leading to the revised ENP in 2015 has not changed power asymmetries.

It should not come as a surprise that part of the literature is engaging with the concepts of hegemony and empire to characterise EU relations, including with its neighbourhood. Building on the Gramscian view of hegemony, scholars such as Haukkala (2008), Holden (2011) and Diez (2013) have shown that the EU imposes its model based on a neo-liberal and secular understanding of state-society and economic relations to countries in the neighbouring regions. This is not done by coercion, but through a subtle process of persuasion, societal transformations and regulatory instruments. Similarly, the idea of the EU as a neo-medieval empire (Zielonka 2008) or a Normative Empire Europe (Del Sarto 2016) recalls similar ideas of domination *via* the promotion of EU rules through bilateral or regional relations. By imposing its rules and norms, the EU has aimed to construct a hub-and-spoke model, in which the interests of the centre are ensured through the political and economic control of the periphery. Instead of resorting to coercion and military power, this new type of empire rests on the use of bureaucratic and economic instruments. The final goal remains the prosperity and security of the centre, which is guaranteed by the stability of the peripheries. But neighbouring peripheries have been often difficult – and at times utterly impossible – to coax towards the European order, be it *via* bilateralism or region-building. The extent to which the revised ENP will be better able to provide an answer to these long-standing questions remains to be seen.

Notes

1. The EMP was not the first regional initiative that the EU developed in the Mediterranean. In the 1970s, the then European Economic Community launched the Global Mediterranean Policy, then relaunched it in 1990–1991 as the Renewed Mediterranean Policy (Bicchi 2007).
2. The UfM includes EU Member States, Turkey, the Western Balkans and all Mediterranean ENP countries plus Mauritania.
3. Later reformed into the Regional Convention on pan-Euro-Mediterranean preferential rules of origin.

References

Adler, E., Bicchi, F., Crawford, B. and Del Sarto, A. (eds.) (2006) *The Convergence of Civilizations: Constructing a Mediterranean Region*, Toronto: University of Toronto Press.

Averre, D. (2009) 'Competing Rationalities: Russia, the EU and the "Shared Neighbourhood"', *Europe-Asia Studies* 61(10): 1689–1713.

Barbé, E. and Herranz-Surrallés, A. (2010) 'Dynamics of Convergence and Differentiation in Euro-Mediterranean Relations: Towards Flexible Region-Building or Fragmentation?', *Mediterranean Politics* 15(2): 129–147.

Bechev, D. and Nicolaïdis, K. (2010) 'From Policy to Polity: Can the EU's Special Relations with Its "Neighbourhood" be Decentred?', *Journal of Common Market Studies* 48(3): 475–500.

Bicchi, F. (2006) '"Our Size Fits All": Normative Power Europe and the Mediterranean', *Journal of European Public Policy* 13(2): 286–303.

Bicchi, F. (2007) *European Foreign Policy Making Toward the Mediterranean*, Basingstoke/New York: Palgrave Macmillan.

Bicchi, F. (2011) 'The Union for the Mediterranean, or the Changing Context of Euro-Mediterranean Relations', *Mediterranean Politics* 16(1): 3–19.

Bicchi, F. (2014) '"Lost in Transition": EU Foreign Policy and the European Neighbourhood Policy Post-Arab Spring', *L'Europe en Formation* 371(1): 26–40.

Börzel, T. and Pamuk, Y. (2012) 'Pathologies of Europeanisation: Fighting Corruption in the Southern Caucasus', *West European Politics* 35(1): 79–97.

Börzel, T. and Risse, T. (eds.) (2009) 'Diffusing (Inter) Regionalism—The EU as a Model of Regional Integration', *KFG Working Paper Series* 7, Berlin.

Börzel, T. and Risse, T. (2016) 'Introduction', in Börzel T. and Risse, T. (eds.) *The Oxford Handbook of Comparative Regionalism*, Oxford: Oxford University Press, 3–15.

Cardwell, P. (2011) 'EuroMed, European Neighbourhood Policy and the Union for the Mediterranean: Overlapping Policy Frames in the EU's Governance of the Mediterranean', *Journal of Common Market Studies* 49(2): 219–241.

Casier, T. (2013) 'The EU–Russia Strategic Partnership: Challenging the Normative Argument', *Europe-Asia Studies* 65(7): 1377–1395.

Cottey, A. (2012) 'Regionalism and the EU's Neighbourhood Policy: The Limits of the Possible', *Southeast European and Black Sea Studies* 12(3): 375–391.

Dandashly, A. (2015) 'The EU Response to Regime Change in the Wake of the Arab Revolt: Differential Implementation', *Journal of European Integration* 37(1): 37–56.

Delcour, L. (2011a) *Shaping the Post-Soviet Space? EU Policies and Approaches to Region-Building*, Farnham/Burlington: Ashgate Publishing.

Delcour, L. (2011b) 'The Institutional Functioning of the Eastern Partnership: An Early Assessment', *Eastern Partnership Review* 1, September, http://papers.ssrn.com/abstract=2276452, accessed on 15 October 2015.

Del Sarto, R. (2016) 'Normative Empire Europe: The European Union, Its Borderlands, and the "Arab Spring"', *Journal of Common Market Studies* 54(2): 215–232.

Del Sarto, R. and Schumacher, T. (2005) 'From EMP to ENP: What's at Stake with the European Neighbourhood Policy Towards the Southern Mediterranean?', *European Foreign Affairs Review* 10: 17–38.

Diez, T. (2013) 'Normative Power as Hegemony', *Cooperation and Conflict* 48(2): 194–210.

Dragneva, R. and Wolczuk, K. (eds.) (2013) *Eurasian Economic Integration: Law, Policy and Politics*, Cheltenham, UK: Edward Elgar Pub.

Dworkin, A. and Wesslau, F. (2015) 'Ten Talking Points from the New ENP', *ECFR Commentary*, 20 November.

European Commission (2013) 'European Neighbourhood Policy (ENP)—Fact Sheet', Memo 13/236, Brussels.

European Commission (2015a) *Black Sea Synergy: Review of a Regional Cooperation Initiative*, SWD (2015) 6 Final, Brussels.

European Commission (2015b) *Review of the European Neighbourhood Policy*, JOIN (2015) 50 Final, Brussels, 18 November.

European Commission and European External Action Service (2012) *Supporting Closer Cooperation and Regional Integration in the Maghreb: Algeria, Libya, Mauritania, Morocco and Tunisia*, JOIN (2012) 36 Final, Brussels.

European Council (2003) *A Secure Europe in a Better World: European Security Strategy*, Brussels, 12 December.

Haukkala, H. (2008) 'The European Union as a Regional Normative Hegemon: The Case of European Neighbourhood Policy', *Europe-Asia Studies* 60(9): 1601–1622.

Heydon, K. and Woolcock, S. (2009) *The Rise of Bilateralism: Comparing American, European, and Asian Approaches to Preferential Trade Agreements*, Tokyo/New York: United Nations University Press.

Holden, P. (2009) *In Search of Structural Power: EU Aid Policy as a Global Political Instrument*, Farnham/Burlington: Ashgate Publishing Ltd.

Holden, P. (2011) 'A New Beginning? Does the Union for the Mediterranean Herald a New Functionalist Approach to Co-Operation in the Region?', *Mediterranean Politics* 16(1): 155–169.

Hyde-Price, A. (2006) '"Normative" Power Europe: A Realist Critique', *Journal of European Public Policy* 13(2): 217–234.

Jolly, C. (2014) *Regional Integration in the Mediterranean—Impact and Limits of Community and Bilateral Policies*, Brussels: European Union.

Kelley, J. (2006) 'New Wine in Old Wineskins: Promoting Political Reforms Through the New European Neighbourhood Policy', *Journal of Common Market Studies* 44(1): 29–55.

Keukeleire, S. and Petrova, I. (2014) 'The European Union, the Eastern Neighbourhood and Russia: Competing Regionalisms', in Telò, M. (ed.) *European Union and New Regionalism: Competing Regionalism and Global Governance in a Post-Hegemonic Era*, Farnham/Burlington: Ashgate Publishing, 263–277.

Korosteleva, E. (2011) 'Change or Continuity: Is the Eastern Partnership an Adequate Tool for the European Neighbourhood?', *International Relations* 25(2): 243–262.

Laatikainen, K. and Smith, K. (eds.) (2006) *The European Union at the United Nations. Intersecting Multilateralisms*, Basingstoke/New York: Palgrave MacMillan.

Langbein, J. and Wolczuk, K. (2012) 'Convergence Without Membership? The Impact of the European Union in the Neighbourhood: Evidence from Ukraine', *Journal of European Public Policy* 19(6): 863–881.

Lavenex, S. (2011) 'Concentric Circles of Flexible "European" Integration: A Typology of EU External Governance Relations', *Comparative European Politics* 9(4): 372–393.

Lavenex, S. and Schimmelfennig, F. (2009) 'EU Rules Beyond EU Borders: Theorizing External Governance in European Politics', *Journal of European Public Policy* 16(6): 791–812.

Legrenzi, M. and Calculli, M. (2013) *Regionalism and Regionalization in the Middle East: Options and Challenges*, Washington, DC: International Peace Institute.

Manners, I. (2002) 'Normative Power Europe: A Contradiction in Terms?', *Journal of Common Market Studies* 40(2): 235–258.

Noutcheva, G. (2015) 'Institutional Governance of European Neighbourhood Policy in the Wake of the Arab Spring', *Journal of European Integration* 37(1): 19–36.

Noutcheva, G., Pomorska, K. and Bosse, G. (eds.) (2013) *The EU and Its Neighbours: Values Versus Security in European Foreign Policy*, Manchester: Manchester University Press.

Pace, M. (2006) *The Politics of Regional Identity: Meddling with the Mediterranean*, London: Routledge.

Pace, M. (2010) 'Paradoxes and Contradictions in EU Democracy Promotion in the Mediterranean: The Limits of EU Normative Power', in Pace, M. and Seeberg, P. (eds.) *The European Union's Democratization Agenda in the Mediterranean*, Abingdon/New York: Routledge, 39–58.

Philippart, E. (2003) 'The Euro-Mediterranean Partnership: A Critical Evaluation of an Ambitious Scheme', *European Foreign Affairs Review* 8(2): 201–220.

Renard, T. (2015) 'Partnerships for Effective Multilateralism? Assessing the Compatibility Between EU Bilateralism, (Inter-)Regionalism and Multilateralism', *Cambridge Review of International Affairs* 29(1): 18–35.

Sasse, G. (2008) 'The European Neighbourhood Policy: Conditionality Revisited for the EU's Eastern Neighbours', *Europe-Asia Studies* 60(2): 295–316.

Seeberg, P. (2009) 'The EU as a Realist Actor in Normative Clothes: EU Democracy Promotion in Lebanon and the European Neighbourhood Policy', *Democratization* 16(1): 81–99.

Tassinari, F. (2006) 'A Synergy for Black Sea Regional Cooperation: Guidelines for an EU Initiative', *CEPS Policy Brief* 105, CEPS, Brussels.

Telò, M. (ed.) (2014) *European Union and New Regionalism: Competing Regionalism and Global Governance in a Post-Hegemonic Era*, Farham: Ashgate Publishing, Ltd.

Triantaphyllou, D. (2009) 'The "Security Paradoxes" of the Black Sea Region', *Southeast European and Black Sea Studies* 9(3): 225–241.

Tsantoulis, Y. (2009) 'Geopolitics, (Sub)Regionalism, Discourse and a Troubled "Power Triangle" in the Black Sea', *Southeast European and Black Sea Studies* 9(3): 243–258.

Tsardanidis, C. (2011) 'The EU and Its Neighbours: A Wider Europe Through Asymmetrical Interregionalism or Through Dependencia Subregionalism', in Warleigh-Lack, A., Robinson, N. and Rosamond, B. (eds.) *New Regionalism and the European Union. Dialogues, Comparisons and New Research Directions*, London/New York: Routledge, 236–254.

Van der Loo, G. (2015) 'Enhancing the Prospects of the EU's Deep and Comprehensive Free Trade Areas in the Mediterranean: Lessons from the Eastern Partnership', *CEPS Commentary*, CEPS, Brussels.

Weber, K., Smith, M. and Baun, M. (eds.) (2007) *Governing Europe's Neighbourhood. Partners or Periphery?*, Manchester: Manchester University Press.

Whitman, R. and Wolff, S. (eds.) (2010) *The European Neighbourhood Policy in Perspective. Context, Implementation and Impact*, Basingstoke: Palgrave MacMillan.

Youngs, R. (2004) 'Normative Dynamics and Strategic Interests in the EU's External Identity', *Journal of Common Market Studies* 42(2): 415–435.

Zielonka, J. (2008) 'Europe as a Global Actor: Empire by Example?', *International Affairs* 84(3): 471–484.

23
THE EU AND CIVILIAN MISSIONS IN THE NEIGHBOURHOOD

Dimitris Bouris and Madalina Dobrescu

Introduction

One of the main objectives of the European Security Strategy (ESS) of 2003 was to work towards a secure neighbourhood, because 'neighbours who are engaged in violent conflict, weak states where organised crime flourishes, dysfunctional societies or exploding population growth on its borders all pose problems for Europe' (European Council 2003). The development of the European Neighbourhood Policy (ENP) added momentum to the EU's role in conflict management and resolution by promoting stability and prosperity through the EU's export of governance models and norms (Lavenex and Schimmelfennig 2010). Inherent in the ENP, is the EU's support for 'democratic institution-building as a conflict prevention/resolution instrument' (Youngs 2004: 531). Although conflict management and resolution gradually gained prominence within the ENP framework and the policy's revisions (2011 and 2015), the ENP was not designed to address these domains. The revision of the policy in 2011, allocated a more ambitious conflict resolution role to the EU, by making explicit the assumption that many of the instruments used to promote economic integration and sectoral cooperation in the neighbourhood could also be mobilised to support confidence-building and conflict resolution objectives between conflicting parties (Schumacher and Bouris 2017: 19). The most recent revision of the ENP, in November 2015, made clear reference to the need for coordination between the ENP (which has largely focused on instruments related to the Commission's competencies) and the Common Foreign and Security Policy/Common Security and Defence Policy (CFSP/CSDP).

The aim of this chapter is to focus on the civilian missions that the EU has deployed in its neighbourhood as instruments of conflict resolution. The civilian missions operating in the EU's southern and eastern neighbourhoods reflect the Union's efforts at addressing complex and pervasive security challenges stemming from long-simmering conflicts, significant levels of organised crime, trafficking and illegal migration. Through its CSDP operations, the EU has tried to address these issues by contributing directly to confidence-building between conflict parties, as well as by exporting EU and international regulatory frameworks and institutional templates meant to reform domestic institutions. The remainder of the chapter provides a cross-regional account of the EU's engagement in conflict resolution, through civilian missions deployed at its southern and eastern neighbourhoods.

The EU and civilian missions in the southern neighbourhood

The first EU civilian missions, deployed in its southern neighbourhood, were in Palestine and they were directly linked to the Israeli–Palestinian conflict. Following the military intervention in Libya, and the subsequent migration crisis in the Mediterranean, the EU deployed a civilian and two military missions in Libya (one of them only on paper). While the first missions in Palestine generated mixed results, the EU's inability to act decisively in Libya has exposed the lack of an integrated civil-military approach on behalf of the EU.

EU Border Assistance Mission for the Rafah Crossing Point (EUBAM Rafah)

The European Union Border Assistance Mission Rafah (EUBAM Rafah) was deployed after Israel's unilateral decision to withdraw from the Gaza Strip. In November 2005, Israel and the Palestinian Authority (PA) signed an 'Agreement on Movement and Access' (AMA) which called for a third-party presence at the border crossing point of Rafah, between the Gaza Strip and Egypt (Agreement on Movement and Access 2015). Although Israel was initially reluctant to accept an active EU role, after the United States' unwillingness to do so, it agreed to the establishment of EUBAM Rafah. The mission had significance regarding EU–Israel relations, as it was the first time that Israel accepted an EU mission on the ground.

EUBAM Rafah started operating at the end of November 2005, and it sought to 'reconcile Israel's security concerns with both the Palestinian demands for an autonomous border management and the requirements of Gaza's economic recovery – which presupposes open borders' (Del Sarto 2007: 70). The mission was of great importance, as it dealt specifically with border control, which is one of the 'final status issues' in the Israeli–Palestinian conflict, and it was hoped that its example could be used at other border crossings as well. Its main aims were to: a) assist the PA to build capacity-training on border management and customs; b) evaluate and assess the PA's application of these procedures; c) contribute to confidence-building between the parties; d) contribute to building institutional capacity in the PA; e) ensure effective border control; and f) contribute to the liaison between the Palestinian, Israeli and Egyptian authorities in all aspects of border management at Rafah (Council of the European Union 2005a).

The mission initially had a one-year mandate, which has been extended to date (Council of the European Union 2015a). EUBAM Rafah had some success until Hamas' takeover of Gaza in June 2007, and it was considered the 'Rolls-Royce of EU CSDP Missions', as it was deployed rapidly and managed to make a quick difference on the ground (EUPOL COPPS official, interview 22 April 2013). The mission has not been operational since 2007, but the EU decided to keep it 'alive' and not close it down formally. The initial argument behind this decision has been that the EU considers the situation in Gaza temporary and, despite ten years having passed since then, this rationale has not changed. There has also been the fear that if the mission was terminated, then Israel would not allow it to be redeployed, should there be a change in its policy towards Gaza. This was confirmed by former Israeli Minister of Foreign Affairs, Avigdor Lieberman, who argued that 'we cannot allow a return to the ineffective EUBAM mission' (Lieberman 2011). EUBAM Rafah is coming to the fore every time a major incident takes place in Gaza, such as the 2008–2009 war on Gaza, the 2010 flotilla incident, and the 2012 and 2014 wars (Bouris 2015a: 34; 2015b), but until now, the EU has failed to persuade Israel to open the Gaza crossing points, which would enable the mission to be reactivated. Although the mission could potentially run some projects and training, the fact that it does not have an executive mandate and that its mandate is restricted to its presence at Rafah crossing point have limited its room for manoeuvre. To 'resurrect' EUBAM Rafah, the EU recently proposed the expansion

Table 23.1 EU CSDP missions in the neighbourhood 2003–2016

Name	Mandate	Date mission was agreed and current status	Staff (as of 2016)	Budget in (EUR million)	Country
EUBAM Rafah	Provide a third-party presence at the Rafah Crossing Point in order to contribute to its opening and to build up confidence between the Government of Israel and the Palestinian Authority	14 December 2005 (ongoing)	4 international staff 7 local staff	€1.54 (until 30 June 2017)	Palestine
EUPOL COPPS	Contribute to the establishment of sustainable and effective policing arrangements as well as other international efforts in the wider context of Security Sector including Criminal Justice Reform	14 November 2005 (ongoing)	114 (69 international staff 45 national staff)	€10.32 (July 2016–June 2017)	Palestine
EUBAM Libya	Support the Libyan authorities to develop capacity for enhancing the security of Libya's land, sea and air borders in the short term and to develop a broader IBM strategy in the longer term	22 May 2013 (ongoing)	17	€17 (22 August 2016–21 August 2017)	Libya (but located in Tunis)
EUJUST Themis	Assistance to the Georgian government in reforming the criminal justice sector: guidance for the new criminal justice reform strategy, support for judicial reform and anti-corruption, support for the planning of new legislation, support for international and regional cooperation in the area of criminal justice	28 June 2004 (completed)	12 international staff 16 national staff	€2.05	Georgia
EUBAM Moldova–Ukraine	Develop appropriate operational and institutional capacity in Moldova and Ukraine, contribute to the resolution of the Transnistrian conflict and improve transnational cooperation on border management	7 November 2005 (ongoing)	80 international staff 116 national staff from Moldova and Ukraine	€14.81 (December 2015–November 2017)	Moldova Ukraine
EUMM Georgia	Contribute to stabilisation, normalisation, confidence-building and informing European policy through civilian monitoring of the parties' actions, including full compliance with the six-point Agreement	15 September 2008 (ongoing)	200 EU monitors	€18.30	Georgia
EUAM Ukraine	Mentor and advise relevant Ukrainian bodies in the elaboration of renewed security strategies and in the consequent implementation of relevant comprehensive and cohesive reform efforts	22 July 2014 (ongoing)	>200 Ukrainian and international staff	€17.67 (1 December 2015–30 November 2016)	Ukraine

of its mandate to include a maritime link which 'could open Gaza to Europe and allow the people of Gaza to unlock their socio-economic potential' (European External Action Service 2014). Since this request has not come from any signatory parties of the AMA, the EU has downsized the mission to three people, based at the EU Delegation in Tel Aviv and has also reduced its budget (see Table 23.1).

The European Union Coordinating Office for Palestinian Police Support (EUPOL COPPS)

EUPOL COPPS was the second mission the EU deployed in Palestine, and was closely linked to another 'final status' issue of the Israeli–Palestinian conflict – that is, security – and to the objectives of the 'Roadmap', which requested that the PA reform its security apparatus and improve its ability to take responsibility for law and order (Bulut 2009: 289). EUPOL COPPS was established in 2006, building on a previous bilateral British initiative, initiated in mid-January 2005 by the Department for International Development (DfID).

While the mission had a three-year mandate, this has been extended ever since. EUPOL COPPS has two main operational pillars – a Police Advisory and a Rule of Law section since 2008 – and it also consists of five sections: police advisory; programme coordination; rule of law; administration; and gender. The mission was deployed in January 2006, and its main tasks are: a) to mentor and advise the Palestinian Civil Police (PCP); b) to coordinate and facilitate EU Member State financial assistance to the PCP; and c) to give advice on politically related criminal justice elements (Council of the European Union 2005b). EUPOL COPPS faced several operational challenges, as its deployment coincided with Hamas' electoral victory in the Palestinian elections on 25 January 2006, and the subsequent non-engagement policy of the international community and the EU with the Hamas-led government (Bouris 2014: 54–56). 'From our first days here we were hostages of the political situation without being able to do our job', argues an official from the mission (EUPOL COPPS official, interview 20 May 2010). The mission resumed its operations after the government of Salam Fayyad was established in 2007, but has limited its operations to the West Bank. Since, similarly to EUBAM Rafah, EUPOL COPPS does not have an executive mandate either, the mission can only be present where the PCP can operate, which is mainly in Area A of the West Bank.[1]

Initially, the mission focused on providing training to the PCP and tackling basic equipment, infrastructure and assessment needs. EUPOL COPPS was instrumental in the building of the Jericho Police Training School which has permitted the PA to have the necessary infrastructure to train its own civil police force. Gradually, the mission started focusing more actively on the strategic level of reforms, and more specifically on the criminal justice sector, by targeting the most important actors in the 'criminal chain' – including prosecution services, courts, the High Judicial Council, penitentiary, the Ministry of Justice (MoJ), the Palestinian bar association, civil society and the scientific legal community.

> We realised that we needed a holistic approach that would help us bridge and merge security and justice because there was a fear that the justice system would be left behind and would not be able to catch up with the security system

argues a Department for International Development (DfID) official (interview 16 April 2013). But the engagement of the mission in the strategic planning by Ministries, and in the preparation of draft laws regarding the civil police and justice system, might potentially have some unintended consequences. This is because there is no parliamentary oversight, since there has been a paralysis after the 2006 elections, and all the laws are being passed by presidential decrees. As a result, while the mission is trying to promote rule of law and good governance, ironically it operates in an environment where there is a clear democratic deficit.

EUPOL COPPS has been 'handicapped' because of the realities of the Israeli occupation on the ground. First, since the mission does not have an executive mandate, it can be present only in Area A of the West Bank where the Palestinian civil police are also allowed to operate. This limits the space, but also the projects that the mission could potentially run and, consequently, also its operational effectiveness. The fact that the mission operates in an environment where everything it does has to be approved by Israel first also poses specific limitations. Henrik Malmquist, a former head of the mission, argued that 'any equipment we bring in has to be approved by the Coordinator of Government Activities in the Territories' (Hass 2011).

European Union Integrated Border Management Assistance Mission in Libya (EUBAM Libya)

On 1 April 2011, the Council of the European Union adopted a decision for the deployment of a military operation in Libya which would contribute to the safe movement and evacuation of displaced persons and support (with specific capabilities) the humanitarian agencies in their activities. EUFOR Libya's activation was made conditional on the receipt of a request from the UN Office for the Coordination of Humanitarian Affairs (OCHA). The decision envisaged an Italian commander with operational headquarters in Rome, a budget of EUR7.9 million and an initial duration of four months (Council of the European Union 2011). The planning had included four different scenarios for action in case of its deployment: 1) escorting humanitarian convoys; 2) evacuating humanitarian aid workers; 3) securing the port of Misrata; and 4) ensuring the security of humanitarian aid provisions in the long-term perspectives (Koenig 2011: 16). Since OCHA never requested its deployment, EUFOR Libya remained a 'ghost CSDP operation' (Hatzigeorgopoulos and Fara-Andrianarijaona 2013: 3), which formally terminated its non-operation in November 2011. The failure regarding the deployment of the mission made Members of the European Parliament characterise it as an 'April fool's mission' (2011), and some other diplomats to argue that 'The CFSP died in Libya – we just have to pick a sand dune under which we can bury it' (Atlantic Council 2011). The failure exposed once more the lack of an integrated civil-military approach on behalf of the EU. At the same time, it represented the first foreign and security policy test for the Lisbon Treaty, as it was 'the most serious international crisis the EU had to deal with after the approval of the Treaty' (Fabbrini 2014: 177). The non-deployment also exposed deeper EU divisions, the EU's inability to speak with 'one voice', and the prioritisation of individual Member States' policies. An EU official, for example, admits that

> Germany was behind the OCHA stipulation and they wanted it, because they knew that such request would not come and as such the mission would never be deployed. It was part of their policy towards Libya and their unwillingness to support any kind of military intervention.
>
> *(EEAS official, interview 23 August 2016)*

Following this, the EU decided to deploy a civilian mission in Libya in May 2013. EUBAM Libya aimed to support the Libyan authorities in improving and developing the security of the country's borders. The mission had an annual budget of EUR30 million and its initial mandate was for two years (until May 2015). Contrary to EUBAM Rafah, EUBAM Libya is supposed to be actively involved in land, sea and air borders, offering a more 'inclusive' approach. The mission did not have an executive mandate and its tasks were to: a) support Libyan authorities, through training and mentoring, in strengthening the border services; b) advise the Libyan authorities on the development of a Libyan national Integrated Border Management (IBM) strategy; and c) support the Libyan authorities in strengthening their institutional operational capabilities.

Due to the continuation of violence between rival militias on the ground, the mission initially relocated to Tunis in July 2014, and since then it was downsized to a minimum of three international and three local staff on hold capacity (Council of the European Union 2015b). The 'on hold' mandate of the mission has been extended to August 2017, as the EU has considered that closing the mission would 'send a negative political signal to Libya, the region, and international community partners' (ibid.). Drawing parallels with EUBAM Rafah, which has been in the same 'on hold' since 2007 – based on the same arguments of 'sending a wrong signal' – it seems that EUBAM Libya is on the same path.

The EU and civilian missions in the eastern neighbourhood

The EU's use of CSDP instruments in its eastern neighbourhood should be understood in the context of the ENP and the Eastern Partnership (EaP), but also against the background of momentous political developments in the region. The European Union Border Assistance Mission (EUBAM) to Moldova and Ukraine, and EUJUST Themis in Georgia, were launched in 2005 and 2004, in the aftermath of the 'colour revolutions' in Eastern Europe, which brought to power pro-European, reform-minded governments. The European Union Monitoring Mission (EUMM) to Georgia was the result of an equally ground-breaking, though far from positive, event in the region: the August 2008 war between Russia and Georgia. Finally, the European Union Advisory Mission (EUAM) to Ukraine is one of the actions undertaken by the EU in response to the crisis in Ukraine.

EUJUST Themis in Georgia

EUJUST Themis represented a novelty in the EU's ESDP repertoire from several points of view: it was the first rule of law mission deployed by the EU under the ESDP, and the first ever ESDP operation in the post-Soviet space (Kurowska 2009: 202). While not contributing directly to conflict resolution, the mission was meant to show the Union's support for Georgia's efforts towards democratisation in the aftermath of the Rose Revolution, as well as contribute to embedding stability in the region (Council of the European Union 2004). As the first operation in the former Soviet Union, Themis was also thought to be a good test for the EU's relations with Russia (Helly 2006: 91).

According to the mission's mandate, a total of eight European rule of law experts were co-located with Georgian authorities and were given one year to assist their local counterparts in evaluating the justice system, drafting a criminal justice reform strategy and elaborating an implementation plan. The European experts were co-located in a variety of rule of law institutions, including the Ministry of Justice, the Ministry of Interior, the General Prosecutor's Office, the Supreme Court of Georgia, the High Council of Justice, the Public Defender's Office, the Court of Appeal Tbilisi and the City Prosecutor's Office Tbilisi (EUJUST Themis 2004). The mission's operative plan envisioned three consecutive phases which focused on specific objectives: 1. the assessment of the Georgian criminal justice system; 2. the drafting of a reform strategy; 3. the formulation of a plan for the implementation of the reform strategy (Kurowska 2009: 206).

The drafting of the criminal justice strategy – Themis' main objective – was plagued by delays in setting up the working groups and their constantly changing membership (EUJUST Themis experts, interviews February–October 2013). The routine replacement of the mission's counterparts resulted in infrequent meetings of the working groups and a general lack of commitment on the Georgian side to engage in the drafting process. This led to large parts of the final document being drafted by the mission experts, with no involvement from Georgian stakeholders (EUJUST Themis expert, interview 10 July 2013). The strategy was eventually adopted by presidential decree, without being formally discussed and adopted by the Georgian Parliament (Helly 2006: 100). The volatile political environment, which characterised the early stages of Saakashvili's post-Rose Revolution rule, posed significant challenges to the mission's effective operation. Under the banner of anti-corruption measures, Saakashvili's regime engaged in a thorough purge of the public administration – targeting ministry personnel, judges and prosecutors associated with the Shevardnadze regime (Merlingen and Ostrauskaite 2009: 22) – and effectively blocking any meaningful reforms which could have strengthened the independence of the judiciary in Georgia. As for the mission's role in embedding regional stability, it is questionable whether such a small-scale and short-lived operation made a difference on the ground.

EU Border Assistance Mission to Moldova–Ukraine (EUBAM)

As the second EU mission deployed in the post-Soviet space, EUBAM is to be regarded as expanding the diversity of the EU's civilian crisis management toolbox. At the time of its deployment in November 2005, the mission not only had an innovative mandate merging border assistance and capacity-building, but represented a unique case of a hybrid mission, which was neither a distinct CSDP operation nor an exclusively Commission-managed project (Dura 2009: 282). EUBAM was deployed due to a joint request by the Presidents of Moldova and Ukraine for assistance with the establishment of an 'international customs control arrangement and an effective border monitoring mechanism on the Transnistrian segment of the Moldovan-Ukrainian State border' (EUBAM 2011: 5). Its contribution to the settlement of the Transnistrian conflict was envisaged as the indirect result of enhanced border control, which was expected to curb illegal cross-border activities and lead to a subsequent improvement in the regional security situation.

Being a purely advisory mission that lacks executive powers, EUBAM is not involved in the political negotiation process under the 5+2 format,[2] but its confidence-building work is coordinated with the overall political effort to settle the conflict. Assisting with the implementation of the Joint Declaration (JD), which introduced a new customs regime at the Moldovan–Ukrainian border in 2006,[3] and contributing to the resumption of railway traffic across Transnistria represent two of EUBAM's most prominent efforts towards conflict resolution. The observance of the JD not only provides a legal framework for Transnistrian businesses to operate under, thus curbing smuggling, but also contributes to a degree to economic integration between Moldova and Transnistria, as well as to improved cooperation between Moldova and Ukraine. At the same time, EUBAM was able to contribute – through its technical proposals and the facilitation of contacts between Moldovan and Transnistrian customs and railway experts – to the breakthrough normalisation of railway transport after a six-year interruption.[4]

While EUBAM played a crucial role in helping to improve border control, reduce illegal trade and facilitate contacts between Moldova and Transnistria, its effectiveness as a conflict resolution instrument remains doubtful. The two conflict parties – although engaged in limited technical and economic cooperation – are not even remotely close to a political agreement and there is very little political will on both sides to reach a negotiated settlement.

EU Monitoring Mission to Georgia (EUMM)

EUMM operates in a highly challenging political environment, having been deployed within less than eight weeks after the outbreak of the August 2008 war, to monitor the implementation of the ceasefire between Georgia and Russia. The mission was given a broad technical mandate 'to contribute to stabilisation, normalisation and confidence-building, while also contributing to informing European policy' (Council of the European Union 2008). Although EUMM is mandated to cover the whole territory of Georgia, within the country's internationally recognised borders, Russia, and the *de facto* authorities in Abkhazia and South Ossetia have so far denied access of the mission to the breakaway territories (International Crisis Group 2011: 5). Therefore, EUMM's patrols are mainly restricted to the areas adjacent to the Administrative Boundary Lines (ABLs), which separate the unrecognised entities from unoccupied Georgian territory.

The mission has deployed a variety of confidence-building measures, ranging from monitoring the compliance of the conflict parties with the ceasefire agreement to encouraging parties to exchange information and give notification of military manoeuvres, as well as establishing information and observation routines between them in the form of regular communication platforms.

As the only on-the-ground mechanism that brings together conflict parties, and facilitates information exchange on local incidents, detentions and human rights violations, the Incident and Prevention Response Mechanism (IPRM) has significant potential as a confidence-building tool. Nonetheless, in practice, the functioning of the IPRM has been hampered by the volatility and obstructiveness of the separatist regimes and Russia. The IPRM for the South Ossetian theatre was suspended for over a year because the *de facto* authorities in Tskhinvali conditioned participation on receiving information on missing or detained South Ossetian residents (Human Rights Watch 2011: 13), while IPRM Gali was boycotted for more than four years over a conflict between Abkhazian authorities and the Head of the Mission, dating back to April 2012.

Although the Geneva negotiations[5] – where EUMM contributes with monitoring reports and analyses – have been unable to move forwards – primarily because of the difficult 'recognition' discussions surrounding the status of South Ossetia and Abkhazia – an important accomplishment with regard to the non-use of force, which can be credited to EUMM, is the signing of two Memoranda of Understanding with the Georgian Ministries of Defence and Interior, which limit Tbilisi's military movements (EUMM 2009). Despite its inability to fully oversee the implementation of the ceasefire agreement – given Moscow's refusal to withdraw from the two breakaway regions – the EUMM has been a critical actor in stabilising the situation in the region, using its monitoring and reporting resources to expose destabilising acts, which in turn acted as a deterrent to the renewal of hostilities. However, the mission's ability to maintain relative calm and stability around the ABLs does not easily translate into a long-term role facilitating confidence-building between conflict parties, and might indicate that the EUMM will find it difficult to transition from a crisis management actor to a conflict resolution instrument.

EU Advisory Mission (EUAM) to Ukraine

As the November 2013 crisis in Ukraine escalated from domestic discontent to an international conflict, triggered by Russia's occupation of Crimea in March 2014, the EU began contemplating the deployment of a CSDP mission to Ukraine. The operation was crucial in supporting the Ukrainian authorities 'on the critical path of civilian security sector reform' (Council of the European Union 2014a), an area of particular concern in light of the abusive crackdown of protests by Ukraine's civilian security services and the specific demands of the Maidan movement for anti-corruption reforms.

EUAM was deployed on 1 December 2014, with an initial two-year mandate to work with law enforcement agencies, such as the police and border guards, as well as rule of law institutions – including the Prosecutor's Office – across a number of good governance areas: anti-corruption, human rights, public administration reform and strategic communication.[6] While not conceived with an explicit conflict resolution mandate in mind, EUAM's presence on the ground aimed at sending a signal of political support to Kiev, as well as acting as a strategy to soft balance Russia (Nováky 2015: 246). By addressing pervasive issues of inefficiency, corruption and a lack of effective command and control of law enforcement agencies – all of which had led to inappropriate responses to the crisis and an inability of the state to use force in an exclusive and legitimate manner (Council of the European Union 2014b) – it was hoped EUAM would contribute to enhancing the resilience of the Ukrainian state, which would minimise the scope for Russian interference in Ukrainian affairs.

EUAM's record so far suggests that the mission has established itself as a well-regarded partner for the Ukrainian law enforcement authorities. EUAM has been consulted on the reform of Ukraine's security services (Rieker and Bátora 2015: 26): it developed, together with international partners, a concept for a new structure designed to assist with the reform of Ukraine's National Police (Emerson and Movchan 2016: 23); and set up a Border Management Assistance Group, as a forum to address border management issues by engaging all stakeholders (EUAM 2015). Significantly, the mission has extended its regional outreach beyond Kiev and now also operates in the Lviv region, where it has personnel based on a full-time basis, and is increasing its activities in the Kharkiv region. Nonetheless, the limitations imposed by EUAM's size and budget – also due to Ukraine's sheer size and on its potential for further geographical expansion – should not be underestimated. An additional challenge for the mission's overall success is, unsurprisingly, 'ministerial resistance' to comprehensive reforms – a common obstacle when it comes to anti-corruption measures, but which will have to be overcome if Ukraine is to 'de-sovietise' its civilian security sector (Chromiec and Koenig 2015: 13).

Conclusions

This brief overview of the CSDP missions deployed by the EU in its southern and eastern neighbourhoods reveals the difficulty of addressing complex security challenges with small-scale, non-executive civilian crisis management instruments. Given their strictly advisory and monitoring roles, the success of CSDP civilian operations hinges on the willingness of local actors to cooperate with EU actors among themselves, and on the EU's broader approach towards the country in question. While each of the missions discussed in this chapter can be commended for a range of achievements, none of them can be said to have successfully fulfilled a conflict resolution role.

The one challenge that keeps emerging across both the eastern and the southern dimensions of the EU's neighbourhood is that civilian missions invariably undertake technical approaches in order to achieve political goals. Although CSDP operations are part of the EU's foreign policy toolkit, and considered to be political instruments, their non-executive and technical mandates afford few opportunities to influence conflict resolution processes. But whereas the political impact of EU missions is minimal, their performance on the ground is inevitably affected by broader political and geopolitical dynamics, to the extent that sometimes they are not able to fully implement their mandates (EUMM Georgia, EUPOL COPPS), or are effectively prevented from operating (EUBAM Rafah, EUBAM Libya). An additional complication associated with the politically sensitive contexts within which missions operate – but which they themselves are unable to influence – is that often they become prisoners of rhetorical commitments, with the EU being reluctant to terminate CSDP missions for fear that this might convey a message of disengagement.

So far, the EU has been inconsistent in providing CSDP civilian missions with adequate political support in Brussels, as well as ensuring that the operations enjoy a high political profile on the ground and are well-received by host countries. This process could potentially be facilitated by a more effective implementation of the EU's comprehensive approach to conflict resolution, the importance of which was reaffirmed by the 2015 ENP Review. In practice, this implies drawing on all the instruments at the EU's disposal to address existing challenges and promote stability, creating synergies between the CSDP and the ENP, and greater involvement of and consensus between Member States.

Notes

1 Under the Oslo Accords, the West Bank was divided into three areas: A, B and C. It was only in Area A that the PA was given full responsibility for civilian and security affairs. In Area B, the PA is responsible for civilian affairs, while Israel is responsible for security control. In Area C, Israel retains full responsibility and control in all aspects.
2 The multilateral 5+2 format includes Moldova and Transnistria as parties to the conflict, Russia, Ukraine and the OSCE as intermediaries, and the United States and the European Union as observers. Negotiations were suspended in March 2006, but resumed in February 2011.
3 At the end of 2005, one month after the deployment of EUBAM, the Prime Ministers of Moldova and Ukraine signed a Joint Declaration on the effective implementation of the customs regime on their common border, in a renewed push to curb illegal trade activities from Transnistria.
4 The Transnistrian authorities suspended railway transport through the separatist region in 2006 in reaction to the enforcement of the new customs regime between Moldova and Ukraine, monitored by EUBAM.
5 The Geneva International Discussions address the consequences of the 2008 conflict in Georgia by bringing together the co-chairs – OSCE, EU and UN, representatives of the conflict parties – Georgia, Russia, and Georgia's breakaway regions, Abkhazia and South Ossetia, and the United States.
6 www.euam-ukraine.eu.

References

Agreement on Movement and Access (2015) www.unsco.org/Documents/Key/AMA.pdf, accessed 16 September 2016.
Atlantic Council (2011) 'Diplomats Mourn "Death" of EU Defence Policy Over Libya', 24 March, www.atlanticcouncil.org/blogs/natosource/diplomats-mourn-death-of-eu-defence-policy-over-libya.
Bouris, D. (2014) *The European Union and Occupied Palestinian Territories: State-Building Without a State*, Oxon: Routledge.
Bouris, D. (2015a) 'EU-Palestinian Security Cooperation after Oslo: Enforcing Borders, Interdependence and Existing Power Imbalance', in Del Sarto, R. (ed.) *Fragmented Borders, Interdependence and External Relations: The Israel-Palestine-European Union Triangle*, Basingstoke: Palgrave Macmillan, 27–47.
Bouris, D. (2015b) 'The Vicious Cycle of Building and Destroying: The 2014 War on Gaza', *Mediterranean Politics* 20(1): 111–117.
Bulut, E. (2009) 'The EU Police Mission for the Palestinian Territories—EU Coordinating Office for Palestinian Police Support (EUPOL COPPS)', in Grevi, D., Helly, D. and Keohane, D. (eds.) *European Security and Defence Policy—The First 10 Years (1999–2009)*, Paris: The European Union Institute for Security Studies, 287–298.
Chromiec, J. and Koenig, N. (2015) 'Supporting Ukraine's Difficult Path Towards Reforms', *Policy Paper* 143, Jacques Delors Institute—Berlin, Berlin.
Council of the European Union (2004) *Council Joint Action 2004/523/CFSP of 28 June 2004 on the European Union Rule of Law Mission in Georgia, EUJUST THEMIS*.
Council of the European Union (2005a) *Council Joint Action 2005/889/CFSP of 12 December 2005 on Establishing a European Union Border Assistance Mission for the Rafah Crossing Point*.
Council of the European Union (2005b) *Council Joint Action 2005/797/CFSP of 14 November 2005 on the European Union Police Mission for the Palestinian Territories*.
Council of the European Union (2008) *Council Joint Action 2008/736/CFSP of 15 September 2008 on the European Union Monitoring Mission to Georgia, EUMM Georgia*.

Council of the European Union (2011) *Council Decision 2011/210/CFSP of 1 April 2011 on a European Union Military Operation in Support of Humanitarian Assistance Operations in Response to the Crisis Situation in Libya (EUFOR Libya)*.
Council of the European Union (2014a) 'EU Establishes Mission to Advise on Civilian Security Sector Reform in Ukraine', *Press Release* ST 11974/14, Brussels, 22 July.
Council of the European Union (2014b) *Revised Crisis Management Concept for a Civilian CSDP Mission in Support of Security Sector Reform in Ukraine*, 10454/1/14, Brussels, 19 June.
Council of the European Union (2015a) *Council Decision (CFSP) 2015/1065 of 2 July 2015 Amending Joint Action 2005/889/CFSP on Establishing a European Union Border Assistance Mission for the Rafah Crossing Point (EU BAM Rafah)*.
Council of the European Union (2015b) *Interim Strategic Review of EUBAM Libya*, Brussels, 13 April.
Del Sarto, R. (2007) 'Wording and Meaning(s): EU-Israeli Political Cooperation According to the ENP Action Plan', *Mediterranean Politics* 12(1): 59–75.
Dura, G. (2009) 'The EU Border Assistance Mission to the Republic of Moldova and Ukraine', in Grevi, G., Helly, D. and Keohane, D. (eds.) *European Security and Defence Policy: The First Ten Years (1999–2009)*, Paris: EU Institute for Security Studies, 275–285.
Emerson, M. and Movchan, V. (eds.) (2016) *Deepening EU-Ukrainian Relations. What, Why and How?*, London: Rowman & Littlefield International.
EUAM (2015) 'EUAM Launches the Border Management Assistance Group with State Border Guard Service and International Organizations', *Press Release*, 15 May.
EUBAM (2011) 'Progress Report 2005–2010. Main Achievements in Border Management by the Partner Services in Five Years of EUBAM Activity'.
EUJUST Themis (2004) *Facts on EUJUST THEMIS*.
EUMM (2009) 'EUMM and Georgian Ministry of Defence Sign Memorandum of Understanding', *Press Release*, 26 January.
European Council (2003) *A Secure Europe in a Better World: European Security Strategy*, Brussels, 12 December.
European External Action Service (2014) 'The EU Pledged Today more than €450 Million Euros for Reconstructing Gaza', *Press Release*, 12 October.
Fabbrini, S. (2014) 'The European Union and the Libyan Crisis', *International Politics* 51(2): 177–195.
Hass, A. (2011) 'For Palestinian Police in West Bank, Israel is Still Laying Down the Law', *Haaretz*, 14 February.
Hatzigeorgopoulos, M. and Fara-Andrianarijaona, L. (2013) 'EUBAM Libya: Story of a Long-Awaited CSDP Mission', *European Security Review*, ESR 66, May.
Helly, D. (2006) 'EUJUST Themis in Georgia: An Ambitious Bet on Rule of Law', in Nowak, A. (ed.) *Civilian Crisis Management: The EU Way, Chaillot Paper* 90, Paris: EU Institute for Security Studies, 87–102.
Human Rights Watch (2011) *Living in Limbo: The Rights of Ethnic Georgian Returnees to the Gali District of Abkhazia*.
International Crisis Group (2011) 'Georgia-Russia: Learn to Live Like Neighbours', *Crisis Group Europe Briefing* 65.
Koenig, N. (2011) 'The EU and the Libyan Crisis—In Quest of Coherence?', *The International Spectator: Italian Journal of International Affairs* 46(4): 11–30.
Kurowska, X. (2009) 'The Rule of Law Mission in Georgia (EUJUST Themis)', in Grevi, G., Helly, D. and Keohane, D. (eds.) *European Security and Defence Policy: The first Ten Years (1999–2009)*, Paris: EU Institute for Security Studies, 201–209.
Lavenex, S. and Schimmelfennig, F. (2010) *EU External Governance: Projecting EU Rules Beyond Membership*, Oxon: Routledge.
Lieberman, A. (2011) 'Europe's Irresponsible Gaza Policy', *The Wall Street Journal*, 11 January.
Merlingen, M. and Ostrauskaite, R. (2009) 'EU Peacebuilding in Georgia: Limits and Achievements', *Working Paper* 35, Leuven Centre for Global Governance Studies: Centre for the Law of EU External Relations.
Nováky, N. (2015) 'Why so Soft? The European Union in Ukraine', *Contemporary Security Policy* 36(2): 244–266.
Rieker, P. and Bátora, J. (2015) 'Towards Multi-level Security Community Building: The EU's External Governance in Ukraine', *Working Paper* 860, Norwegian Institute of International Affairs.
Schumacher, T. and Bouris, D. (2017) 'The 2011 Revised European Neighbourhood Policy: Continuity and Change in EU Foreign Policy', in Bouris, D. and Schumacher, T. (eds.) *The Revised European Neighbourhood Policy: Continuity and Change in EU Foreign Policy*, Basingstoke: Palgrave, 1–33.
Youngs, R. (2004) 'Democratic Institution-Building and Conflict Resolution: Emerging EU Approaches', *International Peacekeeping* 11(3): 526–543.

24
THE EUROPEAN NEIGHBOURHOOD POLICY AND THE POLITICS OF SANCTIONS

Clara Portela

Introduction

Sanctions are no stranger to the European Union's (EU's) neighbourhood. On the contrary, out of the sixteen European Neighbourhood Policy (ENP) partner countries, as many as seven have been at the receiving end of EU sanctions during the application of this policy framework. Seven out of sixteen amounts to 44 per cent of the total population of ENP countries – almost half. The list of neighbours affected by EU sanctions grows if we include sanctions measures taken informally, outside the context of the Common Foreign and Security Policy (CFSP). And if we look at the EU's periphery in a broader sense, encompassing the Balkans in the 1990s, Iran, Russia or Turkey, the list expands even further. A study on the geographical distribution of EU sanctions until the year 2004 concluded that sanctions were not only imposed more frequently at its periphery than further afield, but that they pursued objectives different from those advanced elsewhere (Portela 2005). Yet, despite their frequent use, most recently in the wake of the Arab uprisings, EU sanctions practice has attracted little attention among scholars studying the EU's relations with its vicinity. This chapter introduces the EU's employment of sanctions in the neighbourhood, as well as an assessment of this policy and of its connection to the ENP. It reviews the universe of CFSP sanctions imposed after the launch of the ENP in 2003, or already in force by then. In addition, it includes a case of suspension of direct aid, despite its status as a non-CFSP measure.

EU sanctions: the CFSP toolbox and beyond

Sanctions are defined as politically inspired interruptions of bilateral trade, finance, travel and diplomatic relations imposed by (a) sender(s) against a target, in response to what is perceived as objectionable behaviour (Portela 2010). While it is often believed that sanctions aim at coercing the target into complying with certain demands, senders often pursue a variety of goals, including assuaging an outraged public opinion or lobby groups, denying key technology to the target, slowing its economic performance or consolidating international norms (Lindsay 1986). EU sanctions, officially referred to as 'restrictive measures', are imposed by the Council on states, entities and individuals (Council of the European Union 2004). The political decision to impose sanctions is agreed unanimously by the Council at the initiative of any of the

Member States, and takes the form of a Council Decision under the CFSP. If the Decision calls for Community action, the Council is required to follow up with the adoption of a Council Regulation, acting by a qualified majority on a joint proposal from the Commission and the High Representative of the Union for Foreign Affairs and Security Policy (art. 215 TFEU). Subsequent decisions extending, modifying or lifting sanctions equally require unanimity in the Council.

The EU's practice of imposing sanctions, which originated in the 1980s, was boosted with the creation of the CFSP in 1992. Several types of CFSP sanctions can be distinguished. First, the EU implements sanctions in compliance with the UN Charter obligation to give effect to mandatory sanctions adopted by the United Nations Security Council (UNSC) under its Chapter VII. Since these measures merely implement UNSC resolutions, they are not considered EU sanctions *per se* (Biersteker and Portela 2015). However, the EU sometimes imposes measures that go beyond UN resolutions to reinforce UN sanctions regimes. Second, the EU also applies autonomous sanctions in the absence of a UN mandate. The bulk of EU sanctions fall within this category. This is a 'default' option: for the Council, 'it is preferable for sanctions to be adopted in the framework of the UN' (Council of the European Union 2012: 21). Finally, the EU imposes sanctions outside the CFSP framework (Koch 2015; Nivet 2015). This includes the suspension of agreements with third countries, the withdrawal of trade preferences (Fierro 2003) and the suspension or redirection of aid (Portela 2010).

The use of sanctions is related to political conditionality, as it often constitutes its logical and legal follow-up. The 2003 Commission Communication on 'Wider Europe' foresaw conditionality as a defining feature of the ENP, stating that engagement should 'be conditional on meeting agreed targets for reform' (Commission of the European Communities 2003: 16). Conditionality was strengthened in the 2011 revision, thanks to the introduction of the concept of 'more for more' (Natorski and Soler 2014). It claimed that the ENP should 'provide for increased differentiation, more flexibility, stricter conditionality and incentives for best performers' (High Representative of the Union for Foreign Affairs and Security Policy and European Commission 2011: 20). It even threatened the use of sanctions, announcing that the EU would 'uphold its policy of curtailing relations with governments engaged in violations of human rights and democracy standards, including by making use of targeted sanctions' (ibid.: 20). This trend was reversed with the 2015 revision of the ENP, which de-emphasised conditionality in favour of containing mounting instability (European Commission and High Representative of the Union for Foreign and Security Policy 2015).

The following section provides an overview of the sanctions episodes in the EU's vicinity since the launch of the ENP in 2004, featuring both sanctions regimes that were in force prior to that date or initiated afterwards. Attention is devoted to the formal status of the country affected in the ENP as well as to the previous record of relations with the EU.

Eastern neighbourhood

Belarus

Sanctions against Belarus addressed the country's evolution towards autocracy, which originated in 1996 with the enactment of a new constitution concentrating powers on President Aleksander Lukashenko. In response, the Council ceased high-level contacts and assistance programmes and froze the ratification of an already concluded agreement (Fierro 2003). Both the parliamentary elections and the referendum in Belarus of October 2004 were found to fall short of basic OSCE standards by the OSCE International Election Observation Mission. This conclusion, coupled with the repression of peaceful demonstrations, prompted the EU to impose a visa ban on responsible officials. Following the presidential elections of March 2006, the EU expanded its visa ban, blacklisting President Lukashenko for the first time. An assets freeze was applied to the blacklists shortly after, and its lifting was conditioned on the release of political detainees and the reform of the electoral code (Council of the European Union 2006). A separate sanctions regime was motivated by the disappearance of three Belarusian politicians and a journalist: the EU imposed a visa ban on those responsible for the failure to launch an investigation. Yet, Russia's increase of energy charges to Belarus and the energy crisis that ensued in January 2007 induced a gradual rapprochement. Within weeks, the European Commission and Belarus set up 'discussions' on energy. Belarus authorised the opening of a European Commission Delegation in Minsk, and launched a privatisation programme (Portela 2011). Following the OSCE-supervised parliamentary elections of September 2008, the Council suspended the travel ban on most blacklisted individuals to 'encourage dialogue with the Belarusian authorities and the adoption of positive measures to strengthen democracy and respect for human rights' (Council of the European Union 2008: 7). The Council expressed its readiness to lift sanctions 'provided there [we]re further positive developments' (Council of the European Union 2009: 1) and launched a human rights dialogue, while the Commission set up technical dialogues in fields such as environment and customs. Due to widespread rigging and crackdown on the opposition during the presidential elections of December 2010, sanctions were reapplied.

The short-lived rapprochement was also reflected in moves to allow for some Belarusian participation in the ENP. As only EUR21 million, out of a total ENP budget of EUR600 million, had been allocated to Belarus until 2010, the EU operated on a tight budget (Sahm 2010). The EU included Belarus in the multilateral – not in the bilateral – track of the Eastern Partnership. Yet, tensions soon surfaced on issues such as the representation of Belarus in the EU-Neighbourhood East Parliamentary Assembly and the Eastern Partnership Civil Society Forum. At the Eastern Partnership summit in September 2011, Belarus cancelled participation after learning that President Lukashenko was not allowed to attend (Casier 2012).

New attempts at rapprochement were not launched until 2015. In the context of the dispute that emerged between the EU and Russia over the armed conflict in Eastern Ukraine, President Lukashenko improved his standing *vis-à-vis* the EU because of his role as a host of the peace talks and the resulting Minsk agreements (*The Guardian* 2015). The Council temporarily suspended the asset freeze and travel ban 'in response to the release of all Belarusian political prisoners on 22 August and in the context of improving EU-Belarus relations' (Council of the European Union 2015: 1).

Moldova

The sanctions regime applied on Moldova addresses the 'frozen conflict' in Transnistria, a region that declared independence from the Republic of Moldova in the aftermath of the dissolution of the Soviet Union and that survives as a non-recognised territorial entity. The EU imposed a visa ban against Transnistrian leaders, alleging the leadership's obstructionism of the OSCE-led peace process. Yet, the efforts at rectifying the *de facto* split of Transnistria have made little progress, despite the appointment of an EU Special Representative. The sanctions have been criticised for being 'too limited in scope to impose a serious burden on the leadership to make it reverse its policies' and especially for 'the vagueness with which objectives are formulated' (Popescu 2005: 33). Still, they are held to undermine the position of the Transnistrian leadership and the legitimacy of their claim to independent statehood (Giumelli 2011).

Ukraine

The ousting of the pro-Russian leadership after the Maidan protests of early 2014, and the annexation of Crimea and destabilisation of Eastern Ukraine that followed the ousting of the pro-Russian leadership after the Maidan protests of early 2014, prompted sanctions by the EU. The sanctions regime is primarily directed at Russia and aims at supporting Ukrainian sovereignty. EU sanctions against Moscow banned the supply of certain goods, and limited access to primary and secondary capital markets in the EU for targeted Russian financial institutions, energy and defence companies. In addition, their enactment elicited the imposition of Russian counter-sanctions on perishables. Yet, the costs of sanctions for the European economy have not been severe. After the imposition of sanctions, the EU's share in both Russian imports and exports declined by only 3 per cent in 2015 (Gros and Mustilli 2015). EU sanctions also target some Ukrainian nationals and entities. First, the EU blacklisted officials of the ousted government in Kiev after its downfall. Second, it economically isolated Crimea from Europe (Fischer 2015) by imposing a uniquely comprehensive regime in protest to its annexation by Russia. The long list of restrictions prohibit imports from Crimea and Sevastopol, the provision of tourism services, the calling of European ships at Crimean ports and the export of items for the transport, telecommunications and energy sectors, as well as investment in the region. Third, individuals who bear responsibility for the annexation of Crimea are blacklisted under the sanctions regime, as are individuals responsible for action against Ukraine's territorial integrity. Unexpectedly, the almost automatic blacklisting of individuals upon request of the Ukrainian authorities came under fire. The European Court of Justice annulled the blacklisting of Ukrainian oligarch Andrij Portnov for relying solely on accusations from the Ukrainian public prosecutor's office without corroborating the charges (Hirst 2015).

Southern neighbourhood

Tunisia

Before the outbreak of the Arab uprisings of early 2011, Tunisia was fully participating in the ENP and had been one of the first countries to conclude an Action Plan (in 2005) (Natorski and Soler 2014). After revolutionary protests spread across the country, Tunisian leader Ben Ali fled the country in January 2011. Once Tunisian prosecutors opened an investigation into the finances of Ben Ali and his relatives, the EU imposed an asset freeze on 48 persons, including the deposed Ben Ali. The freezing of assets prevented them from accessing state assets held abroad. High Representative Catherine Ashton justified the measure in the following terms: 'Even with a successful democratic transition, the issue of assets misappropriated by former regimes remains. The frozen assets cannot just be released; first ownership must rightfully be transferred to the new state structures' (Ashton 2012: 2). This measure reflected the EU's intention to reserve access to these funds for the post-revolutionary authorities, thereby ensuring their viability, while implying that the EU no longer regarded the ousted leaders as legitimate. Interestingly, the Council linked the freezing to both economic development and democracy promotion, affirming that those having misappropriated Tunisian state funds were 'depriving the Tunisian people of the benefits of the sustainable development of their economy and society and undermining the development of democracy in the country' (Council of the European Union 2011: 1). The Tunisian assets freeze was unprecedented, as it constituted the first instance in which the EU blacklisted rulers after they had relinquished office, as well as the first time in which an EU asset freeze did not accompany a visa ban (Boogaerts et al. 2016).

Egypt

Like Tunisia, the Egyptian leadership under Hosni Mubarak participated fully in the ENP. An Action Plan had been signed in 2007. Although the protests that erupted in late January 2011 were repressed violently by the security forces, the EU responded with an assets freeze only over one month after President Mubarak was forced to step down. The blacklist featured 19 officials, including Mubarak himself. As with Tunisia, the *ex post* nature of the asset freeze shows that it was meant to prevent the former leader and his entourage from accessing state funds as well as their private assets abroad (Portela 2012) and to gain the support of the Supreme Council of the Armed Forces (SCAF), which had taken control following Mubarak's deposition. President Morsi, the candidate of the Muslim Brotherhood's Freedom and Justice Party, which emerged victorious from the 2012 elections, passed legislation concentrating powers in himself and pushed through a new constitution, which had been boycotted by opposition parties. In the midst of a new wave of protests, the SCAF restored direct rule in July 2013 (Roll 2016). When security forces caused over 800 fatalities when dissolving a largely peaceful protest on Rab'a Square on 14 August 2013, the EU banned the transfer of equipment for internal repression (Council of the European Union 2013b). Yet, this measure was not legally binding. It also constitutes a rare stand-alone embargo of this kind, as it does not accompany a standard weapons embargo, which allows for the delivery of military items unrelated to internal repression, such as warships (Boogaerts et al. 2016).

Libya

EU sanctions against Libya, in early 2011, constitute an example of EU measures supplementing UN sanctions. The regime of Muammar Qaddafi long entertained an adversarial relationship with the West. While antagonism with the US was more pronounced than with Europe, the Member States of the then European Community (EC) imposed sanctions on Libya over its sponsorship of terrorism, following a series of terrorist attacks in the airports of Rome and Vienna and a Berlin club in 1986 (Niblock 2001). Yet, by the time the Arab revolts broke out, Libya was in the process of reversing its traditionally tense relationship with the West (Onderco 2014). While Tripoli remained unprepared to embrace the ENP, negotiations of a Framework Agreement were nearing conclusion by the time anti-Qaddafi protests erupted in February 2011. Their violent suppression soon escalated into a civil war, which compelled the UNSC to enact sanctions against the Qaddafi regime, with explicit backing by the Arab League and military support from some Arab states. UNSC Resolutions 1970 and 1973 applied an arms embargo and blacklisted several high-profile regime members, including Qaddafi himself. The EU, which had been preparing its sanctions in parallel, supplemented UNSC measures with additional designations as well as an autonomous ban on equipment employable for internal repression. In subsequent sanctions rounds, the EU blacklisted Libyan financial entities, the Libyan National Oil Corporation and five of its subsidiaries as well as 26 energy firms accused of financing the regime, thereby imposing a *de facto* oil and gas embargo, and eventually blacklisted six Libyan harbours (König 2011).

Syria

Relations between the EU and Syria were long marred by the Assad regime's sponsorship of terrorism, as well as its involvement in Lebanon. The end of the Lebanese civil war opened the way for a gradual improvement of EU–Syrian relations, which led to the negotiation of an

Association Agreement which was approaching conclusion by 2004. The assassination of Lebanese Prime Minister Rafik Hariri in 2005 compelled the EU to freeze Syrian assets and to blacklist several Syrian terrorist suspects (Santini 2008). When, in February 2011, protests were violently suppressed, a civil war ensued. In the face of UNSC inaction, the EU imposed a travel ban, an arms embargo and assets freeze against the regime of Bashar al-Assad. The official goals of the measures included demands to end repression, withdrawal of the Syrian army and implementation of democratic reforms. High representative Catherine Ashton justified the sanctions against the regime of Bashar al-Assad as follows: 'When countries fail [. . .] as we have seen in Syria in their ability to support their people and indeed turn to violence against their people, we are obliged to act morally and I believe internationally' (Ashton 2012). The Council quickly blacklisted over 150 targets including al-Assad, resulting in one of the EU's most severe sanctions ever enacted against a third country (Seeberg 2015; Portela 2012). Apart from its remarkably broad scope and the speed of its imposition, Syria constitutes one of the few targets on which the EU imposed costly sanctions on the energy sector (Thomas 2013). After the severity of the sanctions regimes reached its peak, the Council changed its approach to the conflict (Seeberg 2015), ultimately abandoning its arms embargo in May 2013 (Council of the European Union 2013a) to allow for the supply of arms to anti-Assad factions.

Palestinian Authority

The suspension of aid to the Palestinian Authority (PA), following the victory of Hamas in the Palestinian elections of 2006, is a case of informal sanctions; it constitutes an instance of redirection of aid rather than a freeze (Portela 2010). The suspension, and a ban on direct contacts, was agreed after Hamas, an organisation included in the EU's terrorism list, obtained a majority in the elections of January 2006. The EU justified the freeze on direct assistance to the Palestinian government pointing to Hamas' lack of respect for the principles for engagement – agreed with the Quartet in the framework of mediation efforts in the Middle East conflict. Then-Commissioner for External Relations and Neighbourhood Policy Benita Ferrero-Waldner pointed to Hamas' refusal 'to renounce violence, recognise the right of Israel to exist or accept existing agreements' (Ferrero-Waldner 2006: 1). The ENP process with the Palestinians was frozen (Tocci 2007). At the same time, the EU signalled its readiness to resume aid as soon as Hamas had accepted the principles formulated by the Quartet. Paradoxically, the suspension of payments to the PA was coupled with an increase in EU aid to Palestinians to soothe the deterioration of the social, economic and humanitarian crisis in the Occupied Territories. In June 2006, a special arrangement was put in place to channel international assistance, circumventing the Hamas-led PA government, a Temporary International Mechanism. As total EU aid to the Occupied Territories rose to EUR700 million in early 2007, UN Special Coordinator for the Middle East Peace Process Alvaro De Soto claimed that Europeans 'actually spent more money boycotting the PA than they did when they were supporting it' (De Soto 2007). The EU resumed direct aid, alongside the US, only after Palestinian president Mahmoud Abbas dismissed the Hamas-led executive and swore in a new cabinet under Fatah in June of 2007 (*The Guardian* 2007).

Conclusions: sanctions and the ENP

One of the first criticisms directed at the 'Wider Europe' communication was that it failed to specify its connection to the pre-existing framework of the Euro-Mediterranean Partnership or to the European Security Strategy (Del Sarto and Schumacher 2005). Something similar can be said about the relationship between CFSP sanctions and the ENP: abundant concept papers and consecutive revisions have failed to articulate the role of CFSP sanctions in the ENP. The ubiquity of sanctions in the EU's periphery appears, on first inspection, to be at odds with the EU's preference for co-operation and engagement over punishment and coercion (Tocci 2007). However, a closer look at these sanctions reveals that they are consonant with the EU's intention to upgrade its crisis management role in the region, as announced in the 'Wider Europe' communication (Commission of the European Communities 2003). The preoccupation with neighbouring countries manifests itself in the sensitivity of the EU to developments in these countries: the EU has sometimes reacted with sanctions to incidents of relatively low intensity (Portela 2005), such as consecutive flawed elections in Belarus. At the same time, the EU is often cautious in the application of its bans. A prime example is the imposition of a non-binding embargo on equipment for internal repression after Egyptian authorities crashed the peaceful Rab'a demonstration in 2013. Because the situation in the country remained fragile in the post-2011 period, the Council was reluctant to antagonise the leadership and diminish the EU's influence over a key player in the region (Boogaerts et al. 2016).

Interestingly, the neighbourhood sanctions often feature unique characteristics, such as the first bans imposed on an ousted leader or the only asset freezes that do not follow visa bans (Boogaerts et al. 2016). These instances are unique in the context of overall EU sanctions practice, suggesting that the EU is most innovative in its vicinity than elsewhere. The ban on equipment for internal repression is the only non-binding embargo agreed under the CFSP.

EU measures discriminate between different actors in the domestic political scenes of the countries in question, and the way in which the EU has used their capacity to discriminate is telling. CFSP sanctions have not been used as a follow-up stage to negative conditionality. Our overview shows that EU sanctions were often wielded to support the leadership in power in the face of challenges to its legitimacy or sovereignty. This applies to the Chisinau and Kiev governments, both confronted with Russian-backed separatist forces in their territories. In the same vein, assets were frozen to prevent their misappropriation by leaders after they had left office in Tunis, Cairo or Kiev. Thus, the measures applied to Egypt, Moldova, Tunisia and Ukraine are not sanctions against the countries' leaderships, but sanctions imposed in their support. Leaders of countries participating in the ENP tend not to be targeted, at least while they remain in office. Thus, while the measures had limited efficacy in changing the status quo, sanctions have not had the effect of antagonising governmental elites in the partner countries.

In turn, rulers under sanctions never activated ENP membership in the first place. The most suggestive finding can be seen in the fate of the neighbours that refused to participate in the ENP framework. Of the sixteen ENP countries, co-operation remained dormant in only three cases: Belarus, Libya and Syria (Casier 2012; Natorski and Soler 2014). Shortly after the launch of the ENP, sanctions on Belarus intensified, and less than a decade later, Libya and Syria had become the targets of some of the most severe sanctions regimes in the history of EU foreign policy. This suggests that involvement in the ENP can be regarded as a trustworthy indicator of the degree of amicability or antagonism in bilateral relations. The freeze on the Palestinian Authority constitutes the only instance of ENP suspension. By contrast, with Damascus and Tripoli, there was no co-operation ongoing when the 2011 uprisings broke out.

Finally, the EU sanctions practice in the ENP countries confirms that, as sometimes expressed in the literature, the priorities of the EU in Eastern Europe differ from those in the Southern Mediterranean. This is most visible in the objectives pursued by the measures. While the EU has wielded sanctions to condemn the non-democratic nature of the Belarusian regime and to support Moldovan and Ukrainian sovereignty in the face of Russian-sponsored separatism, the Southern Mediterranean has only seen the EU imposing sanctions in response to civil wars. The assets freezes targeting the Egyptian and Tunisian leaderships were only enacted after these had been ousted, and at the explicit request of the elites that had replaced them. This tends to confirm the notion that the EU is more serious about democracy promotion in Eastern Europe than in the southern neighbourhood, where international security concerns prevail (Casier 2012; Behr 2014).

References

Ashton, C. (2012) Speech by EU High Representative for Foreign Affairs and Security Policy and Vice President of the Commission Catherine Ashton on the EU's Policy on Restrictive Measures at the European Parliament, Brussels, 1 February.

Behr, T. (2014) 'The European Neighbourhood Policy: Going Full Circle?', in Mason, R. and Emmet, D. (eds.) *The International Politics of the Arab Spring: Popular Unrest and Foreign Policy*, Palgrave: Basingstoke, 61–81.

Biersteker, T. and Portela, C. (2015) 'EU Sanctions in Context', *ISSEU Brief* 26/2015, Paris: ISSEU.

Boogaerts, A., Portela, C. and Drieskens, E. (2016) 'One Swallow Does Not Make Spring: A Critical Juncture Perspective on EU Responses to the Arab Uprisings', *Mediterranean Politics* 21(2): 205–225.

Casier, T. (2012) 'European Neighbourhood Policy: Living up to Regional Ambitions?', in Bindi, F. and Angelescu, I. (eds.) *The Foreign Policy of the European Union*, Washington, DC: Brookings, 99–117.

Commission of the European Communities (2003) *Wider Europe-Neighbourhood: A New Framework for Relations with our Eastern and Southern Neighbours*, COM (2003) 104 final, Brussels, 11 March.

Council of the European Union (2004) *Basic Principles on the Use of Restrictive Measures (Sanctions)*, Brussels, 7 June.

Council of the European Union (2006) *Council Common Position 2006/276/CFSP Adopted on the 10 of April 2006*.

Council of the European Union (2008) *Conclusions of the 2897th External Relations Council Meeting*, Luxembourg, 13 October.

Council of the European Union (2009) *Decision 2009/969/CFSP Extending the Restrictive Measures Against Certain Officials of Belarus Laid Down in Common Position 2006/279/CFSP, and repealing Common Position 2009/314/CFSP*, 15 December.

Council of the European Union (2011) *2011/72/CFSP Concerning Restrictive Measures Directed Against Certain Persons and Entities in View of the Situation in Tunisia*, 31 January, OJ L 28/62, 2 February.

Council of the European Union (2012) *Guidelines on Implementation and Evaluation of Restrictive Measures (Sanctions) in the Framework of the EU Common Foreign and Security Policy*, Doc. 11205/12, Brussels, 15 June.

Council of the European Union (2013a) *Council Decision 2013/255/CFSP of 31 May 2013 Concerning Restrictive Measures Against Syria*, OJ L 147, 1 June.

Council of the European Union (2013b) *Conclusions on Egypt, Foreign Affairs Council Meeting*, Brussels, 21 August.

Council of the European Union (2015) 'Belarus: EU Suspends Restrictive Measures Against Most Persons and All Entities Currently Targeted', *Press Release* 767/15, 29 October.

De Soto, A. (2007) *End of Mission Report*, United Nations, New York, May.

Del Sarto, R. and Schumacher, T. (2005) 'From EMP to ENP: What's at Stake with the European Neighbourhood Policy Towards the Southern Mediterranean?', *European Foreign Affairs Review* 10: 17–38.

European Commission and High Representative of the Union for Foreign and Security Policy (2015) *Review of the European Neighbourhood Policy*, JOIN (2015) 50 Final, Brussels.

Ferrero-Waldner, B. (2006) 'Suspension of Aid to the Palestinian Authority Government', European Parliament Plenary, Brussels, 26 April.

Fierro, E. (2003) *The EU's Approach to Human Rights Conditionality in Practice*, M. Nijhoff: The Hague.

Fischer, S. (2015) 'Sanktionen gegen Russland', *SWP Aktuell* 26, SWP, Berlin.

Giumelli, F. (2011) 'EU Restrictive Measures on the Transnistrian Leaders: Assessing Effectiveness in a Strategy of Divide and Influence', *European Foreign Affairs Review* 16(3): 359–378.

Gros, D. and Mustilli, F. (2015) 'The Economic Impact of Sanctions Against Russia: Much Ado About Very Little', *CEPS Commentary*, CEPS, Brussels.

High Representative of the Union for Foreign Affairs and Security Policy and European Commission (2011) *A New Response to a Changing Neighbourhood. A Review of European Neighbourhood Policy*, COM (2011) 303, Brussels, 25 May.

Hirst, N. (2015) 'EU Suffers Major Court Defeat on Ukraine sanctions', *Politico*, 26 October.
Koch, S. (2015) 'A Typology of Political Conditionality Beyond Aid: Conceptual Horizons Based on Lessons from the European Union', *World Development* 75(1): 79–108.
König, N. (2011) 'The EU and the Libyan Crisis—In Quest of Coherence?, *International Spectator* 46(4): 11–30.
Lindsay, J. (1986) 'Trade Sanctions as Policy Instruments: A Re-examination', *International Studies Quarterly* 30(2): 153–173.
Natorski, M. and Soler, E. (2014) 'Relaciones de la Unión Europea con los Vecinos', in Barbé, E. (ed.) *La Unión Europea en las Relaciones Internacionales*, Madrid: Tecnos, 194–218.
Niblock, T. (2001) *'Pariah States' and Sanctions in the Middle East*, Boulder: Lynne Rienner.
Nivet, B. (2015) 'Les Sanctions Internationales de l'Union Européenne: Soft Power, Hard Power ou Puissance Symbolique?', *Revue Internationale et Stratégique* 97: 129–138.
Onderco, M. (2014) 'From a "Rogue" to a Parolee: Analysing Libya's "De-roguing"', in Wagner, W., Werner, W. and Onderco, M. (eds.) *Deviance in International Relations*, Basingstoke: Palgrave, 171–192.
Popescu, N. (2005) 'The EU and Moldova: Settling Conflicts in the Neighbourhood', *Occasional Paper* 60, ISSEU, Paris.
Portela, C. (2005) 'Where and Why Does the EU Impose Sanctions?', *Politique Européenne* 17: 83–111.
Portela, C. (2010) *European Union Sanctions and Foreign Policy*, London: Routledge.
Portela, C. (2011) 'Belarus and the EU: Sanctions and Partnership?', *Comparative European Politics* 9(4): 486–505.
Portela, C. (2012) 'The EU Sanctions Operation Against Syria: Conflict Management by Other Means?', *Revista UNISCI* 30: 151–158.
Roll, S. (2016) 'Managing Change: How Egypt's Military Leadership Shaped the Transformation', *Mediterranean Politics* 21(1): 23–43.
Sahm, A. (2010) 'Belarus at the Crossroads?', in Institute for Peace Research and Security Policy/IFSH (ed.) *OSCE Yearbook 2009*, Nomos: Baden-Baden, 123–135.
Santini, R. (2008) Policies Towards Syria 2003–2007, in Tocci, N. (ed.) *Who is a Normative Foreign Policy Actor?* Brussels: CEPS, 37–46.
Seeberg, P. (2015) 'The EU and the Syrian Crisis: The Use of Sanctions and the Regime's Strategy for Survival', *Mediterranean Politics* 20(1): 18–35.
The Guardian (2007) 'EU and US Restore Funding to Fatah Government', 18 June.
The Guardian (2015) 'Belarus Poll: EU Lifts Sanctions on Lukashenko—Europe's Last Dictator', 13 October.
Thomas, A. (2013) '"Pariah States" and Sanctions: The Case of Syria', *Middle East Policy* 20(3): 27–40.
Tocci, N. (2007) *The EU and Conflict Resolution*, Routledge: London.

25
UKRAINE IN THE EUROPEAN NEIGHBOURHOOD POLICY
A paradoxical partner

Kataryna Wolczuk[1]

Introduction

Ukraine's participation in the European Neighbourhood Policy (ENP) is characterised by several paradoxes. First, the ENP was conceived (Batt et al. 2003) as a framework for engagement for Ukraine as an alternative to enlargement. This accounts for its frosty reception in Ukraine. The second paradox is that, while critical of the policy, Ukraine successfully used the ENP to upgrade its bilateral relations with the European Union (EU) to that of an Association Agreement (AA). The third paradox is that while Ukraine was a *demandeur* in relations with the EU, the Ukrainian authorities have been slow in implementing domestic reforms – an essential pre-condition for integration with the EU. The ENP did not provide incentives that could sway the incumbent elites in favour of domestic reforms, or even into signing the coveted AA, when presented with a counter-offer and incentives from Russia. The failure by President Yanukovych to sign the AA in 2013 triggered a powerful domestic backlash, ending his regime in early 2014, and generated a response from Russia, which culminated in the annexation of Crimea and support for separatism in eastern Ukraine. It was Russia's actions, and the election of new political forces in Ukraine in 2014, that gave the strongest impetus to reforms since the country obtained independence in 1991. Central to these reforms is a drive for integration with the EU, premised on the broad consensus in Ukraine that the country 'has nowhere else to go'. The fourth paradox is that Russia's punitive actions against Ukraine's European choice vastly increased Ukraine's dependency on the EU, imbuing the latter with disproportionate influence – something that the ENP on its own failed to achieve. This chapter analyses Ukraine's participation in the ENP to illuminate these four paradoxes.

The ENP's reception in Ukraine: symbolism over substance

Until 2014, Ukraine's policy towards the EU was characterised by symbolism rather than substance. Above all, the perception of the ENP in Ukraine was conditioned by aspirations for EU membership, which were further fuelled by the 'Orange Revolution' in 2004. By the time the ENP was launched in 2003–2004, the Ukrainian leadership wanted to move from cooperation to integration and was insisting on a change to the nature of relations both in terms of *finalité* and instruments (Wolczuk 2008). The lack of *finalité* in the ENP diminished the attractiveness of the policy as, in Ukraine, the prospect of membership was defined as a litmus test of the EU's interest in, and commitment to, Ukraine. The term 'European neighbourhood' invoked indignation in Kyiv, as it located Ukraine outside the boundaries of Europe and, even worse, grouped it with the southern neighbours of the EU, whereas Ukraine has consistently emphasised its European identity, history and belonging.

Prospects for relations between the EU and neighbouring countries in the ENP have been defined as 'more than cooperation but less than integration' or 'economic integration and political cooperation' (Council of the European Union 2007). This did not seem to offer much new in comparison to the Partnership and Cooperation Agreement (PCA), ratified in 1998, which had already envisaged the creation of a Free Trade Area (FTA) between the EU and Ukraine. The demand for a membership perspective vastly restricted the appeal and mobilising potential of any alternative policy framework, such as the ENP. The incentive of being offered access to the single market – the key 'carrot' of the ENP – did not satisfy the Ukrainian elites. Though generous from the EU's point of view, the offer fell short of the expectations of Ukrainian elites, with their pre-occupation with symbolism (Wolczuk 2008; Gromadzki et al. 2010).

The disillusionment with the ENP was tangible because the launch of the policy coincided with the 'Orange Revolution' in Ukraine, which raised further expectations *vis-à-vis* the EU. At the time, many observers in Ukraine simply believed that the EU could not continue to refuse membership after its overt expression of European values. Yet despite Ukraine's newfound profile in the European media and public opinion, there was no breakthrough in relations as hoped for in Ukraine.

Ukraine's demand for upgrading relations

While the EU regarded the ENP as a long-term policy framework, the Ukrainian authorities viewed the ENP only as a temporary framework and a means for upgrading relations. Although the ENP was conceived as an alternative to enlargement, Ukraine sought to use the ENP as a 'stepping stone' towards membership through association. This required the EU to adjust the ENP by moving away from soft, political instruments and embark on a review of the actual bilateral legal basis governing the relations.

Ukraine was specifically seeking an AA, modelled on the Europe agreements with Central and Eastern European countries in terms of scope and *finalité*. The Europe agreements, concluded in the 1990s, paved the way to accession negotiations and enlargement. The demand for the new agreement was driven by Ukraine's quest for symbolic recognition of its 'European choice', something which the PCA, ratified in 1998, failed to provide and which was in force at the time of the launch of the ENP. In Ukraine, this symbolic recognition was as important as specific economic benefits. It was hoped that the new agreement would create a stronger sense of differentiation within the ENP, allowing Ukraine to move faster towards the EU than the other ENP participants' partners.

In legal terms, the ENP used 'soft-law' instruments, such as ENP Action Plans and Progress Reports, in addition to the pre-existing legal frameworks with individual countries. The ENP instruments complemented – rather than replaced – the pre-existing 'hard' contractual relations. The ENP instruments were sanctioned by bodies already created in bilateral relations before the ENP (in the case of Ukraine, for example, it was the EU-Ukraine Cooperation Council established in the PCA). This flexible 'layering' of instruments meant that the ENP could accommodate the preferences of the partner countries as the relations evolved. Therefore, in bilateral interactions with the neighbours, the Union tailored the policy to their needs and expectations.

Ukrainian foreign policy-makers sought to shift the relations to a new legal framework from the early 2000s. And, indeed, this was one of the key demands raised during the negotiations on the Action Plan during 2004. The EU institutions and key Member States were not ready for such an upgrade of relations. The Commission regarded the PCA as providing sufficient legal grounding for relations.[2] This reluctance to move beyond the PCA is evident in the vague wording in the ENP Action Plan:

> *Consideration* will be given to the *possibility* of a new enhanced agreement, whose scope will be defined in the *light of the fulfilment of the objectives of this Action Plan* and of the overall evolution of EU-Ukraine relations. The *advisability* of any new contractual arrangements will be considered *in due time* [emphasis added].
>
> (EU-Ukraine PCA Cooperation Council 2005)

The Ukrainian side obtained a vague commitment to open negotiations upon the fulfilment of the Action Plan. And yet, the EU refused to specify how and when Ukraine would be rewarded for pursuing the reforms stipulated in the Action Plan.[3] During the early stages of the ENP, the Commission was keen to adhere to the common ENP instruments and framework and so refused to make any specific and far-reaching exceptions for Ukraine.

However, the democratic aspirations evidenced during the 'Orange Revolution' could not go unrecognised and unrewarded. Due to 'enlargement fatigue' in the EU, membership for Ukraine was off the agenda in the EU (Gromadzki and Sushko 2005). Nevertheless, something tangible was offered to Ukraine. The Commission responded to Ukraine's demands by adopting a List of Additional Measures in February 2005, which, while reasserting the priorities of the Action Plan, included an important caveat: the promise to open negotiations on the new 'enhanced agreement', on the fulfilment of the political criteria of the Action Plan. Informally, the conduct of the free and fair parliamentary 2006 elections was singled out as a key condition, designed to stimulate further democratisation in Ukraine.

Hence, the critical upgrade in Ukraine–EU relations took place in a bilateral context and in an obfuscated fashion in 2005. Over time, this upgrade would become a trailblazer for the Eastern Partnership (EaP). The Partnership's significance lay in the fact that it offered the AA with the Deep and Comprehensive Free Trade Area (DCFTA) to other eastern neighbours (Commission of the European Communities 2008). Subsequently, the EU extended the offer of concluding the DCFTA to the southern neighbours and this offer has been taken seriously by Morocco and Tunisia.

The negotiations on what was termed the 'new enhanced agreement' commenced in 2007, while the negotiations on the economic aspects, the DCFTA, started following Ukraine's accession to the WTO in 2008. Despite the EU's reluctance, Ukraine insisted on naming the new accord an AA. Only in 2008 did the EU acquiesce to the proposed nomenclature, though it was clearly and explicitly dissociated from membership as reflected in the following disclaimer: '[the Agreement] neither precludes nor promotes Ukraine's membership aspirations' (Wolczuk 2008). While agreeing to 'association', the mandate for a new agreement as adopted by the Council was rather vague; it merely asserted that 'through this Agreement, the European Union aims to build an increasingly close relationship with Ukraine, aimed at gradual economic integration and deepening of political cooperation' (Council of the European Union 2007).

In practice, the EU–Ukraine AA was drafted as an ambitious and comprehensive legal framework. While stopping short of membership, the agreement offers an advanced and privileged relationship with the EU. The aim of the AA is to achieve Ukraine's economic integration into the EU internal market. More specifically, the agreement embraced principles, concepts and provisions of EU law, which would be interpreted and applied as if the third state was part of the EU (Van der Loo et al. 2014). There are few agreements that the EU has with third countries which allow for such an advanced nature of economic integration into the single market (ibid.). While the EU–Ukraine agreement is not as extensive as the European Economic Area (EEA) Agreement, many of its provisions are close to legislative approximation of the EEA.

As pointed out by Van der Loo et al. (2014), the challenge with this type of arrangement is to ensure a uniform interpretation and application of EU rules within a shared legal framework. This challenge is reflected in the adoption of the robust institutional system, explicit conditionality, wide-ranging mechanisms for legal approximation and a refined system for dispute settlement in the agreement. To integrate Ukraine into the single market, the agreement contains extensive detailed and binding provisions, which require Ukraine to align its laws and policies with those of the EU and pursue legal and regulatory convergence with EU standards. This is because the pursuit of 'deep' economic integration requires extensive legislative and regulatory approximation to ensure the uniform interpretation and effective implementation of relevant EU legislation. The agreement is a dynamic and future-oriented legal framework, which includes various mechanisms for dealing with the evolution of the incorporated EU *acquis*, as well as sophisticated forms of dispute settlement.

The irrelevance of the Eastern Partnership

With the launch of the EaP in 2009, AAs were offered to other eastern partners, namely Moldova, Armenia and Georgia. The initiative was aimed at 'accelerating political association and further economic integration between the European Union and interested partner countries' not only through an AA with the DCFTA but also by facilitating the mobility of citizens and visa liberalisation (Commission of the European Communities 2008). For Ukraine, the EaP added little and was a retrograde step, as it diminished Ukraine's distinctiveness among the eastern neighbours (Solonenko 2011). Indeed, Ukrainian officials were annoyed by being grouped together with – rather than differentiated from – post-Soviet states, such as Azerbaijan and Belarus, despite their weaker ties with, and lower ambitions *vis-à-vis*, the EU (Wolczuk 2011). For Ukraine as a frontrunner, the multilateral dimension of the EaP – a novelty in the eastern neighbourhood – has been considerably less important than its bilateral ties with the EU. The multilateral track provided an opportunity for a collective dialogue between the EU and the partner countries (Delcour 2011) but it has been difficult to find a common 'denominator' which would satisfy all the participating countries.

Europeanisation as a modernisation agenda

Up to the launch of the ENP, integration with the EU was perceived as a foreign policy agenda to be pursued by the Ukrainian leaders and diplomacy. As Sherr has pointed out, 'Ukraine's political leaders have sometimes acted as if they could achieve integration by declaration, or simply by joining and participating in international organizational and political clubs rather than by undertaking concrete structural changes' (Sherr 1998: 12). While declaring an interest in joining the EU, the Ukrainian authorities paid little attention to domestic reforms, pursuing in effect Europeanisation through declarations (Wolczuk 2004).

In 2005, relations between the EU and Ukraine improved noticeably, thanks to the democratic gains from the 'Orange Revolution', which paved the way for a more open political dialogue. But despite the acceptance of the reform agenda, owing primarily to entrenched vested interests in Ukraine, the overall impetus for change was too weak to make a real difference, something the EU and the ENP were unable to influence.

Nevertheless, the ENP can be credited with Ukraine's acceptance and acknowledgement of the demands of European integration by drawing attention to domestic reforms and legal approximation (that is, alignment with the *acquis*). The ENP created a framework for policy transfer, which, at first, coincided with a stronger interest from the incumbent elites. The elites, which came to power in 2005, and which were energised by the 'Orange Revolution', declared that a new chapter in Ukraine's relations with the EU had opened and promised to close the gap between declarations and domestic policy-making that had been so evident under President Kuchma (Gromadzki and Sushko 2005).

With the Action Plan, the EU provided some preliminary guidelines and a focus for domestic policy-making in Ukraine. At the time, Ukrainians were keen to seize the opportunity provided by the ENP to prove their 'Europe-worthiness'. Mindful of the 'enlargement fatigue' prevailing within the EU, Ukrainian proponents of European integration were eager to make the best of what they regarded as a 'transitional framework'. By implementing the Action Plan, they intended to prove Ukraine's credibility and move closer towards membership.

The reform agenda, as defined in the Action Plan, was wide-ranging, lacking clear priorities and focus. The Action Plan was scant on priorities and specific measures: 'Clearly worded as well as measurable and checkable points in particular (benchmarks) can be looked for in vain' (ENEPO 2007). Despite the adoption of the Action Plan, it was not certain what was required of Ukraine. In this context, the adoption of the 'Road Map on the Implementation of the Action Plan' in the spring of 2005 was the most tangible instance of the 'domestication' of an EU-defined reform agenda. Adopted through a resolution of the Cabinet of Ministers of Yulia Tymoshenko, the Road Map became binding for the agencies within the executive branch. Reflecting the structure of the Action Plan, the 2005 Road Map listed 350 measures indicating how, when and by which institutions the objectives of the Action Plan were to be enacted. Even though the Action Plan was a general political document, the adoption of the Road Map was decisive in terms of its impact on domestic policy-making. Renewed on an annual basis until 2010, the Road Map induced greater openness and transparency than any other government programme before (with key documents being available on the governmental portal).

Nevertheless, it soon became apparent that while the 'Orange' elites were committed to their European vocation, they lacked the political machinery and management skills needed to deliver on their declarations. The lack of effective leadership on European issues soon became evident during the so-called 'Orange' period (2005–2009), compounded by frequent governmental changes.

The tumultuous political dynamics, which prevailed during that time in Ukraine, made domestic and foreign policy-making precarious and vulnerable to recurrent upheavals. The profound uncertainty prevailing as to how political actors operated under the 'new rules of the game' affected all areas of policy-making, including EU-related matters. So, even though – unlike the controversial issue of integration with NATO – the process of moving closer to the EU was not openly contested, its progress became a hostage of vested political and economic interests and administrative inefficiencies.

There was no radical reform of the institutional framework for European integration. Even though successive governments, regardless of their political hue, endorsed the Action Plan, the creation of an efficient institutional framework for dealing with EU matters fell by the wayside. The Action Plan's implementation was left to the discretion of state officials with responsibility for EU-related matters. These newly emerged pro-reform enclaves sought to initiate domestic reforms under the banner of European integration, taking advantage of the political mandate to do so from the respective governments (Wolczuk 2009; Langbein and Wolczuk 2012). In other words, European integration was conducted in Ukraine, by reform-minded bureaucrats, while the political class engaged in fratricide.

Back to declarative Europeanisation under Yanukovych

It was owing to this political turmoil which engulfed the 'Orange' elites that President Yanukovych came to power in 2010. Yet despite his supposedly pro-Russian leanings, he continued with the European vector and his administration can be credited with completing the protracted and difficult negotiations on the AA in the autumn of 2011. At the same time, it became apparent that the ENP and the EaP had a limited sway over the new elites. The EU's long-term, developmental agenda was mismatched with the agenda of the newly elected and deeply corrupt political elites in Ukraine.

Furthermore, there were structural issues within the new-found relations which further hindered relations. Ukraine faced high economic costs of economic integration with the EU as the bulk of adjustments fell on Ukraine. While ultimately beneficial for the Ukrainian consumers and the long-term modernisation of the country, the short-term costs to Ukrainian producers were high. Quite simply, the prospect of market access and assistance was not enough to stimulate Ukraine to engage in a far-reaching and comprehensive process of convergence with the EU (Meloni 2007: 100).

Compounding this was a significant domestic factor – the fact that, having gained power, Yanukovych was determined to stay in power by whatever means necessary, including authoritarian consolidation (Dragneva and Wolczuk 2015). As this became clearer, in 2012, the EU resorted to democratic conditionality to avert growing authoritarian tendencies. The EU used the AA – a key tool at the EU's disposal – to pressurise the Ukrainian authorities to address growing concerns over the deterioration of democratic standards. A primary concern was the politically motivated prosecutions of opposition figures – such as the former prime minister, Yulia Tymoshenko, and a former minister of the interior, Yurii Lutsenko. These prosecutions were condemned by EU officials as a conspicuous breach of democratic standards and European values. The EU made the signing and ratification of the agreement conditional upon ending selective justice and introducing far-reaching democratic reforms.

By making economic integration contingent on upholding democratic standards, the EU introduced significant and undesirable political costs for the Ukrainian authorities: meeting EU conditions would affect the prospects of Yanukovych remaining in power at a time when he was consolidating power to prevent any challenges emerging. The trade-off between relations with Europe and consolidating power meant that the pursuit of association with the EU carried economic costs for Ukraine and political risks for President Yanukovych and his backers. Not only was the EU oblivious to these costs, but it compounded its error by failing to consider the punitive measures that Russia threatened to impose on Ukraine if the AA was signed (Dragneva and Wolczuk 2015).

The Russian counter-offer for integration

At the same time as the EU was focusing on the issue of selective justice in Ukraine, Russia was intensifying its efforts to get Ukraine to join the Eurasian economic regime. In doing so, it had reversed its former policy: Russia had paid little attention to the notion of the AA and the launch of EU–Ukraine negotiations in 2007, nor had it at any time voiced any objections to Ukraine's desire to integrate with the EU – in marked contrast to Russia's vociferous objections to Ukraine's aspirations to NATO membership during Yushchenko's presidency (2005–2009). It was the launch of the EaP in May 2009 – which 'rolled out' the agreements to other post-Soviet states – that triggered Russia's concerns over the EU's policy in the eastern neighbourhood and Ukraine's prospects for integration with the EU. In the early 2000s, the EU's cooperation with eastern neighbours was secondary to cooperation with Russia, but under the ENP and especially the EaP the EU departed from its 'Russia first' approach (Lang and Lippert 2015). Russia realised that not only was the EU intent on offering advanced forms of integration, but some eastern partners were keen to take up this offer, to the detriment of Russia's own hegemonic position in the post-Soviet space and its own integration agenda.

While the negotiations on the AA continued, in 2011 the Russian leadership invited Ukraine to join the newly formed Eurasian Customs Union (ECU) between Belarus, Kazakhstan and Russia. This was conceived as an ambitious integration initiative developed in conjunction with Russia's accession to the WTO. The deep and advanced nature of the integration was designed, with the Customs Union, to evolve into a Single Economic Space (SES) in 2012 and, eventually, into the Eurasian Economic Union (EEU) by 2015. In contrast to post-Soviet integration initiatives, the Eurasian project was conceived as a binding regime with no selectivity and entailed the delegation of significant regulatory powers to a supranational Commission (Dragneva and Wolczuk 2013). Despite Ukraine's cautious stance on post-Soviet integration initiatives, Ukraine was expected and encouraged to join the Eurasian regime (Dragneva and Wolczuk 2016).

For Ukraine, Russia was not an attractive 'integration core'. Owing to the structural distortions of Russia's petro-economy and a weak rule of law, its capacity and readiness to deliver rule-based economic integration beneficial to all partner countries was regarded as low. Yet, in contrast to the EU, Russia offered Ukraine considerable and immediate benefits, most particularly a reduction of energy prices. It was evident that Russia was resolved to attract Ukraine to its own integration project in contrast to the EU's much more laissez faire approach to the conclusion of the AA, which was presented as a 'gift' to Ukraine. Russia applied a whole spectrum of positive and negative conditionality, hitting Ukraine hard with punitive economic measures, which further raised the cost of Ukraine's integration with the EU.

By 2010–2011 Russia's conditionality started to place immense pressure on the Ukrainian leadership, which was already reeling from the effects of the crisis of 2009, when the Ukrainian GDP dropped by 15 per cent, and high energy prices. As a result, the choice between the costs of engaging more closely with the EU, and the benefits from not doing so and moving closer to Russia, was proving to be increasingly hard to make, despite the long-standing rhetoric of the 'European choice' in Ukraine. This was particularly so as the EU failed to respond to any of Russia's moves towards Ukraine. For example, when Russia started to exert pressure on Ukraine to join the ECU in 2011, the EU did not initiate a countervailing response. The EU's position was to stress the long-term benefits of the AA to Ukraine, while relying on the Ukrainian authorities to appreciate and pursue these benefits – even at the cost of economic sanctions from Russia and the prospects for political survival of the incumbent authorities.

In this context, integration with the EU became a kind of luxury for the Ukrainian elites – desirable in the long-term but costly in the short term (Gnedina and Sleptsova 2012). Yanukovych came to power in 2010 on the promise to lift the Ukrainian economy out of the decline caused by the crisis of 2009 and his political survival was conditional upon the performance of the Ukrainian economy. Yanukovych tried to recalibrate relations with Russia to obtain critical concessions, without giving up on integration with the EU, and was partly successful. As the signing of the AA loomed in Vilnius, and Ukraine's economy was sliding into recession, in the autumn of 2013, Russia enhanced its 'integration package' to Ukraine by providing massive and instant financial assistance in return for not signing the AA. Russia offered a US$15 billion loan and promised to lower the gas price, from US$425 to US$268 to stall Ukraine's integration with the EU.

The decision to suspend the AA and accept the Russian offer was taken by a narrow circle of Yanukovych's closest associates in November 2013, and presented to the Ukrainian public as a technical delay because the agreement was a costly proposition for Ukraine, in contrast to the more beneficial package offered by Russia (Dragneva and Wolczuk 2015). The Ukrainian leadership's U-turn on the AA confirms the view that the 'ENP benefits above all those that are already making progress, but that is not powerful enough to break through obstacles put up by those unwilling to reform and to overcome resistance' (Lippert 2008).

External backlash and push towards Europe

Yanukovych's decision to accept the Russian offer triggered mass protests targeted against the regime, its corrupt practices and authoritarian tendencies. During the protests, which became increasingly violent, the EU institutions and its Member States repeatedly called for a peaceful resolution of the crisis but otherwise did not seek to influence its dynamics. This 'wait-and-see' approach was in evidence during the Arab uprisings in early 2011, where the EU faced, but failed to resolve, the dilemma in terms of balancing stability with support for democratisation (Noutcheva 2015). The EU's passivity during the protests was striking considering that the political crisis was triggered by societal demand for further integration with the EU.

Following Yanukovych's escape and change of leadership in Ukraine, Russia's determination to shape Ukraine's foreign and domestic policies took on dramatic proportions: the annexation of Crimea, the war in eastern Ukraine, the downing of a commercial jet airliner – all of which sent shockwaves to the international community (Allison 2014; Freedman 2014). The EU reacted to the violations of Ukraine's territorial integrity by imposing economic sanctions against Russia, which retaliated with sanctions against the EU. As a result, the EU found itself drawn into all aspects of Ukraine–Russia relations, which had major repercussions for EU–Russia relations. This has tested the Member States' unity ever since, as there was significant divergence between Member States about how to respond to Russia's coercive actions. Overall, the 'Ukrainian crisis' amply illustrated the limits of the EU's capacity to deal with crises and contestations, as 'the Union is well outside its comfort zone', as Smith (2013: 653) put it. The military escalation and humanitarian situation in Ukraine forced the Union into crisis management mode, with security issues and the search for short-term diplomatic compromise dominating its agenda (Lang and Lippert 2015). The ENP was not designed to deal with the crises in the neighbourhood.

At the same time, the EU did not radically alter or upgrade its integration offer to Ukraine – the implementation of the AA has been the focus point since 2014. Yet, integration with the EU has become an ever more pressing prerogative for Ukraine owing to Russia's punitive actions. The backlash from Russia imbued the EU with an unprecedented influence in terms of security and reforms, arguably the greatest in any ENP partner country (Delcour and Wolczuk 2015).

On coming to power, the new elites embarked on the most ambitious programme of reform in Ukraine's history. In many respects, integration with the EU became the main reference point and a reform agenda for the new authorities. The prospects for rapid Europeanisation of Ukraine remain remote. The EU's strategy of 'economic integration and political cooperation' is premised on comprehensive reforms in a short period of time, that is, five to eight years, with the impact of these changes emerging further into the future. As during enlargement, the ENP/EaP formula continues to be 'reforms now, benefits later' (Commission of the European Communities 2006). At the same time, the scale and type of domestic adjustments envisaged under the ENP/EaP presents a challenge for the post-Soviet states, including Ukraine. They all suffer from poor governance and insufficient institutional and administrative capacity. In many instances, diffusion of the *acquis* is designed to address the very problems which hamper the convergence with the *acquis*, such as political instability, lack of rule of law, weak administrative capacity, corruption and conflicts (Wolczuk 2010). The limited war with Russia further diverts priorities from reforms, despite their pivotal nature for Ukraine's survival as an independent state.

Conclusions

The ENP was conceived as a way of ensuring policy consistency across a number of participating countries, whereas Ukraine has been seeking to obtain a more distinctive status. As a result, Ukraine's participation in the ENP has been marred by misaligned expectations.

In terms of modernisation, it has been convincingly argued in the academic literature that external actors can influence domestic trajectories if they work in tandem with domestic forces. The EU was not exceptional in this regard. As in all other ENP countries, the EU encountered difficulties in stimulating domestic change in Ukraine: the ENP failed to provide a significant boost to the domestic reform efforts. The ENP could support the reform momentum where it had already existed but could not compensate for any dearth.

Yet the ENP did successfully focus attention on the preconditions of European integration in Ukraine. It was the Action Plan that brought the message home as to what *Evrointegratsia* is about. The discussion on Europe shifted from history, geography and geopolitics to European values, norms and technical standards (Wolczuk 2016). This shift represents a sea change in EU–Ukraine relations. The result was an incomparably better understanding of preconditions for moving closer to the EU, although political will, capacity and resources remain in short supply. Post-Soviet political, economic and administrative structures, institutions and practices in Ukraine make it difficult for the EU's policy guidelines to be acted on (Lough and Solonenko 2016). After two decades of mismanagement, the scale of reforms required and domestic barriers to enacting them, including the war in eastern Ukraine, mean that the challenges lying ahead of Ukraine on the 'road to Europe' are formidable. At the same time, a broad consensus has emerged in Ukraine that the country 'has nowhere else to go'. Russia's coercion against Ukraine's European choice vastly increased the dependency of Ukraine on the EU and granted the EU disproportionate influence, something which, paradoxically, the ENP on its own could not achieve and which Russia failed to prevent.

Notes

1 Funding: writing of this chapter has been facilitated by two research projects funded by the UK Economic and Social Research Council (ESRC): 'Russia and the EU in the Common Neighbourhood: Export of Governance and Legal (In)Compatibility' (Grant No: ES/J013358/1) and 'Exploring the Role of the EU in Domestic Change in the Post-Soviet States', co-funded with the ANR under the 'Open Research Area in Europe' scheme (Grant No: RES-360-25-0096).
2 At the same time, some EU officials, such as Chris Patten and Javier Solana, had already advocated the conclusion of so-called neighbourhood agreements. But because of the very name of the proposed agreement this idea was not well received in Ukraine.
3 Authors' interview with a Ukrainian official in the Ministry of Foreign Affairs, Paris (August 2005).

References

Allison, R. (2014) 'Russian "Deniable" Intervention in Ukraine: How and Why Russia Broke the Rules', *International Affairs* 90(6): 1255–1297.
Batt, J., Lynch, D., Missiroli, A., Ortega, M. and Triantaphyllou, D. (2003) 'Partners and Neighbours: A CFSP for a Wider Europe', *Chaillot Paper* 64, European Union Institute for Security Studies, Paris.

Commission of the European Communities (2006) *Communication from the Commission to the Council and the European Parliament on Strengthening the European Neighbourhood Policy*, COM(2006) 726 final, Brussels, 4 December.

Commission of the European Communities (2008) *Eastern Partnership, Communication to the Council and to the European Parliament*, COM (2008) 823 final, 3 December.

Council of the European Union (2007) *Council Conclusions, Press Release 5463/07*, 2776th Council meeting, General Affairs and External Relations, Brussels, 22 January.

Delcour, L. (2011) 'The Institutional Functioning of the Eastern Partnership: An Early Assessment' *Eastern Partnership Review*, Estonian Centre of the Eastern Partnership.

Delcour, L. and Wolczuk, K. (2015) 'Spoiler or Facilitator of Democratization?: Russia's Role in Georgia and Ukraine', *Democratization* 22(3): 459–478.

Dragneva, R. and Wolczuk, K. (eds.) (2013), *Eurasian Economic Integration: Law, Policy, and Politics*, Cheltenham: Edward Elgar

Dragneva, R. and Wolczuk, K. (2015) *Ukraine Between the EU and Russia: The Integration Challenge*, Houndmills and New York: Palgrave Macmillan.

Dragneva, R. and Wolczuk, K. (2016) 'Between Dependence and Integration: Ukraine's Relations with Russia', *Europe-Asia Studies* 68(4): 677–698.

ENEPO (2007) 'Interim Report: Institutional Convergence of CIS Towards European Benchmarks, EU Eastern Neighbourhood: Economic Potential and Future Development', June.

EU–Ukraine PCA Cooperation Council (2005) *EU–Ukraine Action Plan 21 February*, www.enpi-info.eu/library/content/eu-ukraine-action-plan-0.

Freedman, L. (2014) 'Ukraine and the Art of Limited War', *Survival* 56(6): 7–38.

Gnedina, E. and Sleptsova, E. (2012) 'Eschewing Choice: Ukraine's Strategy on Russia and the EU', *CEPS Working Document* 360, January.

Gromadzki, G. and Sushko A. (2005) 'Between Contentment and Disillusionment—EU-Ukraine Relations a Year After the Orange Revolution', Stefan Batory Foundation.

Gromadzki, G., Movchan, V., Riabchuk, M., Solonenko, I., Stewart, S., Sushko, O. and Wolczuk, K. (2010) *Beyond Colours: Assets and Liabilities of 'Post-Orange' Ukraine*, Warsaw: Stefan Batory Foundation/International Renaissance Foundation.

Lang, K. and Lippert, B. (2015) 'EU Options on Russia and the Eastern Partners', *SWP Comments* 32 (May).

Langbein, J. and Wolczuk, K. (2012) 'Convergence Without Membership? The Impact of the European Union in the Neighbourhood: Evidence from Ukraine', *Journal of European Public Policy* 19(6): 863–881.

Lippert, B. (2008) 'European Neighbourhood Policy: Many Reservations, Some Progress, Uncertain Prospects', FES, International Policy Analyses, Berlin.

Lough, J. and Solonenko, I. (2016) 'Can Ukraine Achieve a Reform Breakthrough?', *Chatham House Research Paper*, London.

Meloni, G. (2007) 'Is the Same Toolkit Used During Enlargement Still Applicable to the Countries of the New Neighbourhood?', in Cremona, M. and Meloni, G. (eds.) *The European Neighbhourhood Policy: A Framework for Modernisation?*, EUI Working Papers, Law 2007/21.

Noutcheva, G. (2015) 'Institutional Governance of European Neighbourhood Policy in the Wake of the Arab Spring', *Journal of European Integration* 37(1): 19–36.

Sherr, J. (1998) *Ukraine's New Time of Troubles*, Camberley: Conflict Studies Research Centre.

Smith, M. (2013) 'Beyond the Comfort Zone: Internal Crisis and External Challenge in the European Union's Response to Rising Powers', *International Affairs* 89(3): 653–671.

Solonenko, I. (2011) 'Added Value? Eastern Partnership and EU–Ukraine Bilateral Relations'. http://library.fes.de/pdf-files/ipg/2011-3/11_solonenko.pdf.

Van der Loo, G., Van Elsuwege, P. and Petrov, R. (2014) 'The EU-Ukraine Association Agreement: Assessment of an Innovative Legal Instrument', *EUI Working Papers, Law* 2014/9.

Wolczuk, K. (2004) 'Integration Without Europeanisation: Ukraine and Its Policy Towards the European Union', *EUI RSCAS Working Papers* 2004/15, Robert Schuman Centre for Advanced Studies, European University Institute.

Wolczuk, K. (2008) 'A Dislocated and Mistranslated EU-Ukraine Summit', *EU-ISS Opinion*, October 2008. www.iss.europa.eu/uploads/media/EU-Ukraine_Summit.pdf.

Wolczuk, K. (2009) 'Implementation Without Coordination: The Impact of the EU Conditionality on Ukraine under the European Neighbourhood Policy', *Europe-Asia Studies* 61(2): 187–211.

Wolczuk, K. (2010) 'Convergence Without *Finalité:* EU Strategy Towards Post-Soviet States', in Handerson, K. and Weaver, C. (eds.) *The Black Sea Region and EU Policy: The Challenge of Divergent Agendas*, Farnham: Ashgate, 45–64.

Wolczuk, K. (2011) 'Perceptions of, and Attitudes Towards, the Eastern Partnership Amongst the Partner Countries' Political Elites', *Eastern Partnership Review* December, No. 5, Estonian Centre of the Eastern Partnership.

Wolczuk, K. (2016) 'Ukraine and Europe: Reshuffling the Boundaries of Order', *Thesis Eleven* 36(1): 54–73.

26
EU–BELARUS RELATIONS IN THE CONTEXT OF THE EUROPEAN NEIGHBOURHOOD POLICY

Giselle Bosse[1]

Introduction

The Republic of Belarus, counting fewer than ten million inhabitants, is located at the EU's eastern frontier, bordering Poland to the west, Lithuania and Latvia to the northwest, Ukraine to the south and the Russian Federation (hereafter Russia) to the northeast. After the dissolution of the Soviet Union, Belarus declared independence on 25 August 1991, and since 1994, President Alyaksandr Lukashenka has headed the government. Under Lukashenka's rule, the country has retained many Soviet-era policies, including state ownership of significant parts of the economy. Because of its staunch resistance to any form of democratisation, Lukashenka's Belarus has acquired the unfavourable image of 'the last dictatorship in Europe'.

Partly due to this image, the EU's relations with Belarus have never reached the level of engagement achieved with other countries in its eastern neighbourhood. The Partnership and Cooperation Agreement (PCA), negotiated in 1995, has remained frozen since 1997 in response to the political situation in the country. Nevertheless, the EU's policy towards Belarus has changed over time and undergone several revisions regarding the goals, modes and intensity of the EU's bilateral engagement.

In the first part of this chapter, a short history of EU–Belarus relations is provided. The different phases of the EU's engagement with Belarus over the past two and a half decades are outlined, with a specific emphasis on the 2004 European Neighbourhood Policy (ENP) and the 2009 Eastern Partnership (EaP). The second part of the chapter zooms in on the driving forces behind EU–Belarus relations and explains continuities and change in the relationship by examining the role of values and principles, as well as economic and geopolitical interests in the development of the policy. The final part of the chapter offers an assessment of the impact and effectiveness of the EU's policy towards Belarus, including a brief outlook of future EU–Belarus relations after the outbreak of the *de facto* war in Eastern Ukraine in 2014.

Overview of EU–Belarus relations: 1991–2015

The first decade: deterioration of relations

After Belarus declared independence in December 1991, the goal of its leaders was a 'return to Europe', including eventual membership in the EU (Piontek 2006). The momentum towards political and economic reforms had hardly begun when the old communist establishment reclaimed control. Once elected, the new president, Alyaksandr Lukashenka, quickly began to consolidate his power. In 1995, he was granted the power to dissolve parliament by way of a referendum, and in 1996 another referendum on amending the constitution assured Lukashenka's control over the Constitutional Court. At the same time, the president reoriented Belarus' foreign policy back to closer relations with Russia. As a result, Belarus' relations with the EU quickly deteriorated. In 1997, the General Affairs Council suspended the ratification of the PCA, froze the previously concluded Interim Trade Agreement, and restricted contacts to Belarus to below ministerial level (General Affairs Council 1997).

The ENP 2004–2006: principled engagement with Belarus

Initially, the EU had only a very limited interest in – and interactions with – Belarus. Belarus was pro forma included in the ENP, but the EU adopted a principled approach, underlining its engagement with Belarus 'without compromising the EU's commitment to common and democratic values' (Commission of the European Communities 2003a: 15). Later in 2004, the Council confirmed this position by imposing targeted sanctions (visa bans) on key actors associated with the disappearance of political activists in 1999 and 2000, and by extending the sanctions against persons responsible for the fraudulent parliamentary elections held in December 2004. The visa bans applied only to six persons. The EU emphasised that it wished Belarus to 'take its rightful place in Europe' (Commission of the European Communities 2003b: 1) but was careful not to translate this objective into concrete actions, to avoid jeopardising its relations with Russia. According to a number of EU officials, the then EU-15 had made the tactical choice in early 2004 to institutionalise the status quo of EU–Belarus relations in the ENP, with the intention to counter pressure by prospective Member States to strengthen relations with Belarus, Ukraine and Moldova.[2]

After their accession to the EU, it did not take long for the new Member States from Central and Eastern Europe to start pushing for a more active eastern policy of the EU, much to the dismay of the 'old' EU-15. In October 2005, for example, a meeting between then Lithuanian Prime Minister, Algirdas Brazauskas, and Belarusian Prime Minister, Syarhey Sidorski, caused considerable anger among the 'old' Member States, who had not been consulted before the meeting and who interpreted the move as a clear violation of the EU's restrictions on ministerial-level contacts with the Belarusian government (General Affairs Council 1997).

Differences between 'new' and 'old' Member States also came to the fore after the fraudulent presidential elections in Belarus in 2006, which were marred by violence against the opposition and resulted in the arrest of almost one thousand protesters. Poland, Slovakia and Lithuania wanted to send a clear signal to the Lukashenka regime and proposed a substantial expansion of the visa ban list to up to 300 persons. Germany, France, Italy and Austria, who favoured a more cautious approach, opposed the proposal. Eventually, in April 2006, the Council decided on a compromise, adding 30 names to the visa 'blacklist', including President Lukashenka. Later, in May, the assets of the persons blacklisted were frozen, and in December, the EU withdrew the Preferential Trade Arrangement for products originating in Belarus.

Towards an active step-by-step engagement in a maturing ENP

A renewed push towards more engagement with the Belarusian government occurred in early 2007 after Lukashenka had released several political prisoners and had finally given the green light to the opening of an EU delegation in Minsk (outstanding since 2005). Together with the Council Secretariat, the German EU presidency – having reconsidered its policy towards

Belarus – began to lobby for a double track, step-by-step approach with Belarus (pressure on the regime, support for Belarusian people/the opposition, willingness to engage with the authorities) (Jarábik and Rabagliat 2007). The reaction of the other EU Member States was unenthusiastic: the United Kingdom, France and Lithuania warned of possible fake moves by the government of Belarus,[3] while the Polish government opposed any step-by-step approach,[4] arguing that similar approaches had failed in the past. As the relations between Georgia and Russia drastically deteriorated, throughout the spring and summer of 2008, a stronger consensus emerged among the EU Member States towards more engagement with the Belarusian government. Shortly after the escalation of the conflict in Georgia in early August 2008, the General Affairs and External Relations Council decided to suspend for six months the targeted sanctions imposed against leading figures in Belarus, including President Lukashenka (General Affairs and External Relations Council 2008).

Belarus within the Eastern Partnership: emphasising 'engagement'

In early 2009, preparations for launching the Eastern Partnership (EaP) initiative were in full swing. The EaP project was largely driven by the Polish and Swedish governments, who became recognised as the main advocates of the full participation of Belarus in the EaP, supporting a policy of 'critical engagement' (Kaminska 2014). In February 2009, the EU's High Representative for the Common Foreign and Security Policy, Javier Solana, visited Minsk to confirm the willingness of the EU to integrate Belarus into the EaP. Subsequently, the diplomatic contacts between the EU and Belarus increased substantially. Next to the invitation to participate in the EaP, the EU's greater engagement with Belarus involved clearing the way for new credits from the International Monetary Fund (IMF) (USD3.5 billion) in the summer of 2009 and the decision by the Council, in early 2010, to approve the mandate of the Commission for the negotiation of a Visa Facilitation and Readmission Agreement with Belarus. In addition, the European Commission started to prepare a Joint Interim Plan to serve as a roadmap for enhanced bilateral relations in the trade and economic sectors. Some Member States had even supported a re-launch of the PCA, but the initiative failed to convince the majority – above all the United Kingdom and the Netherlands, who had objected to any such moves.[5]

Crackdown on the opposition after the 2010 presidential elections: back to a critical engagement

In the run-up to the 2010 presidential elections in Belarus, many top officials visited Minsk, among them the Commissioner for Enlargement and Neighbourhood Policy, Štefan Füle, as well as the foreign ministers Guido Westerwelle (Germany) and Radosław Sikorski (Poland). The two foreign ministers even promised Belarus financial assistance of over EUR3 billion to persuade Lukashenka to hold free elections. The widespread optimism within the EU was quickly shattered when Belarusian riot police violently suppressed a large protest rally the night after the elections, severely beating and injuring large numbers of protesters, and resulting in the arrest of hundreds of protesters and seven presidential candidates by the Belarusian secret service.

Despite the brutality of the government-led crackdown, the EU was remarkably slow to react to the events in Belarus. At the end of January 2011, the Foreign Affairs Council eventually decided to impose visa bans and an asset freeze on 157 persons responsible for the political repression in Belarus (Foreign Affairs Council 2011a). It took until June 2011 for the Council to reach a consensus on tougher sanctions (Foreign Affairs Council 2011b), which included the imposition of an arms embargo and restrictive measures against three companies linked to Belarusian oligarch Vladimir Peftiev, who was one of the financiers of the Belarusian government.

In the first two years following the elections, the relations between the EU and Belarus further deteriorated. In late 2011, the Belarusian government introduced new restrictive legislation against the activities of political parties, NGOs and public associations and imprisoned well-known opposition activist Ales Bialiatski. The EU responded with an expansion of the visa ban and assets freeze in October 2011 (Foreign Affairs Council 2011c). Disappointed with the further extension of the EU sanctions list, Belarus asked the head of the EU delegation and the Polish ambassador in Minsk to leave the capital. In response, all EU Member States recalled their ambassadors from Belarus.

Later in March, two men charged for organising the April 2011 terrorist attack on the Minsk metro were executed, following what was widely perceived as a flawed trial – not only by international observers but also by many Belarusians. In turn, the EU imposed additional restrictive measures against 12 individuals – increasing the total number of blacklisted persons to 231 – and against 32 companies, belonging *inter alia* to Belarusian oligarchs Yuri Chizh and Anatoly Ternavsky (Foreign Affairs Council 2012). At the end of 2012, diplomatic relations between the EU and Belarus suffered yet another blow, when a light aeroplane from Sweden crossed the state border to Belarus and dropped an estimated 800 stuffed teddy bears over Ivianets and Minsk, carrying freedom of speech messages, in response to which Belarus refused to renew the reaccreditation of the Swedish Ambassador in Minsk.

The Ukraine war in 2014: towards normalisation

The outbreak of the undeclared but *de facto* war in Eastern Ukraine in 2014, served as a catalyst for greater rapprochement between the EU and Belarus. In April 2014, the Prime Minister of Poland, Donald Tusk, initiated a phone call with President Lukashenka to discuss the 'international situation in the context of Ukrainian developments' (BISS 2014: 8–9). By early 2015, the majority of EU Member States agreed that restrictive measures against Belarus should be eased, once all remaining political prisoners in Belarus were released and rehabilitated.[6] Only a few EU diplomats still recalled the importance of democratic standards as a precondition for lifting EU sanctions.[7] Speaking in private, one high-ranking European official in Minsk even suggested that Lukashenka should send the remaining political prisoners for medical treatment abroad, to 'solve the problem' of political prisoners, while allowing the president to 'save face'.[8]

Clearly, attitudes of the EU-28 towards the regime in Minsk were changing quickly. In 2015, high-level representatives from the EU, including Latvian Foreign Minister, Edgars Rinkēvičs, and Commissioner for Enlargement and European Neighbourhood Policy, Johannes Hahn, held direct talks with Lukashenka in Minsk. At the same time, the policy approach and focus of the EU Delegation in Minsk began to change. As one EU official pointed out at the time, the delegation was 'finally' turning into a proper 'diplomatic actor' in Belarus, talking to the Belarusian government directly, instead of 'adding names' to a long but apparently futile list of civil society contacts.[9] The EU's efforts to normalise relations with Belarus provoked a positive response from the Belarusian side. In August 2015, Lukashenka authorised the release of several political prisoners, including former presidential candidate Mikalaj Statkievic. Irrespective of the fact that the released persons were not fully rehabilitated, Lukashenka's move triggered much enthusiasm among many EU Member States. Despite the flawed presidential elections on 11 October 2015,[10] the EU decided unanimously to first suspend and then lift almost all[11] restrictive measures against Belarus in February 2016 (Foreign Affairs Council 2016).

Explaining continuity and change in the EU's policy towards Belarus

This section zooms in on the role of the main driving forces behind the EU's policy towards Belarus, including: concerns for values and principles, such as human rights and democracy; economic and business interests; and geopolitical interests.

Concerns for values and principles

It is undeniable that the autocratic character of the Belarusian regime has acted as a constraint on diplomatic and economic engagement of the EU with the country. Retaining credibility in the eyes of the domestic electorate, for example, appears to have been a key motivation behind the German government's strong opposition to inviting Lukashenka to the EaP summit in May 2009. A cable from the US embassy in Berlin, cites officials from the German Chancellery, according to whom, such an invite would have helped 'neither Chancellor Merkel nor FM Steinmeier in a year with multiple European, national and regional elections' (US Embassy Cable 2009). The decision by the EU to impose sanctions on Belarus in 2011 was also clearly a response to the brutal crackdown on the opposition in the aftermath of the 2010 presidential elections. Several EU officials confirmed that the measure was mainly taken because the EU had to be seen to be doing 'something' to satisfy public expectations.[12]

Human rights considerations explain the overall limitations on the scope of EU–Belarus relations. Such considerations hardly explain the variation in the intensity of the EU's engagement with Belarus over the years. All authoritative democracy, human rights, and reform indexes suggest that little (if anything) has changed in Belarus during the past two decades.[13] The Polity IV Index[14] and the Bertelsmann Stiftung's Transformation Index (BTI)[15] have consistently ranked Belarus as an autocracy (repeated score of -7) and hard-line autocracy (repeated score of 5); the Political Terror Index indicates no improvements over the years (repeated score of 2.5) and Belarus' rating in the World Press Freedom Index[16] (154/157 of 180 since 2010) has also remained unchanged.

Economic interests

Trade between the EU and Belarus has been growing gradually over the past two decades, whereby the EU is Belarus's second most important trade partner after Russia. From 2002 until 2012, the value of exports from the EU to Belarus has grown faster than the value of Belarusian exports into the EU. Since 2013, EU exports to Belarus have been declining (Figure 26.1). The overall trends in EU–Belarus trade do not suggest significant correlations between political relations and the volume of imports/exports. The fact that trade with the EU has been growing steadily, regardless of Belarus' autocratic character (and despite the EU's restrictive measures), suggests that economic interests do play a role in the EU's policy towards the country. For example, significant parts of the gross domestic product of Lithuania and Latvia depend on transporting goods from Belarus, and especially on shipping oil products *via* the seaports of Klaipeda and Ventspils. A strong business lobby exists in both countries – led by a small but very influential group of large investors and oligarchs, including from Belarus – which has successfully mobilised public opinion and put pressure on the governments to prevent stricter EU economic sanctions against Belarus (Kłysiński 2013).

Economic interests also led the Slovenian government, in early 2012, to threaten to veto the inclusion of Belarusian oligarch Yury Chizh in the EU's sanction regime, because his companies have guaranteed the involvement of Slovenia's construction industry in lucrative real estate

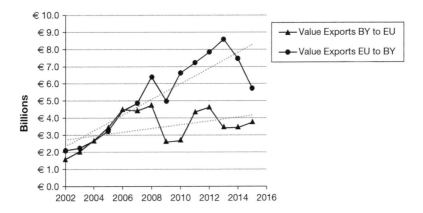

Figure 26.1 Trade volume: EU and Belarus 2002–2015
Source: Author's compilation of data from the European Commission Market Access Database (2016)

projects in Belarus (*The Economist* 2012). Belarusian oligarchs also maintain extensive business links with Latvia, Lithuania, Germany, the Netherlands, Poland and the Czech Republic (Rettman 2012) and have actively engaged in lobbying against the inclusion of certain individuals and entities on the EU sanctions list (Shapovalova 2015).

Economic interests have had a significant influence on EU sanctions against Belarus, ensuring that restrictions are not imposed on the main Belarusian exporters to EU markets (such as companies involved in the export of oil products) or Belarusian companies that do business in or with EU countries (such as construction industries). Yet, the EU's economic interests in Belarus remained limited overall. Between 2009 and 2015, Belarus rarely accounted for more than 0.3 per cent of the EU's total trade with outside partners (European Commission 2016). Economic interests could soften the EU's policy towards Belarus, but they are not sufficiently important to act as game changers in the EU's approach towards Belarus.

Geopolitical interests

The policy of the EU towards Belarus in the 1990s and early 2000s reflected a consensus among the 'old' EU Member States on non-interference into the Russian sphere of interest. That consensus was in large part conditioned by the legacy of the Cold War: a more active policy towards Belarus – either pushing for more democracy or for more engagement with the political elites – would have created unnecessary obstacles to the EU's relationship with Russia. With EU eastward enlargement, a group of states joined the EU who had different historical experiences with Russia, and who were primarily interested in seeking security from, rather than with, Russia. The 'new' Member States had little illusion that Russia would soon turn into a liberal democracy. Expanding NATO and the EU to Ukraine, Moldova and Belarus would at least create a 'pro-Western buffer zone' to what they perceived as an 'increasingly assertive Russia'.[17]

Against this background, the Russia–Georgia conflict, in August 2008, served as a catalyst for greater EU engagement with Belarus. The conflict exacerbated the security fears of the 'new' Member States, and especially the Baltics, while Germany – increasingly taking the lead in the EU's relations with Eastern Europe – grew more supportive of the EaP initiative including Belarus (Babayev 2014). Germany's relationship with Putin's Russia slightly cooled after Angela

Merkel became chancellor, and the war in Georgia prompted her to signal solidarity to the EaP countries, emphasising that they were 'free and independent countries' (Merkel quoted in Szabo 2015: 46). Most EU Member States, including Germany and France, subsequently backed the position that 'Belarusian recognition of the two break-away provinces in Georgia would cross a "red line" foreclosing the potential for Belarus to participate fully in the EaP' (US Embassy Cable 2009), which clearly underlined the relevance of geopolitics in the EU's engagement with Belarus.

Following Russia's annexation of the Crimean Peninsula in February 2014 and the outbreak of a *de facto* war in the eastern provinces of Ukraine, the EU once again moved towards normalising its relations with Belarus, including the decision in early 2016 to lift almost all sanctions against the country. The Baltic States had pushed hard for a greater engagement with Belarus with the aim of strengthening the country's autonomy *vis-à-vis* Russia (and *inter alia* prevent Russia from building an airbase in Belarus on the border with the EU). Germany remained committed to signalling solidarity with those in the EU advocating a tougher stance against Russia (Bierling 2014). At the same time, the German government was keen to control the EU's further engagement with Belarus, in order not to jeopardise the ongoing – and from the German point of view more important – process of normalising relations between the EU and Russia.

The analysis above has shown that values and principles have limited the overall scope for the EU's engagement with Belarus, and that powerful business interests have left a clear mark on the choice and scope of the EU's restrictive measures. Geopolitical interests had the strongest influence on determining the level of intensity of the EU's engagement with Belarus.

Impact and effectiveness of the EU's policy towards Belarus

The following section evaluates the effectiveness of the EU's policy and instruments to promote values and principles in Belarus and the effectiveness of the EU's pursuit of its geopolitical interests in Belarus.

The effectiveness of the EU's instruments for democracy promotion

The EU has developed several policy instruments to foster change in Belarus. It has complemented the restrictive measures imposed on the regime with instruments to support civil society and the people in Belarus.

Support for civil society: The EU, *inter alia*, included Belarus in the EaP Civil Society Forum (CSF)[18] in 2009, initiated the European Dialogue on Modernisation with Belarusian Society (EDM)[19] in 2012, re-engaged Belarus in a Human Rights Dialogue (HRD) in 2015, and financially assisted reform efforts through instruments such as the European Neighbourhood and Partnership Instrument (ENPI)[20] or the European Instrument for Democracy and Human Rights (EIDHR).

The CSF and EDM have been perceived by civil society organisations (CSOs) in Belarus as 'talking shops', lacking real influence,[21] whereas the HRD does not foresee the participation of civil society (Kozhukov 2015). Nevertheless, many civil society activists have confirmed that the CSF, and also partly the EDM, led to greater cooperation among civil society groups within Belarus (Bosse 2012).

EU financial assistance: The reach and impact of the EU's financial assistance on Belarusian civil society have been limited. A survey by the Konrad Adenauer Foundation in 2014 showed that most Belarusian CSOs had never applied for EU funds or been invited by the EU for consultations. Few CSOs believed that European integration (3 per cent) or international donors (11 per cent) had any influence on civil society in Belarus (Konrad Adenauer Stiftung 2014). This is not surprising, given the EU's limited financial assistance to Belarus overall. According to data available from the Commission's Financial Transparency System (European Commission 2015), between 2007 and 2014 a mere EUR20 million of assistance (EUR8 million national/EUR12 million regional allocations) has actually been disbursed to recipients in Belarus (Figure 26.2).[22] Belarusian recipients received no major funds from the EIDHR, except a EUR0.4 million grant disbursed in 2014 (EuropeAid 2015). Few political CSOs have benefited from larger EU funds, mostly channelled through the Office for a Democratic Belarus in Brussels.

EU restrictive measures: Most scholars and commentators agree that the EU's restrictive measures had no discernible impact on the Lukashenka regime (Gebert 2013; Gnedina 2005; Gaidelytė 2010). Others point out, that the sanctions are effective as a symbolic instrument to isolate Lukashenka internationally (Portela 2011), to keep important 'bargaining chips' *vis-à-vis* the regime (Giumelli 2013) or simply – as one EU official put it - to 'irritate' the Belarusian elites.[23] Most analysts highlight that the EU's sanctions have been too light to leave an impression on the regime. In addition, the poor – especially legal – design of the sanctions has damaged their effectiveness to an even greater extent as almost all the measures against Belarusian entities/companies had to be repealed because of successful legal actions taken by Belarusian oligarchs against the EU. In 2014 and 2015, the European Court of Justice (General Court) issued several judgements annulling restrictive measures against all Belarusian oligarchs and (most of) their companies because the Council had failed to present convincing evidence that they had financially supported the Lukashenka regime (Lester and O'Kane 2015).

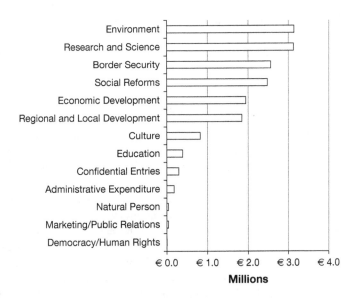

Figure 26.2 EU financial assistance Belarus: 2007–2014

Source: Author's own calculation based on data from the European Commission Financial Transparency System (2015). Funds awarded to beneficiaries in Belarus between 2007 and 2014.

The effectiveness of the EU's regional geopolitics

Evaluating the effectiveness of the EU's geopolitics is above all a question of which Member States – and whose geopolitical vision – prevail in the EU's policy towards the EaP region and, most importantly, towards Russia. Many signs point to the dominance of a pragmatic interest-based engagement with Belarus (Marin 2016), evidenced by the EU's decision to lift almost all restrictive measures on Belarus in early 2016 (Foreign Affairs Council 2016).

Those writing in the realist school of International Relations are likely to judge the pragmatic approach effective, arguing that the 'West' should long have recognised that it has no role to play in Russia's sphere of interest, and that any attempt to change the status quo in the region (through initiatives such as North Atlantic Treaty Organization (NATO) enlargement or the EaP) will upset the great power balance and subsequently lead to greater instability and insecurity in Europe (Mearsheimer 2014).

In contrast, those who argue that European security is best achieved through the gradual expansion of liberal democracy and who see Russia as a 'revisionist power', challenging the liberal internationalist world order (Mead 2014), are likely to regard the pragmatic approach as wholly ineffective: with Russia increasingly challenging the status quo in the EaP countries, it will eventually strive to incorporate Belarus into its sphere of interest unless the EU takes more concerted steps to contain Russian influence in the region overall.

Lukashenka himself prefers a pragmatic engagement with the EU, which is a view partly reflected in public opinion.[24] After the annexation of Crimea and the war in Eastern Ukraine, Lukashenka has been very keen to promote a foreign policy of active neutrality, functioning as a bridge between Russia's and the EU's competing integration projects (Jarábik and Melyantsou 2015; Sahm 2015). From this perspective, the EU's pragmatic approach (no active democratisation but still financial assistance, no substantial economic/legal integration but more trade relations) appears to match Lukashenka's vision of neutrality. Yet, many observers remain unconvinced about Belarus's alleged neutrality and the West's 'general illusion that the Belarusian leadership needs help to fend off the external threat from Russia' (Jurkonis 2015). They argue that Belarus is hardly neutral, given Russia's deeply rooted and profound influence on Belarus' economy and military.[25] Thus, the main function of the 'illusion of neutrality' is to attract the West's attention and (IMF) funds to keep the highly deficient state-run economy afloat.

Conclusions

Belarus's autocratic character and its image as the 'last dictatorship in Europe' have posed significant normative constraints on the EU's relations with the country over the past decades. The EU's emphatic advocacy of a principled approach towards Belarus – an approach partly motivated by the EU's desire to retain credibility *vis-à-vis* domestic publics – has clearly limited its engagement with Lukashenka in general. Yet, it is powerful business interests and especially regional geopolitics *vis-à-vis* the Russian Federation that have influenced the intensity and effectiveness of the EU's relations with the country. The outbreak of the *de facto* war in the eastern provinces of Ukraine in 2014 served as a catalyst for a (limited) normalisation of relations between the EU and Belarus. The future of EU–Belarus relations is, however, inextricably linked to the EU's relations with Russia,[26] on the one hand, and to Russia's policy towards Belarus on the other. If *realpolitik* becomes the sole basis of regional inter-state relations, EU–Belarus relations are likely to remain limited, and will deteriorate further should Russia seek to further integrate Belarus into its sphere of interest. The relationship between the EU and Belarus might therefore best be understood as a relationship *in custodia* (warded) by regional geopolitics.

Notes

1 The author would like to thank the editors of this handbook for their helpful and constructive comments that greatly contributed to improving the final version of this chapter. This work was supported by the Netherlands Organisation for Scientific Research (NWO) under VENI Research Grant Ref. 451-12-015.
2 Interviews by the author with EU officials and EU Member State officials in Brussels, May 2006.
3 Interviews by the author with EU officials and EU Member State officials in Brussels, May 2010.
4 Ibid.
5 Ibid.
6 EU officials have provided different accounts of the number of political prisoners in Belarus, ranging from five to thirteen (Kobzova 2013).
7 Interviews by the author with EU Member State officials in Minsk, February 2015.
8 Interview by the author with a European official in Minsk, February 2015.
9 Interview by the author with an EU official in Minsk, February 2015.
10 The International Election Observation Mission concluded that 'Belarus still has a considerable way to go in meeting its OSCE commitments for democratic elections' (IEOM 2015: 1), thus issuing exactly the same verdict as for the 2010 presidential elections.
11 The EU retained restrictive measures against four members of Lukashenka's security service suspected of involvement in the disappearance of four political opponents in 1999–2000.
12 Interviews by the author with EU officials in Brussels, May 2012, see also Bosse (2012).
13 For a more optimistic outlook on Belarus's future democratisation, see Potocki (2011).
14 The index measures a scale from 10 (full democracy) to -10 (autocracy) (Polity IV Index 2015).
15 The index measures: quality of democracy, market economy, political management (1=democracy in consolidation; 5=hard-line autocracy). Bertelsmann Stiftung's Transformation Index (BTI) (2016).
16 The index measures a scale from 1 (best press freedom scores) downwards. World Press Freedom Index (2014).
17 Polish diplomats quoted in Nielsen (2012: 1).
18 The EaP CSF is a regional platform of 700 Civil Society Organisations (CSOs) from the EaP.
19 The EDM is a platform for the EU and Belarusian CSOs to discuss the modernisation of Belarus.
20 Since 2014, renamed European Neighbourhood Instrument (ENI).
21 Interviews by the author with representatives of Belarusian civil society in Minsk, February 2015.
22 The EU has disbursed funds for Belarus worth EUR50 million between 2007 and 2014: 20 projects (excluding FP7/Horizon, EIDHR, NSA-LA, ENI Civil Society grants), of which EUR8 million was disbursed to recipients in Belarus (EuropeAid 2015).
23 Interview by the author with an EU official in Brussels, May 2012.
24 According to national surveys, Belarusians have a low level of trust towards the 'West'. In 2010–2011 only 20 per cent assessed EU–Belarus relations as equal/mutually beneficial, with over 30 per cent indicating that relations are based on EU interests (Rotman and Veremeeva 2011).
25 For a detailed assessment of Belarus–Russia relations, see Marples (2013), Vysotskaya Guedes Vieira (2014) or Wilson (2014).
26 For an excellent discussion of EU Member States' positions on Russia, see Schmidt-Felzmann (2014).

References

Babayev, A. (2014) 'Democracy Promotion Between the "Political" and the "Developmental" Approach: US and German Policies Towards Belarus', *Democratization* 21(5): 937–957.
Bertelsmann Stiftung's Transformation Index (BTI) (2016) *Report*, Gütersloh: Bertelsmann Stiftung. www.bti-project.org/en/index, accessed 26 May 2016.
Bierling, S. (2014) *Vormacht Wider Willen? Deutsche Außenpolitik von der Wiedervereinigung bis zur Gegenwart*, München: C.H. Beck.
BISS (2014) *Belarus Foreign Policy Index* 19, Vilnius: Belarusian Institute for Strategic Studies.
Bosse, G. (2012) 'A Partnership with Dictatorship: Explaining the Paradigm Shift in European Union Policy towards Belarus', *Journal of Common Market Studies* 50(3): 367–384.
Commission of the European Communities (2003a) *Wider Europe-Neighbourhood: A New Framework for Relations with our Eastern and Southern Neighbours*, COM(2003) 104 final, Brussels, 11 March.

Commission of the European Communities (2003b) Declaration by the Presidency on behalf of the European Union regarding the media situation in Belarus, *Press Release*, 10599/03, Brussels, 25 June.

EuropeAid (2015) Database of 'Calls for Proposals & Procurement Notices' Administered by the European Commission, Brussels. https://webgate.ec.europa.eu/europeaid/online-services/index.cfm?do=publi.welcome&userlanguage=en, accessed 21 March 2016.

European Commission (2015) Database of Beneficiaries of EU Funding Administered by the European Commission. http://ec.europa.eu/budget/fts/index_en.htm, accessed 21 March 2016.

European Commission (2016) *European Union: Trade in Goods with Belarus*, Brussels, 21 June.

European Commission Financial Transparency System (2015) Data on Funds Awarded to Beneficiaries in Belarus 2007–2014. http://ec.europa.eu/budget/fts/index_en.htm, accessed 18 March 2015.

European Commission Market Access Data Base (2016) European Union Trade in Goods with Belarus. http://madb.europa.eu/madb/indexPubli.htm, accessed 21 November 2016.

Foreign Affairs Council (2011a) *3065th Council Meeting: Foreign Affairs*, 5888/1/11 REV 1 (Presse 16), Brussels, 31 January.

Foreign Affairs Council (2011b) *3101st Council Meeting: Foreign Affairs*, 11824/11 (Presse 181), Luxembourg, 20 June.

Foreign Affairs Council (2011c) *3117th Council Meeting: Foreign Affairs*, 15309/11 (Presse 357), Luxembourg, 10 October.

Foreign Affairs Council (2012) *3157th Council Meeting: Foreign Affairs*, 7849/12 (Presse 117), Brussels, 22 and 23 March.

Foreign Affairs Council (2016) *3447th Council Meeting: Foreign Affairs*, 6122/16 (Presse 6), Brussels, 15 February.

Gaidelytė, R. (2010) 'The Link Between the EU Sanctions and Repressions in Belarus', *Lithuanian Foreign Policy Review* 24: 41–80.

Gebert, K. (2013) 'Shooting in the Dark?: EU Sanctions Policies', *Policy Brief* 71, European Council on Foreign Relations, London, January.

General Affairs and External Relations Council (2008) *2902nd Meeting of the Council General Affairs and External Relations*, 15394/08 (Presse 318), Brussels, 10 November.

General Affairs Council (1997) *2027th Council Meeting: General Affairs*, 10368/97 (Presse 269), Brussels, 15 September.

Giumelli, A. (2013) *The Success of Sanctions: Lessons Learned from the EU Experience*, Surrey: Ashgate Publishing.

Gnedina, E. (2005) 'Success and Failure of EU Policies in Ukraine and Belarus', *EuroJournal.org—Journal of Foreign Policy of Moldova* 2(9), Frankfurt am Main: Central and Eastern European Online Library.

IEOM (2015) *Republic of Belarus—Presidential Election 11 October 2015: Statement of Preliminary Findings*, OSCE/ODIHR, Minsk, 12 October.

Jarábik, B. and Melyantsou, D. (2015) 'Is Change on the Way for Lukashenko's Belarus?', Moscow, 14 October. www.themoscowtimes.com/opinion/article/is-change-on-the-way-for-lukashenkos-belarus/539099.html, accessed 18 January 2016.

Jarábik, B. and Rabagliat, A. (2007) 'Buffer Rus: New Challenges for EU Policy Towards Belarus', *Working Paper*, FRIDE, Madrid, March.

Jurkonis, V. (2015) 'The Three Myths Shaping EU Policy on Belarus', Freedom At Issue Blog, 20 May. https://freedomhouse.org/blog/three-myths-shaping-eu-policy-belarus, accessed 17 January 2016.

Kaminska, J. (2014) *Poland and EU Enlargement*, New York: Palgrave Macmillan.

Kłysiński, K. (2013) 'No Other Choice but Co-operation: The Background of Lithuania's and Latvia's Relations with Belarus', *OSW Commentary* 99, Centre for Eastern Studies, Warsaw.

Kobzova, J. (2013) 'Counting Belarus' Political Prisoners', European Council on Foreign Relations, 8 June. www.ecfr.eu/blog/entry/counting_belarus_political_prisoners, accessed 9 June 2016.

Konrad Adenauer Stiftung (2014) *Mapping Study—Belarus Civil Society Organizations in Cross-Sectoral Dialogue: Summary of Legal Environment Research and Expert Survey*, Minsk: Konrad Adenauer Stiftung.

Kozhukov, S. (2015) 'We have Fears that Belarus-EU Dialog on Human Rights will be a Mere Imitation', *EuroBelarus*, Vilnius, 31 June. http://en.eurobelarus.info/news/politics/2015/07/31/aliaksei-kazliuk-we-have-fears-that-belarus-eu-dialog-on-human.html, accessed 17 May 2016.

Lester, M. and O'Kane, M. (2015) 'EU Court Annuls Sanctions on the Belarus Football Club Dinamo Minsk & Yury Chyzh', European Sanctions Blog, London, 7 October. https://europeansanctions.com/2015/10/07/eu-court-annuls-sanctions-on-the-belarus-football-club-dinamo-minsk-yury-chyzh, accessed 17 January 2016.

Marin, A. (2016) 'Belarus: Time for a "Principled" Re-engagement', *Brief* 6/2016, European Union Institute for Security Studies, Paris.

Marples, D. (2013) 'Between the EU and Russia: Geopolitical Games in Belarus', *The Journal of Belarusian Studies* 7(1): 38–68.

Mead, W. (2014) 'The Return of Geopolitics', *Foreign Affairs* 93(3): 69–79.

Mearsheimer, J. (2014) 'Why the Ukraine Crisis Is the West's Fault', *Foreign Affairs* 93(5): 77–89.

Nielsen, N. (2012) 'Belarus: A Look Inside Europe's "Last Dictatorship"', *EU Observer*, Brussels, 20 March. https://euobserver.com/belarus/115635, accessed 17 May 2016.

Piontek, E. (2006) 'Belarus', in Blockmans S. and Lazowski, A. (eds.) *The European Union and Its Neighbours*, The Hague: TMC Asser Press, 531–547.

Polity IV Index (2015) Polity IV Project: Political Regime Characteristics and Transitions: 1800–2013, Authority Trends Belarus, Center for Systemic Peace, Vienna. www.systemicpeace.org/polity/blr2.htm, accessed 10 January 2016.

Portela, C. (2011) 'The European Union and Belarus: Sanctions and Partnership', *Comparative European Politics* 9(4): 486–505.

Potocki, R. (2011) 'Belarus: A Tale of Two Elections', *Journal of Democracy* 22(3): 49–63.

Rettman, A. (2012) 'Slovenia Shields Belarus Oligarch from EU Blacklist', *EU Observer*, Brussels, 24 February. https://euobserver.com/foreign/115361, accessed 17 May 2016.

Rotman, D. and Veremeeva, N. (2011) 'Belarus in the Context of the Neighbourhood Policy: Between the EU and Russia', *Journal of Communist Studies and Transition Politics* 27(1): 73–98.

Sahm, A. (2015) 'Die EU Muss auf Weißrussland Zugehen', *Euractiv*, London, 13 October. www.euractiv.de/sections/eu-aussenpolitik/die-eu-muss-auf-weissrussland-zugehen-318465, accessed 16 May 2016.

Schmidt-Felzmann, A. (2014) 'Is the EU's Failed Relationship with Russia the Member States' Fault?', *L'Europe en Formation* 374: 40–60.

Shapovalova, N. (2015) 'Advocacy and Interest Group Influence in EU Foreign Policy', *Thesis Manuscript*, Coventry: The University of Warwick Institutional Repository.

Szabo, S. (2015) *Germany, Russia and the Rise of Geo-Economics*, London: Bloomsbury Academic.

The Economist (2012) 'Slovenia and Belarus: Heartbreak Hotel', Brussels, 28 February.

US Embassy Cable (2009) 'Germany: Not Pushing for Lukashenka Invite to EU Summit in May', 13 March. https://wikileaks.org/plusd/cables/09BERLIN301_a.html, accessed 16 May 2016.

Vysotskaya Guedes Vieira, A. (2014) 'The Politico-Military Alliance of Russia and Belarus: Re-Examining the Role of NATO and the EU in Light of the Intra-Alliance Security Dilemma', *Europe-Asia Studies* 66(4): 557–577.

Wilson, A. (2014) 'Belarus Wants Out: One of Russia's Closest European Allies Begins to Play the Field', *Snapshot*, Council on Foreign Relations, 20 March.

World Press Freedom Index (2014) *Report*, Reporters Without Borders, Paris. http://rsf.org/index2014/en-index2014.php, accessed 10 January 2016.

27

THE EUROPEAN NEIGHBOURHOOD POLICY AND MOLDOVA

A resilient oligarchic system wedged between the EU and Russia

Florent Parmentier

Introduction

The European Neighbourhood Policy (ENP) was designed to address security, political and economic challenges at the EU's borders by strengthening relations with its eastern neighbours. As the EU Global Strategy asserts, it is in the EU's interests to invest in the resilience of states and societies – the ability of states and society to reform, or to withstand and recover from internal and external crisis (European External Action Service 2016). Moldova, a tiny country sandwiched between Romania and Ukraine, with no previous existence before 1991, has progressively generated security- and stability-related concerns in Brussels. This country has been suffering from an unresolved conflict in the East (Transnistria), weak and corrupted state institutions and organised crime at the EU border, thus undermining the EU's security.

The ENP can be said to be a case of EU external governance, which revolves around the selective extension of certain EU norms, rules and policies – the legal boundary – while precluding possible membership – the institutional boundary (Lavenex 2004). From this perspective, the case of Moldova demonstrates that various factors, such as the interests of the Moldovan government (Hagemann 2013), the state capacity or the regional geopolitical peculiarities of the EU's eastern neighbourhood (linked with Russia's policy and influence) determine the nature of EU–Moldova relations. In other words, local actors have often been supportive of Moldova's European integration process, at least rhetorically, while resisting many of its implications on issues such as 'state capture', transparency or corruption.

The chapter examines how the various domestic and external factors have influenced the emergence of EU–Moldova relations (2003–2009) and how this relationship has evolved in the context of the development of the Eastern Partnership (EaP) (2009–2016).

The ENP and Moldova (2003–2009): an emerging relationship

Before Moldova was among the first countries to be included in the ENP in 2003, the EU and Moldova had limited relations (Shapovalova and Boonstra 2012). The ENP has undoubtedly contributed to the establishment of new and wide-ranging relations between both entities in the realms of economics and security.

Establishing new relations between the EU and Moldova

The initial ENP framework 'Wider Europe-Neighbourhood: A New Framework for Relations with our Eastern and Southern Neighbours' (Commission of the European Communities 2003) proposed an upgraded toolbox and the provision of additional resources in the framework of the EU's emerging relations with Moldova, but ignored the question of EU membership. In June 2001, Moldova has been included in the Stability Pact for South-East Europe, but was denied the implicit 'potential candidate' status enjoyed by the countries of the Western Balkans and the possibility of concluding a Stabilization and Association Agreement. In the ENP framework, membership was neither promised to neighbouring countries nor excluded.

An improvement in cooperation resulted in the adoption of the EU–Moldova Action Plan (Commission of the European Communities 2005), signed in February 2005, shortly before Moldova held its legislative elections in March. This political document outlined a series of strategic objectives and commitments in various spheres and imposed on Moldova reforms in political, security, economic and cultural arenas. Some eighty objectives were defined across seven areas: political dialogue and reform; cooperation for the settlement of the Transnistrian conflict; economic and social reform, as well as development; trade-related issues, market and regulatory reform; cooperation in justice and home affairs; transport, energy, telecommunications, environment and research, development and innovation; and finally people-to-people contacts. The Action Plan introduced the principle of soft conditionality in EU–Moldova relations.

In March 2005, the incumbent Party of Communists of the Republic of Moldova (hereafter PCRM), elected four years earlier on a pro-Russian platform (Quinlan 2004), secured a second victory when it obtained nearly 46 per cent of the votes in the legislative elections and a majority of seats (56 out of 101). Their turn towards deeper cooperation with the EU was supported by several opposition parties at the time, which contributed to the re-election of the incumbent, President Vladimir Voronin (Popescu 2012). A few months later, in October 2005, the European Commission inaugurated a Delegation in Moldova to raise the EU's visibility. In terms of financial aid, trade and freedom of movement, the EU granted significant benefits to Moldova. After the adoption of the EU's new financial instrument – the European Neighbourhood and Partnership Instrument (ENPI) – in 2007, Moldova became the top recipient of EU aid per capita among the EU's eastern neighbours, ranking second overall after the Palestinian Authority (European Commission 2008). One year later, the EU introduced autonomous trade preferences for Moldova, providing unlimited and duty-free access to EU markets for all Moldovan products – except for agricultural products concerned with sanitary and phytosanitary standards – in exchange for an upgrading of Moldova's certification and customs controls systems (European Commission 2007a). About mobility, a crucial issue for Moldova due to the size of its diaspora (Mosneaga 2007),[1] Moldova was the first country in which the EU established a Common Visa Application Centre in 2007 (European Commission 2007b). Subsequently, Moldova was among the first ENP countries to sign a Mobility Partnership in June 2008, whose aim is to ensure a new management of migration flows (Council of the European Union 2008). The same month,

Voronin declared his hope that Moldova would benefit from an Association Agreement (AA) that stipulated a membership perspective (Botan 2008). In October 2008, the two parties signed a visa facilitation agreement along with an agreement on the readmission of illegal migrants (Council of the European Union 2008).

This is when the EU Council agreed to replace the Partnership and Cooperation Agreement (which expired the same year) with an AA that envisages trade and visa liberalisation. The conclusion of such an AA, however, was made conditional on the promise that the Moldovan authorities would ensure free and fair elections in Spring 2009, making these a test case for the reform willingness of the Moldovan political elite.

The case of Transnistria and security cooperation

Beyond the agreed intensification of political and economic cooperation, Moldova and the EU have managed to strengthen their security cooperation, notably on the Transnistrian conflict.

Transnistria is an independent *de facto* state (Pegg 1998; Lynch 2004)[2], located between the left bank of the Dniestr and the eastern Moldovan border with Ukraine, populated by half a million inhabitants. This thin strip of land emerged after a small-scale conflict, which has involved the Soviet Fourteenth Guard Army, and was frozen by the Yeltsin–Snegur agreement of 1992. Transnistria is considered a 'frozen conflict'[3] that has remained unresolved, despite an enduring negotiation process under the aegis of the Organization for Security and Cooperation in Europe (OSCE). Russia officially recognises the integrity of the Moldovan territory, but supports the separatists in Transnistria through several channels (including military presence, diplomatic actions in the framework of the OSCE and elsewhere, financial resources and economic investments and support in building institutions) (Popescu 2006). The region has also been characterised by its 'contraband capitalism' (Luke and Toal 1998; Parmentier 2006), where close links between political, criminal and business elites have led to the status quo. Transnistria has frequently been cited as a hub for all kinds of illicit trafficking, such as arms, human beings and drugs (Molcean and Verständig 2014).

Against this backdrop, the EU started engaging with the Transnistrian conflict only in 2003, taking many steps towards an increased involvement ever since. The main driver of this action was the perspective of EU enlargement in 2004, as well as Romania's accession to the EU in 2007 – supposedly Moldova's most important neighbour. To put some pressure on Transnistrian top officials, the EU started to act coercively with a travel ban imposed on 17 representatives of the Tiraspol leadership (Council of the European Union 2003). To raise its profile and the coherence of its policy, in 2005, the EU appointed a Special Representative for the Transnistrian conflict, Adriaan Jacobovits de Szeged. Later, the EU also became the most important contributor and initiator of confidence-building measures between Chisinau and Tiraspol, implementing a large programme jointly with UNDP Moldova: 'Support to Confidence Building Measures' (Transnistrian Dialogues 2014).

Yet, the most wide-ranging EU initiative regarding the conflict is the creation of the European Union Border Assistance Mission (EUBAM), which was launched in November 2005 (Vahl 2005). Promoting border control, customs, trade norms and practices that meet EU standards, one of EUBAMs main objectives was to control the trafficking occurring at the border with Ukraine, while improving governance through socialisation with EU actors. It has also brought Transnistrian businesses closer to the EU to favour rapprochement with Moldova, attracted by a more comprehensive access to the EU's market (Parmentier 2008). Due to EUBAM operations, several hundred Transnistrian companies have registered with the State Register Chamber of Moldova to gain access to EU markets, thus benefiting from EU trade preferences. Yet, despite the EU's economic attraction and the change of the Transnistrian leadership in December 2011, with Yevgeny Shevchuk replacing the founding President Igor Smirnov and, subsequently in December 2016, with Vadim Krasnosielski replacing Shevchuk, Transnistrian foreign policy has remained unchanged and oriented towards Russia and the Eurasian Economic Union (EEU) (Kosienkowski 2012). Overall, EUBAM is generally considered as a successful mission, but pervasive corruption appears to have been a major obstacle for the mission achieving its aims, while its contribution to the resolution of the Transnistrian conflict is mainly limited to technical – as opposed to political – aspects (Kurowska and Tallis 2009).

Later, in May 2012, Moldova and the EU started to discuss cooperation in the field of Common Security and Defence Policy (CSDP) and Common Foreign and Security Policy (CFSP), as the AA contains a reference to these policies. From this perspective, Moldova agreed to participate in EU civilian and military missions – for example, in the EU Mission to strengthen regional maritime capacity in the countries of the Horn of Africa (Tigui 2013). In exchange for Moldova's participation in the CSDP and CFSP, Moldovan leaders inevitably expect stronger EU involvement in resolving the Transnistrian issue.

The Eastern Partnership (EaP) and Moldova (2009–2016)

The EaP was launched in 2009, with the objective to supplement the ENP and enable political and economic integration in the absence of any perspective of enlargement. In the meantime, EU–Moldova relations have been largely influenced by the evolution of Chisinau's political system and its inability to cope with the various challenges of implementing the (AA), notably the Deep and Comprehensive Free Trade Agreement (DCFTA), arguably the most powerful tool of EU external governance *vis-à-vis* Moldova.

Moldova's hybrid regime and European integration

Political transition is a centrepiece of the EaP, as this framework is based on EaP countries' commitment to political principles and values, such as democracy, rule of law and respect for human rights. Hence, the success of the EaP depends on the nature of neighbours' political system, and – as far as Moldova is concerned – on the role of oligarchic structures in the political system.

Over the last quarter of a century, Moldova's regime trajectory has oscillated between authoritarian and democratic tendencies, being characterised as a 'hybrid regime'. Moldova's hybrid regime has 'acquired some of the characteristic institutions and procedures of democracy, but not others, and, at the same time, [has . . .] retained some authoritarian or traditional features' (Morlino 2008: 7). The Moldovan political and economic landscape should also be understood through the prism of 'state capture', in which 'so-called oligarchs manipulat[e] policy formation and even shap[e] the emerging rules of the game to their own, very substantial advantage' (Hellman Kaufmann 2001; Calus 2015). To date, the oligarchic structures prove resilient in Moldovan policy-making, largely influencing EU–Moldova relations negatively.

In the year preceding the April 2009 parliamentary elections, the government took a series of steps to create an 'uneven playing field' (Levitsky and Way 2010) – applying the use of administrative resources, amending the electoral law or harassing and intimidating opposition candidates. In the end, according to the Central Electoral Commission, the PCRM was declared the winner with 49.48 per cent of the votes (the turnout was 59 per cent), obtaining 60 seats (out of 101). As the presidential elections require a three-fifth majority in the Parliament (61 deputies), the PCRM needed just one representative to secure the vote. Yet, the opposition, as well as thousands of citizens, contested the validity of the results. On 7 April 2009, one day after the elections, rioters attacked the parliament building and the presidential office, starting the so-called 'Twitter Revolution' (Cibotaru 2010). The Communists declared that a *coup-d'etat* was fomented by Romanian authorities and opposition parties and started a series of counter-measures to restore order. While the European Commission recognised the official election results, Members of the European Parliament soon became critical of the government-led campaign of harassment and the systematic violation of human rights (European Parliament 2009).

In the aftermath of the April events, several opposition parties founded the Alliance for European Integration (AEI) and started to work together under the leadership of Vlad Filat; their alliance won a relative majority in July 2009 (53 out of 101, with no possibility of electing a President) and was confirmed after another vote in November 2010. In the meantime, the AEI sent signals to Brussels, increasingly branding Moldova as an EaP 'success story' (Boonstra 2011), thanks to a mix of domestic reforms and a carefully crafted public relations campaign in Brussels. In 2013 and 2014, Moldova ranked first in the European Integration Index for Eastern Partnership Countries (European Integration Index for Eastern Partnership Countries 2014), surpassing Ukraine and Georgia. Yet, the process of reforms has stalled after the demise of Vlad Filat in April 2013, due to endemic elite corruption implicating almost the entire state (Rinnert 2013). Prime Minister Vlad Filat (September 2009 – April 2013) had to step down in April 2013 due to a motion of censure, following charges of corruption, abuse of power and influence peddling. He was replaced by Iurie Leanca (April 2013 – February 2015) who, despite his victory in the parliamentary elections of November 2014, could not maintain his position either. In 2015, political instability reached a peak, with five new heads of government in just a few months: Chiril Gaburici (February 2015), Natalia Gherman (June 2015), Valeriu Strelet (July 2015), Gheorge Brega (October 2015) and Pavel Filip (January 2016) successively became heads of government.

In turn, the self-proclaimed pro-European parties have been part of an oligarchic system, as their interests have not necessarily been in line with the EU model of governance. Under the AEI, state institutions have been subordinated to the leaders of the parties included in the coalition, that is, Vlad Filat (the leader of the Liberal Democratic Party of Moldova) and Vlad Plahotniuc (a billionaire who *de facto* controls the Democratic Party of Moldova) (Calus 2015). The implementation of the AA requires key reforms concerning, among others, the judiciary, the financial sector and the process of de-politicisation of state institutions. Between 2009 and 2014, Moldova fell from 89 to 103 in Transparency International's Corruption Perceptions Index (Transparency International 2014). The extent to which elite corruption is pervasive came particularly to the fore in late 2014, when around US$1 billion (nearly 15 per cent of Moldova's GDP) – in non-performing loans made to people connected with the country's political elite, that is, Vlad Filat, Vlad Plahotniuc and Ilan Shor (Calus 2015) – disappeared from three Moldovan banks (Banca de Economii, Banca Sociala and Unibank). Filat and Plahotniuc have been both business and political competitors, until former Prime Minister Vlad Filat's arrest in Parliament on 15 October 2015. The arrest, supposedly orchestrated by Plahotniuc, has led him to consolidate his dominant position in the Moldovan political system, unprecedented since 1991, through control of the state apparatus, control of part of the Moldovan press, and parts of the political elite and financial power (Calus 2016).

The resilient oligarchic features within the AEI have tarnished the reputation of the European idea in Moldova, linking it with corrupted officials rather than a better model of governance, giving more political space for pro-Russian politicians. As an example, a referendum was organised (illegally according to Chisinau) in Gagauzia[4] in February 2014 on the issues of European integration and relations with Russia. The results showed an overwhelming majority in favour of the EEU (98 per cent); 97.2 per cent were against a closer EU integration; in addition,

98.9 per cent of voters supported Gagauzia's right to declare independence, should Moldova lose or surrender its own independence to Romania (Ursu and Raileanu 2014). In the meantime, support for the EU in Moldova plummeted from 78 per cent in 2007 to 40 per cent in 2015 and to less than 40 per cent in 2016, according to an opinion poll carried out by the Institute for Public Policy (Higgins 2015) and the US-based National Democratic Institute. A significant part of the Moldovan public has a pro-Russian orientation, favouring integration with the EEU. As a result, the Party of Socialists, led by Igor Dodon, who openly met with Vladimir Putin during the Russian presidential campaign in the run up to the November 2014 elections (Russian Presidency 2014), reached first place with more than 20.5 per cent of the vote, while Renato Usatii – a Russian-Moldovan tycoon and leader of Our Party – was elected in June 2015 as mayor of Balti, the second city of the country. The pro-Russian electorate also remains strong in the north of Moldova, in the countryside and among pensioners.

The pro-European segment of Moldovan society proves to be unsatisfied with the pro-European coalition that has been ruling in different formations since 2009. In the context of the 'stolen billion' scandal, 'Dignity and Truth' – a social movement composed of political analysts, journalists and lawyers – emerged in 2015, and ever since has organised large anti-government demonstrations (Solovyev 2015). The paradox of the situation lies in the fact that 'Dignity and Truth', a pro-EU social movement, has contested a self-proclaimed pro-European coalition of parties (AEI), thus indirectly contributing to a situation in which the European idea in Moldova has become increasingly discredited.

The AA, the DCFTA and the transformation of the Moldovan economy

The DCFTA is an essential part of the EU–Moldova AA, aiming at the mutual opening of the two parties' markets for goods and services, based on stipulated and enforceable trade rules. As such, it is considered a powerful tool of external governance, as it is supposed to foster modernisation of the Moldovan economy through legal approximation.

A DCFTA is less about customs tariffs and quotas than about an extensive legal approximation of laws, norms and regulations in various trade-related sectors, including service sector liberalisation, public procurement and competition policy. The Moldovan regulatory system must approximate, adopt, implement and enforce a series of EU norms and standards, including sanitary and phytosanitary norms for agricultural products, competition law, regulations on public procurement and intellectual property rights. The adoption and implementation of standards and norms is costly but, in return, the EU promises to gradually provide Moldova with access to the European Single Market. Moldova, a member of the WTO since July 2001, has also benefited from EU institution-building assistance to strengthen Moldovan state capacity to implement reforms, benefit fully from the EU's autonomous trade preferences regime since 2008, offering Chisinau improved access to EU markets for specific products (such as wine, vegetables and fruits). Thanks to these exceptions, the EU has become Moldova's most important trade partner, even before the AA was provisionally applied in September 2014, accounting for 46.4 per cent, before Russia (21.9 per cent) and Ukraine (11.8 per cent) (European Commission 2015).

The DCFTA offers further access to European markets in exchange for an implementation of EU norms and standards by Moldovan economic and political actors. The reforms should help to improve the business climate, making it more competitive and attractive for European and foreign investments. Though Moldova experienced the highest growth rate in Europe (9.4 per cent) in 2013 (World Bank 2016), it is still characterised according to international organisations by a considerable lack of competitiveness, lacking modern infrastructure in terms of transportation systems (World Economic Forum 2015)[5] and logistics (World Bank 2014)[6]. Its agriculture is largely directed towards the markets of the Commonwealth of Independent States (CIS), as the sector faces difficulties in adapting to EU sanitary and phytosanitary as well as food safety norms and standards. The main natural resources (water, forests and soils), as well as imported resources, are not properly managed.

At the same time, Russia's share in Moldova's exports has decreased both due to Moldova's attempts to diversify its trade partners (already a few years after its independence) and due to 'unclear rules of the game in bilateral trade' (Popa 2015). Yet, Russia remains an important partner for Moldova in several ways. First, Russia is still attracting the highest number of Moldovan migrants, who, *via* their remittances, are crucial contributors to the Moldovan economy and the GDP (Mosneaga 2012), though this share has been in decline in recent years due to the depreciation of the ruble since the beginning of 2014 (Ratha, Wyss and Yousefi 2014). Second, Russia remains a crucial market for several key sectors of Moldova's economy, such as wines and liqueurs, medication and fruit. This explains why Russian authorities have imposed several import restrictions on Moldovan goods (wine, processed pork, fruit and canned vegetables, etc.) even before the AA came into force (Calus 2014). Third, Moldova remains heavily dependent on Russia for its energy mix, as (Russian) gas accounts for 65 per cent of its energy consumption (Barbarosie and Coalson 2014). As domestic gas production covers only 1 per cent of the demand, even though Moldova became a full member of the European Energy Community in May 2010, Moldova has been totally dependent on gas imports from Russia[7] (Puiu 2014). Fourth, Russia is a key source of foreign direct investment in the most important industrial enterprises of the Transnistrian region (Chirila 2013).

Though Moldova has reoriented its trade toward the European Single Market, the transformation of the Moldovan economy along the EU model is still an ongoing process, partly contradicted by Russian policies.

Conclusions: Moldova and the ENP at the crossroads

Since the start of the ENP in 2003, Moldova's political system has been characterised as a case of 'pluralism by default' (Way 2003), as leaders failed to draw sufficiently on state capacities to rig elections, impose censorship or even repress the opposition to impose authoritarianism. At the same time, state capture has thwarted the development of a stable democratic system, based on the rule of law (Parmentier 2014), able to cope with all the obligations required in the framework of the ENP.

Moldova has been considered the 'poster child' of the EaP since 2009 (Rinnert 2013), but the 'stolen billion' scandal of 2014 has tarnished Moldova's reputation in Brussels and its European ambition. The Moldovan presidential elections of November 2016 have resulted in the election of a new president, Socialist Party leader Igor Dodon, who has advocated changes in Moldova's foreign policy regarding Russia, the EU and Transnistria. Yet, given the country's parliamentary system and the political and cultural divides within Moldovan society, any radical change in this regard (such as a full membership of the EEU) would inevitably raise the level of tension among the political elite and the public.

Back in 2001, in the context of the parliamentary elections, President Voronin campaigned on a strong pro-Russia platform, whereas four years later, displaying a great degree of pragmatism, he campaigned on a pro-Europe ticket. Looking towards the future, it is likely that the new Moldovan president will adopt a similar 'multi-vector policy', manoeuvring between Russia and the EU, depending on the respective interests of the different Moldovan stakeholders.

Notes

1 One of the key characteristics of the Moldovan economy is the size of its outward labour migration, which has been having a serious effect on socio-economic stability since the mid-1990s, representing between 600,000 and 700,000 workers temporarily or permanently abroad.
2 'A *de facto* state exists where there is an organised political leadership, which has risen to power through some degree of indigenous capacity; receives popular support; and has achieved sufficient capacity to provide governmental services to a given population in a specific territorial area, over which effective control is maintained for a significant period of time' (Pegg 1998: 26).
3 In the Eurasian context, the term 'frozen conflict' refers to the post-Soviet separatist entities that emerged after the collapse of the USSR: Transnistria in Moldova, South Ossetia and Abkhazia in Georgia, and Nagorno-Karabakh in Azerbaijan. Since 2014, the term is also applied to the situation in the Donbass region in Ukraine. The term is generally misleading as the situation in literally all allegedly frozen conflicts has been evolving in the last years, despite the fact that little progress has been made in finding a resolution (Lynch 2004).
4 Gagauzia is an autonomous region in Southern Moldova, populated by 160,000 inhabitants with mainly Orthodox Russian-speakers of Turkish descent.
5 The Global Competitiveness Report highlights the deficiencies in transport infrastructure: Moldova ranks only 63 for the quality of its railroad system, 91 for air transportation, 129 for its ports and 133 for roads out of a total of 140 countries.
6 In 2014, Moldova ranks 94 in the Logistics Performance Index.
7 The interconnector Iasi-Ungheni opened in March 2015 and is destined to diversify energy sources and routes, thus potentially reducing the monopoly of Moldovagaz and consolidating the country's energy security. However, as Gazprom owns a 50 per cent share of the Moldovagaz company, the interconnector is faced with vested interests in Moldova (Barbarosie and Coalson 2014).

References

Barbarosie, L. and Coalson, R. (2014) 'Empty Pipeline Shows Difficulty of Breaking Moldova's Gazprom Addiction', *Radio Free Europe*, 29 September.
Boonstra, J. (2011) 'Moldova: An EU Success Story?', *Fride Policy Brief* 92, August.
Botan, I. (2008) 'Republic of Moldova Shall Join EU One Day, Somehow . . . ', *E-democracy*, 30 June, www.e-democracy.md/en/monitoring/politics/comments/200806301/.
Calus, K. (2014) 'Russian Sanctions against Moldova. Minor Effects, Major Potential', *OSW Commentary* 152, 6 November.
Calus, K. (2015) 'A Captured State? Moldova's Uncertain Prospects for Modernisation', *OSW Commentary* 168, 22 April.
Calus, K. (2016) 'Moldova: From Oligarchic Pluralism to Plahotniuc's Hegemony', *OSW Commentary* 208, 11 April.
Chirila, V. (2013) 'Why a Strategic Partnership between Moldova and Russia is not a Realistic Option?', *Europa.md*, 24 January, http://2014.europa.md/images/dox4download/societatea_civila/2013-01_vchirila_rm-russia_report.pdf.
Cibotaru, A. (ed.) (2010) *Twitter Revolution: Episode One, Moldova*, Chisinau: Editura Arc.
Commission of the European Communities (2003) *Wider Europe – Neighbourhood: A New Framework for Relations with our Eastern and Southern Neighbours*, COM (2003) 104 final, Brussels.
Commission of the European Communities (2005) *EU/Moldova Action Plan*.
Council of the European Union (2003) *Council Common Position 2003/139/CFSP of 27 February 2003 Concerning Restrictive Measures Against the Leadership of the Transnistrian Region of the Moldovan Republic*, Council Common Position 2003/139/CFSP, 28 February.
Council of the European Union (2008) *Joint Declaration on a Mobility Partnerships between the European Union and the Republic of Moldova*, 9460/08 ADD 1, Brussels, 21 May.
European Commission (2007a) 'European Commission Proposes Additional Autonomous Trade Preferences (ATPs) for Moldova', *Press Release* IP/07/1690.
European Commission (2007b) 'The first EU "Common Application Visa Center" opens in Moldova', *Press Release* IP/07/561.

European Commission (2008) 'European Neighbourhood Policy – MOLDOVA', *MEMO* /08/212.
European Commission (2015) Trade, Moldova, http://ec.europa.eu/trade/policy/countries-and-regions/countries/moldova/.
European External Action Service (2016) *Shared Vision, Common Action: A Stronger Europe. A Global Strategy for the European Union's Foreign and Security Policy*, Brussels.
European Integration Index for Eastern Partnership Countries (2014) www.eap-index.eu/.
European Parliament (2009) 'Resolution on the Situation in the Republic of Moldova', Strasbourg, 7 May.
Hagemann, C. (2013) 'External Governance on the Terms of the Partner? The EU, Russia and the Republic of Moldova in the European Neighbourhood Policy', *Journal of European Integration* 35(7): 767–783.
Hellman, J. and Kaufmann, D. (2001) 'Confronting the Challenge of State Capture in Transition Economies', *Finance & Development* 38(3), www.imf.org/external/pubs/ft/fandd/2001/09/hellman.htm.
Higgins, A. (2015) 'Moldova Eyes Russia's Embrace as Flirtation with Europe Fades', *The New York Times*, 21 May.
Kosienkowski, M. (2012) *Continuity and Changes in Transnistria's Foreign Policy after the 2011 Presidential Elections*, Lublin: The Catholic University of Lublin Publishing House.
Kurowska, X. and Tallis, B. (2009) 'EU Border Assistance Mission: Beyond Border Monitoring?', *European Foreign Affairs Review* 14: 47–64.
Lavenex, S. (2004) 'EU External Governance in "Wider Europe"', *Journal of European Public Policy* 11(4): 680–700.
Levitsky, S. and Way, L. (2010) 'Why Democracy Needs a Level Playing Field', *Journal of Democracy* 21(1): 57–68.
Luke, T. and Toal, G. (1998) 'The Fraying Modern Map: Failed States and Contraband Capitalism', *Geopolitics and International Boundaries* 3(3): 14–33.
Lynch, D. (2004) *Engaging Separatist States: Unresolved Conflict De Facto States*, Washington, DC: United States Institute of Peace Press.
Molcean, A. and Verständig, N. (2014) 'Moldova: The Transnistrian Conflict', in Cornell, S. and Jonsson, M. (eds.) *Conflict, Crime, and the State in Postcommunist Eurasia*, Philadelphia: University of Pennsylvania Press, 129–150.
Morlino, L. (2008) 'Hybrid Regimes or Regimes in Transition', *Working Paper* 70, FRIDE, September.
Mosneaga, V. (2007) 'The Labor Migration of Moldovan Population: Trends and Effects', *Socius Working Paper* 3, http://pascal.iseg.utl.pt/~socius/publicacoes/wp/wp200703.pdf.
Mosneaga, V. (2012) 'Социально-политическое влияние трудовой миграции в Молдове', *CARIM-East Research Report 2012/17*, European University Institute, www.carim-east.eu/media/CARIM-East-2012-RU-17.pdf.
Parmentier, F. (2006) 'Construction étatique et capitalisme de contrebande en Transnistrie', *Transitions* XLV(1): 135–152.
Parmentier, F. (2008) 'The ENP Facing a de facto State. Lessons from the Transnistrian Question', in Delcour L. and Tulmets E. (eds.) *Testing EU Foreign Policy in the Neighbourhood*, Baden Baden: Nomos, 203–216.
Parmentier, F. (2014) *Les chemins de l'Etat de droit. La voie étroite des pays entre Europe et Russie*, Paris: Sciences Po Les Presses.
Pegg, S. (1998) *International Society and De Facto State*, Aldershot: Ashgate.
Popa, A. (2015) 'Moldova and Russia: Between Trade Relations and Economic Dependence', Expert Grup, April, www.expert-grup.org/ro/biblioteca/item/download/1348_10771108a3d22488655de8186bfbb918.
Popescu, N. (2006) '"Outsourcing" de facto Statehood: Russia and the Secessionist Entities in Georgia and Moldova', *CEPS Policy Brief* 109, CEPS.
Popescu, N. (2012) 'Moldova's Fragile Pluralism', *Russian Politics & Law* 50(4): 37–50.
Puiu, V. (2014) 'Moldova Struggles to Escape Russian Gas', *Eurasianet*, 25 September, www.eurasianet.org/node/70161.
Quinlan, P. (2004) 'Back to the Future: An Overview of Moldova Under Voronin', *Demokratizatsiya* 12(4): 485–504.
Ratha, D., Wyss, H. and Yousefi, S. (2014) 'Remittances from Russia to CIS Countries Likely to Fall Sharply', *People Move*, http://blogs.worldbank.org/peoplemove/remittances-russia-cis-countries-likely-fall-sharply.
Rinnert, D. (2013) 'The Republic of Moldova in the Eastern Partnership. From "Poster Child" to "Problem Child"?', *Friedrich Ebert Stiftung*, August.

Russian Presidency (2014) 'Meeting with Leader of the Moldovan Party of Socialists Igor Dodon and Former Prime Minister of Moldova Zinaida Grechany', Moscow, 5 November, http://en.kremlin.ru/events/president/news/46935.

Shapovalova, N. and Boonstra, J. (2012) 'The European Union: A privileged Partnership with Moldova', in Kosienkowski, M. and Schreiber, W. (eds.) *Moldova: Arena of International Influences*, Lanham (Md.): Lexington Books, 51–75.

Solovyev, V. (2015) 'Protests in Moldova: Dignity and Truth vs. Euro-Imitators', *Institute of Modem Russia*, 23 September, http://imrussia.org/en/analysis/world/2422-protests-in-moldova-dignity-and-truth-vs-euro-imitators.

Tigui, E. (2013) 'Republic of Moldova and Common Security and Defence Policy of The European Union: Prospects for Cooperation', *Moldova's Foreign Policy Statewatch* 62, IDIS, February.

Transnistrian Dialogues (2014) *Newsletter* 5, March, www.ape.md/public/files/publication/2014-02-05_Transnistrian_Dialogues_EN.pdf.

Transparency International (2014) 'Corruption Perception Index'.

Ursu, V. and Raileanu, D. (2014) 'Concerned about EU Integration, Moldova's Gagauz Region Holds Disputed Referendum', *Radio Free Europe*, 2 February, www.rferl.org/content/moldova-gagauzia-eu-referendum/25249087.html.

Vahl, M. (2005) 'The Europeanisation of the Transnistrian Conflict', *CEPS Policy Brief* 73, CEPS, May.

Way, L. (2003) 'Weak States and Pluralism: The Case of Moldova', *East European Politics and Societies* 17(3): 454–482.

World Bank (2014) Logistics Performance Index, http://lpi.worldbank.org/international/global.

World Bank (2016) Moldova, Overview, www.worldbank.org/en/country/moldova/overview.

World Economic Forum (2015) 'The Global Competitiveness Report 2015–2016', www3.weforum.org/docs/gcr/2015-2016/Global_Competitiveness_Report_2015-2016.pdf.

28
THE EUROPEAN NEIGHBOURHOOD POLICY AND THE SOUTH CAUCASUS

Licínia Simão

Introduction

At the onset of the European Neighbourhood Policy (ENP), in 2003, the South Caucasus countries, Armenia, Azerbaijan and Georgia,[1] were left out of this initiative due to their 'geographical location' (Commission of the European Communities 2003: 4). This rather simplistic formal explanation obscures the fundamental reasons why, in 2003, the region was considered not eligible for the neighbourhood initiative, namely its complex security relations marked by three protracted conflicts in Abkhazia, South Ossetia and Nagorno-Karabakh,[2] and the understanding among most European Union (EU) Member States that the South Caucasus was part of an area of privileged interests for Russia (Popescu 2011). This naturally created reluctance among some EU Member States on the desirability of an EU policy for the region. Until Georgia's 'Rose Revolution', in October 2003, there were also no clear incentives for the EU to include the region in an initiative focused on the promotion of democratic standards and economic modernisation. Even the energy potential of the South Caucasus, especially in Azerbaijan's Caspian shores, failed to mobilise EU interests in the absence of viable energy transit routes.

The regime change in Georgia, initiated in November 2003, and confirmed with the election of Mikheil Saakashvili as President in January 2004, propelled the EU to take more visible action, dispatching its High Representative to Tbilisi (Solana 2004) and authorising a European Security and Defence Policy (ESDP) rule of law mission, EUJUST THEMIS, to assist the Georgian government in reforming the judiciary system (Council of the European Union 2004a; Helly 2006). Emergency funding was also made available through the Instrument for Stability (IfS) to address the immediate consequences of the political crisis. More structurally, the reluctant voices inside the Council of the EU were now given an important argument as to why the EU needed to support democracy in the region, and why including the three countries in the ENP would be the best way to assure it (Lynch 2006). A regional approach was privileged, as the appointment of an EU Special Representative (EUSR) for the South Caucasus in July 2003 illustrates (Council of the European Union 2003a; 2003b; 2004b; 2005). Georgia was perceived by the European Commission and some Member States as a frontrunner, acting as an incentive for Armenia and Azerbaijan to deepen their relations with the EU (Simão 2013). Moreover, a regional approach was also justified based on the existing security complex in the

Caucasus (Coppieters 1996; Simão and Freire 2008), requiring concerted action in conflict transformation, which greater EU engagement was set to impact.

Thus, the ENP Strategy Paper of 2004 made a recommendation for the inclusion of the three South Caucasus countries as full participants in the ENP, and began to address the individual needs of each country, following the principle of differentiation (Commission of the European Communities 2004). The European Parliament actively promoted a more engaged EU regional policy, namely focusing on conflict issues (European Parliament 2006; 2010). Although the EU had been reluctant to become directly involved in the existing formal peace processes and peacekeeping – namely through the deployment of more muscular ESDP tools – the Commission-led rehabilitation and humanitarian assistance was proving an important incentive in conflict transformation and landed the EU a place in the Joint Control Commission (JCC) for South Ossetia[3] since 2001 (Popescu 2011; Simão 2014). A Crisis Group report issued in 2006 further underlined the conflict resolution potential of the ENP's different tools and policies (International Crisis Group 2006), including the important potential for articulating ENP goals with the work of the EUSR. Following the 2008 war in Georgia, and Russia's veto on the renovation of the mandate of the United Nations Observer Mission in Georgia (UNOMIG), the French EU presidency led the cease-fire negotiations; the Council of the EU approved the deployment of an observer mission, the EUMM (EU Monitoring Mission); and the EUSR led the new peace-talks, under the Geneva International Discussions.[4] With these important steps, Brussels assumed a more prominent role in conflict resolution dynamics in Georgia, and more generally in the South Caucasus (Whitman and Wolff 2010).

EU–Russia relations during this period failed to translate into a solid partnership. Russia declined the EU's offer to participate in the ENP initiative and aimed instead at a strategic partnership, based on four common spaces (Russian Federation and European Union 2003). This initiative, however, was gradually emptied as EU policies in what Russia considers an area of privileged interests became more active. Following the Ukrainian 'Orange Revolution', in 2004, Moscow's relations with Brussels and many European capitals became even more strained, preventing any meaningful action on the South Caucasus regional conflicts and other pressing regional security issues (Samokhvalov 2007). Moreover, the opening of the Baku–Tbilisi–Ceyhan (BTC) and the Baku–Tbilisi–Erzurum (BTE) pipelines, delivering Caspian oil and gas to European markets, and breaking the Russian monopoly on the export of Caspian energy to European markets, further contributed to the accumulation of tensions (Starr and Cornell 2005).

It is in this context that EU relations with the South Caucasus countries have evolved over the last decade. The chapter will first look at the political agreements sustaining these relations, namely the bilateral Action Plans (APs) and Association Agreements (AAs), as well as at the regional initiatives, to understand relations with Brussels. It then addresses the evolving economic relations and visa negotiations, as these are two fundamental aspects shaping external perceptions of the EU, influencing conflict dynamics and driving the EU's export of influence in the shared neighbourhood with Russia. Throughout the analysis, the chapter engages with how these dimensions have impacted conflict management in the South Caucasus and the coherence of EU policies towards the region.

Setting the legal and political background

EU relations with Armenia, Azerbaijan and Georgia are legally grounded on the Partnership and Cooperation Agreements (PCAs) signed in the 1990s. The PCAs are comprehensive agreements focusing on democratic reforms and transition to market economy, as well as the development of multi-sectorial cooperation between the EU and the post-Soviet countries. With the inclusion in the ENP, the PCAs remained the legal frameworks in place, guiding relations between the EU and the three South Caucasus states. The new bilateral ENP APs established concrete steps necessary to bring the neighbouring countries closer to EU standards but did not constitute a new legal basis for relations, leaving the question of the future status of these countries *vis-à-vis* the EU unanswered. Thus, to the extent that inclusion in the ENP created new expectations in the South Caucasus regarding future EU enlargements, this process remained open-ended and rooted in a political and legal basis, which clearly did not reflect the fast-evolving local, regional and international contexts.

The PCAs are extremely vague as regards conflict resolution issues (Council of the European Union and European Commission 1999a; 1999b; 1999c). The ENP APs were only slightly more ambitious in this regard, with conflict-related issues usually mentioned mainly as an obstacle to regional cooperation goals, including in energy and transportation. Moreover, conflict-related conditionality was weak, due to the lack of a strong and binding new political agreement in the framework of the ENP (Sasse 2008). In the case of the South Caucasus, the use of conflict-related conditionality, during the negotiations of the ENP APs, focused on Azerbaijan's commercial flights to the Turkish Cypriot Republic, in violation of the EU's non-recognition policy (Simão and Freire 2008), rather than on the regional conflicts in the South Caucasus. This resulted mainly from the weak institutionalisation of the EU's Common Foreign and Security Policy (CFSP), occasionally taken hostage by certain Member States' concerns, rather than from a coherent and concerted effort to support positive developments in conflict resolution in the neighbourhood, based on the political impulse of the ENP negotiations (Raube et al. 2015). As the latest revision of the ENP in November 2015 underlines, both the EU and ENP countries have expressed a wish for cooperation in the security sector with potential impacts on conflict dynamics (European Commission and High Representative of the European Union for Foreign Affairs and Security Policy 2015b).

The APs were politically weak tools, which addressed conflict dynamics only to the extent that Armenia, Azerbaijan and Georgia perceived it as urgent and necessary. For the Georgian government, the EU's engagement in the Abkhazian and South Ossetian conflicts was a fundamental step to balance what they perceived to be biased and unfavourable frameworks for negotiations. The internationalisation of the Georgian conflicts was a central goal for President Saakashvili as was the objective to have the EU commit to Georgia's territorial integrity (IIFFMCG 2009). Thus, the EU–Georgia ENP AP included a priority area (6) 'Promote peaceful resolution of internal conflicts' (Commission of the European Communities 2006c). In the cases of Armenia and Azerbaijan, a priority area on 'peaceful solution of the Nagorno-Karabakh conflict' was also included, although for Armenia that was priority number seven and for Azerbaijan it was priority number one (Commission of the European Communities 2006a; 2006b). Whereas in the case of Georgia, the EU committed to a series of important steps with potential impact on conflict dynamics, including increased economic assistance and political dialogue with Russia and other relevant actors; in the case of Nagorno-Karabakh, the main efforts were towards supporting the EUSR's work and the OSCE Minsk Group.[5]

Overall, the balance is rather weak in terms of the ability of the EU to use the ENP APs to contribute to conflict resolution (Helly 2007; Sasse 2009). The EU's most significant contribution has been to conflict transformation in the case of Georgia, through its humanitarian and reconstruction assistance (Popescu 2011). However, this has also had negative impacts in conflict dynamics, namely by holding the EU hostage to Georgia's positions within the ENP process. By openly committing to Georgia's territorial integrity, the EU lost the ability to be a neutral mediator between the authorities in Tbilisi and in Abkhazia and South Ossetia (Coppieters 2007), as well as between Georgia and Russia. In the case of Nagorno-Karabakh, the EUSR has been unable to visit the region, due to pressure from Azerbaijan and, overall, the Union has relinquished any meaningful efforts aimed at conflict transformation through rehabilitation or assistance. The most significant contribution is the European Partnership for the Peaceful Settlement of the Conflict over Nagorno-Karabakh (EPNK), funded under the IfS and focused on facilitating dialogue between civil society, media and policy-makers. Looking to keep an equidistant position between Armenia and Azerbaijan, the EU has sought to balance the principles of territorial integrity and self-determination, without explaining how that can help move the peace process forward.

With the negotiation of the new AAs, the EU had an important opportunity to link advances in integration with the EU to conflict resolution. The AAs envision concrete steps towards political association and economic integration, including the establishment of Deep and Comprehensive Free Trade Agreements (DCFTAs) with the Union. They also include important steps towards visa liberalisation, with concrete impact on the lives of the citizens of the South Caucasus. However, due to the increasing competition between the EU and Russia in their overlapping neighbourhoods, including in the South Caucasus, AAs have been signed only with Georgia, whereas Armenia has decided instead to integrate into the Russian-led Eurasian Economic Union (EEU), and in the case of Azerbaijan, negotiations on the AA have been dragging, reflecting Baku's balanced multi-vector foreign policy. Thus, the opportunity to use the AAs to apply conflict-related conditionality has also been lost. The 2015 revision of the ENP further highlighted the need for flexibility and adjustment to each ENP country's needs (European Commission and High Representative of the European Union for Foreign Affairs and Security Policy 2015b), creating further possibilities of overcoming the limitations deriving from the lack of adherence to the AAs in the South Caucasus.

Diffusing regional influence through trade and visa liberalisation

Trade and visa liberalisation have been some of the most appealing incentives for participation in the ENP and Eastern Partnership (EaP). The prospect of a stake in the EU's internal market remains an important element of potential economic growth and modernisation, whereas the possibility of traveling more easily to the EU resonates closely with ordinary citizens. In a regional context of competition with Russia and having the EU's moral, democratic and financial authority diminished by a series of crises hitting the Union since 2008, the ability of the EaP to sustain reforms and promote better social welfare and democratic conditions is highly uncertain.

Georgia[6]

Georgia remains the most advanced and committed partner of the EU in the South Caucasus. Public support for Euro-Atlantic integration remains high and there is a strong consensus among different political forces as to the importance of this foreign policy priority – what one member of government has called 'irreversible Europeanization' (Zalkaliani 2014; see also Kakachia 2015). Despite the difficulties in implementation and the potentially negative effects of trade liberalisation for Georgia (Manoli 2013), Euro-Atlantic integration works as an important element of political cohesion, especially in the face of external threats from Russia (Tsutskiridze 2011). Political and military insecurity has thus been a powerful driver for closer relations between Tbilisi and Brussels, as these are pursued in tandem with NATO integration.

Eleven years after the inclusion of Georgia in the ENP, the parties now stand on renovated and updated political ground, with the signing of the AA. The provisional implementation of the AAs and of the Visa Liberalisation Action Plan (VLAP), even before the ratification process by the

28 Member States was completed, illustrates the commitment by the parties. Trade between the EU and Georgia has increased by 7 per cent since the DCFTA began implementation (European Commission 2015) and Georgia benefits from visa liberalisation from 28 March 2017. Moreover, the EU is Georgia's main donor, providing financial and technical assistance on a broad range of areas,[7] and making EU assistance to Georgia's reforms a crucial element in the country's modernisation, as well as in keeping some level of democratic and human rights-related conditionality.

To move these agendas forward, the 2014 ENP progress report on Georgia underlines the necessary focus on capacity-building, assisting Georgia in developing the institutional and technical competence necessary to implement EU regulations (European Commission and High Representative of the European Union for Foreign Affairs and Security Policy 2015a). This remains a heavy burden for ENP countries, especially in a context of heightened competition between the EU and Russia (Piet and Simão 2016; Delcour 2015). For instance, the changes needed in Georgian customs management have an impact on how trade is conducted with other neighbouring states (such as Armenia, Azerbaijan and Russia), but also with the separatist regions of Abkhazia and South Ossetia. Despite difficult relations, trade across the Enguri river continues and there are important opportunities for regulation, which could promote confidence-building between the parties (Mirimanova 2015). The deepening of economic relations between Georgia and the EU on the one hand, and between the separatist authorities, in Abkhazia and South Ossetia, and Russia on the other, raise issues of compatibility of the rules guiding economic and commercial interaction across borders. If the rules are not made compatible and the EU does not address these issues, this could diminish the potential positive impact of trade and of the ENP on conflict transformation.

A similar argument regarding the potential negative effects on conflict dynamics can be made for the EU's visa policies. As soon as 2007, Georgian authorities expressed their concern that EU visa facilitation negotiations with Russia would negatively affect Georgia's relations with the separatist regions of Abkhazia and South Ossetia (Burjanadze 2007). Due to Russia's policy of passportisation,[8] authorities in Tbilisi feared that facilitated access to the EU to those carrying a Russian passport would remove incentives for approximation with Tbilisi. This argument was an important element in advancing the EU–Georgia visa facilitation dialogue, which resulted in a Mobility Partnership, signed in November 2009. The EU's cooperation on Justice and Home Affairs aiming at visa facilitation has also provided an incentive and active support for the important task of border delimitations in the South Caucasus. In the case of Georgia, delimitation of the border with Russia has a direct impact on conflict dynamics, not only because the territories of Abkhazia and South Ossetia are part of that border but also due to Russia's own borderisation policies (Kakachia 2013).[9] The EUSR Border Support Team[10] further contributes to the development of Georgia's border management capabilities, relevant for addressing these complex issues.

The war in Georgia in 2008 was a turning point in the EU's relations with its eastern neighbours, facilitating the internal consensus on the need to have more significant incentives for closer relations with the Union. Political and economic reforms remain at the core of what the EU expects from its neighbours, and despite Georgia's shortcomings on both matters, the strategic importance of supporting an outspoken Western-oriented government has not been lost among EU institutions. Georgia has been one of the post-Soviet states most severely punished by Russian foreign policy for its pro-Western orientation – including boycotts to Georgian products, forced return of migrants and military intervention among other punitive measures (Nygren 2010). Because of these actions, Georgia has diminished its dependence on the Russian economy, facilitating its withdrawal from the CIS in 2009 (Radio Free Europe/Radio Liberty 2009). Georgia has also ended Russia's military presence in Tbilisi-controlled territory (the leasing of the Akhalkalaki and Batumi Russian military bases was terminated in 2007). These choices came at a heavy price for Georgia, as Russia recognised Abkhazia and South Ossetia's declarations of independence following the war in 2008 and *de facto* integrated both regions into the Russian Federation. In a sense, the EaP has been a weak tool to provide for the security of Georgia's territory (Whitman and Wolff 2010), whereas domestic reforms remain fragile and economic inequalities are still high.

Azerbaijan[11]

EU–Azerbaijan relations remain rooted in the PCA, as negotiations for an AA, ongoing since 2010, have yet to be concluded. Despite the strategic importance of Azerbaijan for the EU's energy diversification – including Baku's interest in Central Asian energy reserves – relations between the two partners have been difficult. In 2006, a Memorandum of Understanding in the field of energy was signed and dialogue has continued in the framework of the bilateral institutions set-up under the PCA. However, the nature of the regime in Baku and tensions over political prisoners and human rights violations have hampered the deepening of relations (Transition Online 2015). Inclusion in the ENP in 2004 and the implementation of the ENP AP have had little leverage over these political and human rights issues. Moreover, the EU has genuinely appreciated the balanced foreign policy of Azerbaijan and its search for autonomy *vis-à-vis* Russia, resulting in weak political conditionality (Yunusov 2007). After the Vilnius summit, in 2013, Azerbaijan advanced the idea of negotiating a Strategic Modernisation Partnership, where balance would be sought between political conditionality and democratic reforms on the EU's side, and support for territorial integrity and access to high-end technology on Azerbaijan's (Rettman 2013), illustrating the divergent understandings underpinning these relations.

EU trade policies with Azerbaijan remain limited, since Baku is not a member of the World Trade Organisation (WTO) and its economy relies mainly on energy exports (Valiyev 2011). Thus, despite the important volume of bilateral trade and investment, Azerbaijan's interest in having a DCFTA with the EU is rather limited. As the Strategic Partnership for Modernisation suggests, the main point of interest is EU funding and support for modernisation and diversification of the economy. Economic relations with Russia are also fundamental for Azerbaijan, both in energy and non-energy goods, and despite the negative impact on bilateral trade of the sanctions imposed on Russia by European and North-American countries since 2014, Baku is set to keep a foreign policy that is not exclusively committed to any regional integration project. Thus, the ENP and the DCFTA envisioned under the EaP have proved limited in anchoring Azerbaijan to European integration.

Regarding visa issues, in 2013, the EU and Azerbaijan established three bilateral agreements on Visa Facilitation, on Readmission and a Mobility Partnership. Border control has been a major concern for Azerbaijan, as stated in its National Security Strategy of 2007. Azerbaijan is located at a strategic juncture, making it a privileged route for organised crime (Ministry of National Security of Azerbaijan Republic 2014). To respond to these challenges, Azerbaijan has devised a new migration policy, upgraded its migration and border services and deepened cooperation with international organisations, including the EU (Ceccorulli 2015). EU support for the creation of an Integrated Border Management strategy has been an important tool for authorities in Baku. Capacity building in this issue is crucial for trade facilitation, but also for security purposes, increasing the exchange of information between the EU and its regional counterparts. Border demarcation with Russia and Georgia has advanced, but due to the dispute with Armenia over Nagorno-Karabakh, no advances have been possible on the demarcation of this common border.

The delicate, yet strategic, relations between Brussels and Baku partly explain the limited EU engagement in the Nagorno-Karabakh conflict. Whereas Armenia has lobbied to maintain the three co-chairs of the Minsk Group, Azerbaijan has been more vocal regarding the potential positive impact of having the EU included in the mediation, since it perceives the current format as being biased towards Armenia (Shiriyev 2013).[12] However, Azerbaijan has yet to authorise the EUSR for the South Caucasus to enter the Nagorno-Karabakh region for the EU to develop a more encompassing confidence-building policy. The EU, on the other hand, has been reluctant to push this issue onto the EU–Azerbaijan agenda, perceiving itself as lacking any significant leverage to exert pressure over the authorities in Baku. As defence budgets increase rapidly in the region (SIPRI 2014) and provocative rhetoric is used to maintain support for the regime, the EU needs to work more closely with its partners on confidence-building to avoid an escalation of these conflicts.

Armenia[13]

Relations with the EU are grounded on the PCA and have been updated by the ENP AP, signed in 2006. Despite advanced negotiations with the EU on a new AA, including a DCFTA, Armenian authorities decided not to initialise the agreement at the EaP Vilnius Summit, in 2013. Instead, they decided to enter the EEU, as of January 2015. This turn of events is significant for the ability of the EU to influence regional dynamics in the South Caucasus, and for the EaP to translate into meaningful influence in the region. In fact, by focusing on sectoral reforms with low political conditionality attached, the EaP has provided a governance-based approach to regional influence. Armenian authorities can benefit extensively from sectoral cooperation with the EU in key areas of administrative and economic reform, without meaningful costs to the ruling elites (Delcour and Wolczuk 2015). Moreover, closer relations with the EU also provided Armenia with important foreign policy alternatives in a difficult geopolitical context. In fact, despite not moving forward with the AA, the EU and Armenia are still looking for ways to enable a new bilateral agreement, respectful of Armenia's new international commitments within the EEU.

Armenia is thus a test case for the ability of the EaP to deliver on regional influence, in the absence of comprehensive and binding trade agreements. Because authorities in Yerevan remain very much interested in pursuing close relations with the EU and in benefiting from the vast array of reform and assistance programmes available, the European Commission has incentives to find ways to develop a trade agreement which is compatible with the EEU. This would be in line with the new focus on flexibility of trade commitments established in the revised ENP and it would contribute to de-escalating tensions in the overlapping neighbourhood with Russia. So far, the EU's profile in Armenia is more of a donor, with limited capacity for political influence, or a long-term partnership with authorities in Yerevan (Babayan 2011). In fact, Armenia's financial, economic and military dependence on Russia is exacerbated by the permanence of the Karabakh conflict, preventing Yerevan from radical foreign policy changes, which would jeopardise the status quo (de Waal 2015). For Armenia, signing an AA with the EU would be a far more complex choice than the economic dimension suggests. In contrast, the security reasons evoked by the Armenian leaders for not signing the AA with the EU and joining the EEU become explicit, considering the level of influence Russia exerts over the country.[14] Bearing a heavy economic cost for this choice, namely due to the economic sanctions imposed on Russia since the annexation of Crimea, Armenia has nevertheless counted on financial assistance from the EU and other international organisations such as the International Monetary Fund and the World Bank.

The Georgian 2008 war had a profound impact on Armenians as their most vital lifeline to Russia through Georgia became disrupted due to the war. Reacting to this situation, the Armenian President invited his Turkish counterpart to attend a football match in Yerevan between the two national teams and used this opportunity to engage in what became known as 'soccer diplomacy'. Although the goal of normalisation of relations between Armenia and Turkey has yet to be achieved, not least due to the issue of the Armenian genocide of 1915 and due to Azerbaijan's pressure, significant changes have taken place in both societies facilitating cross-border exchanges[15] (Hill, Kirişçi and Moffatt 2015; European Stability Initiative 2009). The EU has supported these negotiations,[16] but has failed to use Turkey's accession process and Armenia's participation in the ENP/EaP framework to provide considerable incentives to all parties to change the status quo.

Despite the lack of progress on the political relations with the EU, Visa Facilitation and Readmission Agreements with Armenia entered into force in January 2014, as pre-conditions for the VLAP. For Armenia, visa facilitation with the EU is a very important economic element, as large segments of the population have emigrated abroad, including in EU countries. Moreover, Armenia suffers the consequences of having two closed borders, with Azerbaijan and Turkey, whereas its border with Iran has also been of marginal importance due to the international sanctions imposed on Teheran since 1979. The border with Georgia is open, but subject to fluctuations in Georgian–Russian relations.

Conflict dynamics in the South Caucasus since the launch of the ENP

Since Armenia, Azerbaijan and Georgia were included in the ENP in 2004, the region has become more integrated into Euro-Atlantic structures, particularly the EU. The last decade witnessed an unprecedented western interest in the South Caucasus, driven by Caspian energy, as well as a growing competition with Russia over influence in this strategic region bridging Europe to Central Asia and the Middle East. Besides the institutional weakness of regional states, the protracted conflicts in Abkhazia, South Ossetia and Nagorno-Karabakh further contribute to the hampering of the strategic potential of the region. Transportation corridors, including for energy, can be disrupted in the case of violent conflict, whereas the lack of regional cooperation projects reduces the incentives for peace. The brief war between Russia and Georgia in 2008 illustrated the fragile security of the so-called frozen conflicts. The violence that erupted around Abkhazia and South Ossetia showed the vulnerability of Georgia's status as a transit country and how existing pipelines, namely the BTC, can be targeted in case of hostilities. A similar fear exists in the case of an escalation of violence between Armenia and Azerbaijan over Nagorno-Karabakh, as the BTC is located a few kilometres away from the disputed territories.

The conflicts have also made this a 'broken region' (Semneby 2006), with closed borders between Georgia and Russia, between Armenia and Azerbaijan and Armenia and Turkey. The EU's export of governance, based on trade liberalisation agreements and border management, is hampered by these conditions. The lack of political influence of the EU in the South Caucasus partly reflects the EU's fragmented regional foreign policy: accession talks with Turkey, strategic partnership with Russia, limited relations with Iran and no official relations with the separatist entities. The Union's pan-regional initiatives, including the Black Sea Synergy (Commission of the European Communities 2007) and the EaP's multilateral platforms have sought to overcome some of these limitations, but fundamental shifts in regional perceptions need to happen for the full potential of these initiatives to be harnessed. Also, regional cooperation initiatives, such as the opening of the Baku–Tbilisi–Kars railroad, funded by Turkey and Azerbaijan (Georgia Today 2015), reinforce previously existing exclusion patterns and do not contribute to overcoming the status quo.

More than ten years after the inclusion of the South Caucasus in the ENP, the EU has assumed a significant role in the conflict resolution processes in Georgia (Freire and Simão 2013) and has become an important political and economic partner to Armenia and Azerbaijan. With the Lisbon Treaty, the Union has also made significant institutional changes facilitating an integrated approach to conflicts in the neighbourhood, acknowledging the importance of adding a political dimension to the governance approach underpinning the ENP. These efforts have, nevertheless, faced important challenges as relations with the Russian Federation became more strained. The colour revolutions and the perception in Moscow that the EU was in the business of promoting 'democratic' revolutions in the former Soviet countries (and potentially in Russia) became a major bone of contention. As the EU sought to enlarge an area of regional influence through the export of its governance model, Russia became more engaged in promoting its own model of regional integration and actively contested the EU's normative model. For the South Caucasus, this meant that new dividing lines were being established and that no significant prospects of conflict resolution will be possible in the absence of dialogue among the most important regional powers.

Notes

1 For an introduction to the South Caucasus region see de Waal (2010).
2 For insightful analysis of the frozen conflicts of the South Caucasus see de Waal (2003), Lynch (2004), Cornell (2000) and Welt (2004).
3 This is the format officially mediating the South Ossetian conflict. It was established in 1992, following the cease-fire, and brings together the Georgian government, Russia, South Ossetian authorities and North Ossetian representatives. Since 2008, Georgia has withdrawn from the JCC, considering its format to be unbalanced and outdated.
4 This format is chaired by the Organization for Security and Co-operation in Europe (OSCE), the EU and the United Nations (UN). Representatives from Georgia, South Ossetia and Abkhazia as well as Russia and the United States take part in the discussions.
5 This is the official format for negotiations of the Nagorno-Karabakh conflict, convened in 1992 by the then-CSCE. The Group is co-chaired by France, Russia and the US and the Group's permanent members are Belarus, Germany, Italy, Sweden, Finland and Turkey, as well as Armenia and Azerbaijan. On a rotating basis, the OSCE Troika is also a permanent member. No representatives from Nagorno-Karabakh are included.
6 For an informed analysis of Georgia's post-Soviet political context see Gahrton (2010).
7 Detailed information on the different EU financing schemes available to Georgia is available here: https://eeas.europa.eu/delegations/georgia/1238/eu-projects-with-georgia_en.
8 This policy refers to the practice of attributing Russian passports on a massive scale to citizens of other countries. This was the case of Georgian citizens living in Abkhazia and South Ossetia.
9 This refers to the Russian practice of moving the demarcation signs and installation of barbed-wire fences at the Administrative Border Line between South Ossetia and Abkhazia on the one hand and Tbilisi controlled territory on the other.
10 The Team assists the Georgian Border Police and other relevant Georgian government institutions in the preparation of a comprehensive border management reform strategy. It was deployed in 2005, under the EUSR's authority, following the closing of the OSCE Border Monitoring Mission to Georgia.
11 On post-Soviet Azerbaijan see Swietochowski (1995) and Lussac (2011).
12 Azerbaijani authorities underline the important Armenian diasporas in France, the US and Russia, which prevent these countries from having an unbiased approach to the conflict.
13 For an insightful analysis of Armenia's modern history see Suny (1993).
14 Besides Abkhazia and South Ossetia, Armenia is now the only country in the South Caucasus where Russia has military bases leased, making it a strategic asset in Russian foreign and security policy.

15 Since 1993, Turkey has imposed a unilateral blockage of Armenia, including the closing of the common border, in solidarity with Azerbaijan, over the conflict of Nagorno-Karabakh.
16 The programme 'Support to the Armenia-Turkey Normalisation Process', funded under the IfS is one example of the EU's support. Information available at www.armenia-turkey.net/en/programme, accessed 14 November 2015.

References

Babayan, N. (2011) 'Armenia: Why the European Neighbourhood Policy has Failed', *FRIDE Policy Brief* 68, February.
Burjanadze, N. (2007) 'Non-paper on Visa Facilitation and Readmission Issues between Georgia and the EU', presented by the Speaker of the Georgian Parliament at the IPEX conference, Bratislava.
Ceccorulli, M. (2015) 'Assessing the Role of Mobility and Border Security in EU-Azerbaijan Relations: How Far Can They Go?' *Caucasus International* 5(1) 27–38.
Coppieters, B. (1996) 'The Caucasus as a Security Complex', in Coppieters, B. (ed.) *Contested Borders in the Caucasus*, Brussels: VUB Press, 193–204.
Coppieters, B. (2007) 'The EU and Georgia: Time Perspectives in Conflict Resolution', *European Union Institute for Security Studies Occasional Paper* 70, December.
Cornell, S. (2000) *Small Nations and Great Powers: A Study of Ethnopolitical Conflict in the Caucasus*, London: Curzon Press.
Council of the European Union and European Commission (1999a) *Decision on the conclusion of the Partnership and Cooperation Agreement between the European Communities and their Member States, of the one part, and the Republic of Armenia, of the other part*, (1999/602/EC, ECSC, Euratom), 31 May.
Council of the European Union and European Commission (1999b) *Decision on the conclusion of the Partnership and Cooperation Agreement between the European Communities and their Member States, of the one part, and the Republic of Azerbaijan, of the other part*, (1999/614/EC, ECSC, Euratom), 31 May.
Council of the European Union and European Commission (1999c) *Decision on the conclusion of the Partnership and Cooperation Agreement between the European Communities and their Member States, of the one part, and Georgia, of the other part*, (1999/515/EC, ECSC, Euratom), 31 May.
Council of the European Union (2003a) *Council Joint Action 2003/496/CFSP of 7 July 2003 concerning the appointment of an EU Special Representative for the South Caucasus*.
Council of the European Union (2003b) *Council Joint Action 2003/872/CFSP of 8 December 2003 extending and amending the mandate of the Special Representative of the European Union for the South Caucasus*.
Council of the European Union (2004a) *Council Joint Action 2004/523/CFSP of 28 June 2004 on the European Union Rule of Law Mission in Georgia, EUJUST THEMIS*.
Council of the European Union (2004b) *Council Joint Action 2004/532/CFSP of 28 June 2004 extending and amending the mandate of the Special Representative of the European Union for the South Caucasus*.
Council of the European Union (2005) *Council Joint Action 2005/100/CFSP of 2 February 2005 extending the mandate of the Special Representative of the European Union for the South Caucasus*.
de Waal, T. (2003) *Black Garden: Armenia and Azerbaijan Through Peace and War*, New York: New York UP.
de Waal, T. (2010) *The Caucasus: An Introduction*, Oxford: Oxford UP.
de Waal, T. (2015) 'Losing Control in the Caucasus', *Politico Europe*, 11 October.
Delcour, L. (2015) 'Between the Eastern Partnership and Eurasian Integration: Explaining Post-Soviet Countries' Engagement in (Competing) Region-Building Projects', *Problems of Post-Communism* 62(6): 316–327.
Delcour, L. and Wolczuk, K. (2015) 'The EU's Unexpected "Ideal Neighbour"? The Perplexing Case of Armenia's Europeanisation', *Journal of European Integration* 37(4): 491–507.
Commission of the European Communities (2003) *Wider Europe—Neighbourhood: A New Framework for Relations with Our Eastern and Southern Neighbours*, COM (2003) 104 final, Brussels, 11 March.
Commission of the European Communities (2004) *European Neighbourhood Policy – Strategy Paper*, COM (2004) 373 final, Brussels, 12 May.
Commission of the European Communities (2006a) *EU-Armenia ENP Action Plan*, Brussels.
Commission of the European Communities (2006b) *EU-Azerbaijan ENP Action Plan*, Brussels.
Commission of the European Communities (2006c) *EU-Georgia ENP Action Plan*, Brussels.
Commission of the European Communities (2007) *Black Sea Synergy – A New Regional Cooperation Initiative*, COM (2007) 160 final, Brussels, 11 April.
European Commission (2015) *EU–Georgia Trade: Deep and Comprehensive Free Trade Area Fact-Sheet*, DG Trade.

European Commission and High Representative of the European Union for Foreign Affairs and Security Policy (2015a) *Implementation of the European Neighbourhood Policy in Georgia Progress in 2014 and recommendations for actions*, SWD (2015) 66 final, Brussels, 25 March.

European Commission and High Representative of the European Union for Foreign Affairs and Security Policy (2015b) *Joint Communication to the European Parliament, the Council, the European and Social Committee and the Committee of the Regions – Review of the European Neighbourhood Policy*, JOIN (2015) 50 final, Brussels, 18 November.

European Parliament (2006) *Resolution of 19 January 2006 on the European Neighbourhood Policy*, P6_TA-PROV (2006) 0028.

European Parliament (2010) *Resolution of 20 May 2010 on the Need for an EU Strategy for the South Caucasus*, P7_TA (2010) 0193.

European Stability Initiative (2009) *Noah's Dove Returns: Armenia, Turkey and the Debate on Genocide*, Istanbul: European Stability Initiative.

Freire, M. and Simão, L. (2013) 'The EU's Security Actorness: The Case of EUMM in Georgia', *European Security* 22(4): 464–477.

Gahrton, P. (2010) *Georgia: Pawn in the New Great Game*, New York: Pluto Press.

Georgia Today (2015) 'Azerbaijan to Launch New Passenger Trains on the Baku-Tbilisi-Kars Railway', 21 August.

Helly, D. (2006) 'EUJUST THEMIS in Georgia: An Ambitious Bet on Rule of Law', in Nowak, A. (ed.) *Civilian Crisis-Management: The EU Way*, Paris: EU Institute for Security Studies.

Helly, D. (2007) 'EU's Influence in Its Eastern Neighbourhood: The Case of Crisis Management in the Southern Caucasus', *European Political Economy Review* 7: 102–117.

Hill, F., Kirişci, K. and Moffatt, A. (2015) 'Armenia and Turkey: From Normalization to Reconciliation', *Turkish Policy Quarterly* 13(4): 127–138.

IIFFMCG (2009) *Report of the Independent International Fact-Finding Mission on the Conflict in Georgia* II, September.

International Crisis Group (2006) 'Conflict Resolution in the South Caucasus: The EU's Role', *Europe Report* 173, International Crisis Group, 20 March.

Kakachia, K. (2013) 'The Politics of Insecurity: Cross-Border Conflict Dynamics and Security Challenges in Georgia', in Ergun, A and Isaxanli, H. (eds.) *Security and Cross-Border Cooperation in the EU, the Black Sea Region and Southern Caucasus*, Amsterdam: IOS Press, 152–166.

Kakachia, K. (2015) 'Europeanisation and Georgian Foreign Policy', in *The South Caucasus: Between Integration and Fragmentation*, Baku and Brussels: SAM and EPC, 11–18.

Lussac, S. (2011) 'L'Azerbaïdjan, les hydrocarbures et les pipelines: réseaux sociotechniques et regionalisation', PhD Dissertation, l'Institut d'Etudes Politiques de Bordeaux.

Lynch, D. (2004) *Engaging Eurasia's Separatist States*, Washington, DC: United States Institute of Peace Press.

Lynch, D. (2006) 'Why Georgia matters', *Chaillot Paper* 86, European Union Institute for Security Studies, 01 February.

Manoli, P. (2013) 'Political Economy Aspects of Deep and Comprehensive Free Trade Agreements', *Eastern Journal of European Studies* 4(2): 51–73.

Ministry of National Security of Azerbaijan Republic (2014) 'Combating Organised Crime', www.mns.gov.az/en/pages/47-123.html, accessed 13 November 2015.

Mirimanova, N. (ed.) (2015) 'Regulation of Trade across Contested Borders: The Cases of China/Taiwan, Serbia/Kosovo and Cyprus', International Alert, April.

Nygren, B. (2010) 'Russia and Georgia – From Confrontation to War: What is Next?', in Kanet, R. (ed.) *Russian Foreign Policy in the 21st Century*, Basingstoke: Palgrave Macmillan, 101–120.

Piet, R. and Simão, L. (2016) *Security in Shared Neighbourhoods: Foreign Policy of Russia, Turkey and the EU*, London: Palgrave Macmillan.

Popescu, N. (2011) *EU Foreign Policy and Post-Soviet Conflicts: Stealth Intervention*, London: Routledge.

Raube, K. et al. (2015) 'Supporting European security and defence with existing EU measures and procedures', Study for Directorate-General for External Policies of the Union, Directorate B, Policy Department.

Rettman, A. (2013) 'Azerbaijan and EU Race to Agree "modernisation" Pact', *EUobserver*, 27 September.

Radio Free Europe/Radio Liberty (2009) 'Georgia Finalizes Withdrawal from CIS', 18 August.

Russian Federation and European Union (2003) *300th anniversary of St.-Petersburg – celebrating three centuries of common European history and culture*, EU-Russia Summit Joint Statement, 9937/03 (Presse 154), St.-Petersburg, 31 May.

Samokhvalov, V. (2007) 'Relations in the Russia-Ukraine-EU triangle: "zero-sum game" or not?', *EU Institute for Security Studies Occasional Paper* 68, 1 September.

Sasse, G. (2008) 'The European Neighbourhood Policy: Conditionality Revisited for the EU's Eastern Neighbours', *Europe-Asia Studies* 60(2): 295–316.

Sasse, G. (2009) 'The European Neighbourhood Policy and Conflict Management: A Comparison of Moldova and the Caucasus', *Ethnopolitics* 8(3): 369–386.

Semneby, P. (2006) 'The Role of the EU in the Resolution of the Conflicts in the South Caucasus', *Turkish Policy Quarterly* 5(2) www.esiweb.org/index.php?lang=en&id=291&tpq_ID=8.

Shiriyev, Z. (2013) 'Challenges for the EU in the resolution of the Nagorno-Karabakh conflict: an Azerbaijani perspective', *European Policy Centre Policy Brief*, 17 July.

Simão, L. (2013) 'Region-Building in the Eastern Neighbourhood: Assessing EU Regional Policies in the South Caucasus', *East European Politics* 29(3): 273–288.

Simão, L. (2014) 'The EU's Conflict Resolution Policies in the Black Sea Area', *Journal of Balkan and Near Eastern Studies* 16(3): 300–313.

Simão, L. and Freire, M. (2008) 'The EU's Neighbourhood Policy and the South Caucasus: Unfolding New Patterns of Cooperation', *Caucasian Review of International Affairs* 2(4): 47–61.

SIPRI (2014) SIPRI Military Expenditure Database, www.sipri.org/research/armaments/milex/milex_database, accessed 14 November 2015.

Solana, J. (2004) *Summary of the introductory remarks by the EU High Representative for the CFSP*, press conference in Tbilisi, Georgia, 15 January.

Starr, S. and Cornell, S. (eds.) (2005) *The Baku-Tbilisi-Ceyhan Pipeline: Oil Window to the West*, Washington, DC and Uppsala: Central Asia-Caucasus Institute & Silk Road Studies Program.

Suny, R. (1993) *Looking Toward Ararat: Armenia in Modern History*, Bloomington: Indiana UP.

Swietochowski, T. (1995) *Russia and Azerbaijan: A Borderland in Transition*, New York: Columbia UP.

Transition Online (2015) 'Azerbaijan Halts EU Visit over Human Rights Rebuke', 15 September.

Tsutskiridze, L. (2011) 'Balancing vs. Bandwagoning: Explaining Georgia's Alignments in Security Institutions', in Jafalian, A. (ed.) *Reassessing Security in the South Caucasus: Regional Conflicts and Transformation*, Farnham: Ashgate, 195–208.

Valiyev, A. (2011) 'Azerbaijan's Economic Model and Its Development Since Independence', in *South Caucasus – 20 Years of Independence*, Berlin: Friedrich-Ebert-Stiftung, 218–239.

Welt, C. (2004) 'Explaining Ethnic Conflict in the South Caucasus: Mountainous Karabagh, Abkhazia, and South Ossetia', PhD Dissertation, MIT, Boston.

Whitman, R. and Wolff, S. (2010) 'The EU as a Conflict Manager? The Case of Georgia and its Implications', *International Affairs* 86(1): 87–107.

Yunusov, A. (2007) *Azerbaijan in the Early XXI Century: Conflicts and Potential Threats*, Baku: Adiloglu.

Zalkaliani, D. (2014) 'Georgian Foreign Policy in a New Era', summary of roundtable held at Chatham House on 18 March 2014, Russia and Eurasia Programme Meeting Summary.

29
THE EUROPEAN NEIGHBOURHOOD POLICY AND EU–MAGHREB RELATIONS

Irene Fernández-Molina

Introduction

The target states of the southern dimension of the European Neighbourhood Policy (ENP) include a distinct grouping of countries, the Maghreb states, which can be approached either as a full-fledged regional unit or as a sub-regional setting comprised in the broader regional system of the Middle East and North Africa. The fact that the western part of the Arab world, or north-western Africa, is constructed and recognised as a distinct geopolitical unit owes much to its intimate historical connection with – and external penetration by – European powers. Besides a similarly mixed Arab-Amazigh ethnic and linguistic background, and a common Islamic religious identity, what has drawn the borders of the region as an imagined community is a shared colonial experience under the rule of, first, predominantly France (in the case of the three 'central Maghreb' countries – Morocco, Algeria and Tunisia, as well as Mauritania) and, second, Italy (Libya) and Spain (parts of Morocco and Western Sahara). For the purposes of geopolitical outlining and labelling, this commonality has prevailed over significant divergences between the concerned countries in terms of their contemporary histories (for example, belonging to the Ottoman Empire, form and length of colonial rule, access to independence), their economic, social and demographic structures, and their postcolonial political systems.

This chapter addresses the questions of what the structural characteristics of EU–Maghreb relations are and what factors account for these global features, as well as bilateral differentiation *vis-à-vis* each individual country of the region in the framework of the ENP. The different answers provided are broadly connected to the main theoretical approaches in International Relations (IR), namely realism, liberalism and constructivism, but also incorporate some insights from international political economy and postcolonialism. The following sections will examine: the postcolonial legacies and background of the institutionalisation of EU–Maghreb relations; the debate on the degree of interdependence or dependency that can be observed in this relationship from an international political economy perspective; the realist hindrances to liberal region-building and integration between the Maghreb countries; and the allocation of foreign policy roles and bilateral differentiation between them in the context of the ENP. The focus will be placed on Tunisia, Algeria and Morocco, since Mauritania is not included in the geopolitical scope of the ENP. Libya has so far remained outside most of the ENP structures, despite being recognised as a potential participant, and the Western Sahara conflict has never been directly targeted by this EU policy.

The weight of history: postcolonial legacies half a century later

In 1957, when the European Economic Community (EEC) was created by the Treaty of Rome, one of its six founding members, France, was immersed in the third year of one of the bloodiest decolonisation conflicts of the 20th century, the Algerian war of independence (1954–1962). The paradoxical coincidence of two paradigmatic instances of international cooperation and conflict somehow set the tone of Euro-Maghreb relations for the subsequent decades. Without falling into historical determinism, it can be claimed that colonialism, and the ensuing decolonisation processes, largely shaped the structural features of this relationship as we know it today, over half a century later. First, from the point of view of international political economy, French colonialism established a hub-and-spoke model of economic relations between the metropole and the various territories under its protectorate or direct administration, which foreshadowed the centre-periphery structure of contemporary exchanges between the northern and southern shores of the Mediterranean. Second, in terms of liberal interdependence, the fact that most of the colonial economic, social and cultural flows were channelled through Paris, certainly favoured the regional isolation of the various future North African states and paved the way for a lack of horizontal interdependence between them. Third, from a realist perspective, colonial border redrawing, mainly in favour of French Algeria, played a role in giving rise to bilateral territorial disputes, which provoked intense inter-state mistrust and security dilemmas from the 1960s onwards – even brief open conflict in the case of the 1963 Sands War between Morocco and Algeria (Abed Jabri 1985). At the same time, Algeria's territorial expansion fell short of turning it into an indisputable regional hegemon, paving the way for power balancing and competition to become the prevailing dynamics within the Maghreb system.

Fourth, a constructivist reading would place the focus on two identity-based ideational factors, which were largely forged during the Maghreb countries' anticolonial struggle, but pulled in opposite directions: on the one hand, the norm of regional federation or unification that was embraced by allied Moroccan, Algerian and Tunisian nationalist leaders in the 1940s; on the other, the strong ideological imprint of each young state's own nationalism and the different national role conceptions underlying their respective foreign policies and relationships with Europe (Stora 2003). Fifth, as far as European foreign policy is concerned, the legacy of colonialism also includes the pattern of 'geo-clientelism', or 'patron-client like relationships between EU Member States and certain non-EU countries or groups of countries' (Behr and Tiilikainen 2015: 27), which has marked EU–Maghreb relations for decades, with the former colonisers – France and, to a lesser extent, Spain and Italy – playing the role of patrons. Sixth, this 'geo-clientelism' also extends to scholarship on the relations, which has been comparatively scarce and shown an apparent French-speaking bias. While English-speaking academic literature has often diluted this issue in the wider discussion of Euro-Mediterranean relations, some French-speaking outlets have insisted on defending the distinctiveness and resistance of the Euro-Maghreb 'space' and 'proximity' (Henry 2006) in the form of an exceptional socio-economic interdependence, as well as the successful reactivation of the 5+5 Dialogue between the five Maghreb countries and five southern EU Member States (Portugal, Spain, France, Italy and Malta) in the 2000s.

Going back to 1957, it is also worth considering how the trajectory of the institutionalisation of EEC–Maghreb relations started from a duality, caused by the asymmetric progress of decolonisation in this region. On the one hand, France was interested in preserving and transferring to the EEC the preferential trade conditions it had bilaterally granted to recently – and peacefully – decolonised Morocco and Tunisia. Therefore, it made sure that the Treaty of Rome included two provisions guaranteeing the continuity of the 'special treatment' enjoyed by their goods. On the other hand, Algeria was still part of metropolitan France and hence subject to the intra-Community trade regime that had just been established by the EEC founding members. After it painfully gained independence in 1962, Algeria maintained a provisional trade relationship with the EEC and soon halted the negotiations on an association proposed by the European Commission, because of the latter's perceived neo-colonial connotations. As a result, in 1969, only Morocco and Tunisia entered into a new stage of association with the EEC. They both concluded first-generation bilateral Association Agreements, which were essentially confined to commercial matters – trade concessions qualified by a strong European agricultural protectionism. It was not until 1976 that Algeria joined its neighbours in institutionalising its bilateral relationship with the EEC under the 1972 Global Mediterranean Policy. This new framework, promoted by France, led to the signing of more wide-ranging second-generation Cooperation Agreements, which included financial assistance and social/labour issues in addition to trade provisions (Aghrout 2000).

Meanwhile, Mauritania was dealt with by the EEC under a different, more 'African' cooperation framework, since it was included in the African, Caribbean and Pacific (ACP) group when it became independent in 1960. Libya's foreign policy followed an atypical and idiosyncratic path after the 1969 revolution led by Colonel Muammar Gaddafi, which was to prevent the establishment of any contractual relations with the EEC/EU for decades (Joffé 2001). Western Sahara remained outside the EEC's agenda, even after the Spanish withdrawal, the Moroccan-Mauritanian occupation of the territory, and the outbreak of the conflict between the latter and the pro-independence Polisario Front in 1975-1976 (Vaquer 2004; Fernández-Molina 2016).

The international political economy perspective: interdependence or dependency?

A new era in the institutionalisation of EU–Maghreb relations that lasts until today in bilateral terms started with the launch of the Euro-Mediterranean Partnership (EMP), or Barcelona Process, in 1995. Besides adding a novel multilateral dimension to (bi)regional cooperation across the Mediterranean basin, the EMP framework upgraded the traditional hub-and-spoke pattern of bilateral relations between the EU and individual partner countries, which materialised in a new batch of Association Agreements and respective bilateral institutions set up under each of the latter (Association Councils and Association Committees). Two Maghreb countries, namely Tunisia and Morocco, were, along with Israel, the frontrunners in signing (1995, 1996) and implementing (1998, 2000) their third-generation Association Agreements with the EU. Only negotiations with Algeria were postponed due to the civil war in which terrorist and 'counter terrorist' violence plunged the country during the 1990s – the so-called 'black decade'. The EU–Algeria Association Agreement only saw the light of day in 2002 (in force in 2005) after the domestic situation had stabilised and the international rehabilitation of the Algerian regime was underway (Begga and Abid 2004). In terms of content, the bilateral Association Agreements between the EU and Mediterranean partner countries were presented as multidimensional and going far beyond trade: they envisaged the establishment of regular political and security dialogue, and cooperation in a wide range of sectoral areas, and social and cultural matters. For all partner countries, a standard democracy and human rights clause was included in Article 2. In practice, in keeping with the tradition of EU–Maghreb relations, the aspects that were to take precedence during their implementation were commercial liberalisation – with the prospect of gradually establishing a free trade area over 12 years, yet maintaining the existing 'agricultural exception' – and the accompanying financial support (Aghrout 2000).

In spite of this, from an international political economy perspective, the gradual trade concessions agreed over decades could barely alter the structural nature of the EU–Maghreb relationship. The latter's main constant feature has been a strong asymmetry between the weight of mutual trade for each of the sides. For example, in 2014 the EU-28 was the first trading partner and first supplier of all the five Maghreb countries (see Table 29.1). Exchanges with the northern bloc represented more than 50 per cent of the total trade with the world for all five countries except Mauritania. Conversely, the Maghreb countries occupied quite secondary or even negligible positions (below 1 per cent of total trade) in the ranking of the EU's top trading partners (see Table 29.2). The percentages for Morocco and Tunisia were strikingly similar to those from 50 years earlier, when the EEC had only six members (Aghrout 2000). The only partial exception to this pattern of trade asymmetry was Algeria, the EU's third largest supplier of gas after Russia and Norway.

At the same time, trade balance statistics provide a good indicator of the main differentiating force that has drawn a dividing line between two groups of Maghreb countries: 'oil haves' (Algeria and Libya) have a positive trade balance with the EU, while that of 'oil have-nots' (Morocco, Tunisia and Mauritania) has been consistently negative. This cleavage has also been observed in the sphere of foreign direct investment (FDI), where Tunisia and Morocco have competed for decades to attract EU capital and companies, with each of them trying to distinguish itself from its Maghreb neighbours and project an image of domestic political stability (Murphy 1999: 60). Algeria and Libya were to join this race only in the 2000s.

Against this background, the existing academic literature on EU–Maghreb relations has addressed two major questions stemming from the point of view of international political economy. The first of them concerns the overall structural nature of this relationship. Ahmed Aghrout (2000) assessed whether its main features correspond to the liberal concept of 'interdependence' – which

Table 29.1 Share (%) of trade with EU-28 in the Maghreb countries' total trade with the world (2014)

	Imports	Exports	Total trade
Algeria	50.6	64.3	57.8
Libya	39.4	76.4	57.8
Mauritania	36.7	26.9	33.1
Morocco	51.0	63.4	55.2
Tunisia	61.5	72.8	65.7

Source: European Commission trade statistics (http://ec.europa.eu/trade/policy/countries-and-regions/statistics/index_en.htm); data processed by author.

Table 29.2 Share (%) of trade with Maghreb countries in EU-28's total trade with the world (2015)

	Imports	Exports	Total trade
Algeria	1.2	1.2	1.2
Libya	0.4	0.2	0.3
Mauritania	0.0	0.0	0.0
Morocco	0.7	1.0	0.9
Tunisia	0.6	0.6	0.6

Source: European Commission trade statistics (http://ec.europa.eu/trade/policy/countries-and-regions/statistics/index_en.htm); data processed by author.

highlights the interconnection and mutual reliance between international actors, not necessarily in a symmetrical fashion – or the post-Marxist notion of 'dependency'. He argued that the Maghreb displays some apparent symptoms of dependency on the EU, since the relationship between them involves two economically unequal parties, a centre-periphery pattern of domination and exploitation of the peripheral economy, and common interests between the capitalist centre and the peripheral 'clientele class'. However, he did not find sufficient evidence of a strong historical reliance on foreign investment and penetration by multinational corporations that could be comparable to that of other southern regions, such as Latin America. For this reason, he concluded that the EU–Maghreb relationship is better described as one of 'high asymmetrical interdependence', in which 'both parties would incur costs if the relationship were broken' (ibid.: 14-16). This mixed answer seems more appropriate when taking into account the EU's reliance on Maghreb countries in the energy domain (*vis-à-vis* Algerian natural gas) as well as in non-economic fields such as security and migration control.

The second question interrogates the extent to which natural resource endowment and political economy factors account for the differentiation between the various Maghreb countries' bilateral relationships with the EU. 'Oil have-nots' have certainly followed much more – and more consistent – cooperative trajectories *vis-à-vis* the EU, which they view as their inevitable partner. This cooperative stance includes not only the economic opening (*infitah*) and export-oriented extroversion, which has guided their official development strategies since the 1970s (Tunisia) and 1980s (Morocco) (White 2001; Murphy 1999), but also a permanent political will to strengthen ties with Brussels as much as possible. Also, beyond economic cost–benefit calculations, various authors have discussed how the pro-European orientation of Moroccan and Tunisian elites has led them to accept what were 'sub-optimal agreements' or 'poor deals' from a trade and development perspective (Dawson 2009: 2, 9). The opposite case is Algeria, whose selective and pragmatic – when not reluctant – attitude towards cooperation with the EU has often been attributed to the financial strength provided by energy resources, especially during the boom of oil prices in the 2000s, and the leverage granted by its position as key gas supplier for Spain, Italy, France and Portugal (Darbouche 2008). It can be contended that Algeria is much more dependent on the EU than the other way around, since it exports to that market around 85 per cent of its gas, with few alternatives for diversification, and the sale of hydrocarbons represents over 60 per cent of its budget revenues and 90 per cent of its export earnings (2010–2014) (International Monetary Fund 2016).

Purely economic factors aside, another structural element of asymmetry in EU–Maghreb relations, is the absence of any effective regional integration between the Maghreb countries. The academic discussion of the Maghreb regional system has tended to describe it in realist terms. Security dilemmas and power balancing behaviour by the states that form it have spoiled regional integration since the 1960s, chiefly the Arab Maghreb Union (AMU) launched in 1989. The main economic rationale for this initiative was that Spain and Portugal's 1986 accession to the EEC had substantially deteriorated their southern neighbours' preferential trade conditions to export to the Common Market, which could be theoretically improved by collective bargaining. However, this region-building eagerness was short-lived and the overall activity of the AMU was virtually deadlocked in the mid-1990s. A liberal discourse has developed, denouncing and trying to quantify the high economic 'cost of non-Maghreb' (Ghilès 2010), that is, the development opportunities missed by these countries by not taking advantage of their potential economic complementarity. The EEC/EU has been one of the main external instigators of this debate, although the bilateral practice that took precedence within the EMP actually contributed to 'dividing rather than unifying the sub-region' in the 1990s (Murphy 1999: 119). A joint communication by the European Commission and the High Representative resumed this talk in 2012, examining the ways in which the EU could 'support closer cooperation' in 'one of the least integrated regions in the world' (European Commission/High Representative 2012). The recipes mentioned for this purpose – for example, promoting sub-regional cooperation in existing flexible frameworks such as the Union for the Mediterranean (UfM) and the 5+5 Dialogue, and supporting 'diversified and enhanced south-south trade integration' (ibid.) – hardly sounded new.

Diverging foreign policy roles and bilateral differentiation

The political economy structure and realist spokes in the wheels of liberal region-building have thus concurred in favouring bilateralism and 'geographical differentiation' (Barbé and Herranz-Surrallés 2012: 3) within EU–Maghreb relations. A constructivist analysis would also explain this variation by referring to the influence of the different Maghreb countries' national identities and foreign policy roles, the latter being understood as social constructions resulting from the interaction between their self-definitions ('ego') and external – in this case European – expectations or prescriptions ('alter'). Three divergent roles can be observed in these states' relationships with the EU, which were mainly forged during the decolonisation era and have endured due to a socially constructed path dependence: two competing 'model students' of the EU (Tunisia and Morocco) coexist with a somewhat 'bad student' (Algeria) and a former 'rogue state', which was hastily 'reintegrated' into the international community in the 2000s (Libya). This allocation of roles is reflected in the dissimilar bilateral paths, followed by the Maghreb countries in their relations with the EU, and more particularly in the context of the ENP, a policy that was precisely launched in 2004 in order to encourage bilateral differentiation and thus improve the EU's leverage and positive conditionality *vis-à-vis* individual countries in its periphery.

Table 29.3 EU–Maghreb relations in 2016

	Euro-Mediterranean Partnership (EMP)/ Union for the Mediterranean (UfM)		European Neighbourhood Policy (ENP)	
	Association Agreements (AA) (bilateral legal/contractual framework)			
	Signature	Entry into force	ENP Action Plans	Special bilateral relationships
Morocco	February 1996	March 2000	June 2005 December 2013	Advanced Status 2008
Tunisia	July 1995	March 1998	July 2005 November 2012	Privileged Partnership 2012
Algeria	April 2002	September 2005	No Action Plan *Negotiations launched in 2012	Strategic Energy Partnership 2012
Libya	No Association Agreement *Observer status in EMP/UfM *Negotiations on Framework Agreement 2008–2011		Potential inclusion but no actual participation in most ENP structures *No Action Plan	
Mauritania	No Association Agreement *Member of EMP/UfM since 2007		Not included in ENP (party to EU–ACP Partnership Agreement)	

The 'good'

Morocco and Tunisia both welcomed the ENP's asymmetric and variable-geometry thrust and endeavoured to play the role of 'model students' by immediately negotiating their bilateral ENP Action Plans with the EU. Their Action Plans were adopted in June and July 2005. The two countries' previous trajectories of relations with the EEC/EU had similarly run in parallel, with first-generation Association Agreements (1969), second-generation Cooperation Agreements (1976) and third-generation Association Agreements (1995/1996) having been signed roughly at the same time (see Table 29.3). Rabat and Tunis had also maintained what was viewed as an exemplary commitment to the EMP at multilateral level. This behaviour revealed a consistent willingness and capacity for adaptation to Brussels' expectations, whose origins can be traced back to a mix of the structural constraints of economic extroversion and elite interests, identity and socialisation. Ironically, both countries' official discourses were akin to each other in emphasising the respective national exceptionalism in the regional context and alleged exclusiveness of bilateral ties with the EU.

Three differences can be observed between the Moroccan and Tunisian shared pro-European agency. First, the continuous strengthening of bilateral relations with the EU has been an unparalleled priority for decades for Tunisian foreign policy, while it only appears as the second top objective in Morocco's hierarchy, where it stands behind the international management of the 'national question' of Western Sahara. In practice, the concrete objectives stemming from Morocco's roles as 'territorial champion' and 'model student' of the EU have seldom clashed with each other (Fernández-Molina 2015: 96). Second, from the 1990s onwards, the Tunisian authorities' degree of international adaptation is deemed to have been relatively higher on the economic level, whereas their Moroccan counterparts were more ambitious and skilful politically. Chief among the signs of international endorsement of the proverbial economic reformism (Hibou 2006) of President Zine El Abidine Ben Ali (1987–2011) was repeated praise for the 'Tunisian miracle' by the EU and the International Monetary Fund (IMF): neoliberal privatisation, deregulation and macroeconomic balance were presented as having led to economic growth and an expansion of the middle class, according to what later turned out to be largely manipulated or misleading figures (Kallander 2013). Meanwhile, the Moroccan monarchy raised its pro-European stakes with political statements of intent, such as King Hassan II's formal application for EEC membership in 1987 and Mohammed VI's demand for 'more than association, less than accession' in 2000.

The third difference, in connection to this, is that in October 2008 Morocco achieved the so-called Advanced Status, an upgrade or special relationship with the EU that was similar to what Tunisia also coveted but fell short of reaching, due to growing European human rights concerns. Even though this was a political declaration lacking concrete added value in relation to the opportunities for convergence and integration already created by the ENP (Martín 2009), the Advanced Status still represented a valued qualitative leap and a powerful sign of EU recognition of the merits of Morocco's pro-European foreign policy and domestic 'courageous process of modernisation and democratisation' (EU-Morocco Association Council 2008). By contrast, the increasingly visible Tunisian hindrances to EU democracy assistance (funding for human rights associations), and the freezing of bilateral political dialogue between 2005 and 2007, led the EU to delay the opening of negotiations on the 'reinforced partnership' that Tunis demanded in November 2008. An *ad hoc* bilateral working group was eventually set up to this purpose in March 2010, just a few months before the 2011 Tunisian revolution which overthrew Ben Ali (Van Hüllen 2012).

Beyond these differences and swings, the overall lack of any substantial EU contribution to genuine democratic transformation in either Morocco or Tunisia has opened a scholarly debate on the limits of international socialisation as a mechanism of democracy promotion in the EU's neighbourhood (Powel and Sadiki 2010). The two Maghreb 'model students' share the paradoxical situation of being strongly 'socialised' by the northern power on both macro and micro levels – since their elites have a long history of interaction with, and exposure to, European norms and practices, typically including training or education in France – without having actually exceeded the level of a superficial and rational-choice adoption of EU political standards. This kind of socialisation amounts to a strategic learning of what is socially accepted in the context of their asymmetric relationships with the EU by both state and civil society actors, but it has not resulted in profound change in interests, values and identity (Fernández-Molina 2015; Lacroix 2006). According to critics, EU socialisation has played a problematic role in unwittingly legitimising authoritarian regimes like these (Powel and Sadiki 2010).

The soul-searching and temporary self-criticism shown by the EU in the aftermath of the 2011 Arab uprisings did not ultimately change much in the longstanding patterns of bilateral relations with the Maghreb and the sticking to the socialisation approach *vis-à-vis* the most cooperative partners. Despite the asymmetry between the domestic political processes witnessed in each partner in 2011 – a revolutionary regime change vs a top-down constitutional reform devoid of any structural impact – Tunisia and Morocco were to receive similar preferential treatment from the EU hereafter. They were both chosen by Brussels, along with Egypt and Jordan, as front-running southern neighbours that would benefit from allegedly new EU incentives in terms of 'money' – Support to Partnership, Reforms and Inclusive Growth (SPRING) programme – 'market' – negotiations of Deep and Comprehensive Free Trade Areas (DCFTAs) – and 'mobility' – negotiations of Mobility Partnerships. New ENP Action Plans, replacing those from 2005, were signed with Tunisia and Morocco in November 2012 and December 2013. 'Business as usual' was arguably on the Moroccan side (Colombo and Voltolini 2014). The main distinctive reward granted to post-revolutionary Tunisia was the launch of an EU–Tunisia Task Force to coordinate support for its democratic transition in September 2011. EU Election Observation Missions were subsequently dispatched to monitor the Tunisian Constituent Assembly elections in October 2011 and to the parliamentary and presidential elections held three years later. In the end, the post-2011 context allowed Tunisia to achieve the long-awaited upgrade of its bilateral relations with the EU in the form of a Privileged Partnership established in November 2012. The two Maghreb 'model students' of the EU were standing again on an equal footing.

The 'bad' and the 'ugly'

Meanwhile, Algeria's initial response to the launch of the ENP was even more reluctant than foreseen in Brussels. This country distinguished itself as the only 'normal' Southern Mediterranean partner of the EU that straightforwardly refused to negotiate an ENP Action Plan. This lack of interest was in line with a national identity and a foreign policy role that were essentially at odds with those of Algeria's neighbours, as well as a decades-long history of 'awkwardness' (Darbouche 2008: 371–372) in relations with the EEC/EU. Even in the 2000s, the foreign policy of the former standard-bearer of third-worldism, the Non-Aligned Movement and the 'radical' Steadfastness and Confrontation Front against Israel, was still socially constrained by the norm of opposition to – or at least independence from – the West and maintained a strong emphasis on the principle of non-interference in internal affairs. Having institutionalised its bilateral relationship with the EEC, with a Cooperation Agreement only in 1976 (see Table 29.3), Algeria's insertion into the EMP was largely shaped by the liability of domestic civil war in the 1990s, which made the country's military authorities view the new Euro-Mediterranean cooperation framework as a potential window of opportunity to alleviate their growing international isolation and gather support for their questioned 'counter terrorist' strategy. This rational choice did not fully work, since the negotiations of the EU–Algeria Association Agreement were put off and not resumed until 2000, after Abdelaziz Bouteflika had been elected as president, enacted the 1999 Civil Concord Law and joined the global War on Terror, securing the reintegration of the country into the international community.

Against this backdrop, Algeria's official justification of the dismissal of the ENP in 2004–2005 was one of timing: the new EU policy came too early for a country whose Association Agreement was still not ratified and in force – which only occurred in September 2005 – and needed time and resources to implement it. This was coupled with a more principled questioning of the Eurocentrism, unilateralism and lack of real co-ownership that the ENP approach and the label of 'neighbourhood' implied in comparison to the existing 'partnership', according to this and other Southern Mediterranean states (Jaidi 2005). Beyond the official discourse, observers attributed the Algerian reluctance to political economy factors – the financial strength (in terms of foreign exchange reserves) granted to the country by its gas and oil resources during the 2000s – and identity-related issues encompassing an aversion to conditionality rooted in a long anticolonial and third-world nationalism. Structural and constructivist explanations concurred in accounting for an unusual foreign policy assertiveness, or 'Russian syndrome' (Darbouche 2008), which became explicit in February 2006 when Algeria proposed a Strategic Energy Partnership (SEP) with the EU, reproducing the terminology applied to the EU's relations with great powers and the BRICS. A memorandum of understanding on the SEP was eventually signed in July 2013.

Significantly, this milestone coincided with the adaptive U-turn made by Algiers in its relations with Brussels in the context of the 2011 Arab uprisings, when a new perception of regional fragility and encirclement led the Bouteflika regime to search for external backing (Darbouche and Dennison 2011). 2012 was a historic year, in which Algeria for the first time invited an EU Election Observation Mission to monitor its legislative elections and communicated its readiness to participate in the ENP. Negotiations on a bilateral Action Plan were launched in October (Hernando de Larramendi and Fernández-Molina 2015). However, this cooperative stance was short-lived and the Action Plan talks stretched on without bearing fruit. Algeria recovered its negotiating strength due to European expectations that it play a key role in curbing the security deterioration in the region and its diplomatic mediation in the Malian and Libyan political dialogues (ibid.). Even within domestic instability, Algerian assertiveness reached the point of calling for a renegotiation of the Association Agreement, which was considered to be damaging the country's economy, in August 2015.

Even odder is the situation of Libya, a country that has never established any contractual relations with the EU (see Table 29.3), despite being mentioned as a potential participant in the ENP's framework documents from the outset. Libya's foreign policy role under the Gaddafi regime, and especially during the 1980s and 1990s, was quite akin to the archetype of the 'villain' or 'rogue state'. Being widely tagged as a sponsor of international terrorism made the country subject to international isolation and UN, United States and EC/EU diplomatic (1986) and economic (1992) sanctions. The latter were very severe in the trade and energy domain, and prevented the maintenance of any bilateral political relations or form of multilateral integration within the EMP during this decade. This extreme form of negative conditionality represented the opposite end to the socialisation approach, yet it ended up being equally ineffective. The cooperative turn, made by Libyan foreign policy at the turn of the millennium – with the announcement of the abandonment of the programme of weapons of mass destruction and the payment of compensation to the victims of terrorist attacks previously sponsored by the Gaddafi regime – paved the way for a strikingly swift reintegration of the latter into the international community, irrespective of unchanged authoritarianism in the domestic sphere.

The EU established dialogue in 1999 and launched a new policy of engagement in 2003–2004, which consisted of four elements: the lifting of all economic sanctions, the arms embargo and restrictions on Libyan representatives (diplomats); the admission of Libya as observer into EMP – and later UfM – multilateral fora; the exchange of high-level official visits, including trips to Tripoli by several EU Member States' heads of government and officials of the Commission, as well as Gaddafi's invitation to Brussels in April 2004; and some technical cooperation and financial assistance focusing largely on migration and border management. Observers are divided as to whether the European 'realist' turnaround was driven more by commercial and energy interests – securing oil concessions and arms sales agreements – or by the EU's growing reliance on Southern Mediterranean states for migration control (Zoubir 2009; Lutterbeck 2009). Bilateral relations with certain EU Member States, especially the former coloniser, Italy, also played a major role. The fact that the ENP documents presented this normalisation process as being conditional on Libya's full adoption of the EMP *acquis*, which Gaddafi never accepted, did not make any difference in practice. Even though he dismissed the offer of full membership of the UfM in 2008, negotiations on a bilateral Framework Agreement – a rudimentary form of Association Agreement – that would institutionalise for the first time EU–Libya relations were launched in that same year (Bosse 2011). The 2011 Libyan revolution against Gaddafi put an ironic end to the EU's policy of engagement, in addition to exposing the limits or inadequacies of the ENP for crisis management, when the domestic violence led to an international military intervention led by France and the United Kingdom.

Conclusions

Neither the disruptions caused by the 2011 Arab uprisings and regime changes nor the increased complexity created by the externalisation of EU migration management and the enlargement of the Maghreb's regional security complex to the Sahel have altered the major structural features of EU–Maghreb relations, which were largely inherited from the colonial period. Structural political economy determinants and constructivist identity factors, more closely related to agency, feed into each other in favouring bilateral differentiation. Realist power politics within the Maghreb region has additionally contributed to obstructing any liberal region-building project and thus reinforcing the enduring hub-and-spoke arrangement of EU–Maghreb relations. As a result, each of the Maghreb countries has followed a distinct bilateral path in the context of the ENP. Only those of Morocco and Tunisia show significant parallels, as these two states have consistently played the role of 'model students' of the EU and the EU has rewarded them with similarly privileged treatment – including in post-2011 policy initiatives despite the divergence of their respective domestic political trajectories. Algeria's more limited zig-zag pattern in participating in the ENP only materialised as a matter of necessity in 2012, at a time when the regime felt regionally isolated and weakened. Libya has not become a full-fledged member of the ENP despite the EU's policy of engagement *vis-à-vis* the Gaddafi regime in the 2000s, since the point of departure was one of absence of any contractual relations whatsoever with the EU and the negotiations on a bilateral Framework Agreement were interrupted by the 2011 revolution.

References

Abed Jabri, M. (1985) 'Evolution of the Maghrib Concept: Facts and Perspectives', in Barakat, H. (ed.) *Contemporary North Africa: Issues of Development and Integration*, Washington, DC: Georgetown University, 63–86.

Aghrout, A. (2000) *From Preferential Status to Partnership: The Euro-Maghreb Relationship*, New York: Palgrave.

Barbé, E. and Herranz-Surrallés, A. (eds.) (2012) *The Challenge of Differentiation in Euro-Mediterranean Relations*, Oxon/New York: Routledge.

Begga, C. and Abid, K. (2004) 'The Euro-Algerian Relationship: A Review of its Development', in Aghrout, A. and Bougherira, R. (eds.) *Algeria in Transition: Reforms and Development Prospects*, Oxon/New York: Routledge, 73–86.

Behr, T. and Tiilikainen, T. (eds.) (2015) *Northern Europe and the Making of the EU's Mediterranean and Middle East Policies*, Farnham/Burlington: Ashgate.

Bosse, G. (2011) 'From "Villains" to the New Guardians of Security in Europe? Paradigm Shifts in EU Foreign Policy towards Libya and Belarus', *Perspectives on European Politics and Society* 12(4): 440–461.

Colombo, S. and Voltolini, B. (2014) '"Business as Usual" in EU Democracy Promotion Towards Morocco? Assessing the Limits of the EU's Approach Towards the Mediterranean after the Arab Uprisings', *L'Europe en Formation* 371: 41–57.

Darbouche, H. (2008) 'Decoding Algeria's ENP Policy: Differentiation by Other Means?', *Mediterranean Politics* 13(3): 371–389.

Darbouche, H. and Dennison, S. (2011) 'A "Reset" with Algeria: the Russia to the EU's South', *Policy Brief* 46, European Council on Foreign Relations.

Dawson, C. (2009) *EU Integration with North Africa: Trade Negotiations and Democracy Deficits in Morocco*, London/New York: I.B. Tauris.

EU-Morocco Association Council (2008) *Déclaration de l'Union européenne*, 13 October.

European Commission/High Representative (2012) *Joint Communication: Supporting Closer Cooperation and Regional Integration in the Maghreb: Algeria, Libya, Mauritania, Morocco and Tunisia*, JOIN (2012) 36 final, 17 December.

Fernández-Molina, I. (2015) *Moroccan Foreign Policy Under Mohammed VI, 1999–2014*, Oxon/New York: Routledge.

Fernández-Molina, I. (2016) 'The EU, the ENP and the Western Sahara Conflict: Executive Continuity and Parliamentary Detours', in Bouris, D. and Schumacher, T. (eds.) *The Revised European Neighbourhood Policy: Continuity and Change in EU Foreign Policy*, New York: Palgrave.

Ghilès, F. (2010) 'Le "non-Maghreb" coûte cher au Maghreb', *Le Monde Diplomatique*.

Henry, J. (2006) La Méditerranée occidentale en quête d'un "destin commun"', *'L'Année du Maghreb 2004*, Paris: CNRS, 7–26.

Hernando de Larramendi, M. and Fernández-Molina, I. (2015) 'The Evolving Foreign Policies of North African States (2011–2014): New Trends in Constraints, Political Processes and Behavior', in Zoubir, Y. and White, G. (eds.) *North African Politics: Change and Continuity*, Oxon/New York: Routledge, 245–276.

Hibou, B. (2006) *La force de l'obéissance. Économie politique de la répression en Tunisie*, Paris: La Découverte.

International Monetary Fund (2016) 'Algeria Country Report', 29 April.

Jaidi, L. (ed.) (2005) *La politique de bon voisinage: quelle lecture des pays maghrébins?*, Rabat: Friedrich Ebert Stiftung.

Joffé, G. (2001) 'Libya and Europe', *Journal of North African Studies* 6(4): 75–92.

Kallander, A. (2013) '"Friends of Tunisia": French Economic and Diplomatic Support of Tunisian Authoritarianism', in Gana, N. (ed.) *The Making of the Tunisian Revolution: Contexts, Architects, Prospects*, Edinburgh: Edinburgh University Press, 103–124.

Lacroix, T. (2006) 'Contrôle et instrumentalisation de la société civile maghrébine dans la coopération euro-méditerranéenne: le cas du Maroc et de la Tunisie', *L'Année du Maghreb 2004*, Paris: CNRS, 100–115.

Lutterbeck, D. (2009) 'Migrants, Weapons and Oil: Europe and Libya after the Sanctions', *Journal of North African Studies* 14(2): 169–184.

Martín, I. (2009) 'EU–Morocco Relations: How Advanced is the "Advanced Status"?', *Mediterranean Politics* 14(2): 239–245.

Murphy, E. (1999) *Economic and Political Change in Tunisia: From Bourguiba to Ben Ali*, Basingstoke: MacMillan.

Powel, B. and Sadiki, L. (2010) *Europe and Tunisia: Democratization via Association*, Oxon/New York: Routledge.

Stora, B. (2003) 'Algeria/Morocco: The Passions of the Past. Representations of the Nation that Unite and Divide', *Journal of North African Studies* 8(1): 14–34.

Van Hüllen, V. (2012) 'Europeanisation Through Cooperation? EU Democracy Promotion in Morocco and Tunisia', *West European Politics* 35(1): 117–134.

Vaquer, J. (2004) 'The European Union and Western Sahara', *European Foreign Affairs Review* 9(1): 93–113.
White, G. (2001) *Comparative Political Economy of Tunisia and Morocco: On the Outside of Europe Looking in*, New York: State University of New York Press.
Zoubir, Y. (2009) 'Libya and Europe: Economic Realism at the Rescue of the Qaddafi Authoritarian Regime', *Journal of Contemporary European Studies* 17(3): 401–415.

30
EU–MASHREQ RELATIONS
Differentiation, conditionality and security

Peter Seeberg

Introduction

This chapter presents an overview of key issues in the relations between the European Union (EU) and the countries in the Mashreq region since the launching of the European Neighbourhood Policy (ENP) in 2004. In this chapter, the Mashreq mainly refers to Egypt, Jordan, Lebanon and Syria.[1] Initially, it should be emphasized that the following analysis of EU–Mashreq relations is influenced by the very different political, social and economic realities in the four countries. As stated in a Strategy Paper from the European Commission in 2004, this was, from the beginning, reflected in ENP-related foreign policy considerations: the ENP Action Plans (APs) 'will draw on a common set of principles but will be differentiated, reflecting the existing state of relations with each country, its needs and capacities, as well as common interests' (Commission of the European Communities 2004). In the Mashreq, Jordan, along with the Palestinian Authority and Israel, was the first to negotiate an AP. By mid–2005, AP negotiations with Egypt and Lebanon were ongoing, while Syria still had not signed an Association Agreement (AA).

Connected with the Arab uprisings in 2011, the EU and the Mashreq states were facing new, considerable challenges, not least as a result of the complex political realities in Egypt following the fall of Mubarak and the devastating crisis in Syria, which also brought consequences for the neighbouring states, Lebanon and Jordan. A communication entitled 'A New Response to a Changing Neighbourhood' emphasized that the EU was aware of the unfolding developments (European Commission and High Representative of the European Union for Foreign Affairs and Security Policy 2011) and that a review of the ENP had been carried out with the ambition of strengthening regional partnerships. The developments after the Arab uprisings changed the political conditions in the region in many ways and contributed to the need for the EU to further adjust its policies to new realities.

Following consultations in 2015 with 'EU member states, partner governments, EU institutions, international organizations, social partners, civil society, business, think tanks, academia and members of the public' a presentation of the review of the ENP took place on 18 November 2015 (European Commission and High Representative of the European Union for Foreign Affairs and Security Policy 2015c: 2). The review pointed at recent challenges and mentioned the ongoing conflicts and the rise of extremism and terrorism in the Middle East and that 'the new ENP will take stabilisation as its main political priority in this mandate' (ibid.).

The Mashreq region has for decades been characterized by a lack of stability. All four states have vulnerable economies, high unemployment rates, few natural resources and an inefficient state apparatus (MENA 2015). The continuing critical situation in Syria, and its regional spill-over effects, depict a security environment in which it is difficult for the EU to manoeuvre. In addition, the high numbers of refugees arriving at the European borders and the acts of terror taking place in Europe and the Middle East led to a situation in which 'the EU's own interdependence with its neighbours has been placed in sharp focus' (European Commission and High Representative of the European Union for Foreign Affairs and Security Policy 2015c: 2). The aim of this chapter is to analyse the main aspects of the ENP since 2004 in the context of the Mashreq. The chapter attempts to show that the policies of the EU in relation to the different realities in the Mashreq address the multi-faceted conditions and circumstances by applying pragmatic political practices, while the EU's security interests remain the primary goal.

Egypt: EU cooperation and the restoration of military rule

The EU has for decades worked together with the regime in Egypt, which due to its geostrategic location and its central role in Arab politics is perceived as an actor of considerable importance in the Middle East. An AA between the EU and Egypt came into force in June 2004; later, the cooperation was strengthened by the EU–Egypt AP, adopted in 2007. The AP illustrated the specific role of Egypt in the Arab region and highlighted the significant role of EU–Egyptian cooperation in a security context. The fact that Egypt was considered important by the EU was further underlined when President Husni Mubarak, in 2008, with President Nicolas Sarkozy as European counterpart, was appointed the first co-president of the Union for the Mediterranean (UfM).

The relationship was not without problems, partly, as pointed out by Isaac (2014), because the democracy-stability dilemma played a significant role in the EU's approach to Egypt. The dilemma was obvious, throughout the three-decade long cooperation with Mubarak, in the sense that the EU's ambition of promoting democracy clashed with the EU's belief that Mubarak could provide stability and thus cooperated with the repressive Egyptian regime. During the period of President Muhammad Morsi, the predicament became more complex, because on the one side the EU wanted to support the democratically elected president from the spectrum of Political Islam, but on the other the EU was sceptical about obvious signs that he was not able to secure political and economic progress. The EU commitment to help consolidate political transitions was conditional. Following the 2011 uprising, the EU launched the SPRING (Support for Partnership, Reform and Inclusive Growth) programme under the ENP, which applied the 'more-for-more' principle inherent in the reviewed ENP of the same year, making it possible for the EU to modulate the assistance to Egypt in accordance with the (lack of) progress concerning sustainable democracy and socio-economic development (Amin 2014). Initially, Egypt was the second biggest beneficiary of SPRING (after Tunisia), but later, the conditionality approach led to decreasing allocations to Egypt. Detailed EU assessments of SPRING are not available, but fluctuations within the programme, which reduced financial aid from the EU to Egypt, demonstrated the differentiated approach of the EU regarding aid to the Mashreq states.

The issue of migration plays an important role in EU–Egyptian relations. Egypt delivers human resources to its neighbours; in 2012, together, Libya, the Mashreq states and the Gulf states hosted an estimated four to six million Egyptian work migrants (Amer and Fargues 2014; MPC-Team 2013). Furthermore, Egypt receives refugees and migrants from Syria and Iraq (MPC-Team 2013). The agreements between the EU and Egypt concerning migration are vague and to some degree outdated (Council of the European Union 2005) and – contrary to Jordan and Lebanon – a dialogue with the EU concerning a Mobility Partnership (MP) has not been initiated. From a security perspective, as it is mentioned in the AP, the strategic European interest in controlling migration from Egypt concerns refugees and illegal migrants from Africa, south of the Sahara, refugees from Syria attempting to reach Europe *via* Egypt and, to a lesser extent, work migrants from Egypt (European Commission 2007). Together these phenomena represent significant themes in the EU's revision of the ENP, underlining the security dimension (European Commission and High Representative of the European Union for Foreign Affairs and Security Policy 2015c).

The EU countries together constitute Egypt's largest trading partner, and since the signing of a trade agreement between the EU and Egypt in 2011, the cooperation has focused on how to improve Egypt's general economic situation and the competitiveness of the production sector. The EU is a significant donor for Egypt. Besides the thematic programmes, including those dealing with human rights, civil society, migration and education, the EU's bilateral assistance committed for Egypt under the European Neighbourhood and Partnership Instrument (ENPI) totalled EUR1 billion for 2007–2013. Replacing the ENPI by the European Neighbourhood Instrument (ENI) would mean that the indicative allocation for 2014–2020 is estimated between EUR756 million and EUR924 million, focusing on poverty alleviation, local socio-economic development and social protection, governance, transparency, and quality of life and environment (European Commission 2015b: 7). These areas of intervention seem highly relevant due to the development regarding the political, economic and social conditions in Egypt, which worsened following the ousting of Mubarak in early 2011 and the period in which the Muslim Brotherhood under Muhammad Morsi held a dominant position in Egyptian domestic politics.

Abdel Fatah al-Sisi came to power after a military coup d'état against Morsi in July 2013 and, after being elected in May 2014, was ultimately sworn in as President. The European leaders were sceptical because of the extremely authoritarian character of the new regime, although al-Sisi was received at high level meetings in both Rome and Paris in November 2014. The situation after the takeover by al-Sisi has also been a conflictive period for Egypt. Despite financial support provided by the Arab Gulf states, which to some degree has kept the external fiscal imbalance in check, the Egyptian economy has suffered from serious economic and social problems (European Commission and High Representative of the European Union for Foreign Affairs and Security Policy 2015a: 9).

The cooperation between the EU and Egypt has been affected by the problematic political development in Egypt. The period after the coup was characterized by political, security and economic challenges for Egypt, starting in summer 2013, when the Egyptian military violently dispersed demonstrations in Cairo, which led to the death of more than 1,000 people. A state of emergency was imposed lasting for several months. An extraordinary EU Foreign Affairs Council in August 2013 condemned the violence and called for an end to the state of emergency, the release of political prisoners and the restoration of democratic processes. In short, the political relations between Egypt and the EU cooled down, and due to this development only limited progress took place in addressing agreements within the framework of the ENP. The conditionality-based approach of the ENP was obviously strengthened following the review of 2011, but the European interest in stability in Egypt seemed to be dominant in the democracy-stability equation.

In the ENP Progress Report for Egypt covering 2014, it was stated that 'the formal EU–Egypt dialogue under the ENP remained *de facto* suspended'. However, the report also stated that the EU and Egypt 'agreed to re-launch their cooperation within the framework of the Association Agreement' (European Commission and High Representative of the European Union for Foreign Affairs and Security Policy 2015a: 2). This seemed to indicate that the EU was opening for a return to the kind of cooperation under Mubarak, where the stability of the regime in Cairo was seen as a guarantee for EU's security. This was underlined in the November 2015 review of the ENP, which stressed that 'the new focus on security will open up a wide range of new areas of cooperation under ENP [. . .] security sector reform, border protection, tackling terrorism and radicalisation' (European Commission and High Representative of the European Union for Foreign Affairs and Security Policy 2015c). Under the pressure of a changing security environment in Egypt and in the Mediterranean in general, the EU chose a pragmatic approach regarding its policies *vis-à-vis* the al-Sisi regime, promoting 'stabilisation as its main political priority' (ibid.).

Jordan: a role model ENP partner?

The Jordanian Kingdom is, due to its relative calmness and stability in the middle of an unstable Mashreq region, an important strategic partner for the EU. Historically, Jordan has had good relations with the West, partly as a result of the Peace Treaty of 1994 between Jordan and Israel, which secured a strategic understanding between Jordan and the EU. The treaty furthermore 'underpinned the centrality of Jordan in regional politics' (Shlaim 2008: 546). An AA between the EU and Jordan came into force in 2002. The first EU–Jordan AP was adopted in January 2005 (European Commission 2005). The 2006 ENP Progress Report from the European Commission pointed out that 'Jordan has shown a real commitment to realizing the measures in the Action Plan' (Commission of the European Communities 2006: 2). The report emphasized how the institutional framework of the ENP made it possible to develop cooperation related to political developments within Jordan, but also related to foreign and security policy issues of common interest and to the general situation in the region. Furthermore, the report highlighted areas where the EU evaluated that only limited progress could be registered including progress for democracy, rule of law and social policies. Moreover, other important rights like freedom of assembly, freedom of association, social rights and labour standards (including rights for migrant workers) also left much room for improvement. Despite these shortcomings, the EU recognized that the Jordanian regime was progressing when it came to fighting corruption and transparency in the judiciary. The adoption of an Ombudsman law in April 2008 was also considered a legal and institutional improvement (Commission of the European Communities 2009).

In October 2010, the EU–Jordan Association Council agreed on an 'advanced status' partnership, and, in October 2012, a new AP was adopted which emphasized that 'Jordan has taken bold steps on the path of good governance and political reform; it has shown readiness to take further commitments in the field of democratization, human rights and the rule of law' (European Commission 2012). The main source of EU support to Jordan is the ENI, providing an indicative allocation for 2014–2020 of between EUR 588 million and EUR 714 million. Additionally, Jordan receives funding from EU thematic programmes with a focus on issues like democracy and human rights, stability and peace, migration and asylum totalling EUR 213.7 million since 2011 (European Commission 2015c). Finally, Jordan has been a privileged recipient of the SPRING funds, helping the Kingdom to overcome its challenges related to the Syrian crisis, preserving economic stability and addressing humanitarian and security needs. Yet, Jordanian improvements within several of these policy areas have lagged behind, for instance in the sense that the promised reforms of the election system have only moved forward in small steps (Valbjørn 2013). The Jordanian commitment to developing democracy and good governance and to conducting free, fair and transparent elections have been discussed for years, for instance at EU–Jordan Task Force meetings (European Union 2012). It seems that, regarding these issues, the EU is willing to pursue a pragmatic policy towards the Jordanian regime, hoping that by not insisting on more thorough and rapid reforms the EU can help secure the stability and persistence of the regime. In 2012, Jordan took over the co-presidency of the UfM, which had been held by Egypt, and in September 2014, the UfM senior officials endorsed the renewal of Jordan holding the southern co-presidency.

For the last 10–15 years, environmental issues have been a recurrent theme in EU relations with the Mashreq and have a central position in the APs for Jordan. There is a pressing need to raise environmental awareness in Jordan, not least related to the regionally controversial water issue. Laws concerning violation of water networks, illegal wells and pollution of water have been passed and Jordan participates in EU-financed sustainable water management programmes (European Commission and High Representative of the European Union for Foreign Affairs and Security Policy 2014). A Joint Declaration establishing an MP between Jordan and the EU was signed on 9 October 2014 (European Union 2014), and negotiations are continuing within the framework of a Deep and Comprehensive Free Trade Agreement (DCFTA) (European Commission 2014). The declaration emphasises the specific character of the agreement, since the migration of Jordanians to Europe is limited and that the main interests at stake, in connection with the migration phenomenon, deal with other aspects – first of all 'the specific characteristics of Jordan as major hosting country for refugees in the region and Jordan's significant efforts to support them', but also phenomena like human trafficking and 'prevention of the terrorist threat' (ibid.).

The discussions related to the ENP between the EU and Jordan have touched upon issues of relevance for common security interests, and the development concerning the significant number of refugees arriving in Jordan began to play an increasingly important role in this regard. The refugees and their conditions have been followed closely by the EU as can be seen, for instance, in an ENP implementation document for Jordan (European Commission 2014). According to the UNHCR, in 2016 around 650,000 Syrian refugees were registered in Jordan (UNHCR 2016a). The realities in Jordan point at a development in which Syrians and Iraqis – outside the 'official' context of the UNHCR – are being integrated in Amman's labour market, especially as unskilled workers to some degree replace Egyptian and Asian guest workers.

The official Jordanian narrative not only speaks of the influx of refugees as a huge economic burden for Jordan but also uses the phenomenon as a significant element in attempting to obtain political support from the Jordanian population. The EU acknowledges the official Jordanian narrative (European Commission 2014). This is underlined in the ENI 'Single Support Framework for EU support to Jordan', together with other effects of the Syrian crisis such as expenses to extraordinary public services, lack of income from tourism and increased competition from Syrian migrants at the Jordanian labour market (European Commission 2015c: 3). The specific EU–Jordan cooperation underlines the differentiated relationships between the EU and its Mashreq partners, in particular when it comes to the security dimension. According to the 2014 ENP Progress Report, EU–Jordan relations have improved significantly within the realm of security, and the EU and Jordan have agreed to establish a regular security dialogue to enhance cooperation on counter-terrorism (European Commission 2014).

Lebanon: dual power and EU pragmatism

An EU–Lebanon AP was adopted by the EU and Lebanon in 2006 and 2007. The document reflected the internal situation in Lebanon, for decades a complex, fragile political reality, due to the almost permanent political instability related to the internal sectarian divide and the long-term conflict between Israel and Hezbollah. The devastation resulting from the Israel–Hezbollah war in the summer of 2006, added to the social problems for low-income groups in Lebanon – a field within which a well-functioning cooperation took place between the EU and Lebanon. The EU committed to economic, social and institutional reforms at the Paris III International

Donor Conference in January 2007 and some of the significant fields taken up were local development projects and reforming of civil service, the police and the judiciary. Fostering the Lebanese civil society environment was a further arena where ENP-related activities received financial aid from the EU.

With its significant political and military resources, social activities and media influence, Hezbollah has established a status as an autonomous and very dominant actor, thereby constituting a 'dual power' situation in Lebanon (Seeberg 2009). The EU has had major difficulties in dealing with this reality in Lebanon and has, through indirect measures, attempted to reduce its influence. In July 2013, the EU's foreign ministers agreed to declare the armed wing of Hezbollah as a terrorist organization (EurActiv 2013). This was officially due to an alleged involvement of Hezbollah in a terrorist attack in Bulgaria, but there is hardly any doubt that the direct involvement of Hezbollah militias in the war in Syria, in support of President Bashar al-Assad, shifted the opinion of several EU politicians. At the same time, it was made clear that the EU would maintain contact with Hezbollah's political wing, being part of Lebanon's parliament and an important part of the complicated ethnic-religious realities in Lebanon (Fakhoury 2014).

In recent years, the internal turbulence in Lebanon has increased due to the spill-over effects from the civil war in Syria. The ENP Progress Report for 2014 (published in March 2015) stated that 'Lebanon continued to exercise a high degree of resilience against the challenges and threats that emerged from the turbulence in the region' (European Commission and High Representative of the European Union for Foreign Affairs and Security Policy 2015b). The report notes that Lebanon made only limited progress in implementing the AP and mentions deficits in human rights and fundamental freedoms, trade-related issues and sectoral policies (ibid.).

The war in Syria has produced a large number of Syrian refugees residing in Lebanon, which has a great financial, social and political impact on the small state. According to the UNHCR there were more than one million registered Syrian refugees in Lebanon in 2016 (UNHCR 2016b). Lebanon and the EU share commonalities of interest regarding security, not least due to the long and devastating crisis in Syria. In addition to the EUR 552.1 million earmarked for the refugees in Lebanon, the EU has allocated another EUR 219 million to Lebanon in regular programmed bilateral financial aid under the ENP (European Commission 2015d). The conditionality element does not seem very explicit – rather the EU's focus is to help Lebanon in developing its education sector, health facilities and local infrastructures. Furthermore, the significant aid related to refugees indicates stability and security as important targets. In other words, the EU has obvious interests in improving the security conditions in Lebanon and has obtained good results in assisting with the challenges related to the Syrian refugees, where Lebanon, as described by Lewis Turner, has chosen a constructive, non-encampment based approach (Turner 2015).

The overall security situation in Lebanon has worsened over the past years, since the start of the war in Syria. The European Parliament's delegation for relations with the Mashreq countries noted that it is particularly concerned about the acute security risks that Lebanon is facing, not least related to the expansion of radical Islamist groups, which have also carried out actions in Lebanon. Hence the delegation concluded its visit to Lebanon by stating 'that all tools of the European Neighbourhood Policy should be used to promote closer ties between the EU and Lebanon' (NNA 2015). Initial talks on a possible MP between the EU and Lebanon was called a 'dialogue on migration, mobility and security' (European Commission and High Representative of the European Union for Foreign Affairs and Security Policy 2015b), emphasizing the security dimension. The dialogue was launched in December 2014, with the ambition to develop networks in this respect in the upcoming year (Council of the European Union 2015). Summing up, the EU policies towards Lebanon have, in light of the specifically problematic security situation, focused more on security than on democracy promotion and political reforms.

The Syrian crisis and the ENP

Contrary to the other states in the Mashreq, Syria never signed an AA or an AP with the EU, which means that it is still the Cooperation Agreement of 1977 that governs the relations between the two parties. A draft EU–Syrian AA was negotiated from 1998 to 2004, and in 2008 the AA was updated to consider changes in Syrian customs rules and institutional changes related to the entering into force of the Lisbon Treaty (Council of the European Union 2009). An AA might have given 'Syria the opportunity to benefit from positive dynamic effects of integration such as stimulating investment, promoting transfers of technology and enhancing efficiency' (Dorstal and Zorob 2009), but such perspectives never unfolded. While the EU Member States agreed in October 2009 to sign the AA, the Syrian regime responded with a request for more time to further examine the agreement.

The long negotiation period and lack of progress was linked to a generally poor relationship between Syria and the EU. Attempts at carrying out liberal economic reforms by Syrian President Bashar al-Asad were initially welcomed by the EU, but the foreign policy relations were affected by the collapse of the peace process with Israel, the souring of the relations between Syria and the US and the assassination of Lebanese Prime Minister Rafiq al-Hariri in February 2005, which was blamed on the Syrians (Hinnebusch 2012). Moreover, the inefficient Syrian bureaucracy and the non-competitive Syrian industry contributed to the European reluctance (Zorob 2008). This did not mean, however, that the economic cooperation came to a complete halt.

The EU was the main donor to Syria, aiming at encouraging reforms, especially political reforms. Before the Syrian crisis, the EU criticism of the human rights situation was relatively moderate. Indeed, there had been a few cases, for instance releases of political prisoners, which led the EU to acknowledge positive developments in the country. The EU planned, within the framework of the ENPI, to promote political and economic reforms in Syria. Along these lines, a EUR129 million budget was allocated to a National Indicative Programme beginning in 2011, but in May 2011, considering the brutal clampdown on the opposition by the Ba'athist regime and its military, the EU suspended 'all preparations in relation to new bilateral cooperation programs and [...] the ongoing bilateral programs with the Syrian authorities under ENPI and MEDA instruments' (Council of the European Union 2011). While the bilateral cooperation became suspended due to the severe repression by the regime, a number of projects were maintained related to civil society and refugees – and also programmes for Syrian students and universities.

In the decade up to the crisis, the EU was Syria's largest overall trading partner (European Commission 2015a), but after 2011 EU–Syrian trade fell dramatically and gradually Syria entered a war economy situation (Yazigi 2014). EU leaders had on several occasions declared that they regarded Syria as a country which possessed weapons of mass destruction (WMDs), and in 2013–2014, in accordance with the US, the EU played a role in removing and destroying Syrian chemical weapons. As a result of negotiations with the Syrian regime, which had used chemical weapons against the Syrian population, the leadership accepted handing over the chemical weapons for destruction. UNSC Resolution 2118 bound Syria to a plan which, on 23 June 2014, saw the last chemical weapons being shipped out of Syria (UNSC 2013).

There have been other occasions of EU representatives stating that they considered Syria to be a problematic actor, who contributes to instability in the Mashreq, not least due to its foreign policy position *vis-à-vis* Israel, in which Syria has represented a highly critical position since the wars in 1967 and 1973 (Morris 1999). This general perception influenced the EU's foreign and security policy toward Syria and contributed to the lack of development in Syrian–EU relations. As mentioned before, the standstill concerning the AA became permanent from 2011 on, when the sanctions regime represented the main element in the EU's foreign and security policy toward Syria – a specific kind of 'negative conditionality' resulting from the extraordinary conditions in Syria.

Recent relations between the EU and Syria are very much affected by the decision to suspend all bilateral cooperation with the Syrian government under the ENP since May 2011. Instead the EU launched a comprehensive catalogue of sanctions against the Syrian government within a relatively short period. From an early moment onwards (and before the conflict in Syria had escalated into a war, which also included external actors and terror groups) the EU – *via* Council Regulation No. 442 of 9 May 2011 – took the first step in implementing a series of restrictive measures against the Syrian regime. The first round of sanctions targeted 13 persons and escalated over the next few years so that, by 19 May 2015, 222 persons and 71 entities were included in the EU sanctions on Syria (Seeberg 2015).

In contrast to the US sanctions against Syria since 1979 (by claiming it hosted and supported terror groups), the EU did not launch its comprehensive sanctions regime against Syria until 2011. Four years later, the EU presented a counter-terrorism strategy (January 2015) and a regional strategy (March 2015). The latter entitled 'Syria and Iraq as well as the ISIL/Da'esh threat' underlined the continuance of the EU's sanctions policy against the Syrian regime. Neither of these strategies was meant to stand alone, but should be seen in the context of the EU's wider foreign and security policy toward Syria.

Conclusions and perspectives

The emphasis on the differences between the countries covered in this chapter has highlighted that, confronted with the complex and unstable political realities of the Mashreq, the cooperation in the context of the ENP between the EU and the specific countries is facing severe challenges. The various aspects of this can be grouped in different themes in order to sum up the country-based analyses regarding differentiation, conditionality and security.

The first theme deals with the operational level of the ENP cooperation. Formally the dialogue between Egypt and the EU within an ENP framework has been suspended, but that does not mean that cooperation is not taking place. The EU's assistance to Egypt, in the form of country specific programmes funded under the ENI, is still functioning – so are thematic programmes, for example related to local authorities, human development and education. The differentiation in the EU's approach to the Mashreq states becomes obvious in the case of Jordan, where the 'advanced status' relationship has led to progress within a range of ENP-based activities, whereas, in the case of Lebanon, the focus is on security – due to regional threats and the fragile internal reality because of the sectarian divides and the 'dual power' situation. The cooperation between Lebanon and the EU, based on the ENP, is intact – although on a lower level than in the case of Jordan. Regarding the cooperation between the EU and Syria, there is only limited contact: the AA was never signed and revitalization appears illusionary in the present context.

The second theme refers to the economic cooperation implemented under the umbrella of the ENI as the key EU financial instrument. In absolute terms, Egypt is the largest recipient and the EU's support is concentrating much on poverty and local development, but also productivity and unemployment. Again, the case of Jordan underlines the differentiated EU approach: the Jordanian economy suffers from some of the same issues as the Egyptian, but being generally better off, the EU's support focuses more on developing the public and the private sectors as well as promoting solutions on renewable energy and water issues. Furthermore, additional EU assistance from ENI funds deals with refugees in Jordan, which is related to education. Lebanon is affected even more by this challenge and receives – as already mentioned – ENI support to assist with the refugee crisis. And the fact that some of the Syrian refugees are becoming part of the labour force in Lebanon eases socioeconomic constraints. Regarding Syria, the ENI addresses the needs of the population affected by war, both inside Syria and in neighbouring countries hosting Syrian refugees. The share of ENI funding out of the total EUR 1.1 billion EU development and stabilization assistance amounts to EUR 629 million, of which EUR 150 million go to actions inside Syria.

Migration in a wide sense is the third theme. The challenges within this field are highly differentiated, as is the level of consensus concerning migration between the EU and the Mashreq states and also between the EU Member States. As shown in the case of Jordan, the MP agreement emphasizes the security aspects, while in the case of Lebanon the initial talks explicitly speak of migration, mobility and security. The refugee issue, relevant in all Mashreq states, also underlines this. The analyses above demonstrate that migration, in connection with revision of the ENP policies, will be permanently placed high on the agenda (European Commission and High Representative of the European Union for Foreign Affairs and Security Policy 2015c).

The fourth theme describes the strategic perspectives regarding the relations between the states in the Mashreq region and its regional surroundings. In the aftermath of the Arab uprisings, the balance of power in the MENA region has changed and weakened the states in the Mashreq. EU ambitions of promoting democracy, human rights and the rule of law seem to be replaced by pragmatic cooperation with the regimes in Egypt and Jordan, attempts to support stability in Lebanon and endeavours to contain the chaotic situation in Syria. In reality, conditionality is much less an issue than one might expect from central ENP communications.

The fifth and most significant theme in the context of the Mashreq is security, first for the EU itself. Concerning the refugee issue in the section on Jordan, a relatively high level of correspondence between the EU's policy goals and the policies pursued by the Jordanian regime can be ascertained. Moreover, a similar approach has been undertaken towards Lebanon. The case of Syria adds to this, with the need for policies dealing with counter-terrorism, huge numbers of refugees and disastrous humanitarian conditions behind the Syrian borders. Specifically regarding the Syrian regime, the EU's sanctions policy constitutes a main foreign policy element. Summing up, the analysis has underlined the high level of differentiation concerning the relationships between the EU and the countries in question and that the positive conditionality inherent in the ENP tends to leave the floor for what seems to be the EU's main interests in the Mashreq – security and stability.

Note

1 This chapter, analysing the ENP in the context of the Mashreq, does not focus on EU relations with Israel and Palestine (see Pardo and Müller, this volume). Furthermore, the consequences for the ENP of the war in Syria are dealt with by Koenig (this volume).

References

Amer, M. and Fargues, P. (2014) 'Labour Market Outcomes and Egypt's Migration Potential', *EUI Working Papers*, RSCAS 2014/55.
Amin, K. (2014) 'International Assistance to Egypt after the 2011 and 2013 Uprisings: More Politics and Less Development', *Mediterranean Politics* 19(3): 392–412.
Commission of the European Communities (2004) *Communication from the Commission – European Neighbourhood Policy – Strategy Paper*, COM/2004/0373 final.
Commission of the European Communities (2006) *ENP Progress Report, Jordan*, SEC (2006) 1508, Brussels, 4 December.
Commission of the European Communities (2009) *Progress Report Jordan*, SEC (2009) 517/2, Brussels.

Council of the European Union (2005) *Global Approach to Migration: Priority Actions Focusing on Africa and the Mediterranean*, Brussels: Council of the European Union.
Council of the European Union (2009) *Euro-Mediteranean Agreement Establishing an Association between the European Comunity and Its Member States, on the One Part, and the Syrian Arab Republic, on the Other Part*, Brussels: Council of the European Union.
Council of the European Union (2011) *Council Conclusions on Syria*, Brussels: Council of the European Union.
Council of the European Union (2015) 'Declaration of the High-Level Conference on the Eastern Mediterranean – Western Balkans Route', *Press Release*, Brussels: Council of the European Union.
Dorstal, M. and Zorob, A. (2009) *Syria and the Euro-Mediterranean Relationship*, St Andrews: Lynne Rienner.
EurActiv (2013) 'EU adds Hezbollah's military wing to its terrorist list', Brussels, 22 July, www.euractiv.com/security/eu-adds-Hezbollah-military-wing-news-529502, accessed 22 December, 2016.
European Commission (2005) *EU/Jordan Action Plan*, Brussels: European Commission.
European Commission (2007) *EU/Egypt Action Plan*, Brussels: European Commission.
European Commission (2012) *EU/Jordan Action Plan*, Brussels: European Commission.
European Commission (2014) 'EU–Jordan: A New Partnership to Better Manage Mobility and Migration', *Press Release*, Brussels: European Commission.
European Commission (2015a) 'European Union, Trade in Goods with Syria, Directorate for Trade', Brussels: European Commission.
European Commission (2015b) *Programming of the European Neighbourhood Instrument (ENI) – 2014–2020. Single Support Framework for EU Support to Egypt (2014–2015)*, Brussels: European Commission.
European Commission (2015c) *Programming of the European Neighbourhood Instrument (ENI) – 2014–2020. Single Support Framework for EU Support to Jordan (2014–2015)*, Brussels: European Commission.
European Commission (2015d) *Managing the Refugee Crisis. EU Support to Lebanon and Jordan Since the Onset of the Syria Crisis*, Brussels: European Commission.
European Commission and High Representative of the European Union for Foreign Affairs and Security Policy (2011) *A New Response to a Changing Neighbourhood*, Brussels, 25 May.
European Commission and High Representative of the European Union for Foreign Affairs and Security Policy (2014) *Implementation of the European Neighbourhood Policy in Jordan. Progress in 2013 and Recommendations for Action*, 27 March SWD (2014) 74 final, 2014, Brussels.
European Commission and High Representative of the European Union for Foreign Affairs and Security Policy (2015a) *Implementation of the European Neighbourhood Policy in Egypt. Progress in 2014 and Recommendations for Actions*, Brussels.
European Commission and High Representative of the European Union for Foreign Affairs and Security Policy (2015b) *Implementation of the European Neighbourhood Policy in Lebanon. Progress in 2014 and Recommendations for Action*, 25 March SWD (2015) 68 final, Brussels.
European Commission and High Representative of the European Union for Foreign Affairs and Security Policy (2015c) *Joint Communication to the European Parliament, the Council, the European Economic and Social Committee and the Committee of the Regions. Review of the European Policy*, 18 November JOIN (2015) 50 final, Brussels.
European Union (2012) 'EU–Jordan Task Force – Co-chairs Conclusions', A 74/12. *Press Release*, Brussels.
European Union (2014) *Joint Declaration Establishing a Mobility Partnership between the Hashemite Kingdom of Jordan and the European Union and its Participating Member States*, Brussels: European Union.
Fakhoury, T. (2014) 'The EU and Lebanon in the Wake of the Arab Uprisings', *Middle East Policy* 21(1): 133–143.
Hinnebusch, R. (2012) 'Syria: from "Authoritarian Upgrading' to Revolution"', *International Affairs* 88(1): 95–113.
Isaac, S. (2014) 'The Egyptian Transition, 2011–13: How Strategic to Europe?', *Middle East Policy* 21(1): 154–165.
MENA (2015) *The Middle East and North Africa 2014*, London: Routledge.
Morris, B. (1999) *Righteous Victims. A History of the Zionist-Arab Conflict, 1881–1999*, New York: Alfred a. Knopf.
MPC-Team (2013) *Egypt. The Demographic-Economic Framework of Migration*, Florence: European University Institute.
NNA (2015) 'European Parliament's Delegation for Relations with Mashreq Countries Concludes Its Visit to Lebanon', National News Agency, Lebanese Republic, Ministry of Information.
Seeberg, P. (2009) 'The EU as a Realist Actor in Normative Clothes: EU Democracy Promotion in Lebanon and the European Neighbourhood Policy', *Democratization* 16(1): 81–99.

Seeberg, P. (2015) 'The EU and the Syrian Crisis: The Use of Sanctions and the Regime's Strategy for Survival', *Mediterranean Politics* 20(1): 18–35.
Shlaim, A. (2008) *Lion of Jordan. The Life of King Hussein in War and Peace*, London: Penguin Books.
Turner, L. (2015) 'Explaining the (Non-)Encampment of Syrian Refugees: Security, Class and the Labour Market in Lebanon and Jordan', *Mediterranean Politics* 20(3): 386–404.
UNHCR (2016a) *UNHCR Country Operations Profile – Lebanon*, New York: UNHCR.
UNHCR (2016b) *UNHCR Global Appeal 2016*. Jordan, New York: UNHCR.
UNSC (2013) *Resolution 2118 Adopted by the Security Council at Its 7038th Meeting, on 27 September*, New York: United Nations Security Council.
Valbjørn, M. (2013) 'The 2013 Parliamentary Elections in Jordan: Three Stories and Some General Lessons', *Mediterranean Politics* 18(2): 311–317.
Yazigi, J. (2014) 'Syria's War Economy', *European Council on Foreign Relations Policy Brief*, London: ECFR.
Zorob, A. (2008) 'The Syrian-European Association Agreement and Its Potential Impact on Enhancing the Credibility of Reform', *Mediterranean Politics* 13(1): 1–21.

31
ISRAEL AND PALESTINE AND THE EUROPEAN NEIGHBOURHOOD POLICY

Patrick Müller and Sharon Pardo

Introduction

The European Union's (EU) policy towards Israel and Palestine pre-dates the launching of the European Neighbourhood Policy (ENP). The Arab–Israeli conflict, and especially its Palestinian dimension, has been among the first issues discussed in the framework of the European Political Cooperation (EPC) that was established, in the early 1970s, as the predecessor of the Union's Common Foreign and Security Policy (CFSP). Since then, the EU has progressively developed common positions on key issues pertaining to the Israeli–Palestinian conflict through its declaratory diplomacy, including on the so-called 'final status issues': borders, Israeli settlements, Jerusalem and Palestinian refugees (Ifestos 1987; Allen and Pijpers 1984; Nuttall 1992; Pardo and Peters 2010; 2012; Musu 2010; Müller 2012; Bouris 2014). Making close reference to relevant United Nations (UN) resolutions and public international law, the EU supports an Israeli withdrawal to the 1967 borders (with minor, mutually agreed modifications), emphasizes the illegality of settlement building in the Palestinian Occupied Territories (OT), including in East Jerusalem, and calls for a just, viable and agreed solution for Palestinian refugees. At the same time, the EU has repeatedly stated its support for the right of Israel to exist within secure and recognized borders.

While the EU has initially addressed the Israeli–Palestinian conflict primarily through diplomatic instruments, it has progressively developed a comprehensive approach to conflict resolution that involves (economic) instruments belonging to the 'Community pillar'. In this respect, the ENP provides a 'cross pillar' framework, through which the EU integrates its political objectives in the Middle East Peace Process (MEPP) into its bilateral relations with the parties to this conflict. The ENP, thus, must be considered as a diplomatic framework to develop the Union's bilateral, economic, political and social relations with Israel and the Palestinian Authority (PA), as well as an important political instrument in the EU's conflict resolution toolkit (Crombois 2008). The link between the ENP and the Union's conflict resolution instruments has progressively been strengthened in the strategic documents underpinning the ENP. In 2006, the European Commission declared that addressing conflicts in the neighbourhood is one of the ENP's key purposes and is central for the success of the policy (Commission of the European Communities 2006). Following the Arab uprisings, conflict resolution moved even further up the agenda of the revised ENP (High Representative of the European Union for Foreign Affairs and Security Policy and European Commission 2011). Through the 'more-for-more' principle, the revised ENP offered additional rewards (that is, deeper economic and political integration) to ENP countries committed to conflict resolution, democratic reform, and EU values and norms. Moreover, the 2011 revised ENP placed greater emphasis on security aspects and the role of civil society in bringing about 'deep democracy'. Against the backdrop of severe instability and conflict in the European neighbourhood, the EU became even more concerned about the ENP's appropriate role in conflict resolution, which appeared increasingly out of sync with the profound changes in its neighbourhood. For example, in the Union's consultation paper entitled 'Towards a New European Neighborhood Policy', which critically engages with the EU's traditional approach to the ENP process, the European Commission and the High Representative of the EU for Foreign Affairs and Security Policy raises questions, such as how the ENP should address conflicts and crises in the neighbourhood, whether CFSP and CSDP activities should be better integrated in the ENP framework, and whether the ENP should have a greater role in developing confidence-building measures and post-conflict actions as well as related state- and institution-building activities (High Representative of the European Union for Foreign Affairs and Security Policy and European Commission 2015).

This chapter provides an overview of the EU's relations with Israel and Palestine and of the Union's role in conflict resolution, emphasizing the ENP framework. The chapter shows that the EU has developed close political and economic relations with both Israel and Palestine, while simultaneously developing its role as a political mediator in the conflict. Through the ENP framework, the EU has sought to link its political objectives in the MEPP more closely to its bilateral (economic) relations with Israel and Palestine, an effort that has not been without tensions and contradictions. The conclusions summarize the key arguments.

The EU and the Israeli–Palestinian conflict

Even though the international, European and regional conditions of the EU's conflict resolution policy have changed significantly over the past 46 years, the EU has traditionally considered the Israeli–Palestinian conflict to be closely linked to key European interests. The Union's view of the conflict is shaped by the complex history of individual EU Member States within the region – including diverse experiences, such as the British mandate over Palestine and the Holocaust – as well as by geographic proximity. The EU understands the Israeli–Palestinian conflict to be closely linked to the stability of the wider Middle East and North African (MENA) region, which matters for the containment of political violence and radicalism, the management of migration pressures and European energy security. While the events following the Arab uprisings in 2011 have resulted in profound new challenges to regional stability, the Israeli–Palestinian conflict remained a fundamental policy priority of the EU.[1]

Common European interests notwithstanding, it is also important to emphasize that the EU is not a 'unitary actor' in relation to the Middle East conflict.[2] Despite progressive institutional reforms, the CFSP has remained a heavily intergovernmental process, dominated by Member States with their own national foreign policy interests, models, diplomatic traditions and historic legacies. The EU must reach a compromise between Member States with strong ties to Israel – such as Germany, the Netherlands, Poland and the Czech Republic – and members that have traditionally held positions closer to Arab-views, including France, the UK, Spain, Ireland, Sweden and Malta. The Member States' outlook on the conflict, and their specific ties to the parties to the conflict, have complex reasons, such as Germany's moral debt for its crimes against the Jewish people and the historic involvement of the UK and France in the Arab world and their role as permanent members of the UN Security Council. This has traditionally made the establishment of a common EU policy, from diverse national approaches, a challenging, laborious and time intensive process – with Member States' representatives often arguing substantively before they reach agreement. Often, national diplomats based in Brussels meet informally in groups of like-minded Member States to pre-coordinate their views and gain an advantage in subsequent negotiations. Simultaneously, Member States are subject to significant lobbying activities by the parties to the conflict, with Israel being particularly active in communicating its views to EU countries it considers close friends, as well as lobbying activities by non-state actors (Gordon and Pardo 2015; Voltolini 2015).

The EU's success in progressively narrowing national differences and forging consensus on key issues pertaining to the Israeli–Palestinian conflict is owed to the consensus-based culture prevailing in the increasingly thick institutional web underpinning the CFSP, and the role of previously agreed EU positions as powerful precedents that guide subsequent EU policy (Müller 2013). Yet, this path-dependent logic of EU foreign policy-making does not prevent intra-EU divergences over new policy developments and heated debates over the right way to take EU policy forward (that is, beyond the *acquis* of previously agreed positions) that also impact on the ENP.

EU–Israeli relations and the ENP

Full diplomatic relations between the European Economic Community (EEC) and Israel were established in 1959 (Pardo and Peters 2010; 2012; Pardo 2013; 2015; Rom 1998; Heimann 2015; Harpaz and Heimann 2016). In 1964 the parties signed their first non-preferential agreement (European Economic Community–Israel 1964). Six years later, in 1970, they signed a preferential trade agreement (Kapeliuk-Klinger 1993), and in 1975 Israel and the EC signed their first Free Trade Area (FTA) agreement, which abolished all trade barriers on Israeli-manufactured goods by the end of 1979 (European Economic Community–Israel 1975). For many years, Israel hoped to upgrade the 1975 FTA agreement, but differences over the MEPP rendered this impossible.

EC–Israeli relations were exacerbated by the 1980 Venice Declaration (Pardo and Peters 2012: Document 3/2), which marked a turning point in EC/EU–Israeli relations, adding a charged political undertone to what had previously been a primarily economic relationship.[3] Thirty-seven years on, the Venice Declaration remains a defining moment in Israeli discourse and in the public distrust of the EU as an actor in the MEPP (Peters 2000: 156).

The launch of the Oslo Peace Process in 1993, between Israel and the Palestine Liberation Organization (PLO), led not only to a marked improvement in the tone of EU–Israeli relations but also to a qualitative change in relations between these two partners. In December 1994, EU leaders declared that Israel 'should enjoy a special status in its relations' with the EU (Pardo and Peters 2012: Document 4/6), and in 1995 the EU and Israel signed an Association Agreement (AA; Pardo and Peters 2012: Document 4/23) in the context of the newly established Euro-Mediterranean Partnership (EMP; a.k.a. Barcelona Process). The AA came into force in June 2000, after it was ratified by the national parliaments of the 15 Member States, the European Parliament and the Israeli Knesset, and since then forms the legal basis for EU–Israeli relations.

The implementation of the terms of the AA was not conditioned by the EU on the assurance of continued progress in the MEPP and the end of Israeli occupation of Palestinian territories. What was more, the EU and Israel refrained from identifying the 'territory of Israel' in the AA. Accordingly, both parties interpreted the territorial scope of the AA in line with their respective domestic political understanding and legislation, resulting in follow-up disputes over the correct implementation of the AA (Müller and Slominski 2017). The issue of goods produced in Israeli settlements in the OT led to a protracted dispute between the EU and Israel over the Rules of Origin (ROO) within the terms of the AA. In December 2004, Israel succumbed to EU pressure and the parties reached a 'technical arrangement', under which Israeli customs authorities are required to identify the place of production for all products exported to the Union (Pardo and Peters 2012: Document 5/12; Zemer and Pardo 2003). Eventually the ROO saga found its way to the European Court of Justice (ECJ), and in its 2010 Brita Case (Case C-386/08 2009/2010), the ECJ ruled that the AA must be interpreted as meaning that products originating in the West Bank do not fall within the territorial scope of that agreement and do not therefore qualify for preferential treatment under that agreement (Case C-386/08 2009/2010: Paragraph 53; Pardo and Zemer 2011).

In its November 2015 'Interpretative Notice on Indication of Origin of Goods from the OT' the EU further clarified that 'made in Israel' labels used for products originating from Israeli settlements in the OT would mislead European consumers and therefore are inconsistent with existing EU legislation (European Commission 2015a).

Despite the ROO dispute, since its conclusion, the AA consolidated EU–Israeli relations. Currently, the Union is Israel's largest trade partner. In 2015, 36 per cent of Israel's imports (excluding diamonds) came from the EU and 25 per cent of its exports (excluding diamonds) were directed to the European market (Central Bureau of Statistics 2016). Israel is a much smaller trading partner from the viewpoint of the EU. In 2015, Israel was ranked the EU's 25th major trade partner (European Commission 2016).

Some of the most significant aspects of the AA are the provisions aimed at intensifying scientific and technological cooperation. In October 1995, Israel and the EU concluded a 'Research and Development Agreement', through which Israel became the first non-European country to be fully associated with the Union's research programmes (Pardo and Peters 2012: Document 4/11). Thanks to this agreement the EU is now Israel's second largest source of research funding, second only to the Israel Science Foundation (ISF). In July 2013, the European Commission published the Union's 'Guidelines on the eligibility of Israeli entities in the OT' (European Commission 2013b), according to which, from January 2014, the EU no longer funds or dispenses awards and research grants to Israeli entities operating within the OT (Gordon and Pardo 2015).

As this brief historic overview shows, the EU had traditionally been wary to explicitly link its economic relations with Israel to its policy towards the MEPP, which was to change somehow with the introduction of the conditionality-based ENP. Israel, who was never a big supporter of the EMP, and not yet aware of the conditionality-based ENP, was one of the first Mediterranean countries to welcome the announcement of the ENP. With the new emphasis of the ENP on bilateral relationships, Israel was encouraged by the Union's departure from the regional straitjacket of the EMP that Israel so distrusted. From the late 1990s Israel was completely isolated in the EMP and never enjoyed the EMP's regional advantages. Thus, Israel responded enthusiastically to the possibility of developing a closer relationship with the EU and the opportunities it presented and, already in early 2004, opened discussions over drawing up a joint ENP Action Plan (AP). The EU–Israel AP was adopted in December 2004 and was the first ENP AP to be approved by the European Commission (Pardo and Peters 2012: Document 5/9). Its signing was heralded by both the EU and Israel as a significant achievement and an important step in bringing the Union and Israel together (Pardo and Peters 2010).

The preamble to the AP speaks of the opportunity afforded by enlargement for the two parties to develop an increasingly close relationship. While the AP is based on the 1995 AA, it lays out a much wider and more comprehensive set of jointly developed EU–Israeli ENP priorities, and opens up the possibility of Israel participating progressively in key aspects of EU policies and programmes.

The AP identifies six key areas of cooperation and joint action between Israel and the EU. It places a special emphasis on the 'upgrade in the scope of political cooperation' by calling for a renewed political dialogue based on shared values, including issues such as: the promotion and the protection of human rights and fundamental freedoms; improving the dialogue between cultures and religions; promoting effective multilateralism in the framework of the UN; combating anti-Semitism, racism, xenophobia and Islamophobia (Pardo and Peters 2012 Document 5/9).

A challenging issue during the negotiation process of the EU–Israel AP was the nature of the relationship between the ENP and the Israeli–Palestinian conflict. For Israel, the ENP was mainly an opportunity to associate the country with EU programmes and agencies, and to upgrade its bilateral relations with the EU into a real privileged partnership. During the negotiation process, Israel insisted on de-linking its bilateral relations with the EU to progress in the MEPP. The EU, in turn, was divided over the issue, with pro-Israel Member States, like Germany and the Netherlands, supporting Israel's viewpoint, and members such as Belgium, Greece and Ireland, who considered the ENP to be an instrument to enforce Israel's compliance with its obligations taken in the framework of the MEPP, insisting on linking the bilateral relations to progress in the peace process (O'Donnell 2009).

While the AP refers to various issues related to the peace process, these issues were made subject to non-binding political dialogue, rather than being stated in terms of strict conditionality, specific objectives and obligations (Müller 2012). Accordingly, the link between the ENP and the MEPP was based predominantly on the socializing effects of sustained cooperation and political dialogue, rather than economic leverage and hard conditionality.

The AP calls for containing the spread of weapons of mass destruction and their means of delivery, including ballistic missiles, the question of the illicit trafficking of military equipment and strengthening the fight against terrorism. In the economic sphere, the AP speaks of increasing economic integration by developing trade and investment flows, by liberalizing trade and services, in particular, financial services, with a view to preparing Israel for participation in the EU market – as well as deepening and enhancing the existing economic dialogue and identifying areas relevant for regulatory approximation with EU legislation. The AP also details a range of programmes and common initiatives which cover the following four issues: i) strengthening cooperation on migration-related issues, fighting against organized crime, including trafficking in human beings, and police and judicial cooperation; ii) promoting cooperation in science and technology, research and development, the information society, transport, energy and telecom networks; iii) strengthening the environmental dimension of public policy; and iv) strengthening links and cooperation in people-to-people contacts in education, culture, civil society and public health.

Over the years, the ENP has enabled the EU and Israel to intensify the level of their dialogue in the field of political and security cooperation, to raise significantly the degree of economic integration (through Israeli participation in EU programmes and agencies and the Union's Technical Assistance and Information Exchange programme) and has helped boost socio-cultural and scientific cooperation (through programmes such as the European Peacebuilding Initiative, the European Instrument for Democracy and Human Rights, the Euro-Med Audio-Visual Programme, Erasmus+ and Horizon 2020). While the institutional cooperation through the Association Council, the Association Committee and 10 joint sub-committees have brought together EU and Israeli experts to oversee the implementation of the AP, Israel always rejected the European socialization process and did its utmost to block the diffusion of European norms, mainly in the political dialogue (Pardo 2015).

Be that as it may, without question, the adoption of the AP marks an important turning point in EU–Israeli relations and, all in all, the ENP has bolstered this uneasy relationship. At the same time, the EU – against the backdrop of a severe deadlock in the peace process – carefully moved towards stronger conditionality in its relations with Israel, at least at the level of political rhetoric. In its 2007 progress report, the EU stated that '[a]ny consideration of EU-Israeli relations in the context of the ENP must take into account the persisting Arab-Israeli conflict'

(European Commission 2008: 2). In practice, however, the Union's political management of the ENP with Israel remained subject to careful political manoeuvring and competing interests among EU Member States.

In December 2008, the EU and Israel decided to upgrade their relations within the framework of the ENP (Pardo and Peters 2012: Documents 5/41, 5/55). Yet, in response to Israel's military operation in Gaza that same month, discussions over upgrading relations were put on hold by the Union (Pardo and Peters 2012: Document 5/46). Still, in July 2012, under major Israeli pressure, European foreign ministers 'updated' EU–Israeli relations in 60 concrete activities, in over 15 specific fields within the current AP (Council of the European Union 2012). Finally, in December 2013, the EU Foreign Affairs Council outlined the prospect of a higher status by offering Israel a Special Privileged Partnership (SPP). According to the Foreign Ministers, the Union will provide an unprecedented package of European political, economic and security support to both Israelis and Palestinians in the context of a final status agreement (Council of the European Union 2013). For its part, Israel never reacted to this offer and even refuses to discuss the possible content of the SPP with EU officials, due to its fear that such an 'Israeli wish-list' may be used to put pressure on Israel (Pardo 2015).

The EU's relations with Palestine and the ENP

The EU's political and economic relations with Palestine evolved in close interaction with its declaratory policy on the MEPP. As early as 1973, the EU expressed its support for the 'legitimate rights of the Palestinians' (Pardo and Peters 2012: Document 2/20), calling in subsequent declarations for a 'homeland' for the Palestinians (Pardo and Peters 2012: Document 2/38) and underlining the Palestinian right to self-determination and the necessity to associate the PLO with a peace settlement (Pardo and Peters 2012: Document 3/2). The EU further expressed its full support for a viable and peaceful sovereign Palestinian State (Pardo and Peters 2012: Document 4/21).

While, before the Venice Declaration, the EU had channelled its aid through intermediaries, the Union began to work directly through Palestinian organizations only in the 1980s. In 1986, the EU established direct trade links with the OT (Müller 2013). The EU's decision to involve the OT in the Euro-Mediterranean preferential trading system was not only of economic significance, but it also marked the implicit recognition of an autonomous Palestinian entity (Hollis 1994). Following the launch of the Oslo process, Israel's transfer of administrative powers to the newly established PA provided the EU with a new Palestinian interlocutor. The EU became the biggest international donor to the newly established PA and in 1997 it concluded an interim AA with the PLO in the framework of the EMP.

Besides governing trade-related issues, the EMP involved a commitment to the development of the rule of law and democracy and to the respect of human rights. Yet, initially the EU was reluctant to link its trade relations and generous financial support to the PA to the latter's respect of key principles and values underpinning the EMP. Considering the PA leadership an essential partner in the MEPP, the EU supported the PA, largely irrespective of its severe governance failures, corruption and human rights records, prioritizing swift progress in the peace process over governance reforms (Müller 2012; Tocci 2005). During the Oslo process, the EU had established itself as the main donor to the Palestinian people, providing about half of the total international assistance to the Palestinians through different budgetary lines, including the MEDA mechanism,[4] the UN Relief and Works Agency for Palestine Refugees in the Near East (UNRWA) and the EC Humanitarian Aid Department (ECHO).

It was only against the backdrop of severe setbacks in the Oslo process (which finally collapsed in late 2000), in conjunction with growing external and internal pressure for reforms within the PA, that the EU reconsidered its approach towards the PA and opted for applying more stringent political conditionality (Tocci 2005; Le More 2008). This shift in the Union's political approach towards the PA coincided with the establishment of the so-called Middle East Quartet (the UN, the United States [US], the EU and Russia), which launched the 'roadmap for peace initiative' that placed great emphasis on Palestinian (institutional) reforms.

For the EU, the subsequent establishment of the ENP provided a useful framework to integrate political objectives into its bilateral economic relations with the PA. Accordingly, the EU formulated political conditionality in its 2005 ENP AP with the Palestinians, in a straightforward fashion, making the level of cooperation with the PA dependent on its capacity to implement reforms demanded by the roadmap and the PA's compliance with its obligations under the MEPP (Commission of the European Communities 2005). The 2005 AP also specified clear reform objectives in areas such as human rights, democracy and the rule of law, judiciary reforms and the accountability of public finances, which were made subject to a strict monitoring and review process. The EU, furthermore, became actively involved at the operational level to support Palestinian governance reforms, most notably through its police mission – EUPOL COPPS – that was launched in January 2006, with a staff of more than 30 European police experts and advisors. This Common Foreign and Security Policy (CSDP) mission has a police and rule of law component and has made a valuable contribution to training and professionalization of the Palestinian police and judiciary and to maintaining public order in the West Bank. Through a mix of political incentives and development assistance, the EU assisted in promoting PA reforms in areas such as public finance, transparency and security sector reform (European Commission 2012).

Yet, Palestinian politics soon complicated the reform process. Hamas' 2006 election victory led to a temporary interruption of EU–Palestinian relations, when the new government led by Hamas refused to abide by principles for cooperation established by the Middle East Quartet (Müller 2014). After the violent split of the Palestinian territories into two *de facto* governments in summer 2007 – with Hamas in control of the Gaza Strip and the West Bank being run by the rival Fatah party – the implementation of the AP was resumed with the new Fatah-led government in the West Bank, while the EU opted, together with its Quartet partners, for the isolation of Hamas in the Gaza Strip. From the outset, however, the EU's policy of boycotting Hamas was subject to controversy among the Member States, with France and Scandinavian EU countries reportedly maintaining unofficial contacts with the Islamist movement (Müller 2012).

Due to the intra-Palestinian division, the internationally sponsored reform and development agenda of the PA government was now limited to the West Bank. This also affected the EU's reform efforts, including in the framework of the EUPOL COPPS mission, which not only operated in the context of ongoing Israeli occupation but also now faced the political and institutional division of the Palestinians, with Gaza and the West Bank having different legal, legislative and security systems. In the West Bank, Palestinian Prime Minister Salam Fayyad (2007–2013), an internationally respected economist, placed strong emphasis on good governance and economic development. In December 2007, Fayyad introduced his 'Palestinian Reform and Development Plan', which set out the political and economic reforms central to the Palestinian state-building agenda. The reform initiative enjoyed strong political backing in Brussels, with the EU and other European countries providing more than half of the USD7.7 billion pledged at the 2007 Paris international donors conference (Müller 2012: 66).

The progress achieved in the Palestinian reform process under Fayyad's premiership was acknowledged by the international community, with the EU and other donors like the World Bank expressing the view that the PA has become well-positioned for the establishment of a state in the near future (European Commission 2013a). Negotiations for a new AP were concluded in 2012 (European Commission 2013a), and this new AP now included an offer for a privileged EU–PA partnership, rewarding the PA for the good reform progress it had made in previous years. Yet, the continued deadlock in the MEPP, and the persisting political and territorial division of the Palestinians, increasingly put at risk the process of PA institution building, democratization and governance reforms, which had been set in train in the context of the roadmap. Palestinian disunity clearly undermines democratic and accountable governance, with President Mahmoud Abbas ruling by decree, the Palestinian Legislative Council (PLC) being unable to convene, and the prospects for much overdue Palestinian legislative and presidential elections remaining elusive. At the same time, a 'shadow bureaucracy' of PA officials has been maintained in Gaza – that is on the payroll of the international community – and cannot return to work as long as Hamas maintains its control. After more than ten years of political isolation, two major military conflicts with Israel and a deteriorating humanitarian situation, Hamas remains in control of the Gaza Strip and a relevant force in Palestinian politics.

At the level of its political rhetoric, the EU has remained firmly committed to its democratization and good governance agenda, emphasizing the 'more for more' principle and its commitment to 'deep democracy' of its revised ENP (European Commission 2015b). Behind closed doors, however, EU officials and other international donor representatives voice concerns about pushing for elections that could bring Hamas (back) to power and lead to further political destabilization in an already inflamed region.[5] The EU's focus on President Abbas and the Fatah-dominated PA – in which it has heavily invested for more than two decades as the nucleus of a Palestinian State – has made it even more challenging to facilitate Palestinian reforms and good governance, not least as the EU is anxious to take any step that could undermine the 'moderate camp' (see also Youngs 2014).

At the same time, the EU and other international donors are facing growing criticism by PA officials for not doing enough against Israeli policies that undermine the prospects of a two-state solution and hamper the socio-economic development of Palestine, including the construction of Israeli settlements in the OT and restrictions of Palestinian movement that stifle economic activity.[6] Though the EU has invested heavily in PA institution building and economic development, with Palestine receiving more than EUR6 billion of EU aid since 1994, the PA has become even more dependent on international aid to sustain itself while being unable to develop a viable economy (Abdel-Shafi 2015). In the absence of a credible political strategy, the ENP's focus on Palestinian governance reform and state building thus increasingly appears as a technocratic exercise that almost takes place by default, while the prospects for re-starting peace talks remain dim and the viability of a two-state solution is fading away.

Against this backdrop, the intra-EU debate on the recognition of a Palestinian state has intensified. Sweden officially recognized a Palestinian state in October 2014, countries like Belgium publically stated they are in favour of doing so, while national Parliaments in Spain, Italy, Portugal, France, Ireland and the UK adopted resolutions in which they urge their governments to recognize Palestinian statehood. Conversely, countries like Germany and the Netherlands have declared their position against a unilateral recognition of Palestine (for example, Reuters 2014), with the EU as a bloc lacking consensus to move beyond its 1999 Berlin declaration, that is, support of future recognition of a Palestinian state when appropriate (European Council 1999).

Conclusions

The EU holds that a political resolution of the Israeli–Palestinian conflict is imperative (Müller 2012; Pardo and Peters 2012). The continuation of the conflict is a major source of instability, and the resolution of the Palestinian question is looked on as a critical component in addressing the Arab uprisings in the wider region, and as an important element in tackling the growth of Islamic fundamentalism and international terrorism. The continuation of the Israeli–Palestinian conflict, therefore, is also impacting negatively on the Union's domestic stability.

Yet, as our analysis shows, the EU has traditionally found it difficult to develop a comprehensive and coherent policy towards the Israeli–Palestinian conflict. Historically, the EU has sought to avoid linking its bilateral economic relations with Israel to the MEPP. With the launch of the ENP, the EU's approach has gradually changed, at least at the level of rhetoric and political strategy. Progressively, the EU has integrated the language of conditionality into its ENP relations with Israel, stating its intention to assess the development of bilateral relations due to progress in the MEPP. In practice, however, the EU has been reluctant to implement conditionality in strict terms, not least as such an approach lacked support among key Member States. And while the conflict between Israelis and the Palestinians, and the sustained deadlock in the peace process, have repeatedly complicated EU–Israeli relations, the overall trend has been the progressive deepening of the EU–Israeli relationship. Whether the strong bilateral relationship between these two partners could be sustained once the MEPP – in which the EU has heavily invested politically and financially – is no longer viewed as a credible policy option, remains uncertain. Statements and actions during the past two years by EU institutions and officials suggest that the latest position of the EU is that the MEPP explicitly demands more than merely the resumption of negotiations, but indeed an urgent and comprehensive settlement (European Union External Action Service 2016).

With respect to the EU's policy towards the Palestinians, the ENP was introduced at a time when Palestinian governance reforms had shifted in the focus of the EU and its Quartet partners. Against this backdrop, the conditionality-based ENP was considered a useful tool to incentivize PA reforms, which became a central element of the EU–PA AP and subsequent ENP documents. Yet, continued deadlock in the MEPP and the political and territorial division of the Palestinians – since Hamas took control of the Gaza Strip in 2007 – clearly undermined the EU-promoted reform process, which aimed at building the PA's capacity to run a Palestinian state. Considering the Abbas-led PA government central for political stability – both within the West Bank, as well as in terms of security cooperation with Israel – and valuing its commitment to the moribund peace process, the EU has increasingly turned a blind eye to the growing autocratic tendencies of the Palestinian leadership.

At a more general level, the case of the Israeli–Palestinian conflict reminds us that implementing the ENP is often driven more by context factors – such as the special relations of individual EU Member States with the parties to the conflict, considerations about safeguarding stability or the need to respond to specific conflict-related dynamics – than by the various strategic reforms of the ENP framework.

Notes

1. www.eeas.europa.eu/mepp/index_en.htm, July 2016.
2. It is beyond the scope of this chapter to provide a detailed analysis of the process of Member States' coordination. For this discussion, see Musu (2010) and Müller (2012; 2013).
3. The central parts of the Venice Declaration discuss: (i) the 'Palestinian problem', (ii) the 'question of Jerusalem' and (iii) the Israeli settlements.
4. The MEDA mechanism supported cooperation activities leading to economic transition and strengthening the socio-economic balance in the Mediterranean countries.
5. Interview with a representative of the Local Aid Coordination Secretariat (LAC), Ramallah, 12 August 2015.
6. Ibid., footnote 5.

References

Abdel-Shafi, S. (2015) *Realigning EU Policy in Palestine: Towards a Viable State Economy and Restored Dignity*, London: The Royal Institute for International Affairs.
Allen, D. and Pijpers, A. (eds.) (1984) *European Foreign Policy-Making and the Arab–Israeli Conflict*, The Hague: Martinus Nijhoff.
Bouris, D. (2014) *The European Union and Occupied Palestinian Territories: State-Building Without a State*, London: Routledge.
Case C-386/08 (2009/2010) *Firma Brita GmbH v. Hauptzollamt Hamburg-Hafen*, 2010 ECJ, *EUR-Lex LEXIS*, 63, 29 October; 25 February.
Central Bureau of Statistics (2016) *Israel's Foreign Trade by Countries – 2015*, Jerusalem: Central Bureau of Statistics.
Commission of the European Communities (2005) *EU–Palestinian Authority Action Plan*, Brussels: European Commission.
Commission of the European Communities (2006) *Communication from the Commission to the Council and the European Parliament on Strengthening the European Neighbourhood Policy*, COM (2006) 726, 4 December.
Council of the European Union (2012) *Eleventh Meeting of the EU-Israel Association Council*, Brussels: Council of the European Union.
Council of the European Union (2013) *Council Conclusions on the Middle East Peace Process*, Brussels: Council of the European Union.
Crombois, J. (2008) 'The ENP and EU Actions in Conflict Management: Comparing between Eastern Europe and the Maghreb', *Perspectives* 16(2): 29–51.
European Commission (2008) *Implementation of the European Neighbourhood Policy in 2007. Progress Report Israel*, European Commission, SEC (2008) 394, 3 April.
European Commission (2012) *Implementation of the European Neighbourhood Policy in the Occupied Palestinian Territory. Progress in 2011 and Recommendations for Action*, European Commission, SWD (2012) 120, 15 May.
European Commission (2013a) *European Union – Palestinian Authority Action Plan: Political Chapeau*, Brussels: European Commission.
European Commission (2013b) 'Guidelines on the Eligibility of Israeli Entities and their Activities in the Territories Occupied by Israel since June 1967 for Grants, Prizes and Financial Instruments Funded by the EU from 2014 Onwards', *Official Journal of the European Union*, C 205/9, 19 July.
European Commission (2015a) *Interpretative Notice on Indication of Origin of Goods from the Territories Occupied by Israel since June 1967*, European Commission, C(2015) 7834 final, 11 November.
European Commission (2015b) *Implementation of the European Neighbourhood Policy in Palestine: Progress in 2014 and Recommendations for Actions*, SWD (2015) 71 final, 25 March, Brussels.
European Commission (2016) *Client and Supplier Countries of the EU28 in Merchandise Trade*, Brussels: European Commission.
European Council (1999) *Presidency Conclusions*, Berlin: European Council.
European Economic Community–Israel (1964) 'Accord commercial entre la Communauté économique européenne et l'état d'Israël', *Official Journal of the European Communities*, 64/1518, 4 June.
European Economic Community–Israel (1975) 'Agreement between the European Economic Community and the State of Israel', *Official Journal of the European Communities*, L 136/3, 11 May.
European Union External Action Service (2016) 'Mogherini Promotes EU Role to Recreate Conditions for Middle East Peace Process', 3 June, https://eeas.europa.eu/delegations/un-geneva/4043/mogherini-promotes-eu-role-to-recreate-conditions-for-middle-east-peace-process_en, accessed October 2016.
Gordon, N. and Pardo, S. (2015) 'Normative Power Europe and the Power of the Local', *Journal of Common Market Studies* 53(2): 416–427.
Harpaz, G. and Heimann, G. (2016) 'Sixty Years of EU-Israeli Trade Relations: The Expectations-Delivery Gap', *Journal of World Trade* 50(3): 447–474.
Heimann, G. (2015) 'The Need to Be Part of Europe: Israel's Struggle for an Association Agreement with the EEC, 1957–1961', *Israel Studies* 20(1): 86–109.
High Representative of the European Union for Foreign Affairs and Security Policy and European Commission (2011) *A New Response to a Changing Neighbourhood: A Review of European Neighbourhood Policy. Joint Communication by the High Representative of the Union for Foreign Affairs and Security Policy and the European Commission*, COM (2011) 303, 25 May.
High Representative of the European Union for Foreign Affairs and Security Policy and the European Commission (2015) *Joint Consultation Paper: Towards a New European Neighbourhood Policy*, JOIN (2015) 6, 4 March.

Hollis, R. (1994) 'The Politics of Israeli–European Economic Relations', *Israel Affairs* 1(1): 118–134.

Ifestos, P. (1987) *European Political Cooperation: Towards a Framework of Supranational Diplomacy?*, Aldershot: Avebury.

Kapeliuk-Klinger, D. (1993) 'A Legal Analysis of the Free Trade Agreement of 1975 between the European Community and the State of Israel', *Israel Law Review* 27(3): 415–446.

Le More, A. (2008) *International Assistance to the Palestinians after Oslo: Political Guilt, Wasted Money*, New York: Routledge.

Müller, P. (2012) *EU Foreign Policymaking toward the Middle East Conflict – The Europeanization of National Foreign Policy*, New York: Routledge.

Müller, P. (2013) 'Europe's Foreign Policy and the Middle East Peace Process: The Construction of EU Actorness in Conflict Resolution', *Perspectives on European Politics and Society* 14(1): 20–30.

Müller, P. (2014) 'Informal Security Governance and the Middle East Quartet: Survival of the Unfittest?', *International Peacekeeping* 21(4): 446–480.

Müller, P. and Slominski, P. (2017) 'The Role of Law in EU Foreign Policymaking: Legal Integrity, Legal Spill-Over, and EU's of Differentiation Towards Israel', *Journal of Common Market Studies*, 55(4): 871–888.

Musu, C. (2010) *European Union Policy towards the Arab–Israeli Peace Process: The Quicksands of Politics*, Houndmills: Palgrave Macmillan.

Nuttall, S. (1992) *European Political Co-Operation*, Oxford: Oxford University Press.

O'Donnell, C. (2009) 'The EU's Approach to Israel and the Palestinians: A Move in the Right Direction', *Centre for European Reform Policy Brief*, London, June.

Pardo, S. (2013) The Year that Israel Considered Joining the European Economic Community', *Journal of Common Market Studies* 51(5): 901–915.

Pardo, S. (2015) *Normative Power Europe Meets Israel: Perceptions and Realities*, Lanham, MD: Lexington Books.

Pardo, S. and Peters, J. (2010) *Uneasy Neighbors: Israel and the European Union*, Lanham, MD: Lexington Books.

Pardo, S. and Peters, J. (2012) *Israel and the European Union: A Documentary History*, Lanham, MD: Lexington Books.

Pardo, S. and Zemer, L. (2011) 'Bilateralism and the Politics of European Judicial Desire', *Columbia Journal of European Law* 17(2): 263–305.

Peters, J. (2000) 'Europe and the Arab-Israeli Peace Process: The Declaration of the European Council of Berlin and Beyond', in Behrendt, S. and Hanelt, C. (eds.) *Bound to Cooperate – Europe and the Middle East*, Gütersloh: Bertelsmann Foundation Publishers, 150–172.

Rom, M. (1998) *In the Path of Israel's International Commercial Policy: GSP and the European Common Market*, Tel Aviv: RAMOT.

Reuters (2014) 'Merkel against unilaterally recognizing Palestine as a state', Reuters World News, 21 November, www.reuters.com/article/us-mideast-palestinians-germany-idUSKCN0J51ZJ20141121, accessed October 2016.

Tocci, N. (2005) 'The Widening Gap between Rhetoric and Reality in EU Policy Towards the Israeli-Palestinian Conflict', *CEPS Working Document 217*, January.

Voltolini, B. (2015) 'Non-State Actors and Framing Processes in EU Foreign Policy: The Case of EU–Israel Relations', *Journal of European Public Policy*, 23(10): 1502–1519. doi: 10.1080/13501763.2015.1085429.

Youngs, R. (2014) *The EU and the Israeli–Palestinian Conflict: Action Without a Script*, Carnegie Endowment for International Peace, 21 October.

Zemer, L. and Pardo, S. (2003) 'The Qualified Zones in Transition: Navigating the Dynamics of the Euro-Israeli Customs Dispute', *European Foreign Affairs Review* 8(1): 51–75.

32
LIBYA AND SYRIA

At the crossroads of European Neighbourhood Policy and EU crisis management

Nicole Koenig

If the ENP cannot contribute to addressing conflicts in the region, it will have failed in one of its key purposes.

European Commission

Introduction

In the 2015 review of the European Neighbourhood Policy (ENP), one message clearly stood out: the security dimension needs to be strengthened. This message was timely considering that the EU's neighbourhood has undergone a thorough destabilisation since 2010. As of 2017, eleven of the sixteen ENP partners were subject to some form of frozen, intra- or inter-state conflict. The repercussions of these conflicts have been felt throughout the region and in the EU, as demonstrated by unprecedented migratory flows.

Fostering peace and stability in the neighbourhood have been core objectives of the ENP from the beginning. But despite tireless declarations of intent, the track record of the first decade of implementation is meagre. As Crombois (2008: 2) argues: 'the ENP has contributed for little if anything in the EU actions in conflict management in the neighbourhood'. The literature identifies a range of underlying reasons. Some scholars blame the principle of joint ownership, which has allowed the partners to marginalise sensitive conflict-related issues in their bilaterally agreed Action Plans (Wolff et al. 2007). Others argue that there has simply been a lack of clarity regarding the actions required to foster peace and stability (Crombois 2008). Perspectives differ, but most scholars directly or indirectly refer to the difficulties of ensuring coherence across the EU's institutions and with the Member States (Noutcheva 2014; Sobol 2015; Wolff et al. 2007).

Policy coherence can be defined as the consistent and synergetic use of common instruments and resources geared towards overarching objectives (de Coning 2008). The ENP represents a 'composite policy with multiple objectives (security, economic prosperity and democracy)' that cut across different functional areas and governance levels (Noutcheva 2014: 22). It thus raises horizontal, institutional and vertical coherence challenges (Nuttall 2005). In this chapter, horizontal coherence is understood as the synergetic interaction between the ENP and other EU policies within a broadening scope of comprehensive EU crisis management. Relevant policy areas include: the Common Foreign and Security Policy (CFSP) and Common Security and Defence Policy (CSDP); humanitarian aid; and less conventional crisis management fields, such as migration management and counter-terrorism. A sub-category of horizontal coherence, institutional coherence, refers to collaborative interaction between the responsible EU-level institutional actors. Vertical coherence designates the extent to which national neighbourhood and crisis management policies are in line with (consistency) and positively contribute to (synergy) the EU-level ones.

This chapter analyses the coherence challenges the EU has faced in the implementation of the ENP's security dimension.[1] It focuses on two relevant cases, namely Libya and Syria between 2011 and 2015. Both countries have remained at the margins of the ENP, though having a different formal status. Hopes raised by the Arab uprisings were destroyed by years of violence and continuous or intermittent civil war. Syria and Libya have thus been situated at the intersection of the ENP and comprehensive EU crisis management. Both cases show that the EU has gradually learned its lessons in terms of strengthening horizontal and institutional coherence. However, vertical incoherence and the Member States' inability to agree on collective action are likely to remain important obstacles to the effective implementation of the ENP's security dimension.

Libyan crises: a limited role for the ENP

In the 2000s, the EU was eager to include Libya in the Euro-Mediterranean Partnership (EMP) and the ENP. The Commission initiated negotiations for an EU–Libya Framework Agreement in 2007, with the aim of formalising bilateral relations. However, the negotiations concentrated on economic development and migration management, and less on issues related to human rights and democratisation (Joffé 2011; Zoubir 2009). Libya was thus part of a broader pattern characterising the Union's relations with its southern neighbours, which consisted of prioritising stability and security over sustainable democratisation (Hollis 2012). The 2011 Libyan crisis challenged this pattern.

The 2011 crisis: divided on high politics

The crisis started on 15 February 2011, when human rights activist Fethi Tarbel was arrested in the Eastern Libyan city of Benghazi. The resulting anti-regime protests rapidly spread across the country and were met with massive repression and violence by the regime of Colonel Muammar Gaddafi. On 5 March 2011, Libyan opposition forces established the National Transitional Council (NTC), which they presented as Libya's sole representative. The situation turned into a civil war between opposition forces and pro-Gaddafi loyalists, which caused thousands of casualties and massive internal displacement.

In response to the Libyan crisis, the EU activated a broad range of crisis management instruments. The then High Representative for Foreign Affairs and Security Policy and Vice-President of the Commission (HR/VP) (Ashton 2011a) was quick to condemn the use of violence against civilians on behalf of the EU. The EU suspended all technical assistance under the ENP and froze the negotiations on the EU–Libya Framework Agreement. Its response in the fields of humanitarian aid and economic sanctions was rapid and substantial. Collectively, the EU became the largest humanitarian donor in the Libyan crisis and gradually established a strong sanctions regime (DG ECHO 2011). The EU implemented the sanctions foreseen by UN

Security Council Resolutions 1970 and 1973 and agreed additional autonomous measures targeting Gaddafi's regime, including a *de facto* oil and gas embargo in April 2011.

The EU's initial crisis response was characterised by tensions between the European Commission and the newly established European External Action Service (EEAS) on the one hand, and within the EEAS crisis management structures on the other (Koenig 2011). Tensions arose due to competence overlaps, contested leadership and resource dependencies. While the EEAS was supposed to provide political guidance, most of the resources were in the Commission, which often refused to be coordinated by the EEAS. Yet the cooperation between the HR/VP and the Commissioner for Enlargement and ENP worked reasonably well (EEAS official 2011). A senior Commission advisor (2011) explained that an informal division of labour between the HR/VP and the Commissioner soon emerged. The former was in charge of the ENP's more political aspects, whereas the latter was responsible for the more technical ones.

The biggest challenge during the EU's initial response to the Libyan crisis was vertical coherence, notably in the diplomatic realm. On the day that Ashton condemned the use of violence by the Gaddafi regime, the former Italian Prime Minister Silvio Berlusconi told the press that he had not called Gaddafi, as he did not want to 'disturb' him in a situation that was 'still in flux' (Reuters 2011). Contrasting with the EU's official position, this statement reflected the preferential relations Italy had maintained with the Gaddafi regime in return for its cooperation on energy and migration-related matters (Joffé 2011). The diplomatic approach towards the NTC also became subject to vertical incoherence. France recognised the NTC as sole representative of the Libyan people on 10 March 2011 – one day ahead of an extraordinary European Council meeting on Libya. It intended to push the other Member States closer to its position. The European Parliament (2011) issued a resolution on the same day calling on the Member States to grant the NTC full diplomatic recognition. However, on 11 March, the European Council (2011) merely welcomed the NTC as *a*, and not as the *sole*, representative of the Libyan people. The EU's full diplomatic recognition only followed months later after the UN had given the green light.

The most divisive issue was the use of force. France and the UK were among the main proponents of UN Security Council Resolution 1973, authorising all necessary means 'to protect civilians and civilian populated areas under threat of attack [. . .] while excluding a foreign occupation force of any form on any part of Libyan territory' (UN Security Council 2011). However, Germany – then non-permanent member of the UN Security Council – broke ranks with its European partners and abstained during the respective vote – together with Brazil, Russia, China and India. The EU Member States were also divided on a military contribution in the framework of the CSDP. Some, such as France and Italy, were in favour; others, including Germany and Poland, were reluctant. After difficult discussions, the Member States settled for the lowest common denominator, which was operation EUFOR Libya (European Council 2011). The CSDP operation would have been mandated to facilitate the delivery of humanitarian assistance in Libya. However, its deployment was made dependent on a call by the UN Office for the Coordination of Humanitarian Affairs, which never came.

The EU's crisis management in Libya became more coherent in the course of 2011. Despite divisions on the status of the Libyan opposition, the EEAS established an EU liaison office in Benghazi in May 2011, which amounted to a *de facto* recognition of the NTC. The EU Member States eventually endorsed the Franco-British lead of the NATO operation in Libya. With support by the latter, the Libyan rebels seized Tripoli in August 2011 and Gaddafi fled the city. In October 2011, the rebels held most parts of the country and Gaddafi was captured and killed. The successful termination of the NATO operation on 31 October 2011 marked the transition to post-conflict reconstruction.

Constrained support of complex transition

Hopes were high that the EU would compensate for its relatively incoherent crisis response during transition. At the Paris conference on 1 September 2011, the international community and Libya's transitional authorities agreed that the UN should take the lead in coordinating reconstruction and consolidation. The EU was tasked with border management, civil society and the media (Gottwald 2012).

With a package worth EUR 30 million, the ENP initially focused on civil society support, public administration capacity-building and the management of migration flows (European Commission 2012). In parallel, the EU reactivated its diplomatic efforts to integrate Libya in the ENP. The Commission repeatedly underlined that it was ready to resume negotiations on the EU–Libya Framework Agreement. The Libyan authorities made a step towards the ENP when they decided to opt for an observer status in the Union for the Mediterranean (UfM) in January 2013.

In the field of border management, the EU faced two obstacles. The first was the absence of legitimate and experienced Libyan interlocutors (EEAS official 2013). The EU conducted several needs assessment missions to identify priority sectors with the transitional authorities. However, the latter did not clearly articulate their needs (Gottwald 2012). The second obstacle was the difference in Member State preferences concerning the scope of the envisaged EU Integrated Border Assistance Mission (EUBAM) Libya. France wanted the mission to concentrate on the south-western border whereas others – such as Greece, Malta and Italy – were more interested in a focus on the maritime border (EEAS official 2013). The compromise was a 'crawl–walk–run' approach with an initial focus on the capital and a gradual extension to border 'hotspots'. The EU launched EUBAM Libya in May 2013. However, the mission neglected the south-western border where terrorists, fighters and arms continued to move freely between Libya and the Sahel. The quest for vertical coherence thus produced a collective measure with limited impact on regional stabilisation.

Initially, the EU's activities in the realm of the CFSP and the ENP were largely disconnected. In 2013, there were attempts to raise the degree of horizontal coherence by pooling ENP resources towards security-related goals. ENP funds were used to support activities in the realm of civilian SSR including, for instance, reintegration training into the police forces or the development of the concept for a National Security Strategy (Council of the European Union 2014). In 2013, the Commission programmed a EUR 25 million package under the European Neighbourhood and Partnership Instrument (ENPI) to complement activities in the fields of security and border management (Council of the European Union 2014). This package was to support alternative livelihoods and sustainable employment, protect vulnerable people and foster the development of a rights-based migration management and asylum system. The respective activities were to start in 2014, but most had to be suspended due to the worsening political and security situation.

The resurgence of violence: back to crisis mode

Violence escalated again in June 2014, when the Islamists suffered an important defeat in the parliamentary election. In mid-August an alliance of Tripoli-based Islamists joined forces with militias from Misrata and launched an offensive on Tripoli's airport. Within weeks, they took control of the capital and forced the internationally recognised government to relocate to the Eastern Libyan city of Tobruk. From August 2014 onwards, the country has had two rivalling governments. In January 2015, UN Special Envoy for Libya Bernardino Leon, former EU special envoy for the Southern Mediterranean, initiated peace talks between rivalling factions to reach a lasting ceasefire and form a national unity government.

The relapse of conflict severely curtailed the Union's activities in Libya. EUBAM Libya was downscaled and transferred to Tunis and Brussels. Most aid programmes directed towards governmental authorities were suspended. Only EUR8 million was spent under the European Neighbourhood Instrument (ENI) in 2014, with a focus on capacity building, key democratic institutions and the reconciliation process (European Commission 2015). The ENP implementation report of March 2015 stated that 'it would be unrealistic to expect any progress on the EU agenda' in Libya considering the deterioration of the security situation (European Commission 2015: 2).

Libya thus slipped off the 'ENP radar' as the EU shifted back into a short-term crisis response mode. In October 2014, the Council published the Political Framework for Crisis Approach for Libya, a planning document that was supposed to guide the EU's overall engagement in the country. The document did not even mention the ENP. It explicitly refrained from formulating a medium-term strategy, which would depend on the evolution of the political and security conditions (Council of the European Union 2014). The Framework identified the assistance to the UN-led mediation efforts as the EU's main political priority.

In practice, the EU's focus shifted towards the symptoms of the Libyan conflict. In 2014–2015, Libya was among the main transit countries for migrants and refugees heading towards the EU. In April 2015, the EU and the southern neighbours received an important wakeup call as hundreds of migrants destined for Europe drowned in front of the Libyan coast. At an extraordinary meeting on migration on 23 April, the European Council (2015) decided on a broad package of measures. As part of this comprehensive package, the Council of the European Union (2015a) launched the maritime CSDP operation EUNAVFOR Sophia on 22 June. The operation was mandated to combat human trafficking and smuggling in the Southern Central Mediterranean. With 22 participating Member States and an estimated strength of 2,000 troops, it is among the largest and potentially costliest CSDP operations to date.

Summing up, Libya has been a difficult case in terms of both the ENP and comprehensive EU crisis management. When ENP-related activities and funds were frozen during the 2011 crisis, intergovernmental dynamics prevailed, leading to an incoherent crisis response. Between 2011 and 2013, ENP and CFSP measures co-existed. The level of ENP funding suggests that the EU did not put its full economic weight behind the country's stabilisation. Meanwhile, the lack of experienced local interlocutors, and diverging Member State priorities, prevented substantial CFSP engagement. Subsequent efforts to link the CFSP and ENP activities stalled due to the deteriorating security situation. When violence resurged in 2014, the EU presented a strategic concept for a comprehensive crisis response, which excluded the ENP. In practice, it focused on the conflict's symptoms while it outsourced the more political crisis-management tasks to the UN.

The Syrian tragedy: towards a more conflict-sensitive ENP

In the 2000s, Syria was more integrated in the ENP than Libya. It was a fully-fledged member of the EMP, negotiations on a Syria–EU Association Agreement were ongoing, and the country was a founding member of the UfM. The priorities of EU–Syria cooperation outlined by the Country Strategy Paper and National Indicative Programme (2007–2010) – namely politico-administrative, economic and social reform – were aligned with the EU's values (European Commission 2013). Once more, ENP activities were severely curtailed as the conflict unfolded.

The unfolding conflict: few open divisions

Protests in Syria started on 15 March 2011, after the arrest and torture of children accused of anti-regime graffiti in the southern city of Daraa. The protests soon spread as demonstrators called on President Bashar Al-Assad to step down. The regime responded with large-scale arrests, violent repression and torture. In July 2011, a group of defected officers established the Free Syrian Army, marking the beginning of organised armed resistance. Developments at the start of the Syrian conflict resembled the initial months of the Libyan uprising, but the international response did not. The UN veto powers, China and Russia (a traditional ally of the Syrian regime), refused to go beyond diplomatic condemnations of violence. They rejected attempts to invoke the responsibility to protect as they accused the Western-led coalition in Libya of overstepping their mandate and promoting regime change (Tisdall 2011).

The EU's initial response to the Syrian uprisings was coherent. It reacted to the escalation of violence with diplomatic declarations calling on the regime to protect peaceful demonstrators (Ashton 2011c). Two months into the protests, the EU froze the draft Association Agreement and suspended all bilateral cooperation programmes including those under the ENPI (EEAS 2015). As attempts to impose UN-level sanctions failed, the EU and the US imposed autonomous sanctions and restrictive measures. From May 2011 onwards, the EU gradually strengthened its sanctions regime to include an arms embargo, an oil import embargo, asset freezes and travel bans. In November 2011, the European Investment Bank put all existing loans to Syria on hold. The regime consequently accused the EU (and the US) of waging a 'diplomatic and humanitarian war' against Syria and suspended its membership in the UfM (EurActiv 2011).

In the field of diplomacy, the Member States were less openly divided than in the Libyan case. During the initial months of the Syrian uprising, many in the West still hoped that Assad would agree to an orderly transition or some other form of political compromise. This might explain why the US and the EU waited until 18 August 2011 to urge Assad to step down (Ashton 2011b). On 23 August 2011, the Syrian National Council (SNC) established itself as representative of the Syrian people. Once more, France was the first EU Member State to grant full diplomatic recognition, in November 2011. The EU signalled its willingness to engage with the SNC, but only granted full diplomatic recognition on 27 February 2012.

There was little appetite in the EU (or the US) to engage in a military intervention parallel to that in Libya, without a UN mandate and in a country with a more potent army as well as powerful international allies. In November 2011, France proposed the establishment of a humanitarian corridor in Syria to allow aid groups and observers into the country with the aim of protecting civilians. This was the first time that a major western nation proposed some form of military engagement in Syria since the beginning of the conflict. However, the EU did not endorse the French proposal.

Rising stakes and crumbling unity

Until 2013, the EU was relatively united. It became the most important humanitarian donor in the Syrian crisis and backed the UN-led efforts aiming at a political solution. But while the Syrian conflict turned into the 'worst humanitarian disaster since the end of the Cold War' (Chulov 2013), the EU's unity crumbled. In March 2013, France and the UK started to push for a partial lifting of the arms embargo, to allow for weapon deliveries to moderate rebels. They argued that there was a stark imbalance between the rebels and Assad's forces, which received continuous supplies from Iran and Russia. The easing of the arms embargo was presented as a means to put pressure on Assad ahead of the international peace negotiations.

Other Member States such as Germany, Austria, Sweden and the Czech Republic were sceptical and feared that weapon deliveries would intensify the conflict and turn it into a proxy war (Croft 2013).

France and Britain challenged the EU's vertical coherence, as they threatened to act unilaterally if the EU failed to ease the embargo. This move could have dismantled the whole sanctions regime, which was set to expire on 1 June 2013. The Member States eventually settled on a compromise, which entailed easing the arms embargo without immediate weapon delivery and while maintaining the other sanctions. They also agreed on a common framework to guide future weapon deliveries with the declared aim of protecting civilians. Despite this compromise, the episode was viewed as a serious blow to the EU's foreign policy in general and its approach to the Syrian conflict specifically (Marcus 2013).

Shortly after, the EU institutions made an attempt to increase the coherence of the EU's response to the conflict. On 24 June 2013, the Commission and the HR/VP presented a joint Communication entitled 'Towards a comprehensive EU approach to the Syrian crisis'. The document sought to bring together the 'EU and its Member States' policies and instruments' to support a political solution, prevent regional destabilisation, address the humanitarian crisis and deal with the consequences for the EU (European Commission and HR/VP 2013). While it mentioned intergovernmental policy areas, such as diplomacy and sanctions, the document's key focus was on humanitarian assistance to Syria and neighbouring countries. Accordingly, it reallocated ENPI funds worth EUR145 million for 2013.

In August 2013, another 'high politics' issue divided the Member States. On 21 August, a chemical weapons attack in Ghouta – a rebel stronghold in the Damascus region – killed hundreds of civilians and opposition forces. The US denounced the attack as a grave violation of international law and declared its willingness to conduct limited air strikes against the Assad regime. The EU Member States were united in condemning the attack, but divided on the appropriate response. The UK and France were the only ones signalling support for a US-led air campaign. The UK later withdrew its pledge for military support due to strong opposition by a war-weary British public, reluctant to follow the US lead after the experiences in Iraq and Afghanistan. Due to combined diplomatic pressure by Washington and Moscow, a military intervention could be averted and Assad agreed on the destruction of Syria's chemical weapons arsenal as well as on the accession to the Chemical Weapons Convention.

ISIS and the refugee crisis: horizontal without vertical coherence

In 2014–2015, three interlinked developments further raised the stakes linked to the Syrian crisis. The first was the expansion of the self-styled Islamic State in Iraq and Syria (ISIS). Initially an Al-Qaeda cell in Iraq, the group used the power vacuum to seize control over large parts of Syria and Iraq and to establish a presence in Libya. The second development was a series of ISIS-linked terrorist attacks in neighbouring and European countries, culminating in the tragic Paris attacks of 13 November 2015. The third development was the unprecedented increase of Syrian refugees headed towards Europe. Between January and December 2015, 349,901 Syrians applied for asylum in the EU, raising the total number of applicants since the beginning of the conflict to 579,184 (UNHCR 2015).

On 20 October 2014, the Foreign Affairs Council called for a comprehensive response to the ISIS threat and tasked the European Commission and the HR/VP with the elaboration of a regional strategy. It published an 'EU Regional Strategy for Syria and Iraq as well as the Da'esh threat' five months later (Council of the European Union 2015b). The strategy aimed at enhancing coherence. It called for synergies between the EU and Member State actions and underlined the need for complementarity between diplomacy, humanitarian aid, sanctions and longer-term development cooperation. In line with the call for horizontal coherence, it allocated EUR 1 billion to the regional crisis complex for 2014–2015 from different EU budget lines, amounting to EUR 144 million under the ENI for the Syrian crisis. The ENI funds were supposed to help prevent regional spill-overs, enhance border security, strengthen the moderate opposition, provide basic services and rebuild administration in areas of reduced violence (Council of the European Union 2015b).

The EU used additional ENI funds to complement humanitarian assistance. In December 2014, it established the 'Madad' Regional Trust Fund in Response to the Syrian crisis to implement the priorities set out in the UN Regional Refugee and Resilience Plan (European Commission 2016). The aim of the Fund was to pool financial contributions from the EU budget, the Member States, non-EU donors and private entities and to disburse them flexibly to Syria, Iraq, Jordan, Lebanon and Turkey. In 2015, the EU allocated EUR 300 million under the ENI to the Madad Fund and redirected EUR 200 million to it from the Instrument for Pre-Accession (European Commission 2016).

The flexible use of ENI funds shows that the EU has learned some lessons in terms of increasing horizontal coherence. The same cannot be said for vertical coherence. The EU-level contribution to the Madad Fund was to be matched with another EUR 500 million from the Member States. By November 2015, they had only committed EUR 32.4 million and, thus, little more than 6 per cent (European Parliament 2015). The Member States primarily viewed the Madad Fund as a means for pooling the EU's different budget lines (Hauck et al. 2015). Some were reluctant to channel contributions *via* the Fund as they feared a decrease of their own visibility and political influence. Others believed that the UN should be the primary recipient and that the Fund would just increase transaction costs and cause unnecessary delays (ibid.). The bottom line is that the UN faced important funding gaps, while many Member States failed to contribute their 'fair share' to the international crisis response (OXFAM 2016).

In addition, the Member States had no common collective approach to 'high politics'. They did not agree on military engagement in the fight against ISIS in Syria or Iraq. Their contributions were either unilateral or organised in the framework of the US-led coalition against ISIS. After the Paris attacks, France attempted to Europeanise these contributions when it invoked, for the first time, the EU's mutual assistance clause (Art. 42.7 TEU). After a unanimous and strong pledge of assistance, the Member States' assistance to France's operations in Syria and other theatres were agreed bilaterally instead of being coordinated at the EU level. Though variable, the Europeans' contribution to the military fight against ISIS remained marginal. The US was responsible for strategy and conducted 85 per cent of all air strikes (European Council on Foreign Relations 2015).

Meanwhile, the migratory repercussions of the Syrian conflict became a hard test for vertical coherence. A few Member States such as Sweden and Germany accepted the bulk of the Syrian refugees. Proposals to establish a more equitable distribution met with intense political resistance from national capitals. In September 2015, the EU agreed on a binding mechanism for the redistribution of 160,000 Syrian refugees, but by December only a few hundred had been relocated.

Overall, the EU played a key role as the most important humanitarian donor in the Syrian crisis. It used ENI funds to complement short-term humanitarian assistance and counter-terrorism measures. However, as the UN's funding gaps and the persistent refugee flows illustrated, the EU and the Member States failed to provide the necessary financial bridge between emergency and longer term aid. The EU Member States could not agree on a coordinated political strategy, a collective military contribution or sustainable mechanisms for the management and support of the refugees. Meanwhile, other global and regional players that are far less affected by the repercussions of the Syrian conflict have dominated in the military and diplomatic realm.

Conclusions

The 2015 ENP review shows that the EU has learned some important lessons from the Libyan and Syrian cases. It identified stabilisation as the main political priority for the following three to five years and put a greater focus on the security dimension and migration. It announced the creation of an ENI flexibility cushion for 'conflict and post-conflict needs; refugee support; crises and disaster response; and for security and stabilisation programmes' (European Commission and HR/VP 2015: 20). Trust Funds were mentioned as examples of how the EU can respond more flexibly to short-term financial needs. The review presents the EU Regional Strategy for Syria and Iraq as well as the ISIL/Da'esh threat as a useful tool to ensure coherence (Council of the European Union 2015b). Clearly, the ENP will not turn into a crisis response mechanism. However, as the Libyan and Syrian cases showed, the EU can strengthen the ENP's strategic, financial and institutional links with other fields of comprehensive crisis management.

The review also underlines the need for greater ownership by the Member States. It aims at enhancing vertical coherence through a greater role for the Council. However, the experience with Libya and Syria suggests that this will be a challenging endeavour. While the EU has reacted swiftly and substantially in the fields of humanitarian aid and sanctions, the Member States have often failed to act coherently in areas of 'high politics'. They either deviated from agreed EU positions or failed to agree on a common approach regarding crisis diplomacy, the use of force and migration.

Strengthening the ENP's security dimension and enhancing the focus on migration implies bridging the gaps between supranational and intergovernmental policy areas. This is a traditional challenge in the implementation of EU external action. However, the link between the ENP and comprehensive crisis management magnifies the challenge as the former represents a long-term policy, while the latter suggests a multidimensional short-term approach in a context often marked by urgency, potentially high stakes and risks. This is particularly true for defence and immigration, which are attached to domestic political stakes. There is a chance that the increased visibility of the security- and migration-related implications of the Libyan and Syrian crises for the EU could foster a greater sense of shared and indivisible responsibility and thus enhance the Member States' propensity for collective action. Such a political momentum would be needed to truly bolster the ENP's security dimension.

Note

1 The analysis draws on a range of expert interviews with decision-makers in Brussels and national capitals conducted between 2011 and 2015. Interviews were held under the condition of anonymity. In-text referencing corresponds to generic designations in line with interviewee preferences.

References

Ashton, C. (2011a) *Declaration by the High Representative on behalf of the European Union on Events in Libya (6795/1/11 PRESSE 33)*, Brussels.

Ashton, C. (2011b) *Declaration by the High Representative, Catherine Ashton, on Behalf of the European Union on EU Action Following the Escalation of Violent Repression in Syria (PRESSE 282)*, Brussels.

Ashton, C. (2011c) *Statement by the High Representative on the Crackdown of Demonstrations in Syria (A 114/11)*, Brussels.

Chulov, M. (2013) 'Half of Syrian Population "Will Need Aid by End of Year"', *The Guardian*. www.theguardian.com/world/2013/apr/19/half-syrian-population-aid-year.

Council of the European Union (2014) *Libya, a Political Framework for a Crisis Approach*, Brussels.

Council of the European Union (2015a) *Council Decision (CFSP) 2015/778 on a European Union Military Operation in the Southern Central Mediterranean (EUNAVFOR MED)*, Brussels.

Council of the European Union (2015b) *EU Regional Strategy for Syria and Iraq as well as the ISIL/Da'esh Threat*, Brussels.

Croft, A. (2013) 'EU Divided Over Approach to Syria Conflict', Reuters. www.reuters.com/article/us-syria-crisis-eu-idUSBRE92M0CP20130323.

Crombois, J. (2008) 'The European Neighbourhood Policy and the EU Actions in the Field of Conflict Management: Comparing Eastern Europe and the Maghreb', paper prepared for the Sixth Annual Pan-European Conference on International Relations, Turin.

de Coning, C. (2008) 'The Coherence Dilemma in Peacebuilding and Post-Conflict Reconstruction Systems', *African Journal on Conflict Resolution* 8(3): 85–109.

DG ECHO (2011) *Factsheet Libyan Crisis*, Brussels, 9 November.

EEAS (2015) *Fact Sheet: The European Union and Syria*, Brussels.

EurActiv (2011) 'EU, US Urge Assad to Step Down', Global Europe. www.euractiv.com/global-europe/eu-us-urged-assad-step-news-507045.

European Commission (2012) *ENP Package Syria*, Brussels.

European Commission (2013) *European Neighbourhood and Partnership Instrument: Syrian Arab Republic— Strategy Paper and National Indicative Programme 2007–2013*, Brussels.

European Commission (2015) *Implementation of the European Neighbourhood Policy Partnership for Democracy and Shared Prosperity with the Southern Mediterranean Partners Report*, Brussels.

European Commission (2016) 'EU Regional Trust Fund in Response to the Syrian Crisis'. http://ec.europa.eu/enlargement/neighbourhood/countries/syria/madad/index_en.htm.

European Commission and HR/VP (2013) *Towards a Comprehensive EU Approach to the Syrian Crisis*, Brussels.

European Commission and HR/VP (2015) *Review of the European Neighbourhood Policy*, JOIN(2015) 50 Final, Brussels, 18 November.

European Council (2011) *Declaration at the Extraordinary European Council*, Brussels.

European Council (2015) *Special Meeting—Statement*, Brussels. www.consilium.europa.eu/en/press/press-releases/2015/04/23-special-euco-statement/.

European Council on Foreign Relations (2015) 'European Foreign Policy Scorecard 2015: Syria and Iraq'. www.ecfr.eu/scorecard/2015/mena/39.

European Parliament (2011) *Southern Neighbourhood, and Libya in Particular, Including Humanitarian Aspects, (P7_TA(2011)0095)*, Strasbourg, 10 March. www.ifop.fr/media/poll/1558-2-study_file.pdf.

European Parliament (2015) 'Syria and Africa Funds: Parliament Urges Member States to Pay Up', *Press Release*. www.europarl.europa.eu/news/en/news-room/20151110IPR01805/Syria-and-Africa-Funds-Parliament-urges-member-states-to-pay-up.

Gottwald, M. (2012) 'Options for EU Engagement in Post-Conflict Libya', *TEPSA Brief*, Brussels.

Hauck, V., Knoll, A. and Herrero Cangas, A. (2015) 'EU Trust Funds—Shaping More Comprehensive External Action?', *Briefing Note* 81, European Centre for Development Policy Management. http://ecdpm.org/wp-content/uploads/Briefing_Note_81_EU_Trust_Funds_Africa_Migration_Knoll_Hauck_Cangas_ECDPM_2015.pdf.

Hollis, R. (2012) 'No Friend of Democratization: Europe's Role in the Genesis of the "Arab Spring"', *International Affairs* 88(1): 81–94.

Joffé, G. (2011) 'Libya and the European Union: Shared Interests?', *The Journal of North African Studies* 16(2): 233–249.

Koenig, N. (2011) 'The EU and the Libyan Crisis: In Quest of Coherence?', *The International Spectator* 46(4):11–30.

Marcus, J. (2013) 'Syria Arms Embargo: EU Divided Despite Consensus', BBC Europe. www.bbc.com/news/world-europe-22688997.

Noutcheva, G. (2014) 'Institutional Governance of European Neighbourhood Policy in the Wake of the Arab Spring', *Journal of European Integration* 37(1): 19–36.

Nuttall, S. (2005) 'Coherence and Consistency', in Hill, C. and Smith, M. (eds.) *International Relations and the European Union*, Oxford: Oxford University Press, 90–112.

OXFAM (2016) 'Syria Crisis Fair Share Analysis 2016'. www.oxfam.org/sites/www.oxfam.org/files/file_attachments/bn-syria-fair-shares-analysis-010216-en.pdf.

Reuters (2011) 'Berlusconi Under Fire for Not "disturbing" Gaddafi', 20 February. www.reuters.com/article/us-italy-libya-berlusconi-idUSTRE71J1LH20110220.

Sobol, M. (2015) 'It's the Member States, Stupid! The Deadlock Which Bedevils the European Neighbourhood Policy', *Studia Diplomatica* LYVIII(1): 63–76.

Tisdall, S. (2011) 'The Consensus on Intervention in Libya has Shattered', *The Guardian*. www.theguardian.com/commentisfree/2011/mar/23/libya-ceasefire-consensus-russia-china-india.

UN Security Council (2011) *Resolution 1973*, New York.

UNHCR (2015) 'Europe—Syrian Asylum Applications', *Syria Regional Refugee Response*. http://data.unhcr.org/syrianrefugees/asylum.php.

Wolff, S., Whitman, R. and Krauss, S. (2007) 'Conflict Resolution as a Policy Goal Under ENP in the Southern Neighbourhood', *Briefing Paper*, European Parliament, Brussels.

Zoubir, Y. (2009) 'Libya and Europe: Economic Realism at the Rescue of the Qaddafi Authoritarian Regime', *Journal of Contemporary European Studies* 17(3): 401–415.

PART V

The European Neighbourhood Policy and sectoral cooperation

33
DEEP AND COMPREHENSIVE FREE TRADE AGREEMENTS

Bernard Hoekman[1]

Introduction

Trade agreements have been a central feature of the Association Agreements (AAs) that are a key element of the European Union's (EU's) engagement with countries in its eastern and southern neighbourhood. Trade agreements have also been a pillar of the EU's interaction with countries in the rest of the world, reflecting a long history of using trade as an instrument of foreign policy. Over time both the design and the content of the EU's trade agreements have evolved substantially, moving from a focus on 'shallow' trade agreements – that centre mostly on the liberalization of merchandise trade – towards 'deeper' trade agreements – that also liberalize trade in services, public procurement markets and cross-border investment, and include disciplines on the implementation of national regulatory regimes. This shift is evident in the 2003 European Neighbourhood Policy (ENP), which establishes provisions that allow interested governments to negotiate a Deep and Comprehensive Free Trade Area (DCFTA) between the EU and partner countries.

To date, DCFTAs have not had a very successful track record. As of mid-2016, only four DCFTA negotiations had been concluded, notably with Armenia, Georgia, Moldova and Ukraine. DCFTAs with the Eastern Partnership (EaP) countries became a focal point of contention with Russia, which sought, unsuccessfully, to convince Ukraine to become a member of the Eurasian Customs Union (Dragneva and Wolczuk 2012) – an initiative that was expanded into the Eurasian Economic Union (EEU). In the case of Armenia, Russian pressure led the government to decide to join the EEU, so that the DCFTA that was negotiated as part of the AA in 2013 never entered into force.[2] Following the so-called 'Arab Spring' uprisings in 2011 in the EU's southern neighbourhood, the Council of the European Union agreed to a negotiating mandate for DCFTA talks with Egypt, Jordan, Morocco and Tunisia in December 2011. To date only two of these countries, Morocco and Tunisia, entered negotiations. However, negotiations with Morocco were halted in July 2014 at the initiative of the Moroccan government to assess the potential impacts on its industry, reflecting concerns about the net benefits of a DCFTA and worries that an agreement would not have enough domestic support.

The chapter starts with a brief discussion of elements of the research literature on the economic effects of DCFTAs. The second section considers broader trends in the global economy and developments in the coverage and design of international trade agreements, illustrating that alternative approaches to deepening integration of product markets might be considered by ENP countries and the EU. The final section provides conclusions.

From shallow to deeper integration through DCFTAs

The ENP was intended to provide a framework for deepening economic, as well as non-economic, relations with neighbouring countries that are not EU accession candidates. The primary motivation for the ENP was the 2004 enlargement of the EU to encompass eight former centrally-planned Central and Eastern European countries.[3] The goal was to offer, to neighbours of the newly acceded Member States, opportunities to deepen cooperation with the enlarged EU. The ENP became the umbrella framework for subsequent initiatives targeting cooperation with countries located to the South of the EU – the 2008 Union for the Mediterranean (UfM) – and those to the East of the EU – the 2009 EaP.[4]

Basic principles underpinning cooperation under the ENP are commitment to common values, including democracy, the rule of law, good governance and respect for human rights, and complementing binding treaty-based cooperation with financial and technical assistance from the EU. A key feature is to offer ENP countries the opportunity to converge to EU norms and standards in specific areas of regulation on an *à la carte* basis without giving countries a seat at the table in the elaboration of norms. The approach has been characterized succinctly by the phrase: 'everything but institutions' (Prodi 2002).

The move in the late 2000s to negotiate DCFTAs and focus more specifically on integrating markets was a significant shift in approach by the EU. Much has been written by scholars and civil society groups about the associated reduction in attention and emphasis by the EU on 'exporting' its fundamental values – human rights, political freedoms and the implied turn to focus more on economic policies affecting market access and related regulation (Kausch and Youngs 2009). Less attention has been given in the literature to the political economy of DCFTAs (Monastiriotis and Borrell 2012 is an exception).

DCFTAs are similar to the trade agreements negotiated under the Euro-Mediterranean Partnership (EMP) in terms of issue areas covered, but they differ by establishing specific, binding (enforceable) disciplines and aim at the (gradual) convergence of policies in covered areas with those of the EU. Examples of policy commitments in extant DCFTAs with EaP countries include the following:

- Abolition of import tariffs on both agricultural and industrial products. The extent of inclusion of agricultural products is a major difference compared to the EMP agreements, although coverage of agriculture in DCFTAs depends on the partner country. Thus, for example, the agreement with Ukraine has 10-year transition periods for the EU to remove tariffs on many items, and tariff quotas will remain on sensitive products;
- Provisions on customs and trade facilitation, including the substance and administration of customs laws and regulations, which reflect EU norms;
- National treatment for investors (right of establishment), subject to exceptions;
- Enforcement of competition policy, with alignment of rules and enforcement practices to that of the EU *acquis* in selected areas, applying equally to private and state-controlled enterprises. ENP countries are also to adopt disciplines on state aid (subsidies) that are similar to those in the EU;
- Commitments to apply EU product standards for industrial goods and sanitary and phytosanitary measures for food and animal/plant products and to put in place effective enforcement mechanisms to assure compliance. The aim is to gradually align technical

regulations, standards and related infrastructure with those of the EU, and to negotiate agreements on conformity assessment and acceptance of industrial products in the future. Such agreements would allow trade in covered sectors to occur under the same conditions as those prevailing in the Internal Market, that is, partner country products would be treated as EU products and *vice versa*;
- Requirements to protect intellectual property rights (IPRs) and apply the EU's internal rules in this area, including for geographical indications (GIs) – with transition periods for some products to allow producers to establish trademarks or their own GIs;
- Agreement to open government procurement markets to EU competition (excluding defence-related purchases) through gradual adoption of all EU laws and procedures;
- Measures to open access to services markets. In the case of Ukraine, a process of legislative approximation in financial services, telecommunications services, postal and courier services, and international maritime services involves adoption of both the existing and the future EU *acquis* in these sectors.

Space constraints prohibit a detailed discussion of the content of a DCFTA.[5] Suffice it to say, that the focus is ongoing, beyond the simple reciprocal opening of trade (market access), to also span measures and disciplines to ensure that markets are contestable, by aligning policies to those in the EU in different areas of product market regulation (standards, competition policy and protection of IPRs, as well as certain service sectors). DCFTAs build on WTO rules and practices – the WTO is the baseline – but go beyond the WTO in many of the covered areas.[6]

There is much discussion in the literature on what the EU's specific objectives are in negotiating DCFTAs, with some arguing that they are an exercise in the projection of EU norms, and others arguing that they should mainly be seen through a neo-realist lens – as efforts to ensure the security of the EU Member States by reducing migration incentives, and ensuring access to natural resources (energy). Whatever view is taken, a necessary condition for realizing any of these objectives is that the DCFTAs result in higher growth and rising incomes in partner countries. *Ex ante* analyses of DCFTAs conclude that this will be the case,[7] although specific industries and workers and communities that rely on these industries will be negatively affected because of greater competition from the EU.[8]

Most of what is called for in a DCFTA revolves around national policy reforms by partner countries. Thus, much of what could be achieved through a DCFTA could in principle also be obtained through unilateral, autonomously implemented policy changes. This point is illustrated by Georgia, which was already more open to trade and investment than the EU when it negotiated its DCFTA; it also had already implemented significant economic governance reforms (Messerlin et al. 2011). This raises the question of what the value of a DCFTA is to an ENP country. While better access to the EU is certainly beneficial, EU markets are already relatively open. So far as a neighbourhood country has relatively high barriers to trade, preferential liberalization that extends only to the EU may generate trade diversion and create rents that accrue to EU firms instead of lower prices for consumers.

For the EaP countries, clearly a central factor for pursuing a DCFTA (or, instead, refusing to engage with the EU) was whether on balance they sought to become less susceptible to Russian hegemony. For neighbours where this was (is) the case, the balance of economic costs and benefits of a DCFTA may matter less than whether a DCFTA provides a robust framework that helps deliver greater economic independence. This is not obvious, as making the *acquis* the focal point of sector-specific provisions of the DCFTAs may have impeded progress on the economic independence objective. Indeed, adoption of the *acquis* created a prospect that ENP country firms would have to deal with two incompatible regulatory regimes (EU vs EEU).

More generally, the question is whether a DCFTA provides a useful guidepost and anchor for policy. This has several dimensions. First, does the *acquis* add value relative to a strategy that instead focuses on satisfying international standards for products, internationally agreed norms for good regulatory practices and internationally developed guidelines for public procurement policies? That is, does it have value in and of itself by representing international best practice? If not, it may still make economic sense to adopt the *acquis* if by far the largest share of the country's trade is with the EU. But for countries that have a more diversified set of trading partners, the question should be what the (opportunity) cost is of not converging (completely) with EU norms. This is also a relevant consideration for countries that do trade a lot with the EU. Many non-neighbourhood countries that trade intensively with the EU have not adopted the *acquis*, illustrating that convergence to EU norms is not a necessary condition for deeper trade relations with the EU.

Abstracting from the economic net benefits of adopting the *acquis*, DCFTAs may enhance policy credibility. Adoption of international good practice standards and norms will only be associated with domestic enforcement mechanisms, except in so far as commitments can be made in the WTO.[9] Credibility ultimately requires that there are actors that have an incentive to take a matter to court. Part and parcel of a DCFTA is regular monitoring, dialogue and (potentially) enforcement action, to address instances when an ENP country does not implement relevant provisions that are legally binding. If a neighbour attaches value to this enforcement dimension, it should take that into consideration when deciding whether to adopt elements of EU law as part of a DCFTA. This depends on the extent to which the EU provides the desired monitoring and enforcement services.

A third consideration is that the EU will provide technical and financial assistance to bolster implementation capacity. But such assistance is also available from other sources, including the international development banks, such as the European Bank for Reconstruction and Development, the World Bank and the African Development Bank, as well as bilateral donors. Moreover, the EU is likely to assist independent of signing a DCFTA. Although this may be at a lower level than that associated with *acquis*-based agreements, to some extent this will be offset by the fact that the ENP country will not need to incur all the costs associated with implementing EU rules and norms.

These questions require case-by-case analysis, and the answers will depend on the objectives of every ENP country. As mentioned, in practice, decisions to pursue a DCFTA may have less to do with economics and centre more on political and foreign policy motivations – for example, a hope to eventually accede to the EU (without regard to clear statements from the EU that this is not on offer), or a desire to become less dependent on – and thus vulnerable to – Russia. Even so, an economic perspective should inform the trade strategy of ENP countries, implying a need to assess the potential economic effects of a DCFTA, and comparing this with alternative options that may be available.

The primary tool that has been used to assess possible effects of entering a DCFTA are sustainability impact assessments (SIAs), undertaken for the European Commission.[10] One goal of the SIA exercise is to identify areas where complementary measures may be needed to deal with potential adverse consequences of implementing a DCFTA. SIAs use computational general equilibrium (CGE) models, more qualitative analysis of potential social and environmental effects and consultations with stakeholders. The CGE models are used to simulate the impacts of different scenarios, including a baseline business as usual scenario. The model is used to assess the effects of implementing a DCFTA and mostly focuses on the impacts of lowering trade barriers – the (gradual) removal of most tariffs, expanded access to agricultural markets, measures to increase the contestability of services markets and liberalize cross-border investment (the right of establishment) and actions to adopt the *acquis* in different areas, which are associated with a presumed reduction in trade costs for firms. The standard approach to quantifying the latter dimensions are to convert the effect of prevailing (baseline) policies into ad valorem tariff equivalents (AVEs)[11] and then to apply, based on judgement, a conservative estimate of how much a DCFTA would reduce these AVEs. The models generate information on how the mix of tariff and AVE reductions impact on product prices, which in turn feed into effects on output and wages.

The SIAs are limited in scope. Analysts charged with undertaking SIAs are constrained by the terms of reference given to them and guidelines on how to assess possible impacts in the SIA handbook (European Commission 2006) – for example, SIAs do not assess alternative options in any depth. Although understandable, given the presumption that the aim of the exercise is to conclude a DCFTA, assessing outside options and potential impacts on, and reactions by, other countries is important. This was illustrated by Russia's reaction to DCFTA negotiations with EaP countries, but the broader question of whether there are alternative, potentially superior, trade policy options for partner countries is not asked. Analyses by independent academics and think tanks can complement SIAs by devoting more attention to alternative options.[12]

The SIAs generally point to the importance of liberalization of inflows of foreign direct investment (FDI), trade in services, trade facilitation and logistics. The models show that reducing the incidence of NTBs is particularly important for generating welfare increases, but this is done by assuming convergence towards EU law will result in a certain reduction in estimated AVEs. There is limited empirical evidence on which to base these assumed reductions. Moreover, the costs associated with implementation are essentially ignored, although the models do identify sectors that will win, and potentially lose, from changes in AVEs (and tariffs). More important, empirical research in development economics has shown that what matters for trade liberalization to support higher growth (increasing real incomes) is improving economic governance and related institutions.[13] A basic problem here is that it is not possible to model much of what a DCFTA may do in this regard. This is recognised in the SIA handbook, which notes that modelling trade in services, trade rules and investment can only be done imperfectly, if at all (European Commission 2006). This is even more difficult for changes in regulatory regimes and convergence to the *acquis*.

Towards greater differentiation?

The adoption of elements of EU law may increase costs of domestic production and force less efficient firms to shut down. Firms that can incur the adjustment costs may find it harder to compete in their traditional export markets, if consumers there do not value higher-standard products. Approximation to the EU *acquis* may entail more costs than benefits. For example, a necessary element for EaP countries in converging towards EU norms is to move away from the GOST standards, which may still be in place and continue to apply in Russia. GOST standards are inconsistent with WTO rules because they regulate aspects of products unrelated to safety, are outdated and often are not science-based. Application of EU food standards to sales on the domestic market may impact negatively on the food sector, as well as increase food costs. Messerlin et al. (2011) estimate that harmonization of food safety norms and processes to EU levels could increase food costs in Georgia by 90 per cent.

Reporting on the experience of the Central Eastern European countries that acceded to the EU in 2004 and 2007, the World Bank (2007) notes that despite substantial assistance from the EU, large parts of the food industry were forced to exit the market because of the costs of the upgrades needed to meet EU requirements. The report concludes that harmonization with

EU food safety and agricultural health legislation is neither necessary nor realistic for EEU and other Central Asian countries and that they are best served by carefully prioritising actions in this area based on assessments of costs, benefits and trade opportunities. This recommendation is bolstered given that the scale of financial and technical support that was provided to accession countries is not available for EaP countries. Presumably recognizing the high costs of adjustment, the chapter in the DCFTAs dealing with sanitary and phytosanitary measures refers to adoption of EU standards as a process. Adopting some parts of the *acquis* may be important from an export perspective; for others, it may be better to defer until incomes are higher, thereby providing a domestic market for more expensive products. The general point is that a case-by-case approach may be most appropriate with respect to regulatory reform.

An important area from a growth perspective that is covered by DCFTAs is trade and investment in services. For ENP countries to be competitive on global markets, participate effectively in international supply chains and attract related investments, they must offer efficient transport, financial, logistics and communications services. A DCFTA will usually imply significant reform of services policies. From a DCFTA perspective, service sectors can be divided into three groups: those regulated by comprehensive EU Directives, such as financial services and telecommunications; those subject to Services Directive 2006/123/EC; and other sectors such as public (health, education) and cultural services. In assessing the potential impacts of a DCFTA it is necessary to determine to what extent prevailing policies conform to the applicable EU Directives, including in the case of distribution and professional services, the Services Directive.

Aligning a country's regulatory regime to the EU's is complicated as the agenda spans mobility, licensing and approvals. Cross-border movement of service providers is politically sensitive as it involves people. Countries that are not eligible for accession will never have unfettered access to the EU labour market, but allowing greater movement of suppliers is part and parcel of liberalizing trade in services. The potential for raising incomes in ENP countries through the liberalization of movement of services suppliers is significant (Jensen and Tarr 2012). That said, a focus on the EU *acquis* on services only will not suffice to ensure that policies are most conducive to support substantial productivity improvements. Much will depend on national policy choices on a sector-by-sector basis and the quality of economic governance more generally.

Following the 2015 ENP Review, the EU signalled a move away from the emulation of the accession/enlargement modalities that was the basis of DCFTAs (High Representative of the Union for Foreign Affairs and Security Policy and European Commission 2015). In the future, the approach will be more *à la carte* and case-by-case (Delcour 2015). An example is the pursuit of bilateral Agreements on Conformity Assessment and Acceptance, which would permit free movement of industrial products for covered sectors. The High Representative and the European Commission (2015) make explicit mention of the WTO as a framework for such initiatives – the WTO permits, and encourages, such arrangements while they are open to all WTO members that are interested in participating and able to satisfy the required conditions – which must apply on a non-discriminatory basis.

A less *acquis*-centric approach towards trade cooperation is consistent with the discussion above. DCFTAs are best considered as one element of a broader menu. For countries that do most of their trade with the EU, it may make sense to adopt EU law, but this is not a necessary condition for trading with the EU: Asian exporters to the EU have greatly increased trade without adopting the *acquis*. From the perspective of partner countries, deeper integration with the EU should support greater engagement with the rest of the world as well, not just the near neighbourhood (the EEU, regional integration of Arab countries) but also dynamic countries in Asia. An alternative focal point is cooperation premised on regulatory convergence towards international, as opposed to EU, standards. In some areas, there may be substantial overlap between the *status quo* in the EU and international norms, but in most cases, there will be idiosyncratic dimensions associated with implementing the *acquis* that may not be needed to attain international good practices.

Good regulatory and trade policy practices are increasingly the focus of modern Preferential Trade Agreements (PTAs). These include commitments to open access to FDI (right of establishment), removal of explicit barriers to provision of services by foreign suppliers, elimination of discriminatory government purchasing policies and adoption of international standards. The subject coverage of recent PTAs such as the EU–Korea PTA or Comprehensive Economic and Trade Agreement (CETA) overlaps to a significant extent with DCFTAs, but does not involve agreement to adopt EU regulations. Analysis of other trade agreement contexts and international economic cooperation initiatives involving the EU suggests that, contrary to what is frequently expected, the EU often does not (as it is not able to) export its norms (Young 2015). A more generic PTA approach may well be more appropriate in supporting economic development prospects, since it results in the adoption of norms that (can) also figure in agreements with other trade partners (Hoekman 2011; Messerlin et al. 2011; Dreyer 2012).

There are many potential areas for relations with a broader set of trading partners to be based on intergovernmental agreements. They include deepening cooperation on border control procedures to facilitate trade, permitting foreign investment in services, mutual recognition of product standards and technical regulations, agreements to accept the certification of conformity assessment authorities in the partner country, or mutual recognition agreements of the qualifications of professionals providing services (including, for accountants and engineers). A benefit of using international standards as the focal point for cooperation is that initiatives in these areas may be more easily extended to include additional countries in and outside the EU's neighbourhood to the mutual benefit of all concerned. The potential net welfare gains from trade policy-related reforms are greatest if such reforms apply to all trading partners. DCFTAs cannot maximize welfare because they are discriminatory. Jensen and Tarr (2012), for example, conclude that potential real income gains for Armenia could be tripled if the reforms implied by the (abandoned) DCFTA were applied on a non-discriminatory basis. Adoption of international standards and internationally agreed good regulatory practices may therefore generate much greater benefits than a DCFTA.

Greater engagement with the communities with a strong stake in reducing trade barriers and frictions, as well as with those groups that have concerns that international cooperation to lower barriers to trade may affect them negatively, should inform cooperation. Hoekman et al. (2014) suggest that adoption of an approach that is informed by existing cross-border supply chain-based interactions between firms could help focus attention on how different policy areas – such as border management procedures, product standards, licensing, certification, documentary and data reporting requirements, regulation of transport and distribution (logistics) services – jointly impact on the operation of value chains that are important for a given partner country. The idea is that a supply-chain informed deliberation that includes all groups with a stake in a production network, from suppliers to transporters to distributors, can help to identify areas where significant gains could be achieved through cooperation. Governments may not know enough about how and where deep integration can help attain common growth objectives and what range of possible types of cooperation will generate the greatest gains. Deliberation has been used in a variety of contexts as an instrument to support more informed decision-making by a polity or group of stakeholders. Building in greater space for employing deliberative approaches can contribute to identifying (prioritizing) policy domains where deeper integration should have high payoffs for stakeholders from both the EU and ENP countries.

Conclusions

The original vision underlying DCFTAs was that they would serve as mechanisms through which ENP countries could not only open their markets on a preferential basis to EU suppliers (and in turn obtain access to the EU on a preferential basis) but also gradually adopt the EU *acquis* in specific areas. The presumption was that the *acquis* was a good thing. This approach was recognized as being too limited in the 2015 review of the ENP, and in future a more *à la carte* approach will be pursued to define the content of DCFTAs. Convergence with EU law and regulations may not be the most effective mechanism to support economic growth and development objectives. It is also not necessarily the most efficient instrument to attain greater regulatory coherence. More differentiated approaches that target areas of economic policy and cooperation that have clear payoffs for both sides may be superior in making progress on the fundamental security and development objectives that motivate EU engagement with its neighbourhood.

After all, a DCFTA is a specific type of PTA. What matters from the perspective of both the EU and ENP countries is to identify forms of international cooperation that help provide a good focal point as well as an effective anchor for desirable policy reforms. If EU accession is not on the table, a focus on improving economic governance through adoption of international standards may be more appropriate than one that is centred on EU laws and practices. This can be pursued with the assistance of international development organizations, where there is some evidence that these may be more successful in supporting reforms than the EU (Langbein 2014). Trade agreements have an important potential role to play in reducing policy uncertainty and enhancing the credibility of reforms, but it is not clear whether a DCFTA generates greater credibility than a PTA that is premised on the adoption of international standards and good regulatory practices. Whatever form a PTA takes, it is important to consider that the benefits of reforms will be greater if they are applied to all trading partners. In this regard, more generic trade agreements, and cooperation that is centred on international good practices and standards, may be more easily extended to other countries.

The 2011 and 2015 reviews of the ENP recognize that one size does not fit all (Bouris and Schumacher 2017; Delcour 2015). However, the *acquis* remains the default focal point for the EU. Shifting gears to focus more on international standards and good regulatory practices will therefore require leadership by ENP countries. This can be facilitated through greater engagement with and by other international organizations, such as the Organisation for Economic Co-operation and Development, the United Nations Economic Commission for Europe and the World Bank. In some areas, the *acquis* cannot be avoided – for example, conformity assessment agreements for tradable products will be conditional on a partner country establishing the equivalence of its regime with that in the EU. But even with technical standards, relaxing the constraint of having to adopt the *acquis* may allow greater flexibility and diversity in how EU norms are satisfied. Ultimately, what matters is equivalence – achievement of the regulatory objectives that motivate standards – and this need not require harmonization. The new PTAs between the EU and non-neighbourhood countries illustrate this point: despite a focus on deepening integration of markets, they do not involve partner countries harmonizing their laws and regulations with those of the EU.

Notes

1 I am grateful to Tobias Schumacher and Andreas Marchetti for helpful comments on an initial draft.
2 Armenia formally acceded to the EAEU in December 2015 (Eurasian Economic Commission 2015).
3 In 2004, Cyprus, the Czech Republic, Estonia, Hungary, Latvia, Lithuania, Malta, Poland, Slovakia and Slovenia joined the EU. In 2007, two more Eastern European states acceded: Bulgaria and Romania.

4 The ENP encompasses ten Mediterranean economies – Algeria, Egypt, Israel, Jordan, Lebanon, Libya, Morocco, Palestine, Syria and Tunisia – and six countries located to the East of the EU: Armenia, Azerbaijan, Belarus, Georgia, Moldova and Ukraine. In addition to the southern neighbours covered by the ENP, the UfM also includes Mauretania, Turkey and Western Balkan countries. See Cardwell (2011) for a discussion of the genesis and development of these initiatives and Del Sarto (2016) for an assessment of the EU's underlying goals and references to the literature.
5 See Van der Loo (2016) and Van der Loo et al. (2014) for a comprehensive discussion and assessment of the DCFTA with Ukraine.
6 A precondition for the EU to negotiate a DCFTA is that the partner country is a WTO member. Extant DCFTAs with EaP countries do not include investor protection or investor–state dispute settlement provisions – because this was still a Member State competence at the time they were negotiated.
7 See ECORYS (2013a, 2013b; 2014a, 2014b) and ECORYS and CASE (2007, 2012, 2013).
8 Thus, Jensen and Tarr (2012), Movchan and Giucci (2011) and Shepotylo (2013) concur with the Sustainability Impact Assessment (SIA) undertaken for the EU in estimating substantial net welfare gains from a DCFTA for Ukraine, due mainly to better access to EU markets for exports and productivity gains from the deep integration aspects of the agreement.
9 There is substantial scope for a WTO member to make commitments that go beyond basic tariff bindings and market access and national treatment commitments for services. The WTO gives incentives for countries to use international product standards and permits scheduling of regulatory commitments if countries desire to do so (Hoekman and Mavroidis 2016).
10 See note 7.
11 An alternative is to assume so-called 'iceberg trade costs', which entail modelling non-tariff barriers (NTBs) as a fixed cost that work to 'melt' away a share of the value of a product. This implies that NTBs generate social waste.
12 See, for example, Jensen and Tarr (2012), Institute for Economic Research and Policy Consulting (2011) and Movchan and Giucci (2011).
13 See, for example, Freund and Bolaky (2008) on how the investment climate impacts on the benefits of reducing barriers to trade in goods.

References

Bouris, D. and Schumacher, T. (eds.) (2017) *The Revised European Neighbourhood Policy: Continuity and Change in EU Foreign Policy*, Houndmills Basingstoke: Palgrave Macmillan.

Cardwell, J. (2011) 'EuroMed, European Neighbourhood Policy and the Union for the Mediterranean: Overlapping Policy Frames in the EU's Governance of the Mediterranean', *Journal of Common Market Studies* 49(2): 219–241.

Del Sarto, R. (2016) 'Normative Empire Europe: The European Union, its Borderlands, and the "Arab Spring"', *Journal of Common Market Studies* 54(2): 215–232.

Delcour, L. (2015) 'The 2015 ENP Review: Beyond Stocktaking, the Need for a Political Strategy', *CEPOB 1*, Bruges, December.

Dragneva, R. and Wolczuk, K. (2012) *Russia, the Eurasian Customs Union and the EU: Cooperation, Stagnation or Rivalry?*, London: Chatham House.

Dreyer, I. (2012) 'Trade Policy in the EU's Neighbourhood: Ways Forward for the Deep and Comprehensive Free Trade Agreements', *Study and Research* 90, Notre Europe.

ECORYS (2013a) 'Trade Sustainability Impact Assessment in Support of Negotiations of a DCFTA Between the EU and Tunisia', *Report for DG Trade*.

ECORYS (2013b) 'Trade Sustainability Impact Assessment in Support of Negotiations of a DCFTA Between the EU and Morocco', *Report for DG Trade*.

ECORYS (2014a) 'Trade Sustainability Impact Assessment in Support of Negotiations of a DCFTA Between the EU and Jordan', *Report for DG Trade*.

ECORYS (2014b) 'Trade Sustainability Impact Assessment in Support of Negotiations of a DCFTA Between the EU and Egypt', *Report for DG Trade*.

ECORYS and CASE (2007) 'Trade Sustainability Impact Assessment for the FTA Between the EU and Ukraine Within the Enhanced Agreement', *Report for DG Trade*.

ECORYS and CASE (2012) 'Trade Sustainability Impact Assessment in Support of Negotiations of a DCFTA Between the EU and Georgia and the Republic of Moldova', *Report for DG Trade*.

ECORYS and CASE (2013) 'Trade Sustainability Impact Assessment in Support of Negotiations of a DCFTA Between the EU and Armenia', *Report for DG Trade*.

Eurasian Economic Commission (2015) 'Armenia is Now in the Eurasian Economic Union'. www.eurasiancommission.org/en/nae/news/Pages/02-01-2015-1.aspx.

European Commission (2006) 'Handbook for Trade Sustainability Impact', DG Trade, Brussels.

Freund, C. and Bolaky, B. (2008) 'Trade, Regulations, and Income', *Journal of Development Economics* 87(2): 309–321.

High Representative of the Union for Foreign Affairs and Security Policy and European Commission (2015) *Joint Communication to the European Parliament, the Council, the European Economic and Social Committee and the Committee of the Regions. Review of the European Neighbourhood Policy*, JOIN(2015) 50 Final, Brussels. http://eeas.europa.eu/archives/docs/enp/documents/2015/151118_joint-communication_review-of-the-enp.pdf.

Hoekman, B. (2011) 'North South Preferential Trade Agreements', in Chauffour J. and Maur, J. (eds.) *Preferential Trade Agreements and Development: A Handbook*, Washington, DC: World Bank.

Hoekman, B. and Mavroidis, P. (2016) 'MFN Clubs and Scheduling Additional Commitments in the GATT: Learning from the GATS', *EUI RSCAS Working Paper* 2016/03.

Hoekman, B., Jensen, J. and Tarr, D. (2014) 'A Vision for Ukraine in the World Economy: Defining a Trade Policy Strategy that Leverages Global Opportunities', *Journal of World Trade* 48(4): 795–814.

Institute for Economic Research and Policy Consulting (2011) *Ukraine's Trade Policy Choices: Pros and Cons of Different Regional Integration Options*, Kiev: IER.

Jensen, J. and Tarr, D. (2012) 'Deep Trade Policy Options for Armenia: The Importance of Trade Facilitation, Services and Standards Liberalization', *Economics* 6(1): 1–54. www.economic-ejournal.org/economic/journalarticles/2012-1

Kausch, K. and Youngs, R. (2009) 'The End of the "Euro-Mediterranean Vision"', *International Affairs* 85(5): 963–975.

Langbein, J. (2014) 'European Union Governance Towards the Eastern Neighbourhood: Transcending or Redrawing Europe's East–West Divide?', *Journal of Common Market Studies* 52(1): 157–174.

Messerlin, P., Emerson, M., Jandieri, G. and Le Vernoy, A. (2011) *An Appraisal of the EU's Trade Policy Toward its Eastern Neighbors: The Case of Georgia*, Brussels: SciencesPo and CEPS.

Monastiriotis, V. and Borrell, M. (2012) 'Political and Political Economy Literature on the ENP: Issues and Implications', *SEARCH Working Paper* 01/05.

Movchan, V. and Giucci, R. (2011) 'Quantitative Assessment of Ukraine's Regional Integration Options: DCFTA with European Union vs. Customs Union with Russia, Belarus and Kazakhstan'. www.beratergruppe-ukraine.de/download/Beraterpapiere/2011/PP_05_2011_en.pdf.

Prodi, R. (2002) *A Wider Europe—A Proximity Policy as the Key to Stability*, Brussels, 5 December. europa.eu/rapid/press-release_SPEECH-02-619_en.htm.

Shepotylo, O. (2013) *Export Potential, Uncertainty, and Regional Integration: Choice of Trade Policy for Ukraine*, Kyiv School of Economics. http://ssrn.com/abstract=2288652.

Van der Loo, G. (2016) *The EU-Ukraine Association Agreement and Deep and Comprehensive Free Trade Area: A New Legal Instrument for EU Integration Without Membership*, Leiden: Brill.

Van der Loo, G., van Elsuwege, P. and Petrov, R. (2014) 'The EU-Ukraine Association Agreement: Assessment of an Innovative Legal Instrument', *EUI LAW Working Paper* 2014/09.

World Bank (2007) *Food Safety and Agricultural Health Management in CIS Countries: Completing the Transition*, Washington, DC: World Bank.

Young, A. (2015) 'Liberalizing Trade, Not Exporting Rules: The Limits to Regulatory Coordination in the EU's "New Generation" Trade Agreements', *Journal of European Public Policy* 22(9): 1253–1275.

34
THE EUROPEAN NEIGHBOURHOOD POLICY AND ENERGY

Bernd Weber

Introduction

European Union (EU) energy security is confronted with major challenges, such as the depletion of hydrocarbon reserves within Europe, growing regional competition for fossil fuel resources, the combat against climate change and the need to guarantee affordable energy prices. The combination of the underlying political, economic and environmental constraints has increased the importance of supplies of the least carbon-emitting fuel, natural gas, from and through the EU's neighbourhood. While hydrocarbons make up for two-thirds of the EU's energy mix, more than half of this share comes from neighbouring countries (International Energy Agency 2013). However, Member States' energy mixes differ substantially, as do their path-dependent import dependencies and relations with external suppliers. Based on this, Member States feature divergent interests in the field of energy, which is why a common external energy policy did not find its way into the EU treaties and is not clearly spelled out (Baumann and Simmerl 2011). At the same time, repeated conflicts between Europe's main supplier, Russia, and the major transit states, Ukraine and Belarus, have revealed the vulnerability of EU supply security towards politico-economic conflicts in the neighbourhood. Due to the enduring political uncertainties regarding the future of Russia–Ukraine relations, the risk of supply cut-offs remains high. This is particularly true for Central and Eastern European countries, whose energy supply is characterised by a high dependence on Russian gas imports and limited supply alternatives (Kovacevic 2009). In addition, resource nationalism, as well as turmoil and instability, after the Arab uprisings in 2011, have demonstrated the fragility of hydrocarbon supply chains in the southern neighbourhood, in terms of drops in production and attacks on energy infrastructure (EU Institute for Security Studies 2014). Against this background, pursuing an effective EU external energy policy in the neighbourhood has become a major security concern for the EU.

In this context, the EU has multiplied its instruments to export EU energy key norms to its neighbours to liberalise and modernise their energy sectors. The rationale behind the EU's approach is that reliable supply and affordability of energy are best guaranteed by functioning, interconnected gas and electricity markets, grounded in liberal EU market norms. The major question is, whether and how the EU manages to promote convergence with its energy norms across the neighbourhood.

This chapter provides an overview of the process and outcomes of EU norm export to regulate energy sectors and transnational infrastructure across the neighbourhood. The first section depicts 'EU External Energy Governance' as the *leitmotif* of EU external energy policy in the neighbourhood and its diffusionary logic. The second section unpacks different 'concentric circles of energy co-operation and integration', which have come to emerge in Europe's neighbourhood (Padgett 2011). By analysing the different instruments promoting EU norms through the prism of the two distinct modes of 'EUnilateral' and 'decentred' EU External Energy Governance, the chapter sheds light on the limits of EU norm export in the neighbourhood in terms of convergence. Drawing on this, it is argued that while the EU can transfer its precise norms in the 'inner ring', made up by the Energy Community, it needs to refrain from prescribing pre-defined EU norms to ensure some degree of convergence with its energy norms in the 'outer rings', made up of bilateral partnerships and other regional sectorial cooperation frameworks.

The *leitmotif* of EU energy policy in the neighbourhood

In the absence of a codified EU external energy policy, the EU's strategy to guarantee its energy security in its neighbourhood, and reduce risks along the supply chain, is threefold (European Commission 2011). First, the EU seeks to integrate neighbouring countries into a pan-European market for gas and electricity, based on convergence with EU key norms, rules and standards. The unbundling of gas and electricity sectors, that is, the separation of network operation from production and supply activities, is the linchpin of the EU-envisioned market restructuring. The focus lies on the independent operation of networks, grid access and market-based pricing as opposed to resource nationalism, where the government exerts control over the energy supply chain and prices, as in the cases of Russia, Kazakhstan, Turkmenistan, Algeria and Libya (Fattouh and Stern 2011; Overland et al. 2009). Exporting the underlying EU norms is supposed to stimulate competition and investment of energy companies to guarantee sufficient supply, affordable prices and depoliticise the energy supply chain, thereby contributing to EU supply security and serving as antidote to resource nationalism. The second pillar is the diversification of gas imports and supply routes by strategic projects of 'common European interest' (European Parliament 2009), to reduce European vulnerability, especially *vis-à-vis* its major supplier and transit states. Beyond physical diversification, the EU seeks to prescribe supplies and routes and endow import corridors with a common liberal regulatory transit framework along pipelines, based on EU norms on regulated Third Party Access (TPA), market tariff pricing and investment protection. Third, the EU promotes the deployment of renewable energy sources (RES) and seeks to increase energy efficiency across the neighbourhood. In this context, the EU advocates most for the implementation of European support schemes, which render RES competitive regarding other fuels and increase energy efficiency. Increasing the RES share and the energy efficiency in neighbouring energy sectors can contribute to EU energy security by freeing natural gas and making electricity from RES available for EU imports.

The underlying *leitmotif* of the EU's strategy can be subsumed under the notion of 'EU External Energy Governance', defined as a process that aims at exporting energy related, EU-centred norms and policies to third countries by different bilateral and regional sectorial instruments. As in other policy fields, the overarching goal of the EU External Energy Governance is a far-reaching and preferably legally binding export of EU norms (Lavenex 2011). The guiding concept is that of a '1:1 transfer', in which neighbours, like candidate countries, first assume EU hard norms, that is, precise rules, directives, laws and standards, going beyond more flexible indicative soft norms in the form of best practices and policy recommendations. Subsequently, they commit themselves to these norms formally on the bilateral or multilateral level, before they adopt them without major modification as domestic legislation (Schimmelfennig and Sedelmeier 2005).

However, taking the far-reaching, binding, precise and enforceable outcomes of the norms transfer during the enlargement as the baseline for evaluation of policies in the neighbourhood is misleading, since EU foreign policy faces a very different and far less promising environment in the neighbourhood. First, the bargaining power of the EU is much smaller *vis-à-vis* neighbours, since the EU's main incentive of a credible membership perspective is not on offer (Sasse 2005). Second, the identification of elites with the Union and the legitimacy of its constitutive values is lower (Bafoil and Weber 2014). Although politically intended, empirically, it is rarely accurate to speak of norm transfer in the context of the ENP. Different degrees of export are possible, which involve the diffusion of some policy contents and features without 'copying' EU norms (Dolowitz and Marsh 2000: 13). In order to grasp this conceptually underexposed grey zone between a 1:1 transfer and no norm export at all, one can rely on the concept of 'policy convergence' (Knill 2005). The notion focuses on the 'similarity between one or more characteristics of a certain policy' (ibid.: 768). While taking EU-promoted hard norms as the point of departure, the concept moves the analytical focus to the actual outcomes of EU External Energy Governance. The comparison enables analysts to evaluate the 'degree of convergence', that is, to what extent outcomes in third countries reflect specific contents, principles and institutional features of EU energy norms.

The two modes of EU External Energy Governance

To promote EU norms to ENP countries, the EU has developed comprehensive, sectorial, regional and bilateral instruments. While differing in their institutional design and policy features, all instruments share the same normative 'regulatory core': the EU hard norms and additional soft norms provisions on flexible standards and best practices that are forming the *acquis*, on which the Internal Energy Market (IEM) is grounded.

In order to make sense of the multitude of instruments and grasp their underlying approaches and limits to promote norm export in the neighbourhood, one can analytically distinguish between two different modes of EU External Energy Governance: an 'EUnilateral mode' (Nicolaïdis et al. 2014) leaning towards conditionality and homogeneity; and a 'decentred mode' (Bechev and Nicolaïdis 2010), drawing on joint agency and differentiation.

The EUnilateral mode

Grounded in rational institutionalism and derived from the logic of consequences (March and Olsen 1989), the 'EUnilateral mode' assumes that an asymmetrical bargaining power in its favour allows the EU to coerce ENP countries to adopt its norms (Schimmelfennig 2012). According to the logic of consequences, actors choose strategically between available options, based on the evaluation of the consequences of their decisions. From this perspective, convergence with or rejection of EU norms is the result of rational neighbouring governmental actors maximising their net benefits in their relations with the EU.

The Union can alter cost/benefit calculations of government officials by offering credible and tangible incentives, providing the Commission holds a leverage to coerce governmental actors to adopt EU norms. Drawing upon this, the EU offers incentives to third countries in return for the adoption of non-modifiable EU norms. The EUnilateral mode is further characterised by homogeneity in terms of pre-defined criteria for rewarding more advanced countries and overarching instruments, irrespective of the differences among ENP countries. While the

EUnilateral mode has proved to be conducive to export EU norms during the accession process, its conduciveness in the neighbourhood has been put into question from the very beginning, since the incentives on offer are limited, while political and economic costs for governmental actors in ENP countries adopting liberal EU norms and opening their domestic markets are often high (Kelley 2006).

The decentred mode

The decentred mode of EU External Energy Governance departs from the insight that EU norm export is not only about cost/benefit calculations. Grounded in sociological institutionalism and derived from the underlying logic of appropriateness (March and Olsen 1989), it is assumed that actors' interests are not exogenously given, but vary according to their perceptions of what is appropriate behaviour in specific situations. Seen from this perspective, decision-making deliberations of actors on whether to converge with norms, or not, depends on the appropriateness they attach to these norms, which is influenced by underlying ideas, identities and role perceptions.

The EU can influence the decision-making deliberations of governmental actors in ENP countries by persuading them, based on normative suasion (Checkel 2005). Departing from the insight that the 'access-convergence logic' underlying the EUnilateral mode, that is, the bargain of access to the EU's market, funds and institutions in return for adoption of EU norms might not be conducive in the neighbourhood, the decentred mode explores ways to delink both (Bechev and Nicolaïdis 2010). The underlying assumption is that neighbouring governmental officials consider a more decentred EU External Energy Governance to be more legitimate than the EU's prescriptions based on an access-convergence bargain. Hence, normative persuasion can lead to outcomes, which reflect a certain degree of convergence with EU energy norms, if the EU allows for more joint agency and differentiation.

'Joint agency' provides neighbouring governmental actors with an opportunity to jointly carve out policies and institutions within the cooperation process. In this context, one can distinguish further between 'co-development', which typically involves government officials on the decision-making, and 'co-ownership', which engages experts and bureaucrats on the less politicised operational level. Co-development focuses on the extent to which energy cooperation draws on shared policy goals and broader contents, such as establishing a strategic gas corridor and modernising parts of the supply chain. Hence, it relates to the broader objectives and statements of intention, which denote the direction decision-makers wish to take (Dolowitz and Marsh 2000). Co-ownership raises a second aspect of decentring. It is concerned with the degree to which local actors co-own the processes of shaping specific norms and policies, as well as the instruments and programmes, by which they are promoted. Contrary to the EUnilateral mode, the decentred mode is characterised by differentiation in terms of instruments, institutions and policies, which seek to respond to the specific political and economic importance, capacities and conditions of neighbouring countries.

The concentric circles of EU External Energy Governance in the neighbourhood

The overarching framework: the ENP

The ENP is the overarching framework of EU norm export. Energy is only one policy field among others in the EU's comprehensive approach, but has always been high on the ENP agenda and became the 'driver of the ENP' due to repeated Russo-Ukrainian gas conflicts (Ferrero-Waldner 2006).

The initial communication outlining the ENP approach already stressed the need for interconnected energy infrastructure, additional investment, harmonisation, regulatory approximation and eventually full integration of neighbouring countries into the IEM (Commission of the European Communities 2003). In the context of the first major ENP review in 2011, an emphasis on further sectorial regional cooperation was added to the energy agenda of the ENP 'aiming at further market integration, improved energy security based on converging regulatory frameworks including [. . .] renewable energy sources and energy efficiency' (European Commission and High Representative of the European Union for Foreign Affairs and Security Policy 2011: 10). In its 2015 review, and due to the conception of its Energy Union initiative, the European Union committed itself to give 'pan-European energy security', energy market reforms and cooperation on energy efficiency and renewable energies a 'greater place in the ENP' (European Commission and High Representative of the Union for Foreign Affairs and Security Policy 2015: 11). All major ENP documents reference and stress the intertwining with other bilateral and sectorial regional instruments to achieve the overarching objectives of promoting norm export in the field of natural gas, electricity, renewables and energy efficiency and implementing prioritised regional infrastructure projects. In this context, accession to the Energy Community is depicted as the normative end point of full integration into the IEM.

Overall, the ENP establishes a reference framework for neighbouring countries that is based on the EU's main leverage of improved progressive access to the Internal Market, more investment, tangible rewards, financial support and administrative assistance. Partnership and Cooperation Agreements (PCA) and Association Agreements (AA) form the legal basis of bilateral energy relations between the EU and ENP countries. PCAs and AAs established joint councils, which serve as bodies for decision-makers to supervise the implementation of the agreements. Subcommittees on 'Transport, Energy and Environment' composed of officials from the EU and neighbouring countries are supposed to jointly specify the cooperation in the field of energy. However, they do not set the agendas or hold any decision-making power, as they deal only with procedural matters and report the progress of cooperation within existing frameworks (Padgett 2011).

Further institutional key elements of cooperation in the ENP are the Action Plans, which are not legally binding, but purely political agreements. Jointly developed with representatives from neighbouring countries and the EU, Action Plans set out the broader road map for cooperation. While formally providing for joint agency, the structure of all Action Plans is pre-defined – irrespective of the preferences of ENP countries. In the field of energy and transport, all Action Plans mention the overall objective of approximation towards EU norms and express the commitment of parties towards the development of projects of 'common European interests'. However, Action Plans usually remain vague and do not reference any concrete EU norms and steps to implement projects in the field of energy. The lack of precision renders systematic monitoring and evaluation difficult. This casts doubts on conditionality, although the Commission stipulated that the progress of an ENP country on agreed priorities in the Action Plan should be reflected by the allocation of rewards and financial assistance (Commission of the European Communities 2004). Besides offering a 'stake in the internal market', EU conditionality in the neighbourhood relies additionally on functional support and financial assistance, which are geared at building up and strengthening the capacities of governmental actors in ENP countries in order to empower them to adopt and implement EU norms, policies and projects. Assistance in the field of energy mostly targets public actors on the operational level. Funds are bundled in the European Neighbourhood Instrument (ENI), which amounts to a total budget of EUR15.4 billion for the period from 2014 to 2020. This represents a modest increase from the total budget of the previous European Neighbourhood and Partnership Instrument (ENPI), which was endowed with EUR11.2 billion for the period from 2007 to 2014 for all 16 ENP countries (European Parliament and Council 2014; Council of the European Union 2006).

Although the EU emphasised their 'tailor-made' design, Action Plans reflect more EUnilateralism than decentring, since the overarching goals in terms of EU norm export are predefined – although rather vaguely – and the access-convergence logic is placed at the heart of the process to achieve them. Joint agency and differentiation are proclaimed but are limited to emphasising convergence in the area of gas or electricity. Confronted with this pre-defined structure in the energy sector and beyond, the two major hydrocarbon suppliers in the South, Algeria and Libya, have not signed Action Plans. While Libya has not even signed an Association Agreement with the EU, negotiations on an Action Plan with Algeria started after the Arab uprisings and continued in 2016. Both rentier states have demonstrated a strong preference for far-reaching public involvement in their energy sectors, which are dominated by state-owned National Oil and Gas Companies (NOCs). Being at odds with the underlying EU norms – which would threaten the dominant position of NOCs that account for a major share of their state budgets – Algiers and Tripoli have not aligned with the ENP and its normative regulatory approach in the field of energy (Escribano 2010). In the case of Libya, this situation is further complicated by geopolitical instability, turmoil and weak statehood in the aftermath of the Libya War (EU Institute for Security Studies 2014).

The inner circle: the Energy Community

Parallel and intertwined with the ENP, concentric circles of energy co-operation and integration have evolved during the last decade, which are characterised by different modes and outcomes of EU External Energy Governance.

The 'inner circle' is made up of the Energy Community (EnC), which extends the entire energy *acquis* to third countries. Based on international law, accession to the EnC Treaty involves the far-reaching non-differentiable adoption of all binding, precise and non-modifiable EU energy norms, which prescribe the governance of domestic markets and a transit regime for infrastructure connecting to the EU. Norm adoption and implementation, as well as physical flows, are monitored by a centralised secretariat. Besides carrying out the monitoring and enforcement tasks, the secretariat provides structured assistance for adapting domestic laws and standards and drafts detailed specific road maps for reforms. Furthermore, the EnC's secretariat holds the right to initiate dispute settlement procedures in case of non-compliance (Padgett 2012).

Initially conceived to expand the IEM for gas and electricity to candidate countries and pre-accession states from the mid-2000s onwards, the EnC has enlarged its scope to the neighbourhood with Ukraine and Moldova joining, and Georgia applying for full membership in the early 2010s. While these countries have only vague EU membership perspectives at best, and incentives are limited to technical assistance and capacity building, a major benefit lies in the fact that aligning their domestic sectors to EU norms limits Russia's energy leverage. While Ukraine and Moldova are highly vulnerable towards Russian hydrocarbon deliveries, which account for the major share of their energy mix, Georgia has managed to reduce its overly high dependence on Russian natural gas, but remains dependent on oil supplies from its neighbour. At the same time, all three countries have thorny political relations with Russia and are involved in regional conflicts with their neighbouring energy supplier. Adopting EU unbundling, TPA and market pricing norms prevents Russia's NOC Gazprom from acquiring a dominant position, not only as supplier but also as shipper and seller of gas within the neighbouring energy sectors, and it limits the capacity of Moscow to control the access and prices of energy deliveries (Padgett 2012). Relying on the EUnilateral mode in this context, the EU has managed to include Ukraine, Moldova and Georgia, in the eastern neighbourhood, into the inner ring of EU External Energy Governance. However, neither consumer nor transit countries whose relations with Russia are less conflictual, such as Armenia, or any neighbouring suppliers, have followed.

The outer circles: strategic partnerships and regional sectorial cooperation

Most neighbouring countries maintain less institutionalised energy relations with the EU, which are based on a differentiated, multi-layered system of bilateral and multilateral agreements. EU External Energy Governance in these 'outer circles' provides for a more selective and flexible approximation towards EU norms to regulate certain aspects of the supply chain.

Bilateral energy partnerships with key suppliers

The major bilateral instruments in the outer circles of EU External Energy Governance are Memoranda of Understanding (MoU), which are intended to lay the foundation for strategic energy partnerships with key energy partners. Similar to Action Plans, MoUs are non-binding, jointly agreed political documents, negotiated between high-level representatives of the Commission and neighbouring governments. Contrary to Action Plans, MoUs single out energy as field of cooperation. MoUs can be purely declaratory in nature or highly technical and specific regarding infrastructure projects and *acquis* provisions.

The MoU with Azerbaijan, which was signed in 2006, reflects the highest degree of convergence. It stipulates that this ENP country would establish a fully competent independent energy regulator and Independent System Operator and specifically refers to the adoption of Directive 2003/54/EC on electricity markets, Directive 2003/55/EC on gas markets, and Regulation 1775/2005 on access to gas transmission networks. Indeed, the EU has managed to include precise EU provisions on unbundling, market pricing and TPA in the bilateral memorandum, since Azerbaijan was exposed to strong geopolitical pressure. Russia opposed Azerbaijan's role as significant energy exporter vehemently and engaged on different levels to prevent competing Caspian gas from reaching its markets in Europe. Moscow used its political and military support for the Armenian side in the Nagorno-Karabakh conflict as leverage towards Azerbaijan, sought to purchase large volumes from the Azeri Shah Deniz gas field and increased its gas prices for its exports to the country (Fuller 2013; Kjærnet 2009). Confronted with the need to counterbalance Russia's *realpolitik*, Azerbaijani political leaders pursued the strategy to increase energy interdependence with the EU to engage the Union in the region, and open a Southern Gas Corridor for Azerbaijani supplies to high-priced European destination markets. In this context, governmental decision-makers subscribed to specific regulatory EU provisions in the hope of establishing a strategic partnership on a westbound pipeline and supply security. However, they were never convinced of the appropriateness of the pre-defined, unilaterally prescribed norms, which would have imposed high costs and a loss of control (Weber 2014). As Azerbaijan managed to counterbalance Russia's geopolitical pressure through leaning more towards Turkey as strategic partner, and implemented with the Trans-Anatolian Pipeline (TANAP) the major part of the Southern Gas Corridor to the Greek border, convergence with EU norms stalled (Kardas 2011). In 2011, Presidents Barroso and Aliyev signed a new memorandum on a strategic energy partnership, which delinked the cooperation on the Southern Gas Corridor from stalling convergence in the energy sector, reflecting more co-development with Azerbaijani decision-makers.

No earlier than 2013, the EU managed to conclude a second MoU in the neighbourhood with its third-biggest supplier, Algeria. From 2006 onwards, Algeria had repeatedly rejected EU draft proposals for a MoU based on the blueprint of the EU–Azerbaijani MoU (Darbouche 2011). In the eyes of the Algerian government, the unilateral promotion of EU hard norms was perceived to be inappropriate, in the aftermath of a comprehensive renationalisation of the hydrocarbon sector in the mid-2000s, which restored the dominant position of the NOC SONATRACH along the whole supply chain (Weber 2014). It was not before the early 2010s, that the European Commission opened up to a more decentred mode of EU External Energy Governance towards the southern supplier, which paved the way for eventually signing a MoU. Contrary to earlier drafts, the document refrains from referencing specific EU norms. The agreement reflects more co-development, as it focuses on enabling European investment in the upstream sector based on reciprocal market access.

Regional sectorial cooperation

During the 2000s, the EU has supplemented EU External Energy Governance by regional multilateral instruments. The overarching goal of sectorial regional cooperation is to interconnect sub-regions within the neighbourhood which are characterised by high energy interdependence. Regional frameworks are supposed to transcend the bilateral energy relations with the EU and between individual countries themselves, by pooling the EU's actions in terms of EU External Energy Governance and capitalising on shared functional cooperation interests (Youngs 2009). Achieving sub-regional integration remains the immediate goal, which is supposed to facilitate and lead to an integrated pan-European market functioning on the basis of the binding and precise norms of the IEM.

The major regional sectorial instrument towards eastern neighbours since the early 2000s has been the Interstate Oil and Gas Transportation to Europe (INOGATE). The EU-funded regional network of 21 participant states from Eastern Europe, the Southern Caucasus and Central Asia aims to initiate regional energy cooperation in order to facilitate and secure gas transport to Europe and further convergence of regional energy markets with EU norms. Being demand-driven, it is the ministries from ENP countries which set the priorities together with the EU in terms of concrete EU-funded projects. Cooperation is largely technical, takes place on the level of experts and administrators, and is organised around five fields: the audit of networks, improvement of operational security and efficiency of infrastructure, institutional improvement of trade and transportation of hydrocarbons, facilitating investment, and transfer of regulatory best practices and know-how (Interstate Oil and Gas Transportation to Europe 2016). It is at this technical project level that EU experts seek to introduce EU standards and principles of unbundling and market pricing within discussions during workshops, trainings and projects. Compared to other instruments, INOGATE's project-based approach reflects a comparatively high level of joint agency. Conditionality is not enshrined in the framework, which has much to offer in terms of expertise and technical support, but is endowed with small funds amounting up to EUR61 million for the period between 2007 and 2013 (Theiss 2015). As INOGATE projects are co-developed, the degree of differentiation is particularly high. Since neighbouring public actors often lack experience regarding gas and electricity regulation, EU officials and experts are able to shape the framing of identified problems and the envisioned solutions, based on their advanced knowledge and regulatory expertise without recurring to coercion.[1] Hence, the achieved limited, yet substantial, steps towards more unbundling, market pricing and convergence with technical EU standards – for example, in the field of metering, efficiency and grid-codes – are mostly driven by normative suasion on the operational level, while being supported on the political level.

The Black Sea Synergy (BSS) was introduced in 2007 to provide an additional venue for regional cooperation based on joint technical projects (European Parliament 2010). Within the BSS, jointly proposed projects between Member States and neighbours receive funding from the Commission to be kicked-off, but largely depend on the financial commitment of neighbouring countries. To facilitate the development and funding of projects, multilateral 'sectoral partnerships' engaging officials from the EU and ENP countries have been proposed (ibid.). The agenda of the BSS is neither new nor based on regional joint agency, but simply lists the major issues of the EnC and bilateral energy agendas in the region: engaging in a dialogue over regional energy issues, promoting legal and regulatory harmonisation, upgrading existing and constructing new energy infrastructure, establishing a common legal transit framework and promoting RES and energy efficiency (Weaver and Henderson 2013). Although the BSS repeats mostly unilaterally set objectives from other cooperation instruments, concrete projects provided for more joint agency, since actors from neighbouring countries conceive them.

Just a little more than one year after the BSS was initiated, the Eastern Partnership (EaP) was launched. The EaP addresses the same policy fields as the ENP with all eastern ENP countries, including Belarus. Building on the ENP, the EaP seeks to specify targets, increase incentives and strengthen conditionality. The EaP offers additional mobility partnerships and is designed to provide an added value to access to the Internal Market by offering the prospect of a regional Neighbourhood Economic Community. Furthermore, more comprehensive institution building programmes have been implemented to strengthen state capacities, civil society and the rule of law. So far, EaP countries have benefited from a financial envelope of EUR 3.2 billion, largely based on ENPI and ENI funds, which have been earmarked for the six eastern neighbours (European Commission 2015). In the field of energy, the EaP pursues four objectives, centred around the issue of regional energy security: supporting infrastructure development, interconnections and diversification of supply, paving the way for the accession of all eastern neighbours to the EnC, enhancing RES production and energy efficiency, and increasing energy solidarity. In order to achieve these goals, a joint platform on energy security was established together with a flagship initiative on the Southern Gas Corridor (European External Action Service 2009). Contrary to the platform, which constituted itself in June 2009, the flagship initiative failed to be launched, since Ukraine, Moldova and Armenia were not committed to the opening of the Southern Gas Corridor, which would bypass them.[2]

Considered together, the BSS and EaP reflect more EUnilaterism than INOGATE, since they restate unilaterally set goals with regard to convergence with EU norms and the implementation of the Southern Gas Corridor. However, with the establishment of the sectoral partnership and EaP platform, both instruments paved the way for more co-development in more differentiated regional frameworks. Yet, due to divergent interests and conflicts among neighbouring consumer, transit and supplier states, tangible outcomes in terms of regional convergence with European energy key norms are absent in the field of hydrocarbons, while boosting RES and energy efficiency remain low on the agenda.

In the southern neighbourhood, the Euro-Mediterranean Partnership (EMP) remained the major venue for EU External Energy Governance. Since the launch of the ENP, the EMP has assumed the role of a regional supplement, similar to the EaP in the East. The major sectorial instrument of the EMP in the sphere of energy is the Euro-Mediterranean Energy Partnership (EMEP). Three non-binding EMEP Action Plans have been adopted by the ministerial conference of partner countries, which all emphasise the convergence of energy policies of Mediterranean participants, the convergence with EU energy norms in the mid-term, and the establishment of joint infrastructure projects (Darbouche 2011). Drawing upon the jointly agreed objectives, directors-general and high officials from neighbouring countries, and their counterparts from the EU, formed working groups to specify cooperation agendas. Concrete projects were supposed to be carried out in the context of jointly developed assistance projects financed by the *Mesures d'accompagnement financières et techniques* (MEDA). Since the early 2000s, funding provided by the EMP for sectorial cooperation remained limited and amounted to only EUR 55 million, which was supplemented by EUR 2 billion in form of loans.[3] Although the EMP provided for political conditionality in the form of a clause in the AAs which justifies the suspension of cooperation if human rights are violated, it played no role in the EMEP (Del Sarto and Schumacher 2005). Concrete co-developed policy agendas provided venues for differentiation. However, Mediterranean suppliers mostly perceived the EU's emphasis on the liberalisation of energy markets based on unbundling within the EMEP as a threat. Geared at ending the dominance of state-owned companies and restructuring long-term contracts with European consumers, converging towards EU norms would expose suppliers to financial risks. Furthermore, the political rivalries between southern neighbours themselves prevented actors from engaging in major regional projects.[4]

The only sector where the EU-Mediterranean regional cooperation produced tangible results was the promotion of RES. Contrary to the EMP, its successor instrument, the Union for the Mediterranean (UfM), focuses entirely on RES, while bypassing consumer-supplier and regional conflicts related to hydrocarbons. The centrepiece of the UfM in the field of energy has been the European-Mediterranean Solar Plan (MSP), which seeks to install large photovoltaic capacities in North Africa that are supposed to deliver electricity to Europe and to increase intra-regional electricity trade. The financial feasibility of the MSP hinges upon public and private European funding for the costly infrastructure and bonuses for Mediterranean exports to the IEM. In order to facilitate exports to the EU, Morocco, Algeria and Tunisia converged with unbundling and TPA norms of the IEM for electricity and adopted independent regulators to ensure their implementation (Escribano 2010). However, with the economic crisis hitting Europe, the corresponding massive drop of prices and energy demand, and regional instability in the aftermath of the Arab uprisings, the most advanced MSP-project DESERTEC was abandoned (Frankfurter Allgemeine Zeitung 2014). With the fading perspective for lucrative green energy exports to Europe, regional convergence in the field of RES stalled.

Conclusions

The analysis of its concentric circles has revealed the threefold limits of EU External Energy Governance in the EU's neighbourhood.

First, relying on the EUnilateral export of precise EU norms has only been possible with regard to eastern transit countries. The cases of Ukraine, Moldova and Georgia show that far-reaching convergence with the EU energy *acquis* was less driven by EU incentives than by their confrontation with Russia's regional *realpolitik*. Where Russia's geopolitical pressure was absent, neighbouring countries refused to commit themselves to binding pre-defined EU norms. That is not to say that EU incentives are negligible, but to conceive EU external energy policy as only one external influence among others, which needs to be embedded in the broader geopolitical and energy market context of neighbouring countries.

Second, with regard to EU External Energy Governance towards the other neighbouring transit, consumer and supplier states in the outer rings, decentring seems to be the only way to ensure a certain degree of convergence with EU norms, to regulate parts and specific aspects of the supply chain. In order to achieve tangible sustainable outcomes, public neighbouring actors on the decision-making and operational level need to be engaged. Yet, the insight that decentring does not result in far-reaching, but only quite limited, convergence questions EU External Energy Governance as the *leitmotif* of external energy policy in the neighbourhood.

Third, the mismatch of EU External Energy Governance, seeking to liberalise and unbundle NOCs on one hand and hydrocarbon supplier's vital interest in exerting control over their energy sectors on the other, limits the room for manoeuvre for EU norm export in the gas sector. This is why promoting energy efficiency and RES present themselves as more promising venues for EU norm export towards neighbouring hydrocarbon suppliers.

Notes

1 Interviews with EU officials from INOGATE, conducted on 10/3/2015 and 25/6/2015, INOGATE Secretariat, Tbilisi.
2 Interview with a senior official from the European External Action Service, conducted on 29/1/2013, European External Action Service, Brussels.
3 Interview with a senior official from the European External Action Service, conducted on 29/1/2013, European External Action Service, Brussels.
4 Interview with a senior official from the Directorate-General Energy, conducted on 12/2/2013, Directorate-General Energy, Brussels.

References

Bafoil, F. and Weber, B. (2014) 'Les Temporalités de l'européanisation', *Temporalités* 19: 1–14.
Baumann, F. and Simmerl, G. (2011) 'Between Conflict and Convergence: The EU Member States and the Quest for a Common External Energy Policy', *CAP Discussion Paper*, February.
Bechev, D. and Nicolaïdis, K. (2010) 'From Policy to Polity: Can the EU's Special Relations with its "Neighbourhood" be Decentred?', *Journal of Common Market Studies* 48(3): 475–500.
Checkel, J. (2005) 'International Institutions and Socialization in Europe: Introduction and Framework', *International Organization* 59(4): 801–826.
Commission of the European Communities (2003) *Wider Europe—Neighbourhood: A New Framework for Relations with Our Eastern and Southern Neighbours*, COM(2003) 104 final, Brussels, 11 March.
Commission of the European Communities (2004) *European Neighbourhood Policy: Strategy Paper*, COM(2004) 373 final.
Council of the European Union (2006) *Laying Down General Provisions on the European Regional Development Fund, the European Social Fund and the Cohesion Fund and Repealing Regulation (EC) No 1260/1999*, Regulation 1083/2006.
Darbouche, H. (2011) 'Third Time Lucky? Euro-Mediterranean Energy Co-operation Under the Union for the Mediterranean', *Mediterranean Politics* 16(1): 193–211.
Del Sarto, R. and Schumacher, T. (2005) 'From EMP to ENP: What's at Stake with the European Neighbourhood Policy Towards the Southern Mediterranean?', *European Foreign Affairs Review* 10(2): 17–38.
Dolowitz, D. and Marsh, D. (2000) 'Learning from Abroad: The Role of Policy Transfer in Contemporary Policy-Making', *Governance* 13(1): 5–23.
Escribano, G. (2010) 'Convergence Towards Differentiation: The Case of Mediterranean Energy Corridors', *Mediterranean Politics* 15(2): 211–229.
EU Institute for Security Studies (2014) 'Energy Moves and Power Shifts: EU Foreign Policy and Global Energy Security', Paris.
European Commission (2011) *On Security of Energy Supply and International Cooperation—The EU Energy Policy: Engaging with Partners Beyond Our Borders*, COM(2011), 539 final.
European Commission (2015) 'European Commission Fact Sheet. The Eastern Partnership—A Policy that Delivers'. http://europa.eu/rapid/press-release_MEMO-15-5019_de.htm, accessed 10 December 2016.
European Commission and High Representative of the European Union for Foreign Affairs and Security Policy (2011) *A New Response to a Changing Neighbourhood*, COM(2011) 303.
European Commission and High Representative of the Union for Foreign Affairs and Security Policy (2015) *Joint Communication to the European Parliament, the Council, the European Economic and Social Committee and the Committee of the Regions. Review of the European Neighbourhood Policy*, JOIN(2015) 50 Final, Brussels.

European External Action Service (2009) *Eastern Partnership. Platform 3—Energy Security. Core Objectives and Work Programme 2009–2011*. http://eeas.europa.eu/eastern/platforms/docs/platform3_051109_en.pdf, accessed 7 May 2014.

European Parliament (2009) *An Assessment of the Gas and Oil Pipelines in Europe*, Brussels.

European Parliament (2010) *The EU's Black Sea Synergy: Results and Possible Ways Forward*, Brussels.

European Parliament and Council (2014) *Regulation (EU) No 232/2014 of the European Parliament and of the Council of 11 March 2014 Establishing a European Neighbourhood Instrument*.

Fattouh, B. and Stern, J. (eds.) (2011) *Natural Gas Markets in the Middle East and North Africa*, Oxford: Oxford University Press.

Ferrero-Waldner, B. (2006) *European Neighbourhood Policy*, Speech/06/149, http://europa.eu/rapid/press-release_SPEECH-06-149_en.htm?locale=FR:, accessed 3 September 2015.

Frankfurter Allgemeine Zeitung (2014) 'Desertec am Ende. Der Traum vom Wüstenstrom ist Gescheitert'. www.faz.net/aktuell/wirtschaft/wirtschaftspolitik/wuestenstrom-projekt-desertec-ist-gescheitert-13207437.html, accessed 10 December 2016.

Fuller, E. (2013) 'Azerbaijan's Foreign Policy and the Nagorno-Karabakh Conflict', *IAI Working Papers* 13(12).

International Energy Agency (2013) *Medium-Term Gas Market Report 2013*, OECD, Paris.

Interstate Oil and Gas Transportation to Europe (2016) Project Database. www.inogate.org/projects?collection=ongoing&lang=en, accessed 6 June 2016.

Kardas, S. (2011) 'Turkish–Azerbaijani Energy Cooperation and Nabucco: Testing the Limits of the New Turkish Foreign Policy Rhetoric', *Turkish Studies* 12(1): 55–77.

Kelley, J. (2006) 'New Wine in Old Wineskins: Promoting Political Reforms Through the New European Neighbourhood Policy', *Journal of Common Market Studies* 22(1): 29–55.

Kjærnet, H. (2009) 'The Energy Dimension of Azerbaijani–Russian Relations: Maneuvering for Nagorno-Karabakh', *Russian Analytical Diggest* 56(9): 2–5.

Knill, C. (2005) 'Introduction: Cross-National Policy Convergence: Concepts, Approaches and Explanatory Factors', *Journal of European Public Policy* 12(5): 764–774.

Kovacevic, A. (2009) 'The Impact of the Russia–Ukraine Gas Crisis in South Eastern Europe', *OIES Papers* NG 29.

Lavenex, S. (2011) 'Concentric Circles of Flexible "European" Integration: A Typology of EU External Governance Relations', *Comparative European Politics* 9(4–5): 372–393.

March, J. and Olsen, J. (1989) *Rediscovering Institutions: The Organizational Basis of Politics*, New York: The New Press.

Nicolaïdis, K., Vergerio, C. Fisher Onar, N. and Viehoff, J. (2014) 'From Metropolis to Microcosmos: The EU's New Standards of Civilisation', *Millennium—Journal of International Studies* 42(3): 718–745.

Overland, I., Kjaernet, H. and Kendall-Taylor, A. (2009) *Caspian Energy Politics: Azerbaijan, Kazakhstan and Turkmenistan*, Oxon: Routledge.

Padgett, S. (2011) 'Energy Co operation in the Wider Europe: Institutionalizing Interdependence', *Journal of Common Market Studies* 49(5): 1065–1087.

Padgett, S. (2012) 'Multilateral Institutions, Accession Conditionality and Rule Transfer in the European Union: The Energy Community in South East Europe', *Journal of Public Policy* 32(3): 261–282.

Sasse, G. (2005) 'Conditionality-Lite: The European Neighbourhood Policy and the EU's Eastern Neighbours', in Musu, C. and Casarini, N. (eds.) *The Road to Convergence: European Foreign Policy in an Evolving International System*, Basingstoke: Palgrave, 163–180.

Schimmelfennig, F. (2012) 'Europeanization Beyond Europe', *Living Reviews in European Governance* 7(1): 1–31.

Schimmelfennig, F. and Sedelmeier, U. (2005) *The Europeanization of Central and Eastern Europe*, Ithaca: Cornell University Press.

Theiss, J. (2015) 'Geopolitics vs. Governance in the European Union's Energy Cooperation with its Broader Neighbourhood', in Gstöhl, S. and Lannon, E. (eds.) *The European Union's Broader Neighbourhood. Challenges and Opportunities Beyond the European Neighbourhood Policy*, Oxon: Routledge, 268–295.

Weaver, C. and Henderson, K. (2013) *The Black Sea Region and EU Policy: The Challenge of Divergent Agendas*, London: Ashgate.

Weber, B. (2014) 'Convergence at the Borderline. EU External Energy Governance Towards the Neighbouring Gas Suppliers Azerbaijan and Algeria', *Politique Européenne* 46(4): 142–169.

Youngs, R. (2009) *Energy Security Europe's new Foreign Policy Challenge*, New York: Routledge.

35
MIGRATION
Moving to the centre of the European Neighbourhood Policy

Florian Trauner and Jean-Pierre Cassarino

> The message that migration issues are now at the top of the EU's external relations priorities has not yet been fully communicated to and appreciated by partners. It is essential that in close cooperation with all Member States it is made clear to our partners that a solution to the irregular and uncontrolled movement of people is a priority for the Union as a whole.
>
> *(European Commission 2016a: 3)*

Introduction

A series of migrant boat tragedies in the Mediterranean Sea, and unusually high numbers of new migrants arriving on European soil in late 2015 and early 2016, have stressed the European Union (EU) to the point of a 'crisis' (Trauner 2016). In response, the EU has sought to deepen its cooperation with countries of migrants' origin and transit. In March 2016, Turkey agreed with the EU on a deal in which it agrees to take back all migrants departing irregularly from its shore towards Greece in exchange for financial aid and some other incentives, such as an accelerated visa liberalisation scheme. Contested from a human rights perspective (Greene and Kelemen 2016; Collet 2016), the EU–Turkey deal may become a prototype for a new EU approach on migration in the wider European region. 'Comprehensive partnerships' (or 'compacts') that bring together EU instruments, mechanisms and leverage to 'better manage migration' (European Commission 2016a: 6) are to be signed with Jordan, Lebanon and a range of other priority countries. A third country's willingness to prevent irregular migration into the EU should become a determining element of this country's relation with the Union.

This chapter traces how migration has become a key priority in the EU's relations with neighbouring states subsumed under the European Neighbourhood Policy (ENP). Looking at the EU's external migration agenda *vis-à-vis* southern and eastern neighbours, the chapter seeks to provide a robust overview of the policy evolution and the related academic debates. In terms of structure, it starts by outlining the EU's objective and policy instruments in the neighbourhood. This is followed by an investigation of the reaction of ENP countries and the political dynamics in the EU's eastern and southern neighbourhoods.

EU objectives and instruments in the neighbourhood

Two conceptual approaches have informed the development of the EU's external migration policies (Boswell 2003). The first approach is restrictive and control-oriented. Under it, the EU assists (or puts pressure on) third countries to tighten their entry controls and/or accept provisions for facilitating the removal of irregular migrants and rejected asylum seekers. In the literature, this approach has also been grasped with concepts such as 'policy conditionality', 'externalisation' or 'extra-territorialisation' (Rijpma and Cremona 2007; Trauner 2009; Bigo and Guild 2005). The second approach seeks to tackle the circumstances in the countries of migrants' origin that make people migrate or flee to the EU by using foreign policy tools (such as sanctions for human rights violations), economic cooperation and/or development aid. Officially, this approach aims at eliminating the 'root causes of migration' – a frequent objective in the policy and academic debates.

Migration objectives at the advent of the ENP

The EU has repeatedly emphasised that it seeks to take both approaches into account. However, scholars pointed to the fact that the restrictive approach tended to dominate, notably at the advent of the ENP. Lavenex (2004) proposed an understanding of the 'Wider Europe' initiative of the EU as an attempt to govern externally in order to improve the problem-solving capacities of internal EU policies. 'The EU will expand its sphere of governance in particular in areas which have become securitized inside and where vulnerability is attributed to development in the third countries in question' (Lavenex 2004: 686). There was little doubt that migration would be among these 'securitised' areas (Huysmans 2000; Balzacq 2009).

A key migration-related theme at the beginning of the ENP in 2003 was the prevention of negative externalities stemming from the eastwards expansion of the EU (and its Schengen borders). To align with the EU *acquis*, the candidate countries of Central and Eastern Europe had to introduce new visa requirements for their neighbours to the East, including Russia, Ukraine and other countries from the Commonwealth of Independent States (CIS). The policy debates at the time of the 2004–2007 eastern enlargements revolved around the question of whether the EU would create new dividing lines in Europe and a 'Schengen paper wall' (Grabbe 2002). The Commission was aware of these concerns and promised to ensure that 'the new external border is not a barrier to trade, social and cultural exchange or regional cooperation' (Commission of the European Communities 2003: 11). While fostering good neighbourly relations has been a traditional objective of EU foreign policy actors, the more inward-looking EU ministries of the interior also added their priority: neighbouring countries should do more to curb unwanted migration and cooperate on the removal of irregular migrants. In their debate, a reoccurring theme was the contrast of a safe 'inside' (namely the EU territory) and an unstable and menacing 'outside' (Zhyznomirska 2011).

The instrument of EU visa facilitation agreements was eventually considered a catch-all solution: they gave the EU a strong lever to make some third countries sign readmission agreements and trigger reforms in their justice and home affairs sectors, while they also met major concern from neighbouring countries by relaxing the tight visa regime and offering facilitated travel opportunities (Trauner and Kruse 2008). The visa facilitation-readmission nexus became firmly established in Eastern Europe (Hernández i Sagrera 2010), but less so in the southern neighbourhood. In this region, cooperation on irregular migration has primarily been based on informal arrangements and non-standard bilateral readmission agreements (Cassarino 2007).

The specific objectives of the EU were outlined in the Action Plans for individual ENP countries. They tended to 'offer little space to take into account of the diversity of migrant realities'

(Wunderlich 2010: 255) in the different countries. In most cases, they included comparable priorities relating to migration control, capacity building and alignment with international conventions. There have also been different relevant regional dialogues and consultative processes, aligned with external EU migration objectives such as the Budapest Process, the Söderköping Process, the Prague Process (including an Eastern Partnership panel on Migration and Asylum), the 5+5 dialogue in the Mediterranean and the Africa–EU Partnership on Migration, Mobility and Employment, the Khartoum process and the Rabat Process in the South.

The EU's Global Approach to Migration and Mobility

From 2005, the EU started to make more efforts to go beyond a purely control-oriented external migration approach and put a stronger emphasis on legal migration and development issues (at least in its communications) (Council of the European Union 2005). The reasons for this shift were manifold and included the successful lobbying of ENP countries such as Morocco (Wunderlich 2010), and the dramatic events in Ceuta and Melilla in 2005, when at least fifteen migrants died while seeking to overcome the fences surrounding these two Spanish enclaves. Launched under the British Presidency in 2005, the Global Approach to Migration (GAM) initially had a focus on Africa and the Mediterranean region, but was quickly extended to other regions, notably Eastern and South-Eastern Europe. Its flagship instruments have been 'Mobility Partnerships' seeking to open channels for circular and temporary migration in exchange for cooperation in the prevention and combat of irregular migration and trafficking in human beings (Council of the European Union 2005). The partnerships are legally non-binding, yet they politically commit the participating Member States, and the contracting third country, to implement certain projects and priorities. The priorities of ENP countries should also be considered. For instance, Moldova has been eager to implement measures in support of return migration in order to counter the consequences of its large emigration (Commission of the European Communities 2009). Scholars, however, considered the innovation that Mobility Partnerships offer to be limited. According to Lavenex (2010: 473), 'they largely summarize existing bilateral cooperation programmes with individual member states under a new heading' (for other discussions, see Parkes 2009; Reslow 2012; Weinar 2013).

The 'Arab Spring' exerted an influence on the set-up of the EU migration policy in the neighbourhood. The field of migration and mobility featured high in European debates on how to reinvigorate Euro-Mediterranean relations in the wake of the revolutionary events (European Commission 2011b). In 2011, the term 'mobility' was added to the heading 'Global Approach to Migration', to reflect the EU's intention to promote people-to-people contacts. Other objectives of the renewed approach were to foster legal immigration, focus more on migrants' rights, improve international protection of refugees and create a closer development-migration nexus. Mobility Partnerships 'should be upgraded and promoted as the principle framework for cooperation in the area of migration and mobility between the EU and its partners, with a primary focus on the countries in the EU Neighbourhood' (European Commission 2011b: 10). If an ENP country prefers not to negotiate readmission and visa facilitation agreements, an alternative framework should be the 'Common Agenda on Migration and Mobility' (CAMM). This cooperation framework is less ambitious and committing, because the contracting parties agree to open a dialogue on all migration matters, which is gradually expected to lead to major mutual understanding on such thorny issues as readmission. This explains why a CAMM might be upgraded to a Mobility Partnership at a later stage.

The Mobility Partnerships became more tailor-made regarding the commitments a country was willing to make. The signing of a readmission agreement has become no longer a precondition

Table 35.1 EU Member States and ENP countries participating in EU Mobility Partnerships (as of October 2016)

Third country	Conclusion	Participating Member States (at signature)
Georgia	2009	BE, BG, CZ, DK, EE, FR, DE, GR, IT, LV, LT, NL, PL, RO, SE, UK
Moldova	2008	BG, CY, CZ, FR, GR, HU, IT, LV, PL, PT, RO, SI, SK, SE
Armenia	2011	BE, BG, CZ, FR, DE, IT, NL, PL, RO, SE
Azerbaijan	2013	BG, CZ, FR, LT, NL, PL, SI, SK
Morocco	2013	BE, FR, DE, IT, NL, PT, ES, SE, UK
Tunisia	2014	DE, BE, DK, ES, IT, FR, PL, PT, UK, SE
Jordan	2014	CY, DE, DK, GR, ES, FR, IT, HU, PL, PT, RO, SE
Belarus	2016	BG, LV, LT, HU, PL, RO, FI

Source: Authors' own elaborations based on different Mobility Partnerships. Names of countries refer to ISO 3166-1 (alpha-2 code).

for entering a partnership with the EU – the formal recognition of the willingness to cooperate on the removal of irregular migrants now suffices (European Commission, 2011a). With this renewed approach, Morocco, Tunisia and Jordan, in the southern neighbourhood, accepted a Mobility Partnership, in addition to Georgia, Armenia, Azerbaijan and Belarus in the eastern neighbourhood. At the time of writing (Autumn 2016), the three Common Agendas on Migration and Mobility signed so far did not concern ENP countries but Ethiopia, India and Nigeria (see Table 35.1).

The migration dimension of the ENP post-2015 refugee crisis

The 2015 'refugee crisis', when the numbers of newly arrived migrants reached an unprecedented level, created a sense of urgency in the EU to engage in a more comprehensive and determined way with neighbouring countries. This is also reflected in budgetary allocations. Around half the available ENP funding is now spent on migration-related issues (European Commission 2016b). However, the EU is still struggling to find a balance between the restrictive and the preventive approach of external engagement.

On paper, the restrictive approach clearly dominates. All the EU tools should be mobilised to give readmission 'a central place in all dialogues with countries of origin and transit of irregular migrants' (European Commission and High Representative of the European Union for Foreign Affairs and Security Policy 2015: 17). Pressures stemming from external migration would be 'the new normal', according to the European Commission (2016b: 5), so the EU needs a 'more coordinated, systematic and structured approach to maximise the synergies and leverages of the Union's internal and external policies'. The Partnership Frameworks or 'compacts' should achieve the threefold objectives of saving lives in the Mediterranean Sea, contributing to higher 'return rates', and enabling migrants and refugees to stay closer to their place of origin (ibid.).

The Partnership Frameworks institutionalise a shift to more informal, flexible and *ad hoc* arrangements, notably in the southern neighbourhood and in Africa (Cassarino 2017): 'The paramount priority is to achieve fast and operational returns, and not necessarily formal readmission agreements' (European Commission 2016b: 7). The compacts are to receive a substantial amount of money, up to EUR 8 billion over 2016–2020. In the long-term, an External Investment Fund with up to EUR 62 billion may be devoted to address the root causes of migration (European Commission 2016b). The EU develops country packages for sixteen countries in

North and Sub-Saharan Africa (Afghanistan, Algeria, Bangladesh, Ethiopia, Eritrea, Ghana, Ivory Coast, Niger, Nigeria, Mali, Morocco, Pakistan, Senegal, Somalia, Sudan and Tunisia).

Unsurprisingly, the EU's plan to use all available tools for migration-control purposes (and to present the EU–Turkey deal as an example for engagement in the neighbourhood) has received criticism. A total of 104 NGOs working with refugees signed an open petition to the EU in which they condemned the EU's new approach to contain migration.

> This new Partnership Framework risks cementing a shift towards a foreign policy that serves one single objective, to curb migration, at the expense of European credibility and leverage in defence of fundamental values and human rights.
>
> (PICUM 2016)

Yet the compact with Jordan, the first of its kind, includes many aspects that can be attributed to the 'preventive' rather than the 'restrictive' approach of EU external migration policy (Boswell 2003). The EU has simplified the rules of origin for Jordanian exporters in their trade with the EU. This is expected to create jobs for Jordanians and Syrian refugees in the country. More concretely, the EU will open its market for manufactured goods produced in special industrial areas and development zones – if their producers employ a minimum percentage of Syrian refugees (15 per cent at the outset, progressively increasing to 25 per cent in three years). The overall objective is to provide Syrians with a possibility of a decent life in the country and to improve 'Jordan's resilience in light of the Syria refugee crisis' (European Commission 2016d). The EU's approach in Jordan largely corresponds to what migration scholars have long suggested, namely to 'help refugees help themselves' by facilitating their inclusion into labour markets through a special 'zonal development model' (Betts and Collier 2015). Yet, the credibility of these provisions will be contingent on local social, economic and political preconditions that will shape their rationale and concrete impact. In other words, the inclusion of Syrian refugees in the Jordanian labour market will depend on whether the Jordanian authorities and local business actors can attract substantial foreign investments. More importantly, it will also depend on its capacity to respond to its resilient domestic labour absorption problems, for the sake of social stability. The unemployment rate in Jordan remains reportedly high (14 per cent), especially for youth.

Zooming in on the eastern and southern neighbourhoods

This section looks in more detail at the similarities and differences of the politics of EU migration management in the eastern and southern neighbourhood.

The Eastern Partnership countries and Russia

The Eastern Partnership (EaP) countries have more formalised and closer ties with the EU in the migration field compared to the EU's southern neighbours. Their geographical position and close socio-economic ties with some Member States (for example, between Poland and Ukraine or Romania and Moldova) have contributed to an earlier EU acceptance of the nexus between visa facilitation and readmission (see Table 35.2). The EU's experience of negotiating a readmission agreement with Russia in the early 2000s has also influenced the EU approach towards the entire region. The Russian Federation repeatedly, and successfully, asked for facilitated visa travel as compensation for concluding such an agreement (Hernández i Sagrera 2010; Korneev 2012).

Table 35.2 EU migration agreements with EaP countries and Russia (as of October 2016)

EaP country	Negotiating mandate Readmission	Negotiating mandate Visa facilitation	Agreements signed	Mobility Partnerships	Start of visa-free dialogue	Visa free travel
Belarus	Feb 2011	Feb 2011		Oct 2016		
Ukraine	Feb 2002	Nov 2005	Jun 2007		Oct 2008	Early 2017 (scheduled)
Moldova	Dec 2006	Dec 2006	Oct 2007	May 2008	Jun 2010	Apr 2014
Georgia	Nov 2008	Nov 2008	Nov 2010	Nov 2009	Jun 2012	Early 2017 (scheduled)
Armenia	Dec 2011	Dec 2011	Dec 2012/ Apr 2013	Oct 2011		
Azerbaijan	Dec 2011	Dec 2011	Nov 2013/ Feb 2014	Dec 2013		
Russia	Sep 2000	July 2004	May 2006		Apr 2007	

After the signature of the EU–Russian visa facilitation and readmission agreements in May 2006, the same pattern of cooperation was soon accepted for and by Ukraine and Moldova, with agreements signed in June and October 2007. Moldova and Georgia were the first EaP countries with which the EU negotiated visa facilitation and readmission rights. At first glance, Azerbaijan seemed to be an exception. In January 2011, Commission President José Manuel Barroso promised to quickly grant visa facilitation, in return for an energy deal bringing 10 billion cubic metres of gas to Europe each year (EurActiv 2011). However, not all Member States agreed with the Commission President's assessment that the gas deal justified a more relaxed visa regime. In the end, Azerbaijan and Armenia both signed visa facilitation and readmission agreements with the EU.

The EU has limited relations with the Belarusian regime. Yet, migration has been a tricky question for the EU. On the one hand, the widespread human rights violations of the Lukashenko regime prevent the EU from deepening or even cooperating on sensitive issues such as readmission. On the other hand, more travel opportunities are of high importance for ordinary citizens and may benefit Belarusian society at large (Council of the European Union 2011). Belarus is the country with the highest number of Schengen visas issued per capita in the world and one of the lowest refusal rates (European Commission 2016c). The EU has therefore an interest in a migration cooperation framework with Belarus, as is reflected by the signature of a Mobility Partnership in October 2016.

In addition to Belarus, Mobility Partnerships have been signed with Moldova (May 2008), Georgia (November 2009) and Armenia (October 2011). They ease the way towards 'Visa Liberalisation Dialogues', although they are no prerequisite. Ukraine has entered a visa liberalisation process without committing to a Mobility Partnership. Moldova was the first EaP country to complete a visa liberalisation process. It was removed from Annex I of Regulation 539/2001 in April 2014, implying that the citizens of Moldova no longer needed a visa to enter the Union. In December 2015, the European Commission (2015a, 2015b) considered that Ukraine and Georgia would also meet all the benchmarks set by the EU and qualify for visa-free travel. In October 2016, the EU Member States agreed on visa-free travel for Georgia but demanded Ukraine make further efforts in the fight against corruption. At the same time as this decision, the Council agreed on a facilitated 'suspension emergency mechanism' that allows the re-introduction of restrictions to visa-free travel in case of an abuse (Zalan 2016; for a background on this mechanism, see Trauner and Manigrassi 2014).

Russia also queued for visa-free travel with the EU, but the dialogue was frozen as part of the sanctions imposed in the wake of the annexation of Crimea. The growing EU–Russian competition in the shared neighbourhood has influenced the EU's migration approach in Eastern Europe. Russia's efforts to prevent the EU's eastern neighbours from integrating into the Euro-Atlantic institutions also builds upon migration-related instruments, such as more restrictive access to the Russian labour market or (the threat of) deportations of citizens of cooperation-unwilling neighbours (Ademmer and Delcour 2016). This is of relevance given the large share of foreign workers from Eastern Europe in Russia. Yet research has shown that the question of who influences whom in Eastern Europe does not have an easy and clear-cut answer. At times, Russia's action pushed neighbouring countries towards quicker acceptance of EU policy conditions.

Georgia has been a case in point. Under the ENP framework, Georgia has largely refrained from triggering far-reaching reforms in justice and home affairs. After the EU signed a visa facilitation agreement with Russia in May 2006, Georgia maintained that the EU–Russia visa facilitation agreement would provide Georgian citizens living in the breakaway provinces, South Ossetia and Abkhazia, with an extra incentive to apply for a Russian passport – yet this argument was not strong enough to make the Georgian government accept a readmission agreement or comply with the security-related ENP requirements (Ademmer and Börzel 2013). After the August 2008 war between Russia and the separatist entities of South Ossetia and Abkhazia, on one hand, and Georgia, on the other, Georgia quickly progressed towards meeting the conditions regarding document security and accepting a readmission agreement. In other words, 'the Georgian-Russian conflict and the EU-Russian visa-facilitation agreement reinforced the policy-specific conditionality of the EU for Georgia to engage in visa-facilitation talks with the EU' (Ademmer and Börzel 2013).

The competition between Russia and the EU has become stronger since 2008. Russia has shown its capacity to 'hinder compliance with EU demands in the area of migration and mobility if it links specific rewards to non-compliance with EU demands' (Ademmer and Delcour 2016: 94). A key question for Russia has been whether it perceives the EU's visa liberalisation process (and policies related to it) as a threat to its strategic interests in the shared neighbourhood.

The EU and Russia have tended to operate at different levels. 'While the EU pushes for policy-specific changes, using conditionality and assistance, Russia mostly (dis)incentivizes broader geopolitical choices that challenge its pivotal interests in the region' (Ademmer and Delcour 2016: 108). This can create a situation in which a neighbouring country opts for integration with the Russian-led Eurasian Economic Union but continues to work on the policy-specific EU demands in migration and mobility. In the work of Ademmer and Delcour, Armenia was named as a country that sought to achieve such complementarity. Still striving for closer political ties and economic integration with the EU, Moldova, by contrast, has faced a harsher stance of and challenge by Russia, including in the field of migration. This 'may indirectly hamper continuous compliance with EU requirements in the future' (Ademmer and Delcour 2016: 108).

The EU's cooperation with southern neighbours

A key question regarding the southern neighbours has been how much the EU can, and should, engage with authoritarian regimes to stem unwanted migration. Scholars have highlighted the ethical and human rights-related challenges that the EU faces in terms of working with southern autocrats to establish a buffer zone against uncontrolled migration (Wolff 2008; Cassarino 2010; 2014; Lutterbeck 2006; Klepp 2010; Demmelhuber 2011; Gil-Bazo 2006; Carrera et al. 2016).

Some researchers have noted that Euro-Mediterranean cooperation on migration offers opportunities as well. The EU's involvement may lead to more transparent, accountable and participatory migration governance (Freyburg 2012; Freyburg et al. 2009). Building upon the case study of the 2003 Moroccan reform of migration law, Freyburg (2012) argues that the EU's migration governance may be perceived as 'Janus-faced' – it weakens democratic governance at home but it improves these standards abroad.

As mentioned, the EU has long sought to conclude readmission agreements with southern neighbours as well. The Commission's negotiating mandate for Morocco was given in 2000 and for Algeria in 2002. Even after many years of negotiations, the EU did not manage to make these states accept a formal EU readmission agreement. They particularly opposed the idea of readmitting sub-Saharan African migrants transiting their territory to the EU (Wolff 2014). While the southern ENP partners have refrained from formalising EU level cooperation on readmission, the network of bilateral agreements linked to readmission has intensified, often in the shadow of public debates (Cassarino 2007). Cooperation on removal of irregular migrants has been embedded in broader strategic frameworks of cooperation or other types of arrangements (such as police cooperation agreements and memoranda of understanding). These arrangements are only linked to readmission, and are distinct from standard readmission agreements (Cassarino 2010). Informal patterns of bilateral cooperation on readmission are characterised by four elements, namely their invisibility, flexibility, limited costs of defection and adaptability to security concerns (Cassarino 2007). France, Greece, Italy and Spain have been drivers in developing this non-standard approach towards readmission. EU Member States tend to rely on material and non-material incentives – rather than on conditionalities – for cooperation on readmission and reinforced border controls. Material incentives include financial protocols to improve foreign direct investments and create job opportunities, as well as technical equipment and capacity-building programmes for law-enforcement institutions. Non-material incentives include international recognition of the cooperative governments and stronger support of their political demands in international affairs (Cassarino 2010; 2017).

The dense bilateral cooperation between individual Member States and North African states has paved the way for a stronger EU role. In 2006, Frontex had the first maritime operation to curb irregular migration from West Africa to the Canary Islands, thereby relying on bilateral agreements – for example between Spain and Mauritania – when engaging African states (Carrera 2007). Frontex and Spanish patrols off West Africa seem to have contributed to shifting migration routes, making the route from Libya to Malta and Italy more important (Carling and Hernández-Carretero 2011). Border and migration control in the wider Mediterranean region now built upon many more actors aside Frontex. In May 2015, the EU started a military mission called 'EUNAVFOR Med Operation Sophia' aiming to interrupt the activities of smugglers and traffickers of human beings. While the employment of a EU military mission to curb unwanted migration has been criticised as 'warfare on the logistics of migrant movements' (Garelli and Tazzioli 2016), Operation Sophia saved the lives of some 24,800 migrants crossing the Mediterranean by August 2016 (European External Action Service 2016). In a way, the EU's military operation therefore replaces the live-saving activities of Italy, in the context of the Mare Nostrum operation active between October 2013 and October 2014. The drowning of migrants trying to cross the Mediterranean Sea has not stopped. The year 2016 was even deadlier than the 'crisis' year of 2015 (UNHCR 2016).

At the same time, the migration theme has empowered the EU's Mediterranean neighbours. They tend to capitalise on migration and border controls and exert a kind of 'reverse leverage' on their EU counterparts (Cassarino 2007; 2017). For example, the concessions which Libya's Muammar al-Gaddafi gained from Italy (and the EU) for curbing irregular migration have been well-documented in this context (Paoletti 2011; Wolff 2012). Also, the Tunisian government selectively incorporated elements of the EU's migration policy toolbox to enhance its own strategic options regarding surveillance and control over Tunisian society at large (Cassarino 2014). North African states may exert agency, not only during the negotiation phase of a readmission deal, be it formal or not. By investigating the implementation of the French readmission policy in Morocco, El Qadim (2014) highlights the relevance of mid-level bilateral practices of brokering. The level of Franco-Moroccan cooperation often depended on issue-specific bargains, for instance on a French immigration liaison officer offering technical advice and training in exchange for more operational cooperation on readmission.

Morocco is an interesting case for discussing the feasibility of the EU's 'more-for-more' approach that is supposed to guide the EU's external activities post-refugee crisis. The flow of migrants entering Spanish territory from Morocco has considerably decreased due to intensified cooperation with Spain and the EU (including the signing of a Mobility Partnership). Which lessons can the EU learn from the Moroccan case? According to Carrera et al. (2016), Morocco is becoming more and more a country of destination, yet it struggles to uphold the responsibilities that come with such change. Migrants are often blocked for years in Morocco and face considerable challenges to get along, let alone to integrate into society. This is also the case for refugees fleeing from the Syrian war. They do not face the risk of a *refoulement* from Morocco. However, access to public services, jobs and health is severely limited in the case of Syrians living in Morocco. A (widely reported) practice of 'hot returns' or 'pushback operations' conducted by Spain at the borders of Ceuta and Melilla has been challenged as a human rights violation before the European Court of Human Rights. Overall, Carrera et al. (2016: 10) caution against duplicating the Moroccan model for other ENP countries. 'The "model" of border surveillance and control [. . .] comes at a considerable human cost for migrants, creating a situation of vulnerability, insecurity and human rights violations', as noted by the authors.

Conclusions

This chapter has investigated how migration moved to the centre of the ENP. Migration-related projects now count for half the ENP's spending. Migration issues increasingly influence, if not dominate, the political relations of the EU and its ENP partners.

The chapter has drawn attention to the struggles that the EU faces to balance a more restrictive approach of external engagement, focusing on migration control, with a more preventive one, trying to tackle the 'root causes' as to why people flee or migrate. It is tempting to conclude that the EU focuses primarily on the restrictive approach and short-term interests – notably a reduction of irregular migration from the neighbourhood – if necessary, even at the expense of the human rights and dignity of the migrants concerned. The focus on 'root causes' may only serve as a rhetorical 'add-on' that helps with justifying the external migration control agenda in the EU's neighbourhood, yet *de facto* it lacks substance and prioritisation.

While some scholars referred to in this chapter have argued in this direction, there are two caveats to such a conclusion. First, the argument tends to underestimate the agency of ENP countries. Across the southern and eastern neighbourhoods, migration has become part of the wider geopolitical dynamics. ENP countries' governments and competing regional actors, such as Russia, exploit the salience of the migration issue for their own interests and purposes in their interactions with the EU. They are far from being only the passive 'recipients' of the EU's externalisation agenda. Second, there may also be a gap between the EU's increasingly tough rhetoric *vis-à-vis* countries of migrants' origin and transit and the actual outcome of the external engagement. The latter will predictably remain contingent on local conditions that cannot be dismissed offhand. The EU's 'compact' with Jordan is a case in point. Providing new economic opportunities and facilitating the integration of Syrian refugees into the local labour market constitute daunting challenges when considering Jordan's social economic and political realities.

That said, the EU should have an interest – and probably even has a responsibility – to engage more to safeguard human rights, as well as improve the socio-economic situation of migrants and refugees stuck in neighbouring countries. Based on everything that is known from the past, simply saying 'out of sight, out of mind' will not work for long in the field of migration.

References

Ademmer, E. and Börzel, T. (2013) 'Migration, Energy and Good Governance in the EU's Eastern Neighbourhood', *Europe-Asia Studies* 65(4): 581–608.

Ademmer, E. and Delcour, L. (2016) 'With a Little Help from Russia? The European Union and Visa Liberalization with Post-Soviet States', *Eurasian Geography and Economics* 57(1): 89–112.

Balzacq, T. (ed.) (2009) *The External Dimension of EU Justice and Home Affairs—Governance, Neighours, Security*, Basingstoke: Palgrave.

Betts, A. and Collier, P. (2015) 'Help Refugees Help Themselves. Let Displaced Syrians Join the Labor Market', *Foreign Affairs*, November/December.

Bigo, D. and Guild, E. (ed.) (2005) *Controlling Frontiers: Free Movement Into and Within Europe*, Aldershot: Ashgate Publishing Company.

Boswell, C. (2003) 'The "External Dimension" of EU Immigration and Asylum Policy', *International Affairs* 79(3): 619–638.

Carrera, S. (2007) 'The EU Border Management Strategy: Frontex and the Challenges of Irregular Immigration in the Canary Islands', *CEPS Working Document 261*, Centre for European Policy Studies.

Carrera, S., Cassarino, J.-P., El Qadim, N., Lahlou, M. and den Hertog, L. (2016) 'EU-Morocco Cooperation on Readmission, Borders and Protection: A Model to Follow?', *CEPS Paper* 87, Centre for European Policy Studies.

Carling, J. and Hernández-Carretero, M.H. (2011) 'Protecting Europe and Protecting Migrants? Strategies for Managing Unauthorised Migration from Africa', *The British Journal of Politics and International Relations* 13(1): 42–58.

Cassarino, J.-P. (2007) 'Informalising Readmission Agreements in the EU Neighbourhood', *The International Spectator* 42(2): 179–196.

Cassarino, J.-P. (2010) 'Dealing with Unbalanced Reciprocities: Cooperation on Readmission and Implications', in Cassarino, J.-P. (ed.) *Unbalanced Reciprocities: Cooperation on Readmission in the Euro-Mediterranean Area*, Washington: Middle East Institute, 1–30.

Cassarino, J.-P. (2014) 'Channelled Policy Transfer: EU-Tunisia Interactions on Migration Matters', *European Journal of Migration and Law* 16(1): 97–123.

Cassarino, J.-P. (2017) 'Informalising EU Readmission Policy', in Ripoll Servent, A. and Trauner, F. (eds.) *Routledge Handbook of Justice and Home Affairs Research*, London: Routledge.

Collet, E. (2016) 'The Paradox of the EU–Turkey Refugee Deal', *Migration Policy Institute Commentary*, March, Washington.

Commission of the European Communities (2003) *Communication from the Commission to the Council and the European Parliament. Wider Europe—Neighbourhood: A New Framework for Relations with Our Eastern and Southern Neighbours*, COM (2003) 104, 11 March.

Commission of the European Communities (2009) *Mobility Partnerships as a Tool of the Global Approach to Migration*, SEC(2009) 1240 final.

Council of the European Union (2005) *Global Approach to Migration: Priority Actions Focusing on Africa and the Mediterranean*, 15451/05, 6 December.

Council of the European Union (2011) 'Council Conclusions on Belarus', 5956/11, 31 January 2011.

Demmelhuber, T. (2011) 'The European Union and Illegal Migration in the Southern Mediterranean: The Trap of Competing Policy Concepts', *The International Journal of Human Rights* 15(6): 813–826.

El Qadim, N. (2014) 'Postcolonial Challenges to Migration Control: French–Moroccan Cooperation Practices on Forced Return', *Security Dialogue* 45(3): 242–261.

Euroactiv (2011), 'Barroso Tops Azeri Gas Deal with Visa Faciltiation', 14 January.

European External Action Service (2016) 'European Union Naval Force Mediterranean Operation Sophia', *Press Release* 1/2016, Rome.

European Commission (2011a) *A Dialogue for Migration, Mobility and Security with the Southern Mediterranean Countries*, COM (2011) 292 final.

European Commission (2011b) *The Global Approach to Migration and Mobility*, COM(2011) 743 final of 18 November.

European Commission (2015a) *Fourth Progress Report on Georgia's Implementation of the Action Plan on Visa Liberalisation*, COM(2015) 684 final, 18 December.

European Commission (2015b) *Sixth Progress Report on the Implementation by Ukraine of the Action Plan on Visa Liberalisation*, COM(2015) 905, 18 December.

European Commission (2016a) *Communication from the Commission [. . .] on Establishing a New Partnership Framework with Thrid Countries Under the European Agenda on Migration*. COM(2016) 385 final, 7 June.

European Commission (2016b) *Communication on Establishing a New Partnership Framework with Third Countries Under the European Agenda on Migration*, COM(2016) 385 final, 7 July.

European Commission (2016c) 'EU Launches Mobility Partnership with Belarus', *Press Release* IP/16/3426.

European Commission (2016d) 'EU-Jordan: Towards a Stronger Partnership', *Press Release* IP/16/2570.

European Commission and High Representative of the European Union for Foreign Affairs and Security Policy (2015) *Joint Communication to the European Parliament, the Council, the European Economic and Social Committee and the Committee of the Regions. Review of the European Neighbourhood Policy*, JOIN(2015) 50 Final, Brussels.

Freyburg, T. (2012) 'The Janus Face of EU Migration Governance: Impairing Democratic Governance at Home—Improving It Abroad?', *European Foreign Affairs Review* 17(Special Issue 2012): 289–306.

Freyburg, T., Lavenex, S., Schimmelfennig, F., Skripka, T. and Wetzel, A. (2009) 'EU Promotion of Democratic Governance in the Neighbourhood', *Journal of European Public Policy* 16(6): 916–934.

Garelli, G. and Tazzioli, M. (2016) 'Warfare on the Logistics of Migrant Movements: EU and NATO Military Operations in the Mediterranean', OpenDemocracy, 16 June.

Gil-Bazo, M. (2006) 'The Practice of Mediterranean States in the Context of the European Union's Justice and Home Affairs External Dimension: The Safe Third Country Concept Revisited' *International Journal of Refugee Law* 18(3–4): 571–600.

Grabbe, H. (2002) 'Stabilising the East While Keeping Out the Easterners: Internal and External Security Logics in Conflict', in Lavenex S. and Ucarer, E. (eds.) *Migration and the Externalities of European Integration*, Lanham: Lexington Books, 91–104.

Greene, M. and Kelemen, D. (2016) 'Europe's Lousy Deal with Turkey: Why the Refugee Arrangement Won't Work', *Foreign Affairs*, March.

Hernández i Sagrera, R. (2010) 'The EU–Russia Readmission–Visa Facilitation Nexus: An Exportable Migration Model for Eastern Europe?', *European Security* 19(4): 569–584.

Huysmans, J. (2000) 'The European Union and the Securitization of Migration', *Journal of Common Market Studies* 38(5): 751–777.

Klepp, S. (2010) 'A Contested Asylum System: The European Union Between Refugee Protection and Border Control in the Mediterranean Sea', *European Journal of Migration and Law* 12(1): 1–21.

Korneev, O. (2012) 'Deeper and Wider than a Common Space: EU–Russia Cooperation on Migration Management', *European Foreign Affairs Review* 17(4): 605–624.

Lavenex, S. (2004) 'EU External Governance in "Wider Europe"', *Journal of European Public Policy* 11(4): 680–700.

Lavenex, S. (2010) 'Justice and Home Affairs. Communitarization with Hesitation', in Wallace, H., Pollack, M. and Young, A. (eds.) *Policy-Making in the European Union*, Oxford: Oxford University Press, 458–477.

Lutterbeck, D. (2006) 'Policing Migration in the Mediterranean', *Mediterranean Politics* 11(1): 59–82.

Paoletti, E. (2011) *The Migration of Power and North–South Inequalities: The Case of Italy and Libya*, Basingstoke: Palgrave Macmillan.

Parkes, R. (2009) 'EU Mobility Partnerships: A Model for Policy Coordination?', *European Journal of Migration and Law* 11: 327–345.

PICUM (2016) 'Reject Dangerous Migration Response Plan, More Than 100 NGOs Tell EU Leaders', Platform for International Cooperation on Undocumented Migrants, Brussels. http://picum.org/en/news/picum-news/50797/.

Reslow, N. (2012) 'The Role of Third Countries in EU Migration Policy: The Mobility Partnerships', *European Journal of Migration and Law* 14(4): 393–415.

Rijpma, J. and Cremona, M. (2007) 'The Extra-Territorialisation of EU Migration Policies and the Rule of Law', *EUI Working Paper Law* 2007/01, European University Institute, Florence.

Trauner, F. (2009) 'From Membership Conditionality to Policy Conditionality: EU External Governance in South Eastern Europe', *Journal of European Public Policy* 16(5): 774–790.

Trauner, F. (2016) 'Asylum Policy: The EU's "Crises" and the Looming Policy Regime Failure', *Journal of European Integration* 38(3): 311–325.

Trauner, F. and Kruse, I. (2008) 'EC Visa Facilitation and Readmission Agreements: A New Standard EU Foreign Policy Tool?', *European Journal of Migration and Law* 10(4): 411–438.

Trauner, F. and Manigrassi, E. (2014) 'When Visa-Free Travel Becomes Difficult to Achieve and Easy to Lose: The EU Visa Free Dialogues After the EU's Experience with the Western Balkans', *European Journal of Migration and Law* 16(1): 125–145.

UNHCR (2016) 'Mediterranean Death Toll Sears, 2016 is Deadliest Year Yet', United Nations High Commissioner for Refugees, Geneva.

Weinar, A. (2013) 'Mobility Partnerships—What Impact Do They have on Legal Migration and Mobility?', Migration Policy Centre, European University Institute, Florence.

Wolff, S. (2008) 'Border Management in the Mediterranean: Internal, External and Ethical Challenges', *Cambridge Review of International Affairs* 21: 253–271.

Wolff, S. (2012) *The Mediterranean Dimension of the European Union's Internal Security*, Houndmills: Palgrave.

Wolff, S. (2014) 'The Politics of Negotiating EU Readmission Agreements: Insights from Morocco and Turkey', *European Journal of Migration and Law* 16(1): 69–95.

Wunderlich, D. (2010) 'Differentiation and Policy Convergence against Long Odds: Lessons from Implementing EU Migration Policy in Morocco', *Mediterranean Politics* 15(2): 249–272.

Zalan, E. (2016) 'Georgia Gets Green Light for EU Visa-Free Travel', *Euobserver*, 5 October.

Zhyznomirska, L. (2011) 'The European Union's "Home Affairs" model and its European neighbours: Beyond the "Area of Freedom, Security and Justice?"', *Comparative European Politics* 9(4/5): 506–523.

36
COUNTER-TERRORISM COOPERATION AND THE EUROPEAN NEIGHBOURHOOD POLICY

Chantal Lavallée, Sarah Léonard and Christian Kaunert

Introduction

Although the threat of terrorism was one of the driving factors behind the initiation of internal security cooperation among European states in the 1970s, the European Union (EU) only began to develop its counter-terrorism policy following the terrorist attacks against the United States on 11 September 2001 (Argomaniz 2011; Bossong 2013; Kaunert 2010c). The realisation of the transnational scope and the multifaceted character of the terrorist threat led to an increase in the political will to cooperate among EU Member States, which had been previously rather limited (Kaunert 2010b; Mahncke and Monar 2006; Spence 2007). The bombings in Madrid in 2004, and in London one year later, led to a deepening of the cooperation among EU Member States, epitomised by the establishment of the position of an EU Counter-Terrorism Coordinator in March 2004 (Council of the European Union 2004: 14) and the adoption of the EU Counter-Terrorism Strategy in November 2005 (Council of the European Union 2005). The bombings also resulted in increased counter-terrorism cooperation between the EU and third countries, as policy-makers increasingly acknowledged the strong transnational dimension of the terrorist threat faced by European states (Kaunert 2010a). The EU Counter-Terrorism Strategy of 2005 emphasised the importance of '[combating] terrorism globally' (Council of the European Union 2005: 6). This trend has not been confined to the realm of counter-terrorism, but has characterised the EU's security policies generally. As the linkages between internal and external security have been reinforced, European leaders have repeatedly asserted the necessity of mobilising all the tools at the EU's disposal to tackle internal threats, including in the neighbourhood (Ioannides 2014). One of those has been the European Neighbourhood Policy (ENP).

The ENP has been developed, since 2003, with the ambition of creating a 'ring of friends', that is, an area of political stability, security and economic prosperity, comprising the countries situated to the East (that is, Armenia, Azerbaijan, Belarus, Georgia, Moldova, Ukraine) and the South of the EU (that is, Algeria, Egypt, Israel, Jordan, Lebanon, Libya, Morocco, Palestinian Authority, Syria, Tunisia) (Commission of the European Communities 2003: 4). Thus, one of the aims of the ENP has been to foster security cooperation, including in the fight against terrorism. More than ten years after the launch of the ENP, results have been mixed. Cooperation, notably in the field of security, has not advanced as much as it had been envisaged in the ENP official documents (Kaunert and Léonard 2011).

Moreover, the international environment, notably in the EU's neighbourhood, has considerably changed since the ENP was launched. Political developments, such as the Arab uprisings in the South (Demmelhuber, this volume), and the war in Ukraine in the East (Korosteleva, this volume), have led some observers to argue that the EU is now surrounded by a 'ring of fire', rather than a 'ring of friends' (*The Economist* 2014). As a result, the importance of security concerns on the EU's agenda has been strengthened. The 2015 European Agenda on Security has highlighted the importance of combating terrorism (European Commission 2015: 2) following various terrorist attacks across Europe.

This chapter examines how the EU has attempted to develop counter-terrorism cooperation with its eastern and southern partners and what results it has achieved in practice. It starts by locating counter-terrorism in the broader context of the EU's security policies. It then examines counter-terrorism cooperation between the EU and its neighbours. Having shown that such cooperation has previously remained limited, to a large extent, it examines the obstacles to its development before offering some conclusions. For the purposes of this chapter, counter-terrorism is understood as a broad policy area that comprises a range of responses across various governmental departments (Keohane 2005), including policing, criminal justice, border controls, the freezing of financial assets, intelligence gathering and, more recently, anti-radicalisation measures.

Counter-terrorism as one dimension of the EU's security policies

It is important to recall that the EU's counter-terrorism policy has developed as part of a larger trend of EU involvement in security affairs. This has been supported by the adoption of various strategic documents, which have generally identified terrorism as one of the most acute security threats faced by the EU and its Member States. In 2003, the European Security Strategy (ESS) highlighted terrorism as a major threat requiring national authorities to work closely together (Biscop 2008). The ESS stated that terrorism should be tackled using 'a mixture of intelligence, police, judicial, military and other means' (European Council 2003: 7). It also emphasised the crucial importance of 'better coordination between external action and Justice and Home Affairs policies' in the fight against terrorism (European Council 2003: 13). More generally, the ESS promoted a comprehensive approach to security, which would combine civilian and military tools and would rise above the divide between internal security and external security to tackle multifaceted problems and cross-sectoral threats. The ESS also identified 'building security in our neighbourhood' as one of its three strategic objectives, to be achieved notably through the promotion of good governance and the development of 'close and cooperative relations' (European Council 2013: 8; Biscop 2010; Henökl, this volume).

The necessity to move beyond the divide between the internal and external aspects of European security was also highlighted at the time of the adoption of the EU's Internal Security Strategy (ISS) in 2010. The European Commission notably stated that 'internal security-related priorities should feature in political dialogues with third countries and regional organisations where appropriate and relevant for combating multiple threats, such as [...] terrorism' (European Commission 2010: 3). This point was again emphasised in the recently adopted European Agenda on Security (European Commission 2015: 4), which also highlighted the importance of the 'security dialogues' with a range of partners, including neighbouring countries (European Commission 2015: 4).

Despite this rhetorical commitment by the EU to cooperate with external partners to tackle various security issues in its neighbourhood, in practice, the divide between the internal and external realms of security has been a persistent feature of the EU's involvement in the security domain (Ioannides 2014). This can be aptly illustrated by the relationship between counter-terrorism and the Common Security and Defence Policy (CSDP) (Bouris and Dobrescu, this volume). Despite various official statements on the important contribution that the CSDP could make to counter-terrorism from 2001 onwards (Oliveira Martins and Ferreira-Pereira 2012), it was only in 2012 that the first CSDP mission including a formal counter-terrorism mandate was launched, namely EUCAP SAHEL Niger (Council of the European Union 2012). Such a mission was exceptional in a context that is still marked by a significant divide between the internal and external aspects of security and counter-terrorism.

Counter-terrorism in the relations between the EU and its neighbours

The 2003 Communication of the European Commission (2003: 3) that launched the ENP identified terrorism as one of the 'transboundary threats' that the EU and its neighbourhood have a shared interest in tackling together.

Counter-terrorism in the relations between the EU and its eastern neighbours

The ENP Action Plans drawn up for Armenia, Azerbaijan, Georgia, Moldova and Ukraine[1] contain some objectives in the field of counter-terrorism. However, those objectives are vague and mainly concern the establishment or reinforcement of political dialogue on terrorism-related issues. Nevertheless, some aspects of counter-terrorism cooperation have developed more significantly with some eastern partners. Regarding police cooperation, Europol, the EU's law enforcement agency, signed operational agreements with Moldova in December 2014 and with Ukraine in December 2016.[2] Operational agreements enable the exchange of information, including personal data, contrary to strategic agreements, which are limited to the exchange of strategic and technical information or general intelligence. Concerning judicial cooperation, Eurojust, the European Union's Judicial Cooperation Unit, has only signed agreements on cooperation with Ukraine and Moldova.[3] Contact points for Eurojust have also been appointed in these two countries, as well as in Georgia (Council of the European Union 2015b: 3). When it comes to border controls, which can also contribute to fighting terrorism, working arrangements have been signed by Frontex, which is the European border management agency, with all six eastern ENP partners, namely Armenia, Azerbaijan, Belarus, Georgia, Moldova and Ukraine.[4] However, although border controls can support the fight against terrorism, their contribution to date has been rather limited (Léonard 2015).

The joint declaration, signed in May 2009, that established the Eastern Partnership (EaP) between the EU and its six eastern ENP partners did not make any specific reference to terrorism or even internal security generally (Council of the European Union 2009). Nevertheless, the EU has established a forum for expert discussions on internal security matters, including terrorism, with several of its eastern neighbours. A Subcommittee on Justice, Freedom and Security has been established with Georgia (2008), Armenia and Azerbaijan (2010), Moldova and Ukraine (2011). In addition, whereas the first EaP JHA Ministerial meeting in 2013 did not focus on terrorism, the second meeting, which took place shortly after terrorist attacks had taken place in Paris, was dominated by discussions about counter-terrorism cooperation.

Counter-terrorism in the relations between the EU and its southern neighbours

The legacy of the Euro-Mediterranean Partnership

In the EU's southern neighbourhood, the ENP has built on the experience and legacy of the Euro-Mediterranean Partnership (EMP), or Barcelona Process, which had been launched following the adoption of the Barcelona Declaration in November 1995. The EMP aimed to enhance cooperation between the EU and 12 Southern Mediterranean countries regarding three key areas – political and security issues, economic and financial issues, and social, cultural and human issues – in order to transform the Mediterranean into a common area of peace, stability and prosperity (Euro-Mediterranean Partnership 1995). While the issue of terrorism was already explicitly mentioned in the 1995 Barcelona Declaration, it was cited with many other policy issues, without being given any significant prominence. The signatories merely resolved to 'strengthen their cooperation in preventing and combating terrorism, in particular by ratifying and applying the international instruments they have signed, by acceding to such instruments and by taking any other appropriate measure' (Euro-Mediterranean Partnership 1995: 3).

Over the years, terrorism has increasingly moved towards the top of the agenda of Euro-Mediterranean conferences. This ascension culminated with the adoption of a Euro-Mediterranean Code of Conduct on Countering Terrorism at the 2005 Barcelona Summit (Euro-Mediterranean Partnership 2005). That summit also saw the adoption of the decision to include a fourth key area for cooperation, namely migration and internal security. This new priority has notably been implemented through projects aiming to foster the exchange of good practices and to improve operational cooperation, such as EUROMED Migration and EUROMED Police (European Commission 2014).

However, this reinforced emphasis on security matters was not well-received by all Southern Mediterranean partners, which have not always shared the EU's agenda and political priorities (Bicchi 2011). In that respect, most of the bilateral AA between the EU and the Southern Mediterranean partners do not explicitly mention the issue of terrorism, except the agreements with Egypt and Algeria. Article 59 of the EU–Egypt AA, which entered into force in 2004, anticipates counter-terrorism cooperation between the two parties, particularly regarding the 'exchange of information on means and methods used to counter terrorism; exchange of experiences in respect of terrorism prevention; joint research and studies in the area of terrorism prevention'. Article 90 of the EU–Algeria AA, which entered into force in 2005, also concerns the fight against terrorism. The signatories commit to the implementation of terrorism-related United Nations Security Council Resolutions, the exchange of information on terrorist groups and their support networks, and the sharing of experience in combating terrorism. In other words, these clauses on the fight against terrorism are rather vague (MacKenzie et al. 2013; Kaunert and Léonard 2011).

Counter-terrorism in the ENP

The ENP, with respect to the EU's southern neighbours, was also an attempt at addressing the shortcomings of the EMP. Regarding the relationship between the two policy initiatives, the EU has presented the ENP as a complement to the multilateral framework of the Barcelona Process, which builds on its bilateral dimension. The existing Euro-Mediterranean AAs have provided the legal basis for the development of ENP Action Plans towards Southern Mediterranean states,[5] which have notably included counter-terrorism activities. However, a systematic analysis of these Action Plans reveals that, when it comes to counter-terrorism, only vague and limited objectives have been included in the Action Plans elaborated for the EU's Mediterranean neighbours (Kaunert and Léonard 2011; MacKenzie et al. 2013). As argued by Kaunert and Léonard (2011), counter-terrorism cooperation between the EU and its southern neighbours has remained modest and largely confined to political dialogue. There has been virtually no operational cooperation for counter-terrorism purposes. Concerning police and law enforcement cooperation, Europol, the EU's law enforcement agency, has not signed any agreement with any of the EU's southern neighbours. It has had a mandate to negotiate an agreement with Morocco since 2000, but discussions have been unfruitful to date. Negotiations with Israel, the only other southern ENP country for which Europol has received a negotiation mandate, have not been more successful (Kaunert and Léonard 2011). Concerning judicial cooperation, some of the ENP Action Plans, namely those of Egypt, Jordan, Lebanon and Israel, indicate that judicial cooperation for counter-terrorism purposes should be considered. However, Eurojust has not negotiated an agreement with any of the EU's southern neighbours, although contact points for Eurojust have been appointed in Egypt, Israel and Tunisia (Council of the European Union 2015b). Concerning border controls, Frontex has not signed a working arrangement with any of the EU's southern neighbours, although it has received mandates to negotiate working arrangements with Egypt, Libya, Morocco and Tunisia. Cooperation in the fight against the financing of terrorism has also been rather modest, albeit more advanced than other strands of counter-terrorism cooperation. This is somewhat surprising given the major role that the EU could have played as a provider of technical assistance. However, it might be explained by the very sensitive character of this issue in various Mediterranean and Middle Eastern countries (Kaunert and Léonard 2011).

Counter-terrorism and the financial instruments of the ENP

The implementation of the ENP has been supported by financial instruments. An analysis of those confirms the general lack of ambition when it comes to operational cooperation between the EU and its neighbours in the field of counter-terrorism. Between 2007 and 2013, the financial instrument supporting the ENP was called the 'European Neighbourhood Partnership Instrument' (ENPI). It built on the experience of the previous funding programmes: MEDA (for the Southern Mediterranean countries) and TACIS (for the Eastern European countries). However, counter-terrorism was arguably not identified as a priority area. Article 2 of Regulation (EC) No 1638/2006 listed 'areas of cooperation', among which area 'r' was described as follows:

> supporting reform and strengthening capacity in the field of justice and home affairs, including issues such as asylum, migration and readmission, and the fight against, and prevention of trafficking in human beings as well as terrorism and organised crime, including its financing, money laundering and tax fraud.

Writing in 2010, Wennerholm et al. (2010: 16) argued that, in practice, 'the ENPI [...] [had] never been used for such measures in countries covered by the European Neighbourhood Partnership'.

The ENPI has been replaced by the European Neighbourhood Instrument (ENI), which has received a budget of more than EUR 15 billion for the period 2014–2020. However, Regulation (EU) No 232/2014, which established the ENI, does not mention 'terrorism' once. At most, can it be inferred that terrorism might be alluded to in Article 2.2(j), which establishes the priorities for Union support as follows: 'promoting confidence-building, good neighbourly relations and other measures contributing to security in all its forms and the prevention and settlement of conflicts, including protracted conflicts'. Therefore, this analysis of the financial instruments of the ENP confirms that counter-terrorism cooperation between the EU and its neighbours has mainly consisted of political dialogue and that there is no plan to spend significant amounts of money to foster more practical cooperation.

Recent developments

The terrorist attacks in France, in January 2015, gave a new impetus to the development of the EU's counter-terrorism policy, including its external dimension. The so-called Riga Joint Statement underlined that '[the] joint efforts of the internal and external dimension in fighting terrorism, and in particular the phenomenon of the foreign terrorist fighters, is crucial' (Council of the European Union 2015a: 7). The Council adopted an EU Regional Strategy for Syria and Iraq, as well as the ISIL/Da'esh threat (Council of the European Union 2015c; 2016) (Koenig, this volume). At the Foreign Affairs Council meeting of 9 February 2015, it was decided to '[conduct] targeted and upgraded security and counter-terrorism dialogues' with several of the southern ENP partners – namely Algeria, Egypt, Israel, Jordan, Morocco, Lebanon and Tunisia – in addition to 'developing counter-terrorism action plans starting with Morocco, Tunisia, Algeria, Egypt, Jordan and Lebanon, including measures to dissuade and disrupt foreign terrorist fighters' travel as well as to manage their return' (Council of the European Union 2015d: 7). It was also announced that various capacity-building projects would be launched in MENA (Middle East and North Africa) countries, which could also get involved with the work of the EU's Radicalization Awareness Network (Council of the European Union 2015d: 8). Against this backdrop, in September 2015, the EU held the first so-called 'reinforced political dialogue on security and fight against terrorism' with Tunisia (Délégation de l'Union Européenne en Tunisie 2015). Both parties had been keen to deepen their cooperation after the terrorist attacks that took place in the Bardo museum, in Tunis and in Sousse, in March and June 2015. Moreover, discussions on how best to deal with foreign fighters have been ongoing and have included some of the southern ENP partners. For example, the third Euro-Mediterranean Foreign Fighters meeting, which took place in Baghdad in October 2015, was notably attended by senior officials from Algeria, Egypt, Jordan, Lebanon and Tunisia (National Security Adviser of Iraq/EU Counter-Terrorism Coordinator 2015).

The higher saliency of the terrorist threat and the renewed emphasis on cooperating with neighbouring countries can also be seen in the 2015 Review of the Neighbourhood Policy. This document notably emphasises that '[there] will be a new focus on stepping up work with our partners on security sector reform, conflict prevention, counter-terrorism and anti-radicalisation policies, in full compliance with international human rights law (European Commission/High Representative of the Union for Foreign Affairs and Security Policy 2015: 3). It is envisaged that there will be a greater focus on security, including terrorism and radicalisation, in the ENP in future. At the time of writing, it was not yet possible to assess the extent to which these declarations were to be implemented in practice.

Challenges to counter-terrorism cooperation between the EU and its neighbours

As explained above, to date, counter-terrorism cooperation between the EU and its neighbours has overall remained rather modest. Also, it has mainly consisted of political dialogue, especially with the southern ENP partners. There are several reasons that explain this persistent lack of significant progress. Some of those are general, as they concern difficulties affecting the development and implementation of the ENP as a whole, whereas others are specific to the policy sector of counter-terrorism.

First, there has been a widespread perception that the ENP is an EU policy, which has been imposed by the EU on its neighbours. In the South, most Arab governments have felt excluded from what they largely perceive to be 'a policy adopted by the EU for its neighbours not with them' (League of Arab States 2014: 9). In response to this common criticism, the EU has recently attempted to adopt a more inclusive approach. This was notably evidenced by the fact that the ENP Review was debated within the two regional components of the ENP, the Union for the Mediterranean and the Eastern Partnership in spring 2015 (Delcour 2015). This is likely to encourage a greater sense of ownership of the ENP among the EU's neighbours, although one should not overestimate their influence on the actual contents of the policies given the wide range of stakeholders included in the review. Second, the ENP has generally been weakened by the contradictions that characterise the EU's approach to its neighbours (Pace 2014; Noutcheva et al. 2013; Biscop 2010; Balzacq 2009; Youngs 2003). The EU has sought to simultaneously fulfil its security objectives and promote its values, such as democracy, by encouraging reforms. However, these two objectives can sometimes conflict, since, for example, reforms can lead to instability and insecurity. Likewise, the EU and its Member States have sometimes sought to cooperate on security issues with regimes that may be lacking as far as democratic standards are concerned. Egypt is a case in point. The political dialogue between the EU and Egypt under the ENP has been *de facto* suspended since 2011. This has not prevented various heads of state or governments of various EU Member States – including Germany, France, the United Kingdom and Italy – and the representatives of several EU institutions, such as the President of the European Council, Donald Tusk, and the High Representative of the Union for Foreign Affairs and Security Policy, Federica Mogherini, to meet with representatives of el-Sisi's regime, to discuss the fight against terrorism and the development of security cooperation – in the context of the war in Syria and the rise of ISIS. Moreover, these possible contradictions among the EU's objectives are compounded by the existence, at times, of divergences between the EU's principles and the national interests of some individual Member States (Zajac 2015).

Concerning the challenges that are specific to the terrorism domain, one of them is that counter-terrorism is a particularly sensitive policy, which is very tightly linked to sovereignty. This notably explains that trust can take a long time to develop, while traditional, bilateral channels of cooperation persist or are even preferred to cooperation with the EU. According to Wolff, when it comes to counter-terrorism cooperation, states prefer to cooperate at a bilateral level, such as between France, Spain and North African countries, notably Morocco and Algeria. Historical relationships and trust between the services have proved to be key elements of bilateral cooperation (Wolff 2009: 150).

The enduring importance of these bilateral relations was again recently illustrated by the launch of police training programmes by the German and British governments in Egypt, Libya and Tunisia (German Parliament 2015; Die Zeit 2015; United Kingdom 2015).

Another problem that has hindered the development of counter-terrorism cooperation between the EU and its neighbours, particularly in the South, is the persistence of significant differences between their respective domestic conditions and policies. First, the lack of institutional capacity in the neighbouring countries, especially in the South, has been a significant problem. For example, cooperation in tackling the financing of terrorism has faced important challenges, because of problems of compliance in the southern ENP countries, which have themselves resulted from a lack of financial and technical expertise (Kaunert and Léonard 2011). There have also been persistent differences regarding the general approach to terrorism. The EU has favoured a criminal justice approach to terrorism, whereas the ENP countries have generally favoured a military response (MacKenzie et al. 2013). Operational counter-terrorism cooperation has also been severely restricted with most ENP partners, with some exceptions in the East, such as Moldova and more recently Ukraine, because of the discrepancy between the data protection standards in the EU and those in the partner countries (Kaunert and Léonard 2011; MacKenzie et al. 2013). EU agencies, such as Europol, are only allowed to sign operational agreements with partner countries that fulfil minimum data protection standards. All these obstacles to the development of closer counter-terrorism cooperation between the EU and its neighbours are significant and likely to persist in the foreseeable future, especially in the southern neighbourhood.

Conclusions

Given the transnational nature of the terrorist threat, the EU has sought to develop counter-terrorism cooperation with countries in its neighbourhood. This has been challenging given the persistence of the divide between internal security and external security in the EU. To date, counter-terrorism cooperation between the EU and its neighbours has mainly consisted of political dialogue. Operational cooperation has been very modest for various reasons, including the priority given to bilateral relations and the significant differences between the EU and its partners regarding institutional capacity, the approach to terrorism and data protection standards. It has only been developed with some of the eastern ENP partners, such as Moldova and Ukraine, and has remained virtually non existent with southern ENP partners. Given the important links of the current terrorist threat to the Middle East, the potential benefits of counter-terrorism cooperation for the EU are greater with its southern neighbours than with its eastern neighbours. However, for the reasons already mentioned, counter-terrorism cooperation with the southern ENP countries has been restricted to political dialogue. Any major change in that respect is unlikely given the intractable character of the obstacles to the establishment of operational cooperation.

Notes

1. Although Belarus takes part in the ENP, no Action Plan for Belarus had been drawn up at the time of writing.
2. Full texts of the agreements can be accessed at www.europol.europa.eu/partners-agreements, accessed on 23 January 2017.
3. Full texts of the agreements can be accessed at www.eurojust.europa.eu/doclibrary/Eurojust-framework/Pages/agreements-concluded-by-eurojust.aspx?Page=1, accessed on 23 January 2017.
4. Full texts of the agreements can be accessed at http://frontex.europa.eu/partners/third-countries/, accessed on 23 January 2017.
5. There were no Action Plans in force for Libya and Syria at the time of writing.

References

Argomaniz, J. (2011) *Post-9/11 European Union Counter-Terrorism: Politics, Polity and Policies*, London: Routledge.
Balzacq, T. (ed.) (2009) *The External Dimension of EU Justice and Home Affairs: Governance, Neighbours, Security*, Basingstoke: Palgrave Macmillan.
Bicchi, F. (2011) 'The Union for the Mediterranean, or the Changing Context of Euro-Mediterranean Relations', *Mediterranean Politics* 16(1): 3–19.
Biscop, S. (2008) 'The European Security Strategy in Context: A Comprehensive Trend', in Biscop, S. and Anderson, J. (eds.) *The EU and the European Security Strategy: Forging a Global Europe*, London: Routledge, 5–20.

Biscop, S. (2010) 'The ENP, Security, and Democracy in the Context of the European Security Strategy', in Whitman, R. and Wolff, S. (eds.) *The European Neighbourhood Policy in Perspective: Context, Implementation and Impact*, Basingstoke: Palgrave Macmillan, 73–88.

Bossong, R. (2013) *The Evolution of EU Counter-Terrorism: European Security Policy After 9/11*, London: Routledge.

Commission of the European Communities (2003) *Communication from the Commission to the Council and the European Parliament: Wider Europe—Neighbourhood: A New Framework for Relations with our Eastern and Southern Neighbours*, COM(2003) 104, Brussels.

Council of the European Union (2004) *Declaration on Combating Terrorism*, 7906/04, Brussels.

Council of the European Union (2005) *The European Union Counter-Terrorism Strategy*, 14469/4/05, Brussels.

Council of the European Union (2009) Joint Declaration of the Prague Eastern Partnership Summit, 8435/09 (Presse 78), Prague, 7 May 2009, Brussels.

Council of the European Union (2012) 'Council Decision 2012/392/CFSP of 16 July 2012 on the European Union CSDP mission in Niger (EUCAP Sahel Niger)', *Official Journal of the EU*, L 187/48, 17 July, Brussels.

Council of the European Union (2015a) *Informal Meeting of Justice and Home Affairs Ministers in Riga on 29 and 30 January 2015*, 5855/15, Brussels.

Council of the European Union (2015b) *Meeting with Eurojust Contact Points and Liaison Magistrates appointed by Member States—Outcome Report*, 6417/15, Brussels.

Council of the European Union (2015c) *Council Conclusions on the EU Regional Strategy for Syria and Iraq as well as the Da'esh Threat*, 7267/15, Brussels.

Council of the European Union (2015d) *Outcome of the Council Meeting, 3367th Council Meeting*, Foreign Affairs, 6044/15, Brussels, 9 February.

Council of the European Union (2016) *Council Conclusions on the EU Regional Strategy for Syria and Iraq as well as the Da'esh Threat*, 9105/16, Brussels.

Delcour, L. (2015) 'The 2015 ENP Review: Beyond Stocktaking, the Need for a Political Strategy', *College of Europe Policy Brief* 1.15, College of Europe, Brugges.

Délégation de l'Union Européenne en Tunisie (2015) 'Communiqué de Presse—Premier Dialogue Politique Renforcé "Sécurité et Lute Contre le Terrorisme": l'UE et la Tunisie Renforcent Leur Coopération', Délégation de l'Union Européenne en Tunisie, Tunis.

The Economist (2014) 'Europe's Ring of Fire', 20 September. www.economist.com/news/europe/21618846-european-unions-neighbourhood-more-troubled-ever-europes-ring-fire, accessed 10 September 2015.

Euro-Mediterranean Partnership (1995) *Final Declaration of the Barcelona Euro-Mediterranean Ministerial Conference of 27 and 28 November 1995 and its Work Programme*, 27–28 November 1995.

Euro-Mediterranean Partnership (2005) '10th Anniversary Euro-Mediterranean Summit (Barcelona, 27–28 November 2005)', EURO-MED 2/05, Brussels.

European Commission (2003) 'Communication from the Commission to the Council and the European Parliament – Wider Europe – Neighbourhood: A New Framework for Relations with our Eastern and Southern Neighbours', COM(2003) 104, Brussels.

European Commission (2010) *The EU Internal Security Strategy in Action: Five Steps Towards a More Secure Europe*, COM(2010) 673, European Commission, Brussels.

European Commission (2014) *Commission Implementing Decision of 25.8.2014 on the Annual Action Programme 2014—Part 1 in Favour of the ENI South Countries to be Financed from the General Budget of the European Union*, C(2014) 5948, Brussels.

European Commission (2015) *The European Agenda on Security*, COM(2015) 185, Brussels.

European Commission/High Representative of the Union for Foreign Affairs and Security Policy (2015) *Review of the European Neighbourhood Policy*, JOIN(2015) 50, Brussels, 18 November.

European Council (2003) 'A Secure Europe in a Better World—European Security Strategy', Brussels, 12 December.

German Parliament (2015) 'New Measures on the Part of the Federal Criminal Police Office and the Federal Police to Assist Egyptian Police Authorities', *Bundestag Printed Paper* 18/4784, 15 May. http://statewatch.org/news/2015/may/germany-bundestag-new-measures-to-assist-Egyptian-police.pdf, accessed 23 January 2017.

Ioannides, I. (2014) 'Inside-Out and Outside-In: EU Security in the Neighbourhood', *The International Spectator* 49(1): 113–132.

Kaunert, C. (2010a) 'The External Dimension of EU Counter-Terrorism Relations: Competences, Interests, and Institutions', *Terrorism and Political Violence* 22(1): 41–61.

Kaunert, C. (2010b) 'Europol and EU Counterterrorism: International Security Actorness in the External Dimension', *Studies in Conflict and Terrorism* 33(7): 652–671.

Kaunert, C. (2010c) *European Internal Security: Towards Supranational Governance in the Area of Freedom, Security and Justice?*, Manchester: Manchester University Press.

Kaunert, C. and Léonard, S. (2011) 'EU Counterterrorism and the European Neighbourhood Policy: An Appraisal of the Southern Dimension', *Terrorism and Political Violence* 23(2): 286–309.

Keohane, D. (2005) *The EU and Counter-Terrorism*, London: Centre for European Reform.

League of Arab States (2014) 'Evaluation of European Union Policies towards the Arab World', Political Sector Europe and Europe-Arab Cooperation Department, LEA, June.

Léonard, S. (2015) 'Border Controls as a Dimension of the European Union's Counter-Terrorism Policy: A Critical Assessment', *Intelligence and National Security* 30(2–3): 306–332.

MacKenzie, A., Kaunert, C. and Léonard, S. (2013) 'EU Counterterrorism and the Southern Mediterranean Countries after the Arab Spring: New Potential for Cooperation?', *Democracy and Security* 9(1–2): 137–156.

Mahncke, D. and Monar, J. (eds.) (2006) *International Terrorism: A European Response to a Global Threat?*, Brussels: P.I.E. Peter Lang.

National Security Adviser of Iraq/EU Counter-Terrorism Coordinator (2015) 'Joint Press Release by the National Security Adviser of Iraq and the EU Counter-Terrorism Coordinator at the Occasion of the Third Euro-Mediterranean Foreign Fighters Meeting', Baghdad, 27–28 October. http://eeas.europa.eu/archives/delegations/iraq/press_corner/all_news/news/2015/31102015_01_en.htm, accessed 25 January 2017.

Noutcheva, G., Pomorska, K. and Bosse, G. (2013) *The EU and its Neighbours: Values versus Security in European Foreign Policy*, Manchester: Manchester University Press.

Oliveira Martins, B. and Ferreira-Pereira, L. (2012) 'Stepping Inside? CSDP Missions and EU Counter-Terrorism', *European Security* 21(4): 537–556.

Pace, M. (2014) 'The EU's Interpretation of the "Arab Uprisings": Understanding the Different Visions about Democratic Change in EU-MENA Relations', *Journal of Common Market Studies* 52(5): 969–984.

Spence, D. (ed.) (2007) *The European Union and Terrorism*, London: John Harper.

United Kingdom (2015) '2010 to 2015 Government Policy: Peace and Stability in the Middle East and North Africa', *Policy Paper*, updated 8 May. www.gov.uk/government/publications/2010-to-2015-government-policy-peace-and-stability-in-the-middle-east-and-north-africa/2010-to-2015-government-policy-peace-and-stability-in-the-middle-east-and-north-africa, accessed 23 January 2017.

Wennerholm, P., Brattberg, E. and Rhinard, M. (2010) 'The EU as a Counter-Terrorism Actor Abroad: Finding Opportunities, Overcoming Constraints', *EPC Issue Paper* 60, European Policy Centre, Brussels.

Wolff, S. (2009) 'The Mediterranean Dimension of EU Counter-Terrorism', *Journal of European Integration* 31(1): 137–156.

Youngs, R. (2003) 'European Approaches to Security in the Mediterranean', *Middle East Journal* 57(3): 414–431.

Zajac, J. (2015) 'The EU in the Mediterranean: Between Its International Identity and Member States' Interests', *European Foreign Affairs Review* 20(1): 65–82.

Die Zeit (2015) 'Bundespolizei eröffnet ständiges Büro in Tunesien', *Zeit Online*, 28 August. www.zeit.de/politik/deutschland/2015-08/nordafrika-bundespolizei-tunesien-schleuser-terroristen, accessed 23 January 2017.

37
AID IN THE EUROPEAN NEIGHBOURHOOD POLICY

Fabienne Bossuyt, Hrant Kostanyan, Jan Orbie and BrunoVandecasteele[1]

Introduction

This chapter addresses the aid dimension of the European Neighbourhood Policy (ENP). Following a brief contextualization of the European Union's (EU's) assistance under the ENP, the chapter provides a concise and comprehensive overview of the aid flows from the EU to its eastern and southern neighbourhoods. These two regions have gradually moved up the list of EU aid beneficiaries and now receive a remarkably high amount of aid resources from the EU: in 2014, more than 20 per cent of the Official Development Aid (ODA) granted by the EU institutions went to the 16 ENP countries, compared to 16 per cent in 2007 and 11 per cent in 2000.[2] Thus, although existing research on this topic is relatively limited (Bicchi 2014; Holden 2008; Ratzmann 2012; Reynaert 2011), it is highly relevant to examine aid through the ENP within the wider context of EU external policies, all the more because of the increasingly prominent place of ENP countries among the EU's ODA beneficiaries.

Between development and enlargement models

As mentioned above, an increasingly high proportion of EU aid is directed towards the 16 ENP countries. From a development perspective, this has frequently been criticized (Orbie et al. 2016; Furness and Gänzle 2016). In principle, the EU has committed to prioritizing the least-developed countries (European Commission 2011). Although the ENP beneficiaries do not belong to the group of poorest countries, they are obviously of key interest to the EU. Apart from their strategic importance for the EU, another reason why they receive such a large part of EU aid is that, in the neighbourhood, the Member States have delegated much of their activities to the EU level. This is in contrast to the Global South, where the EU is often 'just another donor' beside traditionally strong Member State donors, such as the United Kingdom, Sweden, the Netherlands, Germany and France. The latter are less actively present in the neighbourhood, where the EU institutions play a more prominent role. This is also reflected in the amount of ODA that the Member States provide to the ENP countries. In 2014, only 5 per cent of the total ODA of the EU-28 went to the ENP countries,[3] compared to more than 20 per cent in the case of the EU institutions. Moreover, this percentage has remained stable over the years for the Member States (ibid., period 2000–2014), while it has significantly increased in the case of the EU institutions, as mentioned above.

This first observation already indicates that, although aid is a key dimension of the ENP, it sometimes sits uneasily with the EU's development policy. The latter has traditionally focused on the countries of the African, Caribbean and Pacific (ACP) group, and on the countries in sub-Saharan Africa. Roughly speaking, two models of EU aid can be distinguished. Each of them has a distinctive background and finality as originated in the history of European integration. On the one hand, the 'Lomé model' focuses on the interaction between trade and aid, with the purpose of economic development. The idea behind the Lomé model is that poverty should be addressed by providing exclusive trade and aid benefits. The ACP countries received preferential access to the European market, and the European Development Fund (EDF) provided aid that was exclusively targeted to these countries (Montana 2003).

Interestingly, a 'light version' of this Lomé model has been applied to the EU's southern ENP countries. In the 1970s, the EU concluded a series of preferential trade agreements with the Maghreb and Mashreq countries as part of the EU's Global Mediterranean Policy (Mishalani et al. 1981). This was accompanied with financial assistance aimed mostly at supporting economic development. The special relationship with the Southern Mediterranean countries was reinvigorated in 1995 with the Euro-Mediterranean Partnership, also known as the Barcelona Process, which included an economic and financial partnership involving preferential free trade agreements, as well as additional funding through the MEDA (*Mesures d'accompagnement*) programme, then a newly established fund exclusively for the Southern Mediterranean region. The fund was targeted explicitly at instigating liberal economic reform and integrating the countries economically with Europe, premised on the idea that economic development is the key driver of poverty reduction (Holden 2008).

On the other hand, there is the 'enlargement model', which focuses on extending the EU *acquis* towards the ENP countries. It finds its origins in the process that led up to the 2004–2007 'big bang' enlargement of the EU. Following the dissolution of the Soviet Union in 1991, the EU extended the already existing assistance programmes 'Poland and Hungary Assistance for Restructuring their Economies' (PHARE) to those countries in Central and Eastern Europe likely to join the EU in the medium-to-long term, notably Slovakia, the Czech Republic, Romania, Bulgaria, Slovenia, Estonia, Lithuania and Latvia. The main purpose was to facilitate the transition from communist systems towards democratic and market-oriented economies (Hughes 2007). This would be done by integrating these countries into the economic and political space of the EU. For the (other) countries of the former Soviet Union, the EU established the 'Technical Assistance to the Commonwealth of Independent States' (TACIS) programme. TACIS is a 'light' version of the enlargement/PHARE model, aimed at facilitating political and economic transition, based on the EU's model, without providing a prospect of membership to the EU (ibid.).

After the launch of the ENP in 2004, bringing together the EU's southern and eastern neighbours under one umbrella framework, the financial instruments for both regions were merged in 2007, with the onset of the new multi annual financial framework. The European Neighbourhood and Partnership Instrument (ENPI) – as well as its successor, the European Neighbourhood Instrument (ENI) – encompasses elements of both 'southern development' and 'enlargement *acquis*' models, although the latter clearly became dominant. Indeed, the basic thrust of the ENP is 'enlargement without institutions' (Kelley 2006), which implies a focus on exporting the EU *acquis* with a view to integration in the European economic and political space, ultimately fostering regional stability and avoiding new dividing lines (Commission of the European Communities 2003).

The influence of both 'models' on ENPI/ENI is also clearly visible at the level of the instrument's aid modalities, in that it relies both on typical enlargement assistance modalities, in particular Twinning, SIGMA[4] and TAIEX,[5] and on typical development aid modalities, namely project-based grants, budget support and concessional loans. Arguably, the imperative of regional stability has become even more important in recent years. In the context of the conflicts in Ukraine, Syria and Libya – as well as the refugee crisis – regional stability has become an explicit objective of the ENP – as can also be witnessed in the 2015 ENP review (Furness and Schäfer 2015). This also influences the spending of aid budgets. As such, it seems that a 'foreign policy model' has become more important.

This resonates with the broader trend of securitization of EU development policy. Despite commitments to poverty reduction and the Millennium Development Goals (and post-2015 the Sustainable Development Goals) as the main objectives, EU development policy has increasingly become aligned with foreign and security policy objectives (Del Biondo et al. 2012). The most obvious example of a diversion of EU development assistance is the financing of the African Peace Facility (APF) for peacekeeping and peace enforcement with money from the EDF. In addition, large amounts of EU funding have gone to strategically important countries, such as Afghanistan, Pakistan and Iraq. At the OECD-DAC, which coordinates the statistical analysis of western donors' aid budgets, several EU Member States have insisted on broadening the definition of ODA to allow for more types of security-related expenses. Institutionally, the creation of the European External Action Service (EEAS) may also enlarge the impact of foreign policy considerations on development policy. The latter was previously located within the European Commission and now must be formulated together with the EEAS. In fact, a very similar evolution could be noticed with the ENP (Furness and Schäfer 2015).

Thus, it seems that foreign policy interests have become more important, both in EU development and neighbourhood policy. However, we must be careful not to draw too generalized conclusions. Beyond general trends, a large diversity of aid spending can be observed regarding the instruments used to finance assistance to the ENP countries. An overview of these instruments is provided in the section below. In the subsequent paragraphs, we will discuss how aid differs across countries, aid modalities, sectors and geographical scope (bilateral, regional and neighbourhood-wide).

Overview of instruments

The ENP, with the Union for the Mediterranean (UfM) and the Eastern Partnership (EaP) as its regional components, has been the overarching framework through which the EU conducts bilateral and multilateral relations with its neighbours since 2004. The lion's share of aid allocated to the ENP countries comes from the ENI,[6] which is used exclusively designed for the 16 ENP countries. The EU's approach of aid allocation for this instrument is incentive-based and differentiated. The latter implies that the EU differentiates its levels of support by tailoring its assistance to the countries' contexts based on five specific criteria: (1) needs, such as level of development and population, (2) progress in political, economic and social reforms, (3) commitment to advancing democracy, (4) the level of cooperation with the EU and (5) absorption capacity of the recipient country (Regulation (EU) No 232/2014). The incentive-based approach means that the EU intends to increase its support for those countries that are genuinely committed to implementing reforms.

The distribution of aid follows the multiannual financial framework of 2014–2020, which is divided into two programming cycles: 2014–2017 and 2018–2020. The ENI regulation provides some flexibility by allowing indicative financial allocations for each country to range up to 20 per cent of the foreseen allocations. For the period 2014–2020, the ENI has been allocated EUR15.4 billion (European Commission 2013b). This is a further increase compared to the EUR11.2 billion allocated through the ENPI to ENP countries in the period 2007–2013, which already was a 32 per cent increase compared to the TACIS and MEDA aid provided to these countries between 2000 and 2006 (European Commission 2014).

Funding through the ENI can be divided into four categories: bilateral support for ENP countries; support for regional programmes in the southern and eastern neighbourhoods through thematic platforms or regional dialogues; ENP-wide horizontal programmes, such as the Neighbourhood Investment Facility (NIF) and Erasmus+; and Cross Border Cooperation Programmes. These programmes are outlined in detail below (see also Tables 37.1–37.4).

Other EU external assistance instruments with a thematic or worldwide coverage, such as the European Instrument for Democracy and Human Rights (EIDHR) and the Instrument contributing to Stability and Peace (IfSP), are also used to assist ENP partner countries. The most widely used of these is the EIDHR, although its overall budget is relatively limited. As the name suggests, this instrument finances activities designed to promote democracy and the respect for human rights. The EU also promotes democracy through the European Endowment for Democracy, but most funds for this instrument are provided by the EU Member States and not by the European Commission. The EIDHR is the EU's specific tool for providing financial support to civil society actors engaged in issues of human rights and democratic development. Unlike the EU's other international cooperation instruments, EIDHR operates without the need for consent from the target countries' governments. The EIDHR funds are disbursed mainly through calls for proposals initiated by the European Commission's headquarters in Brussels – at global level for (cross)regional macro-projects – and by EU delegations – at local level for micro-projects (called Country-Based Support Schemes). A part of the funds is distributed without calls for proposals, *inter alia*, for election observation, but also for individual grants to human rights activists in the countries where they are under most pressure.

For the period 2014–2017, the EU has allocated EUR337.2 million to the EIDHR's Country Based Support Scheme (CBSS), which takes up the largest share of EIDHR's funding (European Commission 2013a). EUR76.9 million has been committed to the ENP countries, which is about one quarter of the total CBSS budget (ibid.). This is a slight decrease compared to 2011–2013, when the ENP countries accounted for about one third of the CBSS budget (European Commission 2010a). In terms of allocations at country level, the EU tends to prioritize countries where the impact of the EIDHR activities has more chance of success, which means that more authoritarian countries such as Azerbaijan and Algeria are allocated less funding than countries with more liberal governments such as Georgia, Israel and Morocco. When it comes to the focus of the projects, research on EIDHR has shown that most of the funding goes to projects centred on relatively uncontroversial issues, such as women's and children's rights (Bicchi and Voltolini 2013).

Finally, the EU has also been providing a substantial amount of humanitarian assistance in its southern and eastern neighbourhoods. As the so-called 'ring of friends' around the EU (Commission of the European Communities 2003) has become more like a 'ring of fire' (*The Economist* 2014), plagued by conflict and war, it is perhaps not surprising that several of the ENP countries are currently among the main beneficiaries of EU humanitarian assistance. Since the outbreak of the ongoing war in Syria in 2011, Syria has been the top beneficiary of EU humanitarian aid. According to Commission calculations, the EU together with its Member States have so far mobilized EUR4.4 billion for humanitarian assistance to Syrians within the country and to Syrian refugees in neighbouring countries (European Commission 2015d). As such, Lebanon and Jordan have been receiving substantial amounts of EU humanitarian assistance for coping with the massive inflows of Syrian refugees. In Libya, meanwhile, the EU has been providing emergency aid to the hundreds of thousands of civilians affected by protracted armed violence involving tribal clashes between militias (European Commission 2015b) and due to the rise of ISIS/Da'esh.

Aid in the ENP

Among the eastern ENP countries, Ukraine has been heading the list of beneficiaries since the conflict in eastern Ukraine erupted in 2014. So far, the European Commission has provided EUR42 million to support Ukrainians affected by the conflict, including refugees in Russia and Belarus (European Commission 2015e). Another major beneficiary of EU humanitarian aid in the neighbourhood is Palestine. In 2015, for instance, the Occupied Palestinian territories received EUR25 million in humanitarian funding from the European Commission (European Commission 2015c). EU humanitarian aid for Palestine consists mostly of 'emergency support to people affected by eviction and/or demolitions, provision of basic services, legal assistance and advocacy for the upholding and respect for International Humanitarian Law and Human Rights Law' (ibid). Another ENP country where the EU has a long tradition of providing humanitarian aid is Algeria, where the EU gives support to the Sahrawi refugees. In 2015, European Commission funding for the Sahrawi refugees in Algeria amounted to EUR10 million (European Commission 2015a).

Diversity in the use of aid instruments

Based on official EU documents[7] as well as official ODA data from the OECD-DAC database,[8] several trends can be observed with regard to countries/regions, aid modalities, sectors and geographical scope (bilateral, regional and neighbourhood-wide instruments). It is also worth noting that the ENP includes aid for cross-border cooperation with non-ENP countries, that is, EU members or Russia. The above-mentioned trends are discussed in the next sections.

ENP countries

Generally, about two thirds of ENPI/ENI funds have been committed to the ten southern neighbourhood partner countries and one third to the six EaP countries (see Figure 37.1 below). This division has remained stable over the past years. When calculated per capita (relative to the GDP/capita (PPP)), however, the EU's funding for the two regions is roughly similar, with the

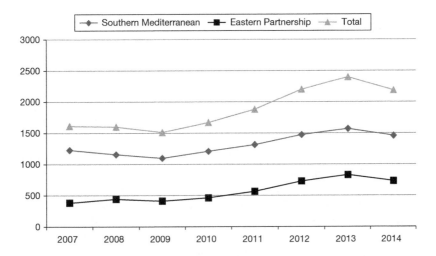

Figure 37.1 ENPI/ENI bilateral and regional allocations (in EUR million) (2007–2014)

Source: Authors' compilation based on figures from the European Commission, DEVCO, http://ec.europa.eu/europeaid/.

EaP region slightly outnumbering the MENA region. For the whole ENP region, a clear increase in aid allocations followed the Arab uprisings in 2011.

Within the eastern and southern neighbourhoods, there are substantial differences in the aid disbursements at country level.[9] In 2014, Ukraine (EUR 490 million), Palestine (EUR 481 million) and Tunisia (EUR 452 million) were the top recipients, while other countries received only a fraction of these sums (for example, Azerbaijan EUR 12 million, Belarus EUR 28 million). When calculated per capita, we see a slightly different picture. For example, in 2014, EU ODA amounted to 2.07 per cent of GDP/capita in Palestine, 1.08 per cent of GDP/capita in Moldova and 0.59 per cent of GDP/capita in Georgia; this stands in sharp contrast with countries like Azerbaijan (0.01 per cent of GDP/capita), Belarus (0.02 per cent of GDP/capita), Egypt (0.03 per cent of GDP/capita) and Libya (0.04 per cent of GDP/capita).

Aid modalities

About 62 per cent of the ENPI/ENI funds are allocated to bilateral assistance. Most of this is granted through budget support, which is also commonly applied under the EDF and the Development Cooperation Instrument (DCI) – the EU's two main development assistance instruments. The remaining ENPI/ENI funds are provided through technical assistance, including through Twinning and other institution-building tools, such as TAIEX and SIGMA. The exact share differs strongly between the ENP countries, in line with their different needs and changing situations. In the case of Moldova, for instance, over 50 per cent of the allocated funding in the period 2007–2011 was reserved for budget support and the other 50 per cent was for Twinning and other technical assistance projects (Ratzmann 2012). In Egypt, the EU has scaled down the use of budget support in recent years due to the government's non-compliance with the agreed conditions and its lack of reform implementation (European Commission 2014). The European Commission argues that it uses budget support to give ownership to the countries and to 'buy' reforms from the neighbouring governments. The counterargument is that once financial assistance enters in the budget it is very difficult to trace, which is problematic considering that many of the ENP countries are still faced with high levels of corruption (Chernikov 2014). Since 2007, the EU has also made use of so-called blending mechanisms to assist the ENP region. Through the NIF, grants from the European Commission and the EU Member States are 'blended' with loans from European Financial Institutions. The 2015 ENP review suggests that the use of blending of finance assistance to the ENP countries will be enhanced in the coming years (European Commission and High Representative of the Union for Foreign Affairs and Security Policy 2015).

Sectors

Looking at the sectors supported under bilateral ENI assistance, there is a large diversity in terms of sectors supported, which fits with the EU's efforts to increase ownership and tailor-made aid (see Table 37.1 below). Some differences can be identified between the eastern and the southern neighbourhoods. For the southern neighbourhood, most support goes to economy-related issues (including diversification, labour market, private sector), support for democracy, good governance and rule of law, and the energy sector. By contrast, in the Eastern Partnership countries, most assistance goes to the strengthening of the justice and police sectors, public administration reform and regional/local development and agriculture. Most ENP countries receive bilateral assistance for civil society support, but the Eastern Partnership countries are allocated less funding for civil society support than the southern ENP countries, where this assistance amounts to approx. 20 per cent.

Table 37.1 EU bilateral support to ENP countries[1,2]

	Priorities for the first period of 2014–2020	2014–2020	2011–2013	2007–2010
Armenia	• Private sector development 35% • Public administration reform 25% • Justice sector reform complementary 20% • Capacity development and institution building 15% • Civil society 5%	EUR252,000,000– EUR308,000,000	EUR157,300,000 • Democratic structures and good governance; • Trade and investment, regulatory alignment and reform; • Socio-economic reform and sustainable development.	EUR98,400,000 • Reform of the justice system; • Economic growth and employment; • Improvements in basic public services.
Azerbaijan	• Regional and rural development 40% • Justice sector reform 20% • Education and skills development 20% • Capacity development and institution building 15% • Civil society 5%	EUR139,000,000– EUR169,000,000	EUR122,500,000 • Democratic structures and good governance; • Socio-economic reform and sustainable development, trade and investment, regulatory approximation and reform; • PCA and ENP AP implementation, including in the area of energy security, mobility and security.	EUR92,000,000 • Democratic development and good governance; • Socio-economic reform (emphasis on regulatory approximation with EU *acquis*), fight against poverty, administrative capacity building; • Legislative and economic reforms in transport, energy and environment sectors.
Belarus	• Social inclusion 30% • Environment 25% • Local and regional economic development 25% • Civil society 10% • Capacity development 10%	EUR129,000,000– EUR158,000,000	EUR56,690,000 • Good governance and people-to-people contacts; • Economic modernization.	EUR30,000,000 • Social and economic development; • Democratic development and good governance.
Georgia	• Public administration reform 25% • Agriculture and rural development 30% • Justice reform 25% • Capacity development and civil society 20%	EUR610,000,000– EUR746,000,000	EUR180,290,000 • Democratic development, rule of law and governance; • Economic development and ENP AP implementation; • Poverty reduction and social reforms; • Peaceful settlement of internal conflicts.	EUR120,400,000 • Democratic development, rule of law and governance; • Economic development and ENP AP implementation; • Poverty reduction and social reforms; • Peaceful settlement of internal conflicts.

(*Continued*)

Table 37.1 (continued)

	Priorities for the first period of 2014–2020	2014–2020	2011–2013	2007–2010
Moldova	• Public administration reform 30% • Agriculture and rural development 30% • Police reform and border management 20% • Capacity development and institution building 15% • Civil society 5%	EUR610,000,000–EUR746,000,000	EUR273,140,000 • Good governance, rule of law and fundamental freedoms; • Social and human development; • Trade and sustainable development.	EUR209,700,000 • Democratic development and good governance; • Regulatory reform and administrative capacity building; • Poverty reduction and economic growth.
Ukraine	Because of special circumstances, there are no priorities identified for Ukraine.	Up to EUR1 billion	EUR470,050,000 • Good governance and the rule of law; • Facilitation of entry into force of Association Agreement (including a DCFTA); • Sustainable Development.	EUR494,000,000 • Democratic development and good governance; • Regulatory reform and administrative capacity building; • Infrastructure Development.
Algeria	• Justice reform and strengthening of citizen participation in public life 25% • Labour market reform and employment creation 30% • Management and diversification of the economy 30% • Capacity development and civil society 15%	EUR221,000,000–EUR270,000,000	EUR172,000,000 • Environmental protection; • Protection and valorization of cultural heritage; • Socio-economic and sustainable development; • Reform of the transport sector; • Fisheries and aquaculture; • Preparation for Association Agreement.	EUR220,000,000 • Reform of the justice system; • Economic growth and employment; • Improvements in basic public services.
Egypt	• Poverty alleviation, local socio-economic development and social protection 40% • Governance, transparency and business environment 20% • Quality of life and environment 40%	EUR756,000,000–EUR924,000,000	EUR449,290,000 • Democracy, human rights, good governance and justice; • Competitiveness and productivity of the economy; • Sustainability of the development process, including social, economic and environmental aspects.	EUR558,000,000 • Democracy, human rights and justice; • Competitiveness and productivity of the economy; • Sustainability of the development process, including social, economic and environmental aspects.

Table 37.1 (continued)

	Priorities for the first period of 2014–2020	2014–2020	2011–2013	2007–2010
Israel			EUR14,000,000 • Higher education: approximation of education and training policies in a global knowledge-based economy, including workshops, exchanges and academic cooperation; • *Acquis*-related activities in key Israeli ministries, including through Twinning/Twinning light in areas such as justice, freedom and security, internal market, networks, environment and people-to-people contacts; • Support to events for the exchange and dissemination of information on *acquis*- and Action Plan-related issues.	
Jordan	• Rule of law for enhanced accountability and equity in public delivery 25% • Employment and private sector development 30% • Renewable energy and energy efficiency 30% • Capacity development and civil society 15%	EUR567,000,000–EUR693,000,000	EUR223,000,000 • Enhanced political dialogue and reform; • Economic and social reform and development; • Trade-related issues, market and regulatory reform; • Justice and home affairs; • Transport, energy, information society and environment; • People-to-people contacts, including education.	EUR265,000,000 • Political reform, democracy, human rights, good governance, justice, co-operation in the fight against extremism; • Trade and investment; • Sustainability of the development process; • Institution building, financial stability and support for regulatory approximation.
Lebanon	• Justice and security system reform 15% • Social cohesion, sustainable economic development and protecting vulnerable groups 40% • Sustainable and transparent management of energy and natural resources 20% • Capacity development and civil society 25%	EUR315,000,000–EUR385,000,000	EUR150,000,000 • Political reform; • Social and economic reform; • Recovery and reinvigoration of the economy.	EUR187,000,000 • Political reform; • Social and economic reform; • Reconstruction and recovery.

(*Continued*)

Table 37.1 (continued)

	Priorities for the first period of 2014–2020	2014–2020	2011–2013	2007–2010
Libya	• Democratic governance 45% • Youth: active citizenship and socioeconomic integration 28% • Health 16% • Capacity development and civil society 11%	EUR126,000,000–EUR154,000,000	EUR60,000,000 • Human capital; • Sustainability of economic and social development; • Managing migration.	
Morocco	• Equitable access to basic social services 30% • Democratic governance, rule of law and mobility 25% • Jobs, sustainable and inclusive growth 25% • Capacity development and civil society 20%	EUR1,323,000,000–EUR1,617,000,000	EUR580,500,000 • Social policy; • Economic modernization; • Good governance and human rights; • Environmental protection.	EUR654,000,000 • Social policy; • Good governance and human rights; • Institutional support; • Economic development; • Environmental protection.
Syria	• Bilateral relations suspended.		EUR129,000,000 • Political and administrative reform; • Economic reform; • Social reform.	EUR130,000,000 • Political and administrative reform; • Economic reform; • Social reform.
Tunisia	• Socio-economic reforms for inclusive growth, competitiveness and integration 40% • Strengthening democracy 15% • Sustainable regional and local development 30% • Capacity development and civil society 15%	EUR725,000,000–EUR886,000,000	EUR240,000,000 • Employment and labour market reform, focus on youth and social protection; • Economic reform, competitiveness (agricultural, industrial and services sectors) and integration in world market; • Implementation of free trade agreement with the EU.	EUR300,000,000 • Economic governance and competitiveness; • Improved graduate employability; • Sustainable development.

[1]The information for this table was retrieved from the Single Support Frameworks 2014–2017, Country Strategy Papers 2007–2013 and National Indicative Programmes 2007–2010 and 2010–2013 for individual ENP countries, available on the website of the EEAS: www.eeas.europa.eu.

[2]Palestine is not included in this table. EU aid to Palestine is not funded through the ENPI/ENI, but through the PEGASE mechanism, which differs from the rest of the ENP and has different budgetary cycles. PEGASE implements the Palestinian Reform and Development Plan (PRDP) and provides two types of aid: on the one hand, it assists the Palestinian Authority to meet recurrent financing needs (salaries, pensions and support to vulnerable families); on the other hand, it allocates aid for long-term development in Palestine. In addition to this, the EU channels aid to Palestinian refugees through UNRWA. EU aid to Palestine between 2008 and 2012 varied between EUR358.5 million and EUR524.9 million per year (European External Action Service 2013). For more information, see: https://ec.europa.eu/europeaid/countries/palestine_en.

Bilateral aid

The ENP – and the Partnership and Cooperation Agreements (PCAs) and Association Agreements (AAs) with neighbouring countries – has been implemented through jointly agreed bilateral Action Plans (APs) and/or Association Agendas. The EU incentivizes neighbourhood partner countries to implement the agreements through bilateral financial assistance (see Table 37.1). Until 2015, the EU annually published Progress Reports to assess progress or regress in the neighbouring countries. Since the most recent ENP review of November 2015, this annual reporting has been abolished in the light of differentiation and flexibility (European Commission and High Representative of the Union for Foreign Affairs and Security Policy 2015). This is a considerable shift from the enlargement methodology of reporting that had so far been central to the ENP.

It should be noted that the actual disbursements are often a lot lower than the allocations. Of the EUR13.2 billion allocated to ENPI for the period 2007-2013, EUR9.8 billion was effectively disbursed (European Commission 2014). Bicchi (2014) found that in the Southern Mediterranean the discrepancy between commitments and disbursements worsened in the period after the Arab uprisings. In 2014, for instance, EUR2.3 billion was committed to ENI, while only EUR1.3 billion was disbursed.

Regional assistance[10]

The ENI-funded regional programmes towards the eastern and southern neighbourhoods (Table 37.2) complement bilateral policies. The multilateral framework of the EaP consists of four thematic platforms: (1) democracy, good governance and stability; (2) economic integration and convergence with EU policies; (3) energy security; and (4) contacts between people. The aim of the platforms is to facilitate the exchange of views and of best practices between EU and ENP countries. To support the work of the platforms, the EaP offers the opportunity to set up expert panels to discuss initiatives, projects and activities in depth, and to report to their respective platforms. Besides assisting the work of the senior civil servants in the platforms, expert panels also support the development and implementation of so-called Flagship Initiatives – for example, small and medium size enterprises; energy; environment; prevention, preparedness and response to natural and man-made disasters; and integrated border management.

The UfM goes beyond the countries included in the ENP and brings in Albania, Bosnia and Herzegovina, Mauritania, Monaco, Montenegro and Turkey. The members of the UfM meet in the 'Platform for Regional and Policy Dialogue' to conduct policy dialogue, exchange ideas and experiences, and to formulate priorities. The jointly identified strategic priority areas are (1) business development, (2) social and civil affairs, (3) higher education and research, (4) transport and urban development, (5) water and environment, and (6) energy and climate action. More information about the regional programmes can be found in Table 37.2.

Neighbourhood-wide aid

Neighbourhood-wide aid includes instruments that are most appropriate for and effectively implementable in the countries of the whole neighbourhood (European External Action Service and European Commission 2014a). The same neighbourhood-wide instruments are deployed to all countries participating in the ENP, but they can be adjusted. The subsidiarity principle is applied here – that is, if a programme is best addressed at the national or regional level, it is not delegated to the neighbourhood-wide instruments.

Table 37.2 EU support to regional programmes in the eastern and southern neighbourhoods

	Current focus	Indicative allocation 2014–2020	Indicative allocation 2011–2013	Indicative allocation 2007–2010
Eastern neighbourhood	• Eastern Partnership including Flagship Initiatives 75% • Regional cooperation frameworks: Northern Dimension and Black Sea Synergy 10% • Energy and transport initiatives involving the wider region 5% • Horizontal and sectoral support to regional cooperation 10%	EUR741,000,000–EUR906,000,000	EUR348,570,000 • Democracy, good governance and stability; • Economic development; • Climate change, energy and environment; • Advancing integration with the EU and regional cooperation.	EUR223,500,00 • Networks; • Environment protection and forestry; • Border and migration management, fight against transnational organized crime, customs; • People-to-people activities, information and support; • Landmines, explosive war remnants, small arms and light weapons.
Southern neighbourhood	• Building a partnership for liberty, democracy and security 20% • Building a partnership for inclusive and sustainable economic development 20% • Building a partnership between the people 25% • Regional and sub-regional institutional cooperation 15% • Complementary support 20%	EUR674,000,000–EUR824,000,000	EUR288,000,000 • Common regional institutions, confidence building measures and media development; • Regional economic integration, investment and regulatory convergence; • Sustainable development; • Social inclusion and cultural dialogue.	EUR343,300,000 • Justice, security and migration cooperation; • Sustainable economic development; • Social development and cultural exchanges.

Table 37.3 Neighbourhood-wide programmes

Current priority areas	Indicative allocation 2014–2020	Indicative allocation 2011–2013	Indicative allocation 2007–2010
• Inclusive and sustainable economic development and integration 55% • Partnership between people: Erasmus+ in the Neighbourhood and Russia 40% • Building capacity for European Neighbourhood countries 5%	EUR3,084,000,000–EUR3,455,000,000	EUR757,700,000 • Promoting reform through European advice and expertise; • Higher education modernization and student mobility; • Cooperation between local actors in the EU and in partner countries: Cooperation in Urban Development and Dialogue II (CIUDAD II); • Investment projects in ENP countries – NIF; • Cooperation between ENP countries and EU agencies; • Inter-regional cultural action.	EUR523,900,000 • Promoting reform through European advice and expertise; • Higher education modernization and student mobility; • Cooperation between local actors in the EU and in ENP countries; • Investment projects in ENP countries – NIF; • Implementation of the ENP and the Strategic Partnership with Russia.

Table 37.4 Funding of cross-border cooperation

Current goals	Indicative allocation 2014–2020	Indicative allocation 2011–2013	Indicative allocation 2007–2010
• Economic and social development in regions on both sides of common borders; • Environment, public health, safety and security; • Better conditions and modalities for ensuring the mobility of persons, goods and capital.	EUR489,000,000–EUR598,000,000	EUR950,516,000 • Economic and social development in regions on both sides of common border; • Environment, public health, safety and security; • Fight against organized crime; • Efficient and secure borders; • Promoting local cross-border people-to-people actions.	EUR583,280,000 • Economic and social development in regions on both sides of common border; • Environment, public health, safety and security; • Fight against organized crime; • Efficient and secure borders; • Promoting local cross-border people-to-people actions.

Neighbourhood-wide support comprises the NIF, which aims to build a partnership for sustainable and inclusive economic development and integration. Erasmus+ is another neighbourhood-wide instrument aiming at building a partnership between people. Finally, the EU supports targeted capacity building through Technical Assistance and Information Exchange (TAIEX) and the Support for Improvement in Governance and Management (SIGMA). Table 37.3 shows the priority areas and allocated/committed funds for neighbourhood-wide support.

Aid for cross-border cooperation

Cross-border cooperation is an integral part of the ENP and the EU–Russia cooperation. The aim is to promote cooperation between EU Member States, ENP countries and Russia (European External Action Service and European Commission 2014b). The cross-border cooperation programmes cover common land borders (for example, Karelia/Russia, Estonia/Russia, Poland/Russia, Latvia/Lithuania/Belarus, Romania/Moldova, Romania/Ukraine, Poland/Belarus/Ukraine, Hungary/Slovakia/Romania/Ukraine), short sea crossings (Italy/Tunisia) and the sea basin (Baltic Sea Region, Black Sea, Mediterranean Mid-Atlantic). Table 37.4 indicates the goals and funding for cross-border cooperation in the ENP/Russia.

Conclusions

The EU's neigbourhood has become an increasingly important destination of EU aid. Therefore, it is remarkable to notice that there have been high 'walls' between the literature on the ENP and on EU development policy. Nevertheless, in political practice, it seems that both external policy domains are converging. Not only have we noticed a general increased coherence regarding the foreign policy orientation of aid, but there are also a number of specific instances where neighbourhood and development policy become more similar. For example, the intention to use more blending in finance assistance to the neighbourhood also characterizes the EU's development policy. Another example concerns the use of budget support to increase ownership, which has also been criticized in the context of both ENP and development policy. Moreover, when looking at aid to the sectors, it can be noticed that jointly identified priorities have become more specific, not only under the ENI but also in development policy, which has been moving towards enhanced sector concentration in view of obtaining increased aid effectiveness and impact (European Commission 2011). However, this is not to say that there are no more distinctions between the ENP and EU development policy. Tensions between both areas of EU external relations and foreign policy will continue to exist, and it would be worthwhile to study these more deeply in further research.

Notes

1 All opinions expressed in the chapter are strictly those of the authors. Its contents have not been reviewed nor approved by the Belgian Federal Public Service Foreign Affairs, Foreign Trade and Development Cooperation.
2 Authors' own calculation based on data from OECD-DAC statistics (https://stats.oecd.org). Total Net ODA from EU Institutions to 16 ENP countries (Belarus, Ukraine, Moldova, Georgia, Azerbaijan, Armenia, Lebanon, Syria (suspended), Israel, Palestine, Jordan, Egypt, Libya, Tunisia, Algeria, Morocco) and total recipients.
3 Authors' own calculation based on data from OECD-DAC statistics (https://stats.oecd.org). Total Net ODA from the 28 EU Member States to the 16 ENP countries (Belarus, Ukraine, Moldova, Georgia,

Azerbaijan, Armenia, Lebanon, Syria (suspended), Israel, Palestine, Jordan, Egypt, Libya, Tunisia, Algeria, Morocco) and total recipients.
4 SIGMA stands for 'Support for Improvement in Governance and Management'.
5 TAIEX stands for 'Technical Assistance and Information Exchange instrument'.
6 In 2014, the European Neighbourhood Instrument (ENI) succeeded the European Neighbourhood and Partnership Instrument (ENPI), which was operational from 2007 until 2013.
7 Single Support Frameworks, Country Strategy Papers 2007-2013, National Indicative Programmes 2007–2010 and 2010–2013, available on the EEAS website: www.eeas.europa.eu.
8 Available at https://stats.oecd.org.
9 Data are retrieved from the OECD-DAC database, available at https://stats.oecd.org.
10 More information on these programmes and related documents can be found on the EEAS website: https://eeas.europa.eu/topics/european-neighbourhood-policy-enp/330/european-neighbourhood-policy-enp_en.

References

Bicchi, F. (2014) 'The Politics of Foreign Aid and the European Neighbourhood Policy Post-Arab Spring: "More for More" or Less of the Same?', *Mediterranean Politics* 19(3): 318–332.

Bicchi, F. and Voltolini, B. (2013) 'EU Democracy Assistance in the Mediterranean: What Relationship with the Arab Uprisings?', *Democracy and Security* 9(1–2): 80–99.

Chernikov, D. (2014) 'EU sectoral budget support', in *EU Budget Support to Eastern Partnership Countries: Cases of Moldova, Georgia and Ukraine*, Kiev: Open Society Foundation, 37–55.

Commission of the European Communities (2003) *Wider Europe–Neighbourhood: A New Framework for Relations with Our Eastern and Southern Neighbours*, COM (2003) 104 final.

Del Biondo, K. Oltsch, S. and Orbie, J. (2012) 'Security and development in EU external relations: Converging, but in which direction?', in Biscop S. and Whitman, R. (eds.) *The Routledge Handbook of European Security*, London, UK: Routledge, 126–141.

European Commission (2010) *European Instrument for Democracy and Human Rights (EIDHR) Strategy Paper 2011–2013*, C (2010) 2432, 21 April, http://by.odb-office.eu/files/eidhr_strategy_paper_2011_2013_com_decision_21_april_2011_text_published_on_internet_en[1].pdf.

European Commission (2011) *Increasing the Impact of EU Development Policy: An Agenda for Change*, COM (2011) 637, 13 October.

European Commission (2013a) *Instrument for Democracy and Human Rights Worldwide, Multiannual Indicative Programme (2014–2017)*, http://eeas.europa.eu/human_rights/docs/eidhr-mip-2014-2017_en.pdf.

European Commission (2013b) *The Multiannual Financial Framework: The External Action Financing Instruments*, http://europa.eu/rapid/press-release_MEMO-13-1134_nl.htm.

European Commission (2014) *European Neighbourhood and Partnership Instrument 2007–2013. Overview of Activities and Results*, http://ec.europa.eu/europeaid/sites/devco/files/overview_of_enpi_results_2007-2013_en_0.pdf.

European Commission (2015a) *ECHO Factsheet Algeria*, http://ec.europa.eu/echo/files/aid/countries/factsheets/algeria_en.pdf.

European Commission (2015b) *ECHO Factsheet Libya*, http://ec.europa.eu/echo/files/aid/countries/factsheets/libya_en.pdf.

European Commission (2015c) *ECHO Factsheet Palestine*, http://ec.europa.eu/echo/files/aid/countries/factsheets/palestine_en.pdf.

European Commission (2015d) *ECHO Factsheet Syria Crisis*, http://ec.europa.eu/echo/files/aid/countries/factsheets/syria_en.pdf.

European Commission (2015e) *ECHO Factsheet Ukraine*, http://ec.europa.eu/echo/files/aid/countries/factsheets/ukraine_en.pdf.

European Commission and High Representative of the Union for Foreign Affairs and Security Policy (2015) *Joint Communication to the European Parliament, the Council, the European Economic and Social Committee and the Committee of the Regions. Review of the European Neighbourhood Policy*, JOIN (2015) 50 Final, Brussels.

European External Action Service (2013) *The European Union and the Palestinians. Real Partners Make a Real Difference*, http://eeas.europa.eu/delegations/westbank/documents/news/2013_generalbrochure_en.pdf.

European External Action Service and European Commission (2014a) *Programming of the European Neighbourhood Instrument (ENI)—2014–2020: Strategic Priorities 2014–2020 and Multi-annual Indicative Programme*

2014–2017 European Neighbourhood-Wide Measures, http://eeas.europa.eu/enp/pdf/financing-the-enp/enp_wide_strategic_priorities_2014_2020_and_multi_annual_indicative_programme_2014_2017_en.pdf.

European External Action Service and European Commission (2014b) *Programming of the European Neighbourhood Instrument (ENI)—2014–2020 Programming Document for EU Support to ENI Cross-Border Cooperation (2014–2020)*, http://eeas.europa.eu/enp/pdf/financing-the-enp/cbc_2014-2020_programming_document_en.pdf.

Furness, M. and Gänzle, S. (2016) 'The European Union's development policy: A balancing act between "A more comprehensive approach" and creeping securitization', in Brown, S. and Grävingholt, J. (eds.) *The Securitization of Foreign Aid*, Palgrave Macmillan, 138–162.

Furness, M. and Schäfer, I. (2015) 'The 2015 European Neighbourhood Policy Review: More Realism, Less Ambition', in *The Current Column of 26*, Bonn: German Development Institute.

Holden, P. (2008) 'Development Through Integration? EU Aid Reform and the Evolution of Mediterranean Aid Policy', *Journal of International Development*, 20(2): 230–244.

Hughes, J. (2007) 'EU relations with Russia: Partnership or asymmetric interdependency?', in Casarini, N. and Muzu, C. (eds.) *The EU's Foreign Policy in an Evolving International System: The Road to Convergence*, London: Palgrave.

Kelley, J. (2006) 'New Wine in Old Wineskins: Promoting Political Reforms Through the New European Neighbourhood Policy', *Journal of Common Market Studies* 44(1): 29–55.

Mishalani, P., Robert, A., Stevens, C. and Weston, A. (1981) 'The pyramid of privilege', in Stevens, C. (ed.) *EEC and the Third World: A Survey*, Great Britain: Overseas Development Institute/Institute of Development Studies, 60–82.

Montana, I. (2003) 'The Lomé Convention from Inception to the Dynamics of the Post-Cold War, 1957–1990s', *African and Asian Studies* 2(1): 63–97.

Orbie, J., Bossuyt, F., Delputte, S. and De Ville, F. (2016) 'Van moreel voorbeeld naar bedreigde wereldmacht: de paradoxen van het Europese externe beleid in een globaliserende wereld', in Carlier, J., Vanhoute, E. and Parker, C. (eds.) *De hermaakbare wereld? Essays Over Globalisering*, Gent: Academia Press.

Ratzmann, N. (2012) 'Securitizing or Developing the European Neighbourhood? Migration Management in Moldova', *Southeast European and Black Sea Studies* 12(2): 261–280.

Reynaert, V. (2011) 'Explaining EU Aid Allocation in the Mediterranean: A Fuzzy-Set Qualitative Comparative Analysis', *Mediterranean Politics* 16(3): 405–426.

The Economist (2014) 'Europe's ring of fire. The European Union's neighbourhood is more troubled than ever', 20 September.

PART VI

The European Neighbourhood Policy and the promotion of EU norms and values

38
PERCEPTIONS OF THE EUROPEAN NEIGHBOURHOOD POLICY AND OF ITS VALUES AND NORMS PROMOTION

Elisabeth Johansson-Nogués

Introduction

Since the European Neighbourhood Policy (ENP) was first proposed in 2003, numerous viewpoints have been offered. Some have judged the policy as a welcome and positive means to further relations between the European Union (EU) and neighbouring countries. The ENP is, according to these observers, seen as an innovative form of foreign policy, representing an attempt to explore mutually beneficial cooperation, and potentially as a tool to project the EU's 'soft' or transformative power beyond its borders (Landaburu 2006a; Lippert 2008; Delcour and Tulmets 2008; Hahn 2015). Yet others have been more sceptical. The policy has been held as an EU-centric, bureaucratic and inflexible exercise representing little added value for ENP countries (Popescu and Wilson 2009; Hollis 2012; Kostanyan 2015). The values and norms promotion component of the ENP, whether political, socioeconomic, cultural or even administrative, has been the feature that has drawn most comments and critique from both practitioners and those in academia. Few fail to note the importance of values and norms as markers of the EU's international identity and thus 'natural' to the ENP as an expression of EU foreign policy (Chaban and Vernygora 2013). However, many also refer to such values and norms export as being conditioned by imposition and power asymmetries (Del Sarto 2007; Korosteleva 2011; Langbein and Wolczuk 2012).

To understand the array of reactions the policy has caused, this chapter will map the perceptions of the ENP among different stakeholders, as well as of the EU's values and norms promotion. The chapter will focus on three key groupings: ENP countries' governments, public opinion and civil society in ENP countries, and the EU, namely the European Commission, the European External Action Service (EEAS), EU Member States and the European Parliament. We will, above all, account for the perceptions reported in the academic literature, although data from opinion polls will also be used when relevant. The result does not cover all actors or issues; however, it provides a snapshot of the predominant attitudes towards the ENP and the values and norms being promoted through it.

The first section of this chapter outlines the main views of ENP countries' governments *vis-à-vis* the ENP, whereas the second section focuses on the opinions of ENP countries' citizens and civil society actors. The third section deals with the EU actors' attitudes towards the ENP.

ENP countries' governments

An overview of scholarly accounts reveals that ENP governments initially greeted the ENP with mixed feelings when it was launched in 2004 (Wolczuk 2009; Bauer 2011; Hollis 2012). Some neighbours' governments saw potential in the policy. For Armenia, Azerbaijan, Belarus and Georgia, the ENP fitted their desire to reduce their dependence on Russia by means of a multi-vector foreign and economic policy (Alieva 2006; Popescu and Wilson 2009; Korosteleva 2014).[1] For Georgia, the ENP also generated a cautious 'hope for a larger EU role in the region' (Nuriyev 2008: 156), support for democratization processes, economic reform and, eventually, an open door to EU accession. In the southern neighbourhood, Jordan was enthusiastic, as the ENP appeared to offer greater access to the EU markets, financial aid and cooperation in specific sectorial areas (Kelley 2006). The Moroccan government gave the policy a similar 'warm reception', as Rabat interpreted it as a step towards the privileged economic relationship the country was seeking with the EU (Baracani 2009: 138). Israel also believed, at first, that the ENP represented a 'genuinely positive opportunity' for furthering bilateral trade relations between Israel and the European Union (Hollis 2012: 86). Both Morocco and Israel were moreover encouraged by the ENP's focus on bilateral relations, as it allowed them to escape the constraints of the multilateral and, by the mid-2000s, stagnant Euro-Mediterranean Partnership (later transformed into the Union for the Mediterranean). Other governments were, however, less convinced about what the ENP had to offer. For determined eastern ENP countries, the policy was going to be a source of disappointment. Ukraine had hoped for a much more advantageous, tailor-made deal and, after the 2004 'Orange Revolution', to be given a firm invitation to future EU membership talks. The Ukrainian government also reacted negatively to the fact that the ENP included non-European southern neighbourhood countries, as this was an impediment for Ukraine's aspirations for EU accession. Korosteleva (2011: 254) reports Ukrainian officials expressing their 'dissatisfaction' and declaring the ENP as 'conceptually unsuited for Ukraine'. In the southern neighbourhood, a majority of Arab governments were largely indifferent to the proposals. Many agreed to participate 'simply because the European market was too important to them to ignore and the ENP promised both greater access and aid' (Hollis 2012: 86), and thus to provide resources to ensure continued regime stability. A couple of governments, such as Algeria or Libya, declined the invitation to participate in the ENP, as the initiative did not seem to hold any added value for their relations with the EU.

The most optimistic perceptions of the policy began to waiver, once the negotiations for the first set of ENP Action Plans began. When some neighbours' governments tried to introduce their own proposals during the ENP Action Plan consultation process, the Commission reportedly deterred such attempts and ENP countries were essentially encouraged to 'take-it-or-leave-it'. Langbein and Wolczuk (2012: 879) argue that the Commission's rationale was to seek 'to minimize changes to the drafts, not only by the neighbouring countries, but also EU Member States, to ensure normative consistency across the whole neighbourhood'. This 'one-size-fits-all' methodology was also evident in the subsequent EEAS- and Commission-led negotiations with the eastern neighbours to conclude Association Agreements (AAs), including Deep and Comprehensive Free Trade Areas (DCFTAs) in the early 2010s. The Ukrainian AA/DCFTA later became the template, with only minor modifications, for similar agreements with Georgia and Moldova and was subsequently also proposed to Egypt, Jordan, Morocco and Tunisia (Schumacher 2012). The insistence on normative consistency during the first decade of the policy, as opposed to a differentiated set of norms mutually agreed to by the EU and each ENP country, gave rise to a persistent perception of the ENP as an essentially EU-centric exercise with questionable added value for most ENP governments (Kostanyan 2015). Popescu and

Wilson (2009: 11) argue that this EU-centrism generated 'frustration with the ENP' and elicited cynical perceptions among the political elite in different ENP countries.

Second, conditionality is another bone of contention for several ENP governments. However, interestingly enough, conditionality as a means for norm promotion was less controversial with these governments for the objectives it was trying to promote (EU values) than for its implications for their status as sovereign countries.[2] Because conditionality is not a feature applied in the EU's more important trade relations (for example, with the United States or with China), the use of financial and technical aid tied to political or economic concessions implicitly reduced ENP countries to a secondary rank. Among the EU's eastern neighbours, Ukraine has been critical over how conditionality undermines its relative status *vis-à-vis* the EU in a way that might be uncalled for outside the context of a proper EU accession process (Korosteleva 2011). Azerbaijan bowed out from the EU's invitation to sign an AA/DCFTA in 2013 and declared its intention to pursue a 'strategic dialogue' with the EU and its Member States, unfettered by conditional requirements (Kostanyan 2015). In the consultation process for the 2015 ENP review, both Algeria and Egypt voiced their resentment for the EU's norm promotion and declared that the use of conditionality is not compatible with the ENP's aim of establishing an equal partnership between the EU and its southern neighbourhood. In the case of Israel, it had expected that the EU would exempt it from political conditionality in its condition of being a democratic country with a working market economy. When the EU insisted on the use of conditionality, the EU–Israeli Action Plan talks became a drawn-out affair. Negotiations only ended successfully when conditional requirements were diluted to a point where the Israelis could 'underscore the agreement's economic advantages' while completely downplaying 'the political provisions, [. . .] particularly the WMD issue, by stressing that the agreement did not change the parameters of the country's positions' (Del Sarto 2007: 70). This allowed the Israeli government to give the appearance of guaranteeing the country's political independence.

Finally, even the most reform-oriented ENP countries' governments were to find the necessary administrative restructuring, to be able to implement the ENP Action Plans, especially challenging. In order to carry out the objectives of ENP Action Plans, extensive changes in the ENP countries' administrative apparatus were often required, such as raising the accountability and efficiency in the national administration and judiciary, and ensuring 'better coordination between different ministries to manage Brussels' cross-sectoral demands' (Pridham 2011: 28). The scale of these normative reforms for some ENP countries was considerable and political will frequently petered out prior to their successful completion (Nuriyev 2008; Popescu and Wilson 2009). Ukraine, the eastern neighbour, which has perhaps attempted the most ambitious administrative reforms to achieve the objectives set out in the ENP Action Plans, has largely failed due to lack of domestic top-level political will and support from successive governments (Wolczuk 2009). The administrative adaptation has been difficult, even in countries with domestic reform plans predating the ENP. For Jordan, the ENP offered an opportunity to gain EU financial and technical assistance for its own ambitious plans for socioeconomic overhaul. Nevertheless, as the Jordanians were soon to find out, they 'simply did not have the capacity in either their public or their private sector to implement all the measures incorporated in the Action Plan they agreed with the EU' (Hollis 2012: 86–87). In general, as a normative objective, administrative reform has become either unviable or outright undesirable for many other ENP countries.

In sum, some governments in ENP countries initially harboured expectations that the ENP could facilitate economic growth and supply substantial financial assistance and thereby ensure political stability in their respective countries. Such hopes vanished, however, once the talks for the ENP Action Plans got under way. The EU's lack of flexibility, use of conditionality, and the complexity of the administrative reforms required for their implementation have put a damper on the policy from the standpoint of ENP countries' governments. These perceptions have led ENP countries' governments to question the added value of the ENP for their respective countries and to issue repeated calls for reform, as was evident from their input to the 2011 and 2015 ENP review processes.

Public opinion and civil society in ENP countries

Citizens' impressions of the policy, EU values and norms promotion, as reflected in public opinion polls in ENP countries and academic literature, paint a varied picture. Overall, the public opinion in the eastern and southern neighbourhood appears to have limited knowledge of the ENP as a policy. Moreover, surveys indicate that a majority of citizens in ENP countries do not feel well-informed about the specific role the EU plays in their country nor about the EU's financial and technical assistance (TNS Opinion 2012; 2013). In terms of the values and norms promoted through the ENP, public opinion in both neighbourhoods tends to identify the EU with values such as human rights, prosperity, solidarity and democracy (ibid.; Chaban and Vernygora 2013). This has led Bengtson and Elgström (2012: 99) to conclude that citizens of Ukraine, Georgia, Armenia, Azerbaijan and Moldova readily recognize 'the attractiveness of [the EU's] normative agenda'. However, surveys in the eastern and the southern neighborhoods also reveal that trade, tackling poverty and peace and security tend to be significantly higher among respondents' priorities in terms of areas where they would like to see more EU involvement in their respective countries, rather than human rights or democracy assistance (TNS Opinion 2012; 2013; Chaban and Vernygora 2013). Moreover, some values promoted by the EU cause ambivalence in ENP countries. A study of public opinion in Algeria, Lebanon, Morocco and the Palestinian Territories points out that they are positively inclined toward democracy as a concept but simultaneously fearful of the real or perceived consequences of democratization, like electoral violence, destabilization in a democratic transition, or socioeconomic downturn (Benstead 2015). As for Israelis, the public tends to take a predominantly negative view of the EU as a norm promoter. The EU is perceived as criticizing Israeli policies designed to safeguard the country's security and for not doing enough to prevent anti-Semitism in EU countries (Pardo 2014).

There are some important geographical exceptions to the conclusion that the EU is not predominantly seen as a normative power. Such perceptions are much more prominent in the EU's eastern and southern neighbourhoods. According to Bengtson and Elgström (2012: 99), Ukraine, Georgia, Armenia, Azerbaijan and Moldova (but not Belarus) 'readily recognize both the great power status of the EU and the attractiveness of its normative agenda. [. . .] the civilizing mission of the EU is perceived in positive [. . .] terms as a contribution to desirable transformation' (2012: 99). Among the general public in these countries, values such as human rights, democracy and freedom of speech are frequently associated with Brussels. The EU is seen as having contributed to developing democracy in these countries and human rights are viewed as an important area of co-operation; however, in line with the general picture, trade and economic development remain the areas where the most important role for the EU is envisaged (TNS Opinion 2013).

A scrutiny of the academic literature on the attitudes of civil society organizations (CSOs) in ENP countries shows that many such actors have a distinct feeling that the ENP is above all an EU-to-governmental affair. Hence, even if engaging with civil society is an explicit aim of the ENP, the EU 'met only occasionally, and only with some NGOs [non-governmental organizations], in the course of consultation over the Action Plans, and rarely against the wishes of the partner government' (Barbé and Johansson-Nogués 2008: 91; cf. Alieva 2006; Bosse 2010). Smith (2011: 396) therefore reports a strong perception among Armenian civil society associations, shared by other activists in the eastern neighbourhood, 'that the EU treated CSOs as inferior to government actors. The government was seen as an equal partner [to the EU] and subsequently had a far greater role in formulating the AP [ENP Action Plan]'. In relation to southern neighbours, Del Sarto and Schumacher (2011: 946) note that 'the buzzword of "co-ownership"' translated into the ENP Action Plans being negotiated with the ENP governments and effectively excluded CSOs from such discussions. Transnational civil society platforms have since either been formed (Eastern Partnership [EaP]) or repurposed (Union for Mediterranean) to provide venues for civil society dialogue with the Commission, the EEAS, the European Parliament and individual Member States. The 2011 ENP review included two new instruments for assisting the work of civil society actors, such as the Civil Society Neighbourhood Facility and the European Endowment for Democracy. Finally, the 2011 and the 2015 ENP reviews have also been opened up to give civil society actors more voice opportunity in the policy design. Notwithstanding, these advances and numerous pledges on the part of the EEAS and the Commission to give civil society a more central role in the ENP appear to have had an uneven impact. Some civil society actors now reportedly feel that their concerns are being heard even at the policy design stage of the ENP/EaP (Kostanyan and Orbie 2013). Other CSOs continue to have the impression that they merely hover in the peripheries of the EU's engagement with ENP countries' governments (Natorski 2016).

Second, in terms of norms promotion, the ENP contains the objective of promoting an extensive array of shared values. A view held by many civil society actors in the EU's neighbourhood is, however, that the EU's norm promotion is far from achieving its full potential due to certain inconsistencies. First, ENP civil society organizations have not failed to notice that the EU's support for CSOs working with sectorial issues such as internal market, environment or migration policy (Bicchi and Lavenex 2015; Natorski 2016) has been much more substantial compared to the support lent to their peers promoting democracy or human rights reforms (including torture and the death penalty). In his study on Armenia, Smith (2011: 396) reports a general perception among NGOs that the EU was prepared 'to compromise its democracy and human rights policies' in favour of its 'more salient economic and strategic policies'. Reynaert (2011: 636), in a quantitative study on the EU's southern neighbourhood, found that

> [e]conomic liberalization is the main goal of the EU's policy in the region and both the state (the executive power and the judiciary) and the civil society are stimulated to support the functioning of the free market. Political and civil rights [...], defined as the core elements of a democracy, are mainly supported [by the EU] if they contribute to the functioning of the market.

It is also worth noting, as Teti et al. (2013) do, that CSOs working on socioeconomic rights or social repercussions arising from economic liberalization rarely figure on the EU's aid radar. Moreover, civil society actors have accused the EEAS and the Commission of being unwilling norm promoters on democracy and human rights. The EEAS and the Commission have at times voluntarily limited their action in these areas. This self-imposed limitation has come in the form of EU Delegations in ENP countries, either not issuing project calls for such projects (Bicchi 2010) or preferring structured dialogues on these issues, also involving representatives of the respective governments (Teti et al. 2013). Finally, the EU and the ENP has done little to undo the great reluctance of ENP countries' governments against independent NGOs working on democracy and human rights in their respective countries. The EU has frequently not even reacted or reprimanded those governments that have erected significant bureaucratic impediments for, or legal persecution of, such civil society organizations' activity (Johansson-Nogués 2006; Smith 2011).

In sum, public opinion and civil society actors in the EU's neighbourhood do not see themselves as very informed or have ambivalent feelings about the ENP. By the broad public, the EU is readily identified as an actor with a normative agenda. However, surveys also show that the citizens in ENP countries generally would prefer the normative accent to be placed on short-term prosperity and solidarity. The civil society actors in the eastern and southern neighbourhoods have been of two minds about the ENP. Some feel supported by the ENP and that their concerns are being acknowledged by the EU, while others continue to have the view of the ENP as too focused on EU-to-governmental relations. Moreover, CSOs working in areas linked to market economic reforms, environment or migration policy are perceived as receiving more attention from the EU compared to human rights and democracy advocates.

European Commission, EEAS, EU Member States and the European Parliament

The European Commission's perceptions of the ENP and the norms and values promoted are portrayed in the scholarly literature as starting off buoyantly at the launch of the ENP, only to subsequently become somewhat subdued (Kelley 2006; Korosteleva 2011). From the Commission's vantage point, the ENP was, in the words of ENP Task Force Director General Eneko Landaburu, 'a truly modern foreign policy, harnessing and integrating instruments from across the spectrum – from support for human rights to judicial reform to elections, support for institution-building, increased political dialogue and cooperation on crisis management' (Landaburu 2006a: 2). Moreover, the Commission appeared to harbour no doubts in the mid-2000s that the values and norms that it was trying to advance through the ENP were the adequate ones. The legitimacy of the ENP's values and norms promotion stemmed from the EU's success with the internal market, as well as from 'the normative power of the *acquis communautaire*' (Landaburu 2006b).

The initially upbeat view of the ENP in the Commission was linked to the fact that the ENP allowed the Commission to continue as a protagonist in the EU's external action, even as enlargement became less prominent on the EU's agenda from 2004. During the eastern enlargement process, 'the Commission came to perceive itself as an important foreign policy actor' (Kelley 2006: 31). When the Commission was entrusted with the conceptualization and implementation of the ENP, before its launch, former Directorate-General (DG) Enlargement officials, reassigned to new positions within the ENP Task Force at the DG External Relations, thus saw the new policy as an 'extension and adaptation of the Commission's active foreign policy role during enlargement' (ibid.). However, by the late 2000s, the Commission woke up to the sober realization that neighbours' governments, citizens, civil society and EU members alike were dissatisfied with the ENP and with the way the Commission was handling the policy (Schumacher 2012). Discontent also began to spread within the Commission itself. One scholar reports that interviewed representatives of the Commission 'were very critical of the ENP/EaP, pointing to the lack of clarity and coherence, the heavy bureaucracy and a reactive (rather than prospective) engagement' (Korosteleva 2011: 249). The European Commissioner for Enlargement and European Neighbourhood Policy, Stefan Füle, and his successor, the Commissioner for European Neighbourhood Policy and Enlargement, Johannes Hahn, have also voiced their criticism of the ENP in the context of the ENP reviews of 2011 and 2015. For example, in 2015 and before the completion of the review process, Commissioner Hahn gave a negative assessment of ENP's one-size-fits-all methodology, its unfocused agenda and its attempt to impose values and norms (Hahn 2015).

The EEAS, which replaced DG External Relations as the principal institutional actor in charge of agenda-setting for and monitoring the ENP after the 2009 Lisbon Treaty, also initially held a favourable view of the policy. High Representative of the Union for Foreign Affairs and Security Policy and Vice-President of the European Commission (HRVP) Catherine Ashton's first impression of the ENP was that it was 'a success story with many examples of concrete achievements on the ground' (European Commission 2010). However, once the Arab uprisings began in 2011, the HRVP and the EEAS, together with other EU institutions and with Member States, offered a *mea culpa* and recognized 'the divorce between "words and deeds" [that] defined the EU's contradictory approach towards its neighbouring countries' (Natorski 2016: 657), in particular when it came to the promotion of values and norms. The level of EEAS satisfaction with the ENP appears still low, as HVRP Federica Mogherini, in the context of the 2015 ENP review, critiqued the ENP for being too EU-centric, disproportionally favouring EU interest and not assiduous enough in pursuing the original objectives of the policy such as equal partnership, differentiation, prosperity and finding ways to 'effectively work together on our common purposes' (EEAS 2015).

The EU Member States' governments' perception of the ENP is unquestionably multifaceted. The EU Member States are the original initiative takers of the ENP and hence initially saw a strong need for the policy's launch. This felt necessity is still present as the literature reports that an overwhelming majority of Member States agree to the idea of the ENP being the main conduit for EU-neighbouring countries and that the *acquis communautaire* should be the basis for the EU's value and norm promotion (Lippert 2007; Korosteleva 2011). However, it is fair to note that the interest for the ENP is not equally strong among all Member States. Some Member States (France, Poland, the Baltic states and Sweden) have over time shown relatively more concern and direct implication in the policy than others (Behr 2015; Kostanyan 2015). Moreover, disagreement exists among EU Member States over how and where the EU's values and norms should be promoted. To a pro-eastern neighbourhood grouping (Northern and Central European Member States) the ENP should be a vehicle for transforming the eastern neighbourhood in the short to medium term and in a proactive way, by upholding democracy and human rights values so central to some of these countries' own post-communist/post-Cold War transitions and by extending an explicit EU membership perspective (Natorski 2007). They have therefore strongly argued for more of the European Neighbourhood and Partnership Instrument (ENPI), and its successor the European Neighbourhood Instrument (ENI), to be geared towards the eastern neighbourhood for norms promotion purposes. This contrasts sharply with the pro-southern neighbourhood coalition (southern EU Member States) that has, since the inception of the ENP, advocated for a more pragmatic approach geared towards promoting norms in the longer term as long as regional stability is not upset. They have also maintained a close eye on the ENPI/ENI to ensure that sufficient funds are allocated to the much more populous southern neighbourhood (Behr 2015). In the 2011 ENP review, a compromise was brokered whereby the pro-southern grouping achieved a greater allocation of ENP funds to the South, while the pro-eastern grouping gained a commitment to placing greater demands for reforms on ENP countries' governments. The use of both positive and/or negative conditionality was therefore backed (Bicchi 2014). In contrast, the 2015 ENP review appears to have caused most Member States to all but abandon the strong normative rhetoric of the 2011 ENP review on promoting substantial human rights and 'deep democracy'. The disjointedness of the EU Member States' attitudes to norms promotion can perhaps be summarized, as

Noutcheva (2015: 24) does, that '[i]n theory, no EU Member State will ever oppose "deep and comprehensive democracy" as an aspiration and goal for the neighbourhood. In practice, they may do little to advance it' (cf. Del Sarto and Schumacher 2011).

The European Parliament's perception of the ENP has varied substantially over the years. When the policy was first launched, the Parliament recognized the need for the policy and approved of its general set-up as well as of the Commission's methodology (Leinen and Weidemann 2007). However, since then, the Parliament has periodically been critical of the lack of support for EU membership aspirations among eastern neighbours and attention to human rights and democratic standards in both neighbourhoods (such as Israel and Azerbaijan). In the 2015 ENP review, the Parliament criticized the methodology applied by the EU – that is, approaching relations as 'technocratic exercises, while overlooking the political consequences' (Kukan 2015). These EU shortcomings, in the words of the Parliament's Special Rapporteur for the ENP, Eduard Kukan, have meant that 'over a decade on, the EU's neighbourhood to the east and south could be described as less democratic, prosperous and secure than it was in 2004' (ibid.).

In sum, the ENP was initially perceived highly positively by the European Commission, as it allowed the institution to maintain the high profile in foreign policy it had acquired during the EU's eastern enlargement. However, by the end of the 2000s, it had begun to come to terms with the fact that the ENP was failing to have the same transformative effect and normative suasion that EU accession had had on Central and Eastern European countries. The EEAS is a relative newcomer in the context of the ENP, but in its short institutional life it has still shown relative lucidity on the shortcomings of the ENP and its norm promotion. As for the Member States and the European Parliament, they agree on having an ENP but they disagree about its norm promotion component.

Conclusions

The ENP has received intense attention in the past decade and many opinions have been offered. Initially, some ENP countries' governments and civil society actors, as well as the European Commission and EU Member States, found reasons for optimism. However, with the passing of time, this sanguinity appears to have faded. Once the Commission translated the ENP concept into concrete Action Plans, the limitations of the offer became clear to ENP governments, citizens and civil society actors, and eventually also to the Commission itself and the Member States. ENP governments have judged the policy to be EU-centric and too complex to implement. The public opinion in ENP countries at large remains fairly unaware of the ENP and its goals. Civil society actors have deemed the ENP mainly as an EU-to-government affair where civil society actors, especially in the area of democracy and human rights, play a largely figurative role. The ENP has therefore failed to gain traction in ENP countries and the EU is perceived as ambiguous on values and norms promotion.

The EU actors have not been unaware of the many problems inherent to the ENP. It is clear that the ENP's performance and value and norms promotion have suffered from a combination of lack of Member States' political will and internal bickering, as well as EU's institutions' – at first the Commission, and later the EEAS and the Commission combined – failure to find a coherent modus operandi for the ENP. In spite of this awareness and various rounds of reform, the overall intra-EU perception appears to be that the ENP has yet to unleash its full potential for organizing EU-neighbourhood relations, a task made more challenging by the changing geopolitical circumstances in the aftermath of the Arab uprisings or the Russian intervention in Ukraine.

Notes

1 The Action Plan for Belarus was later not activated by the EU and it became a 'reluctant observer' of the ENP, only to join the Eastern Partnership's multilateral track in 2009 (Korosteleva 2014: 111).
2 This view is also corroborated by interviews with European Commission officials responsible for the consultations for the ENP Action Plans who 'expressed positive surprise at how willing the first seven partner countries [sic] were to include human rights and democratization issues in the action plans' (Kelley 2006: 33).

References

Alieva, L. (2006) 'EU and the South Caucasus', *CAP Discussion Paper*, Bertelsmann Stiftung, Berlin.
Baracani, E. (2009) 'The European Neighbourhood Policy and Political Conditionality: Double Standards in EU Democracy Promotion?', in Balzacq, T. (ed.) *The External Dimension of EU Justice and Home Affairs. Governance, Neighbours, Security*, London: Palgrave, 133–153.
Barbé, E. and Johansson-Nogués, E. (2008) 'The EU as a Modest "Force for Good": The European Neighbourhood Policy', *International Affairs* 84(1): 81–96.
Bauer, P. (2011) 'The Transition of Egypt in 2011: A New Springtime for the European Neighbourhood Policy?', *Perspectives on European Politics and Society* 12(4): 420–439.
Behr, T. (2015) 'Power and Politics in the Making of Euro-Mediterranean Policies: Exploring the Role of the "North–South Split"', in Behr, T. and Tiilikainen, T. (eds.) *Northern Europe and the Making of the EU's Mediterranean and Middle East Policies: Normative Leaders or Passive Bystanders?*, Farnham: Ashgate, 25–44.
Bengtson, R. and Elgström, O. (2012) 'Conflicting Role Conceptions? The European Union in Global Politics', *Foreign Policy Analysis* 8(1): 93–108.
Benstead, L. (2015) 'Why Do Some Arab Citizens See Democracy as Unsuitable for Their Country?', *Democratization* 22(7): 1183–1208.
Bicchi, F. (2010) 'Dilemmas of Implementation: EU Democracy Assistance in the Mediterranean', *Democratization* 17(5): 976–996.
Bicchi, F. (2014) 'The Politics of Foreign Aid and the European Neighbourhood Policy Post-Arab Spring: "More for More" or Less of the Same?', *Mediterranean Politics* 19(3): 318–332.
Bicchi, F. and Lavenex, S. (2015) 'The European Neighbourhood: Between European Integration and International Relations', in Jorgensen, K. et al. (eds.) *The Sage Handbook of European Foreign Policy*, London: Sage, 868–883.
Bosse, G. (2010) 'The EU's Relations with Moldova: Governance, Partnership or Ignorance?', *Europe-Asia Studies* 62(8): 1291–1309.
Chaban, N. and Vernygora, V. (2013) 'The EU in the Eyes of Ukrainian General Public: Potential for EU Public Diplomacy?', *Baltic Journal of European Studies* 3(2): 68–95.
Delcour, L. and Tulmets, E. (2008) *Pioneer Europe? Testing EU Foreign Policy in the Neighbourhood*, Baden-Baden: Nomos.
Del Sarto, R. (2007) 'Wording and Meaning(s): EU-Israeli Political Cooperation According to the ENP Action Plan', *Mediterranean Politics* 12(1): 59–75.
Del Sarto, R. and Schumacher, T. (2011) 'From Brussels with Love: Leverage, Benchmarking, and the Action Plans with Jordan and Tunisia in the EU's Democratization Policy', *Democratization* 18(4): 932–955.
EEAS (2015) 'ENP Review: Stronger Partnerships for a Stronger Neighbourhood', *Press Release*, 17 November.
European Commission (2010) 'Five Years of European Neighbourhood Policy: More Trade, More Aid, More People-to-People Contacts', IP/10/566, Brussels, 12 May.
Hahn, J. (2015) Speech by Commissioner Hahn on Theorizing the European Neighbourhood Policy, College of Europe, 17 September.
Hollis, R. (2012) 'No Friend of Democratization: Europe's Role in the Genesis of the "Arab Spring"', *International Affairs* 88(1): 81–94.
Johansson-Nogués, E. (2006) 'Civil Society in Euro-Mediterranean Relations: What Success of EU's Normative Promotion?', *Robert Schuman Centre for Advanced Studies Working Paper* 2006/40.
Kelley, J. (2006) 'New Wine in Old Wineskins: Promoting Political Reforms Through the New European Neighbourhood Policy', *Journal of Common Market Studies* 44(1): 29–55.

Korosteleva, E. (2011) 'Change or Continuity Is the Eastern Partnership an Adequate Tool for the European Neighbourhood?', *International Relations* 25(2): 243–262.

Korosteleva, E. (2014) 'Belarus Between EU and Euroasian Economic Union', in Dutkiewicz, P. and Sakwa, R. *Eurasian Integration—The View from Within*, London: Routledge, 111–125.

Kostanyan, H. (2015) 'The Eastern Partnership After Riga: Review and Reconfirm', *CEPS Commentary*, 29 May.

Kostanyan, H. and Orbie, J. (2013) 'The EEAS' Discretionary Power Within the Eastern Partnership: In Search of the Highest Possible Denominator', *Southeast European and Black Sea Studies* 13(1): 47–65.

Kukan, E. (2015) 'EU Needs More Responsive Neighbourhood Policy', *Parliament Magazine*, 12 March.

Landaburu, E. (2006a) 'From Neighbourhood to Integration Policy: Are There Concrete Alternatives to Enlargement?', *CEPS Policy Brief* 95: 1–4.

Landaburu, E. (2006b) 'Hard Facts About Europe's Soft Power', *Europe's World*, Summer: 30–33. http://europesworld.org/2006/06/01/hard-facts-about-europes-soft-power/#.WEfkOLKLTGg, accessed 7 December 2016.

Langbein, J. and Wolczuk, K. (2012) 'Convergence Without Membership? The Impact of the European Union in the Neighbourhood: Evidence from Ukraine', *Journal of European Public Policy* 19(6): 863–881.

Leinen, J. and Weidemann, S. (2007) 'How Does ENP Work? A View from the European Parliament', in Varwick, J. and Lang, K.O. (eds.) *European Neighbourhood Policy: Challenges for the EU-Policy Towards the New Neighbours*, Opladen and Farmington Hills: Barbara Budrich Publishers, 49–60.

Lippert, B. (2007) 'The EU Neighbourhood Policy: Profile, Potential, Perspective', *Intereconomics* 42(4): 180–187.

Lippert, B. (2008) 'European Neighbourhood Policy: Many Reservations—Some Progress—Uncertain Prospects', *International Policy Analysis*, Bonn: Friedrich Ebert Stiftung, June.

Natorski, M. (2007) 'Explaining Spanish and Polish Approaches to the European Neighbourhood Policy', *European Political Economy Review* 7: 63–101.

Natorski, M. (2016) 'Epistemic (un) Certainty in Times of Crisis: The Role of Coherence as a Social Convention in the European Neighbourhood Policy After the Arab Spring', *European Journal of International Relations* 22(3): 646–670.

Noutcheva, G. (2015) 'Institutional Governance of European Neighbourhood Policy in the Wake of the Arab Spring', *Journal of European Integration* 37(1): 19–36.

Nuriyev, E. (2008) 'Azerbaijan and the European Union: New Landmarks of Strategic Partnership in the South Caucasus–Caspian Basin', *Southeast European and Black Sea Studies* 8(2): 155–167.

Pardo, S. (2014) 'Views from the Neighbourhood: Israel', in Chaban, N. and Holland, M. (eds.) *Communicating Europe in Times of Crisis*, London: Palgrave Macmillan, 175–196.

Popescu, N. and Wilson, A. (2009) 'The "Sovereign Neighbourhood": Weak Statehood Strategies in Eastern Europe', *International Spectator* 44(1): 7–12.

Pridham, G. (2011) 'Ukraine, the European Union and the democracy question', *Romanian Journal of European Affairs* 11(4): 18–33.

Reynaert, V. (2011) 'Preoccupied with the Market: The EU as a Promoter of "Shallow" Democracy in the Mediterranean', *European Foreign Affairs Review* 16(5): 623–637.

Schumacher, T. (2012) 'Conditionality, Differentiation, Regionality and the "New" ENP in the Light of Arab Revolts', in Barbé, E. and Herranz Surrallés, A. (eds.) *The Challenge of Differentiation in Euro-Mediterranean Relations: Flexible Regional Cooperation or Fragmentation*, London: Routledge, 142–158.

Smith, N. (2011) 'Europeanization Through Socialization? The EU's Interaction with Civil Society Organizations in Armenia', *Demokratizatsiya* 19(4): 385–402.

Teti, A., Thompson, D. and Noble, C. (2013) 'EU Democracy Assistance Discourse in Its New Response to a Changing Neighbourhood', *Democracy and Security* 9(1–2): 61–79.

TNS Opinion (2012) 'EU Neighbourhood Barometer ENPI South', Fall.

TNS Opinion (2013) 'EU Neighbourhood Barometer ENPI East', Spring.

Wolczuk, K. (2009) 'Implementation Without Coordination: The Impact of EU Conditionality on Ukraine Under the European Neighbourhood Policy', *Europe-Asia Studies* 61(2): 187–211.

39
EUROPEAN NEIGHBOURHOOD POLICY MECHANISMS
Conditionality, socialisation and differentiation

Laure Delcour and Eduard Soler i Lecha

Introduction

This chapter reviews the European Union's (EU) policy mechanisms under the European Neighbourhood Policy (ENP). It seeks to explore the processes through which ENP decisions are adopted and implemented in countries on which the EU cannot hierarchically impose its own rules. It focuses on those mechanisms through which the EU has diffused its norms and influenced domestic change in the neighbourhood, namely conditionality, socialisation and differentiation. In doing so, the chapter investigates how the mechanisms adapted from enlargement policy have evolved since the ENP was launched, the extent to which they have proved effective in transforming the EU's eastern and southern neighbourhoods and how they have been reassessed to respond to a changing political landscape in both 'neighbourhoods'.

What conditionality? From fuzzy to sector-specific conditionality

Conditionality, broadly defined as the provision of incentives tied to the fulfilment of EU demands, was identified as a key policy mechanism in the enlargement process. Premised upon a logic of consequences whereby 'actors choose the behavioural option that maximizes their utility under the circumstances' (Schimmelfennig 2015: 6), the ENP was largely inspired by the perceived success of recent enlargement waves and the toolbox of enlargement policy (Kelley 2006). Hence, conditionality was identified as one of the major policy mechanisms in the ENP. Yet, it soon emerged as a controversial mechanism. In sharp contrast to enlargement policy, scholars have noted the EU's limited leverage *vis-à-vis* non-candidate countries in the absence of a membership perspective, the vagueness of ENP conditionality (Sasse 2008) and the low impact of the EU on political developments in neighbouring countries – given the high costs that compliance with EU political and human rights standards would entail for the ruling elites (Schimmelfennig 2015). However, a closer look at EU policy instruments in the neighbourhood brings important nuances to this understanding.

Both in the eastern and in the southern neighbourhood, debates on political conditionality developed in the EU's policies before the ENP was launched (Schmid 2003). Like the Partnership and Cooperation Agreements (PCAs) signed with post-Soviet countries in the 1990s, the

Association Agreements (AAs), signed in the framework of the Euro-Mediterranean Partnership (EMP or Barcelona Process), included a so-called 'essential element clause', that is, an article stating that

> Relations between the Parties, as well as all the provisions of the Agreement itself, shall be based on respect for human rights and democratic principles which guide their domestic and international policies and constitute an essential element of the Agreement.
> (Bartels 2012)

And yet, despite systematic violations of human rights, this clause was never invoked. Realising that neither the EU institutions nor the Member States were willing to apply negative conditionality measures, the ENP confirmed a policy shift toward 'positive conditionality'. In fact, the EU intended to reward those countries that undertook significant reforms so that they could consolidate this reformist impetus. This approach was confirmed and reinforced with the creation of some specific mechanisms, such as the Governance Facility (Commission of the European Communities 2006). Morocco and Ukraine were the first countries to be rewarded and received additional funds in 2007 to support their respective reform agendas (Youngs 2008).

The eruption of massive protests in Arab countries in the first months of 2011, and the ousting of long-lasting rulers such as Zine el-Abidine Ben Ali in Tunisia and Hosni Mubarak in Egypt, forced the EU to assess why its efforts to promote democratic transformation and good governance among its southern neighbours had ostensibly failed. This assessment gave further impetus to an ongoing policy review of the ENP which, contrary to widespread misconceptions, started before the Arab uprisings. Yet the situation in the EU's southern neighbourhood made this policy review more pertinent, and what could have been an otherwise technical and bureaucratic assessment turned out to be a political exercise (Soler i Lecha and Viilup 2011). This materialised in two different communications, one of which was released in March 2011 resuscitating the concept of partnership based on democracy and prosperity as the main goals (European Commission and High Representative of the Union for Foreign and Security Policy 2011a) and another published two months later, intended to make the ENP more effective (European Commission and High Representative of the Union for Foreign and Security Policy 2011b).

Reinforced conditionality was one of the main prescriptions put forward in the review. According to the two communications released in March and May 2011, the EU aimed to promote 'deep and sustainable democracy' (meaning democracy that goes beyond multi-party elections and includes aspects such as efforts to combat corruption, judicial independence, democratic control over the armed forces and the freedoms of expression, of assembly and of association) through the 'more-for-more' principle. It also identified incentives in terms of financial assistance (money), access to markets and promotion of mobility (the 'three Ms'). Neither the ideas nor the areas of cooperation (with a strong emphasis on trade, border control or technical assistance) were new (Soler i Lecha and Tarragona 2013). What did represent a shift in the EU's orientation, however, is that it adopted not only the 'more-for-more' but also the 'less-for-less' approach. The May 2011 communication mentioned that 'for countries where reform has not taken place, the EU will reconsider or even reduce funding' and that 'the EU will uphold its policy of curtailing relations with governments engaged in violations of human rights and democracy standards, including making use of targeted sanctions and other policy measures' (European Commission and High Representative of the Union for Foreign and Security Policy 2011b).

Although the EU has adopted sanctions on regimes that have been, or are still, repressing its population (sanctions on Gaddafi's Libya and Assad's Syria) since 2011, there are persistent doubts as to the EU's consistency in applying reinforced conditionality. For instance, Balfour (2012: 29) argued that 'political conditionality has few and limited chances of bringing about change because of its problems of delivery and implementation'. In a similar line, Del Sarto and Schumacher (2011) highlighted the deficits of the EU's benchmarking system, which would require clear and predetermined indicators, transparent timetables, decisions on measurement and data collection methods, and commitment from the different actors involved. Closer scrutiny of the EU's application of conditionality in the East reveals similar issues. The EU has only applied political conditionality in two instances: in Belarus[1] and in Ukraine, in late 2012. In the former case, conditionality did not yield effective outcomes (Korosteleva 2016). In the latter case, the EU spelled out political conditions that needed to be fulfilled so that the AA could be signed. However, political conditionality kicked in late, that is, more than two years after democratic and human rights standards started deteriorating. The absence of political conditionality in relation to Azerbaijan (despite growing authoritarianism and a violent crackdown on civil society) also testifies to the EU's low-profile in terms of democracy and human rights in those countries where it has strategic interests (in this case energy imports from Azerbaijan in a context of diversification of EU energy supplies away from Russia) (Merabishvili 2015). Overall, the EU has clearly been reluctant to use sanctions in response to adverse political developments, yet it has not made a more extensive use of positive conditionality in support of those governments effectively engaged in reforms.[2]

However, while in both regions the EU has fallen short of consistently applying political conditionality, in recent years it has clearly shifted toward sector-specific, highly targeted conditionality based upon legal approximation with the EU *acquis* and EU-promoted rules and standards. In Eastern Europe and the South Caucasus, sector-specific conditionality has played a prominent role in the preparation of the AAs, Deep and Comprehensive Free-Trade Areas (DCFTAs) and visa liberalisation offered under the Eastern Partnership (EaP). For instance, the EU formulated specific recommendations to be fulfilled before the negotiations for DCFTAs could be launched (Delcour and Wolczuk 2015a) and listed technical and legal conditions to be met before the obligation of Schengen visas could be lifted; in addition, under the AAs/DCFTAs, approximation with the EU *acquis* is legally binding. Given that approximation with EU sector-specific policies entails the diffusion of democratic principles, scholars have interpreted functional cooperation as a shift in the EU's democracy promotion approach (Lavenex and Schimmelfennig 2011). However, closer scrutiny of ENP implementation reveals that the EU has prioritised safety- and security-related provisions over democratic principles, for instance under the DCFTA (Delcour and Wolczuk 2015b) and the visa liberalisation process (Trauner et al. 2013). This, in turn, questions the nature of transformations that the EU intends to trigger in its neighbourhood. The recent practice of conditionality highlights an emphasis on sector-specific regulatory convergence as a vehicle for increased stability and security and a limited use of political conditionality in support of democratisation (Delcour 2017).

The focus on sector-specific conditionality is also present in the ENP approach towards the southern neighbourhood. And yet, these sector-specific requirements have increasingly been associated with political considerations. For instance, and in principle, DCTFAs will only be offered to those countries which are moving towards 'deep democracy' and which, simultaneously, are willing and able to harmonise their legal frameworks with EU standards. Similarly, the promise to improve mobility between southern neighbours and the EU (in contrast to the eastern neighbourhood, visa liberalisation is not on the agenda) is part of the catalogue of incentives for countries pursuing political reforms, but it is also conditional on solid cooperation in the fight against irregular migration and reinforced border controls. The Mobility Partnership, signed with Morocco in 2014, exemplifies this hybrid technical and political conditionality.

Interestingly, the joint communication about the ENP review, published in 2015 (European Commission and High Representative of the Union for Foreign and Security Policy 2015) does not mention conditionality (neither political nor sector-specific); it merely indicates that the 'more-for-more' approach had been successful when there was a commitment by partners to reform and thereby implicitly acknowledged that conditionality had failed when such commitment was absent. The absence of any reference to the word 'conditionality' speaks volumes about the shortcomings noted during the first twelve years of the ENP, primarily the lack of consistency and the EU-centric nature of conditions (since, as mentioned above, these are based on legally binding approximation with the EU *acquis*). Whether in the East or in the South, the EU has not consistently applied political conditionality. It has not been able to effectively influence political developments where local elites proved resistant to political change. In a similar vein, sector-specific conditionality (mostly based on EU rules and standards and including strong elements of hierarchy) has only worked in reform-minded countries committed to approximating their legal frameworks with the economic and trade-related *acquis*. This is abundantly illustrated by the small number of DCFTAs negotiated with ENP countries. The ENP review eventually acknowledges that partner countries do not follow the same path in their relationship with the EU; therefore, the review seeks to develop 'more effective ways to promote reforms with each partner in mutually agreed formats' (European Commission and High Representative of the Union for Foreign and Security Policy 2015: 5). The ENP's shift toward a tailor-made approach was confirmed in the EU's Global Strategy (European External Action Service 2016: 25).

Socialisation as a long-term instrument

Socialisation, defined as 'a process of inducting actors into the norms and rules of a given community' (Checkel 2005: 804), is a key mechanism for familiarising ENP actors with EU rules and templates and shaping new collective identities in the EU's neighbourhoods. Unlike conditionality, it does not explicitly rely on hierarchy and does not primarily seek to impose EU rules on neighbouring countries. Instead, socialisation is premised on a logic of appropriateness, whereby 'actors choose the behaviour that is appropriate according to their social role and the social norms in a given situation' (Schimmelfennig 2015: 6). Hence, socialisation operates through 'normative rationality' (Börzel and Risse 2012: 6).

Under the ENP, neighbouring countries are socialised into EU rules, norms and practices through networks and capacity-building programmes that operate both bilaterally and multilaterally. While envisaged from the outset of the ENP, socialisation mechanisms have substantially expanded in recent years. This expansion is driven by a functionalist logic reflecting the growing socio-economic interdependences and trans-governmental ties between the EU and its neighbours (Lavenex 2014). In the ENP, socialisation has been channelled through bilateral and multilateral cooperation schemes. Most of these, however, are recent and their effects in terms of socialisation will only be visible in the mid to long term.

As for the bilateral dimension, a major socialisation mechanism has been the gradual opening of EU programmes and the participation in the work of EU agencies to ENP countries. These are key to developing links between the EU and its neighbourhood, based on mutual interest. In March 2007, the Council of the EU agreed to the gradual participation of thirteen ENP countries in EU agencies and programmes[3] to encourage regulatory and administrative reform. These countries, one after the other, have signed framework agreements on the general principles for participation in EU programmes. Their involvement is already effective in specific programmes – for instance, Armenia, Georgia, Moldova, Ukraine and Israel are associate countries with the EU research programme, Horizon 2020. This participation requires capacities and networking resources on the part of ENP countries. In 2012–2014, the EU had allocated EUR3.7 million to promote the participation of ENP countries in the work of EU agencies. Cooperation projects were launched in 2014 between EaP countries and nine regulatory agencies, including the European Environmental Agency (EEA), the European Aviation Safety Agency (EASA), the European Food Safety Authority (EFSA) and the European Border and Coast Guard Agency (FRONTEX).

Regarding the multilateral dimension, southern neighbours have a long record of initiatives. Some of these even pre-date the Barcelona Process, which was launched in 1995. Already, since 1990, embryonic sectoral programmes have been launched under the 'Renovated Mediterranean Policy' to foster cooperation among local governments (MED Urbs), universities (MED Campus) and journalists (Med Media), among others. The Barcelona Process formalised this multilateral dimension and opened new spaces for socialisation at the political level (through ministerial conferences and parliamentary dialogue), at the senior officials level and at the technical level (through multilateral cooperation programmes in various fields such as civil protection, police and judiciary, among others). It also targeted civil society through projects involving civil society organisations. Despite a widespread feeling that the adoption of the ENP would challenge, or even replace, these multilateral efforts, in practice it has preserved these socialisation platforms. Multilateral projects are still supported by the European Neighbourhood Instrument (ENI), formerly the European Neighbourhood and Partnership Instrument (ENPI).

The Union for the Mediterranean (UfM), launched in 2008 as an initiative that was originally promoted by France and progressively Europeanised, introduced some novelties (Bicchi and Gillespie 2011). The UfM intended to boost relations with Mediterranean neighbours, through functional projects in policy areas such as energy, environment, research and higher education, civil cooperation and entrepreneurship (in which not all members are supposed to take part and are instead open to third actors); international financial institutions and Gulf countries were invited to co-sponsor some of those projects. The creation of a permanent secretariat based in Barcelona (with the participation of officials and specialists from several UfM Member States) was also meant to increase the ownership of this initiative and work as a socialisation platform. As also happened with the previous multilateral efforts in the EMP, the UfM suffered since its inception from the deadlocked Middle East Peace Process, the lack of political will of several members to invest politically and financially in this new initiative, and institutional dysfunctions. In parallel, other multilateral cooperation initiatives with a strong socialisation component, such as the Euro-Mediterranean Regional and Local Assembly (ARLEM) and the Parliamentary Assembly of the Union for the Mediterranean (PA-UfM), were launched. And yet, it is doubtful whether these and other initiatives have generated substantial socialisation effects.

The reinforcement of multilateral cooperation frameworks in the South was instrumental in pushing the EU to replicate similar structures in the eastern neighbourhood. Until the late 2000s, the EU had almost exclusively relied on a bilateral approach in the post-Soviet space, given the strong disintegration dynamics that have prevailed there since the collapse of the Soviet Union. The multilateral track of the EaP, established in 2009, constitutes an important framework of networking and exposure to EU norms. It was designed as a multi-layered and participative framework involving the EU, partner countries and international organisations such as the Council of Europe, the European Bank for Reconstruction and Development and others. The multilateral track includes several policy formats and dialogue mechanisms for decision-makers and officials, at both political and technical levels. These combine socialisation, emulation and persuasion mechanisms (for example, exchange of experience and best practices, presentation of EU legislation) with some elements of hierarchy – for instance, the four thematic platforms (the backbone of the governmental format) are chaired by EU institutions that play a key role in defining the agenda. Since the multilateral track was launched, participation in the thematic platforms has proved highly uneven among Eastern Partnership countries, depending upon the resonance of EU governance with domestic norms and preferences; this only confirms earlier scholarly findings (Checkel 2001). The EaP's multilateral track, however, is not confined to governmental actors. It also includes two assemblies, the EURONEST Parliamentary Assembly and the Conference of Regional and Local Authorities of the Eastern Partnership (CORLEAP). However, their work (especially EURONEST's) has been hampered by regional tensions, first and foremost between Armenia and Azerbaijan. In contrast, non-governmental formats (the Civil Society Forum, the Business Forum) have played a crucial role in fostering contacts and dialogue between the EU and Eastern Partnership societies in recent years, as well as monitoring ENP countries' relations (Füle 2013); however, the EU's support for those formats, as part of the multilateral track, has been in sharp contrast to its prioritisation of the relationship with governments and public administration, under the bilateral track.

Under the ENP, the EU has therefore acted as a 'gigantic socialisation agency' (Börzel and Risse 2012: 7). This is likely to develop even further in the coming years, as the 2015 ENP review pinpoints the role of networks and joint activities for pooling resources and experience, especially in research, education and innovation-related policy areas. The ENP review acknowledges the contribution of multilateral cooperation schemes and suggests reinforcing them. The EaP is described as 'a vibrant forum for exchange and cooperation' (European Commission and High Representative of the Union for Foreign and Security Policy 2015: 18). The review also indicates that the EU will 'give priority, wherever suitable, to the UfM in its regional cooperation efforts' (ibid.).

The outcomes of socialisation are likely to be realised in the long-term and the successes have been modest so far. Bilaterally, the participation in EU programmes crucially hinges on ENP countries' capacities and expertise. Regarding the multilateral formats set up by the EU, these are unique fora for ENP countries (both in the East and in the South) to meet and to exchange experiences. However, multilateral formats trigger an uneven interest among ENP countries and they are not well suited to handle the growing differences between ENP countries in their relationship to the EU. Furthermore, they are also affected by regional tensions in both geographical areas covered by the ENP. This only confirms scholarly findings on the limited influence of socialisation due to a lack of joint ownership (Schimmelfennig 2015), poor consistency in the EU's policy and the coexistence with conditionality that is expected to undermine the potential of both mechanisms (Sedelmeier 2007).

Whither differentiation?

Differentiation has been a key principle of the ENP since the policy was launched. As indicated in the ENP initial strategic policy documents, both the scope and pace of EU-ENP countries' relations depend on partner countries' aspirations, commitments to 'shared values' and implementation of reforms (Commission of the European Communities 2004). Hence, differentiation is closely intertwined with the use of conditionality. At the same time, under the neighbourhood policy, the EU has endeavoured to strike a balance between differentiation and coherence, as the ENP operates within a single policy framework based upon a set of common issues. It has also attempted to make differentiation and bilateralism compatible with region-building efforts, in both the eastern and the southern neighbourhoods.

There are several approaches to differentiation when studying the ENP. The first and most evident one is geographic differentiation. Although the ENP is a single policy, it is addressed to two different geopolitical areas, whose countries have different expectations and interests in their relations with the EU. While membership is a possibility (even if a very distant and uncertain one) for at least some Eastern European neighbours of the EU, it is completely discarded for the Mediterranean partners. Hence, at the end of the 2000s, the EU introduced a differentiated regional approach through the UfM in 2008 and the Eastern Partnership in 2009. This was meant to better tailor EU policies to the specific challenges and aspirations of Southern Mediterranean and Eastern European countries. This geographic differentiation can also translate into specific sub-regional focuses, as is the case of relations with the five countries from the Maghreb (through the participation of EU officials in 5+5 meetings and some EU–Maghreb sectorial meetings).

However, the primary factor behind differentiation pertains to the historical trajectories, needs, expectations and capacities of ENP countries. In the southern neighbourhood, it is worth comparing the different attitudes of Morocco and Algeria towards the European integration project. Since its independence, Morocco has tried to preserve a privileged relation with France and by extension with Europe. King Hassan II (1976: 189) once said that Morocco was 'a tree with its roots in Africa and its branches in Europe' and asked for full membership in the European Economic Community (EEC) in 1987. In contrast, Algeria, after a traumatic war for independence, pursued an anti-imperialist foreign policy and distanced itself from France and the EEC. This historical legacy translated into a completely different attitude towards the ENP. While Morocco saw in this new policy an opportunity to obtain a differentiated status and, indeed, succeeded in doing so with the adoption of the Advanced Status in 2008 (Jaidi 2010), Algeria only reluctantly became part of the ENP and, to date, no Action Plan has been adopted with this country (Darbouche 2008). By the end of 2015 this different attitude is palpable in these countries' narratives about their economic relations with the EU. While Morocco was the first Mediterranean country to start negotiations on a DCFTA, the Algerian government negotiated with the EU a postponement of the tariff dismantling to 2020, and the revision of the AA, arguing that it had only benefited EU companies.

In the eastern neighbourhood, while relations with the EU are more recent and only developed in the wake of the collapse of the Soviet Union, ENP countries' attitudes to the EU have been highly diverse from the outset of the ENP, and the EaP only exacerbated this heterogeneity. Three countries (Georgia, Moldova and Ukraine) have long declared their aspirations for EU membership, while the three others (Armenia, Azerbaijan and Belarus) expressed no interest in joining the EU. In fact, the EU's offer triggered diverse responses due to neighbours' aspirations and reforms trajectories. Under the EaP, Azerbaijan and Belarus have not started negotiations for a DCFTA and are unlikely to do so in the short to medium term, the former because it is not a member of the World Trade Organisation (WTO) (a prerequisite to open DCFTA negotiations) and the latter owing to its frozen relationship with the EU since the mid-1990s, its non-membership in the WTO and its membership in the Russian-led Eurasian Economic Union (EEU) (which is in essence incompatible with the conclusion of a DCFTA). In contrast to Azerbaijan and Belarus, Armenia, Georgia, Moldova and Ukraine all completed negotiations for an AA and a DCFTA.

Geographic differentiation is bilateral and country-based. On the one hand, a shared reformist agenda may have, therefore, relations between the EU and Moldova that are seemingly more like those with Morocco than those with Belarus. While some ENP countries have introduced significant reforms in the last decade and, in doing so, have made use of the EU assistance provided under the ENP framework, others have only introduced cosmetic changes in their legislation and practices or, even worse, have gone backwards. This reality could be analysed as one in which a single policy has had different outcomes and this implies responding to questions, such as why the ENP seems to have steered a set of reforms in Moldova or Morocco, while it has not in Egypt or Azerbaijan. But it can also be interpreted as the realisation that this policy has been unable to modify the preferences and the political and administrative dynamics of neighbouring countries and that, whether changes occur in one or another direction, they are more the result of a specific configuration of domestic forces and power struggles than the outcome of (un)successful EU policies. As pointed out by Schumacher (2012: 143), the 2011 events 'forced the Commission to finally acknowledge that political change across its external borders takes place despite rather than because of the ENP'.

On the other hand, whether the incentives the EU is able and ready to offer are attractive enough also determines what the EU may be able to ask in return. For example, while the EaP offered new prospects to South Caucasus countries, such as AAs/DCFTAs, it did not represent a significant step forward for Ukraine, which had already started negotiations for an AA in 2007 and a DCFTA in 2008. Despite the lack of declared membership aspirations (in contrast to neighbouring Georgia, Moldova and Ukraine), the EU's enhanced offer under the EaP resonated strongly in Armenia in a context of increased regional vulnerability: it coincided with the country's need for modernisation and prompted substantial reforms in the framework of negotiations for an AA/DCFTA (Delcour and Wolczuk 2015a). In contrast, Azerbaijan expressed limited interest beyond the prospects for energy cooperation (Franke et al. 2010).

Differentiated treatment in the framework of the ENP also must consider the existence of exceptional situations (for example, the fact that Palestine has not been recognised as a state by most EU members and yet has an interim AA with the EU and has been fully participating in the ENP) or the situation of Turkey, a country that is not part of the ENP but is a member of the UfM. In Eastern Europe and the South Caucasus, Russia's policies have only exacerbated differentiation in terms of integration with the EU (Delcour 2017). Russia's positive and negative incentives (trade and customs war with Ukraine in the summer 2013, financial bailout, trade bans, increasing use of breakaway regions as pressure points) proved ineffective to lure Ukraine into the Eurasian Customs Union and to deter Moldova and Georgia from further integration with the EU. Moreover, Russia's annexation of Crimea and hybrid warfare in eastern Ukraine (in retaliation for president Yanukovych's ousting) only pushed the country towards further integration with the EU. However, Russia's security, energy and political pressure were instrumental in the Armenian President's decision to join the EEU after successfully completing negotiations for a DCFTA (Delcour and Wolczuk 2015a).

Finally, differentiation is also mirroring EU interests and capacities. The ENP has put more emphasis on some areas (trade, environment, energy, justice and home affairs), but even inside each of these sectors, there have been differentiated treatments. For instance, regarding trade, there has been far more progress in tariff reduction for manufactured goods than on non-tariff barriers, agriculture or services (Barbé and Herranz 2010). Similarly, in security cooperation, the focus has been on cooperation with internal security services. The focus on some areas may result from interests (for example, the opposition of the agricultural lobby in some EU countries) or the fact that EU institutions have far more competences in some areas (such as trade or environment) than in others (such as defence).

Differentiation in EU-eastern neighbours' relations has become more visible with the negotiations for AAs and DCFTAs and is even more likely to strengthen with their implementation. In the near future, the three countries that enjoy an enhanced contractual framework will face very different issues in their relationship to the EU (for example, application of EU-approximated legislation) as compared to Armenia, Azerbaijan and Belarus. At the same time, the Eastern

Partnership cannot be reduced to a division between associated and non-associated countries. First, other pillars of the EU's offer, such as visa liberalisation, still cover all six countries – though with marked differences in the pace of implementation. Second, the two 'groups' of countries (associated and non-associated) are by no means homogeneous. In particular, Armenia, Azerbaijan and Belarus have very different expectations *vis-à-vis* the EU; Armenia, for instance, continues to seek closer ties with the EU despite its membership in the EEU. Third, Georgia, Moldova and Ukraine are increasingly fragmented, primarily due to Russia's policies of supporting breakaway regions: for instance, the DCFTAs will *de facto* only apply to the territories controlled by these countries' authorities.

Similarly, in the southern neighbourhood there is a growing gap between the group of countries that were willing to explore the ENP framework and ready to implement some legal or administrative reforms to converge with EU legislation (Morocco, Tunisia and Israel and to a lesser extent Jordan, Lebanon and Palestine) and are willing to intensify relations with the EU and the other countries, and those countries that are not only lagging behind but are openly questioning the current mode of cooperation. In addition, the very philosophy behind the UfM builds on the notion of flexible geometry as it is aimed at promoting projects and cooperation platforms among particular groups of countries. This was one of its main innovations compared to the classical 'Barcelona scheme', where all countries were supposed to participate in all programmes. The 2011 events introduced a new dimension as, for the first time, the EU defined specific support actions for countries in transition or undertaking major reform policies. The clearest example was the launch of a programme to provide 'Support for Partnership, Reforms and Inclusive Growth' (SPRING). Initially, this programme only targeted Tunisia and Egypt (the two countries where uprisings culminated in major political changes) and Morocco and Jordan (both of which presented themselves as reformist countries).

Taking these developments into account, it came as no surprise that the 2015 ENP review singled out differentiation as a hallmark of the new approach. The review also clarifies the EU's understanding of the differentiation principle by indicating that the ENP should reflect 'the wishes of each country concerning the nature and focus of its partnership with the EU' (European Commission and High Representative of the Union for Foreign and Security Policy 2015: 2). Hence, on paper, differentiation is not to be premised on EU interests or conditionality, as has frequently been the case over the past decade. Rather, it is expected to derive from partners' aspirations and therefore to foster their ownership of the reform process.

Conclusions

As revealed by the implementation of the ENP thus far, the assumptions underpinning the use of the enlargement toolbox have proven to be mistaken. In a context of asymmetric relations, conditionality has increasingly mirrored the shadow of hierarchy and focused on EU technical standards, thereby reflecting EU concerns and interests. Yet it has overlooked ENP countries' preferences, needs and constraints, hence falling short of producing any long-lasting effects. The 2015 ENP review suggests reversing the approach underpinning the whole policy, and placing partner countries' aspirations at its centre. In this vein, it departs from a standardised diffusion of EU rules combined with conditionality. Instead, it seeks to expand the opportunities for neighbours to participate in EU initiatives with a view to empowering ENP countries and fostering partnership, while also pursuing the EU's interests. The most direct effect of the shift from an EU-centred to a neighbour-oriented approach, though, is likely to be increased differentiation within the ENP. This is regarded as a driver of effectiveness that will likely serve the interests of both the EU and ENP countries. If it succeeds in reflecting neighbours' aspirations, the ENP will increasingly resemble a policy *à la carte*. For the EU, this is a litmus test as it entails departing from models inspired by previous policies and crafting a new policy at the crossroads of European integration and external action.

Notes

1 The EU did so first by freezing relations in continuation of the policy introduced in the mid-1990s in response to the country's shift toward authoritarianism, and second by introducing sanctions in reaction to the repression that followed the 2010 presidential elections. The 2016 Council conclusions on Belarus, however, recognised 'an opportunity for EU-Belarus relations to develop on a more positive agenda' and decided not to extend the restrictive measures applied to 170 individuals and three companies (Council of the European Union 2016).
2 For instance in the framework of the above-mentioned Governance Facility.
3 Algeria, Armenia, Azerbaijan, Egypt, Georgia, Lebanon, Israel, Jordan, Moldova, Morocco, the Palestinian Authority, Tunisia and Ukraine.

References

Balfour, R. (2012) 'EU Conditionality After the Arab Spring', *EuroMeSCo Papers* 16.
Barbé, E. and Herranz, A. (2010) 'Dynamics of Convergence and Differentiation in Euro-Mediterranean Relations: Towards Flexible Region-Building or Fragmentation?' *Mediterranean Politics* 15(2): 129–147.
Bartels, L. (2012) 'A Legal Analysis of the Human Rights Dimension of the Euro-Mediterranean Agreements', *GREAT Insights* 1.
Bicchi, F. and Gillespie, R. (2011) 'The Union for the Mediterranean: Continuity or Change in Euro-Mediterranean Relations', *Mediterranean Politics* 16(1): 3–19.
Börzel, T. and Risse, T. (2012) 'From Europeanisation to Diffusion: An Introduction', *West European Politics* 35(1): 1–19.
Checkel, J. (2001) 'Why Comply? Social Learning and European Identity Change', *International Organization* 55(3): 553–588.
Checkel, J. (2005) 'International Institutions and Socialization in Europe: Introduction and Framework', *International Organization* 59(4): 801–826.
Commission of the European Communities (2004) *European Neighbourhood Policy. Strategy Paper*, COM(2004) 373 final, Brussels, 12 May.
Commission of the European Communities (2006) *Strengthening the European Neighbourhood Policy*, COM(2006) 726 final, Brussels, 4 December.
Council of the European Union (2016) 'Council Conclusions on Belarus', *Press Release* 61/16, 15 February.
Darbouche, H. (2008) 'Decoding Algeria's ENP Policy: Differentiation by Other Means?', *Mediterranean Politics* 13(3): 371–389.
Del Sarto, R. and Schumacher, T. (2011) 'From Brussels with Love: Leverage, Benchmarking, and the EU Action Plans with Jordan and Tunisia in the EU's Democratization Policy', *Democratization* 18(4): 932–955.
Delcour, L. (2017) *The EU and Russia in Their 'Contested Neighbourhood': Multiple External Influences, Policy Transfer and Domestic Change*, London: Routledge.
Delcour, L. and Wolczuk, K. (2015a) 'The EU's Unexpected "Ideal Neighbour"? The Perplexing Case of Armenia's Europeanisation', *Journal of European Integration* 37(4): 491–507.
Delcour, L. and Wolczuk, K. (2015b) 'Spoiler or Facilitator of Democratization? Russia's Role in Georgia and Ukraine', *Democratization* 22(3): 459–478.
European Commission and High Representative of the Union for Foreign and Security Policy (2011a) *A Partnership for Democracy and Shared Prosperity with the Southern Mediterranean*, COM(2011) 200 final, 8 March.
European Commission and High Representative of the Union for Foreign and Security Policy (2011b) *A New Response to a Changing Neighbourhood. A Review of European Neighbourhood Policy*', COM 303, 25 May.
European Commission and High Representative of the Union for Foreign and Security Policy (2015) *Review of the European Neighbourhood Policy*, JOIN(2015) 50 final, Brussels, 18 November.

European External Action Service (2016) *Shared Vision, Common Action: A Stronger Europe. A Global Strategy for the EU's Foreign and Security Policy*, Brussels.

Franke, A., Gawrich, A., Melnykovska, I. and Schweickert, R. (2010) 'The European Union's Relations with Ukraine and Azerbaijan', *Post-Soviet Affairs* 26(2): 149–183.

Füle, S. (2013) 'Civil Society at the Heart of the Eastern Partnership', Speech/13/79, 4 October.

Hassan II (1976) *Le défi*, Paris: Albin Michel.

Jaidi, L. (2010) 'The Morocco/EU Advanced Status: What Value Does it Add to the European Neighbourhood Policy?', *Mediterranean Yearbook 2009*, IEMED, CIDOB, 149–154.

Kelley, J. (2006) 'New Wine in Old Wineskins: Promoting Political Reforms Through the New European Neighbourhood Policy', *Journal of Common Market Studies* (44)1: 29–55.

Korosteleva, E. (2016) 'The EU and Belarus: Seizing the Opportunity?', *European Policy Analysis* 13, SIEPS, Stockholm.

Lavenex, S. (2014) 'The Power of Functionalist Extension: How EU Rules Travel', *Journal of European Public Policy* 21(6): 885–903.

Lavenex, S. and Schimmelfennig, F. (2011) 'EU Democracy Promotion in the Neighbourhood: From Leverage to Governance?', *Democratization* 18(4): 885–909.

Merabishvili, G. (2015) 'The EU and Azerbaijan: Game on for a More Normative Policy?', *CEPS Policy brief* 329.

Sasse, G. (2008) 'The European Neighbourhood Policy: Conditionality Revisited for the EU's Eastern Neighbours', *Europe-Asia Studies* 60(2): 295–316.

Schimmelfennig, F. (2015) 'Europeanization Beyond Europe', *Living Review of European Governance* 10(1).

Schmid, D. (2003) 'Interlinkages Within the Euro-Mediterranean Partnership. Linking Economic, Institutional and Political Reform: Conditionality Within the Euro Mediterranean Partnership', *EuroMeSCo Papers* 27.

Schumacher, T. (2012) 'Conditionality, Differentiation, Regionality and the "New" ENP in the Light of Arab Revolts', in Barbé, E. and Herranz-Surrallés, A. (eds.) *The Challenge of Differentiation in Euro-Mediterranean Relations: Flexible Regional Cooperation or Fragmentation*, London: Routledge, 142–158.

Sedelmeier, U. (2007) 'The European Neighbourhood Policy: A Comment on Theory and Policy', in Weber, K., Smith, M. and Baun, M. (eds.) *Governing Europe's Neighbourhood*, Manchester: Manchester University Press, 195–208.

Soler i Lecha, E. and Tarragona, L. (2013) 'Self-Imposed Limitations: Why is the EU Losing Relevance in the Mediterranean?', *Notes Internacionals CIDOB* 68.

Soler i Lecha, E. and Viilup, E. (2011) 'Reviewing the European Neighbourhood Policy: A Weak Response to Fast Changing Realities', *Notes Internacionals CIDOB* 36.

Trauner, F., Kruse, I. and Zielinger, B. (2013) 'Values Versus Security in the External Dimension of the EU Migration Policy: A Case Study on the EC Readmission Agreement with Russia', in Noutcheva, G., Pomorska, K. and Bosse, G. (eds.) *Values Versus Security? The Choice for the EU and Its Neighbours*, Manchester: Manchester University Press, 201–217.

Youngs, R. (2008) *Is the European Union Supporting Democracy in Its Neighbourhood?*, Madrid: FRIDE.

40
GEOPOLITICS AND DEMOCRACY IN THE EUROPEAN NEIGHBOURHOOD POLICY

Anna Khakee and Richard Youngs

Introduction

A standard criticism of the European Neighbourhood Policy (ENP) is that it has adopted a 'one size fits all' approach. Analysts routinely admonish the EU for pursuing an overly uniform policy, using similar instruments for virtually identical aims across countries that are radically different from each other. Critics argue that it makes little sense to follow the same set of policy recipes in the eastern neighbourhood as those that are prioritized in the South.[1] The EU has gradually acknowledged these criticisms, most notably since the Arab uprisings. The ENP reviews since then have promised that principles of 'more for more' and 'differentiation' will guide future policy development (European Commission and High Representative for Foreign and Security Policy 2011, 2015). These principles suggest that the EU will begin to make more significant distinction between East and South, and differentiate its strategies within each sub-region. This formally recognizes the reality that Ukraine, Georgia and Moldova want closer relations with the Union and to adopt many EU rules, while Armenia, Azerbaijan and Belarus do not; and it accepts that among Arab states only Tunisia and Morocco appear to be interested in the standard range of ENP instruments and incentives.

In fact, the 'one size fits all' assertion was never entirely correct. It is true that many EU aims are relatively uniform across the whole neighbourhood. The Union's set of generic political goals in the East are defined in a way that is similar to those in the South: to ensure a ring of stability and prosperity on the outer borders of the EU (European Council 2003). The EU seeks to benefit from extensive trade with well-governed, stable and democratic neighbouring states in Eastern Europe and to the South of the Mediterranean. It wants to minimize the spill-over from eastern and southern instability: drugs and contraband, organized crime, terrorism, refugees and economic migrants. The EU has deployed a common set of bilateral tools through the neighbourhood, most notably in the form of Association Agreements. The rhetoric has also remained uniform: market economies and democracies brought stability to Europe and can have the same effect in the neighbourhood (European Commission and High Representative for Foreign and Security Policy 2015). However, as geopolitical challenges have evolved and deepened, variation between East and South has become increasingly apparent – and has also become more notable within each sub-region. In practice, much differentiation has already taken shape as the ENP has evolved since 2004. This is especially evident in the way the EU conceives and approaches the question of democratic reform. Very different geopolitical dynamics have taken root in different parts of the neighbourhood. In some countries, the EU has intensified its support for democratic reform as a geopolitical strategy. In other countries, the Union's geopolitical aims militate against a prioritization of democracy support. Analysts and policy-makers alike have come to focus on 'geopolitical' interests; the 2015 ENP review clearly crystalizes the priority now attached to 'stabilization' and 'security sector reform, conflict prevention, counter-terrorism and anti-radicalization policies' (European Commission and High Representative for Foreign and Security Policy 2015: 2–3). This focus has very different implications for democracy and human rights policies in different parts of the neighbourhood. The EU and its Member States have moulded themselves to a varied set of geopolitical dynamics – and this trend is underplayed by an analysis centred principally on the *de jure* and discursive uniformity of the ENP framework or on the apparently *sui generis* nature of the Union's external policy instruments.

East: the democracy advantage

Between 2004 and 2013 – when the geopolitical scenario abruptly changed – the ENP enshrined a focus on democracy support that was driven by EU strategic aims, but also pursued in a relatively low-key and technocratic fashion. The Eastern Partnership (EaP) began as a relatively low level initiative in 2009. Sponsored initially by Poland and Sweden, it did not engender great enthusiasm or attention from most other Member States. Indeed, their separate national foreign policy engagement in the region remained strikingly modest. Originally, the EaP was in part a trade-off against the newly formed Euro-Mediterranean Union, not primarily an externally or strategically driven initiative. In the aftermath of Russia's 2008 invasion of Georgia, geopolitical concerns were certainly present. But, the policy initiatives launched under the EaP rubric were focused on trade, aid and low-level societal engagement. While the six EaP partners – Armenia, Azerbaijan, Belarus, Georgia, Moldova and Ukraine – welcomed the new framework, they principally noted that the EU was not willing to use the offer of enlargement to underwrite and prompt economic and political reform. The EaP seemed to them more like a poor substitute than an important new umbrella for geopolitical protection. It was a low-level technocratic exercise rather than a high-level political project.

Stressing that the EaP was not overtly geopolitical, the EU expressly insisted it was not about challenging Russian presence in the region or competing in zero-sum terms for influence with Moscow. Yet, the EU clearly saw a deepening of democratic reform as part of EaP states' political reorientation towards the Union's governance orbit. Without wishing to stir Russian hostility, Member States saw the region's modest adoption of EU governance regulations as a helpful means of carving out more strategic manoeuvrability *vis-à-vis* Moscow (Ademmer 2015).

Between 2004 and the tumultuous changes that began in 2013, the EU tried to facilitate and stimulate democratic advances through what became the quintessential set of ENP instruments. Support to civil society increased through a range of programmes. An EaPIC fund started allocating aid as a reward for political reforms – to Moldova, Georgia and Armenia. Reformist EaP governments also benefited from increased sums of direct budget support (Shapovalova and Youngs 2013). By 2013, over 50 twinning arrangements existed with various ministries and regulatory agencies across the EU. Central and Eastern European Member States pushed not only to raise the EaP's profile but also to place democracy support at its heart. Support for democracy was central to these new Member States' strategic vision for the region (Petrova 2014).

The EU saw democracy support as a low cost and low risk means of extending its own circle of influence, and did not foresee a direct clash between this support and Russian 'democracy blocking' tactics (Babayan 2014). Analysts argued that the ENP was essentially about normative ends being pursued through value-shaping persuasion and rules-based influence (Forsberg 2011). The EU aimed to support more accountable governance mainly through technical areas of sectoral cooperation based on its own internal legal rules (Schimmelfennig 2011).

The geopolitical context began to change, of course, with Russia's invasion of Georgia in 2008. But it was the crisis that erupted in late 2013, as Russia pushed back against ENP association agreements and then annexed Crimea, which radically changed the EU's strategic calculus. Since then, the EU and Member States have explicitly sought to adopt a more geopolitical approach to the eastern neighbourhood. This focus has led the European governments to adopt many new decisions that are beyond the scope of this article, but one change that falls within our specific focus here relates to EU support for political reform.

As the crisis deepened after 2013, European governments insisted that increasing support for EaP states offered the most promising means of neutering Russian influence. The EU aimed to become geopolitical in the sense of promoting democratic values with more strategic purpose and tactics (Nitoiu 2015). Diplomats concurred that the EU needed to deploy more strategic heft, precision and agility to create the conditions within which support for democratic and governance reform could prosper. The EU committed itself to a more strategic deployment of its core political norms.

Policy-makers argued that the sharper geopolitical challenge required lighter forms of conditionality (targeted at a selected number of reform requirements) and more direct forms of assistance somewhat detached from heavy requirements of 'approximation' (or convergence) with European rules. The EU was both more insistent that its geopolitical advantage lay in its focus on democratic reforms in EaP partners and less rigid in the tactics through which it pursued that focus. EaP states did not need EU laws so much as they needed basic state capacity, security protection and more organized governance provisions. In the new geopolitical context, they needed resilience rather than Europeanization *per se*.

A general set of incentives were linked to political reforms. The EU accelerated the signing of the Association Agreements with Ukraine, Georgia and Moldova. European Neighbourhood Instrument money was to be made available on terms that were 'more flexible' and 'incentives-based', with lighter forms of conditionality – the EaP states were granted longer transition periods within which to conform to certain aspects of regulatory harmonization with the Union and in some cases, approximation requirements were made more optional than legally binding. This flexibility was particular evident in new trade provisions. The EU stepped up its offers of visa liberalization as perhaps the most attractive carrot for reform.

The EU drew up 'Civil society roadmaps' as vehicles for enhancing support to local civic actors, around their set of own priorities (European Commission and High Representative for Foreign and Security Policy 2014). The Neighbourhood Civil Society Facility was increased from EUR90 million for 2011–2014 to EUR150 million for 2015–2018. Resources were committed to a new StratComm team charged with rebutting Russian propaganda throughout the EaP states. The general spirit of these efforts was that supporting better governance was the EU's best way of approaching geopolitics.

At the same time, geopolitics also explained some limits to EU reform support and to the rewards offered as incentives to democratization. Democratic reformers across the EaP region wanted membership promises and far more money than was offered. Some critics from the region charged the EU with not supporting democracy strongly enough because it now favoured geopolitical engagement and security partnership with elites (Nodia 2014). Compared to the EU,

Russia spent more on supporting its 'civil society links' in the region, through the spread of state propaganda. Yet EU leaders and commissioners insisted there was no contradiction between the 2015 ENP review's focus on stabilization and the commitment to democratic reform.

Strategic variation within the EaP region has become increasingly apparent. The EU has stepped up support for political reforms in Moldova and Georgia, where democratic consolidation is associated with pro-European agendas. The risk is that the EU has overlooked the corruption and nepotism of nominally democratic and pro-European governments in these countries for geopolitical reasons, and geopolitical considerations have led the Union to focus on certain formal elements of political reform but not deep-seated, wide-ranging democratic quality. In Belarus and Azerbaijan, the EU has softened some of its conditionality as it searches diplomatic engagement capable of tempering Russian power in the region.

Ukraine: geopolitical epicentre

It is in Ukraine that the geopolitical thrust behind democracy support has been most apparent. After some prevarication during the 2013–2014 Maidan revolt – when several EU governments focused on negotiating a power-sharing deal with then president, Yanukovich, rather than backing the protestors – the Union increased its support to Ukraine after a pro-democratic government took office.

The EU offered Ukraine EUR11 billion of new funding. Of this, EUR8 billion were loans from the European Investment Bank (EIB) and the European Bank for Reconstruction and Development (EBRD). Of the EUR3 billion in new development aid grants, the largest slice of 1.6 billion was for macro-economic assistance. Another EUR350 million was offered as direct budget support through a state-building contract. The Commission's contribution through this contract was three times more than was originally allocated for 2014 and one of its biggest support packages offered anywhere in the world. The contract was proposed, designed and implemented in the record time of three months, using many derogations from formal EU procedures.

The EU set up a Ukraine Support Group that met for the first time in July 2014. This was an unprecedented initiative to accompany reforms across all major sectors in one country. In early 2015, an EU Advisory Mission added another layer of technical advisory services in the spheres of police reform and law enforcement. The association agreement was to include a coordinating committee with Ukrainian civil society and the Economic and Social Committee. A EUR10 million programme for civil society was introduced to fund groups to monitor government reform commitments. Officials in Kiev stated that a priority would be to support reforms that facilitated reconciliation work. The EU supported the National Reform Council in its efforts to get many different parties agreed on a reform agenda.

In 2015, the EBRD launched an initiative for mentoring reforms, placing technical experts in all the principal ministries. The EU ran a EUR8 million project on judicial reform, taking the form of twinning experts in the Ministry of Justice. This 'super-twinning' project (that involves placing European experts in Ukraine) aimed to prepare the justice sector for budgetary support. The EU and Ukraine jointly put in place an anti-corruption unit of over 30 detectives to investigate the potential misuse of EU funds. The Venice Commission was the main player on rule of law issues. The European Instrument for Democracy and Human Rights allocated around EUR1 million additional funding. The EU defined Ukraine as being subject to a 'crisis declaration' that enabled the delegation in Kiev to identify projects proactively for some funding, outside the scope of calls for proposals. The European Endowment for Democracy supported Maidan activists in the setting up of political parties.

Several Member States also became more active. Germany announced a new EUR500 million package of support to Ukraine, with priorities defined as local elections and constitutional reform linked to the Minsk accord, and training border guards. The Swedish development agency built on a long-standing presence in Ukraine to find a niche role in providing more core support for around a dozen civil society organizations. The UK's development agency returned to Ukraine after being absent for six years, because of the crisis. It launched a GBP10 million programme focusing on economic governance and anti-corruption.

The Donbas conflict reinforced EU support for a process of far-reaching decentralization. Most Member States saw decentralization as the key political process that could assuage Russian concerns and aggression. Many donors now run decentralization projects, as this issue is widely recognized as being the fulcrum for the whole reform process. The EU began to plan for local governance work that might be possible in Donbas on the back of the Minsk peace accords.

Some Member States have pushed president Poroshenko hard on the question of decentralization. They have pressured him to speed up and to deepen the devolution of powers to the Donbas territories controlled by Russian-backed separatists. This has become perhaps the most serious area of contention with the Ukrainian government, which insists that the conflict be resolved before the process of decentralization be extended to Donbas. While not going as far as Russia's calls for federalism, Germany and France have insisted that Poroshenko must agree to a special status for Luhansk and Donetsk. They have also urged him to allow elections to be held in those territories, as soon as basic electoral standards can be achieved, as well as to continue funding the occupied territories from the national budget. The EU and several Member States have begun to fund projects on decentralization, increasingly seen as a priority to create the kind of inclusive governance that might mitigate future tensions. The increased focus on decentralization is seen very much through a geopolitical prism.

EU and Member States' positions on the overarching use of conditionality in Ukraine were informed by strategic goals. The EU and Member States sought to strike a balance between a leniency designed to help the struggling Kiev administration, on the one hand, and pressure for overdue reform, on the other. Some Member States expressly saw the question of conditionality through the lens of their relations with Russia. Their critical stance towards the Poroshenko government was connected to the desire to maintain a balance in their relations with Russia. Germany became more critical of the Poroshenko government's record on reform, and this played into an increasing desire in Berlin for re-normalizing relations with Russia. Conversely, other Member State diplomats expressed the view that the Ukrainian government should not be pushed too hard on economic and political conditions because of the short-term imperative of retaining stability and securing the association agreement. They argued for a flexible implementation of trade liberalization requirements, in anticipation of Russian blaming future economic difficulties on the EU agreement. Diplomats from some Member States worried that the EU was pinning its hopes and credibility too exclusively to the new president. These internal debates showed how perspectives on conditionality were increasingly informed by geopolitical considerations.

South: differentiated caution

The situation in the South has been both similar and different. Similar because differentiation has, here too, become more pronounced over time; different because democracy has rarely been perceived as in the EU's strategic interest – with the notable exception of present-day Tunisia. Between 2004 and late 2010, the EU, even though maintaining a range of governance-related ENP programmes across the Southern Mediterranean, was largely satisfied with the status quo of keeping friendly relations with autocratic leaders (Schlumberger 2006). Its historic distrust of Islamic-leaning actors, relatively staunch support of Israel, interest in containing migratory flows and terrorist threats, and long-standing economic and security ties with countries such as Morocco, Tunisia and Egypt all led the EU to have a consistent geopolitical interest in maintaining more or less tacit support for authoritarian rulers across the Southern Mediterranean (Börzel 2015; Hollis 2012; Powel 2009). Unlike the new Central and Eastern European EU Member States, the countries with the strongest say in determining the southern neighbourhood policy – France and Italy – are also traditionally the least enthusiastic about democracy promotion abroad, perceiving the agenda as dogmatic and going against their national interests (Tassinari and Holm 2015). The ever-increasing presence of the Gulf states in the region also failed to spur the EU to see improved governance through a strategic lens, as European states have focused more on their own commercial interests in the Gulf than the Gulf's increasing role in the southern neighbourhood (Barnes-Dacey 2015; Khalifa 2014).

This difference between East and South has deep roots. During the Cold War, rivalry in the Southern Mediterranean (and elsewhere in the Third World) was not about the choice of the political system. The most important East–West agreement pertaining to civil and political rights of that era, the Helsinki Final Act of 1975, is a case in point. Its focus was squarely on the European heartland. The Mediterranean dimension of that act (only added because of the threat of a Maltese veto) makes no mention of citizens' rights (Maresca 1987; Mastny 1987). Similarly, EU development discourse and practice towards the Third World at the time, focused on economic and social development rather than democratic governance.[2]

The long-standing geopolitical preference for the status quo had an impact on both the form and the content of democracy and governance programming in the region before the Arab uprisings. In implementing the democratization and human rights agenda, the norm of respect for national sovereignty prevailed (Mouhib 2014). Thus, programmes tended to be cautious and non-controversial, eschewing the core of the agenda for democratic change in favour of lower profile human rights projects (Bicchi 2009). Positive conditionality, differentiation and benchmarking, while in principle cornerstones of the ENP, remained non-operational in practice (Del Sarto and Schumacher 2011), as did the negative conditionality contained in the Association Agreements (van Hüllen 2012). The EU kept its distance to moderate Islamist parties, even though it was clear that such parties would be key in determining their countries' democratic future (Pace et al. 2009). Discursively, ENP Action plans and other documents routinely referred to programming aiming to 'guarantee' or 'strengthen' democracy in countries such as Jordan, Morocco and Tunisia, 'as if democratic procedures were already in place' (Del Sarto and Schumacher 2011: 946).

The EU's preference was for modest degrees of political liberalization to help stabilize regime structures, not to push confrontationally for systemic rupture. The context was complicated by Arab regimes' increasing hostility to EU reform initiatives (Cavatorta and Rivetti 2014; Youngs 2014). It is noteworthy that it was mostly in countries where ENP democracy promotion programmes were particularly curtailed or entirely absent (Libya, Syria, Tunisia, Yemen and, to a lesser extent, Egypt), rather than in the most prominent recipients of democracy aid (Jordan, Lebanon and Morocco), that the Arab uprisings led to popular revolts demanding political change. Thus, it seems that if we see the EU's democratization support as a tool aiming for profound changes to existing authoritarian or hybrid regimes, it failed in promoting change. If, in contrast, we perceive it as strengthening existing hybrid regimes in countries such as Jordan and Morocco, it has had some impact.

With the Arab uprisings, there was hope that the EU geopolitical equation would change radically. After all, the popular revolts showed that the old model of supporting authoritarian stability had failed. EU and national European politicians also made their *mea culpa* (Füle 2011; European Parliament 2011). Rapidly, budgets were increased and several new initiatives were launched: the Civil Society Facility, the European Endowment for Democracy, and the SPRING and later Umbrella programmes with their 'more for more' principle of rewarding countries manifesting commitment to, and progress in, deep and sustainable democratic reforms (for a critique of the concept of 'deep democracy', see Teti 2012; Wetzel and Orbie 2012). EIDHR funding also increased significantly in the aftermath of the Arab uprisings. In all programmes, a greater stress was put on EU relations with non-state actors – a recognition of the failures of the previous policy where Southern Mediterranean governments and state bureaucracies were the dominant interlocutors for the EU.

However, with the total breakdown of the democratic experiment in Egypt, the failure of the NATO-led military intervention against Gadhafi to usher in stable and more institutionalized governance in Libya, and the civil wars in Syria and Yemen, the EU has, since 2011, been more preoccupied with stability, containment and conflict resolution than with democratization. Stability has not meant the same thing in all countries however: in Tunisia, EU supports democratic consolidation as a strategic choice. Although levels of support for Tunisia have fallen short of early promises, and have been considerably lower than for Central and Eastern European states during their early transition years (Filiu 2013), several levers have still been pulled. In December 2011, Tunisia was welcomed into the EBRD, which had invested EUR290 million by end-2015 (European Bank for Reconstruction and Development 2016); EIB investments took off, with EUR1.3 billion worth of contracts signed 2011–2015 – by far the largest per capita in the region (European Investment Bank 2016); EU aid in 2011–2014 amounted to EUR614 million, and is estimated to reach EUR725–886 million for 2014–2020. Bilateral aid from EU Member States also increased. There has also been a push towards deepened trade relations, with a first round of negotiations for a Deep and Comprehensive Free Trade Area (DCFTA) in April 2016, and increased cross-border mobility through a so-called Mobility Partnership.

Morocco: strategic variation

Morocco offers an illustration of the EU geopolitical interest in stability over wholesale democratic considerations, and its support of reform that is carefully controlled and bounded. Morocco's softer authoritarianism was clearly an advantage before the Arab uprisings, as it made close relations easier to justify: Morocco had, since the mid-1990s onwards, adopted some of the jargon and terminology of the democratization agenda and made tangible, but not game-changing, reforms in areas such as freedom of the press, electoral processes, the protection of human rights, administrative modernization and the encouragement of civil society (Boukhars 2011). Before 2011, it was thus something of an Arab 'poster boy' for reform.

In per capita terms, Morocco was also, together with Lebanon and Jordan, a main recipient of EU democracy aid until the Arab uprisings. We see the same pattern here as in the rest of the region: a scrupulous respect for sovereignty; a focus on relatively uncontroversial areas, and especially areas pre-selected by the government for reform (Bicchi 2010); fuzzy, if any, use of conditionality – it was, for instance, unclear what precise progress in the governance area led the EU to offer Morocco an Advanced Status in 2008 (Kausch 2009); and a clear distance on the part of the EU towards the moderate Moroccan Islamist party, the Justice and Development Party (PJD) (Cavatorta 2009). Failures to achieve results did not lead to any strong reaction on the part of the EU: key judicial reform projects were postponed several times without any serious consequences (Khakee 2010). Discursively, even though problems were noted, Morocco

Table 40.1 SPRING and Umbrella Programme Funds – application of the 'more for more' principle (in EUR million)

	2011	2012	2013	2014	2015
Egypt	–	90[i]	–	–	–
Morocco	–	80	35	–	–
Tunisia	20	80	40	50	72

[i]Announced in November 2012.
Source: European Commission 2013; European Commission 2016.

has often been praised for sometimes flawed reforms, in what Kristina Kausch calls 'an incoherent "applause policy"' that 'creates a distorted image of what the EU perceives as the reality of Moroccan political life, thereby indirectly bolstering the ruling elite and weakening the position of Moroccan democracy activists' (Kausch 2009: 172).

After the Arab uprisings, Morocco's image as a regional leader of reform was threatened. It made some limited constitutional changes in a top-down, palace-led process ratified by popular referendum (Benchemsi 2012; Bendourou 2012; Ferrié and Dupret 2011). After a few months of tolerance of protests, the regime has clamped down harder on youth movements and subsequently on journalists, scholars and others voicing opposition. This did not trigger much of a reaction from the EU. In fact, since the first days of the Arab uprisings, the EU has often associated Morocco with Tunisia, Egypt and Libya, even though, unlike the others, it had not seen momentous change (Youngs 2014: 97–99). Thus, Morocco received funding envelopes well on par with Egypt and Tunisia under the 'more for more' SPRING envelope, despite the country's lack of any structural change of regime (see Table 40.1). This has changed under the successor to the SPRING programme (the so-called umbrella funds). However, not more than 10 per cent of total funding envelopes are linked to positive conditionality (Koenig 2016).

European democracy support has worked in cooperation with the regime's limited reform agenda, not against it. Thus, for instance, an EIDHR Objective 1 project[3] proposal on human rights in Western Sahara was discarded, although initially shortlisted by the EIDHR unit in Brussels. The reason was reportedly the vociferous opposition of the Head of the EU Delegation in Rabat, who did not want to ruffle Moroccan feathers on the sensitive and contested issue of human rights in Moroccan-controlled Western Sahara (Mouhib 2014). The effects of European democracy aid to Morocco to date have also been decidedly mixed: a growing body of literature is in fact stressing that democracy aid has the direct effect of helping to strengthen the Moroccan hybrid regime (Khakee 2017). The case of Morocco shows that the EU's support for democratic reform is characterized not so much by institutionalized uniformity but by strategic variation – a variation that derives from objectives that are in turn conditioned by the nature of a country's political regime.

Conclusions

Security and geopolitical considerations have increasingly filtered into the balances that the EU strikes in supporting democracy reform across the ENP region. There is no singular relationship between democracy support and geopolitical interest. Often the EU is propelled to do more to support political reforms in neighbourhood states to defend core strategic interests. In other instances, diplomats see support for democracy as potentially useful if encouraged in a low-key and low-cost fashion. At other times, the EU goal has been actively to discourage democratic change. The extent to which the EU supports democracy, and the tactics it uses to such an end, vary according to geopolitical calculation. This is not to say that other variables are unimportant in explaining EU democracy policies; rather, it is to register that geopolitics is far from absent from democracy support variations.

In the East, the EU's response to the Ukraine conflict was not geopolitical in a classical sense. It was about reinforcing support for stable and legitimate political structures and collective security in the eastern neighbourhood, but now accompanied by a heightened recognition that a more competitive strategic context required the EU to reassess the means of achieving such aims. The EU has increased support for democratic norms in those countries where such reforms offered an incipient process for pushing back against Russian influence. But the Union sought to do this without the costs of promising membership. In those states not committed to political reform, the EU sought more pragmatic areas of cooperation. The EU responded to the crisis by supporting milieu improvements that would make EaP states more resilient, while combining these efforts with a concern over relative strategic positioning *vis-à-vis* Russia.

In the South, the EU's response to the Tunisian uprising was not dissimilar to that of Ukraine. Once it seemed evident that Tunisians were serious about democratic reform, the EU made the strategic choice of supporting it – even though the Union's commitment has not been as wholehearted as it was in the case of Central and Eastern Europe and has fallen short of Tunisians' hopes. A well-functioning, stable democracy in the Arab world will, it is hoped, have long-term demonstration effects on the wider region. In other countries to the South, managed political liberalization remains the EU's ideal scenario. In the meantime, however, responses have been more classically geopolitical. In Morocco, the 'more for more' principle is not maintained and the King is supported for reasons of geopolitical stability. The ongoing refugee crisis has led the EU to a rapprochement with an increasingly authoritarian Turkey. The emergence of IS as a fighting force and a terrorist group both in Maghreb/Mashreq and in Europe has led to the military engagement of several EU Member States and to a stepping up of counter-terrorism collaboration with neighbouring states to the South. Support for democratization is set to face challenging times.

Notes

1 This is a general line adopted across the literature, but for a flavour see Börzel and Risse (2008) and Whitman and Wolff (2010).
2 The geopolitical disinterest in promoting democracy continued after the end of the Cold War. Thus, for instance, seeing aid dry up due to Western focus on Central and Eastern Europe, King Hussein of Jordan initially attempted to regain aid funding shares through democratic reform, including holding the first elections in decades and introducing a liberalized media law. This failed, however: neither the US nor the EU re-opened their coffers. Instead, Hussein was more successful in securing (mainly US) aid monies through a peace deal with Israel. As one analyst concluded: 'peace with Israel succeeded where democracy had failed to restore the flow of Western funds to Jordan' (Kassay 2002: 55). Given that this agreement was not popularly anchored, it arguably made democratization more difficult by creating sharper divisions within Jordanian society, magnified by the fact that a large share of the Jordanian population is of Palestinian descent. Thus, in the aftermath of the signature of the peace treaty in 1994, King Hussein clamped down on mounting internal dissent (ibid.). Other more oft-cited instances where democratic gut reactions on the part of the EU have been weak or contested include the aftermath of the Algerian elections in 1991 and the Hamas victory in the Palestinian elections of 2006.
3 Projects falling under EIDHR Objective 1 are considered as concerning at risk contexts which require discretion regarding proposition, selection and implementation. They are handled by the DEVCO EIDHR unit in Brussels, rather than EU Delegations in the target countries.

References

Ademmer, E. (2015) 'Interdependence and EU-Demanded Policy Change in a Shared Neighbourhood', *Journal of European Public Policy* 22(5): 671–689.

Babayan, N. (2014) *Democratic Transformation and Obstruction: The EU, US and Russia in the South Caucasus*, Oxon: Routledge.

Barnes-Dacey, J. (2015) 'Responding to an Assertive Gulf', *European Council on Foreign Relations Brief* 136, Brussels, June.

Benchemsi, A. (2012) 'Morocco: Outfoxing the Opposition', *Journal of Democracy* 23(1): 57–69.

Bendourou, O. (2012) 'La consécration de la monarchie gouvernante', *L'Année du Maghreb* 8(1): 391–404.

Bicchi, F. (2009) 'Democracy Assistance in the Mediterranean: An Overview', *Mediterranean Politics* 14(1): 61–78.

Bicchi, F. (2010) 'Dilemmas of Implementation: EU Democracy Assistance in the Mediterranean', *Democratization* 17(5): 976–996.

Börzel, T. (2015) 'The Noble West and the Dirty Rest? Western Democracy Promoters and Illiberal Regional Powers', *Democratization* 22(3): 519–535.

Börzel T. and Risse T. (2008) 'One Size Doesn't Fit All', in Delcour, L. and Tulmets, E. (eds.) *Pioneer Europe? Testing EU Foreign Policy in the Neighbourhood*, Baden-Baden: Nomos.

Boukhars, A. (2011) *Politics in Morocco: Executive Monarchy and Enlightened Authoritarianism*, London and New York: Routledge.

Cavatorta, F. (2009) 'Divided They Stand, Divided They Fail: Opposition Politics in Morocco', *Democratization* 16(1): 137–156.

Cavatorta F. and Rivetti, P. (2014) 'EU–MENA Relations from the Barcelona Process to the Arab Uprisings: A New Research Agenda', *Journal of European Integration* 36(6): 619–625.

Del Sarto, R. and Schumacher, T. (2011) 'From Brussels with Love: Leverage, Benchmarking, and the Action Plans with Jordan and Tunisia in the EU's Democratization Policy', *Democratization* 18(4): 932–955.

European Bank for Reconstruction and Development (2016) Tunisia Data www.ebrd.com/where-we-are/tunisia/data.html, accessed 7 October 2016.

European Commission (2013) *Summary: Support for Partnership, Reform and Inclusive Growth in Favour of the Southern Neighbourhood for 2013 (SPRING 2013)*.

European Commission (2016) European Neighbourhood Policy and Enlargement Negotiations: Tunisia http://ec.europa.eu/enlargement/neighbourhood/countries/tunisia/index_en.htm, accessed 7 October 2016.

European Commission and High Representative for Foreign and Security Policy (2011) *A New Response to a Changing Neighbourhood, COM (2011) 303*, 25 May.

European Commission and High Representative for Foreign and Security Policy (2014) *Neighbourhood at the Crossroads: Implementation of the European Neighbourhood Policy in 2013, JOIN (2014) 12 final*.

European Commission and High Representative for Foreign and Security Policy (2015) *Review of the European Neighbourhood Policy SWD 500 final*.

European Council (2003) *A Secure Europe in a Better World: European Security Strategy*, Brussels, 12 December.

European Investment Bank (2016) 'Finance Contract Signed—Mediterranean Countries: Breakdown by Country, www.eib.org/projects/loan/regions/5?from=2011&to=2015, accessed 7 October 2016.

European Parliament (2011) *European Parliament Resolution of 17 February 2011 on the Situation in Egypt*, P7-TA-2011-0064, 17 February.

Ferrié, J.-N. and Dupret, B. (2011) 'La nouvelle architecture constitutionnelle et les trois désamorçages de la vie politique marocaine', *Confluences Méditerranée* 78: 25–34.

Filiu, J.-P. (2013) 'Europe and the Arab Revolution: A Missed Opportunity?', in Chopin, T. and Foucher M. (eds.) *Schuman Report on Europe: State of the Union 2013*, Paris: Springer, 111–115.

Forsberg, T. (2011) 'Normative Power Europe, Once Again: A Conceptual Analysis of an Ideal Type', *Journal of Common Market Studies* 49(6): 1183–1204.

Füle, Š. (2011) 'Speech on the Recent Events in North Africa', European Commission Press Release Database, 28 February.

Hollis, R. (2012) 'No Friend of Democratization: Europe's Role in the Genesis of the Arab Spring', *International Affairs* 88(1):81–94.

Kassay, A. (2002) 'The Effects of External Forces on Jordan's Process of Democratization', in Joffé, G. (ed.) *Jordan in Transition 1990–2000*, London: Hurst & Company, 45–65.

Kausch, K. (2009) 'The European Union and Political Reform in Morocco', *Mediterranean Politics* 14(2): 165–179.

Khakee, A. (2010) 'How Seriously Does the EU Take Governance Reform in Morocco? The Test Case of Justice Sector Reform', *IPRIS Maghreb Review* 3: 15–18.

Khakee, A. (2017) 'Democracy Aid or Autocracy Aid? Unintended Effects of Democracy Assistance in Morocco', *The Journal of North African Studies* 22(2): 238–258, DOI: 10.1080/13629387.2017.1279971.

Khalifa, I. (2014) 'Explaining the Patterns of the Gulf Monarchies' Assistance After the Arab Uprisings', *Mediterranean Politics* 19(3): 413–430.

Koenig, N. (2016) 'Taking the ENP Beyond the Conception-Performance Gap', *Jacques Delors Institut Policy Paper* 160, 22 March.

Maresca, J. (1987) *To Helsinki: Conference on Security and Cooperation in Europe, 1973–1975*, Duke Press Policy Studies, Durham, NC: Duke University Press.

Mastny, V. (1987) *Helsinki, Human Rights, and European Security: Analysis and Documentation*, Durham, NC: Duke University Press.

Mouhib, L. (2014) 'EU Democracy Promotion in Tunisia and Morocco: Between Contextual Changes and Structural Continuity', *Mediterranean Politics* 19(3): 351–372.

Nitoiu, C. (2015) 'The Ukraine Crisis is Forcing the EU to Abandon Normative Power and Act More Strategically in its Eastern Neighbourhood', LSE EUROPP Blog, 21 September.

Nodia, G. (2014) 'The Revenge of Geopolitics', *Journal of Democracy* 25(4): 139–150.

Pace, M., Seeberg, P. and Cavatorta, F. (2009) 'The EU's Democratization Agenda in the Mediterranean: A Critical Inside-Out Approach', *Democratization* 16(1): 3–19.

Petrova, T. (2014) *Exporting Democracy in Eastern Europe: A Comparative Study of Postcommunist States*, Cambridge: Cambridge University Press.

Powel, B. (2009) 'The Stability Syndrome: US and EU Democracy Promotion in Tunisia', *Journal of North African Studies* 14(1): 57–73.

Schimmelfennig, F. (2011) 'How Substantial is Substance? Concluding Reflections on the Study of Substance in EU Democracy Promotion', *European Foreign Affairs Review* 16(4): 727–734.

Schlumberger, O. (2006) 'Dancing with Wolves: Dilemmas of Democracy Promotion in Authoritarian Contexts', in Jung, D. (ed.) *Democratization and Development: New Political Strategies in the Middle East*, New York: Palgrave, 33–60.

Shapovalova N. and Youngs, R. (2013) 'Civil Society Support in the Eastern Neighbourhood: A Turn to Civil Society?', *Fride Working Paper* 115.

Tassinari, F. and Holm, U. (2015) 'Values Promotion and Security Management in Euro-Mediterranean Relations', in Marchi, L., Whitman, R. and Edwards, G. (eds.) *Italy's Foreign Policy in the Twenty-First Century A Contested Nature?*, Oxon: Routledge.

Teti, A. (2012) 'The EU's First Response to the "Arab Spring": A Critical Discourse Analysis of the Partnership for Democracy and Shared Prosperity', *Mediterranean Politics* 17(3): 266–284.

van Hüllen, V. (2012) 'Europeanization Through Cooperation? EU Democracy Promotion in Morocco and Tunisia', *West European Politics*, 35(1): 117–134.

Wetzel, A. and Orbie, J. (2012) 'The EU's Promotion of External Democracy: In Search of the Plot', *CEPS Policy Brief* 281, 13 September.

Whitman, R. and Wolff, S. (2010) (eds.) *The European Neighbourhood Policy in Perspective*, Basingstoke: Palgrave Macmillan.

Youngs, R. (2014) *Europe in the New Middle East: Opportunity or Exclusion?*, Oxford: Oxford University Press.

41
DEMOCRACY PROMOTION BY FUNCTIONAL COOPERATION

Tina Freyburg and Sandra Lavenex

Introduction

In response to the regime breakdowns in some Arab countries, the European Commission suggested a 'New Partnership for Democracy and Shared Prosperity with the Southern Mediterranean.' When explaining this strategy in an article published in *The New York Times* on 25 February 2011, Catherine Ashton (2011), then High Representative for Foreign Affairs and Security Policy, emphasised that the European Union (EU) is

> determined to help Tunisia, Egypt and other countries not just to start their journey toward democracy, but to complete it [...] That will involve detailed, unglamorous, work on the ground – with civil servants, local communities, the police, army and judiciary – laying the foundations of deep democracy and then building it up, brick-by-brick.

Democracy promotion by functional cooperation centres precisely on this detailed, technical work on the ground. The 'governance model' of democracy promotion (Lavenex and Schimmelfennig 2011; Freyburg et al. 2015) postulates the transfer of democratic governance as a side effect of functional cooperation, which lies at the heart of the European Neighbourhood Policy (ENP).

While, five years after the ENP was launched, there was some indication that this low-key, depoliticised and technocratic way of transferring democratic principles and practices might indeed present an important complement, if not alternative, to more straightforward strategies of promoting democratic change, ten years later geopolitics appears to paralyse even this soft version of democracy support. The first decade of the ENP has dampened expectations as to its potential to induce democratisation in the EU's East and South. The violent collapse of the so-called 'Arab Spring', the return of armed conflict in Georgia and Ukraine and the internal contestation of the strong pro-EUropean course in Moldova. have deeply shaken the EU's image and efficacy as promoter of democracy, the rule of law and human rights.

Probably much of this image was due to a specific historical context in the late 1980s to early 1990s and the coincidence of a political demand for democratisation on the part of newly liberalising countries with the creation of a more political EU. After the breakdown of communist regimes, the EU contributed successfully to the consolidation of democracy in the region through its policy of accession conditionality (Schimmelfennig et al. 2006; Schimmelfennig and Scholtz 2008) or active leverage (Vachudova 2005). After the completion of its historic eastern enlargement, this foreign policy success has continued to shape expectations towards the EU's ability to trigger and foster democratic change in its neighbourhood. Eventually, the ENP was modelled on the EU's enlargement policy, without providing a membership perspective.

Acknowledging that the EU's leverage in the neighbourhood is limited, we propose a different and much less ambitious perspective on the EU's potential role in democracy promotion that centres on the idea of democratic governance transfer as a side-effect of sectoral cooperation between the EU and its neighbouring partner countries (Freyburg et al. 2009; 2011; 2015). In this chapter, we first argue that the experience of eastern enlargement has suggested an idealised vision of the EU as a transformative power that is ill-suited to understanding the more indirect, partial and subtle effects a policy like the ENP can have in terms of the diffusion of democratic governance. We then present this governance model of democracy promotion, which we deem specific to the EU's ENP, and illustrate its potential with examples taken from a multi-annual research project on the topic conducted with a group of colleagues and published in Lavenex and Schimmelfennig (2011) and Freyburg et al. (2009; 2011; 2015).[1] Finally, and due to recent developments, we contend that the effectiveness of governance-driven democratisation suffers from increased politicisation and geopolitical hardening of the neighbourhood relations. This hardening is mirrored in a diminishing openness of state administrations in ENP countries to external influences, as well as increasing obstacles for civil society organisations to fight for their rights. We conclude that democracy promotion, through functional cooperation, can have a certain impact even in relations with authoritarian regimes but only in a peaceful, interdependent world.

The exception of EU post-communist democracy promotion

The European Neighbourhood Policy (ENP) is directly modelled on the EU's enlargement policy (Kelley 2006). It was designed in the attempt to reproduce the transformative power ascribed to the EU in the context of post-communist enlargement. More than ten years later, it appears to have been falling short of achieving the same degree of democratising influence – partially due to an idealised vision of EU democracy promotion enabled by context-specific factors that do not hold beyond eastern enlargement, as we outline in this chapter.

First, the democratic transition in Central and Eastern Europe (CEE) was primarily driven by strong endogenous forces in populations and elites (Dryzek and Holmes 2002). Some even argue that most domestic changes would have been initiated without EU support (Houghton 2007; Mungiu-Pippidi 2014). Conversely, where strong domestic drivers for genuine change were missing, once the EU had lost most of its leverage, after accession, some originally pro-Europeanisation actors returned to earlier practices, such as clientele-based distribution of spending budget, control of public media and immunity from corruption accusation (Mungiu-Pippidi 2010). As the ill-fated democratisation movements in numerous ENP countries have shown, pro-democratic reforms in these countries face political resistance, and democratic regimes are more difficult to establish and sustain.

Second, 'Europeans first thought about democracy promotion in their neighbourhood after 1989' (Kopstein 2006: 90), that is, after the implosion of the Soviet Union and the initiation of liberalisation processes. Put differently, the EU's strategy is first to build up democracy rather than to break down authoritarian regimes (Freyburg 2014; Magen and McFaul 2009). In the context of enlargement, scholars agree that, as a 'tool of democratization' (Grossmann 2006),

European integration does not have the power to initiate processes of democratisation in (stable) authoritarian regimes. Rather, democratisation support by the EU can increase the speed and quality of domestically driven democratic change. Yet, as demonstrated by both the 'Colour Revolutions' and 'Arab Spring', if authoritarian leaders from within or from outside (namely, Russia) mount powerful counter-attacks, there is little external democracy promoters can do from the outside (Hess 2016).

Third, in the ENP, the EU lacks its strongest incentive for promoting democratic reforms, the membership perspective (Schimmelfennig and Scholtz 2008). In the case of post-Soviet Eastern Europe, the EU has been unwilling to extend the prospect of accession to the aspiring candidates. One may argue that an ENP country that strongly aspires to join the EU, and receives encouraging signals from some Member States, might act as if it was offered a membership perspective and outperform the ENP benchmark (Sasse 2008). Yet, the Council of the EU would need to officially grant a membership perspective to the would-be-candidate by unanimity, which appears unlikely in view of increasing 'enlargement fatigue'. In the case of the Middle East and Northern Africa (MENA) region, third countries have shown no willingness to join the EU.[2] After all, why should the ruling political elite be willing to commit what amounts to political and economic suicide by complying with the EU accession criteria (Schlumberger 2006)? Finally, when the countries that most recently joined have already been rather heterogeneous with the Visegrad group, the Baltics and the Balkan; the sixteen ENP countries are certainly far from forming a homogeneous neighbourhood, not least because some are uninterested in reform – others may even be failed states – and the EU Member States are themselves pursuing divergent interests and goals. Thus, any attempt to assess the ENP's contribution to democracy promotion today through the prism of the exceptional experience with the countries of Central and Eastern Europe in the 1990s is doomed to failure.

Functional cooperation and democratic governance promotion

The 'governance model' is anchored less in an understanding of the ENP as a foreign policy than as a regional structure of functional integration between the EU and its neighbours in different policy sectors such as trade, the environment, energy or migration (Freyburg et al. 2015; Lavenex 2014). The basic idea of this model is reflected in the 2012 EU Communication on the ENP:

> [t]he EU's values of respect of human rights, democracy and the rule of law [. . .] are also reflected in the EU's laws, norms and standards. Taking over EU norms and standards *through sector cooperation* will respond to the partners' wish to come closer to the EU, and, crucially, it will promote such values.
>
> *(European Commission 2012: 18, emphasis added)*

As an extended system of functional regional integration without institutional membership, the ENP is based on the projection of EU policy rules to the neighbourhood as a basis for cooperation. These activities are captured by the concept of external governance, '[which] takes place when parts of the *acquis communautaire* are extended to non-Member States' (Lavenex 2004: 683). When externalising its substantive *acquis* rules for regulating policy in each sector subject to functional cooperation, the EU also transfers procedural rules on how decisions are made and implemented. Given that these procedural rules were developed for advanced democracies, they, in principle, embody provisions of democratic governance, notably participatory, transparent and accountable modes of decision-making at the level of public administration.

By participating in cooperation frameworks, state officials in partner countries can become acquainted with democratic governance (Freyburg 2015). Since partner countries concur with their commitments under their association agreements and ENP Action Plans, and approximate their domestic legislation to the respective EU *acquis*, these provisions can also enter domestic legislation, if not shape, administrative practices, thus contributing – albeit indirectly and only partially – to more democratic governance.

There is evidence that the EU recognised democratising potential of sectoral cooperation already, before launching the ENP in 2004–5. In its 2001 Communication on Democracy and Human Rights Promotion, it declared that

> [t]o promote human rights and democratisation objectives in external relations, the EU draws on a wide-range of instruments [. . .] Some are more innovative, and potentially underused, namely Community instruments in policy areas such [as] the environment, trade, the information society and immigration which have the scope to include human rights and democratisation objectives.
> *(Commission of the European Communities 2001: 6)*

One year after launching the ENP, the European Commission acknowledged that

> [g]overnance in the broad sense is central to [. . . the ENP] action plans, which [. . .] focus on [. . .] introducing sectoral reforms (transport, energy, information society, environment, etc.) in order to improve management and encourage the authorities to account for their decisions to those they administer.
> *(Commission of the European Communities 2006: 16)*

In the same document, the Commission specified that

> [d]emocratic governance is to be approached holistically, taking account of all its dimensions (political, economic, social, cultural, environmental, etc.). [. . .] Accordingly, the concept of democratic governance has to be integrated into each and every sectoral programme
> *(European Commission 2006: 6)*

including cooperation with external actors.

The EU has established numerous policy reform networks aimed at joint problem solving and transfer of best practices in the neighbourhood. Some networks in the eastern neighbourhood evolved in the early 1990s; however, most of the networks evolved with the EU's expansion to the East. Since the mid-2000s, projects such as Twinning, TAIEX and SIGMA, previously available only for candidate states, became available for the ENP countries. In addition, since 2006, ENP countries can participate in the EU regulatory agencies, facilitating policy convergence and increasing linkage (Lavenex 2015). Overall, these networks involve the intensification of contact between administrations and are geared to the approximation of legislative and administrative governance standards.

Support for this kind of democratic governance differs from traditional models of democracy promotion, that is, top-down democratic conditionality and bottom-up democracy assistance, in several respects (Lavenex and Schimmelfennig 2011). First, democratic governance promotion targets states' sectoral legislation, which guides executive action within the different areas of public policy – such as environmental policy, market regulation, welfare regimes or internal security. This approach does not address states' national constitutions and the establishment of core democratic institutions, such as free and fair elections, rule of law or human rights – the traditional elements included in political conditionality, nor does it target the societal basis of democratisation movement – be it through foreign aid or assistance to civil society groups, among other channels. Rather, the primary addressees of democratic governance promotion are public officials working in the administration and ministries of the target countries.

Second, instead of democratic macro-institutions – such as an independent judiciary, universal suffrage, or freedom of association – the model focuses on procedural principles of democratically legitimate political-administrative behaviour embedded in sectoral legislation, notably transparency, accountability and societal participation. Transparency refers both to access to issue-specific data and to governmental provision of information about decision making. Accountability is about public officials' obligation to justify their decisions and actions, the possibility of appeal and sanctioning over misconduct. This can include both horizontal accountability between independent state agencies (such as investigating committees, or ombudsmen) and vertical accountability that emphasises the obligation for public officials to justify their decisions. Participation denotes non-electoral forms of participation such as involvement of non-state actors in administrative decision- and policy-making (Freyburg et al. 2007). Having been developed by democratic countries for democratic countries, the EU sectoral *acquis* abounds with such democratic governance provisions.

Finally, if governance-driven democratisation is successful, democratic governance provisions are transferred into domestic sectoral legislation (that is, formal rule adoption) and applied in everyday administrative practice (that is, rule application). At both stages, the role of an external actor (the EU), consists not only of encouraging the reform process but also of providing the relevant templates or examples of how legal rules should be incorporated into legislation and how to ensure their effective implementation. By participating in cooperative activities, their ENP counterparts can thus also become acquainted with democratic practices of administrative governance (Freyburg 2015). We do not expect an automatic spillover from rule adoption to rule application. A certain law incorporating the elements of democratic governance may be successfully adopted as part of a functional problem-solving strategy but, anticipating high political costs, not implemented.

In sum, the governance model presents a separate model of democracy promotion, which has – due to its indirect and subtle nature – some potential for encouraging democratic developments in countries where more direct forms of external democracy promotion fail. Since functional cooperation is, in most cases, 'actively sought by regimes that see them as unthreatening and offering additional resources to boost policy-implementation capacity' (Youngs 2009: 898), democratic governance promotion can occur within a generally semi-autocratic political system. When intentionally used for political purposes, however, functional cooperation risks losing its political innocence and potential to initiate subtle processes of democratisation (Freyburg 2011). Moreover, an increase in democratic governance is no real substitute for democratic transformation proper. Rules pertaining to transparency provisions in environmental legislation – or to independent judicial review in asylum policy, for instance – are only small drops in the ocean of institutional provisions constituting a democratic order. If included in domestic legislation, provisions of democratic governance can constitute a domestically legitimised point of reference for reform-minded agents that may demand their realisation in practice (Freyburg 2012). Overall, while unlikely to engender, by itself, more profound democratic change, democratic governance plays an important role in preparing the (legal) administrative ground on which eventual political transitions can draw.

Evidence of democratic governance promotion

The conditions for successful democratic governance promotion are conceptualised based on an institutionalist approach (Lavenex and Schimmelfennig 2009). According to this perspective, rules and practices of state administration are shaped through interaction with the external environment. Institutional factors – properties of the EU *acquis* and features of sectoral cooperation – are expected to primarily explain variance in success of EU democratic governance transfer. In total, five factors are suggested as determining the likelihood of democratic governance transfer through sectoral, functional cooperation (Freyburg et al. 2015: Chapter 3): (1) codification of democratic governance provisions in EU legislation; (2) institutionalisation of transgovernmental cooperation between the EU and a third state in a particular policy sector; (3) internationalisation, or reinforcement of transgovernmental cooperation of a third state with the EU in other international fora; (4) sectoral interdependence, or the perceived relative ability of each cooperation party to solve a policy problem individually; and (5) domestic political costs of adopting and implementing democratic governance provisions in sectoral policy-making. In addition, the partner country must be willing to allow external experts and bureaucrats to get involved in policy-making and to accept policy learning from these external actors. Countries that enjoy greater political liberalisation and aspire to EU membership should be more susceptive to EU rule transfer.

In this section, we briefly summarise the key findings of the multi-annual research project, as published in Freyburg et al. (2009; 2011; 2015). This analysis systematically explores the democratising potential of functional cooperation from 2004 to 2012 in 12 cases – two countries from the eastern neighbourhood (Moldova, Ukraine) and two from the southern neighbourhood (Morocco, Jordan), and three policy fields of cooperation. The selected countries were initially among the most active and advanced participants in the ENP and were characterised as 'willing partners' (Emerson et al. 2007: 7). The selected policy fields – competition (state aid control), environment (water governance) and migration policy (asylum) – vary with regard to how strongly democratic governance is prescribed by EU legislation and the domestic political costs associated with effective democratic sectoral governance in (semi-) authoritarian partner countries. The comparative study is based on a wealth of official documents and other published material, and complemented with 199 semi-structured interviews – conducted mostly between 2007 and 2009, and updated with later phone and email conversations – with governmental and non-governmental actors in the four countries and the relevant Commission officials.

The study executed several analytical tasks to explore the EU's influence on modes of decision-making at the level of public administration in the partner countries. It started with juxtaposing the respective sectoral EU *acquis* with the corresponding national legislation in selected ENP countries, with emphasis on provisions of transparent, accountable and participatory governance. The interviews with local and international (non-)governmental actors established whether the existence of provisions can be traced back to cooperative activities by the EU and also the extent to which they are applied in practice. The emerging pattern of democratic governance transfer was then systematically scrutinised using cross-sectional analysis of co-variation to identify similarities and differences across countries and sectors, followed by Qualitative Comparative Analysis (QCA) to cater for potential multiple causalities (Freyburg et al. 2011).

In this chapter, we first demonstrate the analysis by zooming into the transfer of democratic governance provisions through environmental cooperation on water management in Moldova and Morocco, before we then briefly present current knowledge regarding the effectiveness of the governance model of democracy promotion. EU environmental legislation is a policy field that has adopted the democratic governance agenda particularly strongly. Three directives of 2003 and 2006 codified central elements of democratic environmental governance in the EU – partly based on the broader 2001 UNECE Aarhus Convention on Access to Information, Public Participation in Decision-Making and Access to Justice in Environmental Matters. Rules on transparency of documents and access to information, public participation in decision-making processes, mechanisms of accountability – such as the right to an effective 'fair, equitable, timely, and not prohibitively expensive' review procedure before court or tribunal to 'challenge the substantive or procedural legality of decisions' – are regularly included in sectoral environmental legislation (Freyburg et al. 2015: Table 4.3). Overall, the EU environmental *acquis* and international conventions provide developed democratic governance templates, which can be adopted by EU non-members without further specification. To what extent have these provisions found their way into environmental legislation and governance in Moldova and Morocco, which are the two most active and politically liberalised ENP countries in 2004?[3]

While environment has never been salient in EU cooperation with Moldova and Morocco, the management of water resources is one of the top priorities in the EU's environmental cooperation with both ENP countries. Eventually, in solving environmental problems, notably water protection, the EU is bound to Moldova and Morocco through the shared Danube River basin or the Mediterranean Sea. Collaboration existed at the level of experts and policy officials, and in transgovernmental policy networks, such as the EU-coordinated Danube-Black Sea (DABLAS) Task Force or the Eastern European, Caucasus and Central Asia Component of the EU Water Initiative with Moldova, and the Mediterranean component of the EU Water Initiative or the Short- and Medium-Term Priority Environmental Action Programme (SMAP) with Morocco.

Moldova was one of the first countries to ratify the Aarhus Convention but made only partial progress towards the transfer of its provisions into national legislation. If provisions of democratic governance are incorporated in domestic law, the postulated principles remain largely detached from procedures for their implementation. For example, the Regulation on the Ministry of Ecology and Natural Resources in 2004 only states that the Ministry 'informs population about the state of environment and the use of natural resources in the country, ensures access of the public to information and participation in decision making on environmental protection' (Art. 58); it specifies no ways to attain these objectives. Hence, in Moldovan legislation all three principles are adopted but presented as a general goal, which may hinder effective implementation in practice (Freyburg et al. 2015: Chapter 5).

The picture looks similar in Morocco, where all three principles of democratic governance are included in the environmental laws, yet less precise and less strict than the corresponding EU *acquis*, thus leaving ample room for (restrictive) interpretation. For instance, the 2003 Law on Environmental Impact Studies guarantees public access to environmental information and the right to appeal. Yet, it does not specify the quality of environmental information to be provided by public authorities. In contrast to Moldova, Moroccan legislation only granted access to information and public participation that was mediated *via* political institutions, until Article 27 of the constitution was implemented. That is, participation of societal representatives in the planning and monitoring of water policies was moderated through bodies such as the Supreme Council on Water and Climate, a consultative and non-permanent institution consisting of scientific experts and association representatives. In line with this hindrance, democratic governance provisions are partially implemented in transitional Moldova, while in the stable autocratic kingdom, Morocco, they are not.

To what extent is the facilitating effect of political liberalisation and codification supported by comparison across all four country and three sector cases? The aggregated overview in Table 41.1

Table 41.1 Comparative analysis

	Eastern neighbourhood		Southern neighborhood	
Country determinants	Moldova	Ukraine	Jordan	Morocco
Political liberalisation	+/−	+/−	−	−
EU membership aspirations	+	+ to +/−	−	−
Democratic governance				
Legal adoption	+	+/−	− (+/−)	+/−
Application in practice	−/+	−	−	−

Sectoral determinants	Competition	Environment	Migration
Codification	−	+	+/−
Institutionalisation	+/−	+	+/− to +
Interdependence	+	+	+/−
Adoption costs	+	+/−	+/−
Democratic governance			
Legal adoption	+/−	+/− (+)	+/−
Application in practice	−	− to +/−	−

Note: Values: high or present, **+**; medium, **+/−**; low or absent, **−**. Values in brackets correspond to draft legislation. Note that the signs for costs have been reversed for better comparison: high costs, here, have a negative impact on adoption. The study covers the situation from 2004 to 2012.

reveals that country properties – notably the degree of political liberalisation, membership aspirations and geographic region – explain hardly any difference in democratic governance. All four countries show a clear discrepancy between rule adoption and rule application. Whereas the EU has been successful in inducing the four ENP countries to adopt legislation in line with democratic governance provisions, these provisions had generally not been implemented (Freyburg et al. 2015: Tables 8.1 and 8.2).

At the same time, the transfer of democratic governance provisions worked better in the more politically liberalised eastern neighbours, in particular Moldova, than in the less politically liberalised and geographically more distant neighbours, such as Jordan. The transition country Moldova, ruled by a pro-European coalition government between 2009 and 2012,[4] shows the highest degree of both adoption and application of democratic governance, with the latter predominantly being a consequence of severe economic constraints, that is, weak financial capacity of the public sector, involving weak human resource capacity (Freyburg et al. 2015). In Jordan, the comparatively less successful rule transfer appears to demonstrate the significance of political liberalisation, in addition to proximity to the EU (Member States) (Freyburg et al. 2011: Table 3). Jordan's geographic position leads to less interdependence with the EU and a less exclusive focus on the EU as a cooperation partner, whereas trade relations with Moldova, Morocco and Ukraine are asymmetric in favour of the EU and not balanced by other partners. Jordan preserves official neutrality in its cooperation with Europe, the USA and the conservative Gulf states (Bouillon 2002). Overall, the findings suggest that relevant country properties, notably liberalisation and proximity, can facilitate or impair (but not determine) the outcomes of democratic governance promotion. If cooperation is agreed, the extent to which it influences the likelihood of successful promotion of democratic governance appears to primarily depend on sectoral properties.

The lower part of Table 41.1 suggests a sectoral dynamic characterising the transfer of democratic governance provisions into domestic legislation of the selected ENP states. First, the comparison across sectors supports the striking discrepancy between rule adoption and application. In all three sectors, national law grants citizens and stakeholders access to policy-making, including relevant information on substance and procedures, at the discretion of governmental officials, and limited possibilities to hold these officials accountable. Second, the absence of high adoption costs, and at least moderate interdependence, codification and institutionalisation, are associated with rule adoption. Adoption costs vary across sectors, depending on the extent to which the domestic ruling elite perceives the rule transfer as threatening their traditional means of power preservation (high costs), or the sectoral authorities anticipate it to diminish their political influence by causing the loss of undivided influence, exclusive information or opportunities for corruption, among other things (medium costs). For instance, EU rule transfer has been most effective in environment – a policy field with a low degree of politicisation, where transgovernmental cooperation tends to be less impeded by political considerations. None of the sectoral conditions was individually sufficient or necessary, as also confirmed by the QCA (Freyburg et al. 2011).

In sum, although transgovernmental policy networks generally operate without much publicity and are relatively unaffected by the turbulence of political disputes (Pollack 2005; Slaughter 2000), functional cooperation is still embedded in politics and affected by political interests and power. The country- and sector-level findings underpin that the situational context in which sectoral cooperation takes place determines whether the full democratising potential of the governance model becomes manifest. Only if the sector is relatively non-politicised and the political transition of the regime is advanced enough to allow for the necessary leeway and openness, the democratising effect of EU cooperative activities unveils. What do the empirical findings of Freyburg et al. (2015) suggest in terms of the future democratising potential of functional cooperation in the EU's neighbourhood?

Limits of democratic governance promotion

While, in 2004, the ENP was designed to build 'a zone of prosperity and a friendly neighbourhood – a "ring of friends" – with which it enjoys close, peaceful and co-operative relations' (Commission of the European Communities 2003: 4), today's neighbourhood presents itself as a 'ring of fire' (Koenig 2016: 4), affected by a number of intra-state, inter-state or frozen conflicts, some of which are lengthy. To the South, the monumental changes of the 2011 Arab upheavals have deeply destabilised the region, with a violent conflict in Syria, a growing presence of the Islamic State (ISIS) in countries such as Iraq and Libya, and unprecedented flows of refugees to initially relatively stable autocratic monarchies, like Jordan and Morocco, but also the fragile, but comparatively stable, Lebanon with its consensus-driven power-sharing system. The Eastern Partnership (EaP), in turn, is paralysed by Russia's increasing willingness to shield its zone of influence against EU dynamics, as demonstrated with the occupation of Crimea and the military presence in Ukraine. In consequence, the reality of the EU's neighbourhood, and hence the preconditions of the governance model of democracy promotion have dramatically worsened since the empirical analyses of the above-presented pilot study.

While Figure 41.1 cannot depict a return of geopolitics in the neighbourhood, it illustrates the development of key country-level factors in the neighbourhood over time (and as data is available). Precisely, we plot three pivotal variables that can be expected to determine the receptiveness of a country's public administration for functional cooperation, and its potential democratising effect, notably political liberalisation (Freedom House 2016), political participation

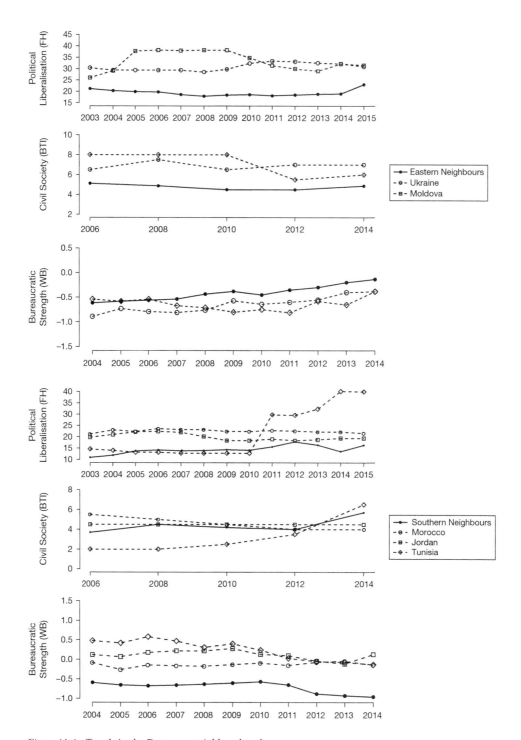

Figure 41.1 Trends in the European neighbourhood

Note: Freedom House (FH) 'Freedom in the world' aggregated scores (political rights and civil liberties) are represented by the y-axis, with 100 = best score (www.freedomhouse.org/report/freedom-world-aggregate-and-subcategory-scores#.U9t-L2BwaP8). Civil society refers to criteria 2.3 'Association/assembly rights' and 2.4 'Freedom of expression' of the Bertelsmann Transformation Index (BTI), combined to a 10-point scale with higher values for greater participation (www.bti-project.org/en/index/). Bureaucratic strength is measured with the Government Effectiveness component of the World Bank's (WB) Worldwide Governance Indicators, ranging from around −2.5 to 2.5 (http://info.worldbank.org/governance/wgi/index.aspx#home). Values of the isolated countries are not included in the regional averages.

(Bertelsmann 2016) and bureaucratic strength (Kaufmann et al. 2010). Political liberalisation combines the scores for political rights and civil liberties, based on a 100-point scale with higher values for greater liberalisation, as weighted and measured by Freedom House. According to the rating body, the scores represent the fundamental components of individual freedom identified by the Universal Declaration of Human Rights. Political participation addresses the extent to which 'the populace decides who rules, and it has other political freedoms'. Specifically, we focus on criteria 2.3 'Association/assembly rights' and 2.4 'Freedom of expression' of the Bertelsmann Transformation Index, combined to a 10-point scale with higher values for greater participation. Finally, we measure the strength of a bureaucracy by a World Bank index that combines analysts' ratings of the quality of bureaucracy, including the independence of the civil service from political pressure.

Figure 41.1 shows that overall, and except the democratising 'showcase', Tunisia, the four countries studied – Moldova, Morocco, Jordan and Ukraine – continue to show higher values of political liberalisation than the average value of their respective neighbourhood. At the same time, the graphs signal that, overall, openness diminished even in these frontrunners. In the South, possibilities for political participation have been curbed in the autocratic regimes, while the quality of bureaucracy continues to be low and likely to hinder the effective implementation of policy and governance reforms, as initiated by EU sectoral cooperation. The picture looks similar in the Eastern Partnership countries: Moldova and Ukraine's bureaucratic strength continues to improve, albeit below the regional average. Recent changes in government, which are not yet captured by these macro indices, may yield not only retrogressions in levels of political liberalisation but also a turn away from an EU focus and, despite the relative autonomy of sectoral cooperation dynamics, declining levels of approximation to EU rules.

In sum, developments after 2011 have shown how precarious democratic governance promotion through functional cooperation is. In the absence of a genuine parallel orientation towards political liberalisation, policy-transfer *via* functional cooperation can strengthen authoritarian governments rather than promote liberal norms. Even if provisions of transparency, participation and accountability have entered the domestic legislation of the ENP countries, our findings seem to suggest that without an active and relatively free civil society demanding implementation, these norms will rarely be enacted, thus remaining dead letters.

Conclusions

EU democracy promotion may operate at many levels and in various forms. Top-down democracy promotion through foreign policy diplomacy and conditionality has not been a stronghold of the European Union, apart from the historical experience of eastern enlargement. The EU is too incoherent as an actor, with the Member States frequently pursuing diverging interests (Geddes and Taylor 2015), and too little leverage to induce political change in third countries, which have no membership perspective (Schimmelfennig and Scholtz 2008). Instead, as a structure of integration, the EU has more indirect resources at its disposal to influence the societal and administrative fabric of interdependent countries. While the exercise and effectiveness of 'linkage' policies through trade, aid and communication with pro-democratic civil society groups has been the object of many studies, the potential of functional cooperation in transgovernmental networks among administrative actors has hitherto received less attention. In this chapter, we have summarised the set-up and the results of a four-year research project that has developed and applied this 'governance model' of democracy promotion through functional cooperation in the realm of the EU's neighbourhood. In the meantime, other authors have also started investigating the indirect democratisation potential of sectoral integration (Delcour and Wolczuk 2015; Dimitrova and Buzogány 2014; Korosteleva 2016; Szent-Iványi 2014).

While up to a few years ago, the ENP seemed fertile ground for this subtle approach of international democracy support, the de-stabilisation that has occurred after 2011, the rise of geopolitical contestations and the general hardening of political regimes across the neighbourhood point at the limits of a transformative approach based on de-politicised, functionalist ties. Looking back to the theoretical scope conditions identified in the studies by Freyburg et al. (2009; 2011; 2015), and reviewing them in the light of more recent data, this chapter has confirmed the complex interplay between general openness towards greater political liberalisation, the empowerment of civil society and democratic governance promotion through transgovernmental ties.

The apparently stable climate of the ENP's initial years and the analysed countries' political will for closer functional integration in the 'wider Europe' were amenable to legislative approximation, even if authoritative state structures were not directly affected. With legislative approximation, democratic governance norms travelled also, thus providing a formal basis for accountability, transparency and participation rules in sectoral laws. Yet, these norms' consolidation, from legislative adoption towards political-administrative application, has been impaired by the hardening political climate and the inability of civil society organisations or the media to mobilise around these alleged entitlements. We therefore conclude that democratic governance promotion through functional cooperation presupposes, next to a peaceful and stable geopolitical context, an ongoing political will for closer interdependence and regulatory approximation 'from above' as well as an activation of pertinent provisions 'from below'.

Notes

1. The research project was funded under the Swiss National Center for Competence in Research (NCCR) 'Challenges to Democracy in the 21st Century' (www.nccr-democracy.uzh.ch). Team members were Sandra Lavenex and Frank Schimmelfennig (the project co-leaders), Tina Freyburg, Tatiana Skripka and Anne Wetzel. We are grateful to the NCCR for funding the research. Much of the synthesis presented in this chapter is based on this common work.
2. Faced with the negative effects of EU southern enlargement on its exports of agricultural products, Morocco applied to the European Economic Community (EC) in 1987. In contrast to today's European Union, the EC back then was no more than an economic union (Bahaijoub 1993: 238).
3. Figure 41.1 (political liberalisation). Our study does not cover Israel. While both countries perform above average in their respective region, Moldova is rated considerably higher than Morocco.
4. In the presented study, we consider the period 2004–2012.

References

Ashton, C. (2011) 'Listening to the Revolution', *The New York Times*, 25 February, www.nytimes.com/2011/02/26/opinion/26iht-edashton26.htmlr.

Bahaijoub, A. (1993) 'Morocco's Argument to Join the EEC', in Joffé, G. (ed.) *North Africa: Nation, State and Region*, London: Routledge, 235–246.

Bertelsmann S. (2016) Transformation Index of the Bertelsmann Stiftung, www.bti-project.org/en/reports/downloads/bti-2016/.

Bouillon, M. (2002) 'Walking the Tightrope. Jordanian Foreign Policy from the Gulf Crisis to the Peace Process and Beyond', in Joffé, G. (ed.) *Jordan in Transition 1990–2000*, London: Hurst, 1–22.

Commission of the European Communities (2001) *The European Union's Role in Promoting Human Rights and Democratisation in Third Countries*, COM (2001) 252 final, 8 May.

Commission of the European Communities (2003) *Wider Europe – Neighbourhood: A New Framework for Relations with our Eastern and Southern Neighbours*, COM (2003) 104 final, 11 March.

Commission of the European Communities (2006) *Governance in the European Consensus on Development: Towards a Harmonised Approach within the European Union*, COM (2006) 421 final, 30 August.

Commission of the European Communities (2012) *Delivering on a New European Neighbourhood Policy*, JOIN (2012) 14 final, 15 May.

Delcour, L. and Wolczuk, K. (2015) 'Spoiler or Facilitator of Democratisation? Russia's Role in Georgia and Ukraine', *Democratisation* 22(3): 459–478.

Dimitrova, A. and Buzogány, A. (2014) 'Post-Accession Policy-Making in Bulgaria and Romania: Can Non-state Actors Use EU Rules to Promote Better Governance?', *Journal of Common Market Studies* 52(1): 139–156.

Dryzek, J. and Holmes, L. (2002) *Post-Communist Democratisation: Political Discourses Across Thirteen Countries*, Cambridge: Cambridge University Press.

Emerson, M., Noutcheva, G. and Popescu, N. (2007) 'European Neighbourhood Policy Two Years On: Time Indeed for an "ENP Plus"', Policy Brief 126, Centre for European Policy Studies, Brussels.

Freedom House (2016) 'Freedom in the World: Aggregate and Subcategory Scores', www.freedomhouse.org/report/freedom-world-aggregate-and-subcategory-scores#.U9t-L2BwaP8.

Freyburg, T. (2011) 'Transgovernmental Policy Networks as Catalysts for Democratic Change? EU Functional Cooperation and Socialization into Democratic Governance', *Democratisation* 18(4): 1001–1025.

Freyburg, T. (2012) 'The Two Sides of Functional Cooperation with Authoritarian Regimes: A Multi-Level Perspective on the Conflict of Objectives between Political Stability and Democratic Change', *Democratisation* 19(3): 103–120.

Freyburg, T. (2014) 'Building-Up Democracies or Breaking-down Autocracies? A Time-Centred Comparison of European and US-American Democracy Assistance, 1990–2008', paper presented at the 2014 EPSA conference in Edinburgh.

Freyburg, T. (2015) 'Transgovernmental Networks as an Apprenticeship in Democracy? Socialization into Democratic Governance through Cross-national Activities', *International Studies Quarterly* 59(1): 59–72.

Freyburg, T., Skripka, T. and Wetzel, A. (2007) 'Democracy between the Lines? EU Promotion of Democratic Governance via Sector-Specific Co-operation', NCCR Democracy Working Paper 5, Zurich.

Freyburg, T., Lavenex, S., Schimmelfennig, F., Skripka, T. and Wetzel, A. (2009) 'EU Promotion of Democratic Governance in the Neighbourhood', *Journal of European Public Policy* 16(6): 916–934.

Freyburg, T., Lavenex, S., Schimmelfennig, F., Skripka, T. and Wetzel, A. (2011) 'Democracy Promotion through Functional Cooperation? The Case of the European Neighbourhood Policy', *Democratisation* 18(4): 1026–1054.

Freyburg, T., Lavenex, S., Schimmelfennig, F., Skripka, T. and Wetzel, A. (2015) *EU Democracy Promotion by Functional Cooperation: The European Union and Its Neighbourhood*, Basingstoke: Palgrave Macmillan.

Geddes, A. and Taylor, A. (2015) 'Those Who Knock on Europe's Door Must Repent? Bilateral Border Disputes and EU Enlargement', *Political Studies* 64(4): 930–947.

Grossmann, J. (2006) 'EU Membership as a Tool for Democratization', Freedom House, 28 September, http://partners.civiced.org/paw/tools/people_download.php?group=event&id=199.

Hess, S. (2016) 'Sources of Authoritarian Resilience in Regional Protest Waves: The Post-Communist Colour Revolutions and 2011 Arab Uprisings', *Government and Opposition* 51(1): 1–29.

Houghton, T. (2007) 'When Does the EU Make a Difference? Conditionality and the Accession Process in Central and Eastern Europe', *Political Studies* 5(2): 233–246.

Kaufmann, D., Kraay, A. and Mastruzzi, M. (2010) 'The Worldwide Governance Indicators: A Summary of Methodology, Data and Analytical Issues', *World Bank Policy Research Working Paper* 5430, 1–31.

Kelley, J. (2006) 'New Wine in Old Wineskins: Promoting Political Reforms Through the New European Neighbourhood Policy', *Journal of Common Market Studies* 44(1): 29–55.

Koenig, N. (2016) 'Taking the ENP beyond the Conception-Performance Gap', *Jacques Delors Institut Policy Paper* 160, Berlin.

Kopstein, J. (2006) 'The Transatlantic Divide over Democracy Promotion', *Washington Quarterly* 29(2): 85–98.

Korosteleva, E. (2016) 'The European Union and Belarus: Democracy Promotion by Technocratic Means?', *Democratisation* 23(4): 1–21.

Lavenex, S. (2004) 'EU External Governance in "Wider Europe"', *Journal of European Public Policy* 11(4): 680–700.

Lavenex, S. (2014) 'The Power of Functionalist Extension: How EU Rules Travel', *Journal of European Public Policy* 21(6): 885–903.

Lavenex, S. (2015) 'The External Face of Differentiated Integration: Third Country Participation in EU Sectoral Bodies', *Journal of European Public Policy* 22(6): 836–853.

Lavenex, S. and Schimmelfennig, F. (2009) 'EU Rules beyond EU Borders: Theorizing External Governance in European Politics', *Journal of European Public Policy* 16(6): 791–812.

Lavenex, S. and Schimmelfennig, F. (2011) 'EU Democracy Promotion in the Neighbourhood: From Leverage to Governance?', *Democratisation* 18(4): 885–909.

Magen, A. and McFaul, M. (2009) 'Introduction: American and European Strategies to Promote Democracy – Shared Values, Common Challenges Divergent Tools?', in Magen, A., Risse, T. and McFaul, M. (eds.) *Promoting Democracy and the Rule of Law: American and European Strategies*, Basingstoke: Palgrave, Macmillan, 1–33.

Mungiu-Pippidi, A. (2010) 'When Europeanization Meets Transformation. Lessons from the Unfinished Eastern European Revolutions', in Bunce, V. et al. (eds.) *Democracy and Authoritarianism in the Postcommunist World*, Cambridge: Cambridge University Press, 59–81.

Mungiu-Pippidi, A. (2014) 'The Legacies of 1989: The Transformative Power of Europe Revisited', *Journal of Democracy* 25(1): 20–32.

Pollack, M. (2005) 'The New Transatlantic Agenda at Ten: Reflections on an Experiment in International Governance', *Journal of Common Market Studies* 43(5): 899–919.

Sasse, G. (2008) 'The European Neighbourhood Policy: Conditionality Revisited for the EU's Eastern Neighbours', *Europe–Asia Studies* 60(2): 295–316.

Schimmelfennig, F. and Scholtz, H. (2008) 'EU Democracy Promotion in the European Neighbourhood. Political Conditionality, Economic Development, and Transnational Exchange', *European Politics* 9(2): 187–215.

Schimmelfennig, F., Engert, S. and Knobel, H. (2006) *International Socialization in Europe: European Organizations, Political Conditionality, and Democratic Change*, Basingstoke: Palgrave, Macmillan.

Schlumberger, O. (2006) 'Dancing with Wolves: Dilemmas of Democracy Promotion in Authoritarian Contexts', in Jung, D. (ed.) *Democratisation and Development: New Political Strategies for the Middle East*, New York: Palgrave Macmillan, 33–60.

Slaughter, A. (2000) 'Government Networks: The Heart of the Liberal Democratic Order', in Fox, G. and B. Roth (ed.) *Democratic Governance and International Law*, Cambridge: Cambridge University Press, 199–235.

Szent-Iványi, B. (2014) 'The EU's Support for Democratic Governance in the Eastern Neighbourhood: The Role of Transition Experience from the New Member States', *Europe-Asia Studies* 66(7): 1102–1121.

Vachudova, M. (2005) *Europe Undivided: Democracy, Leverage, and Integration after Communism*, Oxford: Oxford University Press.

Youngs, R. (2009) 'Democracy Promotion as External Governance?', *Journal of European Public Policy* 16(6): 895–915.

42
HUMAN RIGHTS IN THE EUROPEAN NEIGHBOURHOOD POLICY

Rosa Balfour

Introduction

Human rights have always been an important feature of the European Neighbourhood Policy (ENP), tied to the European Union's (EU's) transformative political and social agenda, which the policy seemed to presuppose. They are part of a conceptual framework in which 'democracy, pluralism, respect for human rights, civil liberties, the rule of law and core labour standards are all essential prerequisites for political stability, as well as for peaceful and sustained social and economic development' (Commission of the European Communities 2003).

Over time, EU human rights policies evolved reflecting a growing sophistication in the conceptualisation of human rights, and acquiring new and more specific tools and financial means to apply them, in EU foreign policy and in the ENP. These developments were a consequence of the debate inside Europe over rights (for example, the recognition in part of Europe of lesbian, gay, bisexual and transsexual (LGBT) rights), and an attempt to respond to demands coming from citizens in Eastern Europe, South Caucasus, the Middle East and North Africa. The dramatic upheavals, which have characterised those parts of the world during the ENP's decade of existence, have brought to the fore the strength of demands for rights and deep connection between the absence of rights and instability.

The Arab uprisings of 2011 saw a partial revision of the ENP, which also affected its human rights components (European Commission 2011a, 2011b), only to be reviewed again in 2014–2015 (European Commission 2015a). By then, Russian destabilisation of Eastern Europe, the war ravaging Syria (and the consequent refugee influx to neighbouring countries), Libya's internal conflict, the return of dictatorship in Egypt and the fragility to which all countries were exposed had cancelled out the optimism generated by the 'Arab Spring' about the prospects of positive political change in North Africa and the Middle East, and were making security first on the political agenda. The EU Global Strategy, drafted between 2015 and 2016, also reflects the search for compromises between maintaining human rights in EU foreign policy and dealing with a European neighbourhood that is increasingly seen as a threat (European Union 2016).

The gap between the role human rights are supposed to play in the ENP and their actual pursuit through policy has been amply commented on from multiple points of view. The differences between the transformation the EU could promote through its enlargement policy and its neighbourhood policy has been one strand of analysis (Schimmelfennig 2005, 2015; Kelley 2006;

Bechev 2013); examinations of the policy framework and the role of human rights (Balfour 2007) have accompanied regional, thematic, and country-based case studies, as well as analyses of the tools at the EU's disposal (Maier 2006; Börzel, Risse & Dandashly 2015; Dimitrovova 2010; Balfour 2012a, 2012b).

This chapter will make a historical overview of over a decade of human rights in the ENP, examining their role in theory and their operationalisation in practice, while tying these to evolving EU conceptions of the role human rights play in foreign policy. This exercise will be divided in two periods, the first covering the first years of the ENP roughly up to the entry into force of the Lisbon Treaty (the second section), which highlights how and through which tools human rights were included in the ENP. The third section examines the changes introduced to human rights promotion in the ENP following the 2011 events, which shook the neighbourhood, those introduced in the EU's global human rights policy, which are of consequence to the ENP, those institutional changes which took place through the shaping of the EU's new diplomatic service – the European External Action Service (EEAS) – and the implications of the EU Global Strategy for human rights in the ENP. The conclusions will explain the travails of pursuing human rights in a changing and troubled landscape, highlighting the discrepancies that have regularly emerged between intentions and practice, and the normative dilemmas and foreign policy problems behind these gaps. The chapter will conclude by offering some prospects for the future due to the 2015 review of the ENP.

Human rights in the European Neighbourhood Policy

The human rights component to the EU's external policy was not introduced by the ENP. It stems from development aid policies of both the Member States and the European Commission, from the 1980s on, and reflects the international principles endorsed by the EU in successive treaties as guidelines for its external action, most explicitly from the 1992 Treaty on the European Union (TEU). The enlargement process to Central Europe linked human rights principles to the establishment of democracy, at the height of the 1990s' optimism around the notion of liberal and democratic peace. A decade later, the ENP was conceived out of the experience of the transformative impact of EU enlargement and the ability of EU institutions to promote democratic change outside its borders.[1]

Human rights, thus, were at the centre of the new policy devised in 2003–2004. As the 2004 strategy document states:

> The privileged relationship with neighbours will build on mutual commitment to common values principally within the fields of the rule of law, good governance, the respect for human rights, including minority rights, the promotion of good neighbourly relations, and the principles of market economy and sustainable development.
> *(Commission of the European Communities 2004)*

Human rights featured in most aspects of European Neighbourhood Policy. The institutionalisation of relations between the EU and individual countries entailed the signature of Association Agreements,[2] which all included a 'human rights or essential elements clause', which allows the use of negative measures in case of breach of fundamental principles. While this clause was included in most agreements with third countries, the ENP also added other commitments from its neighbouring partners through the Action Plans,[3] which are relevant to human rights, such as joining the International Criminal Court (ICC) – whose jurisdiction includes war crimes and crimes against humanity.

The 'human rights' clause allows the EU to make linkages between human rights and other policy areas, such as trade or mobility, by offering the use of negative measures in the fields of cooperation, aid, trade and political dialogue in cases of breaches of human rights. This provision could be a tool to ensure the integration of human rights principles in the overall bilateral relations between the EU and the individual country, helping what the Brussels' jargon calls 'mainstreaming' human rights in foreign policy. Annual progress reports (a procedure that was abolished at the end of 2015) empowered the Commission to monitor the human rights situation in each country.

The human rights clause has never been used, showing a preference towards practices that are more open to dialogue. Furthermore, the decision-making procedures to activate the human rights clause based on a Commission proposal would require lengthy consultations among EU Member States and with representatives of the country involved, making the process cumbersome. Finally, some (rather basic) human rights conditions were exercised *ex ante*: Belarus and Libya were contemplated as ENP partners only if substantive change happened in their regimes, and the agreement with Syria was suspended after the 2005 assassination of former Lebanese prime minister Rafik Hariri.[4]

For those countries that agreed to negotiate new Association Agreements (AAs) – Ukraine, Moldova, Georgia and, initially, Armenia – and were attracted to the possibility of improving trade relations with the EU, Action Plans (AP) were drawn up, negotiated between Brussels and the individual partner country. The language used at the time was one of joint ownership, but recent reviews of the ENP have acknowledged that 'ownership' on the part of the third country was extremely limited (European Commission 2015a). The Action Plans included a number of priority areas and further action areas, which were then broken down into specific points, making the list of priorities very long and lacking prioritisation. The EU–Georgia Action Plan, for instance, listed nine priorities in the field of human rights and fundamental freedoms to be pursued alongside a number of rule of law and good governance reforms. In most cases, there were so many the priorities that they resembled a 'shopping list' of action points rather than real prioritisation. The methodology for monitoring progress on human rights by applying 'benchmarks' was fuzzy, with insufficient reference to international standards and commitments, and lacking clear definitions of the principles expected to be implemented (Del Sarto & Schumacher 2011).

The ENP's financial tool (called ENPI between 2007 and 2011, and ENI thereafter) did not envisage specific human rights support, but a much broader heading of government and civil society, which took up a growing share of funding from about 10 per cent during the first years of the ENP to closer to 20 per cent by 2014, as Table 42.1 demonstrates.

In theory, the ENPI and generally relations with the ENP countries were supposed to be governed by the principle of conditionality: the more the partner country respected the objectives of the AP, the more progress it would make in deepening relations with the EU and achieving the incentives on offer, including the volume of aid. Human rights were supposed to be a key factor in evaluating the partner's commitment. In practice, however, the correlation between improvement of the human rights situation in any given country and aid disbursements, and progress on getting closer to the EU, has been weak and haphazard, especially during the first years of the ENP (Holden 2009; Grigoriadis 2013; Arts & Dickson 2004). In 2012 it was recognised that direct budget support, as it had been applied until then, did not work favourably towards the aim of promoting human rights and was revised to make human rights and democracy principles a 'pre-condition' for receiving external assistance, as an aim of budget support, and as a variable assessing the continuation of such support (European Commission 2012). Today, budget support is no longer offered to those countries with the worst human rights record, such as Egypt.

Table 42.1 Priority areas of ENP

ENPI: finance committed to priority areas (in bilateral cooperation)	ENP South countries			ENP East countries		
	2007–2010	2011–2013	2014 (ENI)	2007–2010	2011–2013	2014 (ENI)
Democratic structures and good governance[5]	10%	18%	17%	46%	23.2%	29%
Trade and investment, regulatory alignment and reform	26%	31%	11%	32%	35.2%	3%
Socio-economic reform and sustainable development	27%	20%	33%	21%	41.4%	16%
Support to PA	23%	15%	15%			
Support to UNRWA	11%	8%	7%			
Other	3%	8%	17%*	2%	0.4%	52%**

*Mainly in context of the response to the Syria crisis.
**Ukraine – Special Measure.

Source: Author's elaboration of data in the Statistical Annex to Progress Reports of March 2015.

The EU did devise some alternative ways to support human rights outside the ENP framework and the logic of institutionalisation and conditionality that it entailed. The European Instrument for Democracy and Human Rights (EIDHR) aimed at supporting human rights initiatives globally, and thus including the ENP countries, by bypassing governments and targeting local, regional or international initiatives directly. EIDHR can support organisations autonomously, without the consent of authoritarian governments, which repress civil society: it allows the financing of non-legal entities and human rights defenders, and is more flexible in terms of re-granting. Its budget has considerably increased over the years, up to EUR 1.5 billion for 2014–2020. The share earmarked for ENP countries has increased from EUR 47.8 million in 2007–2013 to EUR 54.7 million in 2014–2020, from 6.5 per cent to 12 per cent of total EIDHR spending. Since 2013, it can also support non-legal entities in specific circumstances, which represents an asset in countries where registration of non-governmental organisations (NGOs) or human rights organisations can lead to government persecution; and it finances many of its activities through small grants, some through local calls. See Figure 42.1.

Finally, alongside the institutionalisation of relations, which included human rights principles and financial assistance, human rights diplomacy started to play a role with periodic meetings of human rights dialogues, alongside the more general political dialogues held at senior officials' level and the other institutional meetings.

Adjusting the ENP to external shocks and internal changes

The Arab uprisings of 2011 imposed widespread self-criticism of Europe's relationships with neighbouring dictatorships, and these fed into the revision of the ENP. The next section will

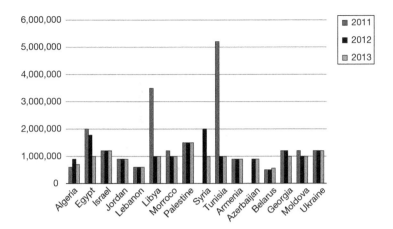

Figure 42.1 EIHDR funding in ENP countries, 2011–2013
Source: Author's elaboration of data in the Statistical Annex to Progress Reports of March 2015.

examine the political and strategic context in which the EU's human rights dimension of the ENP was being played out. Here, the focus will be on examining how human rights tools evolved in the context of the ENP and on the expansion of EU foreign policy tools.

In March 2011, the EU issued a *mea culpa* through a first revision of its policies towards the Southern Mediterranean, and again with a new package unveiled in May of the same year for the whole ENP (European Commission 2011a, 2011b). The latter document was the outcome of a longer reflection period, which had addressed some human rights-related issues, especially with respect to the role of civil society. The two documents made some efforts to revise the problems that had characterised EU engagement, such as the fear of political Islam and the conflation between stability and authoritarianism, both of which had led to consequences harming human rights in the neighbouring countries. They also reflect a growing recognition of some conceptual problems of the ENP, which was constructed on the successful model of enlargement but without offering the traction of accession to the neighbouring countries.

The document also made a claim to a new approach, by insisting that democracy needs to be home-grown and cannot be exported from external actors (European Commission 2011b). This awareness existed at least since the 2003 European Security Strategy (Council of the European Union 2003), though it was never put into practice through policies. Yet, the ENP continued to be based upon assumptions of a 'Eurocentric pull' which could instil democratisation processes. The 2011 revision, despite repeating this recognition of the need for local ownership, did not alter the overall policy set up based on incentives, conditionality for reform and aid (Bouris and Schumacher 2016). The structure of incentives was reviewed, confirming that the principle of conditionality would guide engagement with the countries in the neighbourhood. The slogan 'more for more' indicated that additional incentives were available for countries meeting democracy and good governance objectives. For human rights, the most significant feature was a new attention to civil society, now seen as the essential vehicle for democratisation in general.

Civil society support thus grew since 2011, through the set-up of the Civil Society Facility (see Figure 42.2). This focus was not just intended as a response to the 2011 events in North Africa and the Middle East. To the East, the EU had created the Eastern Partnership (EaP) in 2009, which attempted to give a regional dimension to the otherwise bilateral

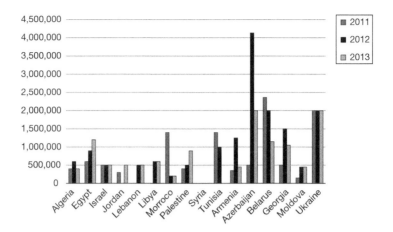

Figure 42.2 Civil Society Facility funding in the ENP region from 2011 to 2013
Source: Author's elaboration of data based on the Statistical Annex to Progress Reports of March 2015.

policies of the ENP. Regular meetings of government and institutional representatives were beginning to be accompanied by consultations with civil society representatives and the creation of civil society platforms. Among other things, this allowed the EU to establish contacts with representatives from Belarus, excluded from the ENP due to its human rights track record. Eager to induce some change in that frozen relationship, the creators of the EaP envisaged alternative forums to engage with non-governmental representatives (Korosteleva 2012; Bosse 2011, 2012).

The Civil Society Facility sponsors the EaP Civil Society Forum and other initiatives, like the Anna Lindh Foundation, for the southern neighbourhood partner countries. The increase of resources in the two regions is notable for certain countries, such as Egypt, Jordan and Palestine, where Civil Society Facility funding doubled from 2011 to 2013, or even quadrupled in Moldova, Georgia and Azerbaijan. In total, most funding went to Ukraine, Belarus and Azerbaijan in the East and to Egypt and Tunisia in the South (see Figure 42.2). These tools accompanied the EIDHR and other instruments, which are not specific to the neighbourhood, such as the Non-State Actors and Local Authorities (NSA-LA).

In parallel to the ENP reviews of 2011 and then of 2014–2015, the EU was also reviewing and strengthening its global external human rights policy. Between 2011 and 2012, the EU produced an ambitious Strategic Framework on Human Rights and Democracy and an Action Plan, which was then revised and updated in 2015 (European Commission 2011c; Council of the European Union 2012, 2015a). An EU Special Representative for Human Rights, Stavros Lambrinidis, was appointed to give diplomatic weight to the EU's positions in bilateral relations as well as in international organisations – a role considered parallel to the US Under Secretary for Civilian Security, Human Rights and Democracy – and to give human rights a high public profile.

This new approach addressed the problem of 'one size fits all', which was also one of the ENP's innate problems, and introduced a commitment towards greater differentiation between countries and situations, developing tailor-made approaches, supporting greater engagement with civil society, better integration with other sectoral objectives (such as security, crisis management or migration), more consistency and coherence between EU actors (including the European Parliament) and improved integration of human rights in EU multilateral work. As Catherine Ashton, the previous High Representative for Foreign Affairs and Security Policy, frequently said, human rights were supposed to constitute the 'silver thread' of foreign policy (Ashton 2010).

The new Strategic Framework thus represented an important step forward after many years of incremental engagement on human rights issues. It also updated human rights to the changing global environment, for instance by including new rights, such as digital ones. The Action Plans (unrelated to the ENP APs) guiding the operationalisation of human rights, show how the EU's global human rights policy was becoming broader, covering a wider range of rights, and deeper, in the sense that rights were more clearly defined. The traditional conceptual clusters of political rights, economic and social rights, and group and minority rights are accompanied by targeted action on lesbian, gay, bisexual and transsexual (LGBT) rights, freedom of religion or belief, freedom of expression (on- and off-line), the rights of indigenous people, and the rights of people with disabilities. At the same time, the Action Plan set out ambitious goals for integrating human rights in other external policies, with a focus on trade, conflict prevention and crisis management, counter-terrorism, freedom, security and justice, employment and social policy. It also indicates clearly the institutions jointly responsible for making progress in these actions, together with a timeframe. This approach represented an attempt to address the long-standing challenge of integrating human rights in all policies (Council of the European Union 2012, 2015a).

One important development is the introduction of Human Rights Country Strategies (HRCS). These are drafted by EU Delegations in third countries, in consultation with Member States' embassies and the human rights units at the European External Action Service.[6] In turn, the EEAS coordinates with the European Commission's Directorate General on Neighbourhood and Enlargement Negotiations. The focus on human rights thus shifted from the Commission to the EU's diplomatic service, even if aid programmes and human rights financial instruments remain managed by the Commission. The EEAS thus conducts human rights dialogues, hosts the EU Special Representative for Human Rights, discusses and negotiates with Member States the HRCSs, while the Commission designs financial assistance. Working together, especially during the first years of the EEAS, was not always easy and relied on the goodwill to cooperate with the officials involved. These distinctions were replicated in the EU Delegations to third countries, which all have human rights focal points, staffed by officials which report back to both Commission and EEAS headquarters.

The new approach attempts not just to support civil society development and empowerment as an aid recipient but also to install a more systematic process of consultation with civil society organisations (CSOs) in bilateral and regional cooperation with the ENP partner countries. CSOs are now consulted regularly before the political dialogue meetings with partner governments. Civil society is acknowledged by the EU to be a capital actor as a reform setter, democracy watchdog and alternative source of monitoring.[7]

These procedural and programmatic improvements have, during the past decade of the ENP, pushed the EU to increase spending on human rights-related issues, to fine-tune the practical implementation of the tools at its disposal, to improve the analysis of political developments on the ground (allowing better formulation of policy and strategic objectives), and to establish better dialogue with a broader range of actors beyond governmental interlocutors.

Yet, as the next section will demonstrate, ensuring that the ENP was fully coordinated and coherent remained a challenge, despite the institutional innovations introduced by the Lisbon Treaty. EU human rights policies in the ENP have become more specialised and relevant, but the overall political strategy of the EU and its Member States has often followed its own logic. While the EU strengthened its support for civil society, for instance, the space for such civil society to operate freely in many of the neighbouring countries has progressively shrunk (see the Table 42.2 below), with little EU diplomacy to oppose these developments.

The recently approved EU Global Strategy (European Council 2016) confirms the commitment to human rights and introduces the concept of 'resilience' of the states and societies of the

Table 42.2 ENP human rights – Freedom House indicators

Country	Political rights 2003	Political rights 2014	Civil liberties 2003	Civil liberties 2014	Status 2003	Status 2014
Armenia	4	5	4	4	PF	PF
Azerbaijan	6	6	5	6	PF	NF
Belarus	6	7	6	6	NF	NF
Georgia	4	3	4	3	PF	PF
Moldova	3	3	4	3	PF	PF
Ukraine	4	3	4	3	PF	PF
Algeria	6	6	5	5	NF	NF
Egypt	6	6	6	5	NF	NF
Israel	1	1	3	2	F	F
Jordan	6	6	5	5	PF	NF
Lebanon	6	5	5	4	NF	PF
Libya	7	6	7	6	NF	NF
Morocco	5	5	5	4	PF	PF
Syria	7	7	7	7	NF	NF
Tunisia	6	1	5	3	NF	F

Scale: 1 (best) to 7 (worst), status: F = free, PF = partly free, NF = not free
Source: based on Freedom House data, https://freedomhouse.org.

eastern and southern neighbourhoods as a strategic priority. The operationalisation of resilience and human rights will be seen through political practices.

The EU's neighbourhood in turmoil: dilemmas in human rights promotion

The EU's neighbourhood has been through most extraordinary change, but none has reflected the transformative path envisaged by the EU when it devised the ENP in 2003–2004. Since Georgia ousted its president in the 2003 'Rose Revolution', the 16 ENP partner countries experienced six more revolutions, five wars, one *coup d'état* and the endurance of five unresolved conflicts which continue to register heavy death tolls. This instability was worsened in 2014–2015 by continuing bloodshed in Syria, Russia's annexation of Crimea, conflict in Eastern Ukraine, the bombing of Gaza by the Israeli Defence Forces, fighting in a divided Libya and the rise of ISIS in the Levant (spreading to the broader Middle East and North Africa). In many countries, basic security and the right to life have deteriorated. Overall GDP growth rates have halved during the decade, while other structural problems which the ENP was designed to address, such as endemic unemployment, have remained dramatically unchanged.

During this period, there have been vital pushes from society for greater political pluralism and personal freedoms, for more dignity and freedom from corruption. These have been followed by uneven processes of opening and, more frequently, by further closure of the political space. In short, except Tunisia, and some improvements in Ukraine and Georgia, the context for normative engagement has changed for the worse, pushing for a further review of the ENP carried out during 2014–2015 (Balfour 2015; Delcour 2015).

The implications for these changes in the political environment for the EU's ability to pursue human rights are numerous, offering policy-makers more acute dilemmas about whether, how and to what extent to continue pursuing human rights in the EU's neighbourhood. Many of these dilemmas were evident during the first decade of the ENP and have become more acute; some reflect general ethical challenges of international politics, others pertain more specifically to the conceptualisation of the ENP (Balfour 2007, 2013; Noutcheva 2015; Tabur 2013).

The first cluster of dilemmas is about the aims of the ENP. The EU had to strike a balance between stimulating political reform and change in its neighbourhood (with uncertain consequences) while, at the same time, pursuing key objectives, such as maintaining stability, avoiding conflict and promoting security, managing migration flows. This is the sphere in which human rights can conflict with other strategic EU foreign policy interests in general – simplified in the 'values vs interests' debate. While this dichotomy is artificial, policy-makers find themselves often struggling with ensuring the complementarity of 'values and interests'.[8]

It is often observed that human rights are frequently trumped by other more compelling interests, such as preserving stability against the potential turmoil of unrest, thus justifying repression in third countries. Often the EU's main interest is in security cooperation of third countries on specific matters, for instance Morocco's traditional role in cooperating on the management of migration flows, or Egypt's role in 'counter-terrorism' (Balfour 2013).

In terms of means, the balance between engagement and the use of coercive measures is not new to foreign policy. In the ENP framework, the relationship between positive and negative engagement was measured through conditionality, with human rights principles (on paper) the key decisive factor for establishing the incentives or their withdrawal. Yet, the EU's application of conditionality has been notoriously haphazard, dependent on a wide variety of considerations, which depended on the real aims the EU was collectively pursuing, and deviation from the standard set out on paper was the most frequent occurrence.

Overall, the ENP has always privileged forms of engagement to forms of coercion. Those countries interested in pursuing relations with the EU essentially could engage, notwithstanding their record on rights. One important consequence was that the ENP proved to be irrelevant for those countries with abysmal track records (Syria) or uninterested in such relations with the EU (Gaddafi's Libya). With Belarus, the EU tried the full spectrum, and after 2009 tried to engage with some parts of the Belarusian establishment. Even with those countries with which a dialogue on human rights is possible, the EU had to strike a balance between pursuing further engagement while putting pressure on them to implement political reforms.

The third dilemma relates to the EU's credibility on human rights: the EU must juggle between ensuring a degree of consistency in the principles and allowing the degree of flexibility necessary to develop policies that address the specific conditions in the countries concerned. On human rights issues, the EU was appealing to the universal principles codified in international treaties and covenants signed by all United Nations members, to avoid accusations of imposing Western or European-based values on third countries at the expense of cultural diversity. For instance, human rights clauses in agreements with third countries have been standardised.

Consistency has been problematic. The ENP standardised the approach for 16 different countries, even if relations were developed bilaterally. This entailed a path dependency between policies and the treatment of countries. For human rights, the implications of path dependency are visible in the comparisons which are inevitably made between the treatment of human rights in one country and that in another. A longstanding critique raised by analysts, journalists and NGO representatives, for example, is in the different treatment of Belarus and Azerbaijan on human rights grounds: the first subject to negative measures since 1997, while the second, an energy exporter, is rarely criticised for its human rights track record, which is equally abysmal to Belarus.

The ENP revision carried out in 2014–2015 further emphasises the need for differentiated policies, reflecting both the interests of the partners and the priorities of the EU. This need not lead to a dilution of human rights objectives, but it could make the dilemmas more acute, especially in the context of turmoil and uncertainty. Differentiation can also enable the EU to build more targeted policies. Due to Tunisia's positive track record in reform, EU institutions have committed to double assistance (Tagba 2016).

The relationship between the ENP and the broader picture of EU foreign policy is another area in which the human rights objectives have been diluted or problematised. The 2011 review underlined how the ENP 'should be a policy of the Union with the Member States aligning their own bilateral efforts in support of its overall political objectives' and 'should serve as a catalyst for the wider international community to support democratic change and economic and social development in the region' (European Commission 2011b). Yet, putting the ENP into practice has suffered from a number of problems which related to the EU's foreign policy set up in general.

The Lisbon Treaty changes (the creation of the post of the High Representative, who is also Vice President of the European Commission and Chairperson of the Foreign Affairs Committee) attempted to connect the dots to make a 'whole of government' policy, such as the ENP, better coordinated, but inter-institutional relations have continued to be a problem. Human rights issues are dealt with by the EEAS as far as diplomacy, the human rights dialogues and reporting are concerned, while the Commission deals with financial support. The EU Delegations have one or two human rights officers, but they report either to the EEAS or the Commission. Finally, ensuring that human rights are integrated into all sectoral policies, such as energy and migration, remains a challenge for most bureaucracies.

Overcoming these coordination issues alone will not suffice if the broader political picture is not addressed. As a framework policy addressing 16 different countries, the ENP suffers from the diverse prioritisation EU Member States have towards individual countries and the different sensitivities are not just about the prioritisation of issues (energy, security, trade) but also about the importance of human rights and the role they should play in foreign policy. Geographical proximity and the current context of insecurity make these dilemmas more intense in relations with neighbouring countries; human rights fall easily to the bottom of the agenda.

Conclusions

'The stabilisation of the neighbourhood in political, economic and security terms will be the main political priority for the EU in the next years. In doing so, the EU will pursue its interests and promote universal values' (Council of the European Union 2015b). With these words the Foreign Affairs Council welcomed the 2015 review of the ENP which outlines a set of principles to govern EU relations with its neighbours in the near future. These suggest that the future will see far more differentiation in the relations between the EU and individual countries, and far more partnership with these countries. Human rights will continue to be part of the agenda, but the importance the EU attaches to it will vary according to the country-by-country situation. In short, the inclusion of human rights in the bilateral agenda will continue to be subject to the dilemmas pointed out in the previous section.

Over a decade, the ENP has no doubt demonstrated that the EU has worked on improving its human rights toolkit. The instruments have become more sophisticated, the understanding of the complexity of rights and their relationship with broader policy areas has improved, the linkages between human rights and political and economic developments in ENP countries have become more evident, more financial resources have been earmarked to support human rights, and better dovetailing between a governance of financial instruments based on human rights principles and disbursement has occurred. There has been a partial shift away from issuing blueprint policies towards supporting the empowerment of societies to build human rights from within. But in parallel with growing specialisation on human rights issues, dilemmas relating to the appropriateness of their pursuit have become, in most cases, more acute – in an environment where human rights are increasingly contested in the EU's neighbourhood, but also inside the EU. This will continue to constitute an obstacle to integrating human rights issues in general policies towards the region.

Notes

1 For a background to the emergence of human rights in the EU's external relations, see Rosa Balfour (2012b) *Human Rights and Democracy in EU Foreign Policy: The Cases of Ukraine and Egypt*, London: Routledge, especially chapter 3.
2 Association Agreements were already under negotiation or agreed between the EU and the Southern Mediterranean states through the Euro-Mediterranean Process launched in Barcelona in 1995; East European states conversely enjoyed an upgrade from previous Partnership and Cooperation Agreements.
3 Action Plans were negotiated between the EU and partner governments and included a roadmap of reform.
4 In 2009 the EU proposed signing the agreement but Damascus did not pick up the offer. In 2011 the whole initiative was buried by the conflict. http://collections.internetmemory.org/haeu/content/20160313172652/http://eeas.europa.eu/delegations/syria/eu_syria/political_relations/agreements/index_en.htm, accessed 26 November 2016.
5 Additional support for Democratic Structures and good governance area came through the post-Arab uprising SPRING programme for partner countries in the South (accounting for 32 per cent all SPRING finance committed.
6 The Lisbon Treaty, which entered into force in 2009, created the HR/VP position and the European External Action Service, and strengthened the EU Delegations.
7 Interviews with EU officials, Brussels, October 2015.
8 Interview with national diplomats, Brussels, October 2015.

References

Arts, K. and Dickson, A. (2004) *EU development cooperation: From model to symbol*, New York and Manchester: Manchester University Press.
Ashton, C. (2010) 'Speech to the European Parliament on human rights', SPEECH/10/317, Strasbourg, France, http://europa.eu/rapid/press-release_SPEECH-10-317_en.htm?locale=en.
Balfour, R. (2007) 'Promoting human rights and democracy in the EU's neighbourhood: tools, strategies and dilemmas', in Balfour, R. and Missiroli, A. (eds.) *Reassessing the European Neighbourhood Policy, EPC Issue Paper* 54, Brussels: European Policy Centre.
Balfour, R. (2012a) 'EU Conditionality after the Arab Spring', *Papers IEMed*, www.epc.eu/documents/uploads/pub_2728_papersbalfour_for_euromesco16.pdf.
Balfour, R. (2012b) *Human rights and democracy in EU foreign policy: The cases of Ukraine and Egypt*, London: Routledge.
Balfour, R. (2013) *EU political dilemmas in North Africa and the Middle East: the logic of diversity and the limits to foreign policy*, Manchester: Manchester University Press.
Balfour, R. (2015) 'Making the Most of the European Neighbourhood Policy Toolbox', 18 November, www.gmfus.org/blog/2015/11/18/making-most-european-neighbourhood-policy-toolbox.
Bechev, D. (2013) 'The EU as a regional hegemon? From enlargement to the ENP', in Noutcheva, G., Pomorska, K. and Bosse, G. (eds.) *The EU and its neighbours: Values versus security in European foreign policy*, Manchester: Manchester University Press, 25–45.
Börzel, T., Risse, T. and Dandashly, A. (2015) 'The EU, external actors, and the Arabellions: Much Ado about (almost) nothing', *Journal of European Integration* 37(1): 135–152.
Bosse, G. (2011) 'From "villains" to the new guardians of security in Europe? Paradigm shifts in EU foreign policy towards Libya and Belarus', *Perspectives on European Politics and Society* 12(4): 440–461.

Bosse, G. (2012) 'A partnership with dictatorship: Explaining the paradigm shift in European Union policy towards Belarus', *Journal of Common Market Studies* 50(3): 367–384.

Bouris, D. and Schumacher, T. (2016) *The revised European Neighbourhood Policy: Continuity and change in EU foreign policy*, London: Palgrave Macmillan.

Commission of the European Communities (2003) *Wider Europe-neighbourhood: A new framework for relations with our eastern and southern neighbours*, COM (2003) 104 final, Brussels, 11 March.

Commission of the European Communities (2004) *European Neighbourhood Policy strategy paper*, COM (2004) 373 final, www.europarl.europa.eu/meetdocs/2004_2009/documents/com/com_com(2004)0373_/com_com(2004)0373_en.pdf.

Council of the European Union (2003) *A secure Europe in a better world: European security strategy*, Brussels, 12 December, https://www.consilium.europa.eu/uedocs/cmsUpload/78367.pdf.

Council of the European Union (2012) *EU strategic framework and action plan on human rights and democracy (11855/12)*, www.consilium.europa.eu/uedocs/cms_data/docs/pressdata/EN/foraff/131181.pdf.

Council of the European Union (2015a) *Council conclusions on the action plan on human rights and democracy 2015–2019 (10897/15)*, https://ec.europa.eu/anti-trafficking/sites/antitrafficking/files/council_conclusions_on_the_action_plan_on_human_rights_and_democracy_2015_-_2019.pdf.

Council of the European Union (2015b) 'Council conclusions on the review of the European neighbourhood policy', *Press release* 926/15, www.consilium.europa.eu/de/press/press-releases/2015/12/14-conclusions-european-neighbourhood/.

Del Sarto, R. and Schumacher, T. (2011) 'From Brussels with love: Leverage, benchmarking, and the action plans with Jordan and Tunisia in the EU's democratization policy', *Democratization* 18(4): 932–955.

Delcour, L. (2015) 'The 2015 ENP review: Beyond stocktaking, the need for a political strategy', *College of Europe Policy Brief* 1.15, www.coleurope.eu/research-paper/2015-enp-review-beyond-stocktaking-need-political-strategy.

Delegation of the European Union to Syria (n.d.) *Agreements*, http://collections.internetmemory.org/haeu/content/20160313172652/http://eeas.europa.eu/delegations/syria/eu_syria/political_relations/agreements/index_en.htm.

Dimitrovova, B. (2010) 'Re-shaping civil society in Morocco: Boundary setting, integration and consolidation', *Journal of European Integration* 32(5): 523–539.

European Commission (2011a) *A partnership for democracy and shared prosperity with the Southern Mediterranean*, COM (2011) 200 final, https://eeas.europa.eu/euromed/docs/com2011_200_en.pdf.

European Commission (2011b) *A new response to a changing neighbourhood*, COM (2011) 303, https://eeas.europa.eu/enp/pdf/pdf/com_11_303_en.pdf.

European Commission (2011c) *Human rights and democracy at the heart of EU external action – towards a more effective approach*, COM (2011) 886 final, www.gov.uk/government/uploads/system/uploads/attachment_data/file/224343/evidence-eeas-joint-communication-dec-11.pdf.

European Commission (2012) 'Budget support guidelines programming, design and management. A modern approach to budget support', Tools and methods series, working document, https://ec.europa.eu/europeaid/sites/devco/files/methodology-budget-support-guidelines-201209_en_2.pdf.

European Commission (2015a) *Joint communication to the European Parliament, the Council, the European Economic and Social Committee and the committee of the regions. Review of the European Neighbourhood Policy*, JOIN (2015) 50 Final, Brussels, https://eeas.europa.eu/enp/documents/2015/151118_joint-communication_review-of-the-enp_en.pdf.

European Commission (2015b) *Implementation of the European neighbourhood policy partnership for democracy and shared prosperity with the southern Mediterranean partners report*, SWD (2015) 75 final, https://eeas.europa.eu/enp/pdf/2015/enp-regional-report-southern-mediterranean_en.pdf.

European Union (2016) Shared vision, common action: A stronger Europe. A global strategy for the European Union's Foreign and Security Policy, https://eeas.europa.eu/top_stories/pdf/eugs_review_web.pdf.

Grigoriadis, T. (2013) 'Aid effectiveness and imperfect monitoring: EU development aid as Prisoner's dilemma', *Rationality and Society* 25(4): 489–511.

Holden, P. (2009) *In search of structural power: EU Aid policy as a global political instrument*, Farnham: Routledge.

Kelley, J. (2006) 'New wine in old wineskins: promoting political reforms through the new European Neighbourhood Policy', *Conference Papers – International Studies Association* 44(1): 29–55.

Korosteleva, E. (2012) 'Questioning democracy promotion: Belarus' response to the "colour revolutions"', *Democratization* 19(1): 37–59.

Maier, S. (2006) 'The European neighborhood policy and the promotion of women's rights as human rights', *Conference Papers - International Studies Association*.

Noutcheva, G. (2015) 'Institutional Governance of European neighbourhood policy in the wake of the Arab Spring', *Journal of European Integration* 37(1): 19–36.

Schimmelfennig, F. (2005) 'European neighborhood policy: Political conditionality and its impact on democracy in non-candidate neighboring countries', *Conference Papers - International Studies Association* 1: 1–29.

Schimmelfennig, F. (2015) 'Europeanization beyond Europe', *Living Reviews in European Governance* 10(1), http://europeangovernance-livingreviews.org/Articles/lreg-2015-1/

Tabur, C. (2013) 'The evolution of EU's neighbourhood policy towards Eastern Europe', *Marmara Journal of European Studies* 21(2): 55–72.

Tagba, K. (2016) 'Tunisia: EU expected to double monetary assistance to €300 million', 30 September, http://northafricapost.com/14345-tunisia-eu-expected-double-monetary-assistance-e300-million.html.

43

THE EUROPEAN NEIGHBOURHOOD POLICY PROMOTION OF CIVIL SOCIETY

Silvia Colombo and Natalia Shapovalova

Introduction

When the European Neighbourhood Policy (ENP) was designed in the early 2000s, there was little on the plate for the European Union's (EU) engagement with civil society. There were separate budget lines to support local and international civil society organisations in their efforts to promote human rights and sustainable development in the neighbouring countries, but the ENP was mainly designed as an instrument for the EU's relations with governments. However, the EU gradually started to put a greater focus on civil society under the ENP. A number of factors contributed to this. First, there was a turn towards civil society participation in the EU's internal governance (Saurugger 2010). Second, top-down Europeanisation through institutional convergence in neighbouring countries was unsuccessful in the absence of a membership perspective (Börzel 2011), and even in countries aspiring to EU membership, like Ukraine, the EU needed to empower other actors beyond the ruling class to promote reforms (Wolczuk 2009). Third, civil societies increasingly raised their voices as agents of change, through a series of protests against fraudulent elections in the East and an unexpected outbreak of popular discontent against the authoritarian, state-centric rule in the South, widely known as the Arab uprisings.

The Eastern Partnership (EaP), launched in 2009, put more emphasis on civil society in the eastern ENP countries. The Commission established the EaP Civil Society Forum, bringing together civil society from the six EaP countries and the EU as one of the pillars of multilateral cooperation, next to the inter-governmental bodies.[1] After the Arab uprisings of 2011, the EU's promotion of civil society moved further up on the ENP agenda. The EU was blamed for missing the major wind of change in its neighbourhood because it had focused too much on the relationship with authoritarian leaders and underestimated the needs and power of societies, despite the fact that the Euro-Mediterranean Partnership/Barcelona Process (EMP), launched in 1995, already envisaged multilateral civil society cooperation in the framework of the Anna Lindh Foundation (Joffe 1997). In reaction to the 2011 developments, the Commission and the newly established European External Action Service (EEAS) introduced new mechanisms of engagement with civil societies in the neighbouring countries and increased the funding when reviewing the ENP in 2011.

This chapter examines the EU's policy discourse and practices of dealing with civil societies in the ENP countries, with particular attention devoted to the post-2011 timeframe. It shows that, on the one hand, there has been a visible change in the EU's discourse on the role of civil society in the framework of the ENP over time and a more nuanced and enhanced support to these actors in the neighbourhood. On the other hand, the EU still has to respond to a number of challenges and pitfalls with respect to its policy towards civil society in the ENP (Pace 2005; Scott and Liikanen 2010; Scott 2011; Bousac et al. 2012).

First, the EU strategy of engagement with, and support of, civil society in the neighbourhood is still in *statu nascendi*. For a long time, the EU's support to civil society has not been a goal in itself, but rather a means to achieve other policy objectives, such as development cooperation, promotion of human rights and democracy (Shapovalova and Youngs 2014), EU enlargement (O'Brennan 2013; Zihnioglu 2013), and conflict management and post-conflict recovery (Marchetti and Tocci 2011; Tocci 2011). This is reflected in the EU's aid to civil society being scattered across different funding instruments, which have their own logic of support. While efforts have been made to overcome such fragmentation by devising a common approach to the EU's engagement with civil society in its external relations – for example, by grouping most of the activities targeting civil society under the umbrella of the Neighbourhood Civil Society Facility (NCSF) – the results are still to materialise.

Second, the EU's support to civil society in the ENP remains driven by the Union's agenda, or the agenda decided in cooperation with the partner governments at best, rather than with civil societies. This has direct implications on whom the EU supports, how and on what issues, and may lead to the establishment of fragmented or divided civil societies in which externally supported civil society organisations are detached from the domestic societies they claim to represent (Challand 2009; Marchetti and Tocci 2011; Hahn-Fuhr and Worschech 2014). In those ENP countries, in which the EU agenda has been primarily driven by interests rather than values (for example, energy, trade, security cooperation), the EU's relations with an ENP country's government have been detrimental to civil society development, such as in the case of Azerbaijan (Gahramanova 2009; Böttger and Falkenhain 2011).

Finally, it is argued here that the EU largely promotes civil society based on its own liberal-democratic model. Whereas this model may work in democratising countries, which aim to be like the EU, it seems rather helpless in non-Western societies and/or authoritarian states. In the Western political tradition, civil society is often viewed as an actor complementary to the state and providing socialisation functions[2] and as an actor controlling the state and protecting civic freedoms[3] (Hahn-Fuhr and Worschech 2014; Beichelt and Merkel 2014). Researchers argue that such conceptualisation may not fit the state of civil society in non-Western countries. While the EU tends to view civil society in the neo-Tocquevillian tradition as 'a single, neutral and harmonious space' (Zihnioglu 2013: 127), in some non-Western cultures, civil society is 'a sphere of political struggle and contestation in which its actors interact in variety of ways' (ibid.). By promoting civil society through the prism of Western concepts, the EU may overlook potent grassroots actors capable of social and political change and instead strengthen domestic cleavages by supporting only organisations that espouse a liberal agenda.

The chapter is divided as follows. First, we overview the EU's policy discourse on the promotion of civil society in the eastern and southern neighbourhood. Then, we discuss the EU's funding mechanisms and other tools and initiatives of engaging with civil society. Lastly, we outline challenges for the promotion of civil society in the framework of the ENP.

The EU's policy discourse on civil society

The EU's engagement with civil society in the neighbourhood countries was neither easy nor straightforward. From the EU's side, it tended to be the subject of several misgivings, as the top priority was to develop effective cooperation instruments, to achieve the goals the Union itself had set alone, or in partnership with the governments. Thus, reaching out to and cooperating with civil society was sometimes pursued as mere window-dressing at best or outright bypassed being perceived as a burden and an obstacle. In addition, the degree of government control over civil society organisations (CSOs) in most countries of the neighbourhood made the notion of offering them input into EU policy-making a nonsense for many EU officials. Civil society was felt to be more an object of support than a partner in its own right (Youngs 2001). As a result, engagement with civil society was limited to those few organisations that were endowed with the resources and the capacity to lobby at the policy-making level, often as a result of co-optation by the regimes in power (Holden 2003). An additional stumbling block to the EU's engagement with civil society was the fact that many local (and international) CSOs were – and to some extent still are – highly critical of the overall EU approach towards the neighbourhood – for example, repeatedly complaining about the mismatch between rhetoric and practice as well as the Union's tendency to focus on short-term rather than long-term initiatives and on its own internal bureaucratic procedures.

The EU's selective and piecemeal engagement with civil society underwent a turbulent shock in 2011, as a result of the Arab uprisings. It could be argued that they were in many respects a wake-up call for the EU: the Union had overlooked an important force – civil society – in its relations with the southern neighbours and discredited itself by relying on authoritarian leaderships for the sake of stability and strategic cooperation. The EU's response to the popular uprisings was outlined in the March 2011 communication, 'A Partnership for Democracy and Shared Prosperity for the Southern Mediterranean' (European Commission and High Representative of the Union for Foreign Affairs and Security Policy 2011b). Partnership with the societies, with an emphasis on the role of CSOs and the youth, has emerged as one of its key pillars. Since then, the EU's rhetoric towards civil society promotion has further strengthened under both the eastern and the southern dimensions of the ENP, whereby the Union seeks to expand support to civil society as '[a] thriving civil society empowers citizens to express their concerns, contribute[s] to policy-making and hold[s] governments to account' and 'can also help ensure that economic growth becomes more inclusive' (European Commission and High Representative of the Union for Foreign Affairs and Security Policy 2011a: 4).

In addition, in September 2012, the EU outlined its vision of engagement, goals and priorities for cooperation with CSOs in external relations (European Commission 2012b; Council of the European Union 2012). The Commission emphasised the role of civil society as 'a crucial component of any democratic system' and 'an asset in itself' (European Commission 2012b: 3). In this respect, the Commission's communication defined CSOs as 'all non-State, not-for-profit structures, non-partisan and non-violent, through which people organize to pursue shared objectives and ideals, whether political, cultural, social or economic', thus clearly exposing its neo-Tocquevillian idea of civil society (ibid.). Three priorities for the EU's support to civil society in external relations were set: a) to enable a favourable environment for civil society actors; b) to promote civil society participation in policy-making, both at the country and international levels; and c) to enhance the role of civil society in development (ibid.). The Commission envisaged a wide range of tools to pursue these goals, starting from political dialogue with third countries, assistance to CSOs and concerted international action to promote civil society.

In concrete terms, in the EaP region, the EU has linked its support to civil society to the promotion of human rights, democratic governance, the rule of law, fight against corruption, sustainable socio-economic development, youth policies and conflict resolution (European Commission and High Representative of the Union for Foreign Affairs and Security Policy 2012a). The EU aims at strengthening the EaP Civil Society Forum's involvement in implementing and monitoring the EaP, including by building capacity and increasing participation in the EaP multilateral track and at the country level. Enhancement of the role of civil society, especially in policy design and implementation monitoring, is one of the strategic objectives of the EU's assistance to the EaP (European External Action Service and European Commission 2014a).

In the southern context, the EU has committed itself to supporting capacity building, advocacy, network and dialogue structures of CSOs, as they are seen as 'agents of change' and 'key actors in democratic and societal transformation' (European Commission and High Representative of the Union for Foreign Affairs and Security Policy 2012b; European External Action Service and European Commission 2014b). The EU has also committed itself to establishing mechanisms for 'structured, sustainable dialogue' between CSOs, the authorities and the EU at the regional level (European External Action Service and European Commission 2014b).

In the ENP review of November 2015, the European Commission and the High Representative have vowed to 'do more to support civil society' at the subnational, national and intra-regional levels by 'developing the capacities of civil society professionals and leadership in the neighbourhood' (European Commission and High Representative of the Union for Foreign Affairs and Security Policy 2015: 6–7). The review also recognised the importance of ethnic, religious and cultural identities and traditions in the neighbouring countries, suggesting that the EU expand its outreach to civil society in its broadest sense (ibid.).

EU aid to civil society in the framework of the ENP

In the early days of the ENP, the EU's aid to civil society in the eastern neighbourhood countries barely existed (Shapovalova and Youngs 2014). The Technical Assistance to the Commonwealth of Independent States (TACIS) programme aimed at trade and investment promotion and government capacity building. The EU lacked specialised instruments and the European Commission's presence in the region necessary for engagement with civil societies, thus, only small funds for micro-projects were distributed in four out of six eastern neighbour countries.[4] In the South, the EU's cooperation with its partners in the framework of the EMP was funded through the MEDA programme, the principal instrument of economic, financial and technical assistance. Launched in 1996 (as MEDA I, with an allocation of EUR 3.43 billion) and amended in 2000 (MEDA II, EUR 5.35 billion), the programme was implemented bilaterally with the Mediterranean countries (European Commission 1996). Civil society groups were very much marginalised at that stage and not involved to a large degree in policy-making and implementation (Holden 2003).

In 2007, the European Neighbourhood and Partnership Instrument (ENPI) was set up as the main financing instrument in the framework of the ENP and as a successor to TACIS and MEDA. A total of around EUR 13.4 billion was committed under the ENPI between 2007 and 2013, while EUR 9.8 billion were disbursed under this instrument during the same timeframe. However, with the exception of EaP Civil Society Forum, up until 2011 this instrument was not used to support civil society (European Commission 2014c).

Instead, the EU's funding to civil society in the neighbourhood has been channelled *via* various aid instruments, reflecting the fact that the ENP integrates various policy goals – ranging from development cooperation, human rights and democracy promotion to conflict resolution, cultural cooperation and education. In the area of sustainable development, the thematic programme 'Civil Society Organisations and Local Authorities in Development' (CSO-LA), funded under the Development Cooperation Instrument, aims at strengthening CSOs and local authorities, so that they can better respond to population needs and participate in policy-making at different levels of governance in support of internationally agreed development goals

(European Commission 2014d). The funds allocated to civil society actors through the country-based schemes have grown from EUR 7.4 million in 2007 to EUR 12.3 million in 2016, peaking at EUR 15.3 million in 2014 (European Commission 2007b, 2014a, 2015a). In the South, the Occupied Palestinian Territories have received the most generous funding. In the East, the support has been more evenly distributed, though Belarus has received more than other countries. This reflects the EU's policy towards this country of supporting the population while having limited cooperation with the Belarusian authorities, due to the non-recognition of their democratic credentials. Apart from the country-based schemes, civil society actors in the neighbourhood can also participate in global programmes, such as the Global Public Goods and Challenges Programme established in 2014 that targets CSOs as key stakeholders in global and multi-regional governance on environment, human development, food security, energy and migration issues (European Commission 2014e).

In the area of democracy and human rights, the European Instrument for Democracy and Human Rights (EIDHR) is the main tool of support to local and international organisations promoting human rights and democratic freedoms through country-based programmes and global calls for projects. The EIDHR takes CSOs as a primary partner in the promotion of human rights, especially in those countries that are undergoing civil unrest and conflict or are likely to fall into them. In this regard, the EIDHR has a special facility to support civil society and human rights defenders where they are at most risk. Such support has been provided through directly awarded grants of up to EUR 1 million in crisis situations, including in the countries of the Arab uprisings, the Occupied Palestinian Territories, Libya and Syria in the South, and Belarus and Azerbaijan in the East.

Through country-based schemes in the ENP countries, the EIDHR provides grants to civil society and human rights defenders working on a wide range of political, civil, economic, social and cultural rights as well as democratisation. The EIDHR funding to the ENP countries has evolved from EUR 7.5 million in 2007 to EUR 14 million in 2016, peaking at EUR 16.8 million in 2012 (European Commission 2007a, 2012a, 2015b). This increase has occurred largely due to a hike in democracy support in the South, especially in the countries of the Arab uprisings. All in all, the EIDHR is meant to be a soft policy instrument, putting emphasis on grassroots activism and local ownership as a means to mitigate the traditional government-to-government approach of the EU.

In the area of conflict resolution and peace-building, the Instrument contributing to Stability and Peace (IcSP), formerly the Instrument for Stability, allocates funding to CSOs in conflict prevention, peace-building and crisis preparedness in third countries. Throughout many years, civil societies from all the eastern neighbours and seven southern neighbours (Egypt, Jordan, Lebanon, Libya, Palestine, Tunisia and Syria) have benefited from this instrument.[5] However, CSOs in the neighbourhood countries receive very limited direct support from the IcSP. Given that this instrument is managed from Brussels, mainly international NGOs and intergovernmental organisations receive direct awards, especially when long-term funding is concerned. For example, since the beginning of the armed conflict in Ukraine in 2014, the IcSP supported international NGOs working on election observation, media freedom, psychosocial rehabilitation and humanitarian support, whereas the main bulk of funds went to intergovernmental organisations.

In the area of culture and education, the Commission has gradually opened participation in its cultural, educational and youth programmes to ENP countries starting from 2006. Through the Erasmus+ programme, the EU supports the youth to study in the EU, but also promotes the modernisation and opening up of higher education institutions in the neighbourhood, by allocating EUR 209 million for ENP South and EUR 131 million for ENP East in 2014–2017 for this purpose. The Commission supports youth exchanges and voluntary services, capacity building and networking for CSOs that work on culture and youth, 'recognising the important role that they can play in the development of civil society in the neighbouring countries' (European Commission 2013: 75). In the South, the Commission also supports the inter-governmental Anna Lindh Foundation that promotes inter-cultural dialogue in view of conflict prevention and resolution. In 2012–2014, the EU provided funds worth EUR10 million from the ENPI, of which EUR3 million were dedicated to the Citizens for Dialogue programme supporting CSOs in the region (European Commission 2014b). A EUR7 million grant for the period 2015–2017 was approved by the European Commission in December 2014 (European Commission and High Representative of the Union for Foreign Affairs and Security Policy 2015).

Established in 2011, the Neighbourhood Civil Society Facility (NCSF) is the only instrument that explicitly aims at civil society development in the ENP. It pursues three main objectives: a) to strengthen non-state actors and contribute to the promotion of an enabling environment for their work; b) to increase non-state actors' involvement in programming, implementation and monitoring of EU assistance and policies in the region; and c) to promote the involvement of non-state actors in policy dialogues and increase interaction between CSOs and authorities at the national level (European Commission 2011). The facility funds projects by non-state actors at the country and regional levels as well as technical assistance programmes to civil societies in the neighbourhood. In general, supported projects have tended to uphold the logic of the EU's cooperation with governments in terms of priority areas (Shapovalova and Youngs 2014). In total, civil society was allocated around EUR73 million in 2011–2013 under the facility financed by the ENPI (European Commission 2014c).

The EU has also proved itself flexible and quick in providing funding to civil society to follow up the political changes in the neighbourhood. In response to the Arab uprisings, the EU increased its support to the countries undergoing transition: EUR449 million to Egypt for the period 2011–2013 and EUR390 million to Tunisia over the period 2011–2012, of which EUR100 million was provided through the SPRING programme – 'Support to Partnership, Reform and Inclusive Growth' – to foster political reform and inclusive economic growth, notably targeting the reform of the justice sector, capacity building of civil society and support for the implementation of the Association Agreements and for the democratic transition. Overall, the EU aimed at strengthening direct engagement with southern CSOs. However, as a result of political and security developments in the region since the Arab uprisings, the conditions under which CSOs operate have changed. Significant differences in the political and legal climate for the functioning of CSOs in Arab countries have emerged. In some countries, like Egypt, the space for CSOs has shrunk considerably, while in others, such as Tunisia, the government pays more attention to and encourages the participation of civil society. In this light, not all the funding pledged by the EU to the southern neighbourhood countries has been disbursed.

Turning to the East, after the Euromaidan revolution, which returned Ukraine on the path of European integration, the EU introduced a State Building Contract with the budget of EUR355 million to help the new government advance democratic reform and consolidate state institutions and envisioned a Civil Society Support Programme of EUR10 million 'to enhance the role of civil society promotion and monitoring democratic reforms and inclusive socio-economic development in Ukraine' (European Commission 2014b). In addition, in 2014, the EU also provided additional funding of EUR60 million to Moldova and Georgia to support the implementation of the Association Agreements, including its free trade components. This special measure included a component of support for civil society organisations.[6]

Since it became operational in August 2013, the European Endowment for Democracy (EED) has provided quick and flexible support to a broader range of actors, including political movements and individual activists, media and non-registered CSOs in an attempt to target those actors that are not financed by other donors or under other EU aid instruments. The EED is supported by the European Commission and 16 EU Member States. During the first two years of the EED, 192 initiatives were supported with over EUR 10 million in 15 neighbouring countries, with Israel being the only ENP country not covered by the EED.[7]

Under the European Neighbourhood Instrument (ENI) that substituted the ENPI in 2014, the EU set to boost its financial support to civil society, by strengthening the capacity of local CSOs to ensure government accountability and local ownership in the domestic reform process. For this purpose, CSOs are to be involved in preparing, implementing and monitoring EU assistance in the priority sectors of cooperation identified with the partner governments, with the ultimate goal of ensuring effective and inclusive policies at the national level. Until now, however, little has been done to institutionalise the participation of civil society in EU assistance programmes to the ENP governments, including budget support (Kaca et al. 2014).

In 2014–2017, the EU has planned to allocate 5 per cent of its bilateral envelopes to the EaP countries to civil society funding through the ENI. This funding is designed as separate actions for civil society and as complementary actions to the budget support. According to the ENI Regional South multi-annual indicative programme for 2014-2017, initiatives aimed at supporting the development of CSOs and the youth will be allocated around 25 per cent of the total funds earmarked for the region (European External Action Service and European Commission 2014b).

To sum up, throughout the evolution of the ENP, more funding has become available for civil society in the ENP countries. Moreover, the EU has quickly reacted to the political developments in its neighbourhood by providing additional support to civil society and introduced a civil society component in its aid to the governments. In relative terms, however, civil societies still receive only a small bit of the EU total funding targeting the ENP countries. An analysis of the ENPI spending shows that if direct budget support to the EaP governments is not taken into account, local CSOs enjoy higher support than other local actors (around 4 per cent of EU aid). However, this share is still less than what goes to EU CSOs (9 per cent), EU public bodies (15 per cent), international organisations (32 per cent) and EU consultancies (40 per cent) (Rihackova 2014).

Moreover, the EU has not always been consistent in providing political backing to civil society and empowering it through dialogue and inclusion in bilateral relations with the ENP governments. In some authoritarian contexts, such as Egypt or Azerbaijan, when the authorities launched attacks on civil society organisations and activists, including those receiving support from the EU and Member States, the Union was too late or too helpless in its attempts to intervene.

Towards a more strategic approach?

The EU has also attempted to adopt a more strategic approach in its support to civil society in the neighbourhood. Following the provisions of the 2012 Commission's communication on engagement with civil society in external relations, the EU Delegations in the ENP countries have developed country roadmaps for engaging with civil society. These three-year strategic frameworks outline the state of civil society development and priorities for engagement, accompanied by a list of actions and benchmarks as well as of mechanisms for inter-donor coordination (beyond the EU). The roadmaps vary in their depth of analysis and priorities for engagement are tailor-made for each country, considering the context and specifics of civil society development in the different contexts. The EU Delegations have been tasked to coordinate civil society funding between the EU, Member States and other international donors. The current mechanisms vary: in some countries, there are working groups dealing with aid to civil society, in others, such donor coordination is *ad hoc* at best. It seems that the domestic political context in each ENP country greatly influences the extent to which cooperation with civil society is possible and channelled through coordinated means.

The EU also pays more attention to investing in knowledge of the civil society environment in the neighbourhood. The EU has financed country mapping studies and a monitoring tool to foster an enabling environment for civil society in the ENP countries. By conceptualising 'enabling environment' broadly, the EU not only focuses on the legal framework but also takes into account socio-cultural and economic conditions, including the membership base of CSOs, coalition building efforts and cooperation with public officials.

In addition, the EU aims to empower civil society by supporting dialogue between governments and CSOs at the country and regional levels as a tool to counter the risk of co-option of the civil society actors by the governments themselves. At the regional level, the EU provides financial support to the EaP Civil Society Forum, funding its annual assemblies, the secretariat in Brussels and activities of national civil society platforms in the EaP countries. In 2014, the Southern Mediterranean Civil Society Forum was established, thus complementing and reinforcing those already in place at the national level in the southern neighbourhood countries. The regional civil society support instruments include an online platform for virtual dialogue and information exchange, regional thematic communities, which meet physically and online to discuss policy-related issues, and knowledge- and trust-building activities.

At the country level, on the basis of the Association Agreements – which were concluded with Georgia, Moldova and Ukraine in 2014 – bilateral civil society platforms are established to contribute to monitoring the implementation of the agreements, which are negotiated with the governments. In the South, the EU's task forces for Tunisia (set up in 2011), Egypt (2012) and Jordan (2012) bring together civil society representatives along with the EU institutions, governments, the private sector and international donors to serve as catalysts for political and economic reform. Furthermore, informal instruments can be deployed occasionally. For example, the EU Delegation in Ukraine launched a civil society–government dialogue on sensitive issues, such as the fight against corruption and the reform of the electoral code.

The EU also increasingly involves CSOs from the ENP countries in consultations on EU policy development and implementation in a more institutionalised way. Such consultations were previously targeting aid tools for civil society only, whereas more recently they also cover other programmes, including budget support. The inclusion of CSOs in planning and supervision of EU budget support is a success of civil society in the neighbourhood that has advocated, for a number of years, a more transparent and accountable distribution of EU aid and evaluation of reform efforts in their countries.[8] Moreover, not only is civil society invited to provide feedback on the implementation of the ENP by submitting its contributions on annual progress reports, but the EU also attempts to incorporate its inputs into earlier stages of the policy-making process. For example, civil society in the EaP countries was consulted in preparing the roadmap to the EaP summit in Vilnius in November 2013. In March 2015, for the first time, the EU opened public consultations on the ENP revision and invited CSOs from the region to submit their views on how the EU should build its relationship with the neighbourhood.

Both institutionalised and *ad hoc* practices of consulting with CSOs have increasingly emerged at the country level, with the EU Delegations in ENP countries playing a key role. However, there seems to be a variation in the level and intensity of engagement of the EU Delegations with civil societies. This appears to depend on various factors: a) the EU's agenda of relations with the ENP governments; b) the state of civil society development and civic freedoms in the country; c) CSOs activism; and d) the openness and capacity of the delegation to include civil society voices. In some countries – such as Tunisia and Lebanon in the South and Georgia, Moldova and Ukraine in the East – civil society is invited to speak on human rights issues, the fight against corruption and democratic reform progress, reforms related to visa liberalization with the EU, conflict management and other domestic developments, whereas in other countries – including Morocco and Jordan in the South and Azerbaijan in the East – EU Delegation consultations are limited to those issues on which such requirement derives from EU planning documents (for example, on EU funding tools).

In conclusion, whereas for a long time support to civil society in the neighbourhood has been a tool to reach various policy goals, as seen in the previous section, a more strategic approach towards civil society in the ENP region is gradually emerging. The EU supports civil society as a watchdog to hold governments to account, especially on human rights and civic freedoms, but also in the fight against corruption, in the promotion of the rule of law and governance reforms, and in fostering economic cooperation. The EU also helps civil society as a service provider, especially in the area of sustainable development. Finally, by investing in cultural and educational activities, as well as in youth mobility, the EU fosters civil society as social capital. While the EU adopts a regional approach towards civil society, more differentiation between civil society needs at the country level is observed. The EU tries to take local contexts into account when devising its approaches. However, the EU's support for civil society is not purely normatively driven. The priorities for the support are often subordinated to the logic of cooperation between the EU and the partner governments and dictated by contingent affairs (for example, implementation of the Association Agreements) or the EU's general approaches to the neighbourhood. The EU sees civil society as an agent in the promotion of Europeanisation reforms and transfer of the EU's *acquis* and also as an implementing partner of its own policy agenda (for example, in the area of conflict resolution). However, if an ENP country government is not interested in European integration or hostile to civil society, this model does not work. Neither does it work for those CSOs that do not espouse Western/liberal values and the EU's interests.

Challenges ahead

Despite the visible improvements in the EU's promotion of civil society in the neighbourhood, a few crucial challenges still remain. First, policy improvements in providing EU's aid and consulting with civil society need to be thoroughly and consistently implemented in practice. Civil society representatives in the neighbourhood repeatedly complain that the EU's funding remains too burdensome in terms of application and reporting procedures and tends to focus on short-term objectives rather than long-term initiatives. Mostly large and professional non-governmental organisations succeed in benefiting from this funding. They are also those most often invited to take part in EU consultations. The Union is seen as failing to strengthen the collective capacity of civil society actors and foster intra-civil society relations. Moreover, participatory methods are not sufficiently developed. The development and implementation of EU policies are largely perceived as a top-down process and not based on a thorough discussion with local civil societies on the actual goals of the EU's initiatives and their local perceptions. Furthermore, the critique that the EU's engagement with civil society in the neighbourhood tends to be 'cloaked in highly normative language' – and therefore sometimes imbued with Western/liberal concepts – is still valid (Marchetti and Tocci 2011: 198–201). A tentative step away from this consolidated rhetoric can be found in the 2015 ENP review that speaks about the need to recognise 'that not all partners aspire to EU rules and standards' as an underpinning for greater differentiation and mutual ownership in the bilateral relations between the EU and the neighbourhood (European Commission and High Representative of the Union for Foreign Affairs and Security Policy 2015: 2).

Second, while devising a strategy of engaging with civil society in the neighbourhood, the EU should deal with other fundamental issues. The Union is better equipped to engage with CSOs in democratising countries that are willing to seek membership in the EU. In such countries, the EU extends its own liberal-democratic model of civil society and state–civil society relations. However, this vision does not work under authoritarian regimes. The EU seems powerless to promote civil society in the countries where it faces repression and crackdown. Beyond providing funding to CSOs and activists (which is often outlawed by the authorities in authoritarian ENP countries), the Union either lacks leverage or is not willing to apply it. Moreover, providing funding to civil society to achieve other policy goals appears to be non-effective in a repressive environment where civil society has no space to engage in policy-making or politics (for example, Belarus, Azerbaijan and some countries in the southern Neighbourhood, particularly Egypt and those countries with ongoing conflicts). The next challenge is how to engage with civil society that is not necessarily 'civil' – at least according to the European notion – but plays an important role in fostering the social fabric. For example, charities run by Islamist movements throughout the Arab world, or even some GONGOs (government-organised non-governmental organisations) and BONGOs (business-organised non-governmental organisations) in the East, which, despite their dependence on authorities or wealthy businessmen, may act as service providers to the population and contribute to sustainable development. More specifically, the EU does not engage with groups perceived as hostile to itself and its liberal-democratic agenda (Islamist and traditionalist religious groups, such as the Orthodox Churches in the East or Russophile groups), despite the fact that they are representative of important segments of the societies in the neighbouring countries. This attitude accentuates the image of a bloc promoting its own interest-based agenda rather than democratic values.

While the EU has recognised the key role society plays in the political, economic and social development of the ENP countries, which has been reflected in the increase of funding and dialogue and consultation initiatives, the Union still needs to crystallise its strategy of engagement with civil society. While maintaining the regional aid tools and supporting intra-regional dialogues between civil societies in the East and the South, the EU approach should be based on the needs and the state of development of civil society in each ENP country. Engagement and aid should be driven by the domestic agendas of civil societies themselves rather than the EU's priorities. The EU should also be more flexible in how it views civil society in the ENP countries, respecting the variety of civil society forms and roles in different cultural contexts. Special attention should be paid to supporting civil society in the countries backsliding towards authoritarianism, societal and political fragmentation, and violent conflicts. This would imply moving beyond developing an agenda for engagement with CSOs and providing them with financial assistance towards addressing the broader conditions that impinge on civil society's role in social transformations.

Notes

1. The inter-governmental bodies of the EaP include a bi-annual Summit, an annual Ministerial Council, four thematic Platforms at the senior officials level (Democracy, good governance and stability; Economic integration and convergence with EU policies; Energy security; and Contacts between people) and numerous Panels at the expert level convening semi-annually.
2. For example, Alexis de Tocqueville's vision of civil society associations as 'schools of democracy' (de Tocqueville, A. (1863) 'Democracy in America', Cambridge) and Robert Putnam's idea of 'social capital' (see Putnam, R. (1995) 'Bowling Alone: America's Declining Social Capital', *Journal of Democracy* 6, 65–78).

3 John Locke's view of freedom from state interference expounded in *Two Treatises of Government* of 1690.
4 In the 1990s, the European Commission only had Delegations in Ukraine and Georgia. The Delegation in Moldova was established in October 2005, while in other eastern neighbourhood countries only in 2008. Thus, in 2002–2006, the Commission Delegations in Ukraine and Georgia ran micro-projects schemes in these countries, extending them to Belarus managed by the Delegation in Kyiv and Armenia managed by the Delegation in Tbilisi in 2005–2006.
5 Based on Annual Reports from the European Commission on the Instrument of Stability in 2010–2013 http://eeas.europa.eu/ifs/docs/index_en.htm. On more recent projects see also www.insighton conflict.org/icsp/.
6 This support amounted to EUR300,000 for Moldovan CSOs engaging on economic competitiveness issues (European Commission, *Commission Implementing Decision of 16.7.2014 on the Annual Action Programme 2014 in favour of the Republic of Moldova to be financed from the general budget of the European Union*, C(2014) 5140 final); EUR3 million for pilot rural development measures in Georgia in which CSOs can participate along with local authorities; EUR3.5 million for CSOs and independent media in the field of anti-discrimination and rights of vulnerable groups in Georgia (European Commission, *Commission Implementing Decision of 14.7.2014 on the Annual Action Programme 2014 in favour of Georgia to be financed from the general budget of the European Union*, C(2014) 5020 final).
7 It has provided more than EUR5.2 million in support for the southern neighbourhood countries and more than EUR5.3 million for the Eastern Partnership countries (European People's Party Group in the European Parliament (2015) 'European Endowment for Democracy - an effective tool for countering anti-European propaganda', Press release, 9 July, http://pr.euractiv.com/pr/european-endowment-democracy-effective-tool-countering-anti-european-propaganda-129751).
8 For an example of civil society advocacy on the participation in ENPI programming and budget support, in particular see Tessier-Stall, S. and Gumeniuk, V. (2009) 'Missing Out: Civil Society and ENPI', Memorandum, Kyiv: International Centre for Policy Studies, www.viitorul.org/public/files/Memo_ENG.pdf, accessed 1 November 2015.

References

Beichelt, T. and Merkel, W. (2014) 'Democracy Promotion and Civil Society: Regime Types, Transitions Modes and Effects', in Beichelt, T. et al. (eds.) *Civil Society and Democracy Promotion*, Palgrave Macmillan, 42–64.

Börzel, T. (2011) 'When Europe hits . . . beyond its borders: Europeanization and the near abroad', *Comparative European Politics* 9(4–5): 394–413.

Böttger, K. and Falkenhain, M. (2011) *The EU's Policy Towards Azerbaijan: What Role for Civil Society?*, Berlin: Institut für Europäische Politik.

Bousac, J., Delcour, L., Rihackova, V., Solonenko, I. and Ter-Gabrielyan, G. (2012) *Improving the EU's Support for the Civil Society in its Neighbourhood: Rethinking Procedures, Ensuring That Practices Evolve*, European Parliament, Brussels.

Challand, B. (2009) *Palestinian Civil Society: Foreign Donors and the Power to Promote and Exclude*, London: Routledge.

Council of the European Union (2012) *Council Conclusions on the Roots of Democracy and Sustainable Development: Europe's Engagement with Civil Society in External Relations, 3191st Foreign Affairs Development Council meeting*, Luxembourg, 15 October.

European Commission (1996) *Council Regulation No 1488/96 of 23 July 1996 on Financial and Technical Measures to Accompany (MEDA) the Reform of Economic and Social Structures in the Framework of the Euro-Mediterranean Partnership*.

European Commission (2007a) *Annual Action Programme 2007. European Instrument for Democracy and Human Rights (EIDHR)*.

European Commission (2007b) *Annual Action Programme for 2007. Thematic Programme 'Non-State Actors and Local Authorities in Development'*.

European Commission (2011) *Action Fiche for Neighbourhood Civil Society Facility 2011*.

European Commission (2012a) *Annual Action Programme 2012. European Instrument for Democracy and Human Rights (EIDHR)*.

European Commission (2012b) *The Roots of Democracy and Sustainable Development: Europe's Engagement with Civil Society in External Relations. Communication from the Commission to the European Parliament, the Council, the European Economic and Social Committee and the Committee of Regions*.

European Commission (2013) *Youth in Action Programme Guide*, Brussels, http://ec.europa.eu/youth/tools/documents/guide13_en.pdf., accessed 1 November 2015.

European Commission (2014a) *Commission Implementing Decision on the Annual Action Programmes for 2014 and 2015 Part 1 'Civil Society Organisations and Local Authorities' to be Financed from the General Budget of the European Union*, C(2014) 7987 final, Brussels.

European Commission (2014b) 'EU announces new support for Ukraine's transition', *Press Release*, http://europa.eu/rapid/press-release_IP-14-501_en.htm, accessed 1 November 2015.

European Commission (2014c) *European Neighbourhood and Partnership Instrument 2007–2013: Overview of Activities and Results*.

European Commission (2014d) *Multiannual Indicative Programme for the Thematic Programme 'Civil Society Organisations and Local Authorities' for the Period 2014–2020*, C(2014) 4865 final, Brussels.

European Commission (2014e) *Programme on Global Public Goods and Challenges 2014–2020: Multi-annual Indicative Programme 2014–2017*.

European Commission (2015a) *Commission Implementing Decision on the Multi-annual Action Programme for years 2015 part II, 2016 and 2017 'Civil Society Organisations and Local Authorities' to be Financed from the General Budget of the European Union*, C(2015) 4574 final, Brussels.

European Commission (2015b) *Commission Implementing Decision on the adoption of the Multi-annual Action Programme 2016 and 2017 for the European Instrument for Democracy and Human Rights (EIDHR) to be Financed from the General Budget of the European Union*. Annex, C(2015) 8548 final, Brussels.

European Commission and High Representative of the Union for Foreign Affairs and Security Policy (2011a) *A New Response to a Changing Neighbourhood: A Review of European Neighbourhood Policy. Joint Communication by the High Representative of the Union for Foreign Affairs and Security Policy and the European Commission of 25 May 2011*.

European Commission and High Representative of the Union for Foreign Affairs and Security Policy (2011b) *A Partnership for Democracy and Shared Prosperity with the Southern Mediterranean. Joint Communication to the European Council, the European Parliament, the Council, [the European] Economic and Social Committee and the Committee of the Regions*.

European Commission and High Representative of the Union for Foreign Affairs and Security Policy (2012a) *Eastern Partnership: A Roadmap to the Autumn 2013 Summit. Joint Communication to the European Parliament, the Council, the European Economic and Social Committee and the Committee of the Regions*.

European Commission and High Representative of the Union for Foreign Affairs and Security Policy. (2012b) *Partnership for Democracy and Shared Prosperity: Report on Activities in 2011 and Roadmap for Future Action. Joint Staff Working Document*.

European Commission and High Representative of the Union for Foreign Affairs and Security Policy (2015) *Review of the European Neighbourhood Policy. Joint Communication to the European Parliament, the Council, the European Economic and Social Committee and the Committee of the Regions*, SWD(2015) 500 final, Brussels.

European External Action Service and European Commission (2014a) *Programming of the European Neighbourhood Instrument (ENI)—2014–2020: Regional East Strategy Paper (2014–2020) and Multiannual Indicative Programme (2014–2017)*.

European External Action Service and European Commission (2014b) *Programming of the European Neighbourhood Instrument (ENI)—2014–2020: Regional South Strategy Paper (2014–2020) and Multiannual Indicative Programme (2014–2017)*.

Gahramanova, A. (2009) 'Internal and external factors in the democratization of Azerbaijan', *Democratization* 16(4): 777–803.

Hahn-Fuhr, I. and Worschech, S. (2014) 'External Democracy Promotion and Divided Civil Society – The Missing Link', in Beichelt, T. et al. (eds.) *Civil Society and Democracy Promotion*, Palgrave Macmillan, 11–41.

Holden, P. (2003) 'The European Community's MEDA Aid Programme: A Strategic Instrument of Civilian Power?', *European Foreign Affairs Review* 8(3): 347–363.

Joffe, G. (1997) 'Southern Attitudes towards an Integrated Mediterranean Region', in Gillespie, R. (ed.) *The Euro-Mediterranean Partnership: Political and Economic Perspectives*, London: Frank Cass, 23–28.

Kaca, E. et al. (2014) *Learning from Past Experiences: Ways to Improve EU Aid on Reforms in the Eastern Partnership*, www.pism.pl/files/?id_plik=17080, accessed 1 November 2015.

Marchetti, R. and Tocci, N. (2011) 'Redefining European Union Engagement with Conflict Society', in Marchetti, R. and Tocci, N. (eds.) *Civil society, Conflicts and the Politicization of Human Rights*, Tokyo; New York; Paris: United Nations University Press.

O'Brennan, J. (2013) 'The European Commission, Enlargement Policy and Civil Society in the Western Balkans', in Bojicic-Dzelilovic, V., Ker-Lindsay, J. and Kostovicova, D. (eds.) *Civil society and Transitions in the Western Balkans*, Palgrave Macmillan, 29–46.

Pace, M. (2005) 'The Impact of European Union Involvement in Civil Society Structures in the Southern Mediterranean', *Mediterranean Politics* 10(2): 239–244.

Rihackova, V. (2014) *Taking Stock of EU Civil Society Funding in EaP Countries*, Brussels.

Saurugger, S. (2010) 'The social construction of the participatory turn: The emergence of a norm in the European Union', *European Journal of Political Research* 49(4): 471–495.

Scott, J. (2011) 'Reflections on EU geopolitics: Consolidation, neighbourhood and civil society in the reordering of European space', *Geopolitics* 16(1): 146–175.

Scott, J. and Liikanen, I. (2010) 'Civil society and the "neighbourhood"—Europeanization through cross-Border cooperation?', *Journal of European Integration* 32(5): 423–438.

Shapovalova, N. and Youngs, R. (2014) 'The Changing Nature of EU Support to Civil Society', in Beichelt, T. et al. (eds.) *Civil Society and Democracy Promotion*, Palgrave Macmillan, 86–109.

Tocci, N. (ed.) (2011) *The European Union, Civil Society and Conflict*, London: Routledge.

Wolczuk, K. (2009) 'Implementation without coordination: the impact of EU conditionality on Ukraine under the European Neighbourhood Policy', *Europe-Asia Studies* 61(2): 187–211.

Youngs, R. (2001) 'European Union democracy promotion policies: Ten years on', *European Foreign Affairs Review* 6(3): 355–373.

Zihnioglu, O. (2013) *European Union Civil Society Policy and Turkey: A Bridge Too Far?*, Basingstoke, UK: Palgrave Macmillan.

PART VII

The European Neighbourhood Policy and future lines of inquiry

44
THE EUROPEAN NEIGHBOURHOOD POLICY AND ISLAMIST ACTORS IN THE SOUTHERN NEIGHBOURHOOD

Michelle Pace and Sarah Wolff

Introduction

Since the European Neighbourhood Policy (ENP) was launched in 2003, the European Union's (EU's) policies have increasingly focused on how the EU can engage with so called 'moderate' Islamist movements. Starting with some reflections about definitions of Islamist actors in the region, this chapter traces the role that Islamists in the Middle East and North Africa (MENA) have been given in the EU's bilateral initiatives, before moving on to a more nuanced analysis of this role in the ENP. It sheds light on the views of such movements and their willingness to become engaged and involved with the EU in its foreign policies at the political and strategic levels. Given the developments in the region since the Arab uprisings, we investigate, more specifically, the role and place of Islamist movements in the EU's democratisation policies. We conclude with a set of policy recommendations on how a revitalised ENP, related to the 2015 ENP review process (European Commission and High Representative of Foreign Affairs and Security Policy 2015), can better integrate Islamist movements through mutual respect, peaceful and non-violent forms of political participation. The chapter focuses on Islamist parties in Morocco, Tunisia, Egypt and Palestine, where the authors have gathered ethnographic data.

Who are the Islamists in the Middle East and North Africa?

In the last decade, 'the nature of the relationship between the West and political Islam has become a defining issue for foreign policy' (Emerson and Youngs 2007: 1). The EU, like other liberal-secular Western powers, has tended to see 'Islamism' or 'Political Islam' either through the 'traditional orientalist views' or through 'realist notions of regional security', thus subsuming the incredibly wide diversity of Islamist actors and movements in the region to a 'monolithic Islamic threat' (Volpi 2009: 20). Western anthropology, following Weberian sociological theory, has tended to treat Islam from a 'traditional practice', devoid of reason and logical discourse, instead of focusing on understanding the historical context conducive to the practice and discourse of Islam (Asad 2009: 23). Following the Arab uprisings, the rise of sectarianism in the region and the governing experience of various Islamist parties, there is a clear need to think outside of the box. As underlined by Schwedler,

> scholars should ask whether these categories continue to provide the kind of analytic traction that made them valuable in the past. The constant pressure on scholars of Middle East politics to respond to a growing wave of Islamophobia has complicated efforts to rethink these categories
>
> (Schwedler 2015)

ENP documents, tend to refer to either 'moderate' or 'radical' Islamist movements, as if this would cover their diversity.[1]

The term 'Islamist' refers to 'highly diverse groups that advocate social, political and economic reform through the application of Islamic teachings to all aspects of life' (Schwedler 2013: 3). Defining Islamist actors and movements has raised significant debate among foreign policy practitioners and academics for many years. While some Western academics such as Varisco (2010) argue that the term 'Islamism' is fuelling Islamophobia by associating Islam with violence, others argue that it designates 'the spectrum of actors who are committed to public action in the name of Islam' (Hegghammer 2012). Without entering this debate, this chapter takes the view that Islamist actors refer to those movements whose public action is driven by principles found in Islam. Since the Arab uprisings, Khalil Al-Anani argues that Islamist politics in the Middle East have been reshaped and that the Islamist architecture is now 'fluid, dynamic and most notably divisive' (Al-Anani 2012: 467). He introduces a distinction between formal and informal Islamists. The former refers to 'Islamist parties, movements and organisations [that] were the only representatives of Islamism' for decades and before the Arab uprisings (ibid.: 468). Informal Islamists are instead

> not officially affiliated with any of the Islamist movements or associations. Nor are they keen to establish their own parties or organisations. Ironically, they eschewed joining the new Islamist parties that have been founded since the Arab 'uprisings'. Thus, they are free from organisational and hierarchical burdens . . . [they] rely heavily on social networks, kinship, friendship links and new technology to disseminate their ideology and widen their influence. They have followers from different social strata; urban and rural, poor and rich, schools and universities, etc.
>
> (ibid: 468)

Some of these movements have been (or are still) prone to violence and extremism, but this needs to be reassessed constantly depending on who defines them as violent and for which purposes. However, movements' stance on violence is not the only selection criteria here (see our note on Hezbollah below). The Muslim Brotherhood (MB), the oldest political Islamist organisation founded in 1928 by al-Banna, entices a negative image due to its violent past, even in spite of being elected democratically in 2011 in Egypt: the MB's Freedom and Justice Party or FJP (officially founded by the MB on 30 April 2011) won the largest number – 235 seats or 47.2 per cent – under Egypt's complex electoral system (Meijer and Bakker 2012: 4). Today, all the different branches of Egypt's Islamist political parties 'now condemn violence' (Meijer and Bakker 2012: 14; see also Ragab 2012) and therefore are included in the review of this chapter. Similarly, al-Adl Wal-Ishane, a Moroccan Sufi association, advocates the establishment of a Caliphate, but through non-violent means and is therefore included in the movements reviewed in this chapter. The authors agree with Al-Anani that the term 'Islamists' covers a wide diversity of actors ranging from conservative parties, such as Ennahda in Tunisia, which was the first Islamic party to lead the drafting of a new democratic constitution, as well as the PJD in Morocco, which is well integrated in the political game, to the Egyptian MB, which was banned in 2013 and declared a terrorist group by the al-Sisi military regime. The Islamic Resistance Movement (Hamas), a nationalist-Islamist spin-off from Egypt's MB, formed the Reform and Change Party and had an iconic victory in the Palestinian Legislative Council 2006 elections. Its participation in these elections was consistent with its dual strategy of directing 'resistance' against Israel, as the occupying power, and building Palestinian support through welfare services (Bhasin and Carter Hallward 2013). In Lebanon, since 1982, Hezbollah evolved from a 'revolutionary vanguard' Islamist organisation, bent on violently overthrowing the Lebanese government, to a hybrid Islamist organisation that uses legitimate political tools to the same end. Today, Hezbollah operates on the civilian plane of *da'wa*, social welfare and religious education, the military-resistance plane and the political plane (Azani 2013).

Islamist actors themselves display different views as to whether they should define themselves as 'Islamist'. In 2013, following the overthrow of the MB in Egypt, Islamist officials elsewhere have been eager to avoid being labelled as such. Some officials from the PJD claim their party has an Islamist frame of reference, but is not an Islamist party.[2] This small, yet significant characterisation is revealing of how labelling and cognitive frames impact upon Islamist actors in the region, their interlocutors and their evolution over time. For Ahmed Yousef, a senior political adviser to the former Hamas prime minister of Gaza, Ismail Haniyeh, Hamas is

> a Palestinian liberation movement that uses traditional Islamic teaching as its point of reference. Hamas is simply a movement resisting (Israeli) occupation and besiegement. Hamas draws inspiration from faith; yet religion has little to do with our struggle. Our faith determines our values, not our platform.[3]

The ENP: politics of engagement or politics of containment? (2004–2011)

The ENP was launched as a 'ring of stability amongst friendly neighbours' (Commission of the European Communities 2003), and aimed at defining the EU's role in its neighbourhood, both to the South and to the East, following the 2004 enlargement. The inauguration of the ENP coincided with the EU acknowledging the need to engage with these 'new' major political Islam forces in the region. In fact, the EU started to show some pragmatism, as the rise of Islamist political parties and their political victories in the region became a constant trend since 2005. The Moroccan PJD gained nine seats in the Parliament as early as 1997, and became the first opposition party in 2002 with 42 seats after the legislative elections and again in 2007 with 46 seats. At the 2005 elections in Egypt, the MB – a key, albeit outlawed, Islamist opposition force – won a fifth of parliamentary seats. In the January 2006 elections in the Occupied Palestinian Territories (OPT), Hamas (Harakat al-Muqawama al-Islamiyya), the Palestinian Islamic Resistance Movement – which is on the EU's list of terrorist organisations – won 74 seats in the 132-seat chamber (56 per cent of the seats). Fatah (a reverse acronym from the Arabic name Harakat al-Tahrir al-Watani al-Filastini, literally Palestinian National Liberation Movement), the Western-backed, secular movement was placed second, with 36 per cent of the seats. These election results created a huge dilemma for external actors like the EU, which had been promoting a liberal form of democracy in the MENA region since the 1990s. But since the events of 9/11 and the US-led 'war on terror', 'Islam' had become the new securitised object in EU discourse on the Middle East. One of the main misunderstandings in EU circles has been that Islamism is incompatible with democracy, and the EU thus found itself in a cul de sac: how does it export its liberal democratic discourse, which worked so well in the European context, to a region that, in the EU's framing, is not yet 'ripe' for democratisation (Pace 2010).

Paradoxically, these electoral victories for the Islamists have 'diminished European (and American) enthusiasm for pushing forward a transformative agenda' in the field of democratisation (Kodmani 2010: 5). Under authoritarian governments, Europeans have had difficulties, or no willingness, to maintain ties with grassroots opposition movements. Since the start of the 1995 Barcelona Process, but also later, under the ENP, the EU has maintained strong ties with civil society, but not necessarily with religious-based organisations. Instead, it has tended to engage with the more secular-oriented civil society (Kodmani 2010: 5). Overall, until the Arab uprisings, no specific strategic role was given to Islamist actors within the framework of the ENP. This is mostly visible in the practice of EU development aid towards the region and access to EU funding, but also in the overwhelming focus on security interests in the region.

Democratisation and dialogue with Islamists

The EU has tended to engage with Islamist political actors mostly when it comes to combating radicalisation (Hamid and Kadlec 2010), particularly since the victory of Hamas in 2006 (Behr 2010). Building on the EMP approach, the EU's internal security has acted as the prime prism through which the EU has constructed its relationship with southern partners, and when it comes to Islamist actors (Wolff 2012). Each of the ENP Action Plans with the EU's southern partners addresses the issues of justice, security and migration. It is within this context that the EU has tended to praise the role of key southern partners, such as Jordan, in the fight against 'extremist interpretations of Islam and the dialogue between cultures' (Council of the European Union 2007a: 6) *via* the Alliance of Civilisation or the Amman Message. The ENP Jordan National Indicative Programme for 2007–2010 thus stressed the role of public education in disseminating 'the vision of a moderate Islam' (Council of the European Union 2007b: 24).

Under the ENP, engagement with Islamist political parties and parliamentarians became more common through parliamentary diplomacy. Members of the Moroccan PJD and the Istiqlal party, a nationalist and conservative party, which advocates Islamism participate in the Mixed Parliamentary Commission EU-Morocco. Created in 2010, it aims at strengthening parliamentary links within the context of the advanced status of Morocco. A similar mixed parliamentary commission between the EU and Tunisia has also been created, in November 2015.[4] Even though, since the Arab uprisings, the role of parliaments has changed (in particular in Tunisia); in the majority of Arab states, parliaments are weak, with 'little influence on the political process' and little legitimacy since 'only 48% of Arab citizens believe their parliaments monitor the activities of government' (Berton and Gaub 2015). German foundations have also been active in linking with political parties and mostly with similarly ideological partners. Thus, the Konrad Adenauer Stiftung, a German political foundation close to the Christian Democrats, cooperates with Nidaa Tounes, the ruling 'secular' party, since the legislative campaign, while its Moroccan branch cooperates with Istiqlal, which was (until 2013) in a coalition government with the PJD. Unfortunately, these initiatives have remained scattered, without providing any 'systematic and formal engagement' with Islamists (Boubekeur 2009: 7). Western diplomats have also been in contact with Hamas but keep these encounters unofficial (Pace interviews in Gaza 2007 and 2014; Abu Amer 2015).[5]

In the Mashreq, the EU missed many opportunities for a systematic engagement with Islamist actors. As already stated above, in Egypt for example, the MB stepped into the political arena by participating in the 2005 elections. Although the MB participated in Egyptian elections in the 1980s through party lists or independent candidates, 2005 was a turning point as they earned 88 out of 444 seats in parliament through MB affiliated independent candidates. Similarly, after facing internal religious disapproval, in 2006, Hamas participated and won the Palestinian Legislative Council (PLC) elections, signalling its decision to fully transition to an Islamic democratic political party. In fact, the MB and the political wing of Hamas have been referred to as 'moderate' Islamists by observers, precisely because they have accepted the framework of elections and pluralism to promote their views. In the case of Hamas, the EU had sent its own electoral observation mission to monitor the election process and found the election results 'free, fair and transparent' (EU Election Observation Mission 2006). But given the constraints placed on the EU by Israel and the US, as well as the other members of the Quartet, the EU refused to accept the election result and insisted that Hamas accepts three conditions set by the Quartet, rather than allowing Hamas time to prove itself in government or to prove the movement's political wing's sincerity (or otherwise) about engaging in the political domain through a democratic mandate. This was a thoroughly missed opportunity (Pace and Pallister-Wilkins 2016) in engaging in a series of diplomatic efforts and in having an open dialogue with Hamas officials on the key issues of concern for the EU including: Hamas's position *vis-à-vis* Israel, women's rights, religious minorities, morals in public life, the application of *Shari'a* and the *Houdud* (or corporal punishment), the use of violence, political pluralism, the religious freedom of minorities, that is, key issues of intense debate within both Hamas and the MB political circles.[6] Although the EU's listing of Hamas on its terrorist list legally allows EU officials to engage in a dialogue with Hamas officials – what it does not permit is the transfer of financial aid directly to Hamas[7] – there has not been any organised, systematic and formal engagement of EU officials with Hamas' political bureau. What we observe instead are many sporadic contacts and encounters between members of both the MB in Egypt and Hamas in Gaza, with officials from the EU and non-EU Member States including officials from the UK, Germany, Sweden, Switzerland and Norway over the last nine years or so.[8]

Despite several calls urging the EU to open talks with Hamas (Bouris 2012; Grant and O'Donnell 2007; Schmid and Dombey 2006; Metro 2009), the authors find no clear evidence of a shift in the EU's policy stance towards engaging in a constructive and direct dialogue with this movement. The problem lies in the way EU officials have lacked a clear understanding of Islamists as political actors. The EU has been attempting to circumvent this constraint by funding research conferences and think tanks that can enhance understandings of the historical trajectory of political Islamist actors and by engaging with academics who have had access to Islamists through their field trips. In this way, the authors observe a recent attempt by EU officials at integrating political Islamist actors into its EU-South neighbourhood policies and objectives through flexible initiatives. After returning from a fieldtrip to Gaza to interview Hamas officials from its political bureau and another fieldtrip to Cairo to interview MB officials back in 2007, one of the authors was struck by the interest shown by EU officials in Brussels in her findings and conversations with interviewed Islamist politicians. It was evidently clear to this author that EU policies thus far had been based on a lack of nuanced information on precisely how these Islamist actors could be brought into the EU's fold of democratisation policy for the MENA region.

No EU money for Islamists

Islamist organisations have been *de facto* excluded from EU funding, the EU pursuing, under the ENP, a policy of containment motivated by concerns about radicalisation and terrorism (Youngs 2014). Access to EU funding for Islamist parties and civil society actors has been made difficult by the choice of budget support, as one of the main policy instruments to channel aid to EU's southern neighbours. The European Commission has overwhelmingly privileged this policy instrument that enables the EU to channel financial aid directly to the national treasury of southern neighbours over grants that would allow civil society to gain access to EU funding. Instead, budget support, supposed to favour ownership, favours power centralisation in authoritarian regimes through a de-politicisation of ENP cooperation (regimes favour less or even non-politicised areas for support) while restricting progress in democratisation and human rights. Budget support has thus favoured a transnational managerial management of EU funding to the region, privileging financial performance over policy objectives (Wolff 2015a).

Thus, in Morocco, the EU opted for sectoral budget support, that is, mainly support to reforming public governance and the financial sector. Although budget support has supported the modernisation of sectoral legislative and regulatory frameworks – principally in the financial sector, public finances and taxation – a joint evaluation report concluded that it did not necessarily address public service reform and therefore the needs of the people, nor did it manage to have any significant impact on regional, gender and urban/rural disparities (European Commission 2014). In the case of Egypt, a 2013 report of the European Court of Auditors concluded that the evaluation of EU support to governance was 'well-intentioned but ineffective'. Out of the EUR1 billion aid disbursed between 2007 and 2013, 60 per cent was disbursed under sectoral budget support (European Court of Auditors 2013a). It suffered, however, from 'endemic corruption' and a 'lack of budgetary transparency' while funds channelled through civil society 'were not sufficient to make a discernible difference' (European Court of Auditors 2013b). Despite difficulties to achieve progress in the field of human rights and democratisation *via* the ENP dialogue, and the main ENPI project allocating EUR90 million to reforms in the areas of democracy, human rights and justice, the Commission continued nonetheless to deliver budget support. For instance, the report notes that

> corruption matters were discussed in the Subcommittee on Justice and Security, which met annually from 2007 to 2010. There was some exchange of information on anti-corruption initiatives but regular calls for cooperation from both sides were not followed up by concrete actions. The dialogue also did not lead to new ENPI projects nor did it address the difficulties faced in starting up the 2008 ENPI project.
> *(European Court of Auditors 2013a: 23)*

The EU 'did little to defend Islamists' basic political rights, but instead funded programmes designed to train "moderate" imams' (Youngs 2014: 51). Where it believed that its funding was serving the purpose of terrorists, sometimes following claims by authoritarian governments, the EU withdrew its financial support, such as in 2003 in Egypt (Behr 2010). In Morocco, under the EMP or ENPI funding, Islamists 'have never benefited from funding' (Wegner and Pellicer 2009: 170). Rather, the EU's policy has been one of 'avoidance' of Islamist actors, the EU preferring to support the regime with 'material and legitimacy resources' (Wegner and Pellicer 2009: 170). Unlike the US, which has pursued a policy of promoting the role of any legal political party in Morocco, the EU has been reticent to engage with Islamists, at least until the Arab uprisings. Support to political parties and technical training to Members of Parliament was nonexistent on the EU's side until the uprisings.

The way the EU has dealt with the legal constraints on transferring financial aid directly to the elected Hamas government – which also happened to be on its terrorist list – was to create the Temporary International Mechanism (TIM). TIM was set up because the EU did not want to deal with the Hamas-led government. In June 2006, TIM was established by the European

Commission, at the request of the Quartet and the European Council, to facilitate need-based assistance to the Palestinian people and to facilitate the maximum level of support by international donors. Emphasis was given to the sectors that enabled the continued functioning of essential public social services. TIM was phased out in March 2008 and replaced by PEGASE. This refers to the EU's mechanism created to continue its support to the Palestinian people. PEGASE was actually launched on 1 February 2008. The programmes that have been financed through PEGASE were designed to support the three-year Palestinian Reform and Development Plan (PRDP), which was presented by the Palestinian Authority Prime Minister, Salam Fayyad, at the Paris Donor Conference of 17 December 2007.

The Arab uprisings, the ENP and the Islamists: from spring to winter?

For many decades, the EU was faced with the so-called 'Islamist dilemma' in the MENA region: how could it continue to promote democracy without risking the rise of Islamists in power? But with the popular uprisings that swept the MENA region from December 2010, the EU did not have a choice. In Tunisia, the government of Zine El Abidine Ben Ali collapsed and Ennahda – a moderate Islamist political party – was granted permission to form a political party by Tunisia's interim government. Following the first free election in the country's history, the Tunisian Constituent Assembly election, on 23 October 2011, with a turnout of 51.1 per cent of all eligible voters, Ennahda won 37.04 per cent of the popular vote and 89 of the 217 assembly seats (41 per cent, according to Feldman 2011). In May 2012, Mohammed Morsi of the MB became Egypt's first democratically elected president (Hamid 2011; Kennemore 2014). Asef Bayat attempted to shed light on these developments and transformations in Islamism through his edited volume on *Post-Islamism: The Changing Faces of Political Islam* (Bayat 2013). He defines 'post-Islamism' both as a condition and a project characterised by the fusion of religiosity and rights, faith and freedom, as well as Islam and liberty. For Bayat, post-Islamism emphasises rights rather than merely obligations, plurality instead of singular authoritative voices, historicity rather than fixed scriptures and the future instead of the past. In Tunisia, Ennahda agreed to resign, in January 2014, to make way for the final drafting of a constitution by a neutral interim government, followed by planned elections based on the new constitution. As Francesco Cavatorta and Fabio Merone explain, the case of the Tunisian Islamist party, Ennahda, shows how the electoral rise of Islamist parties since the Arab uprisings has given rise to different political outcomes in different MENA countries – generating a significant amount of critical engagement with the relevance of thinking about Islamist politics through ideology. Hence, Islamism can be thought of as an evolving ideology that adapts to new circumstances rather than a failure for its acceptance of democratic mechanisms (Cavatorta and Merone 2015).

During the initial protests' period starting from December 2010 and, in a pragmatic turn, following the Arab uprisings and the realisation that the EU did not know its new interlocutors in its southern neighbourhood, the EU started to engage with Islamist actors. First, Stephan Füle apologised and presented an 'unprecedented *mea culpa*' for the EU's approach in the region, saying that the EU should have backed democrats and not dictators' (quoted in Leigh 2011). It published a new communication on a 'Partnership for Democracy and Shared Prosperity with the Southern Mediterranean' (European Commission and High Representative of the Union for Foreign Affairs and Security Policy 2011a) and announced a revised ENP (European Commission and High Representative of the Union for Foreign Affairs and Security Policy 2011b). The idea was also to use 'smart conditionality' and to apply the '3M logic' according to which, 'money, markets and mobility' would open up to southern neighbours who would be doing 'more for more'. Then, in a second step, the EU set up task forces with Tunisian and Egyptian political leaders, including members of Ennahda and the MB, to discuss how to ease democratic transitions. The EU–Tunisia Task Force, co-chaired by EU High Representative/Commission Vice President, Catherine Ashton, and Tunisian Prime Minister, Beji Caid Essebsi, was established to coordinate European and international support to allow quicker and more effective assistance to Tunisia. EU financial support to Tunisia was planned in the region of up to EUR4 billion between 2011 and 2013 (European Commission 2011). The EU also launched an EU/Egypt task force to reiterate EU support for the reform process in Egypt (European External Action Service 2012). When the conclusions of the EU–Egypt task force were being adopted in 2012, Egypt seemed to be following a democratic path: a new constitution had been drafted and elections were being organised (Al-Ali 2012). However, political developments showed how unreal these hopes had been. In 2013, the Egyptian army took power and a new wave of repression against the advocates of the overthrown President Morsi started. The path to stabilisation, democracy, the rule of law and human rights was abandoned, and an ongoing process of re-autocratisation followed (Potyrala et al. 2015).

In the Tunisian case, the situation is different but the outlook is also rather negative. The EU–Tunisia task force met in September 2011 to unveil the 'Jasmin Plan' (Tunisia's ambitious plan for economic growth) on how Tunisia could grow in the next five years by overhauling its financial regulations system: including the encouragement of the development of new public–private partnerships, small businesses and increased microfinance lending throughout the country.[9] The idea behind this plan was that with these changes the economy could experience a 5 per cent economic growth in 2012 and 2013. Yet, growth only reached 2.4 per cent in 2013 and 2.3 per cent in 2014, due to the absence of European demand, a slowdown in domestic demand (affected by strict macroeconomic policies and also the terrorist attacks in the Bardo Museum, in Tunis and nearby Sousse, at the beginning of 2015 (World Bank 2016)). This is in sharp contrast with the plan that aimed for 7 per cent growth between 2013 and 2016 so that Tunisia will be able to converge with the lower end of European Union Member States (Republic of Tunisia, Finance Ministry 2011). At the time of writing, this goal has not been met due to the condition of the global economy as well as the fall in tourist figures, but this level of growth will be needed for sufficient jobs to be created for the annual and additional young Tunisians entering the job market (Unver Noi 2013: 117). In this context, it seems that the EU has not drawn any lessons from the past by retaining a focus on neo-liberal reforms (within the EU–Tunisia task force), which were precisely the origins of discontent among Tunisians, who went out into the streets to protest and who managed to force Ben Ali to flee his country. Similarly, in Morocco, the EU has tended to mostly support neo-liberal reforms, which have matched the agenda of the monarchy and indirectly contributed to disempowering citizens and workers by privileging the technocratisation over the politicisation of the economic agenda (Cavatorta 2015). Combined with the selective funding mechanisms of the EU, these measures can only play in favour of strengthening authoritarianism and socio-economic inequalities.

The post-Arab uprisings experiences of Ennahda in Tunisia, and the MB in Egypt, reveal a great deal about the complex relationship that Islamists have had to develop with power since they were elected. In Tunisia – less than one year after the ouster of President Ben Ali, in November 2011 – the College of Arts and Letters at the Manouba University near Tunis was taken hostage by long-bearded men and veiled women carrying signs reading 'My *niqab* [face veil] is my freedom'. A group of around 50 young Salafi (radical Islamist) men proceeded to occupy the university, until the end of January 2012, in support of two female students kicked out of the classroom for refusing to take off their face veils. Many Tunisians have been concerned about the Salafis' rising influence and what they perceive as timid reactions from

Ennahda, while in government. The events, at Manouba especially, alarmed secularists, liberals and women, who accused Ennahda of turning a blind eye to growing radicalism. However, the party explained that its refusal to enshrine *Sharia* (Islamic Law) in Article One of the (new) Constitution was the ultimate proof of the party's rejection of extremism. With this decision, Ennahda's leaders underscored their political distance from the Salafis and positioned their party as the guarantor of the country's stability (Lusardi 2015). On 6 February 2013, a secular leader, Chokri Belaid, was assassinated, and in late July 2013, the leftist leader, Mohamed Brahmi, was also assassinated. A political crisis evolved, as the country's mainly secular opposition organised several protests against the ruling Troika alliance that was dominated by Rashid al-Ghannushi's Islamist Ennahda.

Although the Arab uprisings constituted a window of opportunity to engage with Islamists, the revised 2011 and 2015 ENP do not foresee connecting more forcefully with key actors in the various countries, including Islamist actors, at various levels. Instead, the EU tends to continue with the same caveats that, as in the past, remain vague and unspecific when it comes to the concept of promoting 'deep democracy', but also lack a full awareness of 'the complexity of current liberalisation and transition processes, whose forms vary greatly from country to country' (Schumacher 2015: 569). Worse, following the 'Jasmine revolution', 'much French funding for [Tunisia] was directed at suppressing Ennahda's popularity' (Youngs 2014: 135). Overall, engagement with the Egyptian MB has been severely limited since the coup, which removed Morsi from power on 3 July 2013, after just over a year in the presidency. In short, succession to the old regime was essentially restored under the leadership of General Abdel Fattah al-Sisi (later elected president) and the Islamist group was repressed. Human Rights Watch has denounced European 'continuous support' to the regime and silence on its repression and the crackdown on the MB (Parker 2015). Even though the EU High Representative, Catherine Ashton, was the only Western diplomat to visit Morsi in prison, European governments have remained silent following his condemnation to the death penalty, posing the question of the prioritisation of its own security interest and short-term stability in the region (El-Sherif 2014; European Parliament 2015; Human Rights Watch 2015; Khalaf 2014; Mandour 2015).

The prioritisation of security and stability is again visible in European governments' support for de-radicalisation programmes. Thus, European governments have been informally supporting the creation of the new Mohammed VI Institute for the Training of Imams that promotes a moderate Moroccan model of Islam.[10] In Morocco, the EU has had little engagement with official political parties and even less with non-official movements such as al-Adl Wal-Ihsane.[11] Despite being extremely popular among Moroccans, this movement – which promotes reform of the monarchic system towards an Islamic state based on *Sharia* and procedural democracy – has never been supported by the EU when it comes to facilitating its legal recognition (Wolff 2015b). In Morocco, most of the EEAS Delegation contacts on the ground go through the various sectoral ministries and one programme that supports capacity-building of the Moroccan parliament. This is seen as due to the de-politicisation of the EU's support to Morocco, favouring non-contentious cooperation on sectoral issues, such as trade or regulation and privileged relations with technocrats (Cavatorta 2015), but also a result of the structural weakness of political parties and the Moroccan parliament.

Conclusions

Are Islamists ready to engage in EU Mediterranean policies? From the Islamists' point of view, the EU's credibility in the region has been severely undermined by its refusal to recognise the electoral victory of Hamas in 2006. The inclusion of Israel in the UfM, launched in 2008, like in the past with the EMP, irritated a number of legalised Islamist parties in the region. Anger was heightened after the EU's meagre response to Israel's military intervention in Gaza during 2008–2009, 2012 and the devastating impact of the war on Gaza of summer 2014. The EU's response to al-Sisi's ousting of Egypt's first freely elected leader, Morsi, through a military coup in July 2013, was further evidence for Islamists that the EU could not be trusted: on the one hand, it seems to promote the value of democracy while, on the other, it supports authoritarian and undemocratic regimes as a way of ensuring its notion of stability in the MENA.

The 2015 ENP review process should have initiated a new approach *vis-à-vis* the role and place of Islamist movements at the EU's democracy policy table, not least because of the evolution in the last decade or so in the behaviour and outlook of some of the Islamist movements in the MENA addressed in this chapter. The 2016 successful re-election of the PJD in Morocco, and the confirmation of a bi-polar system monopolised by, on the one hand the Islamists, and on the other the PAM, their left-wing opponent, show indeed that Islamist parties are now fully part of the political landscape.

Our contention has been that the EU has based its sporadic relations with Islamist movements on a classical security/stability logic, preferring to continue its support of authoritarian regimes, such as al-Sisi, in Egypt – who ensures for Europe a false sense of stability/security in return. Our suggestion is that the EU must rethink its security/stability reasoning and engage with Islamist leaders (in a truly dialogical encounter), with the aim of listening to these partners' concerns, perceptions and views on the everyday political situation in their countries, as a way of knowledge transfer from the South to the North. If the EU is genuinely interested in promoting a sustainable and more effective humanitarian approach to the MENA's development – politically, economically and socially – it needs to accept that Islamist agents are part of the reality of its neighbours to the South and engage with them. To work with Islamist actors in a true partnership requires designing programmes that consider these actors' needs. Only if Islamist actors – especially those that forgo violence, respect pluralism and human rights – are given an opportunity to influence EU external policy can EU foreign assistance efforts for the MENA region become more effective and sustainable. Such engagement of Islamist actors in EU foreign policy-making can then be a way to prevent, mitigate and resolve violent conflict and contribute to the EU's as well as the MENA region's stability and security.

Islamists' attitudes to the use of violence and rejection of what are considered Western democratic values are not sufficient criteria for a categorisation of which Islamist organisations the EU should engage with. As we have shown in this chapter, the programmes of radical Islamist movements can evolve internally, according to their given place in the political process of their countries, as well as externally through interactions with the international community. What is important is that the EU read such developments and keep an eye on the evolution of Islamist movements in their particular domestic and geopolitical contexts.

Notes

1 Council of the European Union (2007a: 8). European Neighbourhood and Partnership Instrument. Regional Strategy Paper 2007–2013 and Regional Indicative Programme (2007–2010) for the Euro-Mediterranean Partnership, http://eeas.europa.eu/enp/pdf/pdf/country/enpi_euromed_rsp_en.pdf.
2 Interview conducted in Morocco, June 2015, by S. Wolff.
3 Interview conducted in Gaza, September 2007, by M. Pace.
4 www.journallapresse.tn/05112015/105997/creation-dune-commission-parlementaire-mixte.html accessed on 18 November 2015.

5 Interviews, in Gaza, September 2007 and October 2014, by M. Pace.
6 Interviews in Cairo, Nablus and Gaza, 2007, by M. Pace.
7 Interview with a Council of the EU official, Brussels, June 2011, by M. Pace.
8 Confidential interviews with officials from these countries and MB and Hamas officials in Cairo and Gaza, 2007–2014, by M. Pace.
9 European External Action Service (2011), http://eeas.europa.eu/tunisia/docs/20110929_taskforce_en.pdf
10 Interview in Morocco, June 2015 by S. Wolff.
11 Interview in Morocco, June 2015, by S. Wolff.

References

Abu Amer, A. (2015) 'Former Hamas Official Speaks Out', *AlMonitor*, May, www.al-monitor.com/pulse/originals/2015/05/hamas-war-gaza-ahmed-youssef-ismail-haniyeh-advisor.html.
Al-Ali, Z. (2012) 'Egypt's Draft Constitution: An Analysis', Open Democracy, 8 November.
Al-Anani, K. (2012) 'Islamist Parties Post-Arab Spring', *Mediterranean Politics* 17(3): 466–472.
Asad, T. (2009) 'The Idea of an Anthropology of Islam', *Qui Parle* 17(2): 1–30.
Azani, E. (2013) 'The Hybrid Terrorist Organization: Hezbollah as a Case Study', *Studies in Conflict and Terrorism* 36(11): 899–916.
Bayat, A. (2013) *Post-Islamism: The Changing Faces of Political Islam*, Oxford: Oxford University Press.
Behr, T. (2010) 'Dealing with Political Islam: Foreign Policy-Making Between the Union and the Member States', Fifth Pan-European Conference on EU Politics, ECPR Porto, 23–26 June 2010, www.jhubc.it/ecpr-porto/virtualpaperroom/158.pdf, accessed 16 March 2015.
Berton, B. and Gaub, F. (2015) *Arab Parliaments: Better Than Their Reputation?*, Paris: European Union Institute for Security Studies Alert.
Bhasin, T. and Carter Hallward, M. (2013) 'Hamas as a Political Party: Democratization in the Palestinian Territories', *Terrorism and Political Violence* 25(1): 75–93.
Boubekeur, A. (2009) *Updating the European Union's Policies Towards Islamist Parties and Radical Actors*, Stockholm: International Institute for Democracy and Electoral Assistance.
Bouris, D. (2012) 'It's High Time for Europe to Engage with Hamas', Council for European Palestinian Relations, 27 February, http://thecepr.org/index.php?option=com_content&view=article&id=293:its-high-time-for-europe-to-engage-with-hamas&catid=2:news&Itemid=15, accessed 22 December 2015.
Cavatorta, F. (2015) 'Authoritarian Stability Through Perpetual Democratisation', *Working Paper* 15, IAI, Rome, October.
Cavatorta, F. and Merone, F. (2015) 'Post-Islamism, Ideological Evolution and 'la tunisianité' of the Tunisian Islamist party al-Nahda', *Journal of Political Ideologies* 20(1): 27–42.
Commission of the European Communities (2003) *Communication from the Commission to the Council and the European Parliament—Wider Europe—Neighbourhood: A New Framework for Relations with Our Eastern and Southern Neighbours*.
Council of the European Union (2007a) *European Neighbourhood and Partnership Instrument. Regional Strategy Paper 2007–2013 and Regional Indicative Programme (2007–2010) for the Euro-Mediterranean Partnership*.
Council of the European Union (2007b) *European Neighbourhood and Partnership Instrument: Jordan Strategy Paper 2007–2013 and National Indicative Programme 2007–2010*.
El-Sherif, A. (2014) 'The Muslim Brotherhood and the Future of Political Islam in Egypt', Carnegie Europe, http://carnegieeurope.eu/2014/10/21/muslim-brotherhood-and-future-of-political-islam-in-egypt.
Emerson, M. and Youngs, R. (2007) 'Political Islam and the European Neighbourhood Policy', in Emerson, M. and Youngs, R. (eds.) *Political Islam and European Foreign Policy. Perspectives from Muslim Democrats of the Mediterranean*, Brussels: Center for European Policy Studies.
EU Election Observation Mission (2006) *West Bank and Gaza. Statement of Preliminary Conclusions and Findings*, https://unispal.un.org/DPA/DPR/unispal.nsf/0/236F02CF539AA9418525710600587785.
European Commission (2011) 'EU/Tunisia Task Force Agrees Concrete Assistance for Tunisia's Transition', *Press Release*, Brussels, 29 September, http://europa.eu/rapid/press-release_IP-11-1137_en.htm?locale=en, accessed 22 December 2015.
European Commission (2014) *Evaluation of Budget Support Operations in Morocco. Directorate-General Development and Cooperation EuropeAid*.

European Commission and High Representative of the Union for Foreign Affairs and Security Policy (2011a) *A Partnership for Democracy and Shared Prosperity with the Southern Mediterranean*, COM (2011) 200 Final, Brussels, 8 March.
European Commission and High Representative of the Union for Foreign Affairs and Security Policy (2011b) *A New Response to a Changing Neighbourhood*, COM (2011) 303, Brussels, 25 May.
European Commission and High Representative of Foreign Affairs and Security Policy (2015) *Review of the European Neighbourhood Policy*, JOIN (2015) 50 Final, Brussels, 18 November.
European Court of Auditors (2013a) 'EU Cooperation with Egypt in the Field of Governance', *Special Report* 4, Luxembourg.
European Court of Auditors (2013b) 'EU Support for Governance in Egypt—'Well Intentioned but Ineffective', Say EU Auditors', *Press Release* ECA/ 13/18, Luxembourg, 18 June.
European External Action Service (2011) *Meeting of the Tunisia-European Union Task Force*, 28–29 September, 2011, Tunis, Co-Chairs Conclusions, dated 29 September 2011.
European External Action Service (2012) 'EU-Egypt Task Force: Supporting the Reform Process in Egypt', *Press*, 14 November, http://eeas.europa.eu/top_stories/2012/141112_eu-egypt-taskforce_en.htm, accessed 22 December 2015.
European Parliament (2015) *European Parliament Resolution of 15 January 2015 on the Situation in Egypt* (2014/3017 (RSP)).
Feldman, N. (2011) 'Islamists' Victory in Tunisia: A Win for Democracy', Bloomberg, 30 October, www.bloombergview.com/articles/2011-10-30/islamists-victory-in-tunisia-a-win-for-democracy-noah-feldman, accessed 22 December 2015.
Grant, C. and O'Donnell, C. (2007) 'The EU Should Talk to Hamas', Centre for European Reform, London, 11 July, www.cer.org.uk/insights/eu-should-talk-hamas, accessed 19 May 2016.
Hamid, S. (2011) 'The Rise of the Islamists', *Foreign Affairs*, May/June.
Hamid, S. and Kadlec, A. (2010) 'Strategies for Engaging Political Islam', FES and Pomed, January.
Hegghammer, T. (2012) 'Islamism: Contested Perspectives on Political Islam'. Edited by Richard C. Martin and Abbas Barzegar, *Journal of Islamic Studies* 23(2): 252–254.
Human Rights Watch (2015) 'Egypt: Year of Abuses Under Al-Sisi. President Gets Western Support While Erasing Human Rights Gains', 8 June, www.hrw.org/news/2015/06/08/egypt-year-abuses-under-al-sisi.
Kennemore, T. (2014) 'The Rise and Fall of the Muslim Brotherhood', *The Jerusalem Post*, 25 November.
Khalaf, R. (2014) 'Too Soon to Embrace Sisi—Egypt is an Unpredictable Place', *Financial Times*, 23 April.
Kodmani, B. (2010) 'Introduction', in Elshobaki, A. and Martín Muñoz, G. (eds.) *Why Europe Must Engage with Political Islam*, Barcelona: European Institute of the Mediterranean & EU Institute for Security Studies.
Leigh, P. (2011) "Europe 'Should Have Backed Democrats Not Dictators,' Commissioner Says", *EU Observer*, 1 March, https://euobserver.com/news/31894, accessed 14 November 2015.
Lusardi, R. (2015) 'Tunisia's Islamists: Ennahda and the Salafis', *Middle East Policy Council*, www.mepc.org/articles-commentary/commentary/tunisias-islamists-are-ennahda-and-salafis-divorcing?print, accessed 22 December 2015.
Mandour, M. (2015) 'EU and the Arab World: 'Cooperation' to Fight Terror is an Excuse', Open Democracy, 25 January, https://www.opendemocracy.net/arab-awakening/maged-mandour/eu-and-arab-world-'cooperation'-to-fight-terror-is-excuse.
Meijer, R. and Bakker, E. (eds.) (2012) *The Muslim Brotherhood of Europe*, New York/London: Hurst/Columbia University Press.
Metro (2009) 'Ministers Urged to Open Hamas Talks', 26 July, http://metro.co.uk/2009/07/26/ministers-urged-to-open-hamas-talks-296419/, accessed 22 December 2015.
Pace, M. (2010) 'Interrogating the European Union's Democracy Promotion Agenda: Discursive Configurations of "Democracy" from the Middle East', *European Foreign Affairs Review* 15(5): 611–628.
Pace, M and Pallister-Wilkins, P. (2016) 'EU-Hamas Actors in a State of Permanent Liminality', *Journal of International Relations and Development*, online first, DOI: 10.1057/s41268-016-0080-y.
Parker, G. (2015) 'David Cameron Pulls Muslim Brotherhood Report', *Financial Times*, 16 March.
Potyrala, A., Przybylska-Maszner, B. and Wojciechowski, S. (eds.) (2015) *Relations Between the European Union and Egypt After 2011: Determinants, Areas of Cooperation and Prospects*, (Logos Verlag Berlin GmbH: The Polish National Science Centre NCN).
Ragab, E. (2012) 'Islamic Political Parties in Egypt: An Overview of Positions on Human Rights and Development and Opportunities for Engagement', Cairo: Netherlands-Flemish Institute.

Republic of Tunisia, Finance Ministry (2011) *Economic and Social Program: The Jasmin Plan*, www.leaders.com.tn/uploads/FCK_files/file/Jasmine%20Plan.pdf.

Schmid, F. and Dombey, D. (2006) 'EU Urged to Make Contact with Hamas', *Financial Times*, 31 August, www.ft.com/intl/cms/s/0/49dad460-390e-11db-a21d-0000779e2340.html#axzz3v30XtEZr, accessed 22 December 2015.

Schumacher, T. (2015) 'The European Union and Democracy Promotion: Readjusting to the Arab Spring', in Sadiki, L. (ed.) *Routledge Handbook of the Arab Spring: Rethinking Democratization*, Oxon and New York: Routledge, 559–573.

Schwedler, J. (2013) 'Islamists in Power? Inclusion, Moderation, and the Arab Uprisings', *Middle East Development Journal* 5(1).

Schwedler, J. (2015) 'Why Academics Can't Get Beyond Moderates and Radicals', in *Islam and International Order. Islam in a Changing Middle East*, Washington: POMEDS, 22 July, http://pomeps.org/2015/07/22/islam-and-international-order/, accessed 12 September 2015.

Unver Noi, A. (ed.) (2013) *Islam and Democracy: Perspectives on the Arab Spring*, Newcastle upon Tyne: Cambridge Scholars Publishing.

Varisco, D. (2010) 'Inventing Islamism: The Violence of Rhetoric', in Martin, R. and Barzegar, A (eds.) *Islamism: Contested Perspectives on Political Islam*, Stanford, California: Stanford University Press, 33–50.

Volpi, F. (2009) 'Political Islam in the Mediterranean: The View from Democratization Studies', *Democratization* 16(1): 20–38.

Wegner, E. and Pellicer, M. (2009) 'Islamist Moderation Without Democratization: The Coming of Age of the Moroccan Party of Justice and Development?', *Democratization* 16(1): 157–175.

Wolff, S. (2012) *The Mediterranean Dimension of the European Union's Internal Security*, New York: Palgrave.

Wolff, S. (2015a) 'EU Budget Support as a Transnational Policy Instrument: Above and Beyond the State?', *Public Administration* 93(4): 922–939.

Wolff, S. (2015b) 'U.S. and EU Engagement with Islamists in the Middle East and North Africa', *Paper Series* 3, 2014–15, Transatlantic Academy, Washington.

World Bank (2016) *Tunisia Overview*, www.worldbank.org/en/country/tunisia/overview, accessed 20 May 2016.

Youngs, R. (2014) *Europe in the New Middle East: Opportunity or Exclusion*, Oxford: Oxford University Press.

45
THE NEIGHBOURS OF THE EU'S NEIGHBOURS
Overcoming geographical silos

Sieglinde Gstöhl and Erwan Lannon

Introduction: reviewing key policies in a deteriorating strategic context

In 2002 and 2003, both the European Neighbourhood Policy (ENP) and the part of the European Security Strategy (ESS) dealing with the EU's neighbourhood aimed to promote 'security, stability and prosperity in a ring of well-governed countries to the East and South of the European Union (EU)' (European Council 2002: point 22; European Council 2003: 8). More than a decade later, the EU's neighbourhood has become politically more unstable and insecure, and both the ENP and the ESS underwent major reviews in 2015. While the review of the ENP was published in November 2015 (European Commission and High Representative 2015b), the High Representative for Foreign and Security Policy and Vice-President of the European Commission, Federica Mogherini, presented the new EU Global Strategy on foreign and security policy – a (thematically) global strategy rather than just a security strategy – in June 2016 (European External Action Service 2016).

Among the questions raised by the joint consultation paper of the European Commission and High Representative (2015a: 4), which prepared the review of the ENP, was the geographical scope of the future policy: 'many of the challenges that need to be tackled by the EU and its neighbours together, cannot be adequately addressed without considering, or in some cases co-operating with, the neighbours of the neighbours'.

The spillover of violence from the civil war in Libya into Mali, in 2013, and from the 'Islamic State' in Iraq into Syria, as well as the waves of migrants and refugees from Africa and Asia crossing the Mediterranean Sea, or following the route through the Balkans, are just a few recent examples to illustrate the regions' interconnectedness. This is also reflected in the strategic assessment presented to the European Council in June 2015 entitled 'The European Union in a changing global environment: A more connected, contested and complex world' (European External Action Service 2015). Two major questions stand out in the ENP review:

> Geographically, the ENP is confronted with the differences between and within each region, as well as the tight interlinkages – for good or ill – between the EU's neighbours and the neighbours' own neighbouring countries and regions. Conceptually,

the ENP was premised on the notion of 'enlargement lite', the relevance and effectiveness of which are now being called into question.

(ibid.:15)

The Council of the European Union (2015a: point 2) called to make the ENP 'more political and responsive to the diverse challenges in the neighbourhood' and to take into consideration the ENP countries' broader geographical context and 'their relations with their neighbours' (ibid. point 5). The European Parliament (2015: point 53) stressed that 'the EU should realistically consider the different policy options that its partners face, as well as how to build bridges with their neighbours on different levels'. In 2006, the European Commission (Commission of the European Communities 2006) had already called for working with the neighbours of the EU's neighbours in Central Asia, the Gulf and Africa. Yet, this appeal gained ground only recently in the policy debate, as well as in the scholarly literature (Gstöhl and Lannon 2014; 2015), and among think tanks (Grevi 2014; Biscop 2014; Lehne 2014).

This chapter asks how the various legal, policy and strategic frameworks designed by the EU for its neighbours, and their neighbours, could be better integrated, or at least linked by developing transnational and cross-regional cooperation initiatives. It argues that, given the rapid development of the trans-regional challenges, which the EU is facing in its broader neighbourhood, and because the ENP and ESS were both under review most recently, there was an opportunity to develop a more consistent cross-regional approach. The ENP is a composite, cross-sector policy, requiring the comprehensive approach that the new Global Strategy aims at also. However, this opportunity was only partially seized. The neighbours of the EU's neighbours are only briefly mentioned in the proposals for the ENP review for the sake of the stabilisation of the broader neighbourhood (European Commission and High Representative 2015b), whereas the EU Global Strategy emphasises the need for the EU to promote resilience in its surrounding regions (European External Action Service 2016), yet without identifying new or innovative instruments to address, in concrete terms, the challenges posed by the neighbours of the EU's neighbours.

The chapter first briefly outlines the challenges that the interconnectedness of many problems in the broader neighbourhood pose. It then presents an overview of the fragmentation of the EU's current frameworks in these regions. It concludes that the review of the ENP could have been better coordinated with the ESS review and that a joined-up approach requires, as stressed by the European External Action Service (2015: 19), 'the end of geographical silos'.

The trans-regional challenges in the EU's broader neighbourhood

Paradoxically, not all direct neighbours of the EU are included in the ENP framework, while some of the ENP partners (Armenia, Azerbaijan and Jordan) are not direct neighbours of the EU. Therefore, the concept of the 'neighbours of the EU's neighbours' should not be interpreted in a strictly geographical sense – as those countries which share a terrestrial or maritime border with a neighbour of the EU – but understood from a broader geopolitical perspective. The following (sub-)regions are, besides Turkey and Russia, of special importance:

- in Africa: the Sahel at large and the Horn of Africa;
- in the Middle East: the Arabian Peninsula with the members of the Gulf Cooperation Council (GCC) and Yemen, as well as Iraq and Iran; and
- in Central Asia: Kazakhstan, Kyrgyzstan, Tajikistan, Turkmenistan and Uzbekistan.

Linkages with other Asian countries, such as Afghanistan and Pakistan, must be taken into consideration, for example in the field of counter-terrorism (Lannon 2014).

The transnational or trans-regional challenges that the EU and its neighbours are currently facing are numerous. With regard to the problems and potential areas of cooperation in the broader neighbourhood, the EU institutions have, among others, identified the following issues: human, drugs and arms trafficking; organised crime; weapons proliferation; terrorism; piracy; regional conflicts; humanitarian crises; environmental pollution; nuclear hazards; communicable diseases; illegal immigration; border management; regional infrastructures; water and energy issues (Commission of the European Communities 2003: 6; European External Action Service 2011: 1; Council of the European Union 2007a: 3). The African sub-region faces numerous challenges related to extreme poverty and food crises, but also fragile statehood.

Among the security challenges in the ENP countries are longstanding conflicts: the Israeli–Palestinian conflict; the Western Sahara; the so-called 'frozen conflicts' in the post-Soviet space – Abkhazia, South Ossetia, Nagorno-Karabakh, Transnistria; alongside the more recent conflicts in Libya, Syria and Ukraine. Although the EU has progressively become more involved in the management of some of the protracted conflicts in its neighbourhood – through diplomacy and different negotiating formats, missions under the Common Security and Defence Policy (CSDP), and sanctions – its engagement has varied considerably across regions (Noutcheva 2015; Popescu 2011). Despite the reinforcement of the CSDP provisions with the Lisbon Treaty, Blockmans and Wessel (2011: 101) identify a 'flagrant lack of common vision on how to tackle and resolve disputes on the borders of the European Union'.

In the EU's broader neighbourhood intra-state conflicts abound, whereas inter-state conflicts are less frequent.[1] According to Kartsonaki and Wolff (2015), there are clear links between conflicts in countries such as Mali, Iraq or Sudan/South Sudan, and conflicts in the more immediate neighbourhood of the ENP. The security challenges that these countries face combine with a range of other challenges related to state fragility and poor living conditions (ibid.).

Many of these challenges are closely interlinked and of a trans-regional nature. Therefore, they should be prioritised when defining inter-regional or cross-border cooperation (Lannon 2015). Despite these many pressing challenges transcending the boundaries of the EU's neighbours, the EU has different policy frameworks in place with the neighbours of its neighbours. The lack of a strategic vision has led to the neglect of the inter-linkages between the EU's direct neighbours and the latter's own neighbours. Yet, the general objectives of the ENP and the ESS – security, stability, prosperity – cannot be achieved if the regional environments and realities of the EU's partners are not properly kept in mind when designing national and (sub-)regional initiatives.

The EU's fragmented policy frameworks

The EU has concluded various types of agreements with the neighbours of its neighbours. It provides them with financial and humanitarian assistance, aims to promote democracy and human rights, as well as trade and development, and has also put a few (sub-)regional strategies in place: for the Sahel, the Horn of Africa and Central Asia. It also carries out a few missions and operations under the CSDP in these regions.

Africa and the Mediterranean

The EU's overall approach to Africa concentrates on development and security issues. The Joint Africa–EU Strategy adopted in 2007 aims 'to bridge the development divide between

Africa and Europe through the strengthening of economic co-operation and the promotion of sustainable development in both continents, living side by side in peace, security, prosperity, solidarity and human dignity' (Council of the European Union 2007b: point 4).

However, the EU's approach towards its direct neighbours in North Africa and the Near East (Israel, Jordan, Lebanon, Palestine and, in principle, Syria) is mainly defined by the ENP frameworks for cooperation (regional, inter-regional and cross-border dimensions) and residuals of the Euro-Mediterranean Partnership (EMP; the Euro-Mediterranean Association Agreements), while the Euro-Mediterranean ministerial meetings, now framed by the Union for the Mediterranean (UfM), are still difficult to relaunch. The EU's relations with the sub-Saharan African countries, including the neighbours of the above-mentioned EU neighbours – Mauritania, Mali, Niger, Chad, Sudan and (by geopolitical extension) South Sudan and Somalia – are formally placed under the Cotonou Agreement concluded with the African, Caribbean and Pacific (ACP) states (Lannon 2014).

At the bilateral level, the EU has concluded Euro-Mediterranean Association Agreements and is negotiating Deep and Comprehensive Free Trade Areas (DCFTAs) with Morocco and Tunisia. At the multilateral level, the 1995 Barcelona Declaration foresaw the establishment of a Euro-Mediterranean Free Trade Area, and Tunisia, Morocco, Jordan and Egypt entered the Agadir Free Trade Agreement (Lannon 2013). For the neighbours of the EU's neighbours, the Economic Partnership Agreements (EPAs) between the EU and regional groupings of the ACP countries are to progressively establish free trade areas. The countries of the Sahel and the Horn of Africa, together with other ACP countries, have been split into four different regional groupings to negotiate EPAs with the EU. These EPA negotiations have encountered many obstacles, because they base trade no longer on the principle of non-reciprocity with the whole ACP group, but on reciprocal, comprehensive Free Trade Areas (FTAs) with several sub-groups (Pape 2013). The least developed countries among the African neighbours of EU's neighbours, profit from the EU's unilateral 'Everything But Arms' initiative and have little incentive to sign up to such EPA.[2] Whereas the Southern Mediterranean partners benefit from the European Neighbourhood Instrument (ENI), the main geographical financial instrument for the ACP countries is the European Development Fund (EDF).

Among the many CSDP missions in the region have been the EUFOR Chad/Central African Republic, the EUCAP Sahel Niger, the EUCAP Sahel Mali, EUCAP Nestor, the EUTM Mali and the EUTM Somalia, as well as the EUAVSEC South Sudan mission and the EUNAVFOR Somalia (Atalanta). The EU also provided assistance to the African Union Mission in Sudan (AMIS) (Bailes and Dunay 2015; Kartsonaki and Wolff 2015). All these missions took place in Sub-Saharan Africa, and mainly in the Sahel and Horn of Africa. In response to the problems in these regions, the EU has in recent years developed specific sub-regional strategies. The EU's 'Strategy for Security and Development in the Sahel' recognises that the challenges faced by the three core Sahel states (Mauritania, Mali and Niger) affect neighbouring countries like Algeria, Libya or Morocco (European External Action Service 2011). It acknowledges that 'the absence of a sub-regional organisation encompassing all the Sahel and Maghreb states [is likely to] lead to unilateral or poorly coordinated action and hamper credible and effective regional initiatives' (ibid.: 3). The 'Horn of Africa Strategy' (Council of the European Union 2011) builds on the earlier 'EU Policy on the Horn of Africa', which emphasised that '[a]ll individual countries of the sub-region have seen their domestic conflicts influenced by, or having implications on, the neighbourhood' (Council of the European Union 2009: 8). The turmoil in Mali in 2013 revealed how closely connected the EU's immediate neighbourhood is to the Sahel. Nevertheless, the EU's free trade projects in the Mediterranean and ACP regions are not (planned to be) linked to each other. The case of Mauritania illustrates the arbitrariness of the cooperation frameworks: this ACP country is a member of the EMP and of the UfM, but – unlike the other countries of the Arab Maghreb Union (Algeria, Libya, Morocco and Tunisia) established in 1989 – it has not been included in the ENP.

The Middle East and the Arab countries

Turning to the Middle East, the EU has – since the ill-fated Euro-Arab Dialogue with the League of Arab States (1973–1990) – divided the Arab countries into different frameworks of cooperation. In addition to the EMP/ENP/UfM, covering most of the Arab Maghreb and Mashreq countries, and the Cotonou Agreement, which includes Arab ACP countries such as the Comoros, Djibouti, Mauritania and, in principle, also Sudan and Somalia,[3] the EU has established an inter-regional relationship with the GCC. The 1988 Cooperation Agreement committed the European Economic Community (EEC) and the GCC to enter 'into discussions concerning the negotiation of an agreement aimed at the expansion of trade' (EEC-GCC Cooperation Agreement 1989: Art. 11). Negotiations regarding an FTA have been initiated, in 1990, but were suspended in 2008 (European Commission 2016). Two other Arab countries, Iraq and Yemen, have been left out of any multilateral institutional arrangement with the European Union, while a Cooperation Agreement was concluded with Yemen in 1998. Two years after the 2003 US-led military intervention in Iraq, the EU established the civilian EUJUST LEX Iraq mission to strengthen the rule of law and to promote the respect for human rights, and in 2012 concluded a Partnership and Cooperation Agreement (PCA) with Iraq. As far as Iran is concerned, negotiations were put on hold from 2005, due to the country's nuclear activities. The three countries benefit from the EU's general Development Cooperation Instrument (DCI), whereas the Partnership Instrument is the framework for financial cooperation between the EU and the GCC countries (as well as other high-income countries).

The EU's relations with the Arabian Peninsula, Iraq and Iran, combine bilateral and inter-regional aspects. The 2004 'EU Strategic Partnership with the Mediterranean and the Middle East' (SPMME) was a first attempt to overcome this fragmentation (European Council 2005). Although it embraced the Arab Mediterranean countries and Israel, the members of the GCC – Yemen, Iraq, Iran and possibly Turkey – it still relied on existing instruments and mechanisms and clearly distinguished between the countries of the EMP and those east of Jordan (ibid.: point 49). Nevertheless, it did consider the progressive future establishment of regional free trade agreements, such as the linking of the Euro-Mediterranean and EU-GCC FTAs. The original proposal from the European Commission and High Representative (2003) to envisage a regional strategy for the 'Wider Middle East' was not followed up in the SPMME. A few years later, instead of embedding the newly created UfM in this Strategic Partnership to connect Europe, the Mediterranean, the Arabian Peninsula, Iran and Iraq, the EU's policies remained compartmentalised (Lannon 2008).

Central Asia and the Black Sea

The EU's relations with Central Asia are mainly based on bilateralism, accompanied by a regional strategy, and a strong focus on energy security. Central Asia is, for the time being, the least conflict-affected area of the EU's broader neighbourhood, but the European Commission supports the Border Management in Central Asia Programme (BOMCA). The EU concluded bilateral Partnership and Cooperation Agreements with Kazakhstan, Kyrgyzstan, Tajikistan and Uzbekistan, while the PCA concluded with Turkmenistan in 1998 has still not been ratified due to human rights concerns. Kazakhstan, a member of the Eurasian Economic Union (EEU), has in December 2015 signed an Enhanced PCA with the EU.

According to the Central Asia Strategy, '[t]he strong EU commitment towards its eastern neighbours within the framework of the European Neighbourhood Policy will also bring Europe and Central Asia closer to each other' (Council of the European Union 2007a: 2). The common challenges notwithstanding, the EU did not pursue a multilateral approach towards the five republics. In June 2015, the Council of the European Union (2015b: point 14) announced that

> [i]n order to support better interconnections of the Central Asian countries with both their immediate neighbours and partners further afield, such as the European Union, the EU will take into account existing regional synergies and links with neighbouring countries in implementing its Strategy, thus recognising the strategic position of the Central Asian countries and possibilities to promote regional stability through stronger trade links. The Council thus encourages sharing European standards, experience and best practices in specific sectors, in accordance with the interest and level of ambition of individual Central Asian countries.

The EU's Black Sea Synergy initiative, launched in 2007, aimed at cooperation with the Organisation of the Black Sea Economic Cooperation, which comprises Albania, Armenia, Azerbaijan, Bulgaria, Georgia, Greece, Moldova, Romania, Russia, Serbia, Turkey and Ukraine. It envisaged 'a close link between the Black Sea approach and an EU Strategy for Central Asia' (Commission of the European Communities 2007: 3). The Black Sea Synergy initiative generated 'rather limited results', and given that 'the Black Sea region is a strategic bridge connecting Europe with the Caspian Sea area, Central Asia and the Middle East', the European Parliament (2011) has been calling for a proper 'EU Strategy for the Black Sea'. Regarding financial assistance, the TACIS programme (Technical Assistance to the Commonwealth of Independent States), from 1991 to 2006, covered Central Asia, the Eastern Partnership countries and Russia. For the Central Asian republics, TACIS was then replaced by the broader DCI, while the eastern ENP countries fall under the ENI and Russia is now included in the Partnership Instrument.

Cross-regional comparison

In comparison, the current policy frameworks in the EU's broader neighbourhood appear to be looser from west to east: while in Africa multilateralism and (emerging) inter-regionalism prevail, cooperation in the Middle East is characterised by inter-regionalism and bilateralism and in Central Asia mainly by bilateralism. Among the main shortcomings are, on the one hand, the divisions within the regions (except for Central Asia) and, on the other, the lack of policy linkages and concrete cooperation projects between the neighbours of the EU's neighbours. Such fragmentation risks leading to 'patchiness and policy vacuums' and 'fails to leverage regional connections' (Youngs and Echagüe 2010: 27). The EU's reaction to the 'Arab Spring', for instance, overlooked the strong relations of Southern Mediterranean countries with the Gulf monarchies, while regional powers, such as Saudi Arabia, Turkey or Iran appear to be engaged in a geopolitical bid seeking to extend their influence across the EU's broader neighbourhood.

Nevertheless, there are first attempts to better connect the policy frameworks. In its 1998 Cooperation Agreement with Yemen, the EU explicitly foresaw that economic and other cooperation may extend to activities under agreements with other countries of the same region.

Two cross-regional programmes are already supported by the ENP's financial instrument and the DCI: the INOGATE programme (Interstate Oil and Gas Transport to Europe), which assists the development of energy cooperation between the EU, the littoral states of the Black and Caspian Seas and their neighbouring countries; and the TRACECA programme (Transport Corridor Europe-Caucasus-Asia), which develops transport between Europe and Asia across the Black Sea, the South Caucasus, the Caspian Sea and Central Asia. The revised Cotonou Agreement of 2010 also contains a clause for cooperation between countries, regions and territories eligible under the ENI, the DCI and the EDF.

On the other hand, the creation of the Eastern Partnership contributed to a more assertive Russia pushing for Eurasian integration in the post-Soviet area, resulting in Armenia and Belarus joining the EEU, Georgia, Moldova and Ukraine searching for closer ties with the EU, and Azerbaijan trying to keep distance from both (Delcour and Kostanyan 2014).

Many events in the ENP area have in fact challenged the assumption of a systematic gradual convergence of the neighbouring countries to the EU. In the context of the ESS review, the European External Action Service acknowledged that the EU's

> diplomatic, economic, migration, asylum and security policies need to account for the deep connections between Europe's southern neighbours and their neighbours in the Gulf and sub-Saharan Africa in order to help put out the fires ravaging the region, from Libya to Syria, and Iraq to Yemen.
>
> *(2015: 9)*

After Russia's annexation of Crimea in March 2014, the intervention of the Russian Federation army in Syria since the end of September 2015 (and notably the launching of missiles from the Caspian and Mediterranean seas) has been shedding light on other connections in the EU's broader neighbourhood. Indeed, Russia and Turkey, two key players in the area, have developed and are developing their own policies and strategies in neighbourhoods partly shared with the EU.

Conclusions: coordinating the implementation of the reviewed ENP and the EU Global Strategy

This chapter examined how the various legal, policy and strategic frameworks designed by the EU for its neighbours and their neighbours could be better integrated, or at least linked by developing transnational and cross-regional concrete cooperation initiatives like the TRACECA programme. It argued that given the rapid development of the trans-regional challenges, which the EU is facing in its broader neighbourhood, the ENP and ESS reviews were opportunities not to be missed to develop a more consistent and coordinated cross-regional approach. Although both documents briefly address the issue of the neighbours of the EU's neighbours, they do so mainly through the perspectives of political dialogue and the few existing sub-regional frameworks (in the Sahel and the Horn of Africa).

Recent events have clearly demonstrated that the EU cannot escape geopolitical rivalry in its neighbourhood and that it largely failed to think strategically ahead. For a broader strategic vision, the EU needs to assess its interests and comparative advantages in a region, while considering coherence with its overall external action. Ignoring the interconnections between the EU's immediate and broader neighbourhood carries the risk of inconsistent and ineffective policies.

While the ENP, for instance, stresses political conditionality regarding democracy and human rights standards in Algeria, the EU needs security cooperation with this pivotal country for its Sahel Strategy (Bello 2012). According to Vines and Soliman (2014), the EU has repeatedly criticised Ethiopia for flawed elections, but nevertheless increased its budget support to the Ethiopian government because the country continues to be a strategic ally in the Horn of Africa. Warkotsch and Youngs (2015) argue that concerns about EU energy security and geopolitical interests in the Middle East and in Central Asia militate against a more ambitious promotion of democracy and human rights *vis-à-vis* political regimes that are not propitious for reforms.

Among the lessons to be drawn from the 'Arab Spring' is that the engagement with authoritarian leaderships, for the sake of political stability, should not sideline the EU's commitment to democracy, rule of law and human rights. In the words of the European External Action Service (2015: 12), 'stability is no substitute for sustainability'. However, given the current crisis situation, generated by several conflicts in the EU's broader neighbourhood or beyond (Afghanistan), a number of EU Member States are willing to promote stability, even if the price to pay is to cooperate with authoritarian – if not dictatorial – political regimes.

The 'values vs. interests' dilemma is at the core of the strategic reflection that is needed at EU level to improve the consistency of its various bilateral and (sub-)regional initiatives (Noutcheva, Pomorska and Bosse 2013). Kartsonaki and Wolff (2015) find that the EU adopts elements of a norms-driven human security approach most consistently in cases where it can also be considered to have significant security interests of its own. 'While undeniably part of the EU's foreign and security policy in the wider neighbourhood, the normative motivations that underpin the human security approach are not a strategic driver of EU action' (ibid.: 224). Whereas the EU pursues a purposeful and institutionalised rule-transfer *vis-à-vis* ENP countries, combined with a conditionality policy, there is no comparable 'external governance' approach in its broader neighbourhood (Lavenex 2011: 386).

The EU could promote bridge-building between the ENP countries and their neighbours on several levels (Gstöhl 2014): unilaterally, through the funding of cross-framework and cross-regional cooperation, for instance on the basis of specific clauses in financial instruments and/or an own cross-border cooperation programme for the neighbours of EU's neighbours, and through the inter-linkage of its regional strategies (while embedding them in a broader common strategic framework); bilaterally, through regional cooperation clauses in agreements and through enhanced political dialogue; and multilaterally, through closer cooperation with the neighbours of the EU's neighbours in regional and global fora. The new trade strategy of October 2015 remains silent on the neighbours of the EU's neighbours, but it recognises that, contrary to earlier assumptions, not all ENP countries are interested in 'closer integration with the EU' and that trade agreements other than the DCFTAs might be needed (European Commission 2015: 34). This demand for more differentiated partnerships was acknowledged by the ENP review a month later (European Commission and High Representative 2015b). The Council of the European Union (2015a: point 5) recognised that 'the broader geographical context of our partners and their relations with their neighbours are important considerations, impacting upon the ENP', but it also stressed immediately afterwards that it was 'the sole right of the EU and its partners to decide in a sovereign way on how they want to proceed in their relations'. The ENP and ESS reviews failed to propose new cross-regional and transnational instruments and programmes to address the manifold concrete challenges (such as migration or terrorism) of the EU's broader neighbourhood. Coordinating the implementation of the reviewed ENP and the EU Global Strategy will thus be of crucial importance. The neighbours of the EU's neighbours are on the EU's political agenda, but what the European External Action Service conceded regarding migration policy applies to external action in general: a joined-up approach 'requires the end of geographical silos' (2015: 19).

Notes

1. For an overview of the conflicts in the EU's wider neighbourhood, within and between the neighbours of the EU's neighbours, see Kartsonaki and Wolff (2015: 205–209).
2. On the EU's trade relations with the ENP countries and with the neighbours of the EU's neighbours, see Gstöhl (2015).
3. On these two specific cases see Lannon (2014: 15).

References

Bailes, A. and Dunay, P. (2015) 'The EU and the Neighbours of its Neighbours: Security Challenges and Strategic Roles', in Gstöhl, S. and Lannon, E. (eds.) (2015) *The European Union's Broader Neighbourhood: Challenges and Opportunities for Cooperation beyond the European Neighbourhood Policy*, Abingdon: Routledge, 53–80.

Bello, O. (2012) *Quick Fix or Quick Sand? Implementing the EU Sahel Strategy*, Madrid: FRIDE.

Biscop, S. (2014) 'Game of Zones: The Quest for Influence in Europe's Neighbourhood', *Egmont Paper* 67, Brussels, June.

Blockmans, S. and Wessel, R. (2011) 'The European Union and Peaceful Settlement of Disputes in its Neighbourhood: The Emergence of A New Regional Security Actor?', in Antoniadis, A., Schütze, R. and Spaventa, E. (eds.) *The European Union and Global Emergencies: Law and Policy Aspects*, Oxford: Hart Publishing, 73–103.

Commission of the European Communities (2003) *Wider Europe-Neighbourhood: A New Framework for Relations with our Eastern and Southern Neighbours*, COM(2003) 104 final, Brussels, 11 March.

Commission of the European Communities (2006) *Communication from the Commission to the Council and the European Parliament on Strengthening the European Neighbourhood Policy*, COM(2006) 726 final, Brussels, 4 December.

Commission of the European Communities (2007) *Communication from the Commission to the Council and the European Parliament, 'Black Sea Synergy—A New Regional Cooperation Initiative'*, COM(2007) 160 final, Brussels, 11 April.

Council of the European Union (2007a) *The EU and Central Asia: Strategy for a New Partnership, 10113/07*, Brussels, 31 May.

Council of the European Union (2007b) *The Africa-EU Strategic Partnership, A Joint Africa-EU Strategy, 16344/07*, Lisbon, 9 December.

Council of the European Union (2009) 'An EU Policy on the Horn of Africa—Towards a Comprehensive EU Strategy', *Annex to the Outcome of Proceedings of the Foreign Affairs Council*, Brussels, 8 December.

Council of the European Union (2011) 'A Strategic Framework for the Horn of Africa', *Annex to the Council Conclusions on the Horn of Africa*, 3124th Foreign Affairs Council meeting, Brussels, 14 November.

Council of the European Union (2015a) 'Council Conclusions on the Review of the European Neighbourhood Policy', *Press Release 188/15*, Brussels, 20 April.

Council of the European Union (2015b) 'Council Conclusions on the EU Strategy for Central Asia', Foreign Affairs Council 10191/15', *Press Release 188/15*, Brussels, 22 June.

Delcour, L. and Kostanyan, H. (2014) 'Towards a Fragmented Neighbourhood: Policies of the EU and Russia and their consequences for the area that lies in between', *CEPS Essay* 17, Brussels, 17 October.

EEC-GCC Cooperation Agreement (1989) 'Cooperation Agreement between the European Economic Community, of the one part, and the countries parties to the Charter of the Cooperation Council for the Arab States of the Gulf (the State of the United Arab Emirates, the State of Bahrain, the Kingdom of Saudi Arabia, the Sultanate of Oman, the State of Qatar and the State of Kuwait) of the other part', *Official Journal of the European Communities*, L 54, 25 February, 3–15.

European Commission (2015) *Trade for All: Towards a More Responsible Trade and Investment Policy*, DG Trade, Brussels, 14 October.

European Commission (2016) *EU-Gulf Cooperation Council trade negotiations*, DG Trade, Brussels, http://ec.europa.eu/trade/policy/countries-and-regions/regions/gulf-region, accessed August 2016.

European Commission and High Representative (2003) *Strengthening EU's Relations with the Arab World, D(2003) 10318*, Brussels, 4 December.

European Commission and High Representative (2015a) *Joint Consultation Paper – Towards a new European Neighbourhood Policy*, JOIN(2015) 6 final, Brussels, 4 March.

European Commission and High Representative (2015b) *Joint Communication to the European Parliament, the Council, the European Economic and Social Committee and the Committee of the Regions 'Review of the European Neighbourhood Policy'*, JOIN(2015) 50 final, Brussels, 18 November.
European Council (2002) *Conclusions of the European Council, 15917/02*, Copenhagen, 12-13 December.
European Council (2003) *European Security Strategy: A Secure Europe in a Better World*, Brussels, 12 December.
European Council (2005) *Final Report on an EU Strategic Partnership with the Mediterranean and the Middle East*, Brussels, 17 June.
European External Action Service (2011) *Strategy for Security and Development in the Sahel*, Brussels, http://eeas.europa.eu/africa/docs/sahel_strategy_en.pdf, accessed August 2016.
European External Action Service (2015) *The European Union in a Changing Global Environment: A More Connected, Contested and Complex World*, Brussels, 30 June.
European External Action Service (2016) *Shared Vision, Common Action: A Stronger Europe – A Global Strategy for the European Union's Foreign and Security Policy*, Brussels, June.
European Parliament (2011) *An EU Strategy for the Black Sea (2010/2087(INI))*, Brussels, P7_TA(2011)0025, 20 January.
European Parliament (2015) *Resolution of 9 July 2015 on the Review of the European Neighbourhood Policy (2015/2002(INI))*, Strasbourg.
Grevi, G. (2014) 'Re-defining the EU's Neighbourhood', in Grevi, G. and Keohane, D. (eds.) *Challenges for European Foreign Policy in 2014: The EU's Extended Neighbourhood*, Madrid: FRIDE, 15–22.
Gstöhl, S. (2014) 'Conclusion: Models of Cooperation with the Neighbours of the EU's Neighbours', in Gstöhl, S. and Lannon, E. (eds.) *The Neighbours of the EU's Neighbours: Diplomatic and Geopolitical Dimensions beyond the European Neighbourhood Policy*, Farnham: Ashgate, 269–289.
Gstöhl, S. (2015) 'EU Trade Relations beyond the "Neighbourhood Economic Community"', in Gstöhl, S. and Lannon, E. (eds.) *The European Union's Broader Neighbourhood: Challenges and Opportunities for Cooperation beyond the European Neighbourhood Policy*, Abingdon: Routledge, 107–129.
Gstöhl, S. and Lannon, E. (eds.) (2014) *The Neighbours of the EU's Neighbours: Diplomatic and Geopolitical Dimensions beyond the European Neighbourhood Policy*, Farnham: Ashgate.
Gstöhl, S. and Lannon, E. (eds.) (2015) *The European Union's Broader Neighbourhood: Challenges and Opportunities for Cooperation beyond the European Neighbourhood Policy*, Abingdon: Routledge.
Kartsonaki, A. and Wolff, S. (2015) 'The EU's Responses to Conflicts in its Wider Neighbourhood: Human or European Security?', *Global Society* 29(2): 1–28.
Lannon, E. (2008) 'The European Union's Strategic Partnership with the Mediterranean and the Middle East: A New Geopolitical Dimension of the EU's Proximity Strategies', in Dashwood, A. and Maresceau, M. (eds.) *Law and Practice of EU External Relations: Salient Features of a Changing Landscape*, Cambridge: Cambridge University Press, 360–375.
Lannon, E. (2013) 'An Economic Response to the Crisis: Towards a New Generation of Deep and Comprehensive Free Trade Areas with the Mediterranean Partners Countries', European Parliament Committee on International Trade (INTA), *The Euromed Region after the Arab Spring and the New Generation of DCFTAs*, PE 433.756, Brussels, 37–63.
Lannon, E. (2014) 'Introduction: The "Neighbours of the EU's Neighbours", the "EU's Broader Neighbourhood" and the "Arc of Crisis and Strategic Challenges" from the Sahel to Central Asia', in Gstöhl, S. and Lannon, E. (eds.) *The Neighbours of the EU's Neighbours: Diplomatic and Geopolitical Dimensions beyond the European Neighbourhood Policy*, Farnham: Ashgate, 1–25.
Lannon, E. (2015) 'Conclusion: Lessons and Policy Proposals', in Gstöhl, S. and Lannon, E. (eds.) *The European Union's Broader Neighbourhood: Challenges and Opportunities for Cooperation beyond the European Neighbourhood Policy*, Abingdon: Routledge, 315–326.
Lavenex, S. (2011) 'Concentric Circles of Flexible "European" Integration: A Typology of EU External Governance Relations', *Comparative European Politics* 9(4/5): 372–393.
Lehne, S. (2014) 'Time to Reset the European Neighbourhood Policy', Carnegie Europe, Brussels, February.
Noutcheva, G. (2015) 'Institutional Governance of European Neighbourhood Policy in the Wake of the Arab Spring', *Journal of European Integration* 37(1): 19–36.
Noutcheva, G., Pomorska, K. and Bosse, G. (eds.) (2013) *The European Union and Its Neighbours: Values versus Security in European Foreign Policy*, Manchester: Manchester University Press.
Pape, E. (2013) 'An Old Partnership in a New Setting: ACP-EU Relations from a European Perspective', *Journal of International Development* 25(5): 727–741.
Popescu, N. (2011) *EU Foreign Policy and Post-Soviet Conflicts: Stealth Intervention*, Abingdon: Routledge.

Vines, A. and Soliman, A. (2014) 'The Horn of Africa: Transnational and Trans-Regional Dynamics in Europe's Broader', in Gstöhl, S. and Lannon, E. (eds.) *The Neighbours of the EU's Neighbours: Diplomatic and Geopolitical Dimensions beyond the European Neighbourhood Policy*, Farnham: Ashgate, 67–95.

Warkotsch, A. and Youngs, R. (2015) 'The Limits of EU Democracy Support: Central Asia and the Gulf Cooperation Council', in Gstöhl, S. and Lannon, E. (eds.) *The European Union's Broader Neighbourhood: Challenges and Opportunities for Cooperation beyond the European Neighbourhood Policy*, Abingdon: Routledge, 187–204.

Youngs, R. and Echagüe, A. (2010) 'Europe, the Mediterranean, the Middle East and the Need for Triangulation', *The International Spectator* 45(3): 27–39.

46
THE EUROPEAN NEIGHBOURHOOD POLICY AND THE CFSP/CSDP

From the European Security Strategy to the Global Strategy

Thomas Henökl

Introduction

On 28 June 2016, after a one-year-long public consultation process, the High Representative of the Union for Foreign Affairs and Security Policy and Vice-President of the European Commission (HRVP) tabled a new European Union Strategy for Foreign and Security Policy (European External Action Service 2016a), replacing the European Security Strategy (ESS) of 2003 (European Council 2003). The first strategy, written by a small team around the EU High Representative, Javier Solana, bore the characteristics of its historical context. It was elaborated during optimism about the Union's evolution, in the euphoric backwash of the successful introduction of the Euro as common currency and on the eve of the 'big bang' enlargement of 2004. A famous and, from today's perspective, overly confident or even self-congratulatory opening statement set the scene: 'Europe has never been so prosperous, so secure nor so free. The violence of the first half of the century has given way to a period of peace and stability unprecedented in European history' (ibid.: 1). With the ESS, Solana and the Council Policy Unit ventured for the first time into strategizing at the level of the EU's Common Foreign and Security Policy (CFSP) in a globally favourable climate for Europe, and, equally important, before the end of the 'permissive consensus' (Norris 1997; Hurrelmann 2007; Hooghe and Marks 2009) within the EU Member States and the negative referenda on the EU Constitution (in France and the Netherlands in 2005) and on the Lisbon Treaty (in Ireland, in 2008). Despite a persisting and heavily debated 'capabilities-expectations gap' (Hill 1993) in the realm of the CFSP, it was then quietly assumed that the European model was the ideal to emulate for the 16 neighbouring countries on their way to association with, or even integration into, the Union (Smith 2004; Lavenex 2004; Manners and Whitman 2003).

The ESS, which also informed the 'old' European Neighbourhood Policy (ENP), stated that '[t]he best protection for our security is a world of well-governed democratic states', and set itself the 'task to promote a ring of well governed countries to the East of the European Union and on the borders of the Mediterranean with whom we can enjoy close and cooperative relations' (European Council 2003: 8). The EU then considered itself a 'normative' or 'civilian power', committed to defend and promote human rights, democracy and the rule of law – also in its neighbourhood (Manners 2002; Aggestam 2008). European self-perception has since evolved: The European Union's Global Strategy (EUGS) adopts an approach of 'principled pragmatism' (European External Action Service 2016a: 8), much more modest and limited in ambition, which was already labelled as a form of European 'Realpolitik' (Biscop 2016). The pragmatic element in this refers to European interests, while principles include the EU's values such as human rights, democracy and the rule of law. Providing a long list of threats and challenges to Europe's security and prosperity, the 2008 Report on the Implementation of the European Security Strategy noted 'that the EU remains an anchor of stability' for its neighbourhood (Council of the European Union 2008: 1). Among the means for playing this role as a partner have been the CFSP, development cooperation, humanitarian action and the EU's trade policy. However, the logical and most prominent place for promoting regional cooperation has been the ENP, together with the EU's enlargement policies. Institutionally, these policy areas and competencies have been neatly separated by, and divided into, different organizational entities. The 2008 Report recognized this and called for 'more coherence, through better institutional co-ordination and more strategic decision-making' in order 'to be more effective – among ourselves, within our neighbourhood and around the world' (Council of the European Union 2008: 9). The report was also an important step in the building of an EU security identity and examined the state of affairs with regard to a number of security objectives, such as the European Defence Agency (EDA), as well as the Helsinki Headline Goals in the area of rapid reaction capacity and civilian response. It also offered an assessment of several sub-strategies, notably regional approaches to East Asia, Latin America – and the EU's neighbourhood. Compared to the ambitious goal setting in earlier documents, such as the Commission Communication 'Wider Europe' of 2003 (Commission of the European Communities 2003), there is now an obvious shift towards an approach of integrated security governance *vis-à-vis* the ENP countries (European Commission and High Representative of the Union for Foreign Affairs and Security Policy 2016; Council of the European Union 2016a, 2016b).

In 2011, then HRVP, Catherine Ashton, jointly with Enlargement Commissioner Stefan Füle, published a communication entitled 'A New Response to a Changing Neighbourhood' (High Representative of the European Union for Foreign Affairs and Security Policy/European Commission 2011). This review did not question the assumptions at the basis of the ENP, nor did it change the original enlargement framework. It was conceived as a reaction to the transformations in the Southern Mediterranean, known as the 'Arab Spring', and offered some, though limited support to democratization in the region. As already acknowledged in the ESS, Europe has inherent incentives to be a point of reference for the establishment of political order in its neighbourhood and an anchor for its stability:

> It is in the European interest that countries on our borders are well-governed. Neighbours who are engaged in violent conflict, weak states where organised crime flourishes, dysfunctional societies or exploding population growth on its borders all pose problems for Europe.
>
> *(European Council 2003: 7)*

The EUGS added a list of governance goals to provide in the medium term, several public goods, such as human security, rule of law, education, health services, investment and a sound income base for neighbouring countries (European External Action Service 2016a).

The question is, whether the EU and its Member States, even taking all their capabilities at the organizational intersection of foreign, neighbourhood and development policies into account, have the legitimacy and the capacity, that is, material means and the instruments, as well as the institutional equipment, to do so. Does the EUGS provide sufficient guidance on how to go about it and, finally, does Europe have the political will and operational capacities to determine the appropriate course of action and to adopt the necessary measures? The chapter will address these questions by first sketching out the parallel evolution from the ESS to the EUGS and of the ENP between 2003 and 2015. In tracing elements of path-dependence in the development of the ESS/EUGS and the ENP, the chapter analyses the extent to which the EU's foreign and security strategy and the ENP have co-evolved into a coherent framework for guiding policy action, before drawing some conclusions on the changing normative dynamics at the institutional intersection of the EUGS and the ENP.

The EU Security Strategy, the Global Strategy and the ENP: path-dependent and co-evolving strategies

Even though the ESS and the old ENP were adopted in the same year and struck a similar chord as to the importance of political stability, democratic governance and economic development in the European neighbourhood, they largely existed in two parallel universes. Wider Europe was conceived as a Commission policy framework for the post–2004 enlargement phase. Some months later, the ESS was published, written by the Council's Policy Unit, a small team of officials around the then EU-HR, Javier Solana. There was little institutionalized communication or consultation between the two realms, neatly separated in their confinements, left and right of the Rue de la Loi in Brussels.

By contrast, the documents presented in November 2015 and June 2016, respectively the Review of the ENP and the EUGS, were the result of institutional learning and communication. Although the EUGS is supposed to be the overarching top-level strategy for the EU's foreign and security policy, it does not introduce hierarchies among other external policy areas. The ENP remains a compatible yet independent field of EU action. Strategies need to be underpinned by institutions able to translate them into concrete policy action. These institutions, especially in the field of the ENP, have only been developed after 2003 and have matured since. In the period since the establishment of the EEAS, the learning curve has been steep: the institutionalization of hybridity in policy-making allows for more and better coordination between Brussels-based (including EU Delegations) and Member States' diplomatic services (Henökl 2015).

More than in the days of the ESS and Wider Europe, today the ENP is the policy area where the Global Strategy is put to a test. The aim is to achieve better coordination of instruments and services, not only administratively but also in view of having stronger political impact. For this purpose, Brussels has endeavored to strike a balance between community instruments, such as trade, aid, migration and the CFSP, as well as actively seeking support by the Member States. This is necessary since the ENP concerns several individual policy areas, theoretically clearly divided but in practice frequently overlapping competencies between administrative units and governance tiers.

Virtually the same Commission officials were dealing with the same policies – the ENP countries to be ever more closely associated with Europe, with practically the same tools, instruments and methods (resources, expertise, rules, drafts and models) readily available. The path for the ENP's evolution was set: for nearly a decade after the entry into force of the Lisbon Treaty in 2009, and two years after the merger of DG ELARG with DEVCO's Directorate F, the new DG NEAR continued what it had been successfully doing, namely trying to get the countries around the EU to reform according to the EU model, comply with its legal order and to conform to the *acquis*. To the 'genetic soup' (Olsen 2010) of enlargement policy, a few new ingredients have been added over time in a way of 'institutional layering' (Streeck and Thelen 2005). Next to the staff and tools from DG DEVCO, some new elements pertaining to mission and tasks were added and reassembled, which determined the shape of the things to come in DG NEAR. Some clarifications about the relations between DG NEAR and DG DEVCO were established in the service-level agreement of 27 February 2015, which regulates the working relations between the services and the administrative support to be provided by DG DEVCO. The ENP also combines financial instruments applying different administrative and operational methodologies inherited from the predecessor structures of DG NEAR (Maass, this volume).

With the Lisbon Treaty, the HRVP has obtained far-reaching powers to formulate, coordinate and implement EU external policies, traditionally a prerogative of the Member States. In the exercise of these delegated powers, since 2010, the HRVP is assisted by a dedicated administrative body, namely the EEAS. Formal decision-making over the EU's CFSP remains with the Council, while the European Neighbourhood and Trade policies, as well as international cooperation, largely remain the competencies of the EU Commission. Being responsible for the implementation of the EUGS, and to achieve coherence between the actions in the different fields of external affairs, the EEAS is situated within several, partly overlapping and conflicting, competence areas and accountability relationships (Henökl 2014a; Henökl 2016). The reform of the ENP in 2015, entailing a readjustment of the EU's approach and ambitions in the two (heterogeneous and diverse) country-groupings, that are frequently lumped together as European neighbourhood(s), has been focusing on problems of consistency and coherence, and is shaped to match established and learned coordination practices. The inter-service consultation between the involved DGs is an example of such learned and institutionalized coordination practices at the EU level.

Sufficient strategic guidance? Translating strategies into action

The EUGS is a strategy document that needs to be broken down into sub-strategies, policy and action plans, with the ENP ideally adding a geographic and operational sub-layer for regions bordering the EU. Connected to both are several agendas, which are being updated and adapted to interact better and articulate with each other and with the EUGS, such as the revision of the European Consensus on Development in 2017 and the future of the ACP–EU Partnership post-2020 (see Figure 46.1). Beyond the EU's own reform processes, there are several global governance undertakings, including the UN 2030 Agenda for Sustainable Development, the Convention on Climate Change with yearly summits, or the G20 process, which under German leadership in 2017 and under the headings 'resilience', 'sustainability' and 'responsibility', focuses on the causes of migration and promotes cooperation with Africa (German Federal Government 2016: 5–13).

As shown in Figure 46.1, the specific multi-level character of the Union, adds complexity to the coordination between governance and administrative levels – involving different EU institutions at several hierarchical layers, as well as political and bureaucratic bodies within Member State governments (Henökl 2014b; Egeberg and Trondal 2015). With the ENP being a central pillar of the ESS and later EUGS, one should expect increased coordination between the two political figures, Commissioner Johannes Hahn and HRVP, Federica Mogherini, as well as between their administrations in charge of the neighbourhood agenda, DG NEAR and the EEAS.

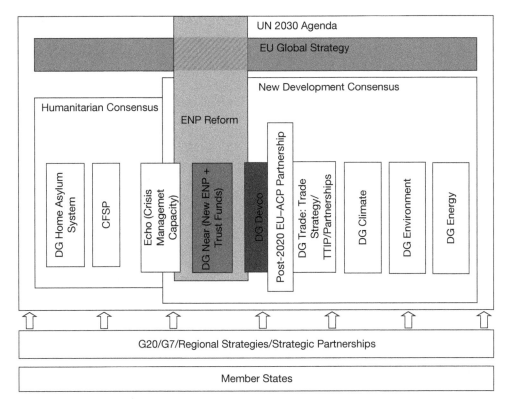

Figure 46.1 EU strategies and reforms affecting ENP – with involved DGs

While the second reform of the ENP has been presented in a Joint Communication by the Commission, spearheaded by Commissioner Hahn and HRVP Mogherini in November 2015, and despite increased inter-organizational exchange between NEAR and EEAS, the ENP is far from being an organic part of EU external action. More than in the ESS, the neighbourhood ranks high on the list of the five priorities that are identified in the EUGS. These are: (1) the security of the EU itself; (2) the neighbourhood; (3) how to deal with war and crisis; (4) stable regional orders across the globe; and (5) effective global governance. While the ENP has always been the EU's most developed regional strategy, the connection from the strategic level to implementation has been further strengthened over the years. Compared to the relation between the ESS and the old ENP, there is an improvement, to the extent to which the EUGS provides strategic guidance for a differentiated and targeted ENP. The main development concerns the degree of convergence of EUGS and the new ENP, propagating similar and compatible approaches and instruments, such as flexibility, differentiation, ownership and resilience. Concomitantly, new agendas targeting migration and security illustrate the actual transformation of EU action and the implementation of the EUGS in the neighbourhood regions. As the institutional structures evolved, the division of tasks at EU level has become clearer and the coordination has increased, also the Global Strategy and the ENP have become more complex, more nuanced and more converging – but not necessarily more ambitious.

Consider the resilience approach, which is central to both documents. The EUGS claims that '[s]tate and societal resilience is our strategic priority in the neighbourhood' (European External Action Service 2016a: 25). Similarly, the ENP Review reads, 'the measures set out in this Joint Communication seek to offer ways to strengthen the resilience of the EU's partners in the face of external pressures and their ability to make their own sovereign choices' (European Commission and High Representative 2015b: 4). Resilience can be an inherently dynamic concept, distinct from 'stability'. Resilience is defined as 'the ability of states and societies to reform, thus withstanding and recovering from internal and external crisis' (European External Action Service 2016a: 23). While the resilience concept may thus be progress *vis-à-vis* the focus on 'stability', the concept has been criticized by scholars for being vague and putting the burden for crisis management on the shoulders of the already distressed countries (or entities), inciting them to build capacities and develop resilience by themselves (Wagner and Anholt 2016). Considering the state of the EU's neighbourhood, the narrative on resilience sounds euphemistic, if not inspired by a neo-liberal idea of self-reliance or self-empowerment, 'whereby the responsibility for security is transferred from the government to (civil) society' (Schmidt 2015: 406). It may be argued that resilience is to some extent the external expression of the subsidiarity principle, leaving responsibility for problems within the jurisdiction where they are best and most efficiently taken care of. This approach may seem adequate for problem-solving in the case of ungoverned spaces, collapsing social contracts and weakened state institutions of the MENA region but the resilience theme makes much less sense in the eastern neighbourhood, since it is not state structures that are missing in the East – during the first years of the ENP it was the neighbours lacking the determination to engage in the prescribed reforms, whereas today it is the power politics of Russia as the regional hegemon that deliberatively undermines EU neighbourhood ambitions.

Putting some flesh to the resilience bone, a draft 'Roadmap on the follow-up to the EU Global Strategy', circulated by the EEAS' Policy Coordination Division to the Antici Group of the Committee of the Permanent Representatives (Coreper), on 19 September 2016, outlines an 'Initiative on resilience', which

> would aim at developing a common narrative on the EU's enhanced approach to state and societal resilience, on governance building and accountability as well as enhancing links with civil society which will be developed in relation to implementation of relevant Sustainable Development Goals.

This initiative 'would target in particular the EU's surrounding regions, in synchronisation with the revised European Neighbourhood Policy' with the consequence that it 'would also contribute to enhancing the EU's own resilience and that of its citizens' (European External Action Service 2016b: 2). In practice, there seems to be a strong emphasis on security related measures, but for the time being, it is not clear how this narrative will be filled with life, other than with stricter measures in the field of migration.

The problem is, of course, that the ENP review of November 2015 (European Commission and High Representative 2015b) was realized before the overarching EUGS was elaborated, with some degree of inconsistency programmed into the process. This is replicating the situation of 2003, when Wider Europe was released by the Commission roughly eight months ahead of Council's publication of the ESS. Strictly speaking, in both cases the ENP should have constituted a regional sub-strategy to the EUGS, but, at least in the case of 2015 ENP review, the document was presented in the form of a Joint Communication by the Neighbourhood Commissioner and the EU High Representative, which suggests that there was better and closer coordination between them.

As an intermission belt to take this coordination further, the Roadmap for Implementation suggests therefore that 'it would be complemented by an update of the relevant sectoral sub-strategies to align relevant EU policies with the goal of a multifaceted and tailor-made approach to resilience' (European External Action Service 2016b: 2). As indicated in the Roadmap, this applies to all strategies that have been elaborated over the last years, and notably to the European Agenda on Security of 2015, which again makes direct references to the EU neighbourhood (Council of the European Union 2015). In 2003, the ESS was more of a 'stand-alone strategy' and did not have such a detailed plan to ensure the follow-up.

Also, in contrast to the ESS, which was less explicit about it, the EUGS now puts the emphasis on Europe's own security, setting the ambitious target of reaching 'strategic autonomy [. . .] to promote peace and security within and beyond its borders' (European External Action Service 2016a: 9). The neighbourhood, next on the list, is a sort of 'resonance room' of the EU's priorities of security, prosperity and democracy – de-emphasising democratization and expressing a certain preference for stability: 'We will take responsibility foremost in Europe and its surrounding regions, while pursuing targeted engagement further afield' (ibid.: 17). Actively promoting democratization is no longer a compulsory part of the package, instead the EU would support democracies where they emerge, for 'their success [. . .] would reverberate across their respective regions' (ibid.: 25).

The idea is that the neighbourhood is the inner most of several 'concentric circles' of the EUGS, closest to its centre – Europe itself. The neighbourhood thus receives strategic priority, ahead of all other partners. The main concern in the neighbourhood is its fragility, a problem intimately linked to the recurring resilience theme of the EUGS (Henökl and Stemberger 2016). 'State and societal resilience to our East and South' (European External Action Service 2016a: 6) and fragile states have been dragged into the centre of EU attention – the word 'resilience' is mentioned forty times in the EUGS. Both concepts, fragility and resilient societies, are of growing importance when dealing with the neighbourhood – certainly in the South but increasingly also in the East. To foster 'resilience in our surrounding regions', it 'will nurture societal resilience also by deepening work on education, culture and youth to foster pluralism, coexistence and respect' (ibid.: 16-17).

Strategic ambiguity in a turbulent environment

While resilience may be a core *topos* for the EU's southern neighbourhood, it is not entirely clear what this approach can do for the eastern neighbourhood. The problem for the countries to the East of Europe is an increasingly assertive and aggressive Russia, actively trying to prevent them from associating with and integrating into the EU. This situation contrasts starkly with the scenario projected in the Wider Europe communication, where Russia was a strategic partner in the region and potentially one of the countries within the ENP. Back in 2003, Russia had also been the single most important recipient of Community assistance under the ENP (Commission of the European Communities 2003). Obviously, neither the reviewed ENP of 2011 or 2015 nor the EUGS can reconcile the fundamental strategic inconsistency of grouping not only different countries, but two geopolitical spaces – embedded in totally different cultural and socio-economic contexts – together in a single policy framework. In the eastern neighbourhood, the EU's 'power-of-attraction' approach proved to be counter-productive and a threat to regional stability (Howorth 2016; Smith 2016).

Based on enlargement and the EU's *acquis communautaire*, the pre-2015 ENP was premised on the assumptions that the EU had all the answers to political and economic organisation, and that neighbouring countries wanted to transform themselves in Europe's image. The image was that of a belt of growing prosperity and democracy around a wealthy and thriving Europe at its centre, ultimately resulting in political stability. Under the umbrella of this superficial assumption, the ENP included too many, and at times contradictory, goals: market-friendly reforms, liberal-democratic transformation, the advancement of human rights, opportunities for investors, energy cooperation, regional stability, migration management and anti-terrorism cooperation. In order to pursue these goals, the ENP assembled a diverse set of policies into a 'tool box', including the 'enlargement carrot', soft-power foreign-policy tools, trade and investment policy and foreign aid (Kelley 2006). Institutionally, this led to a layering of approaches and instruments that were both inadequate and incompatible. The main reason for the ENP's incoherence was that the policy framework reflected too many preferences and tried to pursue them in different country contexts. EU Member States have played a strong role as policy entrepreneurs, while the policy itself has been designed and implemented by the Commission, using the 'golden carrot' of EU membership that later turned into a 'brown carrot', when it became clear that further enlargement of the Union was no longer a realistic scenario (Del Sarto and Schumacher 2005; Bodenstein and Furness 2009). For various geographic, economic and historical reasons, the ENP was divided into two competing zones of influence, characterized by diverging interests and different levels of ambition and ownership. The division into two influence-zones, regrouped under the ENP-roof contributed to unite Member States and consolidate a common EU approach. To the East, Germany, Poland and Sweden together with Lithuania, the Czech Republic and Romania were in the driver's seat, promoting association projects with former Soviet states against growing Russian opposition (Wojna and Gniazdowski 2009). In the South, Mediterranean EU Member States, notably Spain, France and Italy, pushed a broad range of measures, from democracy promotion to self-interested arrangements with the region's authoritarian governments (Schumacher et al. 2016).

With the 2015 refugee crisis, the division of labour between East and South became less self-evident, if not obsolete, since Germany, but also other northern European Member States, got more directly involved in responding to the decomposition in the southern neighbourhood. At least, the EUGS now explicitly recognizes that 'repressive states are inherently fragile in the long term' (European External Action Service 2016a: 16). Managing crises and dealing with the consequences of violent conflict, such as in Libya and Syria, according to the EUGS, requires 'a comprehensive', 'integrated', 'multi-dimensional', 'multi-phased' and 'multi-level approach [. . .] acting at the local, national, regional, and global levels' (ibid.: 18). The security challenges in 2003 were very different – and threats seemed far away. The international community was under the impression of the 9/11 terrorist attacks on the US and the division in Europe regarding the invasion of Iraq. The tone was one of uniting the EU Member States behind a narrative of democracy and governance, contrasting and complementing the US-led global war on terror.

The musings of the ESS seem rather abstract compared to today's fundamental questions of how the EU tackles concrete challenges and how it positions itself *vis-à-vis* key players in its neighbourhoods, most notably Russia (but more recently also Turkey and its position *vis-à-vis* the EU). As the Ukraine conflict demonstrates, this issue has the potential to question the EU's unity and to reduce its response capacity dramatically.

What seems to be an element of continuity between the 'old' and the 'new' ENP – and not repaired by the EUGS – is the strategic ambiguity concerning the question of how precisely to make up for the EU's limited authority and how to bridge its capability gap to reach its lofty targets of peace, security, prosperity, democracy and rule of law.

Conclusions

Among the narratives invoked to mobilize and justify political action at the EU level, the dominant arguments revolve around security and migration being the direct result of conflicts, instability and governance failure in Europe's wider neighbourhood. The rationale behind this refocusing is that, especially after a series of terrorist attacks (notably in Paris 2015 and most recently in London, Berlin and Manchester in 2016 and 2017), in Nice, Brussels and Berlin in 2016, and with record numbers of refugees arriving in Europe, EU leaders perceived as urgent the need to protect the external borders and deliver on citizens' security concerns. Furthermore, the reasoning involves human security in the ENP countries themselves, which has long since been a topic for the EU's international engagement but was not explicitly mentioned in the ESS. More than in 2003, Europe is seen an anchor point for the stability of its surrounding countries as well as a destination for migratory flows, emanating from or transiting through them. Where the ESS stated that 'even in an era of globalization, geography is still important' (European Council 2003: 7), ENP Commissioner Johannes Hahn in a speech, in November 2016, reaffirmed that 'geography is destiny' (Hahn 2016). Quite different from 2003, today's neighbourhood is a global hotspot of war and crisis, and it profoundly challenges the EU's willingness and aptitude not only to co-define regional orders but also to uphold its own European political order (European Commission 2017: 6). To this end, the 'Roadmap on the follow-up to the EU Global Strategy' urges the 'implementation of the Partnership Priorities and Association Agendas' with an emphasis on security cooperation (European External Action Service 2016b). This shift of focus was clearly expressed in the Conclusions of the Foreign Affairs Council of 14 November 2016, where a three-fold priority is outlined: '(a) responding to external conflicts and crises, (b) building the capacities of partners, and (c) protecting the Union and its citizens' (Council of the European Union 2016a: 4).

To give itself a veritable strategy, the EU would need to develop a common understanding of what it is willing and able to invest in regional and global political orders (Howorth 2016). There is also a clear link to other parallel processes of global governance, such as the UN 2030 Agenda or the Paris Agreement on Climate Change. The Sustainable Development Goals feature prominently, under heading 1 of the EUGS, 'Shared Interests and Principles', stating that '[p]rosperity must be shared and requires fulfilling the Sustainable Development Goals worldwide, including in Europe' (European External Action Service 2016a: 5). As demonstrated in the chapter, it is institutional building blocks and organizational boundaries within the EU's governance and administrative system that heavily bear on the content and on the impact of strategy-making and other reform processes. However, the case of EUGS and ENP as intersecting policy fields of EU external action displays the evolving character of both the EU polity and policy-making, resulting over time in institutional emergence transforming normative dynamics. Whereas in the early 2000s the original ENP and the ESS were existing in two parallel, institutionally neatly separated universes, adjustments and reform efforts over the years have led to an increasing convergence of the EUGS and re-jigged neighbourhood policy. In addition, the crisis in the European neighbourhood after 'Arab Spring' in the South, and following the annexation of Crimea in the East, led to a more developed and differentiated policy framework, better harmonized with the EUGS. The implementation plan is now putting security and development, as well as neighbourhood instruments, more directly to use for European interests (European Commission and High Representative of the Union for Foreign Affairs and Security Policy 2015a; Council of the European Union 2016b). The EU's new strategic guidance redirects and extends the EU external action, and particularly the ENP, to include capacity building in security and migration management. Accordingly, the scenario of 'doing much more' in the Commission's White Paper on the Future of Europe presented on 1 March 2017, projects that: '[t]he EU's broad-ranging foreign policy leads it to reinforce its joint approach on migration. Closer partnerships and increased investment in Europe's neighbourhood and beyond help to create economic opportunities, manage regular migration and tackle irregular channels' (European Commission 2017: 27). Considering the overlapping domains of the EUGS and ENP as intersecting policy areas, we may understand the increased security focus as an instance of changing norm dynamics in a gradually or (even abruptly) transforming and increasingly turbulent international environment (Youngs 2004). These changing norm dynamics are the result of combined pressures on the EU polity from both endogenous and exogenous forces, as much as they are the product of the realization of the limits to Europe's power and capacities. Confronted with such pressures, institutional change can occur in two forms, that is, either as gradual, slow and path-dependent adaptation by institutional layering – where transformation is managed and integrated into the political decision-making process – or a radical and unsettling transformation – where, therefore, a polity faces a severe institutional or legitimacy crisis and is unable to adapt. The ENP and the EU as a polity might be at such transformative crossroads. Developing adequate policy responses and combining ambition with realism to address problems in the European neighbourhood will by no means be an easy task.

References

Aggestam, L. (2008) 'Introduction: Ethical Power Europe?', *International Affairs* 84(1): 1–11.
Biscop, S. (2016) 'The Global Strategy: Realpolitik with European Characteristics', *Egmont Security Policy Brief* 75, Brussels.
Bodenstein, T. and Furness, M. (2009) 'Separating the Willing from the Able: Is the European Union's Mediterranean Policy Incentive Compatible?', *European Union Politics* 10(3): 381–401.
Commission of the European Communities (2003) *Wider Europe—Neighbourhood: A New Framework for Relations with our Eastern and Southern Neighbours*, Communication from the Commission to the Council and the European Parliament, COM (2003) 104 Final, Brussels, 11 March.
Council of the European Union (2008) *Report on the Implementation of the European Security Strategy – Providing Security in a Changing World*, S407/08, Brussels, 11 December.
Council of the European Union (2016a) *Council Conclusions on Implementing the EU Global Strategy in the area of Security and Defence*, (OR.en) 14149/16, Brussels, 14 November.
Council of the European Union (2016b) 'Implementation Plan on Security and Defence', Note from the HRVP, (OR.en) 14392/16, Brussels, 14 November.
Del Sarto, R. and Schumacher, T. (2005) 'From EMP to ENP: What's at Stake with the European Neighbourhood Policy Towards the Southern Mediterranean?', *European Foreign Affairs Review* 10(1): 17–38.
Egeberg, M. and Trondal, J. (2015) 'Why Strong Coordination at One Level of Government is Incompatible with Strong Coordination Across Levels (and How to Live with It): The Case of the European Union', *Public Administration* 94: 579–592.
European Commission (2015) 'Communication from the Commission to the European Parliament, the Council, the European Economic and Social Committee and the Committee of the Regions, The European Agenda on Security', Brussels 28 April 2015.
European Commission (2017) *White Paper on the Future of Europe. Reflections and Scenarios for the EU27 by 2025*, Brussels, 1 March.
European Commission and High Representative of the Union for Foreign Affairs and Security Policy (2015a) *Capacity Building in Support of Security and Development – Enabling Partners to Prevent and Manage Crises*, Joint Communication to the European Parliament and the Council, JOIN (2015) 17 Final.
European Commission and High Representative (2015b) *Review of the European Neighbourhood Policy*, JOIN (2015) 50 Final, Brussels.
European Commission and High Representative of the Union for Foreign Affairs and Security Policy (2016) *Elements for an EU-Wide Strategic Framework to Support Security Sector Reform*, Joint Communication to the European Parliament and the Council, SWD (2016) 221 Final.
European Council (2003) *A Secure Europe in a Better World. European Union Security Strategy*, Brussels 12 December.
European External Action Service (2016a) *Shared Vision, Common Action: A Stronger Union. A Global Strategy for the European Union's Foreign and Security Policy*.
European External Action Service (2016b) *Roadmap for Implementation of the Global Strategy*.
German Federal Government (2016) 'Priorities of the 2017 G20 Summit'.

Hahn, J. (2016) Speech by Johannes Hahn at the Press Conference on the EU-Enlargement Package 2016, Brussels, 9 November, https://ec.europa.eu/commission/commissioners/2014-2019/hahn/announcements/speech-johannes-hahn-press-conference-eu-enlargement-package-2016_en.

Henökl, T. (2014a) 'Conceptualizing the European Diplomatic Space: A Framework for Analysis of the European External Action Service', *Journal of European Integration*, 35(5): 453–471.

Henökl, T. (2014b) 'The European External Action Service: Torn Apart Between Several Principals or Acting as a Smart "Double-Agent"?', *Journal of Contemporary European Research* 10(4): 381–401.

Henökl, T. (2015) 'How do EU Foreign Policy-Makers Decide? Institutional Orientations within the European External Action Service', *West European Politics 38*(3): 679–708.

Henökl, T. (2016) 'Conflict and Continuity in European Diplomatic Cultures: Accountability Scrutiny and Control in EU External Affairs', *International Relations and Diplomacy* (4)5: 324–340. doi:10.17265/2328-2134/2016.05.002.

Henökl, T. and Stemberger, A. (2016) 'EU Policies in the Arab World: Update and Critical Assessment', *European Foreign Affairs Review* 21(2): 227–250.

High Representative of the European Union for Foreign Affairs and Security Policy/European Commission (2011) *A New Response to a Changing Neighbourhood*, COM (2011) 303 Final.

Hill, C. (1993) 'The Capability Expectations Gap, or Conceptualizing Europe's International Role', *Journal of Common Market Studies* 31(3): 305–328.

Hooghe, L. and Marks, G. (2009) 'A Postfunctionalist Theory of European Integration: From Permissive Consensus to Constraining Dissensus', *British Journal of Political Science* 39(1): 1–23.

Howorth, J. (2016) 'EU Global Strategy in a Changing World: Approach to the Emerging Powers', *Contemporary Security Policy* 37(3): 1–14.

Hurrelmann, A. (2007) 'European Democracy, the "Permissive Consensus" and the Collapse of the EU Constitution', *European Law Journal* 13(3): 343–359.

Kelley, J. (2006) 'New Wine in Old Wineskins: Promoting Political Reforms Through the New European Neighbourhood Policy', *Journal of Common Market Studies* 44(1): 29–55.

Lavenex, S. (2004) 'External Governance in "Wider Europe"', *Journal of European Public Policy* 11(4): 680–700.

Manners, I. (2002) 'Normative Power Europe: A Contradiction in Terms?', *Journal of Common Market Studies* 40(2): 235–258.

Manners, I. and Whitman, R. (2003) 'The "Difference Engine": Constructing and Representing the International Identity of the European Union', *Journal of European Public Policy* 10(3): 380–404.

March, J. and Olsen, J. (1989) *Rediscovering Institutions: The Organizational Basis of Politics*, New York, NY: The Free Press.

Norris, P. (1997) 'Representation and the Democratic Deficit', *European Journal of Political Research* 32(2): 273–282.

Olsen, J. (2010) *Governing Through Institution Building: Institutional Theory and Recent European Experiments in Democratic Organization*, Oxford: Oxford University Press.

Schmidt, J. (2015) 'Intuitively Neoliberal? Towards a Critical Understanding of Resilience Governance', *European Journal of International Relations* 21(2): 402–426.

Schumacher, T., Bouris, D. and Olszewska, M. (2016) 'Of Policy Entrepreneurship, Bandwagoning and Free-Riding: EU Member States and Multilateral Cooperation Frameworks for Europe's Southern Neighbourhood', *Global Affairs* 2(3): 259–272.

Smith, K. E. (2004) *The Making of EU Foreign Policy: The Case of Eastern Europe*, Springer.

Smith, M. (2016) 'Implementing the Global Strategy Where it Matters Most: The EU's Credibility Deficit and the European Neighbourhood', *Contemporary Security Policy* 37(3): 446–460.

Streeck, W. and Thelen, K. (2005) *Beyond Continuity: Institutional Change in Advanced Political Economies*, Oxford: Oxford University Press.

Wagner, W. and Anholt, R. (2016) 'Resilience as the EU Global Strategy's New Leitmotif: Pragmatic, Problematic or Promising?', *Contemporary Security Policy* 37(4): 414–430.

Wojna, B. and Gniazdowski, M. (eds.) (2009) *Eastern Partnership: The Opening Report*, Warszawa: Polish Institute of International Affairs.

Youngs, R. (2004) 'Normative Dynamics and Strategic Interests in the EU's External Identity', *Journal of Common Market Studies* 42(2): 415–435.

INDEX

9/11 125, 178, 405, 511, 540
5+5 Dialogue 255, 325, 329, 395, 451
2011 ENP review 41, 45, 46, 50, 100, 135, 170, 178, 182, 203–4, 439
2015 ENP review 39, 41, 45, 46, 50, 64, 100, 110–11, 135, 138, 156–9, 178, 182, 219–20, 410, 439, 538; actors and interests 204–6; financial instruments 242; formal and informal processes 206–8; outcomes 208

'A New Response to a Changing Neighbourhood' 6, 45, 203–4, 212, 336, 534
'A Partnership for Democracy and Shared Prosperity with the Southern Mediterranean' 191, 496
Aarhus Convention 473
Abbas, Mahmoud 275, 354, 355
Abkhazia 192, 266, 312, 314, 316–17, 319, 399, 524
acquis communautaire 4, 20, 21, 73, 106, 111–12, 169, 173, 183, 190, 236, 252, 282, 283, 287, 333, 349, 372–8, 383, 416, 440, 441, 447–8, 469–70, 472–3, 502, 536, 539
Action Plans 63, 109, 394–5, 470, 482, 483, 512; Armenia 314, 407; Azerbaijan 314, 407; Georgia 314, 407; Israel 336, 350; Jordan 336, 339, 437; Moldova 303, 307–8, 407; Morocco 331; Palestinian Authority 336; Tunisia 331; Ukraine 280–2, 407, 437
actorness: concept of 29–30; and the ENP 32–4; EU as actor 130–1; European Parliament as actor 223–33
Adenauer, Konrad 53
Africa 524–6
African, Caribbean and Pacific (ACP) group 326, 416, 525, 526
Agadir Agreement 253, 255, 525

aid 415–31; bilateral 425; to civil society 497–500; cross-border cooperation 429; dependence of Palestinian Authority on 354; development/enlargement models 415–17; diversity in use of instruments 419–20; modalities 420; neighbourhood-wide aid 425–9; overview of instruments 417–19; regional assistance 425; sectors 420
Al Khalifa family 181
Algeria 20, 136, 326, 327, 328, 329, 333, 408, 418, 436, 437, 438, 451; Arab Maghreb Union 255, 324; authoritarian resilience 180; counter-terrorism 410, 411; energy 388, 390; EP delegation 227; humanitarian aid 419; readmission agreement 400; response to ENP Action Plan 331–2, 386; war of independence 325
Aliyev, Ilham 387
Amsterdam Treaty 106
approximation: cost/benefits 111, 375; DCFTAs and 108–12, 252, 281–2, 307
Arab League 181, 206, 274
Arab Spring/uprisings 39, 42, 45, 60, 81, 85, 87, 110, 125–6, 135, 146, 177, 181, 191–2, 196, 203–4, 214, 223, 225, 227, 251, 255, 273, 331, 333, 336, 347, 381, 395, 405, 420, 456, 461, 462, 463, 467, 481, 484, 494, 496, 499, 509, 527, 529, 534, 541; human rights and 481; Islamist actors and 515–17
Armenia 6, 20, 42, 73, 112, 192, 254, 398, 399, 449, 450, 452, 453, 457, 527, 528; Association Agreements 282, 483; civil society 438–9; DCFTA 66, 126, 371, 377; EEU membership 171, 173, 315, 371; ENP Action Plan 407, 436; EU relations 312, 313, 314, 315, 318–19, 451, 456; Mobility Partnership 396; political conditionality 194; TACIS 235; visa facilitation and readmission agreement 398

Index

Ashton, Catherine 203, 204, 273, 275, 360, 441, 467, 486, 516, 517, 534
al-Assad, Bashar 181, 274, 275, 341, 363, 364, 447
Association Agreements (AAs) 18, 42, 63, 105, 120, 202, 251, 313, 338, 371, 385, 425, 436, 446, 456, 461, 499; Algeria 326, 332, 408; Eastern Partnership and 168; Euro-Mediterranean Association Agreements (EMAAs) 19, 110, 111, 112, 525; Georgia 108, 458, 501; human rights clause 482–3; Israel 349; MEPs voting on 224; Moldova 108, 304, 305, 458, 501; Morocco and Tunisia 330, 525; Syria 362, 363; three specific features 108–10; Ukraine 108, 126, 127, 193, 279, 458, 501
Azarov, Mykola 229
Azerbaijan 6, 20, 42, 169, 192, 320, 387, 388, 418, 420, 437, 450, 451, 452, 453, 486, 498, 500; Black Sea Synergy initiative 527; civil society 438, 486, 495; conflict resolution 314–15; energy 193, 312, 387–8; energy exporter 387; ENP Action Plans 407; EU relations 312, 313, 317–18, 319, 456, 457, 459, 528; human rights 489; Mobility Partnership 396; political conditionality 194, 447; TACIS 235; visa facilitation and readmission agreements 398

Barcelona Process *see* Euro-Mediterranean Partnership
Barroso, José Manuel 5, 387, 398
Belaid, Chokri 517
Belarus 6, 20, 85, 97, 169, 203, 218, 254, 381, 389, 396, 405, 407, 419, 420, 429, 436, 457, 459, 498, 503, 528; 2010 presidential elections 292–3; deterioration of relations with EU 290–1; Eastern Partnership 213, 292; economic interests 294–5; ECU *versus* EU 171, 173; ENP engagement 291–3; EP delegations 226; EU-Neighbourhood East Parliamentary Assembly 272; EU relations 18, 42, 73, 451, 452, 453, 456; Eurasian Economic Union 112; first decade of ENP 290–1; geopolitical interests 295–6; human rights 483, 486, 489; impact and effectiveness of the EU's policy 296–7; oligarchs 293, 294–5; political conditionality 194–5, 447; regional geopolitics 298; sanctions 271–2, 276; suspension from EURONEST 225; TACIS 235; Ukraine war 293; values and principles 294; visa facilitation and readmission rights 398
Ben Ali, Zine el-Abidine 126, 273, 330, 446, 515, 516, 517
Berlusconi, Silvio 360
Bialiatski, Ales 293
bibliometric mapping exercise 96–9
bilateralism: and region-building 249–58; upgrading legal framework 108–11
Black Sea Synergy 39, 250, 253, 254–5, 319, 389, 527

borders/boundaries: buffering agenda 133–5; colonial frontier strategy 131, 135, 138; conceptualising 130–3; identity and 143–5; regulatory/organizational 20; weak buffer 135–8
Bouteflika, Abdelaziz 332
Brahmi, Mohamed 517
Brazauskas, Algirdas 291
Brega, Gheorge 306
Brexit 142, 154
BRICS 155, 162, 332
budget support 420, 457, 459; human rights and 483; Islamist actors and 513–14
buffer zone 122; ENP countries as weak 135–8
buffering: negative/positive 135–6
Bulgaria 119, 341, 416, 527
Bush, George W. 178, 179

capability-expectations gap 31, 33, 35, 54, 154, 533, 540
Central and Eastern European countries 18, 107, 280, 372, 375, 381, 442
Central Asia 526–7
China 6, 93, 155, 360, 437
civil society 21, 45, 169, 494–506; aid to 497–500; Belarus 296–7; challenges 502–3; Civil Society Facility 439, 458, 462, 485, 486, 495, 499; Civil Society Forum 450; democracy support in the East 458–9; human rights and 485–6, 487; organisations (CSOs) 438, 439, 487, 496, 500, 501, 503; perceptions of values/norms promotion 438–40; policy discourse on 495–7; strategic approach 500–2
civilian missions 259–69; Advisory Mission (EUAM) to Ukraine 261(tab), 266–7; Border Assistance Mission for the Rafah Crossing Point (EUBAM Rafah) 260–2; Border Assistance Mission to Moldova–Ukraine (EUBAM) 265; eastern neighbourhood 264; EUJUST Themis in Georgia 264–5; European Union Coordinating Office for Palestinian Police Support (EUPOL COPPS) 262–3; Integrated Border Management Assistance Mission in Libya (EUBAM Libya) 263–4; Monitoring Mission to Georgia (EUMM) 266; southern neighbourhood 260
coherence/cohesion 33, 35, 42–3, 189–91
Cold War 60, 66, 71, 84, 153, 155, 160, 162, 168, 216, 295, 363, 441, 461, 464n2
'Colour Revolutions' 45, 194, 196, 264, 320, 469
Commissioners, leadership and 52–3
Common Foreign and Security Policy (CFSP) 33, 77, 108, 205, 207, 214, 259, 263, 270, 292, 305, 314, 347, 348, 349, 353, 359, 362, 533–43, 536; Common Strategies 106; sanctions 275–6
Common Security and Defence Policy (CSDP) 205, 207, 215, 259, 260, 263, 264, 265, 266,

545

267–8, 305, 348, 353, 359, 360, 362, 407, 524, 525, 533–43
Commonwealth of Independent States (CIS) 235, 242, 308, 316, 394
computational general equilibrium (CGE) models 374–5
conditionality 22–5, 75–6, 445–8; Armenia 318–19; Association Agreements 109, 112; aversion to in Algeria 332; conflict-related 313–15; democracy support in East 457–9; Eastern Partnership 168–71, 192–5; human rights and 483–4; Mashreq region 336–46; Moldova Action Plan 303; 'more for more' 123–4; norms promotion and 437; Russian in Ukraine 284–6; sanctions and 271
'Conflict Barometer' (Heidelberg Institute for International Conflict Research) 136, 137(tab)
conflict resolution 259–69, 312–23, 347–57
constructivism 70–80; in European studies 71; thick 73, 74–6; thin constructivism I 73, 76–7; thin constructivism II 73, 76–7; three types 71–4
'contraband capitalism' 304
Convention on Climate Change 536
Cooperation Agreements 330, 331, 342, 526, 527
cooperation vs conflict spectrum 70, 71
Copenhagen Criteria 183, 190
Cotonou Agreement 525, 526, 528
Council of Europe 111, 112, 228, 449
Council of the European Union 110, 263, 362, 371, 523, 527, 529
counter terrorism 405–14; Bardo museum attack 410, 516; Berlin terrorist attacks 274, 541; Brussels terrorist attacks 541; challenges to cooperation 410–12; eastern neighbours 407; EU CounterTerrorism Strategy (2005) 405; Euro-Mediterranean Code of Conduct on Countering Terrorism 408; Euro-Mediterranean Partnership legacy 408; financial instruments and 409–10; one dimension of security policies 406–7; recent developments 410; southern neighbours 408–9
Country Based Support Scheme (CBSS) 418
Cox–Kwasniewski mission 224, 229–30, 231
Crimea 60, 66, 81, 87, 126, 127, 160, 193, 204, 234, 266, 273, 279, 286, 296, 298, 318, 399, 452, 458, 475, 488, 528, 541
crisis/conflict management 358–68
Critical Theory 82–3
Cross Border Cooperation Programmes 418, 428(tab), 429
Czech Republic 43, 218, 295, 348, 416, 540

Danielsson, Christian 204
d'Azeglio, Massimo 144
De Gaulle, Charles 53
de Szeged, Adrián Jacobovits 304

decision-making 200–10
Deep and Comprehensive Free Trade Areas/ Agreements (DCFTAs) 5, 19, 21, 24, 63, 105, 108, 111, 120, 208, 217, 219, 371–9, 448, 529; approximation 110; Armenia 66, 126–7, 315, 318, 451, 452; Waves 375; Azerbaijan 315, 317, 437, 451; Belarus 451; conditionality and 109, 447; EaP countries 42; Georgia 66, 112, 252, 316, 451; Jordan 340; Moldova 112, 252, 305, 307–8, 451; Morocco 42, 110, 124, 281, 331, 451, 525; sustainability impact assessments (SIAs) 374–5; Tunisia 42, 110, 281, 331, 462, 525; Ukraine 66, 112, 173, 252, 281, 282, 436, 451, 452; value of 373–4
Delors, Jacques 53
democracy: democratization-stability dilemma 191, 193–5, 196; dialogue with Islamists 512–13; differentiation in South 460–2; geopolitics in Ukraine 459–60; and human rights 85–7; post-communist enlargement 468–9; promotion by functional cooperation 467–80; stability in Morocco 462–3; support in the East 457–9
Democratic Party of Moldova 306
Development Cooperation Instrument (DCI) 205, 420, 497, 526, 527, 528
differentiation 450–3; bilateralism 250–2; DCFTAs 375–7; differentiated integration 18–20; European Neighbourhood and Partnership Instrument (ENPI) 237–8; horizontal 18–19; Mashreq states 343–4
Directorate General for Development and Cooperation (DEVCO) 205, 207, 240, 535–6
Directorate General for European Civil Protection and Humanitarian Aid Operations (ECHO) 240, 352, 359
Directorate General for Neighbourhood and Enlargement Negotiations (DG NEAR) 5, 204, 205, 206–7, 240, 487, 535–6, 537
Directorate General Migration and Home Affairs (HOME) 240
Dispute Settlement Protocols 110
Dodon, Igor 307, 308
Donbas conflict 309n3, 460

Eastern Neighbourhood 32, 41, 66, 87, 111, 126, 127, 167–76, 192–5, 226, 254, 271–3, 441, 449, 451, 539; Belarus 271–2; civilian missions 264–7; Eastern Partnership as EU Governance 168–71; enlargement-light 168–9; Eurasian Union 170, 171–4; Moldova 272; Ukraine 273
Eastern Partnership (EaP) 3, 19, 34, 42, 45, 60, 61, 62, 63, 76, 107, 108, 109, 111, 121, 126, 172, 196, 200, 213, 214, 216, 225, 250, 253–4, 264, 281, 302, 319, 389, 407, 411, 417, 425, 451, 458–9, 485, 528; Belarus 292; Civil Society Forum 272, 296, 486, 494, 496–7, 501;

CORLEAP 450; DCFTAs 110, 371, 375, 447; EaPIC fund 457; as EU governance 168–71; initiative 167, 292; irrelevance for Ukraine 282; and Moldova 305–7; Poland 218; Riga summit 6, 205, 217, 410; and Russia 397–9; trade and visa liberalisation 315; Union for the Mediterranean and 202–3; Vilnius summit 66, 285, 317, 318, 501

effectiveness, concept of 30–1, 43–4; and the ENP 34–5

Egypt 9, 178, 179, 180, 183, 252, 331, 437, 446, 462, 500, 501, 514; Agadir Agreement 255; bilateral agreements 110; budget support 420, 483, 499, 514; Civil Society Facility funding 486; counter-terrorism 408, 409, 410, 411, 489; DCFTAs 110, 371; democracy-stability dilemma 337; ENP 180–1; EP delegation 227; EU assistance 343; EU–Egypt task force 516; European Neighbourhood and Partnership Instrument (ENPI) 338; military government 204, 337–9, 481; 'more for more' approach 203, 463; Muslim Brotherhood 510, 511, 512, 513, 515, 516, 518; political conditionality 195; sanctions 274, 276

election monitoring missions 228–9, 331

energy 381–92; bilateral energy partnerships 387–8; Caspian energy 313, 319, 387; concentric circles of EU External Energy Governance 384–6; decentred mode 384; Energy Community (EnC) 386, 389; EUnilateral mode 383–4; Euro-Mediterranean Energy Partnership (EMEP) 389–90; inner circle 386–7; Internal Energy Market (IEM) 383, 385, 386, 388, 390; regional sectoral cooperation 388–90; renewable energy sources (RES) 382, 389–91; two modes of EU External Energy Governance 383

enlargement 17–27, 133–5, 201–2, 539–40; 'big bang' enlargement 55, 133, 201, 416, 533; 'enlargement fatigue' 281, 283, 469; identity and 142–52

Ennahda 511, 515–17

Erasmus+ programme 351, 418, 429, 498

Essebsi, Beji Caid 516

ethical power, Europe as 52, 64, 154

Ethiopia 529

'EU Strategic Partnership with the Mediterranean and the Middle East' (SPMME) 526

EUAM Ukraine 261(tab), 264, 266, 267

EUBAM 304–5; Libya 261(tab), 263–4, 267, 361, 362; Moldova–Ukraine 261(tab), 264, 265; Rafah 260–2, 263, 264, 267

EUCAP SAHEL Niger 407, 525

EUNAVFOR 362, 400, 525

EUPOL COPPS mission 262–3, 353

Eurasian Customs Union (ECU) 66, 170, 171–4, 172, 285, 371, 452

Eurasian Economic Union (EEU) 112, 126–7, 167, 171, 172, 173, 174, 254, 284, 285, 305, 306, 307, 315, 318, 371, 376, 399, 451, 452, 453, 527, 528

Euro-Mediterranean Free Trade Area 525

Euro-Mediterranean Parliamentary Assembly (EMPA) 225

Euro-Mediterranean Partnership (EMP) 180, 202, 328, 330; Algeria 331–2; civil society 494, 497; counter-terrorism 408; energy governance 389–90; financial instruments 235–6; Islamist actors 512, 514; Israel 349, 350; Libya 333, 359; Mauritania 525–6; multilateral dimension 326; Palestine 352; region building 250, 253–4, 255; Syria 362; trade agreements 372, 416

Euro-Mediterranean Regional and Local Assembly (ARLEM) 449

Euro-Mediterranean Union 457

Eurojust 407, 409, 412

'Euromaidan' 194, 196, 499

EURONEST 207, 225, 450

European Agenda on Security (2015) 406, 539

European Aviation Safety Agency (EASA) 449

European Bank for Reconstruction and Development (EBRD) 374, 449, 459, 462

European Commission, perceptions of ENP 440–1

European Council 63, 203, 206, 326, 360, 362, 515

European Court of Justice (ECJ) 109, 110, 273, 297, 350

European Defence Agency (EDA) 534

European Development Fund (EDF) 416, 417, 420, 525, 528

European Economic Area (EEA) 19, 72, 282

European Economic Community (EEC) 119, 149, 325–6, 327, 328, 330, 331, 349, 451, 526

European Endowment for Democracy (EED) 418, 439, 459, 462, 500

European Environmental Agency (EEA) 449

European External Action Service (EEAS) 9, 44, 45, 133, 155, 201, 203, 204, 209, 230, 231, 240, 241, 255, 263, 417, 435, 436, 439, 440–2, 482, 490, 494, 528, 529, 535, 536, 537, 538; 2015 ENP review 206–7; EEAS Morocco Delegation 517; human rights and 487; Libya tensions 360

European Food Safety Authority (EFSA) 449

European Instrument for Democracy and Human Rights (EIDHR) 86, 296, 297, 351, 418, 459, 462, 463, 464n3, 484, 486, 498

European Investment Bank (EIB) 363, 459, 462

European-Mediterranean Solar Plan (MSP) 390

European Neighbourhood and Partnership Instrument (ENPI) 234, 235, 236–8, 240, 242, 296, 303, 338, 342, 361, 363, 364, 386, 389, 409, 416, 417, 419, 420, 425, 430n6, 441, 449, 483, 497, 499, 500, 514

European Neighbourhood Instrument (ENI) 205, 224, 234, 236, 238–9, 241–2, 338, 339, 343–4,

362, 365–6, 385–6, 389, 409, 416, 417–18, 420, 425, 441, 449, 458, 483, 500, 525, 527, 528
European Parliament (EP) 201, 223–33, 313, 442, 523; 2015 ENP review 207; Committee on Foreign Affairs 226, 228, 231n1; cooperation 225–6; Cox–Kwasniewski mission 229–30; delegations 226–7; diplomacy 225, 229–30; election monitoring missions 228–9; financial instruments 240–1; locating in EU foreign policy 224; perceptions of values/norms promotion 442
European Partnership for the Peaceful Settlement of the Conflict over Nagorno-Karabakh (EPNK) 192–3, 196n1, 315
European Security Strategy (ESS) 10, 53, 63, 66, 134, 177, 182, 207, 249, 259, 275, 406, 485, 522, 523, 524, 528, 529, 533–43
Europeanisation 17–18, 22–5, 32, 44–5, 71; externalization 23; rewards/benefits 24; Ukraine 282–4
Europol 407, 409, 412
Eurozone 45, 149, 217
'Everything But Arms' initiative 525
external governance 20–1

Fatah party 275, 353, 354, 511
Fayyad, Salam 262, 353, 515
Filat, Vlad 306
Filip, Pavel 306
financial instruments 234–45; European External Investment Plan for Africa 242–3; European Neighbourhood and Partnership Instrument (ENPI) 236–8; European Neighbourhood Instrument (ENI) 238–9; institutional advantages and shortcomings 240–2; Madad Trust Fund 239–40; mesures d'accompagnements *(MEDA)* 235–6; Technical Assistance to the Commonwealth of Independent States (TACIS) 235
Finland 18, 43
followers 51, 53; leadership and 54–5
Foucault, M. 82, 83, 84, 86
'Fragile States Index' 2016 (Fund for Peace) 136
France 41, 142, 213, 214–15, 255, 291, 296, 324, 325–6, 348, 353, 354, 360, 361, 363–4, 411, 415, 441, 449, 451, 460, 461, 540; Franco-German competition 43; migrants from North Africa 42; terrorist attacks 365, 410
Free Syrian Army 363
Frontex 400, 407, 409, 449
Füle, Stefan 126, 292, 440, 515, 534
functional cooperation 467–80
'fuzzy borders' 19, 145

G20 process 536
Gaburici, Chiril 306

Gaddafi, Muammar 227, 274, 326, 332–3, 359–60, 400, 447, 462, 489
Gagauzia 306–7, 309n4
Gaza 182–3, 227, 260–2, 352, 353, 354, 355, 488, 513, 518
geopolitics 66–7; Belarus and 295–6, 298; geopolitical vision 120–2; Ukraine as epicentre 459–60
Georgia 45, 76, 88, 124, 126, 167, 169, 170, 172, 192, 195, 227, 314, 373, 418, 436, 438, 451, 456, 459, 467, 499, 527, 528; 2008 war in 193, 203, 216, 268n5, 292, 313, 319, 457, 458; Association Agreement 105, 107, 108, 110, 111, 112, 170, 226, 252, 282, 295, 483, 501; Civil Society Facility funding 486; 'Colour Revolution' 196; conflict resolution 320; counter-terrorism 407; DCFTA 42, 66, 219, 371, 373; energy 386–7, 390; EU–Georgia AP 483; EUJUST Themis 261(tab), 264–5, 312; EUMM Georgia 193, 261(tab) 264, 266, 267; food costs in 375; Mobility Partnerships 396, 398–9; 'Rose Revolution' 194, 264, 265, 312, 488; TACIS 235; Visa Liberalisation Action Plan (VLAP) 315–17
Germany 41, 66, 145, 193, 213, 214, 215–17, 295, 296, 348, 354, 360, 365, 411, 460, 513, 540; Franco-German competition 43; Russia and 216–17; trade with Belarus 42
Gherman, Natalia 306
Global Mediterranean Policy 256n1, 326, 416
Global Public Goods and Challenges Programme 498
Global Strategy (2016) 50, 64, 67, 135, 138, 154, 155, 159, 160, 162, 178, 183, 215, 219, 302, 448, 481, 482, 487–8, 522, 523, 528–9, 533–43
Global War on Terror 179, 332, 511, 540
globalization 145–6
goal attainment 43–4
GOST standards 375
governance model, democracy promotion 469–71
governmentality 83–4, 86
Greece 18, 149, 214, 361, 393, 527
Gulf Cooperation Council (GCC) 181, 523, 526
Gulf states 461

Hahn, Johannes 53, 81, 128, 134, 205, 207, 208, 240, 293, 440–1, 536–7, 541
Hamas 179, 182–3, 275, 353, 354, 355, 511, 512, 513, 518
Haniyeh, Ismail 511
Hariri, Rafik 275, 342, 483
Hassan II, King 330, 451
Helsinki Final Act (1975) 66, 461
Hezbollah 181, 340–1, 510, 511
Horizon 2020 351, 449
Horn of Africa 39, 305, 523, 524, 525, 528, 529
hub-and-spoke model 21, 120, 251, 252, 256, 325, 326, 333

Index

human rights 24, 481–93; Association Agreements clause 482–3; Belarus 294; civil liberties 65; civil society and 485–6, 487; dilemmas in promotion of 488–90
Hungary 43, 183, 218, 416
Hussein, Saddam 179, 182

identity 142–52; borders and 83–5, 143–5; civilizing missions 147, 149; Eurosceptic parties 142; failure of imperial 'dream' 147–9; fuzziness of 145–7; strategic narrative of EU and Russia 161–4
impact, performance of ENP 44–5
imperial mindscape/vision 122–4, 125, 128, 131–3
imperial paradigm 146–9
Incident and Prevention Response Mechanism (IPRM) 266
Instrument contributing to Stability and Peace (IfSP) 418, 498
Instrument for Stability (IfS) 312, 315, 498
integration, differentiated 18–20
Internal Security Strategy (ISS) 406
International Criminal Court (ICC) 482
International Monetary Fund (IMF) 98, 292, 298, 318, 330
internet/social media 160–1, 179
Interstate Oil and Gas Transportation to Europe (INOGATE) 388, 389, 528
Iran 178, 181, 270, 319, 526, 527
Iraq 60, 178, 179, 180, 181, 217, 337, 340, 524, 526; EUJUST LEX Iraq mission 526; invasion of 60, 177, 178–80; IS in 181–2, 364–5, 410, 475, 522; war 182
Ireland 43, 348, 351, 354
Islamic State/IS/ISIS/ISIL 45, 60, 126, 160, 178, 181, 364–5
Islamist actors 509–21; Arab uprisings 515–17; definition/terminology 509–11; democratisation and dialogue 512–13; engagement or containment 511–12; excluded from EU funding 513–15; Islamophobia 510
Israel 76, 88, 110, 111, 206, 227, 260, 263, 326, 336, 340, 342, 347–55, 409, 418, 436–7, 461, 500, 513; EU–Israeli relations 349–52; EU–Israel AP 350–1, 437; Israeli–Palestinian conflict 260, 340, 348–9, 524; Research and Development Agreement 350; settlements 349; Special Privileged Partnership (SPP) 352
Istiqlal party 512
Italy 41, 213, 255, 291, 325, 328, 333, 354, 360, 361, 400, 411, 461, 540
Ivashchenko, Valeriy 229

Jasmin Plan/Revolution 516, 517
Jordan 88, 110, 180, 227, 252, 336, 343, 344, 396, 418, 436, 437, 472, 475, 477, 501, 512, 525, 526; 2006 Progress Report 339; Agadir Agreement 255; DCFTA 371; democratic governance promotion 474; migration and 397, 402; role model 339–40
Juncker, Jean-Claude 42, 204, 205, 207
Justice and Development Party (PJD) 462, 511, 512, 518

Kazakhstan 167, 171, 235, 285, 382, 526–7
Kissinger, Henry 61, 66
Kohl, Helmut 53
Krasnosielski, Vadim 305
Kurds 182
Kwasniewski, Aleksander 229
Kyrgyzstan 171, 235, 526

Lambrinidis, Stavros 486
Latvia 294, 295, 416
leadership 50–9; by example 51; and followership 54–5; four dimensions 52; idealist and materialist interpretations 51; outcomes 53–4; paradox 50–1; person 53; position 53; types of 55–6
Lebanon 110, 274–5, 336, 340–1, 343–4, 410, 418, 511
Leon, Bernardino 361–2
Libya 60, 136, 180, 191–2, 204, 205, 214, 215, 227, 255, 324, 332–3, 358–61, 366, 436, 462, 498; 2011 crisis 359–60; 1969 revolution 326; aid 417, 418; Al-Qaeda 364; civil war 126, 522, 524, 540; civilian missions 260; crisis mode 361–2; energy 386; EUBAM Libya 263–4, 267, 361, 362; EUFOR Libya 263, 360; Framework Agreement 274, 333, 359, 361; human rights 481, 483, 488; migration 400; refugees 475; sanctions 274, 276; transition 361
Lieberman, Avigdor 260
'limes' strategy 131, 132, 138
Lithuania 42, 43, 214, 290, 291, 292, 294, 295, 378n3, 416, 540
Lomé model 416
Lukashenka, Alyaksandr 271–2, 290, 291, 292, 293, 294, 297, 298, 398
Lutsenko, Yurii 230, 284

'3M logic' 515–16
Madad Trust Fund 205, 234, 239–40, 242, 365
Maghreb states 324–35; Arab Maghreb Union (AMU) 253, 255, 328, 526; bilateral differentiation 329; differentiation 451; EP delegation 227; interdependence/dependency 326–9; 'model students' 329, 330–1; postcolonial legacies 325–6; region building 255; trade/aid 416
Maidan protests 266, 273, 459
Mali 214, 215, 522, 524, 525
Malmquist, Henrik 263
Malta 255, 348, 361, 378, 400

549

Manouba University 516–17
Mare Nostrum operation 400
Mashreq region 336–46, 526; Egypt 337–9; EP delegation 227; Islamist actors 512–13; Jordan 339–40; Lebanon 340–1; Syria 342–3; trade/aid 416
Mauritania 255, 256n2, 324, 326, 327, 400, 425, 525–6
Member States 211–22; 2015 ENP review decision-making 206–8; Israeli–Palestinian conflict 348–9; regional tensions 212–14 *see also* entries for individual states
Memoranda of Understanding (MoUs) 251, 266, 387–8
Merkel, Angela 53, 216, 217, 294, 295–6
mesures d'accompagnements (MEDA) 6, 235–6, 237, 242, 342, 352, 390, 409, 416, 418, 497
Middle East and North African (MENA) countries 203, 253, 254, 344, 348, 410, 420, 469, 509, 511, 513, 515, 518, 538
Middle East Peace Process (MEPP) 180, 181, 275, 347, 348, 349, 350, 351, 352, 353, 354, 355, 449
Middle East Quartet 275, 353, 355, 513
migration 191, 192, 393–404; 'Common Agenda on Migration and Mobility' (CAMM) 395; crises 182, 214–15, 216, 255; Eastern Partnership and Russia 397–9; Egypt and 337–8; EU's Global Approach 395–6; management of illegal 42; Mashreq states 344; objectives 394–5; Operation Sophia 400; post-2015 refugee crisis 396–7; southern neighbours 399–401
milieu-shaping 64–5
Millennium Development Goals (MDGs) 239, 242, 417, 538, 541
mindscapes 120–2
Mitterrand, François 53
Mobility Partnerships (MPs) 124, 251, 252, 303–4, 316, 317, 331, 337–8, 389, 395–6, 398, 401, 448, 462
Mogherini, Federica 42, 53, 81, 133, 155, 207, 411, 441, 522, 536–7
Moldova 195, 213, 302–11, 438, 456, 459, 467, 472, 477, 486, 528; aid 420; Association Agreement 105, 107, 108, 110, 111, 112, 170, 172, 226, 252, 303, 307–8, 458, 483, 499, 501; Black Sea Synergy initiative 527; Border Assistance Mission to Moldova–Ukraine (EUBAM) 264, 265; Civil Society Facility Funding 486; Common Visa Application Centre 303; DCFTAs 219, 307–8, 371, 436; democratic governance 474; ECU *versus* EU 173; energy 386–7, 389, 390; ENP Action Plan 407; ENP and 302, 308; environmental legislation 472, 473; EP delegations 227; establishing relations with 303–4; EU relations 42, 76, 88, 124, 169, 203, 449, 451, 452, 456; hybrid regime and European integration 305–7; irrelevance of EP 282; migrants 308, 395; Mobility Partnership 398–9; NATO 295; political reforms 459; public opinion 438; 'ring of friends' 202; sanctions 272; TACIS 235; transformation of economy 307–8; Transnistria and security cooperation 304–5; visa facilitation and readmission agreement 398; and Visgrad group 218
Monnet, Jean 53
'more for more' principle 123, 128, 170, 203, 271, 337, 347, 354, 401, 446, 448, 456, 462, 463, 464, 485, 516
Morocco 20, 76, 180, 183, 205, 418, 448, 456, 464, 473, 489, 509, 516, 517; Advanced Status 330, 512; Agadir Agreement 255, 525; Association Agreement 326; bilateral relations 436; budget support 514; counter-terrorism 409, 410, 411; DCFTAs 21, 42, 110, 252, 281, 371, 451; democratic governance 475, 477; energy 390; ENP Action Plan 330–1, 333; environmental legislation 472, 473; EP delegation 227; EU relations 88, 124, 326–9; geopolitics 462–3, 464; human rights 446; migration and mobility 395–6, 401, 448; PJD 511, 518; readmission agreement 400, 401; Sands War 325; SPRING programme 453
Morsi, Mohamed 181, 195–6, 204, 274, 337, 338, 515, 516, 517, 518
Mubarak, Hosni 274, 336, 337, 338, 446
Multiannual Financial Framework (MFF) 205, 417
Muslim Brotherhood 204, 274, 338, 510–13, 515, 516, 517

Nagorno-Karabakh conflict 193, 194, 312, 314–15, 317–18, 319, 320n5, 321n15, 387, 524
nation states 62–3, 65, 131
Neighbourhood Civil Society Facility (NCSF) 439, 458, 462, 485, 486, 495, 499
neighbourhood clause, Treaty of Lisbon 106–8
Neighbourhood Investment Facility (NIF) 418, 420, 429
neighbours of neighbours: Africa and the Mediterranean 524–6; Central Asia and the Black Sea 526–7; coordinating reviewed ENP and Global Strategy 528–9; cross-regional comparison 527–8; Middle East and the Arab countries 526; trans-regional challenges 523–4
Netherlands 43, 351, 354
network governance 21
Non-Aligned Movement 331
non-governmental organisations (NGOs) 23, 170, 240, 293, 397, 438, 439, 484, 489, 498
non-state actors 62–3, 180–1 *see also* civil society
Nordic Plus 43
Nordstream Gas Pipeline 217

Normative Power Europe (NPE) 28, 52, 56, 71, 74–5, 85, 87, 131, 154, 155, 256
North Atlantic Treaty Organization (NATO) 66, 98, 131, 162, 213, 215, 216, 218, 283, 285, 295, 298, 315, 360, 462
Norway 130, 327

Office for Democratic Institutions and Human Rights (ODIHR) 228
Official Development Aid (ODA) 415, 417, 419, 420
'oil have-nots' 327, 328
oligarchic system, Moldova 302–11
'one size fits all' approach 39, 436, 441, 456, 486
'Orange Revolution' 126, 279–80, 281, 282–3, 313, 436
Organisation for Economic Co-operation and Development (OECD) 237, 417, 419
Organization for Security and Co-operation in Europe (OSCE) 228, 271–2, 304; Minsk Group 193, 314
Ostpolitik 216, 217

Pakistan 183, 417, 524
Palestine 206, 227, 260, 262, 352–4; aid 419, 420; Berlin declaration (1999) 354; Coordinating Office for Palestinian Police Support (EUPOL COPPS) 262–3; differentiation 452; EUBAM Rafah 260–2; Israeli–Palestinian conflict 348–9; Legislative Council 179, 354, 511, 513; Occupied Territories 347, 349, 350, 352, 354, 419, 498, 511; recognition of Palestinian statehood 354, 452; Reform and Development Plan 353, 515
Palestine Liberation Organization (PLO) 349, 352
Palestinian Authority (PA) 110, 227, 260, 275, 276, 303, 336, 347, 515; sanctions 274–5
Paris Charter for a New Europe 66
Parliamentary Assembly of the Union for the Mediterranean (PA-UfM) 225, 449
Partnership and Cooperation Agreements (PCAs) 105, 108, 202, 235, 250–1; Armenia 313–14, 318; Azerbaijan 313–14, 317; Belarus 290, 291; bilateral aid 425; Eastern Partnership and 168; energy relations 385; Georgia 313–14; Iraq 526; Moldova 304; Russia 110, 173; Ukraine 280, 281
Partnership for Democracy and Shared Prosperity with the Southern Mediterranean 191, 467, 496, 515
Partnership Frameworks, migration 396–7
Party of Communists of the Republic of Moldova (PCRM) 303, 305
Peftiev, Vladimir 293
PEGASE 515
performance analysis of ENP: cohesion 42–3; commonly used indicators 40; effectiveness 43–4; impact 44–5; measurement and evaluation 40; not exact science 46; purpose 39–40; relevance 41–2; resilience 45–6
pillar-structure of EU 106
Plahotniuc, Vlad 306
Poland 41, 43, 178, 183, 213, 214, 216, 217, 218–19, 291, 292, 293, 295, 348, 360, 397, 416, 441, 457, 540
'Political Framework for Crisis Approach for Libya' 362
Poroshenko, Pedro 460
Portnov, Andrij 273
Portugal 41, 213, 255, 328, 354
positive othering 168, 174
postcolonial legacies 325–6
postmodern tradition 82–3
power: asymmetries 32, 88, 133, 169, 250, 255–6; European Parliament 224; and leadership 51; realism and 62
Preferential Trade Agreements (PTAs) 377, 378
presence, concept of: definition 29; and the ENP 32
'principled pragmatism' 46, 159, 160, 183, 534
Prodi, Romano 4, 17, 134, 145, 192
Progress Reports 19, 44, 169, 338, 341
Putin, Vladimir 66, 162, 171–2, 295, 307

Qatar 6, 183

Rab'a demonstration 276
Readmission Agreements 251, 252, 319, 394, 396, 398, 400
Realism 64–5, 67, 83; realist international theory 61–2; Realists 51, 61, 64, 71, 74; *Realpolitik* 61, 67, 298, 387, 390, 534
refugees 364–6; aid 418–19; Jordan 340; Lebanon 341; Palestinian 347; Sahrawi 419
region-building 249–50; beyond EU 254–5; at border 253–4
relevance, analysing performance 40, 41–2
research design, ENP studies 94–6
resilience 45–6, 159, 537–9
Riga Summit *see* Eastern Partnership
'ring of fire' 4, 147, 192, 223, 230, 406, 418, 475
'ring of friends' 17, 19, 43, 44, 53, 56, 60, 64, 119, 120, 123, 127, 134, 146, 147, 192, 201–2, 204, 205, 211, 212, 223, 230, 251, 405, 406, 418, 475
ring of instability 39
role theory 54–5
Romania 43, 119, 214, 217, 304, 416, 527, 540
Rose Revolution 194, 264, 265, 312, 488
Rules of Origin (ROO) 349–50
Rumsfeld, Donald 178
Russia 32, 98, 100, 124, 131, 136, 253, 270, 273, 390, 401, 419, 429, 436, 452, 458, 523, 527, 538, 540; annexation of Crimea 60, 81, 87, 193, 204, 234, 266, 273, 279, 296, 488, 528;

Armenia 318–19; Article 8 TEU 107–8; assertiveness of 126–7, 167, 539; Azerbaijan 317, 387; Black Sea Synergy 527; boundaries 145; conflict with Ukraine 39, 159–60, 161–4, 193–4, 218, 219, 229, 272, 273, 460; constructivism 73, 76; counter-offer to Ukraine 279, 284–6; DCFTAs 371, 373, 374, 375; democracy advantage 457–9; Eastern Partnership countries and 397–9; energy 272, 381, 386–7; ENI 238; and ENP 39, 45, 312–15; EU Action Plan 236; Eurasian Customs Union (ECU) 170, 171–4; EU–Russia relations 167–8, 313; geopolitics 66–7, 180, 295, 390; Germany and 216–17; GOST Standards 375; migration and 397–9; Moldova 304, 305, 308; neighbourhood clause 106; PCA 110; region building 253, 254; sanctions 156, 193; special status in ENPI and the ENI 238; strategic narrative of EU and 161–4; TACIS 235; visas 315–16, 394; war with Georgia 193–4, 264, 266, 292, 313, 316–17, 319, 457, 464
Russian Federation 160, 290, 298, 317, 320, 397, 528

Saakashvili, Mikheil 265, 312, 314
Sahel 214, 333, 361, 524, 525, 528
Salafis + 516–17
sanctions: Belarus 42, 271–2, 291, 292–3, 296, 297; cohesion and 42, 189, 193; definition 270; Egypt 274; ENP and 275–7; Libya 274, 359–60; Moldova 272; Palestinian Authority 275; Russia 156, 193, 217; Syria 274–5, 343, 363; Tunisia 273; types of 271; Ukraine 273
Sargsyan, Serzh 6
Sarkozy, Nicolas 193, 202, 213, 337
Saudi Arabia 6, 73, 178, 180–1, 183, 527
Savchenko, Nadiya 226
Schengen Area 19, 84, 142, 145, 252, 394; *acquis* 131; visas 398, 447
Schröder, Gerhard 162, 216
Schulz, Martin 229
Serbia 527
Shevardnadze regime 194, 265
Shevchuk, Yevgeny 305
Sidorski, Syarhey 291
Sikorski, Radoslaw 53, 292
Single Market 190; Moldova and 307, 308; Ukraine and 280, 281–2
al-Sisi, General Abdel Fattah 181, 338–9, 511, 517, 518
Slovakia 43, 218, 378n3, 416
Slovenia 42, 294, 378n3, 416
Smirnov, Igor 305
socialisation 448–50
Solana, Javier 207, 292, 533, 535
South Caucasus 312–23; Armenia 318–19; Azerbaijan 317–18; conflict dynamics 319–20; Georgia 315–17; legal and political background 313–15; trade and visa liberalisation 315–19
South Ossetia 192, 266, 312, 314, 316–17, 319, 399, 524
South Programme 112
Southern Gas Corridor 387–8, 389
Southern Mediterranean Civil Society Forum 501
Southern Neighbourhood 177–85, 191–2; civilian missions 260–4; regional hegemons 180–2; sanctions 273–5
sovereignty, borders and 131
Soviet Union 171, 235, 264, 290, 416, 449, 451, 468
Spain 41, 213, 255, 354, 400, 401, 411, 540
Statkievic, Mikalaj 293
Steinmeier, Frank-Walter 217, 294
'stolen billion' scandal 307, 308
Strategic Framework on Human Rights and Democracy 486, 487
strategic narratives 154–61
Straw, Jack 213
Strelet, Valeriu 306
Sudan 525
Support for Improvement in Governance and Management (SIGMA) 416, 420, 429, 470
Support for Partnership, Reform and Inclusive Growth (SPRING) 331, 337, 339, 453, 462, 463, 499
Supreme Council of the Armed Forces (SCAF) 274
Sustainability Impact Assessment (SIA) 374–5
Sustainable Development Goals *see* Millennium Development Goals (MDGs)
Sweden 18, 41, 43, 213, 214, 216, 217, 218, 293, 354, 364, 365, 415, 457, 540
Switzerland 107–8, 130, 513
Syria 60, 178, 181, 191–2, 204, 205, 214, 215, 276, 336, 337, 410, 462, 481, 483, 488, 489, 522, 524, 528; civil war 126, 136, 180, 234, 242, 341, 411, 418, 462, 475, 481; crisis in 205, 239, 337, 342–3, 344, 362–4; crumbling unity 363–4; EP delegation 227; EU Regional Strategy for Syria and Iraq 364–5, 364, 410; human rights 488; Kurds 182; Madad Trust Fund 239–40; refugees 217, 337–8, 340, 341, 364–6, 397, 402, 418; sanctions 274–5, 447
Syrian National Council (SNC) 363

Tajikistan 235, 526
Tarbel, Fethi 359
Technical Assistance and Information Exchange (TAIEX) 239, 351, 416, 420, 429, 430n5, 470
Technical Assistance to the Commonwealth of Independent States (TACIS) 197, 235–7, 242, 409, 416, 418, 497, 527

Index

Temporary International Mechanism (TIM) 275, 514–15
terrorist attacks 178, 214–15, 274, 293, 364, 365, 405, 407, 410, 516, 541
Transnistria 265, 272, 302, 304–5, 308, 309n3, 524
Treaty of Lisbon 5, 9, 105, 112, 121, 482, 487, 490, 524, 533, 535; cohesion 42; conflict management 320; EEAS 441, 536; effectiveness 43; EP powers 223, 224, 230; EUBAM Libya 263; leadership 53; neighbourhood clause 106–8; Progress Reports 44; shared values 238; Syria AA 342
Treaty of Rome 18, 325
Tunisia 21, 42, 88, 110, 126, 159, 180, 183, 191–2, 195, 204, 227, 252, 255, 281, 324, 325, 326, 327, 329, 330, 333, 371, 396, 409, 410, 456, 462, 486, 488, 490, 499, 501, 509, 511, 515, 525; EU–Tunisia Task Force 331, 516; sanctions 273; uprising 464
Turkey 18, 124, 136, 145, 180, 194, 205, 270, 365, 387, 425, 452, 464, 523, 526, 527, 528, 540; EU accession talks with 183, 202, 319; European credentials 121; EU–Turkey deal 397; migrant deal 393, 397
Turkmenistan 235, 382, 526
Tusk, Donald 293, 411
'Twitter Revolution' 306
Tymoshenko, Yulia 226, 227, 229, 283, 284

Ukraine 45, 55, 76, 85, 88, 136, 169, 174, 196, 202, 203, 213, 223, 228, 234, 279–89, 419, 438, 456, 464, 467, 472, 477, 488, 499, 527, 528; Advisory Mission (EUAM) 261(tab) 264, 266–7; Association Agreement (AA) 4, 105, 107, 108, 109, 110–12, 127, 172, 193, 252, 281–2, 458, 483, 501; Civil Society Facility fund 486; Colour Revolution 196; Common Strategies 106; conditionality 437, 446, 447; conflict in 39, 50, 60, 67, 156, 159–60, 161, 167, 173, 193, 204, 223, 226, 234, 237, 272, 290, 293, 296, 298, 381, 406, 464, 467, 488, 498, 524, 540; Counter-terrorism 407; Cox–Kwasniewski mission 224, 229–30; DCFTA 66, 173, 219, 371, 451, 452; declarative Europeanisation 284; demand for upgrading relations 280–2; energy 217, 386–7, 389, 390; ENP review 242; ENP's reception in 279–80; EU relations 42, 45, 123, 124, 451, 456, 494, 499, 528; Eurasian Customs Union 452; Europeanisation 282–4; geopolitical epicentre 459–60; irrelevance of Eastern Partnership 282; National Police 267; NATO 295; 'Orange Revolution' 126, 279–80, 281, 282–3, 313, 436; political conditionality 194, 195; presidential election 228; push towards Europe 286–7; Russian counter-offer for integration 284–6; sanctions 273; strategic narrative of EU and Russia 161–4; support group 459; TACIS 235; visa facilitation and readmission rights 398; Visa Liberalisation Action Plan 252; Visgrad group 218–19
Union for the Mediterranean (UfM) 3, 5, 19, 34, 42, 43, 63, 121, 180, 196, 200, 202–3, 206, 213, 214, 215, 218, 219, 225, 250, 253, 254, 255, 327, 329, 333, 337, 339–40, 361, 362, 363, 372, 379n4, 390, 411, 417, 425, 436, 449, 450, 451, 452, 453, 457, 518, 525, 526
United Arab Emirates 6, 181
United Kingdom (UK) 43, 142, 178, 201, 202, 213, 292, 333, 348, 354, 360, 363–4, 411, 415, 460
United Nations: 2030 Agenda 536, 541; chemical weapons 342; human rights 489; Israel 347, 348; Libya reconstruction 361, 362; Office for the Coordination of Humanitarian Affairs (OCHA) 263, 360; refugees and 340, 341, 365; sanctions and 271, 274, 275, 359–60; veto powers Syria 363
United States 73, 100, 224, 260, 405, 437
Usatii, Renato 307
Uzbekistan 235, 526

values and norms promotion 54–5, 56, 111–12, 435–44; civil society organizations 438–40; EEAS 441; ENP countries' governments 436–8; EU energy norm export 381–2; 'EUnilateral' 382, 383–4, 386, 387, 389, 390; European Commission 440–1; European Parliament 442; Member States' governments 441–2; milieu-shaping 64–5; public opinion 438
Venice Declaration 349, 352
Verheugen, Günter 17
Visa Facilitation and Readmission Agreement 292, 319
Visa Liberalisation Action Plan (VLAP) 251, 252, 315, 319
visas: bans 271–2, 292–3; Georgia facilitation dialogue 316; liberalisation 250–3, 397–9, 447, 453, 458, 502
Visegrad Group 43, 214, 218–19, 469
Voronin, Vladimir 303, 304, 308

weapons of mass destruction (WMDs) 125, 179, 224, 332, 342, 351, 437
Weber, Max 144
Weimar Declaration 204–5
West Bank 262–3, 350, 353, 355
Western Balkans 88, 106, 107, 303
Western Sahara 110, 227, 324, 326, 330, 463, 524
Westerwelle, Guido 292
'Wider Europe' communication 5, 63, 94, 119, 133–5, 202, 212, 275, 276, 303, 534, 539
World Bank 318, 353, 374, 375, 378, 477

Index

World Trade Organisation (WTO) 98, 109, 281, 285, 317, 374, 375, 376, 451; DCFTAs built on rules 373; Moldova and 307; Russia and 172–3

Yanukovych, Viktor 66, 194, 227, 279, 284, 285–6, 452, 459

Yemen 180, 181, 461, 462, 523, 526, 527, 528
Yousef, Ahmed 511
Yugoslavia 18, 31, 145
Yushchenko, Viktor 285

al-Zarqawi, Abu Musab 182